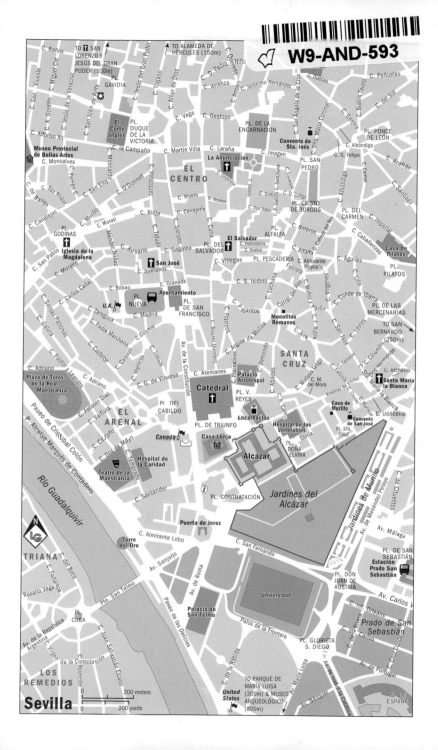

W9-AND-593

Sevilla

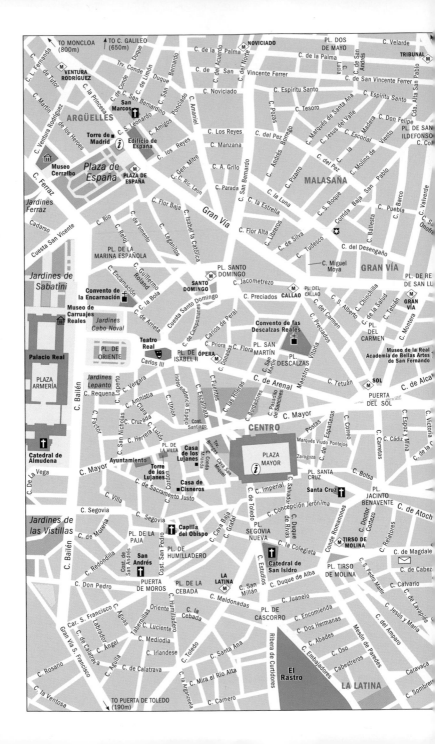

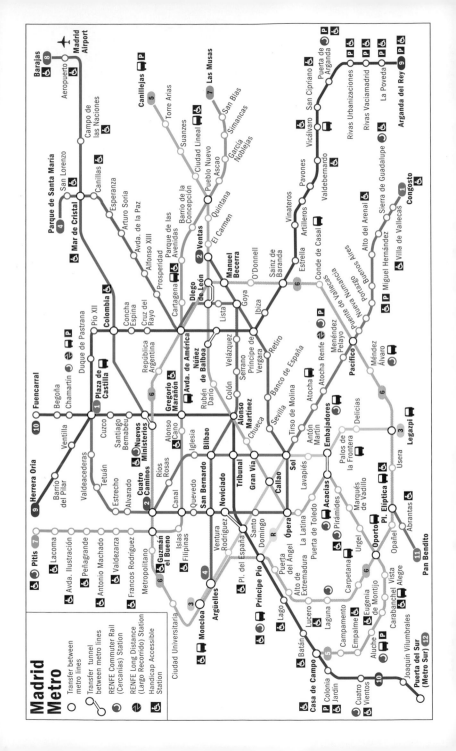

Madrid Metro

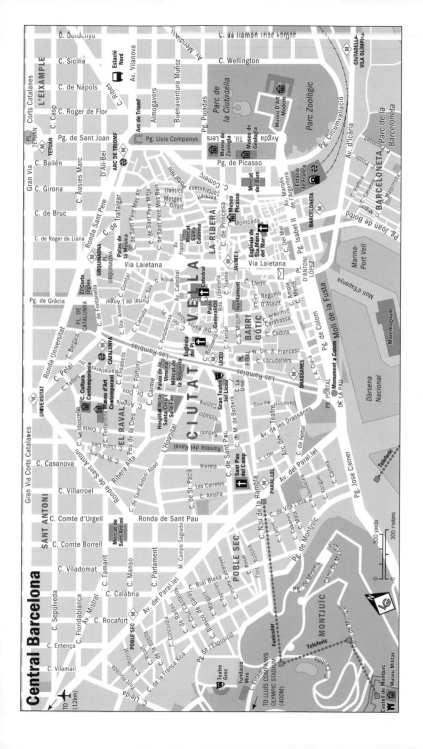

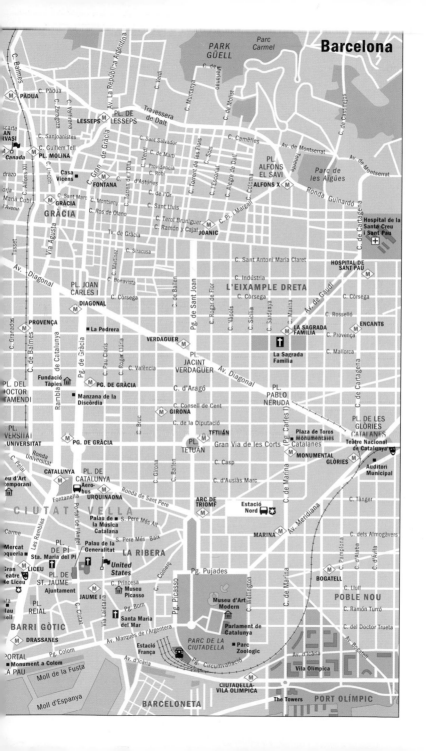

Barcelona Metro

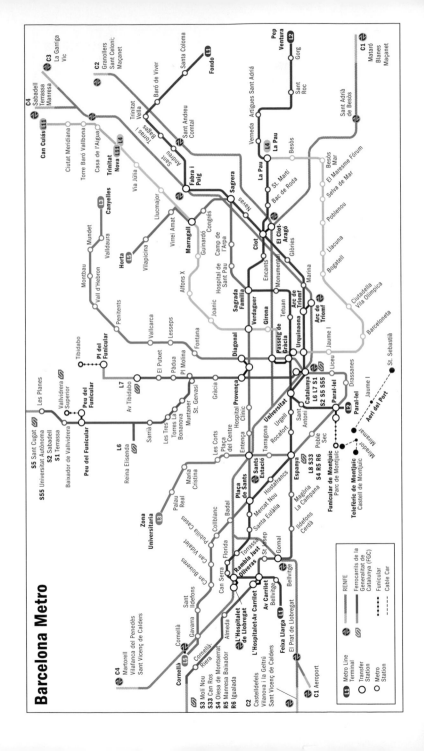

LET'S GO

■ PAGES PACKED WITH ESSENTIAL INFORMATION

"Value-packed, unbeatable, accurate, and comprehensive."

—The Los Angeles Times

"The guides are aimed not only at young budget travelers but at the independent traveler; a sort of streetwise cookbook for traveling alone."

—The New York Times

"Unbeatable; good sight-seeing advice; up-to-date info on restaurants, hotels, and inns; a commitment to money-saving travel; and a wry style that brightens nearly every page."

—The Washington Post

■ THE BEST TRAVEL BARGAINS IN YOUR BUDGET

"All the dirt, dirt cheap."

—People

"Let's Go follows the creed that you don't have to toss your life's savings to the wind to travel—unless you want to."

—The Salt Lake Tribune

■ REAL ADVICE FOR REAL EXPERIENCES

"The writers seem to have experienced every rooster-packed bus and lunar-surfaced mattress about which they write."

—The New York Times

"[Let's Go's] devoted updaters really walk the walk (and thumb the ride, and trek the trail). Learn how to fish, haggle, find work—anywhere."

—Food & Wine

"A world-wise traveling companion—always ready with friendly advice and helpful hints, all sprinkled with a bit of wit."

—The Philadelphia Inquirer

■ A GUIDE WITH A SPIRIT AND A SOCIAL CONSCIENCE

"Lighthearted and sophisticated, informative and fun to read. [Let's Go] helps the novice traveler navigate like a knowledgeable old hand."

—Atlanta Journal-Constitution

"The serious mission at the book's core reveals itself in exhortations to respect the culture and the environment—and, if possible, to visit as a volunteer, a student, or a teacher rather than a tourist."

—San Francisco Chronicle

LET'S GO PUBLICATIONS

TRAVEL GUIDES

Australia 9th edition
Austria & Switzerland 12th edition
Brazil 1st edition
Britain 2008
California 10th edition
Central America 9th edition
Chile 2nd edition
China 5th edition
Costa Rica 3rd edition
Eastern Europe 13th edition
Ecuador 1st edition
Egypt 2nd edition
Europe 2008
France 2008
Germany 13th edition
Greece 9th edition
Hawaii 4th edition
India & Nepal 8th edition
Ireland 13th edition
Israel 4th edition
Italy 2008
Japan 1st edition
Mexico 22nd edition
New Zealand 8th edition
Peru 1st edition
Puerto Rico 3rd edition
Southeast Asia 9th edition
Spain & Portugal 2008
Thailand 3rd edition
USA 24th edition
Vietnam 2nd edition
Western Europe 2008

ROADTRIP GUIDE

Roadtripping USA 2nd edition

ADVENTURE GUIDES

Alaska 1st edition
Pacific Northwest 1st edition
Southwest USA 3rd edition

CITY GUIDES

Amsterdam 5th edition
Barcelona 3rd edition
Boston 4th edition
London 16th edition
New York City 16th edition
Paris 14th edition
Rome 12th edition
San Francisco 4th edition
Washington, D.C. 13th edition

POCKET CITY GUIDES

Amsterdam
Berlin
Boston
Chicago
London
New York City
Paris
San Francisco
Venice
Washington, D.C.

LET'S GO

SPAIN & PORTUGAL
2008

Laura Gordon Editor
Evy Zwiebach Associate Editor
Natalie Sherman Associate Editor

Researcher-Writers
Jesse Barron
Nadav Greenberg
Jake Levine
Courtney Petrouski
Illiana Quimbaya
Erin Riley
Hannah Waight

Drew Davis Map Editor
Sara Culver Managing Editor

St. Martin's Press ⚑ New York

HELPING LET'S GO. If you want to share your discoveries, suggestions, or corrections, please drop us a line. We read every piece of correspondence, whether a postcard, a 10-page email, or a coconut. **Address mail to:**

> Let's Go: Spain & Portugal
> 67 Mount Auburn St.
> Cambridge, MA 02138
> USA

Visit Let's Go at **http://www.letsgo.com,** or send email to:

> feedback@letsgo.com
> Subject: "Let's Go: Spain & Portugal"

In addition to the invaluable travel advice our readers share with us, many are kind enough to offer their services as researchers or editors. Unfortunately, our charter enables us to employ only currently enrolled Harvard students.

HOW TO USE THIS BOOK

COVERAGE LAYOUT. *Let's Go: Spain & Portugal* launches out of Madrid, and follows with a whirlwind tour through Spain. Coverage spirals out counter-clockwise, ending with Las Islas Canarias. Your travels begin anew in Portugal, starting in Lisboa and then sweeping from the south to the north.

TRANSPORTATION INFO. For making connections between destinations, information is generally listed under both the arrival and departure cities. Parentheticals usually provide the trip duration followed by the frequency, then the price. To plan a trip by rail, check out the **Spain and Portugal Transportation** map (p. XII). For more general information on travel, consult the **Essentials** (p. 10) section.

COVERING THE BASICS. The first chapter, **Discover Spain & Portugal** (p. 1), contains highlights of the Iberian Peninsula, complete with **suggested itineraries.** The **Essentials** (p. 10) section contains practical information on planning a budget, making reservations, and other useful tips for traveling in Spain and Portugal. Take some time to peruse the **Life and Times** sections, which introduce each separate country (Spain p. 73; Portugal p. 615) and briefly sum up the history, culture, and customs of each destination. The **Appendix** (p. 759) has climate information, a list of bank holidays, measurement conversions, and a glossary. For study-abroad, volunteer, and work options in Spain and Portugal, **Beyond Tourism** (p. 61) is all you need.

LANGUAGE. Translations of words and phrases in Spanish, Portuguese, and regional languages appear in parentheses directly following them. City and provincial names in this guide are listed in Castilian first, followed by the regional language in parentheses where appropriate. Information within cities is listed in the regional language. For details on Spanish, Portuguese, and regional languages like *català, euskera,* and *gallego,* see the **Language** sections for each country (Spain p. 80; Portugal p. 620), or the **Appendix** (p. 760).

PRICE DIVERSITY. Our researchers list establishments in order of value from best to worst, with absolute favorites denoted by the *Let's Go* thumbs-up (⬛). Since the cheapest price does not always mean the best value, we have incorporated a system of price ranges for food and accommodations; see p. XVII.

PHONE CODES AND TELEPHONE NUMBERS. Area codes for each region appear opposite the name of the region and are denoted by the ☎ icon. Phone numbers in text are also preceded by the ☎ icon.

A NOTE TO OUR READERS. The information for this book was gathered by *Let's Go* researchers from May through August of 2007. Each listing is based on one researcher's opinion, formed during his or her visit at a particular time. Those traveling at other times may have different experiences since prices, dates, hours, and conditions are always subject to change. You are urged to check the facts presented in this book beforehand to avoid inconvenience and surprises.

totally loved my time studing at IH
I got it! fantástico!
Kristin, Iceland

The teachers make learning
Spanish fun. They really love it
and it shows.   Micki, Germany

LOVE OF SPANISH STARTED AT IH
COME BACK TO BRUSH UP ON MY
LLS!   DONALD, CANADA X

After studying at IH I now have lots
of friends from all over the world
Nasim, Sweden

I wasn't expecting such an authentic city in
the heart of Andalusia Cordoba really moved me!
Selina, USA

Todos, desde las secretarias hasta las profesores,
todos nos hicieron sentir como en nuestra casa.
Carl, Group Leader — USA

yo ♥ ihspain

Love to learn Spanish whilst travelling in Spain

Come and study with International House Spain. We offer a wide range of quality Spanish language courses
and accommodation options, wonderful social and cultural activities and an experience you will never forget.

Combine your travels with a Spanish course at one or more schools.
IH Barcelona . IH Cordoba . IH Madrid . IH Palma de Mallorca
IH San Sebastian . IH Seville . IH Valencia . IH Vejer (Cadiz)

www.iloveihspain.com

CONTENTS

IX

CANTABRIAN SEA

Gijón

Asturias and Cantabria
pp. 527-556

ASTURIAS

At Coruña

Oviedo

Cangas de Onís

CANTABRIA

Santander

B

Santiago de
Compostela

Galicia
pp. 557-584

León

Burgos

Castilla y León
pp. 149-189

Valladolid

Viana do
Castelo

Bragança

DOURO AND
MINHO

TRAS-OS-MONTES

Porto

The North
pp. 720-758

Salamanca

Segovia

THE THREE BEIRAS

Aveiro

Guarda

Comunidad de Madrid
pp. 93-148

Coimbra

PORTUGAL

Madrid

Toledo

**Ribatejo and
Estremadura**
pp. 694-719

Cáceres

**Castilla la Mancha
and Extremadura**
pp. 190-218

CAS

Lisboa
pp. 628-666

EXTREMADURA

Lisboa

Setúbal

Mérida

Badajoz

Ciudad Real

ALENTEJO

Évora

Beja

Córdoba

Algarve and Alentejo
pp. 667-693

Sevilla
pp. 219-241

Andalucia
pp. 242-311

Lagos

ALGARVE

Faro

Gran

Málaga

ATLANTIC
OCEAN

Gibraltar

Algeciras

ALBORAN
SEA

Las Islas Canarias
pp. 585-614

MOROCCO

X

Spain and Portugal Chapters

FRANCE

ANDORRA

Vasco
04-526

• Pamplona

NAVARRA

IOJA

• Girona

The Pyrenees
pp. 444-475

• Zaragoza

Cataluña
pp. 414-443

**Aragón, La Rioja,
and Navarra**
pp. 476-503

Barcelona
pp. 372-413

S P A I N

ARAGÓN

• Teruel

• Tarragona

Mallorca

Cuenca •

Castellón •

• Palma

Las Islas Baleares
pp. 343-371

IANCHA

Valencia •

VALENCIA

Ibiza

Eivissa/Ibiza City

Formentera

TO MENORCA →

Menorca

Ciudadela

Mahón

• Alicante

Murcia •

Valencia and Murcia
pp. 312-342

MURCIA

M E D I T E R R A N E A N   S E A

eria

A L G E R I A

N
LG

0 ——————— 75 miles

0 ——————— 75 kilometers

X I

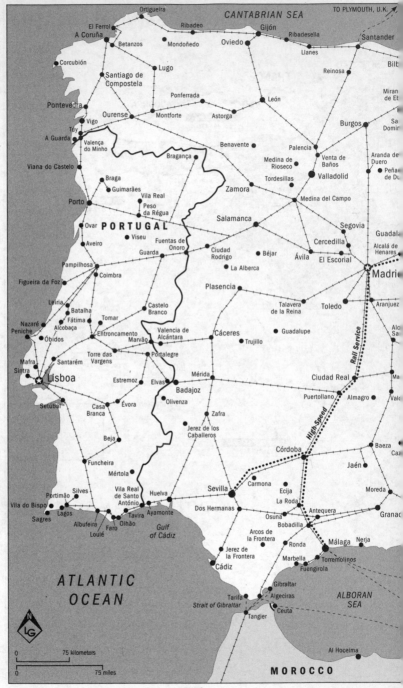

Spain and Portugal Transportation

XIII

RESEARCHER-WRITERS

Jesse Barron *Barcelona, Catalunya, Aragón, La Rioja, and Navarra*

From scoping out the underground music scene in Barcelona, getting intimate with the wines of La Rioja, and learning the intricacies of regional culture in Catalunya, Jesse conquered his route with an all-access pass to the hippest and most-happening events in the northeast. With tales of encounters with municipal mayors, strange languages, and beachfront people-watching, Jesse's stellar copy and candid marginalia kept us laughing all summer.

Nadav Greenberg *Asturias and Cantabria, País Vasco, and the Pyrenees*

Nadav trekked through the Pyrenees, partied in Pamplona, and hung with celebrities in San Sebastián. Nothing could stop Nadav; not even a daunting hike across an entire national park could faze this intrepid researcher. His thorough research and well-written copy never failed to capture the quaint mountain towns, architectural wonders, and hedonistic festivals of his fast-paced route.

Jake Levine *Madrid, Castilla y León, Castilla la Mancha, and Las Islas Canarias*

Fresh off his stint as a researcher for *Let's Go: Hawaii 2007*, Jake morphed into "Jacobo," braving hairpin turns in the Canaries, early morning hours in Madrid, and latter-day fascists everywhere. His college thesis on Spanish artists at the 1937 International Exposition honed his research skills to perfection and his ironic, humourous take on all things in the "Salty Ham Desert" kept his editors happy.

Courtney Petrouski *Andalucía, Extremadura, and the Algarve*

Having just spent a semester in Paris, Courtney braved two more months without peanut butter all in the name of research. She faced angry bus drivers, hostel lockouts and lockins, and scoured southern Spain and Portugal for the best of the best. She reported back with the wit, style, and vintage Petrouski pizzazz that kept us chuckling all summer and put her well on her way to a future in travel writing.

Illiana Quimbaya *Lisboa, Alentejo, Ribatejo, Estremadura, and Northern Portugal*

A Brazil aficionado, Illiana decided to cross the pond and see what Mama Portugal was all about. She traveled the length and breadth of the country, using her anthropology skills and flawless Portuguese to get the real scoop. Even on days that buses never came or that old men were being particularly pesky, Illiana kept her grandmother Wewa, her hero, in mind and did it all with unfailing good humor and enthusiasm.

RESEARCHER-WRITERS

Erin Riley *Valencia, Murcia, and Las Islas Baleares*

Erin's unflappable attitude and evocative descriptions continually amazed her editors. She partied with hardcore clubbers in Ibiza, sought out stunning views in towns along the Costa del Sol, and scootered around remote beaches in Las Islas Baleares, all in the name of fresh and detailed coverage. Even after a week without her pack, Erin refused to call it quits; instead, she made like a local and sipped sangria on the sand.

Hannah Waight *Galicia, Asturias, Castilla y León*

Rock-climber extraordinaire and natural adventurer, Hannah took the Northwest by storm. With equal appreciation for small, sleepy towns, big cities, and national parks, Hannah always found something to love everywhere she went. She overcame stolen notepads, navigated three languages, saw enough scallop shells to last her a lifetime, researched tirelessly, and then partied with Spaniards until dawn. And still she found time to pen punchy copy, and even run with the bulls in Pamplona.

CONTRIBUTING WRITERS

Antonio Córdoba was born in Sevilla, where he earned his B.A. in English Literature. He graduated from Harvard University in 2007 with a Ph.D. in Latin American Literature.

Nicholas Mott attended Institut de Batxillerat Lluis de Peguera, a local high school in Manresa, Cataluña, as part of the American Foreign Service Exchange Program. He graduated from Harvard University in 2007 with a degree in Anthropology

ACKNOWLEDGMENTS

LET'S GO

TEAM S&P THANKS: Our stellar ■ RWs, the best any editors could ever ask for, Sara, Drew, SPAM, YouTube, baked goods, and the Iberian Peninsula.
LAURA THANKS: Team S&P for an unforgettable experience. Evy, for her musical selections, love of Emoland, and infectious laugh. Natalie, for her love of history, impressive sanity, and her spunky edits. Sara, for being too cool for school, for a shared taste in literature, my cheat sheets, and gchat. Drew, for endless patience. Finale and the coffeemaker for always being there, the poltergeist of the Big Yellow, and SPAM, for winning contests and baked goods. Mom, Dad, Beck, and Jonny, for your unconditional love and support.
EVY THANKS: To SPAM Pod for being so good at life. To Frame, for being so...nasty. To Laura, for everything—including Spanish festivals, checklists, Finale sandwiches, Harry Potter, and sanity. To Natalie for sharing mutinous looks, keeping us historically accurate, and quiet hilariousness. To Sara for laugh-out-loud edits and shared appreciation of circules, serpants, and spirles. To the office for baked goods and so much fun. To N for Torito custody wars and loopiness. To MBTA, for never being there. And, to my familia for being so wonderful.
NATALIE THANKS: Mumoo for housing me, feeding me, and putting up with me. Laura and Evy both for thorough edits, overall fun-ness, and willingness to laugh at bad puns. Sara for her careful eye and nononsense edits. Drew for putting up with delays extraordinaire. Mom and Dad for being just a phone call away, all office bakers, for obvious reasons, and the printers for not breaking down completely.
DREW THANKS: Thanks to Bagel/Payday Fridays for saving my life. To the RWs, for all of their hard work. To Laura, Evy, and Natalie for humoring my bizarre work schedule, and for their collective efforts to come up with Tutti Frutti Tuesday. To Mapland, for collective/obsessive calorie counting. Thanks to Mom and Dad for being the greatest. Peace Out.

Editor
Laura Gordon
Associate Editors
Evy Zwiebach and Natalie Sherman
Managing Editor
Sara Culver
Map Editor
Drew Davis
Typesetter
Jansen A. S. Thurmer

Publishing Director
Jennifer Q. Wong
Editor-in-Chief
Silvia Gonzalez Killingsworth
Production Manager
Victoria Esquivel-Korsiak
Cartography Manager
Thomas MacDonald Barron
Editorial Managers
Anne Bensson, Calina Ciobanu, Rachel Nolan
Financial Manager
Sara Culver
Business and Marketing Manager
Julie Vodhanel
Personnel Manager
Victoria Norelid
Production Associate
Jansen A. S. Thurmer
Director of E-Commerce & IT
Patrick Carroll
Website Manager
Kathryne A. Bevilacqua
Office Coordinators
Juan L. Peña, Bradley J. Jones

Director of Advertising Sales
Hunter McDonald
Senior Advertising Associate
Daniel Lee

President
William Hauser
General Managers
Bob Rombauer, Jim McKellar

PRICE RANGES

SPAIN & PORTUGAL

Our researchers list establishments in order of value from best to worst; our favorites are denoted by the Let's Go thumbs-up (🖐). However, because the best value is not always the cheapest price, we have also incorporated a system of price ranges, based on a rough expectation of what you'll spend. For **accommodations,** we base our range on the cheapest price for which a single traveler can stay for one night. For **restaurants** and other dining establishments, we estimate the average amount a traveler will spend. The table tells you what you'll *typically* find in Spain and Portugal at the corresponding price range; keep in mind that no system can allow for every individual establishment's quirks, and you'll typically get more for your money in larger cities. In other words: expect anything.

ACCOMMODATIONS	RANGE	WHAT YOU'RE *LIKELY* TO FIND
❶	under €15	Campgrounds, HI hostels, or basic dorm rooms. Expect bunk beds and a communal bath; you may have to provide or rent towels and sheets.
❷	€15-25	Upper-end hostels or lower-end *pensiones*. You may have a private bathroom, or there may be a sink in your room and a communal shower in the hall.
❸	€26-35	A small room with a private bath, probably in a budget hotel, *hostal*, or *pensión*. Should have decent amenities, such as phone and TV. Breakfast may be included in the price of the room.
❹	€36-50	Similar to ❸, but may have more amenities or be in a more highly-touristed or conveniently-located area. May include mountain *refugios* or *casas de huéspedes*.
❺	over €50	Large hotels or upscale chains. If it's a ❺ and it doesn't have the perks you want, you've paid too much.
FOOD	RANGE	WHAT YOU'RE *LIKELY* TO FIND
❶	under €7	Probably a *kebap* or fast-food stand, a *cafetería*, or bakery. Rarely ever a sit-down meal.
❷	€7-11	Cheap *bocadillos* (sandwiches), tapas, *tostas*, and some set *menús*. May be takeout or sit-down.
❸	€12-16	Typically a sit-down meal. Many *menús* in this price range include a 3-course meal with a drink and dessert.
❹	€17-25	Fancier, more elaborate, or exotic to Iberian palates. Entrees are more expensive than ❸, but you're paying for better service, ambiance, and decor.
❺	over €25	Your meal might cost more than your room, but there's a reason—it's something fabulous or famous, or both, and you'll probably need to wear something other than sandals and a T-shirt.

DISCOVER SPAIN AND PORTUGAL

Spain is a land characterized by unique contrasts: late-night parties segue into the afternoon *siesta*, fast-paced and cosmopolitan cities shut down as citizens linger over lunch, gorgeous palaces of old house modern bureaucratic post offices, and architectural gems recall a past of peaceful coexistence between Jews, Muslims, and Christians. Its regions offer distinctive foods and styles, natural and man-made wonders, unique dialects and traditions, and often fierce pride. Northeastern and central Spain are aesthetic wonders; trendy, quirky Barcelona hugs a rugged coastline characterized by famed architecture like Bilbao's shining Guggenheim Museum and Salvador Dalí's eccentric buildings. The dizzying Pyrenees and Picos de Europa challenge the most intrepid of adventurers, while Spain's miles of silken sands and azure waters entice weary travelers. Architectural enthusiasts explore the Baroque cathedrals of mystical Galicia, the Arab intricacies of Andalucía, and the *Modernista* conjurings in Cataluña, while impressive museums like the Prado and the Reina Sofía showcase the finest works of past and present Spanish painters. The south, land of bullfights, flamenco, and tapas, is the passionate Spain of popular imagination, while the nocturnal energy of Madrid, Barcelona, and Ibiza is enough to challenge the heartiest partiers. Spain is a paradise for partiers, a mecca for art lovers, a kickstart for thrill-seekers, and a rest-stop for the restless. Whether you come in search of *fiesta* fervor, historical rediscovery, tasty tapas, a golden tan, or cultural refinement, Spain's colorful cultural mosaic leaves nothing to be desired.

Often unjustly overshadowed by its Western European neighbors, Portugal's appeal is not limited to its sugary-sweet port wine, nor its past glories of globetrotting explorers. Travelers who come to Portugal today will discover one of Europe's fastest-growing hotspots. Lisboa, the capital and largest city, has the country's most impressive imperial monuments, while the southern Algarve, boasting spectacular beaches and wild nightlife, draws backpackers in droves. Northern Coimbra crackles with the energy of a university town, and Porto surpasses even Lisboa in sophisticated elegance. Portugal's small inland towns have a timeless feel, with medieval castles overlooking rushing rivers and peaceful town squares. The wild northern region, including the land in Trás-Os-Montes, is among the most pristine in all of Europe—some villages have remained unchanged for nearly a millennium.

FACTS AND FIGURES

OFFICIAL NAMES: Kingdom of Spain and Portuguese Republic	**NUMBER OF SPANISH SPEAKERS IN THE WORLD:** 332 million
SPAIN POPULATION: 40.4 million	**AGE OF THE LIGHTHOUSE IN A CORUÑA:** 2026 years old (the oldest lighthouse in the world)
PORTUGAL POPULATION: 10.6 million	
BULLS KILLED PER YEAR IN SPAIN: 30,000	**NUMBER OF UNIVERSITIES IN SPAIN:** 49
PORTUGAL'S MOST FAMOUS INVENTION: The hot air balloon, flown in Lisboa on August 8, 1709	**NUMBER OF CASTLES IN PORTUGAL:** 101

WHEN TO GO

Summer is **high season** *(temporada alta)* for coastal and interior regions in Spain and Portugal; winter is high season for ski resorts and the Islas Canarias. In many parts of Spain and Portugal, high season begins during **Semana Santa** (Holy Week; March 14-23 in 2008) and includes festival days. July and August see some of the hottest weather, especially in the central plains, where the mercury can creep up to 36°C (97°F). Tourism on the Iberian Peninsula peaks in August; the coast overflows as inland cities empty out, leaving closed offices, restaurants, and lodgings. As a general rule, make **reservations** if you plan to travel in June, July, or August.

Traveling in the **low season** *(temporada baja)* has many advantages, most noticeably lighter crowds and lower prices. Many hostels cut their prices by at least 30%, and reservations are seldom necessary. While major cities and university towns may exude energy during these months, many smaller seaside spots are ghost towns, and tourist offices and sights cut their hours nearly everywhere. The weather is also ideal in spring and early summer, when temperatures are around 20-25°C (68-77°F). For a table of temperatures and rainfall, see **Climate**, p. 759. For a chart of **National Holidays** and **Festivals** in Spain, see p. 92; and in Portugal, p. 627.

WHAT TO DO

Two millennia of invaders have swept over these countries, resulting in an edgy and eclectic culture filled with custom, religion, history, and an irrepressible energy. You can see it in **Madrid's** famous nightlife (p. 136), in the sidewalk cafes of **Lisboa** (p. 642), and in the extravagant festivals. There are as many ways to see Spain and Portugal as there are places to go; some choose to search out every Baroque chapel, others spend weeks trekking on some of Europe's best trails, and still more hop from city to city indulging cosmopolitan fantasies.

IMAGES OF IBERIA

The insatiable frenzy of the **Queima das Fitas** in Coimbra (p. 740), **Las Fallas** in Valencia (p. 312), the **Feria de Abril** in Sevilla (p. 219), and the infamous **San Fermín** in Pamplona (p. 498) make it difficult to deny the overwhelming cultural exuberance of the Iberian peninsula. But underneath Iberian fervor is a rich sonority of feeling—the poignant expressions of heartbreak are often as gripping and adrenaline-charged as the celebrations. The ritually tragic emotions of Portuguese *fado* bring tears to the eyes of even the most macho Spanish bullfighters, who in turn create their own tragedies on the bullring sand. Meanwhile, art and architecture like Picasso's powerfully symbolic **Guernica** (p. 127) and the propagandistic **Valle de los Caídos** (p. 143) immortalize the actual tragedies that scarred Spain during a good part of the last century. Lest you feel overwhelmed by the dark emotions of the region's past, ample opportunity exists for peace and quiet in Spain and Portugal: the thin-aired reverence of **Montserrat** (p. 412), the serenity of a rowboat in **El Retiro** (p. 124), and the surreal calm of **Parc Güell** (p. 403) are all placid escapes.

CASAS TO CASTLES

From traditionally conservative to unconventionally decadent, the buildings and monuments of Iberia form a collage of architectural styles. The remains of ancient civilizations are everywhere—from the Celtiberian tower of **O Castro de Baroña** (p. 565) and the Punic walls of **Cartagena** (p. 341). to Roman ruins like the aqueduct in **Segovia** (p. 153) and the amphitheater in **Mérida** (p. 215). Hundreds of years of Moorish rule left breathtaking monuments, including Granada's spectacular **Alhambra** (p. 301), Córdoba's **Mezquita** (p. 248), and Sintra's **Castelo dos Mouros** (p. 663). The Catholic church has spent immense sums of money to build some of the world's most ornate religious complexes, ranging from the pastiche of the **Convento de Cristo** (p. 712) to the imposing **El Escorial** (p. 141), site of the Spanish Inquisition. Spain's magnificent cathedrals are Gothic, Plateresque, or just plain bizarre, as with Gaudí's unfinished *Modernista* **Sagrada Família** in Barcelona (p. 400). Recent additions to the architectural landscape include Lisboa's expansive **Parque das Nações** (p. 654), Bilbao's shining **Guggenheim Museum** (p. 518), and Valencia's huge **Ciudad de las Artes y las Ciencias** (p. 319).

AU NATUREL

Iberia's best-kept secrets are its sprawling national parks and soaring, snowy mountain ranges. **Andorra** (p. 459), in the heart of the Pyrenees, has easily accessible glacial valleys, rolling forests, and wild meadows. In northern Spain, the **Parque Nacional de Ordesa** (p. 467) features well-kept trails, rushing rivers, and thundering waterfalls, while the **Parc Nacional d'Aigüestortes** (p. 451) hides 50 ice-cold mountain lakes in its 24,700 acres of rugged peaks and valleys. The **Picos de Europa** (p. 538) offer some of Europe's best mountaineering. Northern Portugal's **Parque Natural de Montesinho** (p. 757) is probably the most isolated, untouched land in all of Europe. Farther south, greenery-starved *madrileños* hike the **Sierra de Guadarrama** (p. 146), and nature-lovers are drawn to Andalucía's huge **Parque Nacional Coto de Doñana** (p. 257), which protects nearly 60,000 acres of land for threatened wildlife. In the south, **Las Alpujarras** (p. 308) are perfect for hiking among Spain's famous *pueblos blancos* (white towns), while trails in **Mallorca** (p. 345) and the **Canary Islands** (p. 585) juxtapose mountain peaks with ocean horizons.

SUN AND SAND

It would be a shame to spend an entire stay in Spain and Portugal without venturing from the coastline, but the stunning vistas of Iberia's tranquil shores are well-worth a visit. Marc Chagall deemed the red-cliffed shores of **Tossa de Mar** (p. 426) "Blue Paradise." **San Sebastián's** (p. 511) calm, voluptuous Playa de la Concha attracts young travelers from around the world, while **Santander** (p. 548) caters to an elite, refined clientele. The beaches of **Galicia** (p. 557) curve around crystal-green, misty inlets. On the **Islas Baleares** (p. 343) and **Canarias** (p. 585), glistening bodies crowd the chic beaches, and southern Spain's infamous **Costa del Sol** (p. 272) draws tourists to its scorched Mediterranean bays by the planeload. The eastern **Costa Blanca** (p. 327) mixes small-town charm with ocean expanses, and the looming cliffs and turquoise waters of Portugal's southern **Algarve** (p. 667) adorn hundreds of postcards. Thrill-seekers will not be disappointed by the endless opportunities for watersports—surfing, sailing, kiteboarding, scuba diving, and windsurfing are all popular and accessible options.

ALL NIGHT LONG

Nightlife in Spain and Portugal ranges from relaxing to debaucherous, and generally leans toward the latter. Just setting foot outdoors is likely to lead to events of unabashed hedonism unlike anything you've ever experienced. With countless bars and clubs and an incredible, intoxicating energy, **Madrid** (p. 93) has earned international renown as one of the greatest party cities in the world. **Barcelona's** (p. 372) wild, edgy nightlife reflects the city's outrageous sense of style. Residents of **Sevilla** (p. 219) pack discotecas floating on the Río Guadalquivir, and only on **Ibiza** (p. 363) will you find the world's largest club filled with 10,000 decadent partiers. Student-packed **Salamanca** (p. 167) is a crazed, international frat party, and **Lagos,** in Portugal (p. 667), has more bars and backpackers per square meter than any town in the world.

▓ LET'S GO PICKS

BEST PLACE TO STUPIDLY ENDANGER YOUR LIFE: Pamplona, during the infamous Running of the Bulls (p. 499).

BEST PLACE TO GET SPLASHED WHILE DRINKING: Oviedo, where cider is traditionally poured from feet above your cup (p. 528).

BEST REAL-LIFE SHAKESPEAREAN TRAGEDY: The tale of Teruel's star-crossed lovers, who could only be together in death (p. 484).

BEST PRESERVED BODY PARTS: Santa Teresa's finger (p. 155), a treasure of the convent in Ávila; famed singer **Julián Gayarre's larynx** (p. 474), stored in the Casa Museo of Roncal.

BEST PLACE TO SEE A BURNING BUSH: Parque Nacional de Timanfaya, in the Islas Canarias, where volcanic fires burn just below ground (p. 606).

BEST PLACE TO CRY LIKE A BABY: A *fado* house in Lisbon's Bairro Alto district, where melancholy music brings audiences to tears (p. 649).

BEST PLACE TO ATTACK OTHER TOURISTS: Festa de São João, in Porto, where for one evening in June townsmen beat each other over the head with plastic hammers (p. 720).

BEST PLACE TO BE LOUD AND PROUD: Madrid, during Orgullo Gay, one of the biggest gay festivals in the world, with floats, parades, and free concerts (p. 135).

BEST MEDIEVAL RECYCLING PROJECT: The macabre **Capela dos Ossos,** in Évora, made from 5000 unwitting skeletons (p. 686).

BEST PLACE TO SLEEP ON EDGE: The **hanging houses** of Cuenca, which will give you acrophobic dreams (p. 199).

BEST GNARLY WAVE: The Praia do Molho Leste, site of **"Super-tubos,"** also known as the "Portuguese pipeline," comparable to Hawaii's biggest surf (p. 702).

BEST PLACE TO SIT ON THE THRONE: Sintra's Palácio da Pena, where the Queen had a gold-tiled toilet (p. 663).

SUGGESTED ITINERARIES

OFF THE BEATEN CAMINO (4 WEEKS)

Cambados (1 day)
Sweeping vineyard orchards and great shellfish characterize this fishing port (p. 576).

Picos de Europa (3 days)
Hike formidable limestone peaks among wild horses, boars, long-eared owls, and your own deep thoughts (p. 538).

A Coruña (2 days)
They say Hercules built their lighthouse, and who are we to say he didn't? (p. 578).

Logroño (2 days)
A considerably less pious stop on the Camino de Santiago, the town provides access to La Rioja's vineyards and *bodegas* (p. 487).

Zaragoza (1 day)
The best place to perfect that Spanish lisp, founded by Augustus in 14BC (p. 476)

Santiago de Compostela (3 days)
The end of the very beaten path, this city is Galicia's magical, mystical terminus of the Camino de Santiago (p. 557).

Burgos (2 days)
Say "Cheese!" and ye shall receive at the birthplace of El Cid Campeador, Galicia's hero (p. 179).

START

Túy (1 day)
This idyllic town connects Spain with its peninsular companion (p. 571).

Malasaña and Chueca (3 days)
Spend a few days in the funkiest, most eclectic neighborhoods of Madrid (p. 101).

Morella (1 day)
A serpentine ride leads to the medieval town's majestic castle upon the hill (p. 326).

Cáceres (2 days) END
Numerous medieval castles make this city seem like something out of a fairy tale (p. 204).

Valencia (2 days)
The *papier-mâché* madness of Las Fallas has made this spunky, trendy city world-renowned (p. 312).

Las Alpujarras (2 days)
Teeny tiny towns tucked into the Sierra Nevadas remind travelers what Spain was like before tourism (p. 308).

Cuenca (1 day)
"Hanging houses" defy gravity, managing to look picturesque as they teeter over the gorge (p. 199).

Mojácar (1 day)
A postcard-perfect hilltop village that boasts astonishing views of the 17km of smooth, golden coastline below (p. 285).

DISCOVER

BEST OF SPAIN AND PORTUGAL (8 WEEKS

Cabo Finisterre (1 day)
Spain's *finis del terre* (end of the earth) is a lonely, windswept peninsula jutting out from the Costa de la Muerte (p. 564).

Santiago de Compostela (2 days)
Pilgrims and backpackers converge by the thousands on this mystical "city of song" (p. 55

Salamanca (2 days)
The *estudiantes* know how to get down in this ancient college town (p. 159).

Porto (2 days)
Portugal's source of port wine sits on a gorge carved into the earth by the Rio Douro (p. 720).

Coimbra (2 days)
The kids are in charge in this vibrant and fun university town (p. 740).

Aveiro (2 days)
Gondolas and inner tubes float along happily in the "Venice of Portugal" (p. 748).

Parque Natural da Serra da Estrela (1 day)
Site of a beautiful national park and home of the gigantic Serra da Estrela cheese—don't forget your spoon (p. 753).

Lisboa (3 days)
Portugal's capital and cultural center is alive with melancholic *fado* and Europe's most potent Old–World charm (p. 628).

Córdoba (2 d
Once the largest, r decadent city in Eur Córdoba's incredib Mezquita temple com still draws horde tourists to the a (p. 2

Sintra (1 day)
A bougainvillea-filled break from fast-paced Lisboa (p. 660).

Évora (1 day)
Three Franciscan monks made this city's creepy chapel out of thousands of other monks' bones (p. 684).

Sevilla (2 days)
Home to the Spain popular imaginatio flamenco, white houses (and horse and orange tree-lir streets live up to e expectation (p. 21

Sagres (1 day)
Henry the Navigator gazed into the wide beyond from this town's windswept cliffs (p. 674).

Lagos (2 days)
An infamous beach-and-bar town set on the winding, craggy southern coast (p. 667).

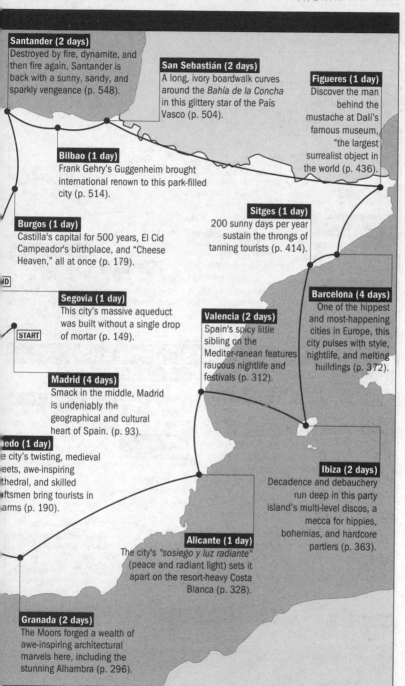

Santander (2 days)
Destroyed by fire, dynamite, and then fire again, Santander is back with a sunny, sandy, and sparkly vengeance (p. 548).

San Sebastián (2 days)
A long, ivory boardwalk curves around the *Bahía de la Concha* in this glittery star of the País Vasco (p. 504).

Figueres (1 day)
Discover the man behind the mustache at Dalí's famous museum, "the largest surrealist object in the world (p. 436).

Bilbao (1 day)
Frank Gehry's Guggenheim brought international renown to this park-filled city (p. 514).

Burgos (1 day)
Castilla's capital for 500 years, El Cid Campeador's birthplace, and "Cheese Heaven," all at once (p. 179).

Sitges (1 day)
200 sunny days per year sustain the throngs of tanning tourists (p. 414).

ND

Segovia (1 day)
This city's massive aqueduct was built without a single drop of mortar (p. 149).

START

Barcelona (4 days)
One of the hippest and most-happening cities in Europe, this city pulses with style, nightlife, and melting buildings (p. 372).

Valencia (2 days)
Spain's spicy little sibling on the Mediter-ranean features raucous nightlife and festivals (p. 312).

Madrid (4 days)
Smack in the middle, Madrid is undeniably the geographical and cultural heart of Spain. (p. 93).

edo (1 day)
e city's twisting, medieval
eets, awe-inspiring
thedral, and skilled
ftsmen bring tourists in
arms (p. 190).

Ibiza (2 days)
Decadence and debauchery run deep in this party island's multi-level discos, a mecca for hippies, bohemias, and hardcore partiers (p. 363).

Alicante (1 day)
The city's *"sosiego y luz radiante"* (peace and radiant light) sets it apart on the resort-heavy Costa Blanca (p. 328).

Granada (2 days)
The Moors forged a wealth of awe-inspiring architectural marvels here, including the stunning Alhambra (p. 296).

DISCOVER

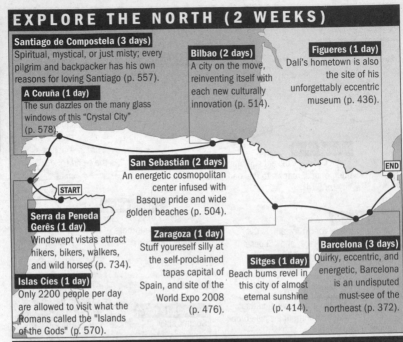

EXPLORE THE NORTH (2 WEEKS)

Santiago de Compostela (3 days)
Spiritual, mystical, or just misty; every pilgrim and backpacker has his own reasons for loving Santiago (p. 557).

A Coruña (1 day)
The sun dazzles on the many glass windows of this "Crystal City" (p. 578).

Bilbao (2 days)
A city on the move, reinventing itself with each new culturally innovation (p. 514).

Figueres (1 day)
Dalí's hometown is also the site of his unforgettably eccentric museum (p. 436).

END

START

San Sebastián (2 days)
An energetic cosmopolitan center infused with Basque pride and wide golden beaches (p. 504).

Serra da Peneda Gerês (1 day)
Windswept vistas attract hikers, bikers, walkers, and wild horses (p. 734).

Zaragoza (1 day)
Stuff yourself silly at the self-proclaimed tapas capital of Spain, and site of the World Expo 2008 (p. 476).

Sitges (1 day)
Beach bums revel in this city of almost eternal sunshine (p. 414).

Barcelona (3 days)
Quirky, eccentric, and energetic, Barcelona is an undisputed must-see of the northeast (p. 372).

Islas Cíes (1 day)
Only 2200 people per day are allowed to visit what the Romans called the "Islands of the Gods" (p. 570).

SOUTHERN COMFORTS (3 WEEKS)

Lagos (2 days)
A surfer haven and party town along the gorgeous, grottoed southern coast of Portugal, Lagos is home to more expats than Portuguese. (p. 667).

Sevilla (3 days)
Spain's third-largest city exudes enough charm to keep you dancing *flamenco* late into the hot, hot night (p. 219).

Córdoba (2 days)
The Moors made this city the magnificent heart of Islam in the West, and *La Mezquita* (p. 242). **END**

Granada (2 days)
You know what they say: "If you die without seeing the Alhambra, you have not lived" (p. 296).

Arcos de la Frontera (1 day)
A idyllic *pueblo blanco* (white town) high above the Río Guadalete considered one of Spain's "most perfect towns."(p. 258).

START

Olhão (2 days)
This fishing port paradise has access to the surrounding islands' pristine beaches and massive flamingo flocks (p. 681).

Jerez de la Frontera (1 day)
Pick a bird, any bird, and you will find it here; spring brings flocks upon flocks of breeding *aves* (p. 251).

Las Alpujarras (3 days)
An adventure-seekers paradise, this string of rustic towns offers the best in climbing, biking, and hiking (p. 308).

Sagres (2 days)
Portugal's southernmost town attracts few tourists with its desolate landscape and end-of-the-world cliffs—but that's the point (p. 674).

Marbella (1 day)
Ten months of summer mean a near-constant bikini beach party in this fancy speedboat paradise (p. 277).

Ronda (2 days)
Centuries-old bridges span this town's 100m El Tajo gorge, a sheer drop from teetering whitewashed houses (p. 288).

THE BEST O' THE FIESTA 2008

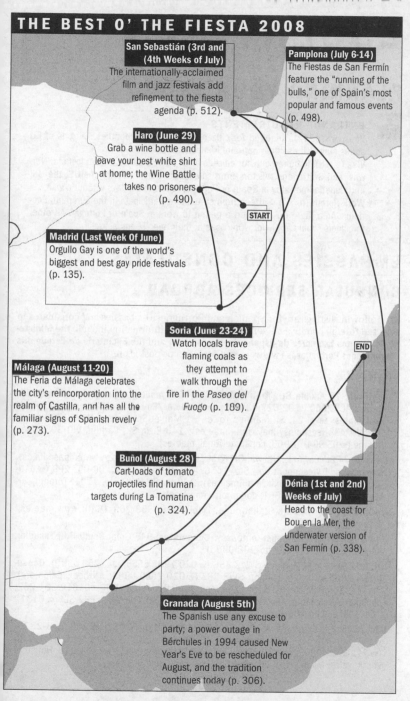

San Sebastián (3rd and (4th Weeks of July)
The internationally-acclaimed film and jazz festivals add refinement to the fiesta agenda (p. 512).

Pamplona (July 6-14)
The Fiestas de San Fermín feature the "running of the bulls," one of Spain's most popular and famous events (p. 498).

Haro (June 29)
Grab a wine bottle and leave your best white shirt at home; the Wine Battle takes no prisoners (p. 490).

START

Madrid (Last Week Of June)
Orgullo Gay is one of the world's biggest and best gay pride festivals (p. 135).

Soria (June 23-24)
Watch locals brave flaming coals as they attempt to walk through the fire in the *Paseo del Fuego* (p. 189).

END

Málaga (August 11-20)
The Feria de Málaga celebrates the city's reincorporation into the realm of Castilla, and has all the familiar signs of Spanish revelry (p. 273).

Buñol (August 28)
Cart-loads of tomato projectiles find human targets during La Tomatina (p. 324).

Dénia (1st and 2nd) Weeks of July)
Head to the coast for Bou en la Mer, the underwater version of San Fermín (p. 338).

Granada (August 5th)
The Spanish use any excuse to party; a power outage in Bérchules in 1994 caused New Year's Eve to be rescheduled for August, and the tradition continues today (p. 306).

ESSENTIALS

PLANNING YOUR TRIP

ENTRANCE REQUIREMENTS
Passport (p. 12). Required for citizens of all foreign countries. Citizens of EU states may also use their national identity card.
Visa (p. 13). Required only for citizens of all non-EU states, except Iceland, Norway, and Switzerland. Visitors from select countries, including the US, the UK, and Canada, may stay in Spain or Portugal for up to 90 days without a visa.
Work Permit (p. 14). Citizens from states that participate in the European Economic Area (EEA) do not need a permit to work in Spain or Portugal. All other foreigners should apply for work visas at their nearest embassy.

EMBASSIES AND CONSULATES

CONSULAR SERVICES ABROAD

The following listings are for Spanish and Portuguese embassies and consulates in selected foreign countries. Useful sources of such information include the **Ministerio de Asuntos Exteriores de España** (www.mae.es) and the **Secretaria de Estado das Comunidades Portuguesas** (www.secomunidades.pt/postos.php).

SPANISH

Australia: 15 Arkana St., Yarralumla, ACT 2600; mailing address: P.O. Box 9076, Deakin ACT 2600 (☎02 627 33 555; www.mae.es/Embajadas/Canberra/es/Home). **Consulates:** Level 24, St. Martin's Tower, 31 Market St., Sydney, NSW 2000 (☎02 926 12 433; cgspainsydney@mail.mae.es); 146 Elgin St., Carlton, VIC 3053 Melbourne (☎03 934 71 966; conspmel@mail.mae.es).

Canada: 74 Stanley Ave., Ottawa, ON K1M 1P4 (☎613-747-2252; www.embaspain.ca). **Consulates:** 1 Westmount Sq., Ste. 1456, Ave. Wood, Montreal, QC H3Z 2P9 (☎514-935-5235; conspmontreal@mail.mae.es); 2 Bloor St. East. Ste. 1201, Toronto, ON M4W 1A8 (☎416-977-1661; cog.toronto@mae.es).

Ireland: 17 Merlyn Park, Ballsbridge, Dublin 4 (☎353 269 1640; www.mae.es/embajadas/dublin).

New Zealand: See Australian embassy. **Consulates:** 345 Great South Rd., Takanini, Auckland (☎9 299 6019; fax 298 9986).

UK: 39 Chesham Pl., London SW1X 8SB (☎020 7235 5555; fax 7259 5392). **Consulates:** 20 Draycott Pl., London SW3 2RZ (☎020 7589 8989; www.conspalon.org); Ste. 1A, Brook House, 70 Spring Gardens, Manchester M2 2BQ (☎01612 361 262; consmanchester@btconnect.com); 63 North Castle St., Edinburgh EH2 3LJ (☎01312 201 843; cog.edimburgo@mae.es.)

US: 2375 Pennsylvania Ave. NW, Washington, D.C. 20037 (☎202-728-2330; www.spainemb.org). **Consulates:** 150 E. 58th St., 30th fl., New York, NY 10155 (☎212-355-4080; cog.nuevayork@mae.es); branches in Boston, Chicago, Houston, Los Angeles, Miami, New Orleans, San Francisco, and San Juan (PR).

PORTUGUESE

Australia: 23 Culgoa Circuit, O'Malley, Canberra, ACT 2606; mailing address: P.O. Box 92, Deakin, ACT 2600 (☎612 629 017 33; www.secomunidades.pt/camberra/). **Consulate:** Level 9, 30 Clarence St., Sydney, NSW 2000; P.O. Box 3309, Sydney, NSW 2001 (☎612 9262 2199; www.consulportugalsydney.org.au).

Canada: 645 Island Park Dr., Ottawa, ON K1Y 0B8 (☎613-729-2270; www.secomunidades.pt/ottawa/). **Consulates:** 438 University Ave., Ste. 1400, Box 41, Toronto, ON M5G 2K8 (☎416-217-0966; www.cgportugaltoronto.com); 904-700 W. Pender St., Vancouver, BC V6C 3S3 (☎604-688-6514; fax 685-7042).

Ireland: Knocksinna Mews, 7 Willow Park/Westminster Park, Foxrock, Dublin 18 (☎353 289 4416; www.secomunidades.pt/dublin).

New Zealand: See Australian embassy.

UK: 3 Portland Pl., London W1B-1HR (☎020 7291 3770; www.secomunidades.pt/londres). **Consulate:** Burlington House, St. Saviours Rd., St. Helier, Jersey, C. I. JE2 4LA (☎01534 877 188); 1 Portland Street Manchester M1 3BE (☎016 1236 0990; www.secomunidades.pt/manchester)

US: 2012 Massachusetts Ave. NW, Washington, D.C. 20036 (☎202-332-3007; www.secomunidades.pt/washington). **Consulates:** 590 5th Ave., 3rd fl., New York, NY 10036 (☎212-221-3245); branches in Boston, New Bedford, New Orleans, Newark, Providence, San Francisco.

CONSULAR SERVICES IN SPAIN

Embassies and consulates are usually open Monday through Friday mornings and late afternoons, with *siestas* in between. Many consulates are only open mornings. Call ahead for exact hours.

Australia: Pl. del Descubridor Diego de Ordás, 3, Madrid 28003 (☎913 53 66 00; www.spain.embassy.gov.au). **Consulates:** Pl. Gala Placidia, 1-3, 1st fl., Barcelona 08006 (☎934 90 90 13); Federico Rubio, 14, Sevilla 41004 (☎954 22 09 71).

Canada: C. Núñez de Balboa, 35, Madrid 28001 (☎914 23 32 50; www.canada-es.org). **Consulates:** Elisenda de Pinós, 10 Barcelona 08034 (☎932 04 27 00; bcncon@sefes.es); Pl. de la Malagueta, 2, 1st fl., Málaga 29016 (☎952 22 33 46; cancon@microcad.es).

Ireland: Po. de la Castellana, 46, 4th fl., Madrid, 28046 (☎914 36 40 93; www.dfa.ie). **Consulate:** Gran Vía de Carlos III, 94, 10th fl., Barcelona 08028 (☎934 91 50 21; cons.irl@webcat.es).

New Zealand: Pinar 7, 3rd fl., Madrid 28006 (☎915 23 02 26; www.nzembassy.com). **Consulate:** Tr. de Gràcia, 64, 4th fl., Barcelona 08006 (☎932 09 03 99; fax 02 08 90).

UK: Po. de Recoletos, 7-9, 4th fl., Madrid 28004 (☎915 24 97 00; www.ukinspain.com). **Consulate-General:** Av. Diagonal, 477, 13th fl., Barcelona 08036 (☎933 66 62 00; barcelonaconsulate@fco.gov.uk). **Consulates** in Alicante, Bilbao, Ibiza, Las Palmas, Málaga, Santa Cruz de Tenerife, and Palma de Mallorca.

US: C. de Serrano, 75, Madrid 28006 (☎915 87 22 00; http://madrid.usembassy.gov). **Consulate General:** Po. Reina Elisenda de Montcada, 23, Barcelona 08034 (☎932 80 22 27; fax 80 61 75). **Consulates** in A Coruña, Las Palmas, Málaga, Palma de Mallorca, Sevilla, and Valencia.

CONSULAR SERVICES IN PORTUGAL

Australia: Embassy: Av. da Liberdade, 200, 2nd fl., 1250-147 Lisboa (☎213 10 15 00; www.portugal.embassy.gov.au).

Canada: Av. da Liberdade, 198-200, 3rd fl., 1269-121 Lisboa (☎213 16 46 00; http://geo.international.gc.ca/canada-europa/portugal/menu-en.asp). **Consulate:** R. Frei

Lourenço de Santa Maria, 1, 1st fl., Apdo. 79, 8001 Faro (☎289 80 37 57; consul.faro.canada@mail.net4b.pt).

Ireland: R. da Imprensa à Estrela, 1-4, 4th fl., Ste. 1, 1200-684 Lisboa (☎213 92 94 40; lisbon@dfa.ie).

New Zealand: Contact New Zealand embassy in Rome: Via Zara 28, Rome 00198, Italy (☎396 441 7171; www.nzembassy.com). **Consulate:** Rua do Periquito, Lote A-13, Quinta da Bicuda, Cascais 2750-712 (☎213 705 779; eduardo.cunha@santander.pt).

United Kingdom: R. de São Bernardo, 33, 1249-082 Lisboa (☎213 92 40 00; www.fco.gov.uk). **Consulates:** Largo Francisco A Mauricio, 7 1st fl., Portimao 8500-535 (☎282 49 07 50; britcon.portimao@mail.telepac.pt); Travessa Barão de Forrester, 10, Vila Nova de Gaia, Oporto 4400-034; (☎226 18 47 89; britcon.oporto@sapo.pt).

United States: Av. das Forças Armadas, 1600-081 Lisboa (☎217 27 33 00; www.american-embassy.pt).

TOURIST OFFICES

IN SPAIN

Spain's official tourist board operates an extensive website at www.tourspain.es.

Canada: Tourist Office of Spain, 2 Bloor St. West, 34th fl., Toronto, ON M4W 3E2 (☎416-961-3131; www.tourspain.toronto.on.ca).

UK: Spanish National Tourist Office, 22-23 Manchester Sq., London W1M 5AP. Mailing address: P.O. Box 4009 - W1A 6NB London (☎0207 486 8077; www.tourspain.co.uk).

US: Tourist Office of Spain, 666 5th Ave., 35th fl., New York, NY 10103 (☎212-265-8822; www.okspain.org). Additional offices in Beverly Hills, CA (☎323-658-7188), Miami, FL (☎305-358-1992), and Chicago, IL (☎312-642-1992).

IN PORTUGAL

The official Portuguese tourism website is located at www.visitportugal.com.

Canada: Portuguese Trade and Tourism Commission, 60 Bloor St. West, Ste. 1005, Toronto, ON M4W 3B8 (☎416-921-7376).

UK: Portuguese Trade and Tourism Office (ICEP), 11 Belgrave Sq., London SWIX 8PP (☎020 7201 6666; www.visitportugal.com).

US: Portuguese National Tourist Office, 590 5th Ave., 4th fl., New York, NY 10036 (☎212-354-4403; www.portugal.com).

DOCUMENTS AND FORMALITIES

PASSPORTS

REQUIREMENTS

Citizens of Australia, Canada, Ireland, New Zealand, the UK, and the US need valid passports to enter **Spain** and to re-enter their home countries. To enter Portugal citizens from EU states need only a national identity card and are not required to present a passport. Neither **Spain** nor Portugal allow entrance if the holder's passport expires in under 6 months; returning home with an expired passport is illegal and may result in a fine.

NEW PASSPORTS

Citizens of Australia, Canada, Ireland, New Zealand, the UK, and the US can apply for a passport at any passport office or at selected post offices and courts of law.

Citizens of these countries may also download passport applications from the official website of their country's government or passport office. Any new passport or renewal applications must be filed well in advance of the departure date, though most passport offices offer rush services for a very steep fee. Note, however, that "rushed" passports still take up to two weeks to arrive.

ONE EUROPE. European unity has come a long way since 1958, when the European Economic Community (EEC) was created to promote European solidarity and cooperation. Since then, the EEC has become the European Union (EU), a mighty political, legal, and economic institution. On May 1, 2004, ten South, Central, and Eastern European countries—Cyprus, the Czech Republic, Estonia, Hungary, Latvia, Lithuania, Malta, Poland, Slovakia, and Slovenia—were admitted to the EU, joining 10 other member states: Austria, Belgium, Bulgaria, Denmark, Finland, France, Germany, Greece, Ireland, Italy, Luxembourg, the Netherlands, Portugal, Romania, Spain, Sweden, and the UK.

What does this have to do with the average non-EU tourist? The EU's policy of **freedom of movement** means that border controls between the first 15 member states (minus Ireland and the UK, but plus Norway and Iceland) have been abolished, and visa policies harmonized. Under this treaty, formally known as the **Schengen Agreement,** you're still required to carry a passport (or government-issued ID card for EU citizens) when crossing an internal border, but once you've been admitted into one country, you're free to travel to other participating states. On June 5, 2005, Switzerland ratified the treaty but has yet to implement it. The 8 of the newest member states of the EU are anticipated to implement the policy in October of 2007. Britain and Ireland have also formed a **common travel area,** abolishing passport controls between the UK and the Republic of Ireland.

For more important consequences of the EU for travelers, see **The Euro** (p. 16) and **European Customs** and **EU customs regulations** (p. 15).

ESSENTIALS

PASSPORT MAINTENANCE

Photocopy the page of your passport with your photo, as well as your visas, traveler's check serial numbers, and any other important documents. Carry one set of copies in a safe place, apart from the originals, and leave another set at home. Consulates also recommend that you carry an expired passport or an official copy of your birth certificate in a part of your baggage separate from other documents.

If you lose your passport, immediately notify the local police and the nearest embassy or consulate of your home government. To expedite its replacement, you must show ID and proof of citizenship; it also helps to know all information previously recorded in the passport. In some cases, a replacement may take weeks to process, and it may be valid only for a limited time. Any visas stamped in your old passport will be irretrievably lost. In an emergency, ask for immediate temporary traveling papers that will permit you to re-enter your home country.

VISAS AND WORK PERMITS

VISAS

As of August 2007, EU citizens do not need a visa to enter Spain or Portugal. Citizens of Australia, Canada, New Zealand, and the US do not need a visa for stays of up to 90 days, though this three-month period begins upon entry into any of the countries that belong to the EU's **freedom of movement** zone. For more information, see **One Europe** (p. 13). Those staying longer than 90 days must apply for a visa in

ESSENTIALS

person at the local embassy or consulate. A visa for long-term stays in Spain costs US$100 for US citizens and US$79.20 for other nationalities. If granted, the visa will allow the holder to spend the requested period of time in Spain. Double-check entrance requirements at the nearest embassy or consulate of **Spain or Portugal** (see **Embassies and Consulates Abroad,** on p. 10) for up-to-date info before departure. US citizens can also consult http://travel.state.gov. Entering **Spain** or Portugal to study requires a special visa (see the **Beyond Tourism** chapter, p. 61).

WORK PERMITS

Admission as a visitor does not include the right to work, which is authorized only by a work permit. For more information, see the **Beyond Tourism** chapter (p. 61).

IDENTIFICATION

When you travel, always carry at least two forms of identification on your person, including a photo ID; a passport and a driver's license or birth certificate is usually an adequate combination. Never carry all of your IDs together; split them up in case of theft or loss, and keep photocopies of them in your luggage and at home.

STUDENT, TEACHER, AND YOUTH IDENTIFICATION

The **International Student Identity Card (ISIC),** the most widely accepted form of student ID, provides discounts on some sights, accommodations, food, and transportation; access to a 24hr. emergency helpline; and insurance benefits for US cardholders (see **Insurance,** p. 23). Applicants must be full-time secondary or post-secondary school students at least 12 years of age. Because of the proliferation of fake ISICs, some services (particularly airlines) require additional proof of student identity. The **International Teacher Identity Card (ITIC)** offers teachers the same insurance coverage as the ISIC and similar but limited discounts. To qualify for the card, teachers must be currently employed and have worked a minimum of 18hr. per week for at least one school year. For travelers who are under 26 years old but are not students, the **International Youth Travel Card (IYTC)** also offers many of the same benefits as the ISIC. Each of these identity cards costs US$22. ISICs, ITICs, and IYTCs are valid for one year from the date of issue. To learn more about ISICs, ITICs, and IYTCs, try www.myisic.com. Many student travel agencies (p. 26) issue the cards; for a list of issuing agencies or more information, see the **International Student Travel Confederation (ISTC)** website (www.istc.org). The **International Student Exchange Card (ISE Card)** is a similar identification card available to students, faculty, and youths aged 12 to 26. The card provides discounts, medical benefits, access to a 24hr. emergency helpline, and the ability to purchase student airfares. An ISE Card costs US$25; call ☎800-255-8000 (in North America) or ☎(480-951-1177 (from all other continents) for more info, or visit www.isecard.com.

CUSTOMS

Upon entering **Spain or Portugal**, you must declare certain items from abroad and pay a duty on the value of those articles if they exceed the allowance established by **the Spanish or Portuguese** customs service. Note that goods and gifts purchased at **duty-free** shops abroad are not exempt from duty or sales tax; "duty-free" merely means that you need not pay a tax in the country of purchase. Duty-free allowances were abolished for travel between EU member states on June 30, 1999, but still exist for those arriving from outside the EU. Upon returning home, you must declare all articles acquired abroad and pay a duty on the value of articles in excess of your home country's allowance. In order to expedite your return, make a list of any valuables brought from home and register them with customs before traveling abroad, and be sure to keep receipts for all goods acquired abroad.

CUSTOMS IN THE EU. As well as freedom of movement of people within the EU (see p. 13), travelers in the 15 original EU member countries (Austria, Belgium, Denmark, Finland, France, Germany, Greece, Ireland, Italy, Luxembourg, the Netherlands, Portugal, Spain, Sweden, and the UK) can also take advantage of the freedom of movement of goods. This means that there are no customs controls at internal EU borders (i.e., you can take the blue customs channel at the airport), and travelers are free to transport whatever legal substances they like as long as it is for their own personal (non-commercial) use—up to 800 cigarettes, 10L of spirits, 90L of wine (including up to 60L of sparkling wine), and 110L of beer. Duty-free allowances were abolished on June 30, 1999 for travel between the original 15 EU member states; this now also applies to Cyprus and Malta. However, travelers between the EU and the rest of the world still get a duty-free allowance when passing through customs.

Spain has a 7% **value added tax** (VAT; in Spain, **IVA**) on all restaurant meals and accommodations. The prices listed in *Let's Go* include VAT. Retail goods bear a 16% VAT, usually included in the listed price. Non-EU citizens who have stayed in the EU fewer than 180 days can claim a refund on the tax paid. **Taxes** are included in all prices in Portugal and are not redeemable, even for non-EU citizens. (See Taxes, p. 18)

MONEY

CURRENCY AND EXCHANGE

The currency chart below is based on August 2007 exchange rates between local currency and Australian dollars (AUS$), Canadian dollars (CDN$), European Union euro (EUR€), New Zealand dollars (NZ$), British pounds (UK£), and US dollars (US$). Check the currency converter on websites like www.xe.com or www.bloomberg.com, or a large newspaper for the latest exchange rates.

It's generally cheaper to convert money in **Spain or Portugal** than at home. While currency exchange will probably be available in your arrival airport, it's wise to bring enough foreign currency to last for the first 24 to 72 hours of your trip.

When changing money abroad, try to go only to banks or casas de cambio/ caixa de cambio that have at most a 5% margin between their buy and sell prices. Since you lose money with every transaction, **convert large sums** (unless the currency is depreciating rapidly), but **no more than you'll need.**

If you use traveler's checks or bills, carry some in small denominations (the equivalent of US$50 or less) for times when you are forced to exchange money at disadvantageous rates, but bring a range of denominations since charges may be levied per check cashed. Store your money in a variety of forms; ideally, at any given time you will be carrying some cash, some traveler's checks, and an ATM and/or credit card. All travelers should also consider carrying some US dollars (about US$50 worth), which are often preferred by local tellers.

EURO (€)		
AUS$1 = EUR€.61		EUR€1 = AUS$1.65
CDN$1 = EUR€.70		EUR€1 = CDN$1.43
NZ$1 = EUR€.51		EUR€1 = NZ$1.95
UK£1 = EUR€1.48		EUR€1 = UK£.68
US$1 = EUR€.73		EUR€1 = US$1.36

ESSENTIALS

THE EURO. The official currency of 13 members of the European Union—Austria, Belgium, Finland, France, Germany, Greece, Ireland, Italy, Luxembourg, the Netherlands, Portugal, Slovenia, and Spain—is now the euro. The currency has some important—and positive—consequences for travelers hitting more than one euro-zone country. For one thing, money-changers across the euro-zone are obliged to exchange money at the official, fixed rate (see below), and at no commission (though they may still charge a small service fee). Second, euro-denominated traveler's checks allow you to pay for goods and services across the euro-zone, again at the official rate and commission-free. At the time of printing, 1€=US$1.36=CDN$1.43=NZ$1.95=AUS$1.65=UK£0.68. For more info, check a currency converter (such as www.xe.com) or www.europa.eu.int.

TRAVELER'S CHECKS

Traveler's checks are one of the safest and least troublesome means of carrying funds. American Express and Visa are the most recognized brands. Many banks and agencies sell them for a small commission. Check issuers provide refunds if the checks are lost or stolen, and many provide additional services, such as toll-free refund hotlines abroad, emergency message services, and assistance with lost and stolen credit cards or passports. Traveler's checks are readily accepted in most part of Spain and Portugal. Ask about toll-free refund hotlines and the location of refund centers when purchasing checks, and always carry emergency cash.

American Express: Checks available with commission at select banks, at all AmEx offices, and online (www.americanexpress.com; US residents only). American Express cardholders can also purchase checks by phone (☎800-528-4800). Also offers the Travelers Cheque Card, a prepaid reloadable card. For purchase locations or more information, contact AmEx's service centers: in Australia ☎61 29 271 8666, in New Zealand 649 367 4567, in the UK 441 273 696 933, in the US and Canada 800-221-7282; elsewhere, call the US collect at 1 336 393 1111. The American Express number in Spain is 902 10 09 56, in Portugal 351 21 427 04 00.

Travelex: Visa TravelMoney prepaid cash card and Visa traveler's checks available. For information about Thomas Cook MasterCard in Canada and the US call ☎800-223-7373, in the UK 0800 622 101; elsewhere call the UK collect at +44 1733 318 950. For information about Interpayment Visa in the US and Canada call ☎800-732-1322, in the UK 0800 515 884; elsewhere call the UK collect at +44 1733 318 949. To call toll-free in Spain, dial ☎900 948971, in Portugal, ☎800 84 4095. For more information, visit www.travelex.com.

Visa: Checks available (generally with commission) at banks worldwide. For the location of the nearest office, call the Visa Travelers Cheque Global Refund and Assistance Center: in the UK ☎0800 895 078, in the US 800-227-6811; elsewhere, call the UK collect at +44 2079 378 091. Checks available in British, Canadian, European, Japanese, and US currencies, among others. Visa also offers TravelMoney, a prepaid debit card that can be reloaded online or by phone. For more information on Visa travel services, see http://usa.visa.com/personal/using_visa/travel_with_visa.html.

CREDIT, DEBIT, AND ATM CARDS

Where they are accepted, credit cards often offer superior exchange rates—up to 5% better than the retail rate used by banks and other currency exchange establishments. Credit cards may also offer services such as insurance or emergency help, and are sometimes required to reserve hotel rooms or rental cars. **MasterCard, EuroCard in Europe,** and **Visa (e.g., Carte Bleue)** are the most frequently accepted; **American Express** cards work at some ATMs and at AmEx offices and major airports. Depending on the system that your home bank uses, you can most likely access your personal bank account from abroad. ATMs get the same wholesale exchange rate as credit cards, but there is often a limit on the amount of money you can withdraw per day (usually around US$500). There is typically also a surcharge of US$1-5 per withdrawal.

The two major international money networks are **MasterCard/Maestro/Cirrus** (for ATM locations ☎800-424-7787 or www.mastercard.com) and **Visa/PLUS** (for ATM locations ☎800-847-2911 or www.visa.com). Most ATMs charge a transaction fee that is paid to the bank that owns the ATM.

> **PINS AND ATMS.** To use a cash or credit card to withdraw money from a cash machine (ATM) in Europe, you must have a four-digit **Personal Identification Number (PIN).** If your PIN is longer than four digits, ask your bank whether you can just use the first four, or whether you'll need a new one. **Credit cards** don't usually come with PINs, so if you intend to hit up ATMs in Europe with a credit card to get cash advances, call your credit card company before leaving to request one.
> PINs may also be thrown off by the lack of letters on European cash machines. The following are the corresponding numbers: 1=QZ; 2=ABC; 3=DEF; 4=GHI; 5=JKL; 6=MNO; 7=PRS; 8=TUV; and 9=WXY. Note that if you mistakenly punch the wrong code into the machine three times, it will swallow your card for good.

GETTING MONEY FROM HOME

If you run out of money while traveling, the easiest and cheapest solution is to have someone back home make a deposit to your bank account. Failing that, consider one of the following options. **Banking hours** in Spain from June through September are generally M-F 9am-2pm; some banks may extend their hours once a week or open on Saturday 9am-1pm. Official banking hours in Portugal are Monday through Friday 8:30am to 3pm.

WIRING MONEY

It is possible to arrange a **bank money transfer,** which means asking a bank back home to wire money to a bank in **Spain or Portugal**. This is the cheapest way to transfer cash, but it's usually takes several days or more. Note that some banks may only release your funds in local currency, potentially sticking you with a poor exchange rate; inquire about this in advance. Money transfer services like **Western Union** are faster and more convenient than bank transfers—but also much pricier. Western Union has many locations worldwide. To find one, visit www.westernunion.com, or call in Australia ☎1800 173 833, in Canada and the US 800-325-6000, in the UK 0800 833 833, in Spain 902 19 91 21 or in **Portugal 213 93 74 62**. To wire money using a credit card (Discover, MasterCard, Visa), call in Canada and the US ☎800-CALL-CASH, in the UK 0800 833 833. Money transfer services are also available to **American Express** cardholders and at selected **Thomas Cook** offices.

US STATE DEPARTMENT (US CITIZENS ONLY)

In serious emergencies only, the US State Department will forward money within hours to the nearest consular office, which will then disburse it according to instructions for a US$30 fee. If you wish to use this service, you must contact the Overseas Citizens Service division of the US State Department (☎202-647-5225, toll-free 888-407-4747).

COSTS

STAYING ON A BUDGET

A bare-bones day in Spain or Portugal (camping or sleeping in hostels/guesthouses, buying food at supermarkets) would cost about €$30 (US$42); a slightly more comfortable day (sleeping in hostels/guesthouses and the occasional budget hotel, eating one meal per day at a restaurant, going out at night) would cost €$50 (US$70); and for a luxurious day, the sky's the limit. Don't forget to factor in emergency reserve funds (at least US$200) when planning how much money you'll need.

TIPS FOR SAVING MONEY

Some simpler ways include searching out opportunities for free entertainment, splitting accommodation and food costs with trustworthy fellow travelers, and buying food in supermarkets rather than eating out. Bring a **sleepsack** (p. 19) to save on sheet charges in European hostels, and do your **laundry** in the sink. Museums often have certain days once a month or once a week when admission is free; plan accordingly. If you are eligible, consider getting an ISIC or an IYTC (p. 14); many sights and museums offer reduced admission to students and youths. For getting around quickly, bikes are the most economical option. Renting a bike is cheaper than renting a moped or scooter. Drinking at bars and clubs quickly becomes expensive. It's cheaper to buy alcohol at a supermarket before going out.

TIPPING AND BARGAINING

IN SPAIN

Tipping is not very widespread in Spain or Portugal. In restaurants, all prices include a service charge. Satisfied customers occasionally toss in some spare change—usually no more than 5%—and while it is purely optional, tipping is becoming customary in restaurants and other places that cater to tourists. Many people give train, airport, and hotel porters €1 per bag while taxi drivers sometimes get 5-10%. **Bargaining** is common at flea markets and with street vendors.

IN PORTUGAL

Tips are customary in fancy restaurants or hotels. Cheaper restaurants include a 10% service charge; if they don't and you'd like to leave a tip, round up and leave the change. Taxi drivers do not expect a tip unless the trip was especially long. **Bargaining** is not customary in shops, but give it a shot at the local *mercado* (market) or when looking for a private room.

TAXES

Both Spain and Portugal have a 7-8% **Value Added Tax,** known as IVA, on all meals and accommodations. The prices listed in *Let's Go* include IVA unless otherwise mentioned. Retail goods bear a much higher 16% IVA, although listed prices are usually inclusive. Non-EU citizens who have stayed in the EU fewer than 180 days can claim back the tax paid on purchases at the airport. Ask the shop where you have made the purchase to supply you with a tax return form, though stores will often provide them only for purchases of more than €50-100. **Taxes** are included in all prices in Portugal and are not redeemable, even for non-EU citizens.

PACKING

Pack lightly: Lay out only what you absolutely need, then take half the clothes and twice the money. The Travelite FAQ (www.travelite.org) is a good resource for tips on traveling light. The online **Universal Packing List** (http://upl.codeq.info) will generate a customized list of suggested items based on your trip length, the expected climate, your planned activities, and other factors. If you plan to do a lot of hiking, also consult **The Great Outdoors,** p. 49. Some frequent travelers keep a bag packed with all the essentials: passport, money belt, hat, socks, etc. Then, when they decide to leave, they know they haven't forgotten anything.

Luggage: If you plan to cover most of your itinerary by foot, a sturdy **frame backpack** is unbeatable. (For the basics on buying a pack, see p. 52.) Toting a **suitcase** or **trunk** is not a great idea if you plan to move around frequently. In addition to your main piece of luggage, a **daypack** (a small backpack or courier bag) is useful.

Clothing: No matter when you're traveling, it's a good idea to bring a warm jacket or wool sweater, a rain jacket (Gore-Tex® is both waterproof and breathable), sturdy shoes or hiking boots, and thick socks. A rain jacket will be important in misty Galicia and northern Portugal, and you'll want more breathable, cotton or linen clothing in Andalucía, Costa del Sol, and the Islas Baleares and Canarias. Flip-flops or waterproof sandals are must-haves for grubby hostel showers, and extra socks are always a good idea. You may also want one outfit for going out, and maybe a nicer pair of shoes. If you plan to visit religious or cultural sites, remember that you will need modest and respectful dress.

Sleepsack: Some hostels require that you either provide your own linen or rent sheets from them. Save cash by making your own sleepsack: fold a full-size sheet in half the long way, then sew it closed along the long side and one of the short sides.

Converters and Adapters: In Spain and Portugal, electricity is 230 volts AC, enough to fry any 120V North American appliance. 220/240V electrical appliances won't work with a 120V current, either. Americans and Canadians should buy an adapter (which changes the shape of the plug; US$5) and a converter (which changes the voltage; US$10-30). Don't make the mistake of using only an adapter (unless appliance instructions explicitly state otherwise). Australians and New Zealanders (who use 230V at home) won't need a converter, but will need a set of adapters to use anything electrical. For more on all things adaptable, check out http://kropla.com/electric.htm.

Toiletries: Condoms, deodorant, razors, tampons, and toothbrushes are often available, but it may be difficult to find your preferred brand; bring extras.

First-Aid Kit: For a basic first-aid kit, pack bandages, a pain reliever, antibiotic cream, a thermometer, a multifunction pocketknife, tweezers, moleskin, decongestant, motion-sickness remedy, diarrhea or upset-stomach medication (Pepto Bismol® or Imodium®), an antihistamine, sunscreen, insect repellent, and burn ointment.

Film: Film and developing in Spain and Portugal are expensive, so consider bringing along enough film for your entire trip and developing it at home. If you don't want to bother with film, consider using a digital camera. Despite disclaimers, airport security X-rays can fog film, so buy a lead-lined pouch at a camera store or ask security to hand-inspect it. Always pack film in your carry-on luggage, since higher-intensity X-rays are used on checked luggage.

Other Useful Items: For safety purposes, you should bring a **money belt** and a small **padlock.** Basic **outdoors equipment** (plastic water bottle, compass, waterproof matches, pocketknife, sunglasses, sunscreen, hat) may also prove useful. **Quick repairs** of torn garments can be done on the road with a needle and thread; also consider bringing electrical tape for patching tears. If you want to do laundry by hand, bring detergent, a small rubber ball to stop up the sink, and string for a makeshift clothes line. Other things you're liable to forget include: an umbrella, sealable **plastic bags** (for damp clothes, soap, food, shampoo, and other spillables), an **alarm clock,** safety pins, rubber bands, a flashlight, earplugs, garbage bags, and a small calculator. A **cell phone** can be a lifesaver (literally) on the road; see p. 40 for information on acquiring one that will work in Spain or Portugal.

Important Documents: Don't forget your passport, traveler's checks, ATM and/or credit cards, adequate ID, and photocopies of all of the aforementioned in case these documents are lost or stolen (p. 12). Also check that you have any of the following that might apply to you: a hosteling membership card (p. 14); driver's license (p. 38); travel insurance forms (p. 23); ISIC (p. 14), and/or rail or bus pass (p. 32).

SAFETY AND HEALTH

GENERAL ADVICE

In any type of crisis situation, the most important thing to do is **stay calm.** Your country's embassy abroad (p. 11) is usually your best resource when things go wrong; registering with that embassy upon arrival in the country is often a good idea. The government offices listed in the **Travel Advisories** box (p. 21) can provide information on the services they offer their citizens in case of emergencies abroad.

LOCAL LAWS AND POLICE

Travelers are not likely to break major laws unintentionally while visiting Spain or Portugal. You can contact your embassy if arrested, although they often cannot do much to assist you beyond finding you legal counsel. You should feel comfortable approaching the police, although few officers speak English. There are three types of police in Spain. The **Policía Nacional** wear blue or black uniforms and white shirts; they deal with crime investigation (including theft), guard government buildings, and protect dignitaries. The **Policía Local** wear blue uniforms, deal with more local issues, and report to the mayor or town hall in each municipality. The **Guardia Civil** wear olive green uniforms and are responsible for issues more relevant to travelers: customs, crowd control, and national security. The *Polícia de Segurança Pública* is the police force in all major Portuguese cities and towns. The *Guarda Nacional Republicana* polices more rural areas, and the *Brigada de Trânsito* is the traffic police, recognizable by their red armbands. All three branches wear light blue uniforms. In **Spain**, contact the **local police** (☎ 092), **national police** (☎ 091), or the **Guardia Civil** (☎ 062) in an emergency.

DRUGS AND ALCOHOL

Recreational drugs are illegal in Spain and Portugal, and police take these laws seriously. The legal minimum drinking age in Spain and Portugal is 16 years old. Spain and Portugal have the highest road mortality rates in Europe, further incentive to refrain from driving while intoxicated and be cautious on the road.

SPECIFIC CONCERNS

TERRORISM

While terrorism is rarely an issue in Portugal, Spain has experienced more than its fair share of troubles in recent years. **Basque terrorism** concerns all travelers in Spain, specifically, the movement's militant wing, the Euskadi Ta Askatasuna (ETA; Basque Homeland and Freedom). March 2006, ETA declared a permanent cease-fire that officially ended in June 2007. ETA's attacks are typically targeted and are not considered random acts of terrorism. The March 11, 2004 train bombings in Madrid have been linked to **al-Qaeda.** In (See **Current Events,** p. 79, for more information.) The box on **travel advisories** lists contacts and websites to visit to get the most updated list of your home country's government's travel advisories.

PERSONAL SAFETY

EXPLORING AND TRAVELING

To avoid unwanted attention, try to blend in as much as possible. Respecting local customs (in many cases, dressing more conservatively than you would at home)

TRAVEL ADVISORIES. The following government offices provide travel information and advisories by telephone, by fax, or via the web:

Australian Department of Foreign Affairs and Trade: ☎612 6261 1111; www.dfat.gov.au.

Canadian Department of Foreign Affairs and International Trade (DFAIT): Call ☎800-267-8376; www.dfait-maeci.gc.ca. Call for their free booklet, *Bon Voyage...But.*

New Zealand Ministry of Foreign Affairs: ☎044 398 000; www.mfat.govt.nz.

United Kingdom Foreign and Commonwealth Office: ☎020 7008 1500; www.fco.gov.uk.

US Department of State: ☎888-407-4747; http://travel.state.gov. Visit the website for the booklet *A Safe Trip Abroad.*

may placate would-be hecklers. Familiarize yourself with your surroundings before setting out, and carry yourself with confidence. Check maps in shops and restaurants rather than on the street. If you are traveling alone, be sure someone at home knows your itinerary, and never tell anyone you meet that you're by yourself. When walking at night, stick to busy, well-lit streets and avoid dark alleyways. If you ever feel uncomfortable, leave the area as quickly and directly as you can.

There is no sure-fire way to avoid all the threatening situations you might encounter while traveling, but a good **self-defense course** will give you concrete ways to react to unwanted advances. Impact, Prepare, and Model Mugging can refer you to local self-defense courses in Australia, Canada, Switzerland and the US. Visit the website at www.modelmugging.org for a list of nearby chapters.

If you are using a **car,** learn local driving signals and wear a seatbelt. Children under 40 lbs. should ride only in specially designed car seats, available for a small fee from most car rental agencies. Study route maps before you hit the road, and if you plan on spending a lot of time driving, consider bringing spare parts. For long drives in desolate areas, invest in a cellular phone and a roadside assistance program (see p. 38). Park your vehicle in a garage or well-traveled area, and use a steering wheel locking device in larger cities. **Sleeping in your car** is the most dangerous way to get your rest, and it's also illegal in many countries. For info on the perils of **hitchhiking,** see p. 39.

POSSESSIONS AND VALUABLES

Never leave your belongings unattended; crime occurs in even the most safe-looking hostel or hotel. Bring your own padlock for hostel lockers, and don't ever store valuables in a locker. Be particularly careful on **buses** and **trains;** horror stories abound about determined thieves who wait for travelers to fall asleep. Carry your bag or purse in front of you where you can see it. When traveling with others, sleep in alternate shifts. When alone, use good judgment in selecting a train compartment: never stay in an empty one, and use a lock to secure your pack to the luggage rack. Use extra caution if traveling at night or on overnight trains. Try to sleep on top bunks with your luggage stored above you (if not in bed with you), and keep important documents and other valuables on you at all times.

There are a few steps you can take to minimize the financial risk associated with traveling. First, **bring as little with you as possible.** Second, buy a few combination **padlocks** to secure your belongings either in your pack or in a hostel or train station locker. Third, **carry as little cash as possible.** Keep your traveler's checks and ATM/credit cards in a **money belt**—not a "fanny pack"—along with your passport and ID cards. Fourth, **keep a small cash reserve separate from your primary stash.** This should be about US$50 (US$ or euros are best) sewn into or stored in the depths of your pack, along with your traveler's check numbers and photocopies of your passport, your birth certificate, and other important documents.

In large cities like Madrid, Barcelona, and Lisbon, **con artists** often work in groups and may involve children. Beware of certain classics: sob stories that require money, rolls of bills "found" on the street, mustard spilled (or saliva spit) onto your shoulder to distract you while they snatch your bag. **Never let your passport and your bags out of your sight.** Hostel workers will sometimes stand at bus and train station arrival points to try to recruit tired and disoriented travelers to their hostel; never believe strangers who tell you that theirs is the only hostel open. Beware of **pickpockets** in city crowds, especially on public transportation. Also, be alert in public telephone booths: If you must say your calling card number, do so very quietly; if you punch it in, make sure no one can look over your shoulder.

If you will be traveling with electronic devices, such as a laptop computer or a PDA, check whether your homeowner's insurance covers loss, theft, or damage when you travel. If not, you might consider purchasing a low-cost separate insurance policy. **Safeware** (☎ 800-800-1492; www.safeware.com) specializes in covering computers and charges $90 for 90-day comprehensive international travel coverage up to $4000.

IN SPAIN

Spain has a low crime rate, but visitors can always fall victim to tourist-related crimes. Tourists should take particular care in Madrid, especially in El Centro, and in Barcelona around Las Ramblas. If visiting the Costa del Sol in a car, be aware of the fact that this area has seen increased **car theft** in recent years. If you happen to experience car problems, be wary of people posing as "Good Samaritans." Drivers should be extremely careful about accepting help from anyone other than a uniformed Spanish police officer or *Guardia Civil* (Civil Guard). Travelers who accept unofficial assistance should keep their valuables at hand. For those travelers using public transportation, it is essential to be aware at all times of your belongings and those around you.

IN PORTUGAL

In Portugal, the highest rates of crime have been in the Lisboa area, especially on buses, in train stations, and in airports. Exercise the most caution in the Alfama district, the Santa Apolonia and Rossio train stations, Castelo de São Jorge, and in Belém. The towns around Lisboa with the most reported crimes in recent years are Cascais, Fátima, and Sintra. Thieves often try to distract people by staging loud arguments, passing a soccer ball back and forth on a crowded street, asking for directions, pretending to dance with their victim, or spilling something on their victim's clothing. Motorists should be wary of "Good Samaritans" who have been known to help ailing motorists by the side of the road and then steal their cars.

PRE-DEPARTURE HEALTH

In your **passport,** write the names of any people you wish to be contacted in case of a medical emergency, and list any allergies or medical conditions. Matching a prescription to a foreign equivalent is not always easy, safe, or possible, so if you take prescription drugs, consider carrying up-to-date prescriptions or a statement from your doctor stating the medication's trade name, manufacturer, chemical name, and dosage. While traveling, be sure to keep all medication with you in your carry-on luggage. For tips on packing a **first-aid kit** and other health essentials, see p. 19.

Spanish and Portuguese names for common drugs are quite similar to their English names (*aspirina, ibuprofen, acetaminofén*), and brand names are generally recognizable in both countries.

IMMUNIZATIONS AND PRECAUTIONS

Travelers over two years old should make sure that the following vaccines are up to date: MMR (for measles, mumps, and rubella); DTaP or Td (for diphtheria, tetanus, and pertussis); IPV (for polio); Hib (for *Haemophilus influenzae* B); and HepB (for Hepatitis B). For recommendations on immunizations and prophylaxis, consult the Centers for Disease Control and Prevention (CDC; see below) in the US or the equivalent in your home country, and check with a doctor for guidance.

USEFUL ORGANIZATIONS AND PUBLICATIONS

The American **Centers for Disease Control and Prevention (CDC;** ☎ 877-FYI-TRIP; www.cdc.gov/travel) maintain an international travelers' hotline and an informative website. Consult the appropriate government agency of your home country for consular information sheets on health, entry requirements, and other issues for various countries (see the listings in the box on **Travel Advisories,** p. 21). For quick information on health and other travel warnings, call the **Overseas Citizens Services** (M-F 8am-8pm from US ☎ 888-407-4747, from overseas 202-501-4444), or contact a passport agency, embassy, or consulate abroad. For information on medical evacuation services and travel insurance firms, see the US government's website at http://travel.state.gov/travel/abroad_health.html or the **British Foreign and Commonwealth Office** (www.fco.gov.uk). For general health information, contact the **American Red Cross** (☎ 202-303-4498; www.redcross.org).

STAYING HEALTHY

Common sense is the simplest prescription for good health while you travel. Drink lots of fluids to prevent dehydration and constipation, and wear sturdy, broken-in shoes and clean socks.

ONCE IN SPAIN OR PORTUGAL

ENVIRONMENTAL HAZARDS

Heat exhaustion and dehydration: Summer temperatures in southern and central Spain can reach a scorching 36°C/97°F. Heat exhaustion leads to nausea, excessive thirst, headaches, and dizziness. Avoid it by drinking plenty of fluids, eating salty foods (e.g., crackers), abstaining from dehydrating beverages (e.g., alcohol and caffeinated beverages), and wearing sunscreen. Continuous heat stress can eventually lead to heatstroke, characterized by a rising temperature, severe headache, delirium and cessation of sweating. Victims should be cooled off with wet towels and taken to a doctor.

Sunburn: Always wear sunscreen (SPF 30 or higher) when spending excessive amounts of time outdoors. If you get sunburned, drink more fluids than usual and apply an aloe-based lotion. Severe sunburns can lead to sun poisoning, a condition that can cause fever, chills, nausea, and vomiting. Sun poisoning should always be treated by a doctor.

Hypothermia and frostbite: A rapid drop in body temperature is the clearest sign of overexposure to cold. Victims may also shiver, feel exhausted, have poor coordination or slurred speech, hallucinate, or suffer amnesia. *Do not let hypothermia victims fall asleep.* To avoid hypothermia, keep dry, wear layers, and stay out of the wind. When the temperature is below freezing, watch out for frostbite. If skin turns white or blue, waxy, and cold, do not rub the area. Drink warm beverages, stay dry, and slowly warm the area with dry fabric or steady body contact until a doctor can be found.

High Altitude: Allow your body a couple of days to adjust to less oxygen before exerting yourself. Note that alcohol is more potent and UV rays are stronger at high elevations. You'll want to be careful in parts of the Pyrenees, the Picos de Europa, the Sierra

Nevada, on Spain's tallest peak, El Teide, on Tenerife in Las Islas Canarias, or in Spain and Portugal's other high-altitude areas.

INSECT-BORNE DISEASES

Many diseases are transmitted by insects—mainly mosquitoes, fleas, ticks, and lice. Be aware of insects in wet or forested areas, especially while hiking and camping; wear long pants and long sleeves, tuck your pants into your socks, and use a mosquito net. Use insect repellents such as DEET and soak or spray your gear with permethrin (licensed in the US only for use on clothing). **Ticks**— which can carry Lyme and other diseases—can be particularly dangerous in rural and forested regions of Spain and Portugal.

Lyme disease: A bacterial infection carried by ticks and marked by a circular bull's-eye rash of 2 in. or more. Later symptoms include fever, headache, fatigue, and aches and pains. Antibiotics are effective if administered early. Left untreated, Lyme can cause problems in joints, the heart, and the nervous system. If you find a tick attached to your skin, grasp the head with tweezers as close to your skin as possible and apply slow, steady traction. Removing a tick within 24hr. greatly reduces the risk of infection. Do not try to remove ticks with petroleum jelly, nail polish remover, or a hot match. Ticks usually inhabit moist, shaded environments and heavily wooded areas. If you are going to be hiking in these areas, wear long clothes and DEET.

FOOD- AND WATER-BORNE DISEASES

Prevention is the best cure: be sure that your food is properly cooked and the water you drink is clean. Watch out for food from markets or street vendors that may have been cooked in unhygienic conditions. Other culprits are raw shellfish, unpasteurized milk, and sauces containing raw eggs. *Salmonella* bacteria, transmitted by raw eggs and egg shells, has been a prevalent problem in Spain in the past decade.

Traveler's diarrhea: Results from drinking fecally contaminated water or eating uncooked and contaminated foods. Symptoms include nausea, bloating, and urgency. Try quick-energy, non-sugary foods with protein and carbohydrates to keep your strength up. Over-the-counter anti-diarrheals (e.g., Imodium) may counteract the problem. The most dangerous side effect is dehydration; drink 8 oz. of water with ½ tsp. of sugar or honey and a pinch of salt, try uncaffeinated soft drinks, or eat salted crackers. If you develop a fever or your symptoms don't go away after 4-5 days, consult a doctor. Consult a doctor immediately for treatment of diarrhea in children.

Giardiasis: Transmitted through parasites and acquired by drinking untreated water from streams or lakes. Symptoms include diarrhea, cramps, bloating, fatigue, weight loss, and nausea. If untreated, it can lead to severe dehydration. Giardiasis occurs worldwide.

OTHER INFECTIOUS DISEASES

The following diseases exist in every part of the world. Travelers should know how to recognize them and what to do if they suspect they have been infected.

Rabies: Transmitted through the saliva of infected animals; fatal if untreated. By the time symptoms (thirst and muscle spasms) appear, the disease is in its terminal stage. If you are bitten, wash the wound, seek immediate medical care, and try to have the animal located. A rabies vaccine, which consists of 3 shots given over a 21-day period, is available and recommended for developing world travel, but is only semi-effective.

Hepatitis B: A viral infection of the liver transmitted via blood or other bodily fluids. Symptoms, which may not surface until years after infection, include jaundice, appetite loss, fever, and joint pain. It is transmitted through unprotected sex and unclean needles. A 3-shot vaccination sequence is recommended for sexually-active travelers and anyone planning to seek medical treatment abroad; it must begin 6 months before traveling.

Hepatitis C: Like Hepatitis B, but differs in the mode of transmission. IV drug users, those with occupational exposure to blood, hemodialysis patients, and blood transfusion recipients blood transfusions are at highest risk, but the disease can also be spread through sexual contact or sharing items like razors and toothbrushes that may have traces of blood on them. No symptoms are usually exhibited. Hepatitis C can lead to liver failure if untreated.

AIDS and HIV: For detailed information on Acquired Immune Deficiency Syndrome (AIDS) in Spain and Portugal, call the 24hr. National AIDS Hotline at ☎800-342-2437.

Sexually transmitted infections (STIs): Gonorrhea, chlamydia, genital warts, syphilis, herpes, HPV, and other STIs are easier to catch than HIV and can be just as serious. Though condoms may protect you from some STIs, oral or even tactile contact can lead to transmission. If you think you may have contracted an STI, see a doctor immediately.

OTHER HEALTH CONCERNS

MEDICAL CARE ON THE ROAD

The public health care system in **Spain** is very reliable; in an emergency, seek out the *urgencias* (emergency) section of the nearest hospital. For smaller concerns, it is best to go to a private clinic to avoid the frustration of long lines. Expect to pay cash up front (though most travel insurance will pick up the tab later; request a receipt) and bring your passport and other forms of identification. A visit to a clinic in Spain can cost anywhere from €70-180, depending on the service. Visit the following site for the most recent updates on travel-related health concerns in Spain: www.mdtravelhealth.com/destinations/europe/spain.html. *'Farmacias* in Spain are also very helpful. A duty system has been set up so that at least one *farmacia* is open at all times in each town; look for a flashing green cross. Spanish pharmacies are not the place to find your cheap summer flip-flops or greeting cards, but they sell contraceptives, common drugs, and many prescription drugs; they can answer simple medical questions and help you find a doctor.

Portugal poses no particular health risks to travelers. The public health system is quite good, and many doctors speak English. A private clinic may be worth the money for convenience and quick service; most travel insurance providers will cover the tab. Portuguese *farmacias* offer basic drugs and advice and are easy to find in most towns.

If you are concerned about obtaining medical assistance while traveling, you may wish to employ special support services. The *MedPass* from **GlobalCare, Inc.,** 6875 Shiloh Rd. East, Alpharetta, GA 30005, USA (☎800-860-1111; www.global-care.net), provides 24hr. international medical assistance, support, and medical evacuation resources. The **International Association for Medical Assistance to Travelers (IAMAT;** US ☎716-754-4883, Canada 519-836-0102; www.iamat.org) has free membership, lists English-speaking doctors worldwide, and offers detailed info on immunization requirements and sanitation. If your regular **insurance** policy does not cover travel abroad, you may wish to purchase additional coverage (see p. 23).

Those with medical conditions (such as diabetes, allergies to antibiotics, epilepsy, or heart conditions) may want to obtain a **MedicAlert** membership (US$40 per year), which includes among other things a stainless steel ID tag and a 24hr. collect-call number. Contact the MedicAlert Foundation International, 2323 Colorado Ave., Turlock, CA 95382, USA (☎888-633-4298, outside US 209-668-3333; www.medicalert.org).

WOMEN'S HEALTH

Women traveling in unsanitary conditions are vulnerable to **urinary tract (including bladder and kidney) infections.** Over-the-counter medicines can sometimes alleviate symptoms, but if they persist, see a doctor. **Vaginal yeast infections** may flare up in hot and humid climates. Wearing loosely fitting trousers or a skirt and cotton underwear will help, as will over-the-counter remedies like Monistat or Gynelotrimin. Bring supplies from home if you are prone to infection, as they may be difficult to find on the road. Tampons, pads, and contraceptive devices are widely available, though your favorite brand may not be stocked—bring extras of anything you can't live without. **Abortion** is illegal in Spain and Portugal, except in the first trimester for health reasons or in the case of rape.

GETTING TO SPAIN OR PORTUGAL

BY PLANE

When it comes to airfare, a little effort can save you a bundle. Courier fares are the cheapest for those whose plans are flexible enough to deal with the restrictions. Tickets sold by consolidators and standby seating are also good deals, but last-minute specials, airfare wars, and charter flights often beat these fares. The key is to hunt around, be flexible, and ask about discounts. Students, seniors, and those under 26 should never pay full price for a ticket.

AIRFARES

Airfares to Spain and Portugal peak between mid-June and early September; holidays are also expensive. The cheapest times to travel are between December and February. Midweek (M-Th morning) round-trip flights run US$40-50 cheaper than weekend flights, but they are generally more crowded and less likely to permit frequent-flier upgrades. Not fixing a return date ("open return") or arriving in and departing from different cities ("open-jaw") can be pricier than round-trip flights. Patching one-way flights together is the most expensive way to travel. Flights between Spain and Portugal's capitals or regional hubs—Madrid, Barcelona, and Lisbon—will tend to be cheaper.

If Spain or Portugal is only one stop on a more extensive globe-hop, consider a round-the-world (RTW) ticket. Tickets usually include at least five stops and are valid for about a year; prices range US$1200-5000. Try **Northwest Airlines/KLM** (☎ 800-225-2525; www.nwa.com) or **Star Alliance,** a consortium of 16 airlines including United Airlines (www.staralliance.com).

Fares for roundtrip flights to Madrid, Barcelona, and Lisbon from the US or Canadian east coast cost US$900-1100, US$500-700 in the low season (December to February, excluding Christmas; from the US or Canadian west coast US$1000-1400/US$700-900; from the UK £150-200/UK£80-150; from Australia AUS$2800-3000/AUS$2500-2800; from New Zealand NZ$5200-6000/NZ$4800-5000.

BUDGET AND STUDENT TRAVEL AGENCIES

While knowledgeable agents specializing in flights to Spain and Portugal can make your life easy and help you save, they may not spend the time to find you the lowest possible fare—they get paid on commission. Travelers holding **ISICs** and **IYTCs** (see p. 14) qualify for big discounts from student travel agencies. Most flights from budget agencies are on major airlines, but in peak season some may sell seats on less reliable chartered aircraft.

STA Travel, 5900 Wilshire Blvd., Ste. 900, Los Angeles, CA 90036, USA (24hr. reservations and info ☎800-781-4040; www.statravel.com). A student and youth travel organization with over 150 offices worldwide (check their website for a listing of all their offices), including US offices in Boston, Chicago, Los Angeles, New York, Seattle, San Francisco, and Washington, D.C. Ticket booking, travel insurance, rail passes, and more. Walk-in offices are located throughout Australia (☎03 9207 5900), New Zealand (☎09 309 9723), and the UK (☎08701 630 026).

Travel CUTS (Canadian Universities Travel Services Limited), 187 College St., Toronto, ON M5T 1P7, Canada (☎888-592-2887; www.travelcuts.com). Offices across Canada and the US including Los Angeles, New York, Seattle, and San Francisco.

USIT, 19-21 Aston Quay, Dublin 2, Ireland (☎01 602 1904; www.usit.ie), Ireland's leading student/budget travel agency has 20 offices throughout Northern Ireland and the Republic of Ireland. Offers programs to work, study, and volunteer worldwide.

Wasteels, Skoubogade 6, 1158 Copenhagen K., Denmark (☎3314 4633; www.wasteels.com). A huge chain with 180 locations across Europe. Sells Wasteels BIJ tickets discounted 30-45% off regular fare, 2nd-class international point-to-point train tickets with unlimited stopovers for those under 26 (sold only in Europe).

FLIGHT PLANNING ON THE INTERNET. The Internet may be the budget traveler's dream when it comes to finding and booking bargain fares, but the array of options can be overwhelming. Many airline sites offer special last-minute deals on the Web. Iberia Airlines (www.iberia.com) serves the entire peninsula, as well as other international destinations.

STA (www.statravel.com) and **StudentUniverse** (www.studentuniverse.com) provide quotes on student tickets, while **Orbitz** (www.orbitz.com), **Expedia** (www.expedia.com), and **Travelocity** (www.travelocity.com) offer full travel services, as does Opodo (www.opodo.com), a foreign equivalent. **Priceline** (www.priceline.com) lets you specify a price, and obligates you to buy any ticket that meets or beats it; **Hotwire** (www.hotwire.com) offers bargain fares, but won't reveal the airline or flight times until you buy. Other sites that compile deals include www.bestfares.com, www.flights.com, www.lowestfare.com, www.onetravel.com, and www.travelzoo.com.

SideStep (www.sidestep.com) and **Booking Buddy** (www.bookingbuddy.com) are online tools that can help sift through multiple offers; these two let you enter your trip information once and search multiple sites.

Air Traveler's Handbook (www.faqs.org/faqs/travel/air/handbook) is an indispensable resource on the Internet; it has a comprehensive listing of links to everything you need to know before you board a plane.

COMMERCIAL AIRLINES

The commercial airlines' lowest regular offer is the **APEX** (Advance Purchase Excursion) fare, which provides confirmed reservations and allows "open-jaw" tickets. Generally, reservations must be made seven to 21 days ahead of departure, with seven- to 14-day minimum-stay and up to 90-day maximum-stay restrictions. These fares carry hefty cancellation and change penalties (fees rise in summer). Book peak-season APEX fares early. Use **Expedia** (www.expedia.com) or **Travelocity** (www.travelocity.com) to get an idea of the lowest published fares, then use the resources outlined here to try to beat those fares. Low-season fares should be appreciably cheaper than the high-season (mid-June to Aug.) ones listed here.

TRAVELING FROM NORTH AMERICA

Basic round-trip fares to Spain and Portugal range from roughly US$450-1000: to Barcelona, US$500-1000; to Lisboa, US$550-900; to Madrid, US$500-900; to Málaga, US$450-900. Standard commercial carriers like **American** (☎800-433-7300; www.aa.com), **United** (☎800-538-2929; www.ual.com), and **Northwest** (☎800-447-4747; www.nwa.com) will probably offer the most convenient flights, but they may not be the cheapest. Check **Lufthansa** (☎800-399-5838; www.lufthansa.com), **British Airways** (☎800-247-9297; www.britishairways.com), **Air France** (☎800-237-2747; www.airfrance.us), and **Alitalia** (☎800-223-5730; www.alitaliausa.com) for cheap tickets from destinations throughout the US to all over Europe. You might find an even better deal on one of the following airlines, if any of their limited departure points is convenient for you.

Finnair: (☎800-950-5000; www.finnair.com). Cheap round-trips from San Francisco, New York, and Toronto to Helsinki; connections throughout Europe.

Spanair: (Spain ☎902 13 14 15; www.spanair.com). Flies out of New York, Boston, Houston, Los Angeles, Philadelphia, and other North American gateways to various cities in Spain and Portugal.

TRAVELING FROM IRELAND AND THE UK

Because of the many carriers flying from the British Isles to the continent, we only include discount airlines or those with cheap specials here. The **Air Travel Advisory Bureau** in London (☎870 737 0021; www.atab.co.uk) provides referrals to travel agencies and consolidators that offer discounted airfares out of the UK. **Cheapflights** (www.cheapflights.co.uk) publishes airfare bargains.

Aer Lingus, Ireland (☎0818 365 000; www.aerlingus.ie). Return tickets from Dublin, Cork, Galway, Kerry, and Shannon to Madrid, Barcelona, Málaga, and the Canarias (EUR€50-244).

bmibaby, UK (☎08702 642 229; www.bmibaby.com). Departures from throughout the UK. London to Alicante (UK£104).

easyJet, UK (☎08712 442 366; www.easyjet.com). London to Barcelona, Madrid, Lisbon, the Canarias, and other Iberian destinations. London to Madrid (UK£13-35).

KLM, UK (☎08705 074 074; www.klmuk.com). Cheap return tickets from London and elsewhere to many destinations in Spain and Portugal, including Madrid, Barcelona, Lisboa, and Porto.

Ryanair, Ireland (☎0818 303 030, UK 08712 460 000; www.ryanair.com). From Dublin, Glasgow, Liverpool, London, and Shannon to Madrid, Barcelona, and Porto.

TRAVELING FROM AUSTRALIA AND NEW ZEALAND

Singapore Air, Australia (☎13 10 11), New Zealand (☎0800 808 909; www.singaporeair.com). Flies from Auckland, Christchurch, Melbourne, Perth, and Sydney to Barcelona.

Thai Airways, Australia (☎1300 65 19 60), New Zealand (☎09 377 38 86; www.thaiair.com). Auckland, Melbourne, Perth, and Sydney to Madrid.

AIR COURIER FLIGHTS

Those who travel light should consider courier flights. Couriers help transport cargo on international flights by using their checked luggage space for freight. Generally, couriers are limited to carry-ons and must deal with complex flight restrictions. Most flights are round-trip only, with short fixed-length stays (usually one week) and a limit of a one ticket per issue. Most of these flights also operate only out of major gateway cities, mostly in North America. Round-trip courier fares from the US to Spain or Portugal run about US$200-500. Most flights leave from Los Angeles, Miami, New York, or San Francisco in the US; and from Montreal, Toronto, or Vancouver in Canada. Generally, you must be over 18 (in some cases 21). In summer, the most popular destinations usually require an advance reservation of about two weeks (you can usually book up to two months ahead). Super-discounted fares are common for "last-minute" flights (three to 14 days ahead). The organizations below provide members with lists of opportunities and courier brokers for an annual fee. Prices quoted below are round-trip.

Air Courier Association, 1767 A Denver West Blvd., Golden, CO 80401 (☎800-211-5119; www.aircourier.org). Ten departure cities throughout the US and Canada to Madrid and throughout Western Europe (high-season US$180-600). One-year membership US$49.

International Association of Air Travel Couriers (**IAATC**; www.courier.org). From 7 North American cities to Western European cities, including Madrid. One-year membership US$45.

Courier Travel (www.couriertravel.org). Searchable online database. Multiple departure points in the US to various European destinations.

STANDBY FLIGHTS

Traveling standby requires flexibility in arrival and departure dates. Companies dealing in standby flights sell vouchers rather than tickets, along with the promise to get you to your destination (or near your destination) within a certain window of time (typically 1-5 days). You call in before your specific window of time to hear your flight options and the probability that you will be able to board each flight. You can then decide which flights you want to catch, show up at the appropriate airport at the appropriate time, present your voucher, and board if space is available. Vouchers can usually be bought for both one-way and round-trip travel. You may receive a monetary refund only if every available flight within your date range is full; if you opt not to take an available (but perhaps less convenient) flight, you can only get credit toward future travel. Read agreements with any company offering standby flights with care; tricky fine print can leave you in the lurch. To check on a company's service record in the US, contact the Better Business Bureau (☎703-276-0100; www.bbb.org). It is difficult to receive refunds, and clients' vouchers will not be honored when an airline fails to receive payment in time.

TICKET CONSOLIDATORS

Ticket consolidators, or **"bucket shops,"** buy unsold tickets in bulk from commercial airlines and sell them at discounted rates. The best place to look is in the Sunday travel section of any major newspaper (such as *The New York Times*), where many bucket shops place tiny ads. Call quickly, as availability is extremely limited. Not all bucket shops are reliable, so insist on a receipt that gives full details of restrictions, refunds, and tickets, and pay by credit card (in spite of the 2-5% fee) so you can stop payment if you never receive your tickets. For more info, see www.travel-library.com/air-travel/consolidators.html.

TRAVELING FROM CANADA AND THE US

Some consolidators worth trying are **Rebel** (☎800-732-3588; www.rebeltours.com), **Cheap Tickets** (www.cheaptickets.com), **Flights.com** (www.flights.com), and **Travel-HUB** (www.travelhub.com). *Let's Go* does not endorse any of these agencies. Be cautious, and research companies before you hand over your credit card number.

CHARTER FLIGHTS

Tour operators contract charter flights with airlines in order to fly extra loads of passengers during peak season. These flights are far from hassle free. They occur less frequently than major airlines, make refunds particularly difficult, and are almost always fully booked. Their scheduled times may change and they may be cancelled at the last moment (as late as 48hr. before the trip, and without a full refund). And check-in, boarding, and baggage claim for them are often much slower. They can be, however, much cheaper.

Discount clubs and fare brokers offer members savings on last-minute charter and tour deals. Study contracts closely; you don't want to end up with an unwanted overnight layover. **Travelers Advantage** (☎800-835-8747; www.travelersadvantage.com; US$90 annual fee includes discounts and cheap flight directories) specializes in European travel and tour packages.

BY TRAIN

You can either buy a **rail pass,** which allows you unlimited travel within a particular region for a given period of time, or rely on buying individual **point-to-point** tickets as you go. Almost all countries give students or youths (usually defined as anyone under 26) direct discounts on regular domestic rail tickets, and many also sell a student or youth card that provides 20-50% off all fares for up to a year.

SHOULD YOU BUY A RAIL PASS? Rail passes were conceived to allow you to jump on any train in Europe, go wherever you want whenever you want, and change your plans at will. In practice, it's not so simple. You still must stand in line to validate your pass, pay for supplements, and fork over cash for seat and couchette reservations. More importantly, rail passes don't always pay off. If you plan to spend extensive time on trains, hopping between big cities, a rail pass will probably be worth it. But in many cases, especially if you are under 26, point-to-point tickets may prove a cheaper option. You may find it tough to make your railpass pay for itself in Spain and Portugal, where train fares are reasonable, distances short, and buses often preferable.

MULTINATIONAL RAIL PASSES

EURAIL PASSES. Eurail is valid in most of Western Europe: Austria, Belgium, Denmark, Finland, France, Germany, Greece, Hungary, Italy, Luxembourg, the Netherlands, Norway, Portugal, the Republic of Ireland, Spain, Sweden, and Switzerland. It is **not valid** in the UK. **Eurail Global Passes,** valid for a consecutive given number of days, are best for those planning on spending extensive time on trains every few days. Other types of global passes are valid for any 10 or 15 (not necessarily consecutive) days within a two-month period, is more cost-effective for those traveling longer distances less frequently. **Eurail Pass Saver** provides first-class travel for travelers in groups of two to five (prices are per person). **Eurail Pass Youth** provides parallel second-class perks for those under 26.

EURAIL GLOBAL PASSES	15 DAYS	21 DAYS	1 MONTH	2 MONTHS	3 MONTHS
Eurail Pass Adult	US$675	US$879	US$1089	US$1539	US$1899
Eurail Pass Saver	US$569	US$745	US$925	US$1309	US$1615
Eurail Pass Youth	US$439	US$569	US$709	US$999	US$1235

OTHER GLOBAL PASSES	10 DAYS IN 2 MONTHS	15 DAYS IN 2 MONTHS
Eurail Pass Adult	US$799	US$1049
Eurail Pass Saver	US$679	US$895
Eurail Pass Youth	US$519	US$679

Passholders receive a timetable for major routes and a map with details on bike rental, car rental, hotel, and museum discounts. Passholders often also receive reduced fares or free passage on many boat, bus, and private railroad lines.

The **Eurail Select Pass** is a slimmed-down version of the Eurailpass: it allows five to 15 days of unlimited travel in any two-month period within three, four, or five bordering countries of 23 European countries. **Eurail Select Passes** (for individuals) and **Eurail Select Pass Saver** (for people traveling in groups of two to five) range from US$429/365 per person (5 days) to US$949/805 (15 days). The **Eurail Select Pass Youth** (second-class), for those ages 12-25, costs US$279-619. You are entitled to the same **freebies** afforded by the Eurail Pass, but only when they are within or between countries that you have purchased.

SHOPPING AROUND FOR A EURAIL. Eurail Passes are designed by the EU itself, and can be bought only by non-Europeans almost exclusively from non-European distributors. These passes must be sold at uniform prices determined by the EU. However, some travel agents tack on a US$10 handling fee, and others offer certain bonuses with purchase, so shop around. Also, keep in mind that pass prices rise annually, so if you're planning to travel early in the year, you can save cash by purchasing before January 1 (you have three months from the purchase date to validate your pass in Europe).

It is best to buy your Eurail before leaving; only a few places in major European cities sell them, and at a marked-up price. You can get a replacement for a lost pass only if you have purchased insurance on it under the Pass Security Plan (US$14). Eurail Passes are available through travel agents, student travel agencies like STA (p. 26), and **Rail Europe** (Canada ☎800-361-7245, US 877-257-2887; www.raileurope.com) or **Flight Centre** (☎1-866-967-5351; www.flightcentre.com). It is also possible to buy directly from **Eurail's** website, www.eurail.com. Shipping is free to North America, Australia, New Zealand, and Canada.

OTHER MULTINATIONAL PASSES. If you have lived for at least six months in one of the European countries where **InterRail Passes** are valid, they prove an economical option. The Inter Rail Pass allows travel within 30 European countries (excluding the passholder's country of residence). The **Global Pass** is valid for a given number of days (not necessarily consecutive) within a 10 day-1 month period. (5 days within 10 days, adult 1st class €329, adult 2nd class €249, youth €159; 10 days within 22 days €489/359/239; 1 month continuous €809/599/399.) The **One Country Pass** limits travel within one European country (€33 for 3 days). Passholders receive free admission to many museums, as well as **discounts** on accommodations, food, and many ferries to Ireland, Scandinavia, and the rest of Europe. Passes are available at www.interrailnet.com, as well as from travel agents, at major train stations throughout Europe, and through online vendors (www.railpassdirect.co.uk).

DOMESTIC RAIL PASSES

If you are planning to spend a significant amount of time within one country or region, a national pass—valid on all rail lines of a country's rail company—may be more cost-effective than a multinational pass. But many national passes are limited and don't provide the free or discounted travel on private railways and ferries that Eurail does. Some of these passes can be bought only in Europe, some only outside of Europe; check with a railpass agent or with national tourist offices.

NATIONAL RAIL PASSES. The domestic analogs of the Eurail Pass, National Rail Passes are valid either for a given number of consecutive days or for a specific number of days within a given time period. Usually, they must be purchased before you leave. A four-day Eurail Spain Pass is US$295-225, and a four-day Eurail Portugal Pass is US$165. For more information on national rail passes, check out www.raileurope.com/us/rail/passes/single_country_index.htm.

RAIL-AND-DRIVE PASSES. In addition to simple rail passes, many countries (as well as Eurail) offer rail-and-drive passes, which combine car rental with rail travel—a good option for travelers who wish both to visit cities accessible by rail and to make side trips into the surrounding areas. Prices range from US$605-2056, depending on the type of pass, type of car, and number of people included. Children under the age of 11 cost $182.50, and adding more days costs $72-105 per day (see **By Car,** p. 36).

FURTHER READING & RESOURCES ON TRAIN TRAVEL.
Info on rail travel and rail passes: www.raileurope.com.
Point-to-point fares and schedules: www.raileurope.com/us/rail/fares_schedules/index.htm. Allows you to calculate whether buying a railpass would save you money.
Railsaver: www.railpass.com/new. Uses your itinerary to calculate the best rail-pass for your trip.
European Railway Server: www.railfaneurope.net. Links to rail servers throughout Europe.
Thomas Cook European Timetable: updated monthly, covers all major and most minor train routes in Europe. Buy directly from Thomas Cook (www.thomascooktimetables.com).

BY BOAT FROM THE UK AND IRELAND

The fares below are **one-way** for **adult foot passengers** unless otherwise noted. Though standard return fares are usually just twice the one-way fare, **fixed-period returns** (usually within five days) are almost invariably cheaper. Ferries run **year-round** unless otherwise noted. **Bikes** are usually free, although you may have to pay up to UK£10 in high season. For a **camper/trailer** supplement, you will have to add UK£20-140 to the "with car" fare. If more than one price is quoted, the quote in UK£ is valid for departures from the UK, etc. A directory of ferries in this region can be found at www.seaview.co.uk/ferries.html.

Brittany Ferries: UK ☎ 08703 665 333, France 0033 298 800; www.brittany-ferries.com. **Plymouth** to **Santander, Spain** (18hr., 2 per week, return UK£80-145).

GETTING AROUND SPAIN AND PORTUGAL

BY PLANE

Many national airlines offer multi-stop tickets for travel within Spain and Portugal. These tickets are particularly useful for travel between the Spanish mainland and the Islas Baleares and Islas Canarias. Outside of the peninsula, the recent emergence of no-frills airlines has made hopscotching around Europe by air increasingly affordable and convenient. Though these flights often feature inconvenient hours or serve less-popular regional airports, with one-way flights averaging about US$80, it's never been faster or easier to jet set across the Continent.

easyJet, UK (☎ 0871 244 2366; www.easyjet.com). Serves 72 destinations in Belgium, the Czech Republic, Denmark, Estonia, France, Germany, Greece, Hungary, Italy, Latvia, the Netherlands, Poland, Portugal, the Slovak Republic, Slovenia, Spain, Switzerland, and the UK.

Ryanair, Ireland (☎ 0818 303 030, UK 0871 246 00 00; www.ryanair.com). Serves 120 destinations in Austria, Belgium, the Czech Republic, France, Germany, Ireland, Italy, Latvia, the Netherlands, Poland, Portugal, Scandanavia, Spain, and the UK.

Vueling, Spain (☎34 902 33 39 33; www.vueling.com). Based in Barcelona, serves major cities in Spain, and also Brussels, Amsterdam, Paris, Rome, Venice, Lisbon, and Milan.

The **Star Alliance European Airpass** offers economy class fares as low as US$65 for travel within Europe to more than 200 destinations in 42 countries. The pass is available to non-European passengers on Star Alliance carriers, including Air Canada, Austrian Airlines, BMI British Midland, Lufthansa, Scandinavian Airlines System, Thai International, United Airlines, and Varig, as well as on certain partner airlines. See www.staralliance.com for more information. In addition, a number of European airlines offer discount coupon packets. Most are only available as tack-ons for transatlantic passengers, but some are stand-alone offers. Most must be purchased before departure, so research in advance.

Europe by Air, (☎888-321-4737; www.europebyair.com). *FlightPass* allows you to country-hop to over 150 European cities. US$99 per flight.

Iberia, (☎800-772-4642; www.iberia.com). *Europass* allows Iberia passengers flying from the US to Spain to tack on a minimum of 2 additional destinations in Europe. US$133 each.

IN SPAIN

All major international airlines offer service to Madrid and Barcelona, most serve Las Islas Baleares and Canarias, and many serve Spain's smaller cities. **AirEuropa** (Spain ☎902 40 15 01, US 888-238-7672; www.aireuropa.com) flies out of New York City, Chicago, and most European cities to Barcelona, Madrid, Málaga, Santiago de Compostela, and Tenerife. Discounts are available for youth and senior citizens. There is no service on Wednesdays or Sundays during the summer. **Iberia** (Canada ☎800 772 4642, Spain 902 40 05 00, UK 0870 609 0500, US 800-772-4642; www.iberia.com) serves all domestic locations and all major international cities. Iberia's less-established domestic competitor often offers cheaper fares and is worth looking into. **SpanAir** (Spain ☎902 13 14 15, US 888-545-5757, general 34 971 74 50 20; www.spanair.com/en) offers international and domestic flights.

SpanAir and Iberia offer the following special flight packages for travel throughout Spain, especially between the islands and the mainland; it may only be possible to add them on to tickets from international destinations.

Iberia Spain Pass: One-way coupons good for all mainland airports and the Islas Canarias and Islas Baleares. Reservations must be made 5 days prior to departure for Spain, and you must purchase your international return ticket before starting your trip. Min. purchase 3 coupons. Call for prices.

SpanAir Spain Pass: Good for flying to any airport within Spain, including Ibiza, Mallorca, and Menorca. Call for prices.

IN PORTUGAL

Most major international airlines serve Lisboa; some serve Faro, the Madeiras, and Porto. **TAP Air Portugal** (US and Canada ☎800-221-7370, UK 08456 010 932, Lisboa 707 20 57 00; www.tap.pt) is Portugal's national airline, serving all domestic locations and many major international cities. **Portugália** (Portugal ☎351 707 78 70 70; www.flypga.pt) is a small Portuguese airline that flies between Faro, Lisboa, Porto, major Spanish cities, and Western European destinations.

BY BUS

Though European trains and rail passes are extremely popular, in some cases buses prove a better option. In Spain, the bus and train systems are on par; in Portugal, bus networks are more extensive, efficient, and often more comfortable. In the rest of Europe, bus travel is more of a gamble; scattered offerings from private companies are often cheap, but sometimes unreliable. Often cheaper than rail passes, **international bus passes** allow unlimited travel on a hop-on, hop-off basis between major European cities. The prices below are based on high-season travel.

Eurolines, 4 Vicarage Rd., Edgbaston, Birmingham B15 3ES, UK (☎08705 143 219; www.eurolines.com). The largest operator of Europe-wide coach services. Unlimited 15-day (high season UK£195, under 26 and over 60 UK£165; low season UK£149/ 129); 30-day (high season UK£290/235; low season UK£209/169); or 60-day (high season UK£333/259; low season UK£265/211) travel passes that offer unlimited transit between 35 major European cities.

Busabout, 258 Vauxhall Bridge Rd., London SW1V 1BS, UK (☎0207 950 1661; www.busabout.com). Offers 5 interconnecting bus circuits covering 60 cities and towns in Europe. Unlimited (consecutive-day) Passes, Flexipasses, and Add On Passes are available. Unlimited standard/student passes are valid for 2 weeks (US$469/419), 4 weeks (US$739/659), 6 weeks (US$919/819), 8 weeks (US$1049/939), 12 weeks (US$1319/1179), or for the season (US$1649/1469).

IN SPAIN

Bus routes, far more comprehensive than the rail network, provide the only public transportation to many isolated areas, and almost always cost less than trains. They are generally quite comfortable, though leg room may be limited. For those traveling primarily within one region, **buses are the best method of transport.**

We list below the major national companies, along with the phone number of their Madrid office; you will likely use many other companies. For more information, see the section for your transportation destination.

ALSA, (☎913 27 05 40; www.alsa.es). Serves Madrid, Galicia, Asturias, and Castilla y León. Runs to many surrounding countries, including France, Germany, Italy, Morocco, the Netherlands, and Portugal.

Alosa, (☎902 21 07 00; www.alosa.es). Operates primarily in northeastern Spain, Alosa serves Barcelona, Huesca, Jaca, Pamplona, and Zaragoza.

Alsina Graells, (☎958 18 54 80; www.alsinagraells.es). Serves Andalucía, including Granada, Córdoba, and Sevilla, and Cataluña, including Barcelona, Huesca, and Lleida.

Auto-Res, (☎902 02 09 99; www.auto-res.net). Runs from Madrid to Castilla y León, Extremadura, Galicia, Valencia, and Portugal.

Daibus, (☎902 27 79 99; www.daibus.es). To Algeciras, Madrid, Málaga, and Marbella.

Linebús, (☎902 33 55 33; www.linebus.com). Runs to France, Morocco, and Bucharest from Almería, Girona, Granada, and Murcia.

Samar, SA, (☎917 23 05 06; www.samar.es). Serves Madrid, Zaragoza, and Sevilla, as well as international routes to Andorra, France, Italy, Morocco, Portugal, and Moscow.

IN PORTUGAL

Buses are cheap and frequent. They connect just about every town in Portugal. **Rodoviária** (☎212 94 71 00; www.rodotejo.pt), the national bus company, has recently been privatized. Each company name corresponds to a particular region of the country, such as Rodoviária Alentejo or Minho e Douro, with a few exceptions such as EVA in the Algarve. Private regional companies also operate, among them **AVIC, Cabanelas,** and **Mafrense.** Be wary of non-express buses in small regions like Estremadura and Alentejo, which stop every few minutes. Express coach service (*expressos*) between major cities is especially good; inexpensive city buses often run to nearby villages. Schedules (*horarios*) are usually printed and posted, but double-check with the ticket vendor to make sure they are accurate.

Portugal's main **Euroline** affiliates are Intercentro, Internorte, and Intersul. **Busabout** coach stops in Portugal are at Lagos, Lisboa, and Porto. Every coach has a guide onboard to answer questions and to make travel arrangements en route.

BY TRAIN

ESSENTIALS

Trains in Spain and Portugal are generally comfortable, convenient, and reasonably swift. Second-class compartments are great places to meet fellow travelers. Trains, however, are not always safe; for safety tips, see p. 20. For long trips, make sure you are on the correct car, as trains sometimes split at crossroads. Towns listed in parentheses on European train schedules require a train switch at the town listed immediately before the parenthesis.

You can either buy a **rail pass,** which allows you unlimited travel within a particular region for a given period of time, or rely on buying individual **point-to-point** tickets as you go. Almost all countries give students or youths (usually defined as anyone under 26) direct discounts on regular domestic rail tickets, and many also sell a student or youth card that provides 20-50% off all fares for up to a year.

RESERVATIONS. While seat reservations are required only for selected trains (usually on major lines), you are not guaranteed a seat without one (usually US$5-30). You should strongly consider reserving in advance during peak holiday and tourist seasons (at the very latest, a few hours ahead). You will also have to purchase a **supple**ment (US$10-50) or special fare for high speed or high quality trains such as Spain's AVE. Supplements are often unnecessary for Eurail pass and Europass holders.

OVERNIGHT TRAINS. On night trains, you won't waste valuable daylight hours traveling and you can avoid the hassle and expense of staying at a hotel. However, the main drawbacks include discomfort, sleepless nights, and the lack of scenery. **Sleeping accommodations** on trains differ from country to country, but typically you can either sleep upright in your seat (supplement about $2-10) or pay for a separate space. **Couchettes** (berths) typically have four to six seats per compartment (supplement about US$10-50 per person); **sleepers** (beds) in private sleeping cars offer more privacy and comfort, but are considerably more expensive (supplement US$40-150). If you are using a railpass valid only for a restricted number of days, inspect train schedules to maximize the use of your pass: an overnight train or boat journey often uses up only one of your travel days if it departs after 7pm.

EURAIL PASSES

There is absolutely no reason to buy a Eurail Pass if you plan to travel only within Spain and Portugal. Trains are cheap, so a pass saves little money. Visit www.raileurope.com for more specific information on the passes below.

Spain Pass: Offers 3 days of unlimited travel in a 2-month period. 1st-class US$253; 2nd-class US$197. Each additional rail-day (up to 7) US$40 for 1st-class, US$33 for 2nd-class.

Portugal-Spain Pass: Good for unlimited 1st-class travel in Spain and Portugal within a 2-month period. Travel may be on consecutive or non-consecutive days. US$289. Each additional rail-day (up to 7) US$40.

Spain Rail 'n Drive Pass: Good for 3 days of unlimited 1st-class train travel and 2 days of unlimited mileage in a rental car within a 2-month period. Prices US$307-806, depending on number of travelers and type of car. Up to 2 additional rail-days and extra car days available; a extra travelers can join in the car using only a Flexipass.

IN SPAIN

Spanish trains are clean, punctual, and reasonably priced, but tend to bypass many small towns. Spain's national railway is **RENFE** (☎902 24 34 02; www.renfe.es).

Avoid *transvía*, *semidirecto*, or *correo* trains—they are very slow. The following list includes types of trains you will find in Spain and their relative speeds. Check the website to find out if reservations are required for a particular train. For the most part, buses are an easier and more efficient means of traveling around Spain.

Grandes Líneas: RENFE's business unit for long-distance travel. A wide range of lines including Euromed, Alaris, Arco, Talgo, and Trenhotel meet every traveler's needs.

AVE (Alta Velocidad Española): High-speed trains dart between Madrid and Sevilla, Ciudad Real, Puertollano, Lleida, Zaragoza, Camp de Tarragona, Huesca, and Córdoba. AVE trains soar above others in comfort, price, and speed. Student discounts available.

Talgo 200: Sleek trains zip passengers in air-conditioned compartments from Madrid to Málaga, Cádiz/Huelva, or Algeciras. They're more comfortable, faster, and twice as pricey as Cercanías-Regionales trains. Changing a Talgo 200 ticket incurs a 10% fine.

Intercity: Cheaper than Talgo, but fewer destinations. Air-conditioned and comfy. Five lines: Madrid-Valencia, Madrid-Zaragoza-Barcelona, Madrid-Alicante, Madrid-Zaragoza-Logroño-Pamplona, and Madrid-Murcia-Cartagena.

Estrella: A fairly slow night train with *literas* (bunks) and showers. Runs from Barcelona across northern Spain to Vigo, from Madrid down to Córdoba and up to Santander, and from Bilbao to Málaga and Alicante.

Cercanías: Commuter trains from large cities to suburbs and towns, with frequent stops.

Regional: Like *cercanías* but older; multi-stop, cheap rides to small towns and cities.

IN PORTUGAL

Caminhos de Ferro Portugueses (☎213 18 59 90; www.cp.pt) is Portugal's national railway, but for long-distance travel outside of the Braga-Porto-Coimbra-Lisboa line, the bus is better. The exception is around Lisboa, where local trains are fast and efficient. Most trains have first- and second-class cabins, except for local and suburban routes. Check the station ticket booth for the departure schedule; trains often run at irregular hours, and posted schedules *(horarios)* aren't always accurate. You can save 10% by buying a return ticket, but unless you own a Eurail pass the return on **round-trip tickets** must be used before 3am the following day. Keep your ticket with you; if you're caught without one, you'll be fined. Children under 12 and adults over 65 receive a 50% discount. **Youth discounts** are only available to Portuguese citizens. Though there is a Portugal Flexipass, it is not worth buying.

BY CAR

Cars offer speed, freedom, access to the countryside, and an escape from the town-to-town mentality of trains. Although a single traveler won't save by renting a car, four usually will. If you can't decide between train and car travel, you may benefit from a combination of the two; RailEurope and other railpass vendors offer rail-and-drive packages. Fly-and-drive packages are also often available from travel agents or airline/rental agency partnerships.

For an informal primer on European road signs and conventions, check out www.travlang.com/signs. The **Association for Safe International Road Travel (ASIRT)**, 11769 Gainsborough Rd., Potomac, MD 20854, USA (☎301-983-5252; www.asirt.org), can provide more specific information about road conditions.

RENTING

You can rent a car from a US-based firm (Alamo, Avis, Budget, or Hertz) with European offices, from a European-based company with local representatives (Europcar), or from a tour operator (Auto Europe, Europe By Car, and Kemwel Holiday Autos) that will arrange a rental for you from a European company at its own rates. Multinationals offer greater flexibility, but tour operators often strike better deals. It is always significantly less expensive to reserve a car from the US than from Europe. Ask airlines about special fly-and-drive packages; you may get up to a week of free or discounted rental. Expect to pay US$80-400 per week, plus tax (5-25%), for a tiny car. Reserve ahead and pay in advance if at all possible. Always check if prices quoted include tax and collision insurance; some credit card companies provide insurance, allowing their customers to decline the collision damage waiver. Ask about discounts and check the terms of insurance, particularly the size of the deductible. At most agencies, all that's needed to rent a car is a license from home and proof that you've had it for a year.

RENTAL AGENCIES

You can generally make reservations before you leave by calling major international offices in your home country. However, sometimes the price and availability information they give doesn't jive with what the local offices in Spain and Portugal will tell you. Try checking with both numbers to make sure you get the best price and the most accurate information possible. Local desk numbers are included in town listings; for home-country numbers, call your toll-free directory.

To rent a car from most establishments in Spain and Portugal, you need to be at least 21 years old. Some agencies require renters to be 25, and most charge those 21-24 an additional insurance fee. Policies and prices vary from agency to agency. Small local operations occasionally rent to people under 21, but be sure to ask about the insurance coverage and deductible, and always check the fine print. Rental agencies in Spain and Portugal include:

Auto Europe (☎888-223-5555 or 207-842-2000; www.autoeurope.com).

Avis (Australia ☎136 333, Canada 800-331-1212, New Zealand 0800 65 51 11, UK 0870 606 0100, US 800-331-1212; www.avis.com).

Budget (Canada ☎800-268-8900, UK 8701 565 656, US 800-527-0700; www.budgetrentacar.com).

Europe by Car (US ☎800-223-1516 or 212-581-3040; www.europebycar.com).

Europcar International, 3 Avenue du Centre, 78 881 Saint Quentin en Yvelines Cedex, France (UK ☎870 607 5000, US 877-940-6900; www.europcar.com).

Hertz (☎800-654-3001 or 800-654-3131; www.hertz.com).

Kemwel (US ☎877-820-0668; www.kemwel.com).

COSTS AND INSURANCE

Renting a car in **Spain** is cheaper than in many other European countries; prices start at around €50 per day from national companies, €25 from local agencies. In **Portugal,** prices start at around €50 per day from national companies, or €35 per day from local agencies. Expect to pay more for larger cars and for 4WD. Cars with **automatic transmission** can cost up to €30 per day more than standard manuals (stick shift), and in some places, automatic transmission is hard to find. It is virtually impossible, no matter where you are, to find an automatic with 4WD. Rental agencies are listed in the **Practical Information** at the start of each city.

Many rental packages offer unlimited kilometers, while others offer a limited number of kilometers per day with a surcharge per kilometer after that. Return the car with a full tank of gasoline (petrol) to avoid high fuel charges at the end. Be sure to ask whether the price includes **insurance** against theft and collision. Remember that if you are driving a conventional rental vehicle on an **unpaved road** in a rental car, you are almost never covered by insurance; ask about this before leaving the rental agency. Be aware that cars rented on an **American Express** or **Visa/MasterCard Gold** or **Platinum** credit card in Spain might *not* carry the automatic insurance that they would in some other countries; check with your credit card company. Insurance plans from rental companies almost always come with an **excess** charge for younger drivers and for 4WD. This means that the insurance bought from the rental company only applies to damages over the excess; damages up to that amount must be covered by your existing insurance plan. Many rental companies in Spain and Portugal encourage you to buy a **Collision Damage Waiver (CDW)**, which will waive the excess in the case of a collision. **Loss Damage Waivers (LDWs)** do the same in the case of theft or vandalism.

National chains often allow one-way rentals (picking up in one city and dropping off in another). There is usually a minimum hire period and sometimes an extra drop-off charge of several hundred dollars.

DRIVING PERMITS AND CAR INSURANCE

INTERNATIONAL DRIVING PERMIT (IDP)

If you plan to drive a car while in Spain or Portugal, you must be over 18 and have an International Driving Permit (IDP). However, in **Spain,** a US licence is valid for six months in a calendar year, after which a driving school can help you apply for a Spanish license. A **driver's license** from any EU member country is valid in **Spain**. In **Portugal,** only a valid license from one's home country is required to rent a car.

It may be a good idea to get an IDP, in case you're in a situation (e.g., an accident or stranded in a small town) where the police do not know English; information on the IDP is printed in 11 languages, including Spanish and Portuguese. The **Jefatura Provincial de Tráfico** (☎913 01 85 00), C. Arturo Soria, 143, in Madrid, is a source for help with such matters.

Your IDP, valid for one year, must be issued in your own country before you depart. An application for an IDP usually requires one or two photos, a current local license, an additional form of identification, and a fee. To apply, contact your home country's automobile association. Be vigilant when purchasing an IDP online or anywhere other than your home automobile association. Many vendors sell permits of questionable legitimacy for higher prices.

CAR INSURANCE

Most credit cards cover standard insurance. If you rent, lease, or borrow a car, you will need a **Green Card**, or **International Insurance Certificate,** to certify that you have liability insurance and that it applies abroad. Green cards can be obtained at car rental agencies, car dealers (for those leasing cars), some travel agents, and some border crossings. Rental agencies may require you to purchase theft insurance in countries that they consider to have a high risk of auto theft.

ON THE ROAD

Spain's highway system connects major cities by four-lane *autopistas* (highways) with plenty of service stations. Traffic moves quickly and drivers can get annoyed if you don't; study your map before you leave. The speed limit in Spain is 31mph/50kph in cities, 55mph/90kph on open roads, and 74mph/120kph on highways. **Speeders beware:** police can "photograph" the speed and license plate of your car and issue a ticket without pulling you over. Purchase **gas** in both Spain and Portugal in super (97-octane), normal (92-octane), diesel, and unleaded. The average price for unleaded gas is approximately $4.55 per gallon in **Spain** and $5.35 per gallon in **Portugal.**

Seatbelts are required in Spain, and drunk driving incurs hefty fines; be aware that allowed blood levels of alcohol are lower than in other countries in Europe.

DANGERS

Portugal has the highest rate of car accidents per capita in Western Europe. The narrow, twisting roads are difficult to negotiate. Speed limits are ignored, recklessness is common, and lighting and road surfaces are often inadequate.

CAR ASSISTANCE

The **Spanish** automobile association is **Real Automóvil Club de España (RACE)**, C. José Abascal, 10, Madrid (☎902 40 45 45; www.race.es). It functions much like AAA, offering roadside assistance and general advice on driving in Spain. **Portugal's** automobile association, the **Automóvel Clube de Portugal (ACP)** (☎213 71 47 20; www.acp.pt) provides **breakdown, towing,** and **first-aid** services.

BY BOAT

Ferries leave from **Valencia** and **Barcelona** for the **Islas Baleares** (p. 343). Ferries are the cheapest, if slowest, way to travel to the **Islas Canarias** (p. 585).

BY BICYCLE

Today, biking is one of the key elements of the budget European adventure. With the proliferation of mountain bikes, you can do some serious natural sightseeing.

Some airlines will count your bike as your second piece of luggage, but others charge extra. The additional fee runs about US$50-75 each way. Airlines sell bike boxes at the airport (US$20-25), although it is easier and cheaper to get one from a local bike store. Most ferries let you take your bike for free or for a nominal fee. You can almost always ship your bike on trains, though the cost varies.

Renting a bike beats bringing your own if your touring will be confined to one or two regions. *Let's Go* lists bike rental shops for larger cities and towns, when they exist. Some youth hostels rent bicycles for low prices. Some train stations rent bikes and often allow you to drop them off elsewhere.

BY MOPED AND MOTORCYCLE

Motorized bikes don't use much gas, can be put on trains and ferries, and are a good compromise between the high cost of car travel and the limited range of bicycles. In Spain, they are a popular method of transportation for locals, and they can be a fun alternative for tourist daytrips. However, they're uncomfortable for long distances, dangerous in the rain, and unpredictable on rough roads and gravel. Always wear a helmet, and never ride with a backpack. If you've never been on a moped, the windy roads of the Pyrenees and the congested streets of Madrid are not the place to start. Before renting, ask if the quoted price includes tax and insurance, or you may be hit with an unexpected additional fee. Pay ahead of time instead—do not hand over your passport.

BY THUMB

Let's Go never recommends hitchhiking as a safe means of transportation, and none of the information presented here is intended to do so.

Let's Go strongly urges you to consider the risks before you choose to hitchhike. Hitching means entrusting your life to a stranger and risking assault, sexual harassment, theft, and unsafe driving. For women traveling alone (or even in pairs), hitching is just too dangerous. A man and a woman are a less dangerous combination; groups of men will have a harder time getting a lift.

In Spain, hitchers report that Castilla and Andalucía are long, hot waits; hitchhiking out of Madrid is virtually impossible. The Mediterranean Coast and the islands are much more promising; remote areas in Cataluña, Galicia, or the Islas Canarias may be best accessible by hitching (if renting a car is not an option). Approaching

ESSENTIALS

people for rides at gas stations near highways and rest stops purportedly gets results. In **Portugal,** hitchhikers are rare. Beach-bound locals occasionally hitch in summer, but otherwise stick to the inexpensive bus system.

KEEPING IN TOUCH

BY EMAIL AND INTERNET

Email is quite easy to access in Spain and Portugal. Internet costs only about €1-3 per hour in most cafes. Many hostels, libraries, and schools also provide free access. In small towns, if Internet access is not listed, check the library or the tourist office, where travelers occasionally get access for a small fee.

Although in some places it's possible to forge a remote link with your home server, in most cases this is a much slower (and thus more expensive) option than taking advantage of free **web-based email accounts** (e.g., www.gmail.com and www.hotmail.com). **Internet cafes** and the occasional free Internet terminal at a public library or university are listed in the **Practical Information** sections of major cities. For lists of additional cybercafes in Spain and Portugal, check out www.cybercaptive.com.

Increasingly, travelers find that taking their laptop computers on the road with them can be a convenient option for staying connected. Laptop users can call an Internet service provider via a modem using long-distance phone cards specifically intended for such calls. They may also find Internet cafes that allow them to connect their laptops to the Internet. And most excitingly, travelers with wireless-enabled computers may be able to take advantage of an increasing number of Internet "hot spots," where they can get online for free or for a small fee. Newer computers can detect these hot spots automatically; otherwise, websites like www.jiwire.com, www.wififreespot.com, and www.wi-fihotspotlist.com can help you find them. For information on insuring your laptop while traveling, see p. 22.

WARY WI-FI. Wireless hot spots make Internet access possible in public and remote places. Unfortunately, they also pose **security risks.** Hot spots are public, open networks that use unencrypted, unsecured connections. They are susceptible to hacks and "packet sniffing"—ways of stealing passwords and other private information. To prevent problems, disable ad hoc mode, turn off file sharing, turn off network discovery, encrypt your e-mail, turn on your firewall, beware of phony networks, and watch for over-the-shoulder creeps. Ask the establishment whose wireless you're using for the name of the network so you know you're on the right one. If you are in the vicinity and do not plan to access the Internet, turn off your wireless adapter completely.

BY TELEPHONE

CALLING HOME FROM SPAIN AND PORTUGAL

You can usually make **direct international calls** from pay phones, but unless you're using a phone card, you may need to feed the machine regularly. **Prepaid phone cards** are a common and relatively inexpensive means of calling abroad. Each one comes with a Personal Identification Number (PIN) and a toll-free access number. You call the access number and then follow the directions for dialing your PIN. To purchase prepaid phone cards, check online for the best rates; www.callingcards.com is a good place to start. Online providers generally send your access number and PIN via email, with no actual "card" involved. You can also call home with prepaid phone cards purchased in Spain and Portugal (see Calling Within Spain and Portugal, p. 41).

PLACING INTERNATIONAL CALLS. To call Spain or Portugal from home or to call home from Spain or Portugal, dial:

1. The **international dialing prefix.** To call from **Australia,** dial 0011; **Canada** or the **US,** 011; **Ireland, New Zealand, Spain, Portugal,** or the **UK,** 00.
2. The **country code** of the country you want to call. To call **Australia,** dial 61; **Canada** or the **US,** 1; **Ireland,** 353; **New Zealand,** 64; the **UK,** 44; **Spain,** 34; **Portugal,** 351.
3. The **city/area code.** Let's Go lists the city/area codes for cities and towns in Spain and Portugal opposite the city or town name, next to a ☎. If the first digit is a zero (e.g., 020 for London), omit the zero when calling from abroad (e.g., dial 20 from Canada to reach London).
4. The **local number.**

Another option is to purchase a **calling card,** linked to a major national telecommunications service in your home country. Calls are billed collect or to your account. To obtain a calling card, contact the appropriate company listed below. Where available, there are often advantages to purchasing calling cards online, including better rates and immediate access to your account. To call home with a calling card, contact the operator for your service provider in Spain and Portugal by dialing the appropriate toll-free access number (listed below).

COMPANY	TO OBTAIN A CARD:	TO CALL ABROAD:
AT&T (US)	800-364-9292 or www.att.com	Spain: 900 99 00 11 Portugal: 800 80 01 28
Canada Direct	800-561-8868 or www.infocanadadirect.com	Spain: 900 99 00 15 Portugal: 800 80 01 22
MCI (US)	800-777-5000 or www.minutepass.com	Spain: 800 09 93 57 Portugal: 800 80 01 23
Telecom New Zealand Direct	www.telecom.co.nz	Spain: 900 99 00 64 Portugal: 800 80 06 40
Telstra Australia	1800 676 638 or www.telstra.com	Spain: 900 99 00 61 Portugal: 800 80 06 10

Placing a **collect call** through an international operator can be expensive, but may be necessary in case of an emergency. You can frequently call collect without even possessing a company's calling card just by calling its access number and following the instructions.

CALLING WITHIN SPAIN AND PORTUGAL

The simplest way to call within the country is to use a coin-operated phone. **Prepaid phone cards** (available at newspaper kiosks and tobacco stores), which carry a certain amount of phone time depending on the card's denomination, may be more convenient, however, and usually save time and money in the long run. The computerized phone will tell you how much time, in units, you have left on your card. Another kind of prepaid telephone card comes with a PIN and a toll-free access number. Instead of inserting the card into the phone, you call the access number and follow the directions on the card. These cards can be used to make international as well as domestic calls. Phone rates typically tend to be highest in the morning, lower in the evening, and lowest on Sunday and late at night.

CELLULAR PHONES

Many travelers find that the availability and usefulness of cell phones in Spain and Portugal make them well worth their moderate cost. Telefónica Movistar (www.movistar.com) and Vodafone (www.vodafone.com) sell cell phones to travelers for €80-100. Calls on these phones cost about €0.75 per minute.

The international standard for cell phones is **Global System for Mobile Communication (GSM)**. To make and receive calls in Spain and Portugal you will need a **GSM-compatible phone** and a **SIM (Subscriber Identity Module) card,** a country-specific, thumbnail-sized chip that gives you a local phone number and plugs you into the local network. Many SIM cards are **prepaid,** meaning that they come with calling time included and you don't need to sign up for a monthly service plan. Incoming calls are frequently free. When you use up the prepaid time, you can buy additional cards or vouchers (usually available at convenience stores or tobacco stores) to "top up" your phone. For more information on GSM phones, check out www.telestial.com, www.orange.co.uk, www.roadpost.com, or www.planetomni.com. Companies like **Cellular Abroad** (www.cellular-abroad.com) rent cell phones that work in a variety of destinations around the world, providing a simpler option than picking up a phone in-country.

 GSM PHONES. Just having a GSM phone doesn't mean you're necessarily good to go when you travel abroad. The majority of GSM phones sold in the United States operate on a different **frequency** (1900) than international phones (900/1800) and will not work abroad. Tri-band phones work on all three frequencies (900/1800/1900) and will operate through most of the world. Additionally, some GSM phones are **SIM-locked** and will only accept SIM cards from a single carrier. You'll need a **SIM-unlocked** phone to use a SIM card from a local carrier when you travel.

TIME DIFFERENCES

Spain is 1hr. ahead of Greenwich Mean Time (GMT), while Portugal and Las Islas Canarias operate at GMT. Both countries observe Daylight Saving Time. The following table relates Spain and Portugal's capitals to other localities at noon GMT.

4AM	5AM	6AM	7AM	8AM	NOON	1PM
Vancouver Seattle San Francisco Los Angeles	Denver	Chicago	New York Toronto	New Brunswick	**LISBOA** London	**MADRID** Sydney Canberra Melbourne

BY MAIL

SENDING MAIL HOME FROM SPAIN AND PORTUGAL

Airmail is the best way to send mail home from Spain and Portugal. **Aerogrammes,** printed sheets that fold into envelopes and travel via airmail, are available at post offices. Write *"airmail," "par avion," "por avión," "por avião,"* or *"via aerea"* on the front. Most post offices will charge exorbitant fees or simply refuse to send *aerogrammes* with enclosures. In Spain, air mail takes from five to eight business days to reach the US or Canada. Standard postage is €0.80 to North America. **Express mail** *(certificado),* is the most reliable way to send a letter or parcel, and takes four to seven business days. Spain's **overnight mail** is not worth the expense, since it isn't exactly "overnight." For better service, try companies like DHL, UPS, or SEUR; look under *mensajerías* in the yellow pages. Their reliability, however, comes at a high cost. Stamps are sold at post offices and tobacconists *(estancos* or *tabacos)*. Mail letters and postcards from yellow mailboxes scattered throughout cities, or from the post office in small towns. Mail in Portugal is somewhat inefficient—Airmail can take from one to two weeks or longer to reach the US or Canada. It is slightly quicker for Europe and longer for Australia and New Zealand. Registered or blue mail takes five to eight business days for roughly three times the price of airmail. **EMS** or **Express Mail** will probably take three to four days for more than double the blue mail price. Stamps are available at post offices *(Correos)*, automatic stamp machines at post offices, and central locations around cities. Fax machines are also available at post offices. In both Spain and Portugal, **Surface mail** is the cheapest but the slowest way to send mail. It takes one to two months to cross the Atlantic and one to three to cross the Pacific—good for heavy items you won't need for a while, such as souvenirs or other articles you've acquired along the way that are weighing down your pack. These are standard rates for mail from Spain and Portugal:

Australia: Allow 14 days for regular airmail home. Postcards/aerogrammes cost €0.57. Letters up to 20g cost €0.78; packages up to 0.35kg €8.90, up to 2kg €35.75.

Canada: Allow 14 days for regular airmail home. Postcards/aerogrammes cost €0.57. Letters up to 20g cost €0.78; packages up to 0.35kg €8.90, up to 2kg €35.75.

Ireland: Allow 4 days for regular airmail home. Postcards/aerogrammes cost €0.57. Letters up to 20g cost €0.57; packages up to 0.35kg €5.45, up to 2kg €15.95.

New Zealand: Allow 14 days for regular airmail home. Postcards/aerogrammes cost €0.57. Letters up to 20g cost €0.78; packages up to 0.35kg €8.90, up to 2kg €35.75.

UK: Allow 4 days for regular airmail home. Postcards/aerogrammes cost €0.57. Letters up to 20g cost €0.57; packages up to 0.35kg €5.45, up to 2kg €15.95.

US: Allow 14 days for regular airmail home. Postcards/aerogrammes cost €0.57. Letters up to 20g cost €0.78; packages up to 0.35kg €8.90, up to 2kg €35.75.

SENDING MAIL TO SPAIN AND PORTUGAL

To ensure timely delivery, mark envelopes *"airmail," "par avion," "por avión,"* or *"por avião."* Sending a postcard or letter (up to 50g) within Spain or Portugal costs €0.78. Service tends to be best between major cities like Barcelona, Lisboa, and Madrid. Rural areas, especially Douro, Minho, and Galicia, often have slower service. In addition to the standard postage system whose rates are listed below, **Federal Express** (Australia ☎ 13 26 10, Canada and the US 800-463-3339, Ireland 1800 535 800, New Zealand 0800 733 339, the UK 08456 070 809; www.fedex.com) handles express mail services from most countries to Spain and Portugal.

There are several ways to arrange pickup of letters sent to you while you are abroad. Mail can be sent via **Poste Restante** (General Delivery; **Lista de Correos (S);** **Lista de Correiros (P)**) to almost any city or town in Spain and Portugal with a post office, **but it is not very reliable.** Address *Poste Restante* letters like so:

Miguel de CERVANTES

Lista de Correos

Salamanca, España

The mail will go to a special desk in the central post office, unless you specify a post office by street address or postal code. It's best to use the largest post office, since mail may be sent there regardless. It is usually safer and quicker, though more expensive, to send mail express or registered. Bring your passport (or other photo ID) for pickup. If the clerks insist that there is nothing for you, have them check under your first name as well. *Let's Go* lists post offices in the **Practical Information** section for each city and most towns.

American Express's travel offices throughout the world offer a free **Client Letter Service** (mail held up to 30 days and forwarded upon request) for cardholders who contact them in advance. Some offices provide these services to non-cardholders (especially AmEx Travelers Cheque holders), but call ahead to make sure. *Let's Go* lists AmEx locations for most large cities in **Practical Information** sections; for a complete list, call ☎800-528-4800 or visit www.americanexpress.com/travel.

ACCOMMODATIONS

HOSTELS

Many hostels are laid out dorm-style, often with large single-sex rooms and bunk beds, although private rooms that sleep two to four are becoming more common. They sometimes have kitchens and utensils for guest use, bike or moped rentals, storage areas, transportation to airports, breakfast and other meals, laundry facilities, and Internet access. There can be drawbacks: some hostels close during certain daytime "lockout" hours, have a curfew, don't accept reservations, or impose a maximum stay. In Spain, a dorm bed in a hostel will average around €14-26 and a private room around €18-26, while in Portugal, a dorm bed in a hostel will average around €12-22 and a private room around €18-26.

 A HOSTELER'S BILL OF RIGHTS. There are certain standard features that we do not include in our hostel listings. Unless we state otherwise, you can expect that every hostel has no lockout, no curfew, free hot showers, some system of secure luggage storage, and no key deposit.

HOSTELLING INTERNATIONAL

Joining the youth hostel association in your own country (listed below) automatically grants you membership privileges in **Hostelling International (HI),** a federation of national hosteling associations. Non-HI members may be allowed to stay in some hostels, but will have to pay extra to do so. HI hostels are scattered throughout Spain and Portugal, and **are typically less expensive than private hostels.** HI's umbrella organization's website (www.hihostels.com), which lists the web addresses and phone numbers of all national associations, can be a great place to begin researching hosteling in a specific region. Other comprehensive hostelling websites include www.hostels.com and www.hostelplanet.com.

Most HI hostels also honor **guest memberships**—you'll get a blank card with space for six validation stamps. Each night you'll pay a nonmember supplement (one-sixth the membership fee) and earn one guest stamp; get six stamps and you're a member. This system works well in most of Western Europe, but in some countries you may need to remind the hostel reception. A new membership benefit is the FreeNites program, which allows hostelers to gain points toward free rooms. Most student travel agencies (p. 26) sell HI cards, as do all of the national hosteling organizations listed below. All prices listed below are valid for **one-year memberships** unless otherwise noted.

Australian Youth Hostels Association (AYHA), 422 Kent St., Sydney, NSW 200 (☎02 9261 1111; www.yha.com.au). AUS$52, under 18 AUS$19.

Hostelling International-Canada (HI-C), 205 Catherine St. Ste. 400, Ottawa, ON K2P 1C3 (☎613-237-7884; www.hihostels.ca). CDN$35, under 18 free.

An Óige (Irish Youth Hostel Association), 61 Mountjoy St., Dublin 7 (☎830 4555; www.irelandyha.org). EUR€20, under 18 EUR€10.

Hostelling International Northern Ireland (HINI), 22-32 Donegall Rd., Belfast BT12 5JN (☎02890 32 47 33; www.hini.org.uk). UK£15, under 25 UK£10.

Youth Hostels Association of New Zealand Inc. (YHANZ), Level 1, 166 Moorhouse Ave., P.O. Box 436, Christchurch (☎0800 278 299 (NZ only) or 03 379 9970; www.yha.org.nz). NZ$40, under 18 free.

Scottish Youth Hostels Association (SYHA), 7 Glebe Cres., Stirling FK8 2JA (☎01786 89 14 00; www.syha.org.uk). UK£8, under 18 £4.

Youth Hostels Association (England and Wales), Trevelyan House, Dimple Rd., Matlock, Derbyshire DE4 3YH (☎08707 708 868; www.yha.org.uk). UK£16, under 26 UK£10.

Hostelling International-USA, 8401 Colesville Rd., Ste. 600, Silver Spring, MD 20910 (☎301-495-1240; www.hiayh.org). US$28, under 18 free.

BOOKING HOSTELS ONLINE. One of the easiest ways to ensure you've got a bed for the night is by reserving online. Click to the **Hostelworld** booking engine through **www.letsgo.com**, and you'll have access to bargain accommodations from Argentina to Zimbabwe with no added commission.

The Spanish Hostelling International (HI) affiliate, **Red Española de Albergues Juveniles (REAJ)**, C. Galera, 1a, Sevilla 41001 (www.reaj.com), runs 165 youth hostels year-round. Prices depend on location (typically some distance away from town center) and services offered, but are generally €9-15 for guests under 26 and higher for those 26 and over. Breakfast is usually included; lunch and dinner are occasionally offered at an additional charge. Hostels usually begin lockout around 11:00am and have curfews between midnight and 3am. As a rule, don't expect much privacy—rooms typically are dorm-style with four to 20 beds in one room. Call in advance to reserve a bed in high season (July-Aug. and during fiestas). A national **Youth Hostel Card** is usually required (see **Hostels**, p. 44). HI cards are available from Spain's youth travel company, **TIVE**. Occasionally, guests can stay in a hostel without one and pay extra for six nights to become a member.

The Portuguese Hostelling International affiliate, **Movijovem** (☎707 20 30 30; www.pousadasjuventude.pt), oversees the country's HI hostels and all bookings can be made through them. A bed in a *pousada da juventude* (not to be confused with plush *pousadas*) costs €9-15 per night (breakfast and sheets included) and slightly less in the low season (Oct.-Apr.). Lunch or dinner usually costs €5, snacks around €2. Rates may be higher for guests 26 and older. Though often the cheapest option, hostels may lie far from the town center. Check-in hours are generally 9am-noon and 6pm-midnight. Some have lockouts 10:30am-6pm, and curfews might cramp club-hoppers' style. The maximum stay is usually eight nights unless you get special permission. An **HI card** is usually mandatory to stay in an affiliated hostel. Although they are sold at Movijovem's Lisboa office, it is more convenient to get an HI membership before leaving home. See **Hostels**, p. 44. To reserve a bed in the high season, obtain an **International Booking Voucher** from Movijovem (or your country's HI affiliate) and send it from home to the desired hostel four to eight weeks in advance. In the low season, double-check to see if the hostel is open. Large groups should reserve through Movijovem 30 days in advance.

OTHER TYPES OF ACCOMMODATIONS

HOTELS, GUESTHOUSES, AND PENSIONS

Spanish accommodations have many aliases, distinguished by the different grades of rooms. The cheapest and barest options are **casas de huéspedes** and **hospedajes**. While **pensiones** and **fondas** tend to be a bit nicer, all are essentially just boarding houses; these establishments provide basic and well-used rooms with a shared bath, possibly a sink, but no A/C. Higher up the ladder, **hostales** generally have sinks in bedrooms and provide sheets and lockers, while **hostal-residéncias** are similar to hotels in overall quality. The government rates *hostales* on a two-star system; even one-star establishments are typically quite comfortable. The system also fixes prices, which are required by law to be posted in the lounge or main entrance. *Hostal* owners invariably dip below official rates in the off season (Sept.-May), so bargain away.

The highest-priced accommodations are **hoteles**, which have a bathroom in each room but are usually on the pricey side, and rated with one to five stars. The top-notch hotels are the government-run **Paradores Nacionales**—castles, palaces, convents, and historic buildings that have been converted into luxurious hotels; they often are interesting sights in their own right. For a *parador*, €75 per night is a bargain. If you have trouble with rates or service, ask for the **libro de reclamaciones** (complaint book), which by law must be produced on demand. The argument will usually end there, since complaints must be forwarded to authorities within 48hr. Report any problems to tourist offices, who may help you resolve disputes.

In Portugal, **pensões**, also called **residencias**, are a budget traveler's mainstay. They're far cheaper than hotels and only slightly more expensive (and much more common) than crowded youth hostels. Like hostels, *pensões* generally provide sheets and towels. All are rated on a five-star scale and are required to post their category and legal price limits. In the high season, many do not take reservations; for those that do, booking a week ahead is advisable.

Hotels in Portugal tend to be pricey. Room prices typically include breakfast and showers, and most rooms that lack a bath or shower have a sink. When business is weak, try bargaining in advance—the "official price" is just the maximum allowed. **Pousadas**, like Spanish *paradores*, outperform standard hotel expectations, but unfortunately have higher rates. Most are castles, palaces, or monasteries converted into luxurious, government-run hotels. "Historical" *pousadas* play up local customs and cuisine and may cost as much as expensive hotels. Most require reservations. Regional *pousadas* are situated in national parks and reserves and are priced much less extravagantly. For info, contact **ENATUR** (☎ 218 44 20 01; www.pousadas.com).

ALTERNATIVE ACCOMMODATIONS

For a cozy alternative to impersonal hotel rooms, B&Bs (private homes with rooms available to travelers) range from acceptable to sublime. Rooms in B&Bs generally cost **€30-50** per person in Spain and €40-60 in Portugal. Check out **Inn-Finder** (www.inncrawler.com), **InnSite** (www.innsite.com), **BedandBreakfast.com** (www.bedandbreakfast.com), or **Pamela Lanier's Bed & Breakfast Guide Online** (www.lanierbb.com) or **BNBFinder.com** (www.bnbfinder.com) for B&B listings.

In less-touristed areas in Spain, **casas particulares** (private residences) are sometimes the only option. Look for signs in windows if you're not accosted by owners in the bus or train station. **Casas rurales** (rural cottages) and **casas rústicas** (farmhouses), referred to as *agriturismo*, have overnight rates from €6-21. In the Pyrenees and Picos de Europa, there are several **refugios**, rustic mountain huts for hikers. In Portu-

HOSTAL ATENAS

The Hostal Atenas offers you accomodation with T.V., central heating and A/C, telephone, and private parking!

Gran Via de Colón, 38
Tlf.: 958 27 87 50 • Fax: 958 29 26 76
18010 Granada (España)
mail: info@hostalatenas.com
www.hostalatenas.com

gal, **quartos** are rooms in private residences, similar to *casas particulares* in Spain. These rooms may be your only option in smaller, less touristed towns, or the cheapest one in bigger cities. The tourist office can usually help you find a *quarto* (room). When all else fails, ask at restaurants for names and addresses, but try to verify the safety and quality of the rooms. Prices are flexible and bargaining is possible.

HOME EXCHANGES AND HOSPITALITY CLUBS

Home exchange offers the traveler various types of homes (houses, apartments, condominiums, villas, even castles in some cases), plus the opportunity to live like a native and to cut down on accommodation fees. For more information, contact HomeExchange.com, P.O. Box 787, Hermosa Beach, CA 90254, USA (☎ 800-877-8723; www.homeexchange.com), **or** Intervac International Home Exchange (in Spain, ☎ 934 53 31 71; www.intervac.com).

   Hospitality clubs link their members with individuals or families abroad who are willing to host travelers for free or for a small fee to promote cultural exchange and general good karma. In exchange, members usually must be willing to host travelers in their own homes; a small membership fee may also be required. **GlobalFreeloaders.com** (www.globalfreeloaders.com) and **The Hospitality Club** (www.hospitalityclub.org) are good places to start. **Servas** (www.servas.org) is an established, more formal, peace-based organization, and requires a fee and an interview to join. An Internet search will find many similar organizations, some of which cater to special interests (e.g., women, GLBT travelers, or members of certain professions). As always, use common sense when planning to stay with or host someone you do not know.

LONG-TERM ACCOMMODATIONS

Travelers planning to stay in Spain or Portugal for extended periods of time may find it most cost-effective to rent an **apartment.** Many students spend time living in sublets, and there are plenty of places to be found. A basic one-bedroom (or studio) apartment in Madrid, Barcelona, or Lisboa will range €250-500 per month. In addition to the rent itself, prospective tenants usually are also required to front a security deposit (frequently one month's rent) and the last month's rent. **Expatriates.com** (www.expatriates.com) has a bulletin board with apartments for rent with extensive listings for Spain and Portugal.

CAMPING

Campgrounds exist throughout Spain and Portugal; their popularity varies by region. They are frequently located on the outskirts of cities and towns, making for inconvenient or extensive commutes. Campers heading to Europe should consider buying an **International Camping Carnet.** Similar to a hostel membership card, it's required at a few campgrounds and provides discounts at others. It is available in North America from the **Family Campers and RVers Association** and in the UK from **The Caravan Club** (see below).

   In Spain, **campgrounds** are generally the cheapest choice for three or more people. Most charge separate fees per person, per tent, and per car; others charge for a *parcela*—a small plot of land—plus per-person fees. Most of these fees will be under €10, but they can pile up; although it may seem like a budget option, prices get high for lone travelers and even for pairs. Campgrounds are categorized on a three-class system, with rating and prices based on amenity quality. Like hostels, they must post fees within view of the entrance. They must also provide sinks, showers, and toilets, and some have a small grocery store or restaurant. Most tourist offices provide info on official areas, including the hefty *Guía de campings*.

   In Portugal, over 150 **official campgrounds** *(parques de campismo)* with amenities. Most have a supermarket or cafe, and many are beach-accessible. Urban and coastal parks may require reservations. Police are cracking down on illegal camping, so don't try it. Tourist offices stock *Portugal: Camping and Caravan Sites*, a free guide to official campgrounds. Otherwise, contact the **Federação de Campismo e Montanhismo de Portugal** (☎218 12 68 90; www.fcmportugal.com). For more information on outdoor activities in Spain and Portugal, see **The Great Outdoors**.

THE GREAT OUTDOORS

The **Great Outdoor Recreation Page** (www.gorp.com) provides excellent general information for travelers planning on camping or spending time in the outdoors.

 LEAVE NO TRACE. Let's Go encourages travelers to embrace the "Leave No Trace" ethic, minimizing their impact on natural environments and protecting them for future generations. Trekkers and wilderness enthusiasts should set up camp on durable surfaces, use cookstoves instead of campfires, bury human waste away from water supplies, bag trash and carry it out with them, and respect wildlife and natural objects. For more detailed information, contact the **Leave No Trace Center for Outdoor Ethics,** P.O. Box 997, Boulder, CO 80306 (☎800-332-4100 or 303-442-8222; www.lnt.org).

USEFUL RESOURCES

A variety of publishing companies offer hiking guidebooks to meet the educational needs of novice or expert. For information about camping, hiking, and biking, write or call the publishers listed below to receive a free catalog.

Automobile Association, Contact Centre, Lambert House, Stockport Road, Cheadle SK8 2DY, UK (☎08706 000 371; www.theAA.com). Publishes Caravan and Camping Europe and Britain & Ireland (UK£10) as well as road atlases for Europe, Britain, France, Germany, Ireland, Italy, Spain, and the US.

Federação de Campismo e Montanhismo de Portugal, Av. Coronel Eduardo Galhardo, 24 D, 1199-007 Lisboa, Portugal (☎218126890/1; www.fcmportugal.com). Provides information on camping and hiking throughout Portugal.

Federación Española de Montañismo, Calle Floridablanca, 75, Arroyo Resno, 28035 Madrid (☎934 26 42 67). Provides local information on hiking and rock climbing.

Federación Española de Deportes de Invierno, Arroyo Fresno 3A, 28035 Madrid (☎913 76 99 30). Helps with ski conditions, ski rentals, and any other winter sport questions you might have.

The Caravan Club, East Grinstead House, East Grinstead, West Sussex, RH19 1UA, UK (☎01342 326 944; www.caravanclub.co.uk). For UK£34, members receive access to sites, insurance services, equipment discounts, maps, and a monthly magazine.

Sierra Club Books, 85 Second St., 2nd fl., San Francisco, CA 94105, USA (☎415-977-5500; www.sierraclub.org). Publishes general resource books on hiking and camping.

The Mountaineers Books, 1001 SW Klickitat Way, Ste. 201, Seattle, WA 98134, USA (☎206-223-6303; www.mountaineersbooks.org). Over 600 titles on hiking, biking, mountaineering, natural history, and conservation.

NATIONAL PARKS

Spain and Portugal have extensive national park systems which offer numerous opportunities for hiking, mountaineering, and generally avoiding the cities. Camp-

ing within national park boundaries is usually illegal, but campgrounds can be found in most nearby towns. The general procedure is to stock up on equipment and supplies, stop by the visitor information center to pick up free maps, and head into the park. More detailed maps, with specific hiking or adventure information, can be purchased both at the Visitors Centers and in nearby towns.

The Spanish government website La Red de Parques Nacionales (www.mma.es/parques/lared) provides information in Spanish about the national park system, including trip-planning tools. Portugal inSite (www.visitportugal.com), the official Portuguese tourist office website, offers some information in English and links to details about the parks, usually in Portuguese.

WILDERNESS SAFETY

Staying **warm, dry,** and **well hydrated** is key to a happy and safe wilderness experience. For any hike, prepare yourself for an emergency by packing a first-aid kit, a reflector, a whistle, high-energy food, extra water, raingear, a hat, mittens, and extra socks. For warmth, wear wool or insulating synthetic materials designed for the outdoors. Cotton is a bad choice as it dries painfully slowly.

Check **weather forecasts** often and pay attention to the skies when hiking, as weather patterns can change suddenly. Always let someone—a friend, your hostel, a park ranger, or a local hiking organization—know when and where you are going. Know your physical limits and do not attempt a hike beyond your ability. See **Safety and Health,** p. 20, for information on outdoor medical concerns.

WILDLIFE

Spain and Portugal are home to a few species of poisonous snakes. When traveling in Northern Portugal, Galicia, León, the Cantabrian coastal strip, and the Basque Country, travelers should be on the lookout for **Seoane's viper,** which grows to be about 75cm long and comes in four color-pattern types: A brown zigzag down the back against a beige or light-gray color, a twin-striped pattern, a uniform brown color with no pattern, and a fragmented zigzag pattern. The snub-nosed or **Lataste's viper** is present throughout the peninsula. This gray, short snake (50 cm) can be recognized by the prominent horn between its eyes, triangular-shaped head, and zig-zag pattern on the back. They tend to live in dry, rocky areas. The 2-metre long **Montpellier snake,** blue with a white underbelly and with prominent ridges over the eyes, is present in Portugal's Algarve and throughout Spain, except for Northern Galicia, Asturias, Cantabria, and the Basque Country. The **False Smooth snake** is found in the Algarve, and the Pyrenees are a home to the **Asp viper,** which grows to an average length of 60-65 cm and has a broad, triangular head.

Snakes hibernate and thus bites are only likely to occur in the spring and summer. Though you should be wary, remember that most snakes will escape at the approach of a human rather than attack. Because snakes cannot open their mouths very wide and the poison is located in the back of the their mouths, a snake bite may not actually be a serious danger. If you are bitten, seek out medical attention immediately.

Travelers should also be aware of the **Mediterranean scorpion.** Wearing boots and thick socks when hiking in dry rocky areas is a good idea. Finally, **Pine Processionary caterpillars** are small but troublesome. When touched, these hairy caterpillars cause an extreme allergic reaction; children have gone temporarily blind from rubbing their eyes after touching them. The caterpillars live in silvery nests in pine trees throughout Spain and Portugal and move in the head-to-tail files which give them their name.

CAMPING AND HIKING EQUIPMENT

WHAT TO BUY

Good camping equipment is both sturdy and light. North American suppliers tend to offer the most competitive prices.

ESSENTIALS

Sleeping Bags: Most sleeping bags are rated by season; "summer" means 30-40°F (around 0°C) at night; "four-season" or "winter" often means below 0°F (-17°C). Bags are made of **down** (warm and light, but expensive, and miserable when wet) or of **synthetic** material (heavy, durable, and warm when wet). Prices range US$50-250 for a summer synthetic to US$200-300 for a good down winter bag. **Sleeping bag pads** include foam pads (US$10-30), air mattresses (US$15-50), and self-inflating mats (US$30-120). Bring a **stuff sack** to store your bag and keep it dry.

Tents: The best tents are free-standing (with their own frames and suspension systems), set up quickly, and only require staking in high winds. Low-profile dome tents are the best all-around. Worthy 2-person tents start at US$100, 4-person tents start at US$160. Make sure your tent has a rain fly and seal its seams with waterproofer. Other useful accessories include a **battery-operated lantern,** a plastic **groundcloth,** and a nylon **tarp.**

Backpacks: Internal-frame packs mold well to your back, keep a lower center of gravity, and flex adequately to allow you to hike difficult trails, while **external-frame packs** are more comfortable for long hikes over even terrain, as they carry weight higher and distribute it more evenly. Make sure your pack has a strong, padded hip-belt to transfer weight to your legs. There are models designed specifically for women. Any serious backpacking requires a pack of at least 4000 cu. in. (16,000cc), plus 500 cu. in. for sleeping bags in internal-frame packs. Sturdy backpacks cost anywhere from US$125 to 420—your pack is an area where it doesn't pay to economize. On your hunt for the perfect pack, fill up prospective models with something heavy, strap it on correctly, and walk around the store to get a sense of how the model distributes weight. Either buy a **rain cover** (US$10-20) or store all of your belongings in plastic bags inside your pack.

Boots: Be sure to wear hiking boots with good **ankle support.** They should fit snugly and comfortably over 1-2 pairs of **wool socks** and a pair of thin **liner socks.** Break in boots over several weeks before you go to spare yourself blisters.

Other Necessities: Synthetic layers, like those made of polypropylene or polyester, and a pile jacket will keep you warm even when wet. A **space blanket** (US$5-15) will help you to retain body heat and doubles as a groundcloth. Plastic **water bottles** are vital; look for shatter- and leak-resistant models. Carry **water-purification tablets** for when you can't boil water. Although most campgrounds provide campfire sites, you may want to bring a small **metal grate** or **grill.** For those places (including virtually every organized campground in Europe) that forbid fires or the gathering of firewood, you'll need a **camp stove** (the classic Coleman starts at US$50) and a propane-filled **fuel bottle** to operate it. Also bring a **first-aid kit, pocketknife, insect repellent,** and **waterproof matches** or a **lighter.**

WHERE TO BUY IT

The online and mail-order companies listed below offer lower prices than many retail stores. A visit to a local camping or outdoors store will give you a good sense of the look and weight of certain items before you buy.

Campmor, 400 Corporate Dr., PO Box 680, Mahwah, NJ 07430, USA (☎800-525-4784; www.campmor.com).

Cotswold Outdoor, Unit 11 Kemble Business Park, Crudwell, Malmesbury Wiltshire, SN16 9SH, UK (☎08704 427 755; www.cotswoldoutdoor.com).

Discount Camping, 833 Main North Rd., Pooraka, South Australia 5095, Australia (☎618 8262 3399; www.discountcamping.com.au).

Eastern Mountain Sports (EMS), 1 Vose Farm Rd., Peterborough, 03458 NH, USA (☎888-463-6367; www.ems.com).

Gear-Zone, 8 Burnet Rd., Sweetbriar Rd. Industrial Estate, Norwich, NR3 2BS, UK (☎1603 410 108; www.gear-zone.co.uk).

L.L. Bean, Freeport, ME 04033, USA (US and Canada ☎800-441-5713; UK 0800 891 297; www.llbean.com).

Mountain Designs, 443a Nudgee Rd., Hendra, Queensland 4011, Australia (☎617 3114 4300; www.mountaindesigns.com).

Recreational Equipment, Inc. (REI), Sumner, WA 98352, USA (US and Canada ☎800-426-4840, elsewhere 253-891-2500; www.rei.com).

ORGANIZED ADVENTURE TRIPS

Organized adventure tours offer another way of exploring the wild. Activities include hiking, biking, skiing, canoeing, kayaking, rafting, climbing, photo safaris, and archaeological digs. Tourism bureaus often can suggest parks, trails, and outfitters. Organizations that specialize in camping and outdoor equipment like REI and EMS (see above) also are good sources for information.

Specialty Travel Index, P.O. Box 458, San Anselmo, CA 94979, USA (US ☎888-624-4030, elsewhere 415-455-1643; www.specialtytravel.com).

ESSENTIALS

ESSENTIALS

SPECIFIC CONCERNS

SUSTAINABLE TRAVEL

As the number of travelers on the road continues to rise, the detrimental effect they can have on natural environments becomes an increasing concern. With this in mind, Let's Go promotes the philosophy of **sustainable travel.** Through a sensitivity to issues of ecology and sustainability, today's travelers can be a powerful force in preserving as well as restoring the places they visit.

Ecotourism, a rising trend in sustainable travel, focuses on the conservation of natural habitats and how to use them to build up the economy without exploitation or overdevelopment. Travelers can make a difference by doing research in advance and by supporting organizations and establishments that pay attention to their impact on their natural surroundings and that strive to be environmentally friendly. Staying at organic farms, campgrounds, or long-established monasteries and convents is one way to minimize your mark in fragile areas. Patronizing local markets instead of tourist restaurants also helps. You can take part in more specialized conservation efforts in the Algarve and the Costa de la Luz, where the government is currently establishing new national parks (**Beyond Tourism,** p. 61).

ECOTOURISM RESOURCES. For more information on environmentally responsible tourism, contact one of the organizations below:
Conservation International, 2011 Crystal Dr., Ste. 500, Arlington, VA 22202, USA (☎800-406-2306 or 703-341-2400; www.conservation.org).
Green Globe 21, Green Globe vof, Verbenalaan 1, 2111 ZL Aerdenhout, The Netherlands (☎31 23 544 0306; www.greenglobe.com).
International Ecotourism Society, 1333 H St. NW, Ste. 300E, Washington, D.C. 20005, USA (☎202-347-9203; www.ecotourism.org).
United Nations Environment Program (UNEP), 39-43 Quai André Citroën, 75739 Paris Cedex 15, France (☎33 1 44 37 14 50; www.uneptie.org/).

RESPONSIBLE TRAVEL

The impact of tourist euros on the destinations you visit should not be underestimated. Travelers who care about the destinations and environments they explore should make themselves aware of the social, cultural and political implications of the choices they make when they travel. Simple decisions such as buying local products instead of globally available ones, paying fair prices for products or services, and attempting to say a few words in the local language can have a strong, positive effect on the community.

Community-based tourism aims to channel tourist money into the local economy by emphasizing tours and cultural programs that are run by members of the host community and that often benefit disadvantaged groups. Portugal in particular is making an effort to direct tourists away from the beach regions of the Algarve and toward places such as Madeira and Azores. The *Ethical Travel Guide* (UK£13), a project of **Tourism Concern** (☎44 020 7133 3330; www.tourismconcern.org.uk), is an excellent resource for information on community-based travel with a directory of 300 establishments for 60 countries.

TRAVELING ALONE

There are many benefits to traveling alone, including independence and a greater opportunity to connect with locals. On the other hand, solo travelers are more vulnerable targets of harassment and street theft. If you are traveling alone, look confident, try not to stand out as a tourist, and be especially careful in deserted or very crowded areas. Stay away from areas that are not well lit. If questioned, never admit that you are traveling alone. Maintain regular contact with someone at home who knows your itinerary, and always research your destination before traveling. For more tips, pick up *Traveling Solo* by Eleanor Berman (Globe Pequot Press, US$18), visit www.travelaloneandloveit.com, or subscribe to **Connecting: Solo Travel Network,** 689 Park Rd., Unit 6, Gibsons, BC V0N 1V7, Canada (☎604-886-9099; www.cstn.org; membership US$30-48).

WOMEN TRAVELERS

Women exploring on their own inevitably face some additional safety concerns, but it's easy to be adventurous without taking undue risks. If you are concerned, consider staying in hostels which offer single rooms that lock from the inside or in religious organizations with single-sex rooms. Stick to centrally located accommodations and avoid solitary late-night treks or metro rides.

Always carry extra cash for a phone call, bus, or taxi. **Hitchhiking** is never safe for lone women, or even for two women traveling together. Look as if you know where you're going and approach older women or couples for directions if you're lost or uncomfortable. Generally, the less you look like a tourist, the better off you'll be. Dress conservatively, especially in rural areas. Wearing a conspicuous

TOP 10 WAYS TO SAVE IN SPAIN AND PORTUGAL

Exchange rate pinching your pocket? Travel in style while sticking to a budget with these tips for cheap eats, low-cost lodgings, and free entertainment.

1. Buy food in **open-air markets** and **grocery stores** instead of restaurants. If you do eat out, opt for a mix of **tapas** in Spain or a *tosta* in Portugal.

2. Stay in **alternative lodgings**, such as monasteries, university dorms, or *refugios*.

3. Be on the lookout for days when you can get into sights and museums for **free**.

4. Clubbing is expensive enough without depending on overpriced *sangria*; start the night off with **market-purchased booze**.

5. Keep an eye out for flyers and coupons (in weekly papers or from promoters) that offer **heavy discounts** at clubs.

6. Take **public transportation** or **walk** as much as possible.

7. Relax on one of the Iberian peninsula's many **beaches** or **parks,** where the scenery is worthwhile and your tan is **free!**

8. Bargain where appropriate, like in Madrid's El Rastro.

9. Enjoy the **great outdoors**; hike in the Pyrenees, or enjoy the view of the Alhambra from the hills of Granada.

10. Get **cheap tickets** for *flamenco* and bullfighting by attending semi-professional shows. They're less touristy, too.

wedding band sometimes helps to prevent unwanted advances.

Your best answer to verbal harassment is no answer at all; simply walking away or feigning deafness, sitting motionless, and staring straight ahead at nothing in particular will usually do the trick. The extremely persistent can sometimes be dissuaded by a firm, loud, and very public "Go away!" in the appropriate language (in Spanish "déjame en paz," in Portuguese "vá-se embora"). Don't hesitate to seek out a police officer or a passerby if you are being harassed. Memorize the emergency numbers in places you visit, and consider carrying a whistle on your keychain. A self-defense course will both prepare you for a potential attack and raise your level of awareness of your surroundings (see **Personal Safety,** p. 20). Also be sure you are aware of the health concerns that women face when traveling (see p. 25).

GLBT TRAVELERS

Attitudes toward gay, lesbian, bisexual, and transgendered (GLBT) people in Spain and Portugal vary by region. GLBT travelers may feel out of place in the smaller, rural areas of Spain and Portugal, given the countries' strong Catholic heritage, but overt homophobia is rare. In Spain, Sitges (p. 414), Benidorm (p. 334), and Ibiza (p. 363) are internationally renowned as gay party destinations, and Madrid (see Chueca, p. 101) hosts the famous party Orgullo Gay (Gay Pride) in June. The website www.guiagay.com has info about gay Spain; www.portugalgay.pt offers listings in Portuguese and English.

Listed below are contact organizations, mail-order catalogs, and publishers that offer materials addressing some specific concerns. **Out and About** (www.planetout.com) offers a weekly newsletter addressing travel concerns and a comprehensive site addressing gay travel concerns. The online newspaper **365gay.com** also has a travel section (www.365gay.com/travel/travelchannel.htm).

Gay's the Word, 66 Marchmont St., London WC1N 1AB, UK (☎44 020 7278 7654; http://freespace.virgin.net/gays.theword/). The largest gay and lesbian bookshop in the UK, with both fiction and non-fiction titles. Mail-order service available.

Giovanni's Room, 345 South 12th St., Philadelphia, PA 19107, USA (☎215-923-2960; www.queerbooks.com). An international lesbian and gay bookstore with mail-order service (carries many of the publications listed below).

International Lesbian and Gay Association (ILGA), Avenue des Villas 34, 1060 Brussels, Belgium (☎32

2 502 2471; www.ilga.org). Provides political information, such as homosexuality laws of individual countries.

> **ADDITIONAL RESOURCES: GLBT.**
> *Spartacus 2005-2006: International Gay Guide.* Bruno Gmunder Verlag (US$33).
> *Damron Men's Travel Guide, Damron Accommodations Guide, Damron City Guide,* and *Damron Women's Traveller.* Damron Travel Guides (US$18-24).
> For info, call ☎800-462-6654 or visit www.damron.com.
> *The Gay Vacation Guide: The Best Trips and How to Plan Them,* Mark Chesnut. Kensington Books (US$15).

TRAVELERS WITH DISABILITIES

Wheelchair accessibility varies widely in Iberia but is generally inferior to that in the US. Handicapped access is common in modern and big city museums. Some Spanish tourist offices abroad can provide useful listings of accessible (but often expensive) accommodations and sights.

Those with disabilities, (*inhabilidades* in Spanish, *inabilidades* in Portuguese) should inform airlines and hotels of their disabilities when making reservations; some time may be needed to prepare accommodations. Call ahead to restaurants, museums, and other facilities to find out if they are wheelchair accessible. **Guide dog owners** should inquire on policies of each destination country.

Rail is probably the easiest form of travel for disabled travelers in Europe: many stations have ramps, and some trains have wheelchair lifts, special seating areas, and specially equipped toilets. All Eurostar, some InterCity (IC), and some EuroCity (EC) trains are wheelchair accessible, and CityNightLine trains and Conrail trains feature special compartments. Some car rental agencies (e.g., Hertz) offer hand-controlled vehicles.

USEFUL ORGANIZATIONS

Accessible Journeys, 35 West Sellers Ave., Ridley Park, PA 19078, USA (☎800 846 4537; www.disabilitytravel.com). Designs tours for wheelchair users and slow walkers. The site has tips and forums for all travelers.

Flying Wheels Travel, 143 W. Bridge St., Owatonna, MN 55060, USA (☎507-451-5005; www.flyingwheelstravel.com). Specializes in escorted trips to Europe for people with physical disabilities; plans custom trips worldwide.

The Guided Tour, Inc., 7900 Old York Rd., Ste. 114B, Elkins Park, PA 19027, USA (☎800-783-5841; www.guidedtour.com). Organizes travel programs for persons with developmental and physical challenges in Canada, Hawaii, Ireland, Italy, Mexico, Spain, the UK, and the US.

Mobility International USA (MIUSA), P.O. Box 10767, Eugene, OR 97440, USA (☎541-343-1284; www.miusa.org). Provides a variety of books and other publications containing information for travelers with disabilities.

Society for Accessible Travel and Hospitality (SATH), 347 Fifth Ave., Ste. 610, New York, NY 10016, USA (☎212-447-7284; www.sath.org). An advocacy group that publishes free online travel information. Annual membership US$49, students and seniors US$29.

MINORITY TRAVELERS

The cities of Spain are increasingly cosmopolitan due to immigration and tourism. The infrequent incidents of racism are rarely violent or threatening. However, after the arrest of Moroccans for the terrorist attack of 11-M (p. 79), travelers who appear Middle Eastern may face some harassment. Portugal, with its rich ethnic composition, is actively anti-racist.

DIETARY CONCERNS

Spain and Portugal can be difficult places to visit as a strict vegetarian; meat or fish are featured in most popular dishes. Markets are a good choice, and Barcelona has over 40 strictly-vegetarian restaurants. Be careful, as many servers may interpret a "vegetarian" order to mean "with tuna or chicken instead of ham." The travel section of the The Vegetarian Resource Group's website, www.vrg.org/travel, has a comprehensive list of organizations and websites that are geared toward helping vegetarians and vegans traveling abroad. For more information, consult *The Vegetarian Traveler: Where to Stay if You're Vegetarian, Vegan, Environmentally Sensitive*, by Jed and Susan Civic (Larson Publications; US$16). Vegetarians will also find numerous resources on the web; try www.vegdining.com, www.happycow.net, and www.vegetariansabroad.com, for starters. The phrase "I don't eat meat," is translated as "Yo no como carne" in Spanish, and "Eu não como a carne," in Portuguese. "Without meat" is translated as "sin carne," and "sem carne," respectively.

Travelers who keep **kosher** should contact synagogues in larger cities for information on kosher restaurants. You can use the worldwide kosher restaurant database at www.shamash.org/kosher. A good resource is the *Jewish Travel Guide*, edited by Michael Zaidner (Vallentine Mitchell; US$18). Travelers looking for **halal** restaurants may find www.zabihah.com a useful resource.

OTHER RESOURCES

Let's Go tries to cover all aspects of budget travel, but we can't put *everything* in our guides. Listed below are books and websites that can serve as jumping-off points for your own research.

USEFUL PUBLICATIONS

The Broadsheet, a monthly magazine for English speakers in Spain. Features current cultural and social events, as well as news. Web edition at www.tbs.com.es.

Contemporary Spain: A Handbook, by Christopher Ross. Broad and informative discussion of Spanish politics, culture, society, and travel (US$25).

Focus Magazine, (www.focusmm.com), a monthly online magazine about the Mediterranean world, with information on Spain.

WORLD WIDE WEB

Almost every aspect of budget travel is accessible via the web. In 10min. at the keyboard, you can make a hostel reservation, get advice on travel hot spots from other travelers, or find out how much a train from Porto to Lisbon costs.

Listed here are some regional and travel-related sites to start off your surfing; other relevant websites are listed throughout the book. Because website turnover is high, use search engines (e.g., www.google.com) to strike out on your own.

THE ART OF TRAVEL

Backpacker's Ultimate Guide: www.bugeurope.com. Tips on packing, transportation, and where to go. Also tons of country-specific travel information.

WWW.LETSGO.COM. Our website features extensive content from our guides; a community forum where travelers can connect with each other, ask questions or advice, and share stories and tips; and expanded resources to help you plan your trip. Visit us to browse by destination and find information about ordering our titles!

BootsnAll.com: www.bootsnall.com. Numerous resources for independent travelers, from planning your trip to reporting on it when you get back.

How to See the World: www.artoftravel.com. A compendium of great travel tips, from cheap flights to self defense to interacting with local culture.

Travel Intelligence: www.travelintelligence.net. A large collection of travel writing by distinguished travel writers.

Travel Library: www.travel-library.com. A fantastic set of links for general information and personal travelogues.

World Hum: www.worldhum.com. An independently produced collection of "travel dispatches from a shrinking planet."

INFORMATION ON SPAIN AND PORTUGAL

A Collection of Home Pages About Portugal: www.well.com/user/ideamen/portugal.html.

CIA World Factbook: www.odci.gov/cia/publications/factbook/index.html. Tons of vital statistics on (your country's) geography, government, economy, and people.

Geographia: www.geographia.com. Highlights, culture, and people of Iberia.

TravelPage: www.travelpage.com. Links to official tourist office sites in Iberia.

PlanetRider: www.planetrider.com. A subjective list of links to the "best" websites covering the culture and tourist attractions of Spain and Portugal.

Portugal-info: www.portugal-info.net. Great source for all types of information, from photos to wine descriptions to Portuguese personals.

Spain Tourism: www.tourspain.es. The **official** Spanish tourism site. Offers national and city-specific info, an information request service, helpful links on all aspects of travel, cultural and practical info including stats on national parks and museums, and links to the biggest Spanish newspapers. In English, French, German, and Spanish.

World Travel Guide: www.travel-guides.com. Helpful practical info.

BEYOND TOURISM

A PHILOSOPHY FOR TRAVELERS

HIGHLIGHTS OF BEYOND TOURISM IN SPAIN AND PORTUGAL

DISCOVER the joys of cooking Basque cuisine in **San Sebastián**, Spain (p. 70).

STOMP your feet in courses on flamenco dance and guitar in **Sevilla**, Spain (p. 70).

BUILD houses in **Braga**, Portugal in between sightseeing (p. 65).

Spain is the world's second most touristed country, and Portugal ranks among the top 20. While certain aspects of Spanish and Portuguese life have benefited from visitors—tourism certainly provides an essential economic boost—other aspects have been jeopardized or damaged. Spain risks becoming economically dependent on tourism, while the Algarve in Southern Portugal has experienced ecological destruction due to massive amounts of visitors. A single tourist can unwittingly participate in cultural and ecological erosion. Responsible and socially-conscious tourism is therefore a must for every traveler.

Some travelers choose to make social and environmental issues the focus of their trip. While hostel-hopping and sightseeing can be great fun, you may want to consider going *beyond* tourism. As a tourist you are always a foreigner, but connecting with a foreign place through studying, volunteering, or working can reduce that stranger-in-a-strange-land feeling. Furthermore, travelers can have a positive impact on the natural and cultural environments they visit, making an experience abroad both more authentic and more rewarding. With this Beyond Tourism chapter, *Let's Go* hopes to promote a better understanding of Spain and Portugal and to provide suggestions for those who want more than a photo album out of their travels. The "Giving Back" sidebar features (p. 301 and p. 679) also highlight regional Beyond Tourism opportunities.

There are several options for those seeking Beyond Tourism activities. Opportunities for **volunteerism** abound, both with local and international organizations. **Studying** can also be very fulfilling, whether through direct enrollment in a local university or an independent research project. **Working** is also a way to immerse yourself in the local culture and to finance your travels.

As a **volunteer** in Spain and Portugal, you can participate in projects ranging from fighting AIDS to ending bullfighting, either on a short-term basis or as the main component of your trip. Later in this chapter, we recommend organizations that can help you find the opportunities that best suit your interests, whether you're looking to pitch in for a day or a year.

Studying at a college or in a language program is another option. You can enroll directly in most Spanish and Portuguese universities or study with American programs that guide you through your foreign travel. Any of these programs can be excellent tools for earnest cultural interaction, as they often organize activities that place you right in the heart of a community. Take an art history class at the Prado or do a homestay with a Portuguese family and you may find yourself having a remarkably authentic experience.

Many travelers also structure their trips by the **work** that they can do along the way, either odd jobs as they go, or full-time stints in cities where they plan to stay for some time. Those staying in a city, particularly one with a university, will find positions teaching English readily available in most of Spain and Portugal. In order to work in either country, you must meet the **legal requirements** for either short- or long-term work (see **Working,** p. 70, for more information).

VOLUNTEERING

Throughout Spain and Portugal, you will find ample opportunities to help out. Volunteers from all over the world work to conserve diverse habitats, reach out to immigrants, AIDS patients, and children in need, or fight for other causes that inspire their passions.

Most people who volunteer in Spain and Portugal do so on a short-term basis, at organizations that make use of drop-in or once-a-week volunteers. Volunteers in Spain include those who work both formally, for organizations like social action NGOs, and those who do more informal work such as environmental cleanup. In Spain, the best way to find opportunities that match up with your interests may be to check with **Plataforma del Voluntariado de España,** C. Fuentes, 10, Madrid (☎902 12 05 12; fax 91 541 21. www.plataformavoluntariado.org). Travelers should also note that each autonomous community in Spain has its own volunteer center.

Those looking for longer, more intensive volunteer opportunities usually choose to go through a parent organization that takes care of logistical details and often provides a group environment and support system for a fee. There are two main types of organizations, religious and non-sectarian, although there are rarely restrictions on participation for either.

WHY PAY MONEY TO VOLUNTEER? Many volunteers are surprised to learn that some organizations require large fees or donations. While this may seem ridiculous at first, such fees often keep the organization afloat, in addition to covering airfare, room, board, and administrative expenses for the volunteers. (Other organizations must rely on private donations and government subsidies.) If you're concerned about how a program spends its fees, request an annual report or finance account. A reputable organization won't refuse to inform you of how volunteer money is spent. Pay-to-volunteer programs might be a good idea for young travelers who are looking for more support and structure (such as pre-arranged transportation and housing), or anyone who would rather not deal with the uncertainty implicit in creating a volunteer experience from scratch.

ENVIRONMENTAL CONSERVATION

Development, the abuse of natural resources, and of course tourism all threaten Spain and Portugal's vast tracts of unspoiled terrain and water. One way to give back to the countries you visit is to help preserve them for future generations and future travelers. An added bonus of working with the following organizations (or any environmental conservation group in Spain or Portugal) is the chance to enjoy the immense beauty of the landscapes you'll be protecting.

Earthwatch, 3 Clocktower Pl., Ste. 100, Box 75, Maynard, MA 01754, USA (☎800-776-0188 or 978-461-0081; www.earthwatch.org). Arranges 1-3-week programs in Spain to assist archaeologists or conservationists conducting field research. Fees vary based on program location and duration; average cost $2000, plus airfare. Earthwatch also arranges 1-2 week programs in Algarve, Portugal where volunteers help scientists monitor the migration of the storm petrol. Fees vary.

Experience Europe by Eurail!

It's not just the Best Way to See Europe, it's also the cleanest, greenest and smartest

If you believe the journey's as important as the destination then rail's clearly the best way to experience the real Europe. Fast, sleek trains get you where you want to go when you want to go and - mile for mile - do less damage to the environment than cars or planes. Even better, you don't have to navigate unfamiliar roads, pay for gas (it's not cheap in Europe!) or find parking - leaving you more time and money to spend simply enjoying your travel.

Eurail has created a range of passes to suit every conceivable itinerary and budget. So whether you want to discover the whole continent, or focus on just one or two countries, you'll find Eurail the smartest way to do Europe, all around.

Welcome to Europe by Eurail!

EURAIL® *The best way to see Europe*

Ecoforest, Apdo. 29, Coin 29100, Málaga, Spain (☎661 07 99 50; www.ecoforest.org). Fruit farm and vegan community in southern Spain that uses ecoforest education to develop a sustainable lifestyle.

Sunseed Desert Technology, Apdo. 9, 04270 Sorbas, Almería, Spain (☎950 52 57 70; www.sunseed.org.uk). Researches methods of preventing desertification in the driest region of Spain. Volunteers can stay from 1 week to 1 year at costs ranging from €137 per week in high season to none at all for a year-long residency. Room and board included. Student discount available.

Volunteers for Peace, 1034 Tiffany Road, Belmont, VT 05730 (☎802-259-2759; www.vfp.org). Organizes 2-3 week projects in both Spain and Portugal, offering volunteers the opportunity to work on a large variety of issues, including environmental ones. Average cost $300 plus transportation.

World-Wide Opportunities on Organic Farms (WWOOF), puts members in contact with independent organic farms in Spain and Portugal, which offer work in exchange for room and board. WWOOF Spain, Chemi Pena, Yainz, 33 Cereceda, Cantabria, Spain (☎902 010 814; www.wwoof.org).

IMMIGRATION ISSUES

Immigration to Spain has been on the rise ever since the *destapeo* (uncovering) that followed the fall of fascism. Today, Spain has the highest rate of immigration of the European Union. The greatest number of immigrants come from North Africa (particularly from Morocco), while most of the rest are from Latin America. Portugal is home to many immigrants from its former African colonies and Brazil. An immigrant's life can be difficult, and legal structures in both countries often fail to provide equal rights for non-citizens. Portugal is much more tolerant of other cultures than Spain, and its attitude toward immigration is less hostile. There are many Spanish organizations working to alleviate the burdens placed on immigrants and eliminate the inequality they face; listed below are just a few of them.

ARSIS, C. General Weyler, 257, 08912 Barcelona, Spain (☎902 88 86 07; www.arsis.org). Opportunities to tutor underprivileged children, work in a women's center, or run food and clothing drives for recent immigrants.

Comisión Española de Ayuda al Refugio (CEAR), C. Noviciado 5, 28015 Madrid, Spain (☎915 55 06 98; www.cear.es). Aims to protect the right to asylum. Opportunities in outreach, legal assistance, translation, and human rights research.

Ecos do Sur, C. Ángel Senra, 25, La Coruña, Spain (☎981 15 01 18; www.ecosdosur.org). Works to ease recent immigrants' transition into Galician society. Teach English, Spanish, or *gallego* language classes (if you're fluent), conduct tests for tuberculosis, or do outreach work in the community.

Federació Catalana de Voluntariat Social, C. Pere Vergès, 1, Barcelona, Spain (☎93 314 19 00; www.federacio.net). Volunteers assist with projects to achieve better standards of living and equality for immigrants to the region.

SOS Racism, C. Hospital, 49, Principal 08001 Barcelona, Spain (☎933 01 05 97; www.sosracisme.org) and Quinta da Torrinha, Lote 11A, 1750 Ameixoeira, Lisboa, Portugal (☎217 55 27 00; www.sosracismo.pt). Volunteers work to combat racism and achieve equal rights for non-citizens and migrant workers.

SOCIAL ACTIVISM

Spain offers opportunities to work for virtually any cause that you're passionate about, with organizations for combating *la SIDA* (AIDS; a growing problem in

Spanish cities and among young people), banning bullfighting, and everything in between. Working for a cause that interests you in Spain or Portugal may give you insight into the global implications of your interests and also provide you with a social network of locals. In order to devote as much of your time as possible to interacting with the people you'll be helping, it's often easier to arrange such activities through established programs.

Abraço, Largo José Luís Champalimaud, 4a, 1600-110 Lisboa, Portugal (☎21 799 75 00; madalena.abraco@netcabo.pt). With multiple offices in Portugal, this non-profit offers support services, fights HIV/AIDS discrimination and works on prevention. Volunteers should contact Madalena Pereira.

Banco Alimentar, Av. de Ceuta, Estação C.P.Alcântara-Terra, Armazém 1, 1300-125 Lisboa, Portugal (☎213 649 655; www.bancoalimentar.pt/index.html). This federation of food banks operates 10 banks throughout Portugal, providing much-needed food for the hungry. Various options for volunteers.

Equanimal, Apartado de Correos, 14454, 28080 Madrid, Spain (☎650 93 10 97; www.equanimal.org). Works for animal rights, including ending bullfighting, through educational efforts. Volunteers participate in demonstrations and help distribute pamphlets and organize events.

Fundación Triángulo, C. Eloy Gonzalo, 25, 28010 Madrid, Spain (☎915 93 05 40; www.fundaciontriangulo.es). Fights discrimination and promotes equality for gay, lesbian, bisexual, and transgendered people in Spain and around the world. Also sponsors a GLBT film festival in Madrid (see **Film,** p. 133). Volunteer for outreach or legal efforts.

Global Village, Habitat for Humanity International, P.O. Box 369, Americus, GA 31709, USA (☎800-422-4828 or 229-924-6935, ext. 2549; www.habitat.org/gv). Volunteers build simple houses in Braga, Portugal and have free days for sightseeing. Programs average 10 days. $1650 plus airfare includes food and accommodations.

Stop SIDA, C. Muntaner, 121, Entresuelo 1, Barcelona, Spain (☎902 10 69 27; www.stopsida.org). A member of the federation of associations Coordinadora GaiLesbian, Stop SIDA helps combat the spread of AIDS by providing info on AIDS prevention and offering support services.

STUDYING

Study abroad programs range from basic language and culture courses to college-level classes, often for credit. In order to choose a program that best fits your needs, research as much as you can before making your decision. Consider costs and duration, as well as what kind of students participate in the program and what sort of accommodations are provided.

Spain is one of the most popular destinations in the world for students studying abroad. To find out more, contact American university programs and youth organizations that send students to Spanish universities and language centers. Madrid, Sevilla, and Salamanca contain numerous programs. While fewer students think of studying abroad in Portugal, most Portuguese universities open their gates to foreign students.

In programs that have large groups of students who speak the same language as you, there is a trade-off. You may feel more comfortable in the community, but you will not have the same opportunity to practice a foreign language or to befriend other international students. For accommodations, dorm life provides a better opportunity to mingle with fellow students, but there is less of a chance to experience the local scene. If you live with a family, there is a potential to build lifelong friendships with locals and to experience day-to-day life in more depth, but conditions can vary greatly from family to family.

BEYOND TOURISM

VISA INFORMATION. Most foreigners planning to study in Spain or Portugal must obtain a student visa. However, those studying for fewer than three months in Spain need only a passport. Visa applications for study in Spain and Portugal can be completed in your home country, at your destination country's consulate (listed under **Consular Services Abroad,** p. 10). Obtaining a visa can be an arduous process; the consulate will often require you to apply in person and demand loads of paperwork (letter verifying enrollment, medical certificate, proof of health insurance, etc.) before they process your application. They are also likely to charge a processing fee of around US$100. To study more than 90 days, you must obtain a student residency card (student visa) once in Spain which is valid for as long as you are enrolled in the university. To study in Portugal for any amount of time, a student visa is required. Make sure to contact the consulate for requirements at least three months before your departure.

UNIVERSITIES

Most university-level study-abroad programs are conducted in the language of the country, although many programs offer classes in English and beginner- and lower-level language courses. Those fluent in Spanish or Portuguese may find it cheaper to enroll directly in a university abroad, although getting college credit may be more difficult. You can search www.studyabroad.com for various semester-abroad programs that meet your criteria, including your desired location and focus of study. The following is a list of organizations that have their own branch in Spain or Portugal and can help place students in university programs abroad.

SPANISH AND PORTUGUESE PROGRAMS

Universities in major cities like Madrid and Lisboa and smaller cities like Salamanca, Granada, and Coimbra also have active study abroad programs and host thousands of foreign students every year. Check with the individual school for specific requirements and enrollment procedures.

Agencia Nacional Erasmus, Vicesecretaría General del Consejo de Universidades, Juan del Rosal, 14, Ciudad Universitaria, 28040 Madrid (☎914 53 98 32; http://wwwn.mec.es/educa/ccuniv/erasmus/). Spanish branch of the European Union's Erasmus program, which offers EU members the opportunity to study within Europe.

Agência Nacional para os Programas Comunitários Sócrates e Leonardo da Vinci, Av. Infante Santo, 2, Piso 1, 1350-178 Lisboa, Portugal (☎21 394 47 60; www.socleo.pt). Portuguese branch of the European Union's study abroad program, which offers the citizens of EU member states the opportunity to study within Europe.

Universidad Complutense de Madrid, Vicerectorado de Relaciones Internacionales, C. Isaac Peral, 28040 Madrid, Spain (☎913 94 69 22/23; www.ucm.es/info/ucmp/index.php). Largest university in Spain. Hosts 3500 foreign students annually. Opportunities for study in a variety of fields.

Universidade de Lisboa, Rectorate Al. da Universidade, Cidade Universitária, Campo Grande, 1649-004 Lisboa, Portugal (☎217 96 76 24; www.ul.pt). Allows foreign students to enroll directly.

OTHER PROGRAMS

Academic Programs International (API), 107 E. Hopkins, San Marcos, TX 78666, USA (☎512-392-8520 or 800-844-4124; www.academicintl.com). Programs available in

another spain

studying abroad in catalunya

The first class I attended at my high school in Manresa, Catalunya, was gym. When the teacher told us in Cat-

"To walk down the boulevard of Manresa speaking Spanish is to be a foreigner."

alán to stretch, I interpreted "meditate" and promptly began. One of my classmates, Dani, who quickly became my best friend, woke me up 15min. later. The only concept I understood the whole first week was "mini-tramp" (miniature trampoline), which apparently has no Catalán equivalent.

I had been accepted by the American Foreign Service Exchange program to spend a year in Spain living with a local host family, attending a Spanish public high school. But when I got on the plane, I still knew nothing about the details, not even in which province I would live. I was placed in Manresa, a small city outside of Barcelona that is often referred to as "al cor de Catalunya," being directly in the center of the region and one of its most fervent strongholds of cultural identity. To walk down the boulevard of this town speaking Spanish is to be a foreigner.

I had never even heard Catalán. Even my Spanish was limited to two years of high school study which, as I learned upon arrival in Madrid, meant little. I arrived in Manresa to meet my host family knowing just two words in Catalán: "Estic cansat" (I'm tired), which after traveling for 8hr. by train from Madrid I certainly was. As it turns out, I could not have been luckier in regard to my host family. My "father," an intelligent, opinionated, but most of all, loving man, worked for the electric company, and was an avid model train enthusiast. My new "mother" was a hairdressing instructor. We reviewed my poor grammar together, and she also gave me free and frequent hair-

cuts. My older "brother," an 18-year-old university student, spoke English well, and my 11-year-old "sister" communicated with funny faces and familiar board games.

At school, Spanish and Catalán were both literature classes; my fellow students were studying Don Quixote and Tirant Lo Blanc. If there were a linguistic equivalent to the mini-tramp, I was on it. Within a month, I could understand most things and communicate on a basic level. Within two months I was communicating in three languages with ease.

Attending school in Spain taught me that the best teachers are often not the ones in front of the class, but the ones in the back, like my friends Dani and Miguel. They showed me what Spanish culture was like in the discos, bars, cafes, restaurants, and in the streets, playing futbolin (foosball) and futbol

"The best teachers are often not the ones in front of the class."

sala (soccer in the plaza).Tired of speaking in Spanish with an obvious American, they pushed me to learn Catalán, and helped me pick out new clothes. Soon I saw people speaking Spanish on the main boulevard and thought of them as foreigners.

I still maintain close ties to Manresa, and although it's been two years since I last visited, I keep in contact with my friends and family there. In another two years, I plan on moving back there, this time for much longer than one year.

A DIFFERENT PATH

Nicholas Mott attended Institut de Batxillerat Lluis de Peguera, a local high school in Manresa, Catalunya, as part of the American Foreign Service Exchange Program. He graduated in 2007 with a degree in anthropology from Harvard University.

Barcelona, Bilbao, Cádiz, Granada, Madrid, Salamanca, and Sevilla. Classes include international business, Spanish literature, and Hispanic studies.

American Institute for Foreign Study, College Division, River Plaza, 9 West Broad St., Stamford, CT 06902, USA (☎800-727-2437; www.aifsabroad.com). Organizes programs for high school and college study in universities in Barcelona, Granada, and Salamanca.

Central College Abroad, Box 0140, 812 University, Pella, IA 50219, USA (☎800-831-3629; www.central.edu/abroad). Offers internships, summer-, semester-, and year-long programs in Granada and a summer ethnographic research program in San Sebastián.

College Consortium for International Study, 2000 P St. NW Ste. 503, Washington, D.C. 20036, USA (☎800-453-6956 or 202-223-0330; www.ccisabroad.org). Offers summer and semester study abroad programs in Spain and Portugal.

Council on International Educational Exchange (CIEE), 7 Custom House St., 3rd fl., Portland, ME 01401, USA (☎800-407-8839 or 207-553-7600; www.ciee.org/study). Sponsors work, volunteer, academic, and internship programs throughout Spain and a new program in Lisbon, Portugal.

Institute for the International Education of Students (IES), 33 N. LaSalle St., 15th fl., Chicago, IL 60602, USA (☎800-995-2300 or 312-944-1750; www.iesabroad.org). Programs in Barcelona, Granada, Madrid, and Salamanca for a year, semester, or summer. Internships available. US$50 application fee. Scholarships available.

International Academic Programs, Study Abroad Resource Room, 250 Bascom Hall, 500 Lincoln Dr., Madison, WI 53706, USA (☎608-265-6329; www.studyabroad.wisc.edu). Affiliated with the University of Wisconsin-Madison. Offers study in Alcala, Granada, Madrid, Seville, and at the University of Coimbra in Portugal.

International Association for the Exchange of Students for Technical Experience (IAESTE), 10400 Little Patuxent Pkwy. Suite 250, Columbia, MD 21044, USA (☎410-997-3068; www.iaeste.org). Offers 8- to 12-week internships in Spain and Portugal for college students who have completed 2 years of technical study.

School for International Training, College Semester Abroad, Kipling Rd., P.O. Box 676, Brattleboro, VT 05302, USA (☎888-272-7881 or 802-258-3212; www.sit.edu/studyabroad). Semester-long, language and culture intensive programs in Spain run US$20,000. Also operates **The Experiment in International Living** (☎800-345-2929; www.usexperiment.org). 3-5-week summer programs that offer high-school students cross-cultural homestays, community service, ecological adventure, and language training in Spain. US$5000-6000.

LANGUAGE SCHOOLS

Language schools are often independently run international or local organizations or divisions of foreign universities. They rarely offer college credit. They are a good alternative to university study if you desire a deeper focus on the language or a slightly less rigorous courseload. These programs are also good for younger high school students who might not feel comfortable with older students in a university program. Some worthwhile programs include:

Amerispan, 117 South 17th St., Philadelphia, PA 19103, USA (☎800-879-6640 or 215-751-1100; www.amerispan.com). Language-immersion programs in Spain and Portugal with homestays and organized activities. 1- to 4-wk. programs $300-$3000.

Center for Cross-Cultural Study, US office at 446 Main St., Amherst, MA 01002, USA (☎413-256-0011; www.cccs.com). Coordinates a variety of study abroad programs in Sevilla and throughout Spain. Programs include summer ($3000), semester ($9000), or year-long ($19,000). Financial aid available.

Don Quijote, C. Placentinos 2, 37008 Salamanca, Spain (☎923 26 88 60; www.don-quijote.org). A nationwide language school offering Spanish courses for all levels in Barcelona, Granada, Madrid, Málaga, Salamanca, Sevilla, Tenerife, and Valencia. Very social atmosphere. 2 week intensive courses (20hr. language plus 5hr. "culture") start at €375. €33 enrollment fee. Discounts for longer sessions.

Eurocentres, Seestr. 247, CH-8038 Zurich, Switzerland (☎41 1 485 50 40; fax 481 61 24; www.eurocentres.com) or in London, 56 Eccleston Square, London SW1V 1PH (☎207 963 84 50). 2-12 week. language programs and homestays in Barcelona and Valencia for beginning to advanced students.

First Step World, 225 Bush Street, 16th floor, San Francisco, California, United States 94104 (☎415-738-8598; www.firststepworld.com). Language immersion programs and homestays in Faro, Lisbon, and Porto, Portugal, as well as in various Spanish cities.

Languages Abroad, 386 Ontario St., Toronto, ON M5A2V9, Canada (☎800-219-9924 or 416-925-2112; www.languagesabroad.com). 1-4 week language immersion programs and homestays with a private tutor in Spain or Portugal. Standard and intensive programs 1-4 weeks ($700-2300) include accommodations and some meals.

OTHER STUDY ABROAD

For those who are looking for something less traditional, these are only a few of the many exciting opportunities available.

Associació per a Defensa i L'Estudí de la Natura (ADENC), Ca l'Estruch, C. Sant Isidre, 08208 Sabadell, Spain (☎937 17 18 87; www.adenc.org). *Català* conservation group offering short summer courses on bird-watching, landscape photography, biology, and other ecotourism-related fields.

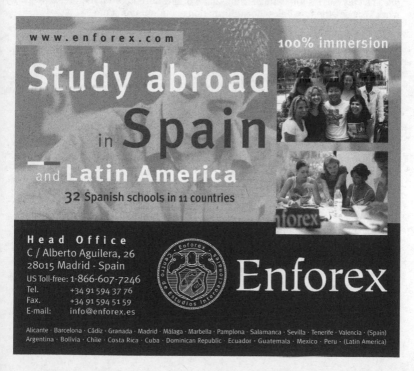

eduVacations, 1431 21st St.NW, Ste. 302, Washington, D.C. 20036, USA (☎202 857 8384; www.eduvacations.com). Language immersion combined with instruction in culinary and fine arts, dance, and sports. Spanish and Portuguese language trips from 1-2 wk. (€400-500) to 12 week (€2,500); 1 week combination trips from €400.

Escuela de Cocina Luis Irizar, C. Mari, 5, 20003 San Sebastián, Guipuzcoa, Spain (☎943 43 15 40; www.escuelairizar.com). Learn how to cook Basque cuisine at this culinary institute. Programs range from week-long summer courses to the comprehensive 2-year apprenticeship. Some of the summer courses may be taught in English.

Taller Flamenco School, C. Peral, 49, E-41002 Sevilla, Spain (☎954 56 42 34; www.tallerflamenco.com). Offers courses in flamenco dance (€180-240 per week) and guitar (€204 per week) with substantial discounts for longer commitments.

WORKING

As with volunteering, work opportunities abroad tend to fall into two categories. Some travelers want long-term jobs that allow them to integrate into a community, while others seek out short-term jobs to finance the next leg of their travels. It is possible to pick up short-term work in the tourist industry, in tasks like bartending. People looking for more lengthy employment should consider teaching English. For either category, the INEM (Instituto de Empleo) in Spain, which has a monopoly on the job market, is a good place to begin. The address and telephone number of regional employment offices *(Oficinas de Empleo)* can be found in any telephone guide or at **www.inem.es.** Many seasoned travelers, however, go straight to a particular town's Yellow Pages *(Páginas Amarillas)* or even go door-to-door. In Portugal, the English-language weekly newspaper *Anglo-Portuguese News* carries job listings. Note that working abroad often requires a special work visa; see the box below for information about obtaining one.

VISA INFORMATION. Travelers from within the European Union can work in any EU member country, but those from outside the EU need a work permit. Obtaining a work permit requires extensive documentation, often including a passport, police background check, and medical records; the cost varies. Contact your nearest consulate (p. 10) for a complete list of requirements.

LONG-TERM WORK

If you're planning on spending a substantial amount of time (more than three months) working in Spain or Portugal, search for a job well in advance. International placement agencies are often the easiest way to find employment abroad, especially for those interested in teaching English. Although they are often only available to college students, **internships** are a good way to segue into working abroad; they are often un- or underpaid, but many say the experience is well worth it. Be wary of advertisements for companies claiming to be able get you a job abroad for a fee—often the same listings are available online or in newspapers. Some reputable organizations include:

Career Journal (www.careerjournaleurope.com). The *Wall Street Journal* publishes this online journal listing thousands of jobs throughout Europe. There are both short- and long-term jobs as well as part- and full-time jobs.

Escape Artist (www.escapeartist.com/jobs/overseas1). Provides information on living abroad, including job listings for Spain and Portugal.

Expat Exchange (www.expatexchange.com). Provides message boards where individuals seeking employment in Spain and Portugal can advertise.

Trabajos (www.trabajos.com). Provides job listings for all regions of Spain.

TEACHING ENGLISH

Teaching jobs abroad are rarely well-paid, although some elite private American schools offer competitive salaries. Volunteering as a teacher is a popular option; even then, teachers often receive some sort of a daily stipend to help with living expenses. In almost all cases, you must have at least a bachelor's degree to be a full-fledged teacher, although college undergraduates can often get summer positions teaching or tutoring. For non-EU citizens, teaching English is one of the few work options that doesn't require a work permit. Though the teaching job market in Spain is one of the world's largest, its growth has tapered off. Non-EU citizens in particular may have difficulty landing a job. It might be easier to find work in Portugal, especially in the north. Before making a commitment to any school, it is a good idea to ask others about their experience there.

Many schools require teachers to have a **Teaching English as a Foreign Language (TEFL)** certificate. You may still be able to find a teaching job without certification, but certified teachers often find higher-paying jobs. Native English speakers working in private schools are most often hired for English-immersion classrooms where no Spanish or Portuguese is spoken. Volunteers or teachers in public schools are more likely to be working in both English and Spanish or Portuguese. Placement agencies or university fellowship programs are the best resources for finding teaching jobs. The alternative is to contact schools directly or to try your luck once you arrive in Spain or Portugal. If you do try the latter, the best time to look is several weeks before the start of the school year. The following organizations are extremely helpful in placing teachers in Spain and Portugal.

International Schools Services (ISS), 15 Roszel Rd., P.O. Box 5910, Princeton, NJ 08543, USA (☎609-452-0990; www.iss.edu). Hires teachers for more than 200 overseas schools including several in Spain; candidates should have experience teaching or with international affairs, 2-year commitment expected.

Teach Abroad (www.teach.studyabroad.com). Sponsored by Study Abroad. Brings you to listings around the world for paid or stipended positions to teach English.

TeachAbroad.com (www.teachabroad.com). Features worldwide job listings including some in Spain and Portugal.

TESOL-Spain (www.tesol-spain.org). Non-profit association of English teachers in Spain. Site features a jobs board among its many resources.

AU PAIR WORK

Au pairs are typically women (although sometimes men), aged 18-27, who work as live-in nannies, caring for children and doing light housework in foreign countries in exchange for room, board, and a small spending allowance or stipend. One perk of the job is that it allows you to get to know Spain or Portugal without the high expenses of traveling. Drawbacks, however, can include mediocre pay and long hours. In Spain, au pairs typically earn upwards of €50 per week. Much of the au pair experience depends on your family placement. The agencies below are a good starting point for looking for employment.

Childcare International, Ltd., Trafalgar House, Grenville Pl., London NW7 3SA (☎+44 020 8906 3116; www.childint.co.uk). With placements in Spain, not Portugal.

InterExchange, 161 Sixth Ave., New York, NY, 10013, USA (☎800-287-2477; fax 924-0575; www.interexchange.org). Lists Spain, not Portugal.

InterExchange, 161 Sixth Ave., New York, NY, 10013, USA (☎800-287-2477; fax 924-0575; www.newaupair.com). Families post messages seeking help. Organized by country for both Spain and Portugal.

SHORT-TERM WORK

Traveling for long periods of time can be hard on the finances. Many travelers try their hand at odd jobs for a few weeks at a time to help pay for their next touring stint. The process for obtaining a work permit is often long, complicated, and bureaucratic. Few short-term workers get work permits, which require a prior job contract; although it is illegal for non-EU citizens to work in Spain or Portugal without a work permit, many establishments hire travelers anyway, particularly in seasonal resort areas. These jobs may include bartending, waiting tables, or promoting bars and clubs. Another popular option is to work several hours a day at a hostel in exchange for free or discounted room and/or board. Many places are eager for help, even if it is only temporary. Most often, these short-term jobs are found by word of mouth, or by expressing interest to the owner of a hostel or restaurant. *Let's Go* lists temporary jobs of this nature whenever possible; look in the practical information sections of larger cities or check out the list below for some of the available short-term jobs in popular destinations.

EcoForest, Apdo. Correos, 29, 29100 Coin, Málaga, Spain (☎661 07 99 50; www.ecoforest.org). Exchanges free camping space for 3hr. of work per day with a €20 initial fee.

Bodega Tour Guide, in Jerez de la Frontera, Spain (p. 251). Many of Jerez's famed sherry *bodegas* hire summer guides. Call the *bodegas* directly for more information.

Intern Jobs (www.internjobs.com). Lists not only internships, but also many ideal short-term jobs like camp counseling and bartending. Applies to Spain, not Portugal.

Transitions Abroad (www.transitionsabroad.com). Lists organizations in Spain and Portugal that hire short-term workers and provides links to articles about working abroad.

FURTHER READING ON BEYOND TOURISM.

Alternatives to the Peace Corps: A Guide of Global Volunteer Opportunities, by Paul Backhurst. Food First Books, 2005 (US$12).

The Back Door Guide to Short-Term Job Adventures: Internships, Summer Jobs, Seasonal Work, Volunteer Vacations, and Transitions Abroad, by Michael Landes. Ten Speed Press, 2005 (US$22).

Green Volunteers: The World Guide to Voluntary Work in Nature Conservation, ed. Fabio Ausenda. Universe, 2007 (US$15).

How to Get a Job in Europe, by Cheryl Matherly and Robert Sanborn. Planning Communications, 2003 (US$23).

How to Live Your Dream of Volunteering Overseas, by Joseph Collins, Stefano DeZerega, and Zahara Heckscher. Penguin Books, 2002 (US$20).

International Job Finder: Where the Jobs Are Worldwide, by Daniel Lauber and Kraig Rice. Planning Communications, 2002 (US$20).

Live and Work Abroad: A Guide for Modern Nomads, by Huw Francis and Michelyne Callan. Vacation-Work Publications, 2001 (US$16).

Overseas Summer Jobs 2002. Peterson's Guides and Vacation Work, 2002 (US$18).

Volunteer Vacations: Short-Term Adventures That Will Benefit You and Others, by Doug Cutchins, Anne Geissinger, and Bill McMillon. Chicago Review Press, 2006 (US$18).

Work Abroad: The Complete Guide to Finding a Job Overseas, by Clayton Hubbs. Transitions Abroad Publishing, 2002 (US$16).

Work Your Way Around the World, by Susan Griffith. Vacation-Work Publications, 2007 (US$22).

SPAIN (ESPAÑA)

A diverse population of over 40 million thrives in Spain, a land marked by foreign invasions, religious crusades, empires, artistic and literary genius, and architectural mastery that stretch back to the time of Cro-Magnon. A collage of autonomous regions, each with its own character (and sometimes its own language), Spain cannot be defined as a single entity. Each of its 15 regions is a product of its own historical DNA, a descendent of a unique line of influences. Spain's geography is as varied as its people, ranging from parched central plateau to lush rolling hills and its glittering white sand beaches. Its diversity provides the opportunity for every traveler to enjoy unique festivals, unbeatable landscapes, and incredible culture.

HISTORY

Spain has been both colony and colonizer, with a history spanning over 50 constitutions. After the rule of the Iberians, Celts, Romans, Visigoths, Arabs, and the French, Spain has emerged economically scarred but culturally enriched. The country began a long and arduous descent from world-class empire to Pyrenean pauper after 1588, though artistic and literary achievements offset constant military defeats. In 1936, democracy disintegrated into civil war, bringing to power Generalissimo Francisco Franco. Now a thriving democracy with the 9th largest economy in the world, Spain surges into the 21st century with a glorious past and a bright future.

RULE HISPANIA (PREHISTORY-AD 711). Spain played host to a succession of civilizations—**Basque, Celtiberian,** and **Greek**—before the **Romans** came for an extended visit in the 3rd century BC. Over the next seven centuries, the Romans left their mark on Spanish culture by introducing their language, architecture, roads, and the cultivation of grapes, olives, and wheat. Following the Romans, a slew of Germanic tribes swept over Iberia, and the **Visigoths**—newly converted Christians—emerged victorious. In AD 419 they established their court at Barcelona and ruled Spain for the next 300 years.

PLEASE, SIR, MAY I HAVE SOME MOORS? (711-1492). A small force of Arabs, Berbers, and Syrians invaded Spain in 711 following Muslim unification. The **Moors** encountered little resistance from the divided Visigoths, and the peninsula fell to the caliph of Damascus, the spiritual leader of Islam. The Moors made their Iberian capital at Córdoba (p. 242), which by the 10th century was the largest city in Europe with over 500,000 inhabitants. During Abderramán III's rule (929-961), many considered Spain the wealthiest and most cultivated country in the world. Abderramán III's successor, Al Mansur, snuffed out opposition in his court and undertook a series of military campaigns that climaxed with the destruction of Santiago de Compostela (p. 557) in 997 and the kidnapping of its bells. It took the Christians 240 years to get them back.

800,000 BC
Homo erectus rises on the Iberian peninsula.

1100 BC
Phoenicians found the ports of Cádiz and Málaga.

500 BC
Celts cross the Pyrenees.

200 BC
The Roman Empire sets up camp.

AD 50
Segovia's aqueduct is constructed without a drop of mortar.

AD 412-718
The Visigoths arrive in Iberia two years after sacking Rome. They fall to a Moorish Alliance 300 years later.

900-1000
Córdoba claims the title of largest city in Western Europe.

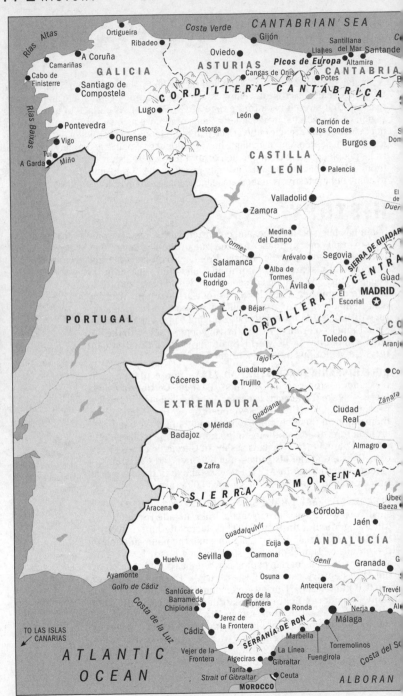

Spain

BAY OF BISCAY

FRANCE

an Sebastián
Hondarribia
Irún
ernica
Roncesvalles
ÍS
SCO
NAVARRA
a
Pamplona
iz
Sangüesa
Ansó Hecho
Toña
Estella
Vielha
Olite
Logroño
Jaca
IOJA
Tudela
Aínsa
La Seu d'Urgell
Soria
Tarazona
Huesca
Catalayud
ARAGÓN
Zaragoza
Cariñera
Daroca
Siguenza
Lleida

PYRENEES

ANDORRA
Andorra
La Vela
Puigcerdà
Núria
Figueres
Ripoll
Girona
Portbou
Empúries
La Bisbal
d'Empordà
Palafrugell
Tossa de Mar
CATALUÑA
Llobregat
Montserrat
Mataró
Costa Brava
Barcelona
Vilanova i la
Geltrú
Sitges
Valls
Reus
Tarragona
Salou
Cambrils de Mar
Costa Dorada

ORDILLERA IBÉRICA
SERRANÍA DE CUENCADOS
ares
Albarracín
AD
Cuenca
Teruel
Mora
de Rubielos
Morella
Castelló

TO MENORCA →

Menorca
Ciutadella
Mahón

SPAIN

Golfo de
Valencia
Costa del Azahar
Alcúdia
BALEARIC
SEA
Palma
Mallorca

STILLA
MANCHA
Júcar
Albacete
Turia
Sagunt
VALENCIA
Valencia
Cullera
Játiva
Gandía
Dénia
Calp
Benidorm
Alicante
Elx
Costa Blanca

LAS ISLAS BALEARES
San Antonio
Ibiza
Eivissa
Formentera

MURCIA
Murcia
Lorca
Manga del
Mar Menor
Águilas
ADA
Mojácar
Almería
Cabo de
Gata
osta de Almería

MEDITERRANEAN SEA

ALGERIA

N
LG

0   75 kilometers
0   75 miles

997
Al Mansur orders Santiago de Compostela destroyed and kidnaps the cathedral bells.

1236
Fernando III takes Córdoba from the Moors and forces captured Muslims to carry the bells back to Santiago.

1478
The Inquisition begins.

1492
Power couple Fernando and Isabel conquer Granada, the last Moorish holdout; Columbus sets sail with royal funding.

1500
A Spanish cardinal reports of Granada that "there is now no one in the city who is not a Christian, and all the mosques are churches."

1506
Juana la Loca drags her dead husband's body through the streets.

1519
Hernán Cortéz lands in Mexico in search of gold, silver, and chocolate.

1559
St. Teresa of Ávila has a vision of Christ that lasts for almost 2 years.

1588
Britain's Elizabeth I defeats Spain's "invincible" Armada.

LOS REYES CATÓLICOS (1469-1516). The marriage of **Fernando de Aragón** and **Isabel de Castilla** in 1469 joined Iberia's two mightiest Christian kingdoms. During their half-century rule, these Catholic monarchs established Spain as the prime European exponent of Catholicism, and as an international power. They introduced the brutal **Inquisition** in 1478, which mandated execution or burning of heretics, principally Jews. The policy prompted a mass exodus, as Jews and Muslims were forced either to convert to Christianity or to leave Spain to avoid being captured and killed. In 1492, the royal couple captured Granada from the Moors (p. 296), victoriously ending the centuries-long *Reconquista* and uniting Spain under Catholic rule. This dominance continued to flourish with lucrative conquests in the Americas, beginning in 1492 when they agreed to finance **Christopher Columbus's** first adventure.

ENTER THE HABSBURGS (1516-1713). The daughter of Fernando and Isabel, **Juana la Loca** (the Mad), married **Felipe el Hermoso** (the Fair) of the powerful Habsburg family. When the young king died, La Loca, a possible schizophrenic, walked his coffin to Granada, opening it occasionally to kiss his corpse. Juana and Felipe secured their genetic legacy with the birth of **Carlos I,** better known as Holy Roman Emperor Charles V (1516-1556).

Under Carlos, the Spanish empire grew exponentially. Royal marriages placed the country in control of European territories in Sicily and Naples, while in the New World conquistadors plundered Mexico, Peru, and Chile, destroying the vast empires of the Aztec and Inca civilizations. They brought their booty back to Spain by the galleon, providing Carlos with funds for his battles and conquests. Gold and silver were complemented by the potatoes, corn, and exotic fruits which were introduced as new crops in Europe.

When Carlos retired to a monastery, **Felipe II** (1556-1598) inherited a handful of rebellious territories in the Protestant Netherlands. His marriage to Mary Tudor, Queen of England, in 1554 created an international Catholic alliance, and Felipe made it his life's mission to create a true Catholic empire. In 1581, a year after Felipe II annexed Portugal, the Dutch declared their independence from Spain, starting a war and becoming embroiled with England's Elizabeth I. The conflict ground to a halt when Sir Francis Drake totaled Spain's "invincible" **Armada** in 1588. With much of his European empire lost and his wealth from the Americas sapped, Felipe retreated to **El Escorial** (p. 141) and sulked in its monastery until his death.

In 1609, **Felipe III** (1598-1621) expelled nearly 300,000 of Spain's remaining Moors. **Felipe IV** (1621-1665) then painstakingly held the country together through his long, tumultuous reign while patronizing the arts (painter Diego Velázquez and playwright Lope de Vega both graced his court) and architecture (he commissioned the Parque del Buen Retiro in Madrid; p. 124). Defending Catholicism began to drain Spain's resources after the outbreak of the **Thirty Years' War** (1618-1648), which ended with the marriage of Felipe IV's daughter María Teresa to Louis XIV of France. Felipe's successor **Carlos II el Hechizado** (the bewitched; 1665-1700), the product of generations of inbreeding, was known to fly into fits of rage and epileptic seizures. From then on, little went right: Carlos II left no heirs, Spain fell into an economic depression, and cultural bankruptcy ensued. Rulers from all over, particularly Habsburg Vienna, battled for the crown, and the **War of Spanish Succession** began.

THE REIGN IN SPAIN (1713-1931). The 1713 Treaty of Utrecht ended the ordeal (and Spain's possession of Gibraltar, which went to the English) and landed **Felipe V** (1713-1746), a Bourbon grandson of **Louis XIV**, on the Spanish throne. Though the new king cultivated a flamboyant, debaucherous court, he competently administered the Empire, at last regaining control of Spanish-American trade. The next century was dominated by the Bourbon effort to create a modern state, as the crown centralized power and stripped the different regions of their historical privileges. Finally, in 1808, **Napoleon** invaded Spain as part of his bid for world domination, inaugurating an occupation as short as the general himself. In the midst of the upheaval, most of Spain's Latin American empire threw off the colonial yoke, and those still beyond Napoleon's reach penned the progressive Constitution of 1812, which established Spain as a parliamentary monarchy. The violence ended when the Protestant Brits defeated the Corsican's troops at Waterloo (1814), placing the reactionary **Fernando VII** (1814-1833) to the throne.

Parliamentary liberalism was restored in 1833 upon Fernando VII's death, and survived the conservative challenge of the first **Carlist War** (1833-1839), a dispute over the monarchy of **Queen Isabel II** (1843-1870). Her successor, **King Amadeo I** (1870-1873) enjoyed a short reign before the **First Spanish Republic** was proclaimed. After a coup d'etat in 1875, the monarchy was restored under **King Alfonso XII** (1875-1885), and the last two decades of the 19th century were marked by rapid industrialization. However, Spain's 1898 loss to the US in the **Spanish-American War** cost it the Philippines, Puerto Rico, Cuba, and any remaining dreams of colonial wealth.

Closer to home, Moroccan tribesmen rebelled against Spanish troops in northern Africa beginning in 1917, resulting in a series of embarrassing military defeats. These events further weakened Spaniard morale and culminated in the **massacre** of 14,000 Spanish troops in 1921, threatening the very survival of the monarchy. The search for those "responsible" for the disaster occupied aristocrats, bureaucrats, and generals for the next decade, throwing the country into chaos. In 1923, **General Miguel Primo de Rivera** sought to bring order to the situation in the form of Spain's first dictatorship.

REPUBLIC AND REBELLION (1931-1939). King Alfonso XIII (1902-1931) abdicated the throne in April 1931, giving rise to the **Second Spanish Republic** (1931-1939). Republican Liberals and Socialists established safeguards for farmers and industrial workers, granted women's suffrage, assured religious tolerance, and chipped away at traditional military dominance. National euphoria, however, faded fast. The 1933 elec-

1605
Cervantes publishes Don Quixote in Madrid.

1701-1714
Europe jockeys for control of the Spanish monarchy in the War of Spanish Succession.

1808
Napoleon occupies Spain and rules for a short 6 years.

1814
Fernando VII is released from prison in France and returns to become king.

1873-1874
The first Spanish Republic forms and quickly dissolves.

1893
Anarchists bomb Barcelona's Liceu, killing 20 opera-goers.

1898
Spain loses the Spanish-American War and its last 3 colonies.

1919
The Christ of Limpias, a statue in Santander, appears to blink and move its eyes, attracting pilgrims from across Europe.

1921
14,000 Spanish troops are massacred in Morocco after their attempt to consolidate Spain's hold on its new protectorate.

SPAIN

1923
Spain's 1st dictator, General Primo de Rivera, rises to power in a coup.

1933-1936
The country is polarized by the increased presence of the military and the Fascist Falange.

1936-1939
Civil War engulfs Spain. Europe joins the fray.

1937
Nazi planes bomb the Basque town of Guernica; Picasso paints his *Guernica* in response.

1939
Franco begins his reign and the country enters a period later known as the "national tragedy."

1959
Twenty years into Franco's rule, the Euskadi Ta Askatasuna (ETA) forms.

1975
Franco dies, and "La Movida" begins: the nation explodes in a burst of creative expression.

1982
Felipe González is elected prime minister and works over the next decade to rejuvenate the economy

SPAIN

tions split the Republican-Socialist coalition, increasing the power of right-wing and Catholic parties in parliament. Military dissatisfaction led to a heightened profile of the **Fascist Falange** (founded by Primo de Rivera's son José Antonio), which only further polarized national politics. By 1936, radicals, anarchists, Socialists, and Republicans had formed a **Popular Front** coalition to win the February elections. Their victory, however, was short lived. Once **Generalísimo Francisco Franco** snatched control of the Spanish army, militarist uprisings ensued, and the nation plunged into war. **La Guerra Civil (The Spanish Civil War;** 1936-1939) fanned ideological flames across the world. Germany and Italy dropped troops, supplies, and munitions into Franco's lap in hopes of getting aid from Franco in the future, while the US and liberal European states hid behind the Non-Intervention Treaty. The Soviet Union organized the **International Brigades,** an amalgamation of Communists and other leftist volunteers from all over Europe and the US, to battle Franco's fascism. But soon after, foreign aid waned as Stalin began to see the benefits of an alliance with Hitler. Bombings, executions, combat, starvation, and disease took nearly 600,000 lives and forced almost one million Spaniards to emigrate. In April 1939, Franco marched into Madrid and ended the war.

FRANCO AND THE NATIONAL TRAGEDY (1939-1975). Franco's dictatorship was based on the church, the army, and the Falange. Thousands of scientists, artists, intellectuals, and sympathizers were exiled, imprisoned, or executed in the name of order and purity. Franco initially pursued an isolationist economic policy, but stagnant economic growth eventually forced him to adopt open economic policies. With prosperity came protest. Dissatisfied workers and students took to the streets, hoping to draw attention to the abominations of Franco's reign. Groups like the **Basque ETA** also provided resistance throughout the dictatorship, often via terrorist acts, producing unrest that undermined the legitimacy of the regime. In his old age, the general tried to smooth international relations by joining NATO, courting the Pope, and encouraging tourism. However, the **national tragedy,** as the tense period under Franco was later called, did not officially end until Franco's death in 1975. **King Juan Carlos I** (1975-), grandson of Alfonso XIII and nominally a Franco protégé, carefully set out to undo Franco's damage.

TRANSITION TO DEMOCRACY (1975-2004). In 1978, under centrist prime minister **Adolfo Suárez,** Spain adopted a new constitution and restored parliamentary government and regional autonomy. The post-Franco years have been marked by progressive social change in the economic and political arenas. The period was also characterized by a movement known in Madrid as "La Movida," which saw an unprecedented outburst of artistic, cultural, and social expression after decades of censorship and inhibition. Suárez's resignation in early 1981 left the country ripe for an attempted coup on February 23rd of that year, when a group of rebels took over parliament in an effort to impose a military-backed government. King Juan Carlos I used his personal influence to convince the rebels to stand down, paving the way for the charismatic **Felipe González** to lead the PSOE (Spanish Socialist Worker's Party) to victory in the 1982 elections. González opened the Spanish economy and championed consensus policies, overseeing Spain's integration into the European Community (now the EU) four years later. Despite unpopular economic policies, González was reelected in 1986 and continued a program of massive public investment to rejuvenate the nation's economy. By the end of 1993, however, recession and revelations of large-scale corruption led to a resounding Socialist defeat at the hands of the Popular Party (PP) in the 1994 European parliamentary elections. The PP's leader, **José María Aznar,** managed to maintain a fragile coalition with the support of the *catalana* and Islas Canarias regional parties. He won an absolute majority in 2000. Since then Spain has moved in a more liberal direction. On July 1, 2005 it legalized gay marriage, eliminating all legal distinctions between same sex and heterosexual couples

GLOBAL TERRORISM. Under the conservative Aznar, Spain became one of the US's most prominent allies in the war on terror, but the relationship has since strained. On **March 11, 2004,** days before the national elections, the country suffered its own grievous attack, often referred to as **11-M** *(el once eme).* In an attack linked to Al-Qaeda, 10 bombs exploded on four trains heading to Madrid from the suburbs, killing 191 passengers and injuring more than 1800. When the conservatives lost the election to **José Luis Rodríguez Zapatero** of the PSOE, many attributed it to reaction against attempt by Aznar and his party to shirk responsibility for the attacks. Under the new government, Spain withdrew its troops from Iraq.

1986
Spain joins the European Economic Community, which will become the European Union.

1996-2004
Popular Party leader José María Aznar is elected president and works to quell terrorism.

2004
Bombings linked to Al-Qaeda rock Madrid and kill 192 people. Days later, the Spanish elect José Luis Rodríguez Zapatero as prime minister.

2005
The Spanish parliament legalizes same-sex marriage.

2006
ETA announces the end of its terrorist tactics.

2007
ETA revokes the cease-fire, dashing hopes of peace.

CURRENT EVENTS

ETA TERRORISM. Spain has a long history of domestic terrorism, due to separatist movements, particularly in the Basque region in northwestern Spain. Since 1968, over 800 people have been killed in bombings planned by the movement's militant wing, the Euskadi Ta Askatasuna (ETA; Basque Homeland and Freedom). Violence continued into 2005, with a series of car bombings in Madrid. In March 2006, ETA declared a permanent cease-fire, promising to promote Basque separation through democratic means, but in December 2006 two bombs exploded in the Madrid airport. In June 2007, the cease-fire officially came to an end. While there may be some danger to travelers, the ETA's attacks are typically targeted and are not considered random acts of terrorism. In more recent years, the organization has tended to provide advance warning.

FURTHER READING. These texts provide additional resources on the history and culture of Spain.

Homage to Catalonia, by George Orwell (1938). A personal account of Orwell's time in uniform during the Spanish Civil War.

Iberia, by James Michener (1968). A bestselling travelogue that continues to captivate audiences with its vivid prose.

South from Granada, by Gerald Brenan (1957). A classic account of Pre-Civil War Spain, including acute observations on the Spanish character.

The New Spaniards, by John Hooper (1995). An excellent introduction to contemporary Spanish society.

The Ornament of the World, by María Rosa Menocal (2003). An insightful account of the peaceful interaction of Moorish, Christian, and Jewish cultures in Toledo.

A FIGHT FOR THE ROCK. For the past 300 years, Spain has fought an uphill battle to regain control of **Gibraltar** (p. 269), a strategic 6km territory in the south currently under British rule. Britain's desire to improve relations with Spain paved the way for a 2002 proposal to share sovereignty of the rock between the two nations, but Gibraltar residents, who remain overwhelmingly loyal to the crown and enjoy salaries almost a third higher than the Spanish average, rejected the measure.

STRAITENED RELATIONS. In July 2002, a handful of Moroccan soldiers "occupied" the goat-infested island of **Perejil** in Spanish territorial waters off Morocco, sparking a minor international event. Amid much fanfare and grandstanding, the soldiers and their Moroccan flag were promptly removed. Its sovereignty and military prowess secured, Spain could once again direct its attention to pressing internal affairs, including increased **immigration** from northern Africa. The Canary Islands and Spain's outposts in Morocco, Ceuta and Melilla, are typical places of entry. In 2005, Spain granted amnesty to 700,000 of the illegal immigrants within its borders, and has continued to experiment with temporary worker programs.

PEOPLE AND CULTURE

LANGUAGE

Castellano (Castilian) Spanish, spoken almost everywhere, is Spain's official language; other languages are official regionally. **Català** (Catalan) is spoken throughout Cataluña in the northeast and is the official language of Andorra. Permutations of *català* gave rise to the dialects **valencià** (Valencian), the regional tongue of Valencia, and **mallorquí,** the principal dialect of the Islas Baleares. Even tiny Asturias has its own dialect, **bable,** spoken mostly among older generations. The once-Celtic northwest corner of Iberia gabs in **gallego** (Galician), which is closely related to Portuguese and is most prevalent in the countryside. **Euskera** (Basque), spoken in País Vasco and northern Navarra, is one of the oldest languages in Europe and known by only about 2% of the nation's population.

City and provincial names in this guide are listed in Castilian first, followed by the regional language in parentheses where appropriate. Information within cities (i.e. street and plaza names) is listed in the regional language. For a **phrasebook, glossary,** and **pronunciation guide,** see p. 759.

RELIGION

The **Roman Catholic Church** has dominated everyday life in Spain since 1492. Though almost the 80 percent of the population still identify as Catholic, like the rest of

Europe, Spain has become increasingly secular, with only 20% claiming to regularly attend church, and 50% saying they almost never go except for weddings and funerals. However, one need only look at Spanish art and architecture to see the influence of the other religions, like **Islam** and **Judaism,** that once thrived in Spain. Before Fernando and Isabel's completion of the **Reconquista** in 1492 (p. 76), the Moors controlled the Iberian Peninsula for seven centuries, leaving buildings such as the 10th-century *mezquita* (mosque) in Córdoba to attest to their once dominant presence. The *Reyes Católicos* (Catholic kings) began the Spanish Inquisition in 1478, even before they had completely reclaimed the Iberian Peninsula from the Moors. Anyone who was suspected of practicing Judaism was tried, usually found guilty, and punished, often with death. The ultimate goal of the *Reyes Católicos* was the expulsion of all Jews and Moors from the peninsula. Many Jews converted to Catholicism or immigrated to North Africa to avoid persecution. The Spanish Inquisition finally ended in 1834 after over 30,000 people died at the hands of the crown.

FOOD AND DRINK

Many of Spain's best meals are served not in expensive restaurants, but in private homes or street-side bars. Alternatively, many opt for tapas barhopping in lieu of a formal meal. Today, Spanish food is becoming increasingly sophisticated and cosmopolitan. Fresh, local ingredients play an integral part of the cuisine, varying according to each region's climate, geography, and history.

LOCAL FARE

ANDALUCÍA. Andalusian cuisine is the oldest in Spain, flavored with spices and prepared according to traditional methods brought by Islamic tribes during the first millennium. Centuries later, it was through **Sevilla** (p. 219) that New World products like corn, peppers, tomatoes, and potatoes first entered Europe. *Andalucianos* have since mastered the art of *gazpacho*, a cold tomato-based soup perfectly suited to the hot southern climate. Andalucía is famous for its olive oil, which is found in a vast number of the region's dishes. The area is also known for its *pescadito frito* (fried fish), *rabo de toro* (bull's tail), egg yolk desserts, sherry wines, and tasty tapas. Spain's best cured ham, *jamón ibérico*, comes from the town of Jabugo, where black-footed pigs are pampered with daily oak acorn feasts.

THE CASTILLAS. Sheep share space with more of the prized black-footed pigs in nearby **Extremadura** (p.

IN RECENT NEWS

A PEACE POSTPONED

After nearly 40 years of violence and the death of over 800 Spanish civilians, security personnel and politicians, the Basque separatist movement, ETA ("Basque Homeland and Freedom" in the Basque language Euskara), announced a permanent cease-fire in early 2006 and began negotiations with the Spanish government. As discussions progressed, there was hope that the organization's bloody campaign for a sovereign Basque state was coming to an end.

That optimism instantly vanished in December 2006, when ETA claimed responsibility for a bombing in Madrid's Barajas Airport. Though ETA announced that it was still fully committed to the cease-fire, the Spanish government flatly announced that ETA had violated the terms of the truce, and declared the peace process as unquestionably over. In June 2007, the cease-fire officially came to an end.

The Spanish public, for its part, has not remained silent on the issue. While Prime Minister Jose Luis Rodriguez Zapatero's attempts to reach a solution with ETA were originally met with support, the airport bombing provoked public outrage, and has caused the government to back away from any further attempts at dialogue. With parliamentary elections looming in March 2008, it seems that at least in the near future, peace is not in the cards.

204), where the pastoral life has inspired *cocidos* (hearty stews), cheeses, and unique meals based on *migas* (bread crumbs). This type of dry-land "shepherd's cuisine" dominates central Spain. **Castilla La Mancha** (p. 190) is famous for its sheep's milk *queso manchego*, the most widely eaten cheese in Spain, and the deliciously vegetarian *pisto manchego*, a mix of zucchini, tomatoes, and eggplant. Spain's most prized spice, *azafrán* (saffron) is also grown in La Mancha. Lamb and roasted game are essential parts of menus both here and in **Castilla y Léon** (p. 149). *Escabeche*, an Arab tradition of sautéing with vinegar, has become a specialty, as has *tortilla española* (potato omelette) and *menestra de verduras*, a succulent vegetable mix. **Madrid** (p. 93) rivals Andalucía with its tapas and renowned *cocido*, a heavy stew of meat, cabbage, carrots, and potatoes.

CANTABRIAN COAST. Farther north, the 800 miles of coastline in **Galicia** (p. 557) provide fresh ingredients for local shellfish dishes. Octopus, spider crab, and mussels are popular here, as is *empanada gallega*, the Galician pastry filled with anything from pork to chicken to fish. In **Asturias** (p. 527), dried beans rule the kitchen; *fabada asturiana*, a hearty bean and sausage stew, is the best way to refuel after a long day of work. Apples, *sidra* (cider), and cow's milk are also especially good here. **Cantabrian** (p. 548) sardines and tuna are among the best in Spain and are often included in a seafood stew. Food in the **País Vasco** (p. 504) rivals that of Cataluña in national prominence. The combination of coastal and mountain cultures has created a unique style of food in the Basque Country. Popular dishes include *bacalao* (salt cod), *angulas* (baby eels), *calamar en su tinta* (squid in its own ink), and suckling lamb.

THE PYRENEES. Navarra (p. 491) boasts the best red peppers in Spain, as well as the famous Roncal cheese; game meats, sausages, and cauldron stews are popular here. Neighboring **La Rioja** (p. 486) is known for its pork, vegetables, and above all its *vino* (wine). The region, which boasts seven different grape varieties, has been host to wineries and vineyards since before the arrival of the Moors. **Aragón's** (p. 476) hearty cuisine reflects the region's varied character. *Migas de pastor* (bread crumbs fried with ham) and lamb are ubiquitous, while sweeter treats include *melocotones al vino* (native peaches steeped in wine) and *adoquines* (caramel-filled pastries wrapped in an image of the Virgen de Pilar).

MEDITERRANEAN COAST. In **Cataluña** (p. 414), the Roman triumvirate of olives, grapes, and wheat dominates, and seafood, grilling, and even pasta play key roles in many meals. Cataluña also houses the avant-garde movement of cooking, led by innovative chef Ferran Adrià of El Bulli. On the Mediterranean coast, **Valencia** (p. 312) has been the home of paella and oranges ever since Arab short-grain rice and American oranges were introduced to the area. Less than 200 years old, paella has evolved from a simple dish to an increasingly elaborate mix of rice, vegetables, seafood, and meat. The island of **Menorca** is known for its *mahón* cheese, which is often grated over meat or vegetables.

DRINKS

VINO. When in doubt, the *vino de la casa* (house wine) is an economical and often delectable choice. Castilla y León's **Ribera del Dueros** are smooth and full-bodied reds, and Biezo has recently been unearthed as a red wine haven. Cataluña's whites and *cavas* (champagnes) and **Galicia's** *Albariños* pack a refreshing punch, while the reds and whites of **La Rioja** are justifiably famous. As the saying goes, the wines taste best in good company: *"El vino, para que sepa a vino, bébelo con un amigo"* (For wine to taste of wine, you must drink it with a friend). *Sidra* (cider) from Asturias and *sangria* (red-wine punch with fruit, seltzer, and sugar) are other delicious alcoholic options. *Jerez* (sherry), Spain's most famous libation, hails from **Jerez de la Frontera** (p. 251) in Andalucía. Try the dry *fino* and *amontillado* as aperitifs, or finish off a rich supper with the sweet *dulce*.

CERVEZAS. A normal-sized draft beer is a *caña de cerveza*, while a *tubo* is a little bigger. Small beers go by different names—*corto* in Castilian, and *zurito* in Basque. Pros refer to mixed drinks as *copas*: beer and Schweppes Limón make a *clara*, *calimocho* is a mix of Coca-Cola and red wine; another famous drink is *tinto de verano*, a mix of red wine and carbonated water or orange soda. Spain whips up non-alcoholic quenchers as well, notably *horchata de chufa* (made by blending almonds and ice) and flavored crushed-ice *granizados*. *Café solo* means black coffee; add a touch of milk for a *nube*; a little more and it's a *café cortado*; half milk and half coffee makes a *café con leche*.

MEALS AND DINING HOURS

TYPICAL SPANISH MEALS. Having a meal, whether at home or at a restaurant, is one of the most popular forms of socializing in Spain. Spaniards start their day with *el desayuno*, a continental breakfast of coffee or thick, liquid chocolate accompanied by *bollos* (rolls), *churros*, or *porros* (dough fritters). Mid-morning they often have another coffee with a tapa to tide them over to the main meal of the day, *la comida*, which is eaten around 2 or 3pm. *La comida* consists of several courses: soup or salad, meat, fish, or, on special occasions, paella, and a dessert of fruit, cheese, or sweets. Supper at home, *la cena*, tends to be lighter— usually a sandwich or *tortilla española* anywhere from 8pm to midnight. Eating out starts anywhere between 9pm and midnight. Going out for tapas is part of the Spanish lifestyle; groups of friends will often spend several hours bar-hopping.

RESTAURANT DINING. While some restaurants are open from 8am to 1 or 2am, most serve meals from 1 or 2 to 4pm only and in the evening from 8pm until midnight. Some hints: eating at the bar is cheaper than at tables or on a terrace, and the check won't be brought to a table unless it is requested. Also, even though a server may bring bread to the table, it is often not free and the unwitting tourist falls prey to the "You touched it, you bought it" policy of most Spanish restaurants. Service is notoriously slow. Spaniards commonly choose the **menú del día**—two or three dishes, bread, a drink, and dessert—a good deal at roughly €7-12. *Raciones* are large tapas, comparable in size to entrees.

ON THE MENU

TAPAS A TO Z

Food on toothpicks and in small bowls? The restaurant isn't being stingy, and your food isn't shrinking; you're merely experiencing an integral part of the Spanish lifestyle. The tapas tradition is one of the oldest in Spain. These tasty little dishes are Spain's answer to hors d'oeuvres, but have more taste, less pretension, and are eaten instead of meals.

To the untrained tourist, tapas menus are often indecipherable, if the bar has even bothered to print any. In order to avoid awkward encounters with tentacles or the parts of the horse you rode in on, keep the following things in mind before *tapeando* (eating tapas).

Servings come in three sizes: *pinchos* (eaten with toothpicks), *tapas* (small plate), and *raciónes* (meal portion). On any basic menu you'll find: *Aceitunas* (olives), *albóndigas* (meatballs), *callos* (tripe), *chorizo* (sausage), *gambas* (shrimp), *jamón* (ham), *patatas bravas* (fried potatoes with spicy sauce), *pimientos* (peppers), *pulpo* (octopus), and *tortilla española* (onion and potato omelette). The more adventurous should try *morcilla* (blood sausage), or *sesos* (cow's brains). Often, bartenders will offer tastes of tapas with your drink and strike up a conversation. Ask for a *caña* (glass) of the house *cerveza* (beer) to guarantee the full respect of the establishment.

CUSTOMS AND ETIQUETTE

Spaniards are generally polite and courteous to foreigners; attempts to be culturally correct will not go unnoticed.

TABOOS. As is to be expected, Spaniards are very proud and take offense to criticism about their country or customs. Foreigners should be careful when
approaching Spanish women; overly *macho* fathers, husbands, or boyfriends can
be aggressive. Be aware that shorts and short skirts are not common in most parts
of Spain, save the coasts. Wearing these and other especially revealing clothing
away from the beaches may garner unwanted attention or at the very least scream
"I am a foreigner!" Women with bare shoulders should carry a shawl to tour
churches and monasteries, and it is considered disrespectful to wear shorts.

PUBLIC BEHAVIOR. Spaniards are very polite in mannerisms and social behavior;
it's a good idea to be as formal as possible in first encounters. Be sure to address
Spaniards as *Señor* (Mr.), *Señora* (Mrs.), or *Señorita* (Ms.), and don't be surprised if you get kissed on both cheeks instead of receiving a handshake.
Machismo is very apparent, especially in Andalucía, and women may be the
object of whistling and catcalling when walking alone or in groups without any
men. The best response to this display of *machismo* is to ignore it.

TIPPING. Though a service charge is generally included in the check at bars
and restaurants, an additional tip is common for good service; 5-10% will generally do the trick. Taxi drivers, theater ushers, and hotel porters may also
expect small tips for their services.

SPAIN

THE ARTS

ARCHITECTURE

ANCIENT AND EARLY MODERN. The earliest art in Spain can be found at the caves at **Altamira**, near Santander in Cantabria, which display some of the oldest Paleolithic cave paintings in the world. **Roman ruins** are scattered throughout the country, with the magnificent **aqueduct** in Segovia (p. 149), the **amphitheater** in Mérida (p. 211), and the town of Tarragona (p. 419) all testifying to six centuries of colonization. Other vestiges of Spain's Roman past include the ruined towns of Itálica (near Sevilla; p. 219) and Sagunt (near Valencia; p. 322).

When the Moors invaded Spain in 711, they built distinctive mosques and palaces throughout the country's southern regions. Because the Qur'an forbids human and animal representation, Moorish architects instead adorned their buildings with geometric designs, red-and-white horseshoe arches, and ornate tiles. The spectacular 14th-century **Alhambra** in Granada (p. 301), maintained even after the *Reconquista* (1492) for its astounding beauty, and the **Mezquita** in Córdoba (p. 248) epitomize the Moorish style. Periods of peaceful coexistence between Muslims and Christians inspired the synthetic **mudéjar** architectural movement, created by Moors living under Christian rule in the years between the Christian resurgence (11th century) and the *Reconquista*. Sevilla's **Alcázar** (p. 231) is an exquisite example of this tradition, featuring brick and complex tiling patterns.

The **Spanish Gothic** style (13th-16th centuries) experimented with pointed arches, flying buttresses, slender walls, airy spaces, and stained-glass windows. Along with those in Toledo (p. 190) and León (p. 169), the cathedral of Burgos is one of the finest examples of Spanish Gothic style. Sevilla boasts the largest Gothic cathedral (p. 229) in the world. Spain also contains important **Romanesque** sculpture; Maestro Mateo's **Pórtico de la Gloria,** completed in 1188 in Santiago de Compostela (p. 562), is considered one of the style's finest specimens.

RENAISSANCE AND BAROQUE. New World riches inspired the **Plateresque** ("silversmith") style, a flashy extreme of Gothic that changed the face of the wealthier parts of Spain. Intricate stonework and extravagant use of gold and silver made 15th- and 16th-century buildings shine; **La Universidad de Salamanca** (p. 162) practically drips with ornamentation. In the late 16th century, Italian innovations in perspective and symmetry arrived in Spain and sobered up the Plateresque style. These innovations influenced **Juan Bautista de Toledo** in his design for the austere **El Escorial** (p. 141), Felipe II's immense palace-cum-monastery. Opulence took center stage in 17th- and 18th-century **Baroque** Spain. The Churriguera brothers pioneered the new, aptly-named **Churrigueresque** style, whose elaborate ornamentation with extensive sculptural detail gave buildings of this period a rich exuberance, most resonant in Salamanca's **Plaza Mayor** (p. 164).

MODERN AND POSTMODERN. In the late 19th and early 20th centuries, Cataluña's **Modernistas** burst on the scene in Barcelona, led by the eccentric geniuses **Antoni Gaudí, Lluís Domènech i Montaner,** and **Josep Puig y Cadafalch.** *Modernista* structures defied any and all previous standards with their voluptuous curves and unusual textures. The new style was inspired in part by *mudéjar*, but more so by organic forms and unbridled imagination. Gaudí's **La Sagrada Família** (p. 400) and **Casa Milà** (p. 401), stand as the best examples of *català Modernisme*.

Spain's outstanding architectural tradition has continued through the 20th and into the 21st century. *Català* architect **Josep Lluís Sert** helped introduce European Modernism throughout the 1900s with his stark concrete buildings. Today Spain boasts stars like **Rafael Moneo,** and **Santiago Calatrava,** who has become the most recent sensation with his elegant steel-and-crystal buildings in Valencia (p. 312) and unmistakable bridges in Sevilla, Mérida, and Bilbao. Spain has also acquired several new landmarks from foreign architects, including Frank Gehry's stunning **Guggenheim Museum** in Bilbao (p. 518).

PAINTING AND SCULPTURE

MEDIEVAL AND RENAISSANCE. Fresco painters and manuscript illuminators adorned churches and their libraries along the Camino de Santiago and in León and Toledo in the 11th and 12th centuries. During Spain's imperial ascension in the 16th century, Spanish painting reached its **Siglo de Oro** (Golden Age; roughly 1492-1650). Felipe II, one of the era's presiding monarchs, imported foreign art and artists to jump-start native production and embellish his palace, El Escorial. One hopeful artist, Crete-born Doménikos Theotokópoulos, a.k.a. **El Greco** (1541-1614), was denied a royal commission by Felipe II because of his intensely personal style. Though misunderstood by his contemporaries, El Greco's haunting, elongated figures and dramatic use of light and color have since garnered widespread appreciation. El Greco is also known for his particular style of painting hands—in many of his portraits, one or two fingers of his subjects are bent down. One of his most famous canvases, *El entierro del Conde de Orgaz* (*The Burial of Count Orgaz*, 1586) graces the Iglesia de Santo Tomé in Toledo (p. 190), the city whose landscape he so vividly painted beginning in 1597.

Felipe IV's foremost court painter, **Diego Velázquez** (1599-1660), is considered one of the world's greatest artists. Whether depicting Felipe IV's family or commoners buying cups of water, Velázquez painted scenes with naturalistic precision; working slowly and meticulously, he captured light with a virtually photographic quality. Nearly half of this Sevilla-born artist's works reside in the Prado, perhaps most notably his famous and somewhat controversial *Las Meninas* (1656; p. 125). Other distinguished Golden Age painters include **Francisco de Zurbarán** (1598-1664) and **Bartoloméo Murillo** (1617-1682).

FROM MODERN TO AVANT-GARDE. While Spain's political power declined, its cultural capital flourished. **Francisco de Goya** (1746-1828) ushered European painting into the modern age. Hailing from provincial Aragón, Goya rose to the position of official court painter under the degenerate Carlos IV. Goya cast flattery aside: his depictions of the royal family come close to caricature, as attests Queen María Luisa's haughty jaw line in Goya's famous *The Family of Charles IV* (1800). His series of etchings, *The Disasters of War* (1810-1814), which includes the landmark *El 2 de mayo* and *Fusilamientos del 3 de mayo*, records the horrific Napoleonic invasion of 1808. Deaf and alone in his later years, Goya painted nightmarishly fantastic visions, inspiring expressionist and surrealist artists of the next century with his free and loose brushstrokes and dramatic presentation. His chilling *Black Paintings* (1820-1823) fill a room in the Prado.

There is perhaps no artist who influenced 20th-century painting so profoundly as did Málaga-born **Pablo Picasso** (1881-1973). During his Blue Period, which began in 1900 and was characterized by somber depictions of society's outcasts, Picasso alternated between Barcelona and Paris. His permanent move to Paris in 1904 initiated the Rose Period, which probed into the engrossing lives of clowns and acrobats. With his French colleague Georges Braque, he founded **Cubism,** a method of abstraction in painting achieved by the geometric fragmentation of form. His huge 1937 painting *Guernica* portrays the bombing of the Basque city (p. 519) by Nazi planes during the Spanish Civil War. A protest against violence, *Guernica* now resides in the Museo Nacional Centro de Arte Reina Sofía in Madrid (p. 127).

Català painter and sculptor **Joan Miró** (1893-1983) is famed for painting simple shapes in bright primary colors. His haphazard, abstract squiggles rebelled against the authoritarian society of the post-Civil War years. Fellow *catalana* **Salvador Dalí** (1904-1989) scandalized society and leftist intellectuals in France and Spain by claiming to support the Fascists. Dalí's name is now synonymous with **Surrealism,** the artistic expression of the liberated imagination. A self-congratulatory fellow, Dalí founded the **Teatro-Museu Dalí** in Figueres (p. 437), the second-most visited museum in Spain after the Prado.

Since Franco's death in 1975 (p. 78), a younger generation of artists has thrived. With new museums in most major cities, Spanish painters and sculptors once again have forums for their work. **Antonio Tápies** (1923-) constructs unorthodox collages and is a founding member of the self-proclaimed "Abstract Generation," while **Antonio López García** (1936-) paints hyperrealist works.

LITERATURE

FROM DARK AGE TO GOLDEN AGE. Spain's literary tradition first blossomed in the late Middle Ages (1000-1500). The 12th-century *El Cantar del Mío Cid (Song of My Cid)* is Spain's most important epic poem. It chronicles the life and military triumphs of national hero Rodrigo Díaz de Vivar, from his exile to his eventual return to grace in the king's court. At the end of the 15th century, **Fernando de Rojas** wrote the especially famous novel *La Celestina* (1499), a tragicomedy beloved for the strong, witch-like female character who serves as a go-between for star-crossed lovers Calixto and Melibea. The anonymous work *Lazarillo de Tormes*, considered the first *novela picaresca* (picaresque novel), is a social satire in the form of a fictional autobiography of an orphan boy's adventurous rise in society. The **Toro Ibérico** statue in Salamanca (p. 159) still stands, depicting several of the characters from this proto-novel. Literature and poetry alike thrived during Spain's literary **Siglo de Oro** (Golden Age; 16th and 17th centuries); some consider the sonnets of **Garcilaso de la Vega** the most perfect ever written in *castellano*. The Golden Age also produced outstanding dramatists, including **Pedro Calderón de la Barca** (1600-1681) and **Lope de Vega** (1562-1635), who collectively wrote over 2,300 plays. **Tirso de Molina's** (1584-1648) famed *El Burlador de Sevilla* (1630) introduced the character of Don Juan into the national psyche. **Miguel de Cervantes's** *Don Quixote de la Mancha* (1605-1615)—often considered the world's first novel—is the most famous work of Spanish literature. This humorous parable tells the story of the hapless Don and his servant Sancho Panza, who fancy themselves a bold knight and squire out to save the world.

ROMANTICS AND INNOVATORS. The 18th century brought a belated Enlightenment, while the 19th century inspired contrasting forms, including **Rosalía del Castro's** lyrical verse and the naturalistic novels of **Leopoldo Alas ("Clarín").** Essayist and philosopher **Miguel de Unamuno** and critic **José Ortega y Gasset** led the **Generación de 1898,** along with novelist **Pío Baroja,** playwright **Ramón del Valle Inclán,** and poets **Antonio Machado** and **Juan Ramón Jiménez.** Reacting to Spain's defeat in the Spanish-American War (1898), they argued that each person must spiritually and ideologically attain peace before society can do the same. This *generación* influenced the **Generación de 1927,** a group of experimental lyric poets like **Federico García Lorca** and **Rafael Alberti** who wrote Surrealist and avant-garde poetry.

MODERN MARVELS. Spanish Nobel Prize recipients include playwright and essayist **Jacinto Benavente y Martínez** (1922), poet **Vicente Aleixandre** (1977), and novelist **Camilo José Cela** (1989). Female writers, like **Mercè Rodoreda, Carmen Martín Gaite,** and **Almudena Grandes** have likewise earned critical international acclaim. Spanish artists flocked to Madrid as they once did earlier in the century, and an avant-garde spirit—known as *La Movida*—was reborn in the capital. **Ana Rossetti** and **Juana Castro** led a new generation of erotic poets into the 80s, placing women at the forefront of Spanish literature for the first time.

FICTION AND NON-FICTION.
Don Quixote de la Mancha, by Miguel de Cervantes (1605). A two-part classic about the adventures of a whimsical knight and his loyal squire.
El Burlador de Sevilla, by Tirso de Molina (1630). A literary staple about the original Don Juan, who steals the virtue of all the ladies in one medieval town.
El Cantar del Mío Cid. A 12th century epic medieval poem recounting the accomplishments of a Castilian hero in ballad form.
La Casa de Bernarda Alba, by Federico García Lorca (1936). A satirical play about women defying tradition and controversial social standards.
San Manuel Bueno, Martír, by Miguel de Unamuno (1933). Unamuno's acclaimed story of a troubled priest who has lost faith in his own religion.
The Sun Also Rises, by Ernest Hemingway (1926). Immortalizes bullfighting, *machismo,* and Spain itself.

MUSIC

FLAMENCO. Spain's most famous form of cultural expression combines *cante* (song), *baile* (dance), and *guitarra* (guitar). True flamenco artists are said to perform with *duende*—the soul or spirit behind any passionate performance. The music originated among Andalusian gypsies in the late 18th century and remains an extremely popular tradition that continues to enrapture audiences around the world. While it is possible to buy flamenco recordings, nothing compares to seeing a live performance. Like any art, flamenco has its heroes: **Andrés Segovia** (1893-1987) was instrumental in giving the flamenco guitar the same renown as the violin and the cello, and singer **Antonio Mairena** (1909-1983) was so significant that flamenco historians often divide the art into pre-Mairena and post-Mairena periods.

CLASSICAL. Spain bred two of the greatest Renaissance composers in **Francisco Guerrero** and **Tomás Luis de Victoria**. Guerrero composed both sacred and secular masterpieces, while Victoria penned a stunning **Requiem Mass** (1603) for the funeral of his longtime patron, Empress Maria. Spain's classical tradition continued centuries later when **Pau (Pablo) Casals** (1876-1973), *català* cellist, conductor, composer, pianist, and humanitarian, became one of the most influential classical musicians of the 20th century. To promote world peace, Casals composed the oratorio *The Manger* (1960) and conducted it throughout the world. Arguably the greatest Spanish composer of the last two centuries, Cádiz native **Manuel de Falla** (1876-1946) wrote the popular opera *El sombrero de tres picos* (*The Three-Cornered Hat*), which premiered in London in 1919 with stage design by Picasso. Another favorite de Falla work is the frequently performed *Noches en los jardines de España* (*Nights in the Gardens of Spain;* 1914). Spain also claims two of the world-famous "Three Tenors," Barcelona-born **José Carreras** and **Plácido Domingo**, who hails from Madrid.

FOLK MUSIC. Nearly every region in Spain celebrates flamenco, but each also offers its own distinctive style of folk music. Accordion-based **trikitrixa** music defines Basque folk, a truly unique cultural product, while the **zambomba drum,** played by pulling on a rope inside the drum, is a staple of the music of Extremadura. Valencia takes pride in its **brass bands,** Cataluña enjoys a good **sardana**, or circle dance, and the Canary Islands hosts Latin American music played by the guitar-like **charanga**. Meanwhile, **Celtic** music can be heard in Spain in Castilla, Madrid, León, and Aragón.

CONTEMPORARY MUSIC. The popular music scene among Spanish youth is primarily dominated by American and Latin American artists, yet several Spanish-born singers, like Julio and Enrique Iglesias, as well as Alejandro Sanz, have recently gained international acclaim.

SPAIN

FILM

FILM UNDER FRANCO. Spain's first film, *Riña en un café* (directed by **Fructu- oso Gelabert**), dates back to 1897, and technically-innovative director **Segundo de Chomón** is recognized worldwide as a pioneer of early cinema. **Luis Buñuel,** close friend of **Salvador Dalí,** produced several early classics, most notably *L'Âge d'or* (1930). Later, in exile from Fascist Spain, he produced a number of brilliantly surrealist films including *Viridiana* (1961), which was denounced by the Cath- olic church as heretical. Meanwhile, Franco's censors stifled most creative ten- dencies and left the public with nothing to watch but cheap westerns and bland spy flicks. As censorship waned in the early 1970s, Spanish cinema showed signs of life, led by **Carlos Saura's** dark, subversive hits such as *El jardín de las deli- cias* (1970) and *Cría cuervos* (1976).

CONTEMPORARY CINEMA. In the wake of Franco's death, domestic censorship laws were revoked in 1977. The move brought artistic freedom and financial hard- ship for Spanish filmmakers, who found their films shunned domestically in favor of newly permitted foreign films. Depictions of the exuberant fervor of a super-lib- erated Spain found increased attention and international respect. Basque director **Eloy de la Iglesia's** *El diputado* (1979) explored the risqué themes on which con- temporary Spanish cinema often focuses. Equally radical are the films of Spain's most highly acclaimed director, **Pedro Almodóvar.** His *Todo sobre mi madre* (1999) and *Hable con ella* (2002) won several major awards, and his recent film *Volver* (2006) won Best Screenplay at the Cannes Film Festival. Chilean-born Spanish director **Alejandro Amenábar** received critical acclaim as well as the Best Foreign Language Film award at the 2004 Oscars for his poignant *Mar adentro*.

Over 12,000 hostels in 165 countries

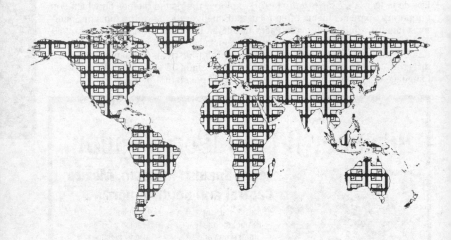

SPORTS

FÚTBOL

Soccer is a nationally unifying and locally divisive passion for Spaniards. Spanish national teams have been shut out of major international success since 1964, but the current Spanish national team, featuring superstars Fernando Torres, Xavi Hernández, and Raúl González, is currently gearing up for an appearance at the European Cup Championships in 2008. Spanish club teams constantly bring back honors from European leagues, led by international icons like Brazilians Ronaldo and Ronaldinho, Argentine Lionel Messi, and Cameroonian Samuel Eto'o. Squads in the Spanish "La Liga" Premier League, such as Real Madrid, FC Barcelona, and Valencia, carry fans' hopes on their skilled feet, and often do Spaniards proud. La Liga competition starts up every September.

BULLFIGHTING

The national spectacle of *la corrida* (bullfighting) dates in its modern form to about 1726, although it derives from earlier Roman and Moorish practices. As bullfighting grew in popularity, Roman amphitheaters like those in Sevilla and Córdoba were restored, and bulls were bred for aggressive instincts. A bullfight is divided into three stages: in the first, *picadores* (lancers on horseback) pierce the bull's neck muscles to lower his head for the kill; next, assistants on foot thrust *banderillas* (decorated darts) into his back to enliven the tiring animal; finally, the *matador* (bullfighter) has ten minutes to kill his opponent with a sword between the shoulder blades, appearing graceful and confident all the while. He can be granted up to five extra minutes if necessary, but after that the bull is taken out alive, to the *matador's* disgrace. If the *matador* shows special skill and daring, the audience waves white *pañuelos* (handkerchiefs), imploring the bullfight's president to award him the coveted ears (and, very rarely, the tail). The techniques of the modern *matador* were refined around 1914 by **Juan Belmonte,** considered one of the greatest *matadores* of all time (others include **Joselito, Manolete,** and **Cristina,** the first female *matadora*). Bullfighting has always had its critics—in the 17th century the Church felt that the risks made it tantamount to suicide. More recently, the challenge comes from animal rights activists who object to the drawn-out slaughter. Cataluña has banned bullfighting, a move tied as much to feelings of *català* nationalism as to cross-species sympathy.

JAI ALAI

Meaning "Merry Festival" in Basque, and also called "*pelota vasca*," this regional sport is promoted by the Basque Government as the "fastest game on earth." Jai Alai is a game played with a wicker *cesta* basket, which is used to hurl a ball against a *fronton* (open-walled arena). Points are awarded when the other team drops, misses, or sends the ball out of bounds. These deadly projectiles have been clocked in at incredible speeds of up to 188 mph.

OTHER SPORTS

Fans fondly remember five-time consecutive Tour de France champion **Miguel Indurain,** a Navarran hero and Spain's most decorated athlete. Old favorites like **Arantxa Sánchez-Vicario** and **Carlos Moya** and up-and-comers like **Rafael Nadal,** one of tennis's top-ranked players, have all made their names on the tennis court.

NATIONAL HOLIDAYS

The following table lists the national holidays for 2008.

DATE	HOLIDAYS
January 1	Año Nuevo (New Year's Day)
January 6	Epifanía (Epiphany)
March 14-23	Semana Santa (Holy Week)
March 20	Jueves Santo (Maundy Thursday)
March 21	Viernes Santo (Good Friday)
March 23	Pascua (Easter)
May 1	Día del Trabajador (Labor Day)
August 15	La Asunción (Feast of the Assumption)
October 12	Día de la Hispanidad (National Day)
November 1	Día de Todos Santos (All Saints' Day)
December 6	Día de la Constitución (Constitution Day)
December 8	La Inmaculada Concepción (Feast of the Immaculate Conception)
December 25	Navidad (Christmas)
December 31	Noche Vieja (New Year's Eve)

SPANISH FESTIVALS IN 2008

The following table lists Spanish festivals for 2008.

DATE	HOLIDAYS
January 26 - February 2	**Carnaval (Canarias)** Hedonism and frivolity at its best—don't miss the "sardine funeral" on Ash Wednesday.
February (entire month)	**Seville Tapas Fair (Sevilla)** Like an all-you-can-eat buffet, but better.
March (entire month)	**Jerez Flamenco Festival (Jerez de la Frontera)** A celebration of the nation's most famous and passionate dancers.
March 17-21	**Fallas de San José (Valencia)** A pyromaniac's dream—fireworks, burning effigies, and a week-long party.
April 27	**Romería de Andújar (Andalucía)** Pilgrims flock to a famous sanctuary.
May 15	**San Isidro (Madrid)** Spain's biggest and most prestigious bullfighting exhibition.
June 23	**Paso do Fuego (Soria)** Fire walking: only the strong (and some say, only the locals) survive this brazen act of courage.
June 29	**Wine Battle (Haro, La Rioja)** Just what it sounds like—wet and wild.
last week of June	**Orgullo Gay (Madrid)** One of Europe's biggest gay pride festivals.
July 6-14	**San Fermín (Pamplona)** Featuring the famous "running of the bulls," this festival was immortalized in Hemingway's "The Sun Also Rises."
1st and 2nd week of July	**Bou en la Mar (Dénia)** The underwater version of *San Fermín*.
August 28	**La Tomatina (Buñol)** An organized food fight—with tomatoes.
September 24	**Festes de la Merce (Barcelona)** The city's biggest all-out demonstration of debauchery.
October 12	**Día de la Hispanidad (Nationwide)** A celebration of the arrival of Christopher Columbus in the Americas.
2nd and 3rd week of October	**Cava Week (Cataluña)** A celebration of the region's champagne.
December 25	**Navidad** (Christmas)
Other Festivals in Spain	**Castellers (Tarragona)** Watch in awe as 7-story human towers rise before your very eyes.

MADRID

Welcome to Spain's political, intellectual, and cultural center—the country's wild, pulsing heart. While theoretically subject to the earth's rotations, Madrid often seems to transcend traditional hours. In this city of ceaseless activity, the morning rush collides with partiers on their way to after-hours clubs, and people only pause for the mid-afternoon siesta. Tourists inundate the city, spending their days absorbed in its monuments, world-renowned museums, and raging nightlife, mixing with the 5.5 million *madrileños* sprawled in the city's many plazas, tapas bars, and parks. Businessmen in suits scoot along on mopeds, old women compare market prices on benches, and teens text furiously in search of the next hip club. Try to stock up on energy with a late afternoon siesta in the Retiro Park or in your hostel; some of the best the city has to offer only opens after the sun has set.

Though Madrid witnessed the coronation of Fernando and Isabel, it did not achieve importance until Habsburg monarch Felipe II moved his court here in 1561. It served as Spain's artistic hub during the *Siglo de Oro* (Golden Age), becoming a seat of wealth, culture, and imperial glory, despite its considerable distance from vital ports and rivers. In the 18th century, Madrid experienced a Neo-classical rebirth when Carlos III embellished the city with wide, tree-lined boulevards and scores of imposing buildings, but things took a turn for the worse during the Peninsular wars against Napoleon (1808-1814), the bloody inspiration of some of Francisco de Goya's most famous canvases. Madrid was the base of the 20th-century Republican government and resisted Franco's troops until the spring of 1939, when the Civil War had already washed most of the peninsula in blood. It was the second-to-last city in Spain to fall; immediately after, the Nationalists took Valencia and brought the four-year conflict to a close. For the next four decades, Madrid served as the seat of Franco's government. When the dictator died in 1975, Madrid, and the rest of Spain, came out in what is known today as *la movida* ("shift" or "movement") or *el destape* ("uncovering"). A 200,000-strong student population took to the streets and stayed there—they haven't stopped moving yet.

Students, families, artists, and immigrants continue to flock to Madrid, mixing ancient sensibilities with modern dreams. Just look to the architecture if you're not convinced: 21st century skyscrapers accent views from narrow alleys and ancient plazas, and palaces house post offices.

HIGHLIGHTS OF MADRID

MUSE over the world-famous museums along the **Avenida del Arte** (p. 125).

RELIVE royal dreams at the luxurious 18th-century **Palacio Real** (p. 122).

RETREAT in kingly fashion to the **Parque de Buen Retiro** (p. 124).

TRIP along the cobblestones in quirky **Malsaña and Chueca** (p. 101).

✈ INTERCITY TRANSPORTATION

BY PLANE

All flights land at **Aeropuerto Internacional de Barajas** (☎902 40 47 04, flight information 35 35 70; www.aena.es.), 16km and 20min. northeast of Madrid. The regional **tourist office** in the international terminal has maps and info. (☎913 05 86 56. Open M-Sa 8am-

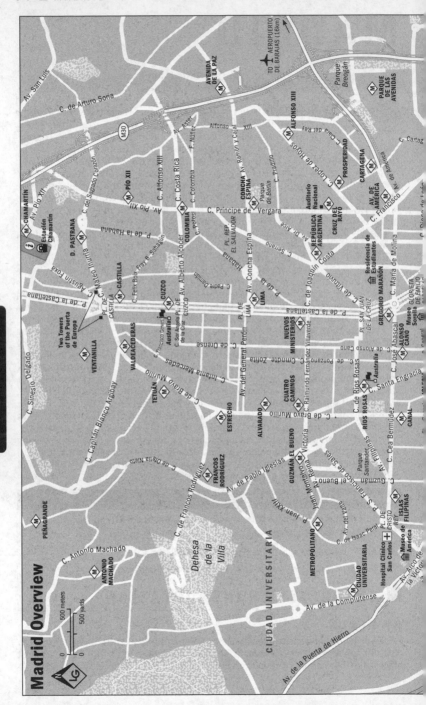

MADRID

Madrid Overview

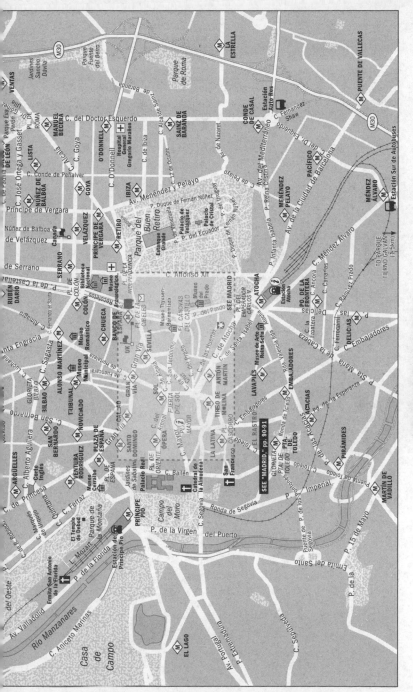

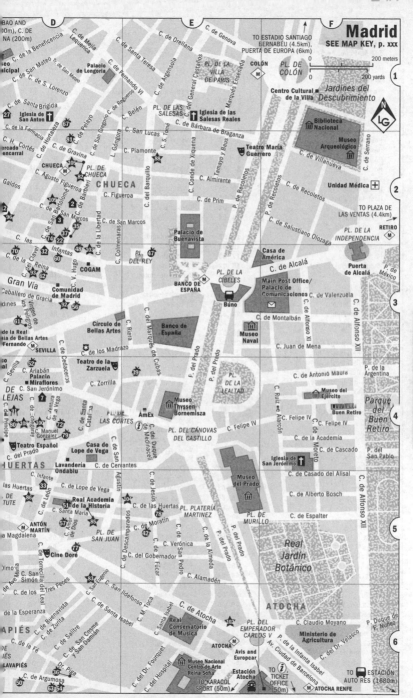

Madrid
SEE MAP, pp. 96-97

🏠 ACCOMMODATIONS

Albergue Juvenil Santa Cruz de Marcenado (HI),	1	B2
Barbieri International Youth Hostel,	2	D2
Casa Chueca,	3	D2
Cat's Hostel,	4	C5
Hostal A. Nebrija,	5	A2
Hostal Abril,	6	D2
Hostal Aguilar,	7	D4
Hostal Alicante,	8	B4
Hostal Los Arcos,	9	C4
Hostal Betanzos,	10	C5
Hostal Cantábrico,	11	D4
Hostal Chelo,	12	D2
Hostal Esparteros,	13	C4
Hostal Gran Via 44,	14	C3
Hostal Lauria,	15	B2
Hostal Margarita,	16	B2
Hostal Oriente,	17	B3
Hostal Palacios/Hostal Ribadavia,	18	C2
Hostal Paz,	19	B3
Hostal Pérez,	20	A1
Hostal Plaza D'Ort,	21	C5
Hostal Rio Miño,	22	D2
Hostal Santillan,	23	B2
Hostal Valencia,	24	A3
Hostal Villar,	25	D4
Hostal-Residencia Cruz-Sol,	26	C4
Hostal-Residencia Domínguez,	27	D1
Hostal-Residencia Lamalonga,	28	B2
Hostal-Residencia Luz,	29	B4
Hostal-Residencia Ríos,	30	A1
Hostal-Residencia Rober,	31	B3
Hotel San Lorenzo,	32	D3
La Posada de Huertas,	33	D5
Mad Hostel,	34	C5

🍎 FOOD

4 de Tapas,	35	D2
Achuri,	36	D6
Al-Jaima,	37	D2
Almendro 13,	38	B5
Al Natural,	39	E4
Ananias,	40	A1
Annalina,	41	C5
Arrocería Gala,	42	E5
Café-Botillería Manuela,	43	C1
Casa Alberto,	44	D5
Casa Amadeo,	45	B6
Cervecería 100 Montaditos,	46	B4
El Circo,	47	E3
Darbar,	48	D3
El Estragón Vegetariano,	49	A5
Eucalipto,	50	D6
La Farfalla,	51	D5
La Finca de Susana,	52	D4
El Fogón de la Abuela,	53	B5
El Granero de Lavapies,	54	D6
La Granja de Saud,	55	C1
Gula Gula,	56	D3

Heladería Giuseppe Ricci,	57	D5
Horno La Santigüesa,	58	A4
Inshala,	59	A4
Isolée,	60	D3
La Mallorquina,	61	D3
Museo Chicote,	62	D3
Museo del Jamón,	63	D6
El Oso y el Madroño,	64	C4
Osteria Il Regno de Napoli,	65	D1
La Piba,	66	A1
Il Pizzaiolo,	67	D1
Pizzeria Maravilles,	68	C1
Pizzeria Mastropiero,	69	C1
Pizzeria Vesuvio,	70	D3
Restaurante Casa Granada,	71	C5
Restaurante Integral Artemisa,	72	D4
Root,	73	D4
La Sacristía,	74	D2
La Sanabresa,	75	D5
Sobrino del Botín,	76	B5
Taberna "Er 77,"	77	D5
Taberna Maciera,	78	E5
La Toscana,	79	C4
La Trucha,	80	D4
Vegaviana,	81	D2

⭐ NIGHTLIFE

Acuarela,	82	D2
Cardamomo,	83	D5
Cafe Central,	84	C5
El Cafe de Schérezad,	85	D5
Cafe Jazz Populart,	86	D5
La Casa de los Jacintos,	87	B6
El Clandestino	88	E2
La Comedia,	89	D4
La Creación,	90	D4
Cuevas de Sésamo,	91	D4
De Las Letras Restaurante,	92	D3
Del Diego,	93	D3
La Ida,	94	C1
Kenthmandío,	95	A4
Mama Inés,	96	D2
Ocho y Medio Club,	97	C3
Palacio Gaviria,	98	B4
The Penthouse,	99	C4
Taberna Viniçola Mentridana,	100	D4
Tapasentao,	101	B5
Teatro Kapital,	102	E6
El Tigre,	103	D3
La Trocha,	104	E5
El Truco,	105	D2
Tupperware,	106	C1
Vía Láctea,	107	C1
Viva Madrid,	108	D4
Why Not?,	109	D2

8pm, Su 9am-1pm.) **Luggage storage** (*consigna*) is sometimes available. (☎913 93 68 05. 1 day €2.85, 2-15 days €3.58 per day. Max. storage 15 days. Open 24hr.)

The **Barajas metro stop** connects the airport to all of Madrid (€1 extra from the airport). From the airport arrivals area, follow signs to the metro, located in Terminal 2 (10min.). Take Line 8 (pink) to Nuevos Ministerios and switch to Line 10 (dark blue, dir.: Puerta del Sur). At Tribunal, change to Line 1 (light blue, dir.: Valdecarros), and two stops later you'll find yourself at Sol, smack in the middle of Madrid's best accommodations and sights. The **Bus-Aeropuerto #200** leaves from the national terminal **T2** and runs to the city center. (☎902 50 78 50. Look for "EMT" signs just outside the airport doors. Daily every 10-15min. 6am-11pm; last bus 11:30pm; €1.) The bus stops in the metro station **Avenida de América**. Line 101 leaves from T1, 2, and 3 and goes to Canillejas, and Line 204 leaves from T4 and goes to Avenida de América as well. Fleets of **taxis** swarm the airport. Taxi fare to central Madrid should cost €30-35, including the €5 airport surcharge, depending on traffic and time of day.

BY TRAIN

Two *largo recorrido* (long-distance) **RENFE** stations, **Chamartín** and **Atocha**, connect Madrid to surrounding areas and the rest of Europe. Both stations are easily accessible by metro. Call RENFE (☎902 24 02 02; www.renfe.es) for reservations and info. Buy tickets at the station or online.

ATOCHA SO. On your way to the Atocha train station? To avoid Lost Tourist Syndrome, make sure to get off the stop called Atocha Renfe, not Atocha.

Estación Atocha, Av. Ciudad de Barcelona (☎915 06 61 37). M: Atocha Renfe. The cast-iron atrium of the original station has been turned into an indoor rainforest, with lush plants and the occasional bird. Galleries, boutiques, and restaurants provide additional diversions. There is a **tourist office** in the station. (☎913 15 99 76; open M-Sa 8am-8pm, Su 9am-2pm.) **RENFE information office** in the main terminal (☎902 24 02 02). Open daily 6:30am-10:30pm. **Luggage storage** (*consignas automáticas;* €2.40-4.50), at the back right corner of the atrium. Open daily 6:30am-11:45pm. Ticket windows open 6:30am-10:30pm, advance purchases 7am-9:30pm. No international service. **AVE** (☎91 506 63 29) offers high speed service to southern Spain, including **Sevilla** (2½hr., 22 per day 6:30am-11:30pm, €63-70) via **Córdoba** (1¾hr., €40-52). Daytime *Grandes Líneas* trains for **Barcelona** leave from Atocha (4½-5hr., 9 per day 7:45am-7pm, €36-63); overnight trains leave from **Chamartín.**

Estación Chamartín, C. Agustín de Foxa (☎913 00 69 69). M: Chamartín. Bus #5 runs to and from Puerta del Sol (45min.); the stop is just beyond the lockers. Alternatively, get off at M: Atocha Renfe and take a red *Cercanías* train (15min., every 5-10min., €1.05) to Chamartín. Be sure to keep your ticket, or you won't be able to exit the turnstiles. Chamartín is a mini-mall of useful services, including a **tourist office** (Vestíbulo, Puerta 14; ☎913 15 99 76; open M-Sa 8am-8pm, Su 8am-2pm), **currency exchange, accommodations service, post office, car rental, police,** and **luggage storage** (*consignas;* €2.40-4.50; open daily 7am-11pm). For international destinations, call RENFE (☎902 24 34 02); for domestic destinations call RENFE (☎902 24 02 02; Spanish only). Ticket windows open 5:30am-midnight, advance sales 8am-9pm. Chamartín serves both international and domestic destinations to the northeast and south. Most *Cercanías* (local) trains stop at both Chamartín and Atocha. Major destinations include: **Barcelona** (9hr., 10 and 11pm, €35-42; express 5½hr., 6 per day 7:45am-7pm, €60.50); **Bilbao** (6½hr., 2:50pm, €31.50; night train 8¾hr., 10:45pm, €40 or €80.50 with cabin); **Lisboa** (9¼ hr., 10:45pm, €54); **Paris** (13½hr., 7pm, €112-129).

BY BUS

Numerous private companies serve Madrid, each with its own station and set of destinations. Most buses pass through **Estación Sur de Autobuses** and **Estación Auto-**

Res, both easily accessible by metro. The Pl. Mayor and any other tourist office in the city has information on the most relevant intercity buses.

ALSA: Headquarters located on C. Alcalá, 478 (☎902 42 22 42; www.alsa.es). International destinations include: **Czech Republic, France, Germany, Holland, Italy, Poland, Portugal, Romania,** and **Switzerland,** but flying can actually be cheaper. Contact **Eurolines** for more information (reservations ☎902 40 50 40). Madrid office in **Estación Sur** bus station (☎915 06 33 60; www.eurolines.es). M: Méndez Álvaro. Open daily 7am-11pm.

Estación Autocares Herranz: Headquarters located on C. Juan de Toledo, 5 (☎918 96 90 28), in the Intercambio de Moncloa. M: Moncloa. To **Valle de los Caídos** (20min.; Tu-Su departs El Escorial 3:15pm, returns 5:30pm; round-trip plus admission €8) via **El Escorial** (1hr., €3.20).

Estación Auto-Res: C. Fernández Shaw, 1 (☎902 02 09 99; www.auto-res.net). M: Conde de Casal. **Luggage storage** €1.45 per bag per day. (Open M-Th 6:30am-10:30pm, F 6:30am-1pm, Sa 6:30am-9pm, Su noon-10pm.) **Info booth** open daily 6:30am-1am. Tickets sold daily 6am-1am. To: **Badajoz** (5¼hr., 9-10 per day 8am-1am, €23.03; express 4½hr., 10am-9pm, €29); **Cáceres** (4hr., 7-10 per day 8am-1am, €18; express 2hr., €22); **Cuenca** (2½hr.; M-F 8-10 per day 6:45am-10, Sa-Su 5-6 per day 8am-8pm, Su last bus 10pm; €9.75; express 2hr.; M-F and Su 10am, 6:30pm, Sa 10am; €13.10); **Mérida** (4¼hr.; M-Sa 9 per day 8am-1am, Su 8 per day 8am-9pm; €20.20; express 4hr., €26); **Salamanca** (3-3¼hr., 9 per day 8:30am-10:30pm, €10.90; express 2½hr.; M-Sa 15-16 per day 7am-10pm, Su 8am-11pm; €16); **Trujillo** (3¼hr., 15-17 per day 8am-1am, €14.90; express 2¾hr., €21); **Valencia** (5hr., 4 per day 1am-2pm, €22; express 4hr., 10-11 per day M-Sa 7am-1am, Su 8am-1am, €29).

Estación Empresa Alacuber: Pl. del Caudillo, 2 (☎913 76 01 04). M: Moncloa. To **El Pardo** (20min.; every 15min. M-F 6:25am-1am, Sa 6:25am-2am, Su 7:15am; €1.10).

Estación Empresa Continental Auto: Av. de América, 9 (☎917 45 63 00). M: Av. de América. To: **Alcalá de Henares** (40min.; M-Sa every 15min. 6:15am-11pm, Su every 20min. 7-11pm; €2.00).

Empresa Larrea: Est. Sur de Autobuses (☎913 98 38 05). To **Ávila** (1½hr.; M-F 8 per day 7am-8:30pm, Sa 6 per day 9:30am-10pm, Su 4 per day 10am-8:30pm; €6.84). M: Méndez Álvaro.

Empresa La Sepulvedana: Headquarters located on C. Palos de la Frontera, 16 (☎915 59 59 55; www.lasepulvedana.es). M: Príncipe Pío (via extension from M: Ópera). To **Segovia** (1½hr.; every 30min. 6:30am-10:30pm; €6.04, round-trip €9.54).

Estación Sur de Autobuses: C. Méndez Álvaro (☎914 68 42 00; www.estaciondeauto-buses.com). M: Méndez Álvaro; metro stop inside station. **Info booth** open daily 6:30am-1am. **ATMs,** food, and **luggage storage** (€1.25 per bag per day). National destinations include: **Algeciras, Alicante, Aranjuez, Benidorm, Cartagena, Gijón, A Coruña, Lugo, Murcia, Oviedo, Santiago de Compostela,** and **Toledo.** Check at the station or call for specific info on routes and schedules. **AISA-Empresa Semar** (☎915 27 12 94) is the best option to **Aranjuez** (45min.; M-F every 30min. 6:30am-11:45pm, Sa-Su every 30min. 7am-11:30pm; €3.20).

■ ORIENTATION

THE NEIGHBORHOODS OF MADRID

EL CENTRO: SOL, ÓPERA, AND PLAZA MAYOR

Puerta del Sol is the center of the city in the center of the country. The "Kilómetro 0" sign in front of the police station marks the intersection of eight of Madrid's most celebrated streets and the starting point of the country's major highways. In the heart of it all, flower-potted balconies, *hostales*, and *pensiones* lie interspersed with most of Madrid's prominent sights, including the **Ópera** and **Plaza Mayor**. Just west of Sol off C. Mayor, Pl. Mayor is a hub of activity for tourists and *madrileños* alike; the plaza houses both contemporary cafes and the churches and historical buildings of **Habsburg Madrid**, also known as **Madrid de los Austrias**. Farther west of Sol, by way of C. del Arenal, lies the chief monument of **Bourbon Madrid**, the Palacio Real. This section of Madrid, also known as **Ópera**, contains fantastic gardens and churches.

LA LATINA AND LAVAPIÉS

South of Sol and west of Huertas is the area around the metro stop **La Latina** and **Lavapiés**, multicultural hot spots whose immigrant roots are starting to attract bohemian gentrification where thousands of immigrants make a home. Trendy *madrileños* socialize in the small markets that line the area's winding streets, perfect for an evening of gourmet treats. Just a 10min. walk down the hill from Huertas, the area is easily accessible and clearly worth the climb back up. **El Rastro**, an ancient, gargantuan flea market, is held here every Sunday morning.

HUERTAS

Huertas is the area between C. de San Jerónimo and C. de Atocha, with C. de las Huertas cutting through the southern portion of the district. Long ago the literary quarter and more recently a seedy area, Huertas has grown into a clean, popular cluster of theater, restaurants, and bars. **Plaza Santa Ana, Calle del Príncipe**, and **Calle de Echegaray** contain some of the best bars in Madrid, and **Calle de Ventura de la Vega** offers some of the best restaurants. The area is home to the city's three great museums along the Avenida del Arte (p. 125) and the lush **Parque del Buen Retiro** (p. 124).

 STAYING SAFE IN MADRID. Madrid is much safer than most major European cities, but Pta. del Sol, Pl. de España, Pl. Chueca, C. Gran Vía, and Malasaña's Pl. 2 de Mayo can be intimidating late at night. As a general rule, avoid parks and quiet residential streets after dark, and always watch out for thieves and pickpockets in crowds.

GRAN VÍA

North of Sol, busy **Gran Vía** is the commercial center of Madrid. Only come here if you must; Gran Vía is littered with American fast-food restaurants, loud traffic, neon lights, and expensive brand-name stores. The massive thoroughfare contrasts sharply with the quaint historical districts and residential neighborhood in the rest of Madrid. A continual parade of flashing cars, swishing skirts, and high-heeled shoes bustles by sex shops and pricey hostels—it might be worth a quick look, but not much more.

MALASAÑA AND CHUECA

Across the Gran Vía to the north, and split down the middle by C. de Fuencarral, **Malasaña** and **Chueca** are the hubs of Madrid's alternative, funky, and queer scene. Small boutiques and delicious restaurants provide ample daytime activities; by night, the GLBT scene blooms into an outrageous and colorful bar and club atmosphere. While clearly the center of Madrid's gay population, the neighborhoods offer something for everyone, including a wide range of excellent eateries, charming plazas, great shopping, and the requisite never-ending nights that characterize Madrid's hard-core parties. Beyond Gran Vía and east of Malasaña and Chueca lies modern Madrid.

ARGÜELLES AND MONCLOA

Just outside the core of the city, north and northwest of the Palacio Real, the neighborhood of Argüelles and the zone around **Calle San Bernardo**, together with

Moncloa, form a cluttered mixture of middle-class homes, student apartments, tranquil parks, and bohemian hangouts. Located near the *Ciudad Universitaria*, the area is full of teenagers wandering its orderly streets.

BILBAO
Located slightly north of the city's cultural nexus, Bilbao is the area north of **Glorieta de Bilbao** (M: Bilbao), in the "V" formed by C. Fuencarral and C. Luchana including Pl. de Olavide. Like its neighbors, Argüelles and Moncloa, Bilbao is a student district filled with cheap eateries and neon nightclubs.

MAPS

The free *Plano de Madrid* (street map) and *Plano de Transportes* (public transportation map) are fantastic. Pick them up at any tourist office. Public transportation info is also available by phone (☎012) or on the web (www.ctm-madrid.es). **El Corte Inglés** (p. 135) offers a free one-page map of Madrid. For a comprehensive map with street index, pick up the *Almax* map (€6) at any newsstand.

🄴 LOCAL TRANSPORTATION

METRO

Safe, speedy, spotless, and almost always under *obras* (improvements), Madrid's metro puts most major subway systems to shame. Trains run frequently; green timers above most platforms show increments of five minutes or less between trains. The free *Plano del Metro* (available at any ticket booth) and the wall maps of surrounding neighborhoods are clear and helpful. Fare and schedule info is posted in every station; trains run daily 6am-2am.

Twelve lines, totaling 317km, connect Madrid's 316 stations, making the city's metro the third most extensive in the world, after London and New York. Line 12, Puerta del Sur, now extends coverage to the Casa de Campo, Móstoles, and Getafe regions south of the city. An individual metro ticket costs €1, or €1.30 if you leave the city limits, but frequent riders opt for the ■metrobus (ticket of 10 rides valid for both the metro and bus system; €6.40). Children under the age of four travel free. Buy them at machines in metro stops, *estancos* (tobacco shops), or newsstands. Remember to keep your ticket until you leave the metro—riding without one can subject you to outrageous fines. There is also the **abonos turísticos** (tourist ticket of unlimited rides for a period of 1, 2, 3, 5, or 7 days; €3.80-39.60). These are available at all metro stations and on the Internet. For more detail, call **Metro info** (☎902 44 44 03) or visit www.metromadrid.es.

Violent crime in metro stations is almost unheard of, and women usually feel safe traveling alone. Be advised, however, that pickpockets do their best work in crowded cars. Metro stations such as Tirso de Molina, La Latina, Lavapiés, Gran Vía, Pl. de España, Chueca, and Sol can be intimidating after midnight if alone. These areas are usually busy all through the night with bar- and club-hoppers, but many crimes are reported in the area; use caution and common sense.

BUS

While the metro makes the most sense for trips across Madrid, buses cover areas inaccessible by metro and are a great way to see the city. Most stops are clearly marked, but if you want extra guidance in finding routes and stops, try the handy *Plano de Transportes* or the English-language *Visiting the Downtown on Public Transport*, free at the tourist office, or *Madrid en Autobús*, free at bus kiosks.

Bus fares are the same as the metro, and tickets are interchangeable. Look for the *Cercanías* transportation. Buses run 6am-11pm, generally at intervals of 10-15min. From midnight-6am the night bus, the **Búho** (owl), travels from Pl. de Cibeles (and other marked routes) to the outskirts of the city (every 30min. midnight-3am, hourly 3-6am; F-Sa every 20min.) Night buses (N1-N24), the cheapest form of transportation for late-night revelers, are listed in the *Plano*. For info, call **Empresa Municipal de Transportes.** (☎902 50 78 50 or 914 06 88 10; www.emtmadrid.es. Open M-F 8am-2pm.)

TAXI

Taxis stream through Madrid around the clock. If you want to summon one, call **Radio Taxi** (☎914 05 55 00), **Radio-Taxi Independiente** (☎914 05 12 13), or **Teletaxi** (☎913 71 37 11; www.tele-taxi.es). A *"libre"* sign in the window or a green light indicates availability. Base fare is €1.85 (or 2.90 after 10pm), plus €0.87-1.00 per km from 6am-10pm and €1-1.10 from 10pm-6am. **Teletaxi** charges a flat rate of €1 per km. Fare supplements include airport (€5) and bus and train stations (€2.50). Official taxis are white with a red stripe on the door; avoid impostors.

Check that the driver starts the meter. If you have a complaint or think you've been overcharged, demand a *recibo oficial* (official receipt) and an *hoja de reclamaciones* (complaint form), which the driver is required to supply. Take down the license number, route taken, and fare charged. Take the forms and information to the **Oficina Municipal del Taxi,** C. Alberto Aguilera, 20 (☎915 88 96 26; fax 88 96 29. Open July-Sept. M-F 9am-1pm; Oct.-June 9am-2pm) or the **Ayuntamiento** (City Hall), Pl. de la Villa, 4 (info ☎010 or 915 88 10 00; M: Ópera) to request a refund. To request **taxi service for the disabled,** call ☎915 47 85 00 or 47 86 00. Rates are the same as other taxis. If you leave belongings in a taxi, visit or call the **Negociado de Objetos Perdidos,** Pl. Legazpi, 7. (☎915 88 43 47. M: Legazpi. Open M-F 9am-2pm.)

CAR RENTAL

There is no reason to rent a car in Madrid. If congested traffic and nightmarish parking don't drive you into hysterics, aggressive drivers, annoying mopeds, and sky-high gasoline prices will. If you do choose to drive, parking permits are available on the street from column-like machines with "P" signs. If you plan to drive to destinations outside of Madrid, a larger car rental chain is the best bet.

Atesa: (Reservations in Spain ☎902 10 01 01, elsewhere 10 05 15; www.atesa.com.) Offices: Gran Vía, 80 (☎915 42 96 10; M: Pl. de España); airport (☎913 29 02 22).

Avis: (Reservations ☎902 13 55 31; http://avis.com.) Offices: Estación de Atocha (☎915 30 01 68); Gran Vía, 60 (☎915 48 42 04; M: Gran Vía); airport (☎902 20 01 62).

Europcar: (Reservations ☎902 10 50 30; www.europcar.com.) Offices: Estación de Atocha (☎915 30 01 94); airport (☎913 93 72 35).

MOPED AND BIKE RENTAL

Fortunately for pedestrians, Madrid is not scarred by the moped mayhem that has taken over most of Europe. Though mopeds are swift, Madrid's stellar public transport system is more than sufficient for getting around. If you choose to ride, you'll need a lock and helmet. **Motocicletas Antonio Castro,** C. Conde Duque, 13, rents mopeds from €45 per day or €150 per week, including unlimited mileage and insurance. (☎915 42 06 57. M: San Bernardo. 21+ with **International Driver's Permit** only (see **Driving Permits,** p. 38). €300 deposit required for 1-day rentals, €650 for 1-wk. rentals. Open M-F 8am-3:30pm and 5-8pm.) For **bike rental,** try **Karacol Sport,** P. de Tortosa, 8. (☎915 39 96 33; www.karacol.com. M: Atocha. €15 per day; €50 deposit and passport required. Open M-F 10:30am-3pm and 5-9pm, Th afternoon 5-9:30pm, Sa 10:30am-2pm.)

⑦ PRACTICAL INFORMATION

TOURIST AND FINANCIAL SERVICES

Tourist Offices: English and French are spoken at most tourist offices. Those planning trips outside the Comunidad de Madrid can visit region-specific offices within Madrid; ask at any tourist office for their addresses. **Regional Office of the Comunidad de Madrid,** C. del Duque de Medinaceli, 2 (☎914 29 49 51, info 902 10 00 07; www.madrid.org). M: Banco de España. Brochures, transportation info, and maps for the Comunidad. Extremely helpful; if you are planning to travel beyond Madrid, make this your first stop. Open M-Sa 8am-8pm, Su 9am-2pm. **Madrid Tourism Centre,** Pl. Mayor, 27 (☎915 88 16 36; www.esmadrid.com). M: Sol. Hands out indispensable city and transportation maps and a complete guide to accommodations, as well as *In Madrid*, a monthly activity and information guide in English. **Branches** at Estación Chamartín (p. 93), Estación Puerta de Atocha (p. 93), and the airport (p. 93), also at Plaza de Cibeles, Plaza de Callao, and Plaza de Felipe II. All open daily 9:30am-8pm.

General Info Line: Turespaña ☎901 30 06 00 or 010. Info on anything about Madrid, from police stations to zoo hours. Ask for *inglés* for an English-speaking operator.

Tours: Tours can be informative but pricey. Read the fine print before signing on. The **Ayuntamiento** offers **walking tours** in English and Spanish called **descubremadrid** (☎915 88 29 06. Open M-F 9:30am-8:30pm. €3.10; students, children, and seniors €2.50) or pick up more info at the municipal tourist office. **Madrid Vision** (☎917 79 18 88; www.madridvision.es) offers tours on double-decker buses. There are 2 routes (Madrid Histórico and Moderno) each of which makes 15-20 stops around the city, featuring monuments and museums. Get off and on the bus as you please. €16, ages 7-16 and seniors €8; 2-day ticket €20.

Budget Travel:

Viajes TIVE, C. Fernando el Católico, 88 (☎915 43 74 12). M: Moncloa. Walk straight down C. Arcipreste de Hita (one street over, parallel to C. Princesa) and turn left on C. Fernando el Católico. A great resource for long-term visitors. Lodging, tourism, and student residence info. Organizes group excursions and language classes. Some English spoken. Non-Spaniards €18.10, students with ISIC €6, HI card €5, over 30 €11. Open M-F 9am-2pm. Arrive early to avoid lines.

Comunidad de Madrid, Dirección General de Juventud, Gran Vía, 10 (☎901 51 06 10; www.madrid.org). M: Gran Vía. Open M-F 9am-2pm and 5-8pm, but occasionally does not re-open in the afternoon.

Consulates: see Embassies and Consulates, p. 11.

Currency Exchange: The airport is the best place to change your cash, but if you need to change more in the city later, head to **Banco Santander Central Hispano,** which does not charge commission on American Express Travelers Cheques, but will charge around a €12 commission on all others. Max. exchange €300. **Main branch,** Po. Castellana, 7 (☎915 58 11 11). M: Sol. Follow C. San Jerónimo to Pl. Canalejas. Open Apr.-Sept. M-F 8:30am-2pm; Oct.-Mar. M-F 8:30am-2pm, Sa 8:30am-1pm. **Banks** usually charge 1-2% commission (min. charge €3). Booths in Sol and Gran Vía, open as late as midnight and on weekends, have poor rates and are not a good deal. **ServiRed, ServiCaixa,** and **Telebanco** machines accept bank cards with the Cirrus, PLUS, EuroCard, or NYCE logos. Withdrawal fees are around $5 per withdrawal and $3 per balance check.

American Express: Currency exchange only at the airport open M-F 9am-7:30pm, Sa 9am-2pm. **Airport Branch** (☎913 93 82 16 or 93 82 16). To report lost travelers checks, call toll free ☎900 99 44 26.

LOCAL SERVICES

Luggage Storage: At the airport and bus and train stations (€2.75 per bag per day).

EXTRA BAGGAGE. Due to heightened security measures, be aware that airports or stations may decide to cancel or reduce this service without notice.

English-language Periodicals: International edition dailies and weeklies available at kiosks everywhere, especially on Gran Vía, Paseos del Prado, Recoletos, Castellana, and around Pta. del Sol. For **English-language Books,** try **Book Sellers,** C. José Abascal, 48 (☎914 42 81 04). M: Gregorio Marañon. Open M-Sa 10am-1pm and 5-9pm.

Language Service: Forocio, C. Mayor, 4, 3rd fl. (☎902 36 36 33; www.forocio.com). M: Sol. An organization dedicated to bringing foreigners and natives together to share languages and good times. Sponsors weekly parties every W with a Mexican theme at The Bourbon Cafe, C. de San Jeronimo, 5. (☎915 32 58 57. €4 with free Coronita.) Also organizes group trips for reasonable prices. Stop by the office for more info. Open M-F 10:30am-7:30pm.

Libraries: The municipal tourist office has a comprehensive list of libraries around the city. These include **Bibliotecas Municipales Especializadas,** numerous branches of the **Bibliotecas Públicas Municipales por Distritos** (23 locations), and **Bibliotecas Públicas de la Comunidad de Madrid** (18 locations). Large branch **Biblioteca Centro-Pedro Salinas** (☎913 66 54 07) at M: Pta. de Toledo, has English-language periodicals. Open M-F 8:30am-8:45pm, Sa 9am-1:45pm.

Women's Resources: For general information on women's services in Spain or to report an incident, call **Instituto de la Mujer,** C. Genova, 11 (☎900 13 10 10; www.mtas.es/mujer).

GLBT Resources: Most establishments in Chueca carry a free guide to gay nightlife in Spain called **Shanguide.** The guide also offers detailed listings and maps of the many gay establishments in and around Madrid. Alternatively, you can purchase **Zero** magazine (€5) at any kiosk. The magazine includes a small pull-out guide to nightlife and gay activities. Support groups and associations: **Colectivo de Gais y Lesbianas de Madrid (COGAM),** C. de las Infantas, 40, 1st fl. (☎915 22 45 17; www.cogam.org). M: Gran Vía. Provides a wide range of services and activities of interest. Reception open daily M-Sa 5-10pm. Free counseling M-Th 7-9pm, AIDS-specific counseling M-F, phone hotline 5-9pm (☎915 23 00 70). Call ahead for hours at new location. **GAY-INFORM,** a gay info line (☎915 23 00 70), provides information in Spanish and English on Thursdays between 7-9pm about gay associations, activities, health issues, sports, dinners, and **Brujulai,** COGAM's weekend excursion group, which organizes hiking and sports expeditions. Open M-F 10am-2pm, 5-8pm. The city of Madrid has its own **GLBT info line** (☎900 72 05 69) open M-F 10am-2pm and 5-9pm.

Laundromat: Lavandería Ondablu, C. León, 3 (☎913 69 50 71). M: Antón Martín, Sol, or Sevilla. Wash €3.50, dry €1. Also available in most hostels for €5 wash and dry. (**Internet** access available.) Open M-F 9:30am-10pm, Sa 10:30am-7pm. Also at C. Hortaleza, 84 (☎915 31 28 73). M: Chueca. Same hours and prices.

EMERGENCY AND COMMUNICATIONS

Police: C. de los Madrazo, 9 (☎ 913 22 11 60 or 900 15 00 00). M: Sevilla. English forms available. Open daily 9am-2pm.

Hotlines: Poison Control (24hr. ☎915 62 04 20). **Rape Hotline** (☎915 74 01 10). Open M-F 10am-2pm and 4-8pm.

Late-Night Pharmacy: Dial ☎098 for locations. One at C. Mayor, 13 (☎913 66 46 16), off Pta. del Sol; another at C. Mayor, 59 (☎915 48 00 14), closer to M: Ópera.

Hospitals: Emergency rooms are the best option for immediate attention. US insurance is not accepted, but if you get a receipt your insurance may pick up the tab. Emergency exams run around €95. For non-emergency concerns, **Unidad Médica Angloamericana,** C. del Conde de Aranda, 1, 1st fl. (☎914 35 18 23; www.unidadmedica.com). M: Serrano or Retiro. Regular English-speaking personnel on duty M-F 9am-8pm, Sa 10am-1pm. Initial visit €110, €75 for students. AmEx/MC/V. Embassies and consulates keep lists of English-speaking doctors.

Emergency Clinics: In a **medical emergency,** dial ☎061 or 112. **Hospital de Madrid,** Pl. del Conde del Valle Suchil, 16 (☎914 47 66 00; www.hospitaldemadrid.com). **Hospital Ramón y Cajal,** Ctra. Colmenar Viejo, km 9100 (☎913 36 80 00). Bus #135 from Pl. de Castilla. **Red Cross** (☎915 22 22 22, info 902 22 22 92). **Centro de Salud Santobal,** C. Santobal, 7 (☎914 45 23 28). M: Bilbao. Free, confidential government clinic specializing in treating HIV/AIDS and other STDs. Open M-F 9am-2pm.

Telephones: Information ☎1003. (For more information, see **Keeping in Touch,** p. 40.)

Internet Access: Hundreds of Internet cafes are spread across the city, and most hostels provide free Internet access as well. The rates are generally consistent (roughly €0.80-1.50 per 30min., €1.30-2.50 per hour). The cheapest spots are in Lavapiés, where mom-and-pop places charge less than €0.02 per min. ◨**SATS XXI,** C. San Jerónimo (☎915 32 09 70). Shares a floor with Asatej travel agency. Fast connections, good music, **printing, fax,** disks, CDs, and a telephone booth. €1.85 per hour. Open daily 10am-midnight.

Post Office: Palacio de Comunicaciones, C. Alcalá, 51, on Pl. de Cibeles (☎902 19 71 97). M: Banco de España. Enormous palace on the far side of the plaza from the metro. Info (main vestibule) open M-Sa 8:30am-9:30pm. Windows open M-Sa 8:30am-9:30pm, Su 8:30am-2pm for stamp purchases. To find a more convenient location near you, check the website at www.correos.es. **Postal Code:** 28080.

⌐ ACCOMMODATIONS

The demand for rooms in Madrid is always high and rises dramatically in summer. Though the city is filled with hostels, good quality at good prices can be hard to find. Most listings below include breakfast and internet, and offer laundry services. Prices range from €15 to €50 per person, depending on location, amenities, and season. Don't be deceived; higher prices don't necessarily indicate nicer accommodations. Try negotiating the price if you plan on staying for over a week. Those staying in Madrid for long periods may want to check out **The Broadsheet** (€2.50), an English periodical listing classifieds and events throughout Spain.

In Madrid, the difference between a one-star *hostal* and a *pensión* is often minimal. In winter, heating is standard; in summer, air-conditioning is not. Unless otherwise noted, communal bathrooms (toilet and shower) are the norm. Reservations are recommended in summer and on weekends, especially in the Pta. del Sol area and at the first few places *Let's Go* lists in each neighborhood. Owners are usually accustomed to opening doors, albeit groggily, at all hours, or providing keys for guests, but ask before club-hopping into the wee hours. *Pensiones* are inexpensive, sometimes have curfews, and often host guests staying for longer periods of time. The tourist office in the airport has a full list of lodgings; also check out www.hosteleriademadrid.com.

ACCOMMODATIONS BY PRICE

A Argüelles and Moncloa **C** El Centro: Sol, Ópera, and Plaza Mayor **E** Elsewhere **GV** Gran Vía **H** Huertas **M** Malasaña and Chueca			
UNDER €15 (❶)		Hostal Abril (110)	M
Albergue Juvenil Santa Cruz (110)	A	Hostal Betanzos (108)	H
Camping Alpha (107)	E	Hostal Chelo (110)	M
Hostal Pérez (110)	A	Hostal Esparteros (107)	C
		◨ Hostal Gran Vía 44 (109)	GV
€15-25 (❷)		Hostal Los Arcos (108)	C
Barbieri International Youth Hostel (110)	M	Hostal Palacios/Hostal Ribadavia (109)	M
Cat's Hostel (108)	H		

Hostal Río Miño (109)	M	**€35-50 (❹)**		
Hostal-Residencia Ríos (110)	A	Casa Chueca (109)	M	
▨ La Posada de Huertas (108)	H	Hostal Aguilar (108)	H	
Mad Hostel (108)	H	Hostal Lauria (109)	GV	
		Hostal Oriente (107)	C	
€25-35 (❸)		Hostal-Residencia Cruz-Sol (107)	C	
Hostal A. Nebrija (109)	GV	▨ Hostal-Residencia Domínguez (109)	M	
Hostal Alicante (108)	C	Hostal-Residencia Lamalonga (109)	GV	
Hostal Cantábrico (108)	C	▨ Hostal-Residencia Luz (107)	C	
Hostal Margarita (109)	GV	Hostal-Residencia Rober (108)	C	
Hostal Paz (107)	C	Hostal Valencia (108)	C	
Hostal Plaza D'Ort (108)	H			
Hostal Santillan (109)	GV	**OVER €50 (❺)**		
Hostal Villar (109)	H	Hotel San Lorenzo (110)	M	

CAMPING

Tourist offices have the *Guía Oficial de Campings*, which provides info on the 22 campsites surrounding Madrid, as well as in the Comunidad de Madrid. For further camping info, contact the Consejería de Educación (☎901 51 06 10).

Camping Alpha (☎916 95 80 69; www.campingalpha.com), on a tree-lined site 12.4km down Ctra. de Andalucía in Getafe. M: Legazpi. From the metro, walk down Vado Santa Catalina, cross the bridge, and bear right. Take the green bus #447, which stops across from the Museo de Jamón (10min., every 20-30min. 6am-10pm, €1.25). Ask for the Camp Alpha stop. Cross the footbridge and walk 1.5km back toward Madrid along the busy highway; signs lead the way. Welcoming reception, paved roads, pool, tennis courts, showers, and laundry. €6.50 per person, €6.70 per tent and per car. Singles €36; doubles €45; bungalows 1-2 people €62, 3-4 people €92. IVA not included. ❶

EL CENTRO: SOL, ÓPERA, AND PLAZA MAYOR

The following listings fall in the area between the Sol and Ópera metro stops. For better deals in quieter spots, stray several blocks from Sol. Price and location in El Centro are as good as they get, especially if you are planning to brave the legendary nightlife. Buses #3, 25, 39, and 500 serve Ópera; buses #3, 5, 15, 20, 50, 51, 52, 53, and 150 serve Sol. The area's proliferation of accommodation options has done little to drive down prices, but good deals can be found slightly outside Pl. Mayor.

▨ **Hostal-Residencia Luz**, C. de las Fuentes, 10, 3rd fl. (☎915 42 07 59; www.hostal-luz.com). M: Ópera. Newly redecorated rooms are clean and cozy. Satellite TV, free Wi-Fi, and A/C. Laundry €5. €36 per person. Singles, doubles, and triples available. Discount for longer stays. MC/V. ❹

Hostal Paz, C. Flora, 4, 1st and 4th fl. (☎915 47 30 47). M: Ópera. Unbeatable hospitality from welcoming owners. Spotless rooms with satellite TV and A/C. Reserve ahead. Laundry €10. Singles €30; doubles €36-38, with shower €42; triples with shower €54; quad €68. Monthly rentals available but must be arranged far in advance. MC/V. ❸

Hostal Esparteros, C. de Esparteros, 12, 4th fl. (☎915 21 09 03). M: Sol. Unbeatable location. Sparkling rooms with balconies or large windows are worth the 4-flight hike; some have private bath, TV, and fans. Laundry €9-10. Singles €25; doubles €35; triples €45. Discount for longer stays. Cash only. ❷

Hostal Oriente, C. de Arenal, 23, 1st fl. (☎915 48 03 14). M: Ópera. Beautiful tiled floors and walls, chandeliers, and immaculate rooms. Friendly owners. 17 rooms have TV, phone, A/C, and bath. Singles €40; doubles €60; triples €80. MC/V. ❹

Hostal-Residencia Cruz-Sol, Pl. Santa Cruz, 6, 3rd fl. (☎915 32 71 97). M: Sol. Colorful hostel with modern rooms and all the amenities: safe, phone, A/C, free Internet access, and bath. Laundry €6. Singles €42; doubles €52; triples €72; quads €75. MC/V. ❹

MADRID

Hostal-Residencia Rober, C. de Arenal, 26, 5th fl. (☎915 41 91 75; hostal-rober@duerme.net). M: Ópera. Quiet *hostal* with balconies. No smoking. Each room has tiny TV and fan. Singles €45; doubles €55; triples €80. MC/V. ❹

Hostal Valencia, Pl. del Oriente, 2, 3rd fl. (☎915 59 84 50; www.hostalvalencia.tk). M: Ópera. Narrow glass elevator lifts you to 7 elegant rooms, each decorated with Old World flair. Ask for a view overlooking the Pl. del Oriente. Rooms have TV and fan. Reserve ahead. Singles €45; doubles €75-95; master suite €110. MC/V. ❹

Hostal Los Arcos, C. Marqués Viudo de Pontejos, 3, 2nd fl. (☎915 22 59 76). M: Sol. Homemade puzzle-art lines the hallways. Basic rooms with bath, phone, and TV. Singles €25; doubles €40. Cash only. ❷

Hostal Alicante, C. de Arenal, 16, 2nd fl. (☎915 31 51 78). M: Ópera or Sol. Clean rooms with TV. Singles €28; doubles €48; triples €66. MC/V. ❸

Hostal Cantábrico, C. de la Cruz, 5 (☎915 31 01 30). M: Sol. Welcoming reception leads to rooms with complete bath, some with balcony views. Restaurant downstairs. Breakfast included. Singles €30-35; doubles €45-55; triples €62. Discounts July-Aug. MC/V. ❸

HUERTAS

Smaller and quieter than nearby El Centro, Huertas has budget accommodations within walking distance of sights, bars and a diverse range of inexpensive and high-quality cuisine. Sol-bound buses stop on C. del Príncipe, C. Núñez de Arce, and C. San Jerónimo; buses #10, 14, 27, 34, 37, and 45 run along Po. del Prado. Buses #6, 26, and 32 run up C. Atocha; get off at C. San Sebastián for Pl. Santa Ana. The closest metro stops are Sol, Sevilla, Antón Martín, and Tirso de Molina.

La Posada de Huertas, C. Huertas, 21 (☎914 29 55 26; www.posadadehuertas.com). M: Antón Martín or Sol. Rooms of 4 or 8 come clean, well-kept, and equipped with comfortable beds. Spotless bathrooms. Kitchen, Wi-Fi, and breakfast included. €5 wash and dry. Check out 10:30am, luggage storage available. Beds from €18. MC/V. ❷

Cat's Hostel, C. Cañizares, 6 (☎913 69 28 07; www.catshostel.com). M: Antón Martín. This renovated 18th-century palace features clean dorms (2-16 beds), small doubles with private baths, an authentic *mudéjar* patio area, bar, and cafe. Cheapest beer in the area (€2-3). Breakfast, luggage storage, and Internet access included. Laundry €5 wash and dry. Reserve ahead and don't forget flip-flops; the bathrooms are not the most pleasant we've ever seen. Dorms €20; doubles with bath €22. MC/V. ❷

Hostal Plaza D'Ort, Pl. del Angel, 13 (☎914 29 90 41; www.plazadort.com). M: Antón Martín. Conveniently located outside the Pl. Santa Ana. Beautifully decorated, comfortable rooms, all with TV, phone, and A/C. Internet access and in-room movies €11. The quality is well worth the price. Singles €30-40, depending on bathroom; doubles €50/60; triples €75-85; suite €110. MC/V. ❸

Mad Hostel, C. Cabeza, 24 (☎915 06 48 40; www.madhostel.com) M: Tirso de Molina. The owners of Cat's Hostel bring the same high-tech flair and relaxed atmosphere to this brand-new hostel, which features sparkling dorms (2-6 beds), a bar area with pool table, free Wi-Fi, gym, rooftop terrace, and kitchen. Breakfast included. Laundry €5 wash and dry. Reserve ahead. Dorms €20-22. MC/V. ❷

Hostal Betanzos, C. Luis de Guevera, 8, 3rd fl. (☎913 69 14 40). M: Antón Martín. Climb the fantastic—and ancient—double staircase to classic rooms with sinks and wooden furniture. Singles €15; doubles €25. Cash only. ❷

Hostal Aguilar, C. San Jerónimo, 32, 2nd fl. (☎914 29 59 26; www.hostalagui-lar.com). M: Sol or Sevilla. Retro artwork in the common area contrasts with clean, large, modern rooms. Large bath, phone, safe, A/C, and TV. Internet available. Singles €39; doubles €51-57; triples €65; quads €78. AmEx/D/MC/V. ❹

Hostal Villar, C. del Príncipe, 18 (☎915 31 66 00; www.villar.es). M: Sol or Sevilla. Rooms with TV and phone, some with A/C. Quiet and peaceful. Big lounge. Singles €26-33; doubles €33-46; triples €46-64. D/MC/V. ❸

GRAN VÍA

🏠 **Hostal Gran Vía 44**, Gran Vía, 44, 8th fl. (☎915 21 00 51; www.hostalgranvia44.com). M: Callao. Well-lit, spacious rooms with great views, high ceilings, and brightly-colored bedspreads. Private bath, TV, fan, and balcony. Lounge area and free Wi-Fi. Breakfast included. Doubles start at €45; triples start at €50. MC/V. ❷

Hostal Santillan, Gran Vía, 64, 8th fl. (☎915 48 23 28; www.hostalsantillan.com). M: Pl. de España. Take the elevator to the top of this gorgeous building. Leaf-patterned curtains and wooden furniture give rooms a homey feel. All have shower, sink, TV, and fan. Doubles €50-55; triples €66. MC/V. ❸

Hostal A. Nebrija, Gran Vía, 67, 8th fl., elevator A (☎915 47 73 19). M: Pl. de España. Management is very friendly and most rooms have spectacular views of the city. Airy rooms feature high ceilings, TV, fan, and shared baths. No smoking. Singles €28; doubles €36; triples €54. AmEx/MC/V. ❸

Hostal Margarita, Gran Vía, 50, 5th fl. (☎/fax 915 47 35 49). M: Callao. Warm and inviting family offers small, simple rooms with large windows, TV, fan, and telephone, most with street views. TV lounge and big kitchen. Laundry €10. Singles €35; doubles with shower €45; triples with bath €55. Reserve ahead. MC/V. ❸

Hostal Lauria, Gran Vía, 50, 4th fl. (☎915 41 91 82; www.geocities.com/hostallauria). M: Callao. Spotless rooms with orange bedspreads, bath, phone, fan, and TV. Lounge has TV. English spoken. Singles €40; doubles €55-60; triples €75-80. MC/V. ❹

Hostal-Residencia Lamalonga, Gran Vía, 56, 2nd fl. (☎915 47 68 94; hlamalonga@hotmail.com). M: Callao or Sto. Domingo. Elegant chandeliers in the common area lead to simple rooms with lots of polished wooden furniture. All with TV, A/C, and Wi-Fi. Singles €47; doubles €53-56; triples €71. D/MC/V. ❹

MALASAÑA AND CHUECA

Hostales and *pensiones* in Malasaña and Chueca are usually located on the upper floors of older buildings, and though accommodations can be a bit pricier here than in other areas, they are reliably clean, comfortable, and welcoming. Newly renovated rooms are chock full of amenities but lack the "traditional Spanish" flavor you might be seeking. Buses #3, 40, and 149 run along C. de Fuencarral and C. Hortaleza. Metro stops Chueca, Gran Vía, and Tribunal service the area.

🏠 **Hostal-Residencia Domínguez**, C. de Santa Brígida, 1, 1st fl. (☎915 32 15 47). M: Tribunal. A modern look at low prices. The doubles on the 2nd and 3rd fl. are immaculate and brand-new. Hospitable young owner provides tips on local nightlife. Singles €39; doubles with bath and A/C €49; triples €59. Cash only. ❹

Casa Chueca, C. de San Bartolomé, 4, 2nd fl. (☎915 23 81 27; www.casa-chueca.com). M: Chueca. Modern rooms, with A/C, bath, satellite TV, free Internet access, and cool tile-muraled walls. "Mini-breakfast" included. Reservations required. Singles €40; doubles €55; triples €70. MC/V. ❹

Hostal Rio Miño, C. de Barbieri, 3, 1st fl. (☎915 22 14 17). M: Chueca. Simple rooms are cheap and of decent quality. All have green bedspreads and A/C, and common baths are very clean. Reserve 2 weeks ahead. Singles €20; doubles €28, with bath €40; triples €26 for extra bed. Cash only. ❷

Hostal Palacios/Hostal Ribadavia, C. de Fuencarral, 25, 1st-3rd fl. (☎915 22 71 35; www.hostal-palacios.com). M: Gran Vía. Both run by the same family. Palacios is a step above, with Wi-Fi, tiled rooms, bath, TV, and A/C; Ribadavia's rooms are comfortable

MADRID

and have TVs and fans. Singles €22, with bath €32; doubles with shower €34, with bath €40; triples €56. Check-out 11:30am. MC/V. ❷

Hostal Chelo, C. de Hortaleza, 17, 3rd fl. (☎915 32 70 33; www.chelo.com). M: Gran Vía. The biggest draw of this *hostal* is the helpful staff, who are well-versed in everything Madrid. Rooms are clean and spacious with TV, fan, and bath. Unique upholstered headboards add to charm. A great location, but very quiet. English spoken. Singles €22, with bath €30; doubles €42; triples €57. Cash only. ❷

Hostal Abril, C. de Fuencarral, 39, 4th fl. (☎915 31 53 38). M: Tribunal or Gran Vía. Rooms like college dorms, but cleaner and cozier; even the ones with balconies are surprisingly tranquil. Phones in every room. Singles €25, with shower €27; doubles with bath €45; triples with bath €60. Cash only. ❷

Barbieri International Youth Hostel, C. de Barbieri, 15 (☎915 31 02 58; www.barbierihostel.com). M: Chueca. Shared rooms with pink and green bunks are cramped but cheap. Lively crew meets in colorful kitchen and common room, then heads out. Internet €0.50 per 15min. Quiet time 11pm-7am. Check-out 10am (€3 penalty for lateness). 8-bed dorms €17; 4-bed dorms €20; 2-bed dorms €29.50. Showers, kitchen, and luggage storage €5. MC/V. ❷

Hotel San Lorenzo, C. del Clavel, 8 (☎915 21 30 57; www.hotel-sanlorenzo.com). M: Gran Vía. Quiet, sparkling rooms with new furniture, baths, A/C, TV, and phone. Also has a lounge, coffee bar, room service, and laundry. Reserve ahead. Rooms €45-65 per person, depending on the season. AmEx/MC/V. ❺

ARGÜELLES AND MONCLOA

Though far enough from the city center to be slightly inconvenient, accommodations in the residential and suburban atmosphere of Argüelles and Moncloa offer relief from fast-paced city life.

Albergue Juvenil Santa Cruz de Marcenado (HI), C. de Santa Cruz de Marcenado, 28 (☎915 47 45 32; fax 48 11 96). M: Argüelles. From the metro, walk 1 block down C. de Alberto Aguilera away from C. de la Princesa, turn right onto C. de Serrano Jóver, then left onto C. de Santa Cruz de Marcenado. Great lounge for mingling. The 72 beds fill quickly, even in winter. Single-sex fl. Breakfast and sheets included. Laundry €2. 6-day max. stay. Quiet hours after midnight. Reception daily 9am-10pm. 1:30am curfew. Reserve in advance. Closed Christmas and New Year's Eve. Dorms €8.50, 26 and over €12.84. €3.50 extra per night without HI card. Cash only. ❶

Hostal-Residencia Ríos, C. de Juan Álvarez Mendizabal, 44, 4th fl. (☎915 59 51 56). M: Ventura Rodríguez or Argüelles. From M: Argüelles, face the shrubbery, walk 3 blocks left (south) down C. de la Princesa to C. del Rey Francisco, go 3 blocks to C. de Juan Álvarez Mendizabal, and turn left again. Nothing fancy: just clean, comfortable rooms close to the park, some with A/C (€5 extra). Singles €17; doubles with shower €33; triples €45. Cash only. ❷ **Hostal Pérez** (☎915 41 91 90; www.hostalperez.com), in the same building, has free Internet access and Wi-Fi. Singles €15, with shower €20; doubles with shower €30. Cash only. ❶

🍴 FOOD

Madrid is chockablock with restaurants and *cafeterías* that cater to all tastes. Vegetarians should check out www.mundovegetariano.com. Even carnivores may appreciate a vegetarian meal, given Madrid's indulgence in meats and fried food.

Hopping from bar to bar gobbling tapas is an alternative to a full sit-down meal and a fun way to sample local food. Most tapas bars *(tascas* or *tabernas)* are open noon-4pm and 8pm-midnight or later. Some, like **Museo del Jamón** (p. 112), double as restaurants, and many cluster around **Plaza Santa Ana** and **Plaza Mayor.**

Bars pack **Calle Cuchilleros** and **Calle de la Cruz.** Madrid's cafes offer ambience as well as caffeine, giving contemplative coffee drinkers a shot of history and atmosphere with their *cafe con leche.* Linger for an hour or two in these historic cafes—an economical way to soak up a little of Madrid's laid-back culture. You won't be bothered with the check until you ask.

FOOD BY TYPE

A Argüelles and Moncloa **B** Bilbao **C** El Centro: Ópera, Sol, and Plaza Mayor **GV** Gran Vía **H** Huertas **L** Lavapiés and La Latina **M** Malasaña and Chueca

CAFES
Café Comercial (119)   B ❶
Café Gijón (113)   C ❷
🍴 Café de Oriente (112)   C ❶
Café-Botillería Manuela (118)   M ❶
Cervecería 100 Montaditos (112)   C ❶
🍴 Eucalipto (113)   L ❶

ITALIAN
🍴 Osteria Il Regno de Napoli (119)   B ❸
Il Pizzaiolo (118)   M ❷
Pizzeria Maravilles (119)   B ❶
Pizzeria Mastropiero (118)   M ❷
Pizzeria Vesuvio (118)   M ❶

LATIN AMERICAN
El Novillo Carioca (115)   GV ❸
La Farfalla (114)   H ❷

NORTH AFRICAN/MIDDLE EASTERN
🍴 Al-Jaima, Cocina del Desierto (115) M ❷
Bar Samara (119)   B ❸
Inshala (112)   C ❸
La Granja de Said (118)   M ❷

OTHER
Swedish: Collage (119)   B ❸
Indian: Darbar (118)   M ❸
French: La Crêperie (119)   A ❶
🍴 Chinese: Rey de los Tallarines (119) B ❷

SPANISH
Ananias (119)   A ❸
Annalina (114)   H ❷
🍴 Arrocería Gala (114)   H ❸
El Fogón de la Abuela (112)   C ❷
El Oso y el Madroño (112)   C ❷
Gula Gula (115)   GV ❹

Isolée (115)   M ❷
🍴 La Finca de Susana (114)   GV ❷
La Piba (119)   A ❸
La Sacristía (118)   M ❸
La Sanabresa (114)   H ❷
Museo del Jamón (112)   C ❶
Museo Chicote (115)   GV ❷
Root (115)   GV ❷
Sobrino del Botín (112)   C ❹
Taberna "Er 77" (113)   L ❷
Taberna Maceira (114)   H ❸

SWEETS
Heladería Giuseppe Ricci (114)   H ❶
Horno La Santiagüesa (112)   C ❶
La Mallorquina (112)   C ❶

TAPAS
4 De Tapas (118)   M ❷
Almendro 13 (113)   L ❷
Casa Alberto (111)   H ❷
Casa Amadeo (113)   L ❷
Casa Maravilla (120)   B ❶
Cáscaras (119)   A ❷
El Circo (118)   M ❷
🍴 El Tigre (118)   M ❶
La Toscana (115)   H ❷
🍴 Restaurante Casa Granada (114)   H ❷
La Trucha (114)   H ❸

VEGETARIAN
Achuri (113)   L ❶
Al Natural (114)   H ❷
🍴 El Estragón Vegetariano (113)   L ❸
El Granero de Lavapiés (113)   L ❷
Restaurante Integral Artemisa (114)   H ❷
Vegaviana (118)   M ❷

MADRID

FOOD SHOPPING

In general, the bigger the market and the farther from the city center, the cheaper the groceries. Specialty items may require a visit to a pricey store, but *supermercados* are generally the best bet. Also look for shops labeled *"alimentaciones"* or *"frutos secos,"* small convenience stores that generally have low prices.

Groceries: Champion and **%Día** are the cheapest city-wide supermarket chains, though they are mostly far from the city center. There is, however, a **Champion,** C.

Toledo, 32, in La Latina at the corner of C. Toledo and C. de la Colegiata. (M: La Latina. ☎914 65 55 22. Open M-Sa 9:30am-9:30pm.)

Markets: Mercado de San Miguel, a covered market on Pl. de San Miguel, off the northwest corner of Pl. Mayor, sells the finest seafood and produce in the city, albeit at high prices. Open M-F 9am-2pm and 4:30-8pm, Sa 9am-2pm.

Pastry Shops: These are everywhere. **La Mallorquina,** C. Mayor, 2 (☎915 21 12 01) is the most famous in all Madrid, and their desserts live up to their reputation (€.90-1.90 each, or €14-22 per kg). Open daily Sept.-July 9am-9:15pm. The sublime **Horno La Santiagüesa,** C. Mayor, 73 (☎915 59 62 14) sells everything from *roscones de reyes* (sweet bread for the Feast of the Epiphany) to *empanadas* (€18-23 per kg) and pastries doused in rich chocolate. Don't pass through without trying the *tarta de Santiago* (almond bread). Open daily 8am-9pm.

Red-Eye Establishments: *Guía del Ocio* lists late-night eateries under *Estilos de la noche*. Street vendors sell sandwiches and drinks to hungry clubbers well in to the late hours; you may see these sandwich-sellers fleeing into the darkness at the first sight of police presence. *Cervecerías* and *kebap* restaurants open until 2am aren't hard to find.

EL CENTRO: SOL ÓPERA, AND PLAZA MAYOR

Tourists flood the *centro*, producing a neighborhood packed with overpriced places serving mediocre fare. A little sifting, however, can lead to some amazing restaurants at decent prices.

RESTAURANTS

Inshala, C. de la Amnistía, 10 (☎915 48 26 32). M: Ópera. Perfect for a fancy date, but cheap enough for a backpacker's meal. Moroccan decor, but decidedly eclectic international fare, ranging from Japanese to Mexican. Weekday lunch *menú* €9. Dinner €10-26. Reservations strongly recommended. Open in summer M-Th noon-5pm and 8pm-1am, F-Sa noon-5pm and 8pm-2am; in winter M-Sa noon-2am. MC/V. ❸

El Fogón de la Abuela, C. Almendro, 9 (☎913 64 18 18). Tasty dishes cater to a friendly, hip, gray-haired crowd and those in search of comfort food. Daily plates feature Spanish classics (€7-7.50) and Grandma's specials (€9.50-11.50). MC/V. ❷

Sobrino del Botín, C. Cuchilleros, 17 (☎913 66 42 17; www.botin.es), off Pl. Mayor. Founded in 1725, Botín has the distinction of being the oldest continuously operating restaurant in the world, which explains the crowds of camera-carrying tourists. Serves a variety of simple but filling Spanish dishes (€8-30; *menú* of roast suckling pig €35.90). Open daily 1-4pm and 8pm-midnight. AmEx/MC/V. ❹

El Oso y el Madroño, C. Bolsa, 4 (☎925 22 77 96). From M: Sol, go up C. Carretas to Pl. Benavente and turn right onto C. Bolsa. A rich *cocido de garbanzos* (chickpea and meat stew; €14) is their specialty. Open M-Th 8pm-midnight, F-Su 8pm-2am. ❷

Museo del Jamón, C. San Jerónimo, 6 (☎915 21 03 46; www.museodeljamon.es). M: Sol. Ten other locations in Madrid, including C. Mayor, 7 (☎915 31 45 50). A vegetarian's nightmare and pork-lover's dream. Hooves and shanks hang around the bar; the restaurant upstairs serves the chef's specialties (€3.75-7). *Menús* €7.30. Cafeteria and store open daily 8am-12:30am, restaurant 1-11:30pm. *Menús* served 1-5pm and 8-11pm. MC/V. ❶

TAPAS BARS AND CAFES

■ **Café de Oriente,** Pl. del Oriente, 2 (☎915 47 98 31). M: Ópera. A glittering, old-fashioned cafe catering to a ritzy older crowd and hungry tourists strolling by the Palacio. Specialty coffees €4-7. Open M-Th and Su 8:30am-1:30am, F-Sa 8:30am-12:30am. AmEx/D/MC/V. ❶

Cervecería 100 Montaditos, C. Mayor, 22 (☎902 19 74 94; www.cerveceria100montaditos.es). M: Sol. One of several other locations in the city, this quick little cafe offers 100 varieties of tiny, creative *bocadillos* (mini-sandwiches; €1.20). Perfect for a snack or extremely light lunch. Open M-Th 10am-12:30am, F-Sa 10am-2am. ❶

Café Gijón, Po. de Recoletos, 21 (☎915 21 54 25). M: Colón. Enjoy thought-provoking conversation and good coffee in this historic landmark, populated by slightly older cof-fee-sippers. A perfect stop along your walking tour of the *paseos*. Coffee €2.80. *Menú del día* €12. Open M-F and Su 7am-1:30am, Sa 7am-2am. AmEx/MC/V. ❷

LA LATINA AND LAVAPIÉS

From the centro, ▨**Calle Almendro** winds down toward **Lavapiés** and **La Latina,** which are quieter, more local, and brimming with exciting new restaurants, tapas bars, and terraces. If you come for a drink, you might stay for dinner; and if you stick around for a meal, you'll probably wander into a wine cellar. There's less caviar and champagne here, but plenty of *menús* for around €8.

RESTAURANTS

▨ **El Estragón Vegetariano,** Pl. de la Paja, 10 (☎913 65 89 82; www.guiadelocio.com/estragonvegetariano). M: La Latina. In the running for the best medium-priced restaurant of any kind in Madrid. Its vegetarian delights could convince even the most die-hard carnivores to switch teams. *Menús* (M-F €10, Sa-Su and evenings €25). Open daily 1:30-4pm and 8pm-midnight. AmEx/MC/V. ❸

Taberna "Er 77," C. Argumosa, 8. M: Lavapiés. In the heart of this young, bohemian neighborhood. A local joint with bar, cozy terrace, and a small kitchen turning out some of the area's most creative and tasty dishes. Try the asparagus with raw salmon (€7). Entrees €5-11. Open Tu-Th 6pm-midnight, F-Sa 1pm-1am, Su 1-6pm. Cash only. ❷

Achuri, C. Argumosa, 21 (☎914 68 78 56). M: Lavapiés. Young crowds come for cheap food and wine. Mostly vegetarian. *Bocadillos* €2.70. *Raciones* €4.80. Wine €0.80-2.20 per glass. Open M-Th and Su 1:30pm-2am, F-Sa 1:30pm-2:30am. Cash only. ❶

El Granero de Lavapiés, C. Argumosa, 10 (☎914 67 76 11). M: Lavapiés. For 18 years, rotating art exhibits and inventive specials have kept this hideaway packed with locals. Vegetarian *menú* with a full range of first courses and fantastic desserts (M-F €8.50, Sa €10). Dinner €5.80-6.90. Open daily 1-4pm and 8:30-11pm. MC/V. ❷

TAPAS BARS AND CAFES

▨ **Eucalipto,** C. Argumosa, 4 (☎629 33 49 98), south of Huertas. M: Lavapiés. Take a break from normal coffee fare for refreshing *zumos tropicales* (fresh juice; €2.60-3.50). Try the amazing Brazilian Lulo berry. The *batidos* (€3-3.50) are delicious. Spike up the night with a *daiquiri* (€4.50-4.80), or enjoy a huge fruit salad (€7). Lively side-walk seating. Open daily 5pm-2am. ❶

Casa Amadeo, Pl. de Cascorro, 18 (☎913 65 94 39). M: La Latina. The jovial owner of 64 years supervises the making of house specialty *caracoles* (snails; €4.50). Good place to rest after a day at El Rastro. *Raciones* €4-11. Open 11am-4pm. Open F-Su 10:30am-8pm. ❷

Almendro 13, C. Almendro, 13 (☎913 65 42 52). M: La Latina. Locals dive into plates of *huevos rotos* (eggs and ham over fried potatoes; €7.80) and the tomato salad (€5) on top of barrels. Open M-F 1-4pm and 7:30pm-12:30am, Sa-Su 1-5pm and 8pm-1am. ❷

HUERTAS

Huertas is, without a doubt, the best place to eat in the center of the city. Popular with locals, Pl. de Santa Ana is perfect for killing some time with a drink and a snack. **Calles de Echegaray, Ventura de la Vega,** and **Manuel Fernández González** offer the best options; quality is high and if you head into the less-crowded streets, prices are low. As the evening grows and wine flows, these streets become the first stop for a night out in Madrid.

RESTAURANTS

▨ **La Finca de Susana,** C. Arlabán, 4 (☎913 69 35 57). M: Sevilla. A swanky, fine-dining establishment affordable enough to be packed every day for lunch. Arrive early to avoid the ever-present line down the street. *Menú* M-F €8.40. Also runs **Bazaar Restaurante** in Malsaña and Chueca. Open daily 1-3:45pm and 8:30-11:45pm. AmEx/MC/V. ❷

▨ **Arrocería Gala,** C. de Moratín, 22 (☎914 29 25 62; www.paellas-gala.com). M: Antón Martín. Decor as colorful as its specialty paella. *Menú* (€13.70) offers paella with salad, bread, wine, and dessert. Excellent *sangria*. Lush, vine-covered interior garden. Reserve ahead on weekends. Open Tu-Su 1-5pm and 9pm-1:30am. Cash only. ❸

Heladeria Giuseppe Ricci (Gelato & Cafe), C. de las Huertas, 9 (☎687 98 96 12; www.heladeriaricci.com). M: Antón Martín. Forget tapas and *jamón;* this gelato is the best relief from a hot Madrid summer's day. Most patrons request 2 flavors, which still counts as 1 scoop. Small cones €2, large €3. Open M-Th and Su 10am-10pm, F-Sa 10am-10:30pm. ❶

Taberna Maceira, C. de Jesús, 7 (☎914 29 15 84), also C. Huertas, 66 (☎914 29 58 18). M: Antón Martín. The funky taverns offer local atmosphere, fantastic seafood, and great prices. 2 people can feast for under €25. Open M 8pm-12:45am, Tu-F 1-4:15pm and 8:30pm-12:45am, Sa-Su 1-4:45pm and 8:30pm-1:30am. Cash only. ❸

La Sanabresa, C. Amor de Dios, 12 (☎914 29 03 38). M: Antón Martín. Incredibly popular with locals. *Menús* offer many delicious options (€8.50-14). Open Tu-Su 1-4pm and 8:30-11pm. MC/V. ❷

La Farfalla, C. Sta. María, 17 (☎913 69 46 91), at the corner of C. de las Huertas. M: Antón Martín. This intimate and colorful restaurant's specialty is Argentine-style grilled meat (*parrilla;* €10.95), but don't miss the thin-crust pizzas (€5.45-6). Open for lunch M-Sa 1-4pm, dinner Tu-Su 9pm-3am. AmEx/MC/V. ❷

Restaurante Integral Artemisa, C. de Ventura de la Vega, 4 (☎914 29 50 92). M: Sol. 2nd location in Pl. del Carmen, Tres Cruces, 4 (☎915 21 87 21). Elegant vegetarian fare caters to an older crowd. Local lunchtime atmosphere. Great food, if a little pricey. Vegetarian *menú* €11.40. Open daily 1:30-4pm and 9pm-midnight. AmEx/D/MC/V. ❷

Al Natural, C. de Zorrilla, 11 (☎913 69 47 09; www.alnatural.biz). M: Sevilla. Vegetarian Mediterranean dishes (€8-12) served in an intimate setting. Open M-Sa 1-4pm and 9pm-midnight, Su 1-4pm. AmEx/D/MC/V. ❷

Annalina, C. Atocha, 21 (☎ 913 69 24 49). Ultra-modern decor makes orange and purple actually work as a color combination. Some of the freshest salads in the city (€6.90-7.50). Daily *menú* €7.95-9. Takeout available. Open M-Th and Su 1-5pm and 8:30pm-midnight, F-Sa 1-5pm and 8:30pm-2am. AmEx/D/MC/V. ❷

TAPAS BARS AND CAFES

▨ **Restaurante Casa Granada,** C. Doctor Cortezo, 17, 6th fl. (☎914 20 08 25). The unmarked door on the left side of C. Doctor Cortezo as you head downhill is easy to miss, but the experience of the rooftop tapas terrace at the top is hard to forget. A favorite with locals. Come around 8pm and stay for the sunset. Don't forget to put your name on the outdoor seating list when you arrive. *Cañas* of beer (€2.20) come with tapas. *Raciones* €5.50-8. Open M-Sa noon-midnight, Su noon-9pm. MC/V. ❷

Casa Alberto, C. de las Huertas, 18 (☎914 29 93 56; www.casaalberto.es). M: Antón Martín. A classic tapas bar founded in 1827, equipped with a manual-wash bar. Sweet vermouth (€1.45) is served with original house tapas. Try the delicious *gambas al ajillo* (shrimp with garlic; €10.50) or the *canapés* (€2.25-3). Open Tu-Sa noon-5:30pm and 8pm-1:30am. MC/V. ❷

La Trucha, C. Manuel Fernández González, 3 (☎914 29 58 33). M: Sol. Also at C. Núñez de Arce, 6 (☎915 32 08 90), without terrace. Vast selection of seasonal vegetables

(€5-9) and daily specials. Grab the *rabo de toro* (bull's tail with potatoes; €11.80). Entrees €12-15. Open daily 12:30-4pm and 7:30pm-midnight. AmEx/MC/V. ❸

La Toscana, C. Manuel Fernández González, 10-12 (☎914 29 60 31). M: Sol or Sevilla. A local crowd hangs out over tapas of *morcilla asado* (€9.60). Antique lettering and wrought-iron decor lend a medieval feel. Open M-Sa 1-4pm and 8pm-midnight. ❷

GRAN VÍA

Good food is hard to find when only McDonalds' golden arches, KFC, and Burger King can compete with the neon of Gran Vía's sex shops. Long lines at fast-food joints demonstrate that convenience often beats out fine dining. Fear not—there are still some culinary diamonds in the rough. Small **markets** can be found in Chueca, a couple streets north of Gran Vía.

Gula Gula, Gran Vía, 1 (☎915 22 87 64; www.gulagula.net). M: Gran Vía. People come for the outrageous drag shows, not the food. They do offer an all-you-can-eat buffet, though (lunch €11; dinner €23). Performances M-Th and Su 11pm, F-Sa 10:30pm and midnight. Reserve 1 week ahead for weekend dinner. Open daily 1-5pm and 9pm-last customer. AmEx/MC/V. ❹

Museo Chicote, C. Gran Vía, 12 (☎915 32 67 37). M: Gran Vía. Recline in green leather chairs amid glamorous black-and-white pictures of silver screen celebrities. Share mixed drinks with Madrid's chic socialites after 11pm. Lunchtime *menú* €10. Lunch served 1-4pm, no dinner. Open M-Sa 7am-3am. AmEx/MC/V. ❷

El Novillo Carioca, C. Mozart, 7 (☎915 48 51 40). M: Príncipe Pío. Pick from 12 different kinds of meat at the buffet. Fresh salad bar with cold dishes and choice of 2 kinds of succulent BBQ (€15). Desserts €3-4.50. *Caipirinhas* €4.50. Open 1:30-4:30pm and 8:30pm-12:30am. AmEx/D/MC/V. ❸

Root, C. Virgen de los Peligros, 1 (☎912 75 81 18). A classy lunchtime crowd meets downstairs to dine on a wide variety of menu options. Mellow environment, sophisticated white leather mixes with a hint of nature-themed decor. M-F 1-3pm *menú* €9.50. Open M-Th 1-4:30pm and 8:30pm-midnight, F 1-4:30pm and 8:30pm-1am, Sa 1:30-4:30pm and 8:30pm-1am, Su 1:30-4:30pm. MC/V. ❷

MALASAÑA AND CHUECA

One could spend several years in Chueca and Malasaña and still discover new eats. Restaurants fill the small corners and colorful plazas of this neighborhood— even if you don't follow the recommendations below, you're sure to stumble into something offbeat. Exceptional vegetarian, Middle Eastern, Italian, and fusion cuisine dominate the scene, and these small and intimate eateries offer high quality and low prices. For some of the freshest fruit in the city, try **Frutas Eloy,** C. Barbieri, 26. Right off the metro in Plaza de Chueca, this fruit stand makes you feel healthier just by walking in. (☎917 01 01 91. Open M-F 9am-9pm, Sa-Su 9am-3pm. Cash.)

RESTAURANTS

🦑 **Al-Jaima, Cocina del Desierto,** C. de Barbieri, 1 (☎915 23 11 42). M: Gran Vía or Chueca. Waltz from Chueca's happy streets into a Maghreb Middle Eastern oasis. Lebanese, Moroccan, and Egyptian food served to patrons seated on pillows on the floor. Specialties include kebabs and tajines (1st courses €4, main courses €8). Try *pollo con higos y miel* (chicken with figs and honey, €6.10). Open daily 1:30-4pm and 9pm-midnight. Reserve ahead. MC/V. ❷

Isolée, C. de las Infantas, 19 (☎915 22 81 38; www.isolee.com). A restaurant, deli, lounge, and fashion boutique combo, this hangout for hipsters screams New Age pretension, but why else would we go? *Menú* €9.50. Free Wi-Fi. Takeout available. Open M-Sa 10:30am-11pm, Su 3:30-10:30pm. MC/V. ❷

MADRID

Madrid's *paseos* are a great starting point for walking tours, since most major sights are loca on these main avenues. Trees in the the grassy medians offer shade and provide a nice bu from the zooming traffic. You may be tempted to head to El Retiro after the Museo del Prado venture to Puerta del Sol once you have reached Pl. de Cibeles. Regardless of the path cho: the *paseos* are a simple way to acquaint yourself with the city and organize a daily itinerary.

1. REINA SOFÍA. Directly across from Estación Atocha, the **Museo Nacional Centro de A Reina Sofía** (p. 127), home to Picasso's *Guernica,* presides over Pl. del Emperador Carlos V glass elevators hint at the impressive collection of modern art within.

2. MUSEO DEL PRADO. Walking up Po. del Prado, you'll pass the **Real Jardín Botánico** on right. Next to the garden is the world-renowned **Museo del Prado** (p. 125); behind it, on C. Ruí Alarcón, stands the **Iglesia de San Jerónimo,** Madrid's royal church. Built by Hieronymite mo the church has witnessed the coronation of Fernando and Isabel and the marriage of King Alfo XIII. These days, only Madrid's social elite wed in the church. *(Open daily 10am-1pm and 5-8:30p*

3. PLAZA DE LA LEALTAD. Back on Po. del Prado, to the north in Pl. de la Lealtad, stands **Obelisco a los Mártires del 2 de Mayo,** filled with the ashes of those who died in the 1 uprising against Napoleon. Its four statues represent constancy, virtue, valor, and patriot Behind the memorial sits the colonnaded classical **Bolsa de Comerico** (Madrid's St Exchange). Ventura Rodríguez's **Fuente de Neptuno,** in Pl. Cánovas de Castillo, is one of tt aquatic masterpieces along the avenue, famous enough to have earned him a Metro stop. Cr ing the plaza brings you to another great museum, the **Museo Thyssen-Bornemisza** (p. 128)

4. PLAZA DE CIBELES. The arts of the Po. del Prado transition into the Po. de Recoleto the flower-encircled **Plaza de Cibeles.** From the plaza, the small **Museo Naval** is to the ri *(Entrance on C. Juan de Mena, 1. ☎913 79 52 99; www.museonavalmadrid.com. Open Tu-Su 10 2pm. Closed Aug. Free.)* In the southeast corner of the plaza sits the spectacular **Palacio Comunicaciones** (p. 106), designed by Antonio Palacios and Julián Otamendi of Otto Wagr Vienna School in 1920, which functions as Madrid's central post office. On the corner oppo the Palacio lies the equally impressive **Banco de España.**

5. CASA DE AMÉRICA. Looking to the right up C. Alcalá from the Palacio de Comunicacion Sabatini's **Puerta de Alcalá,** the 18th-century emblematic gateway and court symbol. On the n eastern corner of the plaza roundabout (behind black gates) is the former **Palacio de Linare** 19th-century townhouse built for Madrid nobility. Proven by a team of "scientists" to be inhab by ghosts, it is now the **Casa de América** with a library and lecture halls for the study of Latin A ican culture and politics. It also sponsors art exhibits and guest lectures. *(Pl. de las Cibeles, 2 Banco de España. ☎915 95 48 00; www.casamerica.es. Open M-F 11am-2pm and 5-8pm.)*

6. BARRIO DE SALAMANCA. Continuing north toward the brown **Torres de Colón** (Towe Columbus), you'll pass the **Biblioteca Nacional** (National Library), which often hosts temporary bitions and celebrations in the summer. *(Entrance at P. de Recoletos, 20-22. ☎915 80 78 www.bne.es. Open M-F 9am-9pm, Sa 9am-2pm. Free.)* Behind the library is the massive **Mu Arqueológico Nacional.** Madrid's display of the history of the Western world, including a 4th-ce urn, Felipe II's astrolabe, and a 16th-century porcelain clock, settled in this huge museum in 1 after countless moves. *(C. Serrano, 13. M: Serrano. ☎915 77 79 12; www.man.mcu.es. Open in mer Tu-Sa 9:30am-8:00pm, Su 9:30am-3pm. €3.01, Sa after 2:30pm and Su free.)* The mus entrance is on C. Serrano, an avenue lined with pricey boutiques in the posh **Barrio de Salaman**

7. PLAZA DE COLÓN. The museum and library huddle just before the modern **Plaza de Colór** *Colón)* and the **Jardines del Descubrimiento** (Gardens of Discovery). On one side loom huge clay

boulders, inscribed with trivia about the New World, including Seneca's prediction of its discovery, the names of the mariners onboard the caravels, and passages from Columbus's diary. A neo-Gothic spire honoring Columbus rises opposite a thundering fountain in the center of the plaza. An inlaid map detailing Columbus's journey covers the wall behind the waterfall. Concerts, lectures, ballets, and plays are held in the **Centro Cultural de la Villa** (☎914 80 03 00; *www.esmadrid.com/ccvilla/jsp/index.jsp. Box office open Tu-Su 11am-1:30pm and 5-7pm or check on www.telentrada.com)*, the municipal art center beneath the statue.

8. PASEO DE LA CASTELLANA. Nineteenth- and early 20th-century aristocrats dislodged themselves from Old Madrid to settle along Po. de la Castellana. During the Civil War, Republican forces used the mansions as barracks, but they weren't so effective, and in 1939, Franco marched his army down the Castellana. Most of the mansions were torn down in the 1960s when banks and insurance companies commissioned more innovative structures. Some notables include: Rafael Moneo's **Bankinter,** #29, the first to integrate rather than demolish a townhouse; the Sevillian-tiled **Edificio ABC,** #34, formerly the office of the pro-monarchy newspaper and now a shopping center; **Banco Urquijo,** known as "the coffeepot"; the pink **Edificio Bankunion,** #46; **Banca Catalana Occidente,** #50, which looks like an ice cube on a cracker; and the famous chandelier-like **Edificio La Caixa,** #61.

9. PLAZA DE LIMA. Just south of the **American Embassy,** between Pl. de Colón and Glorieta de Emilio Castelar, is a very small **open-air sculpture garden** with works by Joan Miró and Eduardo Chillida. Smaller museums, including the **Museo Lázaro Galdiano** (p. 132), are just off the Paseo. At **Plaza de Lima** is the 110,000-seat **Estadio Santiago Bernabéu** (M: Lima), home to the beloved **Real Madrid** soccer club, which won its 9th European Championship in 2002 and its 30th Spanish La Liga Championship in 2007.

Pizzeria Mastropiero, C. San Vicente Ferrer, 34, at 2 de Mayo. M: Tribunal or Bilbao. Revolutionary politics meet gustatory pleasure in this cozy all-natural pizzeria. Friendly owner serves pizza fresh out of the oven (small €8.50-9, large €17-19), as well as huge slices of spinach pie (€3, enough for 2). If you're lucky, you may get a free *postre* (dessert), but it's worth paying for (€2.50). Open daily 9pm-1:30am. Cash only. ❷

Darbar, C. de Barbieri, 1 (☎915 21 31 93), at the corner of C. de Barbieri and C. de las Infantas. M: Chueca or Gran Vía. Cooks up samosas but calls them tapas (€4-6). Curry dishes range from €9-11. Reservations recommended. Open Tu-Sa 12:30-5pm and 8:30pm-2am. MC/V. ❸

La Granja de Said, C. de San Andrés, 11 (☎915 32 87 93). M: Tribunal or Bilbao. Dim yellow lights glow in this Arab-themed restaurant. A youthful crew fills the place at night, feasting on big portions. Lunch *menú* €8.50. Open daily 1pm-2am. MC/V. ❷

Pizzeria Vesuvio, C. de Hortaleza, 4 (☎915 21 51 71). M: Gran Vía. Fresh food, good service, mix and match pastas and sauces, and 30+ varieties of personal pizzas. Lunch rush packs counters with a rowdy crowd. Meals €3.30-5. Open M-Th 1-3pm and 8pm-midnight, F-Sa 1-4pm and 8pm-1am. Cash only. ❶

Il Pizzaiolo, C. de Hortaleza, 84 (☎913 19 29 64). M: Chueca. Authentic thin-crust Italian pizzas made with fresh ingredients. Friendly staff and bright, casual atmosphere. *Menú* €8.90. Pizzas €6.50-9. Open daily noon-4pm and 8:30pm-12:30am. MC/V. ❷

Vegaviana, C. de Pelayo, 35 (☎913 08 03 81; www.accua.com/vegaviana). M: Chueca. Wholesome vegetarian cuisine. Very popular with locals and tourists. Lunch *menú* €8.90. Meals €7.50-8. Pizzas €6.50. No smoking. Open Tu-Sa 1:30-4pm and 9pm-midnight. MC/V. ❷

La Sacristía, C. de las Infantas, 28 (☎915 22 09 45). M: Gran Vía or Chueca. The tasty seafood, including 60 types of *bacalao* (cod, €18), attracts a polished crowd. Lunch *menú* €10. Bar seating has a shorter and cheaper *menú*. Open daily 1:30-4pm and 8:30pm-12:30am. AmEx/MC/V. ❸

TAPAS BARS AND CAFES

▨ **El Tigre,** C. Infantas, 30 (☎915 32 00 72), is the most happening *cañas* (small glass–of beer, usually) spot in Chueca. The tapas—included with your drink—get tastier with each sip. Young and inviting crowd. Beer €1.50. *Raciones* €4-7. Open M-F 12:30pm-1:30am and Sa-Su 1pm-2am. Cash only. ❶

Café-Botillería Manuela, C. de San Vicente Ferrer, 29 (☎915 31 70 37; www.manuela-cafe.com). M: Tribunal. Upbeat music in an inviting Old World atmosphere. Specialty cocktails (€3-5), coffees (€3.50-4.50), and juices, as well as a traditional tapas menu (€2-8). Storytelling, literature reviews, poetry nights, and live music (Sa 9:30pm). Open June-Aug. M-Th 6pm-2am, F-Su 4pm-3am; daily Sept.-May 4pm-2am. ❶

El Circo, Pl. del Rey, 4 (☎915 21 21 04), in Chueca. Full of professionals at lunch or after work. Bright, clean, and pleasant interior. Order a beer and *tapear* (to eat tapas) free. Beer €1.20. Lunch *menú* €8.80. Open M-F 7am-10pm. MC/V. ❷

4 De Tapas, C. Barbieri, 4 (☎915 23 94 64; www.4detapas.com). Dreadlocked bartenders serve hefty tapas portions at this slick and modern variation on traditional food. Beer (€1.20), tapas (€3.60-7). Open M-Sa 8pm-2:30am, Su 9pm-midnight. MC/V. ❷

ARGÜELLES AND MONCLOA

Argüelles and Moncloa, in the heart of a modest Madrid residential area outside of the touristy center, brims with inexpensive markets and picnicking spots. If you miss tourists and overpriced coffees, hit up the chic *terrazas* on Po. del Pintor Rosales overlooking the park.

Ananias, C. de Galileo, 9 (☎914 48 68 01). M: Argüelles, a left off C. Alberto Aguilera. *Torero* paraphernalia covers front room walls, while regulars enjoy *castellano* cuisine, like the classic *queso manchego* (€9), in the back room elegance. Entrees €7-16. Open M-Tu and Th-Sa 1-4pm and 9pm-midnight, Su 1-4pm. Closed Aug. MC/V. ❸

La Crêperie, Po. del Pintor Rosales, 28 (☎915 48 23 58). M: Ventura Rodríguez. Lounging on the terrace on chic Po. del Pintor Rosales, you might as well be on a 19th-century Parisian boulevard. The cherub decorations are almost as sweet as the dessert crepes (€3-5.25). Reserve ahead. Open M-Th and Su 1:30-4:15pm and 8pm-midnight, F-Sa 1:30-4:15pm and 8pm-12:30am. MC/V. ❶

La Piba, C. Martín de los Heros, 10 (☎915 41 36 06). A colorful hole-in-the-wall take-away joint. Salads, soups, paninis, and other snacks. Everything homemade, delicious, and perfect for the neighborhood parks. Expect to pay €3-5 per item. Open M-F 11am-11pm, Sa-Su 2-11pm. ❸

Cáscaras, C. Ventura Rodríguez, 7 (☎915 42 83 36). M: Ventura Rodríguez. A lunchtime hot spot, full of locals and their tapas, *pinchos,* and ice-cold Mahou beer. Intellectual, modern atmosphere. Exotic vegetarian entrees €6.10-11.90. Open M-F 6am-1am, Sa-Su 10am-2am. AmEx/MC/V. ❷

BILBAO

Although discotecas and cheap drinks are easy to find, the student-filled streets and plazas usually empty out after a few cocktails, when the crowd heads to nearby Malasaña or Chueca. **Calle Hartzenbusch, Calle Cisneros, C. de Fuencarral,** and **C. de Luchana** all offer cheap tapas and beers.

RESTAURANTS

🦑 **Osteria Il Regno de Napoli,** C. San Andrés, 21 (☎914 45 63 00). From Gl. de Bilbao, head 1 block down C. Carranza; turn left onto C. San Andrés. Delicious Italian food in an understated, tranquil setting. Lunch *menú* €10. Dinner entrees €9-15. Try the carpaccio with rucola and olive oil (€14). Reservations advisable on weekends. Open M-F 2-4pm and 9pm-midnight, Sa 9pm-midnight, Su 2-4pm. AmEx/MC/V. ❸

🦑 **Rey de Tallarines,** C. Cardenal Cisneros, 33 (☎914 47 68 28). It's no surprise that locals come here in droves for Beijing Cuisine—the portions are huge and the prices tiny. Noodle dishes €3-8. *Menú* €8.25. Open daily noon-midnight. ❷

Pizzeria Maravilles, Pl. 2 de Mayo, 9. (No telephone). Peaceful terrace on the Plaza 2 de Mayo. Fill up on jokes and pizza delivered by a smiling staff. Pizza €6-8. Coffee €1.50. Open M-F 11am-1:30am, Sa-Su 11am-2:30am. MC/V. ❶

Collage, C. Olid, 6 (☎914 48 45 62; www.restaurantecollage.com), 3rd street on the right off C. Fuencarral. Though the all-white decor doesn't evoke the image of a collage, the Swedish menu mixes and matches in style. Entrees €13-22. *Menús* €12-22. Open M-F 1-4pm, Tu-Sa 9pm-midnight. D/MC/V. ❸

Bar Samara, C. Cardenal Cisneros, 13 (☎914 48 80 56). From M: Bilbao, walk up C. Luchana and take a quick left. Middle Eastern staples. Kebaps and other entrees €13-17. Small meat and falafel pockets at bar €4-5. Open M-Th and Su 1:30-4:30pm and 8:30pm-midnight, F-Sa 1:30-4:30pm and 8:30pm-1am. Cash only. ❸

TAPAS BARS AND CAFES

Café Comercial, Glorieta de Bilbao, 7 (☎915 21 56 55). M: Bilbao. Founded in 1887, Madrid's oldest cafe boasts high ceilings, cushioned chairs, and huge mirrors perfect for people-watching. Frequented by artists and liberals alike, Comercial saw the first anti-Franco protests take place. Coffee at the bar €1.20, at a table €1.90. Internet access, 50min. for €1. Open M-Th 7:30am-1am, F 7:30am-2am, Sa 8:30am-2am, Su 10am-1am. ❶

Casa Maravilla, C. Manuela Malasaña 13 (☎914 48 82 59) M: Bilbao. Cheap snacks and a lively local ambience. *Bocadillos* €3-6. Open M-F 2-7pm and 9pm-midnight. Sa-Su 9pm-2am. ❶

◉ SIGHTS

Madrid, large as it may seem, is a walker's city. Its fantastic public transportation system should only be used for traveling between the day's starting and ending points or for granting your feet a rest; you don't want to miss the beauty above the tunnels. Although the word *paseo* refers to a major avenue (such as Paseo de la Castellana or Paseo del Prado), it literally means "a stroll." Soak it all in, strolling from Sol to Cibeles and Pl. Mayor to the Palacio Real.

For hard-core visitors with a checklist of destinations, the municipal tourist office's *Plano de Transportes*, also called *Visiting the Downtown on Public Transport*, is indispensable; it marks monuments as well as bus and metro lines. In this chapter, sights are arranged by neighborhood. If you are trying to design a walking tour of the entire city, it is best to begin in El Centro, the nucleus of Madrid. A good day of sightseeing might move from historic Madrid, to the cafes of Huertas, to the celebrated *paseos*, to a stroll through El Retiro (see **The Paseos: A Walking Tour,** p. 116). El Pardo is best visited as a daytrip.

EL CENTRO
The sunlit buildings in El Centro radiate from the Puerta del Sol (Gate of the Sun), ultimately dividing into two sections named after the families that financed their famous monuments: **Habsburg Madrid** *(Madrid de los Habsburgos)* and **Bourbon Madrid** *(Madrid de los Borbones)*. The directions for most of the sights in Habsburg Madrid are given from Puerta del Sol, and directions for sights in Bourbon Madrid originate in Ópera.

PUERTA DEL SOL
Puerta del Sol bustles day and night with taxis, performers, and countless locals-in-transit trying to evade the luggage-laden tourists. A web of pedestrian-only streets originating at Gran Vía leads a rush of consumers down a gallery of stores, funneling them into Sol. Named for the **Puerta del Sol** (Gate of the Sun) that stood here in the 1500s, today the sun shines over department stores, restaurants, a throng of pedestrians, and the ever-present crowd snapping photos with **El oso y el madroño,** a bronze statue of the bear and "strawberry" tree from the city's heraldic coat of arms. On New Year's Eve, citizens meet here to gobble one grape per clock chime at midnight, ensuring good luck in each month of the coming year.

HABSBURG MADRID
El Centro, the city's central neighborhood, is most densely packed with monuments and tourists. In the 16th century, the Habsburgs funded the construction of **Plaza Mayor** and the **Catedral de San Isidro.** Many of Old Madrid's buildings date from much earlier, some as far back as the Moorish empire. After moving the seat of Castilla from Toledo to Madrid (then only a town of 20,000) in 1561, Felipe II and his descendants commissioned the court architects (including Juan de Herrera, the master behind El Escorial) to update many of Madrid's buildings to the latest styles. Another Juan, Juan de Villanueva, added his architectural mark to the mix under Carlos III, and designed the **Prado.** After only a century of Felipe II's development and expansion of Madrid, the city's population more than doubled.

PLAZA MAYOR. In 1620, the Pl. Mayor was completed for Felipe III; his statue, installed in 1847, graces the plaza's center. Though designed by Juan de Herrera, the same architect who built the stolid El Escorial, Pl. Mayor remains stately, though somewhat richer and softer in style. Its elegant arcades, spindly towers, and pleasant verandas are defining elements of the "Madrid style," which inspired architects across the city and throughout the country. In the 17th century, nobles on horseback spent Sunday afternoons chasing bulls in the plaza; citizens joined the fun on foot. The tradition came to be known as a *corrida*, from the verb *correr* (to run). As the site of the grand *auto-da-fé* (trials, or "acts of faith") during the Inquisition, Pl. Mayor was also the site of a bloodbath of a different kind under the rule of Carlos II.

In the evening, Pl. Mayor awakens as *madrileños* resurface, tourists multiply, and cafe tables fill with lively patrons. Live performances of *flamenco* and music are a common treat. While the cafes are a nice spot for a drink, all goods are overpriced. On Sunday mornings, the plaza holds a rare coin and stamp sale, marking the start of **El Rastro** (p. 135). During the annual **Fiesta de San Isidro** (p. 135), held the Friday before May 15 through the following Sunday, the plaza explodes with celebration and dancing in traditional costume. *(From Pta. del Sol, walk down C. Mayor, 5-10 min. M: Sol.)*

CATEDRAL DE SAN ISIDRO. Though Isidro, patron saint of crops, farmers, and Madrid, was humble, his final resting place is anything but. The church was designed in the Jesuit Baroque style at the beginning of the 17th century, before San Isidro's remains were disinterred from San Andrés and brought here in 1769 at Carlos II's command. During the Civil War, rioting workers burned the exterior—all that survived were the main chapel, a 17th-century banner, and the mummified remains of San Isidro and his wife, María de la Cabeza. The cathedral, which has since been restored, reigned as the cathedral of Madrid from the late 19th century until the Catedral de la Almudena (p. 123) was consecrated in 1993. *(From Pta. del Sol, take C. Mayor to Pl. Mayor, cross the plaza, and exit onto C. de Toledo. Cathedral is at the intersection of C. Toledo and C. de la Colegiata. M: Latina. Open daily in summer 7:30am-1:30pm and 5:30-9pm; in winter 7:30am-1pm and 5:30-8:30pm. Free.)*

PLAZA DE LA VILLA. When Felipe II made Madrid the capital of his empire in 1561, most of the town existed between Pl. Mayor and the Palacio Real; Pl. de la Villa marks the heart of Old Madrid. The horseshoe-shaped door on C. Codo is one of the few examples of the Gothic-*mudéjar* style left in Madrid, and the 15th-century *Torre de los Lujanes* was once the prison for Francisco I, King of France. Across the plaza is the 17th-century *Ayuntamiento*, designed in 1640 by Juan Gómez de Mora as both the mayor's home and the city jail. The neighboring Casa de Cisneros, a 16th-century Plateresque house, has served as a government building since 1907. *(From Pta. del Sol, go down C. Mayor and past Pl. Mayor. About 3min. M: Sol.)*

CONVENTO DE LAS DESCALZAS REALES. In 1559 Juana of Austria, Felipe II's sister, converted the former royal palace into a convent; today it is home to Franciscan nuns who watch over Juana's tomb. Claudio Coello's magnificent 17th-century frescoes line the staircase. The **Salón de Tapices** contains 11 renowned tapestries along with Santa Úrsula's jewel-encrusted bones. The highlights of the tour are in the final rooms, which include a portrait of Carlos II (the final, most terribly inbred Habsburg monarch), an allegorical Flemish painting of demons assaulting society, a dark portrait of San Francisco by Zurbarán, and Titian's *Tributo de la Moneda al César*. Lines are long in the summer; arrive early, and enjoy the mandatory 1hr. tour in Spanish. *(Pl. de las Descalzas, between Pl. de Callao and Pta. del Sol. ☎914 54 88 00; www.patrimonionacional.es; M: Callao, Ópera, or Sol. Open Tu-Th and Sa 10:30am-12:30pm and 4-5:30pm, F 10:30am-12:30pm, Su 11am-1:30pm. €5, students €2.50. The visita de conjunto ticket (€6/3.40) gives a combined entrance to the Convento de la Encarnación. EU citizens free W.)*

CONVENTO DE LA ENCARNACIÓN. Spain's finest reliquary is housed in this monastery, with more than 1500 saintly relics, including a vial of San Pantaleón's blood believed to liquefy every year on July 27. According to legend, if the blood does not liquefy, disaster will strike Madrid. Rumor has it that the blood failed to change states before the Civil War broke out, but the Church insists it has never once remained solid. Artistic highlights include the dramatic *San Juan Bautista* by José Ribera, a contorted wooden Christ by Pedro de Mano, and a dark *Last Supper* by Vicente Carducho. *(Pl. de la Encarnación.* ☎ *915 47 53 50; www.patrimonionacional.es. M: Ópera. From the metro stop, facing the Ópera building, bear diagonally right up C. Arrieta. Mandatory 1hr. tour in Spanish. Open Tu-Th and Sa 10:30am-12:45pm and 4-5:45pm, F 10:30am-12:45pm, Su 11am-1:45pm. €3.60; students, under 18, and over 65 €2. Visita de conjunto with the Convento de las Descalzas Reales €6/3.40. EU citizens free W.)*

ALONG THE RÍO MANZANARES. Madrid's notoriously puny "river" snakes its way around the city past the **Puerta de Toledo.** The triumphal arch was commissioned by Joseph Bonaparte to celebrate his brother Napoleon, but was completed in honor of Fernando VII, the "exterminator of the French usurpers." The Baroque **Puente de Toledo** makes up for the river's inadequacies. Sandstone carvings by Juan Ron on both sides of the bridge depict the martyrdom of San Isidro and his family. The **Puente de Segovia,** which spans the river along C. Segovia, was conceived by Juan de Herrera and constructed in the late 16th century, making it the oldest bridge in Madrid. *(To reach Puente de Toledo from Pta. del Sol, take C. Mayor through the Pl. Mayor and onto C. Toledo; follow C. Toledo to the bridge; approx. 15min. M: Puerta de Toledo or Ópera.)*

OTHER SIGHTS. As the legend goes, **Iglesia de San Pedro,** C. de Nuncio, 14, began as a *mudéjar* mosque. A 17th-century overhaul commissioned by Felipe IV infused the original structure with Baroque intricacies. *(Facing the Palacio, go left on C. de Bailén and right onto C. de Segovia. The church will be on your right when you reach Cost. San Pedro. Open for mass only. Mass F noon and 8pm, Sa 7pm, Su noon.)* Next to Iglesia de San Pedro is the **Museo de San Isidro,** where the saint allegedly lived. His sarcophagus rests here, in the **Capilla de San Isidro,** but his body is in the nearby cathedral. The museum hosts temporary exhibits of archaeological finding and paintings. There is a stunningly beautiful courtyard. *(Cuesta San Andrés.* ☎ *913 66 74 15. M: La Latina. Open Tu-F 9:30am-8pm, Sa-Su 10am-2pm. Free.)*

BOURBON MADRID

Weakened by plagues and political losses, the Habsburg era in Spain ended with the death of Carlos II in 1700. Felipe V, the first of Spain's Bourbon monarchs, ascended the throne in 1714 after the 12-year War of the Spanish Succession. Bankruptcy, industrial stagnation, and moral disillusionment compelled Felipe V to embark on a crusade of urban renewal. His successors, Fernando VI and Carlos III, fervently pursued the same ends, with astounding results. Today, the lavish palaces, churches, and parks that they left are the most touristed in Madrid.

PALACIO REAL. The impossibly luxurious Palacio Real overlooks the Río Manzanares at the western tip of central Madrid. Felipe V commissioned Giovanni Sachetti to replace the Alcázar, which burned down in 1734, with a palace that would dwarf all others—and the architect succeeded. When Sachetti died, Filippo Juvara took over, basing his new facade on Giovanni Bernini's rejected designs for the Louvre. The shell took 26 years to build, and the decoration of its 2000 rooms with a vast collection of porcelain, tapestries, furniture, and art dragged on for over a century. The time was well-spent: although today the palace is used by the royal couple only on official occasions, it continues to stand as one of Europe's most grandiose residences.

The palace's most impressive rooms are decorated in the Rococo style. The **Salón del Trono** (Throne Room) contains the two magnificent Spanish thrones, supported by two golden lions. According to tradition, the thrones are never actually used during state visits, as the king and queen merely stand in front of them. The room also features a ceiling fresco painted by Tiepolo, outlining the qualities of the ideal ruler, while the **Salón de Gasparini,** site of the king's ceremonial dressing before the court, houses Goya's portrait of Carlos IV. Perhaps most beautiful is the **Chinese Room,** whose walls swirl with verdant tendril patterns. The **Real Oficina de Farmacia** (Royal Pharmacy) has crystal and china receptacles used to hold royal medicine. Also open to the public is the **Real Armería** (Armory), which has an entire floor devoted to an impressive collection of knights' armor sitting atop their fully decorated horses. *(From Pl. de Isabel II, head toward the Teatro Real. M: Ópera. ☎914 54 87 88. Open Apr.-Sept. M-Sa 9am-6pm, Su 9am-3pm; Oct.-Mar. M-Sa 9:30am-5pm, Su 9am-2pm. Arrive early to avoid lines. €8, with tour €10; students €3.50/6. Under 5 free. EU citizens free W.)*

PLAZA DEL ORIENTE. The statues in this sculpture garden were originally intended for the palace roof, but were too heavy to support. Because the queen had a nightmare about the roof collapsing, they were instead placed in this symmetrical plaza. Stroll through as if you were a royal guest and check out the intimidating equestrian statue of Felipe IV, sculpted by Pietro Tacca, in the center. *(From Pl. Isabel II, walk past Teatro Real. Across from the Palacio Real. M: Ópera.)*

CATEDRAL DE NUESTRA SEÑORA DE LA ALMUDENA. Take a break from the cherub-filled frescoes of most Spanish cathedrals for refreshingly modern decor. Begun in 1879 and finished a century later, this cathedral is a stark contrast to the gilded Palacio Real. After a 30-year hibernation, the building, dedicated to Madrid's other patron saint, received a controversial face-lift. The reasons for the controversy are apparent, as the cathedral's frescoes and stained glass windows sport a discordant mix of traditional and abstract styles: gray stone walls clash with the ceiling panels of brilliant colors and sharp geometric shapes. *(C. Bailén, 10. ☎915 42 22 00. Left of the Palacio Real on C. Bailén. M: Ópera. Closed during mass. Open daily 9am-9pm. Confession 11am-12:45pm and 5pm-8:30pm. Free.)*

MUSEO DE LA REAL ACADEMÍA DE BELLAS ARTES DE SAN FERNANDO. Fernando VI established a royal academy in 1752 to train the country's most talented artists. The rooms dedicated to Goya display his range, juxtaposing the satirical *Casa de Locos* and macabre *El Entierro de la Sardinera* with portraits of nobility. Other highlights include Ribera's *Martirio de San Bartolomé* and Velázquez's portrait of Felipe IV, as well as 17th-century canvases by Murillo and Rubens. The top floor holds Picasso sketches. The Calcografía Real (Royal Print and Drawing Collection) holds Goya's studio and organizes exhibitions. *(C. Alcalá, 13. ☎915 24 08 64; http://rabasf.insde.org. M: Sol or Sevilla. Open July-Aug. M 9am-2:30pm, Tu-F 9am-7pm, Sa 9am-2:30pm and 4-7pm, Su 9:30am-2pm; Sept.-June M and Sa-Su 9am-2pm, Tu-F 9am-6:30pm. €3, students €1.50. W free. Top 2 fl. often closed; call ahead.)*

OTHER SIGHTS. The **Campo de Moro** lies below the Palacio Real. With its wide, gentle slope of grass and lush, leafy trees, it is a park fit for kings. Walking trails wind through the woods to shady resting places and locals row boats in the small lake or relax on its banks. *(From the palace, turn left onto C. Bailén, left again down Cuesta de San Vicente, and at the bottom of the hill turn left onto C. Puerto. From M: Príncipe Pío, cross the plaza to the entrance on C. del Puerto. Open in summer M-Sa 10am-6pm, Su 9am-6pm; in winter M-Sa 10am-8pm, Su 9am-8pm; last entrance 30min. before closing.)* The **Jardines de Sabatini,** to the right when facing the palace, is the romantic's park of choice; there's a fountain for wading and topiaries to lie among. Be sure to catch the ◙**sunset** from the garden walls. *(Open daily in summer 9am-10pm; in winter 9am-9pm.)*

HUERTAS

Huertas is a wedge bordered by C. de Alcalá to the north, C. de Atocha to the south, and Po. del Prado to the east. Off C. San Jerónimo, streets slope downward, outward, and eastward toward various points along Po. del Prado and Pl. Cánovas de Castillo. **Plaza de Santa Ana** and its *terrazas* are the center of this old literary neighborhood. Huertas's sights, from authors' houses to famous cafes, reflect its artistic past. Home to Cervantes, Quevedo, and Calderón de la Barca during its heyday in the *Siglo de Oro* (see **Literature,** p. 87), Huertas enjoyed a fleeting return to literary prominence when Hemingway dropped by in the 1920s.

PARQUE DEL BUEN RETIRO

With the construction of the 300-acre Parque del Buen Retiro, Felipe IV intended to transform the former hunting grounds into a personal retreat, *un buen retiro*. Today, the magnificent park and its accompanying gardens are filled with palm-readers, sunbathers, soccer players, reflective students, and occasional drug pushers (just ignore them and they should leave you alone). The northeast corner of the park enchants with medieval monastic ruins and waterfalls. The park also houses the spectacular Palacio de Cristal and Estanque Grande. On weekends, the promenades fill with musicians, families, and young lovers; on summer nights (when only the north gate remains open), the lively bars and cafes scattered around the park become quite active. Try to avoid the park after dark if you're alone—it is also home to a slew of shady characters. The park is easily accessible from the Retiro metro stop. There are four entrances: C. Alfonso XII, C. Alcalá, Pl. de la Independencia, and Av. Menéndez y Pelayo.

ESTANQUE GRANDE. Overlooked by Alfonso XII's mausoleum, rowers crowd this rectangular lake in the middle of the park. The lake has been the social center of El Retiro ever since aspiring caricaturists, fortune-tellers, and *pipas* (sunflower-seed) vendors first parked their goods along its marble shores. The colonnaded monument is the perfect spot for relaxation and people-watching. While away the lazy afternoons in a rowboat on the lake. Sundays from 5pm to midnight, over 100 percussionists gather for an immense ▓**drum circle** by the monument on the Estanque; synchronistic rhythms and hash smoke fill the air. *(Boats €5 per 45min. for 4 people. The Pl. de la Independencia entrance leads to Av. de Méjico, the path to the lake.)*

PALACIO DE VELÁZQUEZ. This Ricardo Velázquez creation has billowing ceilings, marble floors, and tiles by Daniel Zuloaga. It exhibits frequently changing contemporary and experimental works in conjunction with the Museo Nacional Centro de Arte Reina Sofía (p. 127). *(From the Estanque, walk straight to Pl. de Honduras and turn left onto Po. Venezuela. The palace will be on your right. ☎915 73 62 45. Open Apr.-Sept. M-Sa 11am-8pm, Su 11am-6pm; Oct.-Mar. M-Sa 10am-6pm, Su 10am-4pm. Free.)*

PALACIO DE CRISTAL. Built by Ricardo Velázquez to exhibit flowers from the Philippines in 1887, this exquisite steel-and-glass structure hosts a variety of art shows and exhibits, with subjects ranging from Bugs Bunny to Spanish portraiture to vocal recognition of bird calls. *(From Palacio de Velázquez, head out the main door until you reach the lake and the palace. ☎915 74 66 14. Open Apr.-Sept. M-Sa 11am-8pm, Su 11am-6pm; Oct.-Mar. M-Sa 10am-6pm, Su 10am-4pm. Free.)*

PUERTA DE ALCALÁ AND CASÓN DEL BUEN RETIRO. Bullets from the 1921 assassination of Prime Minister Eduardo Dato permanently scarred the eastern face of the **Puerta de Alcalá** (1778), outside El Retiro's Puerta de la Independencia. To the south, the **Casón del Buen Retiro,** faces the park; behind it sits the **Museo del Ejército.** *(The permanent collection, normally 19th- and 20th-century works from the Prado, is closed. Information on temporary exhibits ☎915 22 89 77.)* In this stately fragment, is a vast collection of over 27,000 artifacts tracing the history of the Spanish military. Each room is dedicated to a different period or conquest; the most famous contains the *Tizona* sword of El Cid Campeador and a fragment of the cross Columbus was wearing when he arrived in the New World. The two buildings are remnants of Felipe IV's palace, which burned in the Napoleonic Wars. *(C. Méndez Núñez, 1. ☎915 22 89 77. M: Retiro or Banco de España. The museum is currently undergoing renovations, expected to be finished by the end of 2007.)*

OTHER SIGHTS

REAL JARDÍN BOTÁNICO. Opened during reign of Carlos III, the garden show-cases over 30,000 species of plants, ranging from traditional roses to medicinal herbs. The garden's vast collection of imported trees, bushes, and flowers has a universal appeal. *(Pl. de Murillo, 2, next to the Prado. ☎914 20 30 17; www.rjb.csic.es. Open daily in summer 10am-9pm; in winter 10am-6pm. €2, students €1, under 10 and over 65 free.)*

CASA DE LOPE DE VEGA. Golden Age authors Lope de Vega and Miguel de Cervantes were bitter rivals, but Lope de Vega's 17th-century home is ironically located on C. Cervantes (and, of course, Cervantes is buried on C. Lope de Vega). A prolific playwright and poet, Lope de Vega spent the last 25 years of his life writing plays in this house. None of the objects here belonged to him, but they are all period pieces collected using a catalog that he left behind. Although historians were able to reconstruct what his house looked like, they are not as familiar with his amorous exploits—his exact number of children is unknown, but estimates range from 12 to 15. *(C. Cervantes, 11. With your back to Pl. de Santa Ana, turn left onto C. del Prado, right onto C. León, and left onto C. de Cervantes. ☎914 29 92 16. Open Tu-F 9:30am-2pm, Sa 10am-2pm. Entrance and tour €2, students €1. Free on Sa.)*

CÍRCULO DE BELLAS ARTES. The Círculo is the hub of Madrid's performing arts scene, organizing performances and shows around the city. Designed by Antonio Palacios, this building houses two stages and several studios for lectures and workshops run by prominent artists. Their quarterly magazine, *Minerva*, is available at the entrance (€15). Many facilities are for *socios* (members) only, but the galleries are open to the public. Exhibitions range from photography to video art to abstract sculpture. It also sponsors **Radio Círculo**, 100.4 FM, which plays jazz, folk, or whatever guest DJs feel like spinning. They also sponsor concerts, festivals, films, and theater events. Pick up a free program at the front desk. *(C. Alcalá, 42. From Pl. de Santa Ana, go up C. del Príncipe, cross C. San Jerónimo to C. Sevilla, and turn right onto C. Alcalá. ☎913 60 54 00; www.circulobellasartes.com. Open Tu-F 5-9pm, Sa 11am-2pm and 5-9pm, Su 11am-2pm. €1. Cafe open daily 10am-1am.)*

AVENIDA DEL ARTE

Art buffs and apathetic tourists alike will enjoy Madrid's museums, which need no introduction. Considered to be among the world's best art galleries individually, the Museo del Prado, Museo de Thyssen-Bornemisza, and the Museo Nacional Centro de Arte Reina Sofía together form the impressive "Avenida del Arte." From Goya in the Prado and Rothko in the Thyssen-Bornemisza to Picasso in the Reina Sofía, Madrid's museums form one of the most comprehensive collections in the world.

▨ MUSEO DEL PRADO

Po. del Prado at Pl. Cánovas del Castillo. M: Banco de España or Atocha. ☎ 913 30 28 00; www.museoprado.es. Open Tu-Su 9am-8pm. €6, students €3, under 18, over 65 free. Su free 9am-7pm.

One of Europe's finest centers for 12th- to 17th-century art, the Prado is Spain's most prestigious museum and home to the world's greatest collection of Spanish paintings. Following Carlos III's order for a museum of natural history and sciences, architect **Juan de Villanueva** began construction of the Neoclassical building in 1785. In 1819, Fernando VII transformed it into the royal painting archive; the museum's 7000 pieces are the result of hundreds of years of the Royal

Houses of Austria's and Bourbon's art collecting. The walls are filled with Spanish and foreign masterpieces, including a comprehensive selection from the Flemish and Venetian schools. The museum is well-organized: the ground floor houses Spanish painting from the 12th through 16th centuries and 15th- to 16th-century Flemish, German, and Italian works. The first floor contains 17th-century pieces, and 18th-century paintings are located on the second floor. The museum provides a free and indispensable guide upon entry which describes each numbered room. Audio guides in English are available for the best €3 you've yet spent in this city—they are a wealth of lesser-known facts and a fantastic way to see the museum. The sheer quantity of paintings means you'll have to be selective. No matter what it is —Velazquez, Goya, Flemish altarpieces, or Rococo cherubs—come to the Prado with a goal. You may feel guilty sprinting past someone's life work, but push on or you may find yourself wandering until closing time. The museum's guidebooks (€10-25) also offer extensive art history and criticism and can help you sift through the floors.

DIEGO VELÁZQUEZ. The first floor houses Spanish, French, Dutch, and Italian works. The most notable is an collection of works by Diego Velázquez (1599-1660). Known for his unforgiving realism and use of light, Velázquez was the court painter and majordomo to Felipe IV (portraits of the foppish monarch abound). Several of his most famous paintings are here, including *Las hilanderas (The Weavers)*, *El Dios Marte (Mars)*, and *La fragua de Vúlcano (Vulcan's Forge)*. The painter's magnum opus is ▣**Las Meninas** *(The Maids of Honor)*, but some suspect that his was not the only brush to touch the canvas. In the painting, Velázquez sports the cross of the order of Santiago, which was first created in 1658. Since the work was completed two years earlier, in 1656, art historians think that Felipe the IV himself added the mark to enoble his painter. With or without the king's help, the snapshot quality of Velazquez's figures transformed painting in the 17th century.

FRANCISCO DE GOYA. In 1785, Francisco de Goya y Lucientes (1746-1828) became the court portraitist. Despite his rather controversial depictions of the royal family (some argued that Goya manipulated light and shadow to focus the viewer's gaze on the figure of the queen—rather than the king—in *La familia de Carlos IV*, discreetly pointing to the true power behind the monarchy), Goya was never expelled from court. (He didn't escape punishment completely, however, and was hauled before the Inquisition in 1815.) Goya consciously imitated the techniques of his national predecessors, including himself in the shadows of a royal portrait, in a nod to Velázquez and Las Meninas, and employing an unparalleled range of subjects and moods. One room has pastoral hunting scenes and cheery peasant dances, while the other bristles with darker, politically charged scenes. The stark *2 de Mayo* and *Fusilamientos de 3 de Mayo* depict the terrors of the 1808 Napoleonic invasion, and may be Goya's most recognized works, along with the expressionless woman in *La maja vestida* and *La maja desnuda*, thought to be Goya's mistress, the Duchess of Alba. The *Pinturas Negras (Black Paintings)* are the most evocative. These paintings were aptly named for the darkness of both the colors and the subject matter—Goya painted them at the end of his life, when he was deaf and alone. *Saturno devorando a su hijo (Saturn Devouring His Son)* stands out; Goya captures the crazed eyes of Saturn as he bites off the head of his son after a prophesy that one of his children would overthrow him. Another black painting, *Perro semihundido (The Half-drowned Dog)*, mystifies viewers.

ITALIAN, FLEMISH, AND OTHER SPANISH ARTISTS. The ground floor of the Prado displays many of **El Greco's** (Doménikos Theotokópoulos, 1541-1614) religious paintings. *La Trinidad (The Trinity)* and *San Andrés y San Francisco (St. Andrew and St. Francis)* are characterized by El Greco's luminous colors, elongated figures, and mystical subjects. On the first floor are works by Spanish artists like **Bartoloméo Murillo**, **José de Ribera**, and **Francisco Zurbarán**.

The collection of Italian works is formidable, including **Titian's** portraits of Carlos V and Felipe II and his mythologically inspired *Danäe Receiving the Shower of Gold* and **Raphael's** *El cardenal desconocido (The Unknown Cardinal)*. **Tintoretto's** rendition of the homicidal seductress Judith and her hapless victim Holofernes, as well as his awesome *Washing of the Feet*, are also here. Some minor **Botticellis** and a slew of imitations are on display. Among the works by **Rubens**, *The Adoration of the Magi* and *The Three Graces* best show his grand style. Still, **Fra Angelico's** *Annunciation* is the most resplendent of all the Italian works.

As a result of the Spanish Habsburgs' control of the Netherlands, the **Flemish** holdings are also top-notch. **Van Dyck's** *Marquesa de Legunes* is here, as well as landscapes by **Joachim Patinir**. Room 56A, which houses a collection of phantasmagorical Flemish paintings, like **Peter Brueghel the Elder's** terrifying *The Triumph of Death*, is especially amazing. **Hieronymus Bosch's** moralistic ▨**The Garden of Earthly Delights** is a favorite, with pink crystal fountains, other-wordly creatures, hedonistic pleasure-seekers, the hell that awaits them, and the heaven that doesn't.

LA AMPLIACIÓN. The Prado's newest expansion—the biggest in the museums's 200-year history—is poised to open at the end of 2007. Designed by Rafael Moneo, the new building will house the cloisters of the former monastery of Los Jerónimos and a 440-seat auditorium, in addition to space for temporary exhibitions, restorations and painting storage.

▨ MUSEO NACIONAL CENTRO DE ARTE REINA SOFÍA

Pl. Santa Isabel, 52. ☎ 917 74 10 00; www.museoreinasofia.es. M: Atocha. Open M and W-Sa 10am-9pm, Su 10am-2:30pm. €3, students €1.50. Sa after 2:30pm, Su, holidays, under 18, over 65 free.

Since Juan Carlos I declared this renovated hospital a national museum in 1988, naming it after his wife, this collection of 20th-century art has grown steadily. The building is a work of art in itself, with two futuristic-looking glass elevators looking out over the museum's small plaza. With over 10,000 pieces, the museum has an amazing collection of paintings, sculptures, experimental space, and film. The second and fourth floors are mazes of permanent exhibits charting the Spanish avant-garde and contemporary movements. If stark canvases with dots don't do it for you, skip to the rooms dedicated to Juan Gris, Joan Miró, and Salvador Dalí, which display Spain's vital contributions to the Surrealist movement. Miró's works show a spare, colorful abstraction, while Dalí's paintings, including the X-rated *El Gran Masturbador* (The Great Masturbator) and *El enigma sin fin* (Enigma Without End), portray the artist's Freudian nightmares and sexual fantasies.

Picasso's masterpiece, ▨**Guernica**, is the highlight of the Reina Sofía's permanent collection. Now freed from its restrictive glass cover and long exile in New York, it depicts the Basque town bombed by the German and Nationalist air forces during the Spanish Civil War (see **The Tragedy of Guernica**, p. 520). Commissioned to produce a piece large enough for the main wall in the Spanish Pavilion at the Paris World's Fair in August 1937, Picasso began work on the painting May 1st, and completed the mammoth work just weeks later. In a huge, colorless work of contorted, agonized figures, Picasso denounced "the military caste which [had] sunk Spain into an ocean of pain and death." While many have attempted to explain the allegory behind this work and its components, Picasso himself refused to acknowledge its symbolism; still, most critics insist that the screaming horse represents war and the twisted bull represents Spain. Picasso stipulated that the painting was not to return to Spain as long as a Fascist government was in place, and loaned the canvas to the Museum of Modern Art in New York on the condition that it be repatriated when democracy was restored. In 1981, six years after Franco's death, Guernica was delivered to the Prado. The subsequent move to the Reina Sofía sparked an international controversy—Picasso's other request was that the painting hang only in the Prado, where it belonged, among the works of the Old Masters, like El Greco, Goya, and Velázquez.

▨ MUSEO THYSSEN-BORNEMISZA

On the corner of Po. del Prado and C. Manuel González. M: Banco de España or Atocha. Buses #1, 2, 5, 9, 10, 14, 15, 20, 27, 34, 37, 45, 51, 52, 53, 74, 146, and 150. ☎ 913 69 01 51; www.museothyssen.org. Open Tu-Su 10am-7pm. Last entrance 6:30pm. €6, students with ISIC and seniors €4, under 12 free. Audio guides €3.

Unlike the Prado and the Reina Sofía, the Thyssen-Bornemisza covers many periods and diverse media; exhibits range from 14th-century canvases to 20th-century sculptures, and its collection encompasses periods of art lacked in the other two. The museum is housed in the 18th-century **Palacio de Villahermosa** and contains the former collection of the late Baron Heinrich Thyssen-Bornemisza. The baron donated his collection in 1993, and today the museum is the world's most extensive private showcase. In June 2004, a new wing was opened to house the collection of his wife, Baroness Carmen.

A little more manageable and less overwhelming than the Prado and the Reina Sofía, the pieces proceed in chronological order from the second floor down, making it easy to see the art-historical march of time. The top floor is dedicated to the Old Masters, with stars like Hans Holbein's austere *Portrait of Henry VIII* and El Greco's *Anunciación*. You can chart the changing attitudes and representations of the body, from Lucas Cranach's *The Nymph of the Spring* to Titian's *Saint Jerome in the Desert* to Anthony van Dyck's *Portrait of Jacques Le Roy*. The Thyssen-Bornemisza's Baroque collection, with pieces by Caravaggio, Ribera, and Claude Lorraine, rivals the Prado's.

A burst of color characteristic of the 17th century accompanies the descent down a floor. During this period, Dutch works, like Frans Hals's *Family Group in a Landscape*, began to master the depiction of natural light. The Impressionist and Post-Impressionist collections explode with texture and color—look for works by Renoir, Manet, Degas, Monet, van Gogh, Cézanne, and Matisse. The museum is also home to Europe's only collection of 19th-century American paintings, including Winslow Homer's *The Signal of Distress.*

The highlight of the tour is the museum's 20th-century collection, which reflects a diversity of styles and philosophies. You can trace the deconstruction of figurative painting, starting with Picasso, Georges Braque, and Juan Gris. From there, the vibrant colors and action of Frantisek Kupka *(The Machine Drill)* contrast with the sterility of Piet Mondrian and the Constructivists. Room 45, on the ground floor, features some great pieces by Picasso (including *Harlequin with a Mirror*), Marc Chagall, and Wassily Kandinsky. Room 46 ushers in American Abstract Expressionism (Pollack, Mark Rothko, Morris Louis, and Willem de Kooning) with its bold enthusiasm. Look for one of Georgia O'Keeffe's desert flowers. German Expressionist artists are also well-represented, with *Summer Clouds* by Emile Nolde, brooding portraits by Max Beckmann, and *The Dream* by Franz Marc. Of the same era is Egon Schiele's *The Old Town*, in which huddled houses peer out over a frozen river. The second-to-last room chills with an evocative Lucien Freud portrait and *Hotel Room* by Edward Hopper. A peek across the room, however, is cheering—Henri Magritte's games with broken glass in *La Clef de Champs*, Dalí's *Dream Caused by the Flight of a Bumblebee around a Pomegranate*, and Joseph Cornell's poetic boxes are sure to please.

MALASAÑA AND CHUECA

Devoid of the numerous historic monuments and palaces that characterize most of Madrid, the labyrinthine streets of Malasaña and Chueca house countless undocumented "sights," from street performers and sex shops to some of Madrid's best fashion. These streets are a funky, colorful, and relaxing break for travelers weary of crucifixes and brush strokes. Chueca in particular is perfect for people-watching and boutique shopping. By night, both of these districts bustle with Madrid's alternative and gay scene. Although the region between **Calle de Fuencarral** and **Calle de San Bernardo** plays host Madrid's avant-garde—architecture and art galleries included—the streets and people walking them are the real draw.

IGLESIA DE LAS SALESAS REALES. Bourbon King Fernando VI commissioned this church in 1758 at the request of his wife. The Baroque/Neoclassical domed church is clad in granite, with sculptures by Alfonso Vergaza and a dome painting by the brothers González Velázquez. The church's ostentatious facade and interior prompted critics to pun on the queen's name, Bárbara: "Barbaric queen, barbaric tastes, barbaric building, barbarous expense," they said, giving rise to the expression *"¡qué bárbaro!"* Today, the phrase refers to absurdity, extravagance, or any "savage" foreigner in the 4th century. *(C. Bárbara de Braganza, 1. M: Colón. From Pl. Colón, go down Po. de Recoletos and take a right onto C. de Bárbara de Braganza. ☎ 913 19 48 11. Open M-F 8:30am-1pm and 5:30-9pm. Not open to tourists during mass.)*

MUSEO DE HISTORIA (ANTIGUO MUNICIPAL). An intricate facade welcomes visitors to explore Madrid's history through its art. Exhibits feature paintings, prints, and photographs, all of which document the changes and consistencies of this dynamic city over the past four centuries. Though the museum undergoes relatively frequent renovation projects, small, well-curated exhibits are open to the public. Highlights include lithographs of the 1837 revolution and paintings of chivalric festivities in the Pl. Mayor. The 3D model of the city is a lifesaver for the disoriented tourist. *(C. de Fuencarral, 78, right outside M· Tribunal. ☎ 917 01 18 63. Open Tu-F 9:30am-8pm, Sa-Su 10am-2pm. Free.)*

GRAN VÍA

Urban planners paved Gran Vía in 1910 to link C. Princesa with Pl. de Cibeles, creating a cosmopolitan center of life in the city. After Madrid gained wealth as a neutral supplier during WWI, the city funneled much of its earnings into making Gran Vía one of the world's great thoroughfares. In its heyday, Hemingway described it as a cross between Broadway and Fifth Avenue. Today we might simply compare it to the lights and excitement—and touristic excess—of Times Square. While actual sights are few and far between, the best way to experience Gran Vía is to throw yourself into the throngs on the sidewalk and keep up with the pace.

Sol's shopping streets converge at Gran Vía's highest elevation in **Plaza del Callao** (M: Callao). C. Postigo San Martín splits off southward, where you'll find the famed **Convento de las Descalzas Reales** (p. 121). Westward from Pl. de Callao, Gran Vía descends toward **Plaza de España** (M: Pl. de España). Locals relax on the shady grass, but you're better off going to the bottom of the park and turning left toward the Royal Gardens, or right to **El Templo de Debod** (p. 130). Next to Pl. de España are two of Madrid's tallest skyscrapers, the **Telefónica building** (1929) and the **Edificio de España** (1953). Lewis S. Weeks of the Chicago School designed the Telefónica building, the tallest concrete building at the time (81m), which was used as a lookout by Republican forces during the Civil War. The Edificio de España, designed by architects Joaquín and Julián Otomendi during Franco's mid-dictatorial attempt to spur economic growth. The building is in the neo-baroque style, and resembles its contemporaries along Central Park in New York City—

hardly the "fascist" block you might expect from Franco's commission. Tucked between them on C. San Leonardo is the small **Iglesia de San Marcos,** a Neoclassical church composed of five intersecting ellipses—this Euclidean dream of a building does not have a single straight line.

ARGÜELLES AND MONCLOA

▓ **TEMPLO DE DEBOD.** Built by King Adijalamani of Meröe in the 2nd century BC, the Templo de Debod is the only Egyptian temple in Spain. In 1968, The Egyptian government shipped the temple stone by stone to Spain in appreciation of Spanish archaeologists who helped to rescue the Abu Simbel temples from the floods of the Aswan Dam. The temple was originally built to honor Isis and Ammon; the structure was elaborated by Egyptian monarchs and later, Roman emperors Augustus and Tiberius. The **Parque de la Montaña** is home to the temple and two of its three original gateways. At sunset, ascend to one of the park's lookout points for one of the best views of the metropolis. *(M: Pl. de España or Ventura Rodríguez. Buses #1 and 74. From the metro, walk down C. Ventura Rodríguez to Parque de la Montaña; the temple is on the right.* ☎ *913 66 74 15; www.munimadrid.es/templodebod. Guided tours available. Open Apr.-Sept. Tu-F 10am-2pm and 6-8pm, Sa-Su 10am-2pm; Oct.-Mar. Tu-F 9:45am-1:45pm and 4:15-6:15pm, Sa-Su 10am-2pm. Closed M. Free. Park open daily year-round, free.)*

▓ **EL PARDO.** Built as a hunting lodge for Carlos I in 1547, El Pardo was enlarged by generations of Habsburgs and Bourbons. Though Spain's growing capital eventually extended into the old hunting grounds and enveloped the country palace, the Pardo remains one of the nation's most compelling constructions. In 1940, centuries after its heyday as a hunting lodge, El Pardo opened its doors to its most trigger-happy resident when Franco, who fancied himself Felipe II reincarnate, decided to move in, living there until his death in 1975. Though politics have changed, the palace is still the official reception site for foreign dignitaries. Renowned for its collection of vivid pastoral **tapestries**—several of which were designed by Goya—the palace also holds a Velázquez painting and Ribera's *Techo de los Hombres Ilustres* (Ceiling of the Illustrious Men). You can also see Franco's bathroom, and the bedroom cabinet in which he kept Santa Teresa's silver-encrusted arm. Entrance to the palace's **capilla** and the nearby **Casita del Príncipe,** created by Juan de Villanueva of Museo del Prado fame, is free. *(Take bus #601 from the stop in front of the Ejército del Aire building above M: Moncloa; every 15min., €1.* ☎ *913 76 15 00. Palace open Apr.-Sept. M-Sa 10:30am-6pm, Su 9:25am-1:40pm; Oct.-Mar. M-Sa 10:30am-5pm, Su 9:55am-1:40pm. Mandatory 45min. guided tour in Spanish. €4, over 65 and students with ID €2.70. W free for EU citizens. The Casita del Príncipe may be undergoing restorations; call ahead.)*

MUSEO DE AMÉRICA. This underrated museum reopened after painstaking renovations and is now a worthwhile excursion. It documents the cultures of the Americas' pre-Hispanic civilizations and the legacy of Spanish conquest with detail and insight. The wealth of pre-Columbian artifacts include tools, pottery, codices, ceremonial and daily dress, funeral shrouds, and shrunken heads. Colonial accounts and artwork provide a glimpse into the conquistadors' perspectives on the peoples they encountered. Especially fascinating are paintings depicting interracial families and the various ethnic identities assigned to their offspring, which illustrate the stereotypical colonial mindset. *(Av. de los Reyes Católicos, 6, next to the Faro de Moncloa.* ☎ *915 49 26 41; www.museodeamerica.mcu.es. M: Moncloa. Open Tu-Sa 9:30am-3pm, Su 10am-3pm. €3.01, under 18 and over 65 free. Sa after 2:30pm, Su free.)*

ERMITA DE SAN ANTONIO DE LA FLORIDA. Although slightly off the beaten Madrid-tourist-path, the *Ermita* (hermitage) is worth the trouble. It contains

Goya's pantheon—a frescoed dome that arches above his buried corpse. Goya's skull, apparently stolen by a phrenologist, was missing when the corpse arrived from Bordeaux. On June 13th, single *madrileñas* offer their faith (and blood) to San Antonio in exchange for his help in the husband-hunt. The women line the baptismal fount with thirty pins and then press their hands into them; the number of resulting pin-pricks represents how many *novios* (boyfriends) they'll have in the coming year. *(M: Príncipe Pío. From the metro, go right onto Po. de la Florida and walk to the first traffic circle. The Ermita is on the right. ☎915 42 07 22. Open Tu-F 9:30am-8pm, Sa-Su 10am-2pm. Free.)*

CASA DEL CAMPO. Take the **Teleférico** *(☎915 41 11 18; open M-F noon-2pm and 3-9:30pm, Sa-Su noon-9:30pm; one-way €3.25, round-trip €4.65)* from Po. del Pintor Rosales into Madrid's largest park. Or head down from M: Príncipe Pío, left of the traffic circle and over the Río Manzanares. Shaded by pines, oaks, and cypresses, joggers and walkers exercise in the mornings and late afternoons. The Campo feels more local than the Retiro on the other side of town and boasts a lake with paddleboats *(€4 for 45min.)* and vibrant cafes on its banks. Early morning reveals evidence of questionable nighttime activities and their weary participants; it's wise to stay away much after dark. Inside the amusement park, **Parque de Atracciones**, relive your childhood on the roller coaster. One of Madrid's largest **pools** is in the corner of the park, next to M: Lago. *(Take bus #33 or 65 or M: Batán. Turn right out of the metro and walk up the main street away from the lake. ☎914 63 29 00; www.parquedeatracciones.es. €8.20 to enter, €26 to ride. Schedule changes daily, see website for hours.)* The **Zoo/Aquarium,** 5min. away, features gorillas, leopards, and a dolphin show. *(☎915 12 37 70; www.zoomadrid.com. Open M-F 10:30am-8pm, Sa-Su 10:30am-9:30pm. In summer M-W 10:30am-9pm, Th-Sa 10:30am-midnight. Schedule changes daily; check website for details. €15.90, under 7 €12.20.)*

MUSEO CERRALBO. This museum displays the collections of the Marqués de Cerralbo in all their ornate, eclectic, 19th century *fin-de-siècle* glory. Highlights include El Greco's *Ecstasy of St. Francis* in the chapel, collections of battle-scarred European and Japanese arms, a quaint green garden, and a golden ballroom capped by a ceiling fresco of tumbling revelers. *(C. Ventura Rodríguez, 17. ☎915 47 36 46. M: Ventura Rodríguez or Pl. de España. Open Tu-Sa 9:30am-3pm, Su 10am-3pm. €2.40, students €1.20, under 18 and over 65 free. W and Su free.)*

OTHER SIGHTS. The **Parque del Oeste** is a large, sloping park known for the **Rosaleda** (rose garden) at its bottom. A yearly competition determines which rose will be added to the permanent collection. The garden is best viewed in late spring to early summer, when the flowers are at their height. *(M: Moncloa. From the metro, take C. Princesa. Garden open daily 10am-8pm.)* A prime example of Fascist Neoclassicism, the arcaded **Cuartel General del Aire** *(Ejército del Aire;* Air Force Headquarters*)* commands the view on the other side of the Arco de la Victoria (by the Moncloa metro station). The renovation of Felipe V's soldiers' barracks has produced one of Madrid's finest cultural centers, the **Centro Cultural Conde Duque,** which hosts traveling exhibitions and is home to the **Museo Municipal de Arte Contemporáneo.** The museum has an impressive collection—not overly abstract, for those concerned. *(C. Conde Duque, 9. Museo ☎915 88 59 28; www.munimadrid.es/museoartecontemporaneo. M: San Bernardo. Open Tu-Sa 10am-2pm and 6pm-9pm, Su 10:30am-2:30pm. Free.)* Suspended like a UFO 92m above the Plaza de Moncloa, the 1992 **Faro de Moncloa,** built in 1992, is an observation tower near the Museo de América offering vast views, on a good day, clear to El Escorial. *(Av. de los Reyes Católicos. From the Moncloa stop, head towards the Arco de la Victoria. There is a pedestrian path across the busy street. ☎915 44 81 04. Open Tu-Su 10am-2pm and 5-9pm. €1, over 65 and under 10 €0.50.)*

MADRID

FIT FOR A FOREIGNER

The T-shirts that read something like "Spanish Workout: Siesta, Fiesta, Sex," are not too far off. While Let's Go heartily endorses all of the above activities, some tips below for those interested in staying fit in the more "traditional" sense of the word.

1. Parque del Buen Retiro: The only place in Madrid where doing outdoor pull-ups does not guarantee a stare. Test out the jungle gym at the southern tip.

2. masvitalzenter, C. de la Cruz, 28: Exhale like a zen master in a matter of hours. (☎902 10 89 10; www.masvital.org. Yoga and pilates classes €10-20.)

3. Medina Mayrit, C. Atocha, 14: A series of the most indulgent baths you may ever take. Be warned—many locals come with their significant other. (☎902 33 33 34; www.medinamayrit.com. €22.)

4. Excellence, Pza. Del Angel, 6: Will help you shed *peso* in more ways than one. Cyclying classes, lifting, yoga, full spa, and numerous outdoor excursions. (915 23 40 65; www.spaexcellence.es. Day pass €30, monthly €120)

A quick glossary:
footing: jogging
baño turco: steam bath
musculación: weight lifting
body pump: Hahahahaha
ciclo indoor: spinning class
fitball: physio ball

BILBAO

▨ MUSEO SOROLLA. The former residence of the Valencian painter Joaquín Sorolla Bastida (1863-1923) displays his art and that of other late 19th-century painters. The collection also includes centuries of colorful ceramic works.-Sorolla's charming house and garden are as captivating as his work, which includes *Trata de Blancas, Clotilde con Traje de Noche, Mis Hijos,* and *La Siesta. (Po. General Martínez Campos, 37. M: Iglesia or Rubén Darío. ☎913 10 15 84; www.museosorolla.mcu.es. Open Tu-Sa 9:30am-3pm, Su 10am-3pm. Open 9am-11:30pm in the summer. Check dates online. €2.40, students €1.20. Su free.)*

MUSEO LÁZARO GALDIANO. This small palace, once owned by 19th-century financier Lázaro Galdiano, displays a private collection of Italian Renaissance bronzes and Celtic and Visigoth brasses. Paintings include *Young Christ,* a painting unofficially attributed to Leonard da Vinci, and Hieronymus Bosch's *Ecce Homo,* along with the Spanish trifecta: El Greco, Velázquez, and Goya. *(C. Serrano, 122. M: Gregorio Marañón. Turn right off Po. de la Castellana onto C. María de Molina. ☎915 61 60 84; www.flg.es. Open M and W-Su 10am-4:30pm. €4, students €3. W free for EU citizens.)*

🎵 ENTERTAINMENT

Anyone interested in the latest in live entertainment—from music to dance to theater—should stop by the **Círculo de Bellas Artes,** C. Alcalá, 42 (☎913 60 54 00; fax 915 23 28 12) at M: Sevilla or Banco de España. The six-floor building not only houses performance venues and art exhibits, but also is an organizing center for events throughout Madrid; it has current information on virtually all performances. The **Guía del Ocio** is an indispensable guide to all entertainment in the city.

MUSIC

In summer, Madrid sponsors free concerts, ranging from classical and jazz to bolero and salsa, at Pl. Mayor, Lavapiés, Oriente, and Villa de París; check the *Guía del Ocio* for the current schedule. Many night spots also have live music.

The **Auditorio Nacional,** C. Príncipe de Vergara, 146, home to the National Orchestra, features Madrid's best classical performances. (☎913 37 01 40; www.auditorionacional.mcu.es. M: Cruz del Rayo. Tickets €6-100. Box office open M 4-6pm, Tu-F 10am-5pm, Sa 11am-1pm.) **Fundación Joan March,** C. Castelló, 77, hosts summer cultural activities such as a lecture series (usually Tu and Th 7:30pm; free), poetry readings, and free concerts. (☎914 34 42 40; www.march.es. M: Núñez de Balboa. Concerts M, W, Sa; no events June-Oct. Call ahead for details.) **Teatro Monumental,** C. Atocha, 65, is home to Madrid's Symphonic Orchestra. Reinforced concrete—a Spanish invention—was first used in its construction in the 1920s, so be prepared for unusual acoustics. (☎914 29 12 81, tickets 29 12 81. M: Antón Martín. No concerts mid-Apr. to mid-Oct.) For opera and *zarzuela* (light opera native to Madrid), head for the ornate **Teatro de la Zarzuela,** C. Jovellanos, 4. Built in 1856, it was modeled on Milan's La Scala. (☎915 24 54 10; www.teatrodelazarzuela.mcu.es. M: Sevilla or Banco de España. No performances late July to Aug. Box office open daily noon-6pm, or until the beginning of a performance.) The city's principal performance venue is the prestigious **Teatro Real,** Pl. de Oriente, featuring the city's best ballet and opera. (☎915 16 06 06. M: Ópera. Tickets sold M-Sa 10am-1:30pm and 5:30-8pm.) The grand 19th-century **Teatro de la Ópera** is the city's principal venue for classical ballet. Most theaters close in July and August, but many participate in **Veranos en la Villa,** hosting summer events or productions.

FLAMENCO

Flamenco in Madrid is tourist-oriented and expensive, but a few nightlife spots are authentic (see ◼**Cardamomo,** p. 138). **Las Tablas,** Pl. de España, 9 on the corner of C. Bailén and Cuesta San Vicente, has lower prices than most other clubs (€22). Shows start every night at 10:30pm. (☎915 42 05 20; www.lastablas-madrid.com. M: Pl. de España.) **Casa Patas,** C. Cañizares, 10, offers excellent quality for a bit less than usual (*espectáculo* M-Th €25, F-Sa €30), and teaches intensive 4-day scourses in flamenco dance and song for €65. (☎913 69 04 96; www.casapatas.com. M: Antón Martín. Call for reservations. Shows M-Th at 10:30pm, F-Sa at 8pm and midnight.) **Teatro Albéniz,** Po. Pintor Rosales, 11, hosts the *Certamen de Coreografía de Danza Española* (Choreography Competition; 3-4 days in June) with original music and extraordinary flamenco. (☎915 47 69 79; www.certamenflamenco.com. M: Sol.)

FILM

In summer, the city sponsors free movies and plays, often outdoors, all listed in the *Guía del Ocio* and the entertainment supplements of Friday newspapers. During summer months (June-Aug.) watch for the **Fescinal,** (www.fescinal.info) a film festival at the Parque de la Bombilla. From M: Príncipe Pío, turn right and follow the river down Po. de la Florida, off C. de la Florida. Most cinemas show three films per day starting at 10:30pm, on two screens; tickets cost €4.20-7. In mid-November, look for the two-week long **Festival Internacional de Cine Lésbico y Gay de Madrid,** held at venues throughout central Madrid (www.lesgaicinemad.com). Some cinemas offer weekday-only matinee student discounts for €3.90.

In Madrid, Wednesday (or sometimes Monday) is *el día del espectador,* when tickets cost around €4. Show up early as tickets go fast. Check the *versión original (V.O. subtitulada)* listings in the *Guía del Ocio* for English movies subtitled in Spanish. **Princesa,** C. la Princesa, 3 (☎915 41 41 00; www.cinesrenoir.com; €6, weekends €6.20, student matinee €4.50), shows Spanish films and subtitled foreign films. The theater-bar **Golem,** C. Martín de los Héroes, 14 (☎915 59 38 36; www.golem.es; €6, *día del espectador* €3.50), behind Princesa and underneath the patio, shows current alternative foreign and Spanish titles. **Renoir Cuatro Caminos,** C. Raimundo Fernández Villaverde, 10 (☎915 41 41 00; €6, Sa-Su €6.20, student matinee €4.50), shows highly acclaimed films, many foreign and subtitled. Check the *Guía del Ocio* for other cineplexes around the city.

The **Filmoteca Española,** C. de la Magdalena, 10, houses over 70,000 prints of 35,000 titles and a library with more than 25,000 books and periodicals. (☎914 67

26 00; www.mcu.es/cine/mc/fe/index.html. M: Antón Martín. Library open M-F 9:30am-2pm.) The Filmoteca sponsors cheap (€2-2.50) nightly screenings of historic films, rare prints, and art cinema at the nearby **Cine Doré,** C. de Santa Isabel, 3. (☎913 69 11 25. M: Antón Martín. Screenings usually Tu-Su starting at 5:30pm, with the last session usually starting at 11pm.)

THEATER

Huertas, east of Sol, is Madrid's theater district. In July and August, Pl. Mayor, Lavapiés, and Villa de París frequently host outdoor performances. Seeing a play in Madrid is an entertaining way to participate in traditional culture and to improve your Spanish. Tickets range from €3-30; student and senior discounts are often available. Theatergoers should consult the magazines published by state-sponsored theaters, such as **Teatro Español,** C. del Príncipe, 25, in Pl. de Santa Ana (☎913 60 14 80; M: Sol or Sevilla), **Teatro Infanta Isabel,** C. Barquillo, 24 (☎915 19 47 69 or 915 21 02 12; M: Banco de España), and the superb **Teatro María Guerrero,** C. Tamayo y Baus, 4 (☎913 10 15 00; M: Colón or Banco de España). Tickets can be purchased at theater box offices or at ticket agencies. (**El Corte Inglés** ☎902 40 02 22; **FNAC** 915 95 62 00; **Crisol** 902 11 83 12; **TelEntrada** 902 10 12 12; **Entradas.com** 902 48 84 88.)

FÚTBOL

Fútbol (soccer) festivities start hours before matches begin as fans with headphones congregate in the streets, listening to pre-game commentary and discussing it with other die-hard fans. If either **Real Madrid** (in all white) or **Atlético de Madrid** (in red and white stripes) wins a match, count on streets clogged with honking cars. Every Sunday and some Saturdays between September and June, one of these two teams plays at home. Real Madrid plays at **Estadio Santiago Bernabéu,** Av. Cochina Espina, 1. (☎914 57 11 12. M: Santiago Bernabéu.) In the summer, the club offers tours of the stadium. (☎902 29 17 09; www.realmadrid.com. Tours 10:30am-6:30pm. €7-9.) Atlético de Madrid plays at **Estadio Vicente Calderón,** Po. de la Virgen del Puerto, 67. (☎913 64 22 34; www.clubatleticodemadrid.com. M: Pirámides or Marqués de Vadillos.) Tickets cost €22-50 and sell out quickly.

BULLFIGHTS

Some call it animal torture, others tradition; either way, the Plaza de Ventas remains the most important bullfighting arena in the world since its opening in 1931. The ring plays host to the real professionals; you can also catch a summer *Novillado* (beginner), when a younger and less experienced bullfighter takes on smaller bulls. Try to snag a seat in the shade; though they're more expensive, it gets extremely hot in the sunlight.

From early May to early June, the **Fiestas de San Isidro** stage a daily *corrida* (bullfight) with top *matadores* and the fiercest bulls in the largest ring in Spain, **Plaza de las Ventas,** C. Alcalá, 237. (☎913 56 22 00; www.las-ventas.com or www.taquillatoros.com. M: Ventas.) A seat costs €2-115, depending on its location in the *sol* (sun) or *sombra* (shade). Tickets are available, in person only, the Friday and Saturday before and Sunday of a bullfight. Advance tickets recommended for the Fiestas de San Isidro. There are also bullfights every Sunday from March to October and less frequently the rest of the year. Look for posters in bars and cafes for upcoming *corridas* (especially on C. Victoria, off C. San Jerónimo). **Plaza de Toros Palacio de Vistalegre** also hosts bullfights and cultural events. (☎914 22 07 80. M: Vista Alegre. Call ahead for schedule and prices.) To watch amateurs, head to the **Escuela de Tauromaquia,** a bullfighting school which has its own *corridas* on Saturdays at 7:30pm. (☎914 70 19 90. M: Batán. €7, children €3.50. Open M-F 10am-2pm. At the Casa de Campo, Avda. de Portugal Lago.)

FESTIVALS

The city bursts with dancing and processions during **Carnaval** in February, culminating on Ash Wednesday with the beginning of Lent and the *Entierro de la Sardina* (Burial of the Sardine), which commemorates the arrival of a shipload of rotting sardines to Madrid during the reign of Carlos III, who ordered them promptly buried. Goya's painting of these popular feasts and festivals hangs in the **Real Academia de Bellas Artes.** In March, the city gets dramatic for the renowned **International Theater Festival.** The Comunidad de Madrid celebrates its struggle against the French invasion of 1808 during the **Fiestas del 2 de Mayo** with bullfights and concerts. Starting May 15, the week-long **Fiestas de San Isidro** honor Madrid's patron saint with concerts, parades, and Spain's best bullfights. In the last week of June or the first week of July, Madrid goes mad with **⊠Orgullo Gay** (Gay Pride). Outrageous floats filled with drag queens, muscle boys, and rambunctious lesbians shut down traffic between El Retiro and Puerta del Sol on the festival's first Saturday. Free concerts in Pl. Chueca and bar crawls among the congested streets of Chueca are popular weekend activities. Throughout the summer, the city sponsors the **Veranos de la Villa.** Movies play nightly at 10:30pm in **Parque de la Bombilla,** Av. de Valladolid. (M: Príncipe Pío; June 29-Sept. 3. Ticket office opens 9:30pm. €5, students €4.50; schedule at tourist office.) The **Festivales de Otoño** (Autumn Festivals), from September to November, offer more refined music, theater, and film events. In November, an **International Jazz Festival** entices great musicians to Madrid. On New Year's Eve, **El Fin del Año,** crowds gather at Puerta del Sol to countdown to the new year. The brochure *Madrid en Fiestas,* available at tourist offices, contains comprehensive details on Spain's festivals.

⌐ SHOPPING

For upscale shopping, throw on your oversized Gucci sunglasses and sashay down the swanky **Calle Serrano** and **Calle Velázquez** in the famous **Salamanca** district (near Pl. de Colón), where fine boutiques and specialty stores like Pedro del Hierro line the streets next to Mango, Hoss, Armani, and the like. Most major department stores can be found between Puerta del Sol and Callao, with smaller clothing stores scattered along Gran Vía. **El Corte Inglés,** Spain's unavoidable all-in-one store, sports over 10 locations throughout the city. (www.corteingles.es. Some convenient locations include: C. Preciados, 3. ☎913 79 80 00. M: Sol. C. Goya, 76. ☎914 32 93 00. M: Goya. C. Princesa, 56 ☎ 914 54 60 00. M: Argüelles. Open daily 10am-10pm. AmEx/MC/V.) Countless funky boutiques in **Chueca** display hot clubwear, tight jeans, and sexy street clothes. **Mercado Fuencarral,** C. Fuencarral, 45, specializes in funky attire and is home to many tattoo and piercing parlors. (☎915 21 41 52; www.mdf.es. Open M-Sa 11am-9pm.) By law, *grandes almacenes* (department stores) may open only the first Sunday of every month to allow smaller businesses to compete. Many boutiques close in August, when almost everyone flees to the coast. Non-EU residents can shop tax-free at major stores, as long as they remember to ask for their VAT return form and spend more than €100. (☎900 43 54 82 for more info. Don't forget to bring your passport.) The municipal tourist office has the *Rutas de Compras en Areas y Centros Comerciales de la Comunidad de Madrid,* a map with shopping routes.

⊠ EL RASTRO (FLEA MARKET)

For hundreds of years, *El Rastro* has been a Sunday-morning tradition in Madrid. The market begins in La Latina at Pl. Cascorro off C. Toledo and ends at the bottom of C. Ribera de Cortidores. *El Rastro* sells everything from zebra hides to jeans to antique tools to pet birds. As crazy as the market seems, it is actually thematically organized, and for many, a weekly stop. The main street is a labyrinth of clothing, cheap jewelry, leather goods, incense, and sunglasses, branching out into side streets, each with its own repertoire of vendors and wares. Antique-sellers hawk their unique wares on C. del Prado, and in their own shops in small plazas off C. Ribera de Cortidores. Fantastic collections of old books and LPs are sold in Pl. del Campillo del Mundo at the bottom of C. Carlos Arnides. Be careful not to spend your money all at once, or all at first; there are some great buys here, but there are also some broken Barbie dolls. Whatever price you're thinking (or being offered), it can probably be bargained in half. The flea market is a pickpocket's paradise, so leave your camera behind, bust out the money belt, and turn that backpack into a frontpack. Take a hint from the locals and always keep your hand on your bag while walking. Police are available if you need them (p. 105). Open Sundays and holidays 9am-3pm.

BOOKS

Books in English tend to be outrageously expensive in Spain. If you read Spanish, however, it's worthwhile to buy books here and ship or carry them home; you'll save a good deal of money and have access to a much wider selection. Generally, the **Rastro**, **Paseo del Duque Fernán Nuñez,** at the bottom of El Retiro and just across the Paseo del Prado from the Reina Sofia Museum, and the many little shops in **Huertas,** are great places to find antique and more recent books on the cheap. **Altair,** C. Gaztambide, 31, is a comprehensive travel bookstore, with some excellent travel guides and knowledgeable staff. (M: Moncloa or Argüelles. ☎915 43 53 00. Open M-F 10am-2pm and 4:30-8:30pm, Sa 10:30am-2:30pm and 4:30-8pm. AmEx/MC/V.) The **Berkana Librería Gay y Lesbiana,** C. Hortaleza, 64, is a gay and lesbian bookstore with loads of contact info and a free map of the gay Madrid. (M: Chueca. ☎/fax 915 22 55 99.)

▣ NIGHTLIFE

We might as well entitle this section "Life." Nightlife, especially in the summer months, is a Madrid staple, and an activity as standard as your free hostel breakfast. Make sure to get a good *siesta* in if you plan on going out—you'll be out from sunset to sunrise. Partygoers start to the hit the streets around 11pm, when streets, plazas and squares begin to pulse with an intoxicating mix of music, alcohol, and youthful energy. Both gay and straight bar- and club-hoppers will be overwhelmed by their countless options. Proud of their nocturnal offerings, *madrileños* will tell you with a straight face that they were bored in Paris or New York—they insist that no one goes to bed until they've "killed the night" and, in most cases, a good part of the following morning.

A successful night involves several neighborhoods and countless venues; half the party is the hunt. A typical evening might start in the tapas bars of Huertas, move to a discoteca in Malasaña, and then crash the wild parties of Chueca. While bars open their doors around dinner, most clubs and discotecas don't start raging until 1 or 2am; still others don't even bother opening until the real diehards arrive, at 6am. The only (relatively) quiet nights of the week are Monday and Tuesday. For clubs and discotecas, *entrada* (cover) often includes a drink and can be as high as €18; men may be charged up to €3 more than women, who may not be charged at all. Venues often change prices depending on the night; Saturdays are the most expensive. Keep an eye out for *invitaciones* and *oferta* cards—in stores, restaurants, tourist publications, and on the street—that offer a free *chupita* (shot) to lure you in the door.

NIGHT READING. For info on the latest hotspots, scan Madrid's entertainment guides. The **Guía del Ocio,** available behind the counter of any news kiosk, should be your first purchase in Madrid (€1). Although it's in Spanish, alphabetical listings of clubs and restaurants are invaluable even to non-speakers. The *Guía* comes out on Fridays; be sure you're buying the latest issue. For an English magazine with articles on new finds in and around the city, pick up **In Madrid,** free at tourist offices and many restaurants. For articles as well as listings, do what the cool *madrileños* do and check out **Salir Salir Madrid** (€1.80) at any kiosk. Gay travelers can pick up the free magazine **Shanguide,** which lists activities and nightspots, or buy **Zero** magazine at any kiosk (€4).

Walking home alone is clearly not as safe as walking with company, but if you must walk solo, avoid unlit areas like El Retiro, Salamanca, and some of the seedier metro stops around Sol, La Latina, and Lavapiés. Check a bus map for the best **Búho** (p. 102) home from Pl. de Cibeles. Alternatively, taxis are a safe ride home.

EL CENTRO

In the middle of Madrid and at the heart of the action are the spectacular clubs of El Centro. With multiple floors, swinging lights, cages, and disco balls, they meet even the wildest clubber's expectations. Some of the most happening tapas bars in town huddle southwest of Pl. Mayor, closer to M: Latina.

Taberna Vinoçola Mentridana, C. San Eugenio, 9 (☎915 27 87 60) M: Antón Martín. One block from the metro off C. Atocha. This bar's quiet facade hides the energy and amiability inside. Apopular local tapas bar during the day, at night this place revs up with locals thirsty for a glass of wine (€2.50-7). The crowd is sophisticated and somewhat philosophical, so don't forget a thinking cap to top off your nightcap. MC/V.

Palacio Gaviria, C. de Arenal, 9 (☎915 26 60 69; www.palaciogaviria.com). M: Sol or Ópera. Party like royalty in 3 regally decorated ballrooms—don't spill your Red Bull and vodka on the high art all over the walls. Cover €15, includes 1 drink. Mixed drinks €10. Open Tu-W and Su 11pm-3:30am, Th 10:30pm-4:30am, F-Sa 11pm-6am.

Do Los Letras Restaurante, C. Gran Vía, 11 (☎915 23 79 80; www.hoteldelasletras.com). Situated right on the border between El Centro, Chueca, and Gran Vía, this beautiful terrace atop the hotel of the same name is a great place to start the night. Drinks are on the pricey side, but the view's impressive. Open Su-Th 7:30pm-midnight, Fri-Sa 7:30pm-12:30am. MC/V.

La Turuleta Tapas Restaurante, C. Almendro, 25 (☎913 64 26 66). Amid quaint traditional bars, Turuleta's sleek, modern interior attracts a sophisticated crowd. Wine €2.50-5. Mixed drinks €4.50. Open daily 1pm-2am. MC/V.

LA LATINA AND LAVAPIÉS

The diverse and up-and-coming haunts on C. Argumosa (M: Lavapiés) along C. Almendro and C. Cava Baja, are laid-back, but can be much more pleasant and authentically Spanish than El Centro's massive clubs.

La Casa de los Jacintos, C. Arganzuela, 11 (www.lacasadelosjacintos.net). M: La Latina or Puerta de Toledo. More an art gallery than a cafe, this intimate venue hosts workshops, performances, music, and flamenco shows on the cheap. F (9:30pm-midnight) and improv night on Th (10:30pm-midnight). Performances, movies, and mojitos (€3). Check out the drawing, dance, improv, and yoga as well. Open M-Su. Check website for schedule.

Tapasentao, C. Almendro, 27 (☎913 64 07 21). M: La Latina. Right by the Iglesia de San Andrés, this restaurant-bar floods with locals looking to feast on tapas and *tosta-*

MADRID

das (€2.50-12) in a quintessential European café scene. Shots €2.50. Mixed drinks €3. Open Tu 8:30pm-midnight, W-Th 1:30-4pm and 8:30pm-midnight, F 1:30-4pm and 8:30pm-1am, Sa 1:30pm-1am, Su 1pm-midnight.

HUERTAS

Plaza de Santa Ana brims with *terrazas*, bars, and jazz cafes. Many bars convert to clubs as night unfolds, spinning house and techno on intimate dance floors. With its variety of styles, Huertas is one of the best places to party. C. del Príncipe is lined with smaller spots, but check out the discotecas on C. de Atocha. Most locals begin their nights in Huertas and end them in El Centro or Chueca.

▨ **Cuevas de Sésamo,** C. del Príncipe, 7 (☎914 29 65 24). M: Antón Martín. "Descend into these caves like Dante!" (Antonio Machado) is one of the many colorful literary tidbits that welcome you to this smoky, underground gem. Cheap pitchers of sangria (small €6.50, large €10) and live jazz piano draw hipsters of all ages. Chill atmosphere and room for large groups. Open daily 7pm-2am.

▨ **Cardamomo,** C. de Echegaray, 15 (☎913 69 07 57; www.cardamomo.net). M: Sevilla. Flamenco and Latin music spin all night. Those who prefer to relax retreat to the lounge area. Live music at midnight on W nights brings out a crowd for some intoxicating dancing. Beer €4. Open daily 9pm-3:30am.

▨ **Teatro Kapital,** C. de Atocha, 125 (☎914 20 29 06). M: Atocha. 7 fl. of discoteca insanity. From hip-hop to house, open *terrazas* to cinemas, it is easy to lose yourself—and empty your wallet—in the madness. Drinks €12. Cover €12-18 includes 1 drink. Open Th-Su midnight-6am.

The Penthouse, Pl. Santa Ana, 14 (☎917 01 60 20). M: Antón Martín or Sol. Directly across the lively Plaza Santa Ana from the Teatro Español, the Penthouse is a swanky local hangout for late 20s-early 30-somethings. The bar sits atop a fancy hotel and looks over the Plaza for a spectacular bird's eye view of the city's night owls. The line can be long, so try to arrive early. Drinks €10-13. Open daily from 9pm-3am. MC/V.

La Creación, C. Núñez de Arce, 14 (☎915 32 87 05). M: Antón Martín, Sevilla, or Sol. Patrons come to this hip little joint for the cider, dished out from the bar in bottles (€4) and by the glass (€1.50). Classic jazz and people-watching just off Pl. de Santa Ana complement other popular activities, like pouring cider from impressive heights. Fresh fruit tapas in summer. Open M-Th and Su 7pm-1:30am, F-Sa 7pm-2:30am.

Viva Madrid, C. Manuel Fernández González, 7 (☎914 29 36 40), off C. Echegaray. M: Sol or Sevilla. *"Lo mejor del mundo"* (the best in the world) is the humble motto of this daytime cafe/nighttime spot. Locals come for the mojitos and *caipirinhas*. Mixed drinks €8. Open daily 1pm-2am.

Café Jazz Populart, C. Huertas, 22 (☎914 29 84 07; www.populart.es). M: Sevilla or Antón Martín. This intimate, smoke-filled scene hosts local and foreign talent in a relaxed environment. Live jazz, blues, and reggae add a dynamic nighttime note. Shows daily 11pm and 12:30am. No cover. Open daily 6pm-3am.

Café Central, Pl. de Ángel, 10 (☎913 69 41 43; www.cafecentralmadrid.com), off Pl. de Santa Ana. M: Antón Martín or Sol. Art Deco meets Old World cafe in one of Europe's top jazz venues. More formal than Populart. Shows nightly. Beer €2.30. Cover €8-15, cheapest on M. Open M-Th and Su 1:30pm-2:30am, F-Sa 2:30pm-3:30am.

El Café de Schérezad, C. Santa Maria, 18 (☎ 913 69 24 74). M: Antón Martín. Lounge with hookah smoke and Moroccan music. Bangled waitresses serve delicious herbal teas with fresh fruit and small pastries. Tea and hookah €9. Open daily 6pm-3am.

GRAN VÍA

Drum and bass beats pound well into the early morning in the boisterous landmark clubs on the neon-lit side streets of Gran Vía. Subtlety has never been a strong suit of this area, nor is it known for its safety; a mix of seedy tourists and locals makes Gran Vía less than ideal for late-night wandering.

■ **Ocho y Medio Club,** C. Mesonero Romanos, 13 (☎915 41 35 00; www.tripfamily.com). Where the cool kids go for their late-night discoteca fix; the line will probably be long, but the wait is worth it. Local hipsters dance to electronica remixes of their favorite tunes. Each F offers a new DJ or live performance. Sa is Dark Hole, a gothic extravaganza. Check the website for schedule. Drinks €7. Cover €8 includes 1 drink. Open F-Sa 1-6am.

Del Diego, C. de la Reina, 12 (☎915 23 31 06). M: Gran Vía. A classy refuge for the post-work crowd. Frosted glass windows hide a modern bar. Beer €4. Mixed drinks €8. Open M-Sa 7pm-3am. Closed Aug.

MALASAÑA AND CHUECA

By sunset, **Plaza Chueca** and **Plaza Dos de Mayo** are social meccas—places to hang out, meet your friends, and to start, or continue, generous amounts of libation. As you branch out along the smaller radiating streets, the bars appear less frequently. Many partyers eventually migrate away, but the area vibrates deep into *la madrugada* (dawn). Beyond the plazas, most nightlife consists of classy cafes, cruise-y bars, and shady clubs. Much of the dance music is saccharine techno-pop, but rock 'n' rollers and jazz mavens can find their niches too. Though Chueca is largely gay, its establishments are often quite mixed.

The area is ideal for bar-hopping until 2 or 3am, when it's time to hit the clubs near Sol, El Centro, and Gran Vía. A more economical evening might start out with a *"mini"* of sangria (1 liter; €4.50), *Calimotxo* (red wine mixed with cola; €3), or beer (€3.50) from **Bar Nike,** C. de Augusto Figueroa, one street below Pl. Chueca. (Open daily 7am-2:30am.)

■ **La Ida,** C. Colón, 11 (☎915 22 91 07), a few blocks from Pl. Chueca, towards Malasaña. This colorful bar is full of a young and local crowd; birthday cake is as normal here as a mixed drink, and the friendly bartenders and smiling patrons make you feel right at home. Mojitos €6. Open daily 1pm-2am. MC/V.

■ **Acuarela,** C. de Gravina, 10 (☎915 22 21 43). M: Chueca. A welcome alternative to the club scene. Candles surround cushy antique furniture, and conversation flows with the coffee, teas (€1.80-4.50), and liquor (€3.20-5). Open daily 11pm-2am.

El Clandestino, C. del Barquillo, 34 (☎915 21 55 63). M: Chueca. A chill 20-something crowd drinks and debates at the bar upstairs, then heads down to the caves to nod and dance to the DJ's acid jazz, fusion, and funk selections. Beer €3. Mixed drinks €6. Live music most Th-Sa at 11:30pm. Open M-Sa 6:30pm-3am.

El Truco, C. de Gravina, 10 (☎915 32 89 21). M: Chueca. Watch the fogged-up windows from Pl. Chueca for misty shadows of people dancing inside. This gay- and lesbian-friendly bar blasts pop far into the night. The line gets very long and the club gets very packed; luckily, there is some outdoor seating, which also helps avoid the €1 cover. Same owners also run the popular **Escape,** also on the plaza. Open Th 10pm-late, F-Sa midnight-late.

Tupperware, Corredera Alta de San Pablo, 26 (☎925 52 35 61; http://plan-x.tupperware-club.com). M: Tribunal. Where latte sippers go for liquor. The music and the crowd are just as funky as the colorful cartoons on the walls. The mural of hipsters on the wall mirrors the local crowd; soul patches and horizontal stripes galore. DJ plays a great mix of rock and pop favorites from all ages. Mixed drinks €4.50-5. Open daily 9pm-3am.

Vía Láctea, C. de Velarde, 18 (☎914 46 75 81). M: Tribunal. Dive into the Brit punk rock scene nightly 9-11pm, when soft drinks and beer on tap are €2-3.50 each. After midnight, a late 20s crowd gets groovy between the pink walls. The loudspeakers can be deafening. Th offers funk and *afrodisia*, an event with 3 DJs spinning new mixes. Open M-Th 9pm-2:45am, F-Su 9pm-3:15am.

Mama Inés, C. de Hortaleza, 22 (☎915 23 23 33; www.mamaines.com). M: Chueca. Chic cafe-bar with perfect diva lighting. Great for drinks and conversation. Good desserts (€3-4), light meals (€5-8), and teas (€1.60). Food is €0.50-2 more after 10pm. Open daily 10pm-2am.

Why Not?, C. de San Bartolomé, 7. M: Chueca. When in doubt, people flock to Why Not? Small, well-air-conditioned downstairs bar gets packed almost every night starting at 2am with a wild crowd dancing to salsa. Beer €4. Mixed drinks €8. Cover €8 when crowded, includes 1 drink. Open daily 11:30pm-6am. The same owners manage **Polana,** C. de Barbieri, 8-10 (☎915 32 33 05), which gets going around 2:30am, blasting campy Spanish pop music for a mixed crowd. Open daily 10pm-5am.

ARGÜELLES AND MONCLOA

The only reason to leave Madrid's better nighttime areas for Moncloa is **Los Bajos,** a concrete megaplex of diminutive bars serving incredibly cheap *chupitos* (shots €1). The bars tend toward the grimy, and are overpacked with students with raging hormones. Bars are usually only open Fridays and Saturdays and close around 2-3am. From M: Moncloa, align yourself with the center of the imposing Ejército del Aire building on C. de la Princesa and cross the street under the double archway. Walk one block up C. de Hilarion Eslava and turn left onto C. de Fernando el Católico. Los Bajos is a few blocks down on the left.

Clamores Jazz Club, C. Albuquerque, 14 (☎914 45 79 38; www.salaclamores.com), off C. Cardenal Cisneros. M: Bilbao. Swanky neon setting and interesting jazz. The cover (€5-12) is added to the bill if you're there for the music (daily starting around 10pm), though Mondays are usually free to get in. Check posters outside and arrive early for a seat. See website for schedule. Open in summer M-Th and Su 6:30pm-3am, F-Sa 6pm-4am; in winter M-Th and Su 7:30pm-1:30am, F-Sa 7:30pm-3am.

La Musa, C. Manuela Malasaña, 18 (☎914 48 75 78). Hip, chain restaurant-bar made hipper by a funky collection of shadowbox artwork. An older crowd comes here for tapas after work. Wine €2.50 per glass. Open daily 1:30-5pm and 9pm-midnight.

⚑ DAYTRIPS FROM MADRID

SAN LORENZO DE EL ESCORIAL ☎918

El Escorial—half monastery and half mausoleum—is the most popular daytrip from Madrid. Although Felipe II constructed El Escorial primarily for himself and God, the complex, with its magnificent library, palaces, and works of art, seems made for tourists. Visits are popular during the *Fiestas de San Lorenzo* (Aug. 10-20), when parades line the streets and fireworks fill the sky, and on *Romería a la Ermita de la Virgen de Gracia*, the second Sunday in September, when folk dancing contests fill the forests. The whole town shuts down on Mondays.

▣ ⚑ TRANSPORTATION AND PRACTICAL INFORMATION

El Escorial's **train station** (☎918 90 00 15), on Ctra. Estación, is 2km outside of town. Trains run to Atocha and Chamartín stations in Madrid (1hr.; 30 per day M-F and Su 5:47am-10:15pm, Sa 19 per day 5:47am-10:15pm; €2.70). **Autocares Herranz buses**

(☎918 96 90 28) run from Madrid's Moncloa metro station (bus #661, in the bus interchange just above the metro platform; 50min.; every 10-30min. M-F 6:15am-10pm, Sa 8am-8pm, Su 8am-10pm; €3.20) and back (every 15min. M-F 7:15am-10pm, Sa 9am-9:30pm, Su 9am-11pm; €3.20). Shuttles go between the bus and train stations (M-F every 15-20min. 7:23am-10:38pm, Sa-Su every 20min.-1hr. 9:44am-10:38pm; €1.05).

The **tourist office** is located beneath a huge arch near the monastery at C. Grimaldi, 2. (☎918 90 53 13; www.sanlorenzoturismo.org. Open M-F 10am-6pm, Sa-Su 10am-7pm.) With your back to the bus station, turn right down C. Juan de Toledo, then make a right onto C. Floridablanca. Follow C. Floridablanca until the first archway on the left. From the train station, take the shuttle to the bus station or exit the train station, walk straight ahead, and follow the signs uphill (25min.). For a more peaceful walk, exit the train station and enter the Casita del Príncipe main entrance directly in front of you. Start walking uphill and take the C. de los Tilos path, which leads to the monastery (25min.). The **police** are at Pl. de la Constitución, 3 (☎918 90 52 23). On this street there are many 24hr. **ATMs**. There is a **pharmacy** on C. Floridablanca, 16 (☎918 90 15 18).

🛏🍴 ACCOMMODATIONS AND FOOD

Because of its proximity to Madrid, El Escorial makes an easy daytrip. For those wishing to stay the night, **Hostal Cristina ❺**, C. Juan de Toledo, 6, on the same street as the bus station, fits the bill with private bath, TV, and phone. With your back to the station, turn right and walk 100m. (☎918 90 19 61; www.lanzadera.com/hcristina. July-Aug. doubles €51. MC/V.) To reach **Albergue Juvenil El Escorial (HI) ❶**, C. Residencia, 14, from C. del Rey, turn right onto C. de las Pozas, left onto C. Claudio Coello, right onto Po. Unamuno, then right onto C. Residencia. It's a steep uphill climb the whole way, but the price is unbeatable. All dorm rooms have attached bath. (☎918 90 59 24; fax 90 06 20. HI card required. Laundry €2. Reserve at least 2 weeks ahead. Closed Sept. Dorms with breakfast €8.50, with dinner €11.50, with 3 meals €14; over 26 €12/15.50/18.50. Cash only.) **Mercado San Lorenzo**, C. del Rey, 7, is just off the central plaza and sells fruit, meats, and bread. (Open M-Sa 10am-2pm and 5-8pm.)

👁 SIGHTS

EL ESCORIAL

☎918 90 59 03. *Complex open Tu-Su Apr.-Sept. 10am-7pm; Oct.-Mar. 10am-6pm. Last entry to palaces, pantheons, and museums 30min. before closing. Complete*

IN RECENT NEWS

THE UNBURIED DEAD

In July 2006, the Spanish Socialist Workers' Party (PSOE) passed a proposal called the Ley de la Memoria Histórica. The law seeks to excavate new information on the Spanish Civil War (1935-39) and the Franco dictatorship, and supporters have proposed projects as controversial as digging up the mass graves that dot the Spanish landscape.

Most members of the conservartive, right wing, Partido Popular vociferously oppose the law, arguing that the law will only open the "healed" wounds, causing more pain (including, of course, the discomfort of those complicit in the atrocities).

But some Spaniards are getting their hands dirty anyway. Antonio Ontañón, a member of the Association for the Recuperation of Historical Memory, and president of the Asociación Héroes de la República is one example. He has been diligently chipping away at the *Ayuntamiento de Santander* to recover the names of the 850 Republican *desconocidos* (unknowns) who were shot and buried in a common grave (*fosa común*) in Santander between 1937 and 1948. Ontañón's work has allowed families to read the letters their relatives wrote to them as they awaited death. José Manuel Marcano Cobián, who was executed on the 28th of August, 1940, wrote to his family, "*Muero con toda tranquilidad*"—I die with complete tranquility. He was 23.

visit 2hr. Guided tour €9. Spanish tours every 15min.; English times vary. Monastery €7, students and seniors €3.50. Admission to tombs and library €8/4. W free for EU citizens.

MONASTERIO. *El escoria* translates roughly to "scum." Indeed, the regal Escorial (place associated with *escoria*) sits atop a pile of bones and dung that was once a refuse heap. Ironically, the pile of left-overs includes royal bones dating back to Charles V. Felipe II built the **Monasterio de San Lorenzo del Escorial** as a gift to God and his people, and perhaps to alleviate his conscience for sacking a French church at the battle of San Quintín in 1557. He commissioned Juan Bautista de Toledo to design the monastery-mausoleum complex, but Toledo died just four years into the project and the job fell to Juan de Herrera. With the exception of the Panteón Real and minor additions, the monastery was completed in just 21 years. Felipe oversaw the work from a chair-shaped rock, the **Silla de Felipe II**, 7km away.

Considering the resources Felipe II commanded, the building is noteworthy for its symmetry and simplicity. The entire structure is built in a gridiron pattern: four massive towers anchor the corners, and a great dome surmounts the towers of the central basilica. Felipe himself described it as "majesty without ostentation."

GALLERIES AND LIVING QUARTERS. To avoid the worst of the crowds, enter El Escorial through the gateway on C. Floridablanca, where you'll find a collection of Flemish art. Though much of the work is standard religious fare, keep an eye out for some exceptions. In the first room hang lovingly woven replicas of Hieronymus Bosch's paintings; El Greco's *El Martirio de San Mauricio* is nearby. Though these masterpieces and others by Durer, Tintoretto, Titian, Van Dyck, and Zurbarán still adorn the walls, most of the collection is now housed in Madrid's Museo del Prado. The adjacent **Museo de Arquitectura and Pintura** has an exhibition comparing El Escorial's construction to that of other related structures, featuring wooden models of 16th-century machinery and gigantic iron clamps.

Azulejos (tiles) from Toledo line the **Palacio Real,** which includes the **Salón del Trono** (Throne Room) and two dwellings: Felipe II's spartan 16th-century apartments and the more luxurious 18th-century rooms of Carlos III and Carlos IV. As the retreat was only used during religious holidays, Felipe II's rooms were designed so he could listen to and see masses from his own bed. The *Puertas de Marquetería*, German doors inlaid with 18 species of wood, show incredible craftsmanship. The **Sala de Batallas** (Battle Room) links the two parts of the palace with frescoes by Italian artists Grabelo and Castello. The walls and ceiling trumpet first Castilla's and then united Spain's greatest victories—including Juan II's 1431 triumph over the Muslims at Higueruela, Felipe II's successful expeditions in the Azores, and the Battle of San Quintín. Look closer to find comic details of the everyday; bowmen share a laugh during the battle while two peasants look on, passing a wineskin. Maps line the **Salon de Paseo;** the last one on the right portrays the world as (mis)understood by 16th-century Europeans.

LIBRARY. The *biblioteca* on the second floor holds over 40,000 priceless folios and manuscripts. Though several fires have reduced the collection, the extant volumes—some bound as early as 1500—are in remarkably good condition; the bindings, made of scraped hide, can last for hundreds of years. *St. Agustin's De Baptismo*, placed between the 5th and 6th centuries, Alfonso X's *Cantigas de Santa María*, Santa Teresa's manuscripts and diary, the gold-scrolled Aureus Codex of 1039 (by German Emperor Conrad III), and an 11th-century *Commentary on the Apocalypse* by Beato de Liébana are just a sampling of the documents displayed here. Clever allegorical frescoes of the seven fields of knowledge grace the ceiling; note the shriveled hindquarters of the lion that flanks "Rhetoric." Make sure to marvel at the fantastic sphere at the end of the hall.

BASÍLICA. Under the gigantic central dome is the basilica, which for years served as a direct link between the kings and God. Marble steps arrive at an altar adorned by golden sculptures of the royal family, who kneel in perpetual prayer to saints, popes, and Jesus. The *Coro Alto* (High Choir) has a ceiling fresco of heaven. Felipe II's room overlooks Titian's fresco of the martyrdom of San Lorenzo.

PANTHEONS. The impressive—and creepy—**Panteón Real** is filled with the remains of every Spanish king since Charles V (and the lone queen, Isabel II); their stacked green marble tombs are in a circular room. Unlike any other site of royal interment, the pantheon houses over 500 years of monarchial history. The connecting **Pudrería** is where royal bodies are cured for over 25 years in a solution of water and *cal* (limestone) before being interred in the crypt. The Pudrería is currently home to three corpses who are attended to regularly by monks. Out of respect for the dead, tourists are not allowed in. These bodies will fill the three empty tombs that now rest in the *Panteón*. The **Panteón de los Infantes** was built to have space for over 60 children; it is rumored that many illegitimate royal offspring lie within the crypts.

VALLE DE LOS CAÍDOS

The Valle de los Caídos is accessible only via El Escorial. Autocares Herranz runs 1 bus to the monument from C. Juan de Toledo. (☎918 90 41 25 or 96 90 28. 20min.; Tu-Su 3:15pm, returns 5:30pm; round-trip plus admission €8.30.) Mass M-Sa 11am, Su 11am, 12:30, 1, and 5:30pm. Entrance gate open Tu-Su 10am-6pm. €5.30. W free for EU citizens. Funicular to the cross €2.50 round trip, 5min. one way.

In a once-untouched valley 8km north of **El Escorial,** General Franco forced Republican prisoners to build the overpowering monument of Santa Cruz del Valle de los Caídos (Holy Cross of the Valley of the Fallen) as a memorial to those who gave their lives in the Spanish Civil War. As a historical wonder, this site should not be missed—but it also should not be misunderstood. Although ostensibly a monument to both sides, the inscription over the door to the crypt that reads "Caídos por Díos y España" (Fallen for God and Spain) suggests it is more a Nationalist memorial than anything else. The massive granite cross was a mammoth construction project that claimed the lives of at least 14 forced laborers, and decades of the lives of thousands more. To climb to the base of the cross, follow the paved road up to the trailhead just past the monastery on the right (30min.), or take the **funicular.** Apocalyptic tapestries line the vast and austere, cave-like **basílica,** where the ghost of Fascist architecture rests. Muscular warrior monks watch the pews, while gigantic death-angels guard the crucified Jesus. Forty thousand dead Nationalists and many unidentified other soldiers are buried behind the chapel walls; **José Antonio Primo de Rivera** (founder of the Fascist Falange party) and **General Franco** himself rest beside the high altar, underneath the imposing cross with its giant statues. Many tour operators venerate the monument as a testament to the glory of Franco's dictatorship and as a holy site, but for most Spaniards, it persists as a stain on the central Spanish landscape.

COMUNIDAD DE MADRID

The Comunidad de Madrid is an autonomous administrative region smack in the middle of Spain, bordered by Castilla y León to the north and west and Castilla La Mancha to the south and east. Beyond Madrid proper, the Comunidad offers travelers a variety of daytrips to exquisite cultural landscapes and small-town serenity.

ALCALÁ DE HENARES   ☎918

The train station is on Po. de la Estación (☎902 24 02 02). Cercanías trains run to Estación Atocha in Madrid (40min., every 10min. 5:54am-11:26pm, €3). Continental Auto,

Comunidad de Madrid

Av. Guadalajara, 5 (☎*918 88 16 22), runs buses between Alcalá and Madrid (45min.; M-Sa every 15min. 6:10am-11pm, Su every 30min. 7-9am and every 20min. 9am-11pm; €3). To reach the city center from the bus station, turn right onto Paseo de la Estación, then left on C. de Libreros. Taxis can be summoned at* ☎*918 82 21 88.*

The one-time home of Golden Age authors Miguel de Cervantes, Francisco de Quevedo, and Lope de Vega and site of a university dating to 1498, Renaissance Alcalá de Henares (pop. 191,000) is a popular daytrip for travelers seeking to pay homage to Spain's literary greats. The **Plaza de Cervantes,** filled with cafes, rose bushes, and a statue of its namesake, bursts with color in the summertime. At the end of the plaza opposite C. de Libreros lie the **ruinas de Santa María,** the remains of a 16th-century church destroyed during the Spanish Civil War. The **Capilla del Oidor,** where Cervantes was christened, survived. (☎918 79 73 80. Open June-Sept. Tu-Su noon-2pm and 6-9pm; Oct.-May Tu-Su noon-2pm and 5-8pm. Free.) Just before Pl. de Cervantes in Pl. de San Diego, take a left off C. de Libreros onto C. Bedel to see the **Colegio Mayor de San Ildefonso** (☎918 85 64 87). In the **paraninfo** (main hall), where doctorates were once awarded, the king now presents the Premio Cervantes, Spain's most prestigious literary award, during the week-long **Festival de Cervantes.** The *paraninfo* and **Capilla de San Ildefonso** both have spectacular *mudéjar* ceilings. (Mandatory tours in summer M-F 6 per day 11am-2pm and 5-7pm, Sa-Su every 30min. 11am-2pm and 5-7:30pm. €13.) The town's **Cate-dral Magistral,** at the end of C. Mayor in Pl. de los Santos Niños, is one of only two in the world with this title (the other is in Lovaina, Belgium). To be so named, each priest must also be a university professor. (www.catedraldealcala.org. Open M-F 9am-1pm and 5pm-8:30, Sa 9:15-11:30am and 6-8:30pm, Su 10am-1:30pm and 6-8:30pm. Free.) Down C. Mayor from Pl. de Cervantes is the **Casa Natal de Cervantes,** the reconstructed house where the author was born in 1547. The house displays a variety of furniture and editions of *Don Quixote* in languages Cervantes never knew existed. Bronze statues of the delusional knight and his long-suffering squire sit on a bench outside. (☎918 89 96 54; www.museo-casa-natal-cervantes.org. Open Tu-Su 10-6pm. Free.)

Alcalá's famed *almendras garrapiñadas* (honey- and sugar-coated almonds) beg to be sampled. At night, it seems that the whole town comes out to eat on the the *terrazas* on C. Mayor and Pl. de Cervantes. Dinner *menús* can be a bit pricey (€14.50-24), so the tapas that come with your drink at **Rocío Chico ❶,** C. Ramón y Cajal, 3, are a good alternative. (☎918 83 10 75. Drinks €2-3. Open daily 8pm-2am. Cash only.) You can feed two with the fantastically huge *tortilla patata bocadillo* (potato omelette sandwich) for €3.20. **El Gringo Viejo ❸,** C. Ramón y Cajal, 8, offers great Mexican entrees (€6-17) and burgers from €5-6. (☎918 78 89 01. Open M-F 8:30pm-2am, Sa 10pm-1am. MC/V.) The **tourist office,** Pl. de Cervantes, 1, offers a list of local cultural events and has maps and suggestions for accommodations and restaurants. To get there, walk the length of Pl. Cervantes toward the bell tower and turn left down the small street. There is also an office in the Pl. de los Santos Niños. (☎918 89 26 94; www.alcalaturismo.com. Open daily in summer 10am-2pm and 5-7:30pm.)

ARANJUEZ   ☎918

RENFE trains, C. de la Estación (☎902 24 00 42), go to Cuenca (2hr.; M-F 4-5 per day 6:10am-8:14pm, Sa-Su 9:23am-8:14pm; €7.60), Madrid (45min.; to Estación Atocha M-F every 15-30min.; 5:30am-11:30pm, Sa-Su 6am-11:30pm; to Estación Chamartín M-F 8-10 per day 6:57am-9:27pm, Sa-Su 8:57am-9:27pm; €2.75), and Toledo (30min.; M-F 7-10 per day 7:20am-9:12pm, Sa-Su 9:17am-9:12pm; €2.75). AISA, C. de las Infantas, 16 (☎902 190 788, www.alsa-grupo.com) also runs buses to Toledo (8am and 4:15pm, €3, 30min.) and Madrid (45min, every 15min. 5am-midnight, €3.20).

Once a getaway for Habsburg and Bourbon royalty, and recently declared a World Heritage Cultural Landscape by UNESCO, Aranjuez remains a worthwhile retreat thanks to its dazzling gardens and palaces, as well as its famous asparagus and strawberries. Under the direction of Felipe II, the chief architect of the gloomy El Escorial Juan de Herrera designed the resplendent white ▨**Palacio Real** under the direction of Felipe II. Felipe V, Fernando VI, and Carlos III enlarged and embellished the palace, but it was Isabel II who left her mark in the mid-19th century with over-the-top draperies and decor. On your way out, the **Museo de la Vida en Palacio** contains a collection of toys of the royal children. (☎918 91 07 40; www.patrimonionacional.es. Open Apr.-Sept. Tu-Su 10am-6:15pm; Oct.-Mar. Tu-Su 10am-5:15pm. 1-1½hr. tours in English or Spanish approx. every 15min. The 1½hr. tour gives access to 12 extra rooms. €4.50, students €2.50; with guided tour €5, students €3. Museo de la Vida free.) Just outside the palace is a labyrinth of river walkways, freshly trimmed hedges, and mythological statues. The **Jardín del Príncipe,** a short walk from the palace on C. de la Reina, was built for Carlos IV's amusement. (Open daily Apr.-Sept. 8am-8:30pm; Oct.-Mar. 8am-6:30pm. Free.) The **Falúas Museum,** once home to the Tajo's sailing squad, stores royal gondolas. (Open Tu-Su Oct.-Mar. 10am-5:15pm; Apr.-Sept. 10am-6:15pm. €3.40, students and under 16 €1.70. W EU citizens free.) The last weekend in May, when the strawberry harvest reaches its pinnacle, Aranjuez holds parades, concerts, and bullfights.

For a city its size, Aranjuez has a wide variety of choices for accommodations and food. **Hostal Rusiñol ❷**, C. de San Antonio, 76, has bright, open rooms with clean, white beds and TV. Some doubles have A/C. (☎918 91 01 55; www.hostalesaranjuez.com. Singles €22, with bath €38; doubles €40/48. MC/V.) Most dining options around the Palace and gardens cater to tourists and are quite pricey. For cheaper eats, try the indoor **Mercado de Abastos** on Ctra. de Andalucía. With your back to the tourist office, go left through the arch; the market is on the left. (Open M-F 9am-2pm and 6-9pm, Sa 9am-3pm.) Be sure to grab some delicious ▨**fresones con nata** (strawberries and cream) from the vendors just over the small bridge near the main fountain in front of the palace gardens. The 102-year old **El Rana Verde ❸**, C. de la Reina, 1, by the water, specializes in expensive asparagus (€10), *ancas de rana* (frog legs, €10) and small game. (☎918 01 15 71; www.aranjuez.com/ranaverde. Dinner €15-20. Open daily 9am-midnight. AmEx/D/MC/V.)

To get to the city by foot, exit left from the train station parking lot and follow signs to the Palacio Real. With your back to the bus station, head left onto C. de las Infantas toward the main fountain. Alternatively, on the corner outside the palace, climb aboard the **Chiquitren de Aranjuez,** a sightseeing train, to catch all the major sights. (☎918 08 80 89. €4, under 13 €2, not including admission to museums and sights.) The helpful **tourist office** in Pl. San Antonio, 9, stores luggage. (☎918 91 04 27; www.aranjuez.net. Open daily Apr.-Sept. 10am-6pm; Oct.-Mar. 9am-5:30pm.) Services include: **police,** C. de las Infantas, 36 (☎918 09 09 80); **pharmacy,** C. Real, 25, on the corner of C. del Capitán Angosto Gómez Castrillón and C. Real (☎918 91 08 62. Open M-F 9:30am-1:45pm and 5:30-8:30pm, Sa 10am-1:45pm. MC/V). **Internet access** is available at the **Centro de Acceso Público a Internet,** in the Centro Cultural on C. del Gobernador, 81, 2nd fl. (Open M-Sa 9am-3pm. Free.) The **post office** is on C. de Peñarredonda, 3, off C. del Capitán Angosto Gómez Castrillón. (☎918 91 11 32. Open M-F 8:30am-2:30pm, Sa 9:30am-1pm.) **Postal Code:** 28300.

SIERRA DE GUADARRAMA

The Sierra de Guadarrama is a cold, clear, and dry retreat from Madrid's noise and pollution. If Madrid's urbane sophistication has got you down, consider spending an afternoon (or a few days) in the Sierra, a pine-covered mountain range halfway between Madrid and Segovia. With *La Mujer Muerta* (The Dead Woman) to the west, the *Sierra de la Maliciosa* (Mountains of the Evil Woman) to the east, and the less imaginatively named *Siete Picos* (Seven Peaks) along its northern perimeter, the Sierra draws visitors in all seasons to hike and ski.

CERCEDILLA   ☎918

A picturesque chalet town graced with mild summer heat and ample winter snow, Cercedilla (pop. 6,000) is the ideal base for venturing into the Sierra. This unassuming mountain base lures visitors year-round, especially in the summertime, when city-dwellers swelter in nearby Madrid.

▣▨ **TRANSPORTATION AND PRACTICAL INFORMATION.** The **train station** (☎918 52 00 57), at the base of the hill on C. Emilio Serrano, sends trains to: El Escorial (1hr.; M-F and Su 25 per day 5:47am-10:32pm, Sa 17 per day 6:33am-10:32pm; €1.55) via Villalba; Los Cotos (45min.; M-F and Su 8 per day 9:35am-6:35pm, Sa hourly 9:35am-7:35pm except 2:35pm; €3.90) via Puerto de Navacerrada (€3.70); Madrid's Atocha and Chamartín stations (1½hr.; over 20 per day M-F and Su 6:07am-10:35pm, Sa 6:37am-9:35pm; €3.60) via Villalba (30min., €1.55); Segovia (45min., 8-9 per day 7:27am-9:23pm, €2.60). **Larrea** (☎918 52 02 39) sends buses from the bus stop across the street from the *Ayuntamiento* in Plaza Mayor, with a stop by the train station, to Madrid (1-1½hr.; M-F every 20-30min. 5:30am-10:20pm, Sa-Su every 20-30min. 6:20am-10:20pm; €3.40).

Upon arrival in Cercedilla, proceed a few kilometers up the hill to the **Valle de la Fuentría: Centro de Educación Ambiental,** which has **tourist info** and great hiking maps (some in English) and is the starting point for several hikes (**Hiking,** p. 147). To get there from either station, you may want to call a **taxi** (Manolo ☎619 80 64 52; Francisco 650 26 30 43; and Juan 619 226 272; each about €7) or wait for one, though they do not come often. The *centro* is roughly 3km from the train station on **Carretera de las Dehesas,** km 2. By foot (40min.), go straight uphill and bear left at the fork. Local services include the **police** (☎639 35 17 91) and the health center, the **Centro de Salud** (☎918 52 30 31, emergency 52 04 97).

⌂☐ ACCOMMODATIONS AND FOOD. Cercedilla makes an easy daytrip from Madrid and most of the youth hostels in Cercedilla are booked during the summer by camp groups and other organizations. Camping is not allowed, so pack for a day hike. For most *albergues* and *hostales*, reservations should be made at least 15 days in advance. Conveniently located near the trails, **Albergue Juvenil "Las Dehesas" (HI) ❶,** Ctra. de las Dehesas, is a beautiful government-subsidized hostel at the foot of the mountains. Rooms (for two to six people) are bright and clean with shared bath. Guests mingle in the large common spaces and basketball court. (☎918 52 01 35; www.madrid.org/inforjoven. Blankets provided, but not sheets or towels. Open Jan. 2-Aug. 15 and Sept. 21-Dec. 30. HI card required and available for purchase. With breakfast €9.25, with 2 meals €13.25, with 3 meals €14.75; over 26 €12.75/18.25/19.25. Cash only.) **Villa Castora (HI) ❶** is about 1km up Ctra. de las Dehesas on the left, and has rooms with two to four beds and private bath. (☎918 52 03 34; fax 52 24 11. Reception 8am-10pm. Reservations strongly recommended. With breakfast €8.50, with 2 meals €11.50, with 3 meals €14; over 26 €12/15.50/18.50.) **Camping** is strictly controlled throughout the Sierra de Guadarrama and is prohibited in the area surrounding Cercedilla. Since you'll be staying in town, ask the Centro de Educación Ambiental for a list of Cercedilla's restaurants. For groceries, find **Supermarket Gigante,** C. Doctor Cañados, 2, in the town center off Av. del Generalísimo. (☎918 52 23 19. Open M-Sa 9:30am-2pm and 5-9pm, Su 9:30am-2pm.) Convenience stores outside the bus and train stations sell the essentials. Near the train station, the **bar ❶** at Hostal Longino serves large *bocadillos* (€3.60), which can be wrapped for picnics.

⛰ HIKING. The **Valle de la Fuentría: Centro de Educación Ambiental** functions as a **tourist office** and offers hiking information. (☎918 52 22 13. Open daily 10am-6pm. Some English spoken.) The Centro provides detailed maps of six trails and day hikes ranging from the challenging (14.3km, 5-6hr.) **El GR-10** to the more relaxed **▨Camino Puricelli** (4km, 1½hr.), which conveniently leads from the trailhead to the train station. Set aside an afternoon for the orange trail, **Los Miradores** (9.3km, 3hr.), a hike with fantastic views of the valley. Most of the hiking around Cercedilla begins up **Carretera las Dehesas,** near the Centro de Educación Ambiental. At the top of the Carretera, the **Calzada Romana** (about 1.5km from the Centro) offers hiking along a Roman road that connected Madrid to Segovia (1½hr.). Springs marked with a blue dot on the trail map should have potable water, but double check at the Centro. Weather is unpredictable, so bring a rain jacket and sweater. Those who prefer wheels over heels should check out the

MADRID

bike trails. Rentals are rare, but try **Cercedilla Aventura** (☎ 629 60 25 22; www.cercedillaaventura.com). Horses are available at **Hípica La Vaqueriza,** next to Albergue Juvenil "Las Dehesas," uphill from the Consejería. (☎ 637 80 90 35 or 679 44 59 59. Guide and lesson €15 per hour.)

PUERTO DE NAVACERRADA AND LOS COTOS

A year-round magnet for nature-lovers, **Puerto de Navacerrada** offers **skiing** in the winter (late Dec. to early Apr.) and beautiful **hiking** in the summer. Expert skiers will enjoy the challenging bowl trails off **Guarramillas'** ski slope, but there are only four easy trails for beginners. Snowboarders are allowed on five out of eight lifts. (M-F skiers €20, snowboarders €19; Sa-Su skiers €29/€26. On the weekends and holidays, take the Guarramillas Lift up to the top for €3-5.) Those in search of challenging hikes often take the popular **Camino Schmid,** a 7km trail from Navacerrada to **Pradera de los Corralillos;** from there it is another 3km to the Centro in Cercedilla (trail info ☎ 918 52 14 35).

Deporte y Montaña has a main office 1.5km from the train station, next to Residencia Navacerrada on the highway. The business owns and operates most of the lifts in Navacerrada and offers info on many outdoor activities. (Madrid ☎ 915 94 30 34, Navacerrada 918 52 33 02; www.puertonavacerrada.com. Open in winter only 9:30am-4:30pm.) More details can be found at the **Asociación Turística de Estaciones de Esquí y Montaña** (☎ 913 50 20 20) in Madrid. To head for the trails, exit the train station platform, go up the stairs and climb up the dirt path on the hill straight ahead, which will drop you off on the highway next to the ski pass office and the **Residencia Navacerrada ❸,** Ctra. M-601, km 20, a mountainside hotel with a bell tower on its roof. There are two to five beds per room, each with private bath. (☎ 918 52 39 84; fax 52 02 68; residencia.navacerrada@madrid.org. High season €27.20; low season €22.80.) Another housing option is the **Hotel Pasadoiro ❹,** Ctra. M-601, km 20, just across the highway from Residencia Navacerrada. Rooms are a bit pricier here (€35-55), but amenities include breakfast, a gym, a sauna, and a slightly shorter walk to the main lift. (☎ 918 52 14 27; www.pasadoiro.com). From Madrid, **Larrea, S.A.** (☎ 915 30 48 00), runs bus number 691 to Navacerrada and beyond to Valdesquí M-F 7am-10pm, Sa-Su 8am-10pm.

CASTILLA Y LEÓN

Culture and grandeur pervade the province of Castilla y León. Spanish icons like the aqueduct and fairy-tale Alcázar of Segovia, the Gothic cathedrals of Burgos and León, the Romanesque belfries along the Camino de Santiago, the sandstone of Salamanca, and the city walls of Ávila all belong to this ancient region. Well before Fernando of Aragón and Isabel of Castilla were joined in a world-shaking matrimony, Castilla was the political and military powerhouse of Spain. During the High Middle Ages, it emerged from obscurity to lead the Christian charge against Islam. Its nobles, enriched by the spoils of combat, made their success official: *castellano* became the dominant language of the nation. Castilla's comrade in arms, León, though chagrined to be lumped with Castilla in a 1970s provincial reorganization, shares many cultural similarities with its co-province.

HIGHLIGHTS OF CASTILLA Y LEÓN

GUSH over the Roman aqueduct in **Segovia** (p. 153).

LOSE yourself in the medieval library of the **Universidad de Salamanca** (p. 162).

SMILE with the saints on the facade of **León's** stunning cathedral (p. 172).

WIN a golden ticket to the **Museo de Chocolate** in medieval **Astorga** (p. 173).

SEGOVIA   ☎921

Verdant Segovia is most famous for its legendary Roman aqueduct, but the city's modest river and royal gardens are tempting in their own right. Water flows freely along the medieval perimeter and in the lavish fountains distributed throughout. It was here that Columbus charmed the crown into financing his journey to the "New World." Though Segovia is a city of 60,000, you'd hardly notice—stay for a few days and you're sure to recognize a few faces by the end. If you do make it to this "stone ship" (so called because the stone aqueduct resembles a ship's helm), expect to shell out a little more cash; but trust us, Segovia should not be missed.

▐ TRANSPORTATION

Trains: Po. Obispo Quesada (☎902 24 02 02). To **Madrid:** (2hr.; 7-9 per day M-F 5:55am-8:55pm, Sa-Su 8:55am-8:55pm; €5.60) and **Villalba** (1hr., 7-9 per day M-F 5:55am-8:55pm, €3.80). Transfers to **Ávila, El Escorial, León,** and **Salamanca.**

Buses: Estación Municipal de Autobuses, Po. Ezequiel González, 12 (☎921 42 77 07). **Linecar** (☎921 42 77 06) to **Valladolid** (2hr.; M-F 12 per day, Sa 8 per day 6:45am-9pm, Su 6 per day 9am-9pm; €6.72). **La Sepulvedana** (☎921 42 77 07) to: **Ávila** (1hr.; M-Sa 7:45am, 6pm; €4.42); **La Granja** (20min.; 9-15 per day M-Sa 7:40am-9:30pm, Su 10:30am-10:30pm; round-trip €2.42); **Madrid** (1½hr.; every 30min. M-F 6:30am-10:30pm, Sa 8am-10:30pm, Su hourly 8am-10:30pm; €6.26); **Salamanca** (3hr.; M-F 7:45am, 2pm, Sa-Su 9am, 7pm; €9.27).

Public Transportation: Transportes Urbanos de Segovia, C. Juan Bravo, in the Centro Comercial Almuzara (☎921 46 27 27). €0.73; discounted electronic passes available.

Taxis: Radio Taxi (24hr. ☎921 44 50 00). Taxis pull up by the train and bus stations. Stands in the Pl. Mayor and just beyond the Pl. Azoguejo.

Castilla y León

CANTABRIAN SEA

✦ 🛈 ORIENTATION AND PRACTICAL INFORMATION

Take bus #8 from the train station to **Acueducto,** which drops off near **Plaza del Azoguejo** and the **municipal tourist office,** which is just downhill, along **Calle Real** (the main route from the Aqueduct to the Pl. Mayor, composed of C. Cervantes, C. Juan Bravo, and C. Isabel la Católica) from **Plaza Mayor,** the city's historic center (M-F every 15-30min. 7:25am-10:03pm, Sa every 30-45min. 8:18am-10pm, Su every 30min. 8:50am-10pm). On foot from the **train station** (30min.), turn right, cross the street, and walk toward town along Po. Obispo Quesada, which becomes Av. Conde de Sepúlveda and then Po. Ezequiel González, before coming to the **bus station.** From there, (15min.) cross Po. Ezequiel González and follow Av. de Fernández Ladreda to Pl. del Azoguejo, or take bus #4 to the aqueduct.

Tourist Office: Regional office, Pl. Mayor, 10 (☎921 46 03 34). Open July-Sept. 15 M-Th and Su 9am-8pm, F-Sa 9am-9pm; Sept. 16-June 9am-2pm and 5-8pm. **Municipal office (Centro de Recepción de Visitantes),** Pl. del Azoguejo, 1 (☎921 46 67 20; fax 46 67 24). Open daily in summer 10am-8pm; in winter 10am-7pm.

Currency Exchange: Banco Santander Central Hispano, Av. de Fernández Ladreda, 12. Open Apr.-Sept. M-F 8:30am-2pm; Oct.-Mar. M-F 8:30am-2pm, Sa 8:30am-1pm. **ATMs** and other banks, which also exchange cash, line Av. de Fernández Ladreda.

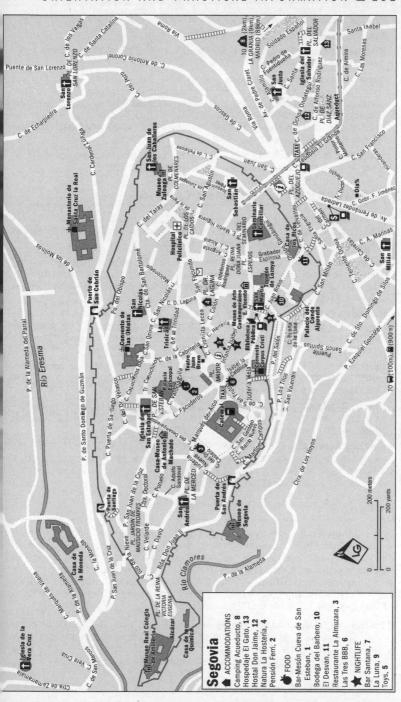

CASTILLA Y LEÓN

Segovia

▲ ACCOMMODATIONS
Camping Acueducto, 8
Hospedaje El Gato, 13
Hostal Don Jaime, 12
Natura La Hostería, 4
Pensión Ferri, 2

🍴 FOOD
Bar-Mesón Cueva de San
Esteban, 1
Bodega del Barbero, 10
El Desván, 11
Restaurante La Almuzara, 3
Las Tres BBB, 6

★ NIGHTLIFE
Bar Santana, 7
La Luna, 9
Toys, 5

Luggage Storage: Lockers at the **train station** (€3 per day). Open daily 6am-10:30pm.

Police: C. Guadarrama, 24 (☎921 43 12 12).

Hospital: Policlínico San Agustín, C. San Agustín, 13 (☎921 46 03 88 or for emergencies 921 41 91 00).

Internet Access: Biblioteca Pública, C. Juan Bravo, 11 (☎ 921 46 35 33). Free and fast. Max. 30min. Passport required. Open July-Aug. M-F 9am-3pm, Sa 9am-2pm; Sept.-June M-F 9am-9pm, Sa 9am-2pm. **Cyber Graphika Internet,** Av. de Fernández Ladreda, 12, 1st fl. (☎921 46 09 66). €1.50 per hr. Open daily 11am-2:30pm and 4:30-10pm. **Locutorio Mundo 2000,** Pl. del Azoguejo, 4 (☎921 44 17 09). €0.90 per 30min. Open daily 11am-11pm.

Post Office: Pl. Dr. Laguna, 5 (☎921 46 16 16), up C. Cronista Lecea from Pl. Mayor. Open M-F 8:30am-8:30pm, Sa 9:30am-2pm. **Postal Code:** 40001.

♠♥ ACCOMMODATIONS AND CAMPING

Segovia's numerous sights and its proximity to Madrid and La Granja make rooms scarce during the summer. Reservations are a must for any hotels in or around major plazas. *Pensiones* are significantly cheaper.

Natura La Hosteria, C. Colón, 5 and 7 (☎921 46 67 10; www.naturadesegovia.com), outside the Pl. Mayor. Rooms are big and beautiful, though they cost a few extra euro. Free Wi-Fi. Prices according to season and time of week–call ahead. Singles €35-40; doubles €70-80. MC/V. ❸

Hospedaje El Gato, Pl. del Salvador, 10 (☎921 42 32 44; fax 43 80 47). Follow the aqueduct uphill to modern rooms with comfortable wooden beds. The bar downstairs fills with locals day and night. All rooms have A/C, satellite TV, and private bath. Singles €23; doubles €38; triples €52. MC/V. ❷

Pensión Ferri, C. Escuderos, 10 (☎921 46 09 57), off Pl. Mayor. Cute cottage-style rooms, some with garden views. Lots of potted plants. Unbeatable central location and hospitality. Shower €2. Singles €18; doubles €25. Cash only. ❷

Hostal "Don Jaime", C. Ochoa Ondátegui, 8 (☎921 44 47 87; hostaldonjaime@hotmail.com). Unbeatable hospitality and location just behind the aqueduct. Some rooms have bath for a higher price. Singles €35; doubles €50. MC/V. ❸

Camping Acueducto, C. Borbón, 49/Highway CN-601, km 112 (☎921 42 50 00; www.campingacueducto.com), 2km toward La Granja. Restaurant, supermarket, showers, pool, and laundry. July-Aug. and *Semana Santa* €5 per person, per tent, and per car; Apr.-June and Sept. €4.50. MC/V. ❶

◖ FOOD

To avoid tourist traps, steer clear of Pl. Mayor, Pl. del Azoguejo, and any menus posted on "parchment." *Sopa castellana* (soup with eggs and garlic), *cochinillo asado* (roast suckling pig), *ponche* (egg-yolk pastry), and lamb are all regional specialties. A **market** comes to Pl. Mayor on Thursdays and next to Av. de la Constitución on Saturdays (9am-2:30pm). Buy groceries at **Día%,** C. Gobernador Fernández Jiménez, 3, off Av. de Fernández Ladreda. (Open M-Th 9:30am-2pm and 5:30-8:30pm, F-Sa 9am-9pm.)

▨ **Restaurante La Almuzara,** C. Marqués del Arco, 3 (☎921 46 06 22), past the cathedral. Scrumptious vegetarian cuisine in an intimate setting with nature frescoes. Large portions. Try one of the soups or "creams" (€6.50-9). Salads €4-10.50. Lunch *menú* €10. Open Tu 8-11:30pm, W-Su 12:45-4pm and 8-11:30pm. MC/V. ❷

La Bodega del Barbero, C. Alhóndiga, 2. (☎921 46 27 70), just off C. Juan Bravo. An easy-to-miss terrace that makes a perfect mid-day break from the sights. Technically a "vinoteca" (winery) with tastings and exhibitions, the bodega also keeps an inventive kitchen year-round. Mouth-watering salads €5.80-8.80 and lunch *menú* €10. Open Tu 11am-3:30pm, W-Su 11am-3:30pm and 7:30-11:30pm. MC/V. ❷

Bar-Mesón Cueva de San Esteban, C. Valdeláguila, 15 (☎921 46 09 82). The owner knows his wines (he's still celebrating his 2002 victory in the national "nose of gold" competition), and his food is excellent as well. *Menú* M-F €9, Sa-Su €10. Entrees €7-18. Open daily 11am-midnight. MC/V. ❸

Las Tres BBB, Pl. Mayor, 13 (☎921 46 21 25). Follow locals here for cheap eats. Specializes in seafood (€2.40-10), but also offers simple *bocadillos* (€2.10-3.20). Lunch *menú* €9. Kitchen open daily 1-4pm and 8-11pm. Bar open 8am-1:30am. MC/V. ❶

El Desvan, C. Juan Bravo, 58 (☎921 46 27 41). Cheap and good. *Revuelta de la Casa* (scrambled eggs with ham, pepper, onion, and cheese) for €5.50. Beer €1.50. Open M-F 9am-11:30pm, Sa 9am-12:30pm, Su 11am-11:30pm. MC/V. ❶

👁 SIGHTS

Segovia rewards the wanderer, so put away the guidebook for the day and explore the city's alleys, museums, churches, and gardens *al gusto.* Often overlooked by visitors are Segovia's northern areas, outside the walls and away from the Alcázar. For a relaxing walk or invigorating run, head downhill from the palace, cross the modest highway, and tour the monasteries and churches along the Río Eresma.

🪨 AQUEDUCT. The Romans built Segovia's aqueduct with 20,000 blocks of granite and not a drop of mortar around 50 BC to pipe in water from the Río Frío, 18km away. The two tiers of 163 arches supported by 128 pillars span 813m and reach a height of 29m near Pl. del Azoguejo. This spectacular feat of engineering, restored by the monarchy in the 1400s, transported 30L of water per second to the Alcázar. It was used until 60 years ago, but today mainly pipes in tourists from Madrid.

🪨 ALCÁZAR. Walt Disney reportedly modeled Cinderella's castle off the Alcázar's spiral towers and pointed turrets, and the similarity is so striking that from Queen Victoria Eugenia's gardens below, you'd swear you lost a glass slipper of your own. Fortifications have commanded the site since Celtic occupation. Alfonso X, who allegedly

LOCAL LEGEND

A DEAL WITH THE DEVIL

Segovia's Roman aqueduct, constructed AD 100-200 under Emperor Nervus, was built with no mortar, but many storied stones.

According to legend, after laboring for years on the cobblestone streets carrying water from the nearby Río Frío (Cold River) to her boss's doorstep in town, a poor servant could take it no more. Desperate, the woman invoked the devil in a stream of tears and promised him her soul if he could cure her unfortunate situation. They made a deal: If the devil could deliver the water from the river to the servant's doorstep before the cock crowed in the morning, she would deliver him her soul.

That night, a storm struck Segovia. Hidden by the heavy clouds, an army of devils set to work constructing stone by stone the aqueduct that Segovia has nurtured for the last 1800 years. But in the middle of the night, the servant was gripped with guilt and terror—she prayed that the devil could not complete his task. Just as the first ray of sun pierced through the dark clouds, and the devil had but one more stone to place, the cock crowed. The poor servant's soul was saved—and the city got a 99.6% complete aqueduct to boot. The women hurried to the priest to confess her sins and to celebrate her salvation, the townspeople placed a statue of the Virgin and Saint Stephen atop the aqueduct.

believed he was God, beautified the original 11th-century fortress. Successive monarchs increased the grandeur; the final touches were added for the coronation of Isabel I in 1474. In the Throne Room, the inscription above the throne reads: *"tanto monta, monta tanto"* (she mounts, as does he), intended to imply that Fernando and Isabel had equal authority. The **Museo Real Colegio de Artillería** commemorates the Alcázar when it was an artillery school. *(Pl. de la Reina Victoria Eugenia. ☎921 46 07 59. Open daily Apr.-Sept. 10am-7pm; Oct.-Mar. 10am-6pm. Tower closed Tu. Buy tickets in the Real Laboratorio de Chimia, to the left of the Alcázar. Palace €4, seniors and students €2.50. Tower €2. Audio tours in English €3.)*

■ **CASA-MUSEO DE ANTONIO MACHADO.** Antonio Machado (1875-1939), literature professor, playwright, and, above all, author of love poems and melancholy verse, never made much money. The poet rented this small *pensión*-turned-museum from 1919 to 1932 for three *pesetas* per day. A short, informative tour details major influences on Machado's poetry, including the 1909 death of his teenage wife and his affair with a married woman. The poet's room, filled with manuscripts and portraits (including a Picasso), has been left untouched. *(C. des Desamparados, 5. ☎921 46 03 77. Open M-Tu 4:30-7:30pm, W-Su 11am-2pm and 4:30-7:30pm. Mandatory guided tour in Spanish every 30min. €1.50, W free.)*

CATHEDRAL. In 1525, Carlos V commissioned a cathedral in Pl. Mayor to replace the 12th-century edifice destroyed in the *Revuelta de las Comunidades*, a political uprising against the crown that lasted from 1520-1521. When the cathedral was finished 200 years later with an impressive 23 chapels, it earned the nickname "The Lady of All Cathedrals." The **Sala Capitular**, hung with 17th-century tapestries, displays an ornate silver-and-gold chariot. Off the cloister (moved from the Alcázar) is the **Capilla de Santa Catalina**, filled with crosses, chalices, and candelabra. *(☎921 46 22 05. Open daily Apr.-Oct. 9am-6:30pm; Nov.-Mar. 9:30am-5:30pm; last entry 30min. before closing. Mass M-Sa 10am, Su 11am and 12:30pm. €3, under 14 free. Guided tours leave from the entrance at 11am, 4:30, 5:30pm.)*

🎸 🌸 NIGHTLIFE AND FESTIVALS

Plaza Mayor is the heart of Segovia's after-hours scene. Do as the locals and branch out toward the Alcázar on one of its many capillaries. Crowded **C. Infanta Isabel** toward the aqueduct, definitely earns its local nickname *calle de los bares*. The bars filling Pl. del Azoguejo, C. Fernandez de Ladreda, and C. Carmen, near the aqueduct, are frequented by the high school set. *Copas* and plastic childhood knick-knacks mix in a fun, eclectic atmosphere at **Toys,** C. Infanta Isabel, 13. Techno music plays on the small dance floor while a diverse crowd sips cocktails under the red lights upstairs. *(☎609 65 41 42. Beer €1. Mixed drinks €4.50-5.50. Open daily 10pm-4am.)* For a casual older crowd try **Bar Santana,** C. Infanta Isabel, 18. Tasty tapas and rock music draw locals. *(☎921 46 35 64. Beer €1.10. Mixed drinks €4.50. Open daily 10:30pm-3:30am.)* Club headquarters is C. Ruiz de Alda, off Pl. del Azoguejo. You can count on a raucous American crowd nearly all year long at **La Luna,** C. Pta. de la Luna, 8. From Pl. Mayor, head down C. Isabel la Católica onto C. Juan Bravo and take the first right. *(☎921 46 26 51. Beer €1.50. Chupitos (shots) €3. Open daily 5pm-4am.)*

June 23rd-29th, Segovia holds a **fiesta** in honor of San Juan and San Pedro, with free open-air concerts on Pl. del Azoguejo, and dances and fireworks on June 29. **Zamarramala,** 3km northwest of Segovia, hosts the **Fiestas de Santa Águeda** (the closest Su to Feb. 5). Women take over the town for a day and dress in period costumes to commemorate a sneak attack on the Alcázar in which women distracted the castle guards with wine and song. The all-female local council takes advantage of its authority to ■ridicule men and, at the festival's end, burns a male effigy.

◪ DAYTRIP FROM SEGOVIA

◪ LA GRANJA DE SAN ILDEFONSO

La Sepulvedana buses (☎921 42 77 07) run from Segovia (20min.; 12-14 per day M-Sa 7:40am-9:30pm, Su 10:30am-10:30pm; return M-Sa 7:20am-9pm, Su 11am-10pm; €2.84 round-trip). From the bus walk uphill through the gates and follow signs. ☎921 47 00 19. Open Apr.-Sept. Tu-Su 10am-6pm; Oct.-Mar. Tu-Sa 10am-1:30pm and 3-5pm, Su 10am-2pm. Spanish tours depart every 15min. €5, with guide €5.50; students and under 16 €3.

La Granja, a must-see located 9km southeast of the city, is the most extravagant of Spain's royal summer retreats (the others being El Pardo, El Escorial, and Aranjuez). Felipe V, the first Bourbon King of Spain and grandson of Louis XIV, detested the Habsburgs' austere El Escorial. Nostalgic for Versailles, he commissioned La Granja in the early 18th century, choosing the site for its hunting and gardening potential. A fire destroyed the living quarters in 1918, but the structure was rebuilt in 1932 to house one of the world's finest collections of Flemish tapestries, as well as four Goya tapestries, and his 16th-century *Triumphs of Petrarch*, and a 17th-century *History of Venus* series. The **Museo de Tapices** may be closed for renovations; call ahead. French architect René Carlier designed the **gardens** around the palace. Hedges surround impressive flowerbeds, but even those are no match for the decadent ◪**Cascadas Nuevas,** an ensemble of illuminated fountains and pools representing the continents and seasons. The **Baños de Diana** fountain is a particularly worthwhile stop. (Gardens open daily 10am-9pm. *Baños de Diana* July 22-Sept. 2 Sa from 10:30am-11:30pm. Other fountains suspended due to lack of water, except for May 30, July 25, Aug. 25; ask at the Segovia tourist office. Palace open daily June 17-Aug. 10am-9pm; May-June 16 and Sept. 10am-8pm; Apr. 10am-7pm; Mar. and Oct. 10am-6:30pm; Nov.-Feb. 10am-6pm.)

ÁVILA   ☎920

Ávila (pop. 50,000) is a popular retreat from Madrid summer heat and winter bustle. It has two main attractions: an impressive set of restored 12th-century stone walls and the former abode of Santa Teresa de Jesús (1515-1582). Within its walls, Ávila is untouched by pollution, advertisements, or traffic, and is accessible via Madrid, or as a daytrip from Salamanca or Segovia.

⊏ TRANSPORTATION

Trains: Po. de la Estación (☎902 24 02 02). Info office open daily 7:30am-1:30pm and 3:30-9:30pm. To: **El Escorial** (1hr.; 6-9 per day M-F 5:30am-8:15pm, Sa-Su 9:15am-8:37pm; €4.05); **Madrid** (1½-2hr.; 15-23 per day M-F 5:30am-8:15pm, Sa-Su 7am-10:15pm; €7.20) via **Villalba** (1hr., €6.40); **Salamanca** (1¾hr., 5-7 per day 7am-11pm, €8.05); **Valladolid** (1½hr.; 10-13 per day M-F and Su 9:53am-10pm, Sa 9:53am-8pm; €7.20).

Buses: Av. de Madrid, 2 (☎920 22 01 54). To **Madrid** (1½hr.; 6-8 per day M-F 6am-8pm, Sa 9am-8:30pm, Su 6 per day 10am-10:15pm; €7.65) and **Segovia** (1hr.; M-F 5 per day 6:30am-7pm; Sa-Su 10:15am and 7:15pm; €4.65).

Taxis: Radio Taxis (☎920 35 35 45), in Pl. Sta. Teresa and the bus and train stations.

◪ ✴ ◪ ORIENTATION AND PRACTICAL INFORMATION

Most tourist sights lie near the city walls. The winding old city streets meet in the **Plaza del Mercado Chico** inside the walls and the recently revamped **Plaza de Santa**

Teresa just outside. Bus #1 (€0.65) runs to Pl. del Mercado Chico from a block from the train station. To get from the bus station to Pl. Sta. Teresa, cross the intersection in front, follow the park, and turn left onto C. Duque de Alba.

Tourist Office: Pl. Pedro Dávila, 4 (☎920 21 13 87). English spoken. Open July-Aug. M-Th 9am-8pm, F-Sa 9am-9pm; Sept.-June 9am-2pm and 5-8pm. **Centro de Recepción de Visitantes,** Av. de Madrid, 39 (☎920 10 21 21), across the street from the northwest tower of the wall. Open daily in summer 9am-8pm; in winter 9am-6pm.

Currency Exchange: Banco Santander Central Hispano, C. Don Gerónimo, 8 (☎920 21 11 39). Open Apr.-Sept. M-F 8:30am-2pm; Oct.-May also Sa 8:30am-1pm.

Luggage storage: At the train station (€3). In summer 2007, it was under indefinite renovation. 24hr. Also at the bus station (€1-2). Open M-F 5:50am-8:30pm, Sa 6:50am-10:15pm, Su 9:15am-12:30pm and 3:45-8:30pm.

Police: C. Molino del Carril, 1 (☎920 35 24 24).

Pharmacy: C. Reyes Católicos, 31 (☎920 21 13 35). Open M-F 9:30am-2pm and 4:30-8pm, Sa 10am-2pm.

Hospital: Hospital Provincial, C. de Jesús del Gran Poder, 42 (☎920 35 72 00). **Ambulance:** ☎920 22 22 22.

Internet Access: Cybernet Locutorio DG, Av. de Madrid, 25 (☎920 253 800). €2 per hour, but you don't have to use all your time at once. Open daily 10am-3pm and 4-10:30pm. Also available at the **Biblioteca Municipal,** Pza. de la Catedral, 3 (☎920 25 46 38). Open M-F winter 9am-9pm, summer 9am-2:45pm.

Post Office: Pl. de la Catedral, 2 (☎920 35 31 06). **Fax** service available. Open M-F 8:30am-8:30pm, Sa 9:30am-2pm. **Postal Code:** 05001.

ACCOMMODATIONS

Comfortable, affordable accommodations can be found within the city walls. Real budget places are along the **Av. de la Juventud,** about 25min. outside of the old city. Those near the cathedral and Pl. de Sta. Teresa fill fast in summer, so call early.

Hostal Casa Felipe, Pl. Mercado Chico, 12 (☎920 21 39 24). Airy rooms with purple walls, some with large tiled bathrooms, TV, and sink overlook the square. Singles €22; doubles €36, with bath €42. MC/V. ❷

Hostal Bellas, C. de Caballeros, 19 (☎920 21 29 10). Clean rooms with TV and bath are tastefully decorated and clean. Breakfast €3.50, 3 meals €16.15. July-Sept. singles €38; doubles €46. Oct.-June €30/37. MC/V. ❹

Residencia Santo Tomás, Pl. de Granada, 1 (☎920 22 25 50), to the right of the monastery's main entrance. University rooms with A/C and Internet access. 3 meals per day. Singles with bath €35-40; doubles with bath €30 per person. Cash only. ❹

Albergue Juvenil Duperier, Av. de la Juventud, s/n (☎920 22 17 16), just next to the Polideportivo Territorial. A student dorm during the school year and a youth hostel July-Aug. €8.50 per person. Cash only. ❶

FOOD

Every Friday, the **market** in Pl. Mercado Chico sells produce 10am-2pm. The supermarket, **Alimentación Gimeco,** C. Juan José Martín, 6, stocks basics. (Open in summer M 10:30am-2pm and 5:30-8:30pm, Tu-Su 9:45am-2pm and 5:30-8:30pm; winter M-Sa 9:45am-2pm and 5-8pm.)

La Taberna del Lagartijo, C. Martín Carramolino, 4 (☎920 22 88 25), just behind Iglesia de San Juan. Decorated with bullfight photos and *matador* garb. A favorite of *abu-*

CASTILLA Y LEÓN

Ávila

▲ ACCOMMODATIONS
Albergue Juvenil Superior, 8
Hostal Bellas, 5
Hostal Casa Felipe, 2
Residencia Santo Tomás, 7

● FOOD
Cafe Barbacana, 3
La Pera Limonera, 1
Restaurante La Posada de la Fruta, 6
La Taberna del Lagartijo, 4

TO ✠ (100m)

Parque de San Antonio

C. de Banderas de Castilla
C. de Reina Isabel Alcázar
C. de Alonso de Montalvo
C. de Alfonso de Montalvo
Castillo de la Mota
C. de Capitán Méndez Vigo
Capitán
C. de Santa Fé
C. de Gran Cisneros
Av. de la Juventud
Monasterio de Santo Tomás

TO ✠ POLIDEPORTIVO TERRITORIAL (100m)

C. de Fernando III El Santo
C. de Fivasa
Toros de Guisando
PL. DE GRANADA
C. de Santo Tomás

Ermita del Cristo de la Luz
Convento de las Gordillas
Convento de Santa Clara
P. de San Roque
Bjda. de Don Alonso
Po. de Santo Tomás
C. S. Provisional
Hospital Provincial

C. del Carmen
Convento de Santa Ana
PL. SANTA ANA
C. de Cristo de la Luz
Capitán Peñas
Félix Hernández
C. de Perpetuo Socorro

Monasterio de San José
Parque de San Roque
C. de Jesús del Gran Poder
C. de Trinidad

Nuestra Sra. de Sonsoles

Ruinas de San Francisco
PL. DE SAN FRANCISCO
Museo de Ávila
PL. DEL DR. BENIGO
PL. DE ITALIA
San Miguel
PL. DE SAN PEDRO
San Pedro
C. de Deán Castor

Basílica de San Vicente
Puerta de San Vicente
PL. DE LEALES
Puerta de la Harina
PL. DE STA. TERESA
Puerta del Alcázar
Santa María de Gracia
C. de Cebreros

Catedral
Puerta de San Segundo
Cruz Vieja
PL. CALVO SOTELO
PL. DE SANTIAGO

C. del Tostado
PL. DE LA CATEDRAL
C. de Alemania
PL. JOSÉ TOMÉ
Puerta del Rastro

Portillo del P. de la Ronda Vieja
PL. FUENTE DEL SOL
Capilla de Mosén Rubí
PL. MERCADO CHICO
San Juan
Puerta de Santa Teresa

Convento de Santa Teresa
PL. DE LA SANTA
Sala de Reliquias

Puerta del Carmen
PL. CONCEPCIÓN
ARENAL
Teso del Carmen
Las Murallas
Ermita de San Esteban
Puerta del Puente
Puerta de la Malaventura

Mercado de Ganados

Atrio de San Isodoro
C. de Burgohondo

0   100 meters
0   100 yards

lenses (Ávila residents). Under renovations; call ahead. Entrees €12-15. Lunch *menú* €12. Open daily 11am-4pm and 8pm-midnight; closed Tu in winter. MC/V. ❸

Restaurante La Posada de la Fruta, Pl. Pedro Dávila, 8 (☎920 25 47 02; www.posadadelafruta.com). 4 different seating locations at different prices—the *terraza* is the most pleasant and the cheapest. *Menú* €10-14. Restaurant open daily 1-4:30pm and 8:30-11:30pm. Bar open 9am-midnight. MC/V. ❷

Café Barbacana, Pl. Santa Teresa, 8. (☎920 22 00 11). Just outside the ancient Roman walls, this beautiful outdoor terrace offers great food and tranquility at reasonable prices. Lunch *menú* €11. Mixed salad €6. Open M-Sa 1-11pm. MC/V. ❷

La Pera Limonera, Pl. Mosén Rubí, 5 (☎ 920 25 04 72) Cool lime-green tablecloths, orchids, and black leather make are a welcome break from the endless "medieval-themed" regional fare in the city. Specializes in rice and seafood dishes. Entrees €13-17. Open Tu-Sa 1:30-4pm and 9pm-midnight, Su 1:30-4pm. MC/V. ❸

ⓖ SIGHTS

▧ **LAS MURALLAS.** These gigantic city walls were originally built to keep foreigners out. They now draw thousands of them in each year, providing tourists with a walk around the ramparts and views of the city from above. Research dates the 2500 battlements, 88 towers, and nine gates to the 12th century, though legend maintains that they are the oldest in Spain, dating back to 1090. **Cimorro,** the most imposing tower, doubles as the cathedral's apse. The walls can be reached from both Puerta del Peso de la Harina and Puerta del Alcázar, on either side of the cathedral. *(☎920 25 50 88. Open daily Apr.-Oct. 15 10am-8pm, night visits M-W and Su 10pm-12:30am, Oct. 16-Mar. 11am-6pm, also July 19-Sept. 18 M-W and Su 10pm-12:30am; theatrical tour June 16-Sept. 17 Th-Sa 10-11:30pm, last entry 45min. before closing. €3.50; students, groups, over 65, and under 8 €3.50. 3-person theatrical tour €4.50.)* The best view of the walls and of Ávila is from the **Cuatro Postes,** past the Río Adaja, 1.5km along the highway to Salamanca. *(From Pl. de Sta. Teresa, walk out the Puerta del Puente. Cross the bridge and follow the road to the right for about 1km. 25min. walk.)*

▧ **CATEDRAL.** Begun in the late 12th century, Ávila's is the oldest Spanish cathedral in the transitional style between Romanesque and Gothic. Look for the **Altar de La Virgen de la Caridad,** where 12-year-old Santa Teresa prostrated herself after the death of her mother. Behind the main altar is the alabaster **tomb** of Cardinal Alonso de Madrigal, a bishop of Ávila and prolific writer whose dark complexion won him the title "El Tostado" (The Swarthy, or "Toasted"). The nickname spread, and during the Golden Age, it became popular to call an aspiring author *un tostado.* The **museum** displays an El Greco portrait, enormous *libros de canti* (hymnals), and Juan de Arfe's silver, six-story **Custodia del Corpus,** complete with swiveling bells. *(Pl. de la Catedral. ☎920 21 16 41. Open July-Sept. M-F 10am-7:30pm, Sa 10am-8pm, Su noon-6pm; Nov.-Mar. M-F 10am-5pm, Sa 10am-6pm, Su noon-5pm; Apr.-June and Oct. M-F 10am-6pm, Sa 10am-7pm, Su noon-6pm. Last entry 45min. before closing. Front entrance only free; full cathedral and museum €4.)*

MONASTERIO DE LA ENCARNACIÓN. The monastery **museum** highlights the sacrifices Santa Teresa made to obtain her sainthood. Possessions from her childhood in the lap of luxury are on display, but she renounced these for a life of asceticism, trading her pillow for a wooden log. The mandatory tour visits Santa Teresa's tiny cell and the main staircase where she had a mystical encounter with the child Jesus; a mannequin on the stairs recreates the experience. Upstairs are personal effects given to the convent by wealthier nuns as bribes to procure entrance. *(Po. de la Encarnación. ☎920 21 12 12. Museum open in summer M-F*

9:30am-1pm and 4-7pm, Sa-Su 10am-1pm and 4-7pm; in winter M-F 9:30am-1:30pm and 3:30-6pm, Sa-Su 10am-1:30pm and 3:30-6pm. Admission and tour €1.70.)

OTHER SIGHTS. Santa Teresa's admirers built the 17th-century **Convento de Santa Teresa** at the site of her birth. *(Inside the city walls, near Puerta de Sta. Teresa. ☎920 21 10 30. Open daily 9:30am-1:30pm and 3:30-7:30pm. Free.)* If you only see one site related to Santa Teresa, visit **Sala de Reliquías,** a building near the convent, where you will find a small scrapbook of Santa Teresa relics, including her 🕮**preserved ring finger,** the sole of her sandal, and the cord she used to flagellate herself. *(Open daily Apr.-Oct. 9:30am-1:30pm and 3:30-7:30pm; Nov.-Mar. Tu-Su 10am-1:30pm and 3:30-7pm. Free.)* For a larger collection of items that Santa Teresa may have touched, looked at, or lived among, as well as artifacts of lesser-known Teresas, visit the **Museo de Santa Teresa,** built into the convent's crypt. *(☎920 22 07 08. Open Apr.-Oct. daily 10am-2pm and 4-7pm; Nov.-Mar. Tu-Su 10am-1:30pm and 3:30-5:30pm. Last entry 30min. before closing. €2.)*

SALAMANCA
☎923

Salamanca (pop. a term-time 363,000) is Spain's golden equivalent to the Emerald City of Oz. The massive buildings and ornate facades exemplify Spanish Plateresque architecture, and because they were built with yellow Villamayor stone, the city seems to literally radiate its own light. Salamanca's location is also golden: while accessible from Spain's major transportation hubs, it is far enough away to qualify as a nice retreat, and its mild summer temperatures provide a haven from the heat that afflicts the rest of Spain's interior. Once a battling ground for Arabs and Christians, Salamanca has since become the home of the prestigious Universidad de Salamanca, in medieval times considered one of the "four leading lights of the world." Salamanca remains a university town; thousands of students flood the streets., creating a brouhaha that rivals Barcelona and Madrid.

TRANSPORTATION

Flights: Aeropuerto de Salamanca, Ctra. Madrid, km 14 (☎923 32 96 00).

Trains: Vialia Estación de Salamanca, Po. de la Estación (☎923 12 02 02). To: **Ávila** (65min., 7-8 per day 6am-7:53pm, €8.05); **Lisboa** (6hr., 4:51am, €47); **Madrid** (2½hr., 6-7 per day 6am-7:53pm, €15); **Palencia** (2hr., 1:50pm, €9-21); **Valladolid** (2hr., 4-6 per day 7:35am-8:35pm, €6.05-13.40). The station offers **luggage storage,** a Champion supermarket, restaurants, and a movie theater.

Buses: Av. Filiberto Villalobos, 71-85 (☎923 23 67 17). Take C. Ramón y Cajal to Po. de San Vicente. Cross this avenue, and C. Ramón y Cajal becomes Av. Filiberto Villalobos. Open M-F 8am-8:30pm, Sa 9am-2:30pm and 4:30-6:30pm, Su 10am-2pm and 4-7:30pm. **Avanza Grupo** (☎902 02 09 99) sends buses to: **Ávila** (1½hr.; M-Th 4 per day 6:30am-8:30pm, F 6 per day 6:30am-8:30pm, Sa-Su 4 per day 8:30am-8:30pm; €5, round-trip €10); **Barcelona** (11hr.; 7:30am, noon; €44.50, ISIC discount); **León** (2½hr.; M-F 5-6 per day 9am-6:30pm, Sa 4 per day 9am-3:15pm, Su 4 per day 8:45am-10pm; €12.60); **Madrid** (2½hr.; M-Sa 16 per day 6am-9:30pm, Su 16 per day 8am-11pm; €11.40-17); **Segovia** (2¾hr.; M-F 6:30am, 1:15pm, Sa-Su 8:30am, 5:30pm; €9.42, round-trip €17.29); **Valladolid** (1½hr.; M-Sa 7-9 per day 7am-8pm, Su 6 per day 9am-10pm; €7, round-trip €13.20); **Zamora** (1hr.; M-F 7 per day 9am-6pm, Sa 4 per day 9am-3:15pm, Su 4 per day 8:45am-7:15pm; €4.40). **El Pilar** (☎923 46 02 17) motors to **Ciudad Rodrigo** (1hr.; M-F 12 per day 7am-9:30pm, Sa 6 per day 8:30am-6pm, Su 4 per day 11am-9:30pm; €5.20).

Taxis: Radio Taxi (☎923 25 00 00). 24hr.

Car Rental: Avis, Po. de Canalejas, 49 (☎923 26 97 53). Open M-F 9:30am-1:30pm and 4-7pm, Sa 9am-1:30pm. **Europcar,** C. Calzada de Medina (☎923 25 02 70). Open M-F 9am-1:30pm and 4:30-7:30pm, Sa 9am-1:30pm.

⚡❓ ORIENTATION AND PRACTICAL INFORMATION

The majestic **Plaza Mayor** is the social and geographical center of Salamanca. Most hostels are to the south on **Rúa Mayor** and **Plaza de Anaya,** as are the **University** and most sights. From the **train station,** catch bus #1 (€0.80) to Gran Vía and get off at the Pl. Mayor (20min. from train station, 15min. from bus station).

Tourist Office: Municipal office, Pl. Mayor, 32 (☎923 21 83 42 or 923 27 24 08). Open June-Sept. M-F 9am-2pm and 4:30-8pm, Sa 10am-8pm, Su 10am-2pm; Oct.-May M-F 9am-2pm and 4-6:30pm, Sa 10am-6:30pm, Su 10am-2pm. **Regional office,** R. Mayor (☎923 26 85 71), in the Casa de las Conchas. Open July-Sept. M-Th and Su 9am-8pm, F-Sa 9am-9pm; Oct.-June daily 9am-2pm and 5-8pm. Look out for *DGratis,* a free listing of goings-on available at tourist offices and distributors in Pl. Mayor. See www.salamanca.es for details.

Currency Exchange: EuroDivisas, R. Mayor, 2 (☎923 21 21 80). Open M-F 8:30am-10pm, Sa-Su 10am-7pm. **ATMs** can be found on every major street.

Luggage Storage: At the **train station** (24hr.; €3-4.50) and **bus station** (open daily 7am-7:45pm; €2).

Women's Resources: Office for the Assistance of Victims of Sexual Assault and Harassment, Gran Vía, 39-31, 4th fl. (☎923 12 68 75). **Association for the Assistance of Victims of Sexual Assault and Domestic Abuse,** Pl. Nueva de San Vincente, 5 (☎923 26 15 99).

Laundromat: Pasaje Azafranal, 18 (☎923 36 02 16), off C. Azafranal. Wash and dry €4. Open M-F 9:30am-2pm and 4-8pm, Sa 9:30am-2pm.

Police: In the *Ayuntamiento,* Pl. Mayor, 2 (☎923 19 44 40 or locally 923 27 91 38).

Red Cross: C. Cruz Roja, 1 (☎923 22 22 22).

Pharmacy: Amador Felipe, C. Toro, 25 (☎923 21 41 24). Open daily 9:30am-10pm.

Hospital: Hospital Clínico Universitario, Po. de San Vicente, 108 (☎923 29 11 00).

Bookstore: Spanning both sides of the street, **Librería Cervantes,** C. Azafranal, 11-13, and Pl. de Santa Eulalia, 13-19 (☎923 21 86 02), is the closest thing to a superstore. Open M-F 10am-1:30pm and 4:30-8pm, Sa 10am-2pm.

Internet Access: Biblioteca Pública, Casa de Las Conchas, C. Compañía, 2 (☎923 26 93 17). Free Internet access and a cool reading room. Open July to mid-Sept. M-F 9am-3pm, Sa 9am-2pm; mid-Sept. to June M-F 9am-9pm, Sa 9am-2pm. **Cyber Place Internet,** Pza. Mayor, 10, 1st fl., is flooded with foreign students calling mom, but has a good rate of €1 per hour. Open M-F 11am-midnight, Sa-Su noon-midnight. **Cyber Anuario,** C. La Latina, 8 (☎923 26 13 54) has comfortable chairs and fast connections (€1.50 per hour). **Photocopying, printing, fax,** CD burning, and long-distance calls (€0.10 per minute to the US). Open daily 9am-1am.

Post Office: Gran Vía, 25-29 (☎923 26 30 11). **Lista de Correos.** Open M-F 8:30am-8:30pm, Sa 9:30am-2pm. **Postal Code:** 37080.

🏠📷 ACCOMMODATIONS AND CAMPING

Thanks to floods of student visitors, reasonably priced *hostales* and *pensiones* pepper the streets of Salamanca, especially off Pl. Mayor, R. Mayor, and C. Meléndez. Make reservations a week in advance in July and August.

Pensión Los Ángeles, Pl. Mayor, 10, 2nd-3rd fl. (☎923 21 81 66; www.pensionlosangeles.com). Colorful rooms with balconies over the stunning Pl. Mayor. Neat and organized, but could use a mopping under the bed. Ask for a room with a view. English spoken. Breakfast €4. €22 per person, with bath €25. MC/V. ❷

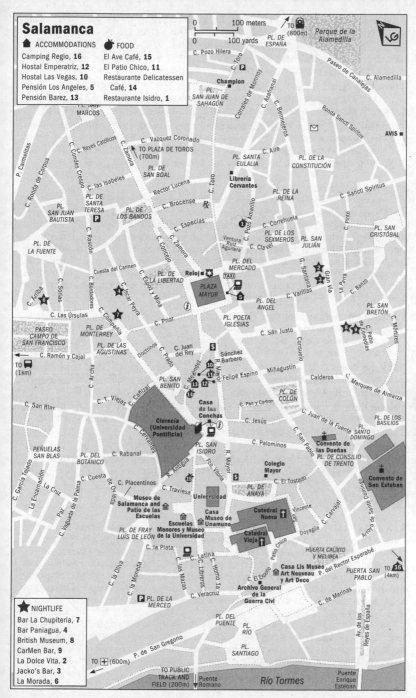

Salamanca

▲ **ACCOMMODATIONS**   🍎 **FOOD**

Camping Regio, **16**   El Ave Café, **15**
Hostal Emperatriz, **12**   El Patio Chico, **11**
Hostal Las Vegas, **10**   Restaurante Delicatessen
Pensión Los Angeles, **5**   Café, **14**
Pensión Barez, **13**   Restaurante Isidro, **1**

★ NIGHTLIFE

Bar La Chupitería, **7**
Bar Paniagua, **4**
British Museum, **8**
CarMen Bar, **9**
La Dolce Vita, **2**
Jacko's Bar, **3**
La Morada, **6**

CASTILLA Y LEÓN

Hostal Las Vegas Centro, C. Meléndez, 13, 1st fl. (☎923 21 87 49; www.lasvegascentro.com). Terraces, TV, and friendly owners make for a great deal. Spotless rooms with white tile floor and shower. Singles €20, with bath €24; doubles €30/36. MC/V. ❷

Pensión Barez, C. Meléndez, 19 (☎923 21 74 95). Clean pink-and-yellow rooms overlook the street. Common room with terrace. €13 per person. Cash only. ❶

Hostal Emperatriz, R. Mayor, 18 (☎923 21 91 56; fax 21 87 83). Operates out of the reception of the hotel by the same name next door. Spacious rooms with bath and phone. Rooms facing R. Mayor have a view but can be noisy. Singles €26; doubles €35. Cash only. ❸

Camping Regio (☎923 13 88 88; www.campingregio.com), on Ctra. Salamanca, 4km toward Madrid. Salmantino buses leave every 30min. from Gran Vía near Pl. de la Constitución (€0.80). First-class sites with hot showers. Laundry €3. Pool €1.30. €3.20 per person; €2.80 per tent, per car, and for electricity. MC/V. ❶

🍴 FOOD

Food in Salamanca is as diverse as its student population. Pork is the city's speciality, with dishes ranging from *chorizo* (spicy sausage) to *cochinillo* (suckling pig). Try the *Salamancas hornazo,* a type of meat-stuffed pie. Cafes and restaurants surround Pl. Mayor, which lights up around 10pm. Try to branch out to the less-touristed north, along **C. Zamorra, C. Toro,** and **Gran Vía** for more local fare. **Champion,** C. Toro, 82 (☎923 21 22 08), is a central supermarket. (Open M-Sa 9am-9:30pm.) Another tactic is to go from bar to bar, ordering drinks which come with *pinchos,* a more filling tapas relative.

Restaurante Delicatessen Café, C. Meléndez, 25 (☎ 923 28 03 09). A dramatic departure from the traditional taverns that dominate the restaurant scene, this funky locale serves up a wide variety of *platos combinados* (€9.50-10), and a lunch *menú* (€11) in a colorful solarium. Open daily 1:30-4pm and 9pm-midnight. MC/V. ❷

El Patio Chico, C. Meléndez, 13 (☎923 26 51 03). *Salmantinos* crowd this joint, but hefty portions are worth the wait. Try the *morcilla picante* (spicy blood sausage). Entrees €5-10. *Menú* €14. Open daily 1-4pm and 8pm-midnight. MC/V. ❷

El Ave Café, C. Libreros, 24 (☎ 923 26 45 11), Pleasant terrace facing the cathedral, and decorative "cubist" interior murals. Delicious lunch *menú* (€10.60) with tons of tasty options. Open daily 8am-midnight. MC/V. ❷

Restaurante Isidro, C. Pozo Amarillo, 19 (☎923 26 28 48), a block from Pl. Mayor. Prompt service, big crowds, and large portions. Numerous vegetable, seafood, and meat entrees (€4-15.50). *Menú* €10. Open M-Sa 1-3:30pm and 8-11:30pm. MC/V. ❷

👁 SIGHTS

🏛 **LA UNIVERSIDAD DE SALAMANCA.** Salamanca's highlight is this renowned university, established in 1218. The entrance is one of the country's best examples of Spanish Plateresque, a style named after the work of *plateros* (silversmiths). But the silver filigree on the stone is only an illusion, created when the region's pliable, iron-rich sandstone ages, hardening and weathering like granite. Sculpted into the facade is a tiny frog atop a skull, now a mascot for Salamanca. Legend has it that if you find the croaker without assistance, good luck or marriage follow—but it's likely your chances will be spoiled by everyone else already pointing at it.

The old lecture halls inside the university are open to the public. The 15th-century classroom **Aula Fray Luis de León** has been left in more or less its original state; medieval students considered the hard benches luxurious, as most students then sat on the floor. The **Biblioteca Antigua,** one of Europe's oldest libraries, is the most spectacular room of all. The magnificent Plateresque staircase represents the perilous path past careless youth, love, and adventure to true knowledge, though as with most things scholarly, is open to interpretation. 800 years ago, the University administered its rigorous oral tests in front of the chapel, *La Capilla del Estudiante.* That evening, the town would host a bullfight in honor of those who passed; the fresh blood of the bull was mixed with flour and used to paint the names of the new doctors on the university and cathedral walls. Look closely and you'll see faded red stamps and text on the sandstone.

Across the street from the university and through the hall on the left corner of the patio is the **University Museum.** The reconstructed **⬛Cielo de Salamanca,** the library's famous 15th-century ceiling fresco of the zodiac by the celebrated Fernando Gallego, is preserved here. Peek at the intricate strongbox with its many locks. *(From Pl. Mayor follow R. Mayor, veer right onto R. Antigua, then left onto C. Libreros; the University is on the left. University ☎ 923 29 44 00, museum 29 12 25. Museum open Tu-Sa 12pm-2pm and 6pm-9pm, Su 10am-2pm. University open M-F 9:30am-1:30pm and 4-7:30pm, Sa 9:30am-1:30pm and 4-7pm, Su 10am-1:30pm. €4, students and seniors €2.)*

CATEDRAL NUEVA. It took 220 years (1513-1733) to build this spectacular Gothic structure. While several architects decided to retain the original late Gothic style, they couldn't resist adding touches from later periods, apparent in the Baroque tower. Modern renovators left their marks too: look for an astronaut and a ⬛**dragon** eating ice cream on the left side of the main door. The church is best viewed first from the ground, but be sure to visit the **Ieronimus,** which allows you to climb the tower for a spectacular artifactual and architectural exhibition of the tower, and an even more stunning ⬛ **view of the city and the New Cathedral.** *(Pl. de Anaya. Cathedral open daily Apr.-Sept. 9am-8pm; Oct.-Mar. 9am-1pm and 4-6pm. Free. Ieronimus open daily 10am-8pm, last entry 7:15pm. €3.)*

CATEDRAL VIEJA. Constructed in 1140, the Romanesque Cathedral Vieja has one of the most detailed cupolas in Spain and was assembled from many intricately carved pieces. The oldest original part of the cathedral is the **Capilla de San Martín,** with frescoes dating from 1242. Look for the image of the Virgen de la Vega, Salamanca's patron saint. The **museum** features works by Fernando Gallego, a Renaissance painter who experimented with deep perspective. Pedro Bello's work is amusing; central figures in his religious paintings are often bored or asleep. Be sure to check out the famed **Patio Chico** behind the cathedral, where students congregate

LOCAL LEGEND

THE SCOUNDREL OF SALAMANCA

Before the crazy nightlife, the all-night cramming, and the hordes of knowledge-thirsty youngsters searching for enlightenment at the Universidad de Salamanca, a different kind of student roamed the streets of the city. A bronze statue at the end of Puente Romano immortalizes a pupil of misbehavior and legendary scoundrel: Lazarillo de Tormes.

The ancestor of scrubby little thieves everywhere, Lazarillo is a creation of an anonymous author, who chronicled the boy's adventures in 1554 with a story entitled, predictably, *Lazarillo de Tormes.* Named for the river that runs through the city, the Tormes, Lazarillo was born to lowly beginnings within the city walls. The story of his life describes his servitude to several different masters, including a blind man, a priest, and a nobleman.

Wickedly funny and cynical, the picaresque novel predates even *Don Quixote.* The ensuing literary tradition has been continued by the likes of Mark Twain, and shades of Lazarillo's character can be seen in the famed *Adventures of Huckleberry Finn.* Today, students and tourists alike are reminded of Lazarillo's failures as well as his glorious successes: the Toro Iberico, the site where Lazarillo received a beating from his blind master, still stands in Salamanca.

and tourists head for a view of both cathedrals. *(Enter through the Catedral Nueva. Museum ☎923 21 74 76. Cathedral open daily Oct.-Mar. 10am-1:30pm and 4-7:30pm; Apr.- Sept. 10am-7:30pm. €4, students €3.25, children €2.50.)*

PLAZA MAYOR. Built on the orders of Bourbon King Philip V, the renowned Plaza Mayor owes its beauty to French taste in architecture. Designed and built by Alberto Churriguera (see **Architecture**, p. 85) between 1729 and 1755, the plaza contains 88 towering arches, the *Ayuntamiento*, and three pavilions. The Pabellón Real, to the right of the *Ayuntamiento*, honors the Spanish monarchy (and, quite controversially, the 20th-century dictator Francisco Franco, behind the blue tarpaulin); the Pabellón del Sur, in front of the *Ayuntamiento*, is dedicated to famous Spanish conquistadors; and the Pabellón del Oeste, to the left of the *Ayuntamiento*, pays homage to important *salmantinos* like San Juan de Sahagún and Miguel de Unamuno. Additional spaces of honor were left intentionally blank for future generations. For modern-day history-makers like yourself, the Plaza Mayor is a common meeting place—right under the *reloj* (clock).

CASA LIS MUSEO ART NOUVEAU Y ART DECO. This early 20th-century stained-glass palace houses an extensive collection of 19th- and 20th- century glassware, statues of flappers in various states of undress, and a set of bottles depicting curmudgeonly old Dickens characters. The ambient music in the background makes it almost like walking into the middle of a F. Scott Fitzgerald novel or Edith Wharton's most animated boudoir. *(C. El Explolio, 14. ☎923 12 14 25; www.museocasalis.org. Open Apr.-Oct. 15 Tu-F 11am-2pm and 5-9pm, Sa-Su 11am-9pm; Oct. 16-Mar. Tu-F 11am-2pm and 4-7pm, Sa-Su 11am-8pm. €3, students €2, under 14 free. Free Th 11am-2pm.)*

EL ARCHIVO GENERAL DE LA GUERRA CIVIL ESPAÑOLA. Once a vital organ in Franco's anti-Communist repression, this early 18th century hospital now houses Spain's most extensive collection of Republican documents and rotating exhbitions. During the Spanish Civil War (1936-1939), Franco converted the building into a storage and work facility for the Office of Anti-Communist Investigation and Propaganda, which accumulated information on Republican forces. In 1938, the office was christened the State Delegation for the Recuperation of Documents. After Franco's death in 1975 and the end of his dictatorship, the collection of documents became a general archive, part of Spain's system of Studies and Documentation. *(C. El Explolio, 2. ☎923 21 28 45; www.mcu.es/archivos/MC/AGC/index.html. Archive open M-F 8am-8:30pm. Museum on ground floor open Tu-Sun 11am-2pm and 5-9pm. To consult documents, bring a passport and acquire a pass from the guards at the front door. Free.)*

CONVENTO DE SAN ESTEBAN. This convent holds Salamanca's gold-encrusted altar, and a magnificent facade depicting the stoning of San Esteban. The beautiful **Claustro de los Reyes** (Kings' Cloister), with its Gothic structure and Renaissance details, is visibly the product of two different eras. José Churriguera's central painting, *The Triumph of the Catholic Church* (1693), in the choir, depicts horses pulling a carriage full of saints and popes trampling less holy figures. *(Off C. San Pablo and C. Palominos. ☎923 21 50 00. Open daily Apr.-Sept. 8:30am-1pm and 4-8pm; Oct.-Mar. 9am-1pm and 4-6pm. €2, free M 10am-noon.)*

MUSEO DE SALAMANCA. Across from the university in the Patio de las Escuelas, the Museo de Salamanca occupies an astounding building that was once home to Álvarez Albarca, physician to Fernando and Isabel. Along with the Casa de las Conchas, this structure is among Spain's most important examples of 15th-century architecture. The museum has an intriguing collection of sculptures and paintings including *Mesa Alegre* (Happy Table) by Vincenzo Camp and *Viejo Bebedor* (Old Drunk) by Esteban March, Juan de Flandes's portrait of San Andrés, and Luis de Morales's *Llanto por Cristo muerto*. *(Patio de las Escuelas, 2. ☎923 21 22 35. Open*

July-Sept. Tu-Sa 10am-2pm and 4-7pm, Su 10am-2pm; Oct.-June Tu-Sa 10am-2pm and 4-7pm, Su 10am-2pm. €1.20; students, children, and over 65 €0.60. Free Sa and Su.)

CASA DE LAS CONCHAS. Follow R. Mayor from the Plaza Mayor until you reach a plaza with an organ-pipe fountain. On the right, you'll find the 15th-century Casa de las Conchas (House of Shells), with over 300 scallop halves on the facade, one of Salamanca's most famous landmarks. Pilgrims who journeyed to Santiago de Compostela (p. 557) traditionally wore shells to commemorate their visit to the tomb of Santiago. Legend has it that the Jesuits bought and leveled every house in the area to build their college—except the Casa de las Conchas, though they offered to pay one gold coin for every shell. *(C. Compañía, 2. Library ☎923 26 93 17. Open M-F 9am-9pm, Sa 9am-2pm. Casa open M-F 9am-9pm, Sa-Su 9am-2pm and 4-7pm, Su 10am-2pm and 5-8pm. Free.)* Directly across from the Casa de las Conchas is **La Clerecía** (Royal College of the Holy Spirit), the main building of La Universidad Pontificia de Salamanca. *(☎923 27 71 00. Open Tu-F 10:30am-12:50pm and 5-7:30pm, Sa 10am-1:20pm and 5-8pm, Su 10am-1:20pm. €2.)*

CASA MUSEO DE UNAMUNO. Miguel de Unamuno, one of the founding figures of the prolific Spanish literary group known as the *Generación de '98*, lived here when he served as the rector of the university during the early 20th century. Unamuno passionately opposed dictatorship and encouraged his students to do so as well. His stand against General Miguel Primo de Rivera's 1923 coup led to his dismissal, though he was triumphantly reinstated some years later. Poet, author, and intellect, Unamuno's extensive library testifies to his ability to read in 14 different languages. *(C. Libreros, 25. To the right of the university's main entrance. Ring bell if house appears closed. ☎923 29 44 00, ext. 1196. Open July-Sept. Tu-F 9:30am-1:30pm, Sa-Su 10am-1:30pm; Oct.-June Tu-F 9:30am-1:30pm and 4-6pm, Sa-Su 10am-2pm. Research room open M-F 9am-2pm. Mandatory tour in Spanish every 30min. €3, students €1.50.)*

PUENTE ROMANO. A 2000-year-old Roman bridge spans the scenic Río Tormes at the southern edge of the city. It was once part of the *Camino de la Plata* (Silver Way), a Roman trade route running from Mérida in Extremadura to Astorga. In medieval times, that was the route most Andalusian and Castilian Christians took to complete their pilgrimage to Santiago de Compostela. A headless granite bull called the **Toro Ibérico** guards one end of the bridge. Though it dates to pre-Roman times, the bull gained fame in the 16th century when it appeared in *Lazarillo de Tormes*, the prototype of the picaresque novel and a predecessor of *Don Quixote*. In one karmic episode, Lazarillo gets his head slammed into the bull's ear after cheating his blind employer. *(To reach the bridge, walk downhill toward the river.)*

▌◧ NIGHTLIFE

Salmantinos claim Salamanca is the best place in Spain ▥**para ir de marcha** (to go out partying). With some 5,000 different bars in this little city, Salamanca is not lacking in supplies. *Chupiterías* (bars selling mostly shots), *barres*, and discotecas line nearly every street, and the party doesn't wind down until the sun starts coming up at 6am. For out-of-towners, *la marcha* (the party) starts in Pl. Mayor, where members of local college or graduate-school *tunas* (medieval-style student troubadour groups) strut around the plaza dressed in traditional black capes, serenading women with mandolins and tambourines in hand. Student nightlife spreads out to **Gran Vía, Calle Bordadores,** and side streets. Spacious disco-bars blast music until dawn. **Calle Prior** and **Rúa Mayor** are full of bars; **Plaza de San Juan Bautista** fills with university students kicking off their evening—date in one hand, infamous *litro* of beer in the other. Late-night revelry occurs off **Calle Varillas** until dawn. On C. Prior and C. Compañía, tipsy young Americans and clubby *salmantinos* mix at clubs like **Niebla,** C. Bordadores, 14 (☎923 26 86 04) with its weekly themed parties and **Gatsby,** C. Bordadores, 16 (☎923 21 73 62); all host to the same tight pants and free-flowing alcohol. Dress to impress; though none of the clubs have cover charges, bouncers can be picky. Look for club promoters in the streets handing out cards for free drinks; if they don't approach to give you one, ask.

Bar La Chupitería, Pl. de Monterrey. Make your way through the crowds to order from *Los Exóticos,* the changing list of specialty shots (€1-1.70). *Chupitos* (large shots) €0.90. Beer €2.50. Open daily 10pm-very late.

Jacko's Bar, C. Iscar Peyra, 22. Cheap shots and *litros* keep students—mostly American—coming to the Michael Jackson-inspired Jacko's. Brand new menu of drinks, colorful expansion underway. *Litro* of beer, sangria, or *tinto de verano* M-Th €2, F-Sa €2.70. Specialty *litros* €3.90-7. *Chupitos* €0.90-1.20. Open daily 9:30pm-4am.

Bar Paniagua, C. Varillas, 1. Smartly dressed student crowd. Rumor has it that Paniagua is the place for foreigners to meet their Salamantino mate. Liters of beer and *Kalimotxo* (wine and coke) €3.50. Open M-Th and Su 8pm-3am, F-Sa 8pm-5am.

CarMen Bar, C. Patio de Comedias, 2, across from the Teatro Breton. A slightly older gay crowd populates this intimate bar. Good music and a comfortable space for dancing. Shots €2.50. Beer €3. Open Th-Sa in summer 11pm-4:30am, in winter 10pm-4:30am.

British Museum, C. San Justo, 36. Despite the nerdy name, this bar attracts a laid-back, local student crowd who dig the Beatles, R.E.M., and American blues. Beer €1.50. Open M-Th 7pm-3am, F-Sa 7pm-4:30am.

La Dolce Vita, Gran Vía, 48. Groove to salsa and pop in a Hollywood-themed disco. Unbeatable weeknight promotions; €4 gets you unlimited beer and sangria. Shots €1. Beer €3. Mixed drinks from €5. Open M-Th 10:30pm-3:30am, F-Sa 11pm-4:30am.

TIP

PINCHING PENNIES. Eating in Salamanca is expensive. The supermarket offers one alternative, but *pinchos,* a close, slightly smaller sized relative of tapas, pack a punch so you don't have to pack a lunch. On C. Van Dyke (north of the city, but worth the walk), they come included with your drink, so a few are sufficient for a light meal—and a lighter bill.

 ♫ ❋ ENTERTAINMENT AND FESTIVALS

Guia del Ocio, a free pamphlet distributed at the tourist office and at some bars, lists movies, special events, and bus schedules. Posters at the **Colegio Mayor,** Pl. de Anaya, advertise university events, free films, and student theater. On June 12, in honor of San Juan de Sahagún, the **Plaza de Toros** hosts a bullfight for charity. Take C. Zamora to Po. Dr. Torres Villarroel; the bullring is just beyond Pl. de la Glorieta. (Seats in the sun from €35.) A **Renaissance fair** runs until June 15. Between the end of July and September, Salamanca puts on **Verano en La Cueva,** a weekend music and theater festival in a cave in the Villena Antigua Muralla, across from the Convento de San Esteban. (Shows start at starts at 9:15pm. For more info www.salamanca.es.) Salamanca celebrates the week-long **Fiestas de Salamanca** in honor of their patroness the Virgen de la Vega; exhibitions abound, most honoring the bullfighting that has made the region's *ganaderías* (bull farms) the best in all of Spain. Salamanca goes all out during **Semana Santa** with local traditions like *Lunes de Aguas,* celebrated the Monday after Easter.

▶ DAYTRIP FROM SALAMANCA

CIUDAD RODRIGO

Buses arrive from Salamanca (1hr.; M-F 14 per day 7am-9:30pm, Sa 7 per day 8:30am-6pm, Su 5 per day 9:30am-9:30pm; last return to Salamanca M-F 9pm, Sa 8pm, Su 8pm;

€5.50). *Buy tickets from El Pilar, windows 23 and 24. Save about 25min. walking from the Plaza Mayor to the bus station, or take the number 4 bus (€0.80).*

The hushed, labyrinthine streets and 18th-century ramparts of Ciudad Rodrigo (pop. 16,000), a sleepy town just 27km from Portugal, harbor sandstone churches, Roman ruins, and medieval masonry. The town was a Roman outpost, but its namesake is Conde Rodrigo González Girón, the count who brought the site back to life in 1100 after Moorish invasions. Fortified during border wars between Spain and Portugal, Ciudad Rodrigo soon grew into an outpost for Spanish military. The **cathedral** is the town's main attraction. Originally a Romanesque church, it was later modified to conform to 16th-century Gothic tastes. The cathedral's **claustro** (cloister) is the highlight of a trip to Ciudad Rodrigo. The capitals of the ruined columns are covered with figures doing everything from making love to playing peek-a-boo to flirting with cannibalism. (Cathedral open July-Sept. Tu-Sa noon-2pm and 4-7pm, Su 1-2pm and 4-6pm; Oct.-June daily 10am-1pm and 4-7pm. €2.50, students €2. Cloister and museum open Tu-Su 10am-2pm and 4-8pm, Sa-Su 10am-8pm. Free; includes tour in Spanish.) Aside from its cathedral, Ciudad Rodrigo makes a worthwhile stop for its daytime tranquility and rollicking festivals.

The **bus station** (☎923 46 10 09) is on Campo de Toledo, 3-25. From the entrance, walk uphill on Av. Yurramendi and through the stone arch; the cathedral is ahead. The many parks and expensive restaurants make this town perfect for picnicking. Stop by **Supermercado El Arbol**, Av. Yurramendi, s/n. (☎923 48 00 56. Open M-Sa 9:15am-9:15pm. MC/V.) The **tourist office,** Pl. de Amayuelas, 5, is to the left through the arch. (☎923 46 05 61; turismociudadrodrigo@jcyl.es. English spoken. Open M-F 9am-2pm and 5-7pm, Sa-Su 10am-2pm and 5-8pm.) There is also a visitor's center just before the arch. (☎923 16 33 73. Open Tu-Su 9am-8pm.) To get to Pl. Mayor from the tourist office, go straight on Pl. de Amayuelas into town, turn left onto C. del Cardenal Pacheco before Pl. de San Salvador, and take a right onto C. Julián Sánchez; Pl. Mayor is at the end of this street.

ZAMORA ☎980

With more than 20 churches, Zamora (pop. 70,000) overflows with monuments of religious fervor. Perched atop a cliff over the Río Duero, the city is a mix of modern and medieval: 11th-century churches rub shoulders with Mango and Zara, and the 12th-century cathedral overlooks modern subdivisions and steel bridges. While locals enjoy the town's modern conveniences, it is Zamora's history as one of the most powerful cities in medieval Castilla that lures tourists. Nearly every plaza venerates Zamora's infamous figures, including the fierce Roman warrior Viriato, who was born here; El Cid, who fled here; and Sancho II, who died here during an attempt to overthrow his sister and claim the House of Castilla as his own. The nearby *pueblo* of Sanabria was also the inspiration for Miguel de Unamuno's famous story *San Manuel Bueno, Mártir*.

◨◪ TRANSPORTATION AND PRACTICAL INFORMATION. The best way to reach Zamora is by **bus.** Buses leave from the station on Av. Alfonso Peña (☎980 52 12 81; 24hr.; lockers €2) to: Madrid (2½-3½hr.; M-F 6 per day 7am-7:30pm, Sa 3 per day 10:30am-5:30pm, Su 6 per day 10:30am-9pm; €13-20), Salamanca (1hr.; M-F 15 per day 6:30am-9:35pm, Sa 10 per day 7:45am-8:30pm, Su 7 per day 8:45am-10:15pm; €4), and Valladolid (1½hr.; M-F hourly 7am-8:30pm, Sa 6 per day 8:00am-6:30pm, Su 4 per day 10:30am-8pm; €6). **Trains** leave C. de la Estación (☎980 52 11 10; 24hr.) at the end of Av. Alfonso Peña and go to Madrid (3hr.; M-F and Su 4am, 8:32am (change in Medina del Campo), 6:20pm; Sa 4am,

8:32am (change in Medina del Campo), 2:30pm; €26) and Valladolid (1½hr., 8:32am, €7.15). Both stations are a 20min. walk from the Pl. Mayor.

The **tourist office** is at Av. Príncipe de Asturias, 1. Exit the bus station through the arrival platform and turn left onto Av. Alfonso Peña, which becomes Av. de Tres Cruces. Take a left at Pl. Alemania onto C. Alfonso IX, and then a left onto Av. Príncipe de Asturias. (☎980 53 18 45. Open July 1-Sept. 15 M-Th and Su 9am-8pm, F-Sa 9am-9pm; Sept. 16-June 30 daily 9am-2pm and 5-8pm.) A **branch** is closer to the monuments at Pl. Arias Gonzalo, 6. (☎987 53 36 94; www.ayto-zamora.org. Open daily Oct.-Mar. 10am-2pm and 4-7pm; Apr.-Sept. 10am-2pm and 5-8pm.) There is a **pharmacy** right in the Pl. Mayor on C. Ramos Carrión, 2. (☎980 53 01 62. English spoken. Open M-F 9:45am-2pm and 5-8pm, Sa 10am-1:45pm.) In a medical emergency, head to **Hospital Virgen de la Concha**, Av. Requejo, 35 (☎980 54 82 00; emergencies 54 82 12). The **Biblioteca Pública**, Pl. Moyano, has free **Internet** access,. (☎980 53 15 51. Max. 1hr. Passport required. Open M-F 9am-9pm, Sa 9am-2pm.)

⚡ ▢ ACCOMMODATIONS AND FOOD. If you stay the night in Zamora, there are a number of options in the old part of the city. ◨**Hostal Siglo XX ❷**, Pl. del Seminario, 3, a few blocks off the Pl. Mayor, has beautiful, antique rooms and a serene location across from a historic seminary. (☎980 53 29 08. Singles €20; doubles €30.) **Hostal La Reina ❷**, C. Reina, 1, conveniently located right off Pl. Mayor, is also a safe bet, with some rooms featuring TVs and private baths for a higher price. (☎980 53 39 39. Singles €15-25; doubles €28-35. Cash only.) The Pl. Mayor also houses a number of inviting restaurants. **Casa Bernardo ❶**, Plazuela de San Miguel, 2, has a terrace right on the Pl. Mayor next to the picturesque Iglesia de San Juan. The entrees (€5-9), tapas (€3-7) and sandwiches (€2.50-4.50) are fit for any traveler's budget. (☎980 53 27 41. Open M and W-Su 1-4pm, 9-11:30pm.) Alternatively, the **El Arbol** supermarket, Av. de las Tres Cruces, 26-28, stocks all the basics. (Open M-Sa 9:30am-9:30pm.)

◙ SIGHTS. The ◨**Museo de Semana Santa**, Pl. Santa María la Nueva, is a rare find. Hooded mannequins guard sculpted floats, used during the *romería* processions of *Semana Santa*, which depict the stations of the cross. The crypt-like setting and collection of pieces ranging from the 16th century to today make this museum one of the eerier stops in town. (☎980 53 22 95. Open Tu-Sa 10am-2pm and 5-8pm, Su 10am-2pm. €3, under 12 €1.) Twelve striking, recently restored **Romanesque churches** remain within the walls of the old city. Almost all date from the 11th and 12th centuries, but their ornate altars were added in the 15th and 16th centuries. In Pl. Mayor, the **Iglesia San Juan** is notable for its marble-veined windows. **Iglesia Santa María la Nueva** was the site of *El Motín de la Trucha;* in 1158 villagers set the church on fire (with the nobles inside) to protest a law giving the nobility priority over the people in buying trout. From the Pl. Mayor, walk up C. Sacramento and turn right onto C. Barandales; the church is in Pl. Santa María la Nueva. (All open Tu-Sa Mar.-Sept. 10am-1pm and 5-8pm; Oct.-Jan. 6 10am-2pm and 4:30-6:30pm. Free.) Beyond its medieval heritage, Zamora also hosts the contemporary **Museo Etnográfico**, C. Sacramento, a seven-story glass building just off the Pl. Mayor. The museum has a collection of over 1000 eclectic works chronicling life in Castilla y León over the last few centuries. (☎980 53 17 08. Open Mar.-Sept. Tu-Su 10am-2pm and 5-8pm; Oct.-Dec. Tu-Su 10am-2pm and 4:30-6:30pm. €3, students €1.) Zamora's foremost monument is its Romanesque **cathedral,** built in the 12th-15th centuries. In the cloister, the **Museo de la Catedral** features the priceless 15th-century **Black Tapestries** that illustrate the story of the Trojan War. From the tourist office, go one block up C. del Obispo. (☎980 53 06 44. Cathedral and museum open Tu-Su 10am-2pm and 5-8pm; mass daily 10am, also Sa 6pm and Su 1pm. €3, students €1.50.) Located directly behind the cathedral is another venerable building of Zamora: **El Castillo.** Built during the middle ages with pre-Roman foundations, the castle of Zamora stands formidably on the cliff overlooking the countryside surrounding Zamora. Although it is not open to the public, the park and area around the castle offer great views of Zamora and its surroundings.

■ HIKING. The tourist office has info on hikes about 25km west of the city. Two popular routes are those from **Muelas del Pan** and **Ricobayo de Alba,** both of which include great views and pass through undisturbed countryside. Vivas runs buses from the Zamora station (M-Th 1:30, 5:45, 6pm; F 1:30, 6pm, Sa 1:30, 5:45pm; return M-Sa 8:30am; €1.10). Trails are well-marked, and the hikes are 8-9km each. Going to either town requires an overnight stay, since buses only return in the morning. **Pensión Tomasita ❶,** Ctra. Alcañices, has rooms along Muelas del Pan (☎980 55 30 07. Doubles €20, breakfast included.) Those traveling to Ricobayo can stay at **Hostal del Rio ❷,** Ctra. Alcañices, 90. (☎980 55 32 45. Singles €20; doubles €36.)

LEÓN   ☎987

León (pop. 165,000) is the last big city along the Camino de Santiago where pilgrims have a chance to rest, enjoy delicious tapas, and visit a gorgeous cathedral. It's easy to feel at home in León; though big, its streets are easy to navigate and its natives are fun, welcoming, and friendly. The Roman Legion named the town *Legio* in AD 68, but derivations over the years have led the name to *León*, or lion. The city was also a stronghold against the Moors during the *Reconquista*. The spectacular blue stained-glass windows of its famous cathedral have earned León the nickname *La Ciudad Azul*. This Gothic masterpiece is only a starting point for exploration of León's parks, bustling cafes, and raucous nightlife.

▐ TRANSPORTATION

Flights: Aeropuerto de León (☎987 87 77 00). **Air Nostrum** (☎902 40 05 00) flies to Barcelona and Madrid. **Lagun Air** (☎902 34 03 00) services Alicante, Ibiza, Málaga, Menorca, Palma, Sevilla, and Valencia.

Trains: RENFE, Av. de Astorga, 2 (☎902 24 02 02). Open 24hr. To: **Barcelona** (9½hr.; 2-3 per day 12:25am-9:28pm, Sa until 1:12pm; €44-57); **Bilbao** (5½hr., 2:54pm, €26); **Burgos** (2-3hr.; 6-7 per day 12:25am-9:38pm, Sa until 6:12pm; €18-24); **La Coruña** (7hr., express 4½hr.; 2-3 per day 5:40am-2:07pm, M, Th, Sa-Su until 4:40pm; €28-37); **Gijón** (3hr.; 5-7 per day M-F 4:45am-7:40pm, Sa until 7pm; Su 8:20am-7:40pm; €9-21) via **Oviedo** (2hr., €7-19); **Madrid** (4½hr.; 7 per day M-Sa 1:12am-6:12pm, Su 7:10am-7:08pm; €21-37); **Valladolid** (2½hr.; 10 per day M-Sa 1:12am-8:35pm, Su 7:10-8:35pm; €9-22). Schedules daily in Diario de León (€0.65).

Buses: Estación de Autobuses, Po. del Ingeniero Sáenz de Miera (☎987 21 00 00). Station open M-Sa 5:15am-2:30am, Su 6am-2:30am. Information open M-F 7:30am-9pm, Sa 8am-1pm, Su 3:30-8:30pm. To: **Madrid** (4½hr.; 9-13 per day 2:30am-10:30pm, Sa until 8:30pm; €20-30); **Salamanca** (2½hr.) via **Zamora** (1½ hr.; M-F 6 per day 8am-6:30pm, Sa 4 per day 8am-5pm, Su 3 per day 10:15am-7pm); **Santander** (5hr.; M-Th 7 per day 3:40am-5pm, F 9 per day 3:40am-7 pm, Sa 6 per day 3:40am-3pm, Su 7 per day 3:40am-7pm; €11-28); **Valladolid** (2hr., 14-18 per day 2:14am-11:59pm, €8);

Taxis: Radio Taxi (☎987 26 14 15). 24hr.

Car Rental: Europcar, Av. de Astorga, next to the train station (☎987 23 02 51; fax 27 19 80). 21+, must have had license for 1 year. From €80 per day with 350km limit. Open M-F 9am-1:30pm and 4-7:30pm, Sa 9am-1pm.

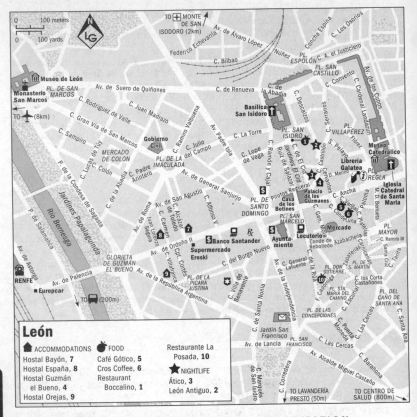

León

🏠 ACCOMMODATIONS
Hostal Bayón, **7**
Hostal España, **8**
Hostal Guzmán
el Bueno, **4**
Hostal Orejas, **9**

🍴 FOOD
Café Gótico, **5**
Cros Coffee, **6**
Restaurant
Boccalino, **1**

Restaurante La
Posada, **10**

★ NIGHTLIFE
Ático, **3**
León Antiguo, **2**

✴️ 🛈 ORIENTATION AND PRACTICAL INFORMATION

Most of León, including the old city (*León Gótico*) and the modern commercial district, lies on the east side of the **Río Bernesga**. The bus and train stations are across the river on the west side. Av. de Palencia leads across the river to **Glorieta de Guzmán el Bueno**, and after the rotary becomes **Avenida de Ordoño II,** which bisects the new city. At Pl. de Santo Domingo, Av. de Ordoño II becomes **Calle Ancha,** a pedestrian street that splits the old town in two and leads to the cathedral.

Tourist Office: Pl. Regla, 3 (☎987 23 70 82; www.turismocastillayleon.com). Free city maps, regional brochures, and accommodations guide. Sept.-June M-F 9am-2pm and 5-7pm, Sa-Su 10am-2pm and 5-8pm. July-Aug. open M-F 9am-7pm, Sa-Su 10am-8pm.

Currency Exchange: ATMs and banks line Pl. de Santo Domingo. **Banco Santander Central Hispano,** Pl. de Santo Domingo (☎987 24 10 12). Open Apr.-Sept. M-F 8:30am-2pm; Oct.-Mar. also Sa 8:30am-1pm. **Citibank,** on Av. de la Independencia at C. Legión VII. Open M-F 8:30am-2pm.

Luggage Storage: At the **train station** (€3). Open 24hr. At the **bus station** (€2). Buy tokens M-F 7:30am-9pm, Sa 8am-1pm, Su 3:30-8:30pm.

English-Language Bookstore: Librería Galatea, C. Sierra Pambley, 1 (☎987 27 26 52). Open M-F 10am-2pm and 5-8:30pm, Sa 10am-2pm.

Police: National C. Villa de Benavente, 6 (☎987 21 89 00). **Municipal** Paseo del Parque (☎987 25 55 00).

Medical emergency: ☎987 22 22 22.

Medical Services: Hospital Monte de San Isodoro, Ctra. Asturias (☎987 22 72 50).

Late-Night Pharmacy: Farmacia Mata Espeso, Av. de Ordoño II, 3, (☎987 20 73 15). Open M-F 9:30am-2pm, 4:30-10pm, Sa 9:30am-2pm, every night 10pm-9:30am.

Internet Access: Cafetería Santo Domingo, Av. de Ordoño II, 3 (☎987 26 13 84). €1.80 per hour, 30min. minimum (€1). Open M-F, Su 8am-11pm, Sa closed. Also at **Locutorio,** C. La Rúa, 8 (☎987 23 01 06). €2 per hour, €3 per 2hr. 15min. minimum (€0.50). Open M-F 9:30am-2:30pm and 4-10:30pm, Sa 10am-2pm and 5-9:30pm.

Laundromat: Lavandería Mito C. Arcipreste de Hita. (☎987 20 08 77). From the Pl. Santo Domingo walk down Ave. de la Independencia. When you reach Pl. San Francisco continue straight onto C. Corredera. After about 5 blocks turn right onto C. Arcipresta de Hita. Open M-F 10am-1pm and 4-8pm, Sa 10am-2pm.

Post Office: Jardín de San Francisco (☎987 87 60 81). **Lista de Correos** (windows #12-13) and **fax.** Open M-F 8:30am-8:30pm, Sa 9:30am-2pm. Winter Sa open 8:30am-8:30pm. **Postal Code:** 24004.

ACCOMMODATIONS

Moderately priced hostels are fairly easy to find here, thanks to the yearly influx of pilgrims on their way to Santiago, but they tend to fill up during the June fiestas. If you plan to on visit León on a weekend, book rooms at least a week in advance. Find rooms on **Avenida de Roma, Avenida de Ordoño II,** and **Avenida de la República Argentina,** which lead into the old town from **Glorieta de Guzmán el Bueno.**

Hostal Bayón, C. Alcázar de Toledo, 6, 2nd fl. (☎987 23 14 46). Wicker chairs, old photos of León, sun-drenched rooms and bright colors make this hostel a good retreat from the hustle and bustle of the city. Hall baths and a dining room with TV. Breakfast €1.50. Singles €15, with shower €25; doubles €28/35. Cash only. ❷

Hostal Orojas, C. Villafranca, 6, 2nd fl. (☎907 25 29 09). Located in the newer parts of the city. Cheery rooms complete with modern fixtures, big, comfy beds, showers and cable TV. Cozy dining hall has free Wi-Fi access. Daily breakfast €2.50. Singles €30, with bath €35-45; doubles €50; triples €62. MC/V. ❸

Hostal España, C. Carmen, 3, 2nd floor (☎987 23 60 14). This hostel features antique-looking rooms with beautiful white fixtures and a friendly staff. Daily meals served in large dining room. Call in advance because this place fills quickly. Singles €15; doubles with shower €35. Cash only. ❷

Hostal Guzmán el Bueno, López Castrillón, 6 (☎987 23 14 62; www.leoncentrogotico.com/hostalguzmanelbueno). Conveniently located in the old city, steps away from the cathedral. Rooms are large and have TV and full bath, but walls are thin. Singles €33; doubles €35-40. AmEx/MC/V. ❸

FOOD

Inexpensive eateries fill the area near the cathedral and the small streets off C. Ancha; also check **Plaza de San Martín** near Pl. Mayor. Meat-lovers will rejoice; many variations of pork top the local menus. The **Eroski Center Supermercado** is on Av. de Ordoño II, 16 (☎987 25 60 53. Open daily 9:30am-9:30pm. AmEx/MC/V.)

Café Gótico, C. Varillas, 5 (☎987 08 49 56). Conveniently located, with a pleasant outdoor patio. Delicious fresh food. The daily *menú* (€10.80) has a vegetarian option. A wide variety of salads, *platos combinados, raciones,* and dessert drinks. Excellent service. Entrees €4-11. Open daily 1-4pm and 8:30-11:30pm. AmEx/MC/V. ❷

▨ **Restaurante La Posada,** C. La Rúa, 33 (☎987 25 82 66). Cheery family restaurant off the beaten path. Savory *raciones* (€3-6) served in front of a stone hearth. Saturday's *menú del día* features a traditional meal from Castilla y León. *Menú* €8.70. Open daily 1-3:45pm M-Th, Su 7-11:45pm, F-Sa 8:30-11:45pm. MC/V. ❷

Restaurante Boccalino, Pl. de San Isodoro, 9 (☎987 22 30 60). Set right next to the picturesque Basílica San Isidoro, this restaurant features an incredibly wide selection of Italian and Spanish dishes: moderately priced salads, pasta, fish, meat, and pizza. Terrace overlooks the church. *Menú* €9. Open daily 7pm-1am. MC/V. ❷

Cros Coffee, C. Varillas, 5 (☎987 21 55 39). Next door to Café Gótico. Great selection of very reasonably priced sandwiches in a relaxed, familiar ambience. Salads, *tostadas,* and paella ranging €3-7.50. *Raciones* €2-10, decadent desserts €2-3. Open daily 10am-midnight. Cash only. ❷

⊙ SIGHTS

León has several historically and religiously significant sights, crowned by its magnificent cathedral. The city still retains a provincial quality, and has many attractive parks where weary travelers can sit and laze away the day.

▨ **IGLESIA CATEDRAL DE SANTA MARÍA.** The 13th-century Gothic cathedral, *La Pulchra Leonina,* arguably the most beautiful in Spain, exhibits the country's best Gothic architecture. The grand facade depicts smiling saints amid monsters munching on the damned. Silhouetted against a clear sky, the cathedral is best seen in the early morning or evening, when the angels and flowers depicted in the stained glass windows dazzle in phenomenal color and detail. Tours allow you to visit the cathedral's museum, which houses an impressive collection of slightly gruesome 7th-16th century religious artwork. *(On Pl. Regla. ☎987 87 57 70; www.catedraldeleon.org. Open July-Sept. M-Sa 8:30am-1:30pm and 4-8pm, festivals 8:30am-2:30pm and 5-8pm; Oct.-June M-Sa 8:30am-1:30pm and 4-7pm, festivals 8:30am-2:30pm and 5-7pm. Free. Tour of Museum in Spanish. Museum open June-Sept. M-F 9:30am-1pm and 4-6:30pm, Sa 9:30am-1pm, Su closed; Oct.-May M-F 9:30am-1pm and 4-6pm. €4, cloisters €1.)*

BASÍLICA SAN ISIDORO. The Romanesque Basílica San Isidoro was dedicated in the 11th century to San Isidoro of Sevilla. After his death, his remains were brought from Muslim-controlled Andalucía to the Christian stronghold of León. The corpses of countless royals rest in the **Panteón Real,** the ceilings of which are covered by vibrant 12th-century frescoes with themes of infancy, passion, and apocalypse. *(On Pl. San Isidoro. Open July-Aug. M-Sa 9am-8pm, Su 9am-2pm; Sept.-June M-Sa 10am-1:30pm and 4-6:30pm, Su 10am-1:30pm. €4, Th afternoons free.)*

OTHER SIGHTS. Casa de los Botines, on C. Ancha just off of Pl. Santo Domingo, is one of the few buildings outside Cataluña designed by Modernist architect Antoni Gaudí, the most famous member of the *Modernista* movement. The building now contains bank offices and is not open to the public.

▣ ▨ NIGHTLIFE AND FESTIVALS

For bars, discos, and techno, head to the *barrio húmedo* ("wet neighborhood," named for the free-flowing alcohol) around **Pl. de San Martín** and **Pl. Mayor.** Walk up C. Ancha toward the cathedral and turn right onto C. Varillas (which becomes C. Cardiles Platerías). Walk to the intersection with C. Carnicerías. To reach Pl. de San Martín, go right; to reach Pl. Mayor, go left onto C. Plegaría. If you're looking for a slightly older crowd, head to the **Pl. Torres de Omaña** and C. Astrilión and C. Cervantes. To reach either area, turn up C. Cervantes from the main pedestrian street C. Ancha, close to the cathedral. Most bars are open Monday through Thursday until 2am and Friday to Sunday until 5-6am. For a relaxed *copa de vino* (glass of wine) or a beer earlier on in the evening, head to **León Antiguo**, Pl. del Cid, 16. (Drinks €2-5. Open M-W 7pm-midnight, Th-Sa 7pm-4am.) For a bigger party later in the evening, head down the street to **Ático,** which features funky dance music and strong drinks. (☎987 24 86 53. Drinks €6, beer €3. Open M-Sa, Su closed.)

In the first week of June, León's 3500km of streams host the **International Trout Festival,** with a *concurso gastronómico* (cooking contest) on Tuesday. Festivals commemorating **San Juan** and **San Pedro** occur June 21-30. Highlights include a *corrida de toros* (bullfight), a massive chess tournament, clowns, artisans, and dance lessons on Pl. Regla. The high point is the feast day of San Juan (June 24). King Juan Carlos I and Queen Sofía have been known to attend.

ASTORGA ☎987

In the 15th century, Astorga was a vital stop on both the Roman silver route and the Camino de Santiago. It became one of the world's main chocolate-making centers in the 17th century, and until the turn of the 20th century there were 49 chocolate factories in Astorga alone. Today *confiterías* still infuse the streets with their sweet aromas. Astorga is one of the oldest towns in Castilla y León, and remnants of its history are everywhere. Modern sights include the fantastically odd Palacio Episcopal, a Gaudí masterpiece sitting atop this hillside city.

◪ TRANSPORTATION. The train station (☎987 61 64 44) is located on Pl. de la Estació and runs to: Barcelona (11hr.; 12:38, 11:48pm, via Lugo and Burgos; €45-58); Burgos (2½hr.; 12:38, 2:20, 11:48pm; €20-27); Gijón (2½hr.; 12:24pm, M-F Su 6:23pm, €12); León (40min., 8 per day 3:02am-11:48pm, €3.05); Madrid (3½-5hr., 3:02am, €40); Vigo (6hr.; 6:09am, 2:44, 5:10pm; €25-34). Buses (☎987 61 91 00) run from the station at Av. las Murallas, 54, to Ponferrada (M-F 10 per day 6:45am-9:15pm, Sa-Su 6 per day 9:15am-9:15pm; €4.60), Madrid (M-Sa 7-9 per day 2:15am-6:15pm, W until 7pm, Su 6 per day 2.15am-7pm; €20-27), Vitoria/Bilbao (3am, €26), and Oviedo and Gijón (4 per day 9:50am-8pm, €10.28).

⁊ ◪ PRACTICAL INFORMATION AND ORIENTATION. There is a **tourist office** at Glorieta Eduardo de Castro, 5. (☎987 61 82 22; www.ayuntamientodeastorga.com. Open Oct.-June daily 10am-1:30pm and 4-6:30pm; July-Sept. 10am-2pm and 4-7pm.) From the train station, head straight uphill onto Av. Estación. Continue uphill until the Pl. de Ponfidio Lopez, and head straight onto C. de las Enfermeras, diagonally across the street. At the Pl. de Obispo Alcolea, turn right onto C. Los Sitios. The tourist office is on your left in the Pl. I. Eduardo de Castro. To get there from the bus station, cross the street into the park with cathedral in front of you and walk straight up to the stairs. Turn left onto the street in front of cathedral. The tourist office will be on your right in the following plaza. A **bank,** Santander Central Hispano, is on Pl. Obispo Alcolea. From the tourist office, go down Los Sitios, which becomes Pl. Obispo Alcolea. (Open M-F 8:30am-2pm, Oct.-March Sa 8:30am-1pm.) Local services include **police** (☎987 61 60 80) and ambulance (☎987 61 85 62). **Internet** access is at Ciber@stoR, C. Manuel Gullón, 2. (☎987 61 80 17. €2 per hr. Open daily 10am-2pm and 4pm-midnight.) **Postal Code**: 24700.

⁊ ◪ ACCOMMODATIONS AND FOOD. Cheap accommodations are scarce in Astorga; some may prefer to stay in León instead. **Pensión Garcia ➋**, Bajada del Postigo, 3, has quaint and moderately-priced rooms with worn pine floors, clean hall bathrooms, and a bright common room. (☎987 61 60 46. Singles €20; doubles €30.) Another option is **Hostal San Narcisco ❷**, Ctra. Madrid-Coruña, km 325. Although a little bit out of the way and located above a noisy bar, this hostal offers spacious, standard rooms on the cheap. To get there, take the C. Leon from the plaza right behind the cathedral out to the highway.. (☎987 615 370. Singles €18, with bathroom €25; doubles €30/36.) Astorga is the one place where no one could blame you for eating dessert first. If you want a full meal, Plaza Mayor and the surrounding streets have plenty of options for the hungry traveler. For fresh meat, cheese, and produce, try **Gadis Supermercado**, Pl. Santocildes, 6. (Open 9am-2:30pm and 5-9pm. MC/V.) **Ruta Romana ❶** and **Cafeteria/Cervecería Imperial ❶**, under the same ownership, are located at Pl. Santocildes, 9, and offer a great selection, friendly service, and a fun atmosphere. Cafeteria has standard tapas fare: ham croquettes (€3) and a variety of salads (€5-7) fill out the menu. The bar is a popular hangout among locals and tourists alike. (☎987 60 30 20. *Menú* €10. Tapas and *raciones* €3-9. Desserts €2-4. Open daily 8am-midnight. MC/V.) **Cervecería Taberna los Hornos ❷**, Pl. de España, 3, serves good and cheap traditional food in a relaxed, tavern-like atmosphere. (☎379 87 61 89. Entrees €8-11, tapas €3-4. Open daily 8am-midnight.)

◪ SIGHTS. Created by Antoni Gaudí, the ◪**Palacio Episcopal (Bishop's Palace)** is Astorga's main distinction. The palace is set upon a section of the ancient Roman wall, and the turrets, main entryway, and beveled stone exterior are pure Gaudí. The palace houses the **Museo de los Caminos**, exhibits historic and contemporary interpretations of the Santiago de Compostela pilgrimage, as well as a permanent exposition of contemporary artwork from Leonese artists. (☎987 61 88 82. Open July-Sept. Tu-Sa 10am-2pm and 4-8pm, Su 10am-2pm; Oct.-June Tu-Sa 11am-2pm and 4-6pm, Su 11am-2pm. €2.50, €1.50 for people over 65 or under 18.) Sugar fiends must stop by the ◪**Museo de Chocolate**, C. José María Goy, 5. This museum chronicles the history of chocolate—from cocoa beans to chocolate wrappers and old chocolate boxes from Granada. In the next room, visitors are welcome to taste free samples. From the Palacio Episcopal, walk up C. los Sitios to Pl. Obispo Alcolea; veer to the right onto C. Lorenzo Segura and C. José María Goy is on the right. (Open Tu-Sa 10:30am-2pm and 4:30-7pm, Su 10:30am-2pm. €2.) The **Museo Romano**, Pl. San Bartolomé, offers a joint ticket (€3), and features artifacts and relics from Astorga's Roman and pre-Roman past. (Open Tu-Sa 10am-1:30pm, 4-6pm, Su 10am-1:30pm. €2.) If you have an hour to spare, walk around the Roman walls encircling the city for magnificent views of Astorga and the far-off mountains.

VALLADOLID   ☎983

When Fernando and Isabel married in Valladolid in 1469, the city stood at the forefront of Spanish politics, finance, and culture. Explorers such as Fernão Magelhães (Ferdinand Magellan) came here to discuss their navigation plans; Miguel de Cervantes, the mind behind Don Quixote, lived here; and in 1506, Christopher Columbus died here. Today, the administrative capital of Castilla y León has a reputation of class, sophistication, and architectural diversity. Wandering through cobblestone streets past outdoor cafes, fountains, statues, and plazas, one experiences both the past majesty of Spain's original capital as well as the lively but laidback culture of what is now a safe and comfortable town.

▌ TRANSPORTATION

Flights: Villanubla Airport, CN-601, km 13 (☎983 41 55 00). Taxi to airport €17-20. Daily flights to **Barcelona, Islas Baleares, Vigo, Brussels, Lisboa, London**, and **Paris**. Info open daily 8am-8pm. **Iberia** (☎983 56 01 62). Open daily 8am-8pm.

Trains: Estación del Norte, C. Recondo (☎902 24 02 02; www.renfe.es), south of Parque del Campo Grande. Info open daily 7am-8:30pm. Trains to: **Barcelona** (9¾-11hr.; daily 9:15am, Sa-Su also 9:40pm; €42); **Bilbao** (4hr.; daily 11:45am, M-Sa 1:40am; €23); **Burgos** (1¾-2½hr.; M-F 10 per day 1:30am-8pm, Sa-Su 8-10 per day 1:30am-5pm; €6.90-14); **León** (2-3hr.; M-Sa 10-11 per day 12:37am-9:08pm, Su 7 per day 10:25am-9:08pm; €9.20-20); **Madrid** (3-3¾hr.; 14-15 per day M-Sa 4am-8:41pm, Su 7am-9pm; €14-24); **Oviedo** (4-5½hr.; 2-3 per day 1:42am-5:25pm, €27); **Paris** (11hr., 9:20pm, €127); **Salamanca** (1¾-2¾hr.; 6-8 per day 3:20am-10:17pm, €7.20-14); **Santander** (3-6hr.; 6-8 per day M-Th and Sa 1:42am-6:54pm, F 1:42am-7:18pm, Su 7:15am-6:54pm; €14-25).

Buses: C. de Puente Colgante, 2 (☎983 23 63 08). Info open daily 8am-10pm. **ALSA** (☎902 42 22 42; www.alsa.es) to: **Barcelona** (10½hr., 11am and 9:30pm, €40); **Bilbao** (4-6hr.; M-Sa 4-5 per day 5:45am-4:15pm, Su 3 per day 5:45am-5pm; €16; Eurobus service 3½hr., 11am, €18); **Burgos** (2-3hr., 5-6 per day 5:45am-9pm, €8); **León** (2hr.; M-Sa 8-9 per day 12:45am-9:45pm, Su 7 per day 2:45am-10:45pm; €8); **Madrid** (2hr.; 19-22 per day M-Sa 12:30am-9:30pm, Su 4:50am-10pm; €12-16); **Oviedo** (3-4hr., 5-6 per day 2am-7:45pm, €16); **Santander** (4hr.; 9:30am, 5:30pm; €10). **La Regional** (☎983 27 15 87; www.laregionalvsa.com) to **Palencia** (45min.; M-F hourly 7am-9pm, Sa 6 per day 8am-8:15pm, Su 3 per day 10am-8pm; €3) and **Zamora** (1½hr.; M-F hourly 7am-8:30pm, Sa 6 per day 8:30am-8:30pm, Su 4 per day 8:30am-8:30pm; €6).

Taxis: Radio Taxi (☎983 29 14 11). 24hr. Train and bus stations to Pl. Mayor €4-5.

Bike Rental: Monta y Pedalea (☎626 70 90 45), Playa de las Morenas. €2.50 for 1hr., €10 per day, €50 per week. Open Tu 5-9pm, W-Su 11:30am-2pm and 5-9pm.

⚡ 🔢 ORIENTATION AND PRACTICAL INFORMATION

The bus and train stations are on the southern edge of town, near the Parque del Campo Grande. To get from the **bus station** to the **tourist office** (15min.), leave the bus station through the left exit as you get off the bus. Turn right onto C. San José and take the first left on Po. del Arco de Ladrillo; keep right onto C. Ladrillo at the rotary and follow it until Po. de Los Filipinos. Turn right and walk along the park until Pl. de Colón. Turn left onto Av. Acera de Recoletos, with the park on your left, and continue to the tourist office. From the front entrance of the **train station** (10min.), walk up the street perpendicular to the station, C. Estación del Norte, and follow it to Pl. de Colón. Follow the rotary to the right; Av. Acera de Recoletos will be the third street on the right. The tourist office is at the top of Av. Acera de Recoletos on your left. From the tourist office, continue up Av. Acera de Recoletos until you reach Pl. de Zorilla. **C.Santiago,** the main pedestrian street, is the second to the right. **Pl. Mayor** is straight up C. Santiago from the tourist office.

Tourist Office: Av. Acera de Recoletos (☎983 34 40 13; www.ava.es). Helpful staff. English spoken. Open daily 9am-2pm and 5-8pm. For general tourism information about Valladolid and Castilla y León, call ☎012 (if calling from within the region) or ☎902 91 00 12 (if outside the region).

Currency Exchange: Citibank, C. Miguel Iscar, 7, off Pl. de Zorrilla. Open M-F 8:30am-2pm. **BBVA,** Av. Acera de Recoletos, 1, on the corner with C. Miguel Iscar. (☎902 22 44 66; www.bbva.es). Open M-F 8:30am-2:15pm, Sa 8:30am-1pm. Banks line Av. Acera de Recoletos; most exchange cash and traveler's checks.

Luggage Storage: At the **train station** at the end of Platform 1. Lockers €3-4.50 per hr. At the **bus station** (€0.70 per bag 1 day; extra days €1). Open M-Sa 8am-10pm.

Police: In the Ayuntamiento (municipal police) (☎983 42 61 07 or 091).

Late-Night Pharmacy: Da. Esther Vicente Reguero Po. de Zorilla, 85 at C. Luna. (☎983 23 15 44). Open M-F 10pm-9:30am; Sa-Su and holidays 10pm-10am.

CASTILLA Y LEÓN

Medical Services: Hospital Pío del Río Hortega, Rnda. de Sta. Teresa (☎983 42 04 00).

Internet Access: Ciberc@fé Segafredo Zanetti, Po. de Zorrilla, 46 (☎983 33 80 63). From Pl. de Zorrilla, walk down Po. de Zorrilla alongside the park; the cafe is on right before Av. García Morato. €0.50 per 10min. Open daily 8am-11pm.

Post Office: Pl. Rinconada (☎983 33 02 31; www.correos.es). 2 blocks from Pl. Mayor, up C. Jesús on the right. Lista de Correos, photocopying, fax, and phone cards available. Open M-F 8:30am-8:30pm, Sa 8:30am-2pm. **Postal Code:** 47001.

⚑ ACCOMMODATIONS

Cheap lodgings and *pensiones* pack the streets off Av. de Recoletos near the train station, the area by the cathedral, and behind Pl. Mayor at Pl. del Val.

Hostal Del Val, Pl. del Val, 6 (☎983 37 57 52; benidiopor@auna.com). Centrally located in a historic building with views of the plaza. At night, you may want to wear earplugs to block out the noisy nightclub downstairs. Rooms with private bathrooms have TVs. Book in advance. Singles €20, with bath €33; doubles €30/42. MC/V. ❷

Hostal Colón, Av. Acera de Recoletas, 22 (☎983 30 40 44). Just a short walk from the train station, Hostal Colón features spacious rooms and great service. The staff is very friendly and happy to help travelers find their bearings in Valladolid. Closed on Sundays. Singles €20-26; doubles without bath €27-38, with bath €34-45. Cash only. ❷

Hostal los Arces, C. San Antonio de Padua, 2, 1st fl. (☎983 35 38 53; benidiopor@auna.com). 3 blocks from Pl. Mayor, just off Pl. de los Arces. Under the same ownership as Hostal del Val. Features cozy rooms with old European charm. Lounge with TV and Playstation. Singles €15, with shower €33; doubles €30/42. MC/V. ❷

⬛ FOOD

An assortment of terraced restaurants and cafes lies between Pl. Mayor and Pl. del Val and near the cathedral. The *castellano* restaurants around Pl. Martí y Monsó, off Pl. Mayor, boast local specialties like *lechazo* (roast lamb) and roast quail. **Mercado del Val,** in Pl. del Val, has fresh fruit and vegetables and lots of fish and meat. (Open M-Sa 9am-3:30pm.) For a supermarket, head to **Supermercados Champion,** on C. Santiago, 13. (☎983 35 92 11. Open M-Sa 9:30am-9:30pm.)

Restaurante Covadonga, C. Zapico, 1 (☎983 33 07 98). This lively establishment with a tastefully decorated interior and reasonable prices will leave you satisfied. *Menú* allows you to select an appetizer, main course, and dessert for €11.90, wine included. Open M-Tu and Th-Sa 1-4pm and 9-11:30pm, W 9-11:30pm. MC/V. ❷

La Toscana, P. de Zorilla, 30 (☎983 35 22 27). This quaint little cafe originally opened in Cuba over 100 years ago. Now Spain also enjoys its all-natural ice cream (€1-3), coffee (€1.10), pastries (€2-5), and frozen drinks (€1-3). Open daily summer 9:30am-11:30pm; winter 10am-9:30pm. Cash only. ❶

El Rincón del Val, Pl. del Val (☎983 33 18 88), a few blocks off the Pl. Mayor. Boasts specialties from the sea (entrees €9-18), vegetarian options (salads €7-12), beer (€2.60), and sangria (€7 per liter). Ask for a table on the romantic terrace. Opens M-F 11am, Sa 12:30pm, Su 12:45pm. Closing time varies. MC/V. ❷

◉ SIGHTS

Valladolid is surrounded by churches, bridges, and pastures. Although the city's sights revolve around art, religion, and culture of centuries past, the attractions gracefully merge medieval with modern to provide a glimpse of both old and new.

■**CASA DE CERVANTES.** The windmill-chasing, barmaid-wooing idealist Don Quixote may be a fictional character, but his presence is almost tangible in the place where he was first created. A serene historical space remains at the house where Cervantes penned *Don Quixote* from 1603 to 1606. Cervantes's vast library is currently not open to the public, but the house itself is; take a tour of Cervantes's living and working spaces, embellished with low ceilings and beautiful woodwork. *(C. Rastro. From Pl. de Zorrilla, walk up C. Miguel Iscar; C. Rastro is 2 blocks up on the right. ☎983 30 88 10. Open Tu-Sa 9:30am-3pm, Su 10am-3pm. €2.40, students with ID €1.20, under 18 and over 65 free. Su free.)*

CATEDRAL METROPOLITANA. Designed by Juan de Herrera, creator of El Escorial (p. 141), this grand cathedral is an excellent example of Herrera's *desornamentado* style of plain masonry, despite some later ornamental additions. The extensive **Museo Diocesano,** in the Gothic addition, houses the remains of the original 11th- to 13th-century structure as well as Herrera's model of the basilica. *(C. Arribas, 1. From Pl. Mayor, walk up C. Ferrari. After 2 blocks, veer left onto Bajada de la Libertad. At Pl. de la Libertad, turn right. ☎983 30 43 62. Open Tu-F 10am-1:30pm and 4:30-7pm, Sa-Su 10am-2pm. Mass Su and festivals 10:45am, noon, 1:30, 6pm. Museum €2.50. Cathedral free.)*

MUSEO NACIONAL DE ESCULTURA. This vast museum boasts a fascinating chronological collection of Spanish sculpture, from an international Gothic *pietà* of the 16th century to more recent Baroque works. It features the works of Renaissance and Baroque masters Alonso Berruguete, Juan de Juni, and Gregorio Fernández. Due to construction on the original museum building, the Colegio de San Gregorio, the museum is currently located in the Palacio de Villena. The collections will be moved back to the Colegio within the year. *(Palacio de Villena, C. San Gregorio, 1. ☎983 25 03 75; www.mne.es. Open Tu-Su Mar. 21-Sept. 20 10am-2pm and 4-9pm; Sept. 21-Mar. 20 10am-2pm and 4-6pm; Su throughout the year 10am-2pm. €2.40, students €1.20, under 18 and over 65 free. Sa afternoon and Su free.)*

🎵 NIGHTLIFE AND ENTERTAINMENT

Lively cafes and drinking establishments are spread throughout the city. Students fill the countless bars on **Calle Paraíso,** near the cathedral. From Pl. de la Universidad at the cathedral, turn left onto C. Duque de Lerma, then right onto C. Marqués del Duero; C. Paraíso will be on the right. **Salobanco,** C. Doctor Cazalla, 4, on **Plaza San Miguel,** is popular among university students and travelers alike. From Pl. Mayor, walk up Pl. Corrillo, turn left onto C. Val; after the plaza, continue onto C. Zapico, and at Pl. los Arces, turn left onto C. San Antonio de Padua, which brings you to Pl. San Miguel. (Beer €2.60. Open M-Tu 10:30pm-2:30am, W-Th 11pm-3:30am, F-Sa 9pm-3:30am.) The area around **Plaza Martí y Monsó,** just off Pl. Mayor, has the most central nightlife. In addition to late-night tapas bars like **El Corcho,** C. Correos, 2 (tapas €1.20-2; beer and wine €1.30; open M-Th and Su 1-4pm and 8pm-midnight, F-Sa until 1am) and chic wine bars like **Vino Tinto Jóven,** C. Campanas, 12 (wine €1.50-2.50; open M-Sa 8pm-6am), this neighborhood also houses Valladolid's dance clubs. **Baqur,** C. Pasión, 13 is has two floors and blasts club and Spanish music. (Open 8:30pm-6am.) **Café España,** Pl. Fuente Dorada, 8, has regular jazz concerts. (☎983 37 17 64; www.cafespa.net. Open M-Th 8:30am-12:30am, F-Sa 8:30am-3am. Cash only.)

🔲 DAYTRIPS FROM VALLADOLID

MEDINA DEL CAMPO
La Regional V.S.A. runs buses to Medina del Campo from Valladolid (45min.-1hr., M-F 4 per day 9:15am-8:15pm, €3). Buses back to Valladolid leave from the bus stop at the

Pl. de San Agustín (M-F 8 per day 7am-7pm, Sa 4 per day 8am-7:30pm; €3.30, round-trip €5.50). Tickets and information are available at the neighboring Bar Punto Rojo (☎983 80 12 98). Open daily 6am-midnight.

Medina del Campo was once the destination of choice for wealthy medieval traders and moneylenders. At its peak, the town was famous for banking and the sheep industry, drawing tens of thousands of visitors every year and serving as the country's gateway for art imports. Today, Medina del Campo's greatest claim to fame is its association with the illustrious Queen Isabel; the town houses her majesty's summer getaway, and Isabel signed her will and died in Medina del Campo. Medina del Campo's most impressive sight is the 15th-century brick **Castillo de la Mota** on a hilltop overlooking the town. To get there, exit Pl. Mayor from the corner opposite the tourist office on C. Maldonado. Turn left at the intersection, cross the bridge over the dry riverbed, walk beneath the highway (access on C. Claudio Moyano), exit on the second stairwell to your right before the tunnel ends, and go uphill onto Av. del Castillo. Queen Isabel and her daughter, Juana la Loca, once lived in the castle, and it has also served as an arsenal and prison. Today, tourists come to see the **chapel** of Santa María del Castillo, and a mural-sized copy of an AD 1500 world map. Only the ground floor is open to visitors, but the Castillo is worth the hike. (☎983 80 10 24. Open M-Sa 11am-2pm and 4-7pm, Su 11am-2pm. Free.) The **Palacio Real Testamentario,** on the corner of the Pl. Mayor, has exhibits on the queen's childhood, reign, and final days, along with copies of her signed will. (☎983 81 00 63; www.palaciorealtestamentario.com. Open M-Sa May-Sept. 10am-1:30pm and 5pm-8pm; Oct.-Feb. 10am-1:30pm and 4pm-7pm. €2, seniors and under 26 €1.80. English audio tours €1.80.)

Medina del Campo is certainly worth a daytrip, though not necessarily an overnight stay. If you do choose to spend the night, a good option is **Hostal Mesón La Plaza ❷,** Pl. Mayor, 34. Call a week ahead in the summer. (☎983 81 12 46; mesonlaplaza@medinacomercial.com. Singles €20; doubles €35; triples €47. MC/V.) There are several quality restaurants located around Pl. Major. **Restaurante Monaco ❸,** Pl. Mayor, 26, has an extensive wine list and a fantastic range of appetizers, entrees, and desserts. *Gambas al ajillo* (shrimp in garlic sauce) is sold as an €8 appetizer, but with free bread and a glass of wine on the side, it is easily a meal. (☎983 80 10 20. Entrees around €16. *Menú* €25. MC/V.)

To get to Plaza Mayor from the bus stop, walk past the bar El Punto Rojo on your right and continue up the street. At the intersection, turn left onto C. de Gamaza and continue straight until you reach the Plaza; the **tourist office,** Pl. Mayor 48, is to your right. (☎983 81 13 57; www.ayto-medinadelcampo.es. Open M 8am-3pm, Tu-F 8am-3pm and 4-7pm, Sa 10am-2pm and 4-7pm, Su 10am-2pm.)

TORDESILLAS

Tordesillas is a 30min. bus ride from Valladolid (M-F 15 per day 7:30am-8:30pm, Sa 9 per day 8:30am-8:30pm; Su 6 per day 8:30am-10:30pm; €2, round-trip €3.65). To get back, go to the bus station on C. de Valdehuertos, 1 (☎983 77 00 72). La Regional V.S.A. runs buses to Valladolid (30min.; M-F 14 per day 7am-9:30pm, Sa 10 per day 7:45am-7:30pm, Su 6 per day 11:30am-11pm; €1.95) and Zamora (1hr.; M-F 7 per day 8am-8:30pm, Sa 6 per day 8am-6:30pm, Su 4 per day 10:30am-8pm; €4.10).

A playing field and building ground for Catholic kings and queens, Tordesillas (pop. 8700) is best known through the 1494 treaty that, rather presumptuously, divided the New World between Spain and Portugal. Inside the old city walls, the town preserves its monasteries and churches with hospitality. Tordesillas is not the most riveting of daytrips, but it does offer some entertainment.

One of the town's unique artistic sights is the **Museo y Centro Didáctico del Encaje de Castilla y León,** C. Carnicerías, 4. This world-renowned needlework museum and research center has an extensive lace collection dating from the 16th century, with an emphasis on the distinct historical designs of Castilla's regions. (☎983 79 60 35;

www.museoencaje.com. Open M-F 5-8pm, Sa noon-2pm and 5-7pm, Su noon-2pm. Mandatory tour €2, students €1.) The **Real Monasterio de Santa Clara**, on C. Santa Clara, was completed in 1363 under Pedro I, who incorporated Moorish designs and dedicated the building to his mistress, María de Padilla. (☎983 77 00 71. Open Apr.-Sept. Tu-Sa 10am-1:30pm and 4-6:30pm, Su 10:30am-1:30pm and 3:30-5:30pm; Oct.-Mar. Tu-Sa 10:30am-1:30pm and 4-5:45pm, Su 10:30am-1:30pm and 3:30-5:30pm. €3.60 including tour, students with ISIC €2. W free for EU citizens.)

The center of town and the old district is the **Plaza Mayor,** a 10min. walk from the bus station; all major sights are within a few blocks. The **tourist office,** C. Tratado, at the top of the hill before C. San Antolín, shares its entrance with the Museo del Tratado. (☎983 77 10 67; www.tordesillas.net. Museum and tourist office open summer Tu-Sa 10am-1:30pm and 5-7:30pm, Su 10am-2pm; winter Tu-Sa 10am-1:30pm and 4-6:30pm, Su 10am-2pm.)

BURGOS   ☎947

By day, Burgos (pop. 346,000) is a city celebrated for its rich history, breathtaking art, and unique cuisine. By night, it is infused with a different kind of energy; behind the magnificently lit cathedral and luminous plazas, narrow streets glow with the neon signs from local bars and clubs. Unlike many other cities of Castilla y Leon, Burgos is cosmopolitan in every sense of the word—as you walk through its cafe and restaurant-filled winding streets, you'll smell cuisines from every corner of the world and hear chatter in foreign languages. Still, Burgos holds fast to its traditions and history. The region's hero, El Cid Campeador, a crusader of medieval lore, was born and eventually buried here. Today you can trace the "Route of El Cid" that begins at his birthplace in Vivar and enters Burgos through the Portal de San Martín south of the city.

◣ TRANSPORTATION

Trains: Pl. de la Estación (☎947 20 35 60). 10min. walk or €3 taxi ride to the city center. Info open 24hr. (☎902 24 02 02). To: **Barcelona** (9-14hr.; M-F and Su 4 per day 2:17am-11:24pm, Sa 3 per day 2:17am-3:07pm; €38-51); **Bilbao** (2½-4hr., 4 per day 3:17am-5:13pm, €16-22); **La Coruña** (6-9hr., 3 per day 3:43am-9:06pm, €36-47); **León** (2-3hr., 6-8 per day 3:43am 7:10pm, €10); **Lisboa** (8-10hr., 2am, €60); **Madrid** (3-5½hr., 5-6 per day 2:20am-7:18pm, €22-34); **Palencia** (45min.; M-F and Su 7-9 per day 3:43am-8:35pm, Sa until 7:18pm; €4.25-11.20); **Valladolid** (1-2hr.; M-Th and Sa-Su 10-11 per day 1:59am-9:06pm, F 11 per day 1:49am-11:13pm; €6.85-14.50).

Buses: C. Miranda, 4 (☎947 28 88 55). Information open 24hr.; if there isn't someone in the booth look around the station for help. **ALSA** (www.alsa.es, ☎902 422 242) runs to: **Bilbao** (2-3hr., M-Th and Sa 4 per day 8:30am-7pm, F 5 per day 8:30am-9pm, Su 5 per day 10:30am-10:30pm; €11); **Gijon** (4½hr.; daily 6:45am, 5:45pm; €17.09) via **Oviedo** (4hrs.; 6:46am, 5:40pm, Sa 2:20am; €15.69); **León** (3½hr.; M-F 4 per day 6:45am-6:15pm, Sa 4 per day 2:20am-4:30pm, Su 3 per day 6:45am-6:15pm; €13); **Salamanca** (3-4hr.; M-Th 4 per day 11:15am-9pm, Tu-W, F-Sa 3 per day 11:45am-9pm, Su 4 per day 12:45pm-9pm; €14-18); **Valladolid** (2-3hr.; M-Th, Sa-Su 5-6 per day 6:30am-9pm, F 6 per day 6:30am-9:45pm; €8). **Continental-Auto** runs to: **Madrid** (2¾hr.; M-Sa 12-15 per day 3:15am-10:30pm, Su 17 per day midnight-10:30pm; €15); **San Sebastián** (4-5hr.; M-Th-Sa 7 per day 3:15am-10pm, F 9 per day 3:15am-11:59pm, Su 7 per day 3:15am-11:59pm; €14.50); **Santander** (3hr., 5-7 per day 3:15am-10pm, €10.50); **Vitoria-Gasteiz** (2hr.; M-Th and Sa 9 per day 3:15am-10pm, F and Su 9-11 per day 3:15am-11:59pm; €7).

Car Rental: Hertz, C. Madrid, 2 (☎947 20 16 75). 23+. Credit card in driver's name required for deposit. Small cars with unlimited mileage from €60 per day. Open M-F 9am-1pm and 4-7pm, Sa 9am-1pm. AmEx/MC/V.

Taxis: Abutaxi (☎947 27 77 77) or **Radio Taxi** (☎947 48 10 10). 24hr.

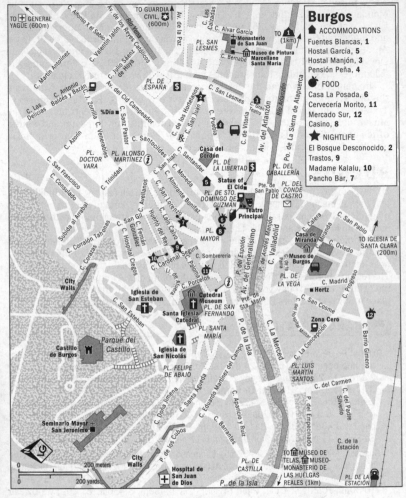

Burgos

⬆ ACCOMMODATIONS
Fuentes Blancas, **1**
Hostal García, **5**
Hostal Manjón, **3**
Pensión Peña, **4**

🍴 FOOD
Casa La Posada, **6**
Cervecería Morito, **11**
Mercado Sur, **12**
Casino, **8**

★ NIGHTLIFE
El Bosque Desconocido, **2**
Trastos, **9**
Madame Kalalu, **10**
Pancho Bar, **7**

CASTILLA Y LEÓN

✦🛈 ORIENTATION AND PRACTICAL INFORMATION

The Río Arlanzón splits Burgos into north and south. While the **train** and **bus stations** are to the south, the **Catedral Santa Iglesia** and most other sights of interest are in the north. To get to the main part of the city from the **train station,** exit out the front of the station and walk straight up C. de la Estación, crossing the small bridge. At the end of the bridge, you will come to a small rotary. Take the second right, C. de Aparicio y Ruiz. Follow it until you come to an intersection with C. de Eduardo Martinez del Campo (right in front of the University building). Turn right onto C. de Eduardo Martinez del Campo, and in about 50m, turn left onto C. Asunción de Ntra. Señora. This street will bring you right into the center of the city, in plain view of the cathedral. From the **bus station,** exit left out of the front entrance onto C. de Miranda. Continue down the street until the intersection and then turn right onto C. de Madrid—you will see the spires of the cathedral ahead. Continue up the street, staying to the left at the rotary and then crossing over a small bridge. Then, go through the arch in front of you into the Pl. del Rey San Fernando.

Tourist Office: Regional Office, Pl. Alonso Martínez, 7 (☎947 20 31 25 or 902 20 30 30). Open July-Sept. M-Th and Su 9am-8pm, F-Sa 9am-9pm; Oct.-June daily 9am-2pm and 5-8pm. The **Municipal Office** is next to the Burgos Cathedral, Pl. de San Fernando, 2 (☎947 28 88 74). Open July-Sept. daily 10am-8pm; Oct.-June M-F 10am-2pm and 4:30-7:30pm, Sa-Su and holidays 10am-1:30pm and 4-7:30pm.

Currency Exchange: Banco Santander Central Hispano, Pl. del Mío Cid, 6 (☎902 24 24 24). Open Apr.-Sept. M-F 8:30am-2pm; Oct.-Mar. also Sa 8:30am-1pm. There are 24hr. **ATMs** on C. San Juan near C. Santander and along C. del Cid.

Luggage Storage: 24hr. lockers at train station €3 per day; bus station €2 per day. Tickets available for purchase at information desk.

Police: Av. Cantabria, 54 (☎947 28 88 39). **Guardia Civil,** Av. Cantabria, 87-95 (☎947 22 22 63).

Medical Services: Ambulance SACYL ☎947 23 75 76. **Hospital General Yagüe,** Av. del Cid Campeador, 96 (☎947 28 18 00). **Hospital de San Juan de Dios,** Po. de la Isla, 41 (☎947 25 77 30).

Internet Access: Zonacero, C. la Concepción, 18 (947 208 649). Internet €1.80 per hour. (€0.50). Open daily 10:30am-2:30pm and 4-10pm. **Biblioteca del Teatro Principal,** Po. del Espolón (☎947 28 88 73). Free 30min. slots. ID required. Open July M-F 8:30am-2:30pm; Aug. M-F 8:30am-9pm; Sept.-June M-F 9am-9pm, Sa 9:30am-2pm.

Post Office: Pl. del Conde de Castro (☎/fax 947 25 66 11). **Lista de Correos** and **fax.** Open M-F 8:30am-8:30pm, Sa 9:30am-12pm. **Postal Code:** 09080.

Laundromat: Presto, C. San Lorenzo, 28. (☎947 20 79 76). Open M-F 9:30am-2pm, 6-8:30pm, Sa 10am-2pm.

⌐ ACCOMMODATIONS

Cheap and desirable accommodations are hard to find in touristy Burgos, but there are some reasonably priced *hostales* and *pensiones* along and near C. San Juan and C. Puebla, leading from the Plaza de la Libertad. Otherwise try hostels on C. Vitoria, at the eastern end of the city, and along Ctr. N-1 toward Irún. Reservations are crucial on summer weekends, given all the festivals from June-August.

Hostal Manjón, C. Gran Teatro, 1, 7th fl. (☎947 20 86 89). A short walk from the city center, this hostel has palatial, well-lit rooms with TV and sink, and an elevator—no luggage lugging here. Single €25, with bathroom €35; doubles €33/42. MC/V. ❷

Pensión Peña, C. Puebla, 18 (☎947 20 63 23). Newly-renovated rooms, only steps away from all-night bars. Shared bath. Single €17; doubles €26. Cash only. ❷

Hostal García, C. Santander, 1, 3rd. (☎947 20 53 53). Located almost on the Pl. del Cid. Sunny rooms, some with balconies overlooking the street. Prices vary with season. Shared bath. Singles €25; doubles €35. Cash only. ❷

Fuentes Blancas, Parque de Fuentes Blancas. (☎947 48 60 16). Catch the #26 bus ("Fuentes Blancas") from Pl. de España June-Aug. (M-F every 30min., 7:45am-10:45pm, €0.70). Sept.-May ride the #7 from the same plaza (4 per day, 9:30am-7:15pm). Showers and restaurant. Open Apr.-Sept. €4.30 per person, €3 per child, €3.50-7 per tent, €4 per car. MC/V. ❶

LOCAL LEGEND

EL CID CAMPEADOR

Whether it's a street name in Leon, a statue in Burgos, or a restaurant in Valladolid, it's hard to escape references to the famous Spanish general of the Reconquista, El Cid Campeador, when visiting the major cities of Castilla y Leon. Who was the man behind the reverential titles and what was his contribution to the Spanish Reconquista?

Rodrigo (Ruy) Díaz de Vivar was born in a small town just north of Burgos in the mid-11th century. Early in his career he led the King of Castille's armies against the Moors. Later he became a mercenary for both Muslim and Christian rulers before conquering Moorish Valencia in 1090, and establishing a kingdom there and making it a Christian city. As Vivar's two titles show, he inspired tremendous respect in both Christian and Muslim groups. El Cid comes from the Andalucían Arabic dialect "al-sid," which derives from the Arabic "sayyid," meaning chief or lord. Campeador, on the other hand, originates in the Latin "campi doctor," meaning "master of the military arts."

El Cid died in Valencia in 1099, but even in death he was victorious. Legend says that his wife strapped his body to his horse and sent it into battle. The troops, seeing the body of their general riding dedicatedly and fearsomely into battle even after death, were rejuvenated and went on to defeat the opposing forces.

◨ FOOD

Burgaleses take pride in their *morcilla* sausage and their *queso de Burgos*, a soft cheese usually served with honey or in a *tarta* as dessert. Look near the cathedral for these staples. C. San Lorenzo is tapas heaven. **Mercado Sur,** on Calle Barrio Gimeno, has fresh meat and bread (Open M-Th 8am-3pm, F-Sa 7:30am-3:15pm). For groceries, try **%Día,** Sanz Pastor, 16 (Open M-Sa 9:30am-2pm and 5-8pm).

Casa La Posada, Pl. Santo Domingo de Guzmán, 18 (☎947 20 45 78). Although a bit pricey, this cozy restaurant is a vegetarian haven, featuring a daily vegetable speciality and an ever-changing *menú* (€15). Fish and meat entrees €7-18. Open daily 1-4pm and 8pm-midnight. AmEx/MC/V. ❸

Cervecería Morito, C. Sombrerería, 27 (☎947 26 75 55). The line for the Cervecería's good, cheap food often snakes out the door. *Raciones* €1-5.30. Sandwiches €2.50-4.50. *Revueltos* €3.60-4.50. Open daily 7pm-midnight. Cash only. ❶

Casino, Pl. Mayor (☎938 05 26 12). Located in the heart of the Plaza Mayor, this cafeteria-restaurant features a variety of paella dishes (€6-8). If you're hankering for classic Spanish cuisine, head here to find it on the cheap. Open daily 9am-midnight. ❷

◉ SIGHTS

CATEDRAL DE BURGOS. The Catedral de Burgos is one of the most stunning in Spain. Its majestic spires, which find their way into every view of the city, are matched only by its Gothic interior. Originally a Romanesque church built by 13th-century *Reconquista* hero Fernando III (El Santo), the cathedral was transformed over three centuries into a Gothic marvel. The cathedral is the product of hundreds of years of work, and its 29 magnificent chambers reflect different time periods, artistic styles, and religious events. Visitors can enter the Chapel of Christ to see the cathedral's holiest and most infamous arch: a crucified Jesus constructed of buffalo skin with human hair and nails. The cathedral has other wonders for those not attending services: the 16th-century stained-glass dome of the Capilla Mayor, the eerily life-like *papamoscas* (flycatcher), and, under the transept, marked by a small brick beneath a star-shaped lantern, the remains of El Cid himself. The cathedral's **museum** displays a Visigoth Bible and El Cid's nuptial documents, as well as chalices, paintings, and tapestries. (☎947 20 47 12; www.catedraldeburgos.es.

Open July-Sept. M-Sa 9:30am-7:15pm; Apr.-June and Oct. M-Sa 9:30am-1:15pm, 4-7:15pm, Nov.-March 10am-1:15pm, 4-6:45pm. Chapel of Christ free. Cathedral and museum €4, students €2.50, pilgrims €1. Audio tour in English €3.50.)

▨ MUSEO-MONASTERIO DE LAS HUELGAS REALES. Built by King Alfonso VIII in 1187, the austere Museo-Monasterio de las Huelgas Reales is slightly out of the way, but certainly worth the trip. Once a summer palace for Castilian kings and later an elite convent for Cistercian nuns, today's monastery-cum-museum allows visitors a glimpse of the glory of medieval Castilian royalty. *(Take the "Barrio del Pilar" bus from Pl. de España to the Museo stop; €0.70. ☎ 947 20 16 30. Open Tu-Sa 10am-1p and 3:45-5:30pm, Su 10:30am-2pm. Mandatory tours in Spanish every 30min. €5, students and under 14 €2.50, under 5 free. EU citizens free W.)*

MUSEO DE BURGOS. This sprawling 16th-century mansion has four floors of provincial Burgalese art and archaeology, with everything from paleolithic skulls to Roman relics from the nearby town of Clunia. The adjacent **Casa de Inigo Angulo** also features four floors of art. Included in the exhibits are a piece of the Santo Domingo de Silos monastery's facade, the sepulchre of Don Juan de Padilla, and paintings from the 14th to 20th centuries. *(C. Miranda, 13. ☎ 947 26 58 75. Open Oct.-June M-Sa 10am-2pm and 4-7pm, Su 10am-2pm; July-Sept. M-Sa 10am-2pm and 5-8pm, Su 10am-2pm. €1.20, under 18, seniors, and students with ID free. Sa and Su free.)*

▨ ❀ NIGHTLIFE AND FESTIVALS

Burgaleses start the night out by sampling *pinchos* and sipping on glasses of wine in tapas bars throughout the city; **Calle San Lorenzo** and **Calle la Puebla** are popular locations. By midnight, C. Avellanos (across from Pl. Alonso Martínez) fills with night owls migrating onto nearby **Calle Huerto del Rey.** Behind the church, **Llanes de Afuera** is lined with hip bars and dance clubs. On Sunday mornings, the crowds will still be dancing at discotecas along **Calle San Juan** and **Calle la Puebla** and in the complex on **Plaza San Lesmes.** During the last week of June, Burgos honors its patron saints with parades, fireworks, and bullfights.

▨ Pancho Bar, C. San Lorenzo, 15. Although this bar just off Plaza Mayor is always packed, the bartenders are relaxed, friendly, and attentive. Full meals are served in the adjacent restaurant. Sangria €1.90. Wine €1.30. Tapas €1.25-3. Open M-Sa 10am-midnight, Su 11am-midnight. AmEx/MC/V.

Madame Kalalu, C. Huerto del Rey, 2. Dance to Cuban pop while rum spills over the counter. Walls covered with posters of old Cuba make for a great atmosphere. Beer €2.20. Open Th-Sa 8pm-5am.

El Bosque Desconocido, C. San Juan, 31 (☎658 64 19 06). This funky bar owes its name to the large tree, hanging with tempting apples, rooted in the very center of the room. A local favorite, it's filled from trunk to wall on weekends. Beer €2. Open Su-Th 3pm-3am, F-Sa 3pm-4am.

Trastos, C. Huerto del Rey, 7. If you're looking for a trance-pumping discoteca, then Trastos is a sure bet. The DJ keeps the hard-core European crowd dancing well into morning hours. Drinks €2-5. Open M-F 11pm-2am, Sa-Su 11pm-5am.

▨ DAYTRIP FROM BURGOS

CARRIÓN DE LOS CONDES

Buses run to Carrión de los Condes from Burgos (1½hr.; M-Sa 11:45am, M-F and Su 6:15pm, return M-Sa 11:15am, M-F also 4:50pm, Su 5:30pm; € 6). Buses also run from Palencia (45min.; M-Sa 7:45am, 1:30, 6:00pm; Su 1:30, 7:15pm; return M-Sa 9am, 2:10, 5:10pm; Su 5 and 6:10pm; €2.30).

Tourists might easily bypass this tiny riverside town, but many pilgrims consider Carrión de los Condes (pop. 2500) to be one of the most important stops on the Camino de Santiago. Carrión makes for a quiet afternoon of church- and monastery-hopping alongside the pilgrims. The **Iglesia de Santiago,** the town's most famous church, was built in the 12th century and rebuilt after *castellano* troops burned it down to prevent the French army from using it as a stronghold in the 1811 War of Independence. The adjacent ▓ **Museo** has a small but impressive collection of embroidered frocks and paintings from the 16th century. (Church and museum open daily 11am-2pm and 4:30-8pm. €1.) On the way to this church from the bus stop, you'll pass by the **Iglesia Santa María del Camino,** the oldest church in Carrión, built in 1130. (Open in summer daily 9am-2pm and 4:30-6pm; in winter M-Sa 11am-1:30am and 6-9pm, Su noon-1:30pm and 6-9pm. Free.) The pretty **Iglesia de Santa Clara** lies just past the bus stop, up the street from the *peluquería* (hairdresser). (Open Tu-Su 10:30am-1pm and 4:30-7:30pm. €2, students €1.20.) Downhill and across the river is the 11th-century **Real Monasterio de San Zoilo,** with one of the most beautiful cloisters of the Spanish Renaissance. (☎979 88 09 02. Open Apr. to mid-Oct. daily 10:30am-2pm and 4:30-8pm; mid-Oct. to Mar. M-F 10:30am-2pm, Sa-Su 4-6:30pm. €1.50, pilgrims €1.)

If you need to spend the night, **Camping El Eden ❶** is in a shaded area on the riverbank, in the Parque Municipal. (☎979 88 01 95. €4 per person; €3.50-3.90 per tent; €4 per car. Electricity €3.50.) Many restaurants along **C. Santa María** offer a three-course *menú del peregrino* (pilgrim menu) for €7-8. **Cervecería "J. M." ❷,** Pl. Marques de Santillana, 10, has all a pilgrim could want for dinner—sandwiches, eggs, salads, meat, and fish. (Open daily noon-4pm and 6-10pm. Cash only.) The **tourist office** is across the street from the bus stop in front of Bar España and offers **Internet** access for €2 per hour. (☎979 88 09 32. Open July-Aug. 10am-2pm, 4:30pm-7pm.) There is also another tourist office located in the Monasterio de San Zoilo open year-round. (☎979 880 902. Open Tu-Su 10am-2pm and 5-8pm.)

PALENCIA
☎**979**

Palencia (pop. 80,000) is celebrated as the birthplace of an unusual insurrection. The Duke of Lancaster attacked the city in the 14th century and met strong resistance from the local women whose men were occupied by battle in distant lands. The women took Palencia's protection into their own hands and launched a successful uprising against the duke. In gratitude, King Juan I granted them the right to wear the gold armor previously reserved for the city's soldiers. Riding a wave of good publicity, Palencia underwent a surge of construction, and as a result, its historic center is studded with 14th- to 16th-century churches. Palencia's lack of notoriety only adds to its charm; you can walk the streets and visit masterpieces such as the Cathedral in Plaza de la Inmaculada among true *Palentinos.*

▐ **TRANSPORTATION. RENFE trains** (☎902 24 02 02; www.renfe.es) depart from Parque Jardinillos de la Estación to: Barcelona (8½-9hr.; daily 1:30 and 2:23pm, M-Sa 10:40pm; €40-53); Bilbao and San Sebastián (4hr., 3:57pm, €20-24); Burgos (1hr.; M-F and Su 8-9 per day 1:30am-10:40pm, Sa 7 per day 1:30am-7:35pm; €4-14); La Coruña (8hr.; daily 4:30am and 1pm; M, Th, Sa-Su also 3:31pm; €33-43); León (1¼hr.; M-Sa 14-15 per day 1:04am-9:42pm, Su 10 per day 4:30am-9:42pm; €7-18); Madrid (3-5hr.; M-Sa 13 per day 2:24am-8:10pm, Su 11 per day 8:15am-8:25pm; €15-30); Salamanca (2½hr.; daily 1:20 pm, M-Sa also 7:57am; €10-21); Santander (3-4hr.; 6 per day M-Sa 3:46am-7:24pm, Su 7:49am-7:24pm; €11-25);

Valladolid (45min.; 20-22 per day M-F 2:29am-9:53pm, Sa 2:29am 11:08pm, Su 8:15am-11:08pm; €3-11). **Buses** depart from the same station (☎979 74 32 22; info open M-F 9:30am-7pm, Sa 9:30am-2pm) to Burgos (1½hr.; M-Th 8:45am and 3pm, F 8:45am, 3, 6:45pm, Su 8:45am; €6) and Valladolid (45min.; M-F hourly 7am-9pm, Sa 6 per day 8am-7:30pm, Su 3 per day 11am-9pm; €3).

⊞⊡ ORIENTATION AND PRACTICAL INFORMATION. Palencian life is centered along **Calle Mayor**. From the bus or train station, head past the Jardinillos de la Estación to Pl. León; from there you can see C. Mayor, the fourth street on the right from the rotary. The **tourist office**, C. Mayor, 105, is a 15min. walk down C. Mayor from Pl. León. (☎979 74 00 68; fax 70 08 22. Open July to mid-Sept. M-Th and Su 9am-8pm, F-Sa until 9pm; mid-Sept. to June daily 9am-2pm and 5-8pm.) There is a smaller office located closer to the train and bus stations right off the Pl. Leon in the Pl. de San Pablo. (☎979 74 00 68. Open daily 10:30am-2pm and 5-8:30pm.) Services include: **Currency exchange**, at **Banco Santander Central Hispano**, on the corner of C. Mayor and C. Martínez de Azcotita (open Apr.-Sept. M-F 8:30am-2pm, Oct.-Mar. Sa 8:30am-1pm); **municipal police**, C. Ortega y Gasset (☎979 71 82 00) and National Ave. Simón Nieto, 10 (☎979 167 400); **taxis**, through **Radiotaxi**, Stops at Estación Renfe or C. Mayor (☎979 72 00 16); a **hospital**, the **Hospital Río Carrión**, Av. Donanter de Sangre (☎979 16 70 00); **Internet** access at the **Biblioteca Pública**, C. Eduardo Dato (☎979 71 11 00; open M-F 8am-9:30pm, Sa 9am-2pm; time limit 30min.; free); and the **post office**, Pl. León, 2 (☎902 19 71 97; fax 74 22 60), by the train station with **Pabellón Postal** (both open M-F 8:30am-8:30pm, Sa 9:30am-2pm). **Postal Code:** 34001.

⊓ ACCOMMODATIONS. Palencia has fewer tourists than many of its neighbors, so its accommodations are less abundant and more expensive. Hostels can be found off C. Mayor. Reserve ahead, as hostels tend to fill up quickly in the summer. One good stop is **Tres de Noviembre ❷**, C. Mancornador, 18, just off C. Mayor across from the tourist office, at the end of C. Los Manteros. This well-maintained hostel has standard rooms with TV and radio, but walls are thin. (☎979 70 30 42. Reception 7am-11pm. Singles without shower €15, with shower €19, with full bath €22; doubles with bath €40. Cash only.) Another option is the conveniently located **Hostal Ávila ❸** on C. Conde de Vallellano, 5. From C. Mayor, turn left onto C. San Bernardo, which becomes C. Empedrada. The hostel features spacious rooms, private bathrooms, telephones, TVs, radios, a common room, parking, and a cafeteria. (☎979 71 19 10; www.hostalavila.com. Singles €33; doubles €49. MC/V.) For a cheaper option, head to the **Pensión El Salón ❷**, Av. República Argentina, 10. From the tourist office on C. Mayor continue down C. Mayor and cross the street onto Av. República Argentina; the *pensión* is on your right after C. Los Tintes. Rooms are basic, but some have sinks, and the staff is very friendly. (☎979 72 64 42. Single room €15; double €25. No private bathrooms. Cash only.)

⊡ FOOD. Cafeterias and restaurants fill the *zona vieja* and the streets branching off C. Mayor. If all else fails, there's always **El Árbol** supermarket, C. Mayor, 99. (Open M-Sa 9:30am-9pm.) **▨La Trebede ❷**, Pl. Mayor, 14, shaded by the white umbrellas and the trees lining Pl. Mayor, offers a pleasant view and delicious food; the *sopa de pescado* (fish soup) is especially good. (☎979 75 01 29. Salads €6-8. Entrees €4-14. *Menú* €9. MC/V.) **Cervecería Gambrinus ❶**, C. Patio Castaño, 1, off C. Mayor from Pl. León, has an outdoor terrace and serves good *raciones* (portions) at reasonable prices. The speciality here is the homemade beer, kept at exactly the right temperature. (☎979 75 08 28. *Raciones* €2.50-11. Open daily 7:30am-1am. AmEx/MC/V.) If you're looking for an escape from Spanish tapas, go

CASTILLA Y LEÓN

to **Rincón de Istanbul ❶**, C. San Bernardo, 4, which has made a name for itself among locals by serving delicious Turkish fare (€3-8). The restaurant's namesake, a vegetarian dish called the *Rincón de Istanbul* (€5), is particularly good, as are the *doner kebap* and *kofte*. (☎979 74 75 33. Open daily noon-2am. Cash only.)

◪ **SIGHTS.** Palencia's biggest attraction is its Gothic ▨**cathedral,** known as *La Bella Desconocida*, where 14-year-old Catherine of Lancaster married 10-year-old Enrique III in 1388. Built between the 14th and 16th centuries with Gothic features, the cathedral has a pastel sandstone interior. Visitors can descend to the spooky **Cripta de San Antolín,** a 7th-century sepulcher containing the remains of the Roman/Visigoth structure upon which the cathedral was built. The cathedral's **museum** contains El Greco's *San Sebastián*, some 16th-century Flemish tapestries, and a tiny caricature of Carlos V. From Pl. León, walk down C. Eduardo Dato and turn left at Pl. Carmelitas onto C. Santa Teresa de Jesús; the cathedral is at the end in Pl. de la Inmaculada Concepción. (☎979 70 13 47. Cathedral is open M-Sa 9am-1:30pm and 4:30-7:30pm, Su 9am-1:30pm. Tours of the museum, crypt and cathedral in Spanish M-Sa hourly 10:30am-12:30pm and 4:30-6:30pm, Su 11:15am. Cathedral free. Museum €3.) Another worthwhile sight is the imposing statue **Cristo del Otero,** located on top of a hill on the outskirts of the city. Built in 1931, it is the second tallest statue of Jesus Christ in the world (Rio de Janiero's Corcovado is taller). The statue itself can be reached by walking up a path that winds to the top of the hill. Besides allowing a closer glimpse of the statue, the short walk (approx. 15min.) to the top also offers fantastic views of Palencia and the surrounding countryside of Castilla y León. To reach the statue, take the B-line bus from Pl. de Leon to Camino La Miranda. Get off at the third stop (Po. de Otero). From the bus stop, continue walking up the street; the enormous statue above you is moments ahead. Follow the street until you reach the park on your right, and take one of the numerous paths to the top. (Bus one-way €0.48.)

▨ ▨ **NIGHTLIFE AND FESTIVALS.** Midweek nightlife is tame, as establishments close by 2:30am, but on weekends, plenty of *palentinos* roam the streets of the *zona vieja*, off C. Mayor, into the wee hours. You will find the college crowd packed in tight at Merlin, C. Conde de Vallellano, 4, where they serve up drinks and dance. (Beer €2. Mixed drinks €4. Open Th-Sa 7pm-4:30am, Su 7pm-2:30am.) Disco-Bar Cendal, another dark, pop music-infused favorite among young crowds, is right across the street. (Beer €1.50. Mixed drinks €4.50. Open M-Th and Su 7:30pm-2:30am, F-Sa until 4:30am.) On C. Estrada, 3, Sábana's has cheap drinks and good service but no dancing. (Beer €1.10. Mixed drinks €3.70. Open M-Th and Su 1pm-1:30am, F-Sa 1pm-4:30am.) Palencia celebrates the Fiesta de San Antolín (Sept. 2) with feasts commemorating their patron saint; some head to the cathedral's crypt to drink the water, anticipating granted wishes.

SORIA
☎975

Known for its raucous Fiesta de San Juan, the poet Antonio Machado, and surrounding architectural sites, Soria (pop. 37,000) is a vibrant small city. Though things really heat up around the fiesta, there is plenty to do in the off-season. In the center of the city lies the lush Parque Alameda de Cervantes, and on the outskirts the intriguing Monasterio de San Juan de Duero and Ermita de San Saturio. Initially built as a fortress to protect against invasions from neighboring Aragón, Soria today is idyllic. Bars with outdoor seating fill Soria's plazas, and the area along the Río Ebro is a serene setting for sunbathing, relaxing, or swimming.

▐ TRANSPORTATION

Trains: Estación El Cañuelo (☎975 23 02 02), Ctra. de Madrid. Buses (€0.45) run from Pl. Mariano Granados to the station 20-25min. before trains depart and return immediately after new arrivals. Trains run to: **Madrid** (3hr.; M-F 7:40am, 5:40pm, Sa 8:45am, 5:40pm, Su 8:45am, 5:40, 6:25pm; €13.35) via **Alcalá de Henares** (2¾hr., €11).

Buses: Av. de Valladolid (☎975 22 51 60). Desk open daily 9am-7pm and 8-10pm. **Continental Auto** (☎975 22 44 01; www.continental-auto.es) sends buses to **Logroño** (1½hr.; M-Th and Sa 6 per day 11am-10:15pm, F and Su 9 per day 11am-12:15am; €6.19), **Madrid** (2½hr.; M-Th and Sa 11 per day 8:15am-3:30am, F and Su 12 per day 8:15am-11:45pm; €12.68-20), and **Pamplona** (2hr.; M-Th and Sa 5 per day 10:45am-10:15pm, F and Su 7-8 per day 10:45am-12:15am, and 4am daily; €11.98). **La Serrana** (☎975 22 20 60) to **Burgos** (2½hr.; M-Sa 1-3 per day 7am-6:30pm, Su 4, 6pm; €9.45). **Therpasa** (☎975 22 20 60) goes to **Zaragoza** (2¼hr.; 6 per day M-Sa 7:30am-8pm, Su 3 per day noon-9pm; €9) via **Tarazona** (1hr., €4.45). **Linecar** (☎975 22 15 55) runs to **Valladolid** (3hr.; M-Sa 3 per day 9:45am-6:45pm, Su 4 per day 11:15am-9:30pm; €12.35).

Car Rental: AVIS, Av. de Mariano Vicén, 1/3 (☎975 21 10 19). 23+. Open M-F 9am-1pm and 4-7pm, Sa 10am-1pm. AmEx/MC/V. **Europcar**, C. Ángel Terrel, 3-5 (☎975 22 05 05). 21+. Open M-F 9:30am-1:30pm and 4-7pm, Sa 10:30am-1pm. AmEx/MC/V.

Taxis: Stands at Pl. Ramón y Cajal (☎975 21 30 34) and bus station (☎975 23 13 13).

▰▰ ORIENTATION AND PRACTICAL INFORMATION

The city center is a brisk 10min. walk from the bus or train station. There's a map just to the left of the traffic circle in front of the **bus station.** Head out from the traffic circle in the direction you're facing while reading the map. Walk along **Avenida de Valladolid** downhill towards the *centro ciudad* for five blocks and bear right at the fork onto Po. del Espolón, which borders the **Parque Alameda de Cervantes.** At the end of the park, the main intersection, **Plaza Mariano Granados,** will be directly in front of you. To reach the center from the **train station,** take the shuttle, or turn left onto **Calle Madrid** and follow the signs to *centro ciudad.* Continue on C. Almazán as it becomes Av. de Mariano Vicén, follow the road for six blocks, and keep left at the fork onto **Av. Alfonso VIII** until you reach Pl. Mariano Granados. **C. Marqués de Vadillo** is the main pedestrian street extending from the city center. It becomes C. El Collado, cutting through the old quarter to **Plaza Mayor.**

Tourist Office: C. Medinaceli, 2 (☎975 21 20 52; www.turismocastillayleon.com). From Pl. Mariano Granados, walk 1 block on Av. Alfonso VIII. It's on the corner to your left. Not well marked. English, French, and German spoken. Open July-Sept. 15 M-Th and Su 9am-8pm, F-Sa 9am-9pm; Sept.-June daily 9am-2pm and 5-8pm; holidays 9am-9pm.

Currency Exchange: Banco Santander Central Hispano, C. El Collado, 56 (☎975 22 02 25), 1 block from the plaza. Open Apr.-Sept. M-F 8:30am-2pm; Oct.-May M-F 8:30am-2pm, Sa 8:30am-1pm. **Branch** at Av. Navarra, 6-8. Several other banks cluster around Pl. Mariano Granados.

Luggage Storage: At the **bus station.** 1st day €0.60, €0.30 each additional day. Open daily 9am-7pm and 8-10pm. At **train station** lockers €3. Open 9am-7:30pm.

Police: Guardia Çivil, C. Eduardo Savedra, 6 (☎975 22 03 50). **Municipal:** C. Obispo Agustín, 1 (☎975 21 18 62). **National:** C. Nicolás Rabal, 9 (☎975 23 93 23).

Hospital: Hospital General Santa Bárbara, Po. de Santa Bárbara (☎975 23 43 00).

CASTILLA Y LEÓN

Pharmacy: Many around Pl. Mariano Granados; check any for listing of *"en guardia"* location for that night.

Internet Access: Cyber Centro, Pje. Tejera, 16 (☎975 23 90 85), up the stairs and on the left in the small tunnel between C. las Casas and C. Caro on Po. Tejera. €2.40 per 30min., €3.60 per hour., €8 per 3hr. Open M-F 10am-2:30pm and 5:30-9:30pm. **Locutorio Nuevo Mundo,** C. Campo, 18 (☎975 23 92 34). Open 11am-2pm and 5pm-midnight. **Locutorio Alô Brasil,** Po. Florida, 4. Open daily 11-3pm and 5-10:30

Post Office: Po. del Espolón, 6 (☎902 24 24 24). Open M-F 8:30am-8:30pm, Sa 9:30am-2pm. **Postal Code:** 42001.

🔏 ACCOMMODATIONS AND CAMPING

Reservations are always a good idea during Fiesta week (June 27-July 2).

Hostal Residencia Alvi, C. Alberca, 2 (☎975 22 81 12; fax 22 81 40). 24 large rooms with simple decor, TV, A/C, full baths, and big beds. Hotel-quality for half the price. Reserve ahead. Breakfast €2.25. Singles €29; doubles €49. MC/V. ❸

Residencia Juvenil Juan Antonio Gaya Nuño (HI), Po. San Francisco (☎975 22 14 66). With your back to Pl. Mariano Granados, take C. Nicolás Rabal left along the park. Take the 2nd left onto C. Santa Luisa de Marillac; look for yellow dorms. TV room. Laundry €1. Reception 24hr. Curfew midnight, but doors open hourly. Open July-Sept. 15. Wheelchair accessible. HI card required. €8.25-11.25 per person. Cash only. ❶

Camping Fuente la Teja (☎975 22 29 67), 2km from town on Ctra. de Madrid. Only accessible by car or long walk on the highway (N-111 km 233). Huge cafeteria, laundry, and playground. Pool open July-Aug. Wheelchair accessible. Open *Semana Santa*-Sept. €4.20 per person, €3.30 per car, €4.20 per tent. IVA not included. AmEx/MC/V. ❶

🍴 FOOD

Countless bars and inexpensive restaurants along C. El Collado and Pl. Mayor offer local specialties like roast lamb and *migas* (bread crumbs fried with garlic and paprika). Buy Soria's famed butter at mantequerías in the town center, or opt for fruits and vegetables at the thriving market in Pl. Bernardo Robles on C. los Estudios, off C. El Collado. (Open M-Sa 8:30am-2pm.) A **SPAR supermarket** is at Av. de Mariano Vicén, 10, four blocks from Pl. Mariano Granados toward the train station. (Open M-Sa 9am-2pm and 5:30-8:30pm. MC/V.)

Collado 58, C. El Collado, 58 (☎975 24 00 53). Huge sandwiches and burgers at this popular, laid-back bar/restaurant. Ice cream concoctions (€4.30-6), shakes (€3.50), and banana splits (€4.30). Combo plates €8-13. Open daily 8am-11pm. Cash only. ❷

Nuevo Siglo, C. Almazán, 9 (☎975 22 13 32), halfway down Av. Mariano Vicén toward the train station. Chinese food served under chandeliers. Entrees €3-8. 4-course lunch weekday *menú* €5.38. Open daily 11:30am-4:30pm and 7:30pm-midnight. MC/V. ❶

TriBeca New York, C. El Collado, 7 (☎975 21 43 95). On the right side just past C. San Juan. This casual bar/restaurant packs in locals. *Menú* €11. Desserts €2.50-3. Open M-Th and Su 8:30am-11:30pm, F-Sa 8:30am-midnight. AmEx/MC/V. ❷

👁 SIGHTS

▨ ERMITA DE SAN SATURIO. Soria's most popular sight is worth the 1.5km trek downstream, and is a nice departure from the more traditional cathedrals found nearby. From ground-level caves with stained-glass windows to passageways carved out of stone, the 17th-century Ermita is a fitting tribute to San Saturio, Soria's patron saint. On foot, take the scenic route through the lush island of **Soto Playa**. Turn right just before the main bridge and cross the first green footbridge, then take the small wooden bridge at the end. Keeping the river to your left, walk off the small island, following small footpaths and boardwalks. After the footpath ends, continue on the black and yellow brick road. The Ermita is on your left, accessed across the bridge and up the stairs. *(Open year-round Tu-Su 10:30am-2pm; also July-Aug. 4:30-8:30pm, Apr.-June and Sept.-Oct. 4:30-7:30pm, Nov.-Mar. 4:30-6:30pm. Free.)*

MONASTERIO DE SAN JUAN DE DUERO. The Monasterio San Juan de Duero sits quietly by the river amid fields of cottonwoods. The church, dating from the 12th century, is one of the most visited in Castilla y León. The graceful arches of its cloister blend Romanesque and Islamic styles. Inside, a few cases display medieval artifacts. *(Turn left after crossing the main bridge. Open Tu-Sa July-Sept. 10am-2pm and 5-8pm, Oct.-June 10am-2pm and 4-7pm; Su year-round 10am-2pm. €0.60; groups of 15 or more €0.30 per person; under 18, over 65, and students free. Sa-Su free.)*

MUSEO NUMANTINO. This museum across from the *alameda* park exhibits a collection of Celtiberian and Roman artifacts excavated from nearby Numancia. *(Po. del Espolón, 8. ☎ 975 22 13 97. Same hours as Monasterio. €1.20; groups of 15 or more €0.60 per person with prior arrangement; under 18, over 65, and students free. Sa-Su free.)*

NIGHTLIFE AND FESTIVALS

For a town of its size, Soria has a vibrant nightlife, especially during fiesta month (almost all of June). As the moon rises, revelers of all ages flood the outdoor seating at bars in **Plaza Ramón Benito Aceña,** a stone's throw from Pl. Mariano Granados and the adjacent **Plaza San Clemente,** off C. El Collado. Late-night discotecas center on the intersection of **Rota de Calatañazor** and **Calle Cardenal Frías,** near Pl. de Toros. Locals tend to move from one discobar to another until sunrise. **Greens,** near the Plaza de Toros, has outdoor seating, and is a good place to have a *calimocho* (wine and coke; €1) and people-watch. Nearby, **Mitos** has loud music and a dance floor, as do many of its neighbors. A few small clubs and a number of bars with a more relaxed atmosphere lie near **Calle Zapatería.** Spend a night surrounded by quirky Irish decor while hanging out with hip *sorianos* at the intimate tables of **Bar Ogham,** C. Nicolás Rabal, 3, on the side of the park opposite Po. del Espolón. *(☎ 975 22 57 71. Open daily noon-3am. Cash only.)*

In summer, Soria hosts concerts and street theater. Pick up the free *Actividades Culturales* at the tourist office for specific dates. Late June brings Soria's biggest celebration, the **Fiestas de San Juan,** which flood the city with celebrants from all over the country, and three weeks of smaller (but equally fun) preceding "prefiestas." Beginning at midnight the morning after Día de San Juan (June 24th), and lasting until Monday, the entire city hits the streets to dance, play music at all hours, drink wine from *botas* (leather wineskins), and, of course, go to bullfights. Patron **San Saturio** is celebrated on Oct. 2 with a more low-key, day-long festival.

CASTILLA Y LEÓN

CASTILLA LA MANCHA AND EXTREMADURA

Castilla La Mancha and Extremadura are the Spanish Outback. Stark and barren compared to the rest of the country, these arid lands hardened New World conquistadors like Hernán Cortés and Francisco Pizarro and inspired some of Spain's greatest fictional characters, including the man of La Mancha himself, Cervantes's Don Quixote. While much of Castilla La Mancha remains unexplored by tourists, Extremadura is undiscovered even by most Spaniards, despite the radiant beauty of its Roman ruins and traditional towns.

HIGHLIGHTS OF CASTILLA LA MANCHA AND EXTREMADURA

REMINISCE in **Toledo** about the days when everyone got along (see below).

ATTACK any windmill you'd like in the world of Don Quixote, **Consuegra** (p. 196).

LIVE on the edge in one of the hanging houses of **Cuenca** (p. 199).

ROAM around the amazingly well-preserved Roman city, **Mérida** (p. 211).

CASTILLA LA MANCHA

Filled with sleepy medieval towns, cliffs, and—of course—windmills, Castilla La Mancha provokes the imagination with its solitary beauty. Drawing its name from the Arabic word *manza* (parched earth) and the Spanish *mancha* (stain), the province remains one of Spain's least-developed regions. Long ago, it was the epicenter of conflict between Christians and Muslims, and so became the domain of military orders modeled after crusading institutions like the Knights Templar, a society of powerful warrior-monks. In the 14th and 15th centuries, the region saw struggles between Castilla and Aragón before they were united in 1492. Castilla La Mancha is Spain's largest wine-producing region, if not its best (*Valdepeñas* is a popular table wine), and the abundant olive groves and wild game influence local recipes, including Toledo's famed partridge dish. Stews, roast meats, and game are all *manchego* staples, as is *queso manchego*, Spain's beloved national cheese.

TOLEDO   ☎ 925

Toledo (pop. 75,500), the pride of Castilla La Mancha, is, like any good medieval city, fraught with myth and legend. Cervantes called the hilltop town the "glory of Spain and light of her cities"; and it is commonly regarded as the "Ciudad de las Tres Culturas" (City of Three Cultures), host to a peaceful coexistence of Muslims, Jews, and Christians. Locals will tell you the history has been a bit romanticized; still, with more monuments per cobblestone than almost any other city in the world, the hometown of El Greco holds a special mystique and charm. The city's numerous churches, synagogues, and mosques share twisting alleyways, and their languages, scripts, and customs melt together inside the walls of the *casco antiguo* (old city). There's so much to do here; try not to dawdle too much over the Damascene swords and knives (used in ancient times and on the set of *Lord of the Rings*), or the sweet marzipan. In June, Toledo's movie-set-like facades come alive with costumed processions during the Corpus Cristi celebration.

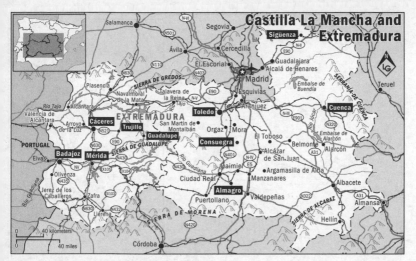

Castilla-La Mancha and Extremadura

TRANSPORTATION

Trains: Po. de la Rosa, 2 (RENFE info ☎902 24 02 02), in an exquisite neo-*mudéjar* station just over Puente de Azarquiel. High speed AVE train to **Atocha** station in **Madrid.** (30min.; M-F 11 per day 6:55am-9:25pm, Sa-Su 9 per day 9:25am-9:25pm; €8.50)

Buses: Av. Castilla La Mancha (☎925 21 58 50), 5min. from Puerta de Bisagra. Open daily 7am-11pm. **Alsina Graells** (in Toledo ☎925 21 58 50, in Valencia 963 49 72 30) goes to **Valencia** (5½hr., M-F 3pm, €23.50; buy ticket on board). **Continental Auto** (in Toledo ☎925 22 36 41, in Madrid 915 27 29 61) runs to Estación Sur in **Madrid** (1½hr.; every 30min. M-F 6am-9pm, Sa 8am-8:30pm, Su 8am-11:30pm; €4.40).

Public Transportation: Buses #5 and 6 serve several city points, mainly the bus and train stations and the central Pl. de Zocodóver. Buses stop to the right of the train station, underneath and across the street from the bus station (€0.95, at night €1.25).

Taxis: Radio Taxi and **Gruas de Toledo** (☎925 25 50 50).

Car Rental: Avis, in the train station (☎925 21 45 35). From €67 per day. 23+. Open M-F 9:30am-1:30pm and 4:30-7:30pm, Sa 9:30am-1pm.

ORIENTATION AND PRACTICAL INFORMATION

Consider yourself warned: the way in Toledo is uphill. To walk from the train station to the **Plaza de Zocodóver** (derived from the Arabic name for the market once held there, "Souk al Dawar") in the center, turn right and follow the left fork uphill to an incredible and ornate stone bridge, the **Puente de Alcántara.** Cross the bridge to the stone staircase; after climbing it, turn left and go up, veering right at C. Cervantes, which leads to Pl. de Zocodóver. The bus avoids the sidewalk-less uphill hike. To get to the Plaza from the bus station, exit via the cafeteria, head toward the traffic circle, and continue on the highway until you reach the bridge on your left. Then, turn right up the stone steps and continue up toward the city.

Tourist Office: Regional office, Puerta de Bisagra (☎925 22 08 43). From the train station, turn right and take the right-hand fork across the bridge (Puente de Azarquiel), following the walls until you reach the 2nd traffic circle; the office is across the road,

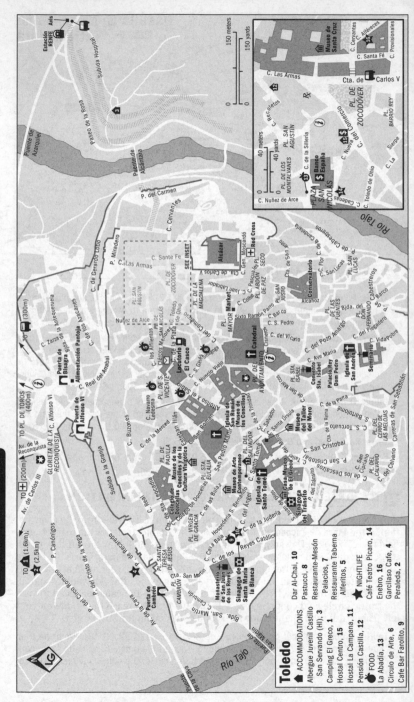

Toledo

▲ ACCOMMODATIONS
Albergue Juvenil Castillo
  San Servando (HI), 3
Camping El Greco, 1
Hostal Centro, 15
Hostal La Campana, 11
Pensión Castilla, 12

♦ FOOD
La Abadía, 13
Círculo de Arte, 6
Cafe Bar Farolito, 9
Dar Al-Chai, 10
Pastucci, 8
Restaurante-Mesón
  Palacios, 7
Restaurante Taberna
  Alfileritos, 5

★ NIGHTLIFE
Café Teatro Pícaro, 14
Enebro, 16
Garcilaso Cafe, 4
Peraleda, 2

outside the walls. Staff offers handy maps. Open July-Sept. M-F 9am-7pm, Sa 10am-6pm, Su 10am-2pm; Oct.-June M-F 9am-6pm, Sa 10am-6pm, Su 10am-2pm. The **municipal office,** Pl. del Ayuntamiento (☎925 25 40 30) is open M 10:30am-2:30pm, Tu-Su 10:30am-2:30pm and 4:30-7pm. **Zococentro,** (☎925 22 03 00) another information office, is just off Pl. de Zocodóver; look for the light green signs. Open daily Apr.-Dec. 10:30am-7pm; Jan.-Mar. 10:30am-6pm.

Currency Exchange: Banco Santander Central Hispano, C. del Comercio, 47 (☎925 22 98 00). No commission and 24hr. **ATM.** Open Apr.-Sept. M-F 8:30am-2pm; Oct.-Mar. M-F 8:30am-2pm, Sa 8:30am-1pm.

Luggage Storage: At the bus station (€3). Open daily 7am-11pm.

Police: (☎925 25 04 12). At the corner of Av. de la Reconquista and Av. de Carlos III.

Pharmacy: Pl. de Zocodóver (☎925 22 17 68). Some English spoken. Open daily 9:30am-2pm and 5-8pm.

Hospital: Hospital Virgen de la Salud, Av. de Barber (☎925 26 92 00), outside the city walls. With your back to Puerta de Bisagra, go left until Glorieta de la Reconquista (200m). Take Av. de la Reconquista to Pl. de Colón; Av. de Barber is to the left.

Internet Access: Options are limited, but access is available at **Locutorio El Casco,** C. La Plata, 25, (☎925 22 61 65), across from the post office. €2 per hour. Open daily 11am-11pm.

Post Office: C. de la Plata, 1 (☎925 22 36 11; fax 21 57 64). **Lista de Correos.** Open M-F 8:30am-8:30pm, Sa 9:30am-2pm. **Postal Code:** 45070.

▖ ACCOMMODATIONS AND CAMPING

Toledo is full of accommodations, but finding a bed in summer can be a hassle, especially on weekends. Reservations are strongly recommended; try the tourist office if you run into trouble. There are also several campgrounds around Toledo.

▨ **Hostal La Campana,** C. de la Campana, 10-12 (☎925 22 16 59 or 925 22 16 62; www.hostalcampana.com). Best location available, monuments at the doorstep, and quintessential Toledo hospitality. Rooms are quaint and clean, and all have bath, TV, phone, A/C, and Wi-Fi. Breakfast included. Singles €36; doubles €60. MC/V. ❹

Albergue Juvenil Castillo de San Servando (HI), C. de San Servando (☎925 22 45 54; reservations 22 16 78; alberguesclm@jccm.es). Cross the street from the train station, then turn right up Subida del Hospital. Continue up the windy, uphill street past Hospital Provincial in the *hostal,* housed in a 14th-century castle. From the bus station, go toward the traffic circle and continue uphill; cross the footbridge to the left and head up to the castle. 38 spacious rooms, each with 2-4 bunks, bath, and wooden floors. Pool in the summer, TV room, and Internet access. Reservations recommended at least 15 days in advance in summer. Lockout from 11am-2pm. Dorms €9.50, with breakfast €11.50; over 30 €12.50/15. MC/V. ❶

Pensión Castilla, C. Recoletos, 6 (☎925 25 63 18). Go down C. Las Armas from Pl. de Zocodóver. Turn left on C. Recoletos. Great prices and location. Midnight curfew. Singles €18; doubles €26, with bath €29. Cash only. ❷

Hostal Centro, C. Nueva, 13 (☎925 25 70 91; hostalcentro@telefonica.net), toward C. del Comercio on Pl. de Zocodóver. Centrally located. Clean, spacious rooms with TV, bath, A/C, phone. Nice rooftop terrace for sunbathing or a view of the cathedral and plaza. Friendly staff. Singles €30; doubles €48; triples €65. MC/V. ❸

Camping El Greco, Ctra. CM-4000 km 0.7 (☎925 22 00 90; www.campingelgreco.es.vg), 1.5km from town. Take bus #7 from Pl. de Zocodóver. Clean, shady site between river and an olive grove. Restaurant, bar, supermarket, and pool. €4.90 per person, per tent, and per car. Pool €3.50. IVA not included. MC/V. ❶

🍴 FOOD

Pastelería windows on every corner in Toledo beckon with *mazapán* (marzipan) of every shape and size, from colorful nuggets to half-moon cookies. For a wide array, stop by the **market** in Pl. Mayor, behind the cathedral. (Open M-Sa 9am-8pm.)

La Abadía, Pl. de San Nicolás, 3 (☎925 25 11 40; www.abadiatoledo.com). From Pl. de Zocodóver, bear left when C. de la Sillería splits; Pl. de San Nicolás is to the right. Dine on tapas (€3.25) or the delicious lunch *menú* (€10) in a maze of cave-like underground rooms. Open daily 8am-midnight. AmEx/MC/V. ❷

Restaurante Taberna Alferitos, 24. C. Alferitos, 24 (☎902 10 65 77; www.alferitos24.com). Despite the aggressively hip music, the post-modern decor at this relatively new spot somehow complements its medieval housing. Ground floor is a popular tapas stop (€5-8), while the 3stories above seat a classy dining crowd. Entrees €12-15. Open daily 8pm-midnight. MC/V. ❸

Restaurante-Mesón Palacios, C. Alfonso X el Sabio, 3 (☎925 21 59 72). Two extravagant *menús* (€7.50-12.90)—including Toledo's famous partridge dish—loaded with good and simple meat, fish, and egg dishes. Entrees €5-12. Open M-Sa 1-4pm and 7-10:30pm, Su 1-4pm. In Aug. closed Su. AmEx/D/MC/V. ❷

Pastucci, C. Sinagoga, 10 (☎925 25 77 42; www.aplinet.com/pastucci). From Pl. de Zocodóver take C. del Comercio; turn right below the underpass just past the Rodier store. Cheerful atmosphere. Pastas €5.60-7.50. Small pizzas €6.50-9.50. Open Tu-Su noon-4pm and 8pm-midnight. MC/V. ❷

CAFES

Dar Al-Chai, Pl. de Barrio Nuevo, 6 (www.daralchai.com). A favorite with local students and young passersby, this *tetería* serves up medicinal tea infusions (€2.30 per person or €10 for 6 people), delicious crepes (€2.50-3.50), and hookah (€9). Just between the 2 synagogues. Open M-Th and Su 9:30am-10pm, F-Sa 4pm-1am. MC/V. ❷

Cafe Bar Farolito, Pl. de Barrio Nuevo, 2 (☎925 25 44 00). A casual and fashionable eatery, specializing in Toledo classics like *pisto manchego* (€6). Daily *menús* from €8.50-11.50. In the summer, sit out in the shaded terrace. Open daily 10am-3pm and 8pm-midnight. MC/V. ❸

Circulo de Arte Toledo, Pl. de San Vicente, 2 (☎925 21 43 29; www.circuloartetoledo.org). A local university and hipster cafe that hosts regular concerts, exhibits, dance recitals, and theater. Beautiful, large, and airy space. Full bar. Tapas €5 and breakfast €1.90-2.30. Open daily, early and late; hours and food availability subject to change according to performance schedule. ❷

👁 SIGHTS

Toledo's many excellent museums, stunning churches, synagogues, and mosques merit more than one day for a thorough visit. Toledo's attractions wrap around its middle within the fortified 7th-century walls. An east-west tour beginning in Pl. de Zocodóver is largely downhill. Most sights are closed on Mondays.

▧ **CATEDRAL.** Built between 1226 and 1498, Toledo's cathedral boasts five naves, delicate stained glass, and unapologetic ostentation. Noteworthy art and sculpture include the 14th-century Gothic *Virgen Blanca* by the entrance and Narciso Tomés's *Transparente*, a Spanish Baroque whirlpool of architecture, sculpture, and painting. Pay your respects (or not) at the tomb of Cardinal Mendoza, one of the early leaders of the Spanish Inquisition, just left of the massive Gothic altarpiece in the **Capilla Mayor.** Beneath the dome is the **Capilla Mozárabe,** the only place in the world where the ancient Visigoth Mass (in Mozarabic) is still held. The newly restored **Capilla de San Blas,** beyond the courtyard, boasts brightly colored intricate designs. The **treasury** flaunts a 400 lb. 16th-century gold monstrosity lugged through the streets during the annual Corpus Cristi procession on June 10th. The **sacristía** holds 18 El Grecos (including *El Espolio*), as well as paintings by other notable Spanish and European masters. The jellyfish-like red hats hanging from the ceiling mark the tombs of every archbishop of Toledo. (☎ 925 22 22 41. *Open M-Sa 10am-6:30pm, Su 2-6:30pm. Audio tour in English, French, and Italian; €8, students €6. Tickets sold at the store opposite the entrance. Modest dress required.)*

EL GRECO SIGHTS. Greek painter Doménikos Theotokópoulos, better known as El Greco, spent most of his life in Toledo. Many works are displayed throughout town, but the majority of his masterpieces have been carted off to the Prado and other big-name museums. The best place to start is the ◪**Casa Museo de El Greco,** the master's former home, which contains 19 of his paintings, among them glowing portraits of a sad-eyed Christ and a San Bartolomé who is poised to kill a *diablito* with a large knife. (*C. Samuel Leví, 2.* ☎ 925 22 44 05. *Open in summer Tu-Sa 10am-2pm and 4-9pm, Su 10am-2pm; in winter Tu-Sa 10am-2pm and 4-6pm, Su 10am-2pm. €2.40; students, under 18, and over 65 free. Sa-Su afternoons free. Closed due to renovation until mid-2008.)* Up the hill and to the right is the **Iglesia de Santo Tomé,** which still houses one of his most famous and recognized works, **El Entierro del Conde de Orgaz** (The Burial of Count Orgaz). The stark figure staring out from the back is El Greco himself, and the boy is his son, Jorge Manuel, architect of Toledo's city hall. (*Pl. del Conde, 4.* ☎ 925 25 60 98; *www.santotome.org. Open daily Mar.-Oct. 15 10am-7pm; Oct.16-Feb. 10am-6pm. €1.90, students and over 65 €1.40.)*

SYNAGOGUES. Only two of the many synagogues once in Toledo's *judería* (Jewish quarter) have been preserved. Samuel Ha Leví, diplomat and treasurer to Pedro el Cruel, built the **Sinagoga del Tránsito** in 1366, which now houses the ◪**Museo Sefardí.** Look up at the Hebrew letters ornately carved into the mudéjar plasterwork and a stunning *artesonado* (coffered) wood ceiling. The museum documents early history of the Sefardic Jews in Spain. (*C. Samuel Leví.* ☎ 925 22 36 65; *www.museosefardi.net. Open Mar.-Nov. Tu-Sa 10am-2pm and 4-9pm, Su 10am-2pm; Dec.-Feb. Tu-Sa 10am-2pm and 4-6pm, Su 10am-2pm. €2.40; students, over 65, and under 18 free. Sa after 4pm and Su free.)* **Sinagoga de Santa María la Blanca,** down the street to the right, is a testament to the dynamic (sometimes not-so-friendly) interfaith relations of Toledo's past. Built by Moorish craftsmen, it served as the city's principal synagogue before the Jews were expelled in 1492. After a period of neglect, it was converted into a church around 1550. Now secular, its Moorish arches and tranquil garden are pleasant for any denomination. (*C. de los Reyes Católicos, 4.* ☎ 925 22 72 57. *Open daily June-Aug. 10am-7pm; Sept.-May 10am-6pm. €1.90.)*

MONASTERIO DE SAN JUAN DE LOS REYES. At the far western edge of the city stands this Franciscan monastery, commissioned by Fernando and Isabel to commemorate their victory over the Portuguese in the Battle of Toro (1476). Over the church's entrance, a grinning skeleton awaits resurrection. The cloister is bright, with a garden melding Gothic and *mudéjar* architecture. The monarchs planned to use the church as their crypt, but decided instead to be interred at Granada, the site of their victory over the Moorish kingdom in 1492. (☎ 925 22 38 02. *Ticket sales stop 20min. before closing. Open daily Apr.-Sept. 10am-7pm; Oct.-Mar. 10am-6pm. €1.90.)*

MUSEUMS. Toledo was the seat of Visigoth rule and culture for three centuries prior to the Muslim invasion in 711. The exhibits at the **Museo de los Concilios y de la Cultura Visigótica** pale in comparison to their beautiful setting: a 13th-century *mudéjar* church. (*C. San Román.* ☎ 925 22 78 72. *Open Tu-Sa 10am-2pm and 4-6:30pm, Su 10am-2pm. €0.60, students free.)* The **Museo del Taller del Moro** features outstanding woodwork, plasterwork, and tiles. *(C. Taller del Moro, 3. Head through Pl. de San Anto-nio and down C. San Bernardo.* ☎ *925 22 71 15. Closed for renovations through 2007; check with the tourist office for updates.)* The impressive and under-touristed **Museo de Santa Cruz** (1504) is a tranquil and impressive example of ornate renaissance architectural embellishment. Inside, explore a handful of El Grecos, temporary shows, and the basement, which holds remains from local archaeological digs; check out the mastodon skull with tusks intact. *(C. Miguel de Cervantes, 3.* ☎ *925 22 10 36; www.jccm.es. Open Tu-Sa 10am-6pm, Su 10am-2pm. Free.)*

◗ NIGHTLIFE

The locals party beyond the city walls. From June to August, just outside the Puerta de Cambrón, on P. de Recaredo, the popular **Garcilaso Café,** C. Rojas, 5, sets up shop and opens a lively summer terrace. (☎925 22 91 60. Drinks €2.50-5. Open Th-Sa 8pm-2am.) For more convenient nightlife, head through the arch and to the left from Pl. de Zocodóver to **Calle Santa Fé,** brimming with beer and young locals. **Enebro,** tucked away on small Pl. Santiago de los Caballeros, 4, off C. Miguel de Cervantes, lures customers with delicious evening tapas, free with every drink. (☎711 35 52 30; www.barenebro.com. Beer €1.50. Open daily 10am-1am. Cash only.) **Calle de la Sillería** and **Calle de los Alfileritos** host a few upscale bars and clubs, including bar at **La Abadía.** (☎925 25 11 40. Open daily 1:30-4pm and 8pm-midnight. For directions, see **Food,** p. 194.) To escape the raucous noise, check out the chill **Café Teatro Pícaro,** C. Cadenas, 6, where lights play on abstract art, and it's just as cool to be sipping on a *batido* (milkshake, €3) as a mixed drink. (☎925 22 13 01; www.picarocafeteatro.com. Mixed drinks €4. Beer €1.50-2.50. Open M-F 4pm-3am, Sa-Su 4pm-5am.) For die-hard partygoers, head past the Hospital, to the summer discos in **Peraleda.** Inquire at the tourist office for more info.

◗ DAYTRIP FROM TOLEDO

CONSUEGRA

Samar buses (☎925 22 12 17) depart from the Toledo bus station (1¼hr.; M-F 12 per day 8am-9pm, Sa 5 per day 9:15am-11pm, Su 4 per day 10:30am-11pm; €4.22) and return from C. Castilla de la Mancha (1¼hr.; M-F 9 per day 6:10am-6:25pm, Sa 5 per day 6:55am-5:55pm, Su 4 per day 6:55am-5:55pm). They also run to Madrid (1½hr.; M-Sa 6:30, 9am, 3:15pm, Su. 3:15, 7:15pm). In Toledo, buy tickets at the office; in Consuegra, the bus office is under renovation, so buy return tickets on board. Plan around departure times to avoid spending the night.

If you're delusionally obsessed with windmills, or at least like taking pictures of them, then of all Manchegan villages, tiny Consuegra, replete with Don Quixote's imagined giants, vast landscapes, and parochial charm, is likely already on your itinerary. Most travelers skip this tiny town for more exciting destinations—but medieval Consuegra is home to a palace, a Franciscan convent, a Carmelite monastery (now a senior citizens home), an olive oil factory, and a winery, making a brief stop worth the effort. The town's 12 windmills, called the *cresteria manchega* by locals for their rooster-like appearance from an aerial view, are a short upward hike from the bus stop. Facing the bus station (under construction as of 2007), turn left, and then take another left under the archway and clocktower. Go straight up C. de la Avanzadilla, (starts on the right side of the plaza) and up the stairs. The village ◼castle, just a few hundred yards down the road, was an Arab, then Castilian fortress. The arid landscape and local snake population supplemented the defense of its turrets. From the 12th to 19th centuries, the castle was held by the *Orden de San Juan Jerusalén,* a powerful order of warrior monks. In the mid-19th century, they were forced to sell most of their riches to raise funds for the War of Independence against Napoleon. Their efforts were in vain; Napoleon's army conquered, sacked, and burned the fortress, causing much of the damage that makes it such a dramatic ruin today. (Open June-Sept. M-F 9am-2pm and 4:30-7pm, Sa-Su 10:30am-2pm and 4:30-7pm; Oct.-May daily 9:30am-2pm and 3:30-6pm. €2.) In 1097, El Cid's only son, Diego Rodriguez, died in battle in the town, and a festival is held in his honor during the weekend closest to August 15; it includes a reenactment of a medieval siege and a reconstruction of a battle using a human chess set with Castilians in white and Moors in black. In September and October this small town hosts two other annual festivals. (For more informations check out Consuegra's website, www.consuegra.es.) The **tourist office,** located halfway up the road to the castle in a windmill, will provide more information on all these sights, and on accommodation options. (☎925 47 57 31. Open June-Sept. M-F 9am-2pm and 4:30-7pm, Sa-Su 10:30am-2pm and 4:30-7pm; Oct.-May daily 9:30am-2pm and 3:30-6pm.)

ALMAGRO   ☎926

Most of the year, sleepy Almagro, an architectural oasis in La Mancha's desert is a quintessential, small Spanish town. For three weeks every July, however, its narrow cobblestone streets and whitewashed, half-timbered houses swell to capacity to host a world-renowned classical theater festival. Even if men in tights aren't your thing, Almagro is a pleasant stop on the way to Andalucía; the town is small and historic—even the post office occupies a building erected in 1614.

▐ TRANSPORTATION. The **train station** is at Po. de la Estación (☎926 86 02 76), outside the city center, at the end of the street. To get from the station to Pl. Mayor, walk down Po. de la Estación and turn left onto C. Rondo de Calatrava; turn right onto C. Madre de Dios (a sign points to Centro Urbano), which becomes C. Feria and leads to the plaza. Trains go to Ciudad Real (15min., 5 per day 8:41am-10:26pm, €2-2.50) and Madrid (2¾hr.; 2:59, 5:39pm; €11.70-14.60). Change at Ciudad Real for Córdoba, Granada, Sevilla, and Valencia. **Buses** (☎926 86 02 50) stop at a brick building at the far end of Ejido de Calatrava, just left of the Hospedería Municipal. **ALSA** (☎926 21 13 42) buses go to Ciudad Real, the connection point for most other cities (30min.; M-F 8 per day 8am-6:15pm, Sa 9:15am, 3pm; €1.50), including Madrid (2¼hr.; 4 per day M-F 7am-4pm, Sa 9:40am-4pm; €11), and has a bus to Damiel (2hr., M-Sa 9:30am, €12) which goes on to Madrid (11:45am, €2). Call for a **taxi:** ☎926 88 20 19 or 616 00 93 93.

▐▐ ORIENTATION AND PRACTICAL INFORMATION. The center of Almagro is the long, arcaded **Plaza Mayor.** From the bus station, walk down the lamppost-lined median, bear left onto C. Rondo de Calatrava, turn left on C. de Madre de Dios, and follow it straight to the plaza. The **tourist office,** Pl. Mayor, 1, is located on the ground floor of the *Ayuntamiento,* directly beneath the clock tower. (☎926 86 07 17; www.ciudad-almagro.com. Open July-Aug. Tu-F 10am-2pm and 6-9pm, Sa 10am-2pm and 6-8pm, Su 11am-2pm; Apr.-June and Sept. Tu-F 10am-2pm and 5-8pm, Sa 10am-2pm and 5-7pm, Su 11am-2pm; Oct.-Mar. Tu-F 10am-2pm and 4-7pm, Sa 10am-2pm and 4-6pm.) **Banks** and **ATMs** line C. Mayor de Carnicerías. Local services include: **police,** C. Mercado, 1 (☎926 86 00 33 or 609 01 41 36), adjacent to the Pl. Mayor; **Centro de Salud,** C. Mayor de Carnicerías, 11 (☎926 86 10 26); **Farmacia Jorreto CB,** Pl. Mayor, 13 (open M-F 9:30am-2pm and 6-9pm, Sa-Su 10am-2pm); **Internet** access at the **Biblioteca Pública,** C. San Agustín (☎926 882 090; limit 1hr.; open M-F 11am-1pm and 5-8pm, Sa 10:30am-1:30pm, closed F afternoons; in summer daily 9am-1:30pm; free); and the **post office,** C. Mayor de Carnicerías, 16 (☎926 86 00 52; open M-F 8:30am-2:30pm, Sa 9:30am-1pm). **Postal Code:** 13270.

⚏☐ ACCOMMODATIONS AND FOOD. Finding a place to sleep during the theater festival, from late June/early July to late July, is a drama in and of itself. Reserve
as early as April, particularly at the **Hospedería de Almagro ❸**, C. Ejido de Calatrava.
Red-tiled rooms with white walls and lanterns for light fixtures overlook the courtyard and echo the austerity of the adjacent monastery. Clean bath, phone, and TV in
each room provide for a comfortable stay. (☎926 88 20 87; fax 88 21 22. July singles
with bath €28; doubles with shower €40, with bath €46; triples €53/61; quads with
bath €61. Aug.-June singles €25; doubles €34/40; triples €44/53; quads €53. MC/V.)
Hostal Rural San Bartolomé ❸, C. San Bartolomé is just off the Pl. Mayor in a quaint
16th-century building. All rooms have bath, TV, A/C. (☎926 26 10 73; www.hostalsan-
bartolome.com. Depending on season, singles €25-35; doubles €40-50. Cash only.)

Outdoor restaurants crowd Pl. Mayor and its offshoots, offering some of the best
(and most expensive) food in town. On a smaller street, **Abrasador ❷**, C. San Agustín,
18, home-cooks all of their meat and specializes in *cerdo ibérico* (Iberian ham,
€15.50 feeds many mouths). (☎926 88 26 56. *Menú* €12. Open daily 11am-5pm and
8pm-midnight. AmEx/D/MC/V.) For groceries, stop at **Dia%**, C. San Agustín. (Open M-
Th 9:30am-2pm and 5:30-8:30pm, F-Sa 9am-2:30pm and 5:30-9pm.) The freshest fruits
and veggies are sold at the outdoor **market.** From Pl. Mayor, walk down C. Mayor de
Carnicerías for one block, then turn left onto Rastro de San Juan. (Open W 8am-3pm.)

◐ ☐ SIGHTS AND ENTERTAINMENT. Plaza Mayor is square one for cultural
sights in Almagro. Here you can find the famous **Corral de Comedias,** Pl. Mayor, 18, an
open-air multi-level theater resembling Shakespeare's Globe. This theater is the only
one left intact from the Golden Age of Spanish drama, and its stage was home to the
works of such literary masters as Cervantes and Lope de Vega. Catch a show during
the Theater Festival and see what it might have been like in *Siglo de Oro*. (☎926 86
15 39; www.corraldecomedias.com. Open Oct.-Mar. Tu-Su 10am-2pm and 4-7pm;
Apr.-June and Sept. Tu-Su 10am-2pm and 5-8pm; July-Aug. Tu-Su 10am-2pm and 6-
9pm. €2.50, children and groups of 15 or more €2.) Directly across the plaza from
the Corral and through a few arches, the **Museo Nacional del Teatro,** C. Gran Maestre,
2, displays the history of Spanish drama. Ticket includes entrance to the museum's
temporary exhibits on different aspects of Spanish theater, such as costumes and
stage design, which are housed separately in the Iglesia de San Agustín, on the corner of C. San Agustín and C. Feria. (☎926 26 10 14. Open Oct.-June and Sept. Tu-F
10am-2pm and 4-7pm, Sa 10am-2pm and 4-6pm, Su 11am-2pm; July-Aug. Tu-F 11-
2pm and 6-9pm, Sa 11am-2pm and 7-9pm, Su 11am-2pm. €2.40; under 18, Sa afternoon, and Su morning free.) Rounding out the theater tour is the **Teatro Municipal,** C.
San Agustín, 20. Follow C. San Agustín out of Pl. Mayor and look for a crimson-and-
white building on the right. Inside is a renovated theater and a small collection of
elaborate costumes. (☎926 86 13 61. Open Oct.-Mar. same hours as Museo Nacional;
Apr.-June and Sept. Tu-F 10am-2pm and 5-8pm, Sa 10am-2pm and 5-7pm, Su 11am-
2pm; July-Aug. Tu-F 10am-2pm and 6-9pm, Sa 10am-2pm and 6-8pm, Su 11am-2pm.
€1.50, students €1.) Teatro Municipal hosts modern Spanish plays on weekends in
September, October, and November for the *Festival de Contemporáneo*.

❀ FESTIVALS. Every summer, prestigious theater companies and players from
around the world descend on the town for the **Festival Internacional de Teatro Clásico
de Almagro.** (Dates vary, but usually between the end of June and the end of July.)
Daily performances of Spanish and international classics take place throughout the
city. The location of the **box office** changes from year to year, so it is best to call the
Caixa Catalunya to book tickets. (☎902 10 12 12; www.telentrada.com, info at
www.festivaldealmagro.com. MC/V.) There are daily productions in July at
10:45pm, and less regularly at 12:30pm or 1pm. Look online or inquire at the tourist

office for specific details. Tickets range from €20-25 (Tu half-price) and should be purchased at the Teatro Municipal in May before the festival begins, as they tend to sell out quickly. The festival also has an office in Madrid at C. Colmenares, 7 (☎915 21 07 20), but you can't buy tickets there. The 2008 program is listed online. From August to December and March to June, there are **classical theater** performances nearly every weekend at the Corral. (☎926 88 24 58; www.corraldecomedias.com. Performances at 7, 7:30, or 9pm, depending on the date. Programs available online.)

CUENCA   ☎969

Cuenca (pop. 50,000) is a quiet hill-top retreat, which owes its fame to the marvelous geological foundations on which it stands. The city spills over a hill and is flanked by two rivers and the stunning rock formations they have carved. This setting, which served the city well as a defense in ancient times, continues to be a backdrop of insurmountable beauty. The enchanting old city safeguards Cuenca's celebrated treasures, including the ██**casas colgadas** (hanging houses), which dangle at a dizzying height above the Río Huécar. The magnificent neo-Gothic facade Catedral de Cuenca dominates the classic Plaza Mayor. Since the 19th century, the city has strained against its natural boundaries, depositing modern and uninspired commercial life downhill in New Cuenca. It's definitely worth a night's stay to see the *casas* lit up at sunrise from the footbridge across the gorge.

▐▀ TRANSPORTATION

Trains: C. Mariano Catalina, 10 (☎902 24 02 02). To **Aranjuez** (2hr., 5-6 per day 7:05am-6:55pm, €7.40), **Madrid** (2½-3hr., 5-6 per day 7:05am-6:55pm, €10.20), and **Valencia** (3-4hr., 3-4 per day 7:35am-6:50pm, €11.15).

Buses: C. Fermín Caballero, 20 (☎969 22 70 87). Info open daily 7am-2:30pm and 4-9pm. **AutoRes** (☎969 22 70 87) to **Madrid** (2½hr.; 8-9 per day M-F 6:45am-10:30pm, Sa 6:45am-9pm, Su 6:45am-12:30am; €10-12). **AISA** to **Toledo** via **Ciudad Directo** (2¼hr.; M-F 6:30am and 4pm, Su 5pm; €11-13). **Samar** buses go to **Barcelona** (9hr., daily 9:30am, €34.52).

Taxis: Radio Taxi (☎969 23 33 43). From the train station to Pl. Mayor €6.

✦▐ ORIENTATION AND PRACTICAL INFORMATION

Upon exiting the train station, the back of the bus station (a large brick building) will be on the street in front of you; head up the steps to C. Fermín Caballero and turn right to enter the bus station. To reach the **Plaza Mayor** in the old city from either station, take a left onto C. Fermín Caballero, following it as it becomes C. Cervantes, C. José Cobo, and, bearing left through Pl. de la Hispanidad, **Calle Carretería**. Street signs point the way. From C. Carretería, head toward the river. The winding route up is more scenic; for a busier route, turn right onto C. Fray Luis de León; it's a long hike uphill to Pl. Mayor and the old city (20-25min.). Alternatively, take bus #1 or 2 (every 30min.; €0.70, Su €0.85) to Pl. Mayor from the bus stop off Pl. de la Constitución, at the intersection of C. Carretería and C. Frey Luis de León.

Tourist Office: Pl. Mayor, 1 or C. Alfonso VII, 2 (☎969 24 10 51; www.cuenca.org). Open July-Sept. daily 9am-9pm; Oct.-June M-Sa 9am-2pm and 4-6:30pm, Su 9am-2pm.

Currency Exchange: Banco Santander Central Hispano, C. Sánchez Vera, 5 (☎969 22 36 51). Open Apr.-Sept. M-F 8:30am-2pm; Oct.-Mar. also Sa 8:30am-2pm.

Luggage Storage: At the **bus station** (☎969 22 70 87; €2 per day; open daily 7am-2pm and 4-9pm).

Cuenca

▲ ACCOMMODATIONS
Hostal Cánovas, **12**
Pensión Central, **14**
Pensión Tabanqueta, **1**
Posada de San José, **4**

🍎 FOOD
Cafetería Gran Vía, **16**
Panadería Miguel
  Rubio, **5**
Mercado Municipal, **13**
Mesón-Bar Tabanqueta, **2**
Posada de San José, **3**
La Venta, **15**

⭐ NIGHTLIFE
Big Red Bus, **11**
People, **9**
Mango, **10**
Nazka, **7**
Noize, **8**
Tascazoco, **6**

Fundación
Antonio Pérez

C. del
Trabuco

■ Casas Colgadas

Río Huécar

Hoz del Huécar

Catedral
and Museo
del Tesoro

Puente de
San Pablo

Museo
Diocesano

Museo
de Cuenca

Canónigos

PL.
MAYOR

C. Obispo
Valero

Ayuntamiento

Museo de Arte
Abstracto Español

PL.
DE RONDA

PL. DE LA
MERCED

Mercado
Miguel
Rubio

Teatro
Auditorio

Paseo del Huécar

San Antón

Puente
San Antón

Hoz del Júcar
Río Júcar

Av. Virgen de la Luz

Cerrito de Santiago

Subida de Santiago

C. de Colón

Hospital de
Santiago

PL.
TRINIDAD

C. San Juan

C. Palafox

C. Andrés de Cabrera

Palacio
de Justicia

Parque
del Huécar

C. Doctor
Galíndez

C. Calderón de la Barca

C. Mateo Aylón

C. Capellán
Moreno

Sto. Domingo

C. González Francés

C. Solera

PL. DEL
CARMEN

San
Felipe

El Salvador

C. de Caballeros

C. del General
Sta. Coloma

C. Alonso de Ojeda

Puerta de
Valencia

BARRIO DE
LOS TIRADORES

C. Fray Luis de León

PL. DE LA
CONSTITUCIÓN

PL. DE LOS
CARROS

PL. DE
ESPAÑA

C. de los Tintes

C. Juan de Corrachel

Hermanos Valdés

Princesa Zaida

C. Sánchez Vera

C. San Agustín

Maestro Prada

Parque de
San Julián

Garcilaso de la Vega

C. Diego Ramírez de Villaescusa

Maestro
Kíelse

C. Martínez

C. C. de
Albornoz

C. Alonso
Chirino

C. Parque de San Julián

C. de las Torres

C. de Segóbriga

C. del General

C. Valería

C. Arcábica

C. Lusones

Carretería

C. Teniente
González

TAXI

PL.
HISPANIDAD

Diputación
Provincial

C. Aguirre

C. Fanjul

C. Menéndez y Pelayo

C. González Falencia

C. B

C. F

C. E

C. D

C. José Cobo

C. de Colón

Cervantes

PL. SAN
ROQUE

C. San Francisco

C. de Ramón y Cajal

C. Doctor Ferrán

Av. de la República Argentina

Hurtado
de Mendoza

■ %Dia

C. Antonio Maura

Tray. Escultor Marco Pérez

Av. Reyes Católicos

Av. de C. de C. San Marcos

C. C. la Mancha

C. San Lucas

C. San Mateo

C. Diego Giménez

C. de Ramón y Cajal

C. Fermín Caballero

C. Teruel

C. M. Catalina Caballero

C. Santa Inés

C. San Antonio

PL. DE LA
AJEDREA

PL. DEL
ROMERO

C. Alférez Rubianes

C. Fausto Culebras

C. Santiago López

C. Tresjuncos

C. Conversa

C. de Sta. María de la Cabeza

C. Jorge Torner

C. Cañete

Parque de
Santa Ana

Camino de la Reguera

Plaza
de Toros

TO ✚
(200m)

100 meters

100 yards

Police: (☎969 22 48 59). At the intersection of C. González Palencia and C. Duque de Alhumada.

Pharmacy: Farmacia Castellanos, C. Cervantes, 20 (☎969 21 23 37), at the corner of C. Alférez Rubianes. Open Apr.-Oct. M-F 9:30am-2pm and 5-8pm, Sa 10am-2pm; Nov.-Mar. M-F 9:30am-2pm and 4:30-7:30pm, Sa 10am-2pm.

Post Office: Parque de San Julián, 16 (☎969 22 10 42). Open M-F 8:30am-8:30pm, Sa 9:30am-2pm. A smaller **branch** with fewer services is right next to the train station. Open M-F 8:30am-2:30pm, Sa 8am-2pm. **Postal Code:** 16002.

ACCOMMODATIONS

Lodging in the old city makes nightlife a bit of an excursion—but the views and clean breezes are definitely worth it. Reserve ahead.

Posada de San José, C. Julián Romero, 4 (☎969 21 13 00; www.posadadesan-jose.com). Rooms with bath, some with balcony. Restaurant attached (see p. 201) Reserve ahead. Breakfast €8. Singles €25, with bath €50; doubles €38/75; triples with bath €83; quads with bath €128. *Semana Santa* higher prices; weeknights and low season lower. AmEx/MC/V. ❷

Pensión Tabanqueta, C. del Trabuco, 13 (☎969 21 12 90), up C. San Pedro from the cathedral past Pl. del Trabuco. Quite a hike from New Cuenca, but the view is worth it. Don't miss the terrace bar. Singles €15; doubles €30. Cash only. ❷

Hostal Cánovas, C. Fray Luis de León, 38, 1st fl. (☎969 21 39 73; www.servinet.net/canovas). Refurbished rooms are elegant and comfortable. Hardwood floors, balconies in all doubles. Private baths and fans justify the price. Some rooms with A/C. Singles €35; doubles €50; triples €65; rooftop terrace suites €65-85. AmEx/MC/V. ❸

Pensión Central, C. de Alonso Chirino, 7, 2nd fl. (☎969 21 15 11). Clean rooms with big windows and high ceilings at the bottom of the hill. Balconies and 2 large common baths. Singles €16; doubles €26; triples €35. Cash only. ❷

FOOD

The area around Pl. Mayor is filled with mid- to high-priced restaurants and only mediocre eats, but side streets near the plaza yield cheaper alternatives. Budget spots line **Calle Cervantes** and **Avenida de la República Argentina**; the cafes off **Calle Fray Luis de León** are even cheaper. Area specialties include *resoli* (a liqueur of coffee, sugar, orange peel, and *aguardiente*) and *alajú* (a nougat of honey, almonds, and figs). The **mercado municipal** is on C. Fray Luis de León (open M-Sa 8:30am-2pm), and groceries are at **%Dia** on Av. Castilla La Mancha. (Open M-Th 9:30am-2pm and 5:30-8:30pm, F-Sa 9am-2:30pm and 5:30-9pm.)

Posada de San José, C. Julián Romero, 4 (☎969 21 13 00). Delicious food at delicious prices. Enjoy an incredible view and relaxing ambience with their *pisto* (tomato, pepper, and onion stew; €4.25). *Bocadillos* and omelettes €4-6. Lamb and fried trout €7-11. Open Tu-Su 8-11am and 6-10:30pm. AmEx/MC/V. ❶

Mesón-Bar Tabanqueta, C. del Trabuco, 13 (☎969 21 12 90). Patrons gorge on views and cheap bites at this bustling little cafe. Several options including a *menú* (€13) and sandwiches (€3.50-5.50). Open Tu-Su noon-2am. Cash only. ❷

La Venta, C. Colón, 81 (☎969 21 29 11). Locals come here for the tasty weeknight *menú* (€9). Main courses include fish (€11-13) and meat dishes (€7-16.50); appetizers offer vegetarian options (€5-12). Open M-F 1-3pm and 9:30-11:45pm, Su 1-3pm. MC/V. ❷

Cafetería Gran Vía, C. Fermín Caballero, 4 (☎969 23 62 26). Well-dressed waiters attend the dining room and scurry among the people-watchers on the outdoor patio. Combo plates of eggs and pork €7-11. Open daily 7:30am-3pm and 7-11pm. MC/V. ❷

Panadería Miguel Rubio, C. Alfonso VIII, 59 (☎969 21 27 07) just down the hill on the left side of the street from the Pl. Mayor. Do as the locals do: get some cheap bread, meat, cheese, and fruit and head for a park. Cuenca's best offering is free: the natural landscape. Open M-F 9am-2pm and 5-8:30pm. Cash only. ❷

◉ SIGHTS

◼ **CASAS COLGADAS.** Cuenca derives its fame from the 14th-century *casas colgadas* that dangle over its riverbanks. These "hanging houses," built precariously on the edges of Cuenca's cliffs, are believed to have been the summer homes of 14th-century monarchs. A walk across Puente de San Pablo at sunset (or sunrise) offers a spectacular ◼ **view** of the casas and the surrounding cliffs. All the *casas* are illuminated at night. For vistas of Cuenca, stroll along two trails flanking Hoz del Júcar and Hoz del Huécar (the steep river gorges on either side of the old city).

◼ **CATEDRAL DE CUENCA.** Constructed under Alfonso VIII six years after he conquered Castilla, the cathedral is a fantastic centerpiece of the Pl. Mayor. A perfect square, it is the only Anglo-Norman Gothic cathedral in Spain and has been cursed by disasters through the ages. A Spanish Renaissance facade and tower were added in the 16th and 17th centuries, only to be torn down when deemed aesthetically displeasing. A 1724 fire prevented a subsequent attempt to rebuild the facade, leaving just the exterior and producing an effect strangely reminiscent of a Hollywood set. Colorful stained-glass windows illuminate the entrance to the **Museo del Tesoro,** which houses late medieval psalters and gold jewelry and is currently closed for renovations. *(Pl. Mayor. Cathedral open July-Sept. M-F 10am-2pm and 4-7pm, Sa 10am-7pm, Su 10am-6:30pm; Oct.-Apr. open daily 10:30am-1:30pm and 4-6pm; May-June Sa 10:30am-2pm and 4-6pm, Su 10:30am-2pm and 4-6:30pm. Cathedral, museum, and audio tour €2.80.)*

MUSEO DE ARTE ABSTRACTO ESPAÑOL. Inside the only *casa colgada* open to the public, the award-winning Museo de Arte Abstracto Español exhibits works by the odd yet renowned Abstract Generation of Spanish painters. All pieces, most by Canogar, Tápies, Chillida, and Fernando Zóbel, were chosen by Zóbel himself. La Sala Blanca (the White Room) and striking views of the gorge are not to miss. *(Pl. de Ronda; follow signs from Pl. Mayor. ☎969 21 29 83. Open July-Sept. Tu-F 11am-2pm and 5-7pm, Sa 11am-2pm and 4-9pm, Su 11am-2:30pm; Oct.-June Tu-F 11am-2pm and 4-6pm, Sa 11am-2pm and 4-8pm, Su 11am-2:30pm. €3, students and seniors €1.50.)*

OTHER SIGHTS. The **Fundación Antonio Pérez,** C. Julian Romero, 20, is near the top of the street. Antonio Pérez, a contemporary writer and critic, has opened his impressively eclectic collection of 20th-century art to the public. Highlights include surrealist collages, Pérez's *objetos encontrados* (found objects), a couple of Warhols, and, notably, Ximo Amigó's "Michelin Man" works, which haunt various nooks and corners of the regal casa. The downstairs gallery hosts exhibits. *(☎969 23 06 19. Open daily 11am-midnight. Free.)* Around the cathedral, down C. Obispo Valero, is the **Museo Diocesano,** whose exhibits include Juan de Borgoña's altarpiece from the local Convento de San Pablo, colossal Flemish tapestries, splendid rugs, and two El Grecos—*Oración del huerto* and *Cristo con la cruz.* *(☎969 22 42 10. Open in summer Tu-Sa 11am-2pm and 4-6pm, Su 11am-2pm; in winter Tu-Sa 11am-2pm. €2.)* Across the street, the **Museo de Cuenca** is a treasure trove of Roman mosaics, coins, and Visigoth jewelry. *(☎969 21 30 69. Open Tu-Sa 10am-2pm and 4-7pm, Su 11am-2pm. €1.20, students €0.60. Sa afternoon and Su free.)*

▐ NIGHTLIFE

Cuenca's nightlife scene extends into the wee hours of the morning from Thursday to Saturday, and bars tend to only open on the weekend. The older, and early-to-bed crowd stays near Pl. Mayor, while teens and twenty-somethings flock to the newer city. Numerous bars with young, well-dressed partiers line **Calle Doctor Galíndez,** off C. Fray Luis de León. It's a hot spot in the new city, but a long, dark walk down the hill from Old Cuenca; a taxi costs about €5.50, but the **Buho** (night bus) #1 runs from nearby Pl. de la Constitución to Pl. Mayor until 3am (€1.15). Locals drink in the Pl. de España before getting down at mirror-lined **Nazka,** C. Dr. Galíndez, 28, at the end of the street. (Open Th-Sa 11:30pm-4am.) The nearby **People,** C. Dr. Galíndez, 8, has a large bar area with chill lime green walls. (Open Th-Sa 11:30pm-4am.) On the same street are **Big Red Bus, Mango,** and **Noize.** Prices can be high, though they're standard at all these bars; beer costs €1-2, mixed drinks €4-5 (€6 at **Nazka**), and shots €1-2. If you're making a night of it, stock up at **%Dia** (open F and Sa until 9pm) and join the locals in the plaza. Most bars provide plastic cups for free. If you stay around the Pl. Mayor, head to the **Pl. de Ronda,** facing the Cathedral. Hug the right side and head downhill to **Tascazoco** (☎969 23 78 87; Pl. de Ronda; open W-Sa 10:30am-4pm and 8-close, Su 11am-4:30pm.), with an airy terrace and impressive wine cellar (glass of wine, €6-12).

SIGÜENZA ☎949

The stone buildings and red-roofed houses of Sigüenza (pop. 5000) surround a stunning Gothic cathedral and storybook castle. In the Civil War, Republicans seized the cathedral and Nationalists took the castle; the bloody standoff ended when Nationalists bombed the church and stormed it with tanks. Since then, Sigüenza's architecture has been restored, and a walk through the streets—from the medieval city to the 18th-century Baroque neighborhoods—makes an enjoyable escape from Madrid, though not for more than a day or two.

From the bottom of the hill, two buildings jut out from Sigüenza's low skyline: the cathedral and the fortified 12th-century castle, restored in the 1970s and now a *parador.* To get to the █**cathedral,** follow Av. de Alfonso VI uphill (it changes to C. del Humilladero), then take a left onto C. del Cardenal Mendoza. Work on the cathedral began in the mid-12th century and continued until the 16th century; 400 years of construction made for a fantastic combination of Romanesque, *mudéjar,* Plateresque, Gothic, Baroque, and Renaissance revival. Renowned for its naturalistic grace is the 15th-century **Tumba del Doncel** (Tomb of the Virginal Youth). The alabaster sarcophagi contain remains of the de Arce family, nobles loyal to the Spanish Crown. Martín Barque de Arce (reclining) died at 25 fighting the Moors in Granada. Centuries later, Miguel de Unamuno dubbed him "El Doncel," and the name stuck. The sacristy's Renaissance ceiling, designed by Alonso de Covarrubias, has 304 stone portraits (3700 counting minor cherubim). The adjoining chapel houses another version of El Greco's *Anunciación.* (☎619 36 27 15. Tour required to enter sacristy and chapel; 6 per day 11am-7pm. Meet by the gated Tumba del Doncel in the back of the church; €4. Cathedral open daily 9:30am-2pm and 4:30-8pm. Free.) Opposite the cathedral, the **Museo de Arte Antiguo** (Museo Diocesano) houses medieval and early modern religious works, including a Ribera and Zurbarán's *La Inmaculada Niña.* (☎949 39 10 23; obsigus.ed.telefonica.net. Closed Jan. 10-Mar. 10. Open Tu-Su 11am-2pm and 4-7pm, in summer 4-8pm. €3.)

Although you can see Sigüenza in a few hours, train schedules might force you to spend the night. One option is the **Hotel El Laberinto ❹,** C. Alameda, 1. From the station, follow Av. de Alfonso VI to the intersection past the Parque de la Alameda; the hotel is on the corner. It offers tidy rooms painted in beach-house colors with TV, telephone, and A/C. (☎949 39 11 65. Single €35; doubles €54. AmEx/MC/V.) Small restaurants offering delicious *menús* for under €8 can be found everywhere.

The **train station** (☎949 39 14 94) is at the end of Av. de Alfonso VI. Trains run to Estación Chamartín in Madrid (1½-2hr., 6-9 per day 7am-10pm, €8.20-€15). **Buses** (☎949 34 72 77) run to Guadalajara (M-F 2 per day, Sa 8am). The **tourist**

office recently moved to a new location, C. Serranzo Sanz. (☎949 34 70 07. Open M-Th 10am-2pm and 5-7pm, F 10am-2pm and 5-8pm, Sa 10am-2:30pm and 5-7pm, Su 10am-2pm.) The tourist office leads guided **city tours,** which take you almost everywhere except the cathedral. (Call ahead for reservations. Tours 11:30-5:15. €7, children €6.) Local services include the **police,** on Ctra. de Atienzo (☎949 39 01 95), and the **Red Cross** on Ctra. Madrid (☎949 39 13 33). Free **Internet** access is available at the Biblioteca Pública, C. de Valencia, on the top floor of the *Ayuntamiento,* in the Torreón de la Muralla. Bear right going uphill on C. de la Humilidero; the building is on the left. (Open M-F noon-2pm and 5-8:30pm.) The **post office,** C. Jose de Villaviciosa, 3, is off Pl. Hilario Yabén. (☎949 39 08 44. Open M-F 8:30am-2:30pm, Sa 9:30am-1pm.) **Postal Code:** 19250.

EXTREMADURA

Extremadura is in no hurry to step into the 21st century. With its endless landscape of thirsty soil, scattered lakes, occasional sunflower fields, and gorgeous stone towns, the region seems to relish in what stays frozen in time. Beyond its unique landscape, Extremadura's hearty pastoral cuisine is particularly appealing; local specialties include rabbit, partridge, lizard with green sauce, wild pigeon with herbs, and *migas extremeñas* (fried bread crumbs). Mérida's ancient Roman ruins and the hushed beauty of Trujillo and Cáceres are only now beginning to draw flocks of admirers looking for the "classic" Spanish countryside.

CÁCERES   ☎927

Stepping into Cáceres's *barrio antiguo* (old city) is a sudden time warp. The bustle of the modern city is silenced by an overwhelming wave of medieval antiquity. Built between the 14th and 16th centuries by rival noble families in a sort of architectural war for prestige and socio-political control, the *barrio antiguo* is comprised of swanky miniature palaces once used to show off each family's power and wealth. Wander through this magnificent maze of tiny streets with palaces on almost every corner, and don't forget to pay your respects to the city's modern sentinels: the storks keep watch from their posts on the roofs and towers. Although the newer areas of Cáceres are less interesting, the cheerful nightlife and intriguing old city provide enough amusement for a one- or two-night stay.

▐ TRANSPORTATION

Trains: RENFE (☎927 23 37 61 or 902 24 02 02), on Av. de Alemania, 3km from the old city. Across the highway from the bus station. Open daily 9am-9pm. To: **Badajoz** (2hr., 3 per day 11:45am-10pm, €7-15); **Lisboa** (6hr.; 3, 8:13am; €35); **Madrid** (4hr., 6 per day 4:10am-6:51pm, €16-35); **Sevilla** (4hr., 8:33am, €15) via **Mérida** (1hr., €4).

Buses: (☎927 23 25 50), on Av. de la Hispanidad. Info open daily 8:30am-7:30pm; Su closed 2-3pm. Fewer buses available in July and August. Buses to: **Badajoz** (1¼hr.; 2-6 per day M-F 7:30am-7:30pm, Sa 8:30am and 2:30pm, Su 2:30pm-9pm; €6.48); **Madrid** (4-5hr., 7-9 per day 1:45am-6pm, €18.35); **Mérida** (1hr.; 2-6 per day M-Th 6:30am-7:30pm, F 6:30am-8:30pm, Sa 1 and 5pm, Su 10am-9:30pm; €4.33); **Salamanca** (4hr.; 7-28 per day M-F 7:15am-9:25pm, Sa 7:15am-10:15pm, Su 9:30am-12:45am; €12.83-12.95); **Sevilla** (4hr., 8-14 per day 4:10am-1:45am, €16.09); **Trujillo** (45min.; M-F 4 per day 11am-5:30pm, Sa 1pm, Su 7:30pm; €2.93); **Valladolid** (5½hr.; noon, 6:15pm; €18.50).

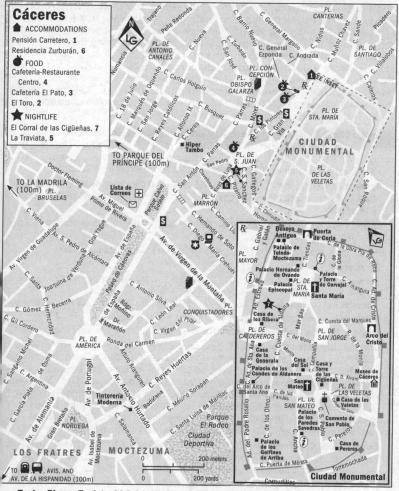

Cáceres

🏠 ACCOMMODATIONS
Pensión Carretero, **1**
Residencia Zurburán, **6**

🍴 FOOD
Cafetería-Restaurante
  Centro, **4**
Cafetería El Pato, **3**
El Toro, **2**

⭐ NIGHTLIFE
El Corral de las Cigüeñas, **7**
La Traviata, **5**

Ciudad Monumental

Taxis: Phono Taxi (☎927 21 21 21) or **Radio Taxi** (☎927 23 23 23) Stands at Pl. Mayor, Pl. de San Juan, and bus and train stations.

Car Rental: Avis (☎927 23 57 21), in the bus station. 23+. 1-day rental from €80. Open summer M-F 9:30am-1pm and 5-8pm, Sa 9:30am-1pm; in winter M-F 5-8pm.

◀🔷 🚹 ORIENTATION AND PRACTICAL INFORMATION

The *ciudad monumental* (also called the *barrio antiguo*) and the commercial Av. de España flank the Pl. Mayor. The plaza is 3km from the bus and train stations, which face each other across the rotary intersection of Av. de la Hispanidad and Av. de Alemania. From the bus or train station, the best way to get to the center of town is via bus #1 (€0.75 per ride, 10 rides for €5.50); from the station, walk out the exit opposite the buses, and turn left uphill. Turn right at the intersection, and the bus stop is past the gas station on the same side of the street. Hop off at Pl. Obispo Galarza. Facing the bus stop, walk right and take the first left down the steps across from the "Pl. Mayor 80m" sign. At the first intersection, turn right, then left to continue downhill and past the next street, following the "Centro Histórico" signs. When you reach the arches, Pl. Mayor will be on the left. Bus #2 stops on Av. de la Hispanidad, around the corner from the bus station, and runs to Pl. de América, the hub of the new downtown. From there, signs point up the tree-lined Av. de España (Paseo de Cánovas) toward the Pl. Mayor. Walking from the bus or train station to Pl. Mayor will take about a half-hour and is not an appealing option in the sweltering Extremaduran afternoon heat.

Tourist Office: Pl. Mayor, 9-10 (☎927 01 08 34; otcaceres@eco.juntaex.es), in the outer wall of the ciudad monumental. Open July-Sept. M-F 8am-3pm, Sa-Su 10am-2pm; Oct.-June M-F 9am-2pm, Sa-Su 9:45am-2pm. **Branch** office at C. Ancha, 7 (☎927 24 71 72). Open Tu-Su summer 10am-2pm and 5:30-8:30pm; winter 4:30-7:30pm.

Currency Exchange: Banks line the Av. de España and the streets leading to Pl. Mayor. **Caja de Extremadura** has a branch on Pl. Mayor near C. Pintores. Open Oct.-Apr. M-F 9am-2pm, Th 5-6:45pm.

Luggage Storage: At the **train station** (€3 per bag per day) and **bus station** (€2 per bag per day).

Police: Municipal (☎092/091, 112 emergency), on C. Diego María Crehuet.

Pharmacies:

  Farmacia Castel, Pl. Mayor, 28A (☎927 24 50 87). Open M-F 9:30am-2pm and 5:30-8:30pm, Sa-Su 9:30am-2pm.

  Farmacia Jiménez Robledo, C. los Pintores, 27 (☎927 24 55 28). Posts the list of 24hr. pharmacies.

  24-Hour Pharmacy: D. Matilde Torres Muñoz, Av. Virgen de la Montaña (☎927 23 73 27).

Hospital: Hospital Virgen de la Montaña (☎927 25 68 00), on Av. de España, 2.

Libraries: Biblioteca Municipal, Pl. de la Concepción, 2 (☎927 26 00 15; fax 927 21 27 94). Located inside the Palacio de la Isla, the 1st fl. exhibits local art. The building is open for tourist visits M-F 9am-9pm, Sa 9am-2pm. The library, on the 2nd fl., has 4 computers with very slow, sometimes nonfunctional **Internet** access. Open M-F 9am-9pm, Sa 10am-2pm. **Biblioteca Pública,** on the corner of Av. Virgen de la Montaña and C. León Leal (☎927 00 68 60). Fortified by a stonewall strangled with ivy, the library has 16 computers on the 2nd fl. or providing free Internet access. Open M-F 10am-2pm and 5-8pm, Sa-Su 9am-2pm and 5-9pm. July-Aug. daily 8:15am-2:45pm.

Laundry: LIMSEC, C. Periodista Sánchez Asensio, 6 (☎927 22 64 78). Open M-F 10am-2pm and 5-8pm, Sa 10am-2pm. Tintorería Moderna, Av. de Antonio Hurtado, 16 (☎927 22 00 66; www.tintoreriamoderna.com). Open M-F 9:30am-2pm and 5-8pm, Sa 9:30am-2pm.

Internet Access: Free **Internet** access at the public and municipal libraries. **Ciberjust,** C. Diego María Crehuet, 7 (☎927 21 46 77). €2 per hour. Free coffee 10am-noon and 4:30-6pm. Open M-F 10:30am-2:30pm and 4:30pm-midnight, Sa noon-2:30pm and 5-11:30pm, Su 5-11:30pm.

Post Office: Av. Miguel Primo de Rivera (☎927 62 66 81). Stamps and **Lista de Correos.** Open M-F 8:30am-8:30pm, Sa 9:30am-2pm. **Postal Code:** 10071.

◤ ACCOMMODATIONS

Hostels are scattered throughout the new city and line Pl. Mayor in the old town. Prices rise during festivals, and advance reservations are recommended on summer weekends, especially for *pensiones* near Pl. Mayor.

  ▨ **Pensión Carretero,** Pl. Mayor, 22 (☎927 24 74 82; pens_carretero@yahoo.es). Spacious rooms with painted tile floors and some with balcony views of the plaza. Hospitable, informative staff. Prime location; the balconies allow you to take in the sounds, not just the views, of the main square. Communal bath. Curfew 1am. Singles €25; doubles €30; triples €40. Before June and after Aug. €15/20/35. AmEx/MC/V. ❷

Residencia Zurbarán, C. Roso de Luna, 11 (☎927 21 04 52). Popular with study-abroad students who live here all semester or summer. Clean rooms are basic, without any particular decor, but have desks and TVs. Hall baths. Singles €20; doubles €38; triples €55. Cash only. ❷

⚡ FOOD

Pl. Mayor overflows with restaurants and cafes serving up *bocadillos, raciones,* and *extremeño* specialties. Side streets and newer parts of the city offer less-touristy bars and pastry shops. **Hiper Tambo,** C. Alfonso IX, 25, has a relatively large selection of wine and groceries and boasts an impressive deli and counters with ready-to-eat meals. (☎927 21 17 71. Open M-Sa 9:30am-9pm. AmEx/MC/V)

El Toro, C. General Ezponda, 2 (☎927 21 15 48). Spanish cuisine in an upscale setting. Animal rights activists may want to ask for a table facing away from the stuffed bull's head. Entrees €8-14. Open Sa-Su 11am-afternoon. MC/V. ❸

Cafetería El Pato, (☎927 24 67 36) in the Pl. Mayor. Co-owned with El Toro. Take in the stork-covered walls of the old city while the friendly staff dishes out everything from ham and eggs to ewe's milk cheese sandwiches. Entrees €6.60-15. *Menú* €10-13. Open Tu-Sa noon-4pm and 8pm-midnight. AmEx/MC/V. ❷

Cafetería-Restaurante Centro, C. Pintores, 34 (☎927 26 00 09). This convenient *extremeño* restaurant has outdoor seating right in the middle of the square. Social atmosphere and a local crowd. Ask for the menu in English to help navigate through the local specialties. Entrees €4-12. Combination plates €7-9. *Menú* €8.50-9.50. Open daily 11am-11pm. AmEx/MC/V. ❷

👁 SIGHTS

The golden **ciudad monumental** is a melting pot of architectural influences: wealthy Spanish families incorporated Roman, Arabic, Gothic, Renaissance, and even Incan influences (brought back by the *conquistadores*) into their palaces. The main attraction is the neighborhood itself, since most buildings don't let tourists in beyond a peek into the patio from an open door. From Pl. Mayor, take the stairs from the left of the tourist office to the Arco de la Estrella, the entrance to the old city.

MUSEO DE CÁCERES. Inside the Casa de los Caballos, the Museo de Cáceres is a must-see, housing a tiny but brilliant Who's Who of Spanish art. It features originals by El Greco, Picasso, Miró, and recent abstractionist stars, along with rotating exhibits. The neighboring **Casa de las Veletas** (House of Weathervanes) displays Celtiberian stone animals, Visigothic tombstones, and an astonishing ▨ **Muslim cistern.** *(Pl. de las Veletas. ☎927 01 08 77. Open Apr.-Sept. Tu-Sa 9am-2:30pm and 5-8:15pm, Su 10:15am-2:30pm. Oct.-Apr. Tu-Sa 9am-2:30pm and 4-7:15pm, Su 10:15am-2:30pm. €1.20; students, seniors, and EU citizens free.)*

IGLESIA CONCATEDRAL DE SANTA MARÍA. A statue of San Pedro de Alcántara, one of Extremadura's two patron saints, eyes Pl. de Sta. María from a corner pedestal outside the cathedral—his shiny toes are the result of many years of good-luck foot rubs. The Gothic cathedral, built between 1229 and 1547, with uncharacteristically visible outlines of its stone composition, looks almost as if it were built inside-out. The red sun painted on the ceiling overlooks the intricate, 16th-century carved wood altar, and the eroded tombstones on the cathedral's floor. *(Pl. de Sta. María. ☎927 21 53 13. Open M-Sa 10am-2pm and 5-8pm, Su 9:30am-2pm and 5-7:30pm. €1. Audio tour near right sub-altar €1.)*

CONVENTO DE SAN PABLO. The convent is late-Gothic eye candy for architecture addicts. Cloistered nuns sell delicious homemade pastries through a peculiar rotating window called a *torno*, which protects them from the unholy gaze of customers. Locals highly recommend the *bocaditos de almendra* (almond-paste cupcakes). Make sure you bring an appetite—these babies only come by the kg (€19). Have your pastry selection ready from the list on the wall, ring the bell by the window, and ask politely during opening hours, even if the door seems closed. *(Pl. de San Pablo. To the left of Casa y Torre de las Cigüeñas. Open M-Sa 9am-1pm and 5-8pm. Pastries €3.50-6.50 per dozen, up to €20 per kilo.)*

CASA Y TORRE DE LAS CIGÜEÑAS. Cáceres's aristocracy was a warring lot, so in the 15th century the monarchy removed all battlements and spires from local lords' houses as punishment. Due to Don Golfín's loyalty to the ruling family, however, his Casa y Torre de las Cigüeñas (House and Tower of the Storks) was the lone estate allowed to keep its battlements. The storks are still grateful. Only the patio is accessible to the public, but it has an imposing collection of medieval arms which are certainly worth a peek. *(From Arco de la Estrella, take a right up the hill, a left onto Adarve de Sta. Ana, then a right and a quick left onto C. de los Condes. Cross Pl. de San Mateo to Pl. de San Pablo; the house and the tower are on the left.)*

PALACIO Y TORRE DE CARVAJAL. This mansion's roof houses a tourist office, museum, and art exhibit inside, but it's real selling point is that it's one of the few *palacios* in the city open to the public. The museum has three rooms of colorful models, stuffed wildlife, photos, and movies of different villages and artisans of Extremadura. The tourist office hands out large maps of the ciudad monumental and information about upcoming festivals and events. Outside, the 500-year-old garden is still lovingly maintained, backed by a wall of roses and centered with a beautiful fig tree. Beware of the grass; sprinklers often go to work without warning. *(From C. Arco de la Estrella, walk up to Pl. Santa Maria la Mayor; it is to the left of the cathedral, on the corner of C. Amargura. Open M-F 8am-8pm, Sa-Su 10am-2pm. Free.)*

OTHER SIGHTS. Most *palacios* and *casas* in the *ciudad monumental* are still inhabited and closed to visitors. The 16th-century **Casa del Sol** is the most famous of Cáceres's numerous mansions; its crest is the city's emblem. The **Casa de Toledo-Moctezuma** was built by the grandson of the Aztec princess Isabel Moctezuma to represent the union of two worlds. *(On Pl. del Conde de Canilleros, to the left as you enter Arco de la Estrella.)* On October 26, 1936, in the **Palacio de los Golfines de Arriba,** yet another Golfín family palace, Franco was proclaimed head of the Spanish state and general of its armies. *(Between C. de Olmos and C. Adarve del Padre Rosalío, just before the Restaurante Los Golfines.)*

◪ NIGHTLIFE

Just follow the noise for a tipsy evening in Cáceres—the nobles never had options this good. The revelry begins in Pl. Mayor and along C. Pizarro, lined with bars showcasing live music. ◪**La Traviata,** C. Sergio Sánchez, 8, is a colorful, artsy, and hip musical cafe that blasts a mix of lounge, techno, and pop, and hosts one-man shows on Thursdays at 10:30pm. *(☎927 21 13 74. Giant espresso €1. Beer €2.50. Mixed drinks €2-4.50. Open M-Th and Su 4pm-3am, F-Sa 4pm-3:30am. Cash only.)* For live jazz, poetry festivals, and free tarot card readings in a backyard setting, head to **El Corral de las Cigüeñas,** Cuesta de Aldana, 6, in the old city. Enclosed by vine-covered walls but open to a star- and sparrow-filled sky and located in the middle of the otherwise sleepy *ciudad monumental*, El Corral offers mellow Spanish music and occasional Friday night concerts for €3-8. (Beer €1.80-2.20. Mixed drinks from €5. Breakfast 8am-1pm. Open M-F 8pm-last customer, Sa-Su from 7pm-last customer. AmEx/MC/V.) Later, the party migrates to **La Madrila,** an area near Pl. del Albatros in the new city, where clubs stay open until the wee hours of the night. From Pl. Mayor, head to main strip Av. de España, take a right onto Av. Miguel Primo de Rivera, and cross the intersection onto C. Dr. Fleming. You'll hear the party from there.

🕙 DAYTRIP FROM CÁCERES

GUADALUPE

Transportation to and from Guadalupe can be somewhat tricky; most visitors arrive via tour bus or in their own cars. Empresa Mirat (☎ 927 23 48 63) sends buses from Cáceres to Guadalupe (2½hr.; M-Sa 1pm, 5:30pm; €7.70) and back (M-Sa 6:45 and 7:30am).

Guadalupe rests on a mountainside in the Sierra de Guadalupe, 2hr. east of Trujillo and 4hr. southwest of Madrid. The **Real Monasterio de Santa María de Guadalupe,** with its eclectic history and decadent architecture, is worth a daytrip, particularly for pilgrims and those with an interest in history, art, and architecture. The fairy-tale monastery has even been nicknamed "the Spanish Sistine Chapel." Its 25,000 square meters host an incredible collection of artwork, including many El Grecos, and a *mudéjar*-style central courtyard. At the Battle of Salado in 1340, Alfonso XI, believed to have been aided by the Virgin Mary, defeated the superior Muslim army. As a token of his gratitude, he commissioned the lavish Real Monasterio. Years later, it became customary to grant licenses for foreign expeditions on the premises; in fact, Columbus finalized his contract with Fernando and Isabel here. In homage to the city, he named one of the islands he discovered Guadalupe (now known as Turugueira). The most prominent object in the basilica is the **Icon of the Virgin,** carved out of wood, blackened with age, and cloaked in robes of silver and gold. (Monastery open daily 9:30am-1pm and 3:30-6:30pm. €3.) The **tourist office** in Pl. Mayor posts information on the door; follow signs from the bus station. (☎ 927 15 41 28. Open June-Aug. Tu-F 10am-2pm and 5-7pm, Sa-Su 10am-2pm; Sept.-May Tu-F 10am-2pm and 4-6pm, Sa-Su 10am-2pm.) Travelers looking for *bocadillos* or beds (singles generally €20) should head to Pl. Mayor.

TRUJILLO   ☎ 927

An enchanting Old World town, hilltop Trujillo is the gem of Extremadura. Often called the "Cradle of Conquistadors," Trujillo furnished history with over 600 explorers of the New World, including Peru's conqueror, Francisco Pizarro, and the Amazon's first European explorer, Francisco de Orellana. Scattered with medieval palaces, Roman ruins, an Arabic fortress, and churches from every era, Trujillo is a hodgepodge of histories and cultures. Today, the city is in no rush to modernize: visitors and locals alike spend evenings sipping *café con leche* (coffee with milk) in the Plaza Mayor's many cafes while relishing the beauty of the town.

🚍 TRANSPORTATION. The **bus station** (☎ 927 32 12 02) is at the bottom of town, on the corner of C. de las Cruces and C. del M. de Albayada; look for the AutoRes sign. Since most buses stop only en route to larger destinations, there are not always seats available—reserve ahead. Buses run to Badajoz (2hr., 10 per day 4:15am-11:55pm, €8.90-13.20); Cáceres (45min., 6-7 per day 7:05am-10:30pm, €2.74); and Madrid (2½hr., 5-8 per day 9:55am-8:30pm, €14-18).

🛈 PRACTICAL INFORMATION. An English-speaking staff sells **bono tickets** (cheap, multi-day tickets) at the **tourist office** in Pl. Mayor, on the left when facing

Pizarro's statue. Info is posted on the windows when it's closed. Guided tours (€6.75) leave from in front of the tourist office at 11am and 5pm. (☎927 32 26 77. Open daily June-Sept. 10am-2pm and 4:30-7:30pm; Oct.-May 9:30am-2pm and 4-7pm.) Local services include: **Currency exchange** and **ATM** at **Banco Santander Central Hispano,** Pl. Mayor, 25 (☎927 24 24 24; open Apr.-Sept. M-F 8:30am-2:30pm; Oct.-Mar. M-F 8:30am-2:30pm, Sa 8:30am-1pm); **police,** C. Carnicería, 2, just off Pl. Mayor (☎927 32 01 08); **Centro de Salud** (☎927 32 20 16) close by for medical emergencies; **Internet** access at **Ciberalia,** C. Tiendas, 18, off Pl. Mayor (☎927 65 90 89; €2 for 1hr., €3.75 for 2hr.; open daily 10:30am-2am); and the **post office,** Po. Ruiz de Mendoza, 28, on the way from the bus station to Pl. Mayor (☎927 32 05 33; open M-F 8:30am-2:30pm, Sa 9:30am-1pm). **Postal Code:** 10200.

▐▌ ACCOMMODATIONS AND FOOD. Get medieval at ▨**Hostal Trujillo ❷,** C. Francisco Pizarro, 4-6. From the bus station, turn left onto C. de las Cruces, right onto C. de la Encarnación, then right again onto C. Francisco Pizarro. The armor, lance, and shield-bedecked halls of this renovated 15th-century hospital lead to rooms with colorful pictures, cushy beds, bath, A/C, and satellite TV. The only downside is the 10min. uphill walk to the sights surrounding Pl. Mayor. (☎927 32 22 74; www.hostaltrujillo.com. Singles €24; doubles €40. AmEx/MC/V.) The pleasant **Pensión Boni ❷,** C. Mingos Ramos, 11, owned and run by a friendly German/Spanish couple, is off Pl. Mayor to the right when facing the church. Rooms have large windows and terraces over a winding stone street. The location, steps away from the major sights, makes this place a steal. (☎927 32 16 04. Laundry €5. Singles €15; doubles €25, with bath €30-35. Extra bed €10. Cash only.)

Meals in Trujillo's historic center are unfortunately overpriced, but cheaper deals hide on the side streets and at the bottom of the hill leading to Pl. Mayor. An authentic and oh-so-delicious *churros* breakfast awaits at **Churrería El Paseo ❶,** P. Ruiz de Mendoza. Made fresh all morning, these *churros* and *porros* are best dipped in *café con leche* or in hot chocolate. (☎927 32 21 67. Open daily 8am-noon. Cash only.) Leave the paella behind and head to **La Tahona ❶,** C. Afueras, 2, for affordable homemade pizzas (€3.50-9), pastas (€4-5.20), and sandwiches (€2.10-3). Exit Pl. Mayor by the church and walk three blocks. (☎927 32 18 49. Open M 7:30pm-midnight, Tu-Su 1-4pm. Cash only.) If all else fails, head to **Consum Supermarket,** Av. Monfragüe at the bottom of the hill. (Open M-Sa 9:30am-10pm. AmEx/MC/V). Many of the stores that sell *extremeño* specialties also sell basics.

◉ SIGHTS. An afternoon stroll through Trujillo's *barrio* offers a general summary of daily life in Extremadura. A ▨*bono* ticket (€4.70), available at the tourist office, allows entrance to the **Casa-Museo de Pizarro,** the **Moorish castle,** and **Iglesia de Santiago,** and includes a guidebook. For €5.30, the *bono* ticket also grants access into the **Iglesia de San Martín** and the **Museo del Queso y el Vino.** The tourist office runs tours of the old city (€6.75), including the Museo del Traje, that leave from the front of the office at 11am and 5pm. (Except where otherwise indicated, sights are open daily June-Sept. 10am-2pm and 5-8pm; Oct.-May 10am-2pm and 4:30-7:30pm. Tours €1.40 without *bono* ticket.)

Far from the other sights, at the bottom of the hill lies the **Museo del Queso y el Vino,** which tells the centuries-old story of the production of wine and shares tips on how to enjoy artisanal wine and cheese. (☎927 32 30 31. Open daily May-Sept. 11am-3pm and 6-8pm; Oct.-Apr. 11am-3pm and 5:30-7:30pm. Tickets €2.40 with tasting, €1.30 without.) Trujillo's **Plaza Mayor** was the inspiration for the Plaza de Armas in Cuzco, Peru, constructed after Francisco Pizarro defeated the Incas. Festooned with stork nests, **Iglesia de San Martín** dominates the plaza's northeastern corner and offers a nice respite from the heat. The church has several historic tombs, but contrary to local lore, Francisco de Orellana does not rest here. (Open

M-Sa 10am-2pm and 5-7:45pm, Su 10am-2pm and 4:30-7pm. €1.40. Mass in summer M-Sa 8:30pm, Su 1 and 8:30pm; in winter M-Sa 7:30pm, Su 1 and 7:30pm. Free.) Across the street, visit the **Palacio de los Duques de San Carlos**, built for the powerful family alliance of Vargas and Carvajal, to see the splendor that fell into the laps of these aristocrats. (Open daily 9:30am-1pm and 4:30-6:30pm. €1.40.)

At the entrance to the *zona monumental*, the 13th-century **Puerta de Santiago** is connected to the **Iglesia de Santiago.** To reach the Gothic **Iglesia de Santa María la Mayor,** take C. de las Cambroneras from the plaza in front of the Iglesia de San Martín and turn right onto C. Santa María. According to legend, the giant soldier Diego García de Paredes picked up the fountain (now located next to the rear door) at age 11 and carried it to his mother to offer her some holy water. After a fatal fall from a horse, the giant was buried here. Commonly known as the "Extremaduran Samson," the giant was immortalized in Cervantes's **Don Quixote.** Above Samson's alleged tomb is the church's intricate 25-panel Gothic altarpiece, painted by master Fernando Gallego in 1480. The steps leading to the top of the Romanesque church tower are a workout, but climb them to feel the Extremaduran winds on your face as you take in the 🐦**panoramic view** of brick rooftops, castle ruins, church towers, distant mountains, and lakes. (Open daily May-Oct. 10am-2pm and 4:30-8:30pm; Nov.-Apr. 10am-2pm and 4-6:30pm. Mass Su 11am. €1.25.) To the left of the church is the restored **Museo de la Coria,** which explores the relationship between Extremadura and Latin America both during the conquest and after the continent's independence. (Open Sa-Su 11:30am-2pm. Free.) Inside a restored convent, the **Museo del Traje** exhibits the spectacular evening gowns worn by royalty and famous actresses from the 17th century on. (Open daily 10:30am-2pm and 4:30-7:30pm. €1.50.) To get to the **Casa-Museo de Pizarro,** walk up the stone road to the right of the Iglesia de Santa María. The bottom floor of the house is a reproduction of a 15th-century nobleman's living quarters, while the top floor is dedicated to the life and times of Francisco Pizarro, with a focus on his time in Peru. (Open daily 10am-2pm and 5-8pm. €1.40.) Crowning the hill are the ruins of a 10th-century **Moorish castle.** Enjoy a view of unspoiled landscape, with Trujillo on one side and fields scattered with ancient battlements on the other.

MÉRIDA ☎924

For quantity of Roman ruins per square foot, it doesn't get better than Mérida (pop. 60,000). In 26 BC, as a reward for services rendered to the Roman Empire, Augustus Caesar granted a group of veteran legionnaires a new city in Lusitania, a province comprising Portugal and part of Spain. The veterans chose a lovely spot surrounded by hills on the banks of the Río Guadiana to found their new home, which they named Augusta Emerita. Itching to gossip with fellow patricians in Sevilla and Salamanca, the soldiers built the largest bridge in Lusitania, the Puente Romano. The nostalgic crew adorned their "little Rome" with baths, aqueducts, a hippodrome, an arena, and a famous amphitheater. Modern Mérida complement the Roman buildings with walkways, small plazas, and the world-class **Museo Nacional de Arte Romano.** In July and August, the spectacular **Festival de Teatro Clásico** offers some of Europe's best classical and modern theater and dance.

▛ TRANSPORTATION

Trains: C. Carderos (☎902 24 02 02). Info open daily 7am-10pm. Tickets sold 9am-9pm. To: **Badajoz** (1hr.; M-Sa 8 per day 7:44am-9:25pm, Su 6 per day 9:48am-10:25pm; €2.80-11.50); **Barcelona** (11hr.; 7:17, 8:20am; €30.60-76.80); **Cáceres** (1hr., 3-6 per day 5:30am-8:45pm, €3.40-12.50); **Madrid** (4-6hr., 4-5 per day 5:30am-3:27pm, €15.30-40); **Sevilla** (4½hr., 9:45am, €11.30).

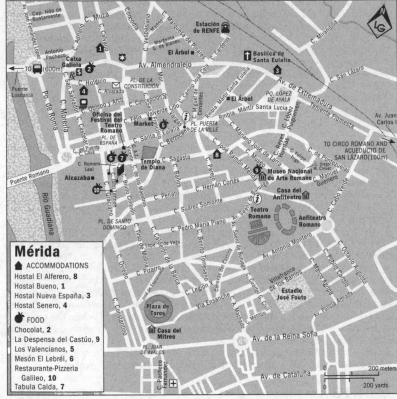

Mérida

🛏 ACCOMMODATIONS
Hostal El Alferero, **8**
Hostal Bueno, **1**
Hostal Nueva España, **3**
Hostal Senero, **4**

🍴 FOOD
Chocolat, **2**
La Despensa del Castúo, **9**
Los Valencianos, **5**
Mesón El Lebrél, **6**
Restaurante-Pizzeria
  Galileo, **10**
Tabula Calda, **7**

Buses: Av. de la Libertad (☎924 37 14 04). Info open M-F 7am-11pm, Sa-Su 7am-1pm and 3:15-11pm. **ALSA** (☎902 42 22 42) to **Sevilla** (3hr., 6-7 per day 2:35am-10:45pm, €11). **AutoRes** (☎924 37 19 55) to **Madrid** (5½hr.; 7-9 per day M-Sa 1:15am-4:45pm, F also at 7:15pm, Su 9:55am-7:15pm; €19-24). **LEDA** (☎924 37 14 03) to **Badajoz** (1hr.; 4-11 per day M-F 6:45am-12:50am, Sa 8:45am-10:50pm, Su noon-10:50pm; €4.03); **Cáceres** (1hr.; 1-4 per day M-F 9:20am-9:15pm, Sa 9:55am and 3:50pm, Su 7:10pm; €4.30); and **Sevilla** (3hr.; 7-9 per day M-F 5:45am-8:30pm, Sa 7am-9:50pm, Su 9am-11:05pm; €11).

Taxis: Teletaxi (☎924 31 57 56) or **RadioTaxi** (☎924 37 11 11). Both 24hr.

Car Rental: Avis (☎924 37 33 11), at the bus station. 23+. From €94.23 per day plus taxes. Insurance included. Open M-F 9am-1pm and 4:30-7:30pm, Sa 9:30am-1pm.

✴🛈 ORIENTATION AND PRACTICAL INFORMATION

Everything in Mérida is relatively close together and easily accessible by foot. **Plaza de España,** the town center, is two blocks up from the Puente Romano and easily accessible from the **Teatro Romano.** Walking outward from the center, cafes and shops around the plaza quickly transform into quiet residential neighborhoods, and streets often lose their signs. To reach Pl. de España from the **bus station,** cross the suspension bridge and turn right onto Av. de Roma. Continue along the river until you reach the Puente Romano, then turn left onto C. del Puente. From the **train station**, take C. Carderos and its continuation, C. Camilo José Cela; bear right onto C. Félix Valverde Lillo and follow it to Pl. de España. Banks and currency exchange line C. Santa Eulalia leading to Pl. de España.

Tourist Office: Municipal Office, C. Santa Eulalia, 64 (☎924 33 07 22). Maps and information on monuments and municipal events. English spoken. Open daily in summer 10am-2pm and 5-8pm; in winter 10am-2pm and 4-7pm. **Centro Cultural Alcazaba,** C. John Lennon, 5 (☎924 33 06 02). Walk up the winding ramp or take the glass tube elevator to the 4th fl. to take advantage of the extensive DVD collection and free **Internet** access at the city library (☎92433 06 02. Open M-F 8:30am-2:30pm in summer; in winter M-F 9am-2:30pm and 5-8pm, Sa 10:30am-1pm). While you're there, peruse the geology museum, municipal historical records, regional collection of prehistory, or walk straight to the back of the building to pull up a free seat next to some Roman ruins, found during the center's construction. Cultural center open until 5pm in summer; in winter 9pm.

Bank: Caixa Galicia: Av. Almendralejo, 12. Open M-F 8:30am-2pm. Banks also line C. Santa Eulalia.

Laundry: Tintoreria Guerrero Lavanderia, Pl. del Rastro, near C. Romero Leal Político (☎ 924 31 42 57). Open M-F 10am-2pm and 5-8pm, Sa 10am-2pm.

Police: Av. Almendralejo (☎092 or 924 38 01 38).

Pharmacy: Juan Vacas Angulo, corner of S. San Salvador and C. Holguín (☎924 31 34 08). Open daily 9:30am-10pm. Several pharmacies are also found on the corner of C. Los Maestros and C. Cuarez Somonte.

Hospital: Residencia Sanitaria de la Seguridad Social Centralita (☎924 38 10 00). **Red Cross,** Ctra. de Caceres (☎924 33 03 53). **Emergencies** (☎112).

Internet Access: Locutorio Ciber-Punto de Encuentro, C. San Juan de Dios, 4. €1 per hour. Open daily 5pm-midnight.

Post Office: Pl. de la Constitución (☎924 31 24 58; fax 30 24 56). Open July 15-Sept. 15 M-F 8:30am-2:30pm, Sa 9:30am-1pm; Sept. 16-July 14 M-F 8:30am-8:30pm, Sa 9:30am-1pm. **Postal Code:** 06800.

ACCOMMODATIONS

Despite the flocks of visor-sporting tourists, finding a reasonably priced room in Mérida won't leave you in ruins. Check the tourist office for complete listings.

Hostal El Alferero, C. Sagasta, 40 (☎924 30 31 83; www.hostalelalfarero.com). Colorful luxury in gorgeously decorated rooms, all with bath (with hydromassage shower), TV, and A/C, and some with balconies. Ceramics and pottery cover every available surface. Check in before 10pm. Apr.-Oct. and Dec. 22-31 doubles €50; triples €61. Nov.-Dec. 21 and Jan.-Mar. €40/55. MC/V. ❷

Hostal Senero, C. Holguín, 12 (☎924 31 72 07; www.hostalsenero.com). A beautifully tiled staircase leads to large, white-walled rooms, all with TV and A/C, some with balconies over the quiet street. English spoken. Reception open 8am-midnight. Singles €23, with bath €26; doubles €32/38. AmEx/MC/V. ❷

Hostal Nueva España, Av. de Extremadura, 6 (☎924 31 33 56). This well-located *hostal*, steps away from the *Basílica*, offers rooms that, while not particularly memorable, are spacious and come with private bath. Ask for a quiet room if traffic noise keeps you up. Singles with A/C €25; doubles €35, with A/C €38; triples €50. MC/V. ❷

Hostal Bueno, C. Calvario, 9 (☎924 30 29 77). The shortest walk from the bus and train stations. Don't stay here for the decor—there isn't very much of it. Rooms have bath, TV, and fan. Singles €20; doubles €30 or €28 for *pequeña* (small; i.e. hardly a place to lay down your backpack); triples €40; quads €50. Cash only. ❷

◧ FOOD

Plaza de España is filled with overpriced cafes. Cheaper options are nearby on **Calle John Lennon** or in cafes near the train station. Buy fresh food at the **Mercado Municipal de Calatrava** on the corner of C. Félix Valverde Lillo and C. Camilo José Cela. (Open M-Sa 8am-2pm.) There are several branches of the supermarket **El Árbol** in town. One is at C. Félix Valverde Lillo, 8. (☎924 30 13 56. Open M-F 9:30am-2pm and 6-9pm, Sa 9:30am-2:30pm. MC/V.) Another is closer to the train station on C. Marquesa de Pinares, and one is on Rambla Sta. Eulalia.

▧ **Restaurante-Pizzeria Galileo,** C. John Lennon, 28 (☎924 31 55 05). A partially glass-floored dining room reveals Roman ruins below. 34 creative varieties of pizza are popular with local families. Desserts either freshly imported from Italy or made fresh in the restaurant. Entrees €3.50-8. Open Tu-Su 1:30-4pm and 8:30pm-12:30am. MC/V. ❶

▧ **Chocolat,** C. Almendralejo, 12 (☎924 31 29 96; chocolatmerida@yahoo.es). Start your day in true Spanish fashion: with a *café con leche* and the buzz of morning conversation in this stylized old world cafe. Filling breakfast for around €2, especially if you opt for the nearly-solid hot chocolate and *churros* (both €1.10); *bocadillos* €1.50-3. Open M-F 8:30am-2pm and 6-10pm, Sa 9:30am-1:30pm and 6-10pm; Sa 9:30am-1pm in summer. Cash only. ❶

Mesón El Lebrel, C. John Lennon, 4 (☎924 31 57 57). Take the hallway to the right of the bar to treat yourself to the shade of cypresses and the stately Alcázar wall, if you don't mind the traffic nearby. A full range of rustic *extremeño* flavors, from just-right gazpacho to rare rabbit *pâté*. Entrees €5-10. *Bocadillos* €2-5. Open M and W-Su noon-4:30pm and 6:30pm-12:30am. MC/V. ❷

Tabula Calda, C. Romero Leal, 11 (☎924 30 49 50; www.tabulacalda.com). The delicious house special, a Sephardic Jewish salad with orange, sugar, and olive oil, comes free with every meal. Eclectic art surrounds tables in an intimate interior garden. Entrees €8. 3-course *menú* €12. Open daily June-Sept. 1-5:30pm and 8pm-12:30am; Oct.-May 1-4:30pm and 7:30pm-midnight. AmEx/MC/V. ❷

Los Valencianos, C. Santa Eulalia, on the right when coming from the Municipal Tourist Office just steps away. This Spanish *heladería* (ice cream shop) scoops up any combination of its 16 flavors for under €2. Order the *cafe granizado*, a frozen coffee-frappe concoction that can bring any Extremaduran day down a few degrees (€1). Open M-F 9am-2:30pm and 4:30-10pm, Sa 9am-2:30pm. ❶

La Despensa del Castuo, C. José Ramón Mélida, 48 (☎/fax 924 30 22 51). After climbing the eroded steps of the Roman theatre, cross the street and reclaim your calories at this grocery store/tapas bar. *Prueba de cerdo, lacon ibérico al pimenton,* and more than 30 other menu items await you. Tapas (€0.60-1 at the bar, €1 at a table) come on fresh bread and bocadillos (€3) include a free drink. Open daily 10am-2 or 3pm and 6pm-around midnight. ❶

◔ SIGHTS

From the **Puente Romano** to astrological mosaics, Mérida offers Spain's best view of the Romans in Iberia. A **combined ticket,** valid for all the listings below except the Museo Nacional de Arte Romano, can be purchased at any of the sights. (Ticket is valid for several days; includes a guidebook to the ruins. €10, EU students €6, seniors and children 9-16 €7. €4 for each individual sight. Ruins open daily June-Sept. 9:30am-1:45pm and 5-7:15pm; Oct.-May 9:30am-1:45pm and 4-6:15pm.)

■ **MUSEO NACIONAL DE ARTE ROMANO.** More than three floors of columns, busts, coins, housewares, and other relics recreate the prestige of the Romans for the 20th-century visitor. While none of the pieces are particularly exceptional, the museum's giant mosaics, almost completely intact, cover the multi-story expanse between statues and ceiling. Downstairs, the crypt gives a roped-off glimpse into parts of an ancient Augusta Emerita street found at the time of the museum's construction. Budget anywhere from 40min. to a couple hours to take in the building's unique architecture and intriguing content. *(C. José Ramón Mélida, 2. ☎924 31 16 90. Open Mar.-Nov. Tu-Sa 10am-2pm and 4-9pm, Su and holidays 10am-2pm; Dec.-Feb. Tu-Sa 10am-2pm and 4-6pm, Su and holidays 10am-2pm. €2.40, students €1.20.)*

■ **TEATRO ROMANO AND ANFITEATRO ROMANO.** The spectacular *teatro* was a gift from Agrippa, a Roman administrator, in 16 BC. Its 6000 seats face a *scaenaefrons*, an incredible marble colonnade built upstage. Today, the stage features performances of Spanish classical theater during the popular *Festival de Teatro Clásico* every July and August. *(Performances on alternate days July-Aug. 10:45pm. Info at the Oficina del Festival, C. Santa Eulalia, 4. ☎924 00 49 30; www.festivaldemerida.com. Tickets €10-40. Combined ticket for all performances €100-250. Consult tourist office Sept.-June for more info.)* Inaugurated in 8 BC, the *anfiteatro* was used for contests between all possible combinations of animals and men. The seats in some of the sections have succumbed to the elements, but the caves where the combatants were kept, now re-enforced with brick, are safe to crawl through. *(In the park across from the Museo Nacional; also accessible by tunnel from the crypt.)*

CASA DEL MITREO AND CASA DEL ANFITEATRO. The Romans knew what they were doing when it came to real estate, and these ruins prove it, showcasing some of the world's most intricate Roman mosaics. Although the **Casa del Mitreo** is a bit of a hike from downtown, you'll thank your lucky stars when you see its *Mosaico Cosmológico*. While the work is world-famous among historians of Rome for its depiction of the Romans' conception of the world and forces of nature, only a third of the mosaic remains. Worth the walk if you have the combination ticket. Do not be deterred by the **Casa del Anfiteatro's** unimpressive entrance; venture a few steps farther downhill, and you will find yourself walking on expanses of beautifully preserved mosaic floors. The site also features foundations, a Roman graveyard, and arrangements of residential quarters in Roman Iberia. Again, this is a great stop with the all-inclusive pass, but much of the Casa can be seen through the fence that runs along it. *(Casa del Anfiteatro is between the Anfiteatro Romano and the Museo de Arte Romano. Casa del Mitreo is on Vía Ensanche opposite the Pl. de Toros.)*

OTHER RUINS. On C. San José at the end of Rambla Mártir Santa Eulalia are the **Museo, Basílica**, and **Iglesia de Santa Eulalia**, all commemorating the child martyr. In 1990, while the 6th-century church was in the midst of repairs, layers of previous construction were uncovered to reveal the ruins of Roman houses dating from the 3rd to 1st centuries BC, a 4th-century AD necropolis, and a basilica dedicated to Santa Eulalia. *(Same hours as ruins but opens at 10am. Church open M-F 7:30am-8:30pm in summer, 7am-8pm in winter. Basilica open for mass M-Sa 9:30am and 7:30pm, Su 9:30am, 11:30am, and 8pm.)* Near the theater complex is the **Circo Romano,** also called the hippodrome or circus. The arena (capacity 30,000) is closed to the public, though the view from outside is still worth the trip. Next to the *Circo* are the remains of the **Acueducto de San Lázaro.** *(From C. Cabo Verde, take the pedestrian walkway under the train tracks.)* Take a stroll around the **Templo de Diana,** the best surprise on the mostly residential C. Sagasta; it is the only surviving Roman temple of worship and displays an impressive colonnaded facade. Built from materials discarded by the Visigoths, the **Alcazaba** was designed by the Moors to guard the Roman bridge. *(Pl. del Rastro near the Puente Romano.)*

CASTILLA LA MANCHA AND EXTREMADURA

BADAJOZ ☎924

Badajoz (pop. 120,000) is generally regarded as a transportation hub on the way into Portugal. However, the city has recently refreshed its ruins, cleared up much of its industrial pollution, and added a tourist office, making forced layovers significantly more pleasant. Free sights and a contemporary art museum provide for an afternoon's distraction, while lively *zonas de pubs* (pub areas) and the hot nightlife entices even Portuguese neighbors to cross the border and join the fun. If you find yourself in Badajoz during the **Feria de San Juan** (June 23-July 1), a one-week festival on the Spanish/Portuguese border with nightly bullfights, you will surely remember it—unless the partying leaves your memory a bit blank.

⌷ TRANSPORTATION

From Badajoz, buses to Portugal are faster and more convenient than trains.

Trains: Av. Carolina Coronado (☎924 27 11 70). Info (☎904 24 02 02) open daily 9am-10pm. From the train station to Pl. de la Libertad, take bus #1. To: **Cáceres** (2½hr.; M-F and Su 7:35am, 2:40pm, Sa 7:35am; €13.75-15); **Madrid** (5hr.; M-F and Su 3 per day 8:15am-2:30pm, Sa 8:15am, 12:30pm; €28-32); and **Mérida** (1½hr., 4-7 per day 6:40am-7:45pm, €3-11).

Buses: Central Station, C. José Rebollo López, 2 (☎924 25 86 61). Info booth open daily 7:45am-12:30am. Buses #3, 6a, 6b, and 9 run between the station and Pl. de la Libertad (€0.65). Schedules are flexible; call ahead or ask the receptionist at your hostel. Intercity buses run more frequently from Sept.-June.

　ALSA to **Cáceres** (1½hr.; M 3 per day 8am-4:30pm, Tu-Sa 9:30am, 4:30pm, Su 4:30pm; €7) via **Salamanca** (5hr., €15.30), and **Lisboa** (3½hr.; 4am, 2:45pm; €17).

　AutoRes (☎924 23 85 15) to: **Cáceres** (1½hr.; M-F 3 per day 8:30am-7:30pm, Sa 8:30am and 2:30pm, Su 8pm; €7); **Lisboa** (2½hr., 4:15am and 7:15pm, €39); **Madrid** (4hr., 5:15am and 8pm, €22-25.50); and **Trujillo** (2hr., 2 per day 3:15pm and 12:15am; €8.40).

　V. Caballero (☎924 25 57 56) to **Cáceres** (1½hr.; M-F 3 per day 8:30am-7:30pm, Sa 8:30am and 2:30pm, Su 8pm; €5.90).

　Damas to **Sevilla** (4½hr.; M-F 6 per day 6:45am-8pm, Sa-Su 3-4 per day 9am-8pm; €12.20).

　LEDA (☎924 23 34 78) to **Mérida** (1½hr.; M-F 9 per day 6:45am-9:30pm, Sa 4 per day 9:30am-9:30pm, Su 3 per day 3-9:30pm; €4.03).

Taxis: At bus and train stations and Pl. de España. **Radio Taxi** (☎924 24 31 01). 24hr.

✳❼ ORIENTATION AND PRACTICAL INFORMATION

Across the Río Guadiana from the **train station** and home to the municipal tourist office, **Plaza de España** is the heart of Badajoz. From the plaza, C. Juan de Ribera and C. Pedro de Valdivia lead to Pl. Dragones Hernán Cortés; one block to the right is **Plaza de la Libertad** and the regional tourist office. Between Pl. de España and Pl. de la Libertad is **Paseo de San Francisco**. To reach the regional tourist office from the **train station,** follow Av. Carolina Coronado straight to Puente de las Palmas, cross the bridge, then continue on C. Prim. Turn left onto C. Juan de Ribera at Pl. Minayo to get to Pl. de España, or right to get to Pl. de la Libertad (35min.). Bus #1 from the train station stops across from the regional tourist office. To get from the bus station to the center of town, walk across the street in front of the station and through the parking lots until you reach C. Damián Téllez la Fuente. Take a left onto this street and go straight through Pl. de la Constitución and Pl. Dragones Hernán Cortés to Pl. de España (20min.).

Tourist Office: Municipal Office, C. San Juan (☎924 22 49 81; www.turismobadajoz.es). Facing the *Ayuntamiento* from Pl. de España, take C. San Juan to its left. English, French, and Portuguese spoken. Open May-Sept. M-F 10am-2pm and 6-8pm, Sa 10am-2pm; Oct.-Apr. M-F 10am-2pm and 4-6pm, Sa 10am-2pm. Depending on staff, sometimes open until 9pm. **Regional Office,** Pl. de la Libertad, 3 (☎924 01 36 58/59; www.turismoextremadura.com). Open M-F 9am-2pm and 5-7pm, Sa 10am-2pm.

Banks: Banks line Av. de Europa, Pl. de España, and every major road in Badajoz.

Luggage Storage: In the bus station (€0.60) and train station (€3).

Police: Pl. de San José, Siglo 1, near Pl. Alta and the Moorish city (☎092 or 924 21 00 72).

Pharmacy: Doctor Camacho, corner of C. Muñoz Torrero and Pl. de España. Open M-F 9:30am-1:45pm and 5:30-8:30pm, Sa 10am-1:45pm.

Hospital: Hospital Infante Cristina, Av. de Elvas, off Ctra. de Elvas (☎924 21 81 00).

Biblioteca Bartolomé Gallardo, Av. de Europa, 2 (☎ 901 60 16 01). Free. Open M-F 9:30am-1:30pm and 5-8pm, Sa-Su 9am-2pm and 5-9pm. During the *feria*, open M-F 9am-2pm, Sa-Su 8:30am-2:30pm.

Internet access: Cyberia, C. Rafael Lucenqui, 22 (☎924 22 93 20), near the bus station. €1.70 per hour until 2:45pm, €2.10 per hour after. Open M-F 11am-2:45pm and 5pm-midnight, Sa noon-2:45pm and 5pm-midnight, Su noon-2:45pm.

Post Office: Po. de San Francisco, 4 (☎924 22 25 48). **Lista de Correos.** Open M-F 8:30am-8:30pm, Sa 9:30am-2pm. **Postal Code:** 06001.

▐ ACCOMMODATIONS

Hostales line the streets radiating out from Pl. de España, which means that even during the *feria*, you're to likely come by a room in the heart of the party. One option is **Pensión Pintor ❷,** C. Arco Agüero, 26. From Pl. de España, take C. San Blas downhill, then the 1st right onto C. Arco Agüero. You may need to ring the bell across the street at #33. Rooms are plain but have huge windows and come with TV, baths, and crucial A/C. (☎924 22 42 28. Singles €25; doubles €40; triples €48. AmEx/MC/V.) **Hostal Niza I and II ❷,** C. Arco Agüero, 34-35, has two locations. Reception is in I, but both I and II (across the street) offer spacious rooms with TV, private bath, and A/C just steps away from Pl. de España. Ask for a room with a terrace—it's worth it for the window and sunlight. Apartments with shared bathrooms are available. (☎924 22 38 81 or 924 22 31 73; www.hostal-niza.com. Singles €25; doubles €42.80; triples €50. Apartments: €15 per day; €220 per month; water, gas, and electricity included. Cash only.)

▐ FOOD

Cafes and eateries crowd Po. de San Francisco and Pl. de España. **La Casona ❶,** Pl. Alta, doesn't need a street number; the pounding dance music and all-Spanish clientele can be heard all the way from the Moorish ruins across the street. Serving up tapas (€0.70-2.50) and main plates (€5-14) all day, this is a restaurant for the traveler that never sleeps or stops eating. (Open M-Sa 11:30am-midnight.) Behind the glitzy bar and fast-food decor of **Bar-Restaurante La Ría ❷,** on Pl. de España, lie large portions of traditional Spanish foods. (☎924 22 20 05. Lunch *menú* €6. Open daily 10am-midnight. MC/V.) With its funkadelic walls and catchy tunes, **La Freskita ❷,** C. Virgen de la Soledad, 14, is hard to miss. Tap your feet to the hottest Spanish tracks, dine on classic fare, and then come back to the bar at night. (Entrees €5-12. Beer €2. Open Tu-Su noon-late. Cash only.) For groceries, head to **Eroski Cen-**

ter, next to the post office on Po. de San Francisco. (Open M-Sa 9:30am-9:30pm. MC/V.) Beyond Pl. de España, cafes and eateries crowd Po. de San Francisco.

◎ SIGHTS

The greatest part about Badajoz is that almost every sight in the city is free. The municipal tourist office has a complete listing of sights as well as recommendations for an afternoon's tour. Work your way back through history by starting at the **Museo Extremeño e Iberoamericano de Arte Contemporáneo (MEIAC).** Recent works from Spain, Portugal, and Latin America are exhibited in what was, until 12 years ago, the site of the city's high-security prison. (☎924 01 30 60. Open Tu-Sa 10am-1:30pm and 5-8pm, Su 10am-1:30pm. Free.) Continue on to Badajoz's **old quarter,** composed of Pl. de España and Paseo de San Francisco and home to the city's 13th-century **cathedral.** This converted mosque is an artistic timeline with one Renaissance, one Gothic, and one Plateresque window. (Open Tu-Sa 11am-1pm and 6-8pm. Free.) Badajoz's 9th-century foundation is still evident in the ruins of the **Alcazaba,** the Moorish citadel atop of the hill on Pl. Alta. Climb the ancient walls to see the rural Extremadura landscape beyond the city limits. (Archaeological museum open Tu-Su 10am-3pm, during the *feria* 10am-2pm. Free.)

◖ NIGHTLIFE

Locals rave about Badajoz's weekend **nightlife** and **pub culture.** City maps proudly display three *zonas de pubs.* The largest and best one is in the old quarter, where every street off Pl. de España has at least three bars. Though usually home to an older crowd, clubs like **Mercantil,** C. Zurbarán, 10, are mainstays of Badajoz's nightlife. Mercantil covers the music scene with live bands every Thursday and Friday starting at 11pm and a DJ spinning a mix of Spanish hip-hop, jazz, and pop on non-concert days. (☎924 220 691. Beer €2.50. Mixed drinks from €4. Open June-Aug. daily 4pm-late; Sept.-May M-Th 8pm-2am, F-Sa 8pm-5am. MC/V.)

University students crowd the area around the intersection of Av. José María Alcaraz y Alenda and Av. de Sinforiano Madroñero. Walking downhill from Pl. de la Constitución on Av. Fernando Calzadilla Maestre, turn right onto Av. Juan Pereda Pila, left onto Av. de María Auxiliadora, and right again onto Av. de Sinforiano Madroñero. The *zona de pubs* is up two intersections straight ahead, a 30min. walk from Pl. de España. Ask for **Cinema Puerta Real** near Ctra. de la Granadilla, a movie theater converted into a student hangout at night, with free Internet access and locals chilling at the bar. (Open Th-Sa 10pm-2am.) The newest *zona de pubs* is located across the river, conveniently near the site of all the *Feria de San Juan* festivities. Crossing Puente de Palmas en route to the train station, turn left onto Av. Adolfo Díaz Ambrona and pass by the Puente de la Universidad on the left. Happening pubs such as **C.K., Flydays,** and **Robinson,** on the right, have similar dance music and drink menus (€3-6) and host 20- to 40-somethings.

SEVILLA

Sevilla (pop. 700,000) is arguably the most charming and romantic of Spain's great cities. Narrow, tangled streets unfold from the center, leading to an awe-inspiring cathedral, the third largest in the world, and the city's tremendous Alcázar, a Moorish and Catholic palace and the official residence of the king and queen of Spain. Once the site of a Roman acropolis founded by Julius Caesar, Sevilla later became the capital of the Moorish empire and a focal point of the Spanish Renaissance. The city is now the guardian of traditional Andalusian culture and embodies the Spain of popular imagination: flamenco, tapas, and bullfighting. Tourists, locals, students, flamenco-lovers, and partiers infuse Sevilla with an energy that is hard to match. The budget traveler's experience here can be one of the best in Spain—with so many students packed in during the academic year, the opportunities for things to do and see on a tight budget are almost overwhelming. For a taste of Sevilla fully unhinged, visit during its most prominent festivals—*Semana Santa* and the *Feria de Abril* are among the most lavish celebrations in Europe.

HIGHLIGHTS OF SEVILLA

FEEL the **duende** and see what the flamenco fuss is all about (p. 237).

SHOUT ¡OLÉ! and cover your eyes at a bullfight in the **Plaza de Toros** (p. 234).

SCREAM with thousands of other crazed fans at a **Betis-Sevilla** *fútbol* game (p. 238).

GET LOST while in the tangled streets of the **Judería** (p. 223).

◪ INTERCITY TRANSPORTATION

BY PLANE

All flights arrive at **Aeropuerto San Pablo,** Ctra. de Madrid (☎954 44 90 00), 12km outside town. A taxi from the center costs about €25. **Los Amarillos** (☎954 98 91 84) runs a bus from outside Hotel Alfonso XIII at Pta. de Jerez (M-F every 30-45min., Sa-Su hourly 6:15am-11pm; €2.40). **Iberia,** C. Guadaira, 8 (☎954 22 89 01, nationwide 902 40 05 00; open M-F 9am-1:30pm) books six flights daily to Barcelona (55min.) and Madrid (45min.). For student fares, head to **Barceló Viajes.**

BY TRAIN

Estación Santa Justa, Av. de Kansas City. (☎902 24 02 02. Info and reservations open daily 4:30am-12:30am.) Services include **luggage storage, car rental,** and **ATM.** In town, the **RENFE** office, C. Zaragoza, 29, posts prices and schedules on the windows and also handles bookings. (☎954 54 02 02. Open in winter M-F 9am-1:15pm and 4-7pm; in summer 9:30am-2pm and 5:30-8pm.)

Altaria and **Talgo** trains run to: **Barcelona** (9-13hr., 3 per day 8:20am-10:22pm, €53.70-88); **Córdoba** (1hr., 6 per day 6:40am-8:30pm, €12.80); **Madrid** (3½hr.; 9:44am, 6:15pm; €52.50); **Valencia** (9hr., 8:20am, €43.50); **Zaragoza** (6½hr., 9:44am, €72.50).

AVE trains run to **Córdoba** (45min., 15-20 per day 6:30am-10pm, €22) and **Madrid** (2½hr., 15-21 per day 6:30am-10pm, €63.60-70).

Regionales trains run to: **Almería** (5½hr., 4 per day 7am-5:40pm, €32.10); **Antequera** (2hr., 3 per day 7am-5:40pm, €11.45); **Cádiz** (2hr., 7-12 per day 6:35am-9:35pm,

SEVILLA

TO PUENTE DE LA BARQUETA (1km)

C. Baños

TO SAN LORENZO Y JESÚS DEL GRAN PODER (100m)

TO ALAMEDA DE HÉRCULES (150m)

TO VIRGEN MACARENA (1.3km)

C. S. J. de la Palma

Av. Torneo

C. Alfaqueque

C. Redes
C. García Ramos
C. Mendoza Ríos
C. San Vicente
C. Miguel Cid
C. A. Gordillo
C. Jesús de la Vera-Cruz

C. Jesús del Gran Poder
C. Trajano
C. Amor de Dios
C. Atienza
C. Jerónimo Hernández
Sta. Ángela de la Cruz

Dìa%

PL. GAVIDIA

Orfila
Arguijo

Mercado de la Encarnación

TO ÍTALICA (9km)

Av. Torneo

Women's Institute of Andalucia

Avenida 5 Cine

C. Gravina
C. Bailén
C. Alfonso XII
C. San Juan de Ávila

El Corte Inglés

PL. DEL DUQUE DE LA VICTORIA

C. la Campana

C. Tarife

PL. DE LA ENCARNACIÓN

Convento d Santa Inés
C. Imagen

Museo Provincial de Bellas Artes

PL. DEL MUSEO

C. Monsalves

C. Martín Villa
C. Laraña

La Anunciación

C. J. L. Luque

PL. PEL

Centro Comercial

PL. de Armas

C. Pedro del Toro

C. San Roque
C. de la Feria

C. O'Donnell

EL CENTRO

C. Goyeneta

C. Cedaceros
C. Puente y Pellón

O. Zúñiga

PL. DEL DE BU

Estación Plaza de Armas

Cines Warner Lusomundo

PL. DE LA LEGIÓN

C. Trastámara
C. Marqués de Paradas
C. Canalejas
C. Gravina
C. Julio César

C. San Pablo

C. San Eloy

C. Murillo

C. Rioja

C. Rivero
C. Cuna

C. de Don A. 'El Sabio'

C. Golfo

PL. ALFALFA

Super

C. Albuera

PL. GODINAS

Iglesia de la Magdalena

C. Moratín

C. Muñoz Olivé
C. Méndez Núñez
C. Rosario
C. Albareda

San José

C. Tetuán
C. Jovellanos
C. Sagasta
C. Villegas

Librería Beta

Iglesia del Salvador

PL. DEL SALVADOR

PL. PESCADERÍA

C. del Rosario

C. Augusto Plasencia

TO EXPO '92 FAIRGROUNDS (2.5km)

C. de los Reyes Católicos

Barceló Viajes

C. Carlos Cañal

C. Bilbao

C. Granada

PL. NUEVA

Ayuntamiento

Chicarreros

C. S. Isidoro
C. Luchana

Corral del Re

C. El Barranca

C. Almansa

RENFE
U.K.
C. Zaragoza

PL. DE C. PADRE MARCHENA

C. Madrid

PL. DE SAN FRANCISCO

Museo del Balle Flamenc

C. Ali

C. Genil

PL. DE C. MOLVIEDRO

Santas Patronas

C. Castelar
C. Canaó
C. Jimios

Av. de la Constitución

C. Alvarez Quintero
C. Francos

C. Argote de Molina
C. Segovias
C. Placentines
C. Guzmán
C. Remondo
C. Abades

SANTA CRUZ

C. Pastor y Landero

Mercado del Arenal

EL ARENAL

C. Adriano

Plaza de Toros de la Real Maestranza

Lavandería Roma

C. Harinas
C. G. de Vinuesa

C. Alemanes

Catedral

PL. V. REYES

C. R. Caire

P. del Alcalde Marqués de Contadero

P. de Cristóbal Colón

C. Antonio Díaz
C. Dos de Mayo
C. Carretería
C. Pavía
C. Rodrigo de Mayo
C. Velarde
C. Temprado

PL. DEL CABILDO

C. Alimirantuzgo

PL. DEL TRIUNFO

Alcázar

PL. G. DOÑA ELVIR

TO C. DE SAN JACINTO (200m), SANTA CECILIA (400m)

Capilla de los Marineros

Río Guadalquivir

Hospital de la Caridad

Cañada

PL. DEL ALTOZANO

TO PL. SAN MARTÍN DE PORRES (900m)

PL. DEL Altozano

San Jacinto

Santa Ana

C. Luca de Tena
C. Pelay Correa
C. Rodrigo de Triana
C. Pagés del Corro

C. del Betis
C. de la Pureza

Teatro de la Maestranza

C. Santander

C. Almirante Lobo

Jardin de lo Reale Alcáza

Universidad de Sevilla

Torre del Oro

ATA Car Rental

Hotel Alfonso XIII

C. San Fernando

Av. de Sanjurjo

Av. de Roma

TRIANA

C. Pilar de Gracia
C. Luz Arriero
C. F. Murillo Herrera
C. M. Champagnat

C. de la Ardilla
C. de la Fortaleza
C. Rosario Vegaza
C. Genova
C. Paraíso

Torre de la Plata

Cines Corona Center

PL. DE CUBA

Palacio de San Telmo

Universidad de Sevilla

C. Palos de la Frontera
SAN

LOS REMEDIOS

C. Salado
C. Virgen Belén
C. Mtra. M. Sánchez Arjona
C. J. Mtra. M. Sánchez Arjona

Av. de la República Argentina
C. Virgen de la Consolación
C. Virgen del Valle
C. Virgen de la Asunción
C. Juan Sebastián Elcano
C. de la Niebla

PL. DE las Delicias

P. de la Rábida

Teatro Lope de Vega

VIPS

TO C. LÓPEZ DE GOMARA (600m)

TO FAIRGROUNDS (800m)

TO (40m), (700m)

United States

TO MUSEO ARQUEOLÓGICO (800m)

C. Turia

Av. de María Luisa

ACARENA   SEE "LA MACARENA," p. 235

Jardines del Valle

C. Salesianos
C. Arroyo
C. Venecia
C. San Juan Bosco
C. Peñuelas
C. Bustos Tavera
C. Sol
C. María Auxiliadora
C. Arroyo
C. Urquiza
C. Dr. Delgado Roig
C. Pérez Hernás
VEGA
PL. PONCE DE LEÓN
C. Alhóndiga
Felipe
PUERTA OSARIO
Av. José Laguillo
C. Esperanza de la Trinidad
Av. Pablo Iglesias
Estación Santa Justa
C. Azafrán
C. Vir. de Gracia y Esperanza
C. José M. Moreno Galván
Ben Saih de Sevilla
C. Santiago
C. Miros de los Navarros
C. Conde Negro
C. Recaredo
C. Arroyo
C. Gonzalo Bilbao
Las Brujas
SAN NDRO
C. Imperial
DE S. ONSOC
Cabalerizas
Casa de Pilatos
C. Guadalupe
C. Amador de los Ríos
C. Júpiter
C. Lope de Vega
C. Padre Méndez Casariego
GLTA. JULIAN BESTEIRO
C. Águilas
C. San Esteban
PL. CARMEN BENÍTEZ
C. Juan de Vera
C. Juan Antonio Cavestany
C. Beata Juana Jugan
TO ✈ 10 (12km)
PL. DE PILATOS
C. Lirio
onde de Ibarra
Vidrio
Tintes
PL. SAN AGUSTÍN
C. Fray Alonso
C. Campo de los Mártires
C. Lictores
C. Pablo Picasso
LA CALZADA
PL. DE LAS MERCENARIAS
C. Levies
C. Céspedes
Av. Menéndez Pelayo
C. la Florida
Av. de Luis Montoto
C. Averroes
C. San Benito
PL. DEL SACRIFICIO
TO ESTADIO SÁNCHEZ PIZJUÁN (1km), 12 (5.6km)
C. José
amalo
C. Sta. María la Blanca
C. San Clemente
SAN BERNARDO
Ruinas ■ Acueducto
C. Vía Crucis
C. S. Florencio
C. Pilar
la Gloria oria
C. Mascaal
C. Cano y Cueto
C. A. Fernández
C. I. María Moreno Galván
Av. de Luis Montoto
Alkimoto ■
Jardines de Murillo
Av. Menéndez Pelayo
C. Demetrio de los Ríos
C. Jiménez Aranda
Av. de la Buhaíra
C. Fernando Prado
C. Juan de Zoyas
ANTA CRUZ," p. 230
PL. DE SAN SEBASTIÁN
C. General Ríos
C. Capitán Vigueras
C. San Bernardo
C. Oscar Carvallo
C. Pirineos
DON N DE STRIA
Av. de Málaga
Estación Prado de San Sebastián
Av. de Cádiz
Juan de Mata Carriazo
Av. de Eduardo Dato
Av. de la Buhaíra
C. José María Osborne
C. Diego Riaño
0   200 meters
0   200 yards
N
LG
Av. Carlos V
Prado de San Sebastián
C. Ciudad de Ronda
Av. De la Burbolla
Av. de Portugal
Isabel
PL. DE ESPAÑA
C. Huestes

Sevilla

⬟ **ACCOMMODATIONS**

Camping Sevilla, **10**
Casa Sol y Luna, **6**
Club de Campo, **12**
Hostal Atenas, **9**
Hostal La Gloria, **5**
Hostal Río Sol, **2**
Oasis Sevilla, **4**
Sevilla Youth Hostel (HI), **16**

🍴 **FOOD**

Café-Bar Jerusalém, **15**
Cerceto, **7**

Confitería la Campana, **3**
Habanita Bar Restaurante, **8**
Restaurante Chino Ciudad de Pekin, **11**
El Rinconcillo, **1**

★ **NIGHTLIFE**

Boss, **13**
Rio Grande: Perto de Cuba, **14**

€9.10); **Córdoba** (1½hr., 6 per day 7:50am-7:55pm, €7.55); **Granada** (3hr., 4 per day 7am-5:40pm, €20); **Huelva** (1½hr., 2-3 per day 9:10am-8:50pm, €7); **Jaén** (2-3hr., 6:46pm, €15.10); **Málaga** (2½hr., 5-6 per day 7:40am-8:10pm, €16).

BY BUS

Estación Prado de San Sebastián, C. Manuel Vázquez Sagastizábal (☎954 41 71 11), serves most of Andalucía. (Open daily 5:30am-1am.) **Estación Plaza de Armas,** Av. Cristo de la Expiración (☎954 90 80 40), primarily serves the regions outside of Andalucía, including many international destinations. (Open daily 5am-1:30am.)

ESTACIÓN PRADO DE SAN SEBASTIÁN

Alsina Graells (☎954 41 88 11). Open daily 6:30am-11pm. To: **Almería** (7hr., 3 per day 7am-midnight, €27); **Córdoba** (2hr., 7-9 per day 7:45am-9:45pm, €9.43); **Granada** (3½hr., 10 per day 8am-11pm, €17.60); **Jaén** (4hr.; M-F 4 per day 9am-6pm, Sa-Su 2-3 per day 1:30-6pm; €16.50); **Málaga** (2½hr., 10-12 per day 7am-midnight, €13.89); **Murcia** (8hr., 3 per day 8am-11pm, €33.30).

Los Amarillos (☎954 98 91 84 or 902 21 03 17). Open M-F 7:30am-2pm and 2:30-8pm, Sa-Su 7:30am-2pm and 2:30-9pm. To: **Arcos de la Frontera** (2hr., 2-3 per day 9:30am-5pm, €7); **Marbella** (3½hr., 2-3 per day 8am-8pm, €15); **Ronda** (2½hr., 3-5 per day 7am-5pm, €10); **Sanlúcar de Barrameda** (2hr.; M-F 12 per day 8am-9pm, Sa-Su 9-10 per day 8am-8pm; €7).

Transportes Comes (☎902 19 92 08). Open M-Sa 6:30am-10pm. To: **Algeciras** (3½hr., 4 per day 9am-8pm, €14.80); **Cádiz** (1½hr., 10-12 per day 7am-10pm, €10.30); **Jerez de la Frontera** (1½hr., 6-9 per day 9am-10:30pm, €6.50); **Tarifa** (3hr., 4 per day 9am-8pm, €14.80).

ESTACIÓN PLAZA DE ARMAS

ALSA (☎954 90 78 00 or 902 42 22 42). Open M-F 5:45am-10:45pm, Sa-Su 7:30am-10:45pm. To: **Cáceres** (4¼hr., 9 per day 6am-9pm, €15); **León** (11hr., 3 per day 6-9pm, €37.80); **Lisboa** (6¼hr., 4 per day 3-11:59pm, €39); **Salamanca** (8hr., 5 per day 6am-9pm, €26.85); **Valencia** (9-11hr., 4 per day 10am-10:30pm, €44-51). Under 26 and seniors 10% discount, under 12 50%.

Damas (☎954 90 77 37). Open daily 6am-10pm. To: **Badajoz** (3½hr., 3-5 per day 6:45am-8pm, €12.55); **Lisboa** (6¼hr., 3 per day 6:30am-4:15pm, €28.25); **Lagos, Portugal** (7hr., 4 per day 6:30am-4:15pm, €18); **Huelva** (1¼hr., 25-28 per day 6am-10pm, €6.54).

Socibus (☎902 22 92 92; socibus@socibus.es). Open daily 7:30-10:30am and 11am-12:45am. To **Madrid** (6hr., 14 per day 8am-1am, €18.15).

■ ORIENTATION

The **Río Guadalquivir** flows north to south through the city, bordered by Po. de Cristóbal, which becomes Po. de las Delicias by the municipal tourist office. Most of the touristed areas of Sevilla, including **Santa Cruz** and **El Arenal,** are on the east bank. The historic *barrios* (neighborhoods) of **Triana, Santa Cecilia,** and **Los Remedios** occupy the western bank. **Avenida de la Constitución,** home of the *Andaluz* tourist office, runs along the cathedral. **El Centro,** a busy commercial pedestrian zone, starts at the intersection of Av. de la Constitución, **Plaza Nueva,** and **Plaza de San Francisco,** site of the *Ayuntamiento.* **Calle Tetuán** and **Calle Sierpes,** both popular shopping areas, run off from Pl. Nueva and through El Centro.

To get to Santa Cruz from the train station, take bus C-2 and transfer to C-3 at the Jardines del Valle; it will drop you off on C. Menéndez Pelayo at the **Jardines de Murillo.** Walk right one block past the gardens; C. Santa María la Blanca is on the left. Without the bus, it's a 15-20min. walk. To reach El Centro from the train station, catch bus #32 to **Plaza de la Encarnación,** several blocks north of the cathedral. Bus C-4 connects the bus station at **Plaza de Armas** to Prado de San Sebastián; from there it's a 5min. walk from the station up Av. Menéndez Pelayo to Santa Cruz.

THE NEIGHBORHOODS OF SEVILLA

SANTA CRUZ

In the very center of the city, Santa Cruz embodies the spirit of Sevilla. The area is called the "Judería" because it was historically the city's Jewish neighborhood, but today its streets are home to more souvenir shops than anything else. Still, it maintains a lively and youthful vibe and is a great place to search for hidden deals.

EL CENTRO

El Centro, a mess of narrow streets radiating from Pl. de la Encarnación and Pl. del Duque de la Victoria, bustles with shoppers during the day, but it is mostly deserted at night. The area near Pl. Alfalfa, a prime tapas location, is more lively.

LA MACARENA

The area north of El Centro doesn't cater to tourist activities. Still, its character ranges from the quirky to the familiar—from tattoo parlors and punk boutiques to authentic bars—and many residents predict that it will be Sevilla's next hot spot.

EL ARENAL AND TRIANA

Immortalized by *Siglo de Oro* writers Lope de Vega, Francisco de Quevedo, and Miguel de Cervantes, Triana was Sevilla's chaotic 16th- and 17th-century mariners' district. Today, it is home to many of the city's best ethnic restaurants and retains a gritty feel, contrasted by the elegant ceramics that are still manufactured in the local *talleres* (studios). Avoid overpriced C. del Betis and plunge down less expensive side streets. El Arenal is the known as the "Plaza de Toros" district and comes to life during the *Feria de Abril.*

▐ TRANSPORTATION

Public Transportation: TUSSAM (☎900 71 01 71; www.tussam.es). Most bus lines run daily every 10min. 6am-11:15pm and converge in Pl. Nueva, Pl. de la Encarnación, and at the cathedral. **Night service** departs from Pl. Nueva (hourly M-Th and Su midnight-2am; F-Sa all night). C-3 and C-4 circle the center and #34 hits the youth hostel, university, cathedral, and Pl. Nueva. €1, **bonobús** (10 rides) €4.50, 30-day pass €26.

Taxis: TeleTaxi (☎954 62 22 22). **Radio Taxi** (☎954 58 00 00). Base rate €1 plus €0.40 per km, Su 25% surcharge. Extra charge for luggage and night taxis.

Car Rental: Hertz, at the airport (☎954 51 47 20) and train station (☎954 42 61 56, info ☎902 40 24 05). 21+. From €60 per day. Open daily 8am-midnight. AmEx/MC/V. **ATA,** C. Almirante Lobo, 2 (☎954 22 09 57 or 954 22 09 58; atasa@logiccontrol.es). 21+. From €45.60 per day plus tax. Also offers 24hr. driver service; prices vary. Open M-F 9am-2pm and 4:30-8:30pm, Sa 9am-2pm. AmEx/MC/V.

Moped Rental: Alkimoto, C. Fernando Tirado, 5 (☎954 58 49 27; www.alkimoto.com). €23 per day. Open M-F 9am-1:30pm and 5-8pm.

▐ PRACTICAL INFORMATION

TOURIST AND FINANCIAL SERVICES

Tourist Offices: There are 4 tourist offices in town: municipal, provincial, and regional.

Centro de Información de Sevilla Laredo, Pl. de San Francisco, 19 (☎954 59 52 88; laredo.turismo@sevilla.org; www.turismo.sevilla.org). English spoken. 1st hour free. **Internet** access M-F 10am-2pm and 5-8pm; sign up at the furthest desk, near the computers. Open M-F 8am-3pm.

Naves del Barranco, C. Aronja, 28, near the bridge to Triana (☎954 22 17 14; barranco@sevilla.org). Takes over when the Centro office is closed. Open M-F 1-8pm, Sa-Su 8am-3pm.

Turismo de la Provincia, Pl. del Triunfo, 3 (☎954 21 00 05; info@dipusevilla.es). Info on daytrips from the city as well as specific itineraries, like *La Ruta del Arroz* (The Rice Route). Sells books on Sevilla and its environs. Open M-F 10am-2:30pm and 3:30-7:30pm, Sa 10am-2pm.

Turismo Andaluz, Av. de la Constitución, 21B (☎954 22 14 04; fax 22 97 53). English spoken. Info on all of Andalucía. Free maps of the region. Open M-F 9am-7pm, Sa 10am-2pm and 3-7pm (until 7:30pm in winter), Su 10am-2pm.

Budget Travel Agency: Barceló Viajes, C. de los Reyes Católicos, 11 (☎954 22 61 31; www.barceloviajes.com). Open June-Sept. M-F 9:30am-1:30pm and 5-8:30pm, Sa 10am-1pm; Oct.-May M-F 9:30am-1:30pm and 4:30-7:30pm, Sa 10am-1pm.

Currency Exchange: Banco Santander Central Hispano, C. Tetuán, 10, and C. Martín Villa, 4 (☎902 24 24 24). Open M-F 8:30am-2pm, Sa 8:30am-1pm. Apr.-Sept. closed Sa. Banks and *casas de cambio* (currency exchange) crowd Av. de la Constitución, El Centro, and the sights in Santa Cruz.

Beyond Tourism: Sevilla is full of language schools; ask at the tourist office. All schools can arrange student accommodations and offer excursions for an additional fee. **Don Quixote** comes highly recommended. For info, see **Beyond Tourism,** p. 61.

LOCAL SERVICES

Luggage Storage: Estación Prado de San Sebastián (€0.90 per bag per day; open 6:30am-10pm); **Estación Plaza de Armas** (€3 per day); **train station** (€3 per day).

English-Language Bookstore: Vertice International Bookstore, C. San Fernando, in front of the university. Best selection of English-language books in Sevilla. Open July-Aug. M-W 10am-2pm and 5-8:30pm, Th-F 9am-3pm; Sept.-June M-F 9:30am-2pm and 5-8:30pm, Sa 11am-2pm. **Trueque,** C. Pasaje de Vila, 2 (☎954 56 32 66). Used books in English and a smattering of other languages. Open M-F 10:30am-1:30pm and 5-8pm, Sa 10:30am-1:30pm. MC/V.

Women's Resources: Women's Institute of Andalucía, C. Alfonso XII, 56 (24hr. toll-free hotline ☎900 20 09 99 or 955 03 59 50, office 954 03 49 53; www.juntadeandalucia.es/institutodelamujer). Info on feminist and lesbian organizations, plus legal and psychological counseling for rape victims. Office open to the public M-F 10am-1pm.

Laundromats: Lavandería y Tintorería Roma, C. Castelar, 2C (☎954 21 05 35). Wash, dry, and fold €6 per load. Open M-F 9:30am-2pm and 5:30-8:30pm, Sa 9am-2pm.

EMERGENCY AND COMMUNICATIONS

Police: Av. Paseo de las Delicias (☎091).

Medical Services: Red Cross: (☎913 35 45 45). **Ambulatorio Esperanza Macarena** (☎954 42 01 05). **Hospital Virgen Macarena,** Av. Dr. Fedriani, 56 (☎955 00 80 00). English spoken.

Library: Paseo de las Delicias, close to Puente de los Remedios. Modern space with free **Internet** access. Open M-F 9am-8:30pm.

Internet Access: It is substantially cheaper to use pre-paid minutes; most places offer Internet *bonos* which amount to whole-sale bulk minutes (most come with a min. of 2hr. or more). Ask about *bonos* at the counter before using the computers. **Distelco,** C. Ortiz de Zuñiga, 3 (☎954 22 99 66; www.distelco.com). €2 per hour min. or 20min. for €0.70 with no minimum; pre-paid cards start at €1.10 per hour. International fax €2.40 for first page, €1.50 per additional page. Open M-F 10:30am-11pm,

Sa-Su 6-11pm. MC/V. **Sevilla Internet Center,** C. Almirantazgo, 1-2, 2nd fl. (☎954 50 02 75; fax 954 50 05 20), in an office building overlooking Av. de la Constitución. Entrance is to the left of the cafe on the corner. If the door is closed, ring the bell. €3 per hour, €1.80 with *bono*, €1.20 per hour with super *bono*. Fax €1.25 per page. Black and white copies €0.10 per page, €1 for color. Expect to wait in line 4-6pm. Open M-F 9am-10pm, Sa-Su 10am-10pm.

Post Office: Av. de la Constitución, 32 (☎954 21 64 76). **Lista de Correos** and **fax.** *Lista de Correos* mail is addressed to the Lista de Correos de la Constitución (otherwise mail may end up in any of the Sevilla post offices). **Internet** access €1.50 per hour. **Photocopying** €0.10 per page. Open M-F 8:30am-8:30pm, Sa 9:30am-2pm. **Postal Code:** 41080.

ACCOMMODATIONS

During *Semana Santa* and the *Feria de Abril,* vacant rooms vanish and prices at least double; reserve several months in advance. The tourist office has lists of *casas particulares* (private residences) that open for visitors on special occasions. Outside of these weeks, you should reserve a few days in advance, and about a week ahead if you're staying for the weekend.

SANTA CRUZ

The narrow streets east of the cathedral around C. Santa María la Blanca are full of cheap hostels, most with virtually identical rooms. The neighborhood is highly touristed; it's best to reserve early, but last-minute rooms are not impossible to come by. Santa Cruz's location is excellent, but many so-called *"hostales"* have the prices of hotels, and cheap lodging rarely shares the neighborhood's charm.

Pensión Vergara, C. Ximénez de Enciso, 11, 2nd fl. (☎954 21 56 68; pensiónvergarasevilla@yahoo.es). Above a souvenir shop at C. Mesón del Moro. Quirky, antique decor and perfect location. Rooms come with A/C. Singles, doubles, triples, and quads, all with common bath; €20 per person. Cash only. ❷

Pensión Bienvenido, C. Archeros, 14 (☎/fax 954 41 36 55). 5 comfortable, cheap rooftop rooms surround a social patio; downstairs rooms overlook inner atrium. All have A/C. Ask for room #101, the largest and classiest in the *pensión*. Singles €20; doubles €38, with bath €50; triples and quads €60-64. MC/V. ❷

Pensión Buen Dormir, C. Farnesio, 8 (☎954 21 74 92). Quilted bedspreads and sunny rooms make "Good Sleep Pension" one of the best deals in town. Rooftop terrace. Singles have fans, all other rooms have A/C. Singles €20; doubles €30, with shower €35, with bath €40; triples with shower €50, with bath €55. Cash only. ❷

EL CENTRO

▨ **Hostal Atenas,** C. Caballerizas 1 (☎954 21 80 47; atenas@hostal-atenas.com), off Pl. de Pilatos. Everything about this hostel is appealing, from the ivy arches and old-fashioned indoor patio to the cheery rooms. All have A/C and bath. Internet access €1 per hour. Singles €35; doubles €58; triples €70. MC/V. ❸

▨ **Oasis Sevilla,** reception at Pl. Encarnación, 29 1/2, rooms above reception and at C. Alonso el Sabio, 1A (☎954 29 37 77; www.hostelsoasis.com). American amenities and young, international companionship. Co-ed dorms on Pl. Encarnación are crowded but centrally located above the client-only Hiro bar. On C. Alonso doubles and 4-person dorms share bathrooms and fridges and are roomier and quieter. Weekly tapas tours, breakfast (8-11am, but get there before 9:30am if you want to eat), free Wi-Fi and desktop Internet access, and jacuzzi-sized pool. Reserve early or show up at 8am with fingers crossed. Dorms €18; doubles €40. MC/V. ❷

Casa Sol y Luna, C. Pérez Galdós, 1A (☎954 21 06 82 or 626 55 96 10; www.casasolyluna2.com). Huge living room with plush crimson couches. The building, with its marble staircase and antique mirrors, outshines the rooms. Beds and rooms vary, so take a survey for the best available fit. Laundry €10. Singles €22; doubles €38, with bath €45; triples €60; quads €80. Min. stay 2-nights. Cash only. ❷

Hostal La Gloria, C. San Eloy, 58, 2nd fl. (☎954 22 26 73), at the end of a lively shopping street. Rooms, with either A/C or fans, are airy and reasonably sized. Singles €25; doubles €40, with bath €50; triples €50. Cash only. ❷

LA MACARENA

Hostal Macarena, C. San Luis, 91 (☎954 37 01 41). Large rooms are painted yellow and green and have matching rainbow-colored bedspreads and curtains. Each comes with A/C and TV. If you're looking for a quiet place to crash, this is it. Singles €20; doubles €30, with bath €40; triples €45/50. MC/V. ❷

Hostal Alameda, Alameda de Hércules, 31 (☎954 90 01 91; hostal_alameda@terra.es.). Standard yet immaculate rooms with A/C, TV, and small roof-top balcony. Singles €25; doubles with bath €45. MC/V. ❷

NEAR ESTACIÓN PLAZA DE ARMAS

Several hostels line C. Gravina, parallel to C. Marqués de las Paradas two blocks from the station. Hostels here tend to be cheaper than those in other neighborhoods and are convenient for exploring El Centro (5min.) and C. del Betis and Triana on the west bank of the river (10-15min.). Be prepared to schlep at least 15min. to the cathedral and the sight-filled Santa Cruz neighborhood.

Hostal Rio Sol, C. Marqués de Paradas, 25 (☎954 22 90 38). Its location right across the street from the bus station makes this perfect for those exhausted upon arrival. Rooms vary in size but, with tiled walls, colorful bed covers, and private baths, are eclectic and a good value. Singles €20; doubles €45; triples €55. AmEx/MC/V. ❷

Sevilla Youth Hostel (HI), C. Isaac Peral, 2 (☎955 05 65 00; sevilla.itj@juntadeandalucia.es). Take bus #34 across from the tourist office on Av. de la Constitución; the 5th stop is the hostel. The doubles, triples, and quads, many with private bath and all with long windows, have a less sterile feel than those in most youth hostels. A/C. Breakfast €1.50, other meals €5. Dorms Mar.-Oct. €13.75, over 26 €18.75; Nov.-Feb. €11.65/16.20. Non-members can pay €3 extra per night for 6 nights to become members. ❶

Club de Campo, C. Libertad, 13 (☎954 72 02 50), Ctra. Sevilla-Dos Hermanas, 8km out of town. Los Amarillos buses leave from C. Infante Carlos de Borbón, at the back of Prado San Sebastián, to Dos Hermanas (every 45min., €0.75). Lots of grass, a pool, and hot showers. Electricity €2.95. €3.90 per 1-person tent, €3.90 per car. MC/V. ❶

Camping Sevilla, Ctra. Madrid-Cádiz, km 534 (☎954 51 43 79), near the airport. Take bus #70 (stops 800m away at Parque Alcosa) from Prado de San Sebastián. Showers, market, and pool. €3.75 per 1-person tent, €3.25 per car. IVA not included. MC/V. ❶

◘ FOOD

Sevilla is a city of tapas. Locals spend their evenings relaxing and socializing over plates of *caracoles* (snails) and fresh seafood, while sipping glasses of sangria and *tinto de verano* (red wine and lemon soda). To dine with Sevilla's working class, head for the intersection of **C. San Jorge** and **C. San Jacinto.** Festive, upscale restaurants can be found nearby on **C. del Betis,** along the Río Guadalquivir. For those on a tighter budget, markets such as **Mercado de la Encarnación,** Pl. de la Encarnación (open M-Sa 8am-2pm), or the more modern **Mercado del Arenal,** on C. Pastor y Lan-

DISTANCE: 3.1km

DURATION: 2-3hr.

WHEN TO GO: Late morning Thursday for the flea market.

1. IGLESIA DE SAN LUIS. The skulls of the side altars and the carved statues of saints, angels, and Christ hovering in the stories-high central dome will leave a bewildered look on your face and a crick in your neck.

2. C. SIERPES AND PL. DE SAN FRANCISCO. Wndow shop or reach into those deep pockets (not so deep if you catch the tri-annual *rebajas*) for some fun in the boutiques on C. Sierpes. Sneak around the back of the *Ayuntamiento* on Pl. de San Francisco to admire the intricate busts and designs carved into the rear facade.

3. C. FERIA AND PL. ENCARNACIÓN. The flea market-bordering-on-a-yard sale on C. Feria (Th 9am-2pm) is the only place you'll find that Ricky Martin cassette tape you've been chasing. Peruse the ¼ mi. of miscellaneous clutter toward Mercado de la Encarnación, where 10 lb. fish and live snails (a favorite here) abound. Who says you shouldn't play with your food?

4. ROMAN RUINS. One minute you're walking down a cramped residential street, the next you're staring at Roman columns jutting out from between two apartment buildings. Talk about location.

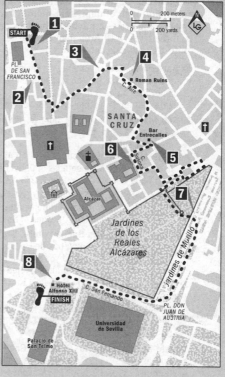

5. BAR ENTRECALLES. Once you get past the massive dried flowers that hang their heads in the windows, you'll be rewarded with some of the best *tinto de verano* in town and a whole lot of gazpacho. Cheap tapas you can actually get full on—now that's thinking.

6. C. SUSONA. Oh, Susona...she did more than cry when her forbidden Christian lover murdered much of her Jewish neighborhood after she revealed their plot to counter the Inquisition. Walk to the very end of the street and look to the right for a ceramic skull commemorating her accidental betrayal.

7. JARDINES. Stroll through the hidden Pl. de Santa Cruz, whose Old World feel carries into the surrounding Jardines de Murillo and Jardines Catalina de Ribera. Get lost in the lulling noise of the fountains in one of the ambrosial side coves.

8. HOTEL ALFONSO XIII. Ogle at the front door of this five-star hotel and soak up the shade from its sprawling front yard gardens. Mentioned in Dan Brown's *Digital Fortress*, Alfonso XIII is the perfect place to begin your own story in Sevilla, ideally one that doesn't involve murder.

dero (open M-Sa 9am-3pm), have fresh meat and produce. For a supermarket, try the mammoth basement of El Corte Inglés in Pl. del Duque de la Victoria (☎954 27 93 97), the **Mercadona** in the Centro Commercial Plaza de Armas next to the bus station, or any of the smaller ones like **%Día, Mas,** and **Super Sol.**

SANTA CRUZ

Restaurants near the cathedral cater almost exclusively to tourists, so beware the unexceptional, omnipresent *menús* featuring gazpacho and paella for €7. Food quality and prices improve in the backstreet establishments between the cathedral and the river in El Arenal and along side streets in Santa Cruz. Despite the droves of tourists, locals can always be spotted sharing mixed drinks at the bars.

■ **Bar Entrecalles,** C. Ximenez de Enciso, 14 (☎617 86 77 52). Situated at the center of the tourist buzz, but the reggae music and relaxed Cuban theme help maintain a local following. Tapas (only available inside, €2) and delicious gazpacho are unusually generous. Open daily 1pm-2am. Kitchen open starting at 1:30 and 8pm. Cash only. ❶

■ **San Marco,** C. Mesón del Moro, 6 (☎954 56 43 90; www.san-marco.net). Serves pizzas, pastas, and Italian desserts in an 18th-century house with old Arab baths. A full menu of salads, including a number of creative vegetarian mixes (€4.30-8.90) and pizza (€6.25-8.50). Open daily 1:15-4:30pm and 8:15pm-12:30am. **Other locations** in equally impressive settings at C. del Betis, 68 (☎954 28 03 10), and C. Santo Domingo de la Calzada, 5 (☎954 58 33 43). AmEx/D/MC/V. ❷

Levíes Café-Bar, C. San José, 15 (☎954 21 53 08; cafelevies@hotmail.com). The bar half of this tapas restaurant dominates, pouring out deliciously liberal and refreshing glasses of sangria (€2.20). Open M-Sa 11:30am-3pm and 8pm-1am. ❶

Histórico Horno San Buenaventura, SA, Av. de la Constitución, 16 (☎954 22 18 19). A melange of restaurant/bar/deli/pastry shop, Histórico Horno is a good choice when you're not sure what food you want; it hosts a delightfully-indulgent selection of everything from ice cream and multi-layered pastries to gourmet jamón. Take-out available. Open M-Sa 8am-11pm, Su 9am-11pm. AmEx/D/MC/V. ❷

Café Cáceres, C. San José, 24 (☎954 21 54 26). Choose from a spread of cheeses, cereals, jams, yogurt, condiments, fresh orange juice, and omelettes. Orange juice, coffee, ham, eggs, and toast (€6). Open M-F 7:30am-5pm, Sa 8am-2pm; in winter Sa-Su 7:30am-7:30pm. MC/V. ❶

Café-Bar Campanario, C. Mateos Gago, 8 (☎954 56 41 89). The Giralda's bells will ring as you sip on the strongest sangria (½liter €12, liter €15) in town. Vegetarian-friendly. Tapas €2.20-3.10. *Raciones* €9-12.40. *Menú* €10. Open daily 11am-midnight. AmEx/D/MC/V. ❷

EL CENTRO

Pl. Alfalfa, Pl. de la Encarnación, and Pl. San Pedro frame a maze of tiny streets full of unassuming tapas bars and affordable international restaurants.

■ **Habanita Bar Restaurante,** C. Golfo, 3 (☎606 71 64 56; www.andalunet.com/habanita), off C. Pérez Galdós. Popular vegetarian/vegan-oriented cafe-restaurant serving Cuban fare, pastas, and salads. Tapas €2.25-3.75. Entrees €7-14.80. Open M-Sa 12:30-4:30pm and 8pm-12:30am, Su 12:30-4:30pm. Reserve ahead. MC/V. ❷

■ **Confitería La Campana,** C. Sierpes 1 and 3 (☎954 22 35 70; www.confiterialacampana.com). Founded in 1885, Sevilla's most famous cafe and dessert stop serves *granizadas de limón* (lemon-flavored crushed ice), ice cream (€2-2.50), and homemade pastries (€1.40-2). Open daily 8am-11pm. AmEx/MC/V. ❶

El Rinconcillo, C. Gerona, 40 (☎954 22 31 83). Founded in 1670 and among the oldest in town, this *bodega* is the epitome of a local hangout, teeming with gray-haired men deep in conversation and locals coming in for a quick glass of wine. The bartender tallies up your tab in chalk on the wooden counter. Tapas €1.70-2.50. *Raciones* €5-14.50. Open daily 1:30pm-1:30am. AmEx/MC/V. ❷

Cereceto, Perez Galdos, 20 (☎954 22 05 67 or 609 32 82 89; www.cerectorestaurant.com). The quick, personal, and attentive service here is a rare gem in Spain, and the food, while not exactly what you'd find in Sicily, is ample. Skip the hallway-like main dining area for the cozier back room. Open M 8:30 or 9pm-midnight, Tu-Sa noon-5pm and 8:30 or 9pm-midnight. ❷

LA MACARENA

Ancha de la Feria, C. Feria, 61 (☎954 90 97 45). Serves tapas (€2; *raciones* from €4) in a breezier version of the traditional *taberna*. The place feels like one big family reunion. Open Tu-Su noon-5pm and 8:30pm-12:30am. Cash only. ❶

La Plazoleta Bodega, C. San Juan de la Palma, (☎954 38 27 91), just past the church on the same side of the street. Serves up generous portions of traditional Spanish fare, including sacred bull's tail (€2.20). Open M-Sa 12:30pm-12:30am, Su 4:30-8pm. ❶

EL ARENAL AND TRIANA

Café-Bar Jerusalém, C. Salado, 6. Neighborhood kebab bar with falafel (€3.50) and chicken, lamb, pork, and cheese *shawarma* (€3.10-4.90). A popular pit stop for a quick bite between discotecas. Open M, W-Th, and Su 8pm-2am, F-Sa 8pm-3am. AmEx/MC/V. ❶

Restaurante Chino Ciudad de Pekin, C. Zaragoza, 6, enter on C. Santas Patrona (☎954 21 84 78; fax 954 22 55 22). Granted, you didn't come to Spain to eat Chinese food, but you also didn't come here to starve, which can happen if your stomach needs more than the ubiquitous snack-like tapas. Steaming bowls of soup (€2.50-3.50), rice (€3-4), and lightly sauced meat (€5-8) are a party for your stomach. Open daily noon-4:30pm and 8pm-midnight. ❶

◉ SIGHTS

While most visits tend to center around the **Catedral** and **Alcázar,** there is much more to Sevilla than these architectural wonders. The streets around these central icons are a winding wonderland, where tapas and *artesanía* dominate. The **Plaza de Toros de la Real Maestranza** is nestled along the riverbank and serves as an ideal place to begin a scenic tour along the Guadalquivir. Heading south toward the **Torre del Oro,** garden oases offer respite from the city center. The **Jardines** behind the Alcázar are flanked by the **Jardines de Murillo,** and from there it's a short jaunt to the **Plaza de España** and nearby **Parque de María Luisa.**

SANTA CRUZ

▨ CATEDRAL

Entrance by Pl. de la Virgen de los Reyes. ☎954 21 49 71; www.catedralsevilla.com. Open M-Sa 9:30am-4pm, Su 2:30-6pm. Last entrance 1hr. before closing. €7.50, seniors and students under 26 €2, under 16 free. Audio tour €3. Mass held in the Capilla Real M-Sa 8:30, 10am, noon, 5pm; Su 8:30, 10, 11am, noon, 1, 5, and 6pm. Free.

Legend has it that in 1401 the *reconquistadores* wanted to demonstrate their religious fervor by constructing a church so great that "those who come after us will take us for madmen." Sevilla's immense cathedral does appear to be the work of an extravagant madman—with 44 individual chapels, it is the third largest in the world, after St. Peter's Basilica in Rome and St. Paul's Cathedral in London, and it is the biggest Gothic edifice ever constructed.

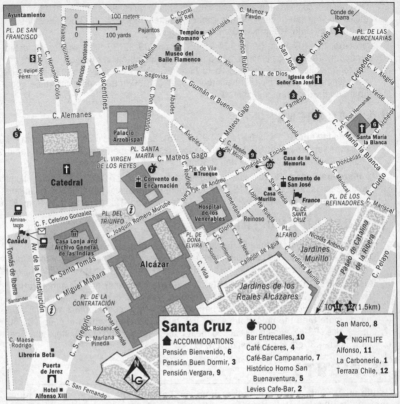

Santa Cruz

FOOD

ACCOMMODATIONS
Pensión Bienvenido, **6**
Pensión Buen Dormir, **3**
Pensión Vergara, **9**

Bar Entrecalles, **10**
Café Cáceres, **4**
Café-Bar Campanario, **7**
Histórico Horno San
   Buenaventura, **5**
Levíes Cafe-Bar, **2**

San Marco, **8**

NIGHTLIFE
Alfonso, **11**
La Carbonería, **1**
Terraza Chile, **12**

In 1401, a 12th-century Almohad mosque was destroyed to clear space for the cathedral. All that remains is the **Patio de Los Naranjos,** where the faithful washed before prayer, the **Puerta del Perdón** entryway from C. Alemanes, and **La Giralda** minaret, built in 1198. The tower and its twins in Marrakesh and Rabat are the oldest and longest-surviving Almohad minarets in the world. The 35 ramps leading to the tower's top were installed to replace the stairs that once stood there, allowing a disabled *muezzín* to ride his horse for the call to prayer. Climbing the ramps will leave you breathless, as will the views from the top—the entire city of Sevilla lies just on the other side of the bells. Be warned that the gong-like iron bells sound every fifteen minutes, and they're loud.

Try every door and follow every hallway to get a full understanding of the cathedral's immensity. While you may easily get distracted by rooms of treasure and eye-level stone tombs, don't forget to look up; paintings hide above the moulding and intricately-carved wooden and stone ceilings lurch toward you. You can get up close and personal with the designs of the more than 135-foot tall central nave (and the incredible angel-adorned organ made of wood) via a well-placed mirror on the nave's floor. In the center of the cathedral, the Renaissance-style **Capilla Real** stands opposite **choir stalls** made of mahogany recycled from a 19th-century Austrian railway. The ◼**retablo mayor,** one of the largest in the world, is a slightly faded golden wall of intricately wrought saints and disciples. Nearby, the **Sepulcro**

de Cristóbal Colón (Columbus's tomb) displays the figures of four robed men towering above the floor, carrying a shrouded coffin. The coffin supposedly holds Columbus' remains, brought back to Sevilla in 1902 after Cuba gained independence (the tomb was in Havana's cathedral until then).

Farther on and to the right stands the **Sacristía Mayor,** which holds gilded panels of Alfonso X el Sabio by Juan de Arefe, works by Ribera and Murillo, and a glittering Corpus Cristi icon, **La Custodia Processional.** Small secrets and treasures can be found in all the cathedral's hundreds of corners; allot enough time to find them all.

ＮＡＬＣＡＺＡＲ

Pl. del Triunfo, 7. ☎ 954 50 23 23. Open Tu-Sa 9:30am-7pm, Su 9:30am-5pm. €7, students, handicapped, over 65, and under 16 free. Tours of private residence every 30min. Aug.-May 10am-1:30pm and 3:30-5:30pm; June-July 10am-1:30pm. Max. 15 people per tour, so buy tickets ahead. €4. English audio tours (€3) offer anecdotes (sometimes difficult to interpret) and a clear route through the complex.

The oldest European palace still used as a private residence for royals, Sevilla's Alcázar oozes extravagance. The palace was constructed by the Moors in the seventh century and embellished in the 1600s. It displays a mix of Moorish, Gothic, Renaissance, and Baroque architecture, but its intricacies are most prominently displayed in the *mudéjar* style of many of the arches, tiles, and ceilings. Fernando and Isabel are the palace's best known former residents; Carlos V also lived here after marrying his cousin Isabel of Portugal in the **Salón Techo Carlos V.**

The Alcázar is a network of splendid patios and courtyards, around which both public and private court life revolved. From the moment you step through the **Patio de la Montería,** the melange of cultures is apparent; an Arabic inscription praising Allah is written in contrasting Gothic writing. Through the archway is the **Patio del Yeso,** an exquisitely geometric space used by Moorish governors before the palace itself was built. The center of public life at the Alcázar, however, was the **Patio de las Doncellas** (Patio of the Maids), a colonnaded quadrangle encircled by archways adorned with still-colorful tile work. The **Patio de las Muñecas** (Patio of the Dolls), one of the drafty palace's more intimate locales, served as a private area for Moorish kings; the room had an escape path so that the king would not have to cross the open space in an attack. Look for the miniature faces at the base of one of the statues, which will explain how the patio got its name. Its columns are thought to have been taken from the devastated palace in Madinat Al-Zahra (near Córdoba), built at the height of the caliph period in the 10th and 11th centuries.

The interior of the Alcázar is sumptuous and elegant, a labyrinth of rooms where the walls themselves are works of art. In the **Sala de los Azulejos del Alcázar,** history's stain is literally visible—the room was the stage of a bloody duel between Pedro I and his half brother, Don Fadrique, and even today the trace of Fadrique's blood can be spotted on the floor. On a more peaceful note, the golden-domed **Salón de los Embajadores** (Ambassadors' Room) is rumored to be the site where Fernando and Isabel welcomed Columbus back from the New World. Their son, Juan, was born in the red-and-blue tiled **Cuarto del Príncipe;** the room was named for him after his untimely death due to, according to legend, a broken heart.

The **private residences** upstairs, the official home of the King and Queen and their lodging on visits to Sevilla, have been renovated and redecorated throughout the years, and most of the furniture today dates from the 18th and 19th centuries. They are accessible only by 25min. guided tours. Fragrant **gardens** adorned with fountains and the not-so-fragrant **Los Baños de Doña María de Padilla** are accessible outside. Save your nose with a sneak peek from the arched entry; walking into the bath caves doesn't allow you to see much more. After chasing the king-sized shadows of carp in Mercury's Pond, walk to the farthest corner of the gardens behind

SEVILLA'S TRAGIC TALE

Among its many legacies, the Judería left Sevilla one of its most tragic legends: that of Susona, La Hermosa Hembra (vulgar for "beautiful woman"). During the 15th century, even as relations between Sevilla's Christian and Jewish populations were increasingly tense, Susona, the daughter of a Jewish merchant, fell in love with a Christian knight. Every night, she would sneak out the window, meet her lover by the army barracks, and make it back home before dawn unnoticed. One night, however, she overheard her father plotting a rebellion against the Christian government and, fearing that she would lose her lover forever, Susona warned him of the plot. The Christian army's retaliation was swift and merciless—Susona's entire family was slaughtered, and their bodies were left to scavengers, which was considered the most dishonorable death. Susona's street thereafter bore the name C. Muerte.

Deeply remorseful, Susona confessed in Sevilla's Cathedral, received baptism, and retreated into a convent. When she died, she asked that her head be placed above her doorway as a symbol of redemption for all and, strangely, nobody touched it for over 100 years. While Susona's skull no longer can be seen on what is now C. Susona, a plaque still bears testimony to her tragic story.

the shrubs to see the three peacock pairs (and babies in July!) that take cover in the less-traveled nook.

CASA LONJA. Between the cathedral and the Alcázar stands the 16th-century Casa Lonja, built by Felipe II as a *casa de contracción* (commercial exchange) for trade with the Americas. In 1785, Carlos III converted it into the **Archivo General de las Índias.** Today, it contains a collection of over 44,000 documents relating to the conquest of the New World. Highlights include Juan de la Costa's wildly inaccurate *Mapa Mundi* (map of the world), letters from Columbus to Fernando and Isabel, and a 1590 letter from Cervantes requesting employment in America. Swing by to eye the magnificent artistry of the casa's exterior. *(☎954 50 05 28. Open M-Sa 10am-4pm. Access to documents is limited to scholars.)*

OTHER SIGHTS. After Fernando III forced Jews who had been exiled from Toledo during the Inquisition to live in Santa Cruz, the area thrived as a lively Jewish quarter. On **Calle Susona,** formerly C. de la Muerte, a ceramic tile with a skull rests above a door, evoking the tale of beautiful Susona, a Jewish girl who fell in love with a Christian knight (see left). C. Susona leads to **Plaza Doña Elvira,** where Lope de Rueda's works, precursors to the dramas of Spain's Golden Age, were staged.

TEMPLO ROMANO. Rising on C. Mármoles are the ruins of the **Templo Romano.** Its two columns ascend 15m from below street level and offer a glimpse of the depth of Sevilla's history; river sediment, accumulated after the construction of the temple, caused the ground level to rise. C. Gloria leads to the **Hospital de los Venerables,** a hospital-church adorned with art from the *Sevillana* School. Though the small garden doesn't have any seating, the adjacent courtyard is a perfect place to read a book or listen to the bubbling tiled fountain *(☎954 56 29 84. Open daily for guided visits 10am-2pm and 4-8pm. €4.75, students €2.40. Children under 12 and Su Free.)*

Calle Lope de Rueda, off C. Ximénez de Enciso, is graced with two noble mansions, beyond which lies the fragrant **Plaza de Santa Cruz,** built on the former site of the neighborhood's main synagogue. South of the plaza are the **Jardines de Murillo,** a shady expanse of shrubbery, benches, and hidden waterworks of art. The **Convento de San José** cherishes a cloak and portrait of Santa Teresa de Ávila. *(C. Santa Teresa, off Pl. de Santa Cruz. Open daily 9-11am. Free.)* The church in Pl. de Santa Cruz houses the grave of artist Bartoloméo Murillo, who died in what is now known as the **Casa Murillo** after falling off the scaffold while he was painting frescoes in Cádiz's Iglesia de los Capuchinos. *(C. Santa Ter-*

esa, 8. ☎954 22 12 72. Closed for renovations in 2007; ask at the tourist office for up-to-date information.) **Iglesia de Santa María la Blanca** was built in 1391 on the foundation of a synagogue and boasts an amazingly elaborate carved plaster ceiling. *(C. Santa María la Blanca. Open M-Sa 10-11am and 6:30-8pm, Su 9:30am-2pm and 6:30-8pm. Free.)*

EL CENTRO

■ **MUSEO PROVINCIAL DE BELLAS ARTES.** This museum contains Spain's finest collection of works by painters of the *Sevillana* School, most notably Murillo, Valdés Leal, and Zurbarán, as well as El Greco and Dutch master Peter Brueghel. Much of the art was cobbled together from decommissioned convents in the mid-1800s and found a stately home amid the traditional tiles and courtyards of this impressive building. Although the art is heavily biased toward religious themes, later works include landscape paintings and portraits of Sevilla, its environs, and its residents. The building alone is worth a visit. *(Pl. del Museo, 9. ☎954 78 65 00; www.museosdeandalucia.es. Open Tu 2:30-8:30pm, W-Sa 9am-8:30pm, Su 9am-2:30pm. €1.50, students and EU citizens free.)*

MUSEO DEL BAILE FLAMENCO. See flamenco as you've never seen it before. Let life-size virtual dancers whisk you away to the heart of a gypsy camp, where screen after screen lights up with color and song to convey the history, music, and technique of this Spanish art. The visual art and photo-heavy exhibitions put the corner-store postcards to shame. *(C. Manuel Rojas Marcos, 3. ☎954 34 03 11. Open daily 9am-6:30pm. €10, students €8. MC/V.)*

CASA DE PILATOS. This large private residence has been inhabited continuously by Spanish aristocrats since the 15th century, and its spaces combine all the virtues of Andalusian architecture and art. On the ground floor, Roman artifacts coexist with tropical gardens in *mudéjar* patios. The second floor features rooms decorated over the centuries with oil portraits, sculptures, painted ceilings, and tapestries. *(Pl. de Pilatos, 1. ☎954 22 52 98. Open daily 9am-7pm. Guided tours every 30min. 10am-6:30pm. Ground level only €5, with upper chambers €8; EU citizens free Tu 1-5pm.)*

IGLESIA DEL SALVADOR. Fronted by a Montañés sculpture, this 17th-century church was built on the foundations of the city's main mosque and still retains the courtyard and the belfry's base of the old building. The church is adorned with Baroque *retablos* and paintings, including Montañés's *Jesús de la pasión*. *(Pl. del Salvador, 1 block from C. las Sierpes. Closed for renovations; check sign on door.)*

OTHER SIGHTS. Calle Sierpes, which starts in Pl. San Francisco, cuts through the Aristocratic Quarter. At the beginning of this pedestrian street, a plaque marks the spot where the royal prison once loomed. Some scholars believe that Cervantes began writing *Don Quixote* here. Legend states that the founder of **Convento de Santa Inés** was pursued so insistently by King Pedro the Cruel that she disfigured her face with boiling oil so he would leave her alone. Today the nuns sell **pastries and cakes** through the courtyard's *torno* (revolving window). *(C. María Coronel. Sweets €2.50-7, sold by the ½kg, kg, and dozen. Mixed box of pastries €10-12. M-Sa 9am-1pm and 5-6:45pm.)* The **Ayuntamiento,** Sevilla's city hall, has 16th-century Gothic and Renaissance interior halls, a decorated domed ceiling, and a sight-worthy Plateresque facade. While art exhibitions take place frequently, the building's beautiful stone work, especially on its back side, is art on its own. *(Pl. de San Francisco, enter from Pl. Nueva. ☎954 59 01 01. Open Sept.-July Tu-Th 5:30-6:30pm, call in advance. Passport or other official documentation required. Free.)* The **Iglesia de la Anunciación** breaks the trend, and features a Roman (not Islamic) pantheon honoring illustrious *sevillanos*, including poet Gustavo Adolfo Bécquer. *(Pl. de la Encarnación; enter on C. Laraña. Open daily 9am-1pm. Mass M-Sa noon, Su 12:30pm; Th and Su also 8:30pm. Free.)*

LA MACARENA

CONVENTO DE SANTA PAULA. Convento de Santa Paula includes a church with Gothic, *mudéjar*, and Renaissance elements, a magnificent ceiling, and Montañés sculptures. The **museum** has religious art, including Ribera's *San Jerónimo*. Nuns peddle ▨homemade marmalade (300g, €2.70) and angel hair pastries. Knock if the door is closed. *(Pl. Santa Paula, 11. ☎954 53 63 30. Museum open Tu-Su 10am-6:30pm. Church open for visits Tu-Su 10am-1pm and 4:30-6:30pm, although visits are randomly not permitted during these times. €2.)*

CHURCHES. A stretch of **murallas** (walls) built in the 12th century runs between Pta. de la Macarena and Pta. de Córdoba on Ronda de Capuchinos. Flanking the west end of the walls, the **Basílica de la Macarena** houses the venerated image of *La Virgen de la Macarena*, which is borne through the streets at the climax of the *Semana Santa* processions. *(C. Bécquer, 1. ☎954 90 18 00. Basílica open daily 9:30am-2pm and 5-8pm. €3, students €1.50. Mass M-F 9, 11:30am, 8, and 8:30pm; Sa 9am and 8pm; Su 10:30am, 12:30, and 8pm.)* Opposite the belfry of the Iglesia de San Marcos rises **Iglesia de Santa Isabel,** featuring an altarpiece by Montañés. Nearby, the Baroque **Iglesia de San Luis** has an unparalleled stained glass altar front-lit by a climbing dome with a life-size Christ sitting crowned on his throne stories above, surrounded by carved angels. The two side altars each hold relics, including two unlabeled skulls. *(C. San Luis. ☎954 55 02 07. Open Tu-Th 9am-2pm, F-Sa 9am-2pm and 6-8pm. Free.)* Toward the river is **Iglesia de San Lorenzo y Jesús del Gran Poder,** with Montañés's lifelike sculpture, *El Cristo del gran poder;* worshippers kiss Jesus's ankle. *(Pl. San Lorenzo. ☎954 91 56 72. Open M-Th 8am-1:30pm and 6-9pm, F 7am-2pm and 5-10pm, Sa-Su 8am-1:30pm and 6-9pm. Free.)*

OTHER SIGHTS. A large garden beyond the *murallas* and the Basílica leads to the **Hospital de las Cinco Llagas,** a spectacular Renaissance building recently renovated to host the Andalusian parliament. Thursday mornings from 9am to 2pm, a large **flea market** is held along C. Feria. The **Alameda de Hércules** is filled with outdoor cafes and the streets on its sides sprout funky restaurants.

EL ARENAL AND TRIANA

The inviting riverside esplanade **Alcalde Marqués de Contadero** stretches along the banks of the Guadalquivir from the base of the Torre del Oro. Somewhat kitschy **boat tours** of Sevilla leave from in front of the tower (1hr., €15).

PLAZA DE TOROS DE LA REAL MAESTRANZA. Bullfighting has been a staple of *sevillano* culture for centuries, as evidenced by the city's beautiful and world-renowned Plaza de Toros. Home to one of the two great bullfighting schools (the other is in **Ronda** p. 288), the plaza fills to capacity (13,800) for the 13 *corridas* of the *Feria de Abril.* Multilingual tours take visitors through a small but informative museum, the chapel where *matadores* pray before fights, and the emergency room used when their prayers go unanswered, though only three matadors have died in the history of bullfighting in Sevilla. *(☎954 22 45 77; www.realmaestranza.com. Open May-Oct. 9:30am-8pm; Nov.-Apr. 9:30am-7pm. Mandatory tours every 20min. in English and Spanish. €5; seniors 20% discount. See Bullfighting, p. 238, for ticket info.)*

TORRE DEL ORO. The 12-sided **Torre del Oro** (Gold Tower), built by the Almohads in the early 13th century, overlooks the river from Po. de Cristóbal Colón. Today, a tiny yellow dome is all that remains of the golden tiles that once covered the tower. Inside is the small **Museo Náutico,** a storehouse of maritime antiquities. Museum officers enthusiastically tend to visitors. Look out for the whale jaw. *(☎954 22 24 19. Open Sept.-July Tu-F 10am-2pm, Sa-Su 11am-2pm. €2, students €1. Tu free.)*

La Macarena

🏠 ACCOMMODATIONS
Hostal Alameda, **4**
Hostal Macarena, **3**

🍴 FOOD
Ancha de la Feria, **5**
La Plazoleta Bodega, **6**

⭐ NIGHTLIFE
Palenque, **1**
Tribal, **2**

OTHER SIGHTS. The **Torre de la Plata** (Silver Tower) was once connected to the Torre del Oro by underwater chains designed to protect the city from river-borne trespassers. Old-fashioned piracy no longer being a concern, the Torre now acts as a bank. One block farther inland, midway between Pte. de Isabel II and Pte. de San Telmo, is the **Iglesia de Santa Ana,** Sevilla's oldest church and the focal point of the fiestas that take over in July. (C. Pelay Correa. Open M and W 7:30-8:30pm.)

OUTER NEIGHBORHOODS

PLAZA DE ESPAÑA. The twin spires of **Plaza de España** gracefully mark the ends of the over 200m-long wonder of a building. Designed by Aníbal González, one of Sevilla's most prominent 20th-century architects, the aristocratic-looking structure hugs a large and beautiful plaza, featuring mosaic floors and a large marble fountain within its semicircle. Mosaics depicting every province in Spain line the crumbling colonnade, and balconies offer a view of the surrounding gardens. The nearby **Parque de María Luisa** is a reminder of Sevilla's 1929 plans for an Ibero-American World's Fair. (Adjacent to Pl. de España. Open daily 8am-10pm.)

NEAR ESTACIÓN PLAZA DE ARMAS

CENTRO ANDALUZ DE ARTE CONTEMPORANEO. If you're interested in the freshest currents flowing through Spain's art scene, the trek is worth it. The interior of this restored monastery is a labyrinth of clean spaces exhibiting everything from optical illusions to a skull made of Christmas lights. Special exhibitions and film series are often featured. *(Av. Américo Vespucio, 2, on Isla de la Cartuja. ☎ 955 03 70 70. Open Tu-F 10am-9pm, Sa 11am-9pm, Su 10am-3pm. Complete visit €3, partial €1.80. Tu free.)*

▣ NIGHTLIFE

Sevilla's nightlife is as hot as its scorching summer afternoons. A typical night of *la marcha* (bar-hopping) begins with visits to several bars for tapas and mixed drinks, continues with dancing at discotecas, and culminates with an early morning breakfast of *churros con chocolate*. Most clubs don't get crowded until well after midnight, and the real fun often starts after 2:30am. Popular bars can be found around **Calle Mateos Gago** near the cathedral, **Calle Adriano** by the bullring, and **Calle del Betis** across the river in Triana; several popular summertime clubs lie along the river near **Puente de la Barqueta**. Many gay clubs cluster around the Pl. de Armas, and some can be found around the **Alameda de Hercules** in the Macarena neighborhood. Sevilla is also famous for its *botellón*, a (mostly student) tradition of getting drunk in massive crowds in plazas or at bars along the river to start the night. A recent crack-down on public drinking laws has the city's plazas vacated (and a lot less odorous) after sunset. In summer, the crowds sweep toward the river in hopes of a breeze, and even on "slow" nights most *terrazas* stay open until 4am. During the school year, bars and clubs are packed regardless of the night; in summer, it takes a bit more searching to find weeknight crowds.

SANTA CRUZ

▣ **La Carbonería,** C. Levies, 18 (☎954 22 99 45). A gigantic bar frequented by students and young summer travelers. Free live flamenco shows nightly at 11pm. *Agua de Sevilla* pitchers €20. Su-W €15. Sangria pitchers €8. Open daily 8pm-3 or 4am. Cash only.

Alfonso, Av. la Palmera (☎954 23 37 35), adjacent to Po. de las Delicias. Avoid longer lines elsewhere and shake it to the DJ's crazy house beats in this spacious outdoor club, amid palm trees and mini-bars. Beer €1.50-2.50. Mixed drinks €4.50-6. Open M-Th and Su 10pm-5am, F-Sa 10pm-7am. AmEx/D/MC/V.

Terraza Chile, Po. de las Delicias. A packed dance club and bar by night with loud salsa and pop, bringing together young *sevillanos*, foreign students, and tourists. Beer €2. Mixed drinks €5. Open June-Sept. daily 8pm-5am; Oct.-May Th-Sa 8pm-5am. MC/V.

LA MACARENA

The area near **Puente de la Barqueta** is the place to go dancing during summer. The near side of the river features several outdoor discotecas, while the far side hosts a more rowdy clubbing scene. From La Macarena, follow C. Resolana to C. Nueva Torneo, by Pte. de la Barqueta. (The A2 night bus runs at midnight, 1, and 2am from Pl. Nueva; ask to be let off near Pte. de la Barqueta. Taxi from Pl. Nueva €5-7.)

▣ **Palenque,** Av. Blas Pascal (☎954 46 74 08). Gigantic dance club, complete with 2 dance floors—one of which is inexplicably called "Alabama"—2 musical choices, and a small ice skating rink (€3, including skate rental; closes at 4am). Beer €3. Mixed drinks €5. F-Sa cover €7, Th free. Open June-Sept. Th-Sa midnight-7am. MC/V.

Tribal, Av. de los Descubrimientos, next to Pte. de la Barqueta. Hip, tropical, tent-like discoteca playing American hip-hop, Latin favorites, and lots of reggaeton. W hip-hop is popular with the international crowd. Drinks served in pitchers €5-10 per person depending on group size. Open W-Sa midnight-6am. MC/V.

EL ARENAL AND TRIANA

▨ **Boss,** C. del Betis. In Sevilla the night is always young, and Boss is...boss. If you pierce its exclusive armor, it will lead you to a crowd that knows how to get fired up. Irresistible beats, a packed dance floor, and hazy blue lights make this a top nocturnal destination. Beer €3.50. Mixed drinks €6. Open daily 9pm-5am. Closed in summer. MC/V.

Rio Grande: Puerto de Cuba, on the right as you cross into Triana on the San Telmo bridge. Planted right on the banks of the river, it's hard to believe this palmy oasis has no cover charge. Recline in one of the intimately placed wicker couches or hop onto a pillow-strewn beached dingy—just watch out for the mist. Dressy casual (i.e. no college tees) will get you past the bouncers and to the bar (drinks €6 and up). Open only in summer daily 11pm-4:30 or 5am.

🎵 ENTERTAINMENT

The tourist office distributes *El Giraldillo* and its English counterpart, *The Tourist*, free monthly magazines with listings on music, art exhibits, theater, dance, fairs, and film. It can also be found online at www.elgiraldillo.es.

THEATERS

Sevilla is a haven for the performing arts. The venerable **Teatro Lope de Vega** (☎954 59 08 67), near Parque de María Luisa, has long been the city's leading stage. Ask about scheduled events at the tourist office or check the bulletin board in the university lobby on C. San Fernando. **Sala la Herrería** and **Sala la Imperdible** put on avant-garde productions in Pl. San Antonio de Padua. (Both ☎954 38 82 19.) **Teatro de la Maestranza,** on the river between the Torre del Oro and the bullring, is a splendid concert hall accommodating orchestral performances, opera, and dance. (☎954 22 65 73. Box office open M-F 10am-2pm and 6-9pm.) On spring and summer evenings, neighborhood fairs are often accompanied by **free open-air concerts** in Santa Cruz and Triana; inquire at the tourist office for schedules and locations. **Avenida 5 Cincs,** C. Marqués de las Paradas, 15 (☎954 29 30 25), and **Corona Center,** in the mall between C. Salado and C. Paraíso in Triana (☎954 27 80 64), screen films from various countries subtitled in Spanish. **Cines Warner Lusomundo (Cinesa),** Co. Comercial Plaza de Armas, theatres on the 2nd fl., shows American films dubbed in Spanish (☎902 33 32 31; www.cinesa.es). For more, look under "Cinema" in *El Giraldillo* or any local newspaper.

FLAMENCO

Sevilla would not be Sevilla without flamenco. As one of the most popular branches in the *gitanos'* (gypsies') musical tradition, flamenco consists of dance, guitar, and songs that express the spontaneity and passion vital to Andalucía. Rhythmic clapping, intricate fretwork on the guitar, throaty wailing, and rapid foot-tapping form a mesmerizing backdrop to the swirling dancers. Flamenco can be seen either in the highly-touristed *tablaos*, where skilled professional dancers perform, or in *tabernas*, bars where locals dance *sevillanas*. Both have merit, but the *tabernas* tend to be free. The tourist office provides a complete list of both *tablaos* and *tabernas;* ask about student discounts.

TABLAOS

Signs advertising *tablao* shows are inescapable—from souvenir shops in Santa Cruz to hotels to banks to Internet cafes, everyone sells tickets for the big shows. As a result, the majority of flamenco *tablaos* in Sevilla cater to the tourist crowd rather than to true flamenco aficionados. Advance reservations can be made online, in person, or in hotels and shops. Many *tablaos* are *tablao-restaurantes,* so you can eat while watching the show, but dinner tends to be very expensive. Less expensive alternatives are the impressive 1hr. shows at the cultural center ⊠**Casa de la Memoria Al-Andalus,** C. Ximénez de Enciso, 28, in the middle of Santa Cruz. Ask at the tourist office or swing by their ticket office for a schedule of different themed performances, including traditional Sephardic Jewish concerts. (☎954 56 06 70; www.casadelamemoria.es. Shows nightly 9pm, in summer also 10:30pm; seating is very limited so reserve your tickets a day or two ahead, and up to four days in advance for weekend shows. €13, students €11, under 10 €6.) **Los Gallos,** Pl. de Santa Cruz, 11, is arguably the best tourist show in Sevilla. Buy tickets in advance and arrive early. (☎954 21 69 81; www.tablaolosgallos.com. Hour-long shows nightly 8 and 10:30pm. Cover €27, includes 1 drink.) **El Arenal,** C. Rodo, 7, is a *tablao*-restaurante and the source of the black-and-white flamenco postcards you'll find around town. (☎954 21 64 92; www.tablaoelarenal.com. Shows nightly 8:30 and 10:30pm. Cover €33, includes 1 drink; €49 includes tapas and a drink; €64 includes a two-course dinner, dessert, and drinks.) **El Patio Sevillano,** Po. de Cristóbal Colón, 11, offers performances at 7:30 and 10pm. (☎954 21 41 20; www.elpatiosevillano.com. €33, includes 1 drink; €55 includes tapas; €65, includes dinner.) **El Palacio Andaluz,** C. María Auxiliadora, 18, has a mixed flamenco and classical dance show. (☎954 53 47 20; www.elpalacioandaluz.com. Shows nightly 7 and 10pm. Advance reservation required. €32, includes 1 drink; €50, includes tapas; €63 includes dinner.) **Casa Carmen Arte Flamenco,** C. Marqués de Paradas, 30, draws a student crowd. (☎954 21 28 89; www.casacarmenarteflamenco.com. Shows nightly 9:30pm and 11pm. Reserve in advance. Cover €14, students €11.) Though further afield in Puerta Osario, **Las Brujas,** C. Gonzalo Bilbao, 10, one of the smaller shows, is worth the trek. (☎954 41 36 51. Shows daily 9:15 and 11:30pm. Buy tickets in advance. Cover €23, includes 1 drink.)

TABERNAS

⊠**La Carbonería,** C. Levies, 18, an open picnic table-filled bar with a courtyard that caters to students and backpackers. **El Tamboril,** Pl. de Santa Cruz, hosts a primarily middle-aged tourist crowd for midnight singing and dancing. (☎954 56 15 90. Open daily June-Sept. 5pm-3am; Oct.-May noon-3am.) Bar-filled **Calle del Betis,** across the river, houses several other *tabernas:* **Lo Nuestro, El Rejoneo,** and **Taberna Flamenca Triana.**

FÚTBOL

Sevilla has two professional teams, and soccer fever engulfs the city, especially when the cross-town rivals play each other. **Real Betis** wears green and white, **Sevilla FC** white and red. Sevilla FC plays at **Estadio Sánchez Pizjuán** (☎954 53 53 53) on Av. de Eduardo Dato, and Real Betis plays at **Estadio Manuel Ruiz de Lopera** (☎954 61 03 40) on Av. de la Palmera. Buy tickets at the stadium; price and availability depend on the quality of the match-up. Both teams struggle against the competitive **Barcelona** and **Real Madrid** clubs. In 2005, Betis won the Copa del Rey trophy for the 2nd time in its history. Not to be outdone, Sevilla FC won the Copa de la UEFA (European Union Football Association) in 2006.

BULLFIGHTING

Sevilla's bullring, one of the most beautiful in Spain, hosts bullfights from *Semana Santa* through October. The cheapest place to buy tickets is at the ring on Po. Alcalde Marqués de Contadero. When there's a good *cartel* (line-up), the booths on C. Sierpes, C. Velázquez, and Pl. de Toros might be the only source to buy tickets in advance. Ticket prices can run from €20 for a *grada de sol* (nosebleed seat in the sun) to €75 for a *barrera de sombra* (front-row seat in the shade); scalpers usually add 20%. *Corridas de toros* (bullfights) and *novilladas* (fights with apprentice bullfighters and younger bulls) are held on the 13 days around the *Feria de Abril* and through early May; Sundays from April to June

sevilla's holy week

party time! the influences of and on sevilla's holy week

For hundreds of years, Sevilla's Holy Week *(Semana Santa)* has demonstrated how tradition, religion, and tourism can create a unique phenome-

> ## "Processions strike outsiders as conventional manifestations of Catholicism."

non. The processions featuring hooded penitents and floats depicting images of the Passion often strike outsiders as conventional manifestations of Catholicism. Things are more complicated (and interesting) than that.

Although some religious brotherhoods were founded around 1400, the Holy Week festival was born around 1550. It was then that dozens of brotherhoods began their activities. The militant Catholicism of the Counter-Reformation welcomed this movement, which sought to take the symbols of the Church to the streets. The brotherhoods also offered Sevillians ways to create affiliated networks to the city and to their peers, as brotherhoods were usually support groups defined by social class, profession, or ethnic background. The result was a complex patchwork of communities that provided Sevilla with some needed social cement. Furthermore, the exuberance toward the cult of the Virgin Mary revealed that the processions were tapping into spiritual energies that went beyond dry precepts to attain salvation. Social and anthropological forces were colliding to create spectacular religious rituals, which gained international recognition by the 16th century.

Declining in importance for two centuries, the festival was revived with a different character in the late 19th century. By then Andalucía had become a frequent destination for European travelers who created an exotic image of a region outside modernity. Andalucíans looked at themselves through the lens of these writings and fashioned themselves according to what they saw. Also of great significance to the changing of the festival was the economic force of tourism, already operating by the turn of the 20th century. Local businessmen and the municipal government in Sevilla decided to actively promote tourism: a revival of the Holy Week festival was part of this effort. Splendor and spectacle were institutionalized for the sake of visitors and natives, and brotherhoods were subjected to more rational arrangements. "Eternal Sevilla" was in the making, and a crucial element was a popular religiosity that manifested itself not in the temple, but on the streets, opening

> ## "Spectacle...was institutionalized...'Eternal Sevilla' was in the making."

the door for alternative ways to be religious. At the same time, modern ways of thought had taken many individuals away from a strict adherence to organized religion.

Nevertheless, the festival's traditional image of the drama of the Passion, with its two protagonists, Christ and his suffering mother, still deeply affected many Sevillians who did not necessarily follow the teachings of the Church.

Today, participation in the brotherhoods still thrives, and individuals who have never set foot in church weep at the passing of the processions. And of course, *Semana Santa* still attracts thousands and thousands of baffled and enraptured tourists.

Antonio Córdoba was born in Sevilla, where he earned his B.A. in English Literature. He is currently a Ph.D. candidate at Harvard University. He plans to graduate in 2007 with a dissertation on Latin American literature.

and September to October, more often during Corpus Cristi in June and early July; and during the *Feria de San Miguel* near the end of September. During July and August, *corridas* occasionally occur on Thursday at 9pm; check posters around town. (For current info and **ticket sales,** call the Plaza de Toros ticket office at ☎954 50 13 82. For more on **bullfighting,** see p. 91.)

SHOPPING

Sevilla is a great place to find Andalusian crafts, such as hand-embroidered silk, lace shawls, and traditional flamenco wear, albeit often at inflated tourist prices. El Centro, the area including C. las Sierpes, C. San Eloy, C. Velázquez, and C. Francos, offers a wide array of crafts, as well as a little bit of everything else, including ceramic shops, the most popular Spanish clothing chains and what seems like hundreds of tiny shoe boutiques and jewelry stores. In Santa Cruz, the streets are packed with identical souvenir shops selling bullfighting and flamenco-themed clothing, trinkets, and postcards. A large, eclectic **flea market** is held Thursday 9am-2pm, extending along C. Feria in La Macarena.

> **TIP** **SMOOTH SALES.** In February, July, and August, all of the stores hold huge ▧**rebajas** (sales), where everything is marked down 30-70%.

FESTIVALS

Sevilla swells with tourists during its fiestas, and with good reason: the parties are world-class. If you're in Spain during any of the major festivals, head straight to Sevilla—you won't regret it (that is, if you remember it at all). Reserve a room a few months in advance, and expect to pay at least twice what you would normally.

▧**SEMANA SANTA.** Sevilla's world-famous *Semana Santa* lasts from Palm Sunday to Easter Sunday. In each neighborhood, thousands of penitents in hooded cassocks guide *pasos* (huge, extravagantly-decorated floats) through the streets, illuminated by hundreds of candles; the climax is Good Friday, when the entire city turns out for a procession along the bridges and through the oldest neighborhoods. Americans should be prepared for the costumes that bear a more than passing resemblance to those of the Ku Klux Klan. Book rooms well in advance and expect to pay triple the usual price. The tourist office has a helpful booklet on accommodations and restaurants during the week's festivities.

▧**FERIA DE ABRIL.** From April 12-17, the city rewards itself for its Lenten piety with the *Feria de Abril*, held in the southern end of Los Remedios. Begun as part of a 19th-century revolt against foreign influence, the *Feria* has grown into a massive celebration of all things Andalusian with circuses, bullfights, and flamenco shows. A spectacular array of flowers and lanterns decorates over 1000 kiosks, tents, and pavilions, collectively called *casetas*. Each *caseta* has a small kitchen, bar, and dance floor. Though there are a few large public ones, most are private, and the only way to get invited is by making friends with the locals. The city holds bullfights daily during the festival; buy tickets in advance.

DAYTRIPS FROM SEVILLA

▧PARQUE DOÑANA
Doñana is accessible from almost any city in Andalucía. Bus schedules vary, but both Empresa Damas (☎954 90 77 37) and Los Amarillos (☎954 98 91 84) run to towns in

the park's boundaries. Buses leave Sevilla's Pl. de Armas station 6 times per day. The easiest way to see Doñana is by car. Take A-483 off of A-92; 45min.

One of Europe's largest national parks, with everything from cork trees to wild buzzards, the immense and diverse Doñana park is both daunting and inspiring. The southern zone is the Parque Nacional, while the northern area is called the Parque Natural, a distinction that often proves confusing for visitors. The Parque Natural is more popular with long-term visitors and nature enthusiasts; there are ample opportunities for horseback-riding and hiking. Like the Marismas del Odiel, Doñana has its fair share of flamingos. The provincial tourist offices in Sevilla provide information on the park, including detailed driving directions, hiking suggestions, campsites, restaurants, and lodging in nearby towns. See www.donana.es for more details. To visit the Parque Nacional, it's necessary to make a reservation for a 4hr., 80km tour that includes a boat ride across the Río Guadalquivir and a trip in an all-terrain vehicle through the three ecosystems of the park—dunes, wetlands, and *pinar*, arid coniferous forrest. (Call ahead to reserve ☎959 43 04 32; www.infodonana.com/donanavisitas. Open daily 9am-7pm. Trips leave Tu-Su May-Sept. 14 8:30am and 8pm; Sept. 15-Apr. 8:30am and 3pm. €23.)

ITÁLICA

Take the Empresa Casal (Área de Sevilla) bus (☎954 41 06 58) toward Santiponce from the Pl. de Armas bus station, platform 34, off to the left of the rest of the platforms. Get off at the last stop (30min.; M-Sa every 10-30min. 6:35am-2:30am, Su hourly 7:35am-midnight; €1.15, pay onboard). The entrance to the ruins is to the left of the gas station, across the street from the bus stop. When returning to Sevilla, wait by the faded bus sign in front of the top of the driveway marking the entrance to Itálica (☎955 99 65 83; italica.ccul@juntadeandalucia.es). Ruins open Apr.-Sept. Tu-Sa 8:30am-8:30pm, Su 9am-3pm; Oct.-Mar. Tu-Sa 9am-5:30pm, Su 10am-4pm. €1.50; free for EU citizens.

Just 9km northwest of Sevilla and right outside the village of Santiponce (pop. 7000) lie the excavated ruins of Itálica, the first permanent Roman settlement in southern Iberia. Founded by general Publius Cornelius Scipio in 206 BC as a kind of "wellness camp" for soldiers injured in the Battle of Ilipa, Itálica was used as a strategic military outpost. The ruins you can visit today are a testament to the cosmopolitan trading center started by emperor Trajan (AD 53) and his son Hadrian (AD 76), a center gradually abandoned and forgotten as Sevilla took over as the regional seat of power. Archaeological excavations, begun in the 18th century, continue today, although the oldest neighborhoods in Itálica and its mysterious forum are still buried under downtown Santiponce and may never be recovered.

The most interesting ruin is the mighty **Amphitheatre**, one of the empire's largest with a seating capacity of nearly 25,000. Follow the fighters' path from the holding room where the rules of the games, carved in metal, still hang on the wall. You can also walk through the musty tunnels under the stands until they spit you into the shadeless ring at the mercy of the unforgiving crowd and Andalusian sun. Treading the grid of ancient streets, you'll find fragments of columns and porticos leading into the intricately patterned floors of dignitaries' homes. There is also a **House of Birds,** with 30 bird species depicted in lightly-restored mosaic, and a **House of the Planetarium,** with seven planetary divinities representing the days of the week. Trajan, the first emperor from a Roman province, left his mark with these impressive works and the construction of the city's **smaller baths,** not quite as well-preserved as the mosaics. Hadrian, however, was motivated to one-up his father, and commissioned the building of **larger baths,** less decayed and not as much of a trek to reach from the main city.

SEVILLA

ANDALUCÍA

Andalucía is Spain at its best. The region is home to bullfighting and flamenco, Moorish arches and church spires, medieval castles and Roman ruins, sun-drenched beaches and expanses of olive groves—in other words, all things quintessentially Spain. This consistently intoxicating mix of Roman, Moorish, and gypsy cultures can be experienced anywhere from the metropolises of Sevilla and Granada to the tiny mountain villages in the Sierra Nevada.

The ancient kingdom of Tartessus—which some say is the same Tarshish mentioned in the Bible for its fabulous troves of silver—grew wealthy off the Sierra Nevada's rich ore deposits. The Greeks and Phoenicians established colonies here and traded up and down the coast, and the Romans later cultivated wheat, olive oil, and wine from the fertile soil watered by the Guadalquivir. In the 5th century AD, the Vandals passed through on their way to North Africa, leaving little more than a name—Vandalusia (House of the Vandals). The Moors, who arrived in 711 and didn't leave until 1492, had a more enduring influence, establishing firm ties to Africa and the Islamic world and developing flamenco and gypsy ballads. The Moors also preserved and perfected Roman architecture, created the distinctive Andalusian patio, furthered the paper industry, and built up the region's greatest cities; Sevilla and Granada reached the pinnacle of Islamic arts, while Córdoba matured into the most culturally influential medieval Muslim city.

Even in the turbulent 20th century, Andalucía retained its strength and solidarity—the region prides itself on having been one of the last strongholds against Franco during the Civil War. Many residents of the area still describe themselves as Andalusian rather than Spanish, and proudly live in the blend of cultures that first made the region famous. As for visitors, whether they come to wander the medieval streets of the *juderías* (Jewish quarters), roast in the sun on the shores of the Atlantic, clap along with a *sevillana*, or eat tons of *jamón* (ham), they are sure to remember Andalucía.

HIGHLIGHTS OF ANDALUCÍA

SCRUB like a sultan in the Arab baths of **Córdoba** (p. 242).

SAMPLE enough sherry to get sufficiently silly in **Jerez de la Frontera** (p. 251).

SIGH like the last of the royal Moors when you too must leave **Granada** (p. 296).

DWELL in caves that double as hotels in **Guadix** (p. 307).

CÓRDOBA ☎957

Abundant courtyards, flowers dripping from balconies, and narrow, winding streets make Córdoba (pop. 310,000) a captivating and unhurried city. Perched on the southern bank of the Río Guadalquivir, it was once the largest city in Western Europe and for three centuries, the hub of the Moorish Empire, and capital of the mighty Umayyad Caliphate, rivaled only by Baghdad and Cairo. Córdoba preserves its past glory with monuments of Roman, Jewish, Islamic, and Christian origin; only in Toledo are the remnants of Spain's colorful heritage as visibly intermixed. The *judería* is one of Spain's oldest Jewish quarters, containing one of the three remaining synagogues on the Iberian peninsula, and the 14th-century Palacio del Marqués de Viana anticipates Spain's Golden Age by two centuries.

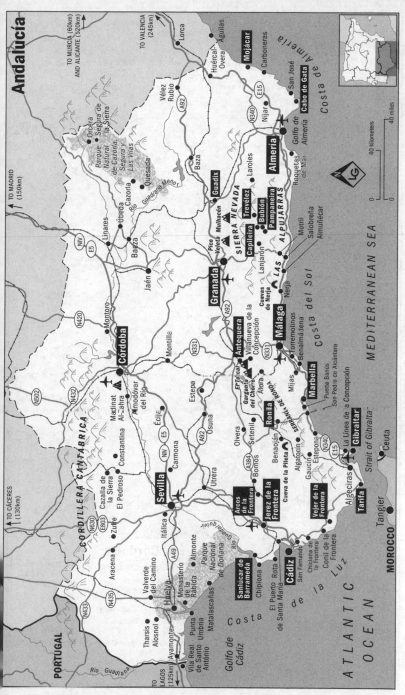

ANDALUCÍA

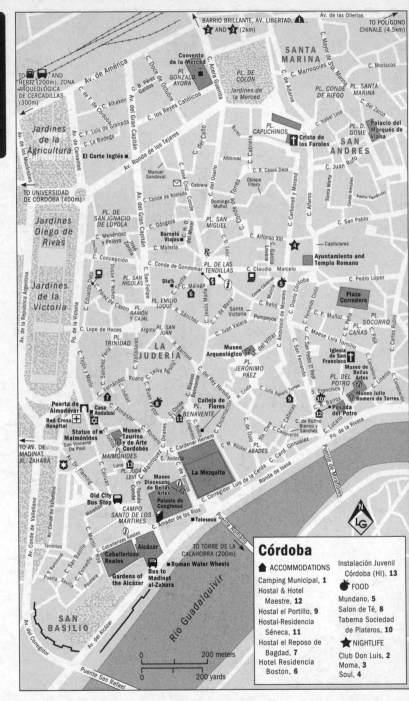

Córdoba

▲ ACCOMMODATIONS

Camping Municipal, **1**

Hostal & Hotel
  Maestre, **12**

Hostal el Portillo, **9**

Hostal-Residencia
  Séneca, **11**

Hostal el Reposo de
  Bagdad, **7**

Hotel Residencia
  Boston, **6**

Instalación Juvenil
  Córdoba (HI), **13**

🍴 FOOD

Mundano, **5**

Salon de Té, **8**

Taberna Sociedad
  de Plateros, **10**

★ NIGHTLIFE

Club Don Luis, **2**

Moma, **3**

Soul, **4**

Spectacular scenery, fountains, and gastronomic specialties such as *salmorejo* (a thicker version of gazpacho) and *rabo de toro* (bull's tail), leave visitors in awe.

TRANSPORTATION

Trains: Pl. de las Tres Culturas (☎957 40 02 02, 902 24 02 02), off Av. de América. To: **Algeciras** via **Bobadilla** (3 per day 10:38am and 7:06pm, €18-39); **Barcelona** (10-11hr., 4 per day 10am-10:52pm, €50-76); **Cádiz** (2½hr., 12:10-6:25pm, €23.60); **Madrid** (2-4hr., 21-33 per day 7:13am-11:44pm, €45.30-46.60); **Málaga** (2-3hr., 5 per day 9:07am-10:12pm, €11.25-22); **Sevilla** (45min., 4-8 per day 6:50am-9:30pm, €7.80-14.20). For tickets, visit the **RENFE** office, Av. Ronda de los Tejares, 10.

Buses: Estación de Autobuses (☎957 40 40 40), on Glorieta de las Tres Culturas across from the train station.

Alsina Graells Sur (☎957 27 81 00) to: **Algeciras** (5hr.; 8am, 3:15pm; €22.57); **Almería** (5hr., 8am, €22.71); **Antequera** (2½hr.; 9am, 4pm; €8.14); **Cádiz** (4-5hr.; M-F 10am, 6pm; Sa-Su 10am; €20.34); **Granada** (3-4hr.; M-Sa 9-10 per day 8am-7pm, Su 11 per day 8am-8:30pm; €11.71); **Málaga** (3-3½hr.; 5 per day 8am-7pm, more frequent June-Aug; €12).

Bacoma (☎902 42 22 42) goes to: **Barcelona** (10hr., 3 per day 5:15pm-12:35am, €62.64); **Baeza** (3½hr.; 12:20, 5:15pm; €9.36); and **Valencia** (4 per day 12:20pm-12:35am, €41-43).

Secorbus (☎902 22 92 92) runs cheap buses to **Madrid** (4½hr., 3-6 per day 1am-6pm, €13.50).

Transportes Ureña (☎957 40 45 58) runs to **Jaén** (2hr.; 7-8 per day M-Sa 7:30am-8pm, Su 6 per day 10am-8pm; €7.76). **Autocares Priego** (☎957 40 44 79), **Empresa Carrera** (☎957 40 44 14), and **Empresa Rafael Ramírez** (☎957 42 21 77) run buses to surrounding towns and campsites.

Local Transportation: 12 bus lines (☎957 25 57 00) cover the city, running from the wee hours until 11pm. Bus #3 makes a loop from the bus and train stations through Pl. de las Tendillas, up to the Santuario, and back along the river and up C. Dr. Fleming. Bus #10 runs from the train station to Barrio Brillante. Buy tickets on board. €0.90.

Taxis: Radio Taxi (☎957 76 44 44). From the bus and train stations to the *judería* €3-5. Night service min. charge €3.80.

Car Rental: Hertz (☎957 40 20 61; www.hertz.com), in the bus station. 25+. Compact car €70 per day. Open M-F 8:30am-2pm and 5-9pm, Sa 9am-2pm.

ORIENTATION

Córdoba is divided into the new city and the old. The modern, commercial northern half extends from the train station on Av. de América down to **Plaza de las Tedillas**, the center of the city. The section in the south is a medieval maze known as the **Judería** (Jewish quarter). This tangle of disorienting streets extends from Pl. de las Tendillas to the banks of the Río Guadalquivir, winding past the **Mezquita** and **Alcázar.** The easiest way to reach the old city from the train or bus station is a 20min. walk. From the train station, with your back to the platforms, exit thought the left doors, then turn right and cross the parking lot. Continue right onto Av. de los Mozárabes. It's best to walk in the middle of the boulevard and through the gardens, **Jardines de la Victoria.** When the gardens end, the **Puerta Almodóvar,** one of the entrances into la Judería, will be on the left.

PRACTICAL INFORMATION

Tourist Offices: Andalucía Regional Office, C. Torrijos, 10 (☎957 35 51 79). From the train station, take bus #3 along the river until the Puente Romano. Walk under the stone arch and the office will be on your left. Free maps. Open July-Aug. M-F 9:30am-7:30pm, Sa 10am-7:30pm, Su 10am-2pm; Sept.-June M-Sa 9am-7:30pm, Su 10am-

2pm. **Turismo de Córdoba** (☎902 20 17 74; www.turismodecordoba.org) has booths in the train station (open daily 9:30am-2pm and 5-8pm), on C. Caballerizas Reales (open daily 9:30am-2:30pm and 5-8pm), and in Pl. de Tendillas (open daily 10am-1:30pm and 6-9:30pm). Offers tours and city-wide audioguide (www.thisis.ws; €15).

Currency Exchange: Banco Santander Central Hispano, Pl. de las Tendillas, 1 (☎902 24 24 24). Open M-F 8:30am-2pm, Sa 8:30am-1pm.

Luggage Storage: At the bus station. €2 per day. Open 24hr.

Laundry: Teleseco, Ronda de Isasa, 10 (☎957 48 33 56), 1 block from La Mezquita, near the river. Coin service and dry cleaning. Washers €4.80, dryers €3. Full service with wash, dry, and fold €10.82.

Budget Travel Agency: Barceló Viajes, C. Historiador Díaz del Moral, 1 (☎957 48 55 55; www.barceloviajes.com), on the corner on C. Morería. Open M-F 9:30am-1:30pm and 5-8:30pm, Sa 10am-1:30pm.

Police: Av. Doctor Fleming, 2 (☎092 or 957 23 87 00).

Medical Services: Red Cross Hospital, Po. de la Victoria, near Puerta de Almodóvar (☎957 42 06 66, emergencies 22 22 22). English spoken.

Library: C. Amador de los Rios, a block from the Mezquita (☎957 35 54 92). Free **Internet** access on 1st and 2nd floors. Open M-F 9am-9pm.

Internet Access: Tele-Click, C. Eduardo Dato, 9 (☎957 94 06 15). New machines, A/C, and assorted refreshments. €1.80 per hour, €0.50 per 15min. Open M-F 10am-3pm and 5:30-10:30pm, Sa-Su noon-11pm. **Ch@t-is,** C. Claudio Marcelo, 15 (☎957 47 45 00). €1.80 per hour; *bonos* from €9 per 10 hours. Fax and copies available (€0.06-0.40, discount for students). Open M-F 10am-2pm and 5:30-9pm.

Post Office: C. José Cruz Conde, 15 (☎957 47 97 96). **Lista de Correos.** Open M-F 8:30am-8:30pm, Sa-Su 9:30am-2pm. **Postal Code:** 14070.

ACCOMMODATIONS

Hostels abound in *la judería* and between La Mezquita and Calle de San Fernando. Córdoba is especially crowded during *Semana Santa*, May, and June, and then dies down during the months of July and August. Still, it is generally advisable to call in advance for reservations. Prices are higher in summer.

IN AND AROUND THE JUDERÍA

The *judería*'s whitewashed walls and proximity to sights make it a great place to stay. During the day, souvenir booths and cafes keep the streets lively, but the area feels more deserted at night. Take bus #5 from the train station to the "Hotel Melia" stop across the street from the Puerta de Almodóvar. Go under the archway to reach the neighborhood.

Instalación Juvenil Córdoba (HI), Pl. Judá Levi, down C. Judios from Puerta Almodóvar (☎957 29 01 66). A mental asylum converted into a backpacker's paradise. Large rooms have bath and A/C. Courtyards surrounded by orange trees and graffiti art. Breakfast included. Lockers €1.80-2 per day. Towels €1.20. Laundry €2.50, dry €1.50. Mar.-Oct. €18.50-€19.50; Nov.-Feb. €2.10 less. HI discount €3.50. MC/V. ❶

Hostal-Residencia Séneca, C. Conde y Luque, 7 (☎957 47 32 34). A beautiful courtyard (and tourists poking through the gate to take pictures) greets you at the entrance. Fans or A/C. Room size differs greatly, so ask to see one first. Breakfast included; special breakfast on Su. Singles €19-25, with bath €32-37; doubles €35-43/42-50; triples and 1 huge quad €89. MC/V. ❷

ANDALUCÍA

BETWEEN LA MEZQUITA AND CALLE DE SAN FERNANDO

■ **Hostal El Reposo de Bagdad,** Fernandez Ruano, 11 (☎957 20 28 54; hostal-el-reposo-bagdad@wanadoo.es). A beautiful Islamic-inspired hostel with large sunlit rooms with bathroom and fan. Pillow-strewn corner where you can eat breakfast in the morning (€3.50) and smoke hookah after dark. Singles €20; doubles €37. ❷

Hostal el Portillo, C. Cabezas, 2 (☎957 47 20 91; www.hostalelportillo.com). A traditional, yet quirkily decorated Andalusian house in a quieter part of the neighborhood. Spacious rooms with wrought-iron beds, bath, and A/C, some have balconies. Singles €18-20; doubles €30-35. MC/V. ❷

Hostal and Hotel Maestre, C. Romero Barros, 6 (☎/fax 957 47 53 95), off C. de San Fernando. Both the hotel and hostal have similar royal-hued decor, but the hostal's corridors, a maze of Spanish trinkets, are more unique. All rooms with private bath and A/C, most with TV. Breakfast buffet €5. *Hostal* singles €23-28; doubles €30-40. Hotel singles €30-38; doubles €42-50. MC/V. ❷

ELSEWHERE

Hotel Residencia Boston, C. Málaga, 2 (☎957 47 41 76; www.hostel-boston.com), a 10min. walk from the *judería*. Plain rooms equipped with A/C, TV, phone, safe, and bath. Breakfast in large dining room and lounge area €4. Internet €1 per 30min. Singles €32-35; doubles €50-57. AmEx/D/MC/V. ❸

Camping Municipal, Av. del Brillante, 50 (☎957 40 38 36). From the train station, turn left on Av. de América, left on Av. del Brillante, and walk uphill (20min.). Bus #10 and 11 from Av. Cervantes stop across the street. Supermarket, restaurant, hot showers. Laundry €3. 1 person and tent €17.66; 2 people and tent €17.66; 2 people, car, and tent €19.05; 2 people and camper €19.05. IVA not included. Cash only. ❷

◘ FOOD

Touristy restaurants have taken over the Mezquita area, but a 5min. walk in any direction yields local spots with reasonable prices. In the evenings, locals converge at the outdoor *terrazao* between **Calle Severo Ochoa** and **Calle Dr. Jiménez Díaz** for drinks and tapas. Cheap eateries are farther from the *judería* in **Barrio Cruz Conde** and around **Avenida Menéndez Pidal** and **Plaza de las Tendillas.** Regional specialties include *salmorejo* (a gazpacho-like cream soup topped with hard-boiled egg and pieces of ham) and *rabo de toro* (bull's tail simmered in tomato sauce). For groceries, try **%Dia,** on C. Sevilla, 4, near Pl. de las Tendillas. (Open M-Sa 9am-3pm and 5:30-9pm.) **El Corte Inglés,** Av. Ronda de los Tejares, 30, has a supermarket on the bottom floor. (Open M-Sa 10am-10pm. AmEx/MC/V.)

■ **Taberna Sociedad de Plateros,** C. San Francisco, 6 (☎957 47 00 42). A mainstay since 1872, this place has the biggest *raciones* for the best price (€4.80-14.80); a half-*ración* of salad can serve as a filling lunch. Open M-F 8am-3:45pm and 8-11:45pm, Sa 8am-3:45pm and 7:30-1:45pm. AmEx/MC/V. ❷

Mundano, C. Conde de Cárdenas, 3 (☎957 47 37 85). Back-alley locale combines homemade fare with funky style and art shows. Breakfast (€1.50-1.80), tapas (gazpacho €1.10), teas, and entrees (€3-5). Vegetarian options. Live music some weekends. Open M-F 10am-5pm and 10pm-2am, Sa noon-6pm and 10pm-2am. Cash only. ❶

Salon de Té, C. Buen Pastor (☎957 48 79 84). Lie back on satin pillows in this recreated 12th-century teahouse while savoring a huge selection of teas, juices, and Arabian pastries. Try the mint-lemonade for a refreshing variation on a summer favorite (€2.30). Open daily 11am-10:30pm. Cash only. ❶

◎ SIGHTS

▨ LA MEZQUITA

☎ 957 47 91 70; fax 957 47 05 12. Open Mar.-Oct. M-Sa 8:30am-7pm, Su 8:30-10:30am and 2-7pm. €8, 10-14 €4, under 10 free. Wheelchair accessible. Last ticket sold 30min. before closing. Mass M-Sa 8:30-10am, Su 11am and 1pm. Take advantage of the free admission M-Sa 8:30-10am (during mass). Silence is enforced; no groups.

Built in AD 784 on the site of a Visigoth basilica, this masterpiece is considered the most important Islamic monument in the Western world. Over the course of two centuries, La Mezquita was enlarged to cover an area the size of several city blocks. With more than 850 columns it was the third-largest mosque in the Islamic world at the time (after Mecca and Medina).

Visitors enter through the **Patio de los Naranjos,** an arcaded courtyard featuring carefully spaced orange trees, palms, and fountains, where the dutiful performed their ablutions before prayer. The **Torre del Alminar** encloses remains of the minaret from which the *muezzin* called the faithful to prayer. The grand **entrances** to the mosque were closed during its conversion to a Gothic cathedral, and today you must enter through the right corner of the facade.

Beginning in the oldest part of the mosque, built under Abd Al-Rahman I, the multiple pillars carved from granite and marble are capped by striped arches. La Mezquita's most elaborate additions—the dazzling **mihrab** (prayer niche) and the triple **maksourah** (caliph's niche)—were created in the 10th century. Holy Roman Emperor Constantine VII gave the nearly 35 tons of intricate gold, pink, and blue marble Byzantine mosaics that shimmer across the arches of the *mihrab* to the caliphs. The *mihrab* formerly housed a gilt copy of the Qur'an and remains covered in Kufic inscriptions reciting the 99 names of Allah. To this day, historians remain stumped as to why the structure does not face Mecca, since Muslim architects had highly precise methods of calculation, and such a "mistake" was unlikely. Nevertheless, prayers continue in the traditional direction.

At the far end of the Mezquita lies the **Capilla Villaviciosa,** which in 1371 was the first Christian chapel to be built in the mosque, thus beginning the transition into a place of Christian worship. In 1523, Bishop Alonso Manriquez, an ally of Carlos V, proposed the construction of a cathedral in the center of the mosque. The town rallied violently against the idea, promising painful death to any worker who helped tear down La Mezquita. The bishop nevertheless erected a towering **crucero** (transept) and **coro** (choir stall), incongruously planting a richly adorned Baroque cathedral amid far more austere environs.

The cathedral's most noteworthy part is the choir, which depicts the entire Bible in mahogany panels. Its maker, Duque Cornejo, died only weeks before completing his masterpiece and lies buried right in the middle of the stall. On one side of the transept, the angel Raphael (the protector of Córdoba), watches over the faithful, proud that his is the most popular male name in the city.

IN AND AROUND THE JUDERÍA

A combined ticket for the Alcázar, Museo Taurino y de Arte Cordobés, and Museo Julio Romero is available at all 3 locations. €7.10, students €3.60. F free.

▨ **ALCÁZAR DE LOS REYES CRISTIANOS.** Along the river, to the left of La Mezquita, lies the Alcázar, built in 1328 during the *Reconquista*. Fernando and Isabel bade Columbus farewell here (commemorated by the towering statue in the gardens), and from 1490 to 1821, it served as a headquarters for the Inquisition. The museum displays first-century Roman mosaics and a marble sarcophagus. Don't leave without visiting the endless gardens with hedges, flowers, dancing fountains, and fish pools. *Cordobeses* come to cool down in this tranquil setting, which also serves as a stage for concerts. *(☎957 42 01 51. Open Tu-Sa 8:30am-2:30pm, Su and holidays 9:30am-2:30pm. €4, students €2; F free. Gardens open June 21-Sept. 8pm-midnight. €2. Free.)*

CASA ANDALUSÍ. A restored 12th-century house, this private museum boasts a Visigothic basement with mosaic floors, a gorgeous flower-filled fountain, old Arabic texts and coins, and an interesting display on Córdoba's role in the rise of paper-making, complete with replicas of the old tools used in the process. *(C. Judíos, 12, near the synagogue. ☎957 29 06 42; sandalus@hotmail.com. Schedule varies, but usually open daily 10:30am-8:30pm. €2.50, students €1.50.)*

SINAGOGA. Built in 1315, the synagogue, where famed philosopher Maimonides (1135-1204) once prayed, is a hollow remnant of Córdoba's once-vibrant Jewish community. Adorned with carved Mozárabe patterns and Hebrew inscriptions, the walls of the small temple have been restored to much of their original intricacy. *(C. Judíos, 20, just past the statue of Maimonides. ☎957 20 29 28. Open Tu-Sa 9:30am-2pm and 3:30-5:30pm, Su 9:30-1:30pm. €0.30, EU citizens free.)*

MUSEO TAURINO Y DE ARTE CORDOBÉS. Get ready for a lot of bull. Dedicated to the history and lore of the bullfight, rooms contain uniforms, posters, and artifacts from decades of bullfighting in Spain. The main exhibit includes a replica of the tomb of Spain's most famous *matador*, the dashing Manolete (1917-1947), and the hide of the bull that killed him. The museum is currently undergoing renovations and is set to reopen in 2008. *(Pl. Maimónides. ☎957 20 10 56. Open Tu-Sa 10:30am-2pm and 5:30-7:30pm, Su 9:30am-2pm. Last entry 15min. before closing. €3, students €1.50; F free.)*

OTHER SIGHTS. Townspeople take great pride in their traditional **patios,** many of which date from Roman times. Among the most beautiful streets are **Calleja del Indiano,** off C. Fernández Ruano at Pl. Ángel Torres, and the **Calleja de Flores,** off C. Blanco Belmonte, where geraniums cluster along the walls of the alley.

OUTSIDE THE JUDERÍA

MUSEO JULIO ROMERO DE TORRES. Romero (1874-1930) mastered the subtleties of mixing a dark palette and applied this talent to renditions of sensual *cordobés* women. Among the dozens of works exhibited here in the artist's former home is the lauded *Naranjas y limones* (oranges and lemons). *(Pl. Potro, 5-10min. from La Mezquita. ☎957 49 19 09. Open Tu-Sa 8:30am-2:30pm, Su and holidays 9:30am-2:30pm. Last entry 30min. before closing. €4, students €2. F free.)*

MUSEO DE BELLAS ARTES. Across the courtyard from Museo Julio Romero de Torres, this museum occupies a building that served as a hospital during the reign of Fernando and Isabel. It hosts a mildly unsettling collection of morbid Renaissance religious art as well as works by more modern *cordobés* artists. *(Pl. Potro, 5-10min. from La Mezquita. ☎957 47 33 45. Open Tu 2:30-8:30pm, W-Sa 9am-8:30pm, Su and holidays 9am-2:30pm. Last entry 20min. before closing. €1.50, EU citizens free.)*

PALACIO DEL MARQUÉS DE VIANA. An elegant 14th-century mansion, the palace displays 12 typical patios complete with sprawling gardens, majestic fountains, tapestries, furniture, and porcelain. *(Pl. Don Gome, 2, a 20min. walk from La Mezquita. ☎957 49 67 41. Open July-Sept. M-Sa 9am-2pm; Oct.-June M-F 10am-1pm and 4-6pm, Sa 10am-1pm. Closed June 1-16. Complete tour €6, garden and courtyards only €3.)*

OTHER SIGHTS. Near the Palacio del Marqués de Viana in Pl. Capuchinos (also known as Pl. de los Dolores) and next to a monastery is the **Cristo de los Faroles** (Christ of the Lanterns), one of the most famous religious icons in Spain and the site of all-night vigils. The eight lanterns lit at night symbolize the eight provinces of Andalucía. Facing the Museo de Bellas Artes and the Museo Julio Romero de Torres is the **Posada del Potro,** a 14th-century inn mentioned in *Don Quixote*. (☎902 20 17 74. *Open daily 9:30am-2pm and 5-8pm. Closed for renovations until 2009. Free.)* Remnants of 2nd-century **Roman water wheels** line the sides of the Río Guadalquivir. Believed to have been used by Romans as mills, they were later used to bring water to the caliph's palace. The mills continued to function until Isabel la Católica demanded they be shut down—they disturbed her sleep.

🎵 NIGHTLIFE

Nightlife is almost nonexistent in the old city, and hip bars and clubs tend to cluster together. Nearest to the old city, **Calle Alfonso XIII** and the adjacent **Calle Alfaros** host a limited number of options. Farther away, the **Barrio Brillante** is a true nightlife hot spot, though its bars and clubs tend to open only on weekends. Bus #10 goes to Brillante from the train station until about 11pm, but the bars are empty until 1am and stay open until 4am. A taxi costs about €3-6. If you're walking, it's a 45min. uphill hike. **Avenida Libertad,** close to the Brillante, offers a more chic (and costly) ambience with its palette of diverse but consistently gorgeous pubs.

In the winter, nightlife centers around the neighborhood where the Universidad de Córdoba used to be, especially in pubs on **Calle Los Alderetes** and **Calle Julio Pellicer,** and near the **Plaza de la Corredera.** An alternative to partying is a stroll (after 10pm) along the 🖼walk-through fountains and falling sheets of water that line Av. de América between Pl. de Colón and the train station, to cool off from the heat.

🖼 **Soul,** C. Alfonso XIII, 3 (☎957 49 15 80; www.bar-soul.com). Spontaneous dancing springs up amidst the late-20- and 30-something crowd. Bring your earplugs or a fever for bass. Free Wi-Fi. Beer €2.10. Mixed drinks €3.60-4.50. Open daily 9am-2pm and 4pm-3am, later on weekends. Cash only.

Moma, Av. Libertad, 4. This ethnic-chic bar has African-styled stools and fake mosaic lamp shades. Beer €2-2.50. Mixed drinks from €5. Open M-W and Su 9am-3am, Th-Sa 9am-5am. AmEx/MC/V.

Club Don Luis, Av. del Brillante, 18. Trendy club draws local university students who dance to Spanish pop. Though there's a large outdoor terrace, most people pack inside. Beer €2.50. Mixed drinks €5. Open Th-Sa midnight-4:30am. Cash only.

🎭 ENTERTAINMENT

For the latest cultural events, pick up a free copy of the *Guía del Ocio* at the tourist office. Though flamenco is not cheap in Córdoba, the shows are high-quality and worth a visit for those not heading to Sevilla. Prize-winning dancers perform at **Tablao Cardenal,** C. Torrijos, 10, facing La Mezquita. Reserve seats there or at your hostel. (☎957 48 33 20; www.tablaocardenal.com. Shows M-Sa 10:30pm. Cover €18, includes one drink.) A cheaper but equally entertaining option is **La Bulería,** C. Pedro López, 3, with nightly shows also at 10:30pm. (☎957 48 38 39. €11, includes 1 drink.) Every July, Córdoba hosts a guitar festival, bringing talent from all over the world. Many concerts are free; check at the tourist office.

🏛 DAYTRIP FROM CÓRDOBA

MADINAT AL-ZAHRA
Bravo buses leave from Po. de la Victoria or in front of the Alcázar on Av. del Alcázar. A video with English subtitles plays on the ride. (30min.; Tu-Sa 11am and 6pm, Sa also 10am, Su 10,

*11am; €6, reserve tickets at a Turismo de Córdoba office or at most accommodations.)
Buses return to Córdoba 1½hr. after arriving in al-Zahra. Visión Córdoba offers transportation
and 1½hr. tour in both Spanish and English (☎957 76 02; natalia@cordobavision.com; Tu-Su
at 10:30am, €28). Alternatively, Bus #1 leaves from Po. de la Victoria; get off at Cruz de
Madinat al-Zahra for a 3km walk to the ruins. (☎957 35 55 06/07; www.juntadeandalu-
cia.es/cultura/madinatalzahra. Open May-Sept. 15 Tu-Sa 10am-8:30pm, Su 10am-2pm;
Sept. 16-Apr. Tu-Sa 10am-6:30pm, Su 10am-2pm. €1.50, EU citizens free.)*

In 940, the self-appointed caliph Abd ar-Rahman III decided to move the region's
seat of power 7km to the northwest of Córdoba. There, with the muscle of an estimated 10,000 workers and 3000 pack animals, the ruler constructed an indulgent
277-acre wonderland of courtyards, gardens, porticos, and salons in a symbolic
effort to strengthen and reunify the steadily diminishing Moorish empire. Legend,
on the other hand, attributes the grand palace-town to the caliph's desire to
impress his favorite concubine, al-Zahra. Weakened by an internal power stuggle,
the medina was soon ransacked by civil mobs and foreign Berber armies; its precious colored marble, swirling columns, and jasper were looted. In less than 80
years, al-Zahra's glory faded completely. Looting continued into the 14th century.

The ruins are worth a visit for the historically intrigued, but don't expect its dazzling former grandeur. The restoration process is ongoing; almost 90% of al-Zahra
is still hidden underground. Once you enter through the gate, you'll be standing
atop the town's third and highest terrace, offering a bird's eye view of the medina
and miniscule Córdoba below. Follow the city wall, reconstructed in 1920s, into
the old town, keeping left until you reach the site where the mosque once stood.
Although you can't reach the lower terrace, you can admire the excavated earthen
foundation paved with flagstones in the caliph's prayer nave. A minaret once stood
high above the sloping landscape, calling those in al-Zahra and Córdoba's Alcázar
to prayer. The most striking part of the ruins is the caliph's royal reception hall.
The High Garden, one terrace above the Lower Gardens, is a structural part of the
hall and is a kind of organic red carpet for any worthy enough to be greeted by the
ruler. Palm trees, hedges, and flowers were replanted in the 1920s to emphasize
the geometrical mazes that once held murmuring fountains and an aviary. Inaccessible to the general public, the gardens are best viewed from the top terrace.

COSTA DE LA LUZ

While most of Andalucía is the domain of foreign tourists seeking wild nightlife
and miles of beaches, the Costa de la Luz remains a destination populated primarily by Spanish vacationers looking for some fun in the sun. Beyond the *bodegas* of
Jerez de la Frontera, the region offers picture-perfect *pueblos blancos* (white
towns), opportunities to catch some wind or waves, and the golden light that is its
namesake. Backed by dry pines and golden-hued dunes of fine sand, the expansive
beaches of Costa de la Luz are home to strong winds and waves that make it a paradise for windsurfers and surfboarders. Less developed than other vacation destinations, this region is also known for its wealth of protected natural reserves.

JEREZ DE LA FRONTERA　　　　　　　☎956

Jerez de la Frontera (pop. 200,000) is the cradle of three staples of Andalusian culture: flamenco, Carthusian horses, and, of course, *jerez* (sherry). The sheer quantity and quality of the third staple draws hordes of tourists, most of whom are
older Europeans. On the other end of the spectrum, the newest generations of flamenco performers take the stage throughout the city and give live rhythmic form
to *el duende* (soul, emotion) itself. Jerez also makes a good departure point for

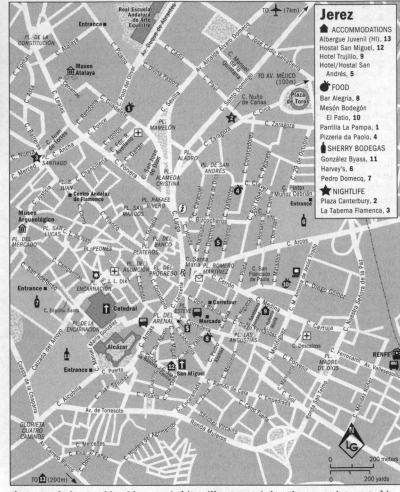

Jerez

🏠 ACCOMMODATIONS
Albergue Juvenil (HI), **13**
Hostal San Miguel, **12**
Hotel Trujillo, **9**
Hotel/Hostal San
Andrés, **5**

🍴 FOOD
Bar Alegría, **8**
Mesón Bodegón
El Patio, **10**
Parrilla La Pampa, **1**
Pizzeria da Paolo, **4**

🍷 SHERRY BODEGAS
González Byass, **11**
Harvey's, **6**
Pedro Domecq, **7**

⭐ NIGHTLIFE
Plaza Canterbury, **2**
La Taberna Flamenca, **3**

the *ruta de los pueblos blancos* (white village route), but those not interested in *bodega* tours or horse shows would be wise to make Jerez a daytrip.

📧 TRANSPORTATION

Flights: Jerez Airport, Ctra. Jerez-Sevilla (☎956 15 00 00; www.aena.es), 7km from town. Taxi to the airport about €15. Airport shuttle (☎96 01 21 00; www.cmtbc.com). **Iberia** (☎956 18 43 94) has an office at the terminal. Most international flights connect to Jerez through Sevilla or Madrid.

Trains: Pl. de la Estación (☎956 34 23 19). **RENFE,** C. Larga, 34 (☎902 24 02 02). To: **Barcelona** (12hr.; 8:22am and 8:10pm; €73); **Cádiz** (45min.; M-F 18 per day 6:30am-10:25pm, Sa 4 per day 8:31am-5:29pm, Su 5 per day 8:31am-5:29pm;

€3.10); **Madrid** (4½hr.; 8:22am and 5:02pm; €53.50); **Sevilla** (1¼hr.; M-F 12 per day 7:39am-10:08pm, Sa 4 per day 7:39am-3:46pm, Su 5 per day 7:39am-3:46pm; €6).

Buses: Pl. de la Estación, recently built next to the train station (☎956 33 96 66).

Linesur (☎956 34 10 63; www.linesur.com) to: **Algeciras** (1¾hr.; 7 M-F 9 per day 7:15am-9:45pm, Sa-Su 7 per day 8:30am-9:45pm; €7.60); **Sanlúcar** (45min.; M-F hourly 7am-9pm, Sa-Su every 2hr. 9am-9pm; €1.50); **Sevilla** (1¼hr., 7-10 per day 6:30am-10:30pm, €5.80).

Secorbus (☎956 34 59 71; www.socibus.es) to **Madrid** (5hr., 6 per day 8:50am-11:50pm, €21.30).

Transportes Generales Comes (☎956 32 14 64 or 902 19 92 08; www.tgcomes.es) service to: **Cádiz** (50min.; M-F 22 per day 7am-11:15pm, Sa-Su 11 per day 7am-11:15pm; €2.75); **Granada** (4½hr., 1pm, €25); **Ronda** (2½hr., 3-6 per day 9:45am-7pm, €9.20); **Sevilla** (1½hr.; M-Sa 5 per day 9am-11:30pm, Su 4 per day 10:30am-11:30pm; €6).

Transportes Los Amarillos (☎956 32 93 47 or 902 21 03 17; www.losamarillos.es) to **Arcos de la Frontera** (30min.; M-F 19 per day 7am-9pm, Sa 9 per day 7:45am-8:15pm, Su 11 per day 9am-9pm; €2.10).

Public Transportation: Most of the 15 bus lines run every 15-20min. (less frequently at night). Most pass through Pl. del Arenal or next to Pl. Romero Martínez. €1. **Info office** (☎956 34 34 46) in Pl. del Arenal.

Car Rental: Niza, Ctra. N. IV Madrid-Cádiz, Km. 634 (☎956 30 28 60 or 956 18 15 75; www.nizacars.es). Take Av. Alcalde Álvaro Domecq to Hwy. N-IV toward Sevilla (next to El Corte Inglés). 21+ and must have had license for at least 1 year. From €67 per day. Open daily 8:30am-8pm. AmEx/MC/V. **Bahía Rent A Car,** in the train station in Pl. de la Estación (☎956 32 25 92 or 669 86 17 89). Open M-F 9:30am-1:30pm and 5-8pm, Sa 9:30am-1:30pm. AmEx/MC/V. There are car rental agencies at the airport.

Taxis: Teletaxi (☎956 34 48 60).

ORIENTATION AND PRACTICAL INFORMATION

The streets of Jerez are difficult to navigate without a map. Get a free one from the tourist office or at any one of the major sights or *bodegas*. **Plaza Romero Martínez** is the city's center. **Calle Lancería/Calle Larga** is the main pedestrian road in the center of the city, and *bodegas* are scattered along the outskirts of the old city.

Tourist Office: Pl. Alameda Cristina (☎956 34 17 11). Open M-F 10am-3pm and 5-7pm, Sa-Su 10am-2:30pm.

Bank: Banco Santander Central Hispano, on the north side of Pl. del Arenal (☎902 24 24 24). Open M-F 8:30am-2pm, Sa 8:30am-1pm. A slew of banks also lines C. Larga.

Police: On Pl. Encarnación (☎092 or 956 33 03 46).

Medical Assistance: Ambulatorio de la Seguridad Social, C. José Luis Díaz (☎956 32 32 02).

Pharmacy: Central, C. Larga, 38 (☎956 34 28 93). Open M-Sa 9:30am-10pm.

Internet Access: The Big Orange, C. M. Antonía de Jesús Tirado (☎956 35 01 01), near the bus station. €1.80 per hour. Open M-Th and Su 11am-1am, F-Sa 11am-3am. **Cyber Jerez,** C. Santa Maria, 3 (www.cyberjerez.com). €0.03 per min. Open M-Sa 10am-2:30pm and 5:30-11pm, Su and holidays 5-11pm.

Post Office: C. Cerrón, 2 (☎956 34 22 95). Open M-F 8:30am-8:30pm, Sa 9am-2pm. **Lista de Correos** open M-Sa 8:30am-8:30pm. **Postal Code:** 11480.

ACCOMMODATIONS

Finding a place to crash in Jerez is as easy as finding a wine cork to sniff, but, like the local wine, it won't come cheap. Prices double during the festivals in the fall.

ANDALUCÍA

Hostal San Miguel, Pl. San Miguel, 4 (☎/fax 956 34 85 62; hostalsm@aena.com), behind the church. Marble embellishments and statues center around a glass-roofed courtyard. Pleasant, spacious rooms with A/C and TV. Ask for a balcony view of the church. Singles €21, with bath €32; doubles €7/42; triples €58/63. AmEx/MC/V. ❷

Hotel/Hostal San Andrés, C. Morenos, 12-14 (☎956 34 09 83; www.hotelsanandres.es). Some of the cheapest digs in the city in a central location. Rooms provide the basics; the adjacent hotel, with TV common room, offers pricier rooms with private baths, A/C, and TV. *Hostal* singles €20; doubles €28. Hotel €24/38. AmEx/MC/V. ❷

Hotel Trujillo, C. Medina, 36 (☎ 956 34 24 38; www.hoteltrujillo.com/net). The friendly staff complements the hotel's quiet locale. Rooms have wooden bed frames, private baths, TV, and enough space to flamenco in. High season singles €35; doubles €50. Low season €28/42. AmEx/MC/V. ❸

Albergue Juvenil (HI), Av. Blase Infante, 30 (☎856 81 40 01; fax 81 40 05), a 25min. walk or 10min. bus ride from downtown (from the bus station, walk past the train station to the rotary and cross at the crosswalk to take bus #9 to Av. Blase Infante). Common bathrooms and bare white walls, but you won't find a better deal anywhere else in Jerez. Pool access. Breakfast included. Wash €2.50; dry €2. Reserve ahead. Pool open July-August from noon-8pm. June-Sept. dorms €13-17. Oct.-May €9.50/12.50. ❶

🍴 FOOD

Food in Jerez is rarely cheap. For deals, tapas-hoppers bounce around Pl. del Arenal, C. Larga, and Pl. del Banco in the old town. For the freshest produce and the aroma of raw fish, head to **Mercado de Abastos,** Pl. Esteve. (Open M-Sa 8:30am-3pm.) For groceries, **Carrefour** is on C. Doña Blanca. (Open M-Sa 9:15am-9:30pm.)

Parrilla La Pampa, C. Guadalete, 24 (☎956 34 17 49), near Pl. Mamelón. The hides dotting the walls hint at this spot's specialty—authentic, imported Argentine beef (€8.75-19.70). Pork, chicken, veal, and ostrich (€16.20-17.70) round out the menu menagerie. Open M-Sa 12:30-4:30pm and 8:30pm-12:30am. AmEx/MC/V. ❸

Mesón Bodegón El Patio, C. San Francisco de Paula, 7 (☎956 34 07 36). Sumptuous traditional fare made with local produce in a refurbished sherry warehouse. Old portraits, antiques, and bear heads fill the dining room. Tapas €1.50-4.25. *Raciones* €5-19. *Menú* €18. Open M-Sa 11:30am-4:30pm and 8pm-12:30am. MC/V. ❷

Entre Vinos y Arte, C. Corredera, 30-32 (☎956 33 38 65), 3 blocks from Pl. del Arenal. Low on tourists, high on hospitality. Don't leave without sampling the bull's tail; a half-*ración* of this delicacy is enough to keep your stomach full. Vegetarian and meat tapas €1.50-2. *Raciones* €6. Open daily 8:30am-4pm and 7pm-midnight. MC/V. ❶

Pizzeria da Paolo, at the corner of C. Clavel and C. Valientes. Like a fancy Italian restaurant, only affordable. Tasty pizzas (€5-8.50) and pastas (€4.50-7.50). Plenty of vegetarian options. Open Tu-Su 1:15-4pm and 9pm-midnight. MC/V. ❷

Pollo Sur, Blvd. Federico Mayo, 1, near Pl. de Abastos (☎956 14 12 60). Lines of locals wind out the doors this tiny chicken shanty, waiting to choose from one of the 5 combination meals (€8.30-14). Forget about napkins and silverware—here, chicken is king. Open daily 8:30-11pm. Cash only. ❷

🎵 SHERRY BODEGAS

People come to Jerez for the *bodegas* (wineries), and while many smaller *bodegas* offer tours, it's worth indulging your inner tourist and checking out the more famous ones. Tour guides explain the city's trademark *solera* (sherry-making process), leading visitors through heavenly-smelling barrel storage rooms and under grape-covered trellises before topping off the tour with free samples. The best time to visit is early September during the harvest; the worst is August, when many *bodegas* close down and wait for the grapes to ripen. Group reservations for tours must be made at least one week in advance. Looking for a job? Many *bodegas* hire English-speaking tour guides for two or three months, depending on need.

■ **Pedro Domecq,** C. San Idelfonso, 3 (☎956 15 15 00; www.domecq.es). Founded in 1730, Domecq is the oldest and most prestigious *bodega* in town. 1½hr. tours include informative 20min. video. Unlimited sampling. Hourly tours in English and Spanish M-F hourly from 10am-1pm, Sa noon. Tour with tapas Tu, Th, Sa 2pm. Tour with tapas and flamenco May-Sept. Th 2pm. Regular tour €6, 2pm tour with tapas €11. AmEx/MC/V.

González Byass, C. Manuel María González, 12 (☎956 35 70 16 or 902 44 00 77; www.gonzalezbyass.es; www.bodegastiopepe.com). The makers of the popular *Tío Pepe* brand. The Disney World of *bodegas*: a bit commercial, but worth visiting and very kid-friendly. Trolleys whisk visitors past the world's largest weathervane and a storage room designed by Gustave Eiffel. June-Sept. tours in English M-Sa hourly 11:30am-2pm and 3:30-5:30pm. Oct.-May tours in English M-Sa hourly 11:30am-5:30pm, Su 11:30am-1:30pm. €8, 2pm tour with tapas €13.50. AmEx/D/MC/V.

Harvey's, C. Arcos, 57 (☎956 15 15 00 or 956 15 15 51; www.bodegasharveys.com). Makers of Harvey's Bristol Cream, the best-selling sherry in the world. Reservations required; call in advance. 1½hr. tours M-F 10am and noon (€5). Tour and technical tasting Th 10am. MC/V.

🅖 SIGHTS

■**ALCÁZAR.** A Moorish foundation, Christian renovations, and 20th-century revisions have made the Alcázar into an architectural mutt. Cruise the outdoor walkways from the mosque through the manicured gardens, well-preserved olive oil mill, and remains of Arab baths. Then make your way to the top of the tallest tower to witness the *Cámara Oscura,* a type of enlarged microscope, displaying images from the city below. (☎956 32 69 23. Open May-Sept. 15 M-Sa 10am-8pm, Su 10am-2:30pm; Sept. 16-Apr. daily 10am-6pm. Alcázar €3, students €1.80; Alcázar and Cámara Oscura €5.40, students €4.20.)

■**PALACIO DEL TIEMPO AND EL MISTERIO DE JEREZ.** The Palacio del Tiempo (Palace of Time) and El Misterio de Jerez (the Mystery of Jerez) make up the Museo de la Atalaya. Inside the Palacio del Tiempo, a collection of 302 rare clocks are kept in working order by one clock keeper, the only person allowed to handle the pieces. The Misterio de Jerez is a journey via a sometimes-confusing video montage to explore the "genuine" Jerez and also has a large wine gallery that showcases Jerez's finest. (C. Cervantes, 3. ☎956 18 21 00 or 902 18 21 00; www.elmisteriodejerez.org. Guided visits only. Tu-Sa 10am-3pm and 5-7pm, Su 10am-3pm. Palacio del Tiempo €6, under 25 €3; El Misterio de Jerez €5/2.50; both museums €9/4.50. MC/V.)

REAL ESCUELA ANDALUZA DE ARTE EQUESTRE. Jerez's love for wine is almost matched by its passion for horses. During May, the Royal Andalusian School of Equestrian Art sponsors the Feria del Caballo—a horse fair with carriage competitions and races of Jerez-bred Carthusian horses. During the rest of the year, weekly shows feature a troupe of horses dancing in choreographed sequences. (Av. Duque de Abrantes. ☎956 31 80 08; www.realescuela.org. Training sessions M and W 11am-2pm, July-Sept. also F, €6. Shows Tu and Th noon; Aug. also F noon. €13-21, depending on seat; children and seniors 40% off. Museum and training session €7, museum only €3. MC/V.)

YEGUADA LA CARTUJA HIERRO DEL BOCADO. Every Saturday at 11am, the horses from the largest Carthusian thoroughbred stud farm in Spain strut their stuff for an appreciative audience. *(Ctra. Medina–El Portal, km 6.5.* ☎*956 16 28 09; www.yeguadacartuja.com. Year-round Sa 11am.)*

🎵 🎭 ENTERTAINMENT AND NIGHTLIFE

Rare footage of Spain's most highly regarded **flamenco** singers, dancers, and guitarists is available for viewing at the **Centro Andaluz de Flamenco,** in Palacio Pemartín, on Pl. San Juan. (☎956 34 92 65; www.caf.cica.es. Open M-F 9am-2pm. Videos hourly 10am-2pm. Free.) Most *peñas* and *tablaos* (clubs and bars that host flamenco) are in the old town and hold special performances in July and August. Occasionally there are free performances in some plazas, especially Pl. de Toros. For more frequent shows, walk over to Pl. Santiago to ◼**La Taberna Flamenca,** Angostillo de Santiago, 3, which hosts some of Jerez's youngest flamenco dancers in an intimate setting that takes you back to the days of the gypsy camps. (☎956 23 26 93; info@latibernaflamenco.com. Mid-May to Oct. shows daily 10:30pm, Tu-Th and Sa also 2:30pm. Nov. to mid-May shows Tu-Sa 10:30pm. Reservations recommended for dinner. Cover €15, includes 2 drinks; with dinner €35. AmEx/MC/V.)

Visitors to Jerez tend to be on the older side, and nightlife in the city center caters directly to them; to get to the more lively, younger scene, head to the outskirts of the city. The Irish-themed bar and disco complex **Plaza Canterbury,** C. Nuño, is a hot spot for tourists and students alike, with two bars (**O'Donoghue's** and **Gambrinus,** the latter serving tapas), an outdoor patio, and a popular club. (Beer at bars €1.25-1.80, mixed drinks €3.50-5; at club €2.50/5. Club cover €8. Gambrinus Bar open M-Sa 9am-1:30pm, Su 4pm-1:30am. O'Donoghue's open daily 6pm-6am. Club open F-Sa 1:30-7am.) A slew of bars and clubs lines the well-lit **Avenida Méjico** between C. Santo Domingo and C. Salvatierra (a 25min. walk from Pl. del Arenal). Bars and pubs also cluster on the lively **Avenida Lola Flores** near the *fútbol* stadium.

Autumn, in addition to being grape harvest season, is festival season, when Jerez showcases its best equine and flamenco traditions. These festivals are collectively known as the Fiestas de Otoño, held from early September until the end of October. In September, the Fiesta de la Bulería and the Festival de Teatro, Música y Baile celebrate flamenco. The largest horse parade in the world, with races in Pl. del Arenal, is the highlight of the final week. Check at the tourist office for details; schedules are available in September for the upcoming year. And, for those with endless amounts of energy, the world-famous Festival Internacional de Flamenco de Jerez electrifies the city each year during February and March.

SANLÚCAR DE BARRAMEDA ☎956

Sanlúcar de Barrameda (pop. 62,000), at the mouth of the Río Guadalquivir, borders both the Parque Nacional Coto de Doñana and a variety of relatively uncrowded beaches. Visitors come to Sanlúcar mostly to get a taste of southern Spain's sherry *bodegas,* fine sands, and sunny weather without all the tourists of nearby Jerez and Cádiz. This seaside corner of the illustrious "sherry triangle" (along with Jerez and El Puerto de Santa María) specializes in *manzanilla,* the saltiest relative in the sherry family. While Sanlúcar makes for a good weekend getaway, there's not enough to entertain visitors for much longer.

🚍 **TRANSPORTATION.** The bus station is on Av. de la Estación, one block from the main Calzada del Ejército. **Transportes Los Amarillos** (☎956 38 50 60) runs **buses** to **Cádiz** (1hr., 5-9 per day 6:15am-6:20pm, €2.90); **Sevilla** (2hr., 6-12 per day 6:45am-9pm, €6.55). **Linesur** (☎956 34 10 63) goes to **Jerez** (45min.; M-F hourly 8:10am-

9:10pm, Sa-Su every 2hr.; €1.53). If ticket booths are closed, you can buy tickets on the bus. For **taxis,** call ☎956 36 11 02 or 36 00 04.

■■ ⊠ **ORIENTATION AND PRACTICAL INFORMATION.** The **tourist office** is on Calzada del Ejército, which runs perpendicular to the beach. Staff has info on the Parque Nacional Coto de Doñana. (☎956 36 61 10. Open daily June-Aug. M-F 10am-2pm and 5-7pm, Sa 10am-2pm; Sept.-May 10am-2pm and 4-6pm.) To hit the beach from the bus station, exit from the stairs facing the supermarket (**Super Sol,** open M-Sa 10am-10pm) and turn left; turn left again at the intersection. Local services include: **Ambulatorio de la S.S.** on Calzada del Ejército (☎956 36 71 65); **police,** Av. de la Constitución (☎956 38 80 11); **Internet** access at **Cyber Guadalquivir,** C. Infanta Beatriz, 11, off Calzada del Ejército (☎956 36 74 03; €1.80 per hour; open M-Sa 10am-1am, Su 11am-1am); and **post office,** C. Correos and Av. Cerro Falcón (☎956 36 09 37; open M-F 8:30am-2:30pm, Sa 9am-1pm). **Postal Code:** 11540.

▐▌▐▌ **ACCOMMODATIONS AND FOOD.** Few bargains exist in Sanlúcar; it may be worthwhile to inquire at doorway signs reading *"se alquilan habitaciones"* (rooms for rent). **Hostal La Blanca Paloma ❷,** Pl. San Roque, 9, keeps clean rooms, some of which have balconies. Its central location makes it a good option. (☎956 36 36 44; hostalblancapaloma@msn.com. Singles €18; doubles €30; triples €45; prices vary with season. Cash only.) At **Los Helechos ❹,** Plaza Madre de Dios, 9, indulge in white arched balconies, spring-hued rooms, and terraces with incredible views. It's quite a splurge, but you'll be patting yourself on the back as you lounge on the patio and sip a cold drink from the bar. All rooms with A/C, personal bath, and satellite TV. (Singles from €40.13; doubles from €53.50.) For a sit-down meal, head for the side streets off C. San Juan or uphill into the *casco antiguo. Terrazas* fill Pl. San Roque and Pl. del Cabildo. Food prices are low across town, and you can find a decent meal for under €8 at any of the cafe-bars off of the two main plazas. Women in flashy pink dresses scoop up endless varieties of the most popular ice cream in town at **Helados Artesanos Toni ❶,** Pl. del Cabildo, 2. (☎956 36 22 13. Small cone €1, large €2. Banana split €4.20. Shakes €2. Open daily 11am-2am.) **Bar El Sur,** C. Alonso Muñez, is a hangout hot spot with a mellow atmosphere. (Beer €1.50. Mixed drinks €4.50. Open M-F 9pm-3am, Sa-Su 9pm-4am.)

◙ ⊡ **SIGHTS AND ENTERTAINMENT.** The enormous 14th-century **Iglesia de Nuestra Señora de la O,** Pl. de la Paz, competes with two impressive palaces for the attention of sun-worshipping tourists. (☎956 36 05 55. Open Tu-Sa 10am-1pm, Su 10am-noon. Free.) Sanlúcar has put its historic buildings to good use; most are still inhabited or have been transformed into offices. The **Palacio Medina Sidonia,** Pl. Condes de Niebla, is the home of the Duque de Medina Sidonia. (☎956 36 01 61. Open Su 10:30am-1:30pm. Free.) The 19th-century **Palacio de Orleáns y Borbón,** C. Cuesta de Belén, now houses the *Ayuntamiento.* (☎956 38 80 00. Open M-F 8am-2:30pm. Free.) Sanlúcar's sandy **beaches** stretch from the mouth of the Río Guadalquivir toward the open Atlantic. Several **bodegas** tower over Sanlúcar's small streets. (Tours M-Sa, more info at tourist office. €1.80-3.) In August, the **Carreras de Caballos** (horse races) thunder along the beach, and the **Festival de la Exaltación del Río Guadalquivir** brings poetry readings, a flamenco competition, and bullfights.

THE MARISMAS DEL ODIEL

The ▧**Marismas del Odiel,** a protected wetland near the Parque Nacional de Doñana, certainly merits a daytrip. An obligatory stop for thousands of migratory birds, including the grey and purple heron, black stork, and 30% of Europe's spoonbill population, the UNESCO reserve is 7185 hectares of marshy estuary at the mouth of the Odiel river. The Marismas are a favored breeding and nesting ground for ■**African flamingos** in winter. Watch for chameleons and lynxes, the park's terrestrial residents. To protect the habitat, only guided visits are permitted, and Erebea offers tours by jeep, boat, mini-train, or foot. Even if bird-watching isn't your passion, the opportunity to see over a thousand flamingos take flight at once doesn't come along every day. (☎660 41 49 20 or 670 70 26 8 to reserve ahead for a tour. Open W-Su 10am-2pm and 6-8pm. €20 per person.)

The tourist office at Marismas can also give you info and make reservations. (☎959 50 90 11. Open M-F 10am-2pm and 3-6pm, Sa 10am-2pm.) The marshes are difficult to reach by public transportation, and are usually accessed from nearby Punta Umbria. Though this small town is best reached by car—a short drive from Huelva down H414—**Empresa Damas** (☎959 25 69 00) also runs buses from Huelva's bus station several times a day (15min.).

ARCOS DE LA FRONTERA ☎956

Arcos de la Frontera (pop. 33,000) has inspired many a poet, including Cristóbal Romero, who described it as a "Town extended in the sun/Winged, raised up in flight..." With its whitewashed houses wrapped around a narrow ridge, Arcos is considered one of the most perfect *pueblos blancos* towns in Spain. Its plazas and churches, huddled in convoluted medieval streets flush with geraniums, make it a historical and romantic gem. The city comes alive in the evening after the heat dies down and locals congregate in the plazas and bars of the old city.

▐ TRANSPORTATION

Buses: Station on C. Corregidores. **Los Amarillos** (☎ 956 32 93 47) runs buses to **Jerez** (30min.; M-F 19 per day 7am-8pm, Sa 9 per day 8am-8pm, Su 11 per day 8am-9pm; €2.20) and **Sevilla** (2hr.; 7am, 3pm; €6.30). **Transportes Generales** to: **Cádiz** (1½hr., 6 per day 7:20am-7:15pm, €4.80); **Costa del Sol** (3-4hr., 4pm, €10-12.80); and **Ronda** (1¾hr., 4 per day 8:15am-4pm, €6). Confirm times and prices at the tourist office, as the bus station is perpetually abandoned. Buy tickets on the bus.

Taxis: C. Debajo del Corral. **Radio Taxi** (☎956 70 13 55/00 66). 24hr.

▄▐ ORIENTATION AND PRACTICAL INFORMATION

To reach the town center from the bus station, exit left, follow the road, and turn left again. Continue uphill for two blocks on C. Josefa Moreno Seguro, taking a right onto C. Muñoz Vázquez. From there it's a 20min. walk uphill. Continue until reaching Pl. de España, then veer left onto C. Debajo del Coral, which quickly changes into C. Corredera; the old quarter is 500m ahead. *Manolo Blanco* minibuses run every 30min. from the bus station to C. Corredera (€1). A taxi costs around €3. If the tourist office is closed when you arrive, make your way to **Bar Hostal Zindicato,** a short climb uphill from the bus stop, where you'll find an invaluable tile map of the city complete with street key.

Tourist Office: Pl. del Cabildo (☎956 70 22 64). Runs **tours** of the old city, monuments, and patios M-F 10:30am, noon, and 6pm, Sa 11am. €5, children free. Call ahead to reserve for Sa and 6pm tours. Open Mar. 15-Oct. 15 M-Sa 10am-2pm and 4-8pm, Su 10am-2pm; Oct. 16-Mar. 14 M-Sa 10am-2pm and 3:30-7:30pm, Su 10am-2pm. Knock if the door isn't open. One computer with **Internet** access (€1 per 15min., €2.50 per hour) and printing (€0.50 per page). An **information kiosk** with a more detailed street map is located on the island between C. Maldonado and C. Boticas near Pl. Boticas.

Bank: Banco Santander Central Hispano, C. Corredera, 63 (☎902 24 24 24). Open M-F 8:30am-2pm, Sa 8:30am-1pm. Apr.-Sept. closed Sa.

Currency Exchange: Caja Sur, C. Corredera, 56, across from Banco Santander Central Hispano (☎901 24 72 47; www.cajasur.es). Open M-F 8:30am-2:30pm.

Laundry: Pressto, C. Debajo del Corral, diagonally across from Hotel La Fonda (☎914 48 58 61; www.pressto.com). Open M-F 9:30am-1:30pm and 5-8pm, Sa 9:30am-1:30pm.

Internet: Ciber-Locutorio "El Barrio," Pl. de las Aguas, 5 (☎956 70 45 69). €0.50 per 30min., €0.90 per hour. International phone service available. Open M-Sa 9:30am-2pm and 5:30-10pm, Su 10am-2pm.

Police: Av. Miguel Mancheño (☎092 or 956 70 16 52).

Medical Emergency: (☎061 or 956 51 15 53).

Hospital: Centro de Salud, C. Rafael Benot Rubio (☎956 70 07 87), in the Barrio Bajo.

Pharmacy: Ldo. Ildefonso Guerrero Seijo, C. Corredera, 34 (☎956 70 02 13). Open M-F 9am-9pm. A list of doctors on call and available after hours is posted in the window.

Post Office: C. Murete, 24 (☎956 70 15 60), overlooking the cliffs and the river. Open M-F 8:30am-2:30pm, Sa 9:30am-1pm. **Postal Code:** 11630.

▐ ACCOMMODATIONS AND CAMPING

Arcos has a few budget hostels, but they are only slightly less expensive than classier hotels in town. Many restaurants on **Calle Corredera** and in the old city also have inexpensive rooms. Call ahead during *Semana Santa* and in the summer.

▨ **Hostal San Marcos,** C. Marqués de Torresoto, 6 (☎956 70 07 21), past C. Deán Espinosa and Pl. del Cabildo. Big rooms with bigger windows, all with private baths, some with A/C and TV. The bar/restaurant downstairs often stays noisy past midnight. Singles €20-25; doubles €30-36; triples €45. AmEx/MC/V. ❷

Pensión Callejon de las Monjas, C. Deán Espinosa, 4 (☎056 70 23 02 or 605 86 84 82; fax 956 70 43 88). Rooms with incredible views, some with TV, bath, and A/C. Singles €20, with bath €25; doubles €33, with terrace €39; 4-person suite €66. MC/V. ❷

Hotel La Fonda, C. Corredera, 83 (☎956 70 00 57; fax 70 36 61), at the bottom of the hill leading to the old city. Originally a 19th-century inn, La Fonda retains refined, old-fashioned feel. Plushly carpeted hallways lead to high-ceilinged rooms with balconies, some with terraces. Singles €30; doubles €45. Prices lower in winter. AmEx/MC/V. ❸

Camping Lago de Arcos, Urbanización El Santiscal (☎956 70 83 33; lagodearcos@ca,pings.net), at the foot of the hill. Enclosed campground with showers, pool, and electricity (€3). €3.60 per person, €3.60-4.25 per tent, €3.25 per car. ❶

▐ FOOD

Cheap cafes and restaurants huddle at the bottom end of C. Corredera, while tapas nirvana can be reached uphill in the old quarter. You can also stock up on fresh fruit and produce at the small **mercado** on Pl. Boticas. (Open M-Sa 9am-3pm.)

Mesón de San Marcos, C. Marqués de Torresto, 6, downstairs of Hostal San Marcos (☎956 70 07 21). Spanish music videos and the occasional ring of the ship's bell set the soundtrack of this restaurant. Vegetarian options. Combo plates €3.50-6. *Menú* €8. Open daily noon-midnight; food served noon-4pm and 9pm-11pm. MC/V. ❷

Los Faraones, C. Debajo del Corral, 8 (☎956 70 06 12), downhill from C. Corredera. Tapas with an Egyptian twist. Extensive vegetarian *menú* €11; normal *menú* €9. Open Tu-Su 9am-5:30pm and 8pm-midnight. Cash only. ❷

Restaurante El Convento, C. Marqués de Torresoto, 7 (☎956 70 32 22), past the church, on the far left, at the end of the street. Admire artifacts and Spanish tiling as you indulge in rabbit, partridge, duck, and deer. Vegetarian salads and soups. Appetizers €4-12. Entrees €5-16. Open 1-4pm and 7:30-10:30pm; closed 2 days of the week, differs by week. Closed first 2 weeks of July. AmEx/MC/V. ❸

Mesón Los Murales, Pl. Boticas, 1 (☎956 70 06 07); turn right at the end of C. Marqués de Torresoto, just before the plaza. Los Murales is on the left. Enjoy delicious *comida típica* (typical food) in the blue-and-white interior or on the peaceful plaza outside. Great *pollo a la plancha* (grilled chicken; €6.40). *Menú* €9. Entrees €7.50-11.50. Open M-Th and Sa-Su 9am-midnight. MC/V. ❷

👁 🌺 SIGHTS AND FESTIVALS

The most beautiful sights in Arcos are the winding alleys, hanging flowers of the old quarter, and the view from the 🏠**Plaza del Cabildo.** The balcony, overlooking the entire region, earned the nickname *Balcón de Coño;* the view is so startling, people often exclaim *"¡Coño!"* ($@#!) in disbelief. In this square is the **Basílica de Santa María de la Asunción,** a blend of Baroque, Renaissance, and Gothic styles built between the 15th and 18th centuries. A symbol of the Inquisition—a circular design within which exorcisms were once performed—is still etched into the ground outside on the church's left side. (Open M-F 10am-1pm and 4-7pm, Sa 10am-2pm. Closed for repairs until 2008. €1.50.) The late-Gothic **Iglesia de San Pedro** stands on the site of an Arab fortress in the old quarter. The gold altar is bookended by lifesized icons, below which lie the "uncorrupted bodies" of two saints removed from the Roman catacombs of St. Calixto. (Open daily 10am-1:30pm. €1. Mass in winter 11:30am. Free.) An artificial **lake** laps at Arcos's feet; although you can't swim in the lake itself, the beach, **El Santisca,** is a popular spot for a stroll. Ask about boat tours and rentals at the tourist office. Buses run there from the bus station (M-Sa 5 per day 9:15am-8:15pm, Su 2-4 per day 12:15-8:15pm; €0.85). **Festivals** are highly spirited and quite popular; a favorite held on Easter Sunday is the **Toro de Aleluya,** in which two bulls run through the streets amid flamenco and general merriment. The arguably more moving **Velada de San Pedro,** is a celebration of the town's patron saint. Following a marching band processional and elaborate mass, 16 men provide the horsepower to move a larger-than-life icon of San Pedro out of the Iglesia de San Pedro and into the streets.

CÁDIZ ☎956

If every city told its story, Cádiz would be spinning yarns well into the night. Founded by the Phoenicians in 1100 BC, Cádiz is thought to be the oldest inhabited city in Europe. Located on a peninsula, the city has a powerful ocean on one side and a placid bay on the other. In the late 16th century, this unique geography triggered the first step in the eventual defeat of the Spanish Armada: Queen Elizabeth's fleet of small, quick ships surprised King Philip II's mighty battalion in Cádiz's harbor, causing significant damage in an event referred to as the "singeing of the King of Spain's beard." Despite Spain's eventual defeat, the Spanish colonial shipping industry transformed Cádiz (pop. 155,000) into one of the wealthiest ports in Europe. Today, the narrow pedestrian streets and soaring

ANDALUCÍA

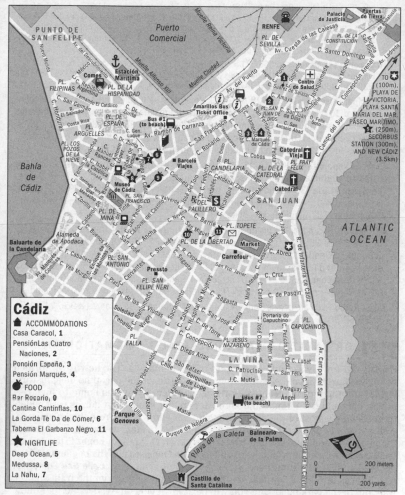

Cádiz

♠ ACCOMMODATIONS
Casa Caracol, 1
PensiónLas Cuatro
   Naciones, 2
Ponsión España, 3
Pensión Marqués, 4

🍎 FOOD
Bar Rosario, 9
Cantina Cantinflas, 10
La Gorda Te Da de Comer, 6
Taberna El Garbanzo Negro, 11

★ NIGHTLIFE
Deep Ocean, 5
Medussa, 8
La Nahu, 7

churches of the old town, the several popular beaches in the new city, and a thriving cafe culture make for a dynamic yet easy-going atmosphere.

⬛ TRANSPORTATION

Trains: RENFE, Pl. de Sevilla (☎956 25 43 01 or 902 24 02 02. Open 7:35am-11:35pm). To: **Barcelona** (12hr., 7:40am and 7:30pm, €73); **Córdoba** (3hr., 7:40am and 7:30pm, €15.50); **Jerez** (40min., 16-22 per day 6:15am-10:10pm, €3.10); **Madrid** (5hr., 8am, €55-85); **Sevilla** (2hr., 7-12 per day 5:45am-8:10pm, €8.50-20).

Buses: Several private companies operate out of small stations in Cádiz.

Transportes Generales Comes, Pl. de la Hispanidad, 1 (☎956 22 78 11 or 902 19 92 08). To: **Algeciras** (3hr., 10 per day 6:45am-8pm, €10); **Córdoba** (5hr., 7am and 3:45pm, €20); **Gran-**

ada (5hr., 4 per day 9am-9pm, €28); **Jerez de la Frontera** (45min., 11-29 per day 5:15am-9pm, €2.60); **La Línea** (3hr., 3 per day 11:30am-5pm, €11); **Málaga** (4hr., 6 per day 6:45am-8pm, €20); **Ronda** (3hr.; M-F 3 per day 9am-6pm, Sa 3 per day 9am-1:45pm, Su 9am and 1:45pm; €13); **Sevilla** (2hr.; M-Sa 10-11 per day 7am-9pm, Su 12 per day 7am-10pm; €10); **Vejer de la Frontera** (1½hr., 6-8 per day 9am-9:15pm, €5).

Transportes Los Amarillos (☎956 29 08 00) depart from beside the port in front of Po. de Canalejas. Purchase tickets on buses or at the Viajes Socialtur office on Av. Ramón de Carranza, 31 (open M-F 9:30am-1:30pm and 5-8:30pm). To **Arcos de la Frontera** (1hr., 2-4 per day 8:30am-8:15pm, €4).

Municipal Buses: (☎956 26 28 06). Pick up a map, schedule, and **bonobus** (discount packet of 10 tickets for €5.70, seniors €2.60) in the cafe at the Transportes Generales Comes bus station. Most lines run through Pl. de España. Bus #1 (Cortadura), a favorite with beach bums, runs along the shore to new Cádiz (every 10min. 6:40am-1:10am, €0.90). Bus #7 runs the same route, leaving from **Playa de la Caleta**.

Ferry: El Vaporcito (☎902 45 05 50. www.cmtbc.es) departs from a dock behind the Estación Marítima near the Transportes Generales Comes station and runs to **Puerto de Santa María** (30-45min.; M-F 18 per day 7:40am-10pm, return 7:10am-9:15pm, Sa 6 per day 11:45am-9pm, return 10am-6pm, Su 5 per day 11:45am-8pm, return 10am-6pm; €3, round-trip €4, bikes €1-2).

Car Rental: Booth located inside the train station. **Bahía Rent A Car** (☎956 27 18 95 or 609 54 29 33; www.bahiarentacar.com. Open M-F 9:30am-1:30pm and 5-8pm, Sa 9:30am-1:30pm). Starting at €52 per day, €190 per week. Prices do not include baby seat (€4 per day, maximum €20 per rental). Delivery out of hours €15 per car. AmEx/MC/V. **Europcar** (☎956 28 05 07. Open M-F 9am-3pm and 5-8pm, Sa 9-3pm). Starting at €54 per day, €172 per week. Personal insurance (PAI) and extras not included.

Taxis: Radio Taxis are across from the library on Av. Ramón de Carranza (☎956 21 21 21 or 26 68 68).

◼❷ ORIENTATION AND PRACTICAL INFORMATION

Cádiz's old town was built on the end of the peninsula. The new town formed behind it, farther inland. The old town hosts most of the cheap hostels, historic sights, and the bus and train stations, while the new town is home to high-rise hotels, bars and restaurants, and kilometers of hot sand. Old Cádiz is very pedestrian friendly—most of the main streets do not allow cars. From the bus station, walk straight and pass through Pl. de la Hispanidad to **Plaza de España**. Walk across the plaza and continue straight tow blocks down C. Antonio López. Turn left on **Calle Isabel la Católica**, which leads to **Plaza San Francisco** and the beginning of the pedestrian district. From there, you can turn left again onto **Calle San Francisco**, which turns into **Plaza San Juan de Dios**, the town center. From the train station, walk out of the parking lot and you will be at Pl. Sevilla on Av. del Puerto. Follow the avenue past the port on your right. Pass Ción. de los Negros on your left and turn left onto the next street, which leads into Pl. San Juan de Dios. When you take the bus into new Cádiz (down the main avenue), hop off at **Glorieta Ingeniero La Cierva** (before the corner with the McDonald's); the beach is directly behind it.

Tourist Office: Municipal, in Paseo de Canalejas (☎956 24 10 01; fax 24 10 05). Has useful maps that include four suggested walking tours. English spoken. Open M-F in summer 9am-2pm and 5-8pm; in winter 9:30am-2pm and 4-7pm. Kiosk in front of the main office open Sa-Su June-Sept. 10am-1pm and 5-7:30pm; Oct.-May 10am-1:30pm and 4-6pm. **Junta de Andalucía,** Av. Ramón de Carranza (☎956 20 31 91; fax 956 20 31 92). Open M-F 9am-7:30pm, Sa-Su 10am-1:45pm.

Currency Exchange: Banco Santander Central Hispano, C. Columela, 13 (☎902 24 24 24). Open M-F 8:30am-2pm, Sa 8:30am-1pm.

Banks: line Av. Ramón de Carranza and C. San Francisco.

Pharmacy: Farmacia Central, Pl. del Palillero (☎956 22 48 01). Open 9am-10pm.

Student Travel Agency: Barceló Viajes, C. San Francisco, 15 (☎956 21 22 23; www.barceloviajes.com). Open M-F 9:30am-2pm and 5-8:30pm, Sa 10am-1:30pm.

Laundromat: Pressto, on the corner of C. San José and C. Benjumeda (☎914 48 58 61; www.pressto.com). Open M-F 9:30am-1:30pm and 5-8pm, Sa 9:30am-1:30pm.

Police: Municipal, C. Campo del Sur, in the new city (☎092). National, Av. de Andalucía, 28, in the new city (☎091).

Medical Services: Ambulatorio Vargas Ponce (☎956 28 38 55). **Centro de Salud,** Pl. Iglesia de la Merced (☎956 28 64 11).

Internet Access: Free **Internet** access (30min. limit) is available at the public library, **Biblioteca Pública Provincial de Cádiz,** Av. Ramón de Carranza, 16 (☎956 20 33 24; www.juntadeandalucia.es/cultura/bibliotecas/bibcadiz/). Open M-F 9am-9pm year-round, Sa 9am-2pm in winter. Free Wi-Fi can also be found in the city's plazas, including Pl. Palillero and Pl. de la Catedral. **Lu@r,** Plaza de Mina, 4, near the art museum (☎956 21 42 05). €0.80 for 30min., €1.50 per hour. Open daily 10:30am-1am.

Post Office: Pl. Topete (☎956 21 05 11). Open M-F 8:30am-8:30pm, Sa 9:30am-2pm. **Postal Code:** 11070.

▛ ACCOMMODATIONS

Most hostels huddle around the harbor, in and around Pl. San Juan de Dios. In the summer, they fill with young beachgoers, so singles and private baths are scarce. Call months in advance to find a room during February's *Carnaval;* calling a few days ahead in summer should be fine. Many owners are willing to bargain a bit.

Casa Caracol, C. Suárez de Salazar, 4 (☎956 26 11 66; www.caracolcasa.com). Where the young beach-loving crowd comes to rest their tired surfer bodies. Hammocks on the rooftop terrace offer the perfect *siesta* (and, if you choose, the cheapest bed in Cádiz), music plays all day, and the staff whips up tasty dinners (€4-5). Free Internet access. Breakfast included. Dorms €13-15; doubles €32; hammocks €10. Cash only ❶

Pensión España, C. Marqués de Cádiz, 9 (☎956 28 55 00). Modern, red leather couches in the lobby contrast with the traditional Spanish interior. Rooms vary greatly in size, but all are brightened by colorful bedspreads, and some have TVs. High season singles €32; doubles €60, with bath €55. Low season €27/40/42. Cash only. ❸

Pensión Marqués, C. Marqués de Cádiz, 1 (☎956 28 58 54). Pleasant rooms, with clean common baths and wrought-iron terraces. High season singles €30; doubles €50, with bath €60. Low season €20/35/45. Cash only. ❸

Pensión Las Cuatro Naciones, C. Plocia, 3 (☎956 25 55 39). White-walled rooms with sinks and balconies. Single beds have enough room for even the most restless sleeper. The common bathrooms are large, well-lit, and well-kept. Call ahead—once the 10 rooms fill up, it's the high-priced hotels or the street corner. High season singles €20; doubles €36. Low season €18/30. Cash only. ❷

◱ FOOD

It's easy to find cafes in any of Cádiz's plazas, but the streets off C. San Francisco have cheaper tapas bars. To stock up for beach trips, head to **Carrefour,** off Pl. Topete (open M-Sa 9:15am-9:15pm), or try the **market** in the same plaza (open Tu-Sa 9am-2pm). Unless you're a Minotaur, you'll want to use the entrance across from Carrefour, where you'll find a detailed layout of the labyrinthian market.

Taberna El Garbanzo Negro, C. Sacramento, 18 (☎956 22 23 17). Bold blue walls, a laid-back atmosphere, and an extensive menu featuring variations on traditional Spanish staples. Tapas €1.30. *Raciones* €4-7. *Menú* €9. Open M-Sa 1:30-4pm and 8:30-11:30pm. AmEx/MC/V. ❶

La Gorda Te Da de Comer, C. General Luque, 1. "The Fat Woman Gives You Food" is a trendy New Age tapas bar that puts a 21st-century spin on age-old cuisine. Tapas €1.40. Open M 9-11:30pm, Tu-Th 1:30-4pm and 9-11:30pm, F-Sa 1:30-4pm and 9pm-midnight. MC/V. ❶

Cantina Cantinflas, C. Javier de Burgos, 19 (☎856 17 17 37 or 699 68 06 73). A Mexican restaurant that delivers, literally and figuratively. Nacho plates (€5.40-7), heaping house specialties, and color-coded vegetarian options will leave you wondering why Spain ever let its Mexican colony go. Don't leave without a margarita (€2.50-5.30). Entrees €2.80-10.30. Open daily 8pm-midnight; closed Tu in winter. ❷

Bar Rosario, Beato Diego de Cádiz, 3 (☎956 22 51 73). The welcoming diner-like atmosphere of this tiny bar/restaurant tends to draw tourists with its €6.50 *menú* (€9 after 7:30pm and on Su and holidays), but the real reason to come here is the churro and coffee breakfast offered until 10am (€1.70). Rise and dine. Open daily 8am-3pm and 7:30-10pm. Cash only. ❶

◉ SIGHTS

▨ CATEDRAL. This gold-domed 18th-century masterpiece was financed by colonial riches. It took 116 years to build, resulting in a mixed Baroque and Neoclassical monument of unusually massive proportions. The treasury bulges with valuables—the *Custodia del Millón* is said to be set with a million precious stones. The chapel holds a gazebo-like main altar encircled by countless side chapels, one of which is the *Capilla de las Reliquia*, full of cases of relics barely visible through the bars that guard the entrance. The crypt below the main altar is eerie but not particularly compelling. Visit the nearby **museum** for treasures and art. *(Pl. de la Catedral. ☎ 956 25 98 12. Mass Su noon. Open Tu-F 10am-6pm, Sa 10am-2pm. Last entrance 30min. before close. Admission to cathedral and museum €4, students €3, children €2.50. Admission to cathedral, museum, Torre de Poniente, Sanctuario Romano, Templos de Apolo, Esculapio, and Hygia €6. Free entrance to cathedral Tu-F 7-8pm and Su 11am-1pm.)*

MUSEO DE CÁDIZ. Cádiz's Fine Arts and Provincial Archaeological Museums merged in 1975, and today Murillo, Rubens, and Zurbarán works reside here alongside Phoenician sarcophagi, ancient jewelry, and blown glass. *(Pl. de Mina. ☎ 956 20 33 68; www.juntadeandalucia.es/cultura/museocadiz. Open Tu 2:30-8:30pm, W-Sa 9am-8:30pm, Su 9am-2:30pm. Guided tours by appointment only Tu 9am-2:30pm. Wheelchair accessible. €1.50, EU citizens and students with ID free.)*

PASEO. Since Cádiz's seaside *paseo* runs around the old city and along the Atlantic, walking the path is a good way to get a feel for the city's layout. Fantastic views of ships leaving the harbor recall Spain's golden age. Exotic trees, fanciful hedges, and a few chattering monkeys enliven the adjacent **Parque Genovés.** *(Paseo accessible via Pl. Argüelles or C. Fermín Salvochea, off Pl. de España.)*

◪ BEACHES

Fortunately for beach-lovers, the exhaust-spewing ships on one coast of Cádiz don't pollute the pristine beaches on the other. **Playa de la Caleta** is the most convenient beach from the old city, at the peninsula's far tip. Better sand and more space can be found in the new city, serviced by bus #1 from Pl. de España (€0.90), or along the *paseo* by the water (20-30min. walk from the cathedral). The first beach beyond the rocks is the unremarkable **Playa de Santa María del Mar.** Next to it is the clean, endless **Playa de la Victoria,** recognized by the EU for its excellence and transformed into a sea of bodies on land and water in the summer. Get off bus #1 at Glorieta Ingeniero La Cierva in front of the McDonald's. A more natural landscape can be found in ■**Playa de Cortadura.** Take bus #1 until just before the highway. The boardwalk ends here, and sunbather density falls steadily.

█ NIGHTLIFE

If you're in the right spot, you'll find that Cádiz's nightlife can't be contained; in winter the scene is situated in the old city, while summer takes the party closer to the beach in the new city. In the old city, look for bars on the side streets off **C. Columela** and **C. San Francisco.** In the new city, **C. General Muñoz Arenillas,** off Glorieta Ingeniero La Cierva, and **Paseo Marítimo,** the main drag along Playa Victoria, have some of Cádiz's best bars. Hard-core clubbers will prefer **Punto de San Felipe,** a strip of bars and clubs north along the sea from Pl. de España (take a right before the tunnel); these spots don't get going until 4 or 5am.

■ **La Nahu,** C. Beato Diego de Cádiz (☎856 07 09 22). An African-themed hookah bar and pub. Beer €1.50. Milkshakes and mixed drinks €4. Hookah €3-7 depending on size. Open daily 8pm-3am, F and Sa until 4am. MC/V.

Medussa, on the corner of C. Manuel Ronces and C. Beato Diego (www.lamedussa.com). A slightly younger bohemian crowd congregates here, where the specialty is *la música*: DJs change daily, providing dance, funk, garage, rock, and retro nights. Beer €2. Mixed drinks €4. W international night with €1 beers. Open Tu-Sa 10pm-4am.

Deep Ocean, Po. Marítimo 28 (☎956 07 80 32; deep-ocean-cadiz@hotmail.com), is a standout among the string of bars and discotecas in Nuevo Cádiz. The two dance floors move to Tu ballroom lessons, Th salsa, F themed parties, and Sa erotic shows. Su drinks include tapas. *Cañas* €1.50. *Copas* €4. Open daily 4:30pm-dawn.

█ FESTIVALS

■**Carnaval** insanity is legendary. The gray of winter gives way to dazzling color as the city hosts one of the most raucous *carnavales* in the world in late February and early March. Costumed dancers, street singers, ebullient residents, and spectators from around the world take to the streets in a week-long frenzy that makes New Orleans's Mardi Gras look like Thursday night bingo at the old folks' home. (www.carnavaldecadiz.com.)

VEJER DE LA FRONTERA   ☎956

Arguably the most charming of the *pueblos blancos*, Vejer (pop. 20,000) is a true village: its pace is steady, its nights are black, its cobblestone alleys are narrow, and its houses are a collection of cozily clustered white buildings. From its perch atop a little mountain, Vejer offers breathtaking views of the unspoiled landscape as well as a workout for the calves. The village is also a good base for exploring the region's many pristine natural reserves and beaches. If simply basking in its quiet charm sounds appealing, plan to spend a night; if you crave a quicker pace and have just a few rushed hours to spare, they might be better spent elsewhere.

█ **TRANSPORTATION.** For **bus** info and tickets, stop by the small **Transportes Generales Comes** office, C. La Plazuela, 2b. (☎956 45 16 80. Open M-F 9am-2:30pm and 6:15-10pm, Sa-Su 11am-2:30pm and 6:15-10pm. When the office is closed,

ANDALUCÍA

buy tickets on the bus.) The office also has snacks for sale, public telephones, and **Internet** access for €2 per hour. From the stop on Av. de Los Remedios near the tourist office, buses leave for **Cádiz** (1½hr., M-F 6 per day 8am-9:30pm, €4.80). For other destinations, take a cab to **Restaurante Venta Pinco Meson Rústico** (the stop name is **La Barca de Vejer**). Buses depart from the parking lot next to the restaurant; be sure to make yourself visible when you see the bus coming or it will pass by. Buses go to: **Algeciras** (2hr., 10 per day 7:50am-10:25pm, €5); **Málaga** (4hr., 7:50am and 5:05pm, €14.50); **Sevilla** (3½hr.; M-Sa 4 per day 7:15am-5:45pm, Su 4 per day 8:30am-5:45pm; €11); **Tarifa** (1hr., 10 per day 7:50am-10:25pm, €3.30). For a **taxi,** call ☎956 45 17 44.

■ ▮ ORIENTATION AND PRACTICAL INFORMATION. While some buses stop at the end of **Avenida de Los Remedios** (which leads uphill into **La Plazuela** (10min.), many leave passengers by the highway at **Restaurante Venta Pinco Meson Rustico** (the stop name is **La Barca de Vejer**) at the base of the hill. The staff at the **tourist office,** Av. de Los Remedios, 2, have information on other towns in the area. (☎956 45 17 36; www.turismovejer.com. Open M-F 10am-2:30pm and 6-8pm, Sa 11am-2pm and 6-8pm, Su 11am-2pm. Hours change frequently, but are always posted in the front window. Get there at least half an hour before closing in case the staff leaves early. Local services include: **Banco Santander Central Hispano,** C. Divino Salvador, 5 (☎902 24 24 24; open M-F 8:30am-2pm, Sa 8:30am-1pm); **Centro de Salud,** Av. de Andalucía (☎956 44 76 25); **police,** Av. de Andalucía (☎956 45 04 00); **Internet** access, free at the **Casa de la Juventud** on La Plazuela (use the entrance on C. Juan Relinque); ask for the username and password at the desk (☎956 44 72 24. Open M-Sa 8am-2pm); and the **post office,** in Pl. Juan Carlos I (☎956 45 02 38; open M-F 8:30am-2:30pm, Sa 9:30am-1pm). **Postal Code: 11150.**

▮ ▮ ACCOMMODATIONS AND FOOD. The most affordable places to stay in Vejer are *casas particulares* (private houses); the tourist office has an extensive list of *hostales* and *casas* if other options are full. Several options line C. San Filmo; to get there, follow C. Juan Relinque from La Plazuela, go right through the Pl. del Mercado, and head left uphill. Each of the rooms at the tranquil *casa rural,* ▮El Cobijo de Vejer ❺, C. Viña, 7, seamlessly blends modern amenities, gorgeous Arabic decor, and warm hospitality. Most rooms have small kitchens, lounges, and terraces with views of the town. All rooms have Internet access, A/C, satellite TV, and a refrigerator. (☎956 45 50 23; www.elcobijo.com. Breakfast included. Reserve at least a month ahead from late July to Sept. Doubles June-Sept. and *Semana Santa* €70-109; Oct.-May €58-75. AmEx/MC/V.) Friendly Señor Trujillo owns **Casa Los Cántaros ❷,** C. San Filmo, 14, a restored Andalusian home with a grape-vined patio. Affordable rooms with private bath are small but comfortable, and the terrace is a perfect for cooking a meal or watching the sunrise. (☎956 44 75 92. June-Sept. singles €20; doubles €30. Oct.-May €20/25. Cash only.)

The cheapest eats are tapas or *raciones* at the bars around La Plazuela; full-service restaurants are more expensive. Relax under a grape trellis and laze away the heat at **La Bodeguita ❶** tapas bar, C. Marqués de Tamarón, 9. (☎956 45 15 82. Tapas €1-1.20. Beer €1. Open daily in winter noon-3pm and 7pm-late, closed M in summer. Cash only.) Renowned for its *jamón ibérico* (Iberian ham), family-run **Mesón Pepe Julián ❷,** C. Juan Relinque, 7, serves reasonably priced entrees (€4.20-8) and tapas (€1-1.50) to a largely local crowd; plan to eat at the bar. An entire page of the menu is dedicated to vegetarian and meat-filled salads. (☎956 45 10 98. Open daily July-Aug. 11:30am-4pm and 7:30pm-midnight; Sept.-June closed Su. MC/V.)

◪ SIGHTS. The best way to enjoy Vejer is to wander along its streets and cliffside *paseos.* Ten kilometers down the road to Los Caños is **El Palmar,** 7km of fine sand and clear waters accessible by car or bus (June-Aug. 4 per day 11:45am-8:45pm, €1). To reach the beach, catch the Cádiz-bound bus to **Conil de la Frontera** and walk along the shore for 3-4km. For info on outdoor activities, consult **Discover Andalucía**, Av. de los Remedios, 45b, across from the bus stop. (☎956 44 75 75; www.discoverandalucia.com. Bicycles €12-15 per day. Surfboards from €6 per day. Open M-F 9am-2pm. AmEx/MC/V.)

FESTIVALS. Vejer throws brilliant fiestas. After the **Corpus Cristi** revelry in June comes the **Candelas de San Juan** on June 23rd, culminating in the midnight release of the **toro de fuego** (bull of fire). A local with a death wish dresses in an iron bull costume and charges the crowd as firecrackers attached to his body fly off in all directions. During the delirious **Semana Santa** celebrations, a *toro embolao* (sheathed bull) with wooden balls affixed to the tips of his horns is set loose through the narrow streets of Vejer on Easter Sunday.

TARIFA   ☎956

Prepare for wind-blown hair—when the breezes pick up in the southernmost city of continental Europe, it becomes clear why Tarifa (pop. 15,000) is known as the Hawaii of Spain. World-renowned winds combined with kilometers of empty, white beaches bring some of the best kite and windsurfers from around the world, while the tropical, relaxed environment beckons to the less adventurous. Location-wise, it doesn't get much better than this. Directly across the Strait of Gibraltar from Tangier, Morocco, Tarifa boasts incomparable views to the south, the Atlantic to the east, and the Mediterranean to the west. From few, other places in the world can you see two continents and two wide open seas at once.

TRANSPORTATION. Transportes Generales Comes buses go to the bus station, a trailer-like building on C. Batalla del Salado, 19. (☎956 68 40 38. Open M-F 7:30-9:30am, 10-11am, and 2:30-6:30pm, Sa-Su 3-7:45pm. Schedule in window; if office is closed, buy tickets from driver.) **Buses** run to: Algeciras (30min., 7-11 per day 6:30am-8:15pm, €1.70); Cádiz (2¼hr., 7 per day 7:25am-8:55pm, €7.44); La Línea (1hr., 6 per day 12:05pm-11:15pm, €3.35); Sevilla (3hr., 4 per day 8am-5:15pm, €14.30). **FRS ferries** (☎956 68 18 30; www.frs.com) leave from the port at the end of Po. de la Alameda for **Tangier** (35min.; daily every 2hr. 9am-11pm, F and Su last ferry at 9pm; return 9:30am-11:15pm, F and Su last return at 9:15pm Morocco time; €29; ages 3-12 €18. Small car €80). For a **taxi**, call **Parada Taxi** at ☎956 68 42 41.

ORIENTATION AND PRACTICAL INFORMATION. The **bus station** is on C. Batalla del Salado. Turn right toward the Repsol gas station and walk 10min. to the intersection with Av. de Andalucía. To reach the center of the old town, cross Av. de Andalucía and pass under the arch. To the left is C. Nuestra Señora de la Luz, which becomes C. Sancho IV el Bravo, the location of many cafes and restaurants. To reach the **tourist office,** don't go under the arch; instead, turn right on Av. de Andalucía. Take the first left onto Av. de la Constitución and then the first left into Parque de la Alameda. The park's only building, the tourist office has detailed maps and information on adventure sports, including kite-surfing. (☎956 68 09 93; www.tarifaweb.com. Open in summer M-F 10:30am-2pm and 6-8pm, Sa-Su 9am-2pm; in winter M-F 10am-2pm and 4-6pm, Sa-Su 9:30am-3pm.) Exchange currency at **Banco Santander Central Hispano,** C. Batalla del Salado, 17 and C. Sancho IV El Bravo in the walled town (☎902 24 24 24. Open M-F 8:30am-2pm, Sa 8:30am-1pm). Local services include the **police** on Pl. Santa María, 3 (☎092 or 956 68 21 74); **Centro Salud,** C. Amador de los Rios, on the left after Punta de Europa when walking from the town center (☎956 02 77 00 or 956 02 77 01); the **pharmacy** on C. Batalla des Salado, 22, is nameless but conspicuous. (☎956 68 05 61. Open M-F 9:30am-10pm, Sa 9:30am-12:30pm.) **Internet** cafes line Av. de Andalucía, but they aren't cheap; 1hr. of online access can cost you anywhere from €2-3. If you have a laptop, look for bars and cafes with signs for free Wi-Fi that'll make your computer worth its weight in cyber minutes. Kill three birds with one stone at **Tarifa Top Clean,** Av. Andalucía, 24, a combination Wi-Fi Internet cafe, coffee/tea bar, and **laundry** service. (☎956 68 03 03; www.topcleantarifa.com. €11 for a large wash, dry, and fold; €18 for extra-large; Internet €1.50 per 30mins., €2.50 per hour. Open M-F 10am-4pm.) The **post office,** C. Coronel Moscardó, 9, is near Pl. San Mateo. (☎956 68 42 37. Open M-F 8:30am-2:30pm, Sa 9:30am-1pm.) **Postal Code:** 11380.

⬛◨ ACCOMMODATIONS AND FOOD. The cheapest rooms line C. Batalla del Salado and its side streets. Prices rise significantly in summer; those visiting in August and on weekends from June to September should call ahead and arrive early. **Hostal Facundo I and II ❶,** C. Batalla del Salado, 47, with its "Welcome backpackers" slogan, draws the young budget crowd, but summer prices can leave your heart heavy and your wallet light. The common kitchen (8am-10pm), small TV room, and spacious common baths provide a place to chat with your fellow travelers. (☎956 68 42 98; www.hostalfacundo.com. Dorms €10-22; singles €25; doubles €22-45, with bath €26-55. Cash only.) Comfortable **Hostal Villanueva ❷,** Av. de Andalucía, 11, has a restaurant and rooftop terrace with an ocean view. Spotless rooms all have bath and TV. (☎956 68 41 49. Breakfast €2.25. Singles €20-25; doubles €35-45. Cash only.) Hard-core windsurfers often stay at one of the several **campgrounds** along the beach several kilometers from town; all have full bath and shower facilities, bars, and mini-supermarkets. Guests must bring their own tents. Although Cádiz-bound buses will drop you off if you ask, flagging one down to get back to town is next to impossible; some surfers call for taxis or befriend fellow surfers with cars. Try the summer camp feel of **Camping Río Jara ❶,** 4km from town (☎956 68 05 70. €6.20 per person, €10 per site including tent, car, and electricity) or **Camping Tarifa ❶,** 6km from town (☎956 68 47 78. €5.60 per person, €9.50 per site including tent, car, and electricity), both on highway CN-340.

For cheap sandwiches (€1.50-3), try any one of the many *bagueterías* lining C. Sancho IV el Bravo and its side streets. Alternatively, C. San Francisco offers a variety of affordable, appetizing options. ⬛**Bamboo ❶,** across from the castle, is a sensory wave of color, music, and both familiar and exotic tastes. Take off your shoes and lounge on eclectic, pillow-covered couches in the open-air seating area. The lounge becomes a bar at night. (☎956 62 73 04. Teas (€1.60-2). Fresh juices (€2.50-3). Panini €2.80-3.50. Full breakfast €4. F-Sa Live DJ. Open M-Th 10am-2pm, F-Sa to 3am, Su to 2pm. MC/V.) **Café Zumo ❶,** C. Sancho IV el Bravo, is a small but lively nook that dishes out plate after plate of vegetarian delight. While you chow down and sip fresh-squeezed juice, read a book from the shelf or make an exchange. (☎956 62 72 51. Meals from €3-7. Books €2 with an exchange, €6 without. Open M-F 10:30am-2pm and 6-8pm, Sa-Su 10am-2pm. Cash only.) **Pizzería Horno de Leña ❷** inside the **Tarifa EcoCenter,** C. San Sebastián, 6, uses only organic local ingredients in its pizzas, staying true to its "Don't panic, it's organic" mantra. Free Wi-Fi, an organic and fair-trade shop, yoga and therapy room, book store, and local crafts complete the EcoCenter and make it a one-stop shop for healthy living. Live music Friday and Saturday. (☎956 62 72 20. Pizzas €4.50-9. Open Tu-Sa 9am-2am, Su and M 9am-1:30pm. Cash only.) **Vaca Loca ❸,** C. Cervantes, is a rare steakhouse in the midst of ham country Iberia. Check the board for daily offerings and have your mind made up by the time you're seated. (Open daily 11am-3am; food served until 1am.

Cash only.) To stock up for your beach trip, go to **Eroski Center** on C. San Jose, parallel to C. Batalla del Salado (open M-Sa 9:30am-9:30pm).

◙ 𝄞 SIGHTS AND OUTDOOR ACTIVITIES. Next to the port and just outside the old town are the facade and ruins of the **Castillo de Guzmán el Bueno.** In the 13th century, the Moors kidnapped Guzmán's son and threatened his life if Guzmán didn't relinquish the castle. The father didn't surrender, even after his son's throat was slashed before his very eyes. (Open Apr.-Oct. Tu-Su 11am-2pm and 6-8pm; Nov.-May Tu-Su 11am-2pm and 4-6pm. €1.80.) Those with something less historical (or less gruesome) in mind can head 200m south to **Playa de los Lances** for 5km of the finest white sand on the Atlantic coast. Bathers should be aware of the occasional high winds and strong undertow. Adjacent to Playa de los Lances is **Playa Chica,** which is tiny but sheltered from the winds. **Tarifa Spin Out Surfbase,** 9km up the road toward Cádiz (ask the bus driver on the Cádiz route to stop, or take a taxi for €6), rents **windsurfing** and **kitesurfing** boards and instructs all levels. (☎956 23 63 52; www.tarifaspinout.com. Book ahead. Windsurf rental €25 per hour, €56 per day; 2hr. lesson including all equipment €50. Kite and board rental €28 per hour, €58 per day; 1½hr. lesson with all equipment €99.) Many campgrounds along CN-340 between km 70 and km 80 provide instruction and gear for outdoor sports; ask at the tourist office for their list of kite- and windsurfing schools and rental shops.

▣ NIGHTLIFE. At night, sunburnt travelers mellow out in the old town's many bars, which range from jazz to psychedelic to Irish. People migrate to the clubs around 1 or 2am. The *terrazas* on C. Sancho IV el Bravo fill with locals and surfers chatting over beer or coffee. Almost every bar and club on C. San Francisco is a hot spot; the street hosts endless places for backpackers and locals to meet, drink, and move to the music. **Moskito,** C. San Francisco, 11, is a combination bar-club with a Caribbean motif, dance music, and tropical cocktails. (Free salsa lessons W night 10:30pm. Beer €2.50. Mixed drinks €4.50-6. Open in summer daily 11pm-3am; in winter Th-Sa 11pm-later.) **La Tribu,** C. Nuestra Señora de la Luz, 7, a favorite among kite surfers, makes some of the most creative cocktails in town, while trance and techno pump energy into this otherwise mellow nightspot. (Beer €2-3. Mixed drinks €4-6. Shots €1.50. Open daily 8pm-2 or 3am.)

GIBRALTAR
☎350 OR 9567

Emerging from the morning mist, the Rock of Gibraltar's craggy face menaces those who pass by its shores. Ancient seafarers referred to the rock as one of the Pillars of Hercules, believing that it marked the end of the world. Today, it is known affectionately to locals as "Gib" and is home to more fish 'n' chips plates and pints of bitter per capita than anywhere in the Mediterranean. Though Gibraltar is officially a self-governing British colony, Spain continues to campaign for sovereignty. When a 1969 vote showed that Gibraltar's populace favored its colonial ties to Britain—at 12,138 to 44—Franco sealed the border. After 16 years of isolation and a decade of negotiations, the border re-opened on February 4, 1985. Tourists and residents cross with ease, but Gibraltar has a culture all its own, one that remains detached from Spain. While the mix of wild primates and unique culture makes Gibraltar worth visiting, it is in many ways a tourist trap, complete with streets of shops, duty-free liquor and tobacco, and pocket-burning prices. Cross the border, explore the Rock, then scurry back to Spain before nightfall.

ANDALUCÍA

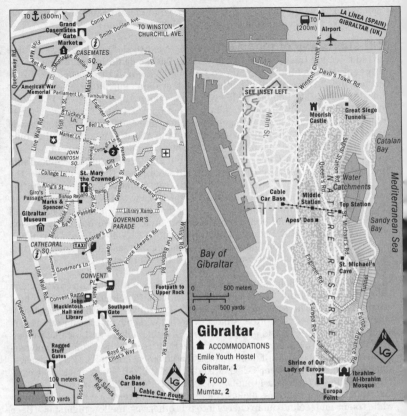

■ TRANSPORTATION

Flights: Airport (☎ 730 26). **British Airways** (☎ 793 00) flies to **London** (2½hr., 2 per day, £168/€233) and **Madrid** (1hr., 2 per day, £142.60/€215).

Buses: From **La Línea,** on the Spanish border, to: **Algeciras** (40min.; M-F every 30min. 7:45am-11:15pm, Sa, Su, and holidays every 45min. 8:45am-11:15pm; €1.82); **Cádiz** (3hr., 4 per day 6:30am-8pm, €12.91); **Granada** (5hr., 7:15am and 2:15pm, €19.43); **Jerez de la Frontera** (4½hr., 9:30am, €12.91); **Madrid** (7hr., 1:10 and 10:15pm, €25.24); **Málaga** (3¼hr., 4 per day 7:15am-5:30pm, Su also 8:45pm; €10.32); **Marbella** (1¾hr., 4 per day 7:15am-5:30pm, €5.20); **Sevilla** (6hr., 4 per day 7am-4:15pm, €19.65); **Tarifa** (1hr., 7 per day 6:30am-8pm, €3.59).

Ferries: Turner & Co., 65/67 Irish Town St. (☎ 783 05; fax 720 06). Open M-F 8am-3pm. To **Tangier, Morocco** (1¼hr.; F 6pm, return Sa 5:30pm Moroccan time; £18/€32, under 12 £9/€16.20).

Public Transport: Most bus lines run from one end of the Rock base to the other. Buses #9 and 10 go between the border and the Rock for £0.60/€1. Round-trip £0.90/€1.50. Unlimited day pass £1.50/€2.50.

Taxis: Gibraltar Taxi Association ☎ 956 77 00 27.

EURO OR POUNDS? Although euro are accepted almost everywhere (except at pay phones and post offices), the pound sterling (£) is the preferred method of payment in Gibraltar. ATMs dispense money in pounds. Merchants and sights sometimes charge a higher price in euros than in pounds. Unless stated otherwise, however, assume that establishments accept euros; change is often given in British currency. The exchange rate fluctuates around £1 to €1.50. As of July 2007, 1£ = €1.48.

ANDALUCÍA

ORIENTATION AND PRACTICAL INFORMATION

Before you head to Gibraltar, make sure you have a valid passport, otherwise you'll be turned away at the border. If you need a visa, the UK embassy in Madrid takes roughly a day to process them. Buses from Spain terminate in the nearby town of **La Línea**. From the bus station, walk directly toward the Rock (it's impossible to miss; the border is 5min. away). Once through customs and passport control, catch bus #9 or 10 or carefully walk across the airport tarmac into town (20min.); stay left on Av. Winston Churchill when the road forks with Corral Ln. Cars take longer to enter and exit Gibraltar—often an hour or more.

Tourist Office: Duke of Kent House, Cathedral Sq. (☎450 00). From Main St., walk behind the cathedral. Open M-F 9am-5:30pm, Sa 10am-3pm, Su 10am-1pm. **Info booth** at Spanish border in the immigration building. Open M-F 9am-4:30pm, Sa 10am-1pm.

Luggage Storage: Bus station in **La Línea.** €3 per day. Buy token for locker at a bus ticket booth. Open daily 7am-10pm.

Bookstore: Gibraltar Bookshop, 300 Main St. (☎718 94). Tons of paperbacks and travel guides. Open M-F 10am-6:30pm. AmEx/MC/V.

Emergency: ☎199. **Police:** 120 Irish Town St. (☎725 00).

Pharmacy: Calpe Centre, Casemates Sq. (☎779 77). Open M-F 9am-7pm, Sa 10:30am-1:30pm.

Hospital: St. Bernard's Hospital, on Hospital Hill (☎797 00).

Internet Access: Call Shop, Main St., 293A (☎496 45). £2.50/€4 per hr. Cheap international calls. Accepts pounds, euros, and dollars; all change given in sterling. Open daily 9am-9pm.

Post Office: 104 Main St. (☎756 62). Open June to mid-Sept. M-F 9am-2:15pm, Sa 10am-1pm; mid-Sept. to May M-F 9am-4:30pm, Sa 10am-1pm. Pounds (£) only.

ACCOMMODATIONS AND FOOD

Gibraltar is best visited as a daytrip. The few accommodations in the area are pricey and often full, especially in the summer, and camping is illegal. At worst, you can crash across the border in La Línea. Back on the Rock, **Emile Youth Hostel Gibraltar ❷,** on Montague Bastian, has bunk beds in cheerfully painted rooms with clean communal baths. (☎511 06; www.emilehostel.com. Breakfast included. Lockout 10:30am-4:30pm. £1 for luggage storage or towels. Dorms £15/€25; doubles £34/€51. Cash only.) International restaurants are easy to find, but you may choke on the prices. Sample the tasty treats of Gibraltar's thriving Hindu community at **Mumtaz ❶,** 20 Cornwalls Ln., where authentic tastes and true *dhaba* style come at the lowest of prices. (☎442 57. Entrees £2.50-6.75, with ample vegetarian selection. Takeout available. Open daily 11am-3pm and 6pm-12:30am. Cash only.) **Marks & Spencer** on Main St. has a small grocery/bakery with relatively decent priced pre-packaged food items and fresh breads. (Open M-F

9am-7pm, Sa 9:30am-5pm. AmEx/MC/V.) The cheapest and freshest can be found at the local **market,** behind Casemates Square. (Open M-Sa 8am-2:30pm.)

◎ SIGHTS

▨THE ROCK OF GIBRALTAR

The top of the Rock Nature Reserve is accessible by car or cable car, or for the truly adventurous, by foot. Cable cars (☎778 26) depart daily every 10min. 9:30am-5:15pm; last return 5:45pm. Tickets sold until 5:15pm. It's possible to buy a ticket for only the cable car (round-trip £8/€13.50), but if you plan on visiting any of the sights, it's better to buy a combined admission ticket (£16/€21.50). The walk down takes 2-3hr., including stops at the sights. Tour operators offer van or taxi tours that take visitors to all attractions in about 1½hr. The official Taxi Tour booth is in the immigrations building across from the tourist booth; make sure you take the official tour sponsored by the Taxi Association. Prices for the Taxi Tour include all sights so it may be slightly cheaper than the cable car. If you drive, there is a £8/€10.50 entrance fee per person, plus £1.50/€3 per car. On foot, take Library St. to Library Ramp from Main St., follow it uphill to the end, and turn right. At the next intersection there is a sign for the footpath to the Rock. Follow the footpath for 20min. until you hit a road, and turn left.

Gibraltar's claim to fame is this legendary **Rock,** and you can't do the city justice without seeing this titanic crag, even if it's just to say you've seen it. Climbing the giant white rock will give you many a photo op to capture the severe cliffs plunging into the ocean. About halfway up the Rock (at the first cable car stop, or a 25min. walk down from the top stop) is the infamous **Apes' Den,** where colonies of Barbary apes cavort atop taxis and tourists' heads. These startlingly tail-less apes have inhabited Gibraltar since the 18th century. When the ape population nearly went extinct in 1944, Churchill ordered reinforcements from North Africa; now they are procreating at such a rate that population control has become an issue. The apes are very tourist-friendly but have been known to steal food and other items from visitors; keep all food hidden and bags closed to avoid unwanted confrontations with the animals. At the northern tip of the Rock, facing Spain, are the **Great Siege Tunnels.** Originally used to fend off a combined Franco-Spanish siege at the end of the American Revolution, the tunnels were expanded during WWII to span 33 miles underground. Nearby, on the way back to town, is the old Moorish castle, rebuilt several times, most recently in 1333. Although the castle is currently under renovation, the exterior still merits a quick look if you're already on the Rock. Thousands of years of water erosion carved the eerie chambers of **St. Michael's Cave.** Ask at the entrance about a guided tour to the lower caves, with an underground lake and stalagmites.

COSTA DEL SOL

The coast has sold its soul to the devil, and now he's starting to collect. Artifice covers its once-natural charms as chic promenades, swanky hotels, and apartment buildings spring up between the small towns and the shoreline. The Costa del Sol extends from Tarifa in the southwest to Cabo de Gata, east of Almería; post-industrial Málaga lies smack in the middle. To the northeast, hills dip straight into the ocean, and rocky beaches enhance the shore's natural beauty. To the southwest, however, waves seem to wash up onto more concrete than sand. Still, nothing can really detract from the coast's major attraction: eight months of spring and four months of summer. News of the fantastic weather has spread, and July and August bring swarms of pale northern Europeans. Reservations are essential in the summer anywhere on the coast, especially at hostels.

MÁLAGA

☎952

Málaga (pop. 550,000) is the busiest city on the coast, and while its beaches are better known for their bars than natural beauty, the city has much to offer. The Alcazaba, commanding on a hill to the west of the city, offers magnificent—and telling—views of Málaga: cranes and industrial ports in the distance contrast with the charming *casco antiguo* and verdant gardens. Known as the birthplace of artist Pablo Picasso, the city finally got its own museum dedicated to the prodigy in 2003. Because it is a critical transportation hub, many see Málaga en route to other coastal stops, but it is well worth a day or two in its own right.

⌐ TRANSPORTATION

Flights: (☎952 04 88 04 or 902 40 47 04). From the airport, bus #19 (every 30min. 6:35am-11:35pm, €1) runs from the "City Bus" sign, stopping at the bus station and at the corner of C. Molina Lario and Postigo de los Abades. RENFE trains connect the city and the airport (12min., €1). **Iberia,** C. Molina Lario, 13 (☎952 13 61 66, 24hr. reservations 902 40 05 00), has daily international flights, mostly to England.

Trains: Estación de Málaga, Explanada de la Estación (☎952 12 80 79). Take bus #3 at Po. del Parque or #4 at Pl. de la Marina to the station. **RENFE** office, C. Strachan, 4 (☎902 24 02 02). To: **Barcelona** (13hr.; 7:20am, 8:20pm; €54.20); **Córdoba** (2hr., 9 per day 6:45am-8:20pm, €15.60); **Fuengirola** (30min., every 30min. 8am-10:30pm, €1.20); **Madrid** (5hr., 7 per day 6:45am-7:45pm, €34.90); **Sevilla** (3hr., 5-6 per day 7:45am-8:10pm, €16.04); **Torremolinos** (20min., every 30min. 5:45am-10:10pm, €1.10). Reservations for long-distance trains are highly recommended.

Buses: Po. de los Tilos (☎952 35 00 61, **ALSA** 902 42 22 42, **Alsina Graells Sur** 952 31 82 95, **Casado** 952 31 59 08, **Daibus** 952 31 52 47, **Portillo** 902 14 31 44), 1 block from the RENFE station along C. Roger de Flor, buses #3, 4, C1 and 19 stop at the station. To: **Algeciras** (3hr., 9-10 per day 5am-7:15pm, €10.70); **Almería** (6-9 per day 3:15am-7pm, €14.05); **Antequera** (1hr.; M-F 13 per day 7am-8:45pm, Sa 8 per day 9:30am-10pm, Su 9 per day 9:30am-11pm, €4.77); **Cádiz** (5hr., 6 per day 6:45am-8pm, €20.21-20.69); **Córdoba** (3hr., 7 per day 9am-8pm, €11.16); **Granada** (2hr., 17-19 per day 7am-10pm, €8.58); **Madrid** (7hr., 8-12 per day 8:30am-1am, €19.05); **Marbella** (1½hr.; M-F 25 per day 6:45am-9:45pm, Sa 22 per day 8:30am-9:45pm, Su 21 per day 9am-9:45pm; €4.52-4.84); **Murcia** (6hr., 5 per day 8:30am-9:45pm, €26); **Ronda** (3hr., 4-12 per day 8am-8:30pm, €9.31-9.63); **Sevilla** (3hr., 11-12 per day 7am-3:15am, €13.89).

Taxis: Radio Taxi (☎952 32 00 00). Town center to waterfront €6; to the airport €15-20; from the train and bus station to town center €4; from Málaga to Balmádena €20.

✴ ⁊ ORIENTATION AND PRACTICAL INFORMATION

The bus and train stations lie a block away from each other along C. Roger de Flor, on the other side of the Río Guadalmedina from the historical center and the majority of other sights. To get to the town center from the bus station, exit right onto Callejones del Perchel, walk straight through the big intersection with Av. de la Aurora, take a right onto Av. de Andalucía, and cross Puente de Tetuán. From here, **Alameda Principal** leads into **Plaza de la Marina** (20min.). Alternatively, take bus #3, 4 or 21 along the same route (€1). From Pl. de la Marina, C. Molina Lario

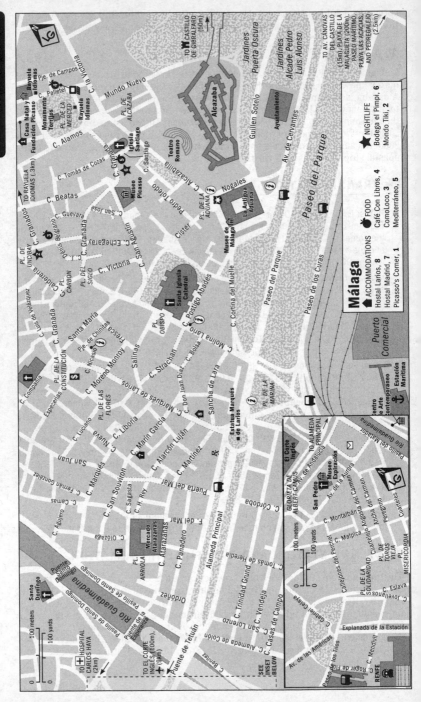

leads to the **cathedral** and the old town. C. Marqués de Larios, the main shopping and pedestrian street, connects Pl. de la Marina to **Plaza de la Constitución.** Behind the latter plaza, C. Granada leads to many good tapas bars and **Plaza de la Merced,** renowned for its *botellón.* Av. Cánovas del Castillo leads to **Playa de la Malagueta** (20min. walk), Málaga's closest beach worth visiting. After dark, be wary of both the neighborhood of **Cruz del Molinillo** (near the market) and desolate beaches.

Tourist Offices: Municipal, Av. de Cervantes, 1, Pl. de la Aduana (☎952 12 20 20; www.malagaturismo.com). Open daily 9am-7pm. **Branch:** Pl. de la Marina (☎952 12 20 20). Open M-F 9am-7pm. **Branch:** Pl. de la Aduana. Open M-F 9am-7pm, Sa 10am-7pm, Su 10am-2pm. **Junta de Andalucía,** Pje. de Chinitas, 4 (☎952 21 34 45). Open M-F 9am-8pm, Sa 10am-7pm, Su 10am-2pm. In winter offices may close earlier.

Currency Exchange: Banks (and **ATMs**) line most major roads and cluster around the intersection of Alameda Principal and C. Marqués de Larios. Most open M-F 8:30am-2pm; some also open Sa mornings.

Luggage Storage: Lockers at the **train station** (open daily 7am-10:45pm) and **bus station** (open daily 6:30am-11pm). Both €2.40-4.50 per day.

English-Language Bookstore: Rayuela Idiomas, Pl. de la Merced, 17 and C. Carcer, 1. (☎952 22 48 10). Open M-F 9:45am-1:30pm and 5-8:30pm, Sa 10am-2pm. MC/V.

Police: Policía Nacional, Plaza de la Aduana, 1 (☎952 04 62 00). **Policía Municipal,** Av. de la Rodaleda, 19 (☎952 12 65 00).

24hr. Pharmacy: Farmacia Caffarena, Alameda Principal, 2 (☎952 21 28 58), at the intersection with C. Marqués de Larios.

Medical Services: ☎952 39 04 00, emergency 952 30 30 34. **Hospital Carlos Haya,** Av. Carlos Haya (☎951 29 00 00).

Internet Access: Internet Meeting Point, Pl. de la Merced, 14. Internet access from €1-2 per hour, depending on time of day. Also has a pool table, video games, and a coffee and liquor bar. Open M-Sa 10am-1am, Su 11am-11pm. MC/V.

Post Office: Av. de Andalucía, 1 (☎902 19 71 97). **Lista de Correos.** Open M-F 8:30am-8:30pm, Sa 9:30am-2pm. **Postal Code:** 29080.

▚ ACCOMMODATIONS

Budget accommodations in Málaga are a little pricier than other Andalusian cities—expect to pay about €18-30 for a single or dorm bed. Most *hostales* are in the old town between Pl. de la Marina and Pl. de la Constitución.

▨ Picasso's Corner, C. San Juan de Letrán, 9, off of Pl. de la Merced (☎952 21 22 87; www.picassoscorner.com). This hostel boasts a large DVD collection, free Internet access, and an elegant bathroom with massaging shower. Dorms are social but sympathetic to weary travelers looking to catch some winks. Breakfast and 24hr. tea and coffee included. 4- to 6-bed dorms €18-19; doubles €22.50 per person. MC/V. ❷

Hostal Larios, C. Marqués de Larios, 9, 3rd fl. (☎952 22 54 90). Don't pay for a room with a private bath; the common ones are clean and new. TV and A/C. Singles €32-37, with bath €35-42; doubles €42-49/53-60; triples with bath €75-89. MC/V. ❸

Hostal Madrid, C. Marín García, 4, 2nd fl. (☎952 22 45 92). Don't let the exterior turn you away from the cheapest beds in the city. Hostal Madrid's sizable rooms have showers and private balconies, some with views of a peaceful street. Singles €15-20; doubles €25-40. During Aug. and *ferias* €30/60. Cash only. ❷

◖ FOOD

Beachfront restaurants specialize in fresh seafood; *málagueños* love *pescaito frito* (fried fish) and sardines roasted over open flames. Restaurants in the streets around C. Granada, Pl. de la Constitución, and Pl. de la Merced tend to lean toward both classic and inventive salad menus. Try your hand at your own salad creation with fresh produce from the **market** on C. Atarazanas (open daily 8am-2pm). There is also a supermarket in **El Corte Inglés,** Av. de Andalucía, 4-6. (☎952 07 65 00. Open M-Sa 10am-10pm. AmEx/MC/V.)

🦪 **Mediterráneo,** C. Santiago, 4 (☎952 21 64 38). Arabic cuisine with a distinctly Greek spin. Pull up a chair and shamelessly indulge in a mojito (€2.50 glass, €6 pitcher) and any of the couscous or combo dishes (€1.80-8.20). Don't leave without a plate of feta in olive oil (€2.20) or a bowl of fried ice cream (€2.80). Open Tu-Su 8pm-midnight. ❶

Café Con Libros, Pl. de la Merced, 19. Sit amid stacks of books and magazines as you sip on milkshakes, smoothies, teas, and coffees (€1.20-3.80), breakfast *menús* (€2.30-3.20), crepes and pastries (€1.90-3). Open daily 11am-2am. Cash only. ❶

ComoLoco, C. Denis Belgrado, 17 (☎952 21 65 71). Specializing in salads and pitas (€4-8), ComoLoco is one of the many trendy restaurants by C. Granada. Salads are large enough to quiet a grumbling stomach, but you'll have to wait the typical 20-70min. for a table. Open daily 1pm-1am. Cash only. ❷

🄶 SIGHTS

ALCAZABA. Towering high above the city, the Alcazaba is Málaga's most imposing sight, offering great views of the harbor and capturing a medieval tranquility within its brick and stone walls. Guarding the east end of Po. del Parque, this 11th-century structure was originally used as both a military fortress and a royal palace by Moorish kings. *(Open June-Aug. Tu-Su 9:30am-8pm; Sept.-May Tu-Sa 8:30am-7pm. €2, students and seniors €0.60, under 7 free. Su free after 2pm.)*

SANTA IGLESIA CATEDRAL DE MÁLAGA. Málaga's commanding cathedral spices up its mostly Renaissance aesthetic with a touch of Baroque. The intricate structure, complete with detailed columns, stained glass windows, and more than 15 side chapels, was built on the site of a former mosque. On the outside, the cathedral looks a bit off balance—it should have two towers, but one of them is only half-built—hence the cathedral's nickname *La Manquita* (One-Armed Lady). The small museum upstairs displays religious art. *(C. Molina Lario, 4. ☎952 22 03 45. Open M-F 10am-6pm, Sa 10am-5pm. Mass daily 9am. €3.50, includes audio tour.)*

CASTILLO DE GIBRALFARO. An Arabic lighthouse was built in this Phoenician castle, which offers sweeping vistas of Málaga and the Mediterranean. After admiring the cityscape, stop by the Centro de Interpretación, which has artifacts from the city's seafaring past. *(Bus #35 leaves every 20min. from the Alameda Principal; otherwise it's a shadeless 30min. uphill hike. Open daily Apr.-Oct. 9am-8pm; Nov.-Mar. 9am-6pm. €1.95, students and seniors €0.60, combined with Alcazaba €3.20. Su free after 2pm.)*

CASA NATAL Y FUNDACIÓN PICASSO. Picasso left Málaga when he was young, but according to local officials, he always "felt himself to be a true *malagueño*." The artist's birthplace now houses the Picasso Foundation, which organizes a series of exhibitions and lectures. The first floor is a seasonal gallery; upstairs is a permanent collection of photographs, drawings, and pottery by the artist. *(Pl. de la Merced, 15. ☎952 06 02 15; www.fundacionpicasso.es. Open daily 9:30am-8pm. €1, seniors, under 17, and students under 26 free.)*

MUSEO PICASSO. Though the collection isn't as impressive as those in Spain's larger museums, this relatively new exhibition dedicated to Málaga's most famous son traces his transition from child prodigy to renowned master. *(C. San Agustín, 8. ☎902 44 33 77; www.museopicassomalaga.org. Open Tu-Th, Su, and holidays 10am-8pm; F-Sa*

10am-9pm. €6 permanent collection, €4.50 for temporary, €8 combined; students, ages 10-16, and large groups €3; under 10 free. Last Su of each month free 3-8pm.)

EL CENTRO DE ARTE CONTEMPORANEO. Some of the best-known artists today, such as Gerhard Richter and the controversial Chapman brothers, have exhibited in this renovated marketplace along the river. In addition to a hefty 400-piece permanent collection, which boasts a noteworthy selection of post-1950s American art, the museum's temporary exhibits maintain its fresh, avant-garde feel. *(C. Alemania. ☎952 12 00 55; www.cacmalaga.org. Open Tu-Su 10am-2pm and 5-9pm. Free.)*

📍🎵 NIGHTLIFE AND BEACHES

Many nightlife spots are only open Thursday through Saturday. 🎵**Bodega El Pimpi** is an ultra-popular traditional *bodega* with lots of little nooks and tiny rooms. The bar fills up early in the evening and stays crowded until about 1am. (Beer €1.50-2. Mixed drinks €4.50. Open daily 11pm-2am.) A standout in a cluster of other trendy bars, **Mondo Tiki**, on Pl. Uncibay, offers a free shot of honey rum with the first drink to get people dancing to the beats of house and techno. (Beer €3. Mixed drinks €6. Open M-W and Su 11pm-3am, Th-Sa 11pm-4am.) For a change in scenery, head to Playa de la Malagueta, a beach that gets even more popular when the sun goes down. Young locals party at *chiringuitos* (beachfront bars). (30min. walk, but a quick and affordable taxi ride; buses don't run during late party hours.)

MARBELLA ☎952

While much of Spain draws visitors looking to engage in the country's history and culture, people come to Marbella (pop. 115,000) looking for something quite different: a tan. Once a sleepy fishing village, the town's 10-month-long swimsuit season has transformed Marbella into a strip of endless umbrellas and seaside cafes. There are more vacationers, it seems, than locals. The city has a long history as a key merchant town occupied by the Phoenicians, Greeks, Romans, and Arabs, and the influence of these groups is still evident in the structure and architecture of the *casco antiguo*, though the old buildings now frequently house upscale restaurants and swimwear shops. So while Marbella serves primarily as a Mediterranean playground for international jet-setters, anyone interested in life beyond yachts and watersports will appreciate the architecture and layout of the old city.

▐ TRANSPORTATION

Buses: Marbella, 56km south of Málaga, can be reached only by bus. Ctra. del Trapiche (☎952 76 44 00). To: **Cádiz** (2¾hr., 6 per day 7:30am-8:45pm, €15.96-16.13); **Fuengirola** (1hr.; approx. every 20min. 6:50am-10:50pm, Su 10.40pm; €2.58); **Granada** (3½hr., 7 per day 8:25am-8:15pm, €13.63-13.95); **Málaga** (1½hr., 22-27 per day 7am-8pm, €4.52-4.84); **Ronda** (1½hr., 7-8 per day 9am-9pm, €5.02); **Sevilla** (4hr.; M-Th and Sa 9am, 4pm, F and Su 9am, 4, 8:30pm; €15.19).

Ferries: To **Puerto Banús** from the port (30min.; hourly; €7, round-trip €10).

Taxis: Taxi Sol (☎952 77 44 88) serves Marbella center (€5) and Puerto Banús (€10). Taxi stands on the corner of Av. Ramón y Cajal and C. Huerta Chica.

▐▌🗲 ORIENTATION AND PRACTICAL INFORMATION

The **bus station** is at the top of Ctra. del Trapiche. To reach the city center, exit the station, walk left, make the first right onto Ctra. del Trapiche, and turn right at the

Marbella

🏠 **ACCOMMODATIONS**
Hostal Paco, **4**
Hostal del Pilar, **3**

🍴 **FOOD**
Cantero, **6**
La Casa del Té, **2**
El Gallo, **1**

⭐ **NIGHTLIFE**
Comedia, **7**
O'Brian's Irish Bar, **5**

Map labels: TO (800m); Museo del Bonsai; Parque Arroyo de la Represa; C. San Francisco; C. Salvador Rueda; C. Bermeja; C. Postigo; C. Lobatas; C. Practicante Manuel Cantos; Av. de Maíz Viñals; C. Alba; C. del San Antonio; C. del Bonijerón; C. San Vicente; C. los Naranjos; Av. del Mercado; Av. de Valenzuela; C. de Francisco de Quevedo; Princesa Príncipe; **Municipal Market**; PL. PUENTE DE RONDA; C. Aduar; C. Ancha; C. Chorrón; C. Portada; Av. Europa; V. del Amparo; Av. de Valencia; C. Padre Salvador; C. Peñuelas; C. Jacinto Benavente; C. Mesones; C. Peral; C. Remedios; Lavomatic; C. Arte; C. Salinas; TO (100m); C. Castillejos; C. de los Caballeros; C. Panadería; C. Escuelas; C. Castillo; PL. DE SAN BERNABÉ; Museo del Grabado Español Contemporáneo; PL. DE LOS OLIVOS; C. Estación; **CASCO ANTIGUO**; PL. DE LOS NARANJOS; C. Trinidad; C. Mendoza; C. Muro; Bus to Puerto Banús; PL. VICTORIA; C. Huerta Chica; C. San Lázaro; C. Buitrago; C. Nueva; C. Álamo; PL. DE LA IGLESIA; C. Viento; PL. C. ALTAMIRANO; C. del Sol; Av. Ricardo Soriano; C. Pedraza; C. Fortaleza; C. Valdés; C. Pandeón; C. Gloria; Alameda; C. Misericordia; C. Soledad; Av. de Nabeul; C. del Río; C. San Cristóbal; C. San Ramón; C. Luna; TAXI; Av. Ramón y Cajal; C. África; C. Tetuán; C. Marq. de Náj.; PL. DE LA ALAMEDA; Trv. Carlos Mackintosh; C. F. Rodríguez de la Fuente; Telekon Locutorio; TO (400m), HOSPITAL COMARCAL (2.5km); Av. Severo Ochoa; Av. de Miguel Cano; Av. del Mar; C. del Fuerte; C. Rafaela Aparicio; Av. Antonio Belón; C. Padres José Vera; J. C. del P20; C. A. Marina; C. Sevillano; Av. Mediterráneo; Av. Puerta del Mar; P. Marítimo; TO MUNICIPAL TOURIST OFFICE (200m), PUERTO BANÚS (7km); Av. Duque de Ahumada; Playa de Venus; **Puerto Deportivo**; **MEDITERRANEAN SEA**; 0–150 meters; 0–150 yards; TO PUERTO BANÚS (7km)

end of the road onto C. Salvador Rueda. Continue downhill on Av. del Mercado and turn left onto C. Castillejos, which leads to the perpendicular **Avenida Ramón y Cajal,** the main street in the new town; this becomes Av. Ricardo Soriano on the way to the swanky harbor of **Puerto Banús** (7km away). C. Peral curves up from C. Huerta Chica off of Av. Ramón y Cajal around the **casco antiguo.** The central hub of the old town, **Plaza de los Naranjos,** is in the middle of a jumble of pedestrian streets. From C. Peral, the most direct route to the plaza is down C. Cabelleros.

Tourist Office: Pl. de los Naranjos (☎952 82 35 50; www.marbella.es). Sells detailed maps of the city and nearby San Pedro de Alcantara (€1); small ones free. Open M-F 9am-9pm, Sa 10am-2pm. **Municipal Office,** Glorieta de la Fontanilla (☎952 77 14 42), across from and several blocks to the right of the main beach when facing the water. English spoken. Open M-F 9:30am-9pm, Sa 10am-2pm.

Currency Exchange: Banco Santander Central Hispano, Av. Ramón y Cajal, 9 (☎902 24 24 24). Open M-F 8:30am-2pm, Sa 8:30am-1pm; Apr.-Sept. closed Sa. **ATMs** abound, especially near the *casco antiguo* and along Av. Ramón y Cajal.

Luggage Storage: At the bus station (€3). Open daily 6:30am-11:30pm.

Laundry: Lavomatic, on the corner of Av. Cánovas del Castillo, 70 (☎952 24 59 02). Boasts that your laundry can be done in under an hour. Wash and dry €13. Open daily 7am-11pm.

Police: Av. Juan de la Cierva (☎952 89 99 00 or 092).

Pharmacy: Farmacia Espejo, Pl. de los Naranjos, 4 (☎952 77 12 91). Open daily 9:30am-midnight; posts list of rotating 24hr. pharmacies.

Hospital: Comarcal, CN-340, km 187 (☎952 86 27 48).

Internet Access: Neotel Locutorios, Pl. Puente de Ronda, 6 (☎952 82 85 24). €2 per hour. Try the €5 bono good for 5 hours. Open M-Sa 9am-1am, Su 10am-1am. MC/V.

Telekom Locutorio, Av. Puerta del Mar, 1 (☎952 82 44 27). €1.50 per hour. Open daily 10am-midnight. Cash only.

Post Office: C. Jacinto Benavente, 26 (☎952 77 28 98), uphill from C. Ricardo Soriano. Open M-F 8:30am-8:30pm, Sa 9:30am-1pm. **Postal Code:** 29600.

ACCOMMODATIONS

The town's popularity has dwindled in recent years, making accommodations a lot easier to find for last-minute arrivals.

Hostal del Pilar, C. Mesoncillo, 4 (☎952 82 99 36; www.hostel-marbella.com). Backpackers enjoy the pool table, bar, and fireplace. Friendly, English-speaking staff. Roof mattresses available when rooms are full (€15). Maximum of 6 people in the dorms (typically same-sex). Wi-Fi. July-Aug. dorms €17.50; doubles €30-35; triples €52.50. Sept.-June €15/25/36. Weekly and monthly rates available in winter. Cash only. ❷

Hostal Paco, C. Isaac Peral, 16 (☎952 77 12 00; www.hostalpacomarbella.com). Near many nightclubs on one of the *casco antiguo*'s main arteries. Reasonably-sized, airy rooms have bath and TV; some have A/C. Singles €33-40; doubles €40-60; triples €60-80; quads €75-95. Highest prices in Aug. and *Semana Santa*. AmEx/MC/V. ❸

FOOD

Terrazas on Pl. de los Naranjos are not particularly budget-friendly—the multilingual menus spell tourist trap. Restaurants farther uphill or hidden in alleys are easier on the wallet and offer more authentic cuisine, although the tapas bars that line these smaller streets are the same price and have more limited menus. The waterfront has similar eateries, but a livelier and younger atmosphere. Locals retreat to Av. Nabeul for cheap eats. The municipal **market,** on Av. del Mercado, uphill from C. Huerta Chica, sells affordable produce and meat. (Open M-Sa 8am-2pm.)

El Gallo, C. Lobatas, 44 (☎952 82 79 98). A truly local restaurant and a perennial favorite with backpackers. Reasonable meals in a family-friendly atmosphere. Tapas from €1. The €8 *menú* is the best bargain, but the rabbit in garlic sauce (€8) steals the show. Open M-W and F-Su 9am-4:30pm and 7-11:30pm. MC/V. ❷

La Casa del Té, C. Ancha, 7 (☎639 16 79 18). Loud music, incense, and low lighting make this place feel like a nightclub crossed with a teahouse. The crepes (€2.30-2.60) and great selection of teas and juices (€1.10-3) are sure to please. Breakfasts €2-3.20. Open May-Sept. 10am-1:30pm and 5-11:30pm; Oct.-Apr. 4-10:30pm. Cash only. ❶

Cantero, C. Castillejo, 7 (☎952 82 21 12). If you're going to do Spanish pastry, you have to do it right, the kind of right that includes enormous cookies and slices of cake for only €1-1.50. Sit at one of the raised tables inside or take your whopping dessert to a nearby park bench. Open M-F 8:15am-2:15pm and 5-9:15pm, Sa 5-9:15pm. ❶

SIGHTS

If you're not staying in the old city, at least relish a stroll through its maze of narrow cobbled streets and white-washed facades trimmed with wild roses. For a break from the beach, head over to the dazzling **Museo del Grabado Español Contemporáneo,** C. Hospital Bazán, in a restored hospital for the poor. It contains a captivating collection of modern artistic styles with works by Miró, Picasso, Dalí, and others. The temporary exhibits, which rotate every few months, are almost always worth visiting as well. (☎952 76 57 41. Open Tu-Sa 10am-2pm and 5:30-8:30pm. €2.50, students €1.25.) To the northeast is the **Museo del Bonsai,** Av. del Dr. Maiz Viñals, a zen experience brought to you by a large and varied collection of centuries-old miniature trees maintained by Rodrigo García, son of famed bonsai artist and museum founder Michael Angel García. (☎952 86 29 26; www.fkbbonsai.com. Open daily 10:30am-1:30pm and 4-7pm. €3, under 12 €1.50.)

🎵 NIGHTLIFE

Marbella nightlife begins and ends late and is scattered throughout town. Except for the busiest weeks of the summer, bars in the *casco antiguo* and along the waterfront only get packed on weekend nights; the expensive bars and clubs in **Puerto Banús** are busy all the time, but also livelier on weekends. The nightlife routine in Marbella means hitting up bars in the *casco antiguo* at midnight or 1am and proceeding to clubbing capital **Puerto Banús** in the early morning, around 3am. **Plaza de los Olivos** contains a handful of bars and clubs, the best of which is **O'Brian's Irish Bar**—popular, and famous for its merging of traditional celtic music with funky new-age beats. It's particularly busy on Tuesdays, and often hosts Ladies' Nights on quieter evenings; check in the window for upcoming theme nights. (☎952 76 46 95. Beer €2.50. Mixed drinks €5. Open M-Th 6pm-3am, F-Sa 6pm-4am, Su 3pm-3am. Cash only.)

After-hours clubbing happens at Puerto Banús, a short drive by taxi (€10) from Marbella's old city. Though open relatively early, the clubs clustered there don't fill up until around 4am. Budget travelers beware—drink prices are exorbitant and many places charge huge covers, even when the bars are mostly empty. One of many options is **Comedia,** C. Ribera, which attracts a dancing crowd with an electrically artistic ambience and high-energy music. (☎952 81 40 04. Beer €8. Mixed drinks €10. Open June-Oct. daily 11pm-5am; Nov.-May Th-Sa 11pm-5am. MC/V.)

🏖 BEACHES

If you like to walk, the 7km stroll from Marbella center to **Puerto Banús,** almost entirely along a boardwalk, is one of the most beautiful ways to spend an hour and a half. If you prefer to sit back and enjoy the ride, city buses along Av. Ricardo Soriano, heading for San Pedro or Hipercor (#6, 7, 25, and 26; €1), bring you to the chic port where brilliant beaches are dominated by imposing white yachts and row upon row of boutiques and restaurants. On clear days, the Moroccan coast is just barely visible. Throngs of well-dressed Europeans mill about the marina in search of well-banked spouses—the port has been frequented by the likes of Sean Connery, King Fahd of Saudi Arabia, Antonio Banderas, and even the late Princess Diana. With 22km of beach, Marbella offers a variety of settings despite its homogenous facade. Shores to the east of the port are popular with British backpackers; those to the west attract a more posh crowd. **Funny Beach,** popular with families, is a 10min. bus ride (take the bus to Fuengirola and ask the driver to stop, €1), or a 2km walk east along the beach. Water-skiing and jet-skiing are especially popular along the strip between Marbella and Puerto Banús, although companies offer an array of watersports. Try calling **Álvaro** (☎686 48 80 68) for lessons. For sailing try **Club Marítimo** (☎952 77 25 04) or **Club de Mar Puerto Banús** (☎952 81 77 50).

ALMERÍA   ☎950

A small, bustling city on the coast, Almería is known as the sunniest place in Europe and has recently become an incredibly popular spot for wealthy weekend travelers and beach-hungry backpackers. Dense and bustling, Almería shows its age with unabashed grace; old stone facades melt into the hillside, streets crack, and colors fade, all beneath a unique hue of sunlight. Busy promenades lined with fountains, sculptures, and palm trees stretch between the shoreline and *casco viejo*. A Moorish fortress, the **Alcazaba**, presides over the city and stands as testament to Almería's historical prowess. Beautiful city aside, visitors argue that the best parts of Almería are its rocking nightlife and kilometers of sand.

E TRANSPORTATION. The **airport** (☎950 21 37 00), 9km outside town, has daily flights to Barcelona (1½hr.; M-Sa 3 per day, Su 1 per day) and Madrid (1hr.; M-F 6 per day, Sa 5 per day, Su 3 per day). The **train station**, Pl. de la Estación (☎902 24 02 02) sends trains to: Barcelona (14hr.; W, F, Su 7:40am; €53.10); Granada (2hr., 4 per day 6am-6:25pm, €13.40); Madrid (7hr.; 7:15am, 4:15pm; €33.90-38); Sevilla (5-5½hr., 4 per day 6am-6:25pm, €32.50); Valencia (9½hr.; W, F, Su 7:40am; €43). **Buses** (☎950 26 20 98) leave from Pl. de la Estación. **ALSA/Enatcar** runs to Barcelona (14hr., 5 per day 9:30am-9:30pm, €56.32; express daily 10am, €68.38); Murcia (2½hr., 6 per day 5:30am-6:30pm, €15.59-18.50); and Valencia (6½-7hr., 6 per day 9:30am-9:30pm, €32.17; 6½hr. express daily 10am, €39.37). **Alsina Graells** sends buses to: Córdoba (6hr., 4:30pm, €21.58); Granada (2hr., 12 per day 7am-8pm, €10.10); Málaga (3½hr.; M-F 9 per day 6:30am-11pm, Sa-Su 8-9 per day 8am-11pm; €14.53); Sevilla (5-9hr.; 9:30am, 1, 11pm; €28). **Almeraya** goes to Madrid (7-7½hr., 5 per day 9:30am-midnight, €21.70).

✦⁊ ORIENTATION AND PRACTICAL INFORMATION. The city revolves around the fountain-laden **Puerta de Purchena,** a six-way intersection ten blocks from the port. The bus and train stations are closer to the port but in a less desirable area of town; the walk to Puerta de Purchena is 15-20 min. To get there, walk straight from either station to the second roundabout (Pl. Barcelona) and take the second left onto Av. de la Estación. From there, walk to Av. Federico García Lorca, an enormous traffic thoroughfare leading straight to the port. Take a right, and then take a left onto Rambla Obispo Orberá. Pta. de Purchena is at the end of the street. **Paseo de Almería,** a landscaped avenue that leads to the port, is lined with 19th century monuments, chic shops, cafes, banks, and pharmacies. This street borders the *casco antiguo* and intersects with Av. Federico García Lorca near the port. The beaches are on the opposite side of the port along **Paseo Maritimo.** The portside area is traversed by the **Parque de Nicolas Salmeron**, site of the municipal **tourist office,** two blocks from where Av. Federico García Lorca meets the port. (☎950 28 07 48; www.almeria-turismo.org. Open M-F 9am-7pm, Sa and holidays 9am-2pm.) The heart of the *casco antiguo* (old city) is just above, bordered by **Calle Real** and **Calle de la Reina**. Other services include: **police,** on C. Santos Zarate (☎950 62 12 05); **Hospital Torre-Cárdenas,** on Paraje Torre-Cárdenas (☎950 21 21 00 or 01 60 00); **Internet** access at **Locutoria PCO,** C. Tiendas 20, near Puerta de Purchena (☎600 82 04 76; €1 per hour; open daily 10:30am-2:30pm, 5:30pm-midnight); and the **post office,** Pl. Juan Cassinello, 1, on Po. de Almería (☎950 28 15 12; open M-F 8:30am-8:30pm, Sa 9:30am-2pm). **Postal Code:** 04080.

⋔ ACCOMMODATIONS. Almería hosts an impressive range of hotels, from rooms in skyscrapers to luxurious suites beside 16th-century monuments. Bargain accommodations are more difficult to come by, though reserving a room is

ANDALUCÍA

typically easy. **Hostal Residencia Nixar ❸**, C. Antonio Vico, 24, is ideally located near the *casco antiguo*, a few blocks along Pl. de Carmen off the Pta. de Puchena. The exterior looks a bit threadbare but the inside does not disappoint; the lobby is a haven of wicker chairs, potted palms, and hidden courtyards. All rooms come with A/C, TV, and bathroom. (☎950 23 72 55. Breakfast €2.50. July-Aug. singles €29; doubles €42; triples €55. Sept.-June €25.50/42/45. MC/V.) **Hostal Delfin Verde ❸**, C. García Cañas, 2, is a merry stucco establishment offering the best budget rooms along the Po. Marítimo. Ocean views, large beds, TV, A/C, and a private bath make for a relaxing stay. (☎950 26 79 27. July-Aug. singles €30; doubles €60; triples €70. Sept.-June €26/45/50. AmEx/MC/V.) **Hostal Americano ❷**, Av. de la Estación, between the train station at Pta. de Puchena, close to Av. Federico García Lorca, has rooms with the bare essentials. (☎950 28 10 15. June-Aug. singles €25, with bath €30; doubles €42, with bath €49. Sept.-May €23/27/39/43. D/MC/V.)

❏ FOOD. While the beaches and Po. de Almería are littered with wallet-denting cafes and gelaterías, the *casco antiguo* is the zenith of cheap tapas restaurants, most in aging taverns overflowing with locals. Most restaurants are located between Po. de Almería and C. Real in the seven blocks below Pta. de Purchena, especially on C. Jovellanos, C. Trajanos, and C. Egea. Locals of all ages congregate at ▨**Casa Puga ❶**, C. Jovellanos, 7, just off C. Real. Faded pictures, walls of liquor, and open doors surround a standing bar, loud and packed until late. Try their sinfully delicious fried popcorn shrimp. (☎950 28 02 43. Tapas €1-6. *Raciones* €6-9 (half), €11-18 (whole). Open M-Sa noon-4:30pm and 9pm-midnight.) **Bodega La Aldea ❶**, C. Mendez Nunez 6 (off Po. de Almeria away from the *casco antiguo*), is a tiny tavern with a ribbed ceiling and roughly hewn rock walls. All sorts of groups stop by for selections from the enormous tapas menu, posted on the wall, or for the night's first glass of wine. (☎960 253 597. Tapas €2-5.) **Taberna El Postigo ❷**, C. Guzmán, is a sizzling tapas bar with packed with a garrulous crowd downing beer in pace with fast-made tapas. (☎950 24 56 52.) The central **market,** on C. Aguilar de Campo, is in an ornate 19th century edifice between P. de Almería and Rambla del Obispo Obrera.(☎950 25 72 95; open daily 9am-3pm.) **Arbol Supermarkets** are located throughout town in Pl. S. Sebastian, Av. Federico García Lorca (by the port), and Po. Marítimo (open daily 9am-2pm and 5-9pm).

◎ SIGHTS. The *casco antiguo* is worth a late afternoon stroll. The ▨**Alcazaba,** a magnificent 14-acre adobe Moorish fortress built in 995 by Abderramán III of Córdoba, is the second largest Muslim edifice in Spain. In the 15th century, the fortress was found partially destroyed by an earthquake; Christian reconstruction left it divided into three definitive parts: the first two Muslim, and the second Christian. The first, now a lush garden, was a residential area during the city's 11th-century peak. The second, still undergoing renovations, was a small palatial city and a governmental hub with public baths and Caliph wells. The third showcases gunpowder towers. The view at sunset is spectacular, when Almería's famed evening lighting bathes the mosaic of rooftops in a golden glow. (☎950 27 16 17. Open Tu-Su 9am-8:30pm. Free. Guided tours Su.) The city's vast **Cathedral** was built after a 1522 earthquake. Don't be fooled by its harsh appearance; the cathedral was built to resemble a fortress as a deterrent against raids by Berber, Turkish, and Moorish pirates. To reach the cathedral, follow the signs leading off C. Real, or take C. de la Reina to the fortress. (☎697 57 24 28. Open M-F 10am-5pm, Sa 10am-1pm, and during mass. €3.) The walk up **Paseo de Almería** from the port reveals an architectural transition from the medieval to the contemporary. Notable spots are the

Teatro Cervantes, a neo-Baroque edifice that still shows movies daily, the open courtyard of the **Escuela de Artes,** which occasionally showcases Andalusian photography in its open courtyard, and the **Casino Cultural,** once an aristocratic mansion. At the cusp of the Pr. de Purchena sit the **Aljibes de Jayran,** Arabic water tanks used in the 11th century to store 630,000L of water channeled from 6.5km away. (Open M-F 10am-2pm. Free.) Around the Puerta, three 16th-century churches fan out amidst Moorish bazaars. A 10min. walk from the Puerta leads up a set of stairs to the **Cerro San Cristobal,** where an exalted white statue of Jesus Christ stands over the town.

◩ **NIGHTLIFE.** Nightlife in Almeria centers on the raucous tapas bars in the upper part of town; relaxed bar-hopping begins early and ends late. Well before sundown, crowds of students buy their own booze at any cheap supermarket and jump-start the night with hundreds of young locals down by the port or along the park-like median of Av. Federico Garcia Lorca. During this mass gathering every weekend, rightfully dubbed ◩ **Botellón** (meaning large bottle), students make merry in the cool night air before hitting bars and clubs. Almería is one of the few cities in Spain where such an outdoor gathering, designed solely for socializing and the consumption of alcohol, is legal. The bar scene is a gradual movement toward the port from the restaurant-heavy areas. Popular spots are never far from the Po. de Almería and are clustered tightly around four winding streets behind the post office in the *casco antiguo*, appropriately called **Cuatro Calles.** Bars are grungy, smoky, and packed. Students have the first drink of the night before dinner at **Mae West,** Parque Nicolás Salmerón, 9, a funky red building with vintage, vampy ambience and seats beneath dark stone archways. Late-night dancing brings crowds back in droves during the wee hours of the night. (☎950 25 35 20. Beer €3. Mixed drinks €5.50. M-F no cover, Sa €10 includes 2 drinks. Open daily 8pm-6am.) The bar is packed at ◩**Chambao,** C. San Pedro, 13, a trendy spot in town that has two sleek bars for mingling, a flat-screen TV for soccer-watching, and a small dance floor for, well, you know. (Beer €2.50. Mixed drinks €6. Shots €2. Open M-W 3:30pm-2am, Th-Su 3:30pm-4am.) A grungy crowd gathers at **Pub Vhada,** C. Real, 54, for games of darts, flagons of beer (you won't find wine here), and rock music. A crowd of regulars flocks to the outdoor tables and bar at **The Irish Tavern,** C. Antonio González Egea, 4. Don't let the word tavern deceive you—music blasts in the background and the large dance floor is jam-packed from wall to wall. (☎950 25 0801; www.theirishtavern.cjb.net. Beer €3. Mixed drinks €6. Open Th-Sa 6pm-4am.) Another popular discoteca is **Teatro Dolce Vita,** C. Marqués de Comillas, 18, designed to look like an old-fashioned theater. (Another entrance on Po. Almería. ☎950 25 33 10. Beer €3. Mixed drinks €5-7. M-F no cover, Sa €5; includes 1 drink. Open daily 3pm-7am. A smaller and hipper crowd dances to the latest Spanish pop at **Underground,** C. Trajano, 23 (☎680 23 28 25. Open Th-Sa 9pm-4am).

◪ **BEACHES.** Tourists swarm Almería's beaches, taking refuge from the city's stifling mid-day heat. The shores may be crowded, but the seaside atmosphere is peaceful—Po. de Marítimo is pedestrian-only, and the town is little more than a swathe of seafood cafes and apartment complexes. Po. de Almería and Av. de Federico García Lorca are only a few blocks left from the shore. The first couple of bays are rocky and churned up by yacht traffic—keep left until the start of Po. de Marítimo, which marks the calm-watered stretch of **Playa Ciudad Luminosa** and **Playa del Zapillo.** If it's seclusion you seek, you're more likely to find it in the *casco antiguo*, or on the vacant shores of Cabo de Gata.

THE LOCAL STORY

SPANISH HOLLYWOOD

The landscape of Almería is a Saharan desert traversed by Egyptian armies. It is an ancient village explored by Indiana Jones. It is vine-dangling jungle where Arnold Schwarzenegger is a barbarian hero. It's all of these things and more, at least in the movies.

They don't call Almería the "Spanish Hollywood" for nothing. With land that can convincingly resemble northern Africa, Arabia, or the American Southwest, acclaimed directors such as Steven Spielberg have chosen Almería's versatile landscape as the setting for their films. It all began in 1961 when Michael Carreras filmed the classic Western *The Savage Guns* in this ideal location, where the days are exceptionally long and the light strangely beautiful. Since then, Almería has been the setting for numerous big budget films, most famously depicting the Saharan landscape in *Lawrence of Arabia* and the arid Egyptian desert in *Cleopatra*. The nearby UNESCO biosphere reserve, Cabo de Gata-Níjar, was also the setting for scenes in *Indiana Jones and the Last Crusade* and Schwarzenegger's *Conan the Barbarian*.

Given its multi-faceted landscape and unique natural lighting, Almería's popularity as a filming hot spot has increased with time. With many music video and films shot here every year, Almería's natural beauty continues to give Hollywood soundstages a run for their money.

CABO DE GATA ☎950

Alsina Graells (☎950 23 81 97) sends buses to San Miguel de Cabo de Gata (1hr.; 6 per day 8am-9:15pm, return 7 per day 7am-10:15pm; €2.13). Autocares Bernardo (☎950 25 04 22) runs to San José (45min.; M-F 10am, 1:15, 6:30pm; Sa 10am, 2:14, 6:30pm; Su 10am, 6:30pm; €3). Buses leave Cabo de Gata from the Estación de Autobuses en route to Salinas. Buses leave from Almería (6 per day 8, 11am, 1, 3, 7, 8:15pm), and Salinas (45-60min.; M-F 7 per day, 7, 9am, noon, 2, 4, 8, 10:15pm; €2.15.)

TIP **TRANSPORTATION TROUBLES?**
Though it's entirely possible to reach the Cabo de Gata region by bus via San José or San Miguel, both towns present difficulties for exploring the park beyond. San José is closer to the reserve, but bus service there is infrequent and often unreliable. San Miguel has reliable bus service from Almería, but is farther from the reserve. The easiest, most reliable, and most efficient way to explore Cabo de Gata is by car. Be sure to ask about return times at the bus station in Almería, as they change frequently.

For a quieter, more relaxed beach experience than Almería, long stretches of pleasant beaches await in the fishing town of **San Miguel de Cabo de Gata** (simply known as Cabo de Gata), which lies at the head of the ◨**Parque Natural de Cabo de Gata-Níjar**, a 60km stretch of protected coast and inland environs 30km east of urban Almería. The near-desolate peninsula features salt marshes, gentle dunes, and phenomenal geographical contrasts. Flamingos flock to the area's tropical salt marshes, while desert and mountains lie farther inland. Bird tracks often collect more thickly along the squashy sand than human footprints, and towns along Cabo de Gata are typically small fishing hubs instead of tourist destinations. Its therefore best to come prepared with food, cash, and anything else you might need for a day of beach-trekking. Most visitors spend little time in the towns—the empty expanses tempts travelers to explore away from crowds. Towns closer to Almería are more commercialized—the quiet resort town of **San José** boasts an unspoiled beach and serves as a base for visiting the park. Contact the **tourist office** in San José for information on water sports, bike and car rentals, and maps for visiting the secluded **calas** (coves) along the coast. (☎950 38 02 99. Some English spoken. Open M-F 10am-9pm, Sa-Su 10am-2pm.) The best beaches begin at **San Miguel de**

Cabo de Gata. The area begins beside a hazy stretch of mountains and peters off into vacant beaches and deep-green marshes. The town itself comprises stilled streets and utilitarian stucco buildings—the only standout feature is an old watchtower by the fishing boats. Savvy beachgoers dive at **Mermaid's Reef** or windsurf off **Playa de San Miguel. Grupo J. 126** (☎950 38 02 99) provides information and tours in English, Spanish, French, and German; contact them a day or two in advance for tours and equipment. Three kilometers from **San Miguel** is **Las Salinas,** a natural salt marsh reserve home to the Laguna de Rosa and miles of sand dunes, where 169 species of birds, including flamingos, storks, and herons, roost in the summertime. **Playa Miramar** is the town's main beach and, though popular, is rarely crowded. Farther up the coast, past the fishing boats, is a secluded and sparsely populated beach, bordered by a small grassy ridge with mountain views. Both beaches have fine gray sands, calm waters, and a nice breeze. **Hostal Las Dunas ❸,** C. Barrionuevo, 5, the only budget option in town, is easy to find—simply follow the weather-worn signs from the bus-stop roundabout. A small marble staircase leads up to clean rooms with A/C, TV, and bath. (☎950 37 00 72. Breakfast €2. Singles €36; doubles €51. Cash only.) **Camping Cabo de Gata ❶** is 6km from the town and has a pool and restaurant. (☎950 16 04 43. €5 per person, €4.40 per child. Electricity €3.85.) The beachfront area offers a string of seafood cafes that quickly gives way to empty kilometers of beach. **Chirribus ❷,** tucked between the watch tower and fishing boats, offers wide ocean vistas underneath craggy mountain shadows. (☎679 18 36 69. Open daily 11am on.) The **tourist office** is on C. Correo. They provide information about the park and Las Salinas. (Open M-F 9am-10:30pm, Sa-Su 10am-2pm and 5:30-8:30pm.) A 24hr. **ATM** is in the same plaza as the **supermarket. Internet** and **phone** access are at **El Cabo Fono,** where C. Emilio Perez and C. La Morena meet. Watch for the yellow sign on the beach. (☎950 06 00 27; €2.50 per 1hr.; open daily 8am-2pm and 4-10pm.)

MOJÁCAR ☎950

Mojácar's postcard-perfect whitewashed buildings spread like snow over the jagged crest of a green hillside. The town's steep knot of rocky, unmarked streets are accented by thick wooden doors and flowered balconies. During the day, the village clears out as tourists escape the heat and trek down the rose-lined path to the turquoise Mediterranean. Later, residents and the small crowd of tourists take to the town's rooftop terraces to enjoy the sunset, while others keep to the beachfront bars and boardwalk. The beachfront resorts fill up quickly in July and August, when hordes of international visitors join the large contingent of German, British, and American expats who have made Mojácar their home—don't be surprised to hear as much English as Spanish from visitors and residents alike.

E TRANSPORTATION. Getting to and from Mojácar is difficult, though it's well worth the effort. The main bus stop (there is no station) on Po. del Mediterraneo connects the many kilometers of Mojácar's coastline (the auxiliary tourist office is just across the street and to the left). The stop is on the beach, around the corner from the stop that takes passengers to the hilltop part of town every half hour (€1). Bus stops list only times for buses running between Mojácar's hilltop town

STUCK IN PARADISE. Once in Mojácar, the city does its best to keep you from leaving—return buses and their schedules are difficult to come by anywhere but the tourist office. Planning your route in advance is imperative.

ANDALUCÍA

and its beaches. Most long-distance buses run from the outdoor ALSA station in Vera, a small neighboring city. Blue "BARAZA" Buses run to Vera every hour from Mojácar's beach stops. **ALSA/Enatcar** buses (☎902 42 22 42) leave for: Almería (from Vera, 1hr.; M-F 2-5 per day 8:05am-8:55pm, Sa 3 per day 7:56am-11pm, Su 3 per day 4:45-11pm; €8.50); Barcelona (leaves from Vera via Alicante; 12hr., 3 per day; to Alicante €50.44); Madrid (9hr., 1-3 per day, €31.96); Murcia (2½hr.; M-F 6 per day, Sa-Su 5 per day 6:55am-8:55pm; €9.56). For a **taxi** call ☎608 33 93 42 or 659 93 69 08, or wait at the Pl. Nueva stop in town. The tourist office has a list of nearly a dozen **car rental** agencies. Try **Mo-Car** (☎950 47 83 07) For **bikes and scooters,** visit Susana's, Po. del Mediterraneo, Pl. del Cantal (☎649 51 03 660).

■ 🖬 **ORIENTATION AND PRACTICAL INFORMATION.** Mojácar is split by the rocky green hills between the town and the 17km stretch of beaches. The town centers around Pl. Nueva; the steep, tangled surrounding streets offer immaculate small-town charm and panoramic ocean vistas framed by flowered terraces. **Paseo de Mediterraneo** seamlessly links the city's 11 beaches. The beach area is decidedly more urban (you will find more banks and supermarkets here). Transportation within Mojácar is a breeze; the yellow **Transportes Urbanos** buses stop at each of the 11 beaches and travels to town mid-loop, beginning at Hotel Indalo at the far right beach (facing the water). (In summer daily 2 per hour except during siesta. 8am-3pm and 5pm-midnight. F-Sa service until 2am; in winter daily 2 per hour 8am-2pm and 3-9pm. €1.) The stop leading to town is in front of the central Playa de las Ventanicas on **Av. de Andalucía,** which diverges from Po. del Mediterraneo at an enormous roundabout. The second stop, in **Pl. Ray Alabez,** is preferable and closest to the town's main square. From the plaza, take a left on **Av. Paris** and head up the steep, slightly-hidden stairs to your immediate right; these lead to **C. Aire,** a rockside street that funnels into **Pl. Nueva,** the only place in town that caters to tourist needs. A few steps below the plaza, a small indoor complex contains the main **tourist office,** C. Glorieta, 1 (☎950 61 50 25; www.mojacar.es. Open M-F 10am-2pm and 5-7:30pm, Sa 10:30am-1:30pm. Beachside branch has the same hours). Services include: **Unicaja Bank,** Pl. Nueva; **Laundry** service at **Bish's Lavandería,** Po. del Mediterráneo, by Playa del Cantal (☎950 47 80 11. €2.75 per kg. Self-serve washers €5-9.50; dryers €1.50 per 15min. Open M-F 9am-5pm, Sa 9am-2pm. Last wash 4pm.); **Internet** access at **Ciber Koko** (€2 per hour; open daily 11:30am-2:30pm and 4:30pm-1am); **police** (☎950 47 20 00); **auxiliary post office** (open M-F 12:30-2:30pm, Sa-Su 10:30-11:30am), and **central post office** is on Po. Mediterráneo. (☎950 47 87 03. Open M-Sa 9am-2pm.) by the main bus stop **Postal Code: 04638.**

🖬 **ACCOMMODATIONS.** Mojácar is not as heavily touristed as the rest of the Costa del Sol. Though this keeps streets quaint and beaches uncrowded, it means finding a bed last minute can be difficult. Reserve well in advance if you plan to visit in late summer or during the summer solstice (end of June) and festival of the Moors and Christians (beginning of June). Hostels in town often provide inexpensive, luxurious rooms with stunning views of the hazy sea horizon. The ideally located 🖬**Hostal Arco Plaza ❸,** Pl. Nueva, offers elegant, blue-walled rooms and fantastic views. All rooms have huge beds, private bathrooms, TV, and A/C, making this *hostal* well worth the price. (☎950 47 27 77. June-July singles €30; doubles €40; triples €50. *Semana Santa* (Holy Week), Aug., and Christmas €36/53/65. Jan-Mar. and Oct.-Nov. €28/35/40. MC/V.) **Pensión Torreón ❷,** C. Jazmín, 4-6, is a toll-house-turned-hostel with rooms surrounding a foyer with stained glass doors. The enormous vine-covered terrace has the best sea view in town. From Pl. Nueva, follow C. Indalo around the church to C. Enmedio, then take a left downhill along C. Unión, and a right at the end of the hill on C. Jazmín. (☎950 47 52 59. Reserve ahead. Breakfast €5. Doubles with shared bath €50. Cash only.) **El Mirador del Castillo ❸**, Mirador del Castillo, is a splurge worth every dollar, where five enormous rooms with mahogany furniture and huge beds surround a tiny pool, bar, and restaurant. (☎950 47 30 22; www.elcastillomojacar.com. Reserve ahead. Doubles €55.) For beachfront accommodations, it's preferable to stay on the stretch from Playa del Cantal to Playa de las Ventanicas, where the shores, boardwalks, and restaurants are best. The cheapest place to stay is **Camping El Cantel Playa de Mojácar ❶**, an enclosed, wooded campground across the highway from Playa del Cantal. (☎950 47 82 04. €4 per person, €3 per child, €4.50 per car, €6.50 per camper. Electricity €2.75. Discounts Oct.-Mar.)

◻ **FOOD.** As with accommodations, you're much better off spending the day at the beach and coming back to eat in town, where you'll find more variety on your plate and better *bocadillos* for your buck. The best beachside eateries are *chirringuitos*, open-air beach bars, though these are better for snacks and peak when night falls. The town, however, offers myriad rooftop restaurants (bring mosquito repellent) that serve creative meals in huge portions. Almost all restaurants are around the Pl.Nueva, Pl. del Sol, and Pl. Fronton or along the streets beneath the church. Not much is open for breakfast save a few cafes around Pl. Nueva and C. Aire just below. **◪JJ's, or Just Jackie's ❸**, C. Enmedio, 24, provides plush indoor seating, romantic ambience, and a variety of daily specials. (☎600 62 58 08. Three separate *menús*: vegetarian (€9-13), regular (€10-17), and a *menú del día* (€9). Reservations recommended. Open daily 7:30pm-1am.) Loud colors, a sunset terrace, and a pool table help **Sinaloa Bar & Grill ❷**, C. Garrucha, just above Pl. Nueva, attract a young crowd hungry for hearty Mexican cuisine and thirsty for the first mojitos of the night. (☎950 13 20 22. Open daily from 11am-late.) For low-key Spanish cuisine at reasonable prices, head to **El Rincón del Embrujo ❷**, C. La Iglesia, around the corner from Pl. Nueva. Don't be put off by the bilingual menu—this place is as local as it gets. (Entrees €6-12. Open 11am-4pm and 7pm-midnight.) **El Cid ❶**, on the Playa del Cantal, is the best spot for a sandwich (€6) and a mojito (€5.50) in the afternoon. (☎950 47 20 63; www.elcidmojacar.com.Open daily 10am-9:30pm.) **La Cantina ❷**, Playa de Ventanicas, has a raucous ambience, sheltered beach view, and authentic Mexican tacos and quesadillas (€7-12) on a wooden deck overlooking the sea. (☎950 47 88 41; www.lacantinamojacar.com. Reserve ahead on weekends. Open daily 7:30pm-midnight.)

◪◪ **SIGHTS AND BEACHES.** Mojácar was the heart of a 1488 pact of free association between Christians, Jews, and Moors. Vestiges of this convivial history are present in several standout sites concentrated around Pl. Nueva. At the lower border of town, along Cuesta de la Fuente, is the **Fuente Mora,** a Moorish fountain from which residents still bottle their daily water. Part of the city's rocky old facade rises from the Jewish quarter by Pl. Flores to C. Enmedio, leading to the arching Puerta de la Ciudad. Along C. Enmedio, the modest **Ayuntamiento** stands in the shadows of the 16th-century Iglesia de Santa Maria, surrounded by flower groves and quiet streets. This bucolic architectural charm is accented by views from the terraces on **Pl. Nueva** and the **Mirador del Castillo,** the highest point in town. **C. Aire** is a rarely-walked stretch leading away from Pl. Nueva that curves beneath the rocky hillside and old facades. Below, Mojácar's string of 11 beaches is the undisputed main attraction: stretches of sands interspersed with small, rocky promontories afford plenty of personal space for the discerning sunbather. Buses run every 30min. between the town and the beaches (see **Practical Information,** p. 245). The choice stretch is between **Playa** del Cantal and **Playa de las Ventanicas,** where traffic is quieter and sands are softer. This is, by no coincidence, also the hub of beachside nightlife. If you're walking from town, take a right from Av. de Andalucia along Po. del Mediterraneo; beaches and bars improve in this direction. **Playa de las Ventanicas** marks the start of a palm-lined path that stretches several kilometers to the south (right at the bottom of the hill from town). If you're craving total seclusion, take a taxi beyond the Macenas Castle (an 18th-century watchtower visible from Pl. de las Ventanicas), where a dirt track leads to ▓**Bordenares** and ▓**Sombrerico.** According to Mojácar Viva, a weekly publication on the city, these beaches were the setting for Orson Welles's film "Treasure Island." Parts of these beaches are now subject to heavy construction due to finish in 2011. For watersports, head to **Samoa Surf/Club** on the Playa del Cantal by Pueblo Indalo. (☎950 47 84 90; samoasurf@vodafone.es. Banana boats €10 per 15min. Sea kayaks for 1 person €6 per 30min., €9 per hour; for 2 people €7/10. Windsurfing €15 per hour, €50 for 5hr. Wakeboarding and waterskiing €35 per 20min.)

▓▐ **NIGHTLIFE AND ENTERTAINMENT.** Nightlife in Mojácar is surprisingly energetic and diverse. The town is dotted with hole-in-the-wall taverns and funky dives filled with loud, mixed crowds. Dozens of tented beach bars *(chirringuitos)* invite a vigorous nightlife crowd to the breezy shores—the "in" place changes constantly, so tourist offices offer helpful lists of the latest hotspots. *Chirringuitos,* offering seaside lounges and mixed drinks, are heavily concentrated at Playa del Cantal and become steadily more upscale and spread out toward Playa de las Ventanicas. Buses stop running at midnight on weekdays and at 1am on weekends, and taxis disappear at sundown—you can call one (see **Transportation,** p. 285), but it will set you back at least €9. Walking the poorly lit road, however, is a dangerous and exhausting alternative. The BuhoBus runs from Hotel Indalo (Playa de las Ventanicas) to the neighboring towns of Garrucha and Vera every two hours (June 14-Sept. 15; every 2hr. 12am-4am; €1).

▓**Lua,** Playa de las Ventanicas, is almost entirely engulfed in lush landscaping, and is accented with an arching mahogany bar, bamboo, and Buddha statues. (Beer €2.50. Mixed drinks €5.50. Open daily noon-4am.) On Playa del Cantal, **El Patio 2000** offers a laid-back atmosphere amid tropical trees and tiki torches. Local rock and salsa bands play in the afternoons and nights on weekends. (Beer €2. Mixed drinks €3-5. Open daily 11am-2:30am.) Right next door, **BBme** is a peeling wooden shack with cool lounges, a crammed dance floor, and delicious Argentine food. Open daily 11am-2:30am. Nearby, **Paradiso,** Po. de Mediterráneo, is a huge, popular discoteca. This white, palm tree-lined palace blasts music until dawn. The other large disco in town, **Skandalo,** Po. de Mediterráneo, across the street from Cueva del Lobo, is crammed with wild black-and-white decor and a huge circular bar. (☎950 47 52 97). **Albatros,** along Playa de Lance, revives crowds with creative mixed drinks and ambience, complete with a talking parrot, pool table, decrepit wooden boat, and a huge seaside deck. (☎661 05 38 20. Open daily 10am-midnight.) Though they're a bit out of the way, **Tito's Beach Bar,** at the end of Playa de las Ventanicas, **Budu Pub,** C. Estacion 9, 23, and **Café Calima,** Pl. Arbollón, 1, are all worth the trek. (Tito's Beach Bar ☎950 61 50 30; open daily 10am-8pm. Bar open 7pm-2:30am. Budu Pub ☎630 23 11 43; open daily 8pm-5am. Café Calima ☎950 47 87 65; open daily 9am-1pm and 7pm-2:30am.)

RONDA
☎952

When you first see picturesque Ronda (pop. 350,000) you'll think you've stumbled onto the pages of a fairy-tale. Its stunning views and delicate beauty combine with the energy of a thriving urban center, and the result is a city many have fallen in love with. Centuries-old bridges and arches span the 100m El Tajo gorge, connecting the *casco antiguo* and most of Ronda's sights to the newer part of town, which is less romantic but full of life. The old city dates from Roman times, when Ronda was a pivotal commercial center. Fortunes dwindled under Moorish rule after Al Mutadid ibn Abbad drowned the ruling lord in his bath and annexed the city for Sevilla. More recently, Ronda—the birthplace of modern bullfighting— attracted such luminaries as Rainer Maria Rilke, who wrote his *Spanish Elegies* here, Ernest Hemingway, who based *For Whom the Bell Tolls* on the city, and Orson Welles, whose ashes are buried on a bull farm outside of town. While Ronda can hold you entranced for days, the city also makes an excellent base for exploring the *pueblos blancos* and the nearby Cuevas de la Pileta.

▛ TRANSPORTATION

The **train** and **bus stations** are in the new city, 3 blocks apart, on Av. de Andalucía.

Trains: Av. Alférez Provisional (☎952 87 16 73, 902 24 02 02). Ticket booth at C. Infantes, 20. Open M-F 7am-10pm. To: **Algeciras** (2hr., 4 per day 7:15am-8:17pm, €7); **Granada** (3hr., 3 per day 9:02am-5:10pm, €12); **Madrid** (4½hr., 10:10am and 6:10pm, €62); **Málaga** (2hr., M-Sa 7:50am, €8); or take the train to **Bobadilla** (1hr., 4 per day 7:52am-5:19pm, €4.25), which has more frequent trains to **Málaga** (1hr., 6 per day 9:17am-9:44pm, €5.05-13).

Buses: Pl. Concepción García Redondo, 2 (☎952 18 70 61). To: **Cádiz** (4hr.; 2-3 per day 9:30am-4:30pm, Sa-Su last bus 6pm; €13); **Málaga** (2½hr., 8-11 per day 7am-7:45pm, €9); **Marbella** (1½hr., 5-6 per day 6:30am-8:15pm, €5.02); **Sevilla** (2½hr., 3-5 per day 7am-7pm, €10.17).

Taxis: (☎952 87 23 16 or 670 20 74 38). From the train station to Pl. de España €4.

◼▟ ORIENTATION AND PRACTICAL INFORMATION

The 18th-century **Puente Nuevo** connects Ronda's old and new sections. On the new side of the city, **Carrera Espinel** (the main street, which includes the pedestrian walkway known as **La Bola**) runs perpendicular to C. Virgen de la Paz, intersecting it between the bullring and Pl. de España. To reach the tourist office and town center, leave the train station and go straight on Av. Martinez Astein. Turn right when the road ends onto the pedestrian C. Espinel. From the bus station, turn left onto C. Naranja, walk four blocks, and then turn right onto pedestrian Carrera Espinel, which leads to the **Plaza de España.**

Municipal Tourist Office: Po. Blas Infante (☎952 18 71 19), near the bullring. English, spoken. Stocked with restaurant listings, accommodations, train and bus schedules, and museum information. Open June-Aug. M-F 9:30am-7:30pm, Sa-Su 10am-2pm and 3:30-6:30pm; Sept.-May M-F 9:30am-6:30pm, Sa-Su 10am-2pm and 3:30-6:30pm. **Regional office,** Pl. de España, 1 (☎952 87 12 72). English spoken. Open June-Aug. M-F 9am-8pm, Sa-Su 10am-2pm; Sept.-May M-F 9am-7pm, Sa-Su 10am-2pm.

Currency Exchange: Banco Santander Central Hispano, Carrera Espinel, 17 (☎902 24 24 24), near C. Virgen de los Remedios. Open M-F 8:30am-2pm; Oct.-May also Sa 8:30am-1pm. If banks are closed, try **Ronda Change,** C. Virgen de la Paz, 2 (☎952 87 96 04), though it gives worse rates. Open M-F 10am-2pm and 4-8pm, Sa 10am-3pm.

Luggage Storage: At the **bus station** (€3 per day). Open daily 9am-8pm.

Police: Pl. Duquesa de Parcent, 3, near the town hall (☎092).

Medical Emergency: ☎952 87 17 73. **Hospital de la Serranía** (☎951 06 50 01), en route to El Burgo.

Pharmacy: Farmacia Homeopatía, Pl. de España, 5 (☎952 87 15 80). Open in summer M-F 9:30am-2pm and 5-8:30pm; in winter M-F 9:30am-2pm and 5-8pm, Sa 9:30am-2pm.

Internet Access: Ciber Locutorio Rondatelecom, C. Jerez, 4-Bajo. Internet €1.40 per hour. Copies €0.20 per page. Public telephones available. Open M-Sa 11am-2pm and 5-10pm.

Laundry: Pressto (☎914 48 58 61; www.pressto.com). Open M-F 9:30am-2pm and 5-8:30pm, Sa 9:30am-2pm.

Post Office: C. Virgen de la Paz, 20 (☎952 87 25 57), across from Pl. de Toros. **Lista de Correos.** Open M-F 8:30am-2:30pm, Sa 9:30am-1pm. **Postal Code:** 29400.

ACCOMMODATIONS

Most hotels in the old city are very expensive, so unless you're willing to shell out over €100 per night for a single, you'll be better off staying in the budget lodgings in the new city. Most *pensiones* are concentrated around the bus station on side streets off Carrera Espinel—try C. Naranja, C. Lorenzo Borrego, or C. Sevilla. Expect room shortages in August and during the *Feria de Ronda* in September.

Hotel Arunda I, C. Espinel, 120 (☎952 19 01 02; www.hotelesarunda.com). Luxurious for a 1-star hotel. Carved-wood furnished rooms have private bath, A/C, TV, and sunny windows. A little classier than its sister hotel. Internet access €2 per hour. **Arunda II,** C. José M.C. Madrid, 10-12 (☎952 87 25 19) has the same white-walled, dark-fixtured decor and Internet prices but offers breakfast. Singles €27, with breakfast €29; doubles €44/47. AmEx/MC/V. ❸

Pensión La Purísima, C. Sevilla, 10 (☎952 87 10 50). Plant-filled hallways lead to bright rooms decorated with tasteful religious art. Some have private bath. Singles €17; doubles €30, with bath €35; triples with bath €45. Cash only. ❷

Hotel Morales, C. Sevilla, 51 (☎952 87 15 38; fax 952 18 70 24). A nature theme carries from the corridor into each room by way of wildlife posters and earth tone bedspreads; singles are small but cozy. All have private bath, A/C, and TV. Singles €23-25; doubles €39-42. MC/V. ❷

FOOD

Restaurants and cafes abound in Ronda, although many are geared to tourists and tend to be overpriced, especially those near Pl. de España. Rabbit and stewed bull's tail *(rabo de toro)* are local specialties.

El Pataton, C. San José, 8 (☎678 87 06 26). Tucked between C. Molino and C. Sevilla. A popular takeout spot with locals. For only €3.50, the friendly chefs prepare a delicious variation of Spanish cuisine: tapas ingredients stuffed into potatoes. Choose from one of 11 options or try the €4.50 "El Pataton" for a giant potato with a filling of your choice. Open Tu-Su 8pm-midnight. Closed one month a year, usually July-early Aug. ❶

Case Ke No, C. Molino, 6B. If choosing one kind of sandwich over another is always an existential struggle, why limit yourself? Serves 50 types of *montaditos* (€1.20), small but substantial sandwiches filled with all possible combinations of Spanish flavors. Open Tu-Su noon-4pm and 7pm-midnight. Cash only. ❶

Los Cántaros, C. Sevilla, 66 (☎952 87 63 23). A small local bar with big food. The bull's tail (€9) is heaping and melts off the bone. A small complimentary pitcher of water if you request it. Open Tu-Sa 9am-5pm and 8-11pm, Su and M 9am-5pm. ❷

Panadería Rondeña, C. Sevilla, 53 (☎952 57 97 86). Lines of sizable fresh pastries (€1-1.40). Pop in for a lemon granizado (small €0.70, large €1.40), a perfect refreshment after a day of sightseeing. Open Tu-Sa 8am-8:30pm, Su and M 8am-8pm. ❶

É Gelato, Av. Carerra Espinel, across from C. Doctor Romón y Cajal (☎952 87 30 71). Stands out among the street's many gelato vendors with over 20 flavors and €1.70 2-scoop cones. Open daily 11am-midnight. ❶

⊙ SIGHTS

▓**CASA DEL REY MORO.** The name of this sight, House of the Moorish King, is rather misleading. Despite its Moorish facade, the house dates from the 18th century and is not the main attraction; you enter it only to pay your admission. Descend the seemingly endless stairways—60m into the depths of a 14th-century mine, which has housed more than its share of prisoners and slaves over the centuries. A strategic defense point, the mine also has a room used to hold cauldrons of boiling oil and a "Room of Secrets," where whispers travel from one corner of the room to the other but are inaudible in the middle. The other main attractions are Forestier's serene gardens, high atop the cliffs and house, designed and constructed in the 1920s by the famous French landscape architect. *(Cuesta de Santo Domingo, 17. Take the first left after crossing the Puente Nuevo. ☎952 18 72 00. Open daily in summer 10am-7pm; in winter 10am-7pm. €4, children €2.)*

▓**PLAZA DE TOROS AND MUSEO TAURINO.** Bullfighting lies at the heart of Ronda's livelihood, as evidenced by the careful construction of this stunning bullring, the oldest in Spain (est. 1785), and its small but comprehensive museum. The museum traces the history of the sport, focusing largely on Ronda's native *matadores*. Original Goya prints of fights and bullfighters, authentic costumes, weapons, and the heads of the bravest bulls grace the walls and glass cases in the museum's hallways, and multilingual posters describe noteworthy fights and explain the exhibits. Ronda has had its share of famous bullfighters, including the Romero dynasty—three generations of fighters from the same family. Pedro, the most famous, killed his first bull at age 17 in 1771; over the course of his career, it is said he fought more than 5600 bulls without a single injury. It also displays the only all-black *matador* costume used in professional bullfighting. Of greater interest than the museum, is the actual bullring and the bull pens and stables. In early September, the Plaza de Toros hosts *corridas goyescas* (bullfights in traditional costumes) as part of the **Feria de Ronda.** The town fills to capacity and rooms are booked months in advance. *(☎952 87 15 39; www.rmcr.org. Open daily Apr. 16-Oct. 10am-8pm; Nov.-Feb. 10am-6pm; Mar.-Apr. 15 10am-7pm. €6. Museum audio tour €3.)*

MUSEO DE LARA. The private collection of Juan Antonio Lara Jurado—who still lives above the museum—is a collection of, well, collections. He covers traditional Spanish culture with fans, bullfighting costumes, and a bodega room, and delves into the more bizarre with a guillotine and roomful of witchcraft and Inquisition torture devices. In the summer, the museum hosts weekend flamenco shows. *(C. Armiñán, 29. ☎952 87 12 63; www.museolara.org. Open daily 10:30am-8pm. €2.50, students and seniors €1.80, children free. Flamenco €23 at 10pm, includes museum admission.)*

OTHER SIGHTS. Carved by the Río Guadalquivir, Ronda's gorge extends 100m below the **Puente Nuevo,** across from Pl. de España. Arrested highwaymen were once held in a prison cell beneath the bridge's center, and during the Civil War, political prisoners were thrown from the top. Supposedly, even as they faced certain death, they were told that if they were to survive the fall they would be free. Take a stroll through Alameda del Tajo for a cliffside walk walled with views. The ✦view from the center is unparalleled. The innovative **Puente Viejo** was rebuilt in 1616 over an Arab bridge with the Arco de Felipe V, built in 1742, presiding over one end of it. Farther down, the **Puente San Miguel** (or Puente Árabe) is an Andalusian hybrid of a Roman base and Arabic arches. To reach them, walk on C. Santo Domingo past the Casa del Rey Moro. The tiny but informative **Museo del Bandolero,** C. Armiñán, 65, is dedicated to presenting "pillage, theft, and rebellion in Spain since Roman time," and recounts the stories of bandits and the men who tracked them. (☎952 87 77 85; www.museoban-dolero.com. Open daily in summer 10:30am-8pm; in winter 10am-6pm. €2.70, students and children €2.40.) Originally inhabited by Don Fernando Valenzuela, a prominent minister under Carlos III, the 17th-century **Palacio de Mondragón** has since been transformed into an anthropological museum. (2 blocks behind Pl. Duquesa de Parcent. ☎952 87 84 50. Open in summer M-F 10am-7pm, Sa-Su 10am-3pm; in winter M-F 10am-6pm, Sa-Su 10am-3pm. €2, students €1, under 12 and disabled free.) Built in the early 20th century, the modernist **Casa de Don Bosco** was a bequest of the Granadino family, who wanted their house to be used as a rest home for sick and elderly priests of the Salesians order. The gardens in the back have an amazing view of the area and feature a fountain surrounded by Nasrid and regional ceramic tiles. (C. Tenorio, 20, near the Puente Nuevo. ☎952 87 16 83. Open daily 9am-2pm and 2:30-6:30pm. €1.50)

◾ NIGHTLIFE

Nightlife in Ronda is fairly low-key, except for weekends. Locals congregate in the pubs and discotecas along C. Jerez and the streets behind Pl. del Socorro, and both local families and young people can be found in *heladerías* (ice-cream parlors) along Carerra Espinel. With cheap drinks and hearty tapas, it's no surprise that **Bar Antonio,** C. San José, 1, is so popular with young Spaniards. (Beer €0.90. Mixed drinks €3. Tapas €1. Giant *bocadillos* €2-2.50. Open M-Sa 7:30am-2am.) A 20-something crowd heads to **Huskies Sport Bar-Café,** C. Molino, 1, for beer and sports. Taking its name from the UConn mascot, the bar is lined with posters of American sports teams—very popular with foreigners. (www.huskiesbar.com. Beer €1.80. Mixed drinks €3.50. Open Tu-Su 4:30pm-3am, M 8:30pm-3am.) For a boisterous and ageless local scene any night of the week, try **Bodeja-Bar 7,** C. Blas Infante, 7. Enjoy the moonlight by the park at one of the outdoor tables that sprawl across the patio. (☎952 87 60 97. Glass of sangria €1.50. Open noon-4pm and 8pm-late)

◾ DAYTRIP FROM RONDA

◾CUEVA DE LA PILETA

By car, take highway C-339 North (Ctra. Sevilla from the new city). The turnoff to Benaoján and the caves is about 22km out, in front of an abandoned restaurant. Taxis will go round-trip from Ronda for €46. A cheaper alternative is the train to Benaoján (20min.; 3 per day 7am-4:33pm, return 3 per day 1:39-8pm; round-trip €3.50). From the train station, it's a tough 1-1½hr. climb to the caves, through the town of Benaoján and then along the highway. Ask locals for the way from Benaoján to the road, and don't stray off the main highway or you might find yourself on an obscure path on the side of the mountain. ☎952 16 73 43. Caves open daily 10am-1pm and 4-6pm. Mandatory 1hr. tours begin on the hr., but call beforehand—there is nothing within reasonable walking distance here if you end up with extra time. €7, groups of 9 or more €6 per person.

The Cueva de la Pileta, 22km west of Ronda, is one of the few remaining privately owned caves in Spain and one of the best preserved. The cave, which stretches over 2km underground, was discovered in 1905 by a local farmer looking for *guano* to use as fertilizer. Although it is now a national monument, the cave has stayed in the family. Gas-lantern tours of this otherworldly expanse of stalactites and stalagmites lead visitors along the 500m long main gallery of the cave, past underground lakes, majestic mineral formations, and cathedral-like chambers. Inside, you'll find remarkably preserved Paleolithic and Neolithic paintings that represent a uniquely wide time frame, with some over 30,000 years old. Ceramics, animal bones, and human skeletons have also been discovered deep in the cave. The lamina formation nicknamed "the organ" is especially fascinating: years of falling water droplets carved its columns out of one giant sheet of rock, and each plays a different tone when struck. Other highlights include a large drawing of a fish, Neolithic calendars, and winged men believed to be representations of tribal shamans. To protect the paintings, all visits are led by guides and are limited to 25 people. Reservations are accepted only in winter, so come early to ensure a spot on a tour. Bring sturdy shoes and a sweatshirt—the caves are cool and slippery.

ANTEQUERA   ☎952

The Romans gave Antequera (pop. 42,000) its name, but older civilizations contributed to making the city a historical and cultural wonder. On the outskirts of town, the *dólmenes* (funerary chambers built from rock slabs) showcase primitive art, and the municipal museum's exhibit of religious art and artifacts tells southern Spain's history since the Moorish conquest. The abundance of beautiful churches in Antequera owes to the fact that this was the first town to be "retaken" for Christianity. With no water in sight, the city has avoided the throngs of beachgoers who flock to the other towns in the area, making Antequera a relaxing one- or two-day detour from the bustling coast.

⌐ TRANSPORTATION

Trains: Av. de la Estación (☎952 84 32 26 or 902 24 02 02). To: **Algericas** (3hr., 3 per day 8:39am-7:15pm, €10.50); **Almería** (4hr., 3 per day 8:42am-7:34pm, €18); **Granada** (1½hr., 3 per day 8:42am-9pm, €6-7); **Ronda** (1¼hr., 3 per day 8:39am-7:15pm, €5); **Sevilla** (1¾hr., 4 per day 9:46am-10:18pm, €11).

Buses: Po. García Olmo (☎952 84 19 57 or 84 13 65). To: **Córdoba** (1¼-1½hr; 4 per day 9:45am-6:15pm, less frequent in Aug.; €8.30); **Granada** (1-1½hr., 9 per day 7:15am-1am, €6.85); **Málaga** (1hr., 9-12 per day 7am-10pm, €5.10); **Murcia** (5hr., 3 per day 9:45am-1am, €24.40); **Sevilla** (1¼-1½hr., 9 per day 4am-1am, €11.70).

Taxis: Taxi Radio Antequera (☎952 84 55 30) services Antequera and will go to Sierra de Torcal. Fare to town center approx. €4, but the walk is manageable.

✳🛈 ORIENTATION AND PRACTICAL INFORMATION

From the train station, it's a 10min. hike up a shadeless hill along Av. de la Estación to reach **Plaza de San Sebastián,** the town center. At the top, continue straight past the market, turn right onto C. de la Encarnación, and pass the Museo Municipal to reach the plaza. Alternatively, from the bus station it's a short 15min. walk down a shadeless hill. Exit the station at the top, cross the intersection, and turn right on Ctra. del Albergue; when you reach Pl. de la Constitución, cross the street at the gas station and walk left along Alameda de Andalucía, which becomes C. Infante Don Fernando and leads to the tourist office and Pl. de San Sebastián.

Tourist Office: Pl. de San Sebastián, 7 (☎952 70 25 05; www.antequera.es). English and French spoken. Open mid-June to mid-Sept. M-Sa 11am-2pm and 5-8pm, Su 11am-2pm; mid-Sept. to mid-June M-Sa 10:30am-1:30pm and 4-7pm, Su 11am-2pm.

Bank: Banco Santander Central Hispano, C. Infante Don Fernando, 51 (☎952 24 24 24). Open M-F 8:30am-2pm, Sa 8:30am-1pm; Apr.-Sept. closed Sa.

Municipal Police: Av. de la Legión (☎952 70 81 04).

Pharmacy: Farmacia Villodres, on the corner of C. Calzada and C. Diego Ponce on Pl. de San Francisco. Open M-F 9:30am-1:30pm and 5-8:30pm, Sa 10:30am-1:30pm.

Hospital: Comarcal, C. Polígono Industrial, 67 (☎952 84 62 63, urgent 06 11 50).

Internet Access: No Problem (NP), C. Merecillas, 17B (☎952 73 90 78). €1.50 per hour. Open M-F 9:30am-2:30pm and 4:30-11pm, Sa 10am-2:30pm and 4:30-11pm, Su 4-11pm.

Post Office: C. Nájera (☎952 84 20 83). Open M-F 8:30am-2:30pm, Sa 9:30am-1pm. **Postal Code:** 29200.

ACCOMMODATIONS

Relative to its size, Antequera offers a good range of accommodation options, many of which are located toward the center of the city.

⬛ Hotel Residencia Colón, C. Infante Don Fernando, 31 (☎952 84 00 10; www.antequerahotelcolon.com). Wicker mirrors, bright bedsheets, huge windows and showers, and a great location make this hotel the best deal in town. Did we mention the A/C and free Internet access? Singles €12, with bath €25; doubles €24/40; triples with bath €55; quads with bath €70. AmEx/MC/V. ❶

Hotel Plaza San Sebastián, Pl. San Sebastián, 4 (☎952 84 42 39; www.hotelplaza-sansebastian.com). Conventional yet spacious rooms with A/C, TV, and roomy bath, and a lounge with cushy leather chairs. Internet access €1.20 per hour. Singles €25; doubles €40. Prices higher end of Aug. and during *Semana Santa*. MC/V. ❷

Pensión Toril, C. Toril, 3-5 (☎952 84 62 71; fax 84 31 84), off Pl. de San Francisco. Clean rooms with fans and TV surround a patio. Filling *menú* at the adjacent restaurant complete with wine €6. Newly installed elevator and free parking make check-in a breeze. Breakfast €1.20. Singles €20, with bath €23; doubles €35. Cash only. ❷

🍴🍷 FOOD AND NIGHTLIFE

Restaurant and nightlife options in Antequera are few and far between. The restaurants at the hostels and hotels listed above are a good bet for an authentic *menú*, as are those lining C. Calzada. Get fresh produce, fish, and meat at the indoor **market** in Pl. San Francisco. (Open M-Sa 8am-3pm.) **Mercadona,** C. Calzada, 18, and C. Infante Don Fernando, 17, has all the basics. (Open M-Sa 9:15am-9:15pm. MC/V.)

La Espuela, C. San Agustín, 1 (☎952 70 30 31). Excellent fusion of Andalusian and Italian cuisine; the menu accommodates most tastes and has a good vegetarian selection. Try the *porra Antequera*, a cold cream soup with ham and tomatoes (€5). Great appetizers €5-14. Entrees €12-16. *Menú* €14-16. Open daily noon-midnight. MC/V. ❸

Manolo Bar, C. Calzada, 14 (☎952 84 10 15). This unique bar is a Spanish take on the old American Western saloon. Ultra-cheap tapas €1. *Raciones* €5-6. *Sangria* €2 per glass and €8 per pitcher. Open W-Th 5pm-1am, F-Sa 5pm-3am. Cash only. ❶

Cafetería Florida, C. Lucena, 44 (☎952 70 10 14). Convenient for a simple breakfast. Lunch is more elaborate; great tapas (try the stuffed artichokes), but you can't beat the filling *menú* (€6-8). Open daily 7am-8pm. MC/V. ❶

Bar-Café Chicón, C. Infante D. Fernando, 1 (☎952 73 90 63). Textured cream-colored walls and leather, wooden, and metal furniture lend a modern flavor to the restaurant's classic fare. A *tostada* and coffee breakfast will only set you back €2-3. Open M-F, Su 7am-10 or 11pm, Sa 7am-3pm. ❶

👁 SIGHTS

LOS DÓLMENES. Antequera's three ancient caves are some of the oldest in Europe. Once burial chambers with storerooms for the riches of the dead, they illustrate the fascinating process of human cultural evolution since the Stone Age on. Although they were looted long ago, the caves are still worth visiting. The 200-ton roof of the **Cueva de Menga** (2500 BC), considered the most important cave of the three, was hauled five miles to its present location. The **Cueva de Viera** (2000 BC), uncovered in 1905, begins with a narrow passageway leading deep into the darkness of the earth. Somewhat farther afield, **Cueva del Romeral** (1800 BC) consists of a long corridor leading to two round chambers; the second was used for funerary offerings. *(1km to the Cuevas de Menga and Viera; follow signs toward Granada from the town center (15-20min.) and look for a small sign past the gas station. To reach Cueva del Romeral from the other caves, continue on the highway to Granada another 3km. After the 4th rotary, across from Mercadona, a gravel road leads to a narrow path bordered by cypress trees; take this across the tracks. Open Tu-Sa 9am-6pm, Su 9:30am-2:30pm. Free.)*

OTHER SIGHTS. All that remains of the **Alcazaba** are its two towers, the wall between them, and some hedges. From the top, visitors get an unparalleled 📷**view** of the city and surrounding countryside. *(Currently closed for repairs; scheduled to reopen in late 2008.)* Next door, the elegant 🏛**Real Colegiata de Santa María la Mayor** was the first church in Andalucía to incorporate Renaissance style. *(☎952 84 61 43. Open July to mid-Sept. Tu-F 10:30am-2pm, W-F also 8:30-10:30pm, Sa 10:30am-2pm, Su 11:30am-2pm; mid-Sept. to June Tu-F 10.30am-2pm and 4:30-7:30pm, Sa 10:30am 2pm, Su 11:30am 2pm. Free.)* To the left of the church are the ruins of **Las Termas de Santa María.** Downhill, one block from the tourist office in the Palacio de Nájera, the **Museo Municipal** includes **Efebo,** a rare bronze statue of a Roman page and the pride of the city. *(☎952 70 40 21. Open Tu 10:30am-2pm, W-F 10:30am-2pm and 8:30-10:30pm, Sa 10:30am-2pm, Su 11:30am-2pm. Mandatory tours leave the entrance every 30min. €3.10.)*

🔲 DAYTRIP FROM ANTEQUERA

🏔 EL TORCAL DE ANTEQUERA

Casado buses (☎952 84 19 57) leave from Antequera (M-F 1pm, €2); the return bus leaves from the turn-off (M-F 4:15pm). Ask the driver to let you off at the turn-off for El Torcal; from there it's a 3km walk. A free service also runs buses from Pl. del Coso Viejo, one block downhill from the tourist office (W-Su 11:30am, return at 1:30pm. ☎952 70 45 31. Reservations recommended.) The standard round-trip price is €30 with a 1hr. wait; for an all-day visit, the fare is €36. Double check taxi fares at the tourist office so you don't get overcharged.

A garden of wind-sculpted boulders, the Sierra de Torcal glows like the surface of a barren and distant planet. The central peak, **El Torcal** (1369m), dominates the horizon, but the surrounding clumps of eroded rocks are even more extraordinary. Declared a natural park in 1978, the Sierra stretches for 11.7km. Several trails circle the summit. The well-traveled green arrow path (1.5km) takes about

45min.; the red arrow path (4½km) takes over 2hr. All but the green path require a guided tour; call the **Centro de Información** for details. (☎952 03 13 89. Open daily 10am-5pm, recently closed for renovation so call ahead before making the trip.) Each path begins and ends at the *refugio* (lodge) at the mountain base. Try to catch a spectacular sunset from the striking ◙**Mirador de las Ventanilas.**

GRANADA ☎958

The splendors of the Alhambra, the magnificent palace that crowns the highest point of this city, have fascinated both princes and paupers for centuries. Granada (pop. 238,000) first blossomed into one of Europe's wealthiest, most culturally advanced cities after being conquered by Muslim armies in AD 711. As Christian armies turned back the tide of Moorish conquest in the 13th century, the city became the last Muslim outpost in Iberia. The relentless Christian onslaught as well as growing disputes and corruption within the ruling dynasty caused Moorish control over Granada to wane by the end of the 15th century. Fernando and Isabel capitalized on the chaos, capturing Boabdil—Granada's last Moorish ruler—and the Alhambra on the momentous night of January 1, 1492. As Boabdil fled, his mother berated him for casting a longing look back at the Alhambra, saying, "You do well to weep as a woman for what you could not defend as a man."

Although the Christians torched all the mosques and the lower city, embers of Granada's Muslim past still linger. The Albaicín, a maze of Moorish houses and twisting alleys, is Spain's best-preserved Arab quarter and the only part of the Muslim city to survive the *Reconquista* intact. Since then, Granada has grown into a university town, surrendering to throngs of international backpackers and Andalusian youth. Two or three days should be enough to begin your discovery of Moorish Spain and to experience the city's energetic nightlife. But do not be surprised if, like Boabdil, you leave longing for more days in this Andalusian gem.

▐ TRANSPORTATION

Flights: Airport (☎958 24 52 00), 17km west of the city. **Autocares J. Gonzales** (☎958 49 01 64) runs a bus from Gran Vía, in front of the cathedral, to the airport (25min., 5 per day 6:50am-9:30pm, €3). A **taxi** costs about €20. **Iberia** (☎902 40 05 00), at the corner of Pl. Isabel la Católica and C. Pavaneras (open M-F 9am-1:45pm and 4-7pm), flies to **Barcelona** (1hr., 3 per day, €135) and **Madrid** (30min., 4 per day, €85).

Trains: RENFE, Av. Andaluces (☎902 24 02 02 or 958 20 40 00). Take bus #3-6, 9, or 11 from Gran Vía to the Constitución 3 stops and turn left onto Av. Andaluces. To: **Algeciras** (4-7hr., 3 per day 7:10am-5:45pm, €17); **Almería** (2½hr., 4 per day 10:09am-9pm, €13.40); **Barcelona** (12-13hr.; 8:40am, 9:25pm; €52.10-53.70); **Madrid** (5-6hr.; 8am, 5:10pm; €31.30-35.40); **Sevilla** (4-5hr., 4 per day 8:18am-8:55pm, €20.05).

Buses: All major intercity bus routes start at the **bus station** (☎958 18 54 80) on the outskirts of Granada on Ctra. de Madrid, near C. Arzobispo Pedro de Castro. Take bus #3 or 33 from Gran Vía de Colón or a **taxi** (€6-7).

ALSA (☎902 42 22 42 or 958 15 75 57) to: **Alicante** (6hr., 11 per day 1am-11:30pm, €25.03); **Barcelona** (14hr., 6 per day 2:31am-11:30pm, €61.86); and **Valencia** (9hr., 9 per day 2:31am-11:30pm, €37.74).

Alsina Graells (☎958 18 54 80) to: **Algeciras** (3½hr., 6 per day 9am-8:15pm, €17.68); **Almería** (2¼hr., 11-12 per day 6:45am-8pm, €9.40); **Antequera** (1½hr., 3-5 per day 3am-7pm, €6.38); **Cádiz** (5½hr., 4 per day 3am-6:30pm, €25.96); **Córdoba** (3hr., 9-10 per day 7:30am-8pm, €10.67); **Jaén** (1½hr., 13-17 per day 7am-9:45pm, €6.44); **Madrid** (5-6hr., hourly 7am-1:30am, €14.74); **Málaga** (2hr., 17-18 per day 7am-9pm, €8.29); **Marbella** (2hr., 6 per day 9am-8:15pm, €12.84-13.13); **Sevilla** (3hr., 10 per day 3am-8pm, €16.46).

Public Transportation: Local buses (☎900 71 09 00). Pick up the bus map at the tourist office. Important buses include: "Bus Alhambra" #30 from Gran Vía de Colón or Pl.

ANDALUCÍA

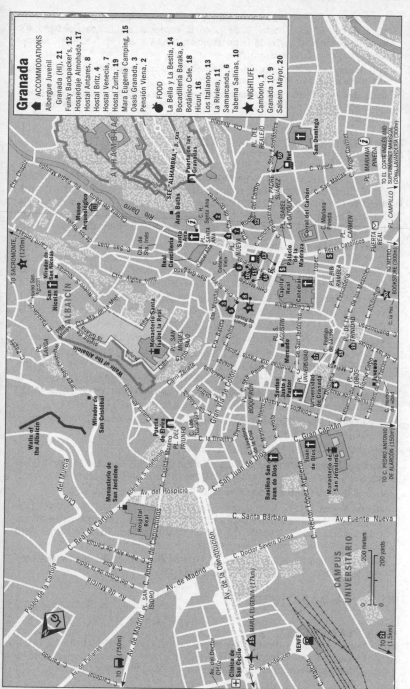

Granada

▲ ACCOMMODATIONS

Albergue Juvenil
Granada (HI), 21
Funky Backpacker's, 12
Hospedaje Almohada, 17
Hostal Antares, 8
Hostal Britz, 4
Hostal Venecia, 7
Hostal Zurita, 19
Mara Eugenia Camping, 15
Oasis Granada, 3
Pensión Viena, 2

🍴 FOOD

La Bella y La Bestia, 14
Bocadillería Baraka, 5
Botánico Cafe, 18
Hicuri, 16
Los Italianos, 13
La Riviera, 11
Samarcanda, 6
Taberna Salinas, 10

★ NIGHTLIFE

Camborio, 1
Granada 10, 9
Salsero Mayor, 20

Nueva to the Alhambra; #31 from Gran Vía or Pl. Nueva to the Albaicín; #10 from the bus station to the youth hostel, C. de Ronda, C. Recogidas, and C. Acera de Darro; #3 from the bus station to Av. de la Constitución, Gran Vía, and Pl. Isabel la Católica. €0.95, *bonobus* (10 tickets) €5.20.

Taxis: Teletaxi (☎958 28 06 54), with service throughout Granada and its environs. Taxi stands in Pl. Nueva and Pl. de la Trinidad 24hr.

Car Rental: Hertz, EuropCar, and Avis in the airport. Hertz has an office in the lobby of Hotel Central Granada, Av. Fuentenueva (☎902 40 24 05). Reservations open 8am-11pm. Office open 9am-1:30pm and 3:30-8:30pm.)

■✸🛈 ORIENTATION AND PRACTICAL INFORMATION

The center of Granada is small **Plaza Isabel la Católica,** at the intersection of the city's two main arteries, **Calle de los Reyes Católicos** and **Gran Vía de Colón.** On Gran Vía, you'll find the **cathedral;** farther down Gran Vía by Pl. de la Trinidad is the **university** area. Two blocks uphill from Pl. Isabel la Católica on C. Reyes Católicos sits Pl. Nueva. The **Alhambra** commands the hill above Pl. Nueva. Downhill, the pedestrian streets off C. de los Reyes Católicos comprise the shopping district.

Tourist Offices: Junta de Andalucía, C. Santa Ana, 2 (☎958 22 59 90). Open M-F 9am-8pm, Sa 10am-8pm, Su 10am-2pm. Posts bus and train schedules and provides a list of accommodations. **Oficina Provincial,** Pl. Mariana Pineda, 10 (☎958 24 71 28). English spoken. Open M-F 9am-8pm, Sa 10am-7pm, Su 10am-4pm.

Currency Exchange: Banco Santander Central Hispano, Gran Vía, 3 (☎902 24 24 24). Open Apr.-Sept. M-F 8:30am-2pm. **American Express:** C. de los Reyes Católicos, 31 (☎958 22 45 12). Open M-F 9am-10pm, Sa 11am-3pm, Su 4-9pm.

Luggage Storage: 24hr. storage at the train and bus stations (€3). Fequently sold out.

English-Language Bookstore: Metro, C. Gracia, 31 (☎958 26 15 65). Vast foreign language section. Open M-F 10am-2pm and 6-8:30pm, Sa 11am-2pm. Bookstores near the university sell English language travel guides and other foreign language books.

Gay and Lesbian Resources: Juvenós, C. Lavadero de las Tablas, 15, organizes weekly activities for gay youth. **Información Homosexual Hotline** (☎958 20 06 02).

Laundromat: C. de la Paz, 19. Wash €6, dry €1 per 10min.; detergent included. Open M-F 10am-2pm and 5-8pm.

Police: C. Duquesa, 21 (☎092). English spoken.

Pharmacy: Farmacia Gran Vía, Gran Vía, 6 (☎958 22 29 90). Open M-F 9:30am-1:30pm and 5-8:30pm, Sa 9:30am-1:30pm and 5:30-9pm. Occasionally stays open later in summer.

Medical Services: Clínica de San Cecilio, C. Dr. Olóriz, 16 (☎958 28 02 00).

Internet Access: Net, Pl. de los Girones, 3 (☎958 22 69 19). €1 per hour. Bono €8 per 10hr. Open M-F 10am-2:30pm and 5-10pm, Sa-Su 5-10pm. **Locutorio Cyber Alhambra,** C. Joaquin Costa, 4 (☎958 22 43 96). €1.20 per hour; €5 bono for 6hr., €10 bono for 13hr. Open daily 9:30am-midnight.

Post Office: Pta. Real (☎958 22 48 35). **Lista de Correos** and **fax** service. Open M-F 8:30am-8:30pm, Sa 9:30am-2pm. **Postal Code: 18009.**

🏠 ACCOMMODATIONS

NEAR PLAZA NUEVA

Hostels line Cuesta de Gomérez, the street leading uphill to the Alhambra, to the right of Pl. Nueva. Crashing in this area is wise for those planning to spend serious time in the Alhambra complex, but these spots tend to fill up very quickly.

> **GRANADA FOR POCKET CHANGE.** Let's face it, you came to Granada for the Alhambra and complimentary tapas, so why not enjoy both for less than a train ride to Sevilla. Haggle vendors along **C. Cría Nueva** for incredible prices on souvenirs, clothing, and jewelry or get your name scribed in Arabic. Refuel at **Oasis Granada** by chowing down at a weekly all-you-can eat dinner for €3.50 with a €15 bed to match. If you're still feeling hungry, stock up on some late-night tapas at **La Riviera** and other bars around **C. Villa** for the price of a drink or grab a €1 treat at **Bocadilleria Baraka.** Walk off the calories with a 15min. walk up to the **mirador** near **Iglesia de San Nicolás** for an unparalleled nighttime view of Alhambra amidst the echo of flamenco crooning. Back in the city, you can dance away your cares at **Salsero Mayor,** where the only cover is the timbered roof aglow with colored lights and undulating shadows.

Funky Backpacker's, Cuesta de Rodrigo del Campo, 13 (☎958 22 14 62; funky@alternativeacc.com). Sizable dorm rooms with a funky kick. Take in the view of the Alhambra, mountains, and rooftops of the city from the bar atop the hostel. The friendly staff hangs out with travelers. Outings to nearby thermal baths. A/C, breakfast, and lockers included. Laundry €7. Free Internet access. Dorms €16.50; doubles €38. MC/V. ❷

Hostal Venecia, Cuesta de Gomérez, 2, 3rd fl. (☎958 22 39 87). Eccentrically decorated with bright colors and Granada paraphernalia, this small hostel has the most character per square foot in town. Homemade herbal tea and conversation available any time of day. Reserve early, especially in summer, since the secret is out. Dorms €18; doubles €32; triples €45. Discounts for longer stays. MC/V. ❷

Pensión Viena, C. Hospital Santa Ana, 2 (☎958 22 18 59; www.hostalviena.com). Rooms, with bare white walls and blinds, aren't particularly memorable but come with A/C and a view of Pl. Nueva. Singles €25, with bath €30-35; doubles €37/45; triples €50/60; quads €57/70; quint €60/90. €5-10 more mid-July-Aug. MC/V. ❷

NEAR THE CATHEDRAL AND UNIVERSITY

Hostels surround Pl. de la Trinidad, at the end of C. de los Mesones when coming from Pta. Real. Many *pensiones* around C. de los Mesones cater to students during the academic year but free up during the summer, offering excellent deals to the diligent stair-climber. The ones listed below are open year-round.

Hospedaje Almohada, C. Postigo de Zárate, 4 (☎958 20 74 46; hospedajealmohada@hotmail.com). Look for double red doors with hand-shaped knockers. Lounge in the TV area, listen to the stereo, use the fridge, cook your own pasta, and peruse the communal music collection and travel guides. Laundry €5 for 8kg. Four-bed dorms €15; singles €19; doubles €35; triples €50. Cash only. ❷

Hostal Zurita, Pl. de la Trinidad, 7 (☎958 27 50 20; www.pensionzurita.com). Soundproof balcony doors allow you to relax in the midst of the busy student-dominated neighborhood. Doubles are spacious, singles are small but adequate; all have TV and A/C. Singles €20; doubles €32, with bath €40; triples €48/60. MC/V. ❷

ELSEWHERE

Hostels are sprinkled along the center of Gran Vía de Colón, though many are expensive. Rooms with balconies on the street are noisier than those that open onto a patio.

Hostal Antares, C. Cetti Meriém, 10 (☎958 22 83 13; www.hostalantares.com). Owner Javier is eager to tell you all about his American idol, Jimi Hendrix, who probably inspired the rooms' motley color schemes. Ask for a room with A/C and TV. Singles €18; doubles €30, with bath €40; €5 more F-Sa. Cash only. ❷

Oasis Granada, Placeta Correo Viejo, 3 (☎958 21 58 48; from Spain free at ☎9001 OASIS; www.hostelsoasis.com). Free Internet, common kitchen, ping-pong table, roof access. Frequented by the under-30 crowd. Weekly parties and daily activities like tapas tours and pub crawls. Breakfast included. Dinner *menús*, €3.50. Dorms €15; doubles €36. If hostel is "full," try showing up early in the morning for a spot. MC/V. ❷

Albergue Juvenil Granada (HI), C. Ramón y Cajal, 2 (☎958 00 29 00). From the bus station, take bus #10; from the train station, #11. Ask the driver to stop at "El Estadio de la Juventud," across the field on the left. The cheapest option in town, but a trek from all of the sights. Dorm-style rooms and relatively clean common baths. Dorms €15 for guests under 26, €19.50 over 26. Non-HI guests extra €3.50 per night. ❶

CAMPING

Buses serve all campgrounds within 5km of Granada. Check the schedules at the bus station or tourist office, and ask the driver to alert you at your stop.

María Eugenia, Av. Andalucía (☎958 20 06 06; fax 20 94 10), at km 436 on the road to Málaga. Take the Santa Fé or Chauchina bus from the train station (every 30min.). Open year-round. Popular with families. €4.50 per person, €3.50 per child. ❶

🍴 FOOD

Though Granada offers a variety of traditional Spanish fare and ethnic restaurants, the best way to eat on a budget is to take advantage of the free tapas, then order a few beers. North African cuisine and vegetarian options can be found around the **Albaicín,** while more typical menus await in Pl. Nueva and Pl. de la Trinidad. The adventurous eat well in Granada—*tortilla sacromonte* (omelette with calf's brains and bull testicles) and *sesos a la romana* (batter-fried calf's brains) are common. Picnickers can gather fresh fruit, vegetables, and meat at the large indoor **market** on Pl. San Agustín. (Open M-Sa 9am-3pm.)

NEAR PLAZA NUEVA

Pl. Nueva abounds with large indoor/outdoor cafes that are adequate but mediocre. Those seeking more authentic fare would do better to comb the small side streets that lead out of the plaza.

🦑 **La Riviera,** C. Cetti Meriem, 7 (☎958 22 79 69). The best place for your choice of delicious free tapas. You can't go wrong with the extensive list of traditional fare. Drinks €1.50-2. Open daily 12:30-4pm and 8pm-midnight. ❶

🦑 **Hicuri,** C. Santa Escolástica, 12 (☎958 22 12 83), on corner of Pl. de los Girones. Your search for healthy, affordable cuisine stops here. This popular eatery's huge selection of vegetarian and vegan dishes will satisfy any tofu craving. Entrees €5.50-6.50. *Menú* €11. Open daily 8:30am-4:30pm. Cash only. ❷

La Bella y La Bestia, C. Carrera del Darro, 37 (☎958 32 55 69), near Granada 10. Huge complimentary tapas proportionate to the number in your party, complete with fries, pasta salad, and *bocadillos*. Drinks €1.40-2. Open M-Th and Su 12:30pm-2am, F-Sa 12:30pm-3am. ❶

ALBAICÍN

Wander the winding streets of the Albaicín and you'll discover many budget bars and restaurants above Pl. Nueva. This is a veritable paradise for connoisseurs of Middle Eastern cuisine; stop anywhere for a cheap falafel sandwich. C. Calderería Nueva, off C. Elvira leading from the plaza, is crammed with teahouses and cafes.

🦑 **Bocadillería Baraka,** C. Elvira, 20 (☎958 22 97 60). Stands out among many Middle Eastern eateries for being the cheapest and the tastiest. Serves delicious traditional pitas (€2.50-3) and addictive homemade lemonade infused with *hierbabuena* (€1). Open daily 1pm-2am. Cash only. ❶

Taberna Salinas, C. Elvira, 13 (☎958 22 14 11). For a light but authentic dinner in this rustic tavern, order a *tabla salinas surtida* (plate of cheeses and pâté; €13.90) to complement a glass of wine. The menu also offers a wide selection of grilled meats and seafood (€8.40-20). Open M-Th and Su 12:30pm-1am. MC/V. ❸

Samarcanda, C. Calderería Vieja, 3 (☎958 21 00 04). Delightful kitchen successfully transplanted from Lebanon. For €43, you can order a huge *Mesa Libanesa* platter to share, complete with a bottle of Lebanese wine. Open M-Tu and Th-Su 1-4:30pm and 7:30pm-midnight. MC/V. ❸

GRAN VÍA AND ELSEWHERE

Filled with little bars and lots of *pastelerías*, Gran Vía is great for finding breakfast on a budget. Busy cafes teeming with students surround Pl. de la Trinidad. Avoid restaurants right next to the cathedral, as they are extremely overpriced; generally, the farther you wander down Gran Vía, the less touristy food becomes.

Botánico Café, C. Málaga, 3 (☎958 27 15 98). Serving self-described "fusion" cuisine, this trendy restaurant throws everything from Italian, Chinese, Spanish, and Mexican into the mix. Converts into a pub Sa-Su nights, but the kitchen is always open. Main dishes €7.40-16.45. *Menú* €11. Open M-Th 1pm-1am, F-Sa 1pm-2am. MC/V. ❸

Los Italianos, Gran Vía, 4 (☎958 22 40 34). Don't just gape at the ridiculously cheap ice-cream prices, get in line and try another flavor. No seating. *Barquillos* (cones) €0.50-2; *tarrinas* (cups) from €1. Mar.-Oct. open daily 9am-2am. Cash only. ❶

👁 SIGHTS

A **bono turístico pass,** which is good for one week and provides direct access to the Alhambra and several other sights throughout Granada, can be useful if you're going to be in the city for several days and are looking to tour the included monuments. The pass also includes 10 free trips on local bus lines to destinations within the city. For reservations, call the Caja Granada information and booking office (☎902 10 00 95); tickets are available for direct sale at the Alhambra Capilla Real or the Parque de las Ciencias. (€24.50. Cash only. Caja Granada also makes reservations. MC/V.)

◪ THE ALHAMBRA

Take Cuesta de Gomérez off Pl. Nueva and be prepared to pant (20min.; no unauthorized cars 9am-9pm), or take the quick Alhambra minibus from Pl. Nueva (every 5min., €0.95). ☎902 44 12 21 or 958 57 51 26; www.alhambra-patronato.es; reservations for entrance

GIVING BACK

A LOAD OF CRAPS

Walking down the streets of Spain, you can't help but notice the circular ONCE booths and ticket easels on every corner and main boulevard. With more than 23,000 vendors in the country, how could you miss them?

Created by Franco in 1938, the Organización Nacional de Ciegos Españoles (ONCE) was initially meant to provide work for the growing number of blind Spaniards, casualties of the Civil War, but has recently grown into a commercial enterprise. Drawn in by the seemingly benevolent charitable contributions of ONCE and other gambling networks, Spaniards are now suffering from widespread gambling addiction, often spending around €100 at a time. Between electronic slot machines, sport wagers, and lotteries, it is estimated that Spain bets over 23 billion euro on legal gambling each year and double that figure on illegal endeavors. The average citizen shells out about 10 times what he allots for his insurance policy. Only the US and the Philippines spend more money seducing Lady Luck.

To help break this inveterate habit, you can volunteer with the Cruz Roja Española as a mediator of a kind of "Gamblers Anonymous" support group.

Visit www.cruzroja.es, or call ☎913 35 46 55 to find a Cruz Roja in your area and learn more about the fight against gambling addiction.

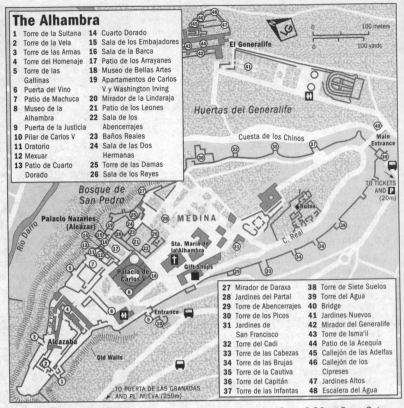

The Alhambra

1 Torre de la Sultana
2 Torre de la Vela
3 Torre de las Armas
4 Torre del Homenaje
5 Torre de las Gallinas
6 Puerta del Vino
7 Patio de Machuca
8 Museo de la Alhambra
9 Puerta de la Justicia
10 Pilar de Carlos V
11 Oratorio
12 Mexuar
13 Patio de Cuarto Dorado
14 Cuarto Dorado
15 Sala de los Embajadores
16 Sala de la Barca
17 Patio de los Arrayanes
18 Museo de Bellas Artes
19 Apartamentos de Carlos V y Washington Irving
20 Mirador de la Lindaraja
21 Patio de los Leones
22 Sala de los Abencerrajes
23 Baños Reales
24 Sala de las Dos Hermanas
25 Torre de las Damas
26 Sala de los Reyes

27 Mirador de Daraxa
28 Jardines del Partal
29 Torre de Abencerrajes
30 Torre de los Picos
31 Jardines de San Francisco
32 Torre del Cadi
33 Torre de las Cabezas
34 Torre de las Brujas
35 Torre de la Cautiva
36 Torre del Capitán
37 Torre de las Infantas
38 Torre de Siete Suelos
39 Torre del Agua
40 Bridge
41 Jardines Nuevos
42 Mirador del Generalife
43 Torre de Isma'il
44 Patio de la Acequia
45 Callejón de las Adelfas
46 Callejón de los Cipreses
47 Jardines Altos
48 Escalera del Agua

☎902 22 44 60; www.alhambratickets.com. Open daily Apr.-Sept. 8:30am-8pm; Oct.-Mar. 8:30am-6pm. Also open June-Sept. Tu-Sa 10-11:30pm; Oct.-May Sa 8-9:30pm. Audio tours are worth the expense and are available in English, French, German, Italian, and Spanish (€3). €10, under 8 and the disabled free. Gardens only €5. Limited to 7700 visitors per day, so get there early or reserve in advance. You must enter the Palace of the Nasrids (Alcázar) during the half-hour time slot specified on your ticket, but you can stay as long as desired. It is possible to reserve tickets in advance at banks for a €0.88 charge; this is recommended July-Aug. and Semana Santa. BBVA branches will also book tickets. Hotels can book tickets, but often take a larger commission.

From the streets of Granada, the Alhambra, meaning "the red one" in Arabic, appears blocky and purely practical—a military base planted in the foothills of the Sierra Nevada. This deceptive appearance conceals a universe of aesthetic and symbolic grandeur born of profound spirituality, artistic skill, and precision. The age-old saying holds true: *"Si mueres sin ver la Alhambra, no has vivido"* (If you die without seeing the Alhambra, you have not lived).

ALCAZABA. The Christians drove the first Nasrid King Alhamar from the Albaicín to this more strategic hill, where he built the series of rust-colored brick towers that form the Alcazaba, or fortress. A dark, spiraling staircase leads to the **Torre de la Vela** (watchtower), where visitors can see all of Granada and the surrounding mountains. The tower's bells were rung to warn of impending danger and to coordinate the Moorish irrigation system. During the annual New Year commemoration of the Christian conquest of Granada, legend holds that local girls who scramble up the tower and ring the bell by hand before January 1 will receive a wedding proposal within a year. Compared to the rest of the Alhambra, the Alcazaba is the most utilitarian and bare-boned structure. Exit through the **Puerta del Vino,** the original entrance to the *medina* (city), where inhabitants of the Alhambra once bought tax-free wine (alas, no more).

ALCÁZAR. Follow signs to the **Palacio Nazaries** to see the Alcázar, a royal palace finished by Moorish ruler Muhammad V (1354-1391) after his father, Yusuf I (1333-1354), was murdered by a political enemy in the palace's isolated basement. Throughout the palace, astonishingly intricate carvings and engravings mark every room. In the **Mexuar,** the first pillared council chamber after the entrance, the glazed tile arrangements reiterate the Nasrid dynasty mantra, "There is no victor but Allah," variations of which you'll see repeated throughout the entire palace. Attached to the Mexuar is a small prayer hall with an intricately decorated *mihrab*, marking the direction of prayer to Mecca. The Mexuar adjoins the **Patio del Cuarto Dorado** (Patio of the Gilded Room). The magnificently carved walls are topped by the shielded windows of the harem, so that the women could see out but no one could see in. The *hammams*, or Arab baths, are behind an iron-grilled door but have been permanently closed for preservation. Off the far side of the patio, leafy horseshoe archways lead to the **Cuarto Dorado,** decorated by Muhammad V. Its carved wooden ceiling, inlaid with ivory and mother-of-pearl, displays colorful, geometric ceramic figures.

Next is the **Patio de los Arrayanes** (Courtyard of Myrtles), an expanse of water filled with goldfish. At the top of the patio, get a glimpse of the 14th-century **Fachada de Serallo,** the palace's elaborate facade. Flanking the courtyard is the **Sala de la Barca,** named not for its inverted boat-hull ceiling, but for the Arabic word "baraka," meaning blessing. The walls are covered with the 99 names of Allah.

Granada was formally surrendered to the *Reyes Católicos* in the elaborate **Sala de los Embajadores** (Hall of Ambassadors), adjoining the Sala de la Barca to the north, and it was here that Fernando and Columbus discussed finding a new route to India. Every surface is wrought with symbolic inscriptions and ornamental patterns. The Mozárabe dome, carved of more than 8000 pieces of wood and inlaid with cedar, forms its own system of constellations and is the most impressive part of the room. A section of the original floor remains in the center. From the Patio de los Arrayanes, the Sala de los Mozárabes leads to the **Patio de los Leones** (Courtyard of the Lions), the grandest display of Nasrid art in the palace. An arcade of marble columns borders the courtyard, and a fountain supported by 12 marble lions (currently under construction). Some believe that this fountain originally belonged to one of the sultan's Jewish advisors, but was transferred to this patio and redecorated with Muslim motifs.

The adjoining **Sala de los Abencerrajes** tells one of the bloodiest chapters in the palace's history. Here, Boabdil, the last Arabic king to rule from the Alhambra, had the throats of 16 sons of the Abencerrajes family slit after one of them allegedly had amorous encounters with his concubine, Zorahayda. The rust-colored stains in the basin are said to mark the indelible traces of the butchering; none of this bothered Holy Roman Emperor Charles V, who dined here during the construction of his **palazzo.** Light filters into the room through the domed ceiling, which features an eight-pointed star representing terrestrial and celestial harmony.

Through archways at the far end of the Patio de los Leones lies the **Sala de los Reyes** (Hall of Kings). The only human representations in the entire palace—the 21 sultans who ruled from the Alhambra, important assemblies, and hunting parties—are depicted on detailed sheepskin paintings fixed to the walls with bamboo pins, and are currently covered up for restoration. On the remaining side of the courtyard, the resplendent **Sala de las Dos Hermanas** (Chamber of the Two Sisters) gets its name from the two matching slabs of marble that comprise most of the floor. It has a *muqarnas* (honeycombed) dome composed of thousands of tiny cells. This stalactite-like structure is typical of Islamic architecture and represents an ascension and the doors of heaven opening. From here, the secluded **Mirador de Daraxa** overlooks the **Jardines de Daraxa** (Gardens of the Sultana).

Passing the room where American author Washington Irving resided in 1829 and wrote the famous *Tales of the Alhambra* (1832), a courtyard leads to the **Baños Reales,** a less ornate 14th-century addition, toward the royal gardens and the exit. Do not leave the Nasrid Palace unless you are satisfied with your visit, because like Boabdil you will not be allowed to return.

TOWERS AND GARDENS. Just outside the eastern wall of the Alcázar in the **Jardines del Partal,** lily-studded pools stand beside rose-laden terraces. The **Torre de las Damas** (Ladies' Tower) soars above it all. A series of six additional towers traverses the area between the Alcazaba and El Generalife.

■ **EL GENERALIFE.** Over a bridge, across the **Callejón de los Cipreses** and the shady **Callejón de las Adelfas** are the lively blossoms, towering cypresses, and streaming waterways of El Generalife, the sultan's vacation retreat. In 1313 Arab engineers changed the Darro's flow by 18km and employed dams and channels to prepare the soil for Aben Walid Ismail's design of El Generalife. Over the centuries, the estate passed through private hands until it was finally repatriated in 1931. The two buildings of El Generalife, the **Palacio** and the **Sala Regia,** connect across the **Patio de la Acequia** (Courtyard of the Irrigation Channel), embellished with a narrow pool fed by fountains that form an aquatic archway. Honeysuckle vines scale the back wall, and shady benches invite long rests. A dead cypress tree stands at the place where the sultana Zorahayda supposedly had amorous encounters with a nobleman from the Abencerrajes tribe.

PALACIO DE CARLOS V. After the *Reconquista* drove the Moors from Spain, Fernando and Isabel restored the Alcázar. Little did they know that two generations later, Emperor Charles V would demolish part of it to make way for his *palazzo*, a Renaissance masterpiece by Michelangelo's disciple Pedro Machuca. The square building, with a circular inner courtyard wrapped in two stories of Doric colonnades, is Machuca's only surviving design. Although the palace is incongruous with the surrounding Moorish splendor, scholars concede that it is one of the most beautiful Renaissance buildings in Spain. Inside, the **Museo de la Alhambra** contains the only remaining original furnishings from the Alhambra, including old doors and the well-preserved *azulejo* tiles. (☎958 02 79 00. Open Tu-Sa 9am-2pm. Free with admission to the Alhambra; free guided visits Tu-Sa 11am-1pm.) Upstairs, the **Museo de Bellas Artes** is currently undergoing renovations to better display its religious sculptures and paintings of the Granada School dating from the 16th century. (☎958 22 14 49. Open Apr.-Sept. Tu 2:30-6pm, W-Sa 9am-6pm, Su 9am-2:30pm; Oct.-Mar. Tu 2:30-7:45pm, W-Sa 9am-7:45pm, Su 9am-2:30pm. €1.50.)

■ **ALBAICÍN**

Although generally safe, the Albaicín is disorienting, so use caution at night. Bus #12 runs from beside the cathedral to C. Pagés at the top of the Albaicín. Bus #30 or 31 go from Gran Vía and Pl. Nueva to the neighborhood.

A labyrinth of steep, narrow alleys, the Albaicín was the only Moorish neighborhood to escape the torches of the *Reconquista*, and remains a key stop in Granada. After the fall of the Alhambra, a small Muslim population remained here until they were expelled in the 17th century. Today, the Albaicín attests to the persistence of Islamic influence in Andalucía—the mosque near Pl. San Nicolás and abundance of North African cuisine, outdoor bazaars blasting Arabic music, and teahouses will leave you wondering if you're actually in Morocco. Spectacular sunsets can be seen from C. Cruz de Quirós, above C. Elvira.

The best way to explore this maze is to proceed along Carrera del Darro off Pl. Santa Ana, climb the Cuesta del Chapiz on the left, then wander through the Moorish ramparts, cisterns, and gates. On Pl. Santa Ana, the 16th-century **Real Cancillería,** with its beautiful arcaded patio and stalactite ceiling, was the Christians' town hall. Farther uphill are the 11th-century **Arab baths.** *(Carrera del Darro, 31. ☎958 02 78 00. Open Tu-Sa 10am-2pm. Free.)* The **Museo Arqueológico** showcases funerary urns, classical sculpture, Carthaginian vases, Muslim lamps, and ceramics. *(Carrera del Darro, 41. ☎958 22 56 40. Open Tu 2:30-8:30pm, W-Sa 9am-8:30pm, Su 9am-2:30pm. €1.50, EU citizens free.)* The ▩**mirador** adjacent to **Iglesia de San Nicolás** affords the city's best view of the Alhambra—it's especially good in winter, when more snow adorns the Sierra Nevada behind it. From C. de Elvira, go up C. Calderería Nueva to C. San Gregorio and continue uphill past Pl. Algibe de Trillo, where it becomes Cta. Algibe de Trillo. At Pl. Camino, make a left onto Cta. Tomasa and another left onto Atarazana Cta. Cabras. The *mirador* is on the right.

SACROMONTE

If you're not up for the 20min. climb from Pl. Nueva, take bus #34 (€0.95), or a night bus Th-Sa 11:25pm-2:30am. Ask at the tourist office for exact schedules and check with the driver that Sacromonte is the destination before you get on. Avoid isolated streets and corners in the neighborhood, as they are somewhat unsafe at night.

Above the Albaicín stands Sacromonte, home to a gypsy community since they took refuge here from the Inquisition. A whole hillside plastered white with the facades of cave dwellings contains a community worth exploring. Though a stroll in the neighborhood is an experience in itself, the **Centro de Interpretación del Sacromonte,** also called the Barranco de los Negros, at the top of the hill, has an informative display of model caves, from a house and kitchen to a stable and caves for iron-working, basket-weaving, and pottery-making; it also does a good job of answering many frequently asked questions—where else could you learn that the gypsies were originally Punjabis? *(☎958 21 51 20; www.sacromontegranada.com. Open Apr.-Oct. Tu-F 10am-2pm and 5-9pm, Sa-Su 11am-9pm; Nov.-Mar. Tu-F 10am-2pm and 4-7pm, Sa-Su 11am-7pm. Access to mirador and outdoor areas €1, museum €4.)* In the summer, there is often impromptu flamenco in some of the caves. Ask at the tourist office or at the entrance to the Centro de Interpretación. Since the Sacromonte sits on a neighboring hill, it also offers magnificent views of the Alhambra.

THE CATHEDRAL QUARTER

CAPILLA REAL. Downhill from the Alhambra, through the Puerta Real off Gran Vía de Colón, on C. Oficios, stands Fernando and Isabel's private chapel, the **Capilla Real.** During their prosperous reign, the Catholic monarchs funneled almost a quarter of the royal income into the chapel's construction (1504-1521) to build a proper burial place. Intricate Gothic masonry and **La Reja,** the gilded grille of Maestro Bartolomé, grace the couple's resting place. Behind La Reja lie the almost lifelike marble figures of the storied royals themselves. Fernando and Isabel are on the right when facing the altar; beside them sleep their daughter, Juana la Loca, and her husband, Felipe el Hermoso. In the adjacent **Sacristía,** Isabel's private **art collection** favors Flemish and German artists of the 15th century. The glittering **royal jewels**—including the queen's golden crown and scepter and the king's sword—shine in the middle. (☎958 22 92 39. *Capilla Real and Sacristía both open M-Sa 10:30am-1pm and 4-7pm, Su 11am-1pm and 4-7pm. Both sights €3.*)

CATEDRAL. Behind the Capilla Real and the Sacristía is Granada's cathedral. Construction of the cathedral began after the *Reconquista* upon the smoldering embers of Granada's largest mosque and was not completed until 1704. The first Renaissance cathedral in Spain, its massive Corinthian pillars support a 45m nave. While the eclectic side chapels and fanning pipes of its gilded organ are beautiful, this cathedral may not impress those who have seen most any other cathedral in Spain. (☎958 22 29 59. *Open Apr.-Sept. M-Sa 10:45am-1:30pm and 4-8pm, Su 4-8pm; Oct.-Mar. M-Sa 10:30am-1:30pm and 3:30-6:30pm, Su 11am-1:30pm and 3:30-6:30pm. €3.*)

◪ NIGHTLIFE

Granada's "free tapas with a drink" tradition lures students and tourists to the many pubs and bars spread across several neighborhoods. Some great tapas bars are found on the side streets off Pl. Nueva. The most boisterous crowds hang out on C. Pedro Antonio de Alarcón, between Pl. Albert Einstein and Ancha de Gracia, while hip new bars and clubs line C. de Elvira from C. Cárcel to C. Cedrán. Gay bars can be found by Carrera del Darro. Check the *Guía del Ocio* (€1), sold at newsstands; it lists clubs, pubs, and cafes.

▨ **Camborio,** Camino del Sacromonte, 48 (☎958 22 12 15), a 20min. walk uphill from Pl. Nueva; night bus #31 runs there until 2am. Pop music spun by live DJ echoes through dance floors to the rooftop patio above. Striking view of the Alhambra. Beer €1.80-3. Mixed drinks €5-6. Cover €7 F-Sa. Open Tu-Sa 11pm-dawn. Cash only.

▨ **Salsero Mayor,** C. la Paz, 20 (☎958 52 27 41; www.salseromayorgranada.com). The name says it all—an ageless group of locals and tourists alike flocks here for crowded nights of salsa, *bachata*, and merengue. Beer €2-3. Mixed drinks €5. Open M-Th and Su 10pm-3am, F-Sa 1pm-4am. Cash only.

Granada 10, C. Cárcel Baja 3 (☎958 22 40 01). Movie theater by evening (shows Sept.-June at 8, 10pm), raging dance club by night. Flashy and opulent. No sneakers or sportswear. Open M-Th and Su 12:30-4am, F-Sa 12:30-5am. MC/V.

♫ ▨ ENTERTAINMENT AND FESTIVALS

The daily paper, *Ideal*, lists entertainment venues in the back under *Cine y Espectáculos;* the Friday supplement highlights bars and special events.

FLAMENCO AND JAZZ. The most "authentic" flamenco performances, which change monthly, are advertised on posters around town. The tourist office provides a list of nightly *tablaos* (flamenco shows), which tend to be expensive and touristy. A smoky, intimate setting awaits at Eshavira, C. Postigo de la Cuna, in a very secluded alley off C. Azacayas, between C. de Elvira and Gran Vía. This joint is the place to go for flamenco, jazz, or a fusion of the two. Photos of Nat King Cole and other jazz greats plaster the walls. Those with musical talent who wish to stage their own impromptu concerts can pick up the guitar or sit down at the piano provided specifically for this purpose. (☎958 29 41 25. *Su-Th 9 or 9:30pm-3:30am, F-Sa until 4am; call for schedule. Min. consumption €3.*)

FESTIVALS. Parties sweep Granada in the summer. The **Corpus Cristi** celebrations, processions, and bullfights in May are world-famous. That same month, avant-garde theater groups from around the world make a pilgrimage to Granada for the **International Theater Festival** (☎958 22 93 44). The **Festival Internacional de Música y Danza** (mid-June to early July) sponsors performances of classical music, ballet, and flamenco in the Palacio de Carlos V and other outdoor venues. *(☎958 22 18 44; www.granadafestival.org. Tickets free €40, senior and youth discounts available.)*

GUADIX What distinguishes Guadix (pop. 20,000) from other cities in Spain and the rest of the world is that almost half its residents live in *casas cuevas* (cave houses). Quite literally dug into the rock basin of what was once a prehistoric lake, Guadix, as has recently been discovered, was a prehistoric graveyard of a people once believed to only have inhabited Africa.

⊡⊠ TRANSPORTATION AND PRACTICAL INFORMATION. From the station on C. Santa Rosa, Maestra buses (☎958 66 06 57) depart for: Almería (1½hr., 2-3 per day 9am-6pm, €6.84); Granada (1hr.; M-F 12 per day 6:45am-10:35pm, Sa 9 per day 7:45am-10:35pm, Su 7 per day 9:45am-10:35pm; €4.05); Jaén (1½hr.; 11am, 6pm; €6.84). Schedules are subject to frequent change. Get off at Pl. de las Américas, in front of the rotary and cathedral, to avoid the easy but unnecessary 15min. walk from the bus station. The tourist office, on Av. Mariana Pineda, is several blocks to the left when your back is to the cathedral. (☎958 69 95 74; otguadix@andalucia.org. Open M-F 8:30am-3:30pm.)

⊓⊡ ACCOMMODATIONS AND FOOD. Despite Guadix's impressive attractions, the city remains relatively untouristed, and while this means a scarcity of accommodations, it's hard to find a more unique, yet still affordable, way to spend a night. Experience cave living at ▓**Chez Jean & Julia ❷**, Ermita Nueva, 67, run by an accommodating staff in the Barriada de Cuevas. Groups can rent authentic cave apartments complete with kitchen and bath, stay in hotel-like cave rooms, or opt for a stay in the main house. The staff is happy to prepare your breakfast early if you have to catch the bus back to Granada. (☎958 66 91 91. Breakfast included. Reserve a day ahead for July-Aug. Non-cave and cave doubles and triples €35. Cave apartments June-Sept., Christmas, and *Semana Santa* €68; Oct.-May €54.) **Cuevas de María ❷**, Ermita Nueva, 52, with rustic cave rooms with TV and heating, is more like a mountaintop hotel than a converted residence. (☎958 66 17 06; www.guadix-

digital.com/cuevasdemaria. Online reservations not recommended. Doubles
€40-50; triples €55-70.) The tourist office has a complete listing of cave
"hotels" and apartments for rent. Great food abounds in Guadix. Walk along
Av. Mariana Pineda for bars and cafeterias during the day, then take advantage
of the Granada tradition of complimentary tapas by wandering C. Tribuna and
nearby side streets. **Calatrava Bodega ❷,** C. Tribuna, is one of the most celebrated bars in town. Locals flock here at night, so be sure to claim a seat at the
bar or outside before 9:15pm. Order one of the cheapest and most delicious
drinks in Spain (€1.20-2), then choose from an extensive list of local tapas
dishes. (☎609 91 23 45. Open M-Sa 1-4pm and 10pm-midnight.) **Café-Bar Los
Arcos ❸,** in the *Ayuntamiento* plaza, treats you with generous *bocadillos* for
each drink, and it's a great place to take in the live performances in the plaza.
(☎958 66 66 29. Open daily 9am-2am.)

🄶 **SIGHTS.** The residential area made up of caves, **Barriada de Cuevas,** behind
the *casco antiguo*, houses the most unique sights in the city. Signs point the
way to the *barriada*, starting in front of the cathedral and on **C. San Miguel** (15-
20min. walk to the caves). Take a break from the climb up to the *barriada* in the
natural coolness of **Museo de Alfarería Cueva La Alcazaba,** C. San Miguel, 47,
underneath the Alcazába. It displays earthenware artifacts and a well dating
from 1650 inside an authentic cave dwelling, along with a large collection of the
town's distinctive decorative and domestic pottery, from the Moorish and modern ages of Guadix, most of it for sale. (☎958 66 47 67. Open M-Sa in summer
10am-1:30pm and 5-8:30pm; in winter 4-7pm. €2, children €1.) In Pl. de la Ermita
Nueva, the main square of the *barriada*, the **Cueva Museo de Costumbres Populares** is a great way to compare older cave dwellings with the more modern ones.
Once a cave home, the building was abandoned in the 1970s. You can witness
how only decades ago, cave dwellers had no running water or bathrooms and
kept their livestock inside, walking them through the kitchen when the animals
returned from pasture. The jester suit and flag of the famed Cascamorras rest in
the museum until September. (☎958 66 07 16 or 618 93 58 95. Open M-Sa 10am-
2pm and 4-6pm, Su 10am-2pm. €1.55, groups €0.90 per person, seniors and children under 14 €0.75.) While these museums offer a glimpse into cave life, modern cave homes give a living picture of life inside the mountains. The home to the
right of the Cueva Museo de Costumbres Populares has a sign explicitly inviting
tourists. To truly get a feel for the *barriada*, continue uphill from the opposite
end of the plaza from the **Cueva Museo** to reach the **Mirador Cerro de la Bala** (on
your left; follow signs or ask a local), where the Sierra Nevadas form a perfect
backdrop to a valley full of chimneys rising out of the surrounding rock.

LAS ALPUJARRAS

Although Andalucía is known for its stretches of sunflowers and grazing cattle,
the Sierra Nevada mountains that peak above the rolling fields are an equally
stunning sight, hard to miss and even harder to forget. In the summer, their white
slopes give way to green gorges, hidden streams, and the *pueblos blancos* (white
villages) of Las Alpujarras, which blanket the southern slopes in an area known
as *la Falda* (the skirt). Although the roads are now paved and the towns more
touristed, a rare sense of tranquility still survives.

These mountain towns are a peaceful escape for the rundown traveler, and an
ideal base for the active tourist. Climbing, biking, horseback riding, and hiking
opportunities abound in the wooded sides of the Sierra Nevada; some backpackers spend months amid the streams, trails, and wild boars. Amateurs can break in

their hiking boots or even sneakers in Pampaneira and Bubión, while seasoned hikers must be well-prepared for sudden climate changes when taking on the most challenging climbs in the higher towns of Capileira and Trevélez. If you're planning a long stay in the mountains, don't forget a good map, compass, warm clothes, cooking and camping equipment, and possibly even a GPS system for GPS-waymarked maps and trails. Whether you're a novice or pro, be sure to research trails before starting out; getting lost in the mountains is never fun. Check out **Discovery Walking Guides'** guidebook for blow-by-blow accounts of every trail in Las Alpujarras (www.walking.demon.co.uk; €15), or simply admire the beauty of the peaks and wildlife from the comfort of a park bench.

⌐ TRANSPORTATION

The "highway" that runs through the Sierra Nevada villages has not quite caught up with the rest of Spain's roads, which makes for a true thrill-ride—higher in the mountains, the two-way road achieves the width of a queen-size bed. Las Alpujarras is best appreciated by **car**, but for those without wheels, **Alsina Graells buses** (☎958 18 54 80) travel from Granada to many of the high-altitude towns, though service is infrequent and not always punctual. The buses trace switchback after unnerving switchback, hugging the scenic road. Bus drivers often stop to let travelers off at intermediate points. Buses run between Granada (3 per day 10:30am-5:15pm) and: Pampaneira (2hr., €4.84); Bubion (2¼hr., €5.30); Capileira (2½hr., €5.35); Trevélez (3½hr., €6.40). Ask in each town for the return schedule. Some hard-core visitors hike from place to place, and locals often sympathize with hitchhikers. *Let's Go* does not recommend hitchhiking.

 WATER, WATER EVERYWHERE. All throughout the villages in the Alpujarras, you'll find fountains of delicious, ice-cold mountain spring water. To save money and treat yourself, bring along an empty water bottle.

▨ BUBIÓN ☎958

Bubión, a steep 3km (1hr.) hike on a dirt trail from Pampaneira, is resplendent with Berber architecture, village charm, and enough *artesanía* (traditional arts and crafts) to make your head spin. The colorful handwoven rugs that line store walls are reminiscent of Berber patterns, another reminder of the multi-cultural traditions of the region. If you begin your hike early, carry some water and snacks with you; everything in this sleepy town opens late. Those not up for the steep hike can catch the "early" bus from Pampaneira at 12:35pm. The town has no tourist office, but locals are glad to assist when they can. **Rustic Blue,** Barrio La Ermita, is a great resource for action-seekers; the intrepid staff specializes in rentals but has been organizing excursions, guided hikes, and horseback rides into the mountains for a decade. (☎958 76 33 81; www.rusticblue.com. Open M-F 10am-2pm and 5-7pm, Sa 11am-2pm.) With its central location and affordable accommodations, Bubion is the best anchor for traveling between the Alpujarras. **▨Las Terrazas de la Alpujarra ➋,** Pl. del Sol, 7, offers rooms with an Alpujarran flair, private baths and breathtaking views of the valley. (☎958 76 30 34; www.terrazasalpujarra.com. Free Internet access. Breakfast €2.50. Singles €20; doubles €29; apartments for 2-10 people €45-120. MC/V.) The *menú* (€8) at **Teide ➋** is limited but generous. (☎958 76 30 84. Entrees €4-13. Open daily 9-11am, 1-4pm, and 7-11pm. MC/V.)

PAMPANEIRA ☎958

Pampaneira (1059m) is the first of a trio of picturesque hamlets overlooking the **Poqueira Gorge,** a massive ravine cut by the Río Poqueira. The town makes a great springboard for climbing to **Bubión** (40min.) and **Capileira** (1¼hr.). But with the biggest and liveliest crowds in Las Alpujarras, why not heed the advice of the sign at the entrance to Pampaneira? *Quédate a vivir con nosotros*, it encourages; "stay and live with us." If settling a homestead isn't on your itinerary, catch the trail to the higher towns by taking any combination of uphill streets to the top of Pampaneira; sporadic signs point the way. Bear right at any fork in the trail, and you will end up in a small plaza behind Bubión's church. Continue uphill until you find the paved road and walk left for a steep but manageable 20min. walk to Capileira. **Nevadensis** offers hiking tours of the Sierra Nevada, sells gear, and even arranges accommodations. Located in the main square, Pl. de la Libertad, they also serve as the town's **tourist office.** (☎958 76 31 27; www.nevadensis.com. Open M and Su 10am-3pm, and random afternoons from 3-5pm; hours vary.) **Hostal Pampaneira** ❷, C. José Antonio Primo de Rivera, 1, off Pl. de la Libertad to the left of the church, has a terrace and large rooms with private baths, TV, and comfortable beds. (☎958 76 30 02; www.hostalpampaneira.com. Breakfast included. Singles €28; doubles €40; triples €46. AmEx/MC/V.) A few doors down, **Restaurante Casa Diego "El Alpujarreño"** ❷, C. José Ant., 15, draws hikers in with its cuisine and shady roof terrace. For a pre-trek protein boost, try the *sopa alpujarreña* (€3.50), a yellow broth with fried bread, hard-boiled eggs, and pork. (☎958 76 30 15. Entrees €5-9. *Menú* €9. Open daily 12:30-4:30pm and 8-11pm. MC/V.) **El Pilon** ❶, under the same ownership as Casa Diego, is a louder, more casual option that serves free tapas with the coldest and tastiest *tinto de verano* in the region (€1.50). (☎958 76 30 15. July-Nov. open daily 10pm-2 or 3am; Dec.-June closed M. MC/V.) Local taverns surrounding Pl. de la Libertad offer pool tables and music, and the locals joke, "Madrid is peaceful. It's all happening in Pampaneira!"

CAPILEIRA ☎958

In Capileira (1436m), looming peaks tower over cobblestone alleys, with the distant valley below. This white-washed town sits perched atop the Poqueira Gorge (2½hr. from Granada, from Bubión a 1hr. hike on the trail or a 20min. walk on the road) and makes a good base for exploring the neighboring villages and the back of la Falda. A tedious ascent to Mulhacén (3479m), mitigated only by views of spectacular gorges, is possible from Capileira via the refugio (shelter); however, novice climbers might prefer to start from the more commonly used base town Trevélez. If that still seems daunting, ride partway and climb Mulhacén with a guide via the national park's **Centro de Información,** on the left side of the main road as you enter Capileira, which offers daily tours. (☎958 76 34 86 or 686 41 45 76; picapileira@oapn.mma.es. Open daily 9am-2pm and 5-8pm; hours vary. €4.50, round-trip €7.50. Reservations required.) This town, while tiny, is full of beautiful places to stay, all with character-filled rooms and great views of the gorge and mountains. Enjoy small luxuries at **El Cascapeñas** ❷, Ctra. de la Sierra, 5, above the restaurant of the same name, where coral and white halls lead to stenciled rooms with balcony, TV, and marble-countered bath; ask for the second floor for the best views. (☎958 76 30 11; www.elcascapenas.com. Singles €20; doubles €36; triples €45. MC/V.) New rooms, a pool, and a filling traditional *menú* (€10-11) can be found at **Mesón Poqueira** ❷, C. Dr. Castillo, 11 and its adjacent hostel. Each room has beds lain with traditional Alpujarra blankets, as well as large wooden furniture and a balcony. (☎958 76 30 48; www.hotelpoqueira.com. Open Tu-Su 1-4pm and 8-11:30pm. One person in a double room €20; double €36; triples €40. MC/V.)

TREVÉLEZ ☎958

■ **Jamón serrano** (mountain-cured ham), and lots of it, distinguishes Trevélez, continental Spain's highest permanent community (1476m). The only "houses" you'll find above this tiny town, however, are the shepherds' lean-tos used in the summer when sheep are led to the top of the peaks. Steep roads weave through three *barrios*, and water rushes through Moorish irrigation systems still intact after 1000 years of use. Above all, Trevélez is a logical base for the ascent to **Mulhacén** (3479m), the highest peak of the Iberian peninsula. Every August, throngs of locals visit Mulhacén to pay homage to the **Virgen de las Nieves** (Virgin of the Snows), who sits on the summit during the festival. Summit-bound travelers should prepare with proper cold-weather equipment (except during summer) and head north on the trail leaving the upper village from behind the church; avoid the trail that follows the swampy Río Trevélez. Continue past the Cresta de los Postreros for a good 3-4hr. until you reach a waterfall. Cross the waterfall and climb up its right side until the top of ridge; on the other side, you should see the **Cañada de Siete Lagunas** (the largest lake, Laguna Hondera, should be directly in front of you); go right to see the **Cueva del Cura** (the Priest's Cave), a famous refuge. To reach Mulhacén, go up the ridge south of the refuge (3-4hr. farther). If you're stocking up on sleep before attempting the climb, budget beds aren't hard to find in Trevélez. **Hostal González ❷**, Pl. Francisco Abellán, behind the restaurant of the same name, has comfortable, clean rooms. (☎958 85 85 31. Singles €15; doubles €25. MC/V.)

VALENCIA AND MURCIA

The whimsical southeast corner of Spain manages to boast a little bit of everything. From the sun-drenched, silky beaches of the Costa Blanca and the unabashed friendliness of Murcia to the cosmopolitan buzz of Valencia, this relatively untouristed area is sure to enchant and impress.

The region's history is rife with power struggles among a cast of usual suspects: Phoenicians, Carthaginians, Greeks, Romans, and Moors, a diverse mix that explains the region's varied architectural influences. It first fell under Castilian control when El Cid expelled the Moors in 1094; he ruled the land in the name of Alfonso VI until his death in 1099. Without El Cid's powerful influence, Valencia and Murcia again fell to the Moors, and remained an Arab stronghold until 1238. After the expulsion of the Moors, Valencia established itself as the forerunner in cultural and technological innovation; in 1492, the *Valencianos* were the first bankers to lend funds to Queen Isabel for her patronage of Christopher Columbus. The region was besieged again in the 1930s, this time by Franco's troops. *Valencianos* resisted with strength—Valencia was the last region incorporated into Franco's Spain, and eventually regained autonomy in 1977.

HIGHLIGHTS OF VALENCIA AND MURCIA

LIGHT 15-foot puppets on fire in **Valencia** during the festival of **Las Fallas** (p. 322).

GO MEDIEVAL by visiting the castle in tiny **Morella** (p. 326).

BURN the midnight oil in sleepless **Alicante** (p. 328).

WHIP OUT your toga at the Roman ruins in **Cartagena** (p. 341).

VALENCIA

Valencia is a hybrid region; pristine nature meets industrial spread and architectural styles vary with each city. Blue-roofed church domes battle new resort developments for skyline prominence, while pristine beaches, quaint coastal towns, and maze-like inland gardens offer a wealth of refuge for weary travelers. Crowded nightlife challenges even the most nocturnal adventurers on the hectic coastline, but it's worth venturing inland for a bit, if only for the unbeatable taste of local oranges. Paella also reaches culinary perfection here in its birthplace, especially the renowned *paella con mariscos* (seafood paella) and the hearty *paella valenciana* (chicken and rabbit). The commonly used regional dialect, *valencià*, is the legacy of Moorish invaders and *català* crusaders who clashed in the northwest hundreds of years ago, and a recent mandate that all students enroll in one course of *valencià* reflects a resurgence of regional pride.

VALENCIA   ☎ 963

Valencia (pop. 800,000) inherited the best genes of its sister cities: the bustling energy of Madrid, the youthful and quirky sophistication of Barcelona, and the friendly warmth of Sevilla. Ancient traditions remain strong despite increasing modernity and commercialism. An evening glance around the central Plaza del Ajuntament reveals a merry mix of classic Spanish architecture, opulent 19th-century palaces, umbrella-crammed cafe patios, Art Deco movie theaters, and modern towers. After a deadly flood in 1957 drowned the streets in almost two meters of water, Valencia drained and diverted the Río Turia southward; now, the dry riverbed that surrounds the city is a

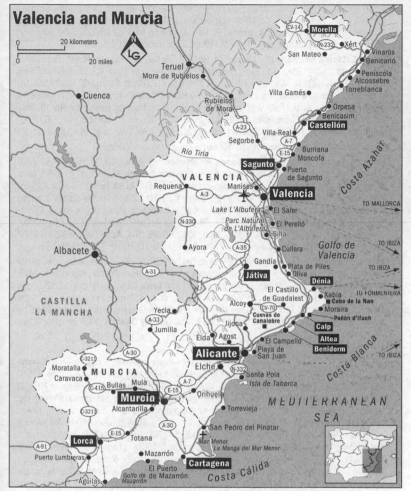

Valencia and Murcia

lush, winding park that offers views of the city's standing fortifications. Beyond these older facades, toward the sea, the riverbed meets the Ciudad de las Artes y las Ciencias, a grandiose scientific complex and architectural marvel. The sudden transition from ancient to avant-guard reflects both the city's duality and its eagerness to modernize competitively. The city's beaches and palm- tree-studded plazas have fewer tourists than Spain's other major destinations, so plan on using your Spanish here.

⊏ TRANSPORTATION

INTERCITY TRANSPORTATION

Flights: Aena, Aeropuerto de Manises/Airport of Valencia (☎961 53 02 29; www.aena.es), 8km from the city. **Aero-Bus** buses run between the airport and train station (35min.; M-Su every 20min., €2.50). Stops: Airport, Av. del Cid, Bailen. Subway line #5 goes straight to C. Colon on the outskirts of Valencia by the Ajuntament. Taxis from airport to city about €14. **Iberia,** C. La Paz, 14 (☎963 52 05 00, 24hr. info and reservations; www.iberia.com). Open M-F 9am-2pm and 4-7:30pm.

Trains: Estación del Norte, C. Xàtiva, 24 (☎963 52 02 02; www.renfe.es). Ticket windows open daily 7am-9pm. 1- to 6-zone distances range from €1.15-3.80. **RENFE** (☎902 24 02 02) to: **Alicante** (2-3hr., 12 per day 7:04am-11pm, €9.40-23.50; Su differs by week); **Barcelona** (3hr., every 1-2hr. 5:50am-8:45pm, €29-37); **Madrid** (3½hr., 12 per day 6:45am-9:15pm, €19.75-39; Su differs by week); **Sevilla** (8½hr., 11:20am, €45.30). **Cercanías** trains run at least 2 per hr. to **Gandía** (1hr., €3.65), **Sagunt** (23min., €2.40), and **Xàtiva** (45min., €2.85). Allot time to go through security.

Metro Valencia C. Colon (☎900 46 10 46; www.metrovalencia.com).

Buses: Estación Terminal d'Autobuses Av. Menéndez Pidal, 13 (☎963 46 62 66), across the riverbed, a 20 min. walk from the city center. Municipal bus #8 runs between Pl. del Ajuntament and the bus station (€1.10). **ALSA** (☎902 42 22 42) to: **Alicante** (4½hr., 1-3 per hr. 4:45am-12:25am, €15.70-17.55) via the **Costa Blanca; Barcelona** (4½hr., 9 per day 9am-10pm, €21); **Granada** (8hr., 9 per day 4:45am-2:30am, €35.45-42.80); **Málaga** (11hr., 9 per day 4:15am-2:30am, €43.60-52.80); **Sevilla** (11hr., 3-4 per day 10:30am-3am, €42.60-49.80). **Auto Res** (☎963 49 22 30) goes to **Madrid** (4hr.; 13 per day 1am, 3am, 7am-10:30pm; €20.40-25.15).

Ferries: Trasmediterránea, Muelle de Poniente (☎902 45 46 45; www.trasmediterranea.es). Take bus #4 from Pl. del Ajuntament or #1 or 2 from the bus station. To: **Mallorca** (5hr., 1 per day 7:45pm, in summer €85) and **Ibiza** (3hr.; 1 per day 12:15pm; in summer €85). One 13hr. ferry to **Menorca** per wk. (Sa 11:30pm; in summer, overnight €56.50, with cot €111.50. Reserve through a travel agency or risk inconvenience by buying tickets at the port on the day of departure. See **By Boat,** p. 343, for more info.

PUBLIC TRANSPORTATION

EMT Office, Pl. Correu Vell, 5 (☎963 15 85 15; www.emtvalencia.es). Open M-F 9am-2pm and 4:30-7:30pm. Bus schedules depend on route and day. Tourist routes 5, 5B, 35, 96. Bus #8 (every 8-9min. 6am-10:30pm) runs to the bus station. Buses #20, 21, 22, and 23 (every 10-20min. 9am-8:40pm) go to Las Arenas and Malvarrosa along Pg. Marítim. Buy tickets (€1.50) on board; combination bus and metro monthly ticket (€33.20, student €24.90), or 1-day pass (€3.10) available at newsstands. No service 10:30-11:30pm. **Late-night buses** N1, N2, N3, N4, N5, N6, and N7 go through Pl. del Ajuntament (every 45min. M-W and Su 11pm-1am, Th-Sa 11pm-3am). **Metro,** P. de Xirivelleta (☎963 97 40 40; www.metrovalencia.com) service loops around the *casco antiguo* (old quarter) and into the outskirts. The most central stop is on C. Xàtiva across the street from the train station, or C. Colón by El Corte Inglés. Buy tickets from machines in any station (€1.20-1.60 depending on distance, 10-ride pass €5.60-8).

Taxis: Onda Taxi (☎963 47 52 52), **Radio Taxi** (☎963 70 33 33), **Tele Taxi** (☎963 57 13 13), and **Buscataxis** (☎902 74 47 47).

Car Rental: C. Xàtiva, 24 (at the Estació del Nord train station). **Europcar** (☎902 10 50 30; www.europcar.es), **Avis** (☎train station 963 52 42 64, airport ☎961 52 18 72; www.avis.es), and **Hertz** (☎963 52 42 64; www.hertz.com) Car prices vary with season, type, and length of rental, but a medium-sized car for 1 week ranges €60-80.

Bike Rental: Orange Bikes, C. Santa Teresa, 8 (☎963 91 75 51; www.orangebikes.net). From the main entrance of the Mercado Central, walk down Av. María Cristina away from Pl. Ajuntamiento, and turn down the 2nd street at the end of the street. From Pl. de la Virgen, take C. Caballeros until it turns into C. Santa Teresas. Bikes €9-15 per day, €45-55 per week. Open M-F 9:30am-2:30pm and 4:30-8pm, Sa 10am-2pm and 7-7:30pm. **Douyoubike,** Corner C. Musico Magenti and Puebla Larga (☎963

VALENCIA AND MURCIA

Valencia

🔺 ACCOMMODATIONS
Home Youth Hostel, 11
Hostal El Cid, 14
Pensión Alicante, 18
Pensión Paris, 17
Purple Nest Hostel, 5
Red Nest Hostel, 13

🍴 FOOD
La Lluna, 2
La Pappardella, 7

El Rall, 9
Sagardi, 15
Sol i Lluna, 10
Zumería Naturalia, 8

⭐ NIGHTLIFE
Akuarela, 16
Bolsería Café, 6
Cafe Negrito, 4
Fox Congo, 3
Radio City, 12
Warhol, 1

Valencia Metro

YELLOW	1
RED	3
BLUE	4
GREEN	5

only runs holidays and weekends

15 55 51 and Movil ☎675 73 02 18; www.doyoubike.com). Also Av. Puerto 21 (☎963 37 40 24) and C. Puebla Larga 13 Junto Guardia Civil (☎963 38 70 28). Student price starting at €2 per hour. Open daily 10am-2pm and 5-8pm.

✦❼ ORIENTATION AND PRACTICAL INFORMATION

The most convenient way to enter the city is to take the new metro line and get off at C. Colon, a central stop near the **Museo Taureu de Valencia** (the giant bull-fighting arena and museum). **Estación del Norte** is also close to the city center, so entrance by train is convenient. **Avenida Marqués de Sotelo** runs from the train station to **Plaça del Ajuntament (Plaza Ayuntamiento)**, in the center of town. At the opposite end of the plaza runs **San Vincente Martir,** which leads to some of the town's most vibrant areas. Take **La Avenida de María Cristina** to **El Mercado,** a bustling fresh-food market, or continue past the shop-laden **C. La Paz** into the **Plaza de la Reina,** central to food, lodging, architecture, and nightlife. To the north of the plaza, streets lead to the bend of the now-diverted **Río Turia,** known today as the **Jardín del Turia,** the verdant park ideal for biking and sightseeing along the way to the port or beaches. Other sights and museums are across the river or on the outskirts of the city. The *casco antiguo* (old quarter) is best explored on foot, but the side-streets can get confusing—keep a map handy.

Tourist Office: Regional office, C. de la Paz, 48 (☎963 98 64 22; www.valencia.es). Open M-F 9am-2:30pm and 4:30-8pm. **Branches** at Estación del Nord, C. Xàtiva, 24 (☎963 52 85 73; open M-Sa 9am-7pm, Su 10am-2pm), and Pl. de la Reina (☎963 15 39 31; www.comunitatvalenciana.com; open M-Sa 9am-7pm, Su 10am-2pm).

Currency Exchange: Banks are easy to find and have decent exchange rates. All have a min. commission of €6 and some will take a small percentage of any money exchanged. Banks are clustered around Pl. del Ajuntament and transportation hubs, and are usually open 8am-2:30pm.

American Express: Duna Viajes, C. Cirilo Amorós, 88 (☎963 74 15 62; fax 34 57 00). Call ahead to cash a check. From the metro stop on C. Colón, walk past the 1st Corte Inglés, turn onto C. Sorní toward a Colón market. C. Cirilo Amorós will be on the left. Open M-F 9:30am-2pm and 4:30-7:30pm.

Luggage Storage: 24hr. storage at the **bus station** (€2.40-4.50) and **train station** (€2.40-4.50). Open daily 4:45am-1am.

English Bookstore: Soriano Librerías, C. Xàtiva, 15 (☎963 51 03 78). Across the street from the train station. Books, maps, posters, magazines. **Fnac** C. San Vicente (☎963 53 90 00).

Laundromat: The L@undry Stop C. Baja, 17 (☎963 91 35 28). This cyber laundromat offers Internet as a distraction while that overdue laundry tumbles. Wash €4, dry €3, soap €0.50, Internet €0.50 for 20min. Open daily 9:30am-10pm. **Lavandería El Mercat,** Pl. del Mercat, 12 (☎963 91 20 10). Wash and dry in 2-3hr. for €10. Open M-F 10am-2pm and 5-9pm, Sa 10am-3pm. MC/V.

Emergency: ☎091, 092, or 112.

Police: Po. de Alameda, 17 (☎963 60 03 50), or C. Maestre, 2 (☎963 15 56 90). General emergencies ☎085.

Late-Night Pharmacy: Rotates daily, check listing in local paper Levante (€1) or the *farmacias de guardia* schedule posted outside any pharmacy around the Pl. de la Virgen and Pl. de la Reina (☎963 91 68 21). *Info Salud* (Health Info) (☎900 20 22 02).

Hospital: Hospital Clínico Universitario, Av. Blasco Ibáñez, 17 (☎963 86 29 00), take bus #81 from Pl. del Ajuntament or take the metro (line 3) at C. Xàtiva to Facultades. **Ambulance:** ☎112 or 96 152 51 59 and **Red Cross Ambulances:** ☎ 96 367 73 75.

Internet Access: ▨ Ono, C. San Vicente Mártir, 22 (☎963 28 19 04; www.ono.com). Close to the Ajuntamento, this 2-story complex is a high-ceilinged technological haven, and it was the first broadband Internet center in Europe. Laptop stations, printing services, Skype, and more. 9am-2pm €2 per 45min., 2-10pm €2 per 30min., 10pm-1am €2 per hr. Cashier closes at 12:30am. Open M-F 9am-1am; Sa-Su and holidays 10am-1am. **Work Center,** C. Xàtiva, 19 (☎961 12 08 30; www.workcenter.es). 24-hour work station across the street from the train station offers office supplies, photocopying, and print services as well as DHL Express. €1.50 per hour. Open daily. AmEx/MC/V.

Post Office: Pl. del Ajuntament, 24 (☎963 512 370; www.correos.es). **Western Union.** Open M-F 8:30am-8:30pm, Sa 9:30am-2pm. **Postal Code:** Changes according to zone. Center: 46002; Renfe: 46007; Ruzafa: 46005.

▛ ACCOMMODATIONS

Well-run hostels and pensions for decent fares abound in Valencia, but finding a room can be a difficult task during travel-heavy summer months or the festival of Las Fallas (Mar. 12-19). The best deals are around **Plaça del Ajuntament** and **Plaça del Mercat,** both in the *casco antiguo.*

▨ **Red Nest Hostel,** C. La Paz, 36 (☎963 42 71 68; www.nesthostelsvalencia.com). A classic, 16th-century Spanish building in a great central location with a busy atmosphere. Free luggage storage. Huge guest kitchen. Internet €1 per hour. 12-person dorms €14 in winter, €20 in summer; 6-person dorm €16.50/22; 4-person dorm €17.50/€25; doubles €50/58, double economy €37/42; quad €84. **Purple Nest Hostel** branch with lounge and bar at P. Tetuan, 5. (☎963 53 25 61). AmEx/MC/V. ❷

Home Youth Hostel, C. de la Lonja, 4 (☎963 91 62 29; www.likeathome.net). 20 rooms surround a funky lobby. Hall baths co-ed, free towels. Internet €0.50 per 15min. 3 or 4-person dorms €23 in summer, €15 in winter; singles €23; doubles €20. 10% ISIC discount. **Branches** at C. Cadirers, 11 (☎963 91 46 91; deluxehostel@likeathome.net), and Pl. Vicente Iborra (☎963 91 37 97; backpackers@likeathome.net). MC/V. ❷

Pensión Paris, C. Salvá, 12 (☎963 52 67 66; www.pensionparis.com). By Universidad de Valencia on a central street. 15 simple, blue and white rooms, most with sink, minute balcony, and hall bath. Does not accept reservations but allows indefinite stays. Singles €22; doubles €32, with shower €38; triples €48. MC/V. ❷

Hostal El Cid, C. Cerrajeros, 13 (☎/fax 963 92 23 23). Off C. San Vicente Mártir near the Plaza de la Reina. In an unassuming, tiled building with 12 airy rooms, some with A/C. Book well in advance. English and French spoken. Doubles €26-28, doubles with TV €35, with bath, shower, and TV €36. MC/V. ❶

Pensión Alicante, C. de Ribera, 8 (☎963 51 22 96). On a lively, cafe-lined street off the Pl. del Ajuntament in the direction of the train station. Rooms are clean and well lit, each with TV. Internet access (€3 per hour) and a small library. Singles €23, with bath and A/C €32; doubles €32/42; triples €52 with bath. MC/V. ❷

FOOD

Valencia is renowned as the birthplace of paella, and a turn down any side-street will often reveal huge crowds of locals sharing this sticky dish from mammoth skillets. *Valencianos* buy heaps of fresh fish, produce, vegetables, snacks, and fruits in the bustling **Mercat Central,** the largest food market in Europe since 1928, located in an Art Nouveau building on Pl. del Mercat (open M-Sa 6am-2:30pm). For **groceries,** stop by **El Corte Inglés** on C. Pintor Sorolla (☎963 15 95 00). For a smaller market, try **La Mercadona** on Calle el Poeta, (open M-Sa 9:15am-9:15pm).

▨ **La Pappardella,** C. Bordadores, 5 (☎963 91 89 15; www.viciositalianos.com). Chic and charismatic 2-story restaurant with some outdoor seating and a serene view of the Plaza. Artistic Italian meals from pizza to spaghetti bolognese and vegetable dishes (€6-14). Ask to sit upstairs. Open daily 2-4pm and 9pm-midnight. AmEx/MC/V. ❷

▨ **El Rall,** C. Tundidores, 2 (☎963 92 20 90). A cheerful 2-room restaurant that spills into an intimate courtyard. Lucky customers may be serenaded by passing accordion players. Paella served in skillets that grow with party size. €11-21 per person, 2 person min. Reserve ahead. Open daily 1:30-4pm and 9-11:30pm. MC/V. ❸

Zumeria Naturalia, C. del Mar, 12 (☎963 91 12 11). This sherbet-colored gem is hidden steps below the cobblestone street outside. Hanging lamps dangle above low tables crammed with cushioned lawn chairs. Offers over 100 fruit drinks and Valencian specialties. Also serves delicious crepes. Open M-W 5pm-12:30am, Th 5pm-1am, F-Sa 5pm-2am, Su 5-10:30pm. ❷

Sol i Lluna, C. del Mar, 29 (☎963 92 22 16; www.solilluna.net). Relaxed Bohemian hang-out and tapas bar. Set *menú* and inventive daily tapas (€3.40-9) in an eclectic restaurant with a cramped bar and ample open-air seating on a slow street just off Pl. de la Reina. Lots of regulars make for lively evenings. Open M 2-4pm, Tu-Sa 2-4pm and 9pm-last customer. Cash only. ❷

La Lluna, C. Sant Ramón, 23 (☎963 92 21 46). Dark wooden beams characterize this underground vegetarian restaurant. Serves a wide variety of traditional Valencian dishes. Appetizers and entrees €3.50-6. 4-course lunch *menú* (€6) on weekdays. Open M-Sa 1:30-3:30pm and 8:30-11pm. MC/V. ❶

Sagardi, San Vincente Martir, 6 (☎963 91 06 68; www.sagardi.com, reservas@sagardi.com). An airy, fast-paced establishment with an old pub feel. Spacious bar downstairs with gigantic cider tap offers elegant skewered tapas (€1.60). Open daily 7-11:30pm, tapas from 10pm-1:30am. ❷

⑥ SIGHTS

The older sights cluster around charming streets around **Plaza de la Reina** and **Plaza del Mercado.** Most museums, gardens, and notable landmarks are east along the Turia Riverbed. The area north of the riverbed is less pedestrian friendly. EMT bus #5 drops off at most of the major sights, but for a full informational tour, the double-decker **Bus Turístic** (☎963 15 85 15) begins in Pl. de la Reina and loops around the old-town sights and along the riverbed toward the **Ciudad de las Artes y Ciencias** (€12).

SANTA IGLESIA CATEDRAL DE VALENCIA. The original cathedral was replaced by a mosque during Muslim rule in the 8th century, but the first stone of the present cathedral was laid after the conquest of Valencia under James I in 1238. The steep 202-step climb up the **Miguelete** (cathedral tower) is worth the sweat; novelist Victor Hugo once counted 300 bell towers in the city from this vantage point. The Gothic **Capilla de Santo Cáliz** is home to a wealth of treasures, from the Crucifijo de Márfil statues, which depict "man's passions," to a chalice which was once claimed to be the Holy Grail used by Christ at the Last Supper. *(Pl. de la Reina. Cathedral ☎963 91 01 89. Open daily 7:30am-1pm and 4:30-8:30pm. Closes earlier in winter. Free. Tower open daily 10am-1pm and 4:30-7pm. €2. Museum ☎963 92 43 02. Open Mar.-Nov. M-Sa 10am-1pm and 4:30-7pm, Su 10am-1pm and 4:30-5:30pm. €3 includes multilingual audio tour. After 6:30pm free.)* Be certain to visit the grandiose gold altar at the neighboring **Basílica Virgen dels Desamparats**. *(In the Pl. de la Virgen, 6, right behind the Catedral. Open for mass M-F 7am-1pm and 4:45-8:30pm, Su 8:30am-1:30pm and 4:45-8:30pm. Free.)*

MUSEO DE BELLAS ARTES. This museum features a manageable array of some of Spain's most important art. Gothic, Renaissance, Baroque, and 19th- and 20th-century paintings are all on display in three straightforward sections. the permanent collection, temporary exhibits, and the remainder of the original building of San Pio V and its more recent (18th-century) facade. One floor is dedicated to 14th-16th century Valencian art taken from the area's convents in the 19th century, while other floors feature El Greco's *San Juan Bautista*, Velázquez's self-portrait, Ribera's *Santa Teresa*, and a slew of Goyas. *(C. Sant Pío V, 9 near the Jardines del Real. Walk toward the riverbed from Plaza de la Reina and cross Puente de la Trinidad; the museum is just right of this bridge and is easily visible. Bus #8 from the Pl. del Ajuntament drops you off across the river; ☎963 60 57 93. Open Tu-Su 10am-8pm. Free. Cafetería, ☎963 69 15 99, serves creative traditional food in large portions for reasonable prices. Entrees €9.)*

CIUDAD DE LAS ARTES Y LAS CIENCIAS. This overwhelming urban citadel, dedicated to the arts and sciences, is a far cry from the blue-tiled church roofs that dominate most of the city skyline. This 350,000 square meter mini-city is Spain's largest museum, divided into four buildings covered with over 4000 panes of glass, all surrounding a vast reflecting pool. **L'Hemisfèric,** hypnotizes spectators with laser shows, a planetarium, and an IMAX theater. **L'Oceanogràfic** showcases 45,500 aquatic creatures in water channeled from the nearby Malvarossa beach. The enormous, glinting **Palau de les Arts** stages opera, theater, and dance performance. The **Museu de Les Ciències Príncipe Felipe,** the insect-like centerpiece, has hands-on exhibits. *(Bus #35 runs from Pl. del Ajuntament. ☎902 10 00 31; www.cac.es. Museum open daily 10am-7pm, high season 10am-9pm. €7.50, students and children €5.80.*

L'Oceanogràfic open high season M-F 9:30am-6:30pm, 8:30pm-1:30am, Sa 9:30am-1:30pm, Su 9:30am-6:30pm. Closed on certain holidays. Prices starting at €17.20. L'Hemisferic open M-Th 10am-7pm. €7.50, children and students €5.80. Combination tickets €18.95-30.50, can be bought at the train station through Cercanias trains.)

INSTITUT VALENCIÀ D'ART MODERN (IVAM). This avant-garde museum includes styles of the 20th and 21st centuries. Its permanent collection on the first floor is famed for abstract works by 20th-century sculptor Julio González and artist Ignacio Pinazo. Temporary exhibits change frequently. *(C. Guillém de Castro, 118. Leaving the Basilica, take C. Caballeros until it turns into C. Quart. Walk under the Torres de Quart and take a right down C. Guillem de Castro; the museum is on the right. Bus #5 from the Pl. del Ajuntament. ☎963 86 30 00; www.ivam.es. Open Tu-Su 10am-10pm. €2, students €1. Su free.)*

MUSEU DE CERÁMICA Y DE LAS ARTES SUNTUARIAS "GONZOLEZ MARTI" EN EL PALACIO DE LOS MARQUESES DE DOS AGUAS. This stunning museum packs two of Valencia's finest attractions into one. The museum, which traces the history of ceramics with special Valencian exhibits, did not move into El Palacio de los Marquese de Dos Aguas until 1954. This building is spectacular, lavish, and unlike anything else to be found in Valencia. The alabaster entrance itself is worth the trip. The first two floors have recreated the palace as it was lived in during the 14th century. Ornate mirrors and marble work adorn each grandiose and breath-taking room. Visitors may choose to breeze through the exhibit, while art enthusiasts can become entranced by the infinite detail of each room. The ceramics exhibits are on the upper floors. *(C. Porta Querol 2 off of C. de la Paz. ☎963 51 63 92. Open Tu-Sa 10am-2pm and 4-8pm. €2.40. Sa free.)*

LONJA DE LA SEDA (SILK EXCHANGE). This Gothic building was once the financial and commercial center of Valencia. It is composed of three distinct parts: the Contract Hall, the tower (used as both chapel and prison), and the Pavilion of the Consolat de Mar. The building became a provisional hospital when waves of cholera hit the city in the 1800s, and was declared a UNESCO World Heritage Site in 1996. Look for the 28 gargoyles surrounding the highest parts of the building. *(Pl. del Mercat. ☎963 52 54 78. Open Tu-Sa 10am-2pm and 4:30-8:30pm, Su 10am-3pm. €2.)*

PARKS. On the other side of the river, next to the Museo de Bellas Artes, off C. Sant Pío, are the **Jardines del Real,** home to oddly shaped ponds, kitschy duck-shaped fountains, labyrinthine paths, and ivy-covered arches. The garden also features an aviary and a small zoo. *(M: Pont de Fuste. Walk to the river, take a left, pass the museum, and enter on C. Sant Pío V. Gardens open Tu-Sa 9:30am-2pm and 4:30-8pm, Su and holidays 10am-10pm. €2, children and students €1. Free Sa-Su and holidays.)* You don't have to be a horticulturist to appreciate the **Jardín Botànic,** a botanical garden that cultivates 43,000 plants of 300 international species, including cacti and tropical palm trees. Benches and friendly felines line the winding paths throughout this site. *(C. Quart, 80, on the western end of Río Turia near Gran Vía Fernando el Católico. M: Turia. Go left out of the Po. de Pechina, exit down Gran Vía, and take a left onto C. Quart. ☎963 15 68 00; www.uv.es/jardibotanic. Open Tu-Su May-Aug. 10am-9pm; Apr. and Sept. 10am-8pm; Mar. and Oct. 10am-7pm; Nov.-Feb. 10am-6pm. Closed Dec. 25 and Jan. 1. €0.60.)*

OTHER SIGHTS. The **Museo Taurino de Valencia** offers a permanent exhibition of Valencian *tauromachia* and a peek inside the formidable 13,000-seat bullfighting arena, the **Plaza de Toros**. *(C. Xàtiva, Open Tu-Su 10am-8pm).* Arena is entered through the museum. Valencia's **Palau de Música** is one of the world's premier concert halls, hosting local orchestras, national and international soloists, and jazz bands throughout the year. *(Bus #35 runs from Pl. del Ajuntament. Po. de la Alameda, 30. ☎963 37 50 20; www.palauvalencia.com. Ticket window open daily 10:30am-1:30pm and 5:30-9pm.)*

NIGHTLIFE

Use your *siesta* wisely; Valencia's nightlife often requires drinking and dancing until sunrise. Bars, pubs, and courtyards start to fill up around midnight around **Pl. de la Virgen and C. Caballeros,** which hosts veritable tides of gung-ho club-hoppers into the wee hours. Follow the street to **Plaza Tossal,** where outdoor terraces, tall-windowed pubs, upbeat music, and *agua de Valencia* (the region's famed alcoholic beverage) energize the masses. A lively local crowd frequents bars along **C. Quart.** The gay and lesbian scene centers on **Calle Quart** and **Plaza Vicente Iborra.**

Discotecas, which feel like ghost towns until at least 1:30 or 2am, dominate the university area, particularly on **Avinguda Blasco Ibáñez.** There are a few calmer pubs with dancing around most of the main plazas. For more info, consult the *Qué y Dónde* weekly magazine (€0.50) or the weekly entertainment supplement, *Valencia City* (€0.50), both available at newsstands and tourist offices. Check out the free monthly *24/7 Valencia,* available in most Internet cafes or tourist booths, for new hotspots.

Radio City, C. Sta. Teresa, 19 (☎963 91 41 51; www.radiocityvalencia.com). Popular bar and discoteca well-suited for casual bar-hopping or wild dancing on the dark dance floor. Pyschadelic lighting effects. Young crowd and high-energy ambience. Beer €3.50. Mixed drinks from €6. Tu flamenco at 11pm. New music and dance/theatre performances M-F. Open daily 7:30pm-3:30am.

Bolsería Café, C. Bolsería, 41 (☎963 91 89 03). Boisterous, beautiful people of all ages pack into this upscale, creatively constructed cafe-bar. Floor-to-ceiling windows give this hot spots a fishbowl effect, so self-conscious dancers better squeeze into the center. Smaller terraces and bars upstairs. Drinks €4-6. Open daily 7:30pm-3:30am.

Fox Congo, C. Caballeros, 35 (☎963 92 55 27). Walls and chunky posts covered in welded metal glint in the limited light of the bar. Fantastic *agua de Valencia.* W and Th hip-hop nights. Beer €4. Mixed drinks €7. No cover. Open Tu-Sa 10pm-3:30am.

Warhol, Av. Blasco Ibáñez, 111 (☎963 71 65 96). An eclectic crowd of students and locals with impressive stamina rock out to a mix of house, 80s, and rock. Hip, pop-art walls. Plan to stay a while if you make the trek. *Festa Brasileira* Tu night, Murray Rock Night Th. Cover M-Th and Su €6, F-Sa €9; includes 1 drink. Open daily 1-7am.

 H₂ORANGE. *Agua de Valencia* is Valencia's ubiquitous drink. Any bartender will make you a pitcher, but each one is a slightly different mix of orange juice, *cava,* and various other liquids and liquors, usually vodka or champagne. The result can be very potent, so go easy!

Akuarela, Pub: C. Juan Llorens, 49, disco: Eugenia Viñes, 152 (☎963 82 29 58), in Pl. Malvarossa. Giant, but less mainstream discoteca with a salsa slant and a variety of music at full blast. Entrance free with purchase of a €7 or more at the pub. Pub open daily 6pm-3:30am. Discoteca open daily midnight-7:30am.

Cafe Negrito, Pl. Negrito 1 (☎963 91 42 33). A bold little cafe in a charming courtyard a few blocks from the Basilica. Dozens of silver tables fill quickly to start off the night. Wide selection of reasonably-priced drinks. Open daily 3pm-3am.

BEACHES

On sunny weekends in Valencia, azure waters meet a sea of beach umbrellas planted in the fine, cream-colored sand. A wide boardwalk connecting the enormous beach is ideal for sun-drenched walks and bike rides. **Avenida del Puerto** has a direct bike path from the riverbed to the port, site of the 2007 America's Cup. From

THE FIERY FALLAS

Valencia's most renowned festival, typically held during the week of March 19, welcomes spring in a fiery fashion. The fiesta of Las Fallas is every pyromaniac's dream—enormous papier-mâché effigies go up in flames, fireworks light up the sky, and a week-long party ensues.

Specialized artists work all year to design and build giant caricatured papier-mâché puppets called *ninots*, which depict anything and everything from pop-culture icons to overtly satirized political figures. During Fallas week, the 10 ft. *ninots* are paraded down the street in a colorful display of artistic mastery, fireworks, gunpowder, and music.

The festival culminates in a massive bonfire, eerily dubbed the *crema*, when the astounding *ninots* are all burned to the ground as a substantial thank you to spring. While their European neighbors may disapprove of such massive destruction of artistry, the *valencianos* see the tradition as a fitting display of the transience of life. Thankfully, one *ninot*, chosen by popular vote, is granted a reprieve from the flames, and is added to the collection on display in the Museo Fallero.

For more information and history on Las Fallas, visit the Museo Fallero, Pl. de Monteolivete, where many salvaged puppets are on display.

here, the beach is only a few blocks north. Buses #20, 21, 22, and 23 all stop nearby and take about 15 minutes from the center of town. The boardwalk connects the most heavily populated beach, **Las Arenas,** to the popular **La Malvarossa.** Equally crowded but more attractive is **Salér,** a smooth stretch of pebbled beach 14km from the city that divides a lagoon from the sea. Cafeterias and snack bars line the shore. The **Autocares Herca** (☎ 963 49 12 50) bus goes to Salér (on the way to El Perello; 30min., hourly 7am-9pm, €1-1.10 depending on destination) from the intersection of Gran Vía de Germanías and C. Sueca. To get to the bus stop, exit the train station and take a right down C. Xàtiva, then turn right onto C. Ruzafa to Gran Vía. Look for a yellow MetroBus post. The ride to Salér can be jammed on weekends. Plan on a day for a worthwhile trip. For a better beach experience, hop the bus or train to **Dénia** (p. 337).

☀ FESTIVALS

Valencia's most famous festival is ◪**Las Fallas** (Mar. 12-19, see left), which features *ninots* (gigantic puppets), gunpowder, and bonfires. During **Semana Santa** in April, monks reenact Biblical scenes and children perform the plays of Sant Vicent Ferrer. **Our Lady of the Forsaken** (May 11), entails masses of worshippers bearing a famous effigy of the Virgin Mary from the basilica to Valencia's main Cathedral. **Corpus Christi,** usually held in June, is a weeklong parade of *Valencianos* dressing as religious characters to reenact scenes from the Old and New Testament. The **Festiu de Juliol,** in July, brings fireworks, concerts, bullfights, and a *batalla dels flors* (battle of flowers), when young girls in carriages blanket the streets with flowers. October 9 celebrates both lovers and the conquest of Valencia by James I in 1238. Valencia's coat of arms is paraded and hoisted outside the *Ajuntament.*

▶ DAYTRIPS FROM VALENCIA

SAGUNTO (SAGUNT)

Cercanías trains (☎ 963 35 74 00; www.renfe.es) run from Valencia to Castellón (C-6 line) via Sagunt (30min.; M-F 3 per hr. 5:55am-10:30pm, Sa-Su 15 per day 7:20am-10:30pm; round trip €2.20-3.70), as do ALSA buses (☎ 964 66 18 50; 45min., daily every 30min. 7am-10:30pm, €2.10) and AVSA buses (daily 7am-10:10pm, €2.60).

The residents of Sagunto are said to be Spain's most courageous. This reputation dates to the 3rd century BC, when the citizens of Phoenician-controlled

Saguntum held out during an eight-month siege by Hannibal's Carthaginians. Some sources say that on the brink of annihilation, Sagunto's women, children, and elderly threw themselves into a furnace, while others insist that they chose starvation over defeat. Perhaps because of their 2000 year history of continual invasion, inhabitants of Sagunto have developed a hard outer shell—no funny business here. Come prepared to explore independently in this tourist-free hideaway.

A stroll through the narrow streets of the old town leads to an ancient **castle,** which survived the battle of Saguntum and Hannibal, and was embellished upon by the Romans, Visigoths, and Moors. The resulting architectural melange lies mostly in ruin above the town and was declared a national monument in 1931. (Open June-Sept. Tu-Sa 10am-8pm, Su 10am-2pm; Oct.-May Tu-Sa 10am-6pm, Su 10am-2pm. Free.) The **Plaza de Armas,** near the official entry to the castle, still displays vestiges of a Roman public square from the 2nd century BC. On the way up to the castle is the **Teatro Romano.** This Roman edifice, built into the hill in the first century and named a national monument in 1896, underwent a controversial, modern restoration in order to accommodate theater festivals in the summer months. By the port, 4km from town, Sagunt's **beaches** attract summer travelers—**Puerto de Sagunt** is the best, but there are three others: **Malvaross a de Corinto, Almardá,** and **Corinto.** Buses to the beaches leave from Av. Sants de la Pedra, along the river. Return buses leave from the beach tourist office (every 30min. 7am-9:30pm, €1).

To get to the old town from the train station, walk out the left hand side of the underpass, take a right, then a left before the overpass onto C. de los Huertos. Continue for 10min. to the far side of the second plaza, Pl. Cronista Chabret. The **tourist office** in Pl. Cronista Chabret is diagonally across the plaza from the *Ayuntamiento* and has maps and walking tours. (☎962 66 22 13; www.sagunt.com/turismo. Open Sept.-May M-F 8am-3pm and 4-6:30pm, Sa 9am-3pm, Su 9am-2pm; June-Aug. usually Tu-F 9:30am-2:30pm and 4-6:30pm, Sa 9am-2pm.) A second **branch** is by the port, at Av. Mediterráneo, 67. (☎962 69 04 02. Open M-F 9:30am-2:30pm and 4-6:30pm, Sa 9am-2pm, Su 10am-2pm and 4:30-7:30pm.)

JÁTIVA (XÀTIVA)

Cercanías (☎902 24 02 02; www.renfe.com/empresa/cercanias) runs from Valencia to Xàtiva (1hr., ovory 30min. 6am-10:30pm, €2.15; return 1-4 per hour 5:30am-3am). To reach the old village and the tourist office from the train station, walk up Baixada de l'Estació and turn left at its end onto Av. Jaime.

Xàtiva bears few marks of tourism, a unique splash of color and culture within the region. It hosts a slew of churches and ruins that date from 30,000 BC, and was also the birthplace of Pope Alexander VI (1431-1503). Xàtiva was burned to the ground by Felipe V in 1707, and reconstruction began the year after. Save plenty of time to explore the impeccably restored ▒**castle,** which has seen a host of occupants, and incorporates Moorish and Roman influences. A patio near the entrance booth provides an impressive panorama over the town to the mountains of Grossa beyond, and divides the two sections of the castle: the **castell machor** and **castell chicotet.** The former, used from the 13th through the 16th centuries, bears the scars of sieges and earthquakes. Its vaulted **prison** has held famous wrongdoers, including Fernando el Católico and the Comte d'Urgell, a would-be usurper of the Aragonese throne who is buried in the castle. The prison's garden also contains the shields and histories of its prisoners. Streets become narrower, steeper, and more residential closer to the castle. (Castle open Apr.-Oct. Tu-Su 10am-7pm, Nov.-Mar. Tu-Su 10am-6pm. €2.10, under 18 €1.10. Tu afternoons free.) The spectacular vistas of the walk up to the castle are wholly worth the 30 min. effort. If you didn't bring your walking shoes, a petite four-car train chugs up the road from the tourist office. (2 per day, 12:30 and 5:30pm, €3.80). To navigate the town, use the **Basilica de Santa Maria** as a landmark. This 500-year-old behemoth was begun in 1612, but

SEEING RED

On the last Wednesday of every August, tens of thousands of tourists descend upon the small town of Buñol, a town in Valencia, to participate in the world's largest food fight: La Tomatina. A tradition since 1944, this tomato battle serves as the culmination of a week-long festival. Although the sloppy free-for-all is followed by a celebration of the town's patron saints, the tomato fight has no significance beyond the primal desire to get dirty and throw food.

Festivities begin when an overgrown ham is placed on a greased pole in the center of town. Locals and tourists scramble up the slippery pole, climbing on top of one another to be the captor of the prized ham. Once a winner is announced, a cannon starts the marinara blood bath.

Throngs of tourists wearing clothes destined for the dumpster crowd around the open-bed trucks that haul 240,000 lb. of tomatoes into the plaza. Over the next 2hr., Buñol becomes an every-man-for-himself battle of oozy carnage. Revelers pelt one another with tomatoes until the entire crowd is covered in tomato guts.

The origins of this food fight are unclear: some say it began as a fight between friends, while others say the original tomatoes were directed at unsatisfactory civil dignitaries. Today, no one is safe from the wrath of tomatoes hurled at friends and foreigners alike.

was not finished until the early 20th century. (Mass M-Sa 10am and 8pm, Su 10:30am, 1, and 8pm. Museum open Tu-Sa 10:30am-1pm, Su 11:30am-1pm. €1.) Budget accommodations are difficult to come by in this quiet and untouristed town. **Hotel Murta ②**, Angel Lacalle, has lovely views and huge, clean rooms, offering one of the best deals in town. (☎962 27 66 11; www.hotelmurta.com. Doubles €43.) Streets are poorly marked, so have plenty of Spanish phrases handy, and plan on getting lost once or twice. To relax, have a drink outside at the marble tables of **El Tiradoret ②**, Pl. del Mercat, 10. (☎96 227 63 540. *Menú* €7.50.) Since 1250, the **Fira de Xàtiva festival** has stormed the city from August 14-20, featuring live music, theater, bullfights, and huge ceramics and livestock fairs. The **tourist office** is at Alameda Jaume I, 50. (☎962 27 33 46; www.xativa.es. English spoken. Open June 15-Sept. 15 Tu-F 10am-2:30pm and 5-7pm, Sa-Su 10am-2pm; Sept. 16-June 14 Tu-F 10am-1:30pm and 4-6pm, Sa-Su 10am-1:30pm.)

CASTELLÓN (CASTELLÓ) ☎964

As the halfway point between Valencia and Barcelona, Castelló (pop. 167,000) can easily seem like little more than a transportation hub brimming with new buildings and the pervasive hum of motorcycles. Its chic shops, bustling plazas, and expansive beaches tell a different story. Home to the large Universidad de Jaime I, this fast-paced and fast-growing city is popular with budget travelers and students; many enjoy Castelló without making a significant dent their wallet.

█ TRANSPORTATION. The combined **train** and **bus station** is on Av. Pintor Oliet, between the University and a 20min. walk to the center of the town. Castelló is most easily reached by train from Valencia, as **Cercanías** trains run there frequently (1hr., 1-4 per hr. 6:10am-10:30pm, €3.75). **RENFE** (☎902 24 02 02) trains run to: Barcelona (2½hr., 16 per day 6:06am-9:30pm, €27.60-53); Granada (9hr.; 10:36am, 11:59pm; €45.30); Málaga (11hr.; 10:36am, 11:59pm; €49-73.50); Murcia (3hr., 3 per day 2:30pm-7:38pm, €30.20). **ALSA** (☎902 42 22 42) sends buses to: Alicante (5½hr., 5 per day 11:35am-10:50pm, €17.48); Almería (9-10hr.; 12:50, 10:50pm; €37); Barcelona (4-5hr., 6 per day 2:45am-6:20pm, €19-37); Gandía (3-4hr.; 9:30, 10:50pm; €8.80); Murcia (6-7hr., 5 per day 11:35am-10:50pm, €22.46); Sevilla (11hr., 8:50pm, €48-58). **Auto-Res** (☎902 02 09 99) goes to Madrid (5hr., 4 per day 6:45am-11:45pm, €24-25). **Autos Mediterráneo** (☎964 22 00 54) departs for Morella (2½hr.; M-F 7:30am and 3:45pm, Sa 1:30pm; €7.75) and other towns in the Castellón province. Bus times and pick-

CASTELLÓN (CASTELLÓ) ■ 325

up locations change throughout the year. **Municipal bus** #9 runs from the train station to Pl. Borrul in the center every 10min. (€0.70). For **taxis,** call **Radio Taxi** (☎964 22 74 74) or **Tele Taxi** (☎964 25 46 46). Bikes can be rented from the university (☎964 73 08 30).

■ ⚡ **ORIENTATION AND PRACTICAL INFORMATION.** The city center is the **Plaza Mayor,** and contains the orange-colored **Ayuntamiento,** the **Catedral de Santa María,** and the **Mercado Central. Po. Morella** is a straight shot to the plaza from the train station, and becomes the plaza's northern border when it turns into C. Colon. **C. Trinidad** and **C. Enmedio** are excellent options for exploring the town, finding a place to stay, or shopping. **Avenida Mar** and **Avenida Hermanos Bou** both have bike lanes and run to the port, 4km east of the town center. Just north of the port stretches the **Parque del Pinar.** Most services, including **banks** and **ATMs,** can be found in and around the Pl. Mayor. The **tourist office** is a few blocks north from the Pl. Mayor at the tip of the **Plaza de María Agustina.** (☎964 35 86 88; castellon@touristinfo.net. Open July-Aug. M-F 9am-7pm, Sa 10am-2pm; Sept.-June M-F 9am-2pm and 4-7pm, Sa 10am-2pm.) There is another **branch** at the port on Po. Buenavista, 28. (☎902 20 31 30; www.castellonturismo.com. Open Tu-Th 10:30am-2:30pm, F-Sa 10:30am-2:30pm and 5-7pm.) The **Hospital General** can be reached at ☎964 72 65 00 or www.gva.es. **24hr. health care** assistance ☎900 16 11 61. The **post office,** in Pl. Tetuán, can be reached at ☎900 50 60 70 or 964 34 03 87. Open M-F 8:30am-8:30pm, Sa 9:30am-2pm. **Postal Code: 12003.**

⌐🏠 **ACCOMMODATIONS AND FOOD.** Budget accommodations are hard to come by in Castelló; try to avoid the expensive hotels across from the train station. **Hostal Corte ❸,** C. Trinidad 23, is a new establishment with colorful walls and a downstairs restaurant. Large, comfy beds occupy almost the entirety of the rooms, each of which has TV, A/C, and a full bathroom. Singles €35; doubles €40. **Pensión La Esperanza ❷,** C. Trinidad, 37, just two blocks off the Pl. Mayor, offers large lace-covered rooms and slightly sagging beds. (☎964 22 20 31. Curfew 1am. Singles €23; doubles €28; triples €40.50; quads €50. MC/V.)

Buy fresh fruit and snacks at the **Mercat Central,** and enjoy the orange groves of the Parque de Ribalta. Around dinner, activity shifts to the **Grau** (port; see **Beaches,** below), where seafood restaurants line Pl. de la Mar. If you opt to stay in the main city, **Avda. Rey Don Jaime** is the best bet for restaurants. Tapas bars and a youthful crowd center around Plaza Santa Clara. Around the port, **Meduse ❷,** Po. Buenavista, 31, has a funky, modern atmosphere and a creative selection of *valenciano* seafood and vegetarian dishes. Try their delicious moussaka. (☎964 06 34 40. Salads and *bocadillos* €1-8. Entrees €6-12. Music and art shows every Sa night at midnight; ask for a schedule. Open summer M and W-Su 6pm-2am. Cash only.) **C. Lagasca** is lined with late-night bars and hang-out spots, and during summer, beach *discotecas* and clubs are open until the wee hours of the morning.

🔲 **SIGHTS.** Castelló's cultural heart beats in the Pl. Mayor, where the free-standing belltower **Torre Campanario de Fadri,** built between the 15th and 18th centuries, stands 58m tall. Next door is the **Concatedral de Santa Maria,** a towering Gothic site built in the 12th century and restored in the 14th. (☎964 22 34 63. Open daily 7:30am-1pm and 5-8pm. Free.) On the pedestrian-friendly C. Caballeros, running perpendicular to the Pl. Mayor, is the **Basilica Santa Maria de Lledo,** dedicated to the patron saint of the city. The lush **Parque de Ribalta** and the neighboring **Plaza de Toros,** which still hosts bullfights during festivals, are worth a mid-afternoon stroll. Toward the port, the avant-garde **Espai D'Art Contemporani de Castelló** features rotating exhibits of contemporary artists. (☎964 72 35 40. Open Tu-Su 10am-8pm. Guided tours Sa 7pm. Free.) One of Castellon's most attractive modern buildings is the ▨**Museu de Bellas Artes,** C. Hermanos Bou, 28, a 7min. walk from the city center. Bus #4 also runs there from Pl. Bou. The museum offers two floors of 14th- to 19th-century sculptures, ceramics, and paintings, including an impressive collection of works by Castilian painter Gabriel Puig Roda. (☎964 72 75 00. Open Tu-Sa 10am-8pm, Su 10am-2pm. Free.)

◢ **BEACHES.** Castelló's **Grau** (port), 4km east of the city between the Avda. del Mar and Av. Hermanos Bou, is a unique, self-contained scene. Buses run from the Pl. Borrul to the port and the beaches (every 15min. in summer, €0.70). Surrounding the port is the **Plaça del Mar,** which houses dozens of restaurants and pubs, as well as a small shopping center. A 10-15min. walk north (left when facing the ocean) along Avda. Ferrandis Salvador leads to **El Pinar,** a giant pine-filled ecosystem, parallel to the soft sands of **Playa del Pinar.** Farther north are **Playa del Gurugú, Playa del Serradal,** and the family-friendly **Benicassim.** All are fairly crowded, and for good reason considering their impressive breadth of smooth sands, sparkling waters, and sports facilities. Playa del Gurugú was recognized by the EU for its quality as a recipient of the 2006 Bandera Azul. The **Paseo Buena Vista** runs from the port to the border of El Pinar, while the **Paseo Marítimo** hugs the shoreline. If you're hungry after sunbathing, check out **Groovy,** a small snack shack close to the Planetarium on Playa del Pinar. Tapas, salads, and combo plates (€3-5) are available, as well as alcoholic and nonalcoholic drinks (€2-5).

MORELLA ☎964

Rising majestically above the fertile valley below, the medieval fortress town of Morella (pop. 2800) is an isolated and idyllic find in the northernmost extremes of the Comunitat Valenciana. The ride to Morella is an experience unto itself, as trees filled with cherries and small, clustered *pueblos* sit on the hills along the serpentine highway. With cobblestone streets, medieval walls, and a castle crowning its highest point, Morella draws in tourists (in small numbers) with soothing vistas and small-town charm. The people you see here are likely to be residents, and prices are generally low enough to allow for a guilt-free and enjoyable stay.

◨◪ **TRANSPORTATION AND PRACTICAL INFORMATION.** Morella is hard to reach. Most visitors arrive via Valencia, though the city is also accessible from Barcelona. Travelers must make a connection at **Castelló** on the **Cercanías** train line from Valencia (1hr., 1-4 per hour 5:11am-9:30pm, €3.75). From Barcelona, the **RENFE** Mediterranean goes to Castelló (2½hr., 16 per day 7am-9:30pm, €16.50-33). **Autos Mediterráneo** (☎964 22 05 36) departs from the bus stop outside of **Castelló's** train station for Morella (2½hr.; M-F 8:30am and 3:30pm, Sa 1:30pm; return M-F 8:05am and 3:45pm, Sa 8:15am; €7.45.) Be at the bus station at least 10min. before the expected departure time. In Morella, the bus drops you off either at the Pta. de San Miguel, or at the Torre Beneito, on C. Muralla. Morella's **tourist office,** Pl. San Miguel, is right through the archway, across the street on the left. (☎964 17 30 32; www.morella.net. Open June-Sept. M-Sa 10am-2pm and 4-7pm, Su 10am-2pm; Oct.-May Tu-Sa 10am-2pm and 4-6pm, Su 10am-2pm.) For **medical assistance,** call ☎964 16 09 62. **Internet** access is at **Ciberlocutori Nou,** C. Sant Nicolas, 2. (☎964 16 10 05; €0.50 per 15min. Open daily 10am-2:30pm and 5:30-10pm.)

◪◨ **ACCOMMODATIONS AND FOOD.** Once you pass through the Gothic archways of Morella, you may never want to leave. Considering the bus schedule, you may not be able to. Fortunately, most lodging here offers luxury standards at budget prices. Live royally at ▨**Hotel El Cid ❸,** Portal Sant Mateu, 3, a block to the right of the bus stop when facing the city wall. Gigantic rooms come with a colorful plaid bedspread, TV, phone, and bathtub, and some have balconies with great views of the countryside. (☎964 16 01 25; www.hotelelcidmorella.com. Breakfast €4. Singles €29.50; doubles €50.50. MC/V.) **Hostal La Muralla ❷**, C. Muralla, 12, has large, bright rooms with TV, private bath, and charming Spanish decor. (☎964 16 02 43. TV lounge. Breakfast €3. High season doubles €36. Low season €40. MC/V.)

The town's local specialty is *trufas* (truffles) dug out of the local turf. Specialties include *paté de trufas* and *cordero relleno trufado* (truffle-stuffed lamb). Most eateries are located on C. Don Blasco de Alagón, Morella's main street. Pastries from Castellón's excellent bakeries are a cheap morning option (around €1.50). At **Restaurante Casa Roque ❸**, Cuesta San Juan, 1, a giant boar's head watches over the dining room. (☎964 16 03 36; www.casaroque.com. Entrees €9-15. *Menú* €12-25. Open Apr.- Dec. Tu-F 1-3:30pm and 8:30-10:30pm, Sa 1:15-4pm and 9-11pm, Su 1:15-4pm; Jan.-Mar. closed Tu and W nights. AmEx/D/MC/V.)

◗ SIGHTS. Perched atop a massive rock, the **▩Castell de Morella** impresses with its rich history and lovely pathways. Celts, Romans, and Moors have all defended Morella's walls as their own. El Cid stormed the summit in 1084, and Don Blasco de Alagón took the town in the name of Jaume I in 1232. Civil wars in the 19th century damaged the castle and added to the intrigue. Inspect the **Cadro guardhouse** and the eerie **Catxo dungeon,** where the prince of Viana was imprisoned in the 15th century. Every step in this castle reveals a different historical oddity and local legend. The highest point, the **Patio de Armas,** provides chilling views of the ancient city through perfectly preserved stone arches. (Entrance at the end of C. Hospital, uphill from the *basílica*. Open June-Sept. 11am-7:15pm; Oct.-May 11am-5:15pm. €1.50, students €1.) In Pl. Arciprestal, on the way to the castle, the ceiling of the Gothic **Basílica Santa María la Mayor** hovers over an intricate stairwell, a gilded organ installed in 1717, and the ghostly statue of Nuestra Señora de la Asunción. Bracketed by chandeliers, the altar is almost as breathtaking as the basilica's stained-glass windows. (Open June-Aug. Tu-Su 11am-2pm and 4-6pm; Sept.-May Tu-Su noon-2pm and 4-6pm. Mass M-F 7pm; Sa 8:15pm; Su 10am, 5, and 6:30pm. Free.) For great views of both the countryside and the castle, stop by the **Mirador de la Plaza Colón** at the end of C. Blasco de Alagón. To see the remnants of the Gothic **aqueduct,** exit the city through the enormous **Portal de San Miguel,** turn left, and walk straight for 5min.

COSTA BLANCA

The "White Coast," named for the color of the fine sand and smooth pebbles that cover its shores, extends from Dénia to Alicante. Jagged mountains, jutting piers, pine trees, cactus-studded rock, and hills covered with cherry trees surround the towns of the Costa Blanca, all of which attract their fair share of tourists. The sparkling beaches and charming towns of Altea, Calp, and Dénia offer relief from the disco droves that energize Alicante and Benidorm, making them ideal for families or travelers seeking tranquil locales. These smaller towns are fast becoming havens for ex-pats, and beachfront hotels come at steep prices; many prefer to spend the night in Alicante or Benidorm and daytrip all over the coast. Fortunately, efficient and cheap modes of transportation make this an easy option.

▐ TRANSPORTATION

Trains: Ferrocarrils de la Generalitat Valenciana (☎965 92 02 02, in Alicante 26 27 31), also known as the "Costa Blanca Express," hits almost every town and beach along the coast on its Alicante-Dénia line. Switch from train to tram (or vice versa) at the **El Campello** station. From **Alicante** trains run to: **Altea** (1½hr., hourly 5:55am-

8:55pm except noon, €4.10); **Benidorm** (1hr., hourly 5:55am-8:55pm, €3.30); **Calp** (1¾hr., 7 per day 5:50am-8:50pm, €4.80); **Dénia** (2¼hr., every 2hr. 5:50am-8:50pm, €7.20). Trains return to Alicante from Dénia and Calp (every 2hr. 6:25am-7:25pm) and from Altea and Benidorm (hourly 6:24am-10:24pm). **Tramsnochador** (☎965 26 27 31), the night train from Alicante, runs in July and August to **Dénia** and **Benidorm**. (Contact the tourist office or call for schedules.)

Buses: ALSA (☎902 42 22 42) runs between Alicante and Valencia, stopping in towns along the Costa Blanca. From **Valencia** buses run to: **Alicante** (2-4hr., 12-20 per day 4:45am-9:45pm, €16.85); **Benidorm** (2-4hr., 15-18 per day 4:45am-9:45pm, €13.15); **Calp/Altea** (2½-4½hr., 8-10 per day 6am-5pm, €10.65); **Dénia** (2-3hr., 11-12 per day 6am-10:45pm, €8.60); **Gandía** (1hr., 9-15 per day 6am-9:45pm, €6.10); **Xàbia/Javea** (2-3hr., 6 per day 6:30am-8pm, €9.45). From **Alicante** buses run to: **Benidorm** (1-1½hr., 3-5 per day, €3.60) **Altea** (1-1½hr., 1-2 per hour 6:30am-8pm, €4.30); **Calp** (1½hr., 1-2 per hour 6:30am-7pm, €5.70); **Dénia** (2½-3½hr., 1-3 per hour 6:30am-9pm, €8.95); **Valencia** (2½hr., 1-3 per hour 6:30am-9pm, €15.90-16.30); **Xàbia** (2½hr., 20 per day 7am-8pm, €7.70).

ALICANTE (ALACANT)   ☎965

Alicante (pop. 320,000) is a city with verve. Though its wild bars, crowded beaches, and busy streets seem decidedly modern, the looming castle-topped crag, 14th-century churches, and marble esplanades declare otherwise. Alicante, once the Roman city "Lucentum," is also home to the remains of a 5th-century Iberian settlement. Alicante is undoubtedly a traditional Spanish city, yet there is extra sparkle and a unique energy here—the locals are friendlier and the nightlife is livelier, making it a worthwhile destination on the Costa Blanca.

▌ TRANSPORTATION

Flights: Aeroport Internacional de L'Altet (☎966 91 91 00 or 966 91 94 00; www.aena.es), 11km south of the city center. **Iberia** (☎902 40 05 00) and **Air Europa** (☎902 40 15 01) have daily flights to **Madrid, Barcelona,** and the **Islas Baleares,** among other destinations. **British Midland Airways** (☎902 11 13 33) flies to **London. Alcoyana** (☎965 26 84 00) bus #C-6 runs to the airport from Pl. Luceros (every 40min., 30 ride, €1). Buses also leave from Pl. Puerta Mar.

Trains: RENFE, Estación Término (☎902 24 02 02 for local destinations or 902 24 34 02 for international destinations), on Av. de Salamanca. Info open daily 7am-midnight. To: **Barcelona** (4½-6hr., 5-6 per day 6:55am-6:20pm, €45); **Elx** (30min., hourly 6:05am-10:05pm, €1.75); **Madrid** (4hr., 4-9 per day 7am-8pm, €42-73); **Valencia** (1½hr., 10 per day 6:55am-8:20pm, €10.80-23.50). **Cercanías** runs to **Murcia** (1½hr., hourly 6:05am-10:05pm, €5.60). **Ferrocarrils de la Generalitat Valenciana (TRAM),** Estació Marina, Av. Villajoyosa, 2 (☎900 72 04 72), by the Mercdo Central, has service along the Costa Blanca. In summer the **Tramsnochador** runs to beaches including **Altea** and **Benidorm,** with some continuing to **Dénia** (hourly 10:55pm-4:55am, €0.95-4.20).

Buses: C. Portugal, 17 (☎965 13 07 00). **ALSA** (☎902 42 22 42 or 965 98 50 03 for booking; www.alsa.es) to: **Altea** (1hr., 1-2 per hour 6:30am-8pm, €4.30); **Barcelona** (9hr., 2 per day 4:45am-2:30am, €38.17); **Benidorm** (1hr., 1-3 per hour 6:30am-10pm, €3.50-4.50); **Calp** (2hr., 1-2 per hour 6:30am-8pm, €5.70); **Dénia** (3hr., 1-2 per hour 6:30am-9pm, €8.95); **Granada** (6hr., 10 per day 6:45am-3am, €25.94-31.79); **Madrid** (5hr., 15 per day 8am-12:45am, €23.81-32); **Málaga** (8hr., 6 per day 2:20am-11:45pm, €34.90-42.60); **Sevilla** (10hr., 11:45pm, €45.19); **Valencia** (3hr., 1-3 per hour 6:30am-9pm, €15.35-17.55); **Xàbia/Javea** (3hr., 20 per day 7am-8pm,

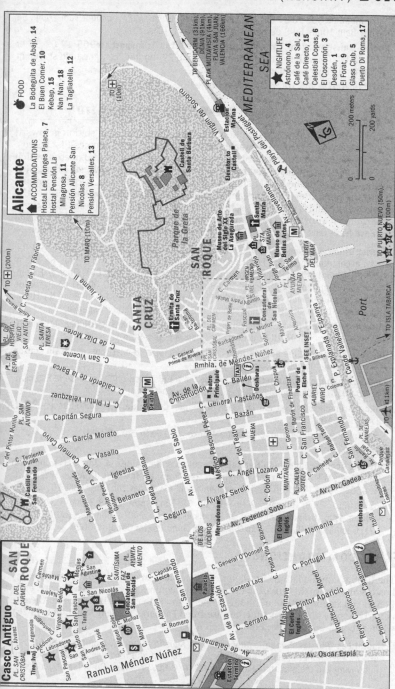

Alicante

★ **ACCOMMODATIONS**
Hostal Les Monges Palace, **7**
Hostal Pensión La
  Milagrosa, **11**
Pensión Alicante San
  Nicolas, **8**
Pensión Versalles, **13**

● **FOOD**
La Bodeguita de Abajo, **14**
El Buen Comer, **10**
Kebap, **15**
Nan Nan, **18**
La Tagliatella, **12**

★ **NIGHTLIFE**
Astrónomo, **4**
Café de la Sal, **2**
Café Directo, **15**
Celestial Copas, **6**
El Coscorrón, **3**
Desdén, **1**
El Forat, **9**
Glass Club, **5**
Puerto Di Roma, **17**

€8). **Mollá** (☎965 26 84 00) runs buses to **Elx** (30min.; M-F 2 per hour 7am-10pm, Sa hourly 8am-10pm, Su 8 per day 9am-9:30pm; €1.70).

Public Transportation: TAM-Alicante Metropolitan Transport (☎965 14 09 36 or 900 72 04 72; www.subus.es). Buses #21 and 22 run from near the train station in Alicante to Playa San Juan (€0.95).

Taxis: Teletaxi ☎965 10 16 11, **Radio-Taxi** ☎965 25 25 11

✦ ? ORIENTATION AND PRACTICAL INFORMATION

Trains to Alicante arrive at the train or TRAM station. The train station is toward the city outskirts at the end of **Avenida de la Estación,** which becomes Pl. Luceros. **Avenida Federico Soto** runs toward the beach, perpendicular to Pl. Luceros, which turns into **Av. Doctor Gadea**. Continuing through Pl. Luceros to **Avenida Alfonso X el Sabio** brings you to the TRAM station by the Mercado Central. A right turn just beyond the market eventually reaches **Rambla Méndez Núñez**, which borders the *casco antiguo* and is full of ATMs, bus-stops, and restaurants. The *casco antiguo* is charming; it provides a pleasant conduit to the beach. The marble **Explanada d'Espanya** traverses the port and links the **Parque de las Canalejas** and the beach.

Tourist Office: Municipal office, C. Portugal, 17, by the bus station (☎965 92 98 02; www.alicanteturismo.com). English spoken. Open M-F 9am-2pm and 5-8pm, Sa 10am-2pm. **Regional office,** Rambla Méndez Núñez, 23 (☎965 20 00 00). Open M-F 9am-8pm, Sa 10am-2pm and 3-8pm. **Beachside branch** (☎965 20 0089) on Paseo de Gomis. **Airport branch** (☎965 28 50 11) open M 9am-3pm, Tu-F 9am-8pm, Sa 10am-8pm. Other branches by the train station and on the Explanada d'Espanya.

Budget Travel: IVAJ (Institut Valencia de la Juventud), Rambla Méndez Núñez, 41. (☎966 47 81 09. www.ivaj.es. HI card €10.80. Open M-F 9am-3pm.)

Luggage Storage: At the **bus station** (€4-7 per bag; open 8am-10pm) and **train station** (€3-6 per bag; open 24hr.).

English-language bookstore: FNAC, just by the train station on Avenida de la Estacion. (☎96 601 01 00, open M-F 10am-10pm, Sat noon-10pm.)

Police: Avenida Julian Bestero 15, open 8am-3pm. **Comisaría,** C. Médico Pascual Pérez, 27 (☎965 10 72 00).

Hospital: Hospital General, C. Maestro Alonso, 109 (☎965 93 83 00).

Red Cross: ☎965 25 25 25.

Internet Access: Fundación BanCaja, Rambla Méndez Núñez, 4, 2nd fl. 1hr. free with ISIC. Open M-F 9am-2pm and 4-9pm, Sa 9am-2pm. **Up Internet,** C. Angel Lozano, 10 (☎965 20 05 77). €1.65 per 1hr.; 4pm-midnight €2.95 per 1hr. Open daily 10am-1am.

Post Office: Bono Guarner, 2 (☎965 22 78 71). Open M-F 8:30am-8:30pm, Sa 9:30am-1pm. **Branch:** Corner of C. Arzobispo Loaces and C. Alemania (☎965 13 18 87). Open M-F 8:30am-8:30pm, Sa 9:30am-2pm. **Postal Code:** 03002.

⌂ ACCOMMODATIONS

The best accommodations in Alicante are in the *casco antiguo*. Though quality hostels abound in this area, ensuring a room requires an early arrival or reservation. If you're not particular, finding a cheap and safe room elsewhere in Alicante is fairly easy, except during the bonfire-filled **Fogueres de Sant Joan** (June 18-25), when accommodations are booked well in advance.

▨ **Hostal Les Monges Palace,** corner of C. San Agustín, 4 and C. Monjas. (☎965 21 50 46; www.lesmonges.net). In an ornate green building, the *hostal* is palatial inside and out, giving you the most bang for your buck. A/C €5. Breakfast €4. Internet access €3 per hour. Singles €29, with bath €40, with jacuzzi €51; doubles €42/56/96; triples €53, with bath €64. AmEx/MC/V. ❸

Hostal-Pensión La Milagrosa, C. Villavieja, 8 (☎965 21 69 18; www.hostallamilagrosa.com). Soft-colored, spacious rooms in the center of the *casco antiguo* and easy walking distance from the beach and TRAM. Some rooms have amazing views of the castle or the Iglesia de Santa Maria. Shared baths and A/C. Internet €1 per 30min. Laundry €2. June-Aug. €15 per person. MC/V. ❶

Pensión Alicante San Nicolás, C. San Nicolás, 14 (☎965 21 70 39, www.alicantesannicolas.com). A new, polished establishment. 7 elegantly decorated rooms with natural, spa-like colors. Full English breakfast offered. A/C. Singles €25, with private bath €35; doubles €40/€50. Additional bed €15. ❷

Pensión Versalles, C. Villavieja, 3 (☎965 21 47 93, 965 32 98 00). 12 small, quirky rooms. Communal atmosphere encouraged by an eclectic outdoor courtyard/kitchen. Great for easy-going groups who want a place to crash or hang out. €18 per person. ❷

🍴 FOOD

Restaurants and *kebap* stops are everywhere, though many are overpriced and on busy streets. Smaller bar/restaurants in the *casco antiguo* are often superior in both atmosphere and tapas selection. **Rambla Méndez Núñez** is full of chic and popular eateries. Cafes can be found along the beach, but the best seaside locales are concentrated in the port, which becomes a raucous nightlife hub as midnight nears. The enormous **central market** is on Av. Alfonso X el Sabio. (Open M-Sa 9am-2pm.) Buy basics at **Supermarket Mercadona,** C. Álvarez Sereix, 5 (☎965 21 58 94; open M-Sa 9am-9pm) or at **El Corte Inglés,** Av. Maisonnave, 53 (☎965 92 50 01; open daily 10am-10pm). Smaller markets are across the street from the **Playa de Postiguet.** Gluten-free products are available at the various 24hr. **Deshoras** shops that dot the city; there's one at C. Bailén, 29. (☎965 21 11 42. Open 24hr.)

☒ Nan Nan, Marina Deportiva, Puerto de Alicante (☎965 20 20 93). A rowdy, port-side tapas bar with a loud staff and comfortable wicker chairs. Nice view of the port, cheap food, and downstairs from a swath of bars and discos. Good place to start the evening with a late dinner. Open daily 12-4pm and 8pm-1am. MC/V. ❷

Kebap, Av. Dr. Gadea, 5 (☎965 22 92 35). Though not unique in name, this slightly off-the-map restaurant offers the best Middle Eastern cuisine in Alicante, and the only Middle Eastern decor with genuine flair. Mouthwatering pitas €2.70. Entrees €5.70-7. Open M-Th and Su 1pm-1am. 2nd location at C. San Fernando, 12. MC/V. ❶

El Buen Comer, C. Mayor, 8 (☎965 21 31 03) Old-town, traditional ambience with patio seating. Wide selection of tapas and fresh seafood. Entrees €10-24. Open daily 7am-midnight. MC/V. ❸

La Bodeguita de Abajo, C. Bailén, 4 (☎965 21 94 80). A cavernous bar/restaurant, dimly lit with wine cellar decor and local artwork. Great appetizer options (€1-4) and *comida típica* (traditional food). Entrees €7-17. *Menú* €13. Th night live music. Open daily 1:30-4pm and 8-11pm. AmEx/MC/V. ❸

La Tagliatella, C. Castaños, parallels Rambla Méndez Núñez, a few blocks from the sea. (☎965 20 87 97, www.latagliatella.es) A romantically decorated Italian restaurant with lavish colors and an upscale ambience; exquisite variety of gourmet salads, pastas (€9-13), risottos, scallops, and pizza (€10), all beautifully prepared. ❷

👁 🧭 SIGHTS AND BEACHES

The **Castell de Santa Bárbara** keeps guard over Alicante's shores and provides an awe-inspiring backdrop to the *casco antiguo* (old town). The castle's drawbridges, dark passageways, and hidden tunnels date from the 9th to the 17th centuries. At 166m tall, Santa Barbara is one of Europe's most sizeable medieval fortresses, and boasts a dry moat, dungeon, and ammunitions storeroom. The **Albacar Vell,** constructed during the Middle Ages, holds a sculpture garden with pieces by Spanish greats. A road from the northern border of the old section of Alicante provides a walk up that is much easier than it looks; otherwise an **elevator** is accessible by a tunnel on Av. Jovellanos, across from Playa Postiguet near the white pedestrian overpass. (☎965 26 31 31. Castle open daily Apr.-Sept. 10am-7:30pm; Oct.-Mar. 9am-6:30pm. Free. Elevator €2.40.) In the old town, the Gothic-styled **Iglesia de Santa Maria** stands over the ruins of an old mosque and is Alicante's oldest church. The neighboring **Concatedral de San Nicolas de Bari** boasts a different flavor of Baroque architecture; a 45m dome allows light to flutter into the dim enclaves of this church. The **Ayuntamiento** on the edge of the *casco antiguo* (near the port) has a stunning 18th century facade with twisted columns and stone sculptures. The ▨**Museo Arqueológico Provincial de Alicante,** Pl. Dr. Gomez Ulla, showcases remains from the Paleolithic, Iberian, Roman, Islamic, and modern periods. (Take the TRAM to the Marq stop. ☎965 14 90 00; www.marqalicante.com. Open Tu-Sa 10am-7pm, Su and festivals 10am-2pm. €3, students €1.50.)

Alicante's **Playa del Postiguet,** near the Ayuntamiento, is a crowded stretch of sand. Sunbathers, ice cream stands, and small cafes dot the wide adjacent boardwalk. For more peaceful shores, the 6km of **Playa de Sant Joan** and **Playa del Mutxavista** are the nearest options, accessible by the tram station at the joint linking the Explanada and the Playa del Postiguet. (The Alicante-Dénia train, TRAM, leaves the main station every 20min. in the summer, hourly in winter, and stops at Playa del Muxtavista and Playa de San Juan; €0.95. To San Juan, take TAM bus #21, 22, or 31. For Mutxavista, take #21. Every 15min., €0.95.)

▣ NIGHTLIFE

Alicante's raucous nightlife can be somewhat capricious; bars that overflow one night are often closed or embarrassingly empty the next. Many of the hit locales are only open weekends only. It's often best to follow the sound of chattering crowds; the most concentrated nightlife areas are the discotecas along the port and the bizarre pubs that spring to life in the *casco antiguo.* For wilder nightlife, **Benidorm,** an hour away (TRAM to El Campello and RENFE train to Benidorm), offers an overwhelming explosion of discotecas, clubs, and bars open all night.

 PARTY ON, WAYNE. Given its long hours and disco destinations, the **Tramsnochador** is a godsend for all-night partiers. The bus runs to cities like Altea, Benidorm, and Dénia, with service until 5am.

CASCO ANTIGUO

The *casco antiguo* is the perfect place to start off the night while the dance floors along the port fill up; though there are plenty of watering holes around **Plaza San Crisóbal** and **Calle Mayor,** the older part of town has the youngest crowd and the quirkiest bars. The cramped patios outside these hotspots accumulate crowds rapidly; the bar-hopping mentality in Alicante is unabashedly follow-the-leader.

▨ **Celestial Copas,** C. San Pascual, 1. Fills up later than surrounding bars but the decor alone makes it worth a visit anytime; the garish bar drips with opulence, and is sinfully offset by kitschy religious artwork. Red velvet curtains, decadent colors, and glinting gold chandeliers overwhelm two tiny rooms.

Astrónomo, C. Virgen de Belén, at C. Padre Maltés (☎965 14 35 22). 2 heavenly fl. of dancing and drinking to Spanish music, pop, house, and everything in between. Escape across the street to a lush, gated outdoor terrace. Beer €3. Mixed drinks from €5. Happy hour midnight-2am. Open Th-Sa 11pm-4am.

El Coscorrón, C. Tarifa, 3. Named after the bump on the head you might receive from the 4 ft. doorframe. Open since 1936, it claims to be the oldest bar in Alicante. Beer €2.50. Mixed drinks €4-6. Open M-W and Su 10:30pm-2:30am, Th-Sa 7pm-4am.

Glass Club, C. de Montegon. Cool medical lab colors and blank mirrored walls let off icy steam in this large air-conditioned, space-age club. Techno and house music seem to reverberate off of every shiny surface. Beer €4. Mixed drinks €5.50. Open 10pm-4am.

El Forat, Pl. Santísima Faz, 4. Decked out with silk flowers, animal-print houses, posters of 1940s movie stars, and plenty of rainbow flags. Diverse gay and straight crowd enjoys an occasional drag show. Beer €3.10. Mixed drinks €5-7. Open Th-Sa 10:30pm-4am.

NEAR THE PORT

Alicante's **main port** houses a complex of cavernous bars and *discotecas* pumping music over the water. Though the music starts early, these bars fill up late and some are only open on weekends. On the way from the old town to the port, be sure to stop by **Havana Cafe,** Rambla Méndez Núñez 26, where a bohemian interior and huge crowds make for a lively feel. Partiers crowd the many huge discotecas on the **Puerto Nuevo,** to the left when facing the water. None of these has a cover charge, though there is sometimes a drink minimum. Beer is almost universally €3.50 and mixed drinks €6. The liveliest spots differ depending on the day of the week, but all have a fairly good crowd any night. **Puerto Di Roma** attracts a young, well-dressed crowd for wild dancing on countertops and the window-lined dance floor. If English is your language of choice, **Coyote Ugly** is just a few doors down, complete with poles on the bar. These clubs are all open midnight-6am. The best choice is **Z-Klub,** C. Coloma, 3. Coming off Rambla Méndez Núñez, go right on Explanada d'Espanya and walk two blocks; C. Coloma is a small side street on the right. This is the only club in Alicante that has a cover charge, but it's well worth it. Spain's top DJs spin house all night long for a gorgeous crowd. (☎965 98 01 36. Cover €10-15, includes 1 drink. Mixed drinks €5-7. Open Th-Sa midnight-6am.)

FESTIVALS AND ENTERTAINMENT

From June 20-24, the **Fogueres de Sant Joan** (Bonfires of St. John) and St. John's Feast Day celebrate the summer solstice in a hedonistic inferno. This rollicking, fire-worshiping blast kicks off with a city-wide parade in traditional garb, and by the third day, every district in the city has its incredible *foguera* (giant papier-mâché structure) on display. Temporary festival halls are erected and feasts take place in open air, punctuated by daily firework shows in the Plaza de los Luceros at 2pm. Parades, flower-offerings, and wild celebrations fill the hours until the festival culminates in a midnight display of fireworks atop Mount Benacantil and a huge bonfire in the Pl. de Ayuntamiento. In June, the **Moors and Christians** festival pays costumed tribute to the Christian battles for Valencian reconquest. The city honors its patron saint, La Virgen del Remedio, from August 3-5 through choral concerts and processions. During late July and early August, Playa de San Juan becomes a stage for ballet and musical performances for the **Plataforma Cultural** series. (Events on Playa de San Juan free.) Monthly schedules for these festivals are on the tourist office website (www.alicanteturismo.com).

BENIDORM ☎965

Many believe Benidorm's name means "good sleep" or "come and sleep"; visitors may sleep well, but they certainly won't sleep long, as Benidorm (pop. 67,000) is hardly the place to pass a peaceful night. The never-ending beams of light over the 5.5km beach boardwalk are the first indication that no one is deterred by the setting sun. Visitors from all over Europe crowd modern, skyscraper-studded streets, some to sunbathe on the city's hot sands, others to engage in raucous revelry until dawn. If it's the tranquility of the Costa Blanca you seek, you may find it here among secluded coves. If you're eager to be swept away by a tidal wave of energy, look no further than the crazy carnival that lights the summer sands of Benidorm.

◪ ⁊ TRANSPORTATION AND PRACTICAL INFORMATION. The **train station** (☎965 85 18 95) is atop a hill above the city on Av. de l'Estacio. The walk down to the city is at least 15min. and not pedestrian-friendly—it's best to take a bus or cab. Local bus #7 departs from the train station for the city center. (☎965 85 43 22. Every 30min. 6:30am-9:50pm, €0.90.) The **ALSA bus station** is on Av. de Europa, at the corner of Av. Gerona about four blocks inland from the beach, close to the city center. For **taxis** call ☎965 86 26 26 (€3-5 to the city center). **Av. Ruzafa** is near the *casco antiguo* (old town) and is full of Internet cafes, banks, accommodations, and taxis. The *casco antiguo* divides Benidorm into two sections: to the north, the boardwalk **Avenida d'Alcoi** runs through the main beach, **Playa de Levante,** site of most big hotels, restaurants, and bars. On the other side of the *casco antiguo* is the seaside **Parque de Elche** and a more secluded beach, **Playa de Poniente.** The **tourist office** is off the beach at Av. de Martínez Alejos, 16. Signs lead to it from Av. Ruzafa. From the bus stop, continue down Av. de Europa toward the beach, take a right at Av. del Mediterráneo, and continue to **Plaza de la Hispanidad,** also called **Plaza Triangular.** Veer left onto C. Dr. Pérez Llorca, and take a left onto Av. de Martínez Alejos. (☎965 85 32 24; www.benidorm.org. Open July-Sept. M-F 9am-9pm, Sa 10am-1:30pm and 4:30-7:30pm, Su 10am-1:30pm; Oct.-June same except M-F 9am-8pm.) **Banks** and **ATMs** line C. Dr. Pérez Llorca. **Internet** access is at **Cybercat Café,** in the bottom floor of **El Otro Mundo de Jaime,** Av. Ruzafa, 2, near the *casco antiguo.* (☎965 86 79 04. €1 per 20min. Open daily 9am-2am.) The **post office** is at Pl. Dr. Fleming, 1, parallel to C. Dr. Perez Llorca. (☎965 85 34 34. Open M-F 8am-8pm, Sa 8:30am-2pm.) **Postal Code:** 03501 or 03502 (depending on zone).

⁊◪ ACCOMMODATIONS AND FOOD. Benidorm's shoreline is a metallic bouquet of upscale hotels (including the tallest hotel in Europe, the Gran Hotel Bali at 186m), making affordable lodging difficult to find. Casually-decorated rooms with balconies and private bathrooms are at **Pensión La Orozca ❷,** Av. Ruzafa, 37. A/C and TVs are available. Street can be noisy at night. (☎965 85 05 25. Open mid-Mar. to Oct. 15. Singles €17; doubles €30. Prices rise July-Aug. MC/V.) Closer to the beach on Av. Ruzafa is **Hostal Tabarca ❷,** Av. Ruzafa, 9, with tiled floors, beaded curtains, and clean hallway bathrooms. (☎965 85 77 08. All have TV and fan. June-Sept. singles €18; doubles €35; triples €40. Oct.-May €15/30/35. Cash only.)

The shoreline is an explosion of gelaterias, pizzerias, and cafes with outdoor seating, loud music, and blinking lights. These cafes are often packed well into the night by an older crowd. **Restaurante L'Albufera ❷,** on the corner of C. Gerona and Av. del Dr. Orts Llorca, offers 14 different *menús del día* (€12) and hearty portions of Italian and Spanish fare at reasonable prices. (☎965 86 56 61. Entrees €8-12. Open daily 11am-midnight.) For a quieter atmosphere, walk through the *casco antiguo* to the restaurants along **el mirador** (see below). The **produce market** (W and F 8am-3pm) is just outside the *casco antiguo* on Vía de Emilio Ortuño and C.

Mercado. The main supermarket, **Mercadona,** is on C. Invierno, one block up C. Mirador, off Vía de Emilio Ortuño. (Open M-Sa 9:15am-9:15pm.)

◨▨ **SIGHTS AND FESTIVALS.** Remnants of the old city have been almost totally engulfed by high-rises and roadways, and most of the ocean is obscured by an vast sea of blue-and-white umbrellas standing guard over sunbathers. A bit of a walk to either end of **Playa de Levante** yields the best views, and, further down the road, secluded lagoons. The hillside panorama of the clear waters of **Tumbona** beach is unforgettable; if you decide to make the trek down, be warned that access costs €3, and most sunbathers are nude. At the end of **El Carrer del Gats,** one of the area's most picturesque streets, protrudes the gleaming **mirador,** also known as "The **Balcony** of the Mediterranean." This gabled blue-and-white prome-nade spans the rocky perimeter of the neighborhood and offers overwhelming views of the Playa del Levante to the north, the Playa de Poniente to the south, and the rocky sea floor below. Straight ahead juts **Benidorm Island,** an enormous slanted-rock formation. The **Balcony** almost entirely conceals the ruins of the **Castillo-Mirador de Benidorm,** built in the 14th century to protect the city from Ber-ber pirates.If it's rowdy beach enjoyment you want, a visit to Benidorm is not com-plete without a stroll along the 2km long **Paseo Marítimo de la Playa de Levante.** This enormous boardwalk is packed nearly 24 hours a day; the place to see and be seen.

In early summer, Benidorm hosts a world-renowned international music festi-val, **Festival de la Canción de Benidorm.** Check out www.festivaldebenidorm.com for more information, tickets, and schedules.

▨ **NIGHTLIFE.** Day or night, Benidorm is one massive party. The club scene is not for the faint of heart. Partygoers follow an exhausting but hedonistically fulfill-ing routine every night in July and August, and on weekends during the rest of the year. Beachside locales start to brim as soon as the esplanade floodlights are lit. The crowd is easy to follow as it moves inland through the night (or morning). Cov-ers at clubs are around €12, but usually include a drink (€6). Promoters outside sometimes offer free admission or deals on drinks. Close to the *Ayuntamiento* in the *casco antiguo* is ▨**La Sal,** C. Costera del Barco, 5. This local favorite is busy on the weekends with an ultra-hip crowd of mainly Spaniards and Germans. (☎066 87 34 94. Beer €3-5. Open F-Su 10:30pm-4am.) C. del Gats, is full of other great places to start the night. Beachside cafes close to the *casco antiguo* promise stiffer prices but great atmosphere. After a few drinks here, partygoers usually head to disco-pubs along Av. de Mallorca. If all you want to do is dance, head to ▨**Penelope,** one of the trendiest venues on the beach, with multiple bars, disco balls, dancers, and a packed dance floor. (www.penelopebeach.com. Mixed drinks €8. Open daily 11pm-5am.) An eclectic crowd grooves to house music at **Ku** (see below for disco), Av. Alcoy, 6, a lounge and club, replete with palm trees and tiki torches. (☎965 86 94 83. Mixed drinks €8. Open daily 10pm-5am.) At **KM,** right next to Penelope on the corner of Av. Bilbao and Av. Alcoy, an international crowd dances to a variety of music. (☎639 12 43 76; www.kmdisco.com. Mixed drinks €8. Open F-Sa 9pm-5am.) Around 5am, the party shifts from the beach to the disco gardens on **Avenida de la Comunitat Valenciana.** It's a good 15min. on foot, but it's best to take a **taxi** (€4). To get to Av. Valenciana from the beach, walk to Av. del Mediterráneo and head towards the *casco antiguo.* Turn right onto C. Esperanto and follow it for about 7min. Turn left on C. Juan Llorca; Av. Com. Valencia is a block ahead. At ▨**Ku (Disco),** Av. Com. Valenciana, 121, a giant double helix stands imposingly outside. Inside, white walls and red lamps surround a dance floor, outdoor terrace, and pool. (Mixed drinks €6. Open midnight-6am.) **Pachá** is Spain's largest *discoteca* chain. (Open midnight-6am. Mixed drinks €6-8.) Later, crowds head to the terrace at **Space,** in the same building as Ku. (☎976 10 80 88. Open nightly midnight-8am.)

ALTEA
☎ 965

Altea's yawning coastline is unique on the Costa Blanca for its absence of sky-scraper hotels and tourist staples. Though apartment complexes and private homes are clustered toward the sea, Altea retains a pristine quality and small-town modesty. A long jetty with a charming walkway protects Altea's stretch of shoreline from large waves, while egg-sized white stones make for a contrast with the turquoise water. Bus #10 runs from Altea to Altea la Vella every hour (€1). **Comte d'Altea,** which runs into **C. La Mar** and **Pl. del Convent,** is the main thoroughfare in Altea. **C. Sant Pere** parallels the beach. The walk past the **Port d'Altea** leads to clearer waters and vistas of **Cap Blanch.** Continuing this walk through a residential area eventually leads to a path that climbs the **Faro de l'Albir,** the peninsula-like peak of the Serra Gelada. The trek takes about an hour, but is not taxing. At the top is an unforgettable vista of the entire shoreline. If there's no time for a hike, be sure to climb the steep stone steps into the old town behind C. del Mar, where the blue dome of the **Plaza de la Iglesia** beckons.

Though Altea isn't very touristy, it certainly won't help you make up for lost euros. Among the cheapest accommodations is **Habitaciones La Mar ❷,** C. La Mar, 82, close to the train station and beach, with 40 decent-sized, simple rooms with bathrooms in a concrete building about 10m from the beach. Look for the neon blue sign. (☎965 84 30 16. Singles €24; doubles €40; triples €40. Cash only.) Past the Port d'Altea is **Camping Cap-Blanch,** Playa Cap Blanch 25, just 2k from downtown Altea and 5km from Benidorm. (☎96 584 59 46, www.camping-cap-blanch.com. €6 per car, tent, and person.) For typical Spanish fare and delicious gazpacho in a cozy setting, try **La Liebre ❷,** Po. Mediterráneo, 39. (☎965 84 45 79. Menú €8.45. Open M-Sa 10am-5:30pm. Kitchen closes at 4pm.) Most bars on the waterfront cater to an older crowd and close early; night owls can be found down the beach toward Faro de l'Albir. Check out the oceanfront lounges and bohemian flair of **Cafe del Mar** along Cap Blanch (Drinks only. Open until 5am.) Many party-goers head to Benidorm and Alicante for nightlife and entertainment.

Both **trains** and **buses** stop at the foot of C. La Mar. The **tourist office** is on C. Sant Pere, 9, parallel to C. La Mar by the water. (☎965 84 41 14. Open June-Aug. M-F 10am-2pm and 5-7:30pm; Sept.-May M-Sa 9:30am-2pm and 5-7:30pm.) **Taxis** can be reached at ☎966 81 00 10. Rent trail, road, or mountain bikes from **Bici Altea** (☎966 88 09 87. Open M-F 10am-2pm and 5-8:30pm, or Sat 10am-2pm). Local services include the **police,** C. La Mar, 91 (☎965 84 55 11), and **ambulances** (☎965 84 31 83).

CALPE (CALP)
☎ 965

The drive into Calp is worth the trip alone; winding roads skirt the brink of a huge valley, while massive rock formations jut into the sea. Upon arrival, Calp may seem like a classic tourist trap; however, exploration of the *casco antiguo* yields hidden gems. Otherwise, as in any other city on the Costa Blanca, flocks of sunseekers descend to enjoy the lovely beaches along with a glut of dining and shopping options. **Avenida Gabriel Miró** is the most central commercial avenue and has direct access to the marbled **Paseo Marítimo Infanta Elena** and the **Playa Arenal-Bol.**

Affordable accommodations are few and far between in Calpe; they are generally found near the *casco antiguo.* Be sure to make reservations well in advance. The tiny but comfortable **Pensión Céntrica ❶,** Pl. Ifach, has charmingly mismatched rooms with sinks, clean hallway bathrooms, and a bar-restaurant downstairs. (☎965 83 55 28; mjpiffet@telefonica.net. Singles €12; doubles €24. MC/V.) **Hostal La Paloma II ❸,** Partida Benicolada 6, is visible from the bus station and offers clean, cream-colored rooms. (☎965 87 54 28. Singles €30; doubles €42.) The most reasonably priced restaurants in Calp can also be found on the plaza: **Bar Buenavista ❶,** Pl. Constitución, offers breakfast (€1.50-3.20) or tapas and bocadil-

los (€2-11) along with coffee, beer, and even slot machines. (☎965 83 13 33. Open
daily 6am-11pm.) Otherwise, try the incredibly stylish **Cambalache ❷**, C. Torreo-
nes, 15, in the *casco antiguo*, for huge entrees. (☎965 83 27 02.)

ALSA buses (☎965 83 90 29) stop 2km from the beach at **Terminal de Autobuses
Alsa**, Av. Diputacion, 51 (see **Transportation,** p. 334). The station is level with the
casco antiguo. The stop is an outdoor parking area with a small ticket office,
next door to a **Mercadona** and **tourist office**. Bus schedules are posted and most
coming through Calp travel between Alicante to Valencia. Several buses leave
daily during the week, but are more infrequent during weekends. The **train station** is about a 15min. uphill walk from the bus stop. Some of the roads do not
have sidewalks. Walking around Calp can be difficult, so make use of the local
transportation. The local buses, **Autobuses Ifach,** head to the beach (in summer
every 30min., winter every hour, €1). If all else fails, call a **taxi** (☎965 83 00 38).
There are three **tourist offices** in Calp. The one located in Calp's urban center
(☎965 83 69 20) is at the beginning of the path to the Peñón at Av. Ejércitos
Españoles, 44. (☎965 83 69 20. Open June-Aug. M-Sa 9am-9pm, Su 10am-1:30pm;
Sept.-May M-F 9am-2pm and 4-8pm, Sa 10am-2pm.) The **police**, Av. Europe, 15
(☎965 83 90 00), are located near the main tourist office. **DIP Internet Center**, C.
Benidorm, 1, is off Av. de Gabriel Miró. (☎965 87 47 65. €1 per 20min., €3 per hr.
Open M-F 10am-11pm, Sa 10am-2pm and 5-7pm, Su 4-11pm.)

DÉNIA   ☎966

Dénia is an ideal family resort destination, featuring a 17km ribbon of smooth
beaches with silken sands, a thriving fishing port, great beaches for watersports,
and a harbor that connects ferries to the Islas Baleares. Catering to an upscale
tourism industry, Dénia's rows of boutiques, beachfront hotels, and tasty restaurants are enough to tempt even the most thrifty travelers to splurge. Fortunately,
the infinite stretches of groomed beaches are available free of charge.

📑🔁 ORIENTATION AND PRACTICAL INFORMATION. The local **train station**
(☎900 72 04 72) is on C. Calderón de la Barca, just off C. Patricio Ferrándiz. The
bus station is an ALSA office on Pl. Arxiduc Carlos and Po. del Saladar, a 10min.
walk to the beaches. For train and bus schedules, see **Transportation,** p. 327. Local
buses (☎966 42 14 08) pick up on the Explanada Cervantes; to get there, head
toward the water from the tourist office and take a left at the Red Cross building.
The stop is about 5min. down from the traffic circle, at the port. Take the bus
marked "Marina" or "Calma" for the more secluded beaches; the bus marked
"Rotas" heads toward great scuba diving sites. To reach the Baleares by sea, consult **Baleária Eurolínes Marítimes** (☎902 16 01 80; www.balearia.net) in Pl. Oculista
Buigues. **Ferries** run from Dénia to Palma and Ibiza (€49-66). For full ferry info,
see **By Boat,** p. 343. For **taxis**, call ☎966 42 44 44 or 96 578 65 65. **Bike rental** is available from **Motos Luís** on C. Abu-Zeyen, 8 (☎965 78 36 02) and **Desnivell Bicicletes** on
Avd. Alicante, 18 (☎ 966 425 230, ciclesdesnivell@hotmail.com).

Local services, including **buses, trains,** and **ferries,** are on **Calle Patricio Ferrándiz,** which runs to the port from the bus station. Orient yourself on the **Calle Marqués de Campo,** the main tourist strip. The **tourist office** is on Pl. Oculista
Buígues, 9, 30m inland from Estació Marítima, at the end of C. Patricio Ferrándiz. Follow the signs to the port from the bus station. (☎966 42 23 67;
www.denia.net. Open July-Aug. daily 9:30am-2pm and 5-8pm; Sept.-June M-Sa
9:30am-1:30pm and 4:30-7:30pm, Su 9:30am-1:30pm.) Contact the **police** at ☎092.
Internet access is available at **Cyber Mon,** on C. Carlos Sentí in the Mon Blau
complex, upstairs in the blue building next to the market on the block between
C. de la Mar and C. Magallanes. (€1.50 per hour. Open daily 10am-11pm.) Also

available at **Locutorio Public Internet,** C. Loreto 52 (M-F, 9:30am-3pm and 4-11pm, Sat 9:30-11pm). The **post office** is on C. Patricio Ferrándiz, 38. (☎965 78 15 33. Open M-F 8:30am-8:30pm, Sa 9:30am-1pm.) Another mail center is across the **Mercadona** on C. Pintor Victoria, 3 (☎965 78 15 33).

ⓘⓒ ACCOMMODATIONS AND FOOD. Dénia's plush hostels fill quickly and don't cater to budget travelers. Be prepared to shell out €30 or more for a single room in the summer, and book in advance, especially during festivals in July. **Hostal L'Anfora ❸,** Explanada de Cervantes, 8, ideally located right on the port, straddles the old and new towns. This spotless find has some of the cheapest rooms in town, all with bath, TV, and A/C. (☎966 43 01 01; www.hostallanfora.com. July-Sept. singles €32; doubles €55; Oct.-June €26/43. AmEx/MC/V.) **Hostal Comerc ❸,** C. La Via, 43, is a giant, spotless hotel-like establishment paralleling Avda. Marques de Campo. A standard and industrial facade leads to rooms with balconies and lots of space. (☎965 78 00 71; www.hostalcomerc.com. Singles €30. MC/V). **Camping Las Marinas ❶,** C. Les Bovetes Nord, 4, is 3km from Platja Jorge Joan. Take the buses marked "Racón" (€1). Hot water, supermarket, restaurant, and the beachside setting are all added bonuses. (☎966 47 41 85. €4.80 per person and per tent.) The **market** is on C. Carlos Sentí, 6 (open M-Sa 7am-2pm). Eateries are found in **Pl. Del Convento,** a courtyard beside a pleasant fountain. At night, crowds move to beachside bars and restaurants. Vegetarian delights like soy burgers and couscous are at **Caña de Azúcar ❶,** C. Fora Mur, 3A. (☎677 09 83 50. Entrees €4-7. 3-course lunch *menú* €9.50. Smoothies and fresh juices €2-4. Offers vegetarian cooking classes; call for details. Open Tu-Su 1-5pm and 8pm-midnight.)

ⓖⓒ SIGHTS AND BEACHES. Away from the beaches, Dénia is best enjoyed in the maze of colorful streets leading up to the **castle;** the walk is steep but short, and passes through the most charming part of town. Access the stairway from **Pl. del Consel** and **Pl. de la Constituto.** Dénia's castle offers amazing panoramas on all sides. The ruins sprawl across the hilltop and exhibit Moorish relics from the 11th and 12th centuries. Within the walls is a small museum of archeology located in what was once the Governor's Palace. (☎966 42 06 56. Open daily June 10am-1:30pm and 4-7:30pm; July-Aug. 10am-1:30pm and 5-8:30pm; Sept. 10am-1:30pm and 4-8pm; Oct. 10am-1pm and 3-6:30pm; Nov.-Mar. 10am-1pm and 3-6pm; Apr.-May 10am-1:30pm and 3:30-6pm. Night hours July to mid-Sept. 10pm-12:30am. €2.15.) A **tourist train** chugs to the castle from the tourist office (☎699 46 88 66. M-F and Su 5pm and 6:15pm, schedule subject to frequent change. Train ticket includes admission to castle; min. 10 passengers). Dénia's biggest draw is its pristine stretch of beaches. Beach bars and volleyball courts are in constant use, and the 17km breadth of coastline rarely gets crowded. Those who crave a beach for relaxation have plenty of options—**Platja Les Marines, Platja Les Bovetes,** and **Platja Punta Raset** are all close to the center of town and well within walking distance from the port. Windsurfers skip over the waves off **Platja Els Molins** (north of the port on the "Marina" bus), while scuba divers explore the depths off **Las Platjas Area de Las Rotes** (south of the port on the "Rotas" bus). The tourist office provides a pamphlet detailing trails in nearby **Montgó Natural Park** (☎966 42 32 05).

⚑ FESTIVALS. Dénia holds a miniature **Fallas Festival** March 16-20, burning puppet effigies at midnight on the final day. During **Festa Major,** or **Las Fiestas de la Santisima Sangre** (first 15 days in July), dances, floats, and fireworks are displayed by the harbor, while locals prove they are as gutsy as their countrymen in Pamplona during the ⚑**bous a la mar** (p. 92), when bulls and fans dive together into the water.

MURCIA ☎ 968

Though Murcia is becoming increasingly urban and fashionable to accommodate its large university, it maintains deep respect for tradition. The old quarter's quiet lanes reveal the Moorish heart of the historic city of Mursiya, founded by Abderramán II in AD 825, but the city's soul rests in its Gothic and Neoclassical plazas. Though the streets connecting these marbled arenas are lined with chic shops and young crowds, daily life in Murcia unfolds to the steady rhythm of the church bells clanging from its many cathedrals. Be warned that the city bakes in the summer heat, and may leave you yearning for the beach. *Murcianos* will tell you that their city is a pleasant place to visit from September to June, from the start of the new school year to the spring explosion of festivals.

█ TRANSPORTATION. Aeropuerto de San Javier (☎968 17 20 00), about 30km to the southeast, has flights to Madrid and London. **RENFE trains** (☎902 24 02 02), at Pl. Industria, across the river from the *casco antiguo*, head to: Alicante (2hr., 6 per day, €5.55); Barcelona (6-8hr., 4 per day, €45.10-47.60); Lorca (1hr., 9:45pm, €13); Madrid (4-6hr., 5 per day, €39.70); Valencia (3½hr., 4 per day, €16-28). **Buses** (☎968 29 22 11) leave from the station on C. Bolos (on the western perimeter of the *casco antiguo*) to: Alicante (1½hr., 14 per day 7am-9pm, €5.20); Almería (4hr., 4-6 per day 5:15am-9:30pm, €16.14-19); Barcelona (8½hr., 9 per day 12:30am-10:00pm, €43.39); Dénia (3½hr., 6 per day 2am-8:50pm, €11.97); Granada (4-5hr.; M-Th 5 per day, F-Su 7 per day 8:30am-10pm; €16.50); Mojácar (2-3 per day, 5:30am-8:30pm; €9.90), La Manga del Mar Menor (1hr.; Sept.-June M-Sa 3 per day, Su 2 per day; July-Aug. hourly 9am-9pm; €5); Lorca (1hr., 6-17 per day 7am-9pm, €3.95); Madrid (5-6hr., 10-12 per day 7am-1am, €21-34); Málaga (7hr., 5 per day 1:25pm-3:35am, €24); Sevilla (7-9hr., 3 per day 10:30am-9pm, €31.50); Valencia (3¾hr., 4-7 per day 5:30am-8:30pm, €11.50). **Municipal buses** (€0.85) cover the city; bus #9 runs past the bus and train stations.

█▌ ORIENTATION AND PRACTICAL INFORMATION. The **Río Segura** is a lateral divide, separating the city sights up north from the train station, cheap accommodations, and mini markets in the south (take bus #9, 17, or 39 between the two). Take **Av. Canalejas** to the Puente Viejo (Old Bridge) across the river to **Gran Vía Escultor Salzillo,** one of the two main streets that cut through the center of town (the other is **Gran Vía Alfonso X El Sabio**), to the Plaza Circular (the former Av. de la Constitución), a giant traffic circle in the city center. G. V. Salzillo is strewn with banks—these may become important once you've stumbled upon the shopping districts. An immediate right off of G. V. Salzillo leads to **Plaza Belluga,** a spectacular grouping of the 14th-century cathedral, Palacio Episcopal, and *Ayuntamiento*: the **tourist office** is amidst this congress of striking architecture, one of the most important (and beautiful) orienting points in the city. (☎968 35 87 49; www.murciaciudad.com. Open daily Apr.-Sept. 10am-2pm and 5-9pm; Oct.-Mar. 10am-2pm and 4:30-8:30pm.) The regional **tourist office** is in Palacio González Campuzano, the red building in Pl. Julián Romea. (☎968 22 06 59. Open M-F 9am-2pm.) Local services include the **police,** Av. San Juan de la Cruz (☎968 26 66 00) and **Hospital de la Cruz Roja,** along the river past the Ayuntamiento and the Plaza de la Cruz Roja. A **24hr. pharmacy** is just across the **Puente Viejo** in the **Plaza Martinez Tornel. Post offices** are on G.V. Salzillo and Pl. Circular, near the intersection with Av. Primo de Rivera. (☎968 27 13 13. Open M-F 8:30am-2:30pm.) **Postal Code:** 30008.

█▐ ACCOMMODATIONS AND FOOD. In Murcia, finding a room without a reservation, especially in the summer, is tricky. Fortunately, the city is well-prepared for travelers with thin wallets. **Universal Pacoche ❸,** C. Cartagena, 21, has simple rooms, off of slightly dark hallways, each with a TV and a tiny private bath. With no A/C or fans, Pacoche's rooms can get muggy in the summer. Just blocks from both the train station and the *casco antiguo*. Friendly hotel/restaurant next door serves breakfast to go. (☎968 21 76 05. June-Aug. Singles €29; doubles €43; triples €60. MC/V.) Similarly, the centrally located **Pensión Hispano I ❷**, C. Trapería, 8, is run by Hotel Hispano. The rooms are clean and well kept, come with a phone and patterned bedspreads, and most have a private bath. (☎968 21 61 52; www.hotelhispano.net. Check in at the Hotel Hispano. Singles €20, with bath €25; doubles with bath €38; triples with bath €48. AmEx/MC/V.)

Enjoy breakfast in the **Plaza de Flores,** a block left of G. V. Salzillo, where tranquil cafes are interspersed with flower shops. **Plaza Apostoles,** behind the cathedral, has outdoor eateries away from tourist traffic. The **Plaza de Santo Domingo,** bordered by an enormous church, offers a wealth of shaded seating, ice cream shops, and cafes. The smaller **Plaza J. Romea** is lit beautifully at night and offers elegant tapas bars beneath the imposing **Teatro de Romea.** The patio seating at **Meson de Jesus ❶** is great for people watching. Indoors, the wood-paneled restaurant has a warm, tavern-like ambience. (☎968 216 869. Tapas €1.50-6.) **Casa Carmelina,** Pl. Puxmarina, 2, is a more elegant option, with silk and gold decor, heavy drapes, and Italian cuisine. (☎968 22 10 17; www.casacarmelina.com) Sample the venerated Murcian harvest at the **Mercado Verónicas,** behind its namesake cathedral on C. de Verónicas (open M-Sa 9am-2pm). A 24hr. walk-through **market** is on C. Puxmanna, paralleling G. V. Salzillo. For other needs, try the **Corte Inglés** at the end of G. V. Salzillo.

◎ SIGHTS. The intricate, Castilian Gothic facade of the 14th-century cathedral in ▧**Plaza Belluga** is one of the city's most unforgettable sights. From the cathedral, walk through the breezy **Jardín El Salitre** and cut across town on C. Acisclo Díaz to the palatial ▧ **Casino de Murcia,** C. Trapería, 18, that served as a gentlemen's club for the city's 19th- and 20th-century bourgeoisie. (Closed indefinitely for renovations. ☎968 21 22 55.) Continue up C. Trapería away from the river and take a right onto C. Andres Bacquero, which becomes C. Dr. Fleming. Take a right onto C. Obispo Frutos and you'll come to Murcia's **Museo de Bellas Artes,** C. Obispo Frutos, 8, containing over 1000 works and a collection of *Murciano* art from the 16th-19th centuries. (☎968 23 93 46; www.museobellasartesmurcia.com. Open May-Sept. Tu-Su 10am-2pm and 5:30-9pm.) Further along is the **Plaza de Toros**. At the opposite end of town, but well worth the walk, is the unassuming **Museo Taurino,** located in the breezy Jardín El Salitre just north of the bus station. This nondescript enclave displays bullfighting memorabilia, matador costumes, and mounted bulls' heads that pay homage to particularly exceptional bulls and those who did them in. Shrines to Spain's best *toreros* exhibit the shredded, bloody shirts worn when they were gored to death by their 1000-pound opponents. (☎968 28 59 76. Open June-Aug. M-F 10am-2pm and 5-8pm; Sept.-May also Su 11am-2pm. Free.)

▧▧ NIGHTLIFE AND FESTIVALS. Though a very young crowd is the lifeblood of Murcia's nightlife, the overall scene is quite calm. Most partygoers congregate in the city's plazas and the main streets connecting them; there's no need to wander aimlessly through any of the darker back-alleys. Just off Pl. de San Juan, a plastic walkway leads to an ornate door opening onto the **La General,** C. Mariano Padilla, 15. (☎692 17 01 29. Beer €1.50. Mixed drinks €2-6. Open M-F 4pm-2am, Sa-Su 4pm-3am.) For a more vivid club scene, the university area near C. Dr. Fleming and Pl. Universidad does the trick on weekends. Unleash your inner animal at **Fauna,** C. Dr. Fleming, 12, among glowing tanks filled with fish and other underwater creatures. (☎658 06 27 50. Beer €3. Mixed drinks €5-6. Open Th-Sa 11pm-3:30am.)

After *Semana Santa,* the six-day **Fiesta de Primavera** descends upon the city, bringing band processions, flower parades, and theater performances. Every June and July, the **Festival Belluga** draws dance and classical music acts from all over Europe to perform outside the cathedral. Check at the tourist office for schedules.

◼ DAYTRIPS FROM MURCIA

LORCA

RENFE Cercanías trains (☎ 902 24 02 02) run to Lorca's Estación Satullena (the 2nd Lorca stop), Ex. de la Estación (1hr., hourly 6:45am-10:05pm except at 8:45pm, €4). The bus station (☎ 968 46 92 70), next to the train station, sends buses to Murcia (1½hr., hourly, €3.80) and Águilas (30min.; M-F 9 per day, Sa-Su 2-3 per day; €2).

Though the dry hills surrounding Lorca (pop 84,000) are blanketed with orchards and cropland, ancient battles stripped the actual town of its foliage and left a host of architectural imprints. Medieval ghettos, Renaissance artistry, post-Franco urbanism, and contemporary elitism all flavor the town's terrain. Atop the rocky hillside is the **Castillo Fortaleza del Sol,** a Moorish fortress with two preserved Christian towers constructed in the 13th and 15th centuries. In summer, the castle hosts shows and concerts at night and medieval festivals on weekends. (☎ 902 40 00 47. Open Tu-F 10am-2pm, Sa-Su 10:30am-6:30pm. Tu-Sa €6, students €4.50; Su and holidays €10, students €6.80.) The awe-inspiring 16th-century **Ex-Colegiata de San Patricio** was built to commemorate the Lorcan battle against the Muslims in 1492. Granada fell in the same year, compelling Lorca's inhabitants to move to the bottom of the slope, leaving behind three churches: **Santa María, San Juan,** and **San Pedro,** all which stand in ruin beneath the castle. The trek up to the castle is a grueling 20-min. climb through a maze of box-shaped, beige homes, followed by paved roads that wind around the desiccated, cactus-strewn rock. When all else fails, just keep walking uphill. A tourist train makes its way up every 40min. or so and is well worth the price (€2).

Food and accommodations are difficult to come by. **Pension Las Palmeras ❶,** at the back of a dead end off of C. Nogalte, is one of the only budget accommodations, and fills quickly. (☎ 968 46 88 93. Singles €15.) It's difficult to find a decent meal here; stock up on snacks at the **Mercadona** off Alameda de la Constitucion (parallel to the train station). Though you may stumble upon the occasional hole-in-the-wall bar in the old part of town, most streets here are residential or historical. Your best bet for a meal is away from the town cultural center near Avenida de Juan Carlos I. **Pl. de Colon, C. Nogalte,** and **C. Lope Gisbert** have quieter cafes.

The **train** and **bus** stations are a block below the town center on Explanada de la Estación. Take Av. Periodista Lopez Barnes from the train station to **Av. de Juan Carlos I,** which traverses the busiest part of town and contains most bank offices. Most cafes and pharmacies are left on Av. de Juan Carlos I; a right turn leads to the cultural center. From Av. de Juan Carlos I, take **C. Presbitero Emilio Garcia Navarro** past lovely churches and the town cultural center; a right turn from there onto **C. Lope Gisbert** leads to the **tourist office,** inside the **Palacio Guevara.** (☎ 968 46 61 57. Open M-F 9:30am-2pm and 5:30-7:30pm, Sa 10am-3pm and 5:30-7:30pm, Su 10am-3pm.) The **post office** is next door, C. Musso Valiente, 1 (☎ 968 46 71 12).

CARTAGENA

RENFE trains (☎ 902 24 02 02) head to: Barcelona (8-10hr., 8:35am, €48.50) via Alicante; Madrid (5hr., 5 per day 5:30am-6:25pm, €41.70); Murcia (1hr., 9 per day 7:35am-9:10pm, €3.60); Valencia (4hr.; 8:35am, €30; 4:43pm, €18.15) from the train station in Pl. de México, several blocks north of the port. Ticket office open 5am-9:30pm. Autocares Costa Azul (☎ 968 50 15 43) runs to Alicante (3hr., 8 per day 7am-8pm, €7.05). Alsina Graells buses go to: Cádiz (10-12hr.; 10:30am, 9pm; €47.43); Gran-

ada (5½hr., 4 per day 8:30am-9pm, €21.16); Málaga (7-8hr.; 8:30am, 3pm; €29.81); Sevilla (9½hr.; 10:30am, 9pm; €37.33).

Cartagena's port-side area is an oasis of dynamic architecture, interspersed with ruins dating back to the 3rd century BC. Though the newer part of the city sprawls to accommodate its 200,000 inhabitants, the historical enclave by the port, embraced by five rolling hills, is a refreshing getaway for art and history aficionados anxious for a reprieve from mainstream tourist treks. Founded in 227 BC by the Carthaginian general Asdrubal, the city of Qart Hadast ("New City"), now Cartagena, was modeled after Carthage itself, and served as the main Punic metropolis in Iberia, rich in natural resources and privileged by its protected interior port. Streets such as **C. Mayor, C. Canon,** and **C. Cuatro Santos** brim with marbled, modernist buildings with intricate ironwork in light colors. The **Ayuntamiento,** 19th century **Iglesia de la Caridad,** and 17th century **Iglesia de Santo Domingo** are standout highlights. The climb up **C. Jara** tenders close-up views of the **Teatro Romano, Byzantine Wall,** and 13th century **Catedral de Sta María La Vieja.** Architecture aside, the modern and informative museums are arguably the best part of the city.

 SHIFTY SCHEDULES. Schedules for sights change on a monthly basis, so ask at the tourist office for updated info. Information on hours can also be found at www.puertoculturas.com or the Cartagena Puerto de Culturas (☎968 50 00 93), which offers substantial discounts for students and children on admission to multiple sights.

The **Centro de Interpretación de la Muralla Púnica (CIMP),** Pl. Bastarreche, just across from the tourist office, provides detailed information about the Punic history of the city, and displays the only remnants of the original defensive wall of Qart Hadast. (€3.50, students and under 16 €2.50.) Continue past Pl. Bastarreche on **C. San Diego,** which becomes **C. Duque** and **C. Cuatro Santos.** This street forms the upper border of the *casco antiguo,* leading past a Byzantine wall, ruins of the Teatro Romano (finished in 1 A.D.), and the Centre d'Interpretation de la Historie de Carthagene. The cross-street **C. Caridad,** becoming **C. Gisbert,** is a lovely walk to the eastern end of the port wall. **C. Cuatro Santos** ends at **C. Aire;** from here the paralleling **C. Canon** leads to the sun-drenched port-side **Pl. del Ayuntamiento,** a central locale for restaurants, sight-seeing, and access to the port. The **Paseo de Alfonso XII** runs along the port, and bus and taxi stops line the way. Perpendicular to the port are the yellowed walls of the **Arsenal Militar,** constructed in the 18th century. Be careful not to stumble in here. Though ruins of the *casco antiguo* are primarily concentrated near the port, Cartagena's sprawl beyond does not feel small or self-contained. To get to the city center and **tourist office,** walk straight on the tree-lined Av. de América to reach Pl. Bastarreche. The **bus station** is next to the tourist office in Pl. Bastarreche. The **tourist office** (☎968 50 64 83; www.cartagena.es) has free walking tours of the city, maps, and an accommodations list. (Open May-Sept. M-F 10am-2pm and 5-7pm, Sa 10am-1pm; Oct.-Apr. M-F 10am-2pm and 4-6pm, Sa 10am-1pm.) For taxis call ☎968 311 515.

Hostal Rosa ❷, Pl. San Agustín, 61, just behind the *Ayuntamiento,* offers 14 minimalist rooms off long carpeted and mirrored hallways. (☎968 52 00 28. Singles €20; doubles €35, with bath €40; triples €45. MC/V.) There is a **market** on C. Gisbert toward the port. Otherwise, relax in the shade of the stone archways at **La Tapería ❷,** C. del Parque 2, which offers a huge tapas menu. (☎968 52 86 14. Tapas and starters €1.50-€7.) Near the Ronda San Juan in a small square is **Entretapas y Vinos ❷,** Portales de la Lonja, 7, which offers creative Spanish fare for reasonable prices, served amid black-and-white decor. (☎968 50 22 56. Tapas and starters €2.50-6.50. Huge wine selection. Open M-Sa noon-4pm and 8pm-midnight.)

LAS ISLAS BALEARES

Ages ago, Spain won a centuries-long race to conquer the Islas Baleares, but the imprints on each island reflect a massive convergence of European culture. T While all four islands—Mallorca, Menorca, Ibiza, and Formentera—share the crowds, each has a unique character that separates it from the rest.

Mallorca, home to the gracefully aging port city of Palma, absorbs the bulk of high-class, package-tour invaders reigns as the cultural hub of the Baleares. Ibiza, a haven for counter-culture since the 1960s, entices bohemians and fashionistas alike with its outlandish parties, transforming crowds into glittering masses grooving to a deafening techno beat. Menorca, wrapped in green fields, staggering sandstone walls, and placid natural harbors, offers tranquility that the other islands do not, with secluded white beaches, fabulous hidden coves, and mysterious Bronze Age megaliths. Formentera, the smallest and most distant island, is a bizarrely-shaped rural expanse containing the calmest and most beautiful beaches in the Mediterranean.

Summers are hot, crowded, fun, and the best time to visit any of the islands; winters are chilly and slow, as nightlife doesn't heat up until early July. Most hours, schedules, and prices listed are for summer only. Low-season prices at hotels can drop by up to half, and hours for sights and attractions are often limited.

HIGHLIGHTS OF LAS ISLAS BALEARES

GOSSIP about Chopin's love life in his home in **Mallorca** (p. 352).

GIGGLE in a laughing gas booth at a *discoteca* in party-town **Ibiza** (p. 363).

PEDAL through the wooden walkways of lovely **Formentera** (p. 371).

CAVE IN to the natural wonders of **Clutadella** (p. 360).

✈ GETTING THERE

Flying to the islands is cheap and faster than taking a ferry. Those under 26 can get discounts with **Iberia/Aviaco Airlines** (in Barcelona ☎902 40 05 00). Many travel agencies in Barcelona and Valencia book special airfare packages that include entrance to nightlife hotspots throughout the islands.

BY PLANE

Scheduled flights are the easiest to book, and flights from Spain to the islands won't break the bank as long as you reserve early. Frequent flights leave from cities throughout Spain and Europe (including Frankfurt, London, Paris, and Rome). Many daily **Iberia** flights (☎902 40 05 00; www.iberia.com) connect Palma and Eivissa to Barcelona, Madrid, and Valencia. The cheapest way to get to Menorca is from Barcelona. Flights from the other cities are infrequent and more expensive. Service from Alicante, Almería, and Bilbao also exists, but is less frequent.

Iberia offers **student fares** (with an ISIC card) on flights from Barcelona (50min., €40-300) and Madrid (1hr., €40-250). **Air Europa** (☎902 40 15 01; www.air-europa.com), **Spanair** (☎902 13 14 15; www.spanair.com), and **Vueling** (☎902 33 39 33; www.vueling.com) also offer very inexpensive flights to the islands if booked well in advance. Schedules and prices are subject to change. Another option is a **charter flight,** which can be the cheapest and quickest means of travel. Most deals entail a stay in a hotel, but some companies (called *mayoristas*) sell unoccupied

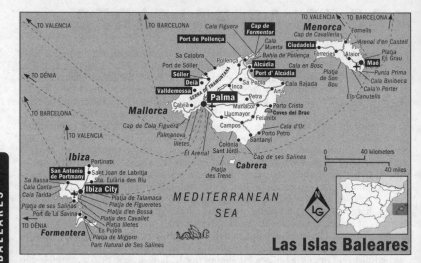

Las Islas Baleares

seats on package-tour flights. The leftover spots ("seat only" deals) can be found in newspaper ads or through travel agencies (check **TIVE** and other budget travel companies in any Spanish city). Prices during summer, San Juan, and *Semana Santa* are higher than in low season (Oct.-May), when tickets are fairly easy to get a week or so before departure. Those traveling in July or August should reserve at least a month in advance, especially to Eivissa and Palma.

BY BOAT

Ferry service is not always less expensive than flying and takes longer. Discotecas and small swimming pools on some boats ease the ride, but beware that not all boats run at the same speed—try to book the high-speed ferry options that take only 2-4hr. Ferries run from Barcelona and Valencia to Palma and Eivissa, and from Dénia (in Alicante) to Eivissa. Seats may be available up to an hour before departure, but reserve tickets a few days in advance.

> **Balearia** (☎902 16 01 80; www.balearia.com) ferries run from **Dénia's** Estació Marítima or **Barcelona** to **Ibiza** (2-4½hr., 2 per day, from €48), continuing on to **Palma** and **Port d'Alcudia** (from €48).

> **Buquebus** (☎902 41 42 42; www.buquebus.com) has super-fast catamaran service between **Barcelona** and **Palma** (4hr., 2 per day, €11-150).

> **Trasmediterránea** (☎902 45 46 45; www.trasmediterranea.com) boats depart daily from **Barcelona's** Estació Marítima Moll and **Valencia's** Estació Marítima to **Ibiza, Mallorca,** and **Menorca.** Fares from the mainland are €50-150, depending on speed and distance. Fares between the islands range €28-75.

▄ GETTING AROUND

INTER-ISLAND TRANSPORT

Iberia flies between Palma and Eivissa (40min., 5 per day, €54-85) and between Palma and Maó, Menorca (35min., 4 per day, from €54-103). **Air Europa, Spanair,** and **Vueling** (see **By Plane,** p. 343) connect the islands at similar prices.

Another option, is to take the **ferry**. Prices and times change with the wind and run very infrequently. It's best to consult with the tourist office or a travel agent. Ferries to and from Mahón can be lengthy (4½hr.), but "fast ferries" now make the journey between the other three islands in under 2½hr. **Trasmediterránea** (☎902 45 46 45) sails from Palma to Mahón (5½hr., Su 8am, €41) and Eivissa (2½hr., Su 8am and 8pm, €31-48). There is no direct Mahón-Eivissa connection. **Trasmapi** (☎902 16 01 80) links Ibiza and Formentera (35min., 6 per day 7:10am-8pm, €10-17; express 25min., 12 per day, €35). **Iscomar Ferries** (☎902 11 91 28; www.iscomar.com) run between Menorca's Port de Ciutadella and Mallorca's Port d'Alcúdia for daytrips.

INTRA-ISLAND TRANSPORT

The three major islands have extensive **bus** systems, although in quieter areas (especially Menorca) transportation nearly comes to a halt on Sundays. Palma and Ibiza are especially easy to navigate by bus. Mallorca has two narrow-gauge **train** systems that are more of a tourist attraction than a major mode of transportation, although most people recommend taking the train at least once for the view. Bus fares between cities range €1.20-7.50 each way. Cars and mopeds are a great way to explore inaccessible remote areas. On Mallorca and Menorca, roads can be confusing and dangerous, so cars are the best option, while in Ibiza and Formentera, a moped is more than adequate. A tiny, standard transmission **car** costs around €45 per day including insurance. **Mopeds** are around €35, and **bicycles** a mere €6-15.

MALLORCA (MAJORCA)

Mallorca has long attracted the rich and famous. The site of the scandalous affair of pianist Frédéric Chopin and novelist George Sand, Mallorca is also a choice vacation spot for Spain's royal family and the world's most glamorous jetsetters. To the northwest, white sand and olive trees adorn the jagged Sierra de Tramontana, where writers and artists have created some of their most impressive work. To the east, expansive beaches sink into calm bays, while to the southeast, phenomenal caves hide natural wonders. Inland, towns retain their own cultures, where creaking windmills power a thriving agricultural economy.

PALMA   ☎971

The streets of Palma (pop. 375,000) are a trip outside of the expected. After a visit to the designer stores near Plaça d'Espanya and the raucous bars and restaurants along the port, it becomes hard to imagine that the city was once a humble devotional retreat for Fernando and Isabel. Head to the beach and the abundance of sunbathing Germans and Brits may make you wonder whether you're still in Spain. Despite the tourist invasion and urban growth, Palma retains a local flavor. In its many cafes and tapas bars, where the native dialect of *mallorquí* is the only language heard, it's clear why Palma reigns as the cultural capital of the Baleares.

▛ TRANSPORTATION

Flights: Aeroport Son San Juan (☎971 78 90 00), 8km from downtown Palma. Bus #1 runs between airport and port, stopping along the way in Pl. d'Espanya (every 20min. 5:50am-2:30am, €1.85). **Air Europa** (☎902 40 15 01), **Iberia** (☎902 40 05 00), and others offer service to Palma. See **By Plane,** p. 343, or **Inter-Island Transport,** p. 344.

Trains: Estacion Plaça Espanya (☎971 752 051), **Ferrocarril de Sóller** (☎971 63 01 30; www.trendesoller.com), Pl. d'Espanya. To: **Sóller** (1hr.; 7 per day 8am-7:30pm; €9, round-trip €14). To **Port Sóller** via a tramway from Sóller (20 per day, €3) **Servicios Ferroviarios**

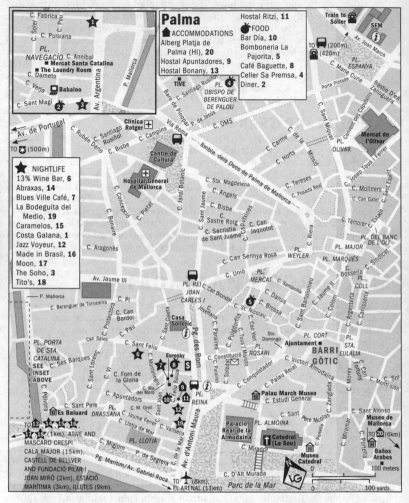

Palma

ACCOMMODATIONS
Alberg Platja de
 Palma (HI), **20**
Hostal Apuntadores, **9**
Hostal Bonany, **13**

Hostal Ritzi, **11**
FOOD
Bar Día, **10**
Bomboneria La
 Pajorita, **5**
Café Baguette, **8**
Celler Sa Premsa, **4**
Diner, **2**

★ NIGHTLIFE
13% Wine Bar, **6**
Abraxas, **14**
Blues Ville Café, **7**
La Bodeguita del
 Medio, **19**
Caramelos, **15**
Costa Galana, **1**
Jazz Voyeur, **12**
Made in Brasil, **16**
Moon, **17**
The Soho, **3**
Tito's, **18**

de **Mallorca (SFM)**, Pl. d'Espanya (☎971 17 77 77), departs to **Inca** (30min., 34 per day
5:50am-10pm, €1.80) and **Sa Pobla** (35min., 16 per day 5:50am-9:25pm, €2.65).

Buses: Palma is a convenient base for bus travel. Nearly all buses stop at the main stop
on C. Eusebi Estada, several blocks down from Pl. d'Espanya; buy tickets on the bus.
The tourist office has a bus schedule. Popular destinations include: **Alcúdia** and **Port
d'Alcúdia** (1hr.; M-Sa 16 per day 8am-9pm, Su 5 per day 9:30am-9pm; €4.50); **Coves
del Drac** (1hr.; M-Sa 2 per day 11:10am and noon, Su 10:15am; €7); **Covetes/Es
Trenc** (1 per day 10:30am, €5.60); **Port Pollença** (1hr.; M-F 12 per day 7am-8:30pm,
Sa-Su 7 per day 7am-8:30pm; €5.25); **Sóller** and **Port de Sóller** via **Palmanyola**
(45min.; M-F hourly 7am-8:30pm, Sa 8 per day 8:30am-6:30pm, Su 6 per day
9:30am-6:30pm; €2.70); **Valldemossa** (30min.; M-F 9 per day 7:30am-7:30pm, Sa 6
per day 8am-7:30pm, Su 6 per day 8am-6:30pm; €1.50).

Ferries: Trasmediterránea, Estació Marítima, 2 (☎902 45 46 45). Ferries dock at Moll Pelaires. Tickets sold M-F 9am-1pm and 5-7pm, Sa 9am-noon. Tickets and info also available at travel agencies. Daily ferries run to **Barcelona, Eivissa,** and **Valencia. Balearia** (☎902 16 01 80) sends ferries to **Dénia.** (See **By Boat,** p. 344.)

Public Transportation: Empresa Municipal de Transportes (☎971 21 44 44; www.emt-palma.es). Pl. d'Espanya is the hub. Buses are easy, clean, and efficient. Stops around town and as far as Cala Major and Arenal. €1.10 (buy tickets on board), 10-ride pass (€8) available at tobacco stands (only in inner-city Palma). Bus #15 runs from Arenal-Can Pastilla-Pl. Reina (every 8min.). Bus #1 goes along Pg. Marítim/Av. Gabriel Roca (every 15min. 6:10am-2:15am, €1.85). Buses run 6am-10pm. The airport bus (#1; €1.85) runs until 2:15am.

Taxis: Radio Taxi (☎971 76 45 45) and **Fondo** (☎971 72 80 81). Airport to center €20. Old town to Estació Marítima €8-10.

Car Rental: Ative, Pg. Marítim, 28 (☎971 45 62 62). €20-45 per day with insurance. Open M-Sa 9am-1pm and 3-7:30pm, Su 10am-1pm. **Mascaro Crespi,** Av. Joan Miró, 9 (☎971 73 61 03). €15-30 per day with insurance. Open M-Sa 8am-1pm and 3-7pm, Su 9am-1pm and 5-7pm. €100 deposit required. Cash only.

■※? ORIENTATION AND PRACTICAL INFORMATION

To get to town from the airport, take bus #1 to Pl. d'Espanya, the busy hub of the city's ground travel (15min., every 15min., €1.90). From the ferry dock, take Pg. Marítim/Av. Gabriel Roca (20min.) or bus #1 to Av. d'Antoni Maura, which leads to Pl. de la Reina and Pg. des Born. The busiest part of the city lies between Pl. d'Espanya and Pl. Reina, by the port. The best street to take from Pl. d'Espanya is **C. Sant Miguel.** Though the street is pedestrian-only, midday crowds of shoppers make for slow going. The street spills into **Pl. Major,** and a right turn from there leads to **Pl. Rei Joan Carlos I,** a spoke-like intersection at the center of the old town. From here **Passeig Des Born** leads toward the port to the town's cultural and culinary nucleus. **Pl. Rei Joan Carlos** can also be reached by **Avinguda Rei Jaume III,** which divides the city's business artery.

Tourist Offices: Palma branch, Pg. des Born, 27 (☎971 22 59 00; www.a-palma.es), in the book shop of Casa Solleric. Open daily 9am-8pm. **Branch** in Pl. d'Espanya by the bus stop. **Island tourist office,** Pl. Reina, 2 services all of Mallorca (☎971 71 22 16). If you need a map, ask for the accompanying street index. Open M-F 9am-8pm, Sa 10am-2pm.

Budget Travel: TIVE, C. Jeroni Antic, 5 bajo (☎971 17 77 88). ISIC and HI cards and tickets. Open M-F 9am-2:30pm and 5-7:30pm.

Currency Exchange: Banco Santander, Pg. des Born, 17 (☎971 72 51 46). Open May-Sept. M-F 8:30am-2:30pm; Oct.-Apr. M-F 8:30am-2pm, Sa 8:30am-1pm.

English Bookstore: The Trading Place, C. Pou 35, in between P. Born and Av. Jaume III (☎871 941 350). New and used books. Open daily 10am-1:30pm and 4:30-8pm.

Laundromat: Self-Press, C. Annibal 18. €9.50 per load. Open M-F 8am-1:45pm. **The Laundry Room,** Pl. Navegació, 9 bajo (☎645 93 63 60). €12 per load. Ironing €20 per hour. Dry cleaning and collection/delivery to boats. Open M-F 8am-3pm. (Both opposite the old town from Av. Argentina, which bisects the port.)

Police: Pg. Mallorca and Av. Sant Ferrà (☎091 or 092 or 010).

Late-Night Pharmacy: Rotates daily; see the local paper, *Diario de Mallorca,* or check *farmàcia de guardia* postings outside pharmacies.

Medical Services: Clínica Rotger, C. Santiago Rusiñol, 9 (☎971 44 85 00), a ways from the port between Pl. Bispe Berenguier de Palou and Pl. Hospital. 24hr.

Internet Access: Babaloo, intersection of C. Verja and C. Sant Magí, a block behind the port off Av. Argentina (☎871 95 77 25). A backpacker-filled haven with fast tech services, cappuccinos (€1), and munchies. €2 per hour. Open M-Sa 10am-10pm, Su 3-10pm. **Vodafone Internet Locutorio,** P. Joan XXIII (☎971 714 658). €2 per hour.

Post Office: C. Constitució, 6 (☎902 19 71 97). Just off Pl. Reina. Packages upstairs. **Fax** service. Open M-F 8:30am-8:30pm, Sa 9:30am-2pm. **Postal Code:** 07003.

ACCOMMODATIONS

The ubiquity of ATMs in Palma is a not-so-subtle hint that travelers are expected to empty their pockets. There are few hostels, most run by expats in cramped buildings close to the port. You won't get much bang for your buck here—rooms offer a lot in character but not much in amenities. Make reservations far in advance.

Hostal Ritzi, C. Apuntadors, 6 (☎971 71 46 10), a ½-block off Pl. de la Reina, flanked by the area's best bars and eateries in the heart of the *casco antiguo*. Tiny, traditional rooms above a Victorian sitting room and kitchen. Full breakfast served at 8:30am. Laundry €7. Singles €30; doubles €45, with shower €48, with bath €52. Cash only. ❸

Hostal Apuntadores, C. Apuntadors, 8 (☎971 71 34 91; www.palma-hostales.com), next door to Hostal Ritzi above the Cafe Art. Spacious singles and 1 huge 6-person dorm. Wi-Fi. Dorms €20 per bed; singles €33; doubles €45, with bath €60. MC/V. ❷

Hostal Bonany, C. Almirante Cervera, 5 (☎971 73 79 24), 3km from town in between the port and Castell de Bellver, close to some of the island's best discotecas. Take bus #3 or 6 from Pl. d'Espanya or Pl. Rei Joan Carles I to the 1st stop on Av. Joan Miró and walk up C. Camilo José Cela. Take the 1st right and then the 1st left. Swimming pool, and rooms with bath, TV, and some with balcony. Singles €28; doubles €40. MC/V. ❸

Alberg Platja de Palma (HI), C. Costa Brava, 13 (☎971 26 08 92), in El Arenal. Clean, single-sex, 4-bed dorms with shower and toilet. HI card required. Breakfast and sheets included. Towel €1.50. Laundry €6.50 wash and dry. 24hr. reception. Dorms (price varies by month) Jan.-Mar. and Nov.-Dec. €8, 26 and over €8.56. Apr.-June 15 €11/12. June 16-Sept. 16 €13/14. Sept. 17-Oct. €11/11.77. MC/V. ❶

FOOD

Palma serves up food with a silver spoon, offering an ethnic selection and round-the-clock service rare in mainland Spain. Make sure to try the *ensaimadas* (pastries smothered in powdered sugar) and the *sopa mallorquina* (stewed vegetables over brown bread). There are two local markets: **Mercat de l'Olivar** in Pl. Olivar by Pl. d'Espanya, and **Mercat Santa Catalina,** across town at the corner of C. Pou and C. Dameto. For groceries, try **AProp** on C. Felip Bauza, just off C. Apuntadors. (☎900 70 30 70; open M-F 8:30am-8:30pm, Sa 9am-2pm).

Celler Sa Premsa, Pl. Obispo Berenguer de Palou, 8 (☎971 72 35 29; www.cellersapremsa.com). An unassuming facade leads to the unexpected—a cavernous restaurant with small, cheery tables dwarfed by floor-to-ceiling wine barrels. Filling half-*raciones* €3.70-6.40. Open M-Sa noon-4pm and 7:30-11:30pm. MC/V. ❶

Bar Dia, C. Apuntadors, 18 (☎971 71 62 64). One of the oldest bars in Mallorca, this hole-in-the-wall taperia is still as popular as when it opened. Delicious tapas (€2-5) and huge *raciones* (€6) devoured at the chaotic standing bar or among the raucous maze of tiny tables. Open Tu-Th and Su noon-midnight, F-Sa noon-1:30am. Cash only. ❶

Diner, C. Sant Magí, 23 (☎971 73 62 22). Ideally situated to satisfy cravings of partiers making the move from old town bars to portside discotecas. American-style burgers in a kitschy diner setting with neon lights and red plastic seats. Burgers (€5), grilled cheese (€3.95), tuna melts (€5.25), and nachos (€4.75) Open daily 24hr. Cash only. ❶

Café Baguette, C. Felip Bauza, 1, off C. Apuntadors (☎617 66 14 61). Tucked away from the foot traffic that tramples its sister streets. Baguette sandwiches (€3), kebabs (€4), and curries (€7.50), to eat in or take away. Open M-F 9am-4pm. MC/V. ❶

Bomboneria La Pajarita, C. San Nicolau 2. If the flourishing, sweet-filled window displays aren't enough to entice you, the cappuccino prices (€1) will. Open M-F 9:30am-2pm and 4:45-8pm, Sa 9:30am-2pm. Cash only. ❶

👁 SIGHTS

Palma's architecture melds Arabic, Christian, and Modernista styles that reflect the island's multicultural past and present. A Mallorcan visit is incomplete without a stroll along **D'Alt Murada,** a fortified boardwalk overlooking a reflecting pool and the sea. The boardwalk also links many of Palma's landmarks and museums.

🖼 CATEDRAL (LA SEU). This Gothic cathedral is Palma's undisputed architectural gem. The cathedral, dedicated to Palma's patron saint San Sebastián, bears the stamp of many centuries—it was begun in the 1300s, finished in 1601, and then modified by Gaudí in his unmistakable Modernista fashion in 1909. The southern facade overlooks a reflecting pool and the ocean, making La Seu the only cathedral in Europe reflected in water. A small **museum** next to the cathedral explores the church's role in Palma's history. *(C. Palau Reial, 29. ☎971 71 31 38. Cathedral and museum open June-Sept. M-F 10am-6:15pm; Apr.-May and Oct. M-F 10am-5:15pm; Nov.-Mar. M-F 10am-3:15pm; year-round Sa 10am-2:15pm. €4. Video guide €4.)*

🖼 ES BALUARD. This forbidding portside stronghold, formerly a 17th-century military fortress, was gutted and transformed into the colossal abode of Palma's contemporary (and well-protected) art museum, which had its grand opening in 2004. An impressive collection features three floors of 20th- and 21st-century paintings, sculptures, and installation pieces with a loyal emphasis on work by local artists. If contemporary artwork isn't your fancy, a visit is still made worthwhile by the portside walk and a tour of the grounds, grassy courtyards accented by bizarre outdoor sculptures. *(At intersection of Av. Gabriel Roca and Pg. Mallorca. Enter through Pl. Santa Catalina. ☎971 90 82 00. Open Tu-Su June-Sept. 10am-10pm; Oct.-May 10am-8pm. Occasional free concerts June-Oct. F 10pm. €6, students €4.50. Tu adult €4.50.)*

ROCKCREATION

Mallorca's terrain is a dramatic mosaic of azure coastline, smooth limestone, vaulting hillsides, and sharp cliffs. While sun-seeking tourists flock to the island's beaches during the summer, in cooler seasons, packs gung-ho daredevils come for an island adventure beyond the disco strips of Palma: a chance to conquer the world-famous rock climbing routes of Mallorca.

Mallorca's efficient bus routes and network of cliffsides make climbing an easy getaway for the determined traveler. The island's climbing terrain includes more than 900 routes and over 20 crags. Difficulty ranges from grades 4 to 8c, accommodating everyone from family groups to intrepid individual climbers.

The eastern part of the island has easier routes, and many travelers who want a mix of the full Mallorcan experience take the vintage train to Soller, were plenty of climbs and hikes are available.

One of the most popular climbing areas is Sa Gubia, a gorge with more routes and variation than anywhere else on the island. Cala Magraner is also a popular destination for climbers with children, and offers routes with a wide range of difficulty. Its beachside locale, caves, and long walls are well-suited for neophytes.

For more information on rock climbing on Mallorca, check out www.rockandsun.com, www.mondaventura.com, or www.tramuntana-pursuits.com.

FUNDACIÓ PILAR I JOAN MIRÓ. Inaugurated in 1992, this small estate hosts rotating exhibitions on the life and work of surrealist Joan Miró, a collection of his paintings and sculptures, and his preserved studio, which houses works in progress at the time of his death. *(Av. Joan Saridakis, 29. Take bus #6 from Pl. Progres to Av. Joan Saridakis. ☎971 70 14 20. Open May 16-Sept. 14 Tu-Sa 10am-7pm, Su 10am-3pm; Sept. 15-May 15 Tu-Sa 10am-6pm, Su 10am-3pm. €4.80, students €2.60.)*

CASTELL DE BELLVER. With austere Gothic turrets rising amidst groves of trees at the end of town, the circular Castell de Bellver offers a unique view of Palma's bustling city and bay. Built in 1300, it served as a summer residence for 14th-century royalty before becoming the prison of Mallorca's most distinguished law breakers. The castle now contains a comprehensive municipal museum and models of archaeological sites. During the summer, the Castell also hosts concerts and theatrical performances. *(Bus #3 from Pl. d'Espanya or #6 from Pl. Rei Joan Carlos I, €1.10. Both drop you off in Pl. Gomila. Walk downhill to C. Bellver and take a left, then a right on C. Drecera. Follow the signs up to the massive staircase. Also accessible by car. The Tourist Bus #50 drives to the top from Pl. de la Reina or Pl. Gomila, €13. ☎971 73 06 57. Open Apr.-Sept. M-Sa 8:30am-9pm, Su 10am-6:30pm; Oct.-Mar. M-Sa 8am-7:15pm, Su 10am-5pm. €2, students €1.)*

PALACIO REAL DE LA ALMUDAINA. Built by the Moors as a fortress, the palace was once a stronghold of Fernando and Isabel. King Jaime II of the 14th century is given credit for transforming the Muslim castle into a Christian stronghold, with a courtyard surrounded by a chapel, queen's quarters, Arab baths, and great hall. *(C. Palau Reial. ☎971 21 41 34; www.patrimonionacional.es. Open Apr.-Sept. M-F 10am-5:45pm, Sa 10am-1:15pm; Oct.-Mar. M-F 10am-1:15pm and 4-5:15pm, Sa 10am-1:15pm. Guided visits €4, unguided €3.20; students and children €2.30. EU citizens free W. Audio tour €2.)*

▣ BEACHES

Mallorca is a huge island, and many of the best beaches are a long haul from Palma. Still, several picturesque (though highly touristed) stretches of sand are accessible by city bus. The beach at **El Arenal** (S'Arenal; Platja de Palma; bus #15), 11km to the southeast (toward the airport), is the prime stomping ground of Mallorca's German tourists. With scores of German-owned restaurants, bars, and hotels, the waterfront is practically Frankfurt on the Mediterranean. Other beaches close to Palma include **Cala Major,** 15km southwest, and **Illetes,** 9km southwest, which are smaller than El Arenal but equally popular (both accessible by bus #3 from Pl. d'Espanya, leaves every 10min.). The tourist office distributes a list of various nearby beaches.

▣ ▣ NIGHTLIFE AND ENTERTAINMENT

Entertainment in Mallorca has a Spanish vim and vigor often missing on the other islands. The tourist office keeps a list of sporting activities, concerts, and exhibits. There is also *cine a la fresca,* an outdoor movie showing held a few nights per week during summer in the Parc de la Mar. For info and events, *El Día del Mundo* (€0.75) has an entertainment supplement every Friday that lists bars and discos, and *La Calle* (€1) offers a monthly review of hot spots. Also check out the free youth guide *(Guías de Ocio)* available in cafes, stores, and restaurants.

BARS

At dusk, the crooked streets between Pl. de la Reina and Pl. Llotja are enlivened by hordes of bar-hoppers, tradesmen, and foot traffic. Elegant eateries and grungy bars fill fast, but a law requiring downtown bars to close by 1am during the week and 3am on weekends has shifted the late-night action to the waterfront.

The Soho, Av. Argentina, 5. This hip "urban vintage" bar has patterned walls and a funky, Warhol-esque interior with black-and-white TV screens. The red-lit den plays alternative music, including 80s hits, classic rock, and underground techno. Beer €1-2.50. Open daily 8pm-2am. MC/V above €5.

Costa Galana, Av. Argentina, 45 (☎971 45 46 58). This swanky bar has white leather chairs and a combo of surfing videos and electro-jazz music. Beer €1.80-2.50. Mixed drinks €5-6. Open M-Th and Su 8am-2am, F-Sa 8am-4am. MC/V.

La Bodeguita del Medio, C. Vallseca, 18, plays great Cuban rhythms in a local tavern. The bar boasts a shrine to Ernest Hemingway's drink of choice: the mojito. Mixed drinks €6. Open M-Th and Su 8pm-1am, F-Sa 8pm-3am. MC/V.

Blues Ville Cafe Bar, C. Ma d'es Moro, 3. This blues and jazz club packs in locals nightly from 11:30pm onward, offering free live music. The boisterous atmosphere is both comfortable and fun. Beer €1-2. Mixed drinks €3-5. Open daily 10:30pm-4am. Cash only.

Jazz Voyeur, C. Apuntadors, 5 (☎971 72 07 80). A gleaming ebony bar with class. Jams with live music weeknights (M-F midnight 3am). Drink min. of €10 for live concerts. Beer €4. Mixed drinks €8-10. Open M-Th and Su 7pm-1am, F-Sa 7pm-3am. MC/V.

13% Wine Bar, C. Sant Feliu 13. A lux, soothing space with walls splashed mint-green and burgundy. Ideal for early evening drinks and lighter meals. Wine €3. Pasta €5.80-9.80. Salad €6.80. Open M-Sa noon-midnight. MC/V.

DISCOTECAS

The center of the club scene is the **Passeig Marítim/Avinguda Gabriel Roca** strip that runs along the water from Av. d'Antoni Maura to the ferry station. Clubbers start the night in *bares-musicales* a little closer to town. Later, the party moves down the block to the giant discotecas. Look for promoters offering reduced cover prices and extra drinks. It's a 20min. walk from Pl. de la Reina, or you can hop on bus #1 from Pl. d'Espanya. (Bus service stops around 2:30am.) There is also the **Bus de Nit** (Night Bus; #41), which runs from the Pl. de Joan Carles I, stopping at key points along the strip (11:40pm-7am, €1.10).

 THE WHEELS ON THE BUS GO 'ROUND AND 'ROUND. On the way back toward town, the Bus de Nit often skips stops, despite attempts to flag it down. You may be better off taking a cab (€7).

Several clubs and bars (many of them gay, especially on Av. Joan Miró) are centered on **Plaça Gomila** and along **Avinguda Joan Miró.** The bars and clubs around the beach at **El Arenal** are German-owned, German-filled, and German-centric, and offer different, fun options. The last bus back to Palma leaves at 1:35am, though, so you'll most likely have to take a cab home.

Tito's, Pg. Marítim/Av. Gabriel Roca. Don't expect any favors from the bouncers at Palma's hippest and most popular discoteca. Beyond the fabulous blue carpet lies an Art Deco palace with a glass elevator, an amazing view of the water, and an occasional fireworks show. Cover €15-18, includes 1 drink. Open daily 11pm-6:30am.

Abraxas, Pg. Marítim, 42, a couple of blocks farther down Av. Gabriel Roca. A versatile cave-like club with massive but cramped dance floor, a smaller salsa club attached, a relaxed tropical terrace, and enthusiastic patrons. Cover €12-21, includes 1 or 2 drinks depending on the night. Open daily 10pm-6am, later on weekends.

Made in Brasil, Pg. Marítim, 27. Takes you right to Río with Brazilian music and a tropical decor. Try their specialty drink, the *caipirinha* (€5.50), a mix of sugar, lime, and the Brazilian liqueur *cachaça,* all blended into an icy slush. Open daily 8:30pm-4am.

Moon and **Caramelos,** both along the Pg. Marítim, offer larger venues than the *bares-musicales* and cheaper covers than the big discos. Moon cover €6, includes 1 drink; Caramelos cover €10, includes 2 drinks. Both open daily 10pm-6am.

WESTERN MALLORCA

Ten minutes beyond the urban lifestyle and high-rises of Palma, the road enters a ravine where the island's first cave-dwellers lived and, above, the land rises in tight, narrow curves amid dramatic green hillsides. This is western Mallorca, one of the most beautiful landscapes in the Mediterranean.

VALLDEMOSSA

TIB buses to Valldemossa leave Palma from the bus station (30min.; M-F 5 per day 7:30am-7:30pm, Sa 3 per day 8am-7:30pm, Su 3 per day 8-6:30pm; €1.80).

Valldemossa is a tiny web of antique, shaded streets dwarfed by the rising slopes of the Sierra de Tramontana. Little in this peaceful village hints at the passion that scandalized townsfolk during the winter of 1838, when Frédéric Chopin and George Sand stayed in the 14th-century monastery **Cartoixa Reial.** The Chopin memorabilia now housed in the monastery includes the *Playel* piano that he carried up the mountain. A ticket (€8) includes access to the **Museu Municipal,** which has a brief history of the city, an 18th-century Cartusian pharmacy, and a contemporary art room with works by Miró and Picasso. The neighboring **Palau del Rei Sancho** was commissioned by King Jaime II in 1309 for his asthmatic son, and is a former retreat of Nicaraguan poet Rubén Darío, who wrote some of his best work here. An open courtyard with gnarled trees and arched doorways is host to folk dances (M and Th 11am-1:30pm), while the music room hosts piano recitals. (☎971 61 21 06. Open Su year-round 10am-1pm; June-Sept. M-Sa 9:30am-6:30pm; Nov.-Jan. M-Sa 9:30am-4pm; Feb. 9:30am-4:30pm; Mar.-May and Oct. M-Sa 9:30am-5:30pm. Recitals hourly on the half-hour in summer. Church attire.) Stop by the **Centro Cultural Costa Nord,** Av. Palma, 6, established by Michael Douglas in an effort to raise awareness about environmental issues. (☎971 61 24 25; www.costanord.com. Open daily 9am-5pm.)

DEIÀ

Buses heading for Port Sóller from Palma stop in Deià after Valldemossa (45min.; M-F 5 per day 7:30am-7:30pm, Sa 3 per day 8am-7:30pm, Su 3 per day 8am-6:30pm; €2.50).

Once a secluded artists' colony, the hillside-village and peaceful cove of Deià now attracts a ritzy, upscale sect of Europe's most fashionable *nouveau riche*. To get to the small, rocky beach, **Cala Deià,** by car, continue along the highway until the second bus stop, then take a left. On the top of the hill behind the church, the flowery **Cementari Municipal** offers a unique insight into this small town as well as one of the best hillside views. English poet Robert Graves, the community's favorite self-exiled expat, is buried there among a few other early 20th-century artists. Graves' hilltop home was recently converted into a **museum,** preserved exactly as it was when the illustrious poet lived there until his death in 1985.

One of the only places to stay is the **Hostal Villa Verde ❹,** on C. Ramón Llull, 19, a hilltop retreat with spectacular rooms and views. Breakfast is served on a flower-filled patio. (☎971 63 90 37. Singles €48; doubles €65, with terrace €83. MC/V.) Expensive restaurants dot the lower town, but the best bet for food is beach-side at **Can Lluc ❷.** (Tapas €3.50-6.50. Entrees €8-14. Open 10:30am-7pm for drinks and snacks. Kitchen open noon-5pm.) End your day on the terrace at **Café Sa Fora ❶,** C.

Archiduque Luis Salvador, 5, right on the main road. (Beer €1.50-2. Mixed drinks €5. Tapas €4. Live Music Sa. Open Mar.-Nov. daily 10am-3am. Cash only.)

SÓLLER

The old-fashioned Palma-Sóller train, run by Ferrocarril de Sóller, Pl. d'Espanya, is a high-light. The ride is longer than the bus (about 70min.) but views of undeveloped lands and orchards are worth it. (☎971 63 01 30, Palma 971 75 20 51; www.trendesoller.com. 7 per day 8am-7:30pm; €9, round-trip €14.)

Located in a fertile valley, every plot of land in Sóller is lined with either citrus groves or sunburnt tourists. The town is all class—quiet streets are lined with tall trees, gourmet delicatessens, and fruit stands rather than typical postcard shops. Restaurants and shops fill the plaza, but quieter streets offer bakeries featuring the *coca mallorquina*, a pizza-like snack (about €1.80). A small central **market** is just beside the tram tracks in Pl. Mercat. Visitors who stay in town or in neighboring farmhouses capitalize on hiking and walking opportunities to **Fornalux, L'Ofre Cuber Els Cornadors,** and the **Port de Soller.** From Sóller it's a 30min. walk or a short ride on the Nord Balear bus (€1.10) or trolley (10min., 1-2 per hr. 7am-8:30pm, €3) to the port, a fantastic turquoise cove book-ended by two pebbly beaches. **Platja D'En Repic,** the beach opposite the port, offers better views and fewer people. The area's famous **coves** are best explored by boat. The best beach meals are at **Marley's ❷,** C. d'es Cingle 1 (at the beginning of Pl. d'en Repic), which offers delicious seafood and cocktails. (☎971 638 186. ½kg shrimp €10. Open daily 10am-10pm.) The **tourist office,** C. Canonge Oliver, 10, has a list of accommodations, car rental agencies, and boat tour companies. (☎971 63 30 42. Open Mar.-Oct. M-F 9:15am-1pm and 2:45-5pm.) The bus station is being remodeled; the temporary stop to return to Palma is on the highway, a 10min. walk from Pl. de la Constitucio.

NORTHERN MALLORCA

The northern gulfs of Mallorca contain droves of older, package-tour crowds in some areas and quieter, family-friendly coves in others. The drive to these sunny beachside towns may be stunning, but can lead to areas are swamped with tourists. If you don't mind a bit of competition for sun spots, don't miss this region—these jagged coves and long beaches are among the most beautiful on the island.

PORT POLLENÇA

Transunion buses connect Palma and Pollença (1hr.; M-F 7 per day 8:30am-9pm, Sa-Su 5 per day 10am-8:30pm; €5.40). Bus/Train combo: take train to Inca and catch a bus from Inca to Port Pollença (1hr.; 7 trains per day M-F 7:20am-6:25pm, 7 buses per day M-F 8:05am-7:10pm; €5.10). Buses stop along the strip and at the end of Pg. Saralegui.

Port Pollença's tranquil coastline, which features a thin man-made beach along a crescent-shaped bay, lures a calm, classy crowd of northern Europeans. The area hosts a **music festival** in July and August, with concerts every Wednesday and Saturday night. A complete schedule of events and list of ticket vendors is available at the tourist office (tickets €15-45). Summer also brings plenty of free events such as the much anticipated **Sons de Nit,** free concerts held either near the water or in the central square. Right next to the *Ayuntamiento,* **Hostal Borrás ❸,** Pl. Miquel Capllonch, 14, offers huge rooms with private bath and old red leather chairs. (☎971 866 647. Open July-Aug. Singles €30; doubles €40, doubles with balcony €50. Cash only.) The **tourist office,** C. Saralegui, is next to the bus station, a block from the port, and has lists of all the restaurants and accommodations in town. (☎971 86 54 67. Open M-F 8am-8pm, Sa 10am-5pm, Su 10am-1pm.) **Rent March,** C. Joan XXIII, 89, rents bikes and mopeds. (☎971 86 47 84. Bikes €9-12 per day; mopeds €35-130 per day. Open Mar.-Nov. M-Sa 9am-1pm and 4-8pm, Su 9am-12:30pm.) The **police** are reachable at ☎971 86 62 67.

CAP DE FORMENTOR

Buses stop 6km away from the end of Cap de Formentor. Autocares Mallorca (TIB), sends one bus from Palma (1hr.; 10:15am, return 3:30pm; €5.60). Autocares Mallorca (☎971 54 56 96) leaves Port Pollença (4 per day 10am-4:30pm, €1.30). A boat (☎971 86 40 14) goes to Platja Formentor from Pollença's Estació Marítima (30min.; hourly 10am-3pm, no boat 2pm; returns hourly 11:30am-6pm, no boat 2:30, 4:30, or 5:30pm; round-trip €8.30).

A trek to Cap de Formentor, 15km northeast of Port Pollença, leads to dramatic seaside cliffs, a lighthouse, and a pristine ocean view—the road is peppered with landings perfect for photo-ops, and all are crowded with cars. Eleven kilometers before the lighthouse, the road drops to **Platja Formentor,** where a canopy of ever-greens seems to sink into the shore's pebbly beach. If you have your own transportation, head to the lighthouse at the top of the steep, winding hill and make a quick stop at the bottom for two of the most beautiful coves in Mallorca. On the left is the small dirt parking lot for **Cala Figuera,** accesible via a practically verti-cal unmarked dirt path. Across the road to your right is a small wooden sign pointing in the direction of ▨**Cala Murta,** perhaps the most secluded cove on the island. From the road, enter through a small wooden gate on your right, then bear left on the dirt path. After a 25min. (2km) walk, you will stumble upon the cove's tiny pebbly beach and crystal-clear turquoise water.

ALCÚDIA AND PORT D'ALCÚDIA

Buses (☎971 54 56 96) run to Alcúdia (€4.10) and Port d'Alcúdia (€4.35) from the bus sta-tion in Palma (1hr.; M-Sa 16 per day 8am-9pm, Su 5 per day 9:30am-9pm). The bus to Port Pollença and Cap de Formentor leaves from the corner of C. del Coral and Pg. Marítim. Munic-ipal buses run between the port and the town every 15min.

Alcúdia and its nearby port are far from undiscovered, but within the city's forti-fied walls awaits an ancient intimacy lacking in Alcúdia's southern sister, Palma. The beach is the main attraction here, but the old town has 14th-century ram-parts, **Roman ruins** dating from 2 BC, and **Parc de s'Albufera,** within walking dis-tance of the beach, is filled with marshes, flowers, and dunes. The interior of the park is only accessible by bike or on foot and the reception is a 1km hike inland. (Open daily in summer 9am-6pm; in winter 9am-5pm. Free.) If you have a car, take the road toward **Artà** and then **Capdepera** from town. About 20km from Port d'Alcúdia, you will see signs leading to **Cala Torta** along a dirt road. If you hike from this beach over the cliffs to the west, you come to **Cala Mitjana,** a cove with crashing waves and tide pools. (Beach chairs and umbrellas €2.) Past Cala Mit-jana is **Es Matzoc,** a white-sand beach that is somewhat tourist-free. Summer brings music, dance, and culture to Alcúdia during the famed **Fiestas de Alcúdia,** celebrating the Día de San Jaime (July 25), in honor of their patron saint.

The recently renovated **Hostal Calma ❸,** C. de Teodoro Canet, 25, offers rooms with A/C, TV, and private bath. There is also a communal kitchen. (☎971 54 84 85; www.hostalcalma.com. Breakfast €4. July-Aug. Singles €30; doubles €48; triples €59. Apr.-June and Oct.-Mar. €22/40/53. Prices decrease with longer stays. MC/V.) **Oceano ❶,** C. dels Mariners, 18B, has fresh sandwiches and salads (€4-5.50) served in a breezy marine setting. (☎971 54 74 14. Open all day. Cash only.) Head to **Supermercats Aprop,** C. dels Mariners, 14, for groceries. (Open M-Sa 9am-9pm.)

There are three **tourist offices,** two at the port, one in town. One is on Pg. Marítim in a plaza at the end of the beach, on the left facing the water. (☎971 54 72 57; open in summer M-Sa 9:30am-8:30pm). **Police** can be reached at ☎971 54 50 66.

SOUTHEASTERN MALLORCA

Signs along the highway of Mallorca's southeast coast might as well read "Welcome Tourist Hordes." Still, the breathtaking scenery, beautiful beaches, and intriguing caves remain relatively unspoiled and well-maintained.

COVES DEL DRAC. Despite its classification as a bona fide tourist attraction, the ▧**Coves del Drac** (Dragon's Caves), just south of Porto Cristo, are among the island's most dramatic natural wonders. The long, dimly lit walkway is dwarfed by scores of striking stalactites and stalagmites reflected in crystal-clear saltwater pools. The tour descends into Lake Martel, one of the largest underground lakes in the world. On the edge of the vast lake, tourists watch in befuddled amazement as classical musicians play soft sultry music from beautifully illuminated rowboats that weave around the lake in a strange nautical dance. Audience members are invited to take boat rides across the lake after the concert. The tour and concert last about an hour and are worth the trip and price. A 10min. walk leads to the turquoise shores of **Porto Cristo,** a calm crescent-shaped bay lined with cafes and shops. (*A bus to the caves runs from the bus station in Palma; 1hr.; M-Sa 4 per day 10am-1:30pm, Su 10am; €7.20. If you're driving, head toward Manacor from Palma and then toward Porto Cristo. Follow the signs through town. Tours daily hourly 10am-5pm. Line up early. €9.50; tickets purchased for entrance at a specific hour are good for 75min.*)

PLATJA DES TRENC. West of Cap de ses Salines and east of Cap Blanc sprawls one of Mallorca's best and longest beaches, Platja des Trenc. In most cases, a 1-2km walk is usually enough to put plenty of sand between you and the thickest crowds; nude bathers often take advantage of the seclusion. (*In summer, buses run to Platja des Trenc from the bus station in Palma; M-Sa 1 per day to ses Covetes 10:30am, Su 10am; €5.50. Driving from Palma, the road to the beaches is off the highway between Llucmajor and Campos. The sign is small, so watch for it. Parking €5.*)

MENORCA

Menorca's fantastic beaches, rustic landscapes, and picturesque towns draw sun-worshippers, photographers, and ecologists alike. When UNESCO declared the island a biosphere reserve in 1993, the government took important strides to emphasize preservation of Menorca's natural harbors, pristine beaches, rocky northern coast, and network of farmlands. Menorca's main cities, Mahón and Ciutadella, located at the east and west ends of the island respectively, serve as gateways to the real attractions: crystal-clear aquamarine water that laps stretches of velvety sand and hidden rocky coves (see **Beaches,** p. 361).

MAHÓN (MAÓ)   ☎971

Mahón (pop. 22,000) exudes authentic energy remarkably unspoiled by its spot on the tourist-heavy island itinerary. Many use Mahón as a launching pad to nearby beaches (via scooters or public buses) but return to candle-lit restaurants in the evening to watch a red sun dip behind the harbour's end.

⌐ TRANSPORTATION

Flights: Airport (☎971 15 70 00), 4.5km out of town. The **Aerobús** (operated by **Torres** ☎902 07 50 66; www.e-torres.net) runs in a loop between the airport, the Pl. de s'Esplanada, and the Port (every 30min., 5:55am-11:15pm, €1.50). **Airport Taxis** are €11 to town. **Iberia/Aviaco** (☎971 36 90 15); **Air Europa** (☎971 15 70

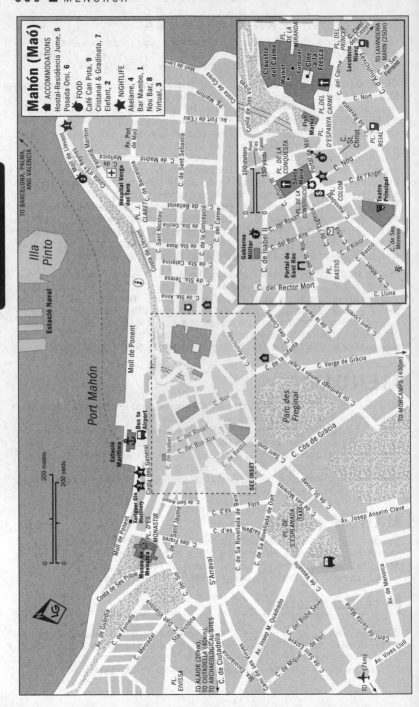

Mahón (Maó)

ACCOMMODATIONS
Hostal-Residència Jume, 5
Posada Orsi, 6

FOOD
Café Can Pota, 9
Cristanal & Gradinata, 7

NIGHTLIFE
Akelarre, 4
Bar Mambo, 1
Elefant, 2
Nou Bar, 8
Virtual, 3

31); **SpanAir** (☎971 15 70 98). Advance booking is essential in summer. See **By Plane**, p. 343, and **Inter-Island Transport**, p. 344.

Buses: The bus station is at the far end of Pl. de s'Esplanada, up C. Vasallo and on the left. The station is the hub for buses to and from Mahón, yet has no ticket or information booths. Check the tourist office or newspapers *Menorca Diario Insular* and *Menorca* for schedules (infomenorcamao@cime.es). **Transportes Menorca (TMSA; ☎**971 35 40 07; www.transportesmenorca.net) to: **Ciutadella** via **Es Mercadal** and **Ferreries** (1hr.; M-F hourly 6:45am-11:15pm, Sa 8 per day 8am-9:30pm, Su 6 per day 8am-7pm; €5); **Es Castell** (20min.; every 30min. M-Sa 7:20am-8:45pm, Su 9:15am-1:45pm and 3:45-8:45pm; €2); **Platja Punta Prima** (20min.; M-Sa 9 per day 8:30am-7:30pm, Su 8 per day 9:30am-7:30pm; €1.30); **Son Bou** (30min., 8 per day 8:30am-7pm, €1.50). **Autobuses Fornells Roca Triay** (☎686 93 92 46; www.autosfornells.com) go to: **Arenal d'en Castell** (30min.; M-Sa 5 per day 9:30am-7pm, Su 11am and 6pm; €1.90); **Fornells** (40min., 2 per day 8:40am and 4pm, €2.65); **Son Parc** (30min., 2-4 per day 10:45am-7pm, €2.05). Buy tickets on board.

Ferries: Trasmediterránea, Moll de Ponent (☎971 36 60 50 or 902 45 46 45; www.trasmediterranea.es; ticket booth open M-F 7am-2pm and 5-8pm, Sa 7am-noon, Su 7-10am and 2:30-5:30pm) sends ferries daily to **Barcelona** and weekly (Su) to **Palma** and **Valencia. Balearia** (☎902 16 01 80; www.balearia.com; ticket booth open M-F 8am-1pm and 5-7pm, Sa-Su 8-9:30am) sends ferries to **Alcúdia, Barcelona,** and **Mallorca.** For more info, see **By Boat,** p. 344, and **Inter-Island Transport,** p. 344.

Taxis: Main stand at Pl. de s'Esplanada (☎971 36 71 11), or **Radio Taxi** (☎971 36 71 11). To: **airport** (€11); **Cala Mesquida** (€15); **Cala'n Porter** (€17); **Es Castell** (€10).

Car Rental: ▨ Morcamps, C. Gobernador Ramírez, 29 (☎971 36 95 94). Fully loaded cars (4 doors, A/C, radio, and CD player), for as little as €25 per day. Tourist office provides a comprehensive list of all car rental agencies in the city.

Scooter Rental: M. Ponent, near the ferry dock. (☎971 36 56 66). 3 days €75. Open M-F 9am-1:30pm and 5-8pm, Sa-Su 9am-1:30pm and 6:30-8pm.

▣ ? ORIENTATION AND PRACTICAL INFORMATION

Plaça de s'Esplanada, a square once used as a parade ground and now lined with chic shops, is the city's transportation hub. **Calle de Ses Moreres** connects the plaza to the five downward-sloping blocks, pedestrian streets at the heart of the old city that lead to the port. Areas to the right of **Pl. Princep** are quieter and more residential. Various serpentine paths lead down to the port, but the central conduit is a set of steps that wind from the **Placa Espanya** and end near the **ferry station** and tourist office. To the right of the port is the **Moll de Llevant,** and to the left is **Moll de Ponent.**

Tourist Office: Moll de Levant, 2, in the Port Authorities Building (☎971 35 59 52; open M-F 8am-1:30pm and 5-8:30pm, Sa 8am-1pm). **Branch** by the bus station (same hours) and at the airport (☎971 15 71 15; open daily 8am-10pm).

Currency Exchange: Banks with 24hr. **ATMs** line C. Hannóver and C. Nou, and dot all the pedestrian streets.

Laundromat: Lavandería Marin, Cami des Castell, 64 (☎971 36 23 79). Wash and dry €11.50 for up to 5kg. Open M-F 9am-1pm and 4-7:30pm.

Police: Municipal, Pl. de la Constitució (☎971 37 37 12) and Pl. de la Miranda.

24hr. Pharmacy: Check the list outside any pharmacy for the *farmàcia de guardia* (all-night pharmacy), which changes every night. Close to Pl. de s'Esplanada is **Landino Pons,** C. Ses Moreres (☎971 36 05 94).

Medical Services: Hospital Verge del Toro, C. Barcelona, 3 (☎971 15 77 00). English spoken. Open 24hr. for emergencies.

Internet Access: V.I.C. Menorca, C. Padronet, 2 (☎971 35 04 48). €0.60 first 12min., €3 per hour. Open daily 10am-midnight. **Locutorio Niang,** C. Cami des Castell 151. €3 per hour. Open daily 11am-2pm and 5-11pm.

Post Office: C. del Bon Aire, 11-13 (€971 36 66 29), at C. de l'Església. Open M-F 8:30am-8:30pm, Sa 9:30am-2pm. **Postal Code:** 07700.

ACCOMMODATIONS

It's easier to find a room in Menorca than on the other islands, but it's still a good idea to call ahead, especially in July and August. █Posada Orsi ❷, C. de la Infanta, 19, is centrally located and has colorful rooms. The residence has a TV room, sitting room, and lovely staff. Fans are available upon request. (☎971 36 47 51. Breakfast €2-4. Singles €20-25; doubles €30-40, with shower €40-50. Cash only.) **Hostal-Residència Jume ❸,** C. de la Concepció, 6, is meters from **Pl. de la Miranda** and **Pl. Princep.** It offers spacious, white-walled rooms with minimal decor and large beds, all with bathrooms. (☎971 36 32 66. July 21-Sept. 10 singles €29.50; doubles €51, extra bed €26.60. Sept. 22-July 20 €25.30/46.60/extra bed €23.50. MC/V.)

FOOD

Cafes and bars spilling into Pl. de la Constitución, Pl. de Reial, and Pl. de s'Esplanada serve *platos combinados* (€2.70-5.10) to throngs of hungry customers during the hot midday hours. Regional specialties include *sobrassada* (a soft sausage and bacon spread) and *camot* (a dark sausage spread made with blood and flavored with fennel). *Mahonesa* (mayonnaise), which was invented in Mahón, and *queso mahon* (strong and savory cheese) are two gastronomic treasures of the island, steeped in pride and tradition. There is a produce **market** in the **Claustre del Carme,** a neoclassical 18th-century building affixed to a church that once housed the town's prison and justice courts. (Open M-Sa 9am-2pm.) Groceries are sold below the produce market at **Eurospar.** (☎971 36 93 80. Open M-Sa 9am-9pm.) █Elefant ❷, Moll de Llevant, 106, a bohemian nook with tiny outdoor tables and ideal sunset views, serves deliciously creative tapas to satisfy any craving. Affordable lunches are €7.50 and tapas run €4.50-5. (☎676 89 24 23. Open M and W-Su noon-4pm and 7pm-midnight. Cash only.) █Cristanal & Gradinata ❶, C. Isabel 11, is an elegantly secluded wine-and-tapas bar with 20s jazz tunes, gleaming wooden floors, warm lighting, and several outdoor tables. (☎971 36 33 16. Open daily 6-11pm.) **Café Can Pota ❶,** Portal de Mar, 11, is an upscale cafe with comfy sitting areas that has been serving delicious coffee, cheap breakfasts, and *bocadillos* (€1.50-3) since 1881. (☎971 36 23 63. Open M-Sa 8am-midnight. MC/V.)

SIGHTS

Though the most awe-inspiring sights in Menorca are outside of its cities, Mahón does have a few attractions. The **Pont de Sant Roc,** up C. Sant Roc from Pl. de la Constitución, straddles the streets of Mahón. The port was heavily damaged after the pirate Barbarossa sacked the city in 1535, and is the last fragment of the medieval wall built to defend the city. The **Església de Santa María La Major,** Pl. de la Constitución, was erected in 1772. The interior trembles with the sound of the 3006 pipes of its über-organ. (Organ concerts daily 11:30am. Open daily 8am-1pm and 6-8:30pm.) The neighboring **Ayuntamiento,** which has stood in some form since the 17th century, exhibits a French baroque interior (Open daily 8am-2pm.) **Museu de Menorca,** Av. Dr. Guàrdia, an old Baroque Franciscan monastery, houses a permanent collection of Menorcan artwork and archaeological relics. (☎971 35 09 55. Open in summer Tu-Sa 9:30am-2pm and 6-8:30pm, Su 9:30am-2pm; in winter M-F 9:30am-2pm, Sa-Su 10am-2pm. €2.40, students €1.20, children under 12 free.) The **Pl. del Carme**, adjoining the **Pl. Espanya**, houses the **Claustre del Carme** (today the public market), **Carme Church,** and **Fish Market.** You can enjoy free liquor samples at the **Xoriguer Gin Distillery,** Moll de Ponent, 93, at the port. Through glass windows at the back of the store, visitors can watch gin bubble and froth in copper vats. (☎971 36 21 97. Open M-F 10am-7pm, Sa 10am-1pm. Free.)

Access to the island's numerous **archaeological sites,** some dating back to 3000 BC, is made simple by Menorca's small size and Mahón's efficient bus system. Highlights feature prehistoric caves, tombs, settlements, and paleochristian basilicas—most are accessible only by car or scooter. See the tourist office for information on a self-guided driving tour. The most famous of the monuments is **Torre d'en Galmes,** off the road to Platges de Son Bou from Alaior. The second largest settlement on Menorca, portions date between 1300 and 1500 BC. Atop a hill overlooking the island's interior are three *talayots* (large watchtowers) and a sanctuary that served as both a religious and commercial center for Menorca's megalithic denizens. **Fort Marlborough,** at the mouth of the harbour by Es Castell, is a remnant of 18th-century British occupation and was one of three fortifications used to protect the city. Across the harbour is **La Mola Fortalessa Isabel II,** a second example of British military architecture of the 19th century.

🔲 🌿 NIGHTLIFE AND FESTIVALS

Mahón's nightlife continues the gentle daytime pace of the city. A string of hip bars and clubs line the **Costa d'els General,** a small street that slopes upwards from the start of Moll de Ponent. One of the more fashionable places on the strip is 🔲**Akelarre,** Moll de Ponent, 41-43, a cavernous bar and dance floor beneath stone archways and bronze art. (☎971 36 85 20; www.akelarrejazz.com. Beer €3-5. Mixed drinks €5-6. Open daily June-Oct. 8am-5am; Nov.-May 7pm-3am.) A few doors down is **Virtual,** Moll de Ponent, 46, where standing crowds are illuminated by two small floors of neon lights, lasers, and rows of TV screens. (Mixed drinks €3-7. Open in summer M-Th and Su 7pm-4am; F-Sa midnight-4am.) At the opposite end of the port, **Bar Mambo,** Moll Levante 209, is a sophisticated wine bar with an outdoor terrace lit by giant candles and enlivened by New Age music. (☎971 35 67 82.) Away from the port, **Nou Bar,** C. Nou, 1, 2nd fl., overlooks Pl. de la Constitución and serves drinks (€4-6) and beer (€2.50) to a calm crowd of older locals. Wicker chairs outside are popular seats for late-afternoon drinks or *cafe con leche.* (☎971 36 55 00. Open daily 7:30pm-3:30am.)

Film-lovers should check out the weekly screening (all films dubbed in Spanish) at **cine a la fresca** in the open-air center of Claustre del Carme (M-W and Sa 10pm, Th 10:30pm). Look for the posters advertising the current selection or ask at the tourist office for a copy of the schedule. (Enter from Pl. de la Miranda. €6.) From May to September, merchants sell shoes, clothing, and bizarre trinkets in *mercadillos* located in the Pl. de s'Esplanada on Tuesday and Saturday. On July 16, Maó's **Verge del Carme** celebration brings a colorfully-trimmed armada into the harbor and an equestrian procession into the streets. The **Festival de Música de Maó** in July and August showcases Església Santa María's Swiss organ and brings renowned classical musicians to the city's **Teatro Principal,** Costa d'en Deià, 40, built in 1829. Check the tourist office or the box office of the theater for schedules and prices. (Box office ☎971 35 57 76; www.teatremao.org. Open Tu-Sa 11:30am-1:30pm, Th-F also open 6:30-8:30pm, and 1hr. before performances.)

CIUTADELLA (CIUDADELA) ☎971

Ciutadella's (pop. 21,000) narrow, cobblestoned paths weave between neighborhoods nearly undisturbed by tourists, while only blocks away, restaurants, shops, and postcard vendors compete for attention in the crowded plazas. Below, a narrow, glassy harbour reflects the tourist traffic of private boats and a strip of bars carved into rough, russet rock. There's a seductive charm in the city's ancient streets, broad plazas, and hectic port. The rugged beauty of the surrounding countryside and nearby beaches provides an easy escape from city heat.

▐ TRANSPORTATION

Bus information: Estación Mahón (☎971 36 04 75). **Transportes Menorca** (TMSA) runs from Pl. dels Pins (☎971 38 03 93), to **Mahón** (1hr.; hourly M-F 6:40am-11:40pm, Sa 8am-9:30pm, Su 8am-7pm; €4.75). **Autocares Torres** (☎971 38 64 61) offers daily service from the ticket booth in Pl. de los Pinos to surrounding beaches: **Cala Blanca** and **Santandria** (15min.; 1-2 per hour M-Sa 7am-12:15am, Su 7am-8:55pm; €2); **Cala Blanes, Los Delfines,** and **Cala Forcat** (10-20min.; 1-2 per hour M-Sa 7:15am-11:30pm, Su 8:40am-9:45pm; €2); **Sa Caleta** and **Cala En Bosc** (25-30min.; 1-3 per hour M-Sa 7am-12:15am, Su 7am-10:30pm; €2); **Cala Morell** (15min.; 3 per day 8:45, 11am, 6:30pm; €2).

Ferries: Balearia (☎902 16 01 80; www.balearia.com) runs between Ciutadella and **Alcúdia, Mallorca** (1hr.; Tu-Th 5 per day 8am-9:50pm; M, F, Su 8am, 9:50pm; Sa 8am, 9:45pm; €69). **Cape Balear** (☎902 10 04 44) links Ciutadella to **Cala Ratjada, Menorca** (55min., May-Oct. 4-5 per day 7:30am-7:30pm, €50-60).

Taxis: (☎971 38 28 96). Pl. de s'Explanada is a prime hailing spot.

Car Rental: Europcar, Av. de Jaume I, 59 (☎971 38 29 98). 21+. From €39 per day and €210 per week. Open daily 9am-8pm. The tourist office provides an extensive list of all rental car agencies in the city.

✈ ▐ ORIENTATION AND PRACTICAL INFORMATION

The **bus stop** and **tourist office** are at the head of Pl. dels Pins (also called Pl. de s'Explanada), which leads directly into the city's harbor-side nucleus, **Pl. d'es Born.** The **port** and its accompanying street, C. Marina, lie below the rest of the city and are reached via the stone steps just off the corner of Pl. d'es Born. The *casco viejo* begins in line with the harbor's end and winds several blocks away from the port.

The **tourist office,** at Pl. de la Catedral, 5, provides maps and info on archaeological sights. (☎971 38 26 93; www.ciutadella.org. English spoken. Open M-F 9am-1pm and 5-7pm, Sa 9am-1pm.) There is a **branch** at the port. (☎971 48 09 35. Open Tu-Sa 8am-8:30pm, Su 8am-1pm.) **BBVA,** at Pl. d'es Born, 14, has **currency exchange.** (☎902 22 44 66. Open M-F 8:30am-2:15pm; Oct.-Mar. also open Sa 8:30am-1pm). Other banks with 24hr. **ATMs** can be found around the Pl. de s'Explanada and Pl. d'es Born. Other services include: **police** (☎971 38 07 87), in Pl. d'es Born; **Clínica Menorca** (☎971 48 05 05; open 24hr.), C. Canonge Moll; **Internet** access at **C@fe Acceso Directo,** Pl. de s'Explanada, 37 (☎971 38 42 15; www.elcafenet.net. €1 per 20min., €6 per 4hr; also offers tapas and sandwiches; open M-Sa 9am-11pm); and the **post office,** Pl. d'es Born (☎971 38 00 81; open May-Oct. M-F 8:30am-8:30pm, Sa 9:30am-1pm). **Postal Code:** 07760.

▐ ◖ ACCOMMODATIONS AND FOOD

Hostels here are few and far between during peak season (June 15-early Sept.). Always reserve ahead in the summer. Relax in the quiet floral courtyard of **Hostal**

Residència Oasis ❷, C. Sant Isidre, 33. From Pl. de s'Explanada, take Av. del Capità Negrito, take the third left onto Av. Alcantara, and turn right onto C. Sant Isidre. (☎971 38 21 97. Breakfast included. Open June-Oct. Doubles with bath €50; doubles for single use €25; triples €75. Cash only.) **Hostal Sa Prensa ❷**, Pl. de Madrid, is by the harbor's mouth and mandates more of a trek into town, but offers simple and spacious rooms close to a phenomenal stretch of coastline. (☎971 38 26 98; www.saprensa.com. Internet €2 per 30min. Doubles €48, with terrace €55).

There's a **market** (open M-F 9am-2pm) on Pl. de la Libertat, and a **Supermarket Super Avui** in C. Sant Onofre, 12. (☎971 38 27 28. Open M-Sa 8am-2pm and 5-9pm.) For traditional island cuisine in a hidden nook of the old town, descend into the dungeon-esque **La Guitarra ❸**, C. Nuestra Sra. dels Dolors, 1. Sample the *sopa mallorquina* (a traditional meat and veggie stew), or the *caldereta de langosta* (lobster stew). (*Menú* €15. Entrees €6.60-24. Open June-Sept. M-Sa 12:30-5:30pm and 7:15-10:15pm. MC/V.) **Es Molí ❶**, C. de Maó, 1, is a local bar inside a giant windmill across from the Pl. de ses Palmeres—it's definitely worth the hike. (☎971 38 00 00. Open M-Th and Su 6am-1:30am, F-Sa 6am-3am. Cash only.)

🇬 🎵 SIGHTS AND ENTERTAINMENT

Pl.des Born and the *casco viejo's* churches offer an exemplary array of Spanish architecture and stonework. Past the mouth of the port and to the left stands the hexagonal **Castel San Nicolau**, a watchtower with channels burrowed into the stone. (Open daily 10am-1pm and 5-9pm. €1.50.) Dating from the Bronze Age, the ancient settlement of ▓**Naveta des Tudons** (near the 40km marker from Maó) was built in 1500 BC, making it one of the oldest pre-talayotic structures in Europe. A mere 4km from the city, these perfectly preserved ruins of communal tombs contain the remains of over 100 people. The archaeological sites of **Torre Trencada** and **Torrellafuda** display the remains of prehistoric settlements. Both protect Stonehenge-like formations that have stood for over 3000 years. If you don't have a rental car, consider **hiking** (about 8km, 3hr.) along C. Vell de Maó, the old road to Maó, or **biking** along the highway (at least 1hr. one-way). The descriptive Archaeological Guide to Menorca is available at the tourist office.

Nightlife in Ciutadella is spirited but tame, focused around the harbor. Funky bars cluster near the port's end and several discotecas around the parking lot attract small crowds. Most enjoy the free live music near the port almost every night and romantic candlelit dinners along the water. From the first week in July to the start of September, Ciutadella hosts the **Festival de Música d'Estiu**, featuring some of the world's top classical musicians. Tickets (€10-24) are sold at the box office. Concerts take place in the cloisters of the seminary. (☎971 38 17 54. Box office open daily 9:30am-1:30pm and 5-8pm.)

BEACHES

Even the most enticing postcards of Menorca's satin sands and turquoise waters cannot do its beaches justice. The island has over 80 beaches, each as breathtaking and varied as the island's rolling terrain. Most are accessible by bus from Maó and Ciutadella (situated around harbors, not beaches), though the island's easygoing pace often muddles bus schedules. With beauty comes popularity; in addition to crowds of tourists, many of the most beautiful beaches are overrun by resort hotels, hokey bars, restaurants, and postcard shops. Other beaches are located in small coves and are naturally more secluded; these are best explored with a rental car or ▓**scooter** and the *Let's Go to the Beach* map (not affiliated with *Let's Go* guides) available at any tourist office. Be careful when driving at night. You may discover your own hidden treasure by choosing at random from the map or off the highway. Nearly all beaches are clothing-optional, providing a relaxed setting to work on a full-body tan.

NORTH SHORE BEACHES

PLATGES D'ALGAIARENS. This stretch east of **Cala Morell** is home to some of the best beaches on the island, including **Cala en Carabó, Penyal de l'Anticrist, Sa Falconera,** and **Cala Pilar Ets Alocs,** all in a lush valley accessible via a path through the woods and over the rocks. Though not as secluded as they used to be, these beaches allow swimmers and sunbathers to forget the outside world for a few hours. The huge waves are great for surfers but not for waders. *(Beaches only accessible by car, moped, or a long bike ride from Ciutadella. Parking €5, mopeds €2. A taxi from Ciutadella costs €16, but there are no pay phones, and cell phones may lose service.)*

ALBUFERA ES GRAU. A diverse natural reserve, Albufera Es Grau allows secluded exploration of the island's lagoons, pine woods, and farmland, as well as flora and fauna. Recreational activities include biking or hiking to the coves across the bay. The best swimming areas are across from the main lagoon and uphill from town. *(☎ 971 35 63 02. Autocares Fornells leave from Maó. 20min.; M-Sa 3 per day 10:15am-6pm, Su 5 per day 10am-6pm; Free. A taxi from Maó is €17.)*

ARENAL D'EN CASTELL. This deep, yawning cove is one of the north shore's most beautiful and accessible—predictably, it entices hordes of daytrippers from Mahón and vacationing families who fill the upscale resorts and cheesy bars dotting the steep slope above the beach. A tourist train, "Arenal Na Macaret Express" (€4), makes the short trip from the bus stop in Arenal across a narrow strip of land to **Macaret,** a tiny fishing village with an even tinier beach. *(Autocares Fornells leaves from Maó. 30min.; M-Sa 5 per day 10:30am-7pm, Su 11am and 6pm; €1.85.)*

FORNELLS. This plain, white-washed fishing village, known primarily for its lobster farms (and lobster dinners), attracts a quiet crowd of adventurous tourists. Windsurfers and kayakers career about Fornells's shallow port, and a walk along the town's hushed boardwalk leads to a rocky oasis with unspoiled vistas of the Torre de Fornells, a massive British watchtower built in 1801. True beach gurus make excursions to the deserted golden sands of **Cala Tirant,** only a few kilometers to the west on a dusty unpaved road that's difficult to trek on foot. *(Autobuses Fornells leaves from Maó to Fornells. 30min.; M-Sa 5 per day 10:30am-7pm, Su 11am and 6pm; €2.65. Buses directly to Cala Tirant leave Maó M-Sa 4 per day 10:45am-7pm; €2.85.)*

SOUTH SHORE BEACHES

CALA MITJANA. Thirty minutes by car or moped from Maó, this small beach overlooks a dramatic cove bordered by limestone cliffs that plunge into the turquoise sea. Climb the staircase on your right upon entering the cove and head down the dirt path for about 5min. to reach **Cala Mitjaneta,** a smaller cove with a tiny beach and even more dramatic views. While some visitors wade into the water here, others prove their bravery (or recklessness) by diving from the rocks. *(On the main highway from Maó to Ciutadella, head toward Ferreries, and then take the road to Santa Galdana. Directly on the left before reaching the roundabout above the town is the dirt road that leads to Cala Mitjana. Park in the small dirt lot and continue on foot.)*

CALA BINIBECA. The trek here is well worth the hassle—Cala Binibeca is the southern coast's most stunning cove, a tiny beach overlooking hidden underwater caves exposed with the tide. Near the cove is **Pueblo Pescadores,** a tourist complex built in 1972 to simulate an old fishing village, with corridors that wind in all directions around white Mediterranean-style houses. To get to Cala Binibeca, enter the village near Pueblo Pescadores and walk all the way around it, staying right. Walk along the subtly marked dirt path that leads around another tourist complex and continue down the dirt path until you reach an unmarked parking area. A small dirt path leads down to the cove after a 20-25min. walk. *(From Maó, take the bus to Sant Lluis, and get off at Pueblo Pescadores. 20min., hourly 8:10am-8:15pm, €1.20.)*

ELS CANUTELLS. Situated near Cala'n Porter (a 15min. drive from Maó), Els Canutells is a secluded cove with azure waters, good for swimming and snorkeling and dotted with the boats of loyal visitors. *(TMSA buses run to and from Maó. 15min., 4 per day 8:45am-7pm, €1.20.)*

CALA'N PORTER. Cala'n Porter greets thousands of visitors each summer, and caters to a young, wild crowd. *(TMSA buses run to and from Maó. M-Sa 7 per day 9:30am-7:40pm, €1.80.)* Its whitewashed houses, orange stucco roofs, and red sidewalks (a 15min. walk away, following the clearly marked signs) lead to the main attraction: the unbelievable ▓**Covas d'en Xoroi,** caves etched into the cliffs hundreds of feet above the sea. These natural caves have been turned into an amazing network of bars and chill-out areas that turn into phenomenal discos by night. *(☎971 37 72 36; www.covadenxoroi.com. Cover for bars before 6:30pm €5.80; 6:30-10:30pm €8.90, includes 1 drink. Children €3.50. Cover for disco F €17, Sa €21-25. Th foam parties. Bars open Apr.-Oct. daily 10:30am-10:30pm. Disco open daily 11pm-late.)*

PLATGES DE SON BOU. Son Bou offers an arrow-straight, 4km expanse of sand, the longest and silkiest stretch on the island. As the most popular of Menorca's beaches, it is frequently covered with throngs of sunburned tourists. The town's cheesy tourist attractions are removed from the beach, though frequent bus service to and from Maó and Ciutadella, ample parking, endless beach chairs, umbrellas for rent, and cafes make it quite visitor-friendly. There are even discotecas only two blocks from the sand. *(TMSA buses to the beaches leave from Maó. 30min., 7 per day 8:45am-7pm, €1.85.)* For those who choose to stay late, **Disco Pub Copacabana,** in the Nuevo Centro Comercial, on the left when heading away from the water, has a huge dance floor, pool tables, and a full arcade, all with a great view of the water. *(Beer €3.50. Mixed drinks €6. Open daily May-Oct. 11pm-3.30am.)* After 7pm, there is no public transportation back to Maó until morning.

IBIZA (EIVISSA)

Nowhere on Earth are decadence, opulence, and downright hedonism celebrated as religiously as on the turquoise shores of the island of Ibiza (pop. 84,000). A hippie enclave in the 1960s, Ibiza has forgone its bohemian roots in favor of a techno beat and a glittering, extravagant crowd. Disco fiends, fashion gurus, movie stars, and party-hungry backpackers arrive in droves to be swept up in the island's outrageous party culture and to bake on its warm sands. A thriving gay community lends credence to Ibiza's image as a center of tolerance, but the island's high price tags preclude true diversity.

IBIZA CITY (EIVISSA) ☎971

Eivissa (pop. 42,800) is the world's biggest 24hr. party, a glam, come-one-come-all blur. During the day, Eivissa is a boutique-laden portside town beneath a 16th century walled city. Come sunset, however, flashy bars and a flashier crowd seem to appear out of nowhere, flooding the port with neon lights, drag queens, pumping music, street stands, and fast-talking club promoters. Come 3am, the scene

IBIZA'S FLOWER POWER

The hundreds of hippies that flocked to Ibiza in the 1960s and 70s brought with them free love, rock star groupies, and copious amounts of psychedelic drugs. The formerly tranquil island was suddenly invaded by droves of nudist peace-lovers who shaped the cultural clay of the island today.

Famous rock stars, including Mick Jagger and Jim Morrison, ran rampant in this bohemian playground during the 60s and 70s. Bob Dylan set up house in a windmill and Nico, frequent collaborator with The Velvet Underground, intently frequented the island's party scene and eventually died here. The island became notorious for its free-wheeling Saturday afternoon jam sessions, when famous rock 'n' rollers would indulge listeners with impromptu concerts while the free spirits in the audience passed joints and marinated in good vibes.

Though the turbulent 60s are long behind the island, Ibiza still retains much of the era's bohemian charm. Hippie markets selling organic produce and macramé trinkets still dot the island, and John Lennon Street graces Ibiza's urban center. Bob Dylan's windmill, which later appeared on a Pink Floyd album cover, is now a popular pilgrimage for latter-day hippies. The 60s are over, but travelers can still "turn on, tune in, and drop out" on this island of peace, love, and rock 'n' roll.

migrates to the colossal *discotecas* outside of town, where parties last until dawn (and often well into the next day). Then, it all begins again.

TRANSPORTATION

Flights: Airport (☎971 80 90 00), 7.5km southwest of the city, near Ses Salinas. Bus #10 runs between airport and Av. d'Isidor Macabich, 20 (30min.; summer every 30min. 6:50am-11:50pm, winter hourly 7:30am-11:35pm; €1.85). Taxis cost €12. **Iberia**, Pg. Vara de Rey, 15 (☎902 40 05 00), flies to **Alicante, Barcelona, Madrid, Palma,** and **Valencia. Air Europa** (☎902 40 15 01), **Vueling** (☎971 80 90 00), and **Spanair** (☎902 13 14 15) offer similar options. See **By Plane,** p. 343, or **Inter-Island Transport**.

Ferries: Estació Marítima. Trasmediterránea (☎902 45 46 45) sells tickets for ferries to **Barcelona, Palma,** and **Valencia.** Office open M-F 9am-1pm and 4:30-7:30pm, and 2hr. before departures. **Trasmapi-Balearia** (☎971 31 07 11) runs daily to **Dénia,** near **Alicante, Palma,** and **Formentera.** Office open M-F 9am-2:15pm, 4:30-8pm, and midnight-1:15am; Sa 9am-2:15pm and 6-8pm; Su 9am-2:15pm and midnight-1:15am. **Umafisa Lines** (☎971 19 10 88) sends boats to **Barcelona** 3-4 times per week. For rates and schedules, see **By Boat,** p. 344, or **Inter-Island Transport,** p. 344.

Buses: Eivissa has an extensive bus system, but buses to remote areas run only a few times per day. The **bus station** is on Av. d'Isidor Macabich, past Pl. d'Enric Fajarnés i Tur walking away from the port. For an exact schedule, check at a tourist office or the *Diario de Ibiza*. **Intercity buses** leave from Av. d'Isidor Macabich, 42 (☎971 31 21 17), to **Sant Antoni** (M-Sa in summer every 15min., Su every 30min. 7:30am-midnight; €1.60) and **Santa Eulària des Riu** (#13 M-F every 30min., Sa-Su hourly 7am-11:30pm, after 11pm hourly; €1.60). Buses to the beaches (☎971 34 03 82) cost €1.35 and leave from Av. d'Isidor Macabich, 20, and Av. d'Espanya to: **Cala Tarida** (in summer 5 per day 10:10am-6:45pm); **Cap Martinet** (in summer hourly M-F 8:15am-11:15pm; in winter M-Sa 9 per day 8:15am-7:30pm); **Platja d'en Bossa** (every 30min. 8:30am-11pm, also 7:45am); **Ses Salinas** (#11; in summer hourly 9:30am-1:30pm and 4:30pm-7:30pm also 3:45pm; in winter M, W, F 10am and 1pm).

Taxis: ☎971 39 84 83.

Car and Moped Rental: Casa Valentín, Av. B.V. Ramón, 19 (☎971 31 08 22 or 30 35 31 for the branch on C. Galicia 35; www.welcome.to/casavalentin). Mopeds €35 per day. Cars from €60 per day. Open daily 9am-1pm and 4-8pm.

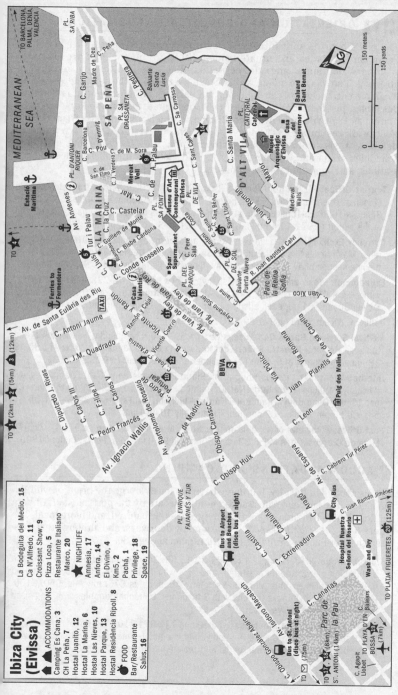

Ibiza City (Eivissa)

▲ ACCOMMODATIONS
Camping Es Cana, **3**
CH La Peña, **7**
Hostal Juanito, **12**
Hostal La Marina, **6**
Hostal Las Nieves, **10**
Hostal Parque, **13**
Hostal Residència Ripoll, **8**

● FOOD
Bar/Restaurante
Salus, **16**

La Bodeguita del Medio, **15**
Ca N'Alfredo, **11**
Croissant Show, **9**
Pizza Loca, **5**
Restaurante Italiano
Marco, **20**

★ NIGHTLIFE
Amnesia, **17**
Anfora, **14**
El Divino, **4**
Km5, **2**
Pachá, **1**
Privilege, **18**
Space, **19**

⚡🔧 ORIENTATION AND PRACTICAL INFORMATION

The city's heart is split into three sections, clustered south of the port. **Sa Penya** and **La Marina** are situated side-by-side on the port and are crammed with bars, boutiques, and trinket stands. Rising behind this packed grid of streets is **D'alt Vila,** the steep, walled town overlooking the sea. There are four available entrances to D'alt Vila, but the easiest and most central is **Portal de Ses Taules,** just behind the market off C. Constitució. **Pg. Vara de Rey** leads to La Marina an D'alt Vila from **Avinguda d'Espanya,** which runs to **Platja Figuretas** and boardwalk restaurants. The local paper *Diario de Ibiza* (€1; www.diario-deibiza.es) has an *Agenda* page with essential info, including bus and ferry schedules, water and weather forecasts, the island's 24hr. pharmacies and gas stations, and important phone numbers.

Tourist Office: Pl. d'Antoni Riquer, 2 (☎971 30 19 00), across from the Estació Marítima. Open June-Nov. M-F 9am-9pm, Sa 9:30am-7:30pm; Dec.-May M-F 8:30am-3pm, Sa 10:30am-1pm. **Booths** at the end of Pg. Vara de Rey, at Platja Figuretes, and at the airport (☎971 19 43 93). Open May-Oct. Tu-Su 10am-2pm and 5-8pm.

Currency Exchange: *Casas de cambio* are all over town; banks and ATMs offer better rates. Major banks like **La Caixa, BBVA, Sa Nostra,** and **Deutsche Bank** huddle around the intersection of Av. d'Espanya and Av. Ignasi Wallis, at the end of Pg. Vara de Rey.

Laundromat: Wash and Dry, Av. d'Espanya, 53 (☎971 39 48 22). Self-service €12, with service €14, dry cleaning €4-11 (2-day wait). **Internet** access €0.50 first 15min., €1 per 30min., €1 per each ensuing hour. Open M-F 10am-2pm and 5-9pm. MC/V.

Police: C. Vicent Serra (☎971 39 88 31 or 092).

Medical Services: Barrio Can Misses (☎971 39 70 00), a hospital west of town, and the large **Hospital Nuestra Señora del Rosario,** C. de Vía Romana, s/n (☎971 30 19 16), near the corner of C. Juan Ramón Jiménez. **Ambulance:** (☎971 39 22 32).

Internet Access: *Locutorios* abound by Platja Figueretes and streets paralleling Av. d'Espanya. Otherwise, try **Surf@Net,** C. Riambau, 4 (☎971 19 49 20), on the port. €1 per 15min. Open daily 10am-2am. **Touba Khelkom,** Av. Espanya, 32 (☎971 39 84 54). €0.50 per 15min., €2 per hour. Open daily 10am-1am.

Post Office: At the end of Av. d' Isidor Macabich away from the port (☎971 19 71 97). **Lista de Correos.** Open M-F 8:30am-8:30pm, Sa 9:30am-2pm. **Postal Code:** 07800.

▌ ACCOMMODATIONS AND CAMPING

Hostels abound in the city, but many have obviously borne the brunt of wild Ibizan nights. The best and safest accommodations are by the port, most off of Vera del Rey. Others by Platja Figueretas are grungier, urbanized, and more local. The letters "CH" *(casa de huéspedes)* mark many doorways, and although these are often cheaper than *hostales,* prices still remain above €30.

▨ **Hostal Parque,** Pl. del Parque 4 (☎971 30 13 58). Ideally located below D'Alt Vila in a charming plaza. Rooms are bright and new with TV and A/C. Singles with shared bath, all doubles ensuite. Mar.-June singles €40; doubles €70. July-Aug. €50/€100. Upstairs terrace overlooks the city with 3 luxurious, bohemian doubles with king-sized beds and flat screen TVs. €150-€170. ❹

Hostal La Marina/Los Caracoles, C. Barcelona 7 (☎971 310 172) Rooms are some of the best in town—each double has individual character, amenities, and price. All with gauzy, beachy decor, tidy white beds, and private bathrooms. €45-110. MC/V. ❸

Otel.com

Are you aiming for
a budget vacation**?**

DO NOT
DISTURB

US & CANADA
1-800-820-4171 OR 1-212-594-8045
EUROPE
00-800-468-35482 OR 44-207-099-2035

CH La Peña, C. La Virgen, 76 (☎971 19 02 40). Clean rooms for low prices. Nestled into a cobblestoned alley right next to the port, this house has flowered bedspreads and giant closets. Open June-Sept. Singles €23; doubles €32; triples €48. MC/V. ❷

Hostal Residència Ripoll, C. Vicent Cuervo, 10-14 (☎971 31 42 75). Fan-cooled, older rooms with communal baths and scant amenities. July-Sept. singles €30; doubles €55; triples €65; 3-person apt. with TV, patio, balcony and kitchen €80. Cash only. ❸

Hostal Juanito/Hostal Las Nieves, C. Joan d'Austria, 17-18 (☎971 19 03 19). Across the street from each other and under the same ownership, both hostels offer cheap housing in a central area. Twin beds aside, rooms are largely bare but will suffice for the few hours slept there. Singles €24; doubles €45, with bath €60. MC/V. ❷

Camping Es Cana (☎971 33 21 17; www.ibiza-spotlight.com/campescana). Pool and clubhouse, complete with game room and bar. Close to restaurants and bars by the beach *Des Canar*. Reserve by phone. €6.50 per person, €7-12 per tent (depending on the size). Bungalows €30-75; cabins €30. MC/V. ❶

◨ FOOD

Ibizan dishes include *sofrit pagès*, a deep-fried lamb and chicken dish, *flao*, a lush lemon- and mint-tinged cheesecake, and *graxonera*, cinnamon-dusted pudding made from eggs and bits of *ensaimada* (sugar-coated bread). The small **Mercat Vell,** at the mouth of the Portal de ses Taules leading to D'Alt Vila, sells meat, fruit, and vegetables (open M-Sa 7am-7pm). For groceries, try **Spar Supermarket,** near Pl. del Parc (open M-Sa 9am-9pm).

La Bodeguita Del Medio, C. Sta. Cruz, 15 (☎971 39 92 90) Tiny blue tables amidst lime green walls, hanging hams, red wax candles, and intriguing antiques. The few merry outdoor tables are ideal for the restaurant's cheap drinks (beer €3) and hot plates of paellas, *tortillas* (€6.40), and tapas. Cash only. ❶

Restaurante Italiano Marco, Po. de ses Pitiuses (☎971 30 10 69). This elegant boardwalk establishment offers candlelit patio seating above the sea on Platja Figuretas. Fantastic spaghetti bolognese (€6.50), soups (€4.50), and pizzas (€5-6). Open 8pm-midnight. MC/V. ❶

Croissant Show, Mercat Vell (☎971 31 76 65), on C. Antoni Palau. Bright cafe serves creative sandwiches (€4.50-6), quiches, salads, pastries, and *platos del dia* (€7.50). Popular for "breakfast" after a hard night of clubbing. Open daily 6am-2am. MC/V. ❶

Pizza Loca, C. Lluís Tur i Palau, 15. Oven-warmed pizza in all varieties is popular among young bar-hoppers at this happy hole-in-the-wall. Toppings include veggies, tuna, and salami. Slices €2.70-4. Open daily 11am-4:30am. Cash only. ❶

Ca N'Alfredo, Pg. Vara de Rey, 16 (☎971 31 12 74). A huge, filling menu offers fish, meat, and heavenly desserts (€6-15). Entrees €10-25. Reserve at least a day in advance. Open Tu-Sa 1-5pm and 8:30pm-midnight, Su 1-5pm. MC/V. ❸

Bar/Restaurante Salus, Pl. del Sol (☎664 71 76 51). Sit over the city beneath gnarled trees and a white-washed wall cluttered with antique brass instruments. Meals feature pizzas (€6.50-8), paella (€10-11), and salads (€8). MC/V. ❷

◎ SIGHTS

Eivissa offers a sharply contrasting selection of sights: the better known ones are portside—the glittery dose of drag queens, disco publicity stunts, and vacationers-gone-wild makes people-watching a worthwhile endeavor. The second selection rises just behind, enclosed in the 16th-century walls of **D'alt Vila** (Old Town), declared a UNESCO World Heritage site in 1999. The center of town offers a breezy array of phenomenal sea views against a small castle and a 14th-century **cathedral,** originally a Carthaginian temple. (Open daily 9:30am-1:30pm.) Across the small plaza in front of the cathedral is the **Museu Arqueològic d'Eivissa,** home to a variety of regional artifacts dating from the Phoenician and Carthaginian days of the island. (☎971 30 12 31. Open in summer Tu-Sa 10am-2pm and 6-8pm, Su 10am-2pm; in winter Tu-Sa 9am-3pm. €2.40, students €1.20, under 18 and over 65 free.) Near the entrance to D'Alt Vila is the small **Museu d'Art Contemporani d'Eivissa,** which displays art exhibitions ranging from video installations to photography, including a wide array of work by local artists and traveling international collections. (Ronda de Narcís Puget, at the base of the old city. ☎971 30 27 23. Open Tu-F 10am-1:30pm and 5-8pm, Sa-Su 10am-1:30pm. €1.20, students free.) The archaeological museum, **Puig des Molins,** Vía Romana, between Platja Figueretes and D'Alt Vila, displays Punic, Roman, and Iberian artifacts. (☎971 30 17 71. Open Tu-Sa 10am-2pm and 6-8pm, Su 10am-2pm. €1.20.)

◪ BEACHES

In Eivissa, if you're not at a disco, you're at the beach. Beaches feature satin sands, pale shores, and seas of umbrellas shading exhausted droves. ◪**Platja de ses Salinas** does the beach as only Eivissa can. Come to see and be seen among masses of beautiful bodies and groove to the New Age music pulsating from **Sa Trincha** bar at the end of the beach. Reserve a beach chair for €10 in front of **The Jockey Club** (☎971 39 57 88; www.jockeyclubibiza.com) and receive full bar and restaurant service right from the sand as top DJs warm up for their club gigs. (Bus #11 runs hourly to Salinas from Av. d'Isidor Macabich.) **Platja Figueretes,** a short stretch of sand connected by a pedestrian boardwalk lined by large hotels, restaurants, and street-stands. A 15min. walk from Pl. Vera Rey down Av. d'Espanya and a left on C. Murcia leads straight there. Farther down, and most efficiently reached by bus, **Platja d'en Bossa** is the longest and liveliest of Eivissa's beaches, with thumping bars and throngs of sun-seeking tourists. After tanning all day, take a dance break at the famous open club ◪**Bora Bora** right on the beach where an outside platform, a beachside bar, and blasting techno bring half-naked dancers all day and into the night. (Bus #14 runs every 30min. from Av. d'Isidor Macabich.) **Platja de Talamanca** is on the opposite side of the port from town (30min. walk). **Platja des Cavallet** attracts a largely gay crowd showing off their bodies—in some cases, their entire bodies. To get there, take bus #11 from Eivissa to Salinas; get off before Salinas (Can Tixedo) and follow the signs (10min.), or just walk from Salinas (20min.).

More private coastal stretches lie in the northern and southwestern parts of the island and are accessible by car or moped, though all attract a large following (true beach snobs head to the island of Formentera). Among these, the German enclave at **Cala de Sant Vicent** (past Santa Eulària des Riu on the road to St. Carles de Peralta) offers white sands and breathtaking views. **Cala Xarraca** is a beautiful cove popular with families, who fight for spots on its small beach. **Cala Carbó,** south of St. Antoni and west of St. Josep, is a small but beautiful beach with awe-inspiring cliffs and a fantastic beachfront seafood restaurant.

◪ NIGHTLIFE

Bars in Eivissa are crowded between 11pm and 3am and are the place to meet, greet, see, and be seen. The scene centers on **Carrer de Barcelona** and spills into the side streets, which can be jammed to the point of immobility, especially around midnight, when the area is flooded with *discotecas* promoters. All discos, except for **Eden** and **Es Paradis** in St. Antoni which are accessible by foot, are outside of town. The **Discobus** runs to most of the hot spots but can be slow and unpredictable (leaves Eivissa from Av. d'Isidor Macabich every hour in summer 12:30am-6:30am, schedule for other stops available at tourist office and hotels; €1.75). The main taxi line to the discos is at the end of the port on Av. Bartolome de Rosello—the line is usually long but moves quickly.

The island's ▓discos are unbelievable, unequaled, and full of the unexpected; veterans claim that you will never experience anything half as wild or fun. Drinks at Eivissa's clubs are outrageously expensive—beers are generally more than €10, and mixed drinks are about €18, while cover runs €35-65.

GET THE MOST OUT OF YOUR DISCO DOLLAR. If you know where you're going ahead of time, buy your disco tickets from a promoter at bars or stores in town—you'll pay €6-20 less than what you would at the door, and it's completely legit. Beach and portside promoters (usually glistening and half-clothed) sometimes give out wristbands that will get you in for free or at least get you serious discounts and lots of extras with your cover.

▓ **Amnesia** (☎971 19 80 41; www.amnesia.es/index2.html), on the road to Sant Antoni. This converted warehouse has a phenomenal sound system, often accented by a live electric violinist. The central dance floor is flooded with psychedelic lights, vents spewing liquid nitrogen, acrobatic go-go dancers, and lasers. W drag performances take over the left room. Cover from €20-50. Open daily midnight-8am.

Space, Platja d'en Bossa (☎971 39 67 93; www.space-ibiza.es). Starts hopping around 8am, peaks mid-afternoon, and doesn't wind down until after 5pm. ▓ **"We Love Sundays"** on Su mornings rocks out nonstop for a full 22 hours until 6am the next morning. Sa mornings "Matinee Group," W "I a Troya" and Tu after-parties with Carl Cox are also popular. Cover €30-60.

Pachá (☎971 31 36 00; www.pacha.com), 15min. from the port by foot. The most famous club chain in Spain, and the most elegant of Eivissa's discos. "Release Yourself" on M brings the best up-and-coming DJs, and fabulous parties on F attract a rowdy crowd. Only club open year-round. Cover €45-60. Open daily midnight-7:30am.

Privilege (☎971 19 80 86; www.privilegeibiza.com), in the Urbanizacion San Rafael, on the Discobus to Sant Antoni, close to Amnesia. There is a free Privilege bus that leaves from the Estacion Maritim every 30min. Taxi €9. One of the world's largest clubs, filled with laughing gas booths, drag queens, and erotic dancers. Th cover from €30-50. Open June-Sept. daily midnight-8am. MC/V.

El Divino, Puerto Ibiza Nueva (☎971 31 83 38; www.eldivino-ibiza.com), a 20min. walk from the port (keep right at the round-about), €6 taxi, or a shuttle boat ride (runs until 4am, look for El Divino signs; €2). Small, energetic club on the water—worth it just for the view, although exotic dancers and the thumping house aren't too shabby either. Cover €25-45. Open mid-June to mid-Sept. daily midnight-7:30am.

Anfora, C. Sant Carles, 7, in the D'alt Vila. A gay disco built into the hillside of the old city, the club's sunken dance floor sits beneath a small maze of bohemian lounges, tiled bars, and terraces. Don't miss Th "Night Fever" and Tu "Madonna." Cover €10, after 2am €15; includes 1 drink. Open daily midnight-6am.

Kilometro Cinco (Km5), Ctra. San Jose (☎971 39 63 49). Appropriately located 5km from the city, this stunning starry garden offers 5 bohemian bars, candlelit tables, gauzy lounges, and plush Arabic tents bathed in golden light. Beer €5. House wine €6/glass. Dinner reservations recommended. Open Apr. 29-Oct. 8 M-Su 8pm-2am. MC/V.

SAN ANTONIO DE PORTMANY (SANT ANTONI)

Every summer, masses of youths migrate from the British Isles to Sant Antoni in search of fun, sun, and relaxation. The rowdy nightlife, easy-going pace, and glam boardwalk lounges with wide ocean vistas have turned the town into a flashy twenty-something enclave. Quieter streets and tranquil sunspots aren't difficult to find, providing a relaxing alternative to the island's fast-moving atmosphere.

🖪🔁 TRANSPORTATION AND PRACTICAL INFORMATION. Sant Antoni's flashy, shop-laden streets lie on a grid behind **Passeig de la Mar,** which traverses the port. An arching boardwalk beyond the port leads to rocky coves and luxe lounges, while **Av. Dr. Fleming** runs perpendicular to the grid amidst a mass of beach bars and discos. Buses run from the end of **Passeig de la Mar** in Sant Antoni to: **Cala Bassa** (20min., 8 per day 9:10am-6:30pm, €1.35); **Cala Conta** (15min., 7 per day 9:10am-6pm, €1.35); **Cala Tarida** (10min., 8 per day 9:15am-7:05pm, €1.35); **Eivissa** (25min.; every 15min. M-Sa 7am-9:30pm, Su every 30min. 7:30am-11pm; €1.65); **Santa Eulària** (35min., M-Sa 5 per day 10:15am-6:45pm, €1.10). Ferries leave Sant Antoni for **Dénia** (see **Inter-Island Transport,** p. 344). Smaller companies run daily boats to nearby beaches; prices average €15-25 round-trip. Signs posted along the port have schedules. For a **taxi,** call ☎971 34 37 64. For car and moped rental, try **Motos Luis,** Av. Dr. Fleming. (☎971 34 05 21. Mopeds from €30. Cars from €45. Open M-Sa 9am-2pm and 5-8pm, Su 9am-2pm.) The **tourist office** is a tiny center in Pg. de ses Fonts, between Pg. de la Mar and Av. Dr. Fleming. (☎971 34 33 63. Open M-F 9:30am-2pm and 3-8:30pm, Sa 9am-1pm, Su 9am-1pm.) Local services include: **police,** Av. Portmany, km 14 (☎971 34 08 30); a **health center,** C. d'Alacant, at the corner of Av. d'isidor Macabich (☎972 07 90 79); a **pharmacy** on C. Barcelona (☎971 34 12 23); and **Internet** access at **Surf@net,** C. B.V. Ramón, 5 bajo (☎971 80 39 47; €1 per 15min., €1.20 per 30min.; open daily 10am-midnight).

🔁🖸 ACCOMMODATIONS AND FOOD. *Hostales* in Sant Antoni are numerous, high-tech, and full of Brits. **Hostal Roca ❷,** C. San Mateo, 7, is in a great location close to the port. The hostal offers plain doubles with TV and private baths. (☎971 34 00 67, ibiza@hotelgransol.net. €14-30 per person depending on the season. MC/V.) **Hostal Mari ❹,** C. Progrés, 42, has spick-and-span white doubles with TV and private bath. (☎971 34 19 74; www.hostalmari.com. Singles €38; doubles €67.)

Restaurants pervade Sant Antoni but are markedly different depending on the area. **Paseo de la Mar** runs along the port and connects the two most important culinary areas: **Paseo del Rey,** a winding boardwalk traversing the rocky coves beyond the port, and **Avenida Dr. Fleming,** the garish disco strip along the sandy **S'Arenal.** The former consists of chic poolside lounges with bikini-clad customers, the latter a rowdier, disco-esque cluster of beach bars. A more trendy beachfront establishment, **🖾The Orange Corner ❷,** Av. Dr. Fleming, 24, serves cheap sandwiches, salads, fruit drinks, milkshakes, and alcoholic favorites on a tented terrace. The popular restaurant also hosts pre-club parties and sells tickets to many of the discotecas. (www.theorangecorner.com. Entrees €6-9. Alcoholic milkshakes €7, non-alcoholic shakes and smoothies €4.50. Open daily 10:30am-4am.)

🔁🖺 BEACHES AND NIGHTLIFE. The town and **Passeig de la Mar** straddle the side of the port, perpendicular to the disco strip and packed sands of Av. Dr. Fleming. The opposite side of Pg. de la Mar leads to slanted, rocky coves where chic youngsters spend hours basking on rocks or lazing about in poolside lounges. Check out **Cala Bassa,** one of the more popular tanning spots, for a gorgeous (and often nude) beach that's accessible by bus. **Cala Gració,** a calm, sunsoaked cove, is 1.5km from Sant Antoni, and is easily reached on foot. **Santa**

Eulària des Riu is more urbanized and substantially larger than some of the other beaches nearby but provides excellent tanning opportunities. Just north of town, accessible by car or moped, the beautiful **Cala Salada** boasts calm waters.

Like restaurants, the nightlife in San Antoni is evenly segmented by Pg. de la Mar. The smooth boardwalk beyond P. de la Mar winds around tiny, sloping coves and is full of swanky lounges with sunset vistas and room for dancing. Breezy **Café Mambo,** Ses Variades, a seductive poolside bar with blue mosaic decor, is packed morning until night and is the unofficial pre-Pachá stop. (☎971 34 66 38. Beer €5. Mixed drinks €7-9. Open daily 11am-3am.) A bit closer to town along the boardwalk, **Spacious Savannah** attracts a well-dressed, older crowd with its pale elegance, calm music, and chic liquor list. (☎971 34 80 31.) Near the end of the boardwalk is **Kanya,** also known as the **Sunset Cafe,** a bright poolside lounge with an energetic, young crowd day and night. (☎971 80 57 89; www.ibiza-kanya.com.) Flashy dance clubs pack **C. Santa Agnes** in the middle of town and are popular preludes to the two neighboring discos along Av. Dr. Fleming, **Envy** and **Es Paradis.**

FORMENTERA

Formentera is heaven for the snobbiest of beach snobs craving a reprieve from the hungover crowd on Ibiza. The silky sands, crystal clear waters, and small towns that pepper the island cater to a glamorous, older crowd. Some of the most beautiful beaches are ▨**Platja Migjorn,** where clear water laps velvety white sands, and ▨**Es Calo,** a fisherman's village with wooden walkways and cerulean waves. The most popular beaches are **Platja des Illetes,** (30min. walk from the port) featuring golden sands and shallow shores, and the nearby **Platja des Pujols,** a protected expanse with deeper waters and a restaurant-filled town.

Formentera is best visited as a day trip. The **tourist office,** located in the port complex, offers a list of Green Tours for hikers and cyclists. (☎971 32 20 57. Open M-F 10am-2pm and 5-7pm, Sa 10am-2pm.) Ferries (35-90min., depending on the boat) drop travelers at **Port de la Savina,** a simple town with a wealth of transportation rental agencies. Inexpensive charters also leave in the morning from Platja Figueretes. Though buses run to all of the beaches, they leave infrequently and can be unreliable. The easiest way to travel is by ▨**scooter** (€20-30) or bike (€6-16). For more info on transportation to Formentera, see **Inter-Island Transport,** p. 344.

BARCELONA

Nobody owns Barcelona. Home to innumerable expats from the US, South America, and a host of other countries, this is a unique city in which there are no outsiders. In the 15 years since the Olympics on the waterfront, Barcelona has rocketed into prominence as a destination for travelers drawn to the beaches, clubs, and first-rate restaurants. Between the urban carnival of La Rambla, the melting buildings of La Manzana de la Discórdia, and Gaudí's mad Sagrada Família cathedral in l'Eixample, the city pushes the limits of style in everything, and gets away with it.

The center of the whimsical and daring Modernista architectural movement and once home to Pablo Picasso and Joan Miró, Barcelona has a brand new bag today, with more art and music than ever. Yet the draw of the city extends beyond its shows and its art. Its residents exhibit the same energy and attention to detail when it comes to fashion, food, and, above all, hospitality. In the quarter-century since the end of Franco's oppressive regime, Barcelona has led the autonomous region of Cataluña in a cultural resurgence. The result is a vanguard city squeezed between the mesmerizing blue waters of the Mediterranean and the green Tibidabo hills, flashing with such vibrant colors and shapes that you'll see Barcelona long after you've closed your eyes. Barcelona is a gateway, not only to *català* art and culture, but to the Mediterranean and the Pyrenees. Don't worry if you don't speak *català*, or Spanish for that matter—Barcelona understands every language.

HIGHLIGHTS OF BARCELONA

REFLECT on your true self in the Hall of Mirrors in the **Gran Teatre del Liceu** (p. 395).

CHILL at an outdoor jazz concert on the rooftops of the fantastical **Casa Milà** (p. 401).

RAMBLE along **La Rambla** (p. 395) and absorb the energy of the **Barri Gòtic** (p. 378).

IMAGINE what the future will bring to the unfinished **La Sagrada Família** (p. 400).

◼ INTERCITY TRANSPORTATION

Flights: Aeroport El Prat de Llobregat (**BCN**; ☎902 40 47 04; www.aena.es and choose Airport: Barcelona from the dropdown on the left), 13km southwest of Barcelona. To get to Pl. Catalunya, take the **Aerobus** (☎ 934 15 60 20) in front of terminals A, B, or C (approx. 40min.; every 6-13min.; to Pl. Catalunya M-F 6am-1am, Sa-Su 6:30am-1am; to the airport M-F 5:30am-12:15am, Sa-Su 6am-12:30am; €3.90, round-trip €6.45). For early-morning flights, the Nitbus **N17** runs from Pl. Catalunya to all three terminals (from Pl. Catalunya hourly 11pm-5am; returns from airport hourly 10:05pm-5:05am; €1.20). The cheaper, faster option is the new **RENFE train** (L10; 20min. to Estació Sants, 25min. to Pg. de Gràcia; every 30min., from airport 6am-11:44pm, from Estació Sants to airport 5:25am-10:55pm; €2.40). To reach the train, take the pedestrian overpass in front of the airport, on the left with your back to the entrance. **Taxis** (☎932 23 51 51) are in front of terminals A, B, and C; €13 to Pl. Espanya; €15.50 to Pl. Catalunya; €19 to Sagrada Família.

Trains: Barcelona has 2 main train stations. For general info call ☎902 24 02 02. **Estació Barcelona-Sants,** in Pl. Països Catalans (M: Sants Estació), is the main terminal for domestic and international traffic. **Estació de França,** on Av. Marquès de l'Argentera (M: Barceloneta), services regional destinations, including Tarragona, Zaragoza, and some international places. Note that trains often stop before the main stations; check the schedule. **RENFE** (☎ reservations 902 24 02 02, general info 902 24 34 02, international 24 34 02) to: **Bilbao** (9-10hr.; 12:30, 10:20pm; €38-50.10); **Madrid** (5-9hr., 10 per day 7:30am-11pm, €36.50-65.30); **Sevilla** (10-12hr., 3 per day 8am-10:30pm, €33-85); **Valencia** (3-5hr., 12-15 per day, €21-38). International destinations include **Milan, Italy** (via Figueres and Nice) and **Montpellier, France** with connections to Geneva, Paris, and the French Riviera. 20% discount on round-trip tickets.

Buses: Arrive at the **Barcelona Nord Estació d'Autobusos**, C. Alí-bei, 80 (☎902 26 06 06; www.barcelonanord.com for ticket and schedule info). M: Arc de Triomf or #54 bus. Info booth open 7am-9pm. Buses also depart from Estació Sants and the airport. **Sarfa** (☎902 30 20 25; www.sarfa.es). Bus stop and ticket office also at Ronda Sant Pere, 21 (☎933 02 52 23). To: **Cadaqués** (2½hr.; 9:45, 11:30am, 8:30pm; €19); **Palafrugell** (2hr., 10-14 per day 8:30am-9pm, €14.30); **Tossa del Mar** via **Lloret de Mar** (1½hr., 10 per day, €9.35). **Eurolines** (☎933 67 44 00; www.eurolines.es) goes to **Paris** via Lyon (15hr., M-Sa 8:30pm, €84) or from June 24-Sept. 9 also via southern France (M, W, Sa 12:30am; €84), and **Naples, Italy** (24hr; M, W, F 5:30pm; €120); 10% discount under 26 or over 60. **ALSA/Enatcar** (☎902 42 22 42; www.alsa.es) goes to: **Alicante** (8-9hr., 3 per day, €37-42); **Bilbao** (7-8hr., 6 per day, €40); **Madrid** (8hr., 20 per day 7am-1am, €26-34); **Sevilla** (14-16hr.; 4:30, 10pm; €71-83); **Valencia** (4-5hr., 14 per day, €23-28); **Zaragoza** (3½hr., 22 per day, €12.20).

Ferries: Trasmediterránea (☎902 45 46 45; www.transmediterranea.es), in Terminal Drassanes, Moll Sant Bertran. **Catamaran** €75; round-trip €142. **"Superferry"** €46/88 June-Aug. to: **Ibiza** (5-9hr., 2 per day M-Sa); **Mahón** (3½-9hr., 1 per day); **Palma** (3½-7hr., 2-3 per day).

◢ ORIENTATION

Barcelona's layout is relatively simple. Imagine yourself perched on Columbus's head at the **Monument a Colom** (on Pg. de Colom, along the shore), viewing the city with the sea at your back. From the harbor, the city slopes upward to the mountains. From the Columbus monument, **La Rambla,** the main thoroughfare, runs up to **Plaça de Catalunya** (M: Catalunya), the city center. **Ciutat Vella** is the heavily touristed historic neighborhood, anchored by La Rambla and encompassing the Barri Gòtic, La Ribera, and El Raval. The **Barri Gòtic** is east of La Rambla (to the right, with your back to the sea), enclosed on the other side by **Via Laietana.** East of Via Laietana lies the maze-like neighborhood of **La Ribera,** bordered by Parc de la Ciutadella and Estació de França. To the west of La Rambla is **El Raval,** Barcelona's most multicultural neighborhood, with a healthy dose of museums and bars.

Beyond La Ribera—farther east, outside Ciutat Vella and curving out into the water—are **Poble Nou** and **Port Olímpic,** which boast the two tallest buildings in Barcelona, not to mention an assortment of discotecas and restaurants on the beach. To the west, beyond El Raval, rises **Montjuïc,** a hill crammed with sprawling gardens, museums, the 1992 Olympic grounds, and a fortress. Directly behind your perch on the Monument a Colom is the **Port Vell** (Old Port) development, where a wavy bridge leads to the ultra-modern (and tourist-packed) shopping and entertainment complexes **Moll d'Espanya** and **Maremàgnum.** North of Ciutat Vella is upscale **l'Eixample,** a gridded neighborhood created during the expansion of the 1860s that sprawls from Pl. de Catalunya toward the mountains. **Gran Via de les Corts Catalanes** defines its lower edge, and the **Passeig de Gràcia,** l'Eixample's main tree- and boutique-lined avenue, bisects this chic neighborhood. **Avinguda Diagonal,** the expansion's largest non-gridded street, marks the border between l'Eixample and the **Zona Alta** ("Uptown"), which includes Pedralbes, Gràcia, and other older neighborhoods in the foothills. The peak of **Tibidabo,** the northwest border of the city, offers the most comprehensive view of Barcelona.

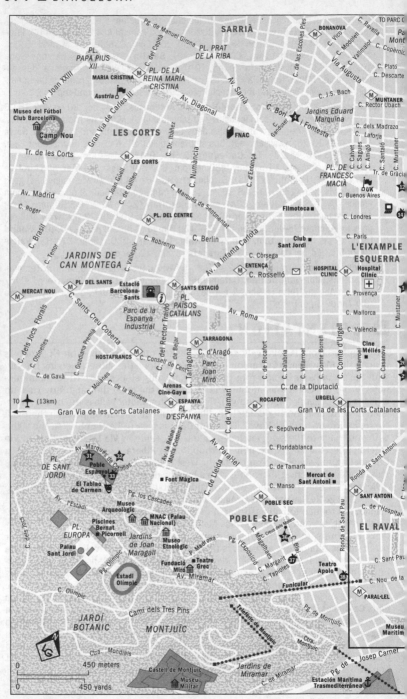

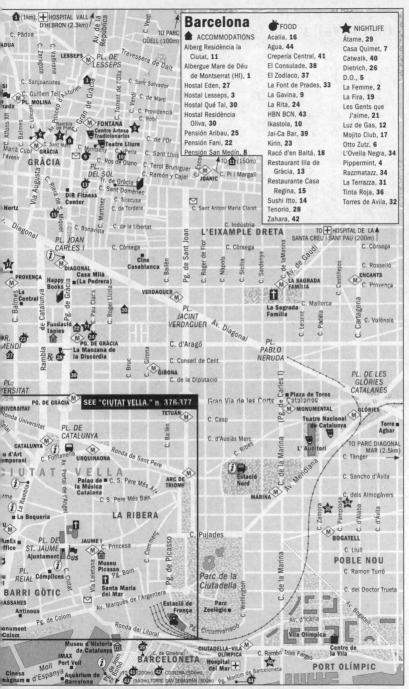

Barcelona

▲ ACCOMMODATIONS
Alberg Residència la
  Ciutat, **11**
Albergue Mare de Déu
  de Montserrat (HI), **1**
Hostal Eden, **27**
Hostal Lesseps, **3**
Hostal Qué Tal, **30**
Hostal Residència
  Oliva, **30**
Pensión Aribau, **25**
Pensión Fani, **22**
Pensión San Medín, **8**

🍎 FOOD
Acalia, **16**
Agua, **44**
Crepería Central, **41**
El Consulade, **38**
El Zodíaco, **37**
La Font de Prades, **33**
La Gavina, **9**
La Rita, **24**
HBN BCN, **43**
Ikastola, **10**
Jai-Ca Bar, **39**
Kirin, **23**
Racó d'en Baltá, **18**
Restaurant Illa de
  Gràcia, **13**
Restaurante Casa
  Regina, **15**
Sushi Itto, **14**
Tenorio, **28**
Zahara, **42**

★ NIGHTLIFE
Átame, **29**
Casa Quimet, **7**
Catwalk, **40**
Dietrich, **26**
D.O., **5**
La Femme, **2**
La Fira, **19**
Les Gents que
  J'aime, **21**
Luz de Gas, **12**
Mojito Club, **17**
Otto Zutz, **6**
L'Ovella Negra, **34**
Pippermint, **4**
Razzmatazz, **34**
La Terrazza, **31**
Tinta Roja, **36**
Torres de Avila, **32**

SEE "CIUTAT VELLA." p. 376-377

B A R C E L O N A

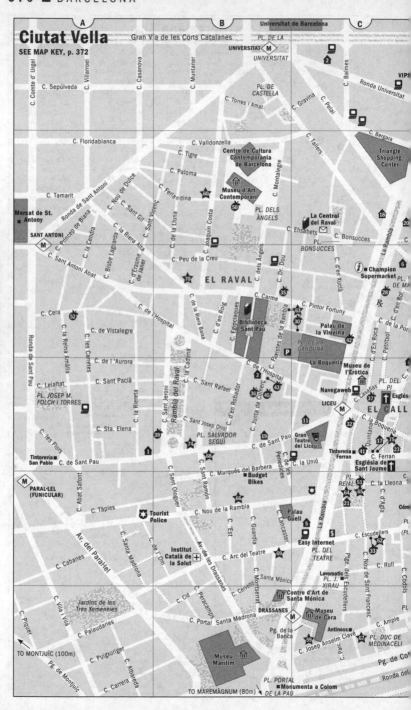

Ciutat Vella

SEE MAP KEY, p. 372

Gran Via de les Corts Catalanes

Universitat de Barcelona

BARCELONA

D PASSEIG DE GRÀCIA
E Gran Via de les Corts Catalanes
F PL. TETUÁN

Ds de la Victòria

Pg. de Gràcia

C. Pau Claris

C. Roger de Llúria

C. Bruc

C. Girona

C. Bailèn

TETUÁN

C. Casp

1

L'EIXAMPLE

0   200 meters
0   200 yards

t de aletes

Ronda de Sant Pere

El Corte Inglés

URQUINAONA

C. d'Ausiàs Marc

DE UNYA

AeroBus

C. Fontanella

Ronda de Sant Pere

TO ESTACIÓ NORD (300m)

2

CATALUNYA (RENFE)

C. Estruc

C. les Moles

Via Laietana

C. les Jonqueres

Ronda de Sant Pere

C. d'Alí Bei

Pg. de St. Joan

ARC DE TRIOMF

C. d'Ortigosa

C. Trafalgar

C. Trafalgar

Corte glés

C. Comtal

Av. Portal de l'Àngel

C. Méndez Núñez

Arc de Triomf

auda

C. Montsió

C. Magdalenes

Palau de la Música Catalana

C. Sant Pere Més Alt

C. S. Pere Més Alt

C. Argenter

C. Sant Pere Monec

PL. SANT PERE

3

C. Durán i Bas

Biblioteca Francesca Bonnemaison

C. Verdaguer i Callís

C. Mare de Déu

C. Sant Pere Mitjà

C. Rec Comtal

Boters

C. Sagristans

C. Dr. J. Pou

C. Sant Pere Més Baix

Gral. Álvarez

C. Jaume Giralt

C. en Cortines

PL. DEL COMERÇ

PL. NOVA

Av. de la Catedral

ANTONI MAURA

Av. de Francesc Cambó

C. Metges

C. Tàstics

C. Portal Nou

la Palla

PL. DE LA SEU

dels Mercaders

C. Feixures

C. Tantarantana

LA RIBERA

Pg. de Pujades

Esglèsia Catedral de la Santa Creu

Palau Reial Major

C. Colomines

C. Flassaders

Museu de la Xocolata

Museu de Zoologia

Mau de la neralitat

Museu d'Història de la Ciutat

C. Corders

C. Assaonadors

Hivernacle

4

C. Bisbe

C. Llibreteria

PL. DEL ÁNGEL

C. Princesa

C. Comerç

Pg. de Picasso

C. Sant Jaume

JAUME I

C. Vigatans

C. Fusina

PL. DE SANT JAUME

C. Jaume I

C. Montcada

Museu Picasso

C. del Rec

BARRI GÒTIC

Via Laietana

C. Banys Vells

Antic Mercat del Born

5

ayuntament

C. Ciutat

C. Manresa

C. Argenteria

C. la Nau

Esglèsia de Santa Maria del Mar

PL. COMERCIAL

C. Comercial

ervantes

C. Regomir

C. Bda. de Viladecols

C. Sots

Pg. del Born

C. Antic St. Joan

C. la Ribera

Parc de la Ciutadella

C. d'Actuari

C. Canvis Nous

C. del Rec

mtessa

C. Gignàs

C. la Fusteria

C. de Agudells

PL. MORERES

Lavomatic

C. Consolat de Mar

Av. Marquès de l'Argentera

6

C. la Mercè

PL. D'ANTONI LÓPEZ

Pg. d'Isabel II

PL. DEL PALAU

Estació de França

Parc Zoològic

C. Simó Oller

ssway tunnel

de la Fusta

Museu d'Història de Catalunya

Canvis Vells

BARCELONETA

Pg. Circumvalació

TO MOLL D'ESPANYA (50m)

TO BARCELONETA AND BEACHES (100m)

Av. d'Icària

TO VILA OLÍMPICA (800m)

Ciutat Vella

SEE MAP, p. 376-377

🏠 ACCOMMODATIONS

Barcelona Mar Youth Hostel,	1	A4
BCN Hostal Central,	2	C1
Center Ramblas,	3	B4
Gothic Point Youth Hostel,	4	E4
Hostal Benidorm,	5	C5
Hostal Campi,	6	C3
Hostal Levante,	7	C5
Hostal Maldà,	8	C4
Hostal Mariluz Youngsters,	9	D5
Hostal Nuevo Colón,	10	F5
Hostal Ópera,	11	C4
Hostal Plaza,	12	D2
Hostal-Residència Lausanne,	13	D2
Hostal Residència Rembrandt,	14	C3

Hostal de Ribagorza,	15	E2
Hostal San Remo,	16	E2
Hostel Sun & Moon,	17	C4
Hotel Lloret,	18	C2
Hotel Peninsular,	19	B4
Hotel Toledano/Hostal Residència Capitol,	20	C2
Kabul Youth Hostel,	21	C5
Pensión Ciudadela,	22	F5
Pensión Fernando,	23	C4
Pensión Port-Bou,	24	F5

🍎 FOOD

Els 4 Gats,	25	D3
L'Antic Bocoi del Gòtic,	26	D5
Arc Café,	27	D6
Attic,	28	C3
The Bagel Shop,	29	C3
Bar Ra,	30	C3
Bunga Raya,	31	E4
Café de l'Ópera,	32	C4
Los Caracoles,	33	C5
La Colmena,	34	D4

DosTrece,	35	B3
Hello Sushi,	36	B4
Juicy Jones,	37	C4
Laie Llibreria Café,	38	D1
Madame Jasmine,	39	B4
Maoz Vegetarian (a),	40	D4
Maoz Vegetarian (b),	41	C4
Maoz Vegetarian (c),	42	C3
Mendizabal,	43	B4
Mi Burrito y Yo,	44	D4
Organic,	45	B4
Orígen 99.9%,	46	E5
El Pebre Blau,	47	E5
Petra,	48	E5
La Pizza del Born,	49	E5
Pla dels Àngels,	50	B2
Les Quinze Nits,	51	C5
Restaurant Can Lluís,	52	A3
Têxtil Cafè,	53	E5
Va de Vi,	54	E5

Vildsvin,	55	C4
Xaloc,	56	C4
El Xampanyet,	57	E5

⭐ NIGHTLIFE

El Born,	58	E5
El Bosq de les Fades,	59	C6
Casa Almirall,	60	B2
El Copetín,	61	E5
Fonfone,	62	C5
iposa,	63	C3
Jamboree,	64	C5
Karma,	65	C5
London Bar,	66	B5
Margarita Blue,	67	C6
Marsella Bar,	68	B4
Moog,	69	B5
Muebles Navarro (El Café que Pone),	70	B3
Palau Dalmases,	71	E5
Pas del Born,	72	E5
Salvation,	73	E2
Sant Pau 68,	74	B4
Schilling,	75	C4

THE BARRIS (NEIGHBORHOODS) OF BARCELONA

BARRI GÒTIC AND LA RAMBLA

The oldest sections of Barcelona, the Barri Gòtic and La Rambla are the city's tourist centers. Originally settled by the Romans in the 3rd century BC, the Barri Gòtic is built on top of the original Roman city, Barcino. Subsequent periods of medieval Catholic rule and design covered Barcino in a maze of narrow streets, dense with historic and artistic landmarks. The modern tourist industry has added shops, hostels, and bars to these *barris* of medieval monuments. Stroll down **Carrer d'Avinyó** and you'll see some of Barcelona's most treasured architectural landmarks, just meters away from the area's most popular nightlife hotspots.

LA RIBERA

As the stomping ground of Barcelona's many fishermen and merchants, La Ribera has always had a working-class feel. Its confines bore witness to some of the most important events to shape Barcelona's history; in the 18th century, Felipe V demolished much of La Ribera, then the city's commercial hub, to make space for the impressive Ciutadella fortress. Originally the center of Madrid's oppressive control, the area is now the site of a beautiful park. The city government has cleaned up La Ribera in the last few years, even demolishing many of the area's legendary haunts (and putting an end to their legendary parties). The result is a neighborhood that locals still love for its intimate restaurants and bars, its free art galleries, and its nightly transformation, come sunset, back to its exciting old self.

EL RAVAL

Located next to La Rambla and the Barri Gòtic, the northern part of El Raval tends to be a favorite of Barcelona's natives rather than its tourists. The southern portion, meanwhile, is home to many immigrants from India and the Middle East. This diverse and mostly working-class neighborhood has a special charm, with small, quirky shops and eateries, welcoming bars, and hidden historical attractions. In the late 19th and early 20th centuries, overcrowding led to an urban nightmare of rampant crime, prostitution, and drug use. Revitalization efforts, especially since the 1992 Olympic Games, have worked wonders; new museums and cultural centers—not to mention plenty of bars and restaurants—have made El Raval a neighborhood with lots of character.

L'EIXAMPLE

Barcelona's l'Eixample (luh-SHOMP-luh; Enlargement) is notable for the unusual circumstances that led to its development. Around the time when the oppressive Bourbon walls of the old city were demolished in 1854, the *catalana* cultural *Renaixença* was picking up. As the number of wealthy beneficiaries of industrialization grew, utopian socialist theories spread like wildfire through philosophical circles, including those of l'Eixample urban planner **Ildefons Cerdà i Sunyer.** The gridded streets wound up filled with relatively wealthy residents (not a blending of classes as he'd imagined), designer shops, corporate buildings, and great eateries from around the world. Most tourists only see the Pg. de Gràcia and Sagrada Família areas, but it's worth your while to stray; L'Eixample is a lesson in Modernism and a treasure trove of small bars, cafés, and museums.

MONTJUÏC

Montjuïc (mon-joo-EEK), the hill at the southwest end of the city, is one of the oldest sections of Barcelona. Throughout Barcelona's history, whoever controlled Montjuïc's peak controlled the city. Dozens of despotic rulers have occupied and modified the **Castell de Montjuïc,** built atop the ancient Jewish cemetery (hence the name Montjuïc, Hill of the Jews). In the 20th century, Franco made the Castell de Montjuïc one of his "interrogation" headquarters; somewhere deep in the recesses of the structure, his *beneméritos* ("honorable ones"; the militia) shot Cataluña's former president, Lluís Companys, in 1940. The fort was not rededicated to the city until 1960. Since reclaiming the mountain, Barcelona has given Montjuïc a new identity, transforming it from a military stronghold into a peaceful park by day and a debaucherous playground by night. Today, it is one of the city's most visited attractions, with world-famous art museums and theater, Olympic history and facilities, botanical gardens, walking and bike trails, a substantial dose of nightlife, and an awe-inspiring historical cemetery.

THE WATERFRONT

The piers of **Barceloneta** and **Port Vell, Poble Nou,** and **Port Olímpic** are also part of Barcelona's coastline. In 1718, La Ribera was butchered to make room for the enormous **Ciutadella** fortress; the destruction of this historic neighborhood left thousands homeless, and it was not until 30 years later that the city created Barceloneta to house the displaced refugees. Because of its seaside location, Barceloneta became home to the city's sailors, fishermen, and their families. Barcelona's drive to refurbish its waterfront resulted in the expansion of Port Vell. After moving a congested coastal road underground, the city opened Moll de la Fusta, a wide pedestrian zone that leads to the beaches of Barceloneta and connects the bright **Maremàgnum** and the **Moll d'Espanya.** Today, the entire stretch, from in front of the Columbus monument to the rejuvenated **Port Vell** (Old Port) to Port Olímpic, is as hedonistic as Barcelona gets. The Olympic bid in 1986 presented a two-sided challenge: comfortably housing 15,000 athletes while beautifying the city's long-ignored coastline. Oriol Bohigas, Josep Martorell, David Mackay, and Albert Puig Domènech designed the solution: the **Vila Olímpica,** a residential area with wide streets, symmetrical apartment buildings, pristine parks, and open-air art. Most social activity in the area takes place in the L-shaped **Port Olímpic,** home to docked sailboats, over 20 restaurants, a large casino, and a long strip of nightclubs.

ZONA ALTA: GRÀCIA AND OUTER BARRIS

Zona Alta (Uptown) is the section of Barcelona that lies at the top of most maps: past l'Eixample, in and around the Collserola Mountains, and away from the low-lying waterfront districts. The Zona Alta is made up of several formerly independent towns, each of which still exhibits its own distinctive character. The most visited part of Zona Alta is Gràcia, incorporated into Barcelona in 1897 despite the protests of many of its residents. Calls for Gràcian independence continue even today, albeit with less frequency, and the area has always had a political streak, evident in names like Mercat de Llibertat ("Liberty Market") and Pl. de la Revolució ("Revolution Plaza"). After incorporation, the area continued to be a center of left-wing activism and resistance, even during the oppressive Franco regime. Gràcia packs a surprising number of *Modernista* buildings and parks, international cuisine, and chic shops into a relatively small area, making it a fascinating district to explore. Relatively untouched by tourism, Gràcia still has that local charm; a stay here is worth the short commute to the center of the city.

MAPS

El Corte Inglés distributes a good free map, as do a variety of guide/map companies, such as **CitySpy** and **BCN.Guide;** check out hotel lobbies to find one you like. The Barcelona **tourist office** (Pl. de Catalunya and Pl. Sant Jaume; p. 382) has maps with an enlarged inset of the Barri Gòtic, although the better ones (which will have street numbers and one-way streets marked, and may include a full index of the city) will cost you between €1-4. There are also maps for almost every theme: Bici i Vainants with bicycle lanes marked, an official gay and lesbian tourist guide, a hotel map, an ethnic food map, a shopping map, an art gallery map, and perhaps most importantly, an excellent *plànol turístic ciutat vella* (map of the old city), stretching from Gran Via out past Barceloneta, with Metro stops, services, museums, landmarks, a street index, and more. Bus and Metro maps, one with tourist sights and landmarks (the **metro&bus touristmapbcn**), and one with hours for each bus line (the **plànolbusbcn**), are both free at tourist offices and metro stations.

⨎ LOCAL TRANSPORTATION

METRO AND BUS

Barcelona's public transportation (info ☎010) is quick and cheap. If you plan to use public transportation extensively, there are several *Autoritat del Transport Metropolità* (ATM) *abonos* (passes) available, which work interchangeably for the Metro, bus, and urban lines of the FGC commuter trains, RENFE Cercanías, Trams, and Nitbus. The **T-10 pass** (€6.90) is valid for 10 rides and saves you nearly 50% off single tickets. The **T-Dia pass** (€5.25) is good for a full day of unlimited travel, and the **T-mes** (€44.35) is good for a month. If you just plan to use the Metro and daytime buses, there are 2-5 day passes at **Transports Metropolitans de Barcelona** (TMB; ☎933 18 70 74; www.tmb.net; **2-Dies** €9.60, **5-Dies** €20.80). These will save you money if you plan to ride the Metro more than three times per day, but they don't work on the Nitbus.

Metro: (☎932 98 70 00; www.tmb.net). Vending machines and ticket windows sell passes. Red diamonds with the letter "M" mark stations. Hold on to your ticket—riding without one can incur a fine of €40. Trains run M-Th 5am-midnight, F-Sa 5am-2am, Su and holidays 6am-midnight. Extended holiday hours. €1.25 per *sencillo* (1-way ticket).

Ferrocarrils de la Generalitat de Catalunya (FGC): (☎932 05 15 15; www.fgc.es). Commuter trains to local destinations with main stations at Pl. de Catalunya and Pl.

d'Espanya. Note that some destinations within the city (parts of Gràcia and beyond) require taking the FGC. Blue symbols resembling 2 interlocking "V"s mark Metro connections. The commuter line costs the same as the Metro (€1.25) until Tibidabo. After that, rates go up by zone: Zone 2 €1.85, Zone 3 €2.60, etc. Metro passes are valid on FGC trains. Info office at the Pl. de Catalunya station open M-F 7am-9pm.

RENFE Cercanías (Rodalies): (☎902 24 02 02; www.renfe.es/cercanias). The L10 to the **airport** (Zone 4; €2.50) is the most popular. Destinations include **Sitges** (Zone 4) and **Blanes** (Zone 6; €3.95). Main connections at Sants and Pg. de Gràcia, marked by either the RENFE double arrows or a funny-looking red circle with a backwards C.

Buses: Go just about anywhere, usually from 5am-10pm (many leave for the last round at 9:30pm). Most stops have maps posted, and you can easily figure out which bus to take. Most buses come every 10-15min. in central locations. €1.25.

Nitbus: 18 different lines run every 20-30min. 10:30pm-4:30am, depending on the line; a few run until 5:30am. All buses depart from around Pl. de Catalunya, stop in front of most club complexes, and work their way through Ciutat Vella and the Zona Alta. Maps are available at *estancos* (tobacco shops), posted on some bus stops, online (www.tmb.net), and marked by signs in Metro stations.

Bus Turístic: Hop-on, hop-off tours of the city. Passes sold for 1-2 days. See p. 395.

TAXIS

About 11,000 taxis swarm the city and you can usually hail one in any relatively central location. A *lliure* or *libre* sign or a green light on the roof means vacant; yellow means occupied. On weekend nights, you may wait up to 30min. for a ride; long lines form at popular spots like the Port Olímpic. To call a cab, try **RadioTaxi033** (☎933 033 033; www.radiotaxi033.com; AmEx/MC/V) or **Servi Taxi** (☎933 30 03 00). **Disabled travelers** should call for Taxi Amic's adapted vehicles (☎934 20 80 88).

CAR RENTAL

Avis, C. Corcega, 293-295 (☎932 37 56 80). Open M-F 9am-9pm, Sa 8am-8pm, Su 8am-1pm. 3 other locations. **Branch** at airport (☎932 98 36 00; open M-Sa 7am-12:30am, Su 7am-midnight), and **Estació Sants,** Pl. dels Països Catalans, s/n. (☎933 30 41 93; fax 91 41 07. Open M-F 7:30am-10:30pm, Sa 8am-7pm, Su 9am-7pm.)

Budget, in El Prat de Llobregat airport (☎932 98 36 38; fax 98 36 42). Open daily 7am-midnight.

Cooltra, Ptge. de Vilaret, 6 (☎932 47 28 34; www.cooltra.com). M: Encants. Mopeds from €30 per day and €260 per month. Open daily 10am-2pm and 4-8pm.

Europcar, Pl. Països Catalanes, s/n (☎934 91 48 22; www.europcar.es), near Sants. Open M-F 7am-11pm, Sa-Su 8am-8pm. Branch at El Prat de Llobregat airport (☎932 98 33 00). Open daily 24hr.

Hertz, C. Tuset, 10 (☎932 17 80 76; www.hertz.es). M: Diagonal or FCG: Gràcia. Open M-F 9am-2pm and 4-7pm, Sa 9am-2pm. **Branch** at airport (☎932 98 36 38) and by **Estació Sants,** C. Viriat, 45 (☎934 19 61 56).

BIKE RENTAL

Budget Bikes, C. Marquès de Barberà, 15 (☎933 04 18 85; www.budgetbikes.eu), down C. Unió from La Rambla. €15 per day, €25 for 2nd day, extra days €7.

Barcelona Bici (☎932 85 38 32). Offers 10hr. rentals. Customized. 3 rental points: Pl. Catalunya, Mirador de Colom, and Pg. Joan de Borbó.

Baja Bikes, Pg. Maritim de Barceloneta, 34 (☎646 25 21 99; www.bajabikesbarcelona.com). Offers a tour and tapas bar combo for €27.95, min. 4 people.

🅰 PRACTICAL INFORMATION

TOURIST AND FINANCIAL SERVICES

Tourist Offices:

Plaça de Catalunya, Pl. de Catalunya, 17S, underground on the bottom left-hand corner facing south (toward La Rambla). M: Catalunya. The main office, along with Pl. de Sant Jaume, has free maps, brochures on sights and transportation, booking service for last-minute accommodations, a gift shop, money exchange, and a box office (Caixa de Catalunya). Open daily 9am-9pm.

Plaça de Sant Jaume, C. Ciutat, 2. M: Jaume I. Open M-F 9am-8pm, Sa 10am-8pm, Su and holidays 10am-2pm.

Oficina de Turisme de Catalunya, Pg. de Gràcia, 107 (☎932 38 40 00; www.gencat.es/probert). M: Diagonal. Open M-Sa 10am-7pm, Su 10am-2pm.

Institut de Cultura de Barcelona (ICUB), Palau de la Virreina, La Rambla, 99 (☎933 16 10 00; www.bcn.cat/cultura). Info office open M-Sa 10am-8pm, Su 11am-3pm.

Estació Barcelona-Sants, Pl. Països Catalans. M: Sants-Estació. Info and last-minute accommodations booking. Open in summer daily 8am-8pm; in winter M-F 8am-8pm, Sa-Su 8am-2pm.

Aeroport El Prat de Llobregat, terminals A and B. Info and last-minute accommodations bookings. Open daily 9am-9pm.

Tourist Office Representatives booths dot the city in the summer. Open July-Sept. daily 10am-8pm; many are open weekends or shorter hours in winter.

Tours: In addition to the Bus Turístic (p. 395), the Pl. de Catalunya tourist office offers 2hr. **walking tours** of the Barri Gòtic daily at 10am (English) and Sa at noon (*català* and Spanish). Group size limited; buy tickets in advance. (☎932 85 38 32 for info. €9, ages 4-12 €3.) 2hr. **Picasso tour** of Barcelona Tu-Su 10:30am (English) and Sa 11:30am (*català* and Spanish). Ages 4-12 €5; includes entrance to the Museu Picasso. **Self-guided** tours of Gothic, Romanesque, *Modernista,* and Contemporary Barcelona available; pick up pamphlets with maps at the tourist office. **Bike tours** abound; see **Bike Rental** (p.381). **Barcelona Segway Glides** offers 2hr. tours ("glides") for €60, M-Sa 10am and 5pm. Call for reservations. (☎678 77 73 71; www.barcelonasegwayglides.com. Cash only.)

Currency Exchange: ATMs give the best rates. The very best are those marked **Telebanco;** they report the exchange rate on the receipt and on-screen rather than leaving you guessing. The next-best rates are at banks. General banking M-F 8:30am-2pm. La Rambla has many exchange stations open late, but the rates are not as good and they will take a commission.

American Express: La Rambla, 74 (☎933 42 73 11). M: Liceu. Open M-F 9am-9pm, Sa 9am-2pm.

LOCAL SERVICES

Luggage Storage: Estació Barcelona-Sants, M: Sants-Estació. Lockers €3-4.50 per day. Open daily 5:30am-11pm. **Estació de França,** M: Barceloneta. Lockers €3/4.50 per day. Open daily 7am-10pm. **Estació Nord,** M: Arc de Triomf. Lockers €3/4.50/5 per day, 90-day limit. Also at the **El Prat Airport,** €4.60 per day.

English-Language Bookstores: See Books, p. 406.

Libraries: The **Biblioteques de Barcelona** (www.bcn.cat/biblioteques) might be located in ancient buildings and have very odd hours, but the A/C and free Internet (and free Wi-Fi with library card) make them well worth figuring out. Excellent map/guide to opening hours and services of all 30 locations. To check out books or use the Wi-Fi, get a library card, a fast and easy process if you have an address in Barcelona.

Biblioteca Francesca Bonnemaison, C. Sant Pere més Baix, 7 (☎932 68 73 60). M: Urquinaona. Walk toward the water, then turn left past the Palau de Música de Catalana and C. Sant Pere més Alt. Open M and Th 4-9pm, Tu and F 10am-2pm and 4-9pm, W 10am-9pm, Sa 10am-2pm.

Biblioteca Barceloneta-La Fraternitat, C. Comte de Santa Clara, 8-10 (☎932 25 35 74), 2 blocks from the beach in Port Vell. Open M-Tu and F 4-9pm, W 10am-2pm and 4-9pm, Th 10am-9pm, Sa 10am-2pm. Closed Aug. 1-15, longer hours during academic year.

Religious Services: Comunidad Israelita de Barcelona (Jewish services), C. Avenir, 24 (☎932 09 31 47; www.cibonline.org). **Comunidad Musulmana** (Muslim services), Mosque Tarek Ben Ziad, C. de l'Hospital, 91 (☎934 41 91 49). Services daily at prayer times. **Església Catedral de la Santa Creu** (Catholic services), Pl. de la Seu, 3 (☎933 42 82 60; www.catedralbcn.org). M: Jaume I. Cloister open daily 9am-1pm and 5-7pm. Mass at 9, 10, 11am, noon, and 7pm; Su 9, 10:30am, noon, 1, 6, and 7pm (in Spanish). **Parròquia María Reina,** Av. d'Esplugues, 103 (☎932 03 55 39). Mass offered in English. **Iglesia Evangélica Pablo Nuevo,** C. Llull, 161 (☎934 85 48 41; www.iepoble9.org). **Testigos de Jehová: Salón Reino,** Consell de cent, 83 (☎934 23 26 68). **Casa del Tíbet,** C. Rosselló, 181 (☎932 07 59 66; www.casadeltibet-bcn.org). **Hare Krishna,** Pl. Reial, 12 (☎933 02 51 94; www.iskcon.org). Contact the tourist office or check out the online directory at www.bcn.es for info on other services.

Gay and Lesbian Resources: Antinous, C. Josep Anselm Clavé, 6 (☎933 01 90 70; www.antinouslibros.com). M: Drassanes. Specializes in gay and lesbian books and films. Decent selection in English. Open M-F 11am-2pm and 5-9pm, Sa noon-2pm and 5-9pm. AmEx/DC/MC/V. **Cómplices,** C. Cervantes, 2 (☎934 12 72 83). M: Liceu. A small bookstore with gay and lesbian books in English and Spanish, as well as a decent selection of films. Also provides a **map** of Barcelona's gay bars and discotecas. Open M-F 10:30am-8pm, Sa noon-8pm. AmEx/MC/V.

Laundromats:

Lavomatic, Pl. Joaquim Xirau, 1, 1 block to the right off La Rambla and 1 block below C. Escudellers; **branch** at C. Consolat del Mar, 43-45 (☎932 68 47 68), 1 block north of Pg. Colon and 2 blocks right off Via Laietana. Wash €4.75, dry €0.85 per 5min. Both open M-Sa 9am-9pm.

Wash @ Net, C. les Carretes, 56, in El Raval. Wash €4-6, dry €1 per 10min. Internet €0.50 per 30min. Open 10am-11pm.

Lavamax, C. Junta de Comerç, 14 (☎933 01 59 32). Wash €5-8, dry €2 per 20min. Self-service open daily 9:30am-9:30pm. Drop-off service M-Sa 9:30am-1:30pm, M-F also 5-9pm.

Orange Laundry, Pl. del Sol, 11-12 (☎934 15 03 61). Wash €4, dry €4. Open 7am-11pm.

EMERGENCY AND COMMUNICATIONS

Local police: ☎092. **National police:** ☎091. **Mossos d'Esquadra:** ☎088. **Medical Emergency:** ☎061.

Tourist Police: La Rambla, 43 (☎932 56 24 30). M: Liceu. Multilingual officers. This is where to go if you've been pick pocketed. Open 24hr.

Late-Night Pharmacy: Rotates; check any pharmacy window for the nearest on duty, or contact the police. Or call **Información de Farmacias de Guardia** (☎93 481 00 60).

Hospital: Hospital Clínic i Provincial, C. Villarroel, 170 (☎932 27 54 00). M: Hospital Clínic. Main entrance at C. Roselló and C. Casanova. **Hospital de la Santa Creu i Sant Pau** (☎932 91 90 00, emergency 91 91 91). M: Hospital de Sant Pau. **Hospital General de la Vall d'Hebron** (☎932 74 61 00). M: Vall d'Hebron. **Hospital del Mar,** Pg. Marítim, 25-29 (☎932 48 30 00), before Port Olímpic. M: Ciutadella or Vila Olímpica.

Telephones: Buy phone cards at tobacco stores and newsstands; the lowest denomination is usually €6, and this promises 45min. of international calling. Rates sometimes require you to use all your minutes up in a single call. A much better option is to use **Locotorios** (international call centers), which dot the streets on either side of La Rambla. A short call to the US will cost only a few cents. **Directory Assistance:** ☎1003 within Spain, 1008 within Europe, 1005 outside Europe.

Internet Access:

■ **Easy Internet Café,** La Rambla, 31 (☎933 01 7507; www.easyinternetcafe.com). M: Liceu. With fairly reasonable prices and over 200 terminals in a bright, modern center, this is Internet heaven. **CD burning** (€5), **faxing** (€1-2.50), **copying,** and **scanning** (€1.30). €2.20 per hour, 1-day unlimited pass €7, 1 week €15, 1 month €30. Open 8am-2:30am. **Branch** at Ronda Universitat, 35. M: Catalunya. €2 per hour, 1-day pass €3, 1 week €7, 1 month €15. Open 8am-2am.

Navegaweb, La Rambla, 88-94 (☎933 17 90 26; navegabarcelona@terra.es). M: Liceu. Located in the basement of a large video arcade, so an air hockey table is never far away. Good rates for international calls ($0.17 per min. to USA). Internet €1.60 per hour. Open M-Th and Su 9am-midnight, F 9am-1am, Sa 9am-2am.

Bcnet (Internet Gallery Café), C. Barra de Ferro, 3 (☎932 68 15 07; www.bornet-bcn.com), down the street from the Museu Picasso. M: Jaume I. €2.90 per hour; 10hr. ticket €19. Open M-F 10am-11pm, Sa-Su noon-11pm.

MS Internet, C. Pintor Fortuny, 30 (☎933 17 55 62), 3 blocks off Las Ramblas in El Raval. M: Liceu or Catalunya. €1 per hour. Open M-Sa 9am-9pm.

Contacta, Gran Via, 600 (☎933 18 73 51). M: Universitat. €1 per hour. Open M-F 9am-11pm, Sa-Su noon-11pm. **Branch** at C. Villarroel, 199 (☎934 19 35 39).

Interspace, C. San Miguel, 41-43 (☎932 21 40 58), right off Pl. la Barceloneta. €1.50 per hour. Open M-F 11am-11pm, Sa-Su 3-11pm.

Post Office: Pl. d'Antoni López (☎902 197 197). M: Jaume I or Barceloneta. **Fax** and **Lista de Correos.** Open M-F 8:30am-10pm, Su (access on side street) noon-10pm. Also dozens of branches; consult www.correos.es. **Postal Code:** 08003.

⚑ ACCOMMODATIONS

While accommodations in Barcelona are easy to spot, finding an affordable bed or room can be more difficult. During one of the busier months (June-Sept. or Dec.), wandering up and down La Rambla looking for a place to stay can turn into a frustrating experience. If you want to stay in the touristy areas, reserve weeks ahead. Consider staying outside heavily trafficked Ciutat Vella; there are plenty of hostels in the Zona Alta, particularly in Gràcia, that have more vacancies. For the best rooms, l'Eixample has good deals and is also quiet at night. La Ribera and El Raval are good Ciutat Vella alternatives to the hectic Barri Gòtic; they're just as close to the action and often cheaper. On the side streets farther from La Rambla, there are some less reputable parts of El Raval, so choose wisely. Accommodations booking can be found at www.hotelsbcn.com or www.hostelworld.com.

 ALTERNATIVE ACCOMMODATIONS. Barcelona is not a cheap city, and a decent hostel will cost at least €23 a night. Those passing through Barcelona for a short time, and carrying no valuables, sometimes turn to another option: the so-called "illegal hostels" that offer rooms for less than half the normal prices (€8-11). Backpackers looking to stay illegally sometimes ask around at Travel Bar (C. Boqueria, 27). Illegal hostels can be dangerous and unpredictable, and Let's Go does not recommend them.

CAMPING

A handful of sites lie in the outskirts of the city, accessible by intercity buses (20-45min.; €1.50). The **Associació de Càmpings de Barcelona,** Gran Via de les Corts Catalanes, 608 (☎934 12 59 55; www.campingsbcn.com), has more info. A good choice is **Càmping Tres Estrellas ❶,** Autovía de Castelldefells, km 13.2. Take bus L95 (€1.60) from Pl. de Catalunya to the stop just 300m from the campsite, 13km south. (☎936 33 06 37; www.camping3estrellas.com. €7 per person, €8 per 2-person tent, €8 per vehicle. Equipped with Internet access, BBQ, pool, ATM, supermarket, and more. Open Mar. 15-Oct. 15. AmEx/MC/V.)

ACCOMMODATIONS BY PRICE

B Barri Gòtic **E** Elsewhere **G** Gràcia **L** La Ribera **R** El Raval **X** L'Eixample

UNDER €15 (❶)			Hostal Benidorm (386)	B
Cámping Tres Estrellas (384)	E		Hostal Campi (386)	B
🏠 Camping Montserrat (412)	E		🏠 Hostal Eden (388)	X
Cel·les Montserrat (412)	E		🏠 Hostal Levante (385)	B
			Hostal Nuevo Colón (387)	L
€15-25 (❷)			🏠 Hotel Peninsular (387)	R
Alberg Residència La Ciutat (388)	G		Hostal de Ribagorza (387)	R
Albergue Mare de Déu de Mont. (388)	G		🏠 Hostal-Residència Rembrandt (386)	B
🏠 Barcelona Mar Youth Hostel (387)	R		Hostal San Remo (387)	X
Center Ramblas (387)	R		Hotel Toledano/Hostal Res. Cap. (386)	B
🏠 Gothic Point Youth Hostel (386)	L		Pensión Aribau (388)	X
🏠 Hostal Mariluz Youngsters (385)	B		Pensión Port-Bou (387)	L
🏠 Hostal Maldà (386)	B		Pensión San Medín (388)	G
Hostal Residència Lausanne (386)	B			
Hostel Sun & Moon (385)	B		**€36-50 (❹)**	
Kabul Youth Hostel (385)	B		Hostal Lesseps (388)	G
Pensión Ciudadela (387)	L		Hostal Ópera (387)	R
Pensión Fani (388)	X		🏠 Hostal Residència Oliva (387)	X
Pensión Fernando (385)	B		🏠 Hostal Qué Tal (387)	X
			Hotel Lloret (386)	B
€26-35 (❸)			**ABOVE €50 (❺)**	
BCN Hostal Central (388)	X		🏠 Hostal Plaza (386)	B

BARRI GÒTIC AND LA RAMBLA

LOWER BARRI GÒTIC

The following hostels are between C. Ferran and the water. Backpackers flock here to be close to the late-night revelry at hip La Rambla. Beware of the cheapest options if you want breathing room.

🏠 **Hostal Mariluz Youngsters,** C. Palau, 4 (☎933 17 34 63; www.pensionmariluz.com), up 3 flights. M: Liceu or Jaume I. Gorgeous renovations turned this hostel into a modern and natural light-filled space around a historic courtyard. All new baths. Offers short-term apartments nearby. Free Wi-Fi. Dorms €20, with bath €21; singles €30/38; doubles €35/50; triples €42/63; quads €56/80, with bath 70/84. MC/V. ❷

🏠 **Hostal Levante,** Baixada de San Miquel, 2 (☎933 17 95 65; www.hostallevante.com). M: Liceu. The best deal in Barri Gòtic. Large, tasteful rooms with light wood furnishings and fans; some have balconies. TV lounge. Ask for a newly renovated room. Apartments have kitchen, living room, and laundry machine. Spacious doubles. Singles €33-43; doubles €56-65; apartments €30 per person per night. MC/V. ❸

Pensión Fernando, C. Ferran, 31 (☎933 01 79 93; www.hfernando.com). M: Liceu. This clean hostel is conveniently located. Dorms with A/C and lockers. Common kitchen with dining room and TV on 3rd fl. Towels €2. Dorms with lockers €16-21; singles €30-36, with bath €40-45; doubles with bath €52-64; triples with bath €58-70. MC/V. ❷

Kabul Youth Hostel, Pl. Reial, 17 (☎933 18 51 90; www.kabul.es). M: Liceu. Legendary among backpackers; squeezes in up to 200 travelers in rooms of 4-20. Lounge with pool table and terrace. Breakfast included. Laundry €2.50. Key deposit €15. Reservations only on website with credit card. Check-out 11am. Dorms €18-24. MC/V. ❷

Hostel Sun & Moon, C. Ferran, 17 (☎932 70 20 60; www.smhostel.net). M: Liceu. Low prices close to La Rambla. Communal kitchen. Includes breakfast and blanket. Sheets

€2. 2 computers in lobby with free Internet access. Parking €20 per day. 6- and 8-bed dorms €20. Singles €40, with bath €60; doubles €65/70; triples €75/80. Discounts for stays longer than 2 days. AmEx/MC/V. ❷

Hostal Benidorm, La Rambla, 37 (☎933 02 20 54; www.hostalbenidorm.com). M: Drassanes or Liceu. One of the best values on La Rambla. Phone, bath, A/C, and balconies overlooking the street. Vending machines in lobby. Internet €1 per 15min. Singles €35.40; doubles €55.65; triples €75.80; quads €90; quints €105. MC/V. ❸

UPPER BARRI GÒTIC

This section of the Barri Gòtic is between C. Fontanella and C. Ferran. **Portal de l'Àngel,** a chic pedestrian avenue, runs through the middle. Rooms are pricier but more serene than in the lower Barri Gòtic. Reservations are advised in summer.

▦ **Hostal-Residència Rembrandt,** C. de la Portaferrissa, 23 (☎933 18 10 11; www.hostrembrandt.com). M: Liceu. Rooms superior to others in the area; all unique, some with large bath, patio, sitting area, and TV. Breakfast (€5). Fans. Reception 9am-11pm. Reservations require credit card. Singles €28; doubles €45-55; triples €70-80. MC/V. ❸

▦ **Hostal Maldà,** C. Pi, 5 (☎933 17 30 02). M: Liceu. Enter inside the small shopping center. The friendly owner keeps the hostel occupied year-round. 26 quality rooms with shared baths at unbeatable prices. No reservations; claim your space 9-11am. Returning guests can call ahead. Doubles €30; triples with shower €45. Cash only. ❸

▦ **Hostal Plaza,** C. Fontanella, 18 (☎933 01 01 39; www.plazahostal.com). Superfriendly owners, brightly painted rooms decorated with colorful art, many with A/C. Free Internet access in the lobby and a great location. Singles €45-50, with bath €60-70; doubles €40-55/60-75; triples €75-90. AmEx/MC/V. ❺

Hostal Campi, C. Canuda, 4 (☎933 01 35 45; www.hostalcampi.com). A centrally located bargain with friendly service. Most rooms have balconies. Prices vary, but generally singles €27; doubles €50, with bath €58; triples €69/78. MC/V. ❷

Hotel Lloret, La Rambla, 125 (☎933 17 33 66; fax 933 17 33 66). M: Catalunya. Modern rooms with large, newly renovated baths, tasteful furniture, A/C, TV, and phone. Worth the splurge for large groups. Breakfast €5. Singles €48-51; doubles €75-84; triples €84-98; quads €108. AmEx/MC/V. ❹

Hostal Residència Lausanne, Av. Portal de l'Àngel, 24 (☎933 02 11 39). M: Catalunya. Great central location. Go up 2 flights at the back of the entrance foyer. White walls, posh lounge with marble staircase, and TV. Free Internet. Doubles €48-53, with bath €68, for 1 person €35; quads with balcony €120; quints €140. Cash only. ❷

Hotel Toledano/Hostal Residència Capitol, La Rambla, 138 (☎933 01 08 72; www.hoteltoledano.com). M: Catalunya. Rooms with cable TV and phones; outer rooms with balcony, interior with A/C. Free Internet access in lobby; free Wi-Fi throughout. 4th-fl. hotel (all but cheapest singles have bath): singles €39; doubles €64; triples €85; quads €100. 5th-fl. hostel: €30/44/62/75. AmEx/MC/V. ❸

LA RIBERA

Less tourist activity in this neighborhood translates into fewer lodging choices. Still, consider La Ribera for a quieter, but still charming, alternative to the *barris*.

▦ **Gothic Point Youth Hostel,** C. Vigatans, 5 (☎932 68 78 08; www.gothicpoint.com). M: Jaume I. Colorful lounge area has free Internet and TV. Beds with curtains in jungle-gym rooms with A/C. Rooftop terrace. Lots of events, including a weekly crafts fair. Breakfast included. Lockers €1.50 per day. Sheets €2, towels €2. Refrigerator access. High-season dorms €22; mid-season €19; low-season €17. €2 credit card fee. AmEx/MC/V. ❷

Hostal de Ribagorza, C. Trafalgar, 39 (☎933 19 19 68; www.hostalribagorza.com). M: Urquinaona. Rooms in a *Modernista* building complete with marble staircase and tile floors. TV, fan, and homey decorations. Doubles €45-60; triples €60-70. Lower prices in winter. MC/V. ❸

Pensión Ciudadela, C. Comerç, 33 (☎933 19 62 03; www.pension-ciudadela.com). M: Barceloneta. Climb 5 flights of stairs to this small hostel with 6 spacious rooms. All have A/C, TV, and balcony. Doubles €43, with bath €54; 1 triple €66. AmEx/MC/V. ❷

Hostal Nuevo Colón, Av. Marquès de l'Argentera, 19 (☎933 19 50 77; www.hostalnuevocolon.com). M: Barceloneta. 26 modern rooms in a hotel-quality building with common area and TV. Reservations recommended in high season. Singles €35; doubles €46, with bath €65; triples €67/85; quads with bath €105. 3- to 6-person apartments with kitchens €105-150 per day. MC/V. ❸

Pensión Port-Bou, C. Comerç, 29 (☎933 19 23 67). M: Barceloneta. Spacious rooms in this old building feel like home. TV, desk, stained-glass windows, and some with balconies. Singles €35; doubles €53; triples €63; quads with bath €73. Cash only. ❸

EL RAVAL

Be careful in the areas nearer to the port and farther from La Rambla; they can be dark and eerily deserted late at night. El Raval, however, is a good lodging alternative to the more crowded zones.

Hotel Peninsular, C. de Sant Pau, 34 (☎933 02 31 38; http://hotelpeninsular.net). M: Liceu. This *Modernista* building arrays 80 beautiful rooms with phone and A/C around its 4-story interior courtyard festooned with plants. Excellent breakfast included. Singles €30, with bath €52; doubles with bath €75. MC/V. ❸

Barcelona Mar Youth Hostel, C. de Sant Pau, 80 (☎933 24 85 30; www.barcelonamar.es). M: Paral·lel. Crams in 120 dorm-style beds; 4-16 per room, with curtains. A/C; free Internet access in the lounge area. Breakfast and locker included. Sheets €2.50, towels €2.50, both €3.50. Self-serve laundry €4.50. Dorms in summer €22-23; in winter €16-19. Double beds €5, F-Sa add €1.50. AmEx/MC/V. ❷

Center Ramblas (HI), C. de l'Hospital, 63 (☎934 12 40 69; www.center-ramblas.com). M: Liceu. Young, friendly staff, and the cheapest beds in Barcelona. Breakfast and sheets included. Free Internet access. Laundry €5. Towels €2. Lockers €2 deposit; A/C advertised. Dorms in summer €20-24. In winter €15-19. HI card required. MC/V. ❷

Hostal Ópera, C. de Sant Pau, 20 (☎933 18 82 01; www.hostalopera.com). M: Liceu. Renovated rooms feel new; bath, phone, and A/C in every one. Cafe downstairs. Free Internet access in the small common room. Singles €46; doubles €66. MC/V. ❹

L'EIXAMPLE

Pricier than those of other *barris*, l'Eixample's lodgings are usually elegant and nicely equipped. At night, the streets are much quieter than in the Ciutat Vella.

Hostal Residència Oliva, Pg. de Gràcia, 32, 4th fl. (☎934 88 01 62; www.lasguias.com/hostaloliva). M: Pg. de Gràcia. Classy ambience; elegant wooden bureaus, mirrors, and a light marble floor. All rooms have high ceilings, TV, and fan, some with a view. Singles €36; doubles €60, with bath €75; triples with bath €84. Cash only. ❹

Hostal Qué Tal, C. Mallorca, 290 (☎934 59 23 66; www.quetalbarcelona.com), near C. Bruc. M: Pg. de Gràcia or Verdaguer. This high-quality gay- and lesbian-friendly hostel has one of the best interiors in the city, with murals, a plant-filled terrace, and snazzy decor in all 13 rooms. Singles €45; doubles €65, with bath €84. Cash only. ❹

Hostal San Remo, Ausiàs Marc, 19 (☎933 02 19 89; www.hostalsanremo.com). M: Urquinaona. 8 spacious rooms have TV, A/C, and windows; 4 have terraces, and some have stained-glass windows. Free Internet access. Reserve early. Singles €20, with bath €36; doubles €50/60; triples €60/72. Nov. and Jan.-Feb. reduced prices. MC/V. ❸

BCN Hostal Central, Ronda Universitat, 11, 1st fl. (☎933 02 24 20; www.hostalcentral.net). M: Universitat. Some rooms with balconies and inviting nooks. Breakfast, coffee, and fruit included. Free Internet. Reception 24hr. Singles with shared bath €25-38; doubles €35-45, with bath €50-62; triples €60/78; quads €60/85. MC/V. ❸

Hostal Eden, C. Balmes, 55 (☎934 52 66 20; www.hostaleden.net). M: Pg. de Gràcia. Modern rooms with high ceilings have TV and fan or A/C; most have new bathrooms. Apr.-Oct. singles €27, with bath €48; doubles €48/69; triples €80; quads €90. Nov.-Mar. singles €22/37; doubles €37/48; triples €64; quads €75. AmEx/MC/V. ❸

Pensión Fani, C. València, 278 (☎932 15 36 45). M: Catalunya. Oozes quirky charm. Rooms rented by month; single nights available only in doubles. Doubles €22 per person per day; singles €375 per month; doubles €500-per month. Cash only. ❷

Pensión Aribau, C. Aribau, 37, 1st fl. (☎934 53 11 06; www.hostalaribau.com). M: Pg. de Gràcia. Most of the hostel's 11 rooms have TV and A/C. Ask for one of the balconies overlooking a terrace. Reserve months ahead in summer. Singles €25-40, with bath €35-50; doubles €40-55, with bath €45-60, triples with bath €65-85. AmEx/MC/V. ❸

ZONA ALTA: GRÀCIA AND OUTER BARRIS

Gràcia is Barcelona's "undiscovered" quarter, so last-minute arrivals may find vacancies here, even though options are few.

Hostal Lesseps, C. Gran de Gràcia, 239 (☎932 18 44 34; www.hostallesseps.com). M: Lesseps. The 16 spacious rooms have TV and bath; 4 have A/C (€5 extra). Rooms facing the street are a bit noisy. Cats and dogs allowed. Free Internet access and Wi-Fi. Singles €45; doubles €75; triples €80, with extra bed €90. MC/V. ❹

Pensión San Medín, C. Gran de Gràcia, 125 (☎932 17 30 68; www.sanmedin.com). M: Fontana. Embroidered curtains and ornate tiling adorn this family-run pensión's 12 rooms, 4 with balcony, all with TV. Small common room with TV. Reception 8am-midnight. Singles €32, with bath €42; doubles €62. MC/V. ❸

Albergue Mare de Déu de Montserrat (HI), Pg. Mare de Déu del Coll, 41-45 (☎932 10 51 51; www.xanascat.net). M: Vallcarca. Take the #92 or #28 bus from the station, right when facing the mountain. Once home to a wealthy *catalana* family, this palatial building is a dazzling alternative to hostels in the Ciutat Vella. Breakfast included. Max. stay 5 days. Dorms €19.55-23.45; under 25 €16-20. MC/V. ❷

Alberg Residència La Ciutat, C. L'Alegre de Dalí, 66 (☎932 13 03 00; http://laciutat.nnhotels.es). M: Joanic. Follow C. Escorial for 5 blocks, then cross over to C. L'Alegre de Dalí. Lounge areas with satellite TV and kitchen. Private rooms have TV, phone, and bath. Breakfast included. Sheets €1.80. Laundry €5.40. Free Internet. Reception 24hr. 4- to 10-bed dorms €15-20; singles €35-50; doubles €48-60. MC/V. ❷

🍴 FOOD

Barcelona offers every kind of food and ambience imaginable. Whether Basque, Chinese, Indian, or American, restaurants here will exceed your culinary expectations. As a proud and distinct region within an already food-happy country, Barcelona boasts a double-edged entourage of "local specialties." Beware of touristy restaurants offering "traditional" specialties—good "authentic" food can be hard to find. Our best advice is to look to the *català* option: *fideuà* unseats paella, *cava* champagne complements every meal, and *crema catalana* satisfies the local sweet tooth. Barcelona's tapas (sometimes called *pintxos*) bars, concentrated in La Ribera and Gràcia, often serve *montaditos*, thick slices of bread topped with all sorts of delectables from sausage to *tortilla* (omelette) to anchovies. Hopping from one tapas bar to another can be a fun, social, and often cheap way to pass the evening. Most tapas bars are self-serve and standing room only. Plates in hand, ravenous customers help themselves to the toothpick-skewered goodies that line the bars. The bartender calculates the bill by tallying up the toothpicks on the way out, and then it's on to another bar. Though vegetarian options in general have never been easier to find, vegetarian tapas are rare. Pick up the extensive *Guía del Ocio* (€1) at a newsstand for a list of most restaurants in Barcelona, including listings by type of food, with hours, reviews, and contact information.

Markets: ▓**La Boqueria (Mercat de Sant Josep),** off La Rambla. M: Liceu. Wholesale prices for vegetables, fruit, cheese, meat, and wine. Open M-Sa 6am-8pm. **Mercat de la Concepi,** C. València, between C. Bruc and C. Girona. M: Girona. Open M-Sa 8am-3pm. **Mercat Santa Caterina,** Av. Francesc Cambó, s/n, just off Via Laietana. Recently remodeled, and now has Wi-Fi. (€1 per hour.) Open M-Sa 7:30am-2pm.

Supermarkets: Champion, La Rambla, 113. M: Liceu. Open M-Sa 10am-10pm. MC/V. **El Corte Inglés,** Pl. de Catalunya, 14. M: Catalunya. Supermarket in basement. Open M-Sa and occasionally Su 10am-10pm. AmEx/MC/V.

FOOD BY TYPE

B Barri Gòtic **G** Gràcia **L** La Ribera **M** Montjuïc **R** El Raval **W** Waterfront **X** l'Eixample

ASIAN
Bunga Raya (391)   L❸
Hello Sushi (392)   R❷
Kirin (392)   X❷
Sushi Itto (394)   G❸

CAFES AND PASTRY SHOPS
Arc Café (390)   B❷
Café de l'Òpera (390)   B❶
Crepería Central (393)   W❷
El Consulade (393)   M❶
La Colmena (390)   B❶
Juicy Jones (391)   B❷
Laie Llibreria Café (393)   X❶
Mendizabal (392)   R❶
Zahara (394)   W❷

CATALAN AND SPANISH
Acalia (392)   X❸
Agua (393)   W❸
DosTrece (392)   R❸
▓ Els 4 Gats (390)   B❹
▓ Ikastola (394)   G❶
La Font de Prades (393)   M❸
▓ La Rita (392)   E❷
▓ L'Antic Bocoi del Gòtic (390)   B❷
▓ Les Quinze Nits (390)   B❶
Los Caracoles (390)   B❸
Madame Jasmine (392)   R❶

Mi Burrito y Yo (390)   B❹
▓ Restaurant Can Lluís (392)   R❸
Xaloc (391)   B❷

INTERNATIONAL
▓ Attic (390)   B❸
▓ El Pebre Blau (391)   L❸
▓ HBN BCN (393)   W❶
La Gavina (394)   G❷
▓ Orígen 99'9% (391)   L❶
▓ Racó d'en Baltà (392)   X❸
Tenorio (393)   X❸
Vildsvin (390)   B❸
La Pizza del Born (391)   L❶
▓ Petra (391)   R❷

TAPAS
▓ Jai-Ca Bar (393)   W❶
Tèxtil Cafè (391)   L❸
Va de Vi (391)   L❷
El Xampanyet (391)   L❶
Zodiaco (393)   M❶

VEGETARIAN
▓ Bar Ra (392)   R❷
Maoz Vegetarian (390)   B❶
▓ Organic (392)   R❸
Pla dels Àngels (392)   R❷
Restaurante Casa Regina (394)   G❸
Restaurante Illa de Gràcia (394)   G❶

BARRI GÒTIC AND LA RAMBLA

Barcelona's nucleus contains all types of eateries. Classic *català* cuisine is juxtaposed with fast-food options and every species of bar imaginable. Choose carefully; anything along La Rambla is likely to be overpriced.

LOWER BARRI GÒTIC

▨ **Les Quinze Nits,** Pl. Reial, 6 (☎933 17 30 75). M: Liceu. Popular restaurant with lines halfway through the plaza every night; get there early to have dinner in this beautiful setting. *Català* entrees at shockingly low prices. Pasta and rice €4-7. Fish €7-9. Meat €6-10. Open daily 1-3:45pm and 8:30-11:30pm. MC/V. ❶

▨ **L'Antic Bocoi del Gòtic,** Baixada de Viladecols, 3 (☎933 10 50 67; www.bocoi.net). M: Jaume I. Formed in part by an ancient 1st-century Roman wall. Excellent salads (€6.50-7.50), *pâtés* (€9-12), and cheese platters (€11.50-16) feature *jamón ibérico* and local produce. Open M-Sa 8:30pm-midnight. Reserve in advance. AmEx/MC/V. ❷

Mi Burrito y Yo, C. del Pas de l'Ensenyança, 2 (☎933 18 27 42). M: Jaume I. Not a Mexican joint (*burrito* means "little donkey"); instead offers *català* specialties. Sit on the balcony or in booths downstairs. Live music at 9:30pm. Entrees €13-24. Paella €20 per person. Weekday lunch *menú* €10.25. Open daily 1pm-midnight. MC/V. ❹

Los Caracoles, C. Escudellers, 14 (☎933 02 31 85). M: Drassanes. Once a 19th-century snail shop, now a bustling restaurant with Old World charm. Specialties include *caracoles* (snails; €10.50) and rabbit. Open daily 1:15pm-midnight. AmEx/MC/V. ❸

Arc Café, C. Carabassa, 19 (☎933 02 52 04; www.arccafe.com). M: Drassanes. This secluded cafe serves curries, soups, and salads. Entrees €8-13. *Platos del mediodía* €5.50. Thai menu W-Th. Open M-Th 1pm-1am, F-Sa 1pm-3am. AmEx/MC/V. ❷

Vildsvin, C. Ferran, 38 (☎933 17 94 07, reservations 902 52 05 22; reservas@sagardi.es). M: Liceu. Oysters and international beers (€4-8) are this central-European bar's specialties. Chic restaurant downstairs has salads, salmon, and homemade cheese and sausage. Tapas €1.20-4.60. Entrees €8-15. Desserts €3-5.20. Open M-F 8:30am-1am, F-Sa 9am-2am, Su 9am-1am. AmEx/MC/V. ❸

Maoz Vegetarian, 3 locations: at C. Ferran, 13; La Rambla, 95; and C. Jaume 1, 7 (www.maozvegetarian.com). Vegetarian chain and Barcelona institution staffed by friendly 20-somethings. Falafel €2.90-4.70. Open M-Th and Su 11am-2:30am, F-Sa 11am-3am. MC/V. ❶

UPPER BARRI GÒTIC

▨ **Els 4 Gats,** C. Montsió, 3 (☎933 02 41 40; www.4gats.com). M: Catalunya. Picasso's old *Modernista* hangout with lots of bohemian character. Cuisine includes Mediterranean salad (€9.50) and Iberian pork with apples (€17.10). Entrees €12-26. M-F lunch *menú* (€11.97) is the best deal and comes with epic desserts; try the *crema catalana*. Live piano 9pm-1am. Open daily 1pm-1am. AmEx/MC/V. ❹

▨ **Attic,** La Rambla, 120 (☎933 02 48 66; www.angrup.com). M: Liceu. It's hard to believe this chic, modern restaurant has such reasonable prices right on touristy La Rambla. Mediterranean fusion cuisine, including fish (€9-13), meat (€6-14), and rice (€6-9) dishes. Open daily 1-4:30pm and 7pm-midnight. AmEx/MC/V. ❸

Café de l'Òpera, La Rambla, 74 (☎933 17 75 85; www.cafeoperabcn.com). M: Liceu. Antique mirror-covered cafe used to be a post-opera bourgeois tradition; now it's a hidden favorite. The hot chocolate (€1.80) is as thick as a melted candy bar. *Churros* €1.30. Tapas €3-6. Salads €3-8. Open daily 8am-3am. Cash only. ❶

La Colmena, Pl. de l'Àngel, 12 (☎933 15 13 56). M: Jaume I. No one can resist this busy dessert shop, appropriately named "the Beehive." Take a number and don't walk in unless you're prepared to buy. Pastries €1-4. Open daily 9am-9pm. AmEx/MC/V. ❶

Xaloc, C. de la Palla, 13-17 (☎933 01 19 90). M: Liceu. Classy, local-favorite. Features a friendly staff and a butcher counter with pig legs hanging from the ceiling. Meat and poultry sandwiches—hot and cold—on tasty baguettes or *català* bread (€4-12). Lunch *menú* €10.50. Open M-F 9am-midnight, Sa-Su 10am-midnight. AmEx/MC/V. ❷

Juicy Jones, C. Cardinal Casañas, 7 and C. Hospital, 74. Create your own juice or try one of the house combinations, like an orange/white grape/pineapple smoothie (€4). A tasty vegan lunch *menú* (€8.50) draws a young crowd to the playfully decorated dining room in the back. Open daily 11:30am-11:30pm. ❷

LA RIBERA

Eclectic, gourmet restaurants in La Ribera cater to a younger crowd. There is a relatively high concentration of Asian restaurants, tapas bars, and wineries.

▨ **Orígen 99.9%,** C. Enric Granados, 9 (☎934 53 11 20; www.origen99.com), C. Vidrieria, 6-8 (☎933 10 75 31), Pg. de Born, 4 (☎932 95 66 90), and C. Ramón y Cajal, 12 (☎932 13 60 31). Delectable entrees such as the beef-stuffed onion (€4.85) and the rabbit with almonds (€4.95) are made with 99.9% local ingredients and served in a hip dining room. Small soups and vegetarian and meat dishes €5-6. Open 12:30pm-1am. AmEx/MC/V. ❶

▨ **Petra,** C. Sombrerers, 13 (☎933 19 91 99). Serves some of the best food in the area at amazingly low prices. Quirky details, like menus printed on wine bottles and lights made of silverware, make the experience pure pleasure. Try the duck with brie and apple and pork with banana salsa. Entrees €7.25. Salads €4. Open Tu-Sa 1:30-4pm and 9-11:30pm, Su 1:30-4pm. Cash only. ❷

▨ **El Pebre Blau,** C. Banys Vells, 21 (☎933 19 13 08). M: Jaume I. Nouveau gourmet restaurant serves Mediterranean and Middle Eastern fusion dishes in a quiet room. Attentive waiters. Salads €9-17. Kitchen open 9-11:30pm.Reserve ahead. MC/V. ❸

La Pizza del Born, Pg. del Born, 22 (☎933 10 62 46). M: Jaume I. The best of Chicago meets the best of Spain, with toppings like artichoke hearts, *jamón serrano*, or goat cheese. You can take anything to go. Slices €1.70. Lunch *menú*: 2 slices and drink €3.70. Open M-Th and Su 1pm-1am, F-Sa 1pm-2am. Cash only. ❶

El Xampanyet, C. Montcada, 22 (☎933 19 70 03). M: Jaume I. Next to the Museu Picasso. Overflows with a crowd that spills onto the street, drinks in hand. The house special, *cava* (champagne in 25 varieties), is served with anchovies and *pa amb tomàquet* (bread with tomato; €1.20). Less crowded weekday afternoons. Bottles from €7. Open Tu-Sa noon-4pm and 7-11:30pm, Su noon-4pm. Closed Aug. MC/V. ❶

Va de Vi, C. Banys Vells, 16 (☎933 19 29 00). M: Jaume I. A romantic restaurant in a candlelit 16th-century Visigoth stone tavern. This hidden gem is easy to miss from the street. Choose from over 300 varieties of wine and *cava* (€2.40-5.75). Wide selection of cheeses €4-18. Tapas €1.80-13. Wheelchair accessible. Open M-W and Su 6pm-1am, Th 6pm-2am, F-Sa 6pm-3am. MC/V. ❷

Bunga Raya, C. Assaonadors, 7-9 (☎933 19 31 69). M: Jaume I. Decorated with bamboo awnings and Southeast Asian art. Bunga's owner cooks up delicacies like *rendang* (beef cooked with milk and coconut butter). The *menú* (€14.50) includes chicken, beef, squid, and fruit. Entrees €5-7. Open Tu-Su 8pm-midnight. Cash only. ❸

Tèxtil Cafè, C. Montcada, 12-14 (☎932 68 25 98; www.textilcafe.com). M: Jaume I. This charming terrace cafe, surrounded by art and flowers, serves mostly tapas and sandwiches with *cava* and wine. Live music in summer: W 8:30-11pm DJ, Su 9-11pm jazz. Lunch *menú* €11; dinner €17.50. Tapas €4.90. Wheelchair accessible. Open Tu-Th 10am-midnight, F-Sa 10am-1am. MC/V. ❸

EL RAVAL

Trendy fusion spots and authentic *català* mainstays contrast with the many Middle Eastern restaurants and a growing number of vegetarian-friendly alterna-

BARCELONA

tives. The Rambla del Raval is a good place to hunt for food or to have tea under the white tents that spring up in summer.

■ **Bar Ra,** Pl. de la Garduña (☎933 01 41 63, reservations 615 959 832; www.ratown.com). M: Liceu. Lots of vegetarian options. Enjoy creative cuisine, like grilled tuna with avocado (€12), on the shady terrace overlooking La Boqueria. Entrees €9-15. Lunch *menú* €10.99. Dinner *menú* €12.50; reservations required. Open daily 9:30am-1:30am. Kitchen open 1:30-4pm and 9:30pm-midnight. AmEx/MC/V. ❷

■ **Organic,** C. Junta de Comerç, 11 (933 01 09 02). Everything at this vegan-friendly eatery lives up to its name—right down to the filtered water used to prepare the food. Vegan salad bar and lunch *menú* (€13) served under exposed ceiling and candlelight. Second location in La Boqueria market has a €10 *menú* and *bocadillos.* Open daily 12:30-midnight. Cash only in both locations. ❷

■ **Restaurant Can Lluís,** C. Cera, 49 (☎934 41 11 87). M: Sant Antoni. The menu is filled with traditional *català* favorites, but the best deal is the unbelievable lunch *menú* (M-F, €7.90). Dinner *menús* €25-40 including wine. Open M-Sa 1:30-4pm and 8:30-11:30pm. MC/V. ❸

Pla dels Àngels, C. Ferlandina, 23 (☎933 49 40 47). M: Universitat. The decor of this colorful, inexpensive eatery is fit for its proximity to the contemporary art museum. Creative, healthy dishes and a large vegetarian selection served on a terrace. Entrees €7-15. Open M-Sa 1:30-4pm and 9-11:30pm. MC/V. ❷

Madame Jasmine, Rbla. del Raval, 22. Eclectic red decorations, a spirited staff, and an array of wonderfully mismatched chairs overlook Fernando Botero's fat cat sculpture. Delicious *bocadillos* (€2.50-4) and the best salads in El Raval (€5.50) made in open kitchen. Kitchen open daily 1pm-midnight. Bar open until 2:30am. Cash only. ❶

DosTrece, C. Carme, 40 (☎933 01 73 06; www.dostrece.net). M: Catalunya. Young locals dine in this artsy bar with a retro diner feel. Lunch *menú* €9. Entrees €7-15. Open M-Sa 1pm-3am; kitchen open 1-4pm and 9pm-midnight, Su brunch 1-4pm; terrace open until midnight. AmEx/MC/V. ❸

Hello Sushi, C. Junta de Comerç, 14 (☎934 12 08 30; www.hello-sushi.com). M: Universitat. Eclectic red-and-blue decor and small tea area with floor cushions. Tempura €8-16. Lunch *menú* €8.50, students €4. Open Tu-Sa 12:30-4:30pm and 8:30pm-12:30am, Su 8:30pm-12:30am. Reservations required F-Su. AmEx/MC/V. ❷

Mendizabal, Junta de Comerç, 2. Try the *zumo del día* (juice of the day) at this colorful student favorite, right near the school of fine arts. Need something to wash down all that juice? No problem: the beer is cheap (€1) and so are the *bocadillos* (€2-3), which are grilled behind the counter. Open daily 8-10pm. ❶

L'EIXAMPLE

Good deals on *bocadillos* and tapas can be found at every street corner.

■ **Racó d'en Baltá,** C. Aribau, 125 (☎934 53 10 44; www.racodenbalta.com). M: Hospital Clínic. Founded in 1900, this treasure offers innovative Mediterranean dishes like duck sirloin with rosemary caramel (€13). Entrees €12-18. Lunch *menú* €9.40. Open M-W 8am-1am, Th-Sa 8am-3am. Kitchen open 1-4pm and 9-11:30pm. AmEx/MC/V. ❸

■ **La Rita,** C. Aragó, 279 (☎934 87 23 76; www.laritarestaurant.com). A killer afternoon lunch *menú* has made Rita a local favorite for a cheap mid-day meal. Their bright red seats are full of people enjoying everything from gazpacho to salmon in orange-and-dill sauce. *Menú* €8.20. Open daily 1-3:45pm and 8:30-1130pm. MC/V. ❷

Kirin, C. Aragó, 231 (☎934 88 29 19; www.restaurantjaponeskirin.com). All-you-can-eat buffet of sushi, *edamame,* and other Asian delicacies rolls by on a conveyer belt. Buffet €8.90-€13.90. Open daily 1-4pm and 8:30pm-midnight. MC/V. ❷

Acalia, C. Rosselló, 197 (☎932 37 05 15). Sculptural light fixtures inside and a terrace outside complement the nouveau-cuisine offerings from this classy restaurant. Meat entrees and green salads with fresh fruit. Lunch *menú* €9.81. Dinner entrees €14-23. Open M-F 1-4pm, Tu-Sa also 8:30pm-11:30pm. MC/V. ❸

Tenorio, Pg. de Gràcia, 37 (☎932 72 05 92). M: Pg. de Gràcia. International fusion cuisine at reasonable prices. Entrees €9-19. Reserve ahead for inside or line up for patio seating. Open daily 9am-12:30am. Kitchen open 12:30pm-12:30am. AmEx/MC/V. ❸

Laie Llibreria Café, C. Pau Claris, 85 (☎933 18 17 39; www.laie.es). M: Urquinaona. This urban oasis offers a modest buffet and a lunch *menú* (€12.95) above a bookstore with a great English selection. Open M 9am-9pm, Tu-F 9am-1am, Sa 10am-1am. Kitchen open 1-4pm and 9pm-1am. AmEx/MC/V. ❸

MONTJUÏC

Dining options are not as plentiful in Montjuïc as elsewhere in the city, but the Fundació Miró, MNAC, Castell de Montjuïc, and Teatre Grec all have pleasant cafes. **Poble Espanyol,** an artisan village set in a 1929 World Expo castle, has a number of more substantial restaurants. *Menús* run €10-15. An up-and-coming neighborhood, **Poble Sec** has lots of restaurants, bars, and grocery stores lining Av. Lleida and Av. Paral·lel, but the real hot spot is the pedestrian zone around C. Blai.

La Font de Prades, Pl. de la Fuente, 4-6 (☎934 26 75 19). M: Espanya. In a quiet area of the *Poble Espanyol*, with an outdoor terrace and large dining room. Make reservations to avoid paying the €7.50 complex admission fee. *Menú* €16. Open June-Sept. Tu-Th 1-4pm and 8:30-10:30pm, F-Sa 1-4pm and 8:30-11:30pm, Su 1-4pm. MC/V. ❸

Zodiaco, C. Margarit, 17, on the corner with Blai. Serves beer, mixed drinks, and fresh *bocadillos* (for a salt fix, try the salmon with anchovies, €3.50) in a relaxed red polka-dotted dining room. Open M-Th 6pm-1am, F-Su 10am-1am. Cash only. ❶

El Consulade, C. Nou de la Rambla, 95 (☎934 41 98 28). The neighborhood headquarters of bacon cheeseburgers (€5), beer (€2), and 60s jazz on the stereo—not to mention one of the friendliest waitstaff around. Th is paella night. Open Tu-F 9pm-midnight, Sa 1pm-1am. Cash only. ❶

THE WATERFRONT

Aside from the dozens of raucous beach bars, there are a handful of tamer establishments for a meal by the beach. Stop by **Spar Express,** P. Juan de Borbon, 74 (☎932 21 83 15) for beachside groceries.

🔲 **HBN BCN,** C. Escar, 1 (☎932 25 02 63; www.habanabarcelona.com), right on Platja San Sebastián in Barceloneta, at the end of Pg. Joan de Borbó on the right. M: Barceloneta. Try the *picadillo* and *arroz congrí*, or the plate of Cuban tapas (plantains, yucca, avocado, shredded beef, rice, and beans; €8). Lunch *menú* €9. Dinner reservations recommended. Kitchen open daily 1pm-midnight. Th salsa lessons €30. MC/V. ❷

🔲 **Jai-Ca Bar,** C. Ginebra, 13 (☎933 19 50 02), 2 blocks down Pg. Joan de Borbó and 3 blocks toward the beach, on the corner with C. Baluard. Hugely popular tapas bar centered around 2 things: Fútbol Club Barcelona and Estrella Damm. Open Tu and Su 9am-10:30pm, W-Sa 9am-1am. MC/V. ❶

Crepería Central, C. Baluart, 54 (☎932 21 40 10), across from the market building. This small breakfast joint and creperie is as close as it gets to beachfront dining. If crepes aren't your thing, there's a full menu of fresh juices, not to mention free Wi-Fi. Breakfast €1-3. Crepes €5-9. Open M, W-Su 10am-midnight. Cash only. ❶

Agua, Pg. Marítim de la Barceloneta, 30 (☎932 25 12 72; www.grupotragaluz.com), the last building on the ocean side of Pg. Marítim before Barceloneta. Tourists, trendy *barceloneses*, and GQ business-types enjoy seafood and rice dishes from the beachfront terrace. Vegetarian options. Entrees €7-16. Wheelchair accessible. Open daily 1-3:45pm and 8-11:30pm, later on weekends. Reserve ahead. AmEx/MC/V. ❸

Zahara, Pg. Joan de Borbó, 69 (☎932 21 37 65; www.zaharacocktails.com). This hip bar is a diamond in the rough of mainstream bar-cafes. The menu uses color-coding and icons to show the contents and potency of each cocktail. Try a "shocktail" (€7-12). Beer €2-3.50. Salads €8-9. Sandwiches €4-5. Open daily 1pm-3am. MC/V. ❷

ZONA ALTA: GRÀCIA AND OUTER BARRIS

Gràcia's restaurants typically serve fresh food amid hip decor, and most of their *menús* run below €10. Vegetarian options abound, as do places for *bokatas* (huge, cheap sandwiches with thinly sliced meat, cheese, or veggies) and beer.

▨ **Ikastola,** C. Perla, 22, has the best *bokatas* in the city, and all the locals know it; the young hip crowd overflows into the street and onto the small backroom terrace every night. Try the fresh pesto/parmesan/basil combination. *Bokatas* €4, salads €6, beer €2. Open M-Th and Su 7pm-midnight, F-Sa 7pm-1am. Cash only. ❶

▨ **Restaurant Illa de Gràcia,** C. Sant Domènec, 19 (☎932 38 02 29). M: Diagonal. Follow Gran de Gràcia for 5 blocks and turn right onto C. Sant Domènec. Huge vegetarian menu. Nothing over €7. Open Tu-Th 1-4pm and 9pm-midnight, F-Su 2-4pm and 9pm-midnight. Closed last 2 weeks of Aug. MC/V. ❶

Restaurante Casa Regina (El 19 De La Riera), C. Riera de Sant Miquel, 19 (☎932 37 86 01). M: Diagonal. Serves only organic food, including vegetarian options. Menú €16. Entrees €10. Wheelchair accessible. Open M-Sa 10am-5pm. AmEx/MC/V. ❸

Sushi Itto, C. Londres, 103 (☎932 41 21 99; www.sushi-itto.com). A classy sushi place combining Japanese cuisine with Western flavors in eclectic roll options. *Nigiri* €1.40-3. Entrees €7-18. Delivery €2. Open daily 1:30-4:30pm and 8:30-11pm. AmEx/MC/V. ❸

La Gavina, C. Ros de Olano, 17 (☎934 15 74 50), at the corner of C. St. Joaquím. Funky Italian pizzeria complete with a life-sized patron saint. Pizzas with fresh meat and veggies €5.50-11. Open Tu-Th and Su 2pm-1am, F-Sa 2pm-2am. Cash only. ❷

⑤ SIGHTS

Barcelona has always been on the cutting edge of the art world. Visitors cross continents not only to see the paintings in the fantastic museums, but also to admire imaginative modern architecture and parks designed by world-renowned artists. The streets are the galleries for Barcelona's artistic spirit; intricate lampposts and murals light up even the most drab neighborhoods. You'll find the classics—Picasso, Miró, Mir, etc.—but also modern shows at museums like the Tàpies that make Barcelona relevant, not just historical. The main architectural attractions are the *Modernista* treasures spread throughout the city, concentrated in l'Eixample. Parc Güell and Parc Diagonal Mar allow for contemplation surrounded by innovative designs and sculptures. Sprinkled throughout the entire city lie plazas, tree-lined avenues, and corner parks, each with their own character to discover.

RUTA DEL MODERNISME

For those with a few days in the city and an interest in seeing some of the most popular sights, the Ruta del Modernisme is the cheapest and most flexible option. The pass provides discount admission to dozens of *Modernista* buildings in the city. The tour is free with the purchase of a guidebook (€12) and additional adult passes are €5, under 18 free. Passes provide a 25-30% discount on the Palau de la Música Catalana, Fundació Antoni Tàpies, the Museu de Zoología, tours of l'Hospital de la Santa Creu i Sant Pau and the facades of La Manzana de la Discordia (Amatller, Lleó i Morera, and Batlló), and map tours of Gaudí, Domènech i Montaner, and Puig i Cadafalch buildings, among other attractions. The pass comes with a map and a pamphlet giving the history of different sights, which is helpful for prioritizing visits. Purchase passes at the Pl. Catalunya tourist office, the Modernisme Centre at **Hospital Santa Creu i Sant Pau**, C. Sant Antoni Maria Claret, 167, or **Pavellons Güell**, Av. de Pedralbes, 7. Centralized info can be found at ☎ 902 07 66 21, 933 17 76 52, or www.rutadelmodernisme.com. Many sights have tour times and length restrictions; visiting all of them on the same day is virtually impossible.

BARCELONA CARD

Another discount option is the **Barcelona Card.** The card is good for 2-5 days and includes free public transportation (on Metro and daytime buses) and over 80 discounts (and free admission to a few attractions and walking tours) at museums, cultural venues, theaters, and a few bars and clubs, shops, and restaurants. They are sold at tourist offices or at Casa Batlló, El Corte Inglés, the Aquarium, and Poble Espanyol. Prices for 2-5 days range €24-36 for adults and €20-31 for ages 4-12. Keep in mind that for students (usually with ISIC card; ISOS accepted less often), it may be cheaper just to use student discounts to get into attractions.

BUS TURÍSTIC

Sit back and let the sights come to you. The Bus Turístic stops at 44 points of interest along three different routes (red for the north, blue for the south, and green for the eastern waterfront). Tickets come with an eight-language brochure with information on each sight. A full ride on each route takes 2½-3hr., but the idea is to get off at any place of interest and use the bus (as many times as you want in your allotted days) as a convenient means of transportation. Multilingual guides stationed in every bus help orient travelers and answer questions. You can buy tickets once on board, or ahead of time at **Turisme de Catalunya**, Pl. de Catalunya, 17, in front of El Corte Inglés, or at www.barcelonaturisme.com. Many of the museums and sights covered by the bus offer discounts with the bus ticket; keep in mind that some are closed on Mondays. (Buses run daily every 5-30min. 9am-9:30pm; no service Dec. 25 and Jan. 1. 1-day pass €19, ages 4-12 €11; 2-day pass €23/15.)

BARRI GÒTIC AND LA RAMBLA

LA RAMBLA

La Rambla, a pedestrian strip roughly 1km long, is a world-famous cornucopia of street performers, fortune-tellers, pet and flower stands, and artists. There is also no shortage of tourists and the restaurants and shops that cater to them. Watch your wallet; this is a pick-pocketer's paradise. The tree-lined thoroughfare consists of five distinct *ramblas* (promenades). Each boasts its own specialty—one stretch is lined by cages of exotic birds. Together, the Ramblas form one boulevard starting at the Pl. de Catalunya and the **Font de Canaletes**—visitors who want to come back to Barcelona are supposed to sample the fountain's water. Halfway down La Rambla, **Joan Miró's** pavement mosaic brightens up the already colorful street. Pass the **Mirador de Colom** on the way out to Rambla del Mar for a spectacular view of the Mediterranean.

■ **GRAN TEATRE DEL LICEU.** After burning down for the second time in 1994, the Liceu was rebuilt and expanded dramatically; a tour of the building includes not just the original 1847 Sala de Espejos (Hall of Mirrors), but also the 1999 Foyer (a curvaceous bar/lecture hall/small theater). The five-level, 2292-seat theater is considered one of Europe's top stages, adorned with palatial ornamentation, gold facades, and sculptures. (*La Rambla, 51-59, by C. Sant Pau. M: Liceu, L3. ☎ 934 85 99 13, for tours 85 99 14; www.liceubarcelona.com. Box office open M-F 2-8:30pm and Sa 1hr. before show or by ServiCaixa. Short 20min. semi-guided visits daily 10am-1pm, €4. 1¼hr. tours 10am by reservation only; call 9am-2pm or email visites@liceubarcelona.com; €8.50.*)

CENTRE D'ART DE SANTA MÓNICA. Once a nunnery, this museum now houses rotating and contemporary, edgy exhibitions. Because it rebuilds its space between shows, call and make sure the galleries are open before you visit. *(La Rambla, 7. M: Drassanes. ☎933 16 28 10. Open Tu-Sa 11am-8pm, Su 11am-3pm. Free.)*

MONUMENT A COLOM. Ruis i Taulet's monument to Columbus towers at the port end of La Rambla. Nineteenth-century *Renaixença* enthusiasts convinced themselves that Columbus was *català*, not Italian. The statue points proudly in a mysterious direction—not to the Americas, but out over the horizon toward Libya—which some take as error, and others as directions to what would have been Columbus's first refueling point. Take the elevator for a view of the city, including the cathedral, Sagrada Família, and the even more futuristic-looking Torre Agbar. *(Portal de la Pau. M: Drassanes. Elevator open June-Sept. 9am-8:30pm; Oct.-May 10am-6:30pm. €2.30, children and over 65 €1.50, large groups €1.90 per person.)*

LA BOQUERIA (MERCAT DE SANT JOSEP). Just the place to pick up that hard-to-find animal part you've been looking for, plus any other random food you've been craving. A traditional *català* market located in a giant, all-steel *Modernista* structure, La Boqueria is a sight in itself. Specialized vendors sell produce, fish, and meat from a seemingly infinite number of independent stands inside. A number of cafés have terraces outside. *(La Rambla, 89. M: Liceu. Open M-Sa 6am-8pm.)*

MUSEU DE L'ERÒTICA. This unique museum has an odd assortment of pictures and figurines that spans human history and depicts a variety of seemingly impossible sexual acrobatics beyond the limits of human flexibility. The 7ft. wooden phallus is a tempting photo-op. *(La Rambla, 96. M: Liceu, L1/3. ☎933 18 98 65; www.erotica-museum.com. Open daily 10am-10pm; winter 10am-9pm. €7.50, students €6.50.)*

PALAU DE LA VIRREINA. Once the residence of a Peruvian viceroy, this 18th-century palace now houses the Institute of Culture, which displays contemporary photography, music, and graphics exhibits. The ground floor is the permanent residence of several *gigantes* (giant floats). *(La Rambla, 99. M: Liceu. ☎933 16 10 00. Open Tu-Sa 11am-8:30pm, Su 11am-3pm. Ground fl. free, exhibits €3 and up.)*

MUSEU DE CERA (WAX MUSEUM). Some 300 wax figures form an endless parade of celebrities, fictional characters, and rather obscure European historical figures. The most recognizable ones have distinctive facial hair, like Fidel Castro and Chewbacca from *Star Wars*. Picasso's there, too. *(La Rambla, 4-6 or Passatge de la Vanca, 7. M: Drassanes. ☎933 17 26 49. Open July-Sept. daily 10am-8pm; Oct.-June M-F 10am-2:30pm and 4-8pm, Sa-Su and holidays 11am-2:30pm and 4:30-9pm. Last entrance 30min. before closing. €7.50, ages 5-11 and seniors €4.50.)*

BARRI GÒTIC

Brimming with cathedrals, palaces, and unabashed tourism, Barcelona's oldest neighborhood masks its old age with 24hr. energy. The Barri Gòtic took shape during Roman times, before the use of the grid layout, and continued to develop during the medieval period. Today it is the political and historical center of the city, with a split personality that is alternately quaint and overwhelming. *Català* commercialism persists in all its glory with store-lined streets and fine restaurants, but the soul of the neighborhood lies deeper than these attractions.

■MUSEU D'HISTÒRIA DE LA CIUTAT. Buried some 20m below a seemingly innocuous old plaza lies one of the two components of the Museu d'Història de la Ciutat: the subterranean excavations of the Roman city of Barcino. This **archaeological exhibit** displays incredibly well-preserved first- to sixth-century ruins; through glass sections, you can see huge ceramic wine casks, intricate Roman floor mosaics, and reused cornerstones forming part of the Roman walls. Built on top of the 4th-century walls, the **Palau Reial Major,** served as the residence of the Catalan-Aragonese monarchs. The Gothic **Saló de Tinell** (Throne Room) is supposedly the place where Fernando and Isabel received Columbus after his journey to America. *(Pl. del Rei. M: Jaume I. ☎ 932 56 21 00; www.museuhistoria.bcn.cat. Wheelchair accessible. Open Apr.-Sept. Tu-Sa 10am-8pm, Su 10am-3pm; Oct.-March Tu-Sa 10am-2pm and 4-7pm, Su 10am-3pm. Pamphlets available in English. Museum €5, students €3.50. Exhibition €1.50/1. Museum and exhibition €5.50/3.50.)*

■ **ESGLÉSIA CATEDRAL DE LA SANTA CREU.** This must-see cathedral is one of Barcelona's most popular and recognizable monuments. The altar holds a cross designed by Frederic Marès in 1976, and beneath lies the Crypt of Santa Eulàlia, while the courtyard arcades surround a duck pond and fountain. The museum in La Sala Capitular holds Bartolomé Bermejo's *Pietà. (In Pl. Seu, up C. Bisbe from Pl. St. Jaume. M: Jaume I. Cathedral open daily 8am-12:45pm and 5:15-7:30pm. Cloister open 9am-12:30pm and 5:15-7pm. Elevator to the roof open M-Sa 10:30am-6pm; €2. Choir area open M-F 9am-12:30pm and 5:15-7pm, Sa-Su 9am-12:30pm; €1. Special guided tours daily 1-5pm include everything for €4.)*

PLAÇA DE SANT JAUME. Pl. de Sant Jaume has been Barcelona's political center since Roman times. Two of Cataluña's most important buildings have dominated the square since 1823: the grandiose **Palau de la Generalitat,** headquarters of Cataluña's government, and the **Ajuntament,** or city hall. *(Generalitat open 2nd and 4th Su of the month 10:30am-1:30pm. Closed Aug. Mandatory tours in català, English, and Spanish every 30min. starting at 10:30am. Free. Ajuntament open 2nd and 4th Su 10am-1:30pm. Free.)*

EL CALL (JEWISH QUARTER). For centuries El Call was Barcelona's center of intellectual and financial activity. Now, one of the synagogues has been transformed into a church, the **Església de Sant Jaume,** C. Ferran, 28. The only tangible remaining evidence of Jewish inhabitants is the ancient **Hebrew plaque** on tiny C. Marlet; the rest of the area has been commercialized. *(M: Liceu.)*

PLAÇA REIAL. This is the most crowded, happening *plaça* in the Barri Gòtic; tourists and locals congregate to eat and drink at night, and to buy and sell at the Sunday morning flea market. Near the fountain in the center of the square are two street lamps designed by Antoni Gaudí—if only he could have witnessed the antics of the drunk backpackers that flood the plaza until sunrise. *(M: Liceu or Drassanes.)*

LA RIBERA

■ **PALAU DE LA MÚSICA CATALANA.** The Graceland of Barcelona. In 1891, the Orfeó *català* choir society commissioned *Modernista* master Luis Domènech i Montaner to design this must-see concert venue. By day, the music hall glows with tall stained-glass windows and an ornate stained-glass skylight, which comes alive again after dark with electric lights. Sculptures of wild horses and busts of the seven muses come out of the walls flanking the stage. Don't miss the Sala de Luis Millet, with an up-close view of the intricately decorated "trencadis" pillars of the breathtaking facade. *(C. Sant Francesc de Paula, 2. ☎ 932 95 72 00; www.palaumusica.org. M: Jaume I. Mandatory 50min. tours in English almost every hour. Open daily July-Sept. 10am-7pm, but call ahead for hours; Oct.-June 10am-3:30pm. €9, students and seniors €8, with Barcelona Card €6.40. Check the Guía del Ocio for concert listings. Concert tickets €6-330. MC/V.)*

■ **MUSEU PICASSO.** The most visited museum in Barcelona traces Picasso's development as an artist with the world's best collection of work from his early Barcelona period. He donated over 1700 works to the museum himself, and it now boasts 3600 pieces of his collage, painting, and sculpture. The pieces display the transition from his classical techniques to the stylistic developments that made him an icon. Crucial works include *Portrait of Aunt Pepa,* the most important from

BARCELONA

his formative period; *First Communion*, his first large exhibited piece; and the 57 canvases of the *Las Meninas* series. Complementing the main attraction are rotating supplemental exhibitions. *(C. Montcada, 15-23.* ☎ *933 19 63 10; www.museupicasso.bcn.es. M: Jaume I. Open Tu-Su 10am-8pm. Last entrance 30min. before closing. €6, students and seniors €4, under 16 free. Temporary exhibit €2.50/1. 1st Su of the month free.)*

PARC DE LA CIUTADELLA. Host of the 1888 Universal Exposition, the beautiful park contains several museums, well-labeled horticulture, wacky fountains, a pond, and a zoo. Buildings of note include Domènech i Montaner's *Modernista* **Castell dels Tres Dracs** (Castle of the Three Dragons, now the **Museu de Zoología**), which houses a large dinosaur exhibit, the geological museum, and Josep Amergós's **Hivernacle**. The kid-friendly **Parc Zoològic** (zoo) has all kinds of animals and even dolphin shows. *(M: Ciutadella or Marina. Park open daily 8am-9pm. Zoo open daily June-Sept. 10am-7pm; Oct.-May 10am-5pm. Park €14.75, children 3-12 €9, over 65 €7.90.)*

MUSEU DE LA XOCOLATA. If you can halt the inevitable salivation for a few moments, this chocolate museum presents gobs of information about the history, production, and ingestion of the sensuous treat. Perhaps more interesting are the exquisite chocolate sculptures, particularly of the Sagrada Família. The small cafe offers workshops on chocolate sculpting for children up to 12 years old, and chocolate tasting (€7.70) for the rest of us. *(Pl. Pons i Clerch, by C. Comerç.* ☎ *932 68 78 78; www.museudelaxocolata.com. M: Jaume I. Open M and W-Sa 10am-7pm, Su 10am-3pm. Workshops for kids from €6.50; reservations required. €3.90, students and seniors €3.40, with Barcelona Card €2.80, under 7 free.)*

ESGLÉSIA DE SANTA MARIA DEL MAR. This architectural wonder was built in the 14th century. The impossibly high ceiling's supporting columns are set 13m apart—farther than in any other medieval building in the world. *(Pl. Santa María, 1. M: Jaume I. Open M-Sa 9am-1:30pm and 4:30-8pm, Su 10am-1:30pm and 4:30-8pm. Free.)*

EL RAVAL

▨ PALAU GÜELL. Gaudí's recently renovated 1889 Palau Güell—the *Modernista* residence built for wealthy patron Eusebi Güell (of Parc Güell fame)—has one of Barcelona's most spectacular interiors. Güell spared no expense on this house, considered to be the first true representation of Gaudí's revolutionary style. *(C. Nou de La Rambla, 3-5. M: Liceu.* ☎ *933 17 39 74. Mandatory tour every 15min. Open Mar.-Oct. M-Sa 10am-8pm, Su 10am-2pm, last tour 6:15pm; Nov.-Dec. M-Sa 10am-6pm. €3, students €1.50.)*

MUSEU D'ART CONTEMPORANI (MACBA). The MACBA has received worldwide acclaim for its focus on post-avant-garde art and contemporary works. The main attractions are the highly innovative rotating exhibits and the brand-new "Nits MACBA," which keep the museum open 'til midnight and let you in cheap, too. *(Pl. dels Àngels, 1. M: Catalunya.* ☎ *934 12 08 10; www.macba.es. Open M and W-F 11am-7:30pm, Sa 10am-8pm, Su 10am-3pm. Th-F open until midnight. Tours in català, English, and Spanish M 6pm; català and Spanish W-Sa 6pm, Su noon. €7.50, students €6, under 14 free; single exhibition floor €4/3. W €3.50 for everything. Nits MACBA Th-F, €3 after 8pm.)*

CENTRE DE CULTURA CONTEMPORÀNIA DE BARCELONA (CCCB). The center stands out for its mixture of architectural styles, incorporating an early 20th-century theater with its 1994 addition, a sleek wing of black glass. CCCB now has a café, gallery space, screening room, and bookstore, and is also the main daytime venue for the Sonar music festival. Check the *Guía del Ocio* for scheduled events. *(Casa de Caritat. C. Montalegre, 5. M: Catalunya or Universitat.* ☎ *933 06 41 00; www.cccb.org. Open Tu-Su 11am-8pm. €6.60, students €4.40, under 16 free. First W of the month free.)*

DISTANCE: 2.5km/1.6 mi.
DURATION: 3-4hr.
WHEN TO GO: Any time.

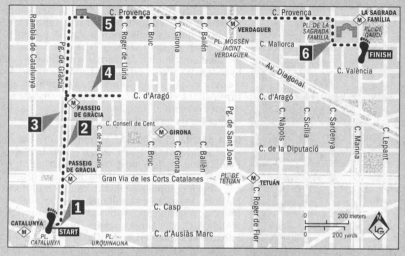

The spacious, right-angled streets L'Eixample (expansion in *Catalán*) provided the perfect setting for 19th-century *Modernista* architecture's bright colors and playful curves.

1. PL. CATALUNYA. Start off in Pl. Catalunya, on the lower border of l'Eixample. Make sure to get your **free map** at El Corte Inglés.

2. PG. DE GRÀCIA. Walk along the wide, tree-lined Pg. de Gràcia and **resist the temptation** to enter (or at least spend money in) the endless array of designer boutiques. You may notice a significant difference from the cramped, old buildings of the Barri Gòtic.

3. LA MANZANA DE LA DISCÒRDIA. The block between C. Aragó and C. Consell de Cent, is known as *La Manzana de la Discòrdia,* ("block of discord"), due to the clash among three designs: **Casa Amatller, Casa Lleó,** and **Casa Batlló,** p. 400. In **Casa Amatller,** you can buy a **Ruta del Modernisme** pass (p. 394).

4. C. ARAGÓ. C. Aragó, to the east of Pg. de Gràcia, has affordable quality restaurants and is a great spot to admire the parade of perfectly dressed *barceloneses.*

5. CASA MILÀ (LA PEDRERA). Three long blocks up Pg. de Gràcia is perhaps Gaudí's best-known work. This building, designed to mimic the ocean's waves and seaweed, and its ⬛ **whimsical rooftop** are definitely worth a visit.

6. LA SAGRADA FAMÍLIA. The last stop is well worth the long walk. Take a right on C. Provença and follow it for 11 blocks (stay straight and don't turn on Av. Diagonal). You cannot miss Gaudí's masterpiece, which after 119 years and counting is still nowhere near finished.

*Metro lines L5 and L2 will transport you back to the city center. Other Gaudí works not in the immediate area include **Parc Güell** (p. 403), **Palau Güell** (p. 398), the **Calvet House,** the **Teresianes Order School,** the **Bellesguard Tower,** the **Güell Pavillions,** and the **Vicenç House.***

3 9 9

SLOW TRAIN COMING

Architect and artist Antoni Gaudí never lived to see the completion of his masterpiece, *La Sagrada Familia*. When he died in 1926, there was hope that the basilica would someday fulfill his original plans, which call for, among other things, a 550 ft. cross.

A team of architects, led by 81-year-old Jordi Bonet, has been working on the Sagrada Familia non-stop in recent years, and a variety of computer models already exist for the finished structure. It's slow going, but, as Gaudí once joked, "the client is not in a hurry."

The cathedral's projected date of completion is 2026—100 years after Gaudí's death. The reality of this goal is up for debate, yet time constraints have recently been replaced by a different threat to the Sagrada's progress: high-speed transportation.

Government plans for a tunnel just meters under the basilica's foundation would allow for a speedier commute from Barcelona to Madrid. Unfortunately, for concerned citizens and Bonet's team, the tunnel will mean equally speedy destruction of the monument, as vibrations underground could damage mosaics, windows, and even the structure.

The Sagrada Familia, the second most visited monument in Spain, attracts millions of visitors every year. Unfortunately, while God may wait an eternity for His house to be built, these other clients are in a hurry.

L'EIXAMPLE

Ildefons Cerdà drew up designs for a new neighborhood where people of all social classes could live side by side; contrary to plan, l'Eixample did not thrive as a utopian community, however, but rather as a playground for the bourgeoisie. Despite gentrification, l'Eixample remains Barcelona's most innovative and beautiful neighborhood. Among the seemingly endless square blocks and wide-open plazas that were the bedrock of this planned community, *Modernista* oddities sit side-by-side with recent additions like **Torre Agbar,** Jean Nouvel's spaceship-like blue- and red-lit glass tower that's visible from just about everywhere. It doesn't take much to guess the nickname that Barcelona locals have given to the Torre.

■ **LA SAGRADA FAMÍLIA.** Antoni Gaudí's masterpiece is far from finished, which makes La Sagrada Família the world's most visited construction site. Only the shortest eight of the 18 planned towers have been completed and the church still doesn't have an "interior," yet millions of people make the touristic pilgrimage to witness its work-in-progress majesty. Of the three facades, only the Nativity Facade was finished under Gaudí. A new team of architects, led by Jordi Bonet, hopes to lay the last stone by 2026 (the 100th anniversary of Gaudí's death), and the affiliated museum displays plans and computer models of the fully realized structure. *(C. Mallorca, 401, across from the Pizza Hut. ☎932 07 30 31; www.sagradafamilia.org. M: Sagrada Família. Open daily Apr.-Sept. 9am-8pm, elevator open 9am-7:45pm; Oct.-Mar. 9am-5:45pm, elevator €2. Guided tours 11am and 1pm in English, 6pm in Spanish. In summer, also at 3 and 5pm in English, 4pm in Spanish. Tours €3. Entrance €8, with ISIC €5. Combined ticket with Casa-Museu Gaudí €9.)*

■ **LA MANZANA DE LA DISCORDIA.** A short walk from Pl. de Catalunya, the odd-numbered side of Pg. de Gràcia between C. Aragó and C. Consell de Cent has been leaving passersby scratching their heads for a century. The Spanish nickname, which translates to the "block of discord," comes from the stylistic clash of its three most extravagant buildings. **Casa Lleó i Morera,** 35, by Domènech i Montaner, lies on the far left corner of the block. Sprouting flowers, stained glass, and legendary doorway sculptures adorn the interior. Two buildings down is **Casa Amatller,** 41, perhaps the most beautiful building on the block, due to Puig i Cadafalch's geometric, Moorish-influenced pattern on its facade. The real discord is next door at **Casa Batlló,** 43, where greenish sparkle and an off-center cross are trumped only by Gaudí's rippling balconies (the house was built using shapes from nature, particularly from the ocean). The most popular interpretation of Casa Batlló is that it represents Cataluña's patron Sant Jordi (St. George) slaying a dragon; the chimney plays the lance, the scaly roof is the dragon's back, and the bony balconies are the remains of his victims. (☎934 88 06 66; www.casabatllo.es. Open daily 9am-8pm. €16.50, students €13.20. Call for group discounts. Free multilingual audio tour.)

■ **FUNDACIÓ ANTONI TÀPIES.** Less than 20 years old, this contemporary museum has a floor devoted to Tàpies, a *barcelonese* sculptor and painter. But the real attractions are the rotating exhibitions on the two lower floors—some of the best modern photography and video art in the city, as well as film screenings and lectures. Keep your eyes peeled in summer for DJ nights on the terrace, with free drinks and after-hours gallery access. (C. Aragó, 255. ☎934 87 03 15. M: Pg. de Gràcia. Museum open Tu-Su 10am-8pm. Guided tours by arrangement only. No temporary exhibitions July-Sept. €6, students and seniors €4.)

CASA MILÀ (LA PEDRERA). From the outside, this Gaudí creation looks like the sea—the undulating walls are the waves and the iron balconies are seaweed. Chimneys resembling armored soldiers sprout from the roof, and the roof is complete with views of every corner of Barcelona. The entrance fee entitles visitors to tour one well-equipped apartment, the roof, and the winding brick attic, now functioning as the **Espai Gaudí,** a multimedia presentation of Gaudí's life and works. The summer concert series transforms the roof into a jazz cabaret on weekend nights. (Pg. de Gràcia, 92. ☎902 40 09 73. Open daily in summer 9am-8pm, last admission 7:30pm; Nov.-Feb. 9am-6:30pm. €8, students/seniors €4.50. Free audio tour. Concerts last weekend of June-July F-Sa 9pm-midnight. €12, drink included. Tickets only through Tel Entrada.)

HOSPITAL DE LA SANTA CREU I SANT PAU. This is not your ordinary hospital. Designated a UNESCO monument in 1997, this is Europe's second-oldest functioning hospital and Domènech i Montaner's lifetime *Modernista* masterpiece. The entire complex covers nine l'Eixample blocks with whimsically decorated pavilions resembling gingerbread houses or little Taj Mahals. (Sant Antoni M. Claret, 167. ☎932 91 90 00; www.santpau.es. M: Hospital de St. Pau, L5. Hospital open 24hr. Free. Guided tours daily 10:15am-1:15pm, €5. Info open daily 10am 2pm.)

MONTJUÏC

■ **FUNDACIÓ MIRÓ.** An extensive collection of sculptures, drawings, and paintings from Miró's career, ranging from sketches to wall-sized canvases, immerses visitors in the work of this Barcelona-born artist. His best-known pieces here include *El Carnival de Arlequín, La Masia,* and *L'or de l'Azuz,* and special treats like Calder's *Mercury Fountain.* The downstairs gallery displays experimental work by young artists and a few famous contributors. The Fundació also sponsors music and film festivals. From the sculpture garden on the side garden, paths run down the hill to the Palau Nacional. (Take the funicular from M: ParaHel or catch the Park Montjuïc bus from Pl. Espanya. ☎934 43 94 70; www.bcn.fjmiro.es. Open July-Sept. Tu-W and F-Sa 10am-8pm; Oct.-June Tu-W and F-Sa 10am-7pm; all year Th 10am-9:30pm, Su and holidays 10am-2:30pm. Doors close 15min. early. Library open same hours as museum. €7.50, students and seniors €5, under 14 free. Temporary exhibitions €4/3. Concert tickets €10.)

■ **MUSEU NACIONAL D'ART DE CATALUNYA (PALAU NACIONAL).** Designed by Enric Català and Pedro Cendoya for the 1929 International Exposition, the beautiful Palau Nacional has housed the Museu Nacional d'Art de Catalunya (MNAC) since 1934. Its main hall is a public event space, while the wings are home to the world's finest collection of *català* Romanesque art and a wide variety of Gothic pieces. Highlights include works by Joaqim Mir, a second-generation *Modernista*

BARCELONA

known for color-saturated landscape, Miró's giant "Gorg Bleu" stained glass, and the gallery of Romanesque cathedral apses. The museum also recently acquired the entire holdings of the Museu d'Art Modern, formerly located in the Parc de la Ciutadella—MNAC is now the principal art museum of Cataluña. In front, the **Fonts Luminoses** (Illuminated Fountains) and the central **Font Màgica** (Magical Fountain) come alive during weekend laser shows. *(From M: Espanya, walk up Av. Reina María Cristina, away from the twin brick towers, and take the escalators to the top. ☎936 22 03 76; www.mnac.es. Open Tu-Sa 10am-7pm, Su and holidays 10am-2:30pm. Temporary exhibits €3-5; both temporary exhibits €6; all exhibits €8.50. 30% discount for students and seniors. Under 14 free. First Su of the month free. Audio tour included.)*

CASTELL DE MONTJUÏC. This historic fortress and its **Museu Militar** sit high on the hill, and from the external ▨**mirador**, guests can enjoy a multitude of panoramic jaw-droppers and photo-ops. The *telefèric* (funicular) to and from the castle is usually half the fun. Even if military history isn't your thing, the view from the roof of the castle makes it well worth entering. *(From M: ParaHel, take the funicular to Av. Miramar and then the cable car to the castle. ☎933 29 86 13. After renovations, Telefèric de Montjuïc open M-Sa 10am-9pm; low season 10am-7pm. €5.50, round-trip €7.50. Parc de Montjuïc bus runs up the slope from in front of the telefèric, or walk up the steep slope on C. Foc from the same spot. Open daily 9am-10pm. Museum open Tu-Sa Mar.-Nov. 9:30am-8pm; Dec.-Feb. 9:30am-5pm. €3 for museum, fortress, Plaza de Armas, and mirador. €1 without the museum.)*

THE WATERFRONT

▨ **MUSEU D'HISTÒRIA DE CATALUNYA.** The last gasp of the old city before entering the tourist trap of Barceloneta, the Museu provides an exhaustive and patriotic introduction to *català* history, politics, and culture. There is a particularly good section devoted to Franco. Recreations of a 1930s Spanish bar, an 8th-century Islamic prayer tent, and other intriguing dioramas make the museum a full sensory experience. *(Pl. Pau Vila, 3. Near entrance to the Moll d'Espanya; left as you walk out toward Barceloneta. ☎932 25 47 00; mhc.cultura@gencat.net. Open Tu and Th-Sa 10am-7pm, W 10am-8pm, Su 10am-2:30pm. €3; students €2.10; EU students, under 7, over 65 free.)*

TORRE SAN SEBASTIÀ. An easy way to see the city from (high) above is from these cable cars, which span the entire Port Vell, connecting beachy Barceloneta with mountainous Montjuïc. *(Pg. Joan de Borbó. M: Barceloneta. In Port Vell, as you walk down Joan de Borbó and see the beaches to the left, stay right and look for the high tower. Open daily 11am-8pm. To Montjuïc one-way €9, round-trip €12.50; just the elevator to the top €4.)*

L'AQUÀRIUM DE BARCELONA. Barely a decade old, this kid-friendly aquarium features sharks, a cafeteria, and exhibits on marine creatures. *(Moll d'Espanya. M: Drassanes or Barceloneta. Advance tickets ☎932 21 74 74; www.aquariumbcn.com. Open daily July-Aug. 9:30am-10pm; June and Sept. 9:30am-9pm; Oct.-May 9:30am-9:30pm. €16, students with ISIC €13.40, under 12 and seniors €12.50. Mini-guide available in English. AmEx/MC/V.)*

VILA OLÍMPICA. The Vila Olímpica, beyond the east side of the zoo, was built to house 15,000 athletes and entertain millions of tourists for the 1992 Summer Olympics. It's home to several public parks, a shopping center, and offices. In **Barceloneta,** beaches stretch out from the old port. *(M: Ciutadella or Vila Olímpica. Walk along the water on Ronda Litoral toward the 2 towers.)*

MUSEU MARÍTIM. The **Drassanes Reiales de Barcelona** (Royal Shipyards of Barcelona) consists of a series of huge indoor bays in which entire ships could be constructed and stored over the winter. The Maritime Museum traces (a bit dryly, considering the subject matter) the evolution of shipbuilding and life on the high seas. Make sure you look in the portside window of the submarine in the courtyard. *(Av. Drassanes, s/n, off the rotary around the Monument a Colom. M: Drassanes. ☎933*

42 99 20; www.museumaritimbarcelona.org. Open daily 10am-7pm. Free audio tour and entrance to a small museum. €6.50; under 16, students, and seniors €3.25. Museum and 1½hr. ride on TriMar beyond the harbor €13.60/9.50. Temporary exhibitions €6, with museum €9.75.)

PARC DIAGONAL MAR. Enric Miralles's innovative design weaves a sprawling gray sculpture around high-rise apartment buildings and labyrinthine gardens; the park is perfect for relaxing and escaping the masses. *(At the end of Av. Diagonal, where it meets the sea. Walk 1 block toward the water. M: Selva de Mar.)*

ZONA ALTA: GRÀCIA AND OUTER BARRIS

⧆ PARC GÜELL. This fantastical park was designed entirely by Gaudí, but—in typical Gaudí fashion—was not completed until after his death. Gaudí intended Parc Güell to be a garden city, with dwarfish buildings and sparkling ceramic-mosaic stairways designed to house the city's elite. However, only one house, now known as the **Casa-Museu Gaudí**, was built. Two staircases lead to a towering *Modernista* pavilion originally designed as an open-air market but now occasionally used as a stage by street musicians. The longest park bench in the world, a multicolored serpentine wonder made of tile shards, decorates the top of the pavilion. *(Bus #24 from Pl. Catalunya stops at the upper entrance. Open daily 10am-dusk. Park free. Museum open daily Apr.-Sept. 10am-8pm; Oct.-Mar. 10am-6pm. €4, with ISIC €3.)*

⧆ MUSEU DEL FÚTBOL CLUB BARCELONA. A close second to the Picasso Museum as Barcelona's most visited museum, the FCB merits all the attention it gets from soccer fanatics. Sports fans will appreciate the storied history of the team. The high point is the chance to enter the stadium and take in the enormity of 100,000-seat Camp Nou. *(Next to the stadium. M: Collblanc. Enter through access gate 7 or 9. ☎934 96 36 08. Open M-Sa 10am-6:15pm, Su and holidays 10am-2pm. €7, students and seniors €5.60. Museum and tour €11/8.80.)*

🎵 ENTERTAINMENT

MUSIC, THEATER, AND DANCE

Barcelona offers many options for theater aficionados, though most performances are in *català* (*Guía del Ocio* lists the language of the performance). Reserve tickets through **Tel Entrada** (24hr. ☎902 10 12 12; www.telentrada.com), **ServiCaixa** at any branch of the Caixa Catalunya bank (24hr. ☎902 33 22 11, for groups 88 80 90; www.servicaixa.com; open M-F 8am-

SCANNING THE SCENE

ScannerFM, Barcelona's three-year-old independent radio station, provides a trilingual agenda of underground shows, exhibits, and festivals.

ScannerFM was created as a response to the gap between the music on the radio and the music people actually listened to—a gap that defined the Barcelona radio of the 90s. Today, their airtime is filled with everything from pop to post-punk. There are no outsiders here; Scanner is a meeting ground for listeners, bands, travelers, and locals.

Get to know Scanner during your stay here ("escanner" to locals). A few minutes spent listening to their live stream online, or 100.5FM on the radio, will educate you about Barcelona's music in a way few other things can. Scanner DJs are increasingly relevant and connected within the city's music scene, and are featured at late-night museum events and music festivals alike.

If you're looking to see how Barcelona art lives and breathes just below the surface of its tourist-friendly sheen, this is where you should begin to snoop.

Forget what you were going to do tonight and spend a few minutes on www.bcn.es/scannerbcn. For more information, try www.scannerfm.com, or look for Scanner's friends at www.maumauunderground.com or www.lecool.com, two more sites to help you take independent art while you're in Barcelona.

2:30pm), or www.ticktackticket.com—the Spanish Ticketmaster. The **Grec** summer festival turns Barcelona into an international theater, music, and dance extravaganza. For information about the festival, ask at the tourist office, check out www.barcelonafestival.com, or, during the festival, stop by the booth at the bottom of Pl. de Catalunya, on Portal de Angel. The **Sónar** music festival comes to town in mid-June, attracting renowned DJs and electronica enthusiasts from all over the world for three days of concerts and partying. Besides Sónar, major music festivals include Summercase (indie and pop) and Jazzaldia. Check www.mondosonoro.com or pick up the Mondo Sonoro festival guide at hostels and bars. For information on cultural activities in the city, swing by the **Institut de Cultura de Barcelona (ICUB)**, Palau de la Virreina, La Rambla, 99. (☎933 16 10 00; www.bcn.es/cultura. Info office open M-Sa 10am-8pm, Su 11am-3pm. Ticket sales Tu-F 11am-1:30pm and 4-8pm, Sa 11am-8pm, Su 11am-2:30pm. Most performances around €18-30.) Check www.barcelonaturisme.com for occasional 10% discounts. **Palau de la Música Catalana**, C. Sant Francese de Paula, 2 (☎932 95 72 00; www.palaumusica.org; M: Jaume I), to the right off Via Laietana at the level of Pl. Urquinaona, also sells concert tickets. (Concert tickets €6-330. Box office open M-Sa 9:30am-3pm, Su from 1hr. prior to the concert. No concerts in Aug.; check the *Guía del Ocio* for listings. MC/V.)

 HIGH CULTURE, LOW BUDGET. The Gran Teatre del Liceu sells nosebleed seats at low prices. Beware of the cheapest tickets (€8-10) unless you want to sit behind an obstruction. Students with ID can arrive at the theater 2hr. before showtime (1hr. on weekends) and pick up remainder seats at a 30% discount. This is best attempted on weekdays, when seats more frequently go unsold. On weekends, arrive exactly 1hr. before curtain.

Centre Artesà Tradicionàrius, Tr. de Sant Antoni, 6-8 (☎932 18 44 85; www.tradicionarius.com), in Gràcia. M: Fontana. *Catalana* folk music concerts Sept.-June F 10pm. Tickets €6-8. Also dance, music workshops, and summer festivals; ask for details. Open M-F 11am-2pm and 5-9pm. Closed Aug. Cash only.

Gran Teatre del Liceu, La Rambla, 51-59 (☎934 85 99 13; www.liceubarcelona.com). M: Liceu. Founded in 1847, destroyed by fire in 1994, and recently reopened, Liceu has regained its status as the city's premier venue for opera and popular music. Reserve tickets in advance. Box office open M-F 2-8:30pm, Sa and holidays 1hr. before showtime. 24hr. ticket sales at ServiCaixa. AmEx/MC/V.

L'Auditori, C. Lepanto, 150 (☎932 47 93 00; www.auditori.com), in l'Eixample between M: Marina and Glòries. Home to the city orchestra (the BOC), and host to visiting chamber, choral, and jazz groups. Concerts from late Sept. to mid-July, with performances generally F 7pm, Sa 9pm, and Su 11am; confirm times in advance. Tickets €16-45; special performances up to €120. Available by phone, through ServiCaixa or TelEntrada, or at ticket windows (open M-Sa noon-9pm, Su 1hr. before show starts). MC/V.

For cheaper rock, pop, and jazz, there are three big venues that invite foreign and local artists. **Apolo,** Nou de la Rambla, 113 (☎934 42 40 02), hosts major indie shows. **Jamboree,** Plaça Reial, 17, has a jazz series that's been active since the 60s and still brings relevant musicians. **Sidecar,** Plaça Reial, 7, hosts American and European rock and roll. Tickets for Apolo and Jamboree through TelEntrada (www.telentrada.com), Sidecar tickets normally €7 at the door on show night.

FILM

Most screens show the latest Hollywood features, some in English. The *Cine* section in the *Guía del Ocio* denotes subtitled films with *V.O.* (original version) *subtitulada*; other foreign films are dubbed *(doblado)*, usually in *català*. Many

BEYOND THE GUÍA DEL OCIO. For the lowdown on both mainstream and underground shows in Barcelona, check out the following helpful sites: **(http://www.agendaconcertscatalunya.com)** Concert listings from ASACC, an umbrella organization for *català* venues; **(http://www.maumaunderground.com)** Local music news, reviews, and a daily agenda of shows and other happenings; **(www.lecool.com)** Register to receive weekly arts updates.

theaters have a discount day (usually Monday or Wednesday). **Filmoteca,** Av. Sarrià, 31-33, screens classic, cult, and other films in the original language with subtitles in Spanish or *català*. (M: Hospital Clínic. ☎934 10 75 90. €2.70, students and seniors €2.) **Méliès Cinemas,** C. de Villarroel, 102 (www.cinesmelies.com), shows classics. (M: Urgell. ☎934 51 00 51. M €2.70, Tu-Su €4.) **Icària-Yelmo,** C. Salvador Espriu, 61, in the Olympic Village, boasts 15 screens and V.O. (☎932 21 75 85; www.yelmocineplex.es. M matinees €5, Tu-Su €6.50.) **Casablanca-Kaplan** shows foreign films in their original languages, and **Casablanca-Gracias,** shows contemporary independent cinema. (☎934 59 03 26, €4.50-6) The brand-new **Cinesa Maremàgnum,** Port Vell, in Moll d'Espanya next to the Aquàrium, has eight screens. (M: Drassanes. Tickets by phone ☎902 33 32 31 or ServiCaixa. €5.80, W €4.20.) Next door, the new **IMAX Port Vell** has an IMAX screen, an Omnimax 30m in diameter, and 3D projection. Get tickets at the door, through ServiCaixa, or by phone. (☎932 25 11 11. €10, matinees €7. Showtimes 10:30am-12:30am.) **Arenas Cine-Gay,** C. Disputació, 5, off of C. Tarragona just below Princep Jorgi, shows contemporary gay-themed films, 10:30am-10pm. (M: Espanya. ☎934 23 11 69. €7.)

FÚTBOL

For the record, the lunatics covered from head to toe in red and blue stripes didn't just escape from an asylum—they are **F.C. Barcelona (Barça)** fans. Grab some face paint and join them in the 120,000-seat **Camp Nou,** Europe's largest *fútbol* ground. On game days, the stadium is packed with thousands of passionate fans cheering one of the world's most popular teams. The box office is on C. Arístedes Maillol, 12-18 (☎902 180 900; www.fcbarcelona.com). Get tickets (€30-60) early; Barça lost to its rival Real Madrid in 2006-7, but is still a true *català* institution. Its motto, *El Barça és més que un club*, "Barça is more than a club," says it all. **R.C. Deportivo Espanyol,** a.k.a. *los periquitos* (parakeets), Barcelona's second professional soccer team, spreads its wings in blue-and-white stripes at **Estadi Olímpic,** Pg. Olímpie, 17-19 (☎932 927 700; www.rcdespanyol.es). This team isn't as renowned as Barça, but the games are fun and cheaper (€20-45). Get tickets from Banca Catalana or call ServiCaixa (☎902 33 22 11; www.servicaixa.com).

BEACHES

The entire strip between Vila Olímpica and Barceloneta is a long, public beach accessible from M: Ciutadella or Barceloneta. The closest and most popular is **Platja Barceloneta,** off Pg. Marítim. Be aware of nudity on **Platja San Sebastià;** however, the only official nude beach is **Platja de la Nova Mar Bella.** Barcelona's beaches, although good for a city, are crowded at almost any time of day. Nicer beaches can be found past the Mapfre tower to the east, or take the commuter rail along the coast and get off when you see one you like.

RECREATIONAL SPORTS

The tourist offices or the online directory (www.barcelonaturisme.com) can provide info about swimming, cycling, tennis, squash, sailing, hiking, scuba diving, whitewater rafting, kayaking, and most other sports.

BARCELONA

DiR Fitness Club, 12 branches throughout Barcelona, including one at C. Gran de Gràcia, 37 (branch ☎934 15 55 50; central ☎902 10 19 79; www.dir.es). A popular Barcelona gym chain with every amenity imaginable, from steam bath, solarium, and personalized fitness programs to a fingerprint-scan entrance. Prices depend on time of day, age, and number of days per week, but generally €4.25 per day (plus €2 membership card, purchased once); monthly passes range €40-200 depending on location and services. Open M-F 7am-10:15pm, Sa-Su and holidays 9am-7:15pm. MC/V.

Piscines Bernat Picornell, Av. Estadi, 30-40 (☎934 23 40 41; www.picornell.com), to the right when facing the stadium. Test your backstroke in the Olympic pools with stadium seating overlooking the city. €4.70 for outdoor pool (long-term passes available); €8.50 for workout facilities including sauna, massage parlor, and gym. Sa and winter M are nude days. Outdoor pool open June-Sept. M-Sa 9am-9pm, Su 9am-8pm; Sept.-May daily 7:30am-4pm. Workout facilities open M-F 8:45am-11:30pm, Sa 7am-8:45pm, Su 7:30am-3pm. MC/V.

BULLFIGHTING

Although the best *matadores* rarely venture out of Madrid, Sevilla, and Málaga, Barcelona's **Plaça Monumental de Toros,** Gran Via de les Corts Catalanes, 743 (☎932 45 58 02; fax 32 71 58; M: Monumental), is an excellent facility. Cataluña is currently considering a ban on bullfighting, so this venue may see a fate similar to the one by Pl. Espanya: conversion into a shopping mall. Bullfights take place during the summer tourist season, since tourists are about the only people who go (Apr.-Sept. Su 6:30pm). Tickets (€24-70) are available at travel agencies, ServiCaixa, or at the office on C. Muntaner, 24. (L'Eixample. ☎934 53 38 21; fax 51 69 98. Open W-Sa 11am-2pm and 4-8pm. MC/V.) The box office at the Plaça de Toros sells tickets from 11am until the fight (cash only).

▣ SHOPPING

A shopaholic's paradise, cosmopolitan Barcelona is littered with trendy stores for all audiences. Those on the prowl for typical European women's clothing should check out C. Portaferrissa, C. Pelai in front of Pl. Catalunya, and Av. Portal de l'Àngel. A stroll down C. d'Avinyó and its smaller side streets will prove beneficial for anyone into underground fashion, as will a trip to La Ribera's hip boutiques. Less expensive jewelry, accessories, and other knick-knacks can be found on C. Boqueria. For more legitimate jewelry, meander into one of the treasure chests on C. Call. The fashionista mecca is still **Pg. de Gràcia** in l'Eixample. One place for bargains is **Carrer Girona,** between C. Casp and Gran Via, in l'Eixample, home to a small string of discount shops offering clothing, shoes, bags, and accessories. (M: Tetuán. Walk 2 blocks down Gran Via and take a left on C. Girona.) **Carrer Bruc,** one street over, offers more retail delights for bargain hunters. Be aware that stores marked "Venta al Mejor" are wholesalers who don't take kindly to browsing. Another area to try for discounts is the **Mercat Alternatiu (Alternative Market)** on C. Riera Baixa in El Raval. (M: Liceu. Take C. de l'Hospital—a right off La Rambla facing the ocean—and follow it to C. Riera Baixa, the 7th right, shortly after the stone hospital.) This short street is crammed with second-hand and thrift stores.

BOOKS

Come in Librería Inglesa, C. Balmes, 129 (☎934 53 12 04; www.libreriainglesa.com). English books and a selection of classic novels. Bulletin boards feature ads for travel partners or language instructors. Open M-Sa 9:45am-2pm and 4:30-8:15pm. MC/V.

Documenta, C. Cardenal Casañas, 4 (☎933 17 25 27; www.documenta-bcn.com), just steps off La Rambla, located in the old Cu-Cut! publishing house, forcibly shut down by the army in the 1930s. Decent selection of English novels and travel guides. Open M-Sa 9:30am-8:30pm, Su and holidays 11am-2:30pm and 5-8:30pm. AmEx/MC/V.

FNAC (www.fnac.es) has 3 locations: Triangle mall in Pl. Catalunya, M: Catalunya (☎933 44 18 00; open M-Sa 10am-10pm); Av. Diagonal, 3-35, M: Besòs Mar (☎935 02 99 00; open M-Sa 10am-10pm); L'Illa Centre Comercial, Av. Diagonal, 557, M: María Cristina (☎934 44 59 00; open M-Sa 10am-9:30pm). AmEx/MC/V.

La Central del Raval, C. Elisabets, 6 (☎933 17 02 93; www.lacentral.com), off La Rambla in El Raval. M: Catalunya. Literature and nonfiction in 7 languages in a spacious bookstore and cafe, born in 1693 as the Gothic-style Església de la Misericòrdia. Pocket *català*/English and *català*/Spanish dictionaries (€11). Open M-F 10am-9:30pm, Sa 10am-9pm. AmEx/MC/V.

🔋 NIGHTLIFE

Barcelona truly lives by night. Its wild and varied nightlife treads the precarious line between slick and kitschy. In many ways, the city is a tourist's clubbing heaven: things don't get going until late (don't bother showing up at a club before 1am) and keep going for as long as you can handle it. Yet for every full-blown dance club, there are a hundred more relaxed bars, from Irish pubs to gay clubs to absinthe dens. Check the *Guía del Ocio*, available at newsstands, for even more up-to-date listings of nighttime fun, as the hot spots change often. *Barcelona Week*, the English arts weekly, also has listings.

BARRI GÒTIC AND LA RAMBLA

Traditional *cervecerías* and bar-restaurants can be found every five steps on main streets such as C. Ferran. C. Escudellers is a lively location for post-bar dancing, and Pl. Reial remains packed until early morning. La Rambla becomes questionable late at night, as prostitutes emerge where families roam in the daylight.

▧ Jamboree, Pl. Reial, 17 (☎933 19 17 89; www.masimas.com). M: Liceu. A disorienting maze of stone arches and swirling lights thumps with hip-hop; 2nd fl. plays 80s and 90s music. Drinks €8-10. Jazz 9-11pm, €3-10. Cover M €3, Tu-Su €10; look for flyers with discounts. Open daily 8pm-1am; nightclub open 2-5am. Upstairs, **Tarantos** hosts flamenco shows (€5). Open M-Sa 8-11pm.

Fonfone, C. Escudellers, 24 (☎933 17 14 24; www.fonfone.com). M: Liceu or Drassanes. Trippy orange and red bubbles protruding from the wall combined with funky music draw crowds from 1-3am. Different DJs every night from all over the world; check the website. Beer €3. Mixed drinks €6-8. Open daily 10pm-2:30 or 3am.

Schilling, C. Ferran, 23 (☎933 17 67 87). M: Liceu, L3. One of the more laid-back and spacious wine bars in the area, with dim lighting and velvet seat cushions. Often attracts British and gay crowds. Excellent *sangria* (pitcher €17). Wine €2-3, bottle from €13. Serves breakfast and sandwiches (€3-6) during the day. Open M-W 10am-2:30am, Th-Sa 10am-3am, Su noon-3am.

Karma, Pl. Reial, 10 (☎933 02 56 80; www.karmadisco.com). M: Liceu. Quite a change from the dive upstairs and the airy terrace outside, this multicolored tunnel of a club and bar with fountain view keeps a Pl. Reial crowd dancing and drinking. Beer (€3) and mixed drinks (€4-6) are less expensive than at other clubs. Club cover €8-10. Bar open Tu-Su 6pm-2:30am; club open Tu-Su midnight-5am.

El Bosq de les Fades, Pg. de la Banca, 16 (☎933 17 26 49), near the Wax Museum. M: Drassanes. This downright ghoulish bar/cafe used to be the horror section of the Wax

BARHOPPING IN BARÇA

To aid you on your late-night adventures, here are our favorite places to bar-hop in Barcelona:

1 **Plaça Reial.** The center of the Barri Gòtic, you can begin your evening here with dinner and stay until the clubs get out the next morning. Try not to fall into the fountain.

2 **Passeig del Born.** The Ribera's main drag is a relaxed good time from dusk to dawn. Every kind of bar (and lots of tapas) draw a young crowd every night of the week.

3 **C. Gran de Gràcia.** From this short stretch in L'Eixample, turn off onto a sidestreet and enjoy some of the best dancing in Barcelona right alongside some of its best *bokatas* (sandwiches) and beer.

4 **Rambla del Raval.** This neighborhood offers terraces and tea during the day and laid-back bars at night. Venture onto C. Sant Pau to have just one more drink.

5 **La Boqueria.** Once the pesky market crowd has gone home, you'll find colorful bars with lit-up terraces that serve elaborate cocktails.

6 **C. Ferran.** This often-gritty offshoot of La Rambla features Irish bars, Maoz Vegitarian (providers of the finest late-night falafel in the city), and everything in between.

Museum; it's now a great place to chill before a club, if the shadowy groves don't scare you away. Open M-Th 2pm-1am, F 2pm-2am, Sa 11am-2am, Su 11am-1am.

Margarita Blue, C. Josep Anselm Clavé, 6 (☎933 17 71 76; www.margaritablue.com). M: Drassanes. Popular with locals. Draws crowds with mojitos and Mexican food. Margaritas €3.50. Entrees €6-12. W and Su magic shows 11:30pm. W-Su DJ 10pm-1am. Open M-W and Su 7pm-2am, Th 7pm-2:30am, F-Sa 7pm-3am. AmEx/MC/V.

LA RIBERA

Besides its wealth of intriguing dinner options, La Ribera has a nightlife scene that is both more local and more varied than the scene on La Rambla. When the gas lantern goes on in front of *Eglesia de Santa Maria*, as it does every night, people begin the nightly migrations from small back-street bars to second-floor sheesha lounges, and everywhere in between.

El Copetín, Pg. del Born, 19 (☎607 20 21 76). M: Jaume I. Cuban rhythm invades this casual, dimly-lit nightspot full of young and old alike. Copetín fills up before some places open, making it a good place to start the night. Awe-inspiring mojitos *("cócktail de la casa")* €7. Open M-Th and Su 7pm-2:30am, F-Sa 7pm-3am. Cash only.

El Born, Pg. del Born, 26 (☎933 19 53 33). M: Jaume I. Sit at the marble counter over basins where fish were once sold, or go up the spiral staircase for a meal. Mixed drinks €4-6. Fondue with a number of different meats €12-16. Open M-Sa 7pm-2am. MC/V.

Palau Dalmases, C. Montcada, 20 (☎933 10 06 73). M: Jaume I. A 17th-century palace filled with lavish paintings and statues. Its large wooden doors, watched over by a guard, make it all the more exclusive. It's whispered that *"quisiera cenar"* (I'd like to have dinner) is the password sometimes required to get in. Mixed drinks €7-10. Live opera Th 11pm; €20, includes 1 drink. Open Tu-Sa 8pm-2am, Su 6-10pm. MC/V.

Pas del Born, C. Calders, 8. M: Barceloneta or Jaume I. This bar's bright pink exterior is an indication of the stylish, yet unpretentious, clientele and interior decoration. Weekends find a couple of trapeze artists swinging, to music, through Pas's modest balcony. Open M-Th 7pm-2am, F-Sa 7pm-3am. Cash only.

EL RAVAL

The streets are densely packed with a bar for every variety of bar-hopper, and true to the artsy nature of the area, El Raval's specialty is a hip, creatively decorated, colorful bar with a young, laid-back crowd. Be sure to check out the area between C. Joaquim Costa and C. Carme, around the Museum of Contemporary Art.

Marsella Bar, C. de Sant Pau, 65. M: Liceu. Don't be deterred by the tarnished mirrors of Barcelona's oldest bar (built in 1820)—they merely add to its charm. Religious figurines grace the walls; perhaps they're praying for the souls of the *absenta* (absinthe; €3.30) drinkers. Beer €3.20. Mixed drinks €4-6. Open M-Sa 10pm-2am. Cash only.

London Bar, C. Nou de la Rambla, 34 (☎933 18 52 61). M: Liceu. Don't let the name fool you: this *Modernista* tavern is for locals and expats alike. Beer, wine, and absinthe €2-3. Live music (usually rock or blues) nightly at 11:30pm with no cover. Mixed drinks €6-7. Open Tu-Sa 8:30am-3:15am. AmEx/MC/V.

iposa, C. Floristes de la Rambla, s/n, one block north-west of La Boqueria. A terrace for tea during the day and a young, international crowd at night make iposa (short for "butterfly") a great place for cheap beer (€1.60) and mixed drinks (€3-5). Open daily 1pm-3am, or until people leave. Cash only.

Casa Almirall, C. Joaquín Costa, 33. M: Universitat. Cavernous space with weathered couches, cool, dim lights, and equally laid-back clientele. It's house policy to stop you after your third absinthe (€5-8), but the staff is fond of saying that you won't make it there anyway. Beer €2-4. Mixed drinks €5-7. Open M-Th 5pm-2:30am, F-Sa 7pm-3am, Su 7pm-2am. Cash only.

Muebles Navarro (El Café que Pone), C. la Riera Alta, 4 (☎934 42 39 66). Enjoy the mellow ambience and relax as you and your friends sink into the comfy couches. Beer and wine €2-3. Mixed drinks €5-6. Open Tu-Th 6pm-1am, F-Su 6pm-3am.

Sant Pau 68, C. de Sant Pau, 68 (☎934 41 31 15). M: Liceu. The red lighting and flowered wallpaper create a relaxed atmosphere in one of El Raval's smoothest bars. Drinks €2-6. Open M-Th and Su 8pm-2:30am, F-Sa until 3am. MC/V.

Moog, C. Arc del Teatre, 3 (☎933 01 72 82; www.masimas.com/moog). M: Liceu or Drassanes. Industrial metal walls and floor betray this as the techno headquarters of Barcelona, though the upstairs dance floor blasts music from the 80s and 90s. Look for discount flyers on the street. Cover €9. Open daily midnight-5am, weekends until 6am.

L'EIXAMPLE

L'Eixample has upscale bars and some of the best—though not exclusively—gay nightlife in Europe, as evident in the area's nickname, "Gaixample." Some clubs can be difficult to get to, or get back from; you may want to check ahead of time which NitBus route will take you home.

Mojito Club, C. Rosselló, 217 (☎932 37 65 28; www.mojitobcn.com). M: Diagonal. This club lures a fun-loving crowd with Latin beats. Free samba lessons W 11pm; salsa F-Sa 11pm-1:30am; 10-week courses available. Brazilian party W with live salsa all night. Th and Su free drink with entry. F-Sa cover €10 cash after 2:30am, includes 1 drink. Open daily 11pm-4:30am. MC/V.

Dietrich, C. Consell de Cent, 255 (☎934 51 77 07; www.dietrichcafe.com). M: Pg. de Gràcia. An unflattering caricature of a semi-nude Marlene Dietrich greets patrons at this inclusive gay bar. Beer €5. Mixed drinks €6-8. Nightly trapeze show 1:30am, drag shows some weekends. Open M-Sa 11pm-2:30am. MC/V.

La Fira, C. Provença, 171 (☎650 85 53 84). M: Hospital Clínic or FGC: Provença. A hip crowd surrounded by carousel swings, mirrors, and a fortune teller. F dance show/dance class 2, 3, 4am. Open W-Th 11pm-2:30am, F-Sa until 5am. Cash only.

Les Gents que J'aime, C. València, 286, downstairs (☎932 15 68 79). M: Pg. de Gràcia. Background soul, funk, and jazz soothe patrons enjoying drinks like Les Gents (kiwi, lime, and pineapple juice) and lounging in the red velvet armchairs. Beer €3.50. ½-bottles of wine €12. Open M-Th and Su 7pm-2:30am, F-Sa later. AmEx/MC/V.

Átame, C. Consell de Cent, 257 (☎934 54 92 73). M: Pg. de Gràcia. Next door to Dietrich, with an industrial gray interior, this bar is frequented mainly by gay men. It's not as scandalous as its name ("tie me up") might imply. Beer €3. Mixed drinks €4-6. Happy hour (free tapas) Tu 7-10pm. Open daily 7pm-2:30am. Cash only.

Luz de Gas, C. Muntaner, 244-246 (☎932 09 77 11; www.luzdegas.com). M: Diagonal. Live music every night, from local rock bands to 60s classics. Beer €6. Mixed drinks €10. Cover €18, includes 1 drink. Concerts up to €35; call for info. Open daily 11:30pm-5am. MC/V.

Salvation, Ronda de Sant Pere, 19-21 (☎933 18 06 86). M: Urquinaona. A popular gay club in the heart of the city. Beer €5. Mixed drinks €8. Cover €16, includes 1 drink. Look for flyers to get discounts. Open F-Sa midnight-6am.

MONTJUÏC

Lower Montjuïc is home to Poble Espanyol, a recreation of famous buildings and sights from all regions of Spain. The courtyards host performances, and the entire complex is filled with interesting craft shops. (Av. Marquès de Comillas, 13. M: Espanya or bus #13 or 50. ☎935 08 63 00. Open M 9am-8pm, Tu-Th 9am-2am, F-Sa 9am-4am, Su 9am-midnight. Ticket booth closes 1hr. before park. €7.50, students and seniors €5.50, after 8pm €4. Prices may vary when there are concerts. Audio tours available 9am-8pm, €3.) When **Terrazza** closes, buses take the most serious party animals to "los afters"—clubs open 6am-7pm. **Merci** and **Souvenir** are the most popular, but ask around when Terrazza lets out.

▨ Tinta Roja, C. Creus dels Molers, 17 (☎934 43 32 43; www.tintaroja.net). Located just off Av. Paral·lel in a newly pedestrian section of Poble Sec. The best combination bar and dance floor in the city. Open Th 9pm-1:30am, F-Sa 9pm-2:30am, Su 7pm-midnight. Cash only.

Torres de Ávila, just around to the right of Tinta Roja, off C. Creus dels Molers. Coffee and beer run €3, and tapas run €4-9, but the real prize is the 180° view of the city. Open noon-6:30pm. Cash only.

La Terrazza, Avda. Marquès de Comillas, s/n (☎934 23 12 85). An outdoor madhouse and the undisputed king of Poble Espanyol nightlife. Cover €10; €3 with flyer. Open June-Oct. Th-Sa midnight-6am.

THE WATERFRONT

Every night Barcelona's biggest mall, **Maremàgnum,** opens one rooftop terrace with a half-dozen clubs; names like **Goldeneye** (open daily 11pm-4:30am) and **Sunset** (open daily 1pm-4:30am) attract throngs of tourists and the occasional Spaniard. Though these clubs are not the most authentic experience in Barcelona, crowds are guaranteed all week. None charge cover; clubs make their money from exorbitant drink prices (beer €5, mixed drinks €8-10).

L'Ovella Negra (Megataverna del Poble Nou), C. Zamora, 78. M: Bogatell or Marina. (☎933 09 59 38; www.ovellanegra.net). On the corner of C. Pallars. What was once a warehouse is now the place to come for the first few beers of the night. Large beers €2, 2L pitchers €8.50. Mixed drinks €4-5. Open Th 10pm-2:30am, F-Sa 5pm-3am, Su 7-1am. Kitchen open all night. Cash only.

Razzmatazz, C. Pamplona, 88, and Almogàvers, 122 (☎932 72 09 10; www.salarazzmatazz.com). M: Marina. A warehouse complex that houses 5 clubs: Pop, The Loft, Razz Club, Lo*Li*Ta, and Rex Room, each with its own live music specialty. Concert prices vary; call ahead or check website. Beer €3.50. Mixed drinks €7. Cover €12-15, includes access to all 5 clubs. Open F-Sa and holidays 1-5am. AmEx/MC/V.

Catwalk, C. Ramón Trias Fargas, 2-4 (☎932 24 07 40). M: Port Olímpic. The sleek interior makes this one of the hottest places in town, with hanging red couches and a crowd dressed to the nines. Cover €18. Open W-Su midnight-6am. MC/V.

ZONA ALTA: GRÀCIA AND OUTER BARRIS

The area around C. Marià Cubí has great nightlife unspoiled by tourists, but you'll have to take a taxi (or the NitBus). For more accessible fun in Gràcia, head to Pl. del Sol to find the popular musical **Eldorado,** Pl. del Sol, 4 (☎932 10 59 00; www.eldoradobcn.com; open daily 10pm-2:30am; terrace from 7pm), or the more relaxed **Café del Sol,** Pl. del Sol, 16 (☎934 15 56 63; open daily 12:30pm-2:30am).

▨ **Otto Zutz,** C. Lincoln, 15 (☎932 38 07 22). FGC: Pl. Molina or M: Fontana. Japanimation lighting and three distinct dance floors make this one of Barcelona's most famous clubs. Beer €6. Mixed drinks €6-12. Cover €10-15, includes 1 drink; look for flyers at bars and hotels to get in free before 2am. Open Tu-Sa midnight-6am. AmEx/MC/V.

▨ **D.O.,** C. Verdi, 36 (932 18 96 73). Late crowd reads a long tapas menu off chalkboards at this between-club snack stopover. Extensive wine list. Tapas €3-7, mixed drinks €3-8. Open M and W-Su 6pm-2am. Cash only.

La Femme, C. Plató, 13 (☎932 01 62 07), on the corner of Muntaner. FCG: Muntaner. A welcoming haven for lesbians of all ages. Couches along shiny silver walls are the perfect place for conversation, or a little something else. Beer €5. Mixed drinks €7. Open F 11pm-3am, Sa 11:30pm-last customer. Cash only.

Pippermint, C. Bori i Fontestà, 20 (☎932 08 00 00), has the largest drinks you'll ever see. *Cuba libre* (6L) €37.40. Beer (13L) €70. Also has normal-sized drinks for tamer, or smaller, groups. 1L €10-12. Open daily 4pm-about 3am). MC/V.

Casa Quimet, Rambla de Prat, 9 (☎932 17 53 27). Don't be deceived: what looks like a music store from the outside is actually the best place around to hear soul music and eat Basque snacks. Beer €3. Open Th-Su 6pm-1am. Cash only.

▧ FESTIVALS

While Barcelona is quite different from other parts of Spain, the city shares at least one thing in common with the rest of the country: it knows how to have fun. For information on all festivals, call the tourist office (☎933 01 77 75; open M-F 10am-2pm and 4-8pm) or check the "Agenda" or "Diary" on www.bcn.es. Double-check sight and museum hours during festival times, as well as during the Christmas season and *Semana Santa.* The **Festa de Sant Jordi** (St. George; Apr. 23) is the *català* take on Valentine's Day, and officially celebrates Cataluña's patron saint with a feast. Men give women roses, and women give men books. In the last two weeks of August, city folk jam at Gràcia's **Festa Mayor;** lights blaze in *plaças* and music plays all night as two dozen streets compete to be the best decorated. On September 11, the **Festa Nacional de Catalunya** brings out traditional costumes, dancing, and *catalana* flags hanging from balconies. Strangely, the *català* national day celebrates the military defeat that subjected the region to years of Bourbon oppression. Barcelona's main festival, the **Festa de Sant Joan,** takes place the night of June 23. You might as well surrender to the all-night beachside partying (and erratic nightclub hours); ceaseless fireworks and bonfires in the street will keep your eyes wide open anyway. The largest Barcelona celebration, however, is the **Festa de Mercè,** the weeks before and after September 24. To honor the patron saint of the city, *barceloneses* revel with fireworks, *sardana* dancing, and concerts. **Santa Eulàlia,** the city's other patron saint, is celebrated February 12-13.

BARCELONA

⚡ DAYTRIP FROM BARCELONA

MONTSERRAT   ☎938

A 1235m peak of limestone, quartz, and slate protruding sharply from the Río Llobregat Valley, Montserrat (Sawed Mountain) is an inspiration to its 2.5 million annual visitors. A millennium ago, one wandering mountaineer claimed to have spotted the Virgin Mary; as the story spread, pilgrims flocked to the mountain. The Monastery of the Virgin, founded in 1025 by the opportunistic Bishop Oliba, is tended today by 80 Benedictine monks. Today, the site attracts those who come to see the Virgin of Montserrat, her ornate basilica, the art museum, and panoramic views of Cataluña from the mountain's distinctive, stunning rocks.

▤⚡ TRANSPORTATION AND PRACTICAL INFORMATION

FGC (☎932 05 15 15) line R5 runs to Montserrat from M: Espanya (1hr.; hourly 8:36am-5:36pm; return from Montserrat 10:33am-10:33pm; round-trip including cable car €13.20); get off at Montserrat-Aeri. From there, catch the **▨Aeri cable car** right by the station, the coolest way to ascend to the monastery. (Runs daily July-Aug. every 15min. 9:27am-6:27pm; price included in bus combo fare or €8 round-trip by itself. Additional times in summer; call ☎938 77 77 01 to check.) Another option is to take the FGC's new train, the **Cremallera de Montserrat.** (☎902 31 20 20; www.cremallerademontserrat.com.) From Barcelona, this requires a combined R5 train plus the Cremallera (Rack Railway) instead of the cable car (Cremallera €6.30, children €3.50, retired €5.70; combined, including train from Pl. Espanya, €13.20/10.40/12.60). Get off the FGC one station later, at Monistrol de Montserrat, and take the railway up (every 20-30min.). Autocars Julià **buses** run to the monastery, from near Estació Sants. (Leaves Barcelona daily 9am and returns June 25-Sept. 14 at 6pm, Sept. 15-June 24 at 5pm. Call ☎934 90 40 00 for reservations. €10. MC/V.) If you plan to use the funiculars, consider buying the **Tot Montserrat** (€32.50) at tourist offices or in M: Espanya; it includes tickets for the FGC, cable car, funiculars, Museu de Montserrat, and a meal. Also available is the **Trans Montserrat** (€19.50), same as the Tot but without the Museu and the meal. Free parking for cars. Call ☎938 35 03 84 for a taxi (fixed price from Barcelona €81.18).

Visitor services are in Pl. Creu, the area straight ahead from the top of the Aeri cable car steps and the Cremallera station. The **info booth** in Pl. Creu provides free maps, schedules of religious services, and advice on mountain navigation. An audioguide with a booklet to Montserrat is €5, and an audio guide with headphones for two is €6.50. (☎938 77 77 77. Open April-Sept. daily 9am-7:50pm; Oct.-Mar. M-F 9am-5:30pm, Sa-Su 9am-7pm.) For more information, buy the *Official Guide to Montserrat* (€7.30) or the museum guide (€4). Services include: **ATMs** and bank at La Caixa, next to the info booth (open M-F 9:15am-2pm; Oct.-May also Sa 9:15am-1:30pm); **public bathrooms** to the left up the stairs from the tourist office; **ambulance** (inquire at info booth); the **Patronat del Parc Natural** (☎938 35 05 91); and the **post office** (open M-F 10am-1:30pm, Sa 10am-noon).

▤▢ ACCOMMODATIONS AND FOOD

Cel-les Abat Marcet ● has beautiful apartments with bath, kitchen, and heating. (☎938 77 77 01; ask for Cel-les. Reception 9am-1pm and 2-6pm. From €14-27 for one person, €24-40 for two. Min. 2 nights; discounts for longer stays.) **Camping Montserrat ●** is a 5min. walk past the funiculars on the road that goes uphill. Its library has climbing books for Montserrat that are no longer in print, and the mountain-savvy staff can put you in touch with climbing guides. (☎938 77 77 77; ask for camping. No parking at the site, but parking near Pl. Creu €5 for 3 days. Open Apr. 1-Oct. 31. €3 per person, €2 for kids under 12, and €2.50 per tent. Cash only.)

Food options in Montserrat are limited and aimed entirely at tourists trapped on a mountainside with no other alternatives. Pack food for your hike before coming or else descend into buffet hell. You can pick up some snacks at the small **Queviures supermarket** in Pl. Creu. For a quick meal, **Bar de la Plaça ❶** is an option. (*Bocadillos* and hamburgers €3-4. Open M-F 9:30am-5pm, Sa-Su 9:30am-6:40pm. Cash only.) A new **cafetería ❶**, in Pl. Creu, has limited self-service food options. (Sandwiches €3-4. Salads €4. Steak and fries €5. Open M-F 8:45am-7:30pm, Sa-Su 8:30am-8pm. MC/V.) There's a **self-service cafetería ❷** up the hill to the right from the cable car steps (in the building with the red "Mirador" sign), included in the price of the Lucky Tot Montserrat card. (2 dishes, chosen from paella, pasta, and meat, plus dessert and bread, drinks not included, for €10, Sa-Su €10.50; under 12 €6.95. Open daily noon-4pm.) A fancier alternative, **Restaurant de Montserrat ❷**, is located in the same building. (*Menú* €18.90, Su €14.80-21.90; children €6.95. Open Mar. 15-Nov. 15 daily noon-4pm. AmEx/MC/V.)

👁 SIGHTS

Above Pl. Creu (from the info booth, take the stairs up and to the right), the beautiful **basilica** looks onto Pl. Santa Noría. Inside the courtyard, next to the main chapel entrance, a marble hallway through side chapels leads to an elevated shrine with the 12th-century Romanesque **La Moreneta** (the black Virgin), an icon of Mary. (Hallway open daily 8-10:30am and noon-6:30pm; in summer also Sa-Su 7:30-8:15pm.) For many years it was revered as a black Virgin, until it was discovered that the statue was merely very dirty; the custom stuck, however, and it was painted black. The **Escalonia boys' choir** performs in the basilica (M-F 1pm; Su noon and 7:30pm, except June 25-Aug. 20; schedules may change; check www.escalonia.net). Also in Pl. Santa María, closer to the stairs up from Pl. Creu, the small **Museo de Montserrat** has art ranging from a mummy to Picasso's *Old Fisherman* and Dalí's *El Mariner*. (Open daily June 26-Sept. 15 10am-7pm; Sept. 16-June 25 10am 5:15pm. €6.50, students and over 65 €5.50, ages 6-12 €3.50, under 8 free.)

🅷 HIKES

Some of the most beautiful areas of the mountain are accessible only by foot. The steep **Santa Cova funicular** descends from Pl. Creu to the **Rosario Monumental,** which winds along the face of the mountain past 15 religious sculptures by notable *catalan* artists, culminating at the ancient hermitage **Santa Cova** where the Virgin Mary sighting took place. (Funicular daily every 20min. 10am-1pm and 2-5:30pm. Round-trip €2.60, students and over 65 €2.40, ages 3-14 €1.35. Santa Cova Chapel open Apr.-Oct. daily 10:30am-5:15pm; Nov.-Mar. M-F 11:30am-4:15pm, Sa-Su 10:30am-4:30pm.) Take the **Sant Joan funicular** up the hill for inspirational views of Montserrat, the monastery, and the surrounding towns. (Daily every 20min. 10am-6pm; in summer 10am-7pm. Check the signs for the last return. Round-trip €6.30, over 65 €5.70, ages 10-14 €3.20; joint round-trip ticket with the Sta. Cova funicular €7.10/6.40/3.60.) Upstairs in the upper station you'll find an exhibit on the funiculars and the **Nature Hall,** containing a model of Montserrat and some of the mountain's history. The **Sant Joan monastery** and **shrine** are only a 20min. tromp from here, and **Sant Jerónim** (the area's highest peak at 1236m), with its views of Montserrat's jagged, mystical rocks, is worth the 1½hr. trek from Pl. Creu (1hr. from the terminus of the Sant Joan funicular). The paths are long and winding but not difficult— after all, they were made for guys wearing very long robes.

BARCELONA

CATALUÑA (CATALUNYA)

Catalunya is the most prosperous region in Iberia—and one of the proudest. The region's linguistic identity, rich natural resources, and cultural tradition have set it apart from the rest of Spain. Colonized first by the Greeks and then the Carthaginians, Catalunya later became one of Rome's favored provinces. Only briefly subdued by the Moors, the region achieved independence in AD 987, growing more powerful after it united with the throne of Aragón in 1137. Still, while this pact allowed Catalunya to pursue her own empire for a time, it ultimately meant one thing: surrender to Spanish rule. The *català* Nationalist Movement that resulted from the subjugation has been a contentious political issue for centuries.

Catalunya's achievements have lent credence to the region's fierce sense of autonomy. In the late 18th century, the region became one of Europe's premier textile manufacturers and pursued a robust trade with the Americas. Nineteenth-century industrial expansion nourished the arts and sciences, ushering in an age known as the *catalana Renaixença* (Renaissance). The turn of the century gave birth to the *Modernista* movement and an all-star list of wildly innovative artists and architects including Picasso, Miró, Dalí, Gaudí, Domènech i Montaner, and Puig i Cadafalch. Despite all of its achievements, Catalunya was the site of merciless persecution under Franco's dictatorship after the Spanish Civil War in the 20th century. Many *catalans* were imprisoned or killed, injustices still fresh in the minds of the older generations. Dictatorship brought suppression of *català* language instruction (except in universities) and limited *català* publications, degrading the very foundation of the population's identity: its beloved tongue, a Romance language—not a dialect—closely related to Spanish and French. There is no "Spanish" here, only *castellano*, (literally, "language spoken in Castilla"), a distinction that allows *catalans* to differentiate themselves from the capital.

Since Catalunya regained regional autonomy in 1977, its media and arts have flourished; *català* is once again the official language. While some worry that its prevalence will discourage talented Spaniards from working or studying in Catalunya, effectively isolating the region and further decentralizing the nation, others argue that increased autonomy has generally led to progressive politics. After you've been to Catalunya, you may understand why many here call their state "A Nation Of Europe"—Catalunya isn't quite like anywhere else in Spain.

HIGHLIGHTS OF CATALUNYA

IMMERSE yourself in the Mediterranean on the Costa Brava (p. 426)

UNCOVER the secrets of the Kabbala at its birthplace in **Girona's** El Call (p. 434).

SURRENDER to Dalí's egotism at the Teatre-Museu Dalí in **Figueres** (p. 437).

COME OUT of your culinary shell at the snail festival in **Lleida** in May (p. 441).

COSTA DORADA

SITGES ☎938

Forty kilometers south of Barcelona, the beach town of Sitges just might deserve its self-proclaimed title as the "jewel of the Mediterranean." Composed of crystalline water, sweeping bays, and beautiful tanning grounds baked by 300 sunny days

Cataluña (Catalunya)

per year, Sitges gained prominence in the late 19th century as one of the principal centers of the *Modernista* art movement. Today, it's swarmed by young and fun-loving tourists who come for the thriving gay community and pulsating nightlife. Sitges makes an ideal daytrip along the coast, but it also merits a few nights' stay.

▐▀ TRANSPORTATION

Cercanías trains (a.k.a. Rodalies; RENFE ☎902 24 02 02) run from Estació Barcelona-Sants to Sitges (Line 2 toward St. Vicenç de Calders or Vilanova; 45min., every 15-30min. 5:27am-11:52pm, €2.50). Trains also run from Sitges to Cambrils (1hr., €4.30) via Tarragona (€3.60). **Mon Bus** (☎938 93 70 60) connects the Barcelona airport to Pg. de Villafranca in Sitges (M-F hourly 7:40am-11:40pm, Sa every 2hr. 8:40am-10:40pm, Su every 4hr., 9:40am-9:40pm; €2.85). **Late-night buses** operate from Pg. de Villafranca to Rambla de Catalunya in Barcelona and back (12:11am-4am, €2.85). Bus Urbà (☎938 14 49 89) runs three **local bus** lines (all leave from the train station, every 30min. M-F 8am-9pm, Sa-Su 9:30am-9pm; earlier in winter; €0.90-0.95). A **taxi** (☎938 94 13 29) between Barcelona and Sitges costs €55-60. To reach the beaches and the *cales* (caves), rent a car in Barcelona or Sitges at **Europcar** (☎938 11 19 96), on the first floor of the Mercat to the right from the train station (open daily 7am-9pm; credit card only, AmEx/MC/V).

CATALUÑA

■ ⚡ ❷ ORIENTATION AND PRACTICAL INFORMATION

Most people arrive at the train station on **Carrer Carbonell** in the north part of town. The town center is 5min. by foot, and the beach 10min. To reach either, take a right as you leave the station and the third left onto **Carrer Sant Francesc.** This leads to the old town and intersects **Carrer de les Parellades,** the main strip of stores and restaurants running parallel to the ocean. Any street off Parellades will lead to the waterfront. **Passeig de la Ribera** runs along the central and most crowded beaches.

For a free map and info, stop by the **tourist office,** C. Siria Morera, 1. From the station, turn right on C. Carbonell and take the next right at the roundabout, onto Pg. de Vilafranca. The office is one block up on the left—look for the sign with the big "i." Make sure to ask for the monthly bulletin of events, expositions, and tours called ⬛**Sitges Daily,** as well as the *Guía del Ocio.* (☎902 94 50 04; www.sitges-tur.com. Open July-Sept. daily 9am-8pm; Oct.-June M-F 9am-2pm and 4-6:30pm.) There are smaller **branches** at the train station and beside the church. (☎938 11 06 11. Open July-Sept. daily 10:30am-1:30pm and 5-9pm; Oct.-June W-F 10:30am-2pm, Sa 11am-2pm and 4-7pm, Su 11am-2pm.) **Agis** offers guided **tours** of the city (☎619 79 31 99; www.sitges.com/agis; €8), while **Jafra Natura** takes visitors through the bordering Garraf Natural Park (☎938 96 84 65; www.jafranatura.com; €4, children €3). Local services include: **medical services** (☎938 94 64 26); **police** in Pl. Ajuntament (from C. Parellades, take C. Major toward the coast); **Internet** access at **Cafe Cappuchino,** C. Sant Francesc, 44 (open daily 9am-11pm; €1 per 15min.); and the **post office** in Pl. d'Espanya (☎938 94 12 47; open M-F 8:30am-2:30pm, Sa 9:30am-1pm; no package pickup Sa). **Postal Code:** 08870.

⛏ ACCOMMODATIONS

Accommodations are difficult to find on summer weekends; call well in advance. The nightlife is crazy enough that you may not need a bed of your own.

⬛ **Hotel El Cid,** C. Sant Josep, 39 (☎938 94 18 42; www.hotelsitges.com). From the train station, pass the rotunda, and take the 4th left off C. Carbonell. One of the best deals in town and popular with young travelers. All 74 rooms come with bath, safe, and fan. Small pool, bar, and garden in back. Reserve a month ahead. Breakfast included. July-Sept. singles €46-69; doubles €67-83; triples €97-121. Oct. and Apr.-June €31-39/46-62. Deals for stays longer than 6 nights. Closed Nov.-Mar. MC/V. ❹

Hostal Parellades, C. de les Parellades, 11 (☎938 94 08 01; hostalparellades@hotmail.com), 1 block from the beach. Well-kept rooms, a terrace, and a piano. Easy entry after late nights (or early mornings). Singles €30; doubles with bath €50; triples with bath €72. MC/V. ❸

Hostal Bonaire, C. Bonaire, 31 (☎938 94 53 26). 12 rooms a block from the beach. Ask for one of the rooms with a terrace overlooking party-prone C. Bonaire. 24hr. reception. In summer singles with bath €42; doubles €58-65. In winter €35/50. MC/V. ❹

Hostal Termes, C. Termes, 9 (☎938 94 23 43). A young staff offers doubles and triples with bath, TV, and A/C. Some have balcony. Doubles in high season €80; triples €100; quads €120. MC/V. ❹

◪ FOOD

The restaurants in Sitges are mostly tourist traps, especially on the beachfront, but the food here is world-class. Venture far down C. de les Parellades or on the pleasant side streets to escape the generic scene. Sitges isn't cheap. You'll pay at least €20 for dinner, but expect to get your money's worth. Groceries are available at **Suma,** C. Carbonell, 24, across from the train station. (☎938 94 12 00. Open M-Sa

9am-9pm, Su 10am-2pm. MC/V.) Alternatively, swing by the **Mercat de Sitges,** C. Carbonell, 26, next door to the train station, which has fruit and vegetable, meat, fish, and cheese vendors, as well as several cafes and bakeries and even a clothing store. (open M-Th 8am-2pm, F-Sa 8am-2pm and 5-8:30pm).

Izarra, C. Major 24 (☎938 94 73 70), behind the museum area. Basque tapas bar good for a quick fix or a leisurely meal. Ask for a *plato* and grab whatever looks tasty, from Basque seafood concoctions to more traditional Spanish *croquetas.* Big entrees (€5-12.50) and great *sidra* (€1.30). Bar open daily 8:30am-1am, *menú* available 1:30-4pm and 8:30-11pm. MC/V. ❷

Ma Maison, C. Bonaire, 28 (☎938 94 60 54). Couscous is the specialty at this gay-friendly restaurant, but all of the Mediterranean entrees are good, and the menu changes every 2 months. Su is paella day. Dinner entrees €21.50. Open daily 8:30pm-midnight, Sa-Su also 1:30pm-4pm. MC/V. ❹

Restaurante La Oca, C. de les Parellades, 41 (☎938 94 79 36). Chicken roasting on an open fire, pasta, and pizza attract lines of hungry tourists to the "Goose Restaurant." Try the house specialty *pollo a la cava* (chicken in a champagne sauce; €6.75). Oct.-Mar. lunch *menú* €9. Open M-F and Su 1pm-midnight, Sa 1pm-1am. MC/V. ❷

El Xalet Restaurant, C. de l'Illa de Cuba, 35 (☎938 11 00 70; www.elxalet.com), inside a *Modernista* hotel garden. An upscale break from the beachfront crowds—the beautiful courtyard seating is reason enough to come. Delicate appetizers (€7.75-16.50) and more substantial meat and fish entrees (€14.25-26.75). *Menú* €21-35. Open May-Sept. M and W-Su 8:30-11:30pm. MC/V. ❹

🔆 SIGHTS

Tourists flock to the shopping, eating, and drinking on the pedestrian walkway **Carrer de les Parellades,** but wise locals stick the side streets and the peaceful beaches farther up the coast. Visitors may come just for the beach, but Sitges has some not-to-be-missed sights, including Morell's whimsical **Modernista clock tower,** Pl. Cap de la Vila, 2. As soon as you come into the Plaça at the intersection of C. de les Parellades and C. Sant Francesc, stop and look high up above the Òptica store. It's easy to miss, and worth ogling for a while.

Sitges has neatly united all of its museums under one consortium; they all have the same hours and prices and combo tickets are available. Seven blocks from the clock on C. Fonollar, the **Museu Cau Ferrat** (☎938 94 03 64) hangs high over the water's edge. Once the home of a driving force of *Modernista* architecture, Santiago Rusiñol (1861-1931), and a

THE LOCAL STORY

CAT GOT YOUR TONGUE?

Whether Catalunya is a state or a nation depends on whom you ask. As far as the Spanish government is concerned, Catalunya is an autonomous region, like Aragón or Navarra. But many *cataloneses* (Catalonians) consider themselves an independent nation, and not entirely without reason.

Catalunya is home to 6,000,000 people. Their identity as a group has everything to do with *Catalán,* a language that emerged when Spain was Roman, and Latin threw a curve ball at the local tongue.

Many young *cataloneses* still speak Spanish (or *castellano*) only begrudgingly, partly a result of the fierce pride that resurfaced after years of cultural oppression by Franco.

Spain does not speak one language (just ask anyone from the País Vasco)—a speaker of *catalán* or *Euskadi* will tell you that there is no such thing as a Spanish language. *Castellano,* literally "the language spoken in Castilla," is a name that reminder of this quirk of Spain's national identity. Castilla is the state that contains Madrid, thus the *español/castellano* divide is symbolic of the split between the nationalist capital and the separatist Catalunya.

If this whets your appetite for catalán, pick up the colorful yellow phrasebook, "Vocabulari en imatges," published by the Secretary of Linguistic Policy of Catalunya, from any catalán tourist office.

meeting place for the young Pablo Picasso and Ramón Casas, the building is a shrine to *Modernista* iron and glass work, sculpture, ceramics, and painting, featuring pieces by El Greco and Picasso. Rusiñol amassed the collection of wrought iron in an effort to preserve various 18th-century traditions. Farther into town, the **Museu Romàntic,** C. Sant Gaudenci, 1, off C. de les Parellades, is an immaculately preserved 19th-century house filled with period pieces like music boxes and two surprising collections: over 400 17th- to 19th-century dolls from all over the world, and over 25 intricate dioramas of 19th- century life in Sitges. (General info ☎938 93 04 64 or 938 94 29 69; www.diba.es/museus/sitges.asp. All museums open July-Sept. Tu-Sa 9:30am-2pm and 4-7pm, Su 10am-3pm; Oct.-June Tu-Sa 9:30am-2pm and 3:30-6:30pm, Su 10am-3pm. Guided tours in summer 4 per day 10am-1pm and 4-6pm, in winter 3 per day; hourly in Museu Romàntic. €3.50 per museum, students and seniors €1.75; combo ticket €6.40/3.50.) Across the street from the waterfront museums, fragments of Spanish artistic culture unite with *Modernista* ceramics in the amazing ▧**Palau Maricel,** on C. Fonollar, built in 1910 for American millionaire Charles Deering. Prepare to be wowed by its sumptuous halls and rooftop terraces. Guided tours are available on some summer nights (July-Sept.) and include a glass of *cava* (sparkling wine) and a castanet concert in, incredibly, the rooftop *claustro*. Days and times vary; call ahead for reservations. (☎938 11 33 11. €10.)

◧ BEACHES

Sitges's sky-blue waters and proximity to Barcelona make it a viable alternative to the crowded sands of Barceloneta and Port Olímpic. At **Platja de la Fragata,** the main beach farthest to the left as you face the sea, sand sculptors create new masterpieces every summer day. By midday, the beaches close to downtown can become almost unbearably crowded; the best beaches, with calmer waters and more open space, like **Platja de la Barra** and **Platja de Terramar,** are a 1-2km walk away (or catch the L2 bus from the train station to the stop next to Hotel Terramar, and walk a bit back toward town; every 30min. 9am-9pm, €0.95). If you decide to walk, you will pass several small beaches, including **Platja de la Bassa Rodona,** popular with gay sunbathers. Rocks partly shield these beaches from waves, creating a shallow ocean swimming pool that extends far into the water and is ideal for children. Farther down, the water is bluer and there's more open sand to claim. Sitges is also well-known for its peaceful **nude beaches. Platja de l'Home Mort** can be reached by walking past Terramar until you hit a golf course at the end of the sidewalk. Walk on the beach past the golf course, and l'Home Mort is in a small cove behind the hills where the train tracks run by the coast. A tamer nude beach is **Platja dels Balmins,** on the opposite side of the city. To reach it, walk past the church and **Platja de Sant Sebastià,** go around the first restaurant you come to, and then take the dirt walkway between the coast and the high white walls of the cemetery. The path will go up and down a slope; the beach is a quiet cove before the port. Clear water is ideal for snorkeling.

◧ ❋ NIGHTLIFE AND FESTIVALS

Sitges makes an easy daytrip, and an (arguably) better night-trip. The wild clubs are the perfect escape from the confines of Barcelona's decidedly more cosmopolitan atmosphere. The places to be at sundown are ▧**Carrer Primer de Maig** (which runs directly from the beach and Pg. de la Ribera) and its continuation, **Carrer Marquès Montroig,** off C. de les Parellades. Bars and clubs line both sides of the small streets, overflowing onto the roads and blasting pop and house from 10pm until 3am. The clubs here are wide open and accepting, with a vibrant mixed crowd of people, gay and straight. Even better is the legendary **Pachá,** the first of the chain in Spain, on Pg. de Sant Didac in nearby Vallpineda, which plays

80s, 90s, and house music, and has a Latin room. (☎938 94 22 98; www.pachasitges.com. Th night "Scandal" with a mixed crowd. Su "Flower Power" with 70s and 80s theme. Cover €20, includes one drink. Open Th-Su midnight-6am. AmEx/MC/V.) For a crowded and sweaty (even shirtless) "disco-beach" scene, check out **Atlàntida**, Platja les Coves, s/n. It's about 3km from the city, but buses run all night from Hotel Canmar (2 blocks down the beach from C. Primer de Maig). On busier nights they stop a 10min walk from the club. (☎934 53 05 82; www.clubatlantida.com. Th foam party. Cover €10-20, flyer discount €5. Open W-Su midnight-6am. MC/V.) Other popular spots can be found on C. Bonaire and C. Sant Pau, but most open only on weekends. **Gay clubs** and cafes include **Trailer,** C. Àngel Vidal, 36 (☎600 55 94 40; cover €20-25, flyer discount €5; open daily June-Sept. 1-6am; in winter only Sa and holidays; MC/V), with infamous foam parties Wednesdays and Sundays, and **Bar Perfil,** C. Espalter, 7 (☎656 376 791; open daily 10:30pm-3am), just half a block down from C. San Francisco. The tourist office has a **Gay Map Sitges,** a guide to gay hotels, restaurants, bars, clubs, and sex shops.

When celebrating holidays, Sitges spares no extravagance and pushes the boundaries of style. During the **Festa de Corpus Cristi** (late May or early June), townspeople collaborate to create intricate carpets of fresh flowers in the **Concurs de Catifes de Flors.** To see papier-mâché dragons, devils, and giants dancing in the streets, visit during the **Festa Major,** held August 23-24 in honor of the town's patron saint, Bartolomé. Nothing compares to **Carnaval,** a preparation for fasting during the first week of Lent (Jan. 31-Feb. 6, 2008). Spaniards crash the town for a frenzy of parades, dancing, outrageous costumes, and vats of alcohol. Saturday and Tuesday nights are the wildest. A pistol shot starts the **Rallye de Coches de Época** in March, an antique-car race from Barcelona to Sitges. July or August brings the **Festival Sitges Jazz Internacional** (part of the larger Sitges Music Festival, €10 per concert). In September, competitors tread on fresh grapes on the beach for the annual **Festa de la Verema,** or grape harvest, and September 22-23 brings the **Festivitat de Santa Tecla.** The famous **Festival Internacional de Cinema de Catalunya** runs through October and November, and is perhaps Sitges's biggest event.

TARRAGONA   ☎977

The strategic position of Tarragona (pop. 130,670) on the Mediterranean coast made the city a provincial Roman capital under Augustus; today, an amphitheater and other ruins harken back to its imperial days. Down the hill from the old city, wider avenues host the best in shopping and dining. Less overwhelming than Barcelona, less sleepy than many coastal towns, and more sophisticated than its beachy neighbors, Tarragona is the perfect anchor of a Costa Dorada vacation.

▐ TRANSPORTATION

Trains: ☎902 24 02 02, on Pl. de la Pedrera by the water, downhill from the old city. Wheelchair accessible. Ticket booth open daily 4:30am-midnight. Customer service open daily 6am-8pm. The best transportation option. Trains run to: **Alicante** (4hr., 8 per day 7:54am-6:54pm, €43-72.10); **Barcelona** (1¼hr., 54 per day 5:20am-11:05pm, €5-29); **Bilbao** (8½hr.; 1:27, 11pm; €35-47); **Madrid** (8hr., 9:41pm, €35-46); **Pamplona** (5-6hr.; 1:27, 11pm; €29.30-38.80); **Salou** (15min., 19 per day 7:07am-10:24pm, €1.30-13); **Sitges** (4 per day 5:52am-10:25pm, €2.95); **Valencia** (2-3hr., 15 per day 7:54am-10:24pm, €15.30-52.70); **Zaragoza** (2½-4hr., 5 per day 10:09-9pm, €16.45-32.10).

Buses: Pl. Imperial Tarraco (☎977 22 91 26). Follow Rambla Nova away from the water; the station is to the left of the roundabout. **ALSA/Enatcar** (☎902 42 22 42) goes to **Valencia** (4hr., 8 per day, €17.25). **HIFE** (☎977 38 10 44; www.hife.es)

and **Plana** (☎977 21 44 75; www.autocarsplana.com) to **Barcelona** (1½hr., 17 per day, €6.91-8.55) also leave from the station.

Public Transportation: EMT Buses (☎977 54 94 80) run daily 7:30am-10pm. Convenient for trips to beaches and ruins in the outskirts. €1.10, 10-ride *abono* ticket €5.40.

Taxis: Radio Taxi (☎977 22 14 14).

Car Rental: AVIS (☎977 23 47 72), by the train station at Pl. de la Pedrera, 2. Open M-F 9am-1pm and 4-7:30pm, Sa 10am-12:30pm.

◢◣ 🛈 ORIENTATION AND PRACTICAL INFORMATION

Most sights are clustered above the train station, but reasonably close to shore, on a hill surrounded by remnants of Roman walls. On the slope of the hill, **Rambla Vella** and **Rambla Nova** (parallel to one another and perpendicular to the sea) are the main thoroughfares of the new city. Rambla Nova runs from **Passeig de les Palmeres**, a walkway overlooking the sea, to **Plaça Imperial Tarraco**, the largest rotunda and home of the bus station. To reach the old quarter, or *casc antic*, from the train station, turn right and follow the shoreline up the hill.

Tourist Office: C. Major, 39 (☎977 25 07 95; www.tarragonaturisme.cat), half a block downhill from the bottom of the cathedral steps, in the center of the old quarter. Open June 21-Sept. M-Sa 9am-9pm, Su 10am-3pm; Oct.-June 20 M-Sa 10am-2pm and 4-7pm, Su and holidays 10am-2pm. **Catalunya Regional Tourist Office:** C. Fortuny, 4, (☎977 23 34 15; www.catalunyaturisme.com). 1 block off Rambla Nova. Info on the whole Catalunya region. Open M-F 9:15am-2pm and 4-6:30pm, Sa 9:15am-2pm. Summer **branches** at L'Imperi Romà, Rambla Nova, Unió with same hours.

Tourist Information Booths: Glass-and-steel kiosks at 3 locations: Pl. Imperial Tarraco, at the end of Rambla Nova by the bus station, and the end of Rambla Vella where Av. de Catalunya meets Via de l'Imperi Romà. Open June 21-Sept. 26 daily 10am-1:30pm and 5-8:30pm; Sept. 27-June 20 Sa 10am-2pm and 4-7pm, Su 10am-2pm.

Luggage Storage: At the train station. €3-4.50 for 24hr. Open daily 4:30am-midnight.

Police: Comissaria de Policia, Pl. Orleans (☎977 24 98 44). From Pl. Imperial Tarraco, walk down Av. President Lluís Companys and take the 3rd left to the station.

Hospital: Hospital de Sant Pau i Santa Tecla, Rambla Vella, 14 (☎977 25 99 00).

Internet Access: Netgaming Tarragona, C. Méndez Núñez, 7 (☎977 23 45 52). Half a block down from Rambla Nova. €1.50-1.80 per hour. Open daily 11am-10pm.

Post Office: Pl. Corsini, 12 (☎902 197 197), 6 blocks from the coast and 2 blocks below Rambla Nova, off C. Cañellas. Open M-F 8:30am-8:30pm, Sa 9:30am-1pm. **Postal Code:** 43001.

🏠 ACCOMMODATIONS AND CAMPING

Most of the city's accommodations are two- to four-star hotels near the center and on the water. Charismatic Pl. de la Font, in the *casc antic* (old city) by the *Ajuntament* (a long plaza parallel to Rambla Vella), and the area around Pl. Imperial Tarraco uptown are filled with cheaper, more pleasant lodgings. Several campsites line the road toward Barcelona (Via Augusta or CN-340) along the northern beaches, around km 1. Take bus #9 (every 20min., €1) from Pl. Imperial Tarraco.

Hostal Noria, Pl. de la Font, 53 (☎977 23 87 17), in the heart of the historic town. Enter through the restaurant on the plaza. 29 rooms, all with bath, some with plaza-facing balconies. June-Sept. singles €27; doubles €44, with bath €58. Oct.-May €21/34/48. Cash only. ❸

Pensión Forum, Pl. de la Font, 37 (☎977 23 17 18), upstairs from the restaurant of same name. 21 cozy rooms, with ceiling fans and pink bathrooms at swell prices. Exterior rooms overlook the plaza. Singles €24; doubles €40-44. Cash only. ❷

Hostal Mediterrani, C. Orosi, 11 (☎977 24 93 53; www.hostalmediterrani.com), just 2 blocks from the train station. Very friendly management offers hotel-quality rooms with full bath, A/C, TV, and phone at affordable prices. Breakfast included. July-Aug. singles €38; doubles €54; triples €74. Sept.-June €30/48/68. AmEx/MC/V. ❹

Platja Llarga (☎972 20 79 52; www.campingplatjallarga.com) is the closest campsite, along the 3km-long beach. Open *Semana Santa* to Sept. €4.50-5.90 per adult, per tent, and per car; €4.10-5.25 per child. Bungalows €55 and up. MC/V. ❶

❑ FOOD

Ramblas Nova and Vella and the streets in between, especially C. Mendéz Nuñez, are full of restaurants serving cheap *menús del día* and greasy *platos combinados* (€6-8). The narrow streets of the *casc antic*, especially in and around Pl. de la Font, have more personal restaurants, but they're more expensive. Tarragona's **Mercat Central** is in a large building in Pl. Corsini next to the post office. (☎977 23 15 51. Open M-Th and Sa 8am-2pm, F 8am-8pm. Flea market Tu and Th.) For regular **groceries,** head to **Opencor,** Pl. Imperial Tarraco, 2. (☎977 24 91 37. Open daily 8am-2pm. AmEx/MC/V). **El Serrallo,** the fishermen's quarter, next to the harbor, has excellent and pricey seafood. It's a bit of a walk, but well worth it. Try your fish with Tarragona's typical ▓**romesco sauce,** made with red peppers, garlic, toasted almonds, and hazelnuts simmered in olive oil.

La Teula, C. Merceria, 16 (☎977 24 86 00), half a block in the direction of the cathedral from Pl. del Fòrum in the old city. Phenomenal salads (€5-8) and toasted *entrepans* with vegetarian and meat combos (€8-16). Lunch *menú* €9.90. Open Tu-Sa 1-4pm and 8pm-midnight, Su 1-4pm. MC/V. ❷

Giuseppe, C. St. Domènec, 28 (☎659 79 81 49), behind Pl. de la Font. Outdoor tables under a giant mural are the perfect setting for delicious flatbread pizzas, salads, and beer. Menú €7.50 with ice cream. Open Tu-Su 6pm-1am. Cash only. ❶

Ca'l Brut, C. Sant Pere, 14 (☎977 24 14 05), right next to Ca'l Marti. Delicious seafood entrees, all with typical local sauces such as Romesco or Zarzuela. 3-course *menú* €9.62. Open Tu-Sa 1-4pm and 8-11pm, Su 1-4pm. MC/V. ❷

El Apapacho, C. Major, 13 (☎977 24 95 57). On the steep main street of the old quarter, near the cathedral. Fresh, flavorful Mexican food awaits you in a wood-floored space. The tacos (€2.70), while small, pack a punch. Open Tu-Th 8-11pm, F 8pm-midnight, Sa 1:30-3:30pm and 8pm-midnight. MC/V. ❷

❍ ❑ SIGHTS AND BEACHES

Tarragona's status as a Roman provincial capital transformed the small military enclosure into a glorious imperial port. Countless Roman ruins stand amid the 20th-century hustle and bustle, all just minutes uphill from the beach.

▓**ROMAN RUINS.** Below Pg. de les Palmeres between Ramblas Vella and Nova, set in the gardens above Platja del Miracle, is the **Amfiteatre Romà.** Gladiators once killed wild animals and each other for captivated audiences in this massive structure. It was also a site for public executions; in AD 259, the Christian bishop Fructuosus and his two deacons were burned alive here. In the AD 6th century, these martyrs were honored with a basilica built in the arena.

Up the hill from here, between the theater and the city, is the entrance to a double-shot attraction: the **Pretori Romà,** former administrative center of the region, and the **Circ Romà,** built in the AD first century for chariot races and other spectacles. The only part of the praetorium still standing is this stair tower, which connects the level of the commoners (the circ) to that of the politicians (the praetorium). Visitors descend into the long, dark tunnels that led fans to their seats, and marvel at medieval houses built in the center of the circus.

The heavily weathered **Fòrum Romà**, with reconstructed Corinthian columns, is near the post office on C. Lleida, three blocks below Rambla Nova and six from the coast, an area with otherwise few remaining ruins. Remember that this forum was the center of town; its distance from the other ruins demonstrates how far the walls of the ancient city extended. To see the remnants of the second-century-BC walls that stretched all the way to the sea, stroll through the **Passeig Arqueològic** in the inland part of the city, near the cathedral. *(Amphitheater ☎ 977 34 25 79; Praetorium 22 17 36; Circ 23 01 71; Forum 24 25 01; Passeig 24 57 96. All ruins open May-Sept. Tu-Sa 9am-9pm, Su 9am-3pm; Oct.-Apr. Tu-Su 9am-7pm. Admission to each €2.40, students and seniors €1.20, all ruins €4.50, under 16 free.)*

MUSEUMS. The **Museu Nacional Arqueològic**, at Pl. del Rei just above the praetorium, displays ancient Roman architecture, sculptures, bronze tools, and mosaics (including the famous "Head of Medusa"), and offers insight into daily life in the Roman Empire. It is considered the most important collection of Roman artifacts in Catalunya. *(Pl. del Rei, 5. ☎ 977 23 62 09. Wheelchair accessible. Open June-Sept. Tu-Sa 9:30am-8pm, Su 10am-2pm; Oct.-May Tu-Sa 9:30am-1:30pm and 3:30-7pm. €2.40, students and seniors €1.20, under 18 or over 65 free. Tu free. Includes entrance to the necropolis.)* Tarragona's historical offerings are not limited to Roman ruins. To see the beautiful house where the Viscounts of Castellarnau and other local nobility lived from the 15th-19th centuries, go up C. Nau (which turns into C. Cavallers) seven blocks from the Museu Nacional Arqueològic and the Circ Romà; the **Museu Casa Castellarnau** will be on your left before the dead end. Although the interior and facades were altered in the 18th century, the courtyard is original. *(C. Cavallers, 14. ☎ 977 24 22 20. Open May-Sept. M-Sa 9am-9pm, Su 9am-3pm; Oct.-Apr. M-Sa 9am-7pm, Su 10am-3pm. €2.20, students €1, under 16 free.)* If you'd prefer to get a feel for the Tarragona of recent years, there is the small but interesting **Museu d'Art Modern de Tarragona**, C. Santa Anna, 8, featuring 20th-century photography, painting, and sculpture from famous and local artists, with a focus on art from the past few decades. They recently acquired a Miró/Josep Royo textile, the "Tapís de Tarragona," exhibited with photos of Miró weaving it in his studio. *(Between Pl. del Fòrum and Pl. del Rei. ☎ 977 23 50 32; www.altanet.org/MAMT. Open Tu-F 10am-8pm, Sa 10am-3pm and 5-8pm, Su and holidays 11am-2pm. Free.)*

BEACHES. The hidden access to **Platja del Miracle**, the main beach visible from the hill, is along Baixada del Miracle, starting from Pl. Arce Ochotorena. Walk left from the amphitheater until the underpass. Then continue under the train tracks to the beach. Perhaps not on par with the region's other beaches, this secluded spot (with generous sand space) is not bad for a few hours of relaxation. A bit farther away are the larger beaches: **Platja Llarga** and the favorites for those in the know, **Platja de l'Arrabassada** and **Platja de la Mora**. *(Take bus #1 or 9 from Pl. Imperial Tarraco or any of the other stops.)*

OTHER SIGHTS. Located in the center of the old quarter and lit by octagonal windows flanking the transept, the gigantic Romanesque-Gothic ⬛**cathedral**, dating back to 1171, is one of the most magnificent buildings in Catalunya. It was at one point an Arab mosque. The dark interior holds the tomb of Joan d'Aragó, and the outside cloister is a perfect place to relax. The adjoining **Museu Diocesà** has a handful of rooms showcasing religious relics from the last 700 years. *(Entrance to both on C. Claustre, near Pl. La Seu. Open M-Sa Mar. 16-May 30 10am-1pm and 4-7pm; June-Oct. 15 10am-7pm; Oct. 16-Nov. 15 10am-5pm; Nov. 16-Mar. 15 10am-2pm. €3.50, students and seniors €1, under 7 free.)* The **Pont del Diable** (Devil's Bridge), a Roman aqueduct 10min. from the city, is visible on the way out of town. Take municipal bus #75 (every 20min., €1.10) from the corner of C. Cristòfor Colom and Av. Prat de la Riba or from Pl. Imperial Tarraco.

NIGHTLIFE AND FESTIVALS

Weekend nightlife in Tarragona takes place on a much smaller scale than in Sitges or Barcelona. Between 5 and 10pm, Ramblas Nova and Vella are packed with strolling families, and the outside seating at restaurants dotting the *casc antic* begins to get crowded. After 10pm, the pedestrian streets liven up, and fireworks brighten the sky, especially during the first week of July. Even later, the place to be is **Port Esportiu**, a seaside plaza near the train station and loading docks that is full of restaurant-bars and little discos; the flow of people from the city center to the port along the streets is a party in itself. Heading up Rambla Nova away from the beach, take a left onto C. la Unió; bear left at Pl. de General Prim and follow C. Apodaca six blocks. Cross the tracks; the fun awaits on the port to the left.

Early July ushers in the **Festival Estiu Tarragona,** which goes through the first week of August (info ☎977 24 47 95, tickets 33 22 11). One week later, the unique **Festa de Sant Magí** for the town's minor patron saint brings waterfront processions and human *castells* (towers), as well as music and theatre for everyone. Pyromaniacs shouldn't miss the end of the first week of July, when fireworks light up the beach in the **Concurs Internacional de Focs Artificials** (International Fireworks Display Contest; www.piroart.com). On even-numbered years, the first Sunday in October brings the ◪**Concurs de Castells,** a competition of tall human towers, as high as seven to nine "stories," called *castells*. More *castells* appear during the annual **Fiesta de Santa Tecla** (Sept. 14-24), Tarragona's *festa major*, featuring not just *castells*, but also *gigantos* (giant puppets that dance and play *grallas*, which are like recorders, medieval treats, 'spoken dances,' *dracs* (dragons), and much more. If you're unable to catch the *castellers* in person, don't miss their life-size monument on Rambla Nova, two blocks from Pl. Imperial Tarraco. Dates vary for all these festivals; check with the tourist office for details.

REUS   ☎977

Reus (pop. 107,000) lacks the splendid coastlines of nearby towns, but still attracts visitors looking to learn more about the birthplace of Antoni Gaudí, the iconic *català* architect. Locals are proud of Reus's influential role during his formative years, and take credit for inspiring the genius. Before Gaudí, a period of industrial growth in the 19th century put Reus on the map as a major trader of *aguardent* (firewater). Around the turn of the century, the *Modernistas* swept its city blocks, and the architectural fruits of that period remain. Reus is *català* Modernism at its most refined, and a subdued alternative to Catalunya's coastal havens.

TRANSPORTATION

Flights: Aeroport de Reus (☎977 77 98 32), Autovia Reus, km 3. Reus Transport Públic runs 8 buses per day from the airport to the train and bus stations 8:35am-10:10pm.

Trains: (☎902 24 02 02), on Pl. de l'Estació. Customer service open 9am-2pm and 4-7pm. Station open 24hr. By far the best method of transportation to Reus. Trains to: **Barcelona** (1½hr., 15 per day 4:51am-9:18pm, €6.45-23.9) via **Tarragona** (15min., €1.35-10.80); **Madrid** (7½hr., 1 per day 9:56pm, €34); **Pamplona** (5hr.; 2 per day 1:41, 9:14pm; €28.10-37.90).

Buses: Stations at Av. Jaume I and Av. President Macià Fortuny. **Hispano Igualadina** (☎977 77 06 98) goes to **Tarragona** every 30min. during the day on weekdays and hourly on weekends. **Autocars Plana** (☎977 54 72 90; www.autocarsplana.com) runs to Salou (July-Aug. every 30min. 6:30am-11pm, Sept.-June hourly). **Nocturn** service runs 7 per night July-Aug. daily 10:45pm-5:15am, Sept.-June F-Sa and nights before festivals, to Cambrils (2-6 per day). Buses leave from the station but stop at Pl. de les Oques in the city before leaving town.

Public Transportation: Reus Transport Públic (☎977 30 00 06; www.reustransport.com) runs 5 bus lines daily 6am-10pm; some every 10-20min. others 1 per hour. Stop by the tourist office for the *Nova Guia Transport Urbà*, with routes and schedules. €1, 10-ride *abono* €6.

Taxis: Radio Taxi (☎977 34 50 50).

■✴ 🛈 ORIENTATION AND PRACTICAL INFORMATION

Reus's sights are concentrated in the city center anchored by **Plaça Prim** and **Plaça Mercadal**. From the train station, walk straight out past the small **Plaça Joan Rebull** onto **Passeig Sunyer,** a wide tree-lined promenade, and follow it for four blocks until **Plaça de les Oques.** Then, turn left on **Carrer de Sant Joan,** one of the city's main streets, which leads to the tourist office and the center of town.

Tourist Office: Plaça Mercadal, 3 (☎902 36 02 00; www.reus.net/turisme). Next to the *Ayuntamiento* in the central plaza. Free map and *Guia del Modernisme*. Guided **walking tours** of the city daily July-Sept. 6pm in *català* and English, noon in French and Spanish. Contact for more info or group reservations (€8 for combined Modernista and IPM tour). Open M-Sa July-Sept. 9:30-8pm; Oct.-June 9:30am-2pm and 4-8pm.

Luggage Storage: At the train station. €3-4.50 for 24hr. Open daily 4:30am-midnight.

Police: Comissaria de Policia, C. General Moragues, 54 (☎977 32 80 00), a block from Pl. Llibertat.

Pharmacy: Farmàcia Monteverde, Plaça Mercadal, 8, (☎977 12 70 84) across from the tourist office. Open daily 9-1:30pm and 5-10pm. 24hr. pharmacies alternate; check the window of any pharmacy.

Medical Services: Hospital de Sant Joan, C. Sant Joan (☎977 32 04 24).

Internet Access: Biblioteca Publica Central, C. Escorxador, 1 (☎977 01 00 25). Free, reserve up to an hour. Open July-Sept. M-F 10am-2:30pm, Oct.-June M-F 10am-8pm, Sa 10am-2pm and 4-8pm.

Post Office: Pl. Llibertat, 12 (☎977 31 46 62). Open M-F 8:30am-8:30pm, Sa 9:30am-2pm. **Postal Code:** 43201.

⌂ ACCOMMODATIONS

Reus has a surprisingly high number of accommodations, all of which are within the city center, and cover a wide range of prices and amenities. **Hotel Ollé ❸,** Pg. de Prim, 45, by Pl. La Pastoreta, offers 30 spacious, hotel-quality rooms at hostel prices, all with big windows, TV, A/C, and bath. (☎977 31 10 90; www.hotelolle.com. Wheelchair accessible. Singles €28; doubles €48; triples €65; quads €72. MC/V.) For a younger feel, check **Hostal Santa Teresa, residència d'estudiants ❷,** C. Santa Teresa, 1. Open July to mid-September with 15 tastefully decorated rooms with fans and clean full baths. (☎977 31 62 97. Laundry €2, terrace with clotheslines. €22 per person. Cash only.) A cheaper, but totally adequate, option is **Hostes Potau ❷,** at C. del Vidre, 13. From the tourist office, walk two blocks after crossing Pl. Prim. Potau has rooms with sink and big beds. (☎977 34 50 01; www.hostalpotau.com. Singles €16; doubles €30, with bath €40. Cash only.)

🔲 FOOD

The narrow streets around Pl. Prim and Pl. Mercadal are filled with bakeries and small tapas bars in between the stores. Reus prides itself on its Siurana olive oil, a special oil extracted from the *arbequina*, a small olive of concentrated flavor very typical of the region. For a delicious local dessert, try the *menjablanc* (almonds and sugar). The **Mercat Central**, in the center of the city, offers a colorful array of fresh produce as well as other delicacies. (Open M-Th 8am-2pm, F 7:30am-2:30pm and 5:30-8:30pm, Sa 7:30am-2pm.) Outrageously popular flea markets shut down this part of the city Mondays and Saturdays 9am-2pm. ▨**El Rincón del Guayabero ❷**, Pl. de les Peixeteries Velles, 1, behind the Prioral de Sant Pere, serves hearty Cuban cuisine with attentive and personal service. The *arroz cubana* (Cuban rice) is meaty and rich, and the *púdin de coco* (coconut pudding) is the perfect end to a meal. (☎977 34 14 71. Open daily noon-4pm and 8-11pm, F-Sa until midnight. MC/V.) **La Ferreteria ❸**, Pl. de la Farinera, 10, behind the *Ayuntamiento*, has a delicious lunchtime *menú* as well as plentiful local tapas in a gorgeous old ironworking shop. (☎977 34 03 26. *Menú* €15 M-F 1-4pm. Open daily 10am-2am. AmEx/MC/V.) **La Bajoqueta ❷**, C. de la Mar, 5, right off Pl. Mercadal, is one of the best-priced restaurants among the shopping streets. The *Bajoqueta* salad consists of artfully displayed tomato slices, green beans, olives, and eggs, and the *pa amb tomàquet* (tomato-rubbed bread) drips with flavor. (☎977 34 54 53. Entrees €10-12. *Menú* M-F €10, Sa €11. Open M-Sa 9am-5pm and 8pm-midnight. MC/V.) **Le Bon Profit ❸**, C. Cristófor Colom, 5, on a side street walking to town from the train station, serves snails cooked on an open grill (with a large fire) in the middle of a packed dining room. (☎977 32 13 17. Snail entrees €12-18. Appetizers €4-10. Reservations recommended. Open M-Tu and Th-Su 1-3:30pm and 8-11pm. MC/V.)

👁 SIGHTS

Reus attracts visitors for two reasons: Gaudí's legacy and the insane amount of shopping. The entire *Tomb de Reus* is packed with shops, but the block along C. Monterols leading down from Pl. Prim is particularly noteworthy. Check out the *Guia Comercial* at the tourist office: a color-coded map of the numerous modern boutiques selling clothes and shoes. They cater to all tastes and ages, with an emphasis on young and innovative fashion. Walking through these streets—except during the *siesta* shutdown—can fill a day (and empty your wallet).

A visit to Reus is not complete without walking ▨**La Ruta del Modernisme de Reus.** Either with a guide or following the pamphlet (available at the tourist office) and the various signs, this walk ambles past the beautiful and uniquely detailed *Modernista* buildings scattered throughout the old town. It starts and ends at the tourist office and conveniently passes through the main shopping streets. One highlight is the **Casa Navàs** (1901), Pl. Mercadal at the corner with C. de Jesús, by Lluís Domènech i Montaner, one of the most significant *Modernista* architects and the figurehead of Reus's *Modernista* movement. Casa Navàs was inhabited until 1999, and retains the character of its past: all furniture and fixtures are original and untouched. (Privately owned; occasional guided tours. Contact the tourist office ☎977 77 81 49.) Domènech i Montaner's biggest work in town is the **l'Institut psiquiàtric Pere Mata**, a multi-pavilion complex that recalls his hospital project in Barcelona, and is also still a functional hospital. (2km west of the city. Guided tours daily July-Sept. 11:30am in *català* and English, 5:30pm in French and Spanish; €8 for combined IPM and *Modernista* tours, €5 for individual tickets. Bus #32 runs there and back 22 per day; for the tour catch the 11:14am bus from Pl. Oques and the 12:51pm bus back.) The greatest number of buildings on the trail belong to Pere Caselles i Tarrats, a local star who received less international attention than his peers. Most of the rest of the *Modernista* buildings on the trail are privately held and only viewable from the outside. Some, such as the **Casa Natal de Gaudí** (C. Sant Vicenç 4 and C. Amargura, between 7 and 9) have sculptures you can play with, like the "Gaudí adolescent" sculpture, erected in 2002 to commemorate the 150th anniversary of his birth, which occurred here. The brand-new **Gaudí Centre** museum, Plaça Mercadal, 3, in the tourist office building, satisfies your appetite for Gaudí audio/visuals and hands-on models of his materials, as well as childhood notebooks and other curiosities. (Open daily July-Sept. 10am-8pm; Oct.-June 10am-2pm and 4-8pm. Su year-round 10-2pm. €6.)

■ ■ NIGHTLIFE AND FESTIVALS

Reus has more quiet plazas than crazy parties; however, an increasing number of entertaining pubs dot the city. A couple are in front of the train station, including **La Fàbrica,** with an older crowd, and **Suau** at Pg. Mata, 18. The real partiers, locals and tourists alike, prefer to hop on the bus and head to Salou. The biggest festival in Reus is **La Festa de Sant Pere,** around June 29. The town builds *gegants* (giant puppets) for the festivities, featuring concerts, dances, and the famous *castells* (human towers). More *castells* appear for the **Festes de Misericòrdia** (around Sept. 25th), with exhibitions on Pl. del Mercadal. For additional festival information, contact the tourist office or the **Oficina de Festivals,** C. Sant Joan, 27. (☎977 77 81 11. Open M-F June-Sept. 10am-2pm; Oct.-May 9am-2pm and 5-7pm.)

COSTA BRAVA   ☎975

Skirting the Mediterranean Sea from Barcelona to the French border, the Costa Brava's cliffs and beaches draw throngs of European visitors, especially in July and August. Early June and late September can be remarkably peaceful; the water is warm and the beaches much less crowded. In winter, the "Wild Coast" lives up to its name, as fierce winds batter quiet, nearly empty beach towns. These rocky shores have attracted romantics and artists like Marc Chagall and Salvador Dalí, a Costa Brava native. No wonder, then, that the Costa Brava is distinctively *català* in everything it does —this is a region that prides itself on its history and on the architectural and artistic treasures it holds. Among these, Dalí's house in Cadaqués and his museum in Figueres display the largest collections of his work in Europe. Certain towns have survived the summer-tourist onslaught better than others (Cadaqués has fared well), but there are still clear waters and pine-covered cliffs almost everywhere you turn.

TOSSA DE MAR   ☎972

"Tossa," with 12th-century medieval ruins abutting long stretches of beach, has been a magnet for artists and romantics since French artist Marc Chagall fell in love with it in 1934. Shortly after in 1951, actress Ava Gardner fell for Spanish bullfighter Mario Cabrera during the filming of *The Flying Dutchman* here, much to the chagrin of her then-husband, Frank Sinatra. Like many coastal towns, Tossa (pop. 5893) suffers from the blemishes of tourism, but the beaches and good *catalana* food leave no doubt as to why Chagall called Tossa "blue paradise."

▶ TRANSPORTATION

Buses: On Av. Pelegrí at Pl. de les Nacions Sense Estat. Ticket booth open daily 7:15am-12:40pm and 3:30-7:40pm. **Pujol** (☎972 34 03 36) takes the scenic route to **Lloret del Mar** (20min.; June-Aug. every 30min. 8:40am-9:10pm, Sept.-May hourly 7:40am-8:40pm; €1.25). **Sarfa** (☎972 34 09 03; www.sarfa.com) goes to **Barcelona** (2hr.; M-Sa 24 per day, Su 17 per day 7:25am-8:40pm; €9.35) and **Girona** (1½hr.; 10:25am, 7:25pm; €4.60).

Boats: Slow service to towns and otherwise inaccessible *cales* (coves) along the coast, including Lloret and Sant Feliu. **Viajes Marítimos** (☎972 36 90 95; www.viajesmaritimos.com) and **DofiJet Boats** (☎972 37 19 39; www.dofijetboats.com) depart hourly 9:35am-5:30pm (€10-15.30). 30min. to Lloret; 1hr. to Blanes. Buy tickets and board on Pg. de Mar, on the beach in front of the First Aid stand.

Car Rental: Viajes Tramontana, Av. Costa Brava, 23 (☎972 34 28 29). Rentals provided by **Olimpia** and **SACAR.** 21+. Credit card, driver's license, and passport required. From €42 per day. Open daily July-Aug. 9am-9pm; Apr.-June and Sept.-Nov. 9am-1pm and 4-8pm. AmEx/MC/V. Also **Viajes Internacional,** C. Peixaterias, 1 (972 34 02 41).

Taxis: Stand outside the bus station (☎972 34 05 49).

⚡🛈 ORIENTATION AND PRACTICAL INFORMATION

Buses arrive at **Plaça de les Nacions Sense Estat** where **Avinguda del Pelegrí** and **Avinguda Ferran Agulló** meet; the town slopes down to the waterfront. From the station, make a right onto Av. del Pelegrí, and go straight until making a left onto C. La Guardia. The street narrows, curving around to become C. Socors and then C. Portal; any street downhill to the left will lead to the beach, while staying on C. Portal will take you to the old quarter, known as the **Vila Vela** (5min.). Running back along Tossa's main beach, the **Platja Gran**, is the hyper-touristy **Passeig del Mar.**

Tourist Office: Av. del Pelegrí, 25 (☎972 34 01 08; www.infotossa.com), in the bus terminal at Av. Ferran Agulló and Av. del Pelegrí. English and French spoken. Hiking info and a posted schedule of upcoming events. Weekend guided hikes and walks (usually Sa-Su 8am). Open June-Sept. M-Sa 9am-9pm, Su and holidays 10am-2pm and 5-8pm; Oct. and Apr.-May M-Sa 10am-2pm and 4-8pm; Nov.-Mar. M-Sa 10am-2pm and 5-8pm. **Branch** at Av. Palma, s/n, right on Platja Gran. Open June-Sept. daily 10am-2pm and 4-8pm; Apr.-May and Oct. Tu-Su 10:30am-1:30pm and 4-7pm.

Currency Exchange: Banco Santander Central Hispano, Av. Ferran Agulló, 2 (☎972 34 10 65). **ATM** on the street. Open M-F 8:30am-2pm, Oct.-May also Sa 8:30am-1pm.

Police: Municipal Police, Av. del Pelegrí, 14 (☎972 34 01 35). English spoken. They'll escort you to a **24hr. pharmacy** at night if necessary.

Pharmacy: Farmàcia Castelló, Av. Ferran Agulló, 12 (☎972 34 13 03). Open daily 9:30am-1:30pm and 4:30-9pm; Oct.-June closes at 8pm.

Medical Services: Casa del Mar, Av. de Catalunya s/n (☎972 34 18 28). Primary care and immediate attention. The nearest hospital is in Blanes, 30min. south.

Internet Access: Tossa Bar Playa, C. Socors, 6, on the main beach. €1 per 15min. Open May-Oct. daily 10am-11:30pm.

Post Office: C. María Auxiliadora, 4 (☎972 34 04 57), down Av. del Pelegrí from the tourist office. Open M-F 8:30am-2:30pm, Sa 9:30am-1pm. **Postal Code:** 17320.

🏠 ACCOMMODATIONS AND CAMPING

Tossa is a seasonal town; many hostels, restaurants, and bars are open only from May to October. The tourist office website (www.infotossa.com) also lists rooms. To get to **Fonda Lluna ❷**, C. Roqueta, 20, from Pg. del Mar, turn right onto C. Peixateries, veer left onto C. Estolt, walk uphill and go left. It has immaculate singles, doubles, and triples with bath and roof access. (☎972 34 03 65; www.fondalluna.com. Breakfast included. Book ahead in summer. Lunch €10. June-July €22 per person. Aug. €24; Sept.-June €20. MC/V.) **L'Hostalet de Tossa ❹**, Pl. de l'Església, 3, in front of the Església de Sant Vicenç, has 32 hotel-quality doubles, foosball and pool tables, and a TV in common areas. (☎972 34 18 53; www.hostalettossa.com. Breakfast buffet included. July 15-Aug. and *Semana Santa* singles with bath €42-44; doubles €64-72. Sept. and June-July 14 €33-35/50-58. Oct. and Apr.-May €28-30/42-50. MC/V.) **Camping Can Martí ❶**, at the end of Rambla Pau Casals, off Av. Ferran Agulló, is a popular, friendly campsite near a wildlife reserve. Amenities include hot showers, telephones, pool, and restaurant. (☎972 34 08 51. June 25-Aug. 9 €8 per person, €8 per tent, €4 per car. May 14-June 19 and Sept. 1-19 €5/5/3. Accepts traveler's checks but not credit cards.)

🌮 FOOD

Tossa's old quarter has the best cuisine and ambience in town. Most restaurants specialize in seafood and have reasonably priced *menús*. For groceries, head to **Can Palou,** C. La Guardia, 25. (Open Apr.-Oct. M-Sa 9am-9pm, Su 9am-2pm. MC/V.) For the most flavorful *català* specialties served in the coziest of dining rooms (and terraces), try ▧**La Lluna ❶**, C. Abat Oliva, 10. The *carxotes amb formatge* (artichokes with local cheese) are the perfect way to begin a meal. Follow them up with one of the fruit *pâtés*, from the mountain region of Cataluña. (☎972 34 25 23. Tapas €3-9. Open daily in summer 11am-3pm and 6-11pm. Cash only.) **Restaurant Santa Marta ❸**, C. Francesc Aromi, 2, is in a medieval dwelling inside the old fortress, just 20m up from C. Portal. They serve innovative cuisine with dishes like salmon with raspberry and kiwi sauce. (☎972 34 04 72. Entrees €10-31. *Menú* €15.50. Open *Semana Santa* to Sept. daily 12:30-4pm and 7:30-11pm. AmEx/MC/V.) **Taberna de Tossa ❷**, C. Sant Telm, 24-26, serves house wine (€5.95 per L), traditional tapas (€3-4), and provincial specialties in a large Old World dining room. (☎972 34 19 39. Entrees €3.70-15. *Menú* 8.50-16.50. Open Apr.-Sept. daily 1-4pm and 7:30pm-midnight; Oct.-Mar. F-Su 1-4pm and 7pm-1am. MC/V.) The more family-oriented **Restaurant Marina ❷**, C. Tarull, 6, has delicious vegetarian *fideuà* (vermicelli with garlic; €10). They also serve meat, fish, and lots of paella. (☎972 34 07 57. Entrees €3.50-12.30. All-included *menús* €8-17, including a vegetarian one. Open daily 10am-11:30pm. MC/V.)

👁🌮 SIGHTS AND BEACHES

Inside the walled fortress of the **Vila Vella,** an escalating spiral of medieval alleys and steep stairways lead all the way to a picture-perfect view of the city and the surrounding *cales* (small coves), as well as the recently opened **Centre d Interpretació dels Fars de la Mediterrània.** At this museum, a series of wordless audio/visuals depict the history and culture of lighthouses. (☎972 34 33 59. Open Mar.-Oct. daily 10am-10pm; Nov.-Feb. Tu-Su 10am-6pm. €3, students and children €1.50.) At the tiny Pl. Pintor J. Roig y Soler is the **Museu Municipal,** which has a collection of 1920s and 30s modern art. There is a room dedicated to Marc Chagall, holding *El violinista celest,* one of his only works remaining works in Spain, as well as letters he wrote to the mayor of Tossa. Tossa's Roman mosaics (dating from the AD 4th to 5th century), and other astonishingly well-preserved artifacts from the ancient Villa dels Ametllers are displayed in a former 14th-century palace. (☎972 34 07 09; museu.tossa@ddgi.es. Open June-Oct. 11 M and Su 10am-2pm and 4-8pm, Tu-Sa 10am-8pm; Oct. 12-May Tu-Sa 10-2pm and 4-6pm, Su 10-2pm. €3, students and seniors €1.80. Under 12 free.) Tossa's main beach, **La Platja Gran,** draws the majority of beachgoers and is surrounded by cliffs and the Vila Vella. To escape the crowds, visit some of the neighboring coves, accessible by foot. The tiny ■Es Codolar sits under the tower of Vila Vella, hugged by wooded cliffs.

NIGHTLIFE

Bars line the narrow streets of the old quarter and occasionally offer live music. They are packed closely together, so you can stroll down C. Portal and Pg. del Mar and take your pick. At ■Bar Trinket, C. Sant Josep, 9, flirt amid dripping candles and romantic chandeliers or stare at the stars in the ivy-covered courtyard. (Open Apr.-Sept. daily 10:30pm-3am; Oct.-May F-Sa. Cash only.) The same owners have a disco called Sibas on C. Eglesia, with rock and roll from 2-6am weekends. The small Bar El Pirat, C. Portal, 32, and its companion bar Piratín, C. Portal, 30, have outdoor tables overlooking the sea below at Es Codolar. (☎972 34 14 43. House sangria €4. Open Apr.-Oct. daily 1pm-3am. Cash only.) For live music and a dance floor, try Don Pepe, C. Estalt, 6, one block up from C. Peixeteries, a small bar that hosts a flamenco guitarist or a rumba musician every night. (☎972 34 22 66. Open June-Oct. daily 10pm-4am. Cash only.) If you don't mind a bit of an uphill walk, then check out the brand-new Bar del Far del Mar, nestled romantically at the foot of the functioning lighthouse on the crest of the Vila Vella. The bar offers tart mojitos and a sweet view. (☎972 34 12 97. Free Wi-Fi. Mixed drinks €3.50-5. Appetizers €3-10. Open June-Sept. daily 10pm-3am; Oct.-May Tu-Su 10am-6pm. MC/V.)

CALELLA DE PALAFRUGELL AND LLAFRANC

Calella de Palafrugell (not to be confused with Calella, a different town) and Llafranc harbor some of the most beautiful stretches of beach. The beaches draw people here, and they don't disappoint.

> **■TIP■ BAY WALK.** Beaches lining the boardwalk are small and often very crowded, but a walk farther to the right when facing the water will get you more space in the sand. Strolls on the walkways along the coast are a must. From Calella to Llafranc, walk left along the beach, through Passeig del Canadell, Passeig de la Torre, and ■Passeig de Xavier Miserachs.

Hotel prices in Calella range from expensive to outrageous—many budget travelers choose to stay in nearby Palafrugell. The Hotel Mediterrani ❺, C. Francesc Estrabau, 40, is, believe it or not, the most reasonable and features a beautiful view of the bay. (May-Oct. ☎972 61 45 00, Nov.-Apr. 932 09 91 13; www.hotelmediterrani.com. Breakfast included. Singles €52-73; doubles €76-142. MC/V.) For camping, go to Moby Dick ❶, C. Costa Verda, 16-28 (☎972 61 43 07; www.camping-mobydick.com). Look for the white whale made of ship's line to find this convenient campsite close to the water. (Open Apr.-Sept. Also offers bungalows. Reception July-Aug. 8am-midnight; Sept.-June 10am-1pm. €2.95-5.25 per adult, tent, and car; €1.60-2.90 per child. Cash only.) Pizzeria Sol Ixent ❷, C. dels Canyers, 24, is a small pizzeria on the rightmost end of the bay facing the water. Salads, pizzas, and other items run €5-15, with good vegetarian options. (☎972 61 50 51. Menú €14.50. Open daily 11am-4pm and 7-midnight. Cash only.)

Nightlife in Calella consists mostly of pubs that close relatively early. There are some festivals, such as Festival Jardins de Cap Roig (formerly the Costa Brava Jazz Festival) held in July and August, which features a series of concerts by big-name international artists like Cesária Évora. (For more information, contact Fundació Caixa de Girona; ☎972 20 98 36. Tickets €15-65.) The Festa de Sant Pere takes place mainly in Calella; the Cantada de Havaneres is celebrated the first Saturday in July in Calella and the first Saturday in August in Llafranc. Llafranc holds its Festa

CATALUÑA

Major de Santa Rosa with dances and activities around August 30th. If you are here the first Saturday of September, check out the **Mercat Boig** in Pl. del Promontori, where anything and everything is sold (but mostly crafts and antiques).

Buses run from Palafrugell to Calella and Llafranc (15-20min.; July-Aug. 24 per day, June and Sept. 12-16 per day, Oct.-May 4-5 per day 7:40am-4pm; €1.25).

GIRONA (GERONA) ☎972

On June 27th, 1980, the *Ayuntamiento* of Gerona (pop. 92,000) passed a law that read, in part: "The government of Gerona hereby changes the name of this municipality back to the original *català*; Girona." GI-rona today is *català* through and through, but it's been almost everything else over the course of its long history. A Roman municipium and then an important medieval center, the "city of four rivers" was an exemplar of the Spanish settlements where Christians, Jews, and a small number of Arabs were able to coexist in peace. Girona was the home of the renowned *cabalistas de Girona*, a group of 12th-century rabbis credited with founding the school of mystic thought called the Kabbala. Although they, along with all other Jews, were banned from the city in 1492, you can still walk the streets (or, more accurately, the staircases) of *El Call*, the old Jewish quarter. In recent years, this many-splendored *català* metropolis has gained international recognition as a cyclist's paradise—former Tour de France hero Lance Armstrong called the city home during training season.

▐ TRANSPORTATION

Flights: Aeropuerto de Girona-Costa Brava, Termino Municipal de Vilobi d'Onyar (☎972 18 66 00; www.aena.es and choose Girona from the dropdown on the left), is small and services a few regular flights on **Iberia** (☎902 40 05 00; www.iberia.com) and **Ryanair** (☎972 47 36 50; www.ryanair.com). **Barcelona Bus** (☎902 36 15 50; www.sagales.com) runs shuttles from Girona, Barcelona, and the Costa Brava to the airport (from the Girona bus station hourly 5am-10pm, return hourly 5:30am-12:30am; €2; from Barcelona 23+ per day 3:45pm-7:30pm, return 28 per day 8:30am-12:10am; €12). A **taxi** to Girona's old city is roughly €20 (12km).

Trains: RENFE (☎902 24 02 02), in Pl. d'Espanya to the west of the city center. Open M-Sa 5:30am-11pm, Su 6:30am-11pm, info 6:30am-10pm. To: **Barcelona** (1½hr., 25 per day 7:27am-9:23pm, €7), change at **Maçanet** for coastal train; **Figueres** (30-40min., 13 per day 7:40am-10:11pm, €2.50-5.60) via **Flaçà** (15min., €1.30-1.50); **Madrid** (10½hr., 9:18pm, €41-51); **Milan, Italy** (11½hr.; 9:47pm; €141, under 26 €106); and **Paris, France** (11hr.; 10:17pm; €138, under 26 €104).

Buses: Next to the train station, 5min. from the city center. **Sarfa** (☎972 20 17 96). Info open M-F 7:30am-8:30pm, Sa-Su 8:45am-noon and 4:30-8:30pm. To: **Cadaqués** (2hr.; 9am, 6:30pm; €9); **Palafrugell** (1hr., 15 per day 8am-9pm, €4.55), for connections to **Calella** and **Llafranc; Tossa de Mar** (40min.; July-Aug. 10:30am, 7pm; €4.60). **Teisa** (☎972 20 02 75; www.teisa-bus.com) info open M-F 9am-7:15pm with 20min. breaks throughout, Sa-Su 9am-1pm, Su 4:30-5:30pm. To: **Lérida** (3½hr.; M-F 3 per day 7:30am-7:15pm, Sa-Su 8:30am, 5:30pm; €18.15); **Ripoll** via **Olot** (2½hr.; M-F 1:15pm, 5:15pm, Sa-Su only 1:15pm; €9.30). **Barcelona Bus** (☎902 36 15 50; www.barcelonabus.com). Buy tickets on bus. Express buses to **Barcelona** (1¼hr.; M-F 5 per day 7am-7:15pm, Sa-Su 3 per day; €11.50) and **Figueres** (50min.; M-F 6 per day 8:05am-8:30pm, Sa-Su 3 per day; €4.60).

Car Rental: Europcar (☎972 20 99 46; www.europcar.es), in the train station. Also in the airport (☎972 18 66 18). Open M-F 9am-1:30pm and 4:30-7pm, Sa 9am-2pm. 21+, must have had driver's license for 1 year. From €60 per day, €8 extra for under

Girona (Gerona)

ACCOMMODATIONS
Alberg de Joventut
   Cerverí de Girona (HI), **17**
Pensión Residència
   Bellmirall, **10**
Pensión Viladomat, **18**

FOOD
Boira Restaurant, **12**
Cafè Le Bistrot, **15**
Cafè La Llibreria, **16**
La Crêperie Bretonne, **13**
Vinil, **14**

MUSEUMS
Centre Bonastruc Ça Porta/
Museu d'Història dels
   Jueus, **11**
Museu d'Art, **7**
Museu del Cinema, **19**
Museu d'Història de la
   Ciutat, **6**

NIGHTLIFE
La Bohim, **4**
La Catedral, **20**

Las Carpas, **5**
La Platea, **8**
La Sala del Cel, **1**
Siddharta, **3**
El Supreme, **9**
La Via Habana, **2**

TO HOSPITAL
DE GIRONA "JOSEP
TRUETA" (1km)

TO (150m)

Riu Ter

Ronda de Pedret

Pg. de Montjuïc

C. Palanfuell

C. de Sant Pau

PL. DE
SANT PERE

Jardins
d'en John
Lennon

Museu
d'Arqueologia
de Catalunya

St. Pere de
Galligants

PL. DELS
JURATS

Banys
Àrabs

Riu Galligants

Pg. Arqueològic

Pg. de la Reina Joana

Sant
Feliu

PL. DE
SANT
FELIU

Pont de
Pedret

Pont de
Sant Feliu

Pg. de la Devesa

Parc
de la
Devesa

Riu Onyar

C. Berenguer Carnicer

PL. José Canaleias

Pont
Pedra
Gómez

VIÇENS
VIVES

La Planeta

TAXI

Av.

Ramon
Folch

C. Fontclara

C. de les Ballesteries

PL. DE LA
CATEDRAL

Catedral

PL. DELS
APÒSTOLS

PL.
LLEDONERS

dels Alemanys

C. Força

St. Llorenç

PL. SANT
DOMÈNEC

EL CALL

PL.DE LA
INDEPENDÈNCIA

Pont de
Sant Agustí

C. Argenteria

C. P. Velles

Correiteil

PL. de
Sant Domènec

Universitat
de Girona

PL. DE
L'OLI

BARRI VELL

C. Figuerola

C. Artillers

Gran Via de Jaume I

C. Anselm Clavé

C. Nord

C. de les Hortes

Pont de Perro

Santa Clara

Riu Onyar

C. Mercaders

PL. Sant Martí

Esc. de la Llebre

Portal Nou

Pg. fora Muralla

C. Bonastruc de Porta

Miquel Blay

C. 20 de Juny

PL.
CONSTITUCIÓ

Caprabo

PL. SANTA
SUSANNA

C. Sèquia

C. Obra

19

PL. DEL
VI

PL. del
BELL-LLOC

C. Sant Josep

C. Ramon Turró

C. Ferran

C. Francesc Roâgas

C. Bernat Boadas

C. Tomàs Mieres

C. de Ferran Soldevila I Zubiburu

C. Sèquia

C. Cristòbal Grober

C. Nou

Av. de Sant Francesc

Pont de Pedra

C. Nou del Teatre

Trav.
Auriga

PL. DEL
MARQUÈS
DE CAMPS

Gran Via de Jaume I

C. Ginesta

PL. DE
CATALUNYA

Passeig de
la Muralla

Jardins de
les Pedreres

TO ANGLES
(8km), SALT
(1km)

C. Santa Eugènia

Centre
Cultural
l'Estació

PL. POETA
MARQUINA

C. Barcelona

C. Àlvarez
de Castro

PL. DE
L'HOSPITAL

PL. POMPEU
FABRA

C. Joan Maragall

Pg. General Mendoza

Pont de
l'Alferes Huarte

PL.
D'ESPANYA

Avis

Europcar

C. Barcelona

C. Juli Garreta

Ronda Sant Antoni M. Claret

C. Bacià

PL. DE SIBIL • LA
DE FORTIÀ

Mercat
Municipal

PL. CALVET I
RUBALCABA

C. del Carme

C. Ferrandiz I Bellès

C. de la
Ribera

C. Muntanya

C. Sol

C. Unirers

C. de Pere Vilar

N
LG

C. Bailèn

Maragall

C. Joan

C. Ullònia

C. Bisbe Lorenzana

PL. MIQUEL
SANTALÓ
I PARVORELL

C. Sant Joan Baptista de la Salle

C. Rutlla

Riu Onyar

C. Isabel la Catòlica

C. Vista Alegre

Pge. Picapedrers

Vista
Alegre

0   200 meters

0   200 yards

TO 20 (6km), GIRONA AIRPORT (13km)

TO QUART (6km)

CATALUÑA

25. AmEx/MC/V. **Avis** (☎972 22 46 64; www.avis.es) across from Europcar. Also at airport (☎972 47 43 33). 23+. Must have had driver's license for at least 1 year. From €80 per day, €10 extra for under 25. Open M-F 8am-9pm, Sa 8am-1pm. AmEx/MC/V.

Bike Rental: Alberg Cerverí, C. Ciutadans, 9 (☎972 21 80 03). €16 per day. **Bicicletes TRAFACH** (☎972 23 49 43) in Salt (2km). Open M-F 9am-1:30pm and 4-8:30pm. €14 per day. **Centre BTT** (☎972 46 82 42), in Quart (3km). Open Sa-Su 8am-3pm.

Taxis: Taxi Girona (☎972 20 33 77 or 972 22 23 23) has 24hr. service. Taxis are scarce on the street except at Pl. Independencia and the train station.

◼✱ 🛈 ORIENTATION AND PRACTICAL INFORMATION

The Riu Onyar divides the city into old and new sections. Eleven bridges, mostly pedestrian, connect the two banks. The **Pont de Pedra** leads into the old quarter by way of C. dels Ciutadans, one block off the bridge, which turns into C. Bonaventura Carreras i Peralta and then C. Força, leading to the cathedral and **El Call,** the historic Jewish neighborhood. The **train** and **bus terminals** are situated off **Calle Barcelona,** in the modern neighborhood. To get to the old city, walk across the parking lot and Pl. Espanya, turn left onto C. Barcelona and go straight for three blocks, then bear right through a plaza and right again onto the small C. Nou; it will take you straight across Pond de Pedra to the old town. The iron bridge to the right was built by the Eiffel Company.

Tourist Offices: Rambla de la Llibertat, 1 (☎972 22 65 75; www.ajuntament.gi), by Pont de Pedra in the old town. English spoken. Pick up the biweekly *La Guia*, in *català* but with clear listings of events. Also has listings of hotels, hostels, and restaurants, with maps and prices. Open M-F 8am-8pm, Sa 8am-2pm and 4-8pm, Su 9am-2pm. The **Punt de Benvinguda** office, C. Berenguer Carnicer, 3 (☎972 21 16 78) is 7 blocks up on the other side of the river. Open M-Sa 9am-2pm and 3-5pm, Su 9am-2pm.

Luggage Storage: Lockers in the train station €3-4.50 per 24hr. Open daily 6:30am-10pm.

Police: Policia Municipal, C. Bacià, 4 (☎972 41 90 92). To report a pick pocketing, contact the Mossos d'Esquadra, C. Vista Alegre (☎972 18 16 00).

Hospital: Hospital de Girona "Josep Trueta," Av. França, 60 (☎972 94 02 00).

Internet Access: Centre Cultural l'Estació, C. Santa Eugènia, 16 (☎972 22 00 70; www.ajuntament.gi/espaisinternet), the red building visible from the train station. Free with a passport or ID. Wi-Fi also offered. Open daily 10am-2pm and 4-8pm.

Post Office: Av. Ramón Folch, 2 (☎902 19 71 97), a brick building with a golden dome. **Lista de Correos.** Open M-F 8:30am-8:30pm, Sa 9:30am-2pm. **Postal Code:** 17007

🛏 ACCOMMODATIONS

There are enough hostels in Girona to find a room without much trouble, but some are no less expensive than the hotels in the new city. The best locations are within a couple of blocks of the river on either bank. Call ahead in the summer.

▨ **Pensión Residència Bellmirall,** C. Bellmirall, 3 (☎972 20 40 09). Expensive but worth it. Delightful rooms, all with private bath, in a 14th-century house by the main cathedral. Breakfast included and served on the plant-filled garden patio. Closed Jan.-Feb. Singles €35; doubles €65; triples €80. €10 extra in high season. Cash only. ❸

Pensión Viladomat, C. Ciutadans, 5 (☎972 20 31 76). Many rooms with balconies, all with high ceilings and large windows, and the price is right. Quiet at night and at the center of the action during the day. Singles with shared bath €22; doubles €40, with bath €60. Cash only. ❷

Alberg de Joventut Cerverí de Girona (HI), C. dels Ciutadans, 9 (☎972 21 80 03; www.xanascat.net). Whitewashed walls and metal bunks, but good price, location, and amenities. Sitting rooms with TV/VCR, board games, videos, and ping-pong. Rooms of 2, 3, 8, and 10 beds with lockers. Unlimited Internet access €1. Breakfast included; other meals €5.70. Sheets included. Wash €2.50, dry €1.50. 24hr. check-in. Reception 8:30am-2:30pm, 3:30-9:30pm, and 10-11pm. Dorms July-Sept. €18.60-€21.25; Oct.-June €14.85-17.30. Non-HI members €2 more. AmEx/MC/V. ❷

▶ FOOD

Girona boasts exciting local cuisine, both savory and sweet. Local specialties are *botifarra dolça* (sweet sausage made with pork, lemon, cinnamon, and sugar) and *xuixo* (sugar-sprinkled pastries filled with cream). A good place for moderately priced food is on C. Cort-Reial at the top of C. Argenteria. Rambla de la Llibertat has several tourist cafes with terrace seating, and Pl. de la Independència, Girona's restaurant hub, offers both high-end and cheaper options, most of which have tables on the square. The covered **mercat municipal** is located in Pl. Salvador Espriu, three blocks upstream from the tourist office (☎972 20 19 00; open M-Sa 6:30am-2:30pm; cash only). Get your **groceries** at **Caprabo,** C. Sèquia, 10, a block off the Gran Via. (☎902 11 60 60. Open M-Sa July-Aug. 9am-9pm; Sept.-June 9am-2pm and 5pm-9am. MC/V.)

La Crêperie Bretonne, C. Cort-Reial, 14 (☎972 21 81 20; www.creperiebretonne.com). Proof of Girona's proximity to France, this popular crepe joint combines a youthful atmosphere with great food right in the historic district. The food is cooked in a small bus bound for the town of Cerbère, but you can eat it on the cozy alley terrace. Lunch *menú* €8-10.50. Crepes €2.50-7. Unusual salads €7-8. Open Tu-Sa 1:30-3:30pm and 8-11:30pm; Aug. also open M. MC/V. ❷

Vinil, C. Cort Reial, 17 (972 21 64 40). If you took Vinil's mantra, "you are what you eat," to heart, then you'd be a salad with honey-soy dressing and paper-thin slices of ham, a knockout hamburger, or a potato purée drizzled in raspberry sauce; green chairs, green walls, and lounge music round out the experience. Lunch menú €9.60. Open M-F 9am-1am, Sa 1pm-1am, Su 7pm-1am. Cash only. ❷

Cafè La Llibreria, C. dels Ciutadans, 15 (☎972 20 48 18; lallibreria@teleline.es), serves mixed drinks (€5), beer (€1.70), *bocadillos* (€2.50-3), and various entrees (€6-11). Also a bookstore (specializes in fiction and Jewish literature). Internet €2 per 20min. Cocktail bar at night, with occasional live music and poetry readings. Open daily 9am-midnight. MC/V. ❷

Cafè Le Bistrot, Pjda. Sant Domènec, 4 (☎972 21 88 03). Eat on the stone steps of the old university, with a view of the old city below. Lunch *menú* M-F €12, Sa-Su €19. Specialty creations are the *pizzas de pagès* (farmer's bread pizzas) made on typical *català* roundbread. Open M-Th 1-4pm and 8pm-1am, F-Sa 1-4pm and 7pm-2am, Su 1-4pm and 8pm-midnight. MC/V. ❸

Boira Restaurant, Pl. de la Independència, 17 (☎972 21 96 05). Fine cuisine served on the terrace by the plaza or in the colorful restaurant with a view of the river. Fresh, simple dishes such as lentil salad with salmon, or cold stewed tomato with a parmesan mousse and basil oil. Vegetarian options available. M-F lunch *menú del día* €12. Entrees €7-16. Open daily 1-4pm and 8:30pm-midnight. AmEx/MC/V. ❸

◉ SIGHTS

Start your self-guided historical tour of the city at the **Pont de Pedra** and turn left down the tree-lined **Rambla de la Llibertat.** Continue on C. Argenteria, bearing right across C. Cort-Reial. C. Força begins on the left up a flight of stairs.

■**EL CALL.** The part of the old town around C. Força and C. Sant Llorenç was once the center of Girona's thriving medieval Jewish community ("call" comes from *kahal*, Hebrew for "community"). The site of the last synagogue in Girona now serves as the Centre Bonastruc Ça Porta, named for Rabbi Moshe Ben-Nachman, a scholar of Jewish mysticism (Kabbala) and the oral tradition. The center includes the prominent **Museu d'Història dels Jueus,** with an excellent audioguide that explains the old Hebrew tombstones and text, as well as the story of the Jews in Girona before and after the Inquisition. *(The entrance is at C. Força, 8, halfway up the hill. ☎972 21 67 61; ajgirona.org/call. Center and museum open May-Oct. M-Sa 10am-8pm, Su 10am-3pm; Nov.-Apr. M-Sa 10am-6pm, Su 10am-3pm. Wheelchair accessible. Museum €2, students and over 65 €1.50, under 16 free. The tourist office offers guided tours of El Call June 15-Sept. 15. €15, under 16 free.)*

MUSEU DEL CINEMA. This unusual collection of artifacts, clips, and heavy machinery documents the rise of cinema from the mid-17th to 20th centuries, with a few Asian shadow theater pieces from as early as the 11th century. The exhibit chronicles the invention of the camera obscura (9th-12th centuries), the "magic lantern," and eventually daguerreotypes, 35mm, Edison, and TV, as well as the viewing culture that developed around each new advance. With several hands-on displays and short films, this is an interactive, multi-sensory experience. A must for movie buffs, given Cataluña's central role in the early Spanish cinema. *(C. Sèquia, 1. ☎972 41 27 77; www.museudelcinema.org. Open May-Sept. Tu-Su 10am-8pm; Oct.-Apr. Tu-F 10am-6pm, Sa 10am-8pm, Su 11am-3pm. Wheelchair accessible. €4, students and over 65 €2, under 16 free. AmEx/MC/V.)*

CATHEDRAL COMPLEX. The imposing Gothic **Catedral de Girona** rises 90 steps from the plaça. Its tower, along with that of **Sant Feliu,** defines the Girona skyline. The **Torre de Charlemany** and cloister are the only structures left from the 11th and 12th centuries; the rest of the building dates from the 14th-17th centuries. Look at the keystone of the world's widest Gothic **nave** (23m); the builders eschewed solid stone in favor of a hollow rock with a wooden "cork" for fear of weighing the structure down and collapsing it. A door on the left leads to the trapezoidal cloister and the **Tresor Capitular** museum, which holds some of Girona's most precious paintings, sculptures, and decorated Bibles. Its most famous piece is the **Tapis de la Creació,** an 11th-century tapestry depicting the events of Genesis. *(Tresor ☎972 21 44 26; www.lacatedraldegirona.com. Open daily Apr.-Oct. 10am-8pm; Nov.-Mar. 10am-7pm. Wheelchair-accessible with advance notice. Cathedral €1; tresor and cloister €3, students and over 65 €2, ages 7-16 €0.90, under 7 free.)*

SCENIC WALKS. Girona's renowned ■**Passeig de la Muralla,** a 2km trail along the fortified walls of the old city, can be accessed at several points: at the Jardins de la Francesa (behind the cathedral), the Jardins d'Alemanys (behind the Museu d'Art), and the main entrance at the bottom of the Rambla in Pl. de la Marvà. *(Open daily 8am-10pm.)* Behind the St. Pere de Galligants church (by the Museu d'Arqueologia), you can go up on a *mirador* for great views of the city. Behind the cathedral, the walk coincides with the equally beautiful **Passeig Arqueològic.** Partly lined with cypresses and flower beds, this path skirts the northeastern medieval wall and also overlooks the city. For the less athletically inclined, a small green train gives a 30min. guided tour of the main sights of the old town, including the town hall, cathedral, Església de Sant Feliu, El Call, and the walls. *(In summer tour leaves daily from the Pont de Pedra every 40-45min. 10am-noon and 3-7pm. Less frequently in the winter; check at the tourist office. Available in English. €4.50, children €4.)*

OTHER MUSEUMS. The **Museu d'Art** has enchanting pieces from the Romantic to the modern; look for the Saints' Day book, the pregnant virgin, and the temporary exhibition space in an old prison cell. *(Pujada de la Catedral, 12. ☎972 20 95 36;*

www.museuart.com. Open Mar.-Sept. Tu-Sa 10am-7pm, Su 10am-2pm; Oct.-Feb. Tu-Sa 10am-6pm, Su 10am-2pm. Wheelchair-accessible. €2, students, under 19 and over 65 free.) The well-done **Museu d'Història de la Ciutat** showcases 2000 years of Girona's history and prominent figures. The exhibit on the *sardana*, Catalunya's national dance, features some interesting old musical instruments and a diagram of the steps. *(C. Força, 27. ☎972 22 22 29; www.ajuntament.gi/museuciutat. Open Tu-Sa 10am-2pm and 5-7pm, Su and holidays 10am-2pm. Some descriptions in English. €2, students €1, under 16 free.)* The small **Banys Àrabs,** inspired by Muslim bath houses, once contained saunas and baths of varying temperatures; now the graceful 12th-century structure hosts outdoor art exhibits in the summer. The walls are bare, so you'll have to buy an audioguide (€3) to appreciate the architecture of the space. *(C. Ferran el Catòlic, s/n. ☎972 19 07 97; www.banysarabs.org. Open Apr.-Sept. M-Sa 10am-7pm, Su 10am-2pm; Oct.-Mar. daily 10am-2pm. €1.60, students €0.80.)*

🔊 🎵 NIGHTLIFE AND FESTIVALS

Nightlife in Girona is extensive and ranges from finger-snapping coffeehouses to rock bars and crowded discotecas. In the summer there is really only one nightlife alternative, and that is ▓**Las Carpas** ("the tents"), an outdoor circus of dance floors, bars, and lights in the middle of the **Parc de la Devesa.** Many clubs close in summer and operate only from their *Carpa* (tent), though some change shape a bit and remain open in both guises. *Las Carpas* is so dazzling, though, that locals don't head inside until the park shuts down (Drinks from €3-6. Open Apr.-Sept. 15 M-Th and Su 11pm-3:30am, F-Sa 11pm-4am.) The artsy bars and cafes in the old quarter are particularly mellow and a good place to start the evening. **El Supreme,** C. Fontclara, 4, with 40 ft. ceilings and chandeliers, plays house to a big crowd when its tent closes. This new club's older sister, **La Platea,** opens only in winter (☎972 22 72 88; www.localplatea.com. Open Th-Sa midnight-6am. Mixed drinks €6-8.) Across the street in Pl. Viçens Vives, 6, **La Bohim** is a trendy bar for a drink.

Just a 10min. walk down the Riu Ter lies another popular nighttime destination, known as La Pedret. **La Sala del Cel,** C. Pedret, 118, (☎972 21 46 64; www.lasaladel-cel.cat) is worth the walk with its labyrinthine dance floors, massage parlor, game room, pool-side terrace, and, yes, ▓**pool.** (Cover €12 and up, drink included. Open F-Sa and nights before fiestas midnight-6am. Cash only.) **Siddharta,** C. Pedret, 116, next door, specializes in pitchers of *Tisane,* fruity concoctions with cognac and other liquors, served in a maze of old stone arches. (1.5L pitchers €15. Open daily 8pm-3am. Cash only.) **La Via Habana,** C. Pedret, 66, down the street, plays salsa and gives lessons. Make like a local and drink only mojitos (€6). (Open Th-Su 11pm-5am. Cash only.) **La Catedral,** does business from a *Carpa* in summer and opens inside for the winter. It's located on the fringe of Girona on Ctra. Santa Coloma; you'll have to take a taxi (€7-8). (Cover around €12. Open Th-Sa midnight-6am.)

Starting on the second Saturday in May and lasting through the following two weeks, government-sponsored **Temps de Flors** (www.gironatempsdeflors.net) exhibitions spring up all over the city; local monuments and pedestrian streets swim in blossoms, and the courtyards of Girona's finest old buildings are open to the public (ask for the "mapa de flors" from the tourist office). Summer evenings often inspire spontaneous *sardana* dancing in the *plaças.* Girona, along with the rest of Cataluña, lights up for the **Focs de Sant Joan** on the night of June 23, featuring outdoor parties of fireworks and large bonfires. On this night, try the traditional Coca de Sant Joan dessert—with *cava,* of course. For Viernes Santo, the Friday of **Semana Santa,** Cofrarías, or church groups, dress up in old-world costumes. Keep an eye out for the men from San Luc decked out in full Roman soldier gear, including horses and weapons. From the end of June into July, the **Festival de Músiques Religioses del Món** (☎872 08 07 09; www.ajuntament.gi/musiquesreligioses) draws choirs and artists from all over the world to perform in the cathedral and on its grand steps, while local restaurants sell cheap food from stands. The patron saint, **Sant Narcís**, is celebrated during the five days surrounding Oct. 29-Nov. 1.

FIGUERAS (FIGUERES) ☎972

Sprawling Figueres (pop. 42,000) is functional, not beautiful. It is the capital of Alt Empordà county and a major gateway city to France and the rest of Europe. In 1974, the mayor of Figueres asked native Salvador Dalí to donate a painting to an art museum the town was planning. Dalí saw his chance and took it, and donated an entire museum. With the construction of the Teatre-Museu Dalí, Figueres was catapulted to international fame; ever since, a multilingual parade of Surrealism fans has been entranced by Dalí's mind-bending and erotic works.

▛▟ TRANSPORTATION AND PRACTICAL INFORMATION

Trains: Pl. de l'Estació (☎902 24 02 02). To: **Barcelona** (2hr.; M-F 22 per day, Sa-Su 14 per day; €7.90-9.10), via **Girona** (30min., €2.40-2.70).

Buses: All buses leave from the **Estació d'Autobusos** (☎972 67 33 54), on the other side of Pl. de l'Estació from the train station. **Sarfa** (☎972 67 42 98; www.sarfa.com) is open 7:45am-8:30pm. If closed, buy tickets on bus. To **Cadaqués** (1hr.; July-Aug. 7 per day 9am-8pm, Sept.-June 6 per day; €4.25) and **Palafrugell** (1½hr.; 12:15, 8pm; €6.45). **Barcelona Bus** (☎972 50 50 29; www.barcelona-bus.com) runs to **Barcelona** (2¼hr.; 2-5 per day M-F 7:45am-6:15pm, Sa 11am-4:15pm, Su 8am-6:15pm; €14.90) via **Girona** (1hr., €4.10).

Taxis: Taxis line the *rambla* (☎972 50 00 08) and the train station (☎972 50 50 43).

Car Rental: Hertz, Pl. de l'Estació, 9 (☎972 67 28 01). 23+, must have had driver's license for 2 years. All-inclusive rental from €59 per day. Open M-F 9am-1pm and 4-8pm, Sa 9am-1pm. AmEx/D/MC/V. **Avis,** Pl. de l'Estació (☎972 51 31 82), in the train station. 23+, credit card only. Rental from €60 per day (€10 underage surcharge). Open M-Sa 9am-1pm and 4-8pm. AmEx/D/MC/V.

◢▟ ORIENTATION AND PRACTICAL INFORMATION

From **Plaça de l'Estació,** bear left on C. Sant Llàtzer, walk six blocks to C. Nou (the third main road), and take a right to get to Figueres's tree-lined Rambla. To reach the **tourist office,** walk all the way up La Rambla and continue on C. Lasauca straight out from the left corner. The blue, all-knowing "i" beckons across the rather treacherous intersection with Ronda Firal.

Tourist Offices: Main Office, Pl. Sol s/n. (☎972 50 31 55; www.figueresciutat.com). Dalí-themed tours M-Sa 11am, noon, 2, 3, 5pm. €16; includes museum. Open July-Sept. M-Sa 8am-8pm, Su 10am-3pm; Apr.-June and Oct. M-F 8:30am-3pm and 4:30-8pm, Sa 9:30am-1:30pm and 3:30-6:30pm; Nov.-Mar. M-F 8am-3pm. 2 **branches** in summer, in the train station (open July-Sept. 15 M-Sa 10am-2pm and 4-6pm), and in front of the Teatre-Museu Dalí (open July-Sept. 15 M-Sa 9am-8pm, Su 10am-3pm).

Currency Exchange: Banco Santander Central Hispano, La Rambla, 21. Open Apr.-Sept. M-F 8:30am-2pm; Oct.-Mar. M-F 8am-2pm. **ATMs** on La Rambla, Pl. Catalunya.

Luggage Storage: Lockers (€3-4.50) at the train station. Open daily 6am-11pm. At the bus station €2. Open daily 6am-10pm.

Police: Av. Salvador Dalí, 107 (☎972 51 01 11). To report a crime, contact the **Mossos d'Esquadra,** C. Ter s/n (☎972 54 18 00).

CATALUÑA

Hospital: Hospital Comarcal de Figueres, Ronda Rector Arolas s/n (☎972 50 14 00), behind the Parc Bosc to the left of the Dalí museum.

Internet Access: Biblioteca Fages de Climent, Pl. Sol, 11 (☎972 67 70 84) offers free 15min. Internet access. Open M-F 10am-1:30pm and 4-8:30pm.

Post Office: C. Santa Llogaia, 60-62 (☎972 50 54 31). Open M-F 8:30am-2:30pm, Sa 9:30am-1pm. **Postal Code:** 17600.

ACCOMMODATIONS

Many visitors to Figueres make the journey a daytrip from Barcelona, but quality, affordable accommodations in Figueres are easy to find. Most hostels tend to be on upper floors above bars or restaurants. Others are located closer to **La Rambla** and **Carrer Pep Ventura.** The tourist office has a list of all pensions and hostels.

Hostal San Mar, C. Rec Arnau, 31 (☎972 50 98 13). Follow C. Girona off La Rambla (from the station, at the beginning on the right) and continue as it becomes C. Jonquera; take the 5th right on C. Isabel II (the plaza with trees after Museu Dalí), then the 2nd left on C. Cadaqués. Clean, modern rooms with adequate bath and TV at very low prices. Singles €16-20; doubles €30; triples €45; quads €60. Cash only. ❷

Hostal La Barretina, C. Lasauca, 13 (☎972 67 64 12; www.hostalbarretina.com). From the train station, walk up La Rambla to its end; look for C. Lasauca on the left; the hostel is a block up on the left. Hotel-like luxury—each room has TV, A/C, heat, and bath. Reception in the restaurant downstairs. Breakfast €3, other meals €8.50. Reservations recommended. Wheelchair-accessible. Singles €27; doubles €45. AmEx/MC/V. ❸

FOOD

Restaurants near the Teatre-Museu Dalí serve overcooked paella to the masses; better choices surround La Rambla on the small side streets—except C. Girona, which is crowded and touristy. The **market,** at Pl. Gra, has an amazing fruit and vegetable selection. (Open Tu, Th, Sa 5am-2pm.) Another option is to buy groceries at **Donpreu,** Pl. Sol, 5. (☎972 50 51 00. Open M-Sa 9am-2pm and 5-9pm. MC/V.)

Cafè Hotel París, La Rambla, 10 (☎972 50 07 13). This chic, thoroughly modern spot is a great deal if you opt for the combination plates (€8-12). Chicken with sesame salad (€8.10) or vegetables au gratin with goat cheese (€6.20). All natural and homemade, down to the coffee ice cubes for iced coffee. Desserts from €2.70. By night, has red leather chairs and a low-key feel. MC/V. ❷

Restaurant Hotel Duran, C. Lasauca, 5 (☎972 50 12 50; www.hotelduran.com). Walk up La Rambla to the end and look for C. Lasauca. One of Dalí's haunts; you can eat in the dining room where he once held court. Delicious *canelones* (canneloni) €15. Meat and seafood entrees €9-26. Open daily 1-4pm and 8:30-11pm. AmEx/MC/V. ❸

Mandarin Restaurant Xinès, C. Lasauca, 11 (☎972 50 00 73). Right by Hotel Duran, this unassuming yet satisfying Chinese spot offers a filling *menú* (€6.80) all day amid dragon-and-tiger decor. The flavorful dishes a la carte are a similarly smashing deal. Open daily 12:30-3:30pm and 8-11:30pm. MC/V. ❶

SIGHTS

🎭 TEATRE-MUSEU DALÍ. Welcome to the world of the definitive Surrealist master. This building, the self-proclaimed "largest surrealistic object in the world," was the municipal theater for the town of Figueres before it was destroyed at the end of the Spanish Civil War. Dalí's personal mausoleum/museum/monument is

CATALUÑA

ego worship at its finest. Naughty cartoons, trippy sculptures, a dramatic, traditional tomb, and many paintings of Gala, his wife and muse, immerse the audience in his world. The collection includes *Self-Portrait with a Slice of Bacon*, *Poetry of America*, *Galarina*, *Meditating Rose*, and *Galatea of the Spheres*. A small number of hand-selected works by other artists, including El Greco, Marcel Duchamp, and architect Peres Piñero, round out the collection. The museum is large and takes several hours to see regardless of your chosen route. *(Pl. Gala i Salvador Dalí, 5. ☎972 67 75 00; www.salvador-dali.org. From La Rambla, take C. Sant Pere 3 blocks up. Or just follow the crowds and signs at every street corner. Open July-Sept. daily 9am-7:45pm; Oct.-June Tu-Su 10:30am-5:45pm. Open Aug. also 10pm-12:30am. Last entry 30min. before close. €11, students and seniors €7, groups over 30 €6 per person, under 9 free.)*

OTHER SIGHTS. Museu Empordà, La Rambla, 2, features works varying from archaeological objects of the region to Medieval, Baroque, and contemporary *català* art. Look for canvases by Modest Cuixart and Ramon Pujol Boira. Cleverly curated temporary exhibitions ("Recto/Verso" in 2007 displayed the backs of famous canvases) keep visitors on their toes. *(☎972 50 23 05; www.museuemporda.org. Open Tu-Sa 11am-7pm, Su and holidays 11am-2pm. Free with entrance to Dalí Museum, temporary exhibitions always free. €2, students €1, seniors free.)* Down the street, delight in the wonders of your favorite childhood toys at the **Museu del Joguet de Catalunya,** winner of Spain's 1999 National Prize of Popular Culture. *(Sant Pere, 1, off La Rambla. ☎972 50 45 85; www.mjc.cat. Open June-Sept. M-Sa 10am-7pm, Su 11am-6pm; Oct.-May Tu-Sa 10am-6pm, Su 11am-2pm. €5, students and under 12 €4.)*

▌ NIGHTLIFE

A bit removed from touristy Rambla, **Plaça Sol,** behind the tourist office, contains nearly all of the town's nightlife. **Cafè de Nit,** C. Mestre Fallan, 2, in Pl. del Sol, offers pool in the back (€2 per game) and cocktails for €5.50. Crowd onto the terrace row out front, or enjoy your sweet *caipirinha* under the starry lights inside. *(☎972 50 12 25. Open daily 5pm-4am. Cash only.)* The popular dance club **La Serradora,** Pl. Sol, 6, features a disco ball, long twisting bar, and maze-like dance floor. *(Cover F-Sa €10. Open W-Su 11pm-3:30am. Cash only.)*

CADAQUÉS AND PORT LLIGAT ☎972

Forty years ago, Cadaqués (pop. 2900) was practically undiscovered. Only a trickle of French tourists visited every summer, and the town had closer diplomatic relations with Cuba than with the rest of Cataluña. The distinctive variety of *català* still spoken here is testament to the enduring individuality of this drop-dead gorgeous beach town. The whitewashed houses and small but deep bay have attracted artists, writers, and musicians ever since Dalí built his summer home on the neighboring beach, Port Lligat, in the 1930s. From September to May, the town is best experienced as a daytrip, as most food and entertainment establishments close in the low season (Oct.-Apr.); however, keep in mind the limited transportation options for a same-day return.

▐ TRANSPORTATION AND PRACTICAL INFORMATION. Cadaqués has no train station. Sarfa **buses** (☎972 25 87 13; ticket office open July-Aug. daily 7:20-9am, 10am-2pm, and 4-8:30pm; Sept.-June opens 15min. before every departure) run to Barcelona (2½hr.; July-Aug. 4-5 per day 7:45am-8:45pm, Sept.-June 7am, 4:15 or 7pm; €19), Figueres (1hr.; July-Aug. 7 per day 9am-8pm, Sept.-June 3 per day 7:15am-5pm, weekends only 2:25pm; €4.25), and Girona (2hr.; July-Aug. daily 8:40am and 5:10pm; Sept.-June M-F 7am; €8.25). The bus stop is in the parking lot across from the ticket office. On your way there, stop at the indexed map on the wall to your right. Then head left past the ticket office and turn right onto Av. Caritat Serinyana; the waterfront **Plaça Frederic Rahola** (known to locals as **Ses Herbes**) is four blocks from this roundabout. **Rent@Bit,** Av. Caritat Serinyana, 9, rents scooters and bikes for exploring the remote areas around Cadaqués. (☎972 25 82 26; www.rentabit.net. Open daily 9:30am-8pm. Bikes from €18 per day, scooters from €45; hourly rates available. Internet access €0.50 per 5min., €4 per 1hr. MC/V.) **Bikes & Boats Cadaqués,** Riera Pianc, 1, in Platja es Poal, rents—you guessed it—bikes and boats. (☎972 25 80 27. Scooters from €26 per 2hr. or €45 per day. Boats from €100 per 4hr. or €180 per 8hr. Open Apr.-Sept. 9am-7pm. MC/V.)

The **tourist office,** C. Cotxe, 2, off Pl. Frederic Rahola, is on a street opposite the beach. They have an excellent *plànol turístic* as well as a listing of hotels and hostels. (☎972 25 83 15. Open July-Aug. M-Sa 9am-2pm and 3-9pm, Su 10:30am-1pm; Sept.-June M-Sa 9am-2pm and 4-7pm.) **Banco Santander Central Hispano** is at Av. Caritat Serinyana, 4. (☎972 25 83 62. Open Apr.-Sept. M-F 8:30am-2pm; Oct.-Mar. M-F 8:30am-2pm, Sa 8:30am-1pm. **ATMs** line the last few blocks of Av. Caritat Serinyana and Pg. Llorens.) Local services include: **police,** C. Carles Rahola, 9 (☎972 15 93 43); **medical services,** C. Nou, 6 (☎972 25 88 07); **Internet** access at **Telecomunicaciones Cadaqués,** Riera de Sant Vicenç, 4, a block off Pl. Frederic Rahola (☎972 15 92 09; €1.50 per 30min.; open daily 9:30am-2pm and 4-11pm) and **Casino,** Pl. Ses Herbes s/n, €1 per 30min.; the **post office,** on Av. Rierassa off Av. Caritat Serinyana, two blocks from the bus station (☎972 25 87 98; open M-F 9am-2pm, Sa 9:30am-1pm). **Postal Code:** 17488.

▐▐ ACCOMMODATIONS AND FOOD. As Cadaqués is a beach town, many accommodations only open during the summer, and often require reservations. ◪**Hostal Cristina ❸,** on Riera de Sant Vicenç, is by the water, to the right of Av. Caritat Serinyana on the plaza. Cristina offers cheerful, newly renovated rooms with great views of the plaza, and even has a few apartment-style rooms around the corner from the church, complete with blue-tiled showers and free incense. (☎972 25 81 38. Reception July-Sept. 9am-3pm; Oct.-June 9am-9pm. Summer prices include breakfast. May-Sept. singles €30; doubles €40, with bath €50; Oct.-Apr. €25/35/45. Apartment rooms €5 less. MC/V.) **Hostal Vehi ❸,** C. de l'Esglesia, 6, is across from the tall white church and a short walk from the water. (☎972 25 84 70. Breakfast €6. Reserve ahead. Singles €25-30; doubles with sink €35-45, with bath €45-55, apartments 60-75; triples €75; quads €90. AmEx/MC/V.) **Camping Cadaqués ❶,** Ctra. Port Lligat, 17, is 100m from the beach on the way to Dalí's house; follow the signs for Hotel Port Lligat. The campground is crowded, but it's clean and not far from the beach or the center of town. (☎972 25 81 26. Open Apr.-Sept. Reception 8am-10pm, quiet hours midnight-8am. €6.70 per person, €8.45 per tent, €6.80 per car. MC/V.)

Cadaqués tourists (many of them French) are more demanding than most, which means that even seaside restaurants with trilingual menus serve respectable food. Still, wander into the back streets for more interesting options. C. Miquel Rosset, off Pl. Frederic Rahola, has some good ones. Picnicking on the beach is always a good idea; **groceries** can be purchased at **Valvi,** on Riera de Sant Vicenç, a block from Pl. Frederic Rahola. (☎972 25 86 33. Open June-Sept. M-Sa 8am-1:45pm and 4:30-8:45pm. Oct.-May 8:30am-1:30pm and 4:30-8:15pm, Su and holidays closed in the evening. MC/V.) **Canshelabi ❹,** C. Riera, 9, like its name, is a fusion of Cataluña and Morocco ("can" is "house" in *català,* "Shelabi" is the owner's Moroccan nickname). Tajine (couscous stew served in a ceramic chimney pot) is the house specialty, and many stop by in the afternoons for the sweet mint tea. (☎972 25 89 00. Entrees €15-25. Open daily 11am-2am. MC/V.) At **Algianni ❷,** C. Riera s/n, the owner has been preparing the freshest food, by hand, for 15 years. A shady terrace invites diners to enjoy pastas with greens, colorful risottos, and freshly caught fish. (☎972 25 83 71. Pasta €7-9, meat and fish €11-15. Open daily in summer 1:30-4:30pm and 7:30pm-1am. Closed Tu in winter. MC/V.)

SIGHTS AND ENTERTAINMENT. Església de Santa María, the defining feature of the Cadaqués landscape, is a small 16th-century Gothic church with an enormous Baroque altar, with 365 carved faces. Listen for the organist, who practices in the afternoons from his special elevated cabin. (Open M-Sa 10am-1pm and 4pm-7pm, Su and holidays 10am-noon.) Two blocks up and to the right, the **Museu de Cadaqués,** C. d'en Narcis Monturiol, 15, displays rotating exhibits that almost always revolve around Dalí. (☎972 25 88 77. Open mid-June to Sept. daily 10am-8pm, except W closed 1:30-3pm; Oct.-June M-Sa 10:30am-1:30pm and 4-7pm. €4.) From the museum, it's a pleasant walk (20min.) to **Casa-Museu Salvador Dalí,** in Port Lligat, the house where Dalí and his wife Gala lived until her death in 1982. Follow the signs at C. Miranda or take the **trolley** that leaves from Pl. Frederic Rahola for the scenic 10km route to Port Lligat via Cap de Creus, the farthest point on the peninsula (1hr.; 6 per day 11am-6pm; €7, children €5). The house is actually seven fisherman's houses that Dalí bought and transformed one by one. While only two unfinished original paintings remain in the house, the stuffed bear and innumerable trinkets that decorate the interior are enough to keep anyone's interest. Catch a glimpse of one of his famous lip-shaped sofas and a pool inspired by the Alhambra, guarded somewhat inexplicably by a plastic Michelin Man. (☎972 25 10 15; pllgrups@dali-estate.org. Open mid-June to mid-Sept. daily 10:30am-9pm, last entry 8:10pm; mid-Sept. to Jan. and mid-Mar. to mid-June Tu-Su 10:30am-6pm, last tour 5:10pm. Visits are supervised and space is limited: call 4-5 days in advance. €10; students, seniors, and children €8.) **Boat rides** in Dalí's own Gala depart from the dock in front of the house on the hour for a 55min. trip to Cap de Creus or Cadaqués. (☎617 46 57 57. Open daily 10am- 8pm, depending on weather. Min. 2 people. €10.)

Back on the Cadaqués beach, **Escola d'en Mar,** on C. Sa Riera, rents kayaks, sailboats, and windsurfing gear, and also runs 3hr. kayak tours. (☎680 80 75 85. €25 per person, min. 5 people, reserve in advance. Open daily June-Sept. 15 9:30am-8pm. Cash only.) **Diving Center Cadaqués,** C. de la Miranda (☎652 31 77 97; www.divingc-cadaques.com) offers 45min. dives 9am and 4pm for €40. Certain routes depend on wind direction and weather: call for information on special offers.

Nightlife in Cadaqués is limited to summer weekends and focused on C. Miguel Rosset, off Pl. Frederic Rahola. A local and international crowd of all ages heads **Café Tropical,** C. Miguel Rosset, 19, for mouth-watering mojitos and dancing in a jungle-like atmosphere—plants hang from the ceiling, and the roof of the terrace is made of tree branches. (☎972 25 88 01. Open M-Th and Su 10:30pm-2:30am, F-Sa 10:30pm-3am. Beer €4. Cocktails €8. MC/V.) Also popular is the **L'Hostal,** at Pg. Llorens, 8, right by the plaza, with a Dalí-designed logo and delicious tequila sunrises. Live music is featured daily in summer (midnight-2am), ranging from rumba to jazz to rock. (☎972 25 80 00. Open May-Dec. daily 5pm-5am; Jan.-Apr. F-Sa 5pm-5am. Cash only.)

Cadaqués certainly does not neglect festivals, however, and the first weekend in September brings dozens of old-fashioned sailboats to the harbor for the renowned **Trobada de Barques de Vela Llatina.** On the weekend before September 11th, the **Festa Major d'Estiu** fills the streets with *sardanas, fútbol,* dances, concerts, and more. December 18th brings more of the same at the **Festa Major d'Hivern.** From late June through August, the **Festival Internacional de Música de Cadaqués** brings big-name international musicians.

INLAND CATALUNYA

LÉRIDA (LLEIDA)   ☎973

Modern Lleida (pop. 115,000) is in the constant presence of history: trendy boutiques are framed by old churches and palaces, and well-kept parks and plazas compete with the fashion retail frenzy of C. Major. Founded in the 6th century BC by the Llergete tribe, Lleida's strategic location has produced a past defined by struggle. The city was destroyed by Germanic tribes in the 3rd century, but by the 15th century, had recovered enough to produce great architectural works. In the 16th and 17th centuries, unrest returned with *català* peasant uprisings, and Napoleon's invasion in the early 1800s. The Spanish Civil War nearly leveled it again, but Lleida is currently undergoing a cultural renovation, with new galleries, a new theater, and the La Panera modern art center set to open in 2012.

TRANSPORTATION. RENFE trains, Pl. Berenguer IV (☎902 24 02 02). Trains to: Barcelona (3-4hr., 7 per day 5:58am-10pm, €9.25-26.10); Madrid (5hr., 8 per day 8:41am-1:25am, €35.50-54); Tarragona (1½-2hr., 9 per day 5:58am-7:20pm, €5-22); Zaragoza (2½hr., 7-8 per day 6:20am-12:15am, €9.90-11.35). **AVE** or **Altaria high-speed trains** run to: Barcelona (2-3hr., 7 per day 8:03am-8:10pm, €20.30-26.10); Calatayud (1½hr., 4 per day 9:50am-8:55pm, €29-33.30); Guadalajara (2½hr., 4 per day 9:50am-8:55pm, €47.90); Madrid (3hr., 12 per day 7:12am-8:59pm, €53-59); Zaragoza (1hr., 15-18 per day midnight-6pm, €19.80-38.60). **Central Bus Station** (☎973 26 85 00; open daily 6am-10pm), on Av. Catalunya half a block up from the river, sends buses to: Andorra (2-3hr.; M-F 5 per day 9:30am-7:30pm, Sa Su 4 per day; €17); Barcelona (2¼-2¾hr.; M-F 14 per day 6am-7:30pm, Sa 10 per day, Su 5 per day starting at 9:10am; €16.70); Girona (3½hr.; M-F 3 per day 6:15am-5:30pm, Sa-Su 2 per day after 8:30am; €18.15); Tarragona (2hr.; M-F 6 per day 7:30am-9pm, Sa-Su 9:30am and 9:15pm; €5); Zaragoza (2¼hr.; M-F 6 per day 6:45am-6pm, Sa-Su 4 per day 8am-6pm; €8-9). Yellow **city buses** (☎973 27 29 99; www.sarbus.com) run throughout the city; the tourist office has a map/schedule. The most useful lines are the Exterior bus (#10, 7am-9:45pm) from the train station to the center, which stops along Av. de Madrid, and the *Centre Històric-Universitats* bus (#12, M-Sa 7:30am-9pm) that runs between the bus station and Seu Vella (€0.85; 10-ride passes €6 at tobacco shops). For a **taxi,** call **Radio Taxi** (☎973 20 30 50).

ORIENTATION AND PRACTICAL INFORMATION. There is a **map** posted on C. Cardenal Remolins (to the right of the traffic circle in front of the train station) to help you navigate to the main tourist office. There is also a small outpost of the Catalunya tourist office in the traffic circle itself. Bordered by the **Río Segre,** Lleida sprawls up the hill toward Seu Vella, the imposing cathedral. **Rambla de Ferran,** the wide street which heads straight out from the train station, runs parallel to the river and changes its name every few blocks, becoming Av. de Francesc Macià/Av. de Blondel/Av. de Madrid. **Carrer Major,** the main commercial street, runs parallel to Ferran, one block inland. The city center stretches from Av. de Madrid/Blondel/Francesc to Rambla d'Aragó, and is bordered on the west by Av. de Catalunya and on the east by Seu Vella massif. Tourism centers on **Plaça Sant Joan,** at the end of C. Major, is the tourist center, with several hostels and cafes right at the foot of the stairs to the cathedral. From the **bus station**, take Av. de Blondel to C. Cavallers, go one block away from the river (to your left) and you'll be on C. Major, or go four blocks straight from the train station (starting on C. Cardenal Remolins, which becomes C. Sant Joan). Lleida has two **tourist offices.** The main one is at C. Major, 31, three blocks past Pl. Sant

Joan when coming from the train station. Make sure to get a free **map** and the very useful **Guía de Turismo,** with information on museums and festivals. (☎902 25 00 50; www.turismedelleida.com. Open M-Sa 10am-2pm and 4-7pm, Su and holidays 10am-1:30pm. Second location in Plaza Beringuer.) The Catalunya tourist office, in a kiosk in front of the train station, has regional information. (Open M-F 10am-2pm and 3:30-7:30pm, Sa 10-2pm.) **Banks** with 24hr. **ATMs** line Rambla de Ferran and C. Major. Other services include: **luggage storage** at the train station (€4.50 per 24hr., €2.40-3 for smaller lockers; open 3pm-1am), but none at the bus station; **police,** Gran Passeig de Ronda, 52 (☎088); **Arnan de Vilanova Hospital,** Av. de l'Alcalde Rovira Roure, 80 (☎973 24 81 00); **Internet** access at **Cyber Jordi,** C. Sta. Marta, 1 (☎973 22 95 98; €1 per 1hr., €1.50 per 2hr.; open M-Sa 9am-11pm), at **Cafetó Internet,** C. del Bonaire, 8 (☎973 72 51 48; €2 per 1hr.; open M-Sa 9am-2pm and 4pm-midnight, Su 4pm-midnight), and at the **public library,** Rambla d'Aragó, 10 (☎973 27 90 70; cultura.gencat.net/bpl; drop by to reserve up to 1hr.; open M-F 10am-8pm, Sa 10am-2pm); and the **post office,** Rambla de Ferran, 16, four blocks toward town from the train station (☎973 24 70 00; open M-F 8:30am-8:30pm, Sa 9:30am-2pm). **Postal Codes:** 25001-25007.

⌂ ACCOMMODATIONS. Most budget accommodations (including those listed) double as student housing, so term-time (Oct.-June) space is limited. Sunny, freshly painted rooms at the centrally located ▨**Hostal Mundial ❷,** Pl. Sant Joan, 4, provide abundant floor space, large beds, shower or bath, sink, and desks in every room. The best ones have balconies overlooking the plaza. (☎973 24 27 00; fax 24 26 02. Breakfast €2-3. M-F *menú* €9. Some rooms with free Internet access. Singles with bath or shower €20; doubles with shower €30, with bath and TV €36. AmEx/MC/V.) **Alberg Sant Anastasi (HI) ❷,** Rambla d'Aragó, 11, offers a social atmosphere with clean four-person rooms, free Internet access, washer (€2.50) and dryer (€1.50), two TV lounges, and a game room. Very few rooms are available— about 125 of their 142 beds are filled year-round with students. (☎973 26 60 99; www.tujuca.com. Breakfast and sheets included. Towels €2.25. Reception 24hr. Wheelchair accessible. IVA not included. Must have HI card. Dorms June-Sept. €16.45, Oct.-May €13.65; over 25 €23.45/19.55. €3 extra with bath. Cash only.) **Hotel Goya ❸,** C. Alcalde Costa, 9, a block up Av. Catalunya from the bus station and then a block and a half left on Alcade Costa, presents a great alternative to overcrowded student housing. Full bath, A/C, TV, and telephone in each of the 18 impeccably clean rooms, some of which have balconies. The hotel only has three singles; reserve ahead. (☎973 26 67 88. Singles €26; doubles €42; Cash only.)

❒ FOOD. Lleida's local specialty is *caragoles* (snails), and the city consumes over 12 slimy tons of them each year, most notably during their popular food festival, the **Aplec del Caragol.** Held the third weekend in May (F-Su night), the festival features ▨**feasting and snail races** in the Parque dels Camps Elisis. The tourist office has a list of restaurants that serve snail-based dishes—some of the more popular ones include snails cooked on a *llauna* (metal sheet), served with *ali-oli* (mayonnaise and garlic), *a la vinagreta* (cooked with veggies on a stone tile), and *a la gormanta* (fried with seasonings). **El Celler del Roser ❷,** C. Cavallers, 24, offers an elegant, almost hip country setting, and serves typical cuisine. Delicate snail, fish, and meat entrees run €10-18. (☎973 23 90 70. *Menú* €11. Appetizers €7-12. Open M-Sa 1-4:30pm and 8:30-11:30pm, Su 1-4:30pm. AmEx/MC/V.) For those who would rather chop off a finger than eat a snail, the area surrounding C. del Bonaire and Av. de l'Alcalde Rovira has the majority of Lleida's restaurants, and the area west of Seu Vella has several establishments serving African cuisine. **Bar Iruña ❷,** Pl. de Sant Llorenç, 3, is a local favorite, with a 17th-century farmhouse exterior and huge courses of Navarran and Basque specialties, served with plenty of fries. (☎973 27 47 55. *Menú* €8.95. Tapas €1-6. Open Tu-Su 11am-4pm and 7:30pm-midnight. MC/V.) Across from the bus station on Av. de Catalunya, the supermarket **Esclat** meets all your grocery needs. (☎902 16 09 25. Open M-Sa 9:15am-9:15pm.) There are also markets on Rambla Aragó and some on C. Mayor.

◪ SIGHTS. Perched atop the hill above the city, **◪Seu Vella** (nicknamed *el castillo* by *leridanos* because of its fortress-like appearance) was used as a military barracks until 1948. For an excellent historical and architectural account of the austere 14th-century cathedral and cloister, get the audio tour for €0.60. The long climb up to the **bell tower** is worth each of the steep 238 steps; two of the seven bells (with names like Bárbara) are Gothic originals from the 15th century, and the view is incomparable. To reach the cathedral, ride the escalator up from Pl. Sant Joan, then the elevator (€0.20 each way), or take the path and stairs to the left of it. (☎973 23 06 53. Open Tu-Su June-Sept. 10am-1:30pm and 4-7:30pm; Oct.-May 10am-1:30pm and 3-5:30pm. Bell tower closes 30min. before the rest of complex. Guided tours in Spanish July 15-Sept. 15; brochures available in English. €2.40, under 21 and students €1.80, under 6 and over 65 free. Tu free.) You can still find several beautiful churches without climbing the hill, most notably the 19th-century **Església de Sant Joan** in Pl. Sant Joan and the 18th-century **Catedral Nova,** in the Pl. de la Catedral at the end of C. Major.

The new **Centre d'Art de la Panera,** Pl. de la Panera, 2, was created in the 13th-century market building to house rotating temporary exhibitions of edgy contemporary and mixed-media art, as well as to foster outreach and resource-building for the burgeoning art scene in Lleida. It will eventually be the site of Lleida's modern art complex, scheduled for completion in 2012. It's easy to get lost finding the Panera: from Plaza Sant Joan, walk down C. Mayor with the river on your left, make a right on C. Cavallers, another right at C. Universitat, a left on C. Sant Martí, and the second left. Panera is the grey building with the staircase. (☎973 26 21 85; lapanera@paeria.es. Open Tu-F 10am-2pm and 4-8pm, Sa 11am-2pm and 4-8pm, Su 11am-2pm. Free tours by appointment. Free.) In a temporary space until it joins the Panera complex in 2012, the **Museu d'Art Jaume Morera** houses a rotating display of 19th- and 20th-century work: painting, sculpture, and photography; the permanent collection begins with realist landscapes by Morera himself (check out the *Picos de Nájarra*), and depicts the evolution to more contemporary *leridano* art. (Temporary exhibitions Avda. Blondel, 40. Permanent collection C. Mayor, 31, 2nd fl. ☎973 70 04 19. Open Tu-Sa 11am-2pm and 5-8pm, Su 11am-2pm. Free.)

◪◪ NIGHTLIFE AND FESTIVALS. The area around C. del Bonaire and Av. de Catalunya is the best place for bar-hopping in Lleida, with popular spots like **Can-Can** and **Maracas.** Pl. de Ricard Vinyes has countless terraced restaurants, like **O'Sullivan's.** The **Guía del Ocio,** available at most bars and pubs, lists various nightlife alternatives, which are abundant considering the small city's size.

The month of May is chock-full of festivals, in addition to the **Aplec del Caragol** (see **Food,** p. 442). The **Festa Major** (weekend of May 11) is held in honor of hometown hero St. Anastasius, a *leridano* who served in the Roman army until he was martyred in 303 by order of emperor Diocletian. The *festa* offers colorful parades which culminate in a floral offering to the saint and the *batalla dels flors,* a flower battle between onlookers and participants on floats. Locals delight in the omnipresent *Lo Marraco,* Lleida's resident 8.5m long dragon, built in 1957, and giant puppets of Marc Anthony and Cleopatra built in 1840 (the oldest puppets in Cataluña). On May 15th, there is a reenactment of the victory over the Moors, while the week of Sept. 29 is a celebration of **Sant Miquel,** Lleida's patron saint.

THE PYRENEES

Nowhere in Spain is the wear of time more marked than along the sprawling stretch of the Pyrenees. Throughout the region, antique cobbled towns exist quietly among steep snow-capped mountains and gently eroded green valleys, and vast nature preserves welcome travelers fleeing the throngs of tourists and manic pace in nearby Pamplona, San Sebastián, and Barcelona. In many of the hills and valleys, *català* is spoken more frequently than Spanish. The French portion of the Camino de Santiago crosses into Spain at Roncesvalles, and pilgrims on their way to Santiago de Compostela in Galicia rest in mountainside refugios. A calm, tempered pace governs life throughout the day, leaving ample time to take in the splendor of the surroundings. For those seeking adventure, vast national parks teeming with natural beauty beg to be explored, and the dramatic landscape provides endless opportunities for excursions and adventure sports of all kinds. During the summer, the mountain air and breezes offer welcome respite from Spain's sweltering heat, and come winter, world-class ski resorts await in the high mountains of Aragón and Cataluña. Early June to late September is the best time for trekking—any earlier and avalanches are a potential danger, and any later the cold can be a problem. The Pyrenees are best explored by car, as public transportation is as common as the area's endangered bears.

HIGHLIGHTS OF THE PYRENEES

RAFT down **La Seu d'Urgell's** Olympic park rapids (p.457).

TRIPLE your fun by skiing in three countries at **Puigcerdà** (p. 449).

INDULGE in a sumptuous cake at one of **Jaca's** bakeries (p. 463).

ROUGH IT in the glorious **Parque Nacional de Ordesa** on the French border (p. 467).

CATALAN PYRENEES

While beachgoers and city-dwellers flock to Barcelona and the Costa Brava, Cataluña's Pyrenees draw a different breed of tourist. Bikinis are tossed aside in favor of better insulation as hikers and high-brow skiers, mostly from Spain and France, come for the refined ski resorts and some of Spain's wildest mountain scenery. Meanwhile, history and architecture buffs, notebooks in hand, eagerly explore the tranquil mountain towns filled with well-preserved Romanesque buildings. Don't expect to hear much English around here—foreign tourists can be extremely rare in some parts, and Spanish is a second language for many locals.

 ACCESS ADVENTURE. The website **www.pirineo.com** is a fantastic resource (for both skiing and hiking) for those who can read Spanish.

RIPOLL
☎972

Just under two hours from Barcelona, Ripoll (pop. 10,800) marks the beginning of another world, where carefully preserved, thousand-year-old monasteries nestle among chic ski resorts. Ripoll is a guardian of Spain's Romanesque architectural legacy; the elaborately carved portal of the Monasterio de Santa María is

The Pyrenees

PYRENEES

FRANCE

PYRENEES

CATALUÑA

ANDORRA
★ Andorra la Vella

Val d'Aran

NAVARRA

ARAGÓN

LA RIOJA

Roncesvalles
Auritz
Burguete
Otsagabia
Zuriza
Izaba
Roncal
Anso
Echo
Javier
Sangüesa
Lumbier
Ujué
Olite
Tafalla
Puente la Reina
Estella
Pamplona/Iruña
Puente la Reina de Jaca
Santa Cilia de Jaca
Jaca
Torla
Sabiñánigo
L'Ainsa
Benasque
Bol
Baqueta
Beret
Salardú
V·elha
Espot
Sort
La Seu d'Urgell
Puigcerdà
Núria
Camprodón
Ripoll
Ribes de Fresер
Queralbs
Sant Joan de les Abadesses
Figueres
Besalú
Banyoles
Girona
Céret
Perpignan
Céret
Lloret de Mar
Blanes
Calella
Mataró

San Juan de la Peña
Castillo de Loarre
Huesca
Ayerbe
Grañén
Sariñena
Barbastro
Monzón
Fraga
Lleida
Tremp
Àger
Balaguer
Cervera
Tàrrega
Manresa
Montserrat
Terrassa
Sabadell
Vic
Berga
Cardona
Pont de Suert
Graus
Benabarre

Parque Nacional de Ordesa y Monte Perdido
Parque Nacional d'Aigüestortes / Estany de Sant Maurici
Mt. Aneto (3404 m)

Ejea de los Caballeros
Arguedas
Zaragoza
Muel
Cariñena
Catalayud
Veruela
Tarazona
Tudela
Alfaro
Caparroso
Cascastillo
Río Gallego
Río Ebro
Río Segre
Río Noguera
Río Ter
Río Fluvià
Río Cardener

THE PYRENEES

40 kilometer
40 mile

one of Spain's most famous examples. Set in a charming green valley framed by two rivers, this serene town offers views of snow-capped mountains and serves as a good base for excursions. Despite its tourist-attraction status, the town maintains a genuine feel, complete with locals gathering in the afternoons to chat and relax in the main square. Be sure to book ahead during summer weekends, when *catalans* flock in to escape the heat.

🖳 🖪 TRANSPORTATION AND PRACTICAL INFORMATION. RENFE, C. Progres (☎972 70 06 44; www.renfe.es) runs **trains** to Barcelona (1¾hr., 9-12 per day 6:34am-8:34pm, €5.65) and Puigcerdà (1hr., 7 per day 8:55am-8:59pm, €2.95). The **bus stop** (across a small park to the left as you exit the train station) sends **Teisa** buses (☎972 26 01 96; www.teisa-bus.com) to Barcelona (1½hr.; M-F 7am, Su Oct. 1-Mar. 31 5pm; Apr. 1-Sept. 30 6pm; €6.30) and Sant Joan de les Abadesses (15min., 8-12 per day M-F 8:15am-9:15pm, Sa-Su and holidays 9:05am-9:05pm €1.25). **Mir S.A.** (☎972 70 30 12) runs buses to Ribes (30min.; 4-15 per day, M-F 7:50am-7:55pm, Sa 9:10am-6:10pm, Su 9:15am-4:15pm; €1.60). **Taxis** are available at ☎609 33 29 94 or 659 43 74 30. Rent bikes at **Bicicletes Pirineu,** Ctra. Ribes, 11B (From the tourist office, take a right on to C. Berenguer El Vell and then left on to Ctra. De Ribes. ☎972 70 36 30. €10 per day. Includes lock and helmet. Open daily 9am-1pm and 4-8pm.) The **tourist office,** next to the monastery on Pl. Abat Oliba, has free maps with listings of accommodations, food, and essential services. (☎972 70 23 51. Open Sept.-June M-Sa 9:30am-1:30pm and 4-7pm; July-Aug. M-Sa 9:30am-1:30pm and 4-8pm, Su year-round 10am-2pm.) Local services include a **laundromat,** Limpid, Pg. el Regull 10, next to the gas station (open M 5-8pm, Tu-F 9:30am-1pm and 5-8pm, Sa 9:30am-1pm; €3.60 per kg, next-day pickup); **municipal police,** Pl. Ajuntament, 3 (☎972 71 44 14); **Guardia Civil** (☎972 70 00 82); and a **pharmacy,** Pl. St. Eudald 2 (☎972 70 02 61; open daily 9am-10pm). Several **locutorios** (telephone centers) have Internet access: one on Pg. el Regull 2, on the right side of the Pont l'Arquer where it bridges the Riu Fresser (☎972 70 42 70; €1.50 per hour; open daily 10am-2pm and 3-5pm) and another on the tiny C. Llupions, near the Pont D'olot (€1.80 per hour. Open daily 10:30am-2pm and 4-10pm). Free Wi-Fi is also available in the **library** C. Vinyes, 6 (☎972 70 07 11; open M-Tu,Th 4-8:30pm, W 9am-2pm, F 10am-2pm and 4-8:30pm, Sat 10am-2pm). The **post office,** C. d'Estació 1, faces the park (☎972 70 07 60; open M-F 8:30am-2:30pm, Sa 9:30am-1pm). **Postal Code:** 17500. There are multiple 24hr. ATMs scattered throughout the town, and most of the main banks are located in the Placa Gran.

🖪 🖸 ACCOMMODATIONS AND FOOD. For more information on accommodations in the entire Ripolles valley, visit www.elripolles.com. The friendly Habitaciones **Paula ❷,** C. Pirineus, 6, on Pl. Abat Oliba, is just past the tourist office. All rooms have an adjoining bathroom and shower, as well as a small TV. (☎972 70 00 11. Doubles €42.80; triples €59.92. MC/V.) **La Piazetta ❹,** Pl. Nova, 11, has spacious and well-appointed rooms with TV and private baths overlooking Pl. Nova. The restaurant downstairs, while providing some of the best food in town (*Menú* €8.50), can be fairly noisy for the rooms on the first floor until around midnight. (☎972 70 02 15. Restaurant open M-Th 1-3:15pm and 8-10pm, F 1-3:15pm and 8-11pm, Sa 1:30-3:15pm and 8-11pm. MC/V. Breakfast included. Singles €36. Discounts for stays longer than three days. AmEx/MC/V.) Many bars around Pl. Ajuntament serve everyday *català* food, such as fried cod and various *boccatas* (sandwiches), offering local ambience. If exquisite *català* fare chased by unique desserts sounds good to you, try **Reccapolis ❸,** Ctra. Sant Joan, 68, about a 25min. walk down Ctra. Sant Joan from Pl. Ajuntament on the way to Sant Joan de Abadesses. (☎972 70 21 06; www.reccapolis.com. Entrees €15-20. Open M-Tu and Th-Su 1-4pm and 8:30-10:30pm, W 1-4pm. AmEx/MC/V.) Stock up on groceries at the **supermarket** across from the bus station, Condis, C. Progrés, 33-37. (☎972 70 31 69. Open M-Sa 9am-9pm, Su 10am-3pm. AmEx/MC/V.)

 SIGHTS. Most visitors to Ripoll come to see the intricate 12th-century portal of the **Monasterio de Santa María.** Founded in AD 880 by Count Guifré el Pelós (Wilfred the Hairy), the Santa María monastery was once one of the most important cultural centers in all of Medieval Europe. The curved doorway, nicknamed the "Stone Bible," depicts scenes from the Old and New Testaments as well as a hierarchy of the cosmos. The portal leads to the **church** that contains the tomb of the Count and several other important figures from the monastery's past. Adjoining the church is a two-story Romanesque and Gothic **cloister,** built between the 12th and 16th centuries. Take a left on C. Progrés toward town from the train and bus stations, following it to the Pont d'Olot on the left, cross the river, then continue straight on C. Bisbe Morgades to Pl. Ajuntament and Pl. Abat Oliba. (Church open daily 10am-1pm and 3-6pm, June-July open until 7pm. €3, students €2. Free information in English available at the nearby tourist information office.) Check out the Farga Palau, on Pg. De La Farga Catalana, where you can peer into a 15th-century iron and copper forge that was transformed in to a museum. Ripoll has some great hiking and biking options that start right inside town. Ask the tourist information office for the green *El Nostre Entorn* brochure that has a map and information about all trails in the area.

▶ DAYTRIP FROM RIPOLL

CAMPRODON

Camprodon is accessible by Teisa bus (☎972 26 01 96) from Ripoll (35min.; M-F 14 per day 8:15am-9:15pm, Sa-Su 7 per day 9:05am-9:05pm; return M-F 14 per day 7am-8pm, Sa-Su 7 per day 8:15am-7:55pm, €2.80).

In up-and-coming Camprodon (pop. 2500), narrow streets meander around a 12th-century monastery, **Monestir de Sant Pere,** and a picturesque Romanesque bridge, the Pont Nou. There is a small **museum** dedicated to renowned Spanish musician Isaac Albéniz, who was born in Camprodon. (C. Sant Roc, 22, near the Pont Nou. ☎972 74 11 66. Open Tu-Sa 11am-2pm and 4-7pm, Su 11-2am. €2.40, students €1.50.) During July and Aug., the town hosts the Isaac Albéniz music festival that features local musicians in classical and jazz concerts. **Cook Robin ❸,** on the Pl. Dr. Robert, serves up brick-oven pizza (☎972 74 04 49; pizzas €8-12). The entire Vall de Camprodon is a paradise for outdoor lovers of all kinds. The best hiking in the Ripolles area can be found along the 900km of trail in the **Vall de Camprodon,** 20min. up the highway from Sant Joan de les Abadesses. The tourist office sells an excellent packet of maps detailing the hiking routes in the valley (€3.60; individual routes free). One of the more popular routes is the loop from **Camprodon** to the **Chapel of Sant Antoni.** (Ruta 3, 1¾hr., low difficulty). Even more challenging is the **Núria** hike (Ruta #26, 4hr., high difficulty, especially in winter), which offers spectacular views from Picos de la Vaca over the Valle de Carança, though a new variant (Ruta #27) is less crowded and has a hut halfway for overnight trips. There are also many **mountain biking** trails in the valley; **bike rental** is available at **Esports VIVAC,** Ctra. C-38, across from the tourist office at the entrance to the town. (☎972 13 04 26. Open M-F 10am-1pm and 5-8pm, Sa 10am-2pm and 4:30-8:30pm, Su 10am-2pm and 5-7pm. ½-day €10, full-day €15.) **Bastiments Aventura** also provides a outdoor options like archery, climbing, and paintballing for groups of 10 or more. (☎629 03 15 82; www.bastimentsaventura.com.) The **ski** resort **Vallter 2000,** several kilometers uphill from Camprodon, also has summer activities run by **Nordsud Esports de Muntanya** (☎605 22 79 78;

www.guiesnordsud.com) ranging from horseback riding to mountain biking to guided excursions. (☎972 13 60 57; www.vallter2000.com. Ski lessons offered. €26 per day, afternoon pass €23; reduced rates for children under 12.) There are two **tourist offices** in Camprodon. The regional office for the Vall de Camprodon area is located at the entrance to town nearest Ripoll, in the middle of a traffic rotary. The helpful staff provides extensive information on outdoor activities. (☎972 74 09 36. Open Tu-F 9:30am-1:30pm and 3-6pm, Sa 10am-2pm and 4-7pm, Su 10am-2pm.) The second, for Camprodon, is located in the Pl. D'Espanya. From the rotary at the entrance to town, follow the Carretera de Sant Joan until it becomes C. Josep Morrer and leads in to the square. (☎972 74 00 10. Open M-Sa 10am-2pm and 4-7pm, Su 10am-2pm.)

VALLE DE NÚRIA   ☎972

Legend has it that around AD 700, Sant Gil lived in the ◼Valle de Núria, preaching the gospel to mountain shepherds. Before he left to spread his teachings, he carefully hid several items that would eventually become hallmark symbols of the valley: the bell he used to call the shepherds, the pot from which he spooned his dinner, his cross, and a wooden statue he had carved known as the Virgen de Núria. The once-remote sanctuary has grown into a full-blown ski resort and summer hiking base, the church and hermitage now overshadowed by the restaurants and hordes of tourists. Núria is accessible only by foot or by the rail known as the ◼Cremallera, or Zipper, which starts in **Ribes de Freser** and stops in **Queralbs.** The 40min. ride up the mountainside costs a hefty €15.80 (round-trip) from Ribes, but the awe-inspiring cliffside ride and pastoral valley above is worth the price. (Open June 25-Sept. 15 and weekends hourly 8:30am-5:40pm, return 8:30am-6:30pm; Sept. 16-June 22, M-F 7 per day 7:30am-5:40pm, return 8:30am-6:30pm. Price includes free cable car ride on top.) The more intrepid can hike up to Núria from **Queralbs,** which is accessible by car, or from Ribes via the Cremallera train (€4.90 round-trip). The 3½hr. hike is somewhat difficult, with a 731m elevation gain, but those who brave it will be rewarded with dazzling vistas and refreshing waterfalls. The Núria **tourist office,** located in the lobby of the hotel in the main sanctuary complex, gives out basic hiking information and sells a map (€2) with descriptions of over 40 hiking routes in the valley of all difficulty levels. (☎972 73 20 20; www.valldenuria.cat. Open daily 8:30am-5:45pm.) Serious hikers should get *Editorial Alpina* Puigmal sector map. (€8 in the hotel lobby shop or in the Ribes bookstore or outdoors shop.) During winter, full ski equipment rental is available.

Núria itself has few accommodations. Families and individuals are welcome at the **Albergue Pic de l'Àliga (HI) ❷,** reached by an 20min. walk up the hill from the upper Cremallera station, or by taking the free cable car. (☎972 73 20 48. Reception 9am-1pm and 5-8pm. 4- to 25-bed dorms €16-19.75, over 26 €19.55-23.45. All rooms with shower and bathroom. Non HI members €2 extra. Breakfast included. Closed Nov. AmEx/MC/V.) Limited **camping ❶** is available behind the sanctuary complex. (☎972 73 20 30. €2 per person and per tent. Register at the reservations desk before pitching your tent. Advance reservations accepted.) The best budget option for food on weekends is **Finestrelles ❶,** which serves delicious sandwiches for under €5. (Open Sa-Su 8:30am-6pm.) Dish up your own cafeteria fare (€6-10) at the **Autoservei ❷,** under the hotel restaurant. (Open daily 1-3:30pm.)

RENFE trains run to Ribes from Puigcerdà (50min.; 6 per day 9:32am-9:35pm, return 6:12am-7pm; €1.30) and Ripoll (30min.; 7 per day 8:55am-8:53pm, return 7:24am-7:48pm; €2.40). **Buses** also run to Ribes from Ripoll (30min.; M-F 16 per day 7:50am-7:55pm, Sa 10 per day 9:10am-6:10pm, Su 4 per day 9:15am-4:15pm, return M-F 16 per day 7:25am-10:05pm, Sa 10 per day 8:45am-5:45pm, Su 4 per day

9:45am-4:45pm; €1.60). **Taxis** can be reached at ☎616 64 48 84. The Cremallera station in Ribes is next to the train station. To get to the center of town, pass behind the Cremallera station and follow C. Pedrera, which becomes C. St. Quinti. As the road crosses the river, veer right into the Pl. Ajuntament (about 60m). The Ribes **tourist office**, with info on accommodations, transportation, and local sights, is to the left. (☎972 72 77 28. Open Tu-Sa 10am-2pm and 5-8pm, Su 11am-1pm; July and Aug. 10am-2pm and 5-8pm.) Local services in Ribes include: **police** (☎627 41 75 35); **medical services** at **Centro Assisténcia Primaria** (☎970 72 77 09); and the local **Cinema Catalunya**, 19 C. Major (☎972 72 74 69). **Internet** access is at **Televall**, on C. Major, about one block from the tourist office toward the church. (€3 per 1hr. Open M-F 9:30am-2pm and 4-8:30pm, Sa 10am-2pm and 4-8pm, Su 10am-2pm.) The **post office** is on C. St. Quinti between the train station and tourist office. (☎902 19 71 97. Open M-F 8:30am-2:30pm, Sa 9:30am-1pm.) **Postal Code:** 17534.

PUIGCERDÀ   ☎972

Puigcerdá (pooh-chair-DAH; pop. 7000) is blessed with the unbeatable surroundings: wheat-sewn valleys, stunning mountains, and incredible views. Puigcerdà's location near the French and Andorran border also makes it a cheap base for hiking, biking, or skiing in three different countries.

▐ **TRANSPORTATION. RENFE trains** (☎972 88 01 65) run to Barcelona (3½hr.; 6 per day 7:58am-6:54pm, €7.90) and Ripoll (1¼hr., 6 per day 7:58am-6:54pm, €3.05). **Alsina Graells buses** (☎973 35 00 20) go to Barcelona (3hr.; M-F 5:15am and 1:15pm, Sat 7:26am and Su 4:11pm; €15) and La Seu d'Urgell (1hr.; M-F 5 per day 7:30am-5:30pm, Sa-Su 9:15am, 12:15, 7pm; €5.30). **Teisa** (☎972 20 02 75) goes to Girona (3½hr., M-F 6.05am). Buses leave from Pl. Barcelona and then stop outside the train station; buy tickets onboard. Schedules are at Bar Estació, in the station and in Pl. Barcelona. **Taxis** (☎972 88 00 11) are on Pl. Cabrinetty.

▐▐ **ORIENTATION AND PRACTICAL INFORMATION.** Puigcerdà's center is at the top of the hill. The **train station** is at the foot of the western slope. Buses stop at the train station and then Pl. Barcelona, get off at the second stop. To reach **Plaça Ajuntament** from the train station, walk past the stairs in the station's *plaça* until you reach the first flight of stairs between two buildings. To save your legs, take the free **cable car**, which leaves from a station about 50m straight in front of the train station. Look for the elevator, in front of the upper station and to the left, that will take you up to Pl. Ajuntament. From the *plaça*, walk one block on C. Alfons I to **Carrer Major.** Turn left on C. Major to Pl. Santa María. Reach Pl. Barcelona from the end of Pl. Santa María farthest from the bell tower.

If you're traveling outside of the month of August, note that most services and stores shut down on Mondays. The **tourist office** is on C. Querol, 1, off Pl. Ajuntament, to the right. English, Spanish, and French are spoken. (☎972 88 05 42 or 14 15 22. Open Tu-Sa 10am-1pm and 4-7pm.) The regional **Comarcal tourist office** is on the junction of the N-152 and N-160, about a 10min. walk down the highway towards Barcelona from the train station. (☎972 14 06 65. Open M-Sa 9am-1pm and 4-7pm and Su 10am-1pm.) Local services include: **Banco Santander Central Hispano,** on Pl. Cabrinetty, 15, which has a 24hr. **ATM** (open M-F 8:30am-2pm, Sa 8:30am-1pm); **municipal police** on Pl. Ajuntament, 1 (☎972 88 19 72); **Hospital de Puigcerdà** in Pl. Santa María (☎972 88 01 50), behind the bell tower; **public library,** Pg. 10 d'Ábril, 2, next to Eglésia de Sant Domènech, 2nd floor, with free **Internet** access, printing €0.10 per page, and lots of helpful tourist info (☎972 88 03 02; open M, W, F 4-8:30pm and Tu, Th 10am-2pm); **Internet** access at **Locutorio Corami,** Pl. Cabrinetty, 10 (☎972 40 31 40; open daily

10:30am-1:30pm and 3-10:30pm; €2 per 1hr.); and the **post office,** Av. Coronel Molera, 11, 1½ blocks down from Pl. Barcelona (☎972 88 08 14; open M-F 8:30am-2:30pm, Sa 9:30am-1pm). **Postal Code:** 17520.

▟ ▛ **ACCOMMODATIONS AND FOOD.** Most *pensiones* are off Pl. Santa María in the old town. The friendly owner of **Hostal Cerdanya ❷,** C. Ramon Cosp, 7, has basic rooms with all the essentials, including a small TV. (☎972 88 00 10. Singles €20, with bath €25. Cash only.) The main virtue of **Hotel Alfonso ❸,** C. D'Espanya, 5, is its location in the streets just below Pl. Santa Maria. (☎972 88 02 46. Singles €25; doubles €45; triples €60. Cash only.) Just 500m from the RENFE station and 4km from the slopes, **Mare de Déu de les Neus (HI) ❷,** Ctra. de Font Canaleta, is perfect for skiers who don't need the amenities or location of town. In winter a bus runs to the slopes every 30min. (☎972 89 20 12, reservations ☎934 83 83 63. Breakfast included. Sheets and towels €2.25 each. Laundry €3; no detergent. Reserve ahead. Jan.-Mar. dorms €19.75, over 25 €23.45; Apr.-Dec. €16/19.55. €2 extra for non-HI members. MC/V.) **Camping Stel ❶,** 1km from Puigcerdà on the road to Llivia, offers full-service camping with a chalet-style restaurant, bar, and lounge. (☎972 88 23 61. €5.50 per person, site with tent €10.30, with car €20. Electricity €3.75. Open daily June 1- Sept. 30, weekends only during ski season. MC/V.)

For cheap produce, try the weekly **market** at Pl. 10 d'Ábril. (Open Su 6am-2pm.) Get **groceries** at **Bonpreu,** Av. Coronel Molera, 12, diagonally across from the post office. (Open M-Sa 9am-9pm, Su 10am-2:30pm. MC/V.) ▨**Central ❷,** Pl. Santa Maria, 6, serves a good selection of tapas and pizzas. (☎972 88 25 53. Open daily 10am-2:30am. Entrees €8. Free Wi-Fi. MC/V). The rustic and secluded **El Pati de la Tieta ❷,** C. Ferrers, 20, serves delicious fresh homemade pasta (€10-12) and pizzas (€7-11) on an ivy-covered patio. (☎972 88 01 56. Fish and meat entrees €15-22. Call for opening hours. MC/V.) For a cheap, quick bite try **L'Auró ❶,** C. Alfons I, 40, where locals like to play cards on Sunday afternoons. (☎972 88 00 90. From the post office, walk downhill. Sandwiches €3-4; tapas €3-6.)

▟ ▟ **SIGHTS AND SLOPES.** **Cercle Aventura** offers a formidable list of outdoor activities in the summer and winter. (☎902 17 05 93. Open daily 9am-2pm and 4-8pm. Daily activities €30-€90. Half-day bike rental €12; full day €20.)**Ski** in your country of choice (Spain, France, or Andorra) at one of 19 ski areas within a 50km radius. The closest and cheapest on the Spanish side is **Alp 2500,** a conglomerate of **La Molina** (☎972 89 20 31; www.lamolina.cat) and nearby **Masella** (☎972 14 40 00; www.masella.com), which offers the longest run in the Pyrenees at 7km. For cross-country skiing, the closest site is **Guils-Fontanera** (☎972 19 70 47). A little farther out, try **Lles** (☎973 29 30 49) or **Aránsa** (☎973 29 30 51). In the spring and summer, the Puigcerdà area is also popular for **biking;** the tourist office has a map with 17 routes. The town of **Llívia,** a Spanish enclave surrounded by France, makes for the perfect afternoon excursion. Try Ruta 9 (7km, 1½hr., low difficulty) or Ruta 10 (23km with steep ascent, 2½hr., high difficulty). Be sure to stop by Rìgolisa on the way back for a view of the ▨**wheat fields at sunset.** The **Lovers' Path,** around a wheat field off a small trail 200m from the Rigolìsa church (15min. walk from the Pl. Barcelona), is, unsurprisingly, very romantic. **Sports Iris,** Av. de França, 16, rents bikes and skis. (☎972 88 23 98. ½-day €15, full-day €20. Open Tu-Sa 10am-2pm and 4-8pm, Su 10am-2pm, open M in ski season. MC/V.) For horseback riding, call **Pica Sant Mare** (☎972 88 00 07). Try piloting or ballooning at **Globos de Pirineu** (☎972 14 08 52; www.globospi.com) or **Cerdanya Globus** (☎609 83 29 74; www.osanaglobus.com). Other adventure sports such as 4X4 and motorbike rental can be arranged with **La Molina** or **Alp 2500 Viatges** (☎972 89 20 29).

THE PYRENEES

PARC NACIONAL D'AIGÜESTORTES I ESTANY DE SANT MAURICI

Cataluña has only one national park, and its snow-capped peaks and lush valleys are well worth a visit. The **Estany de Sant Maurici,** the park's largest lake, in the east and the winding cascades of the **Ribera de Sant Nicolau** in the west have earned the park the nickname "Aigües Tortes" (Twisted Waters). With more than 200 glacial lakes and over 102,300 acres to explore, the park and its surrounding protected reserves merit at least two days.

◄✻ 🔽 ORIENTATION AND PRACTICAL INFORMATION

The two main gateway towns to the park are **Boí** to the west and **Espot** to the east. To drive from Boí, take the main highway (L-500) north for about 2km, then turn right in to the park. The public **taxi** service (☎ cell 629 20 54 89, office 973 69 63 14) runs from the main plaza in Boí to the last information booth 6km past the official park entrance. (20min.; office open daily July 1-Sept. 15 8am-1pm and 3-7pm. In winter call the cell number for service. Taxis leave when there are groups of four or more and arrangements are made for return service. One-way €4.40, round-trip €8.80.) From the Espot side, drive up the main road that goes through Espot to the park entrance or take a **jeep taxi** into the park, leaving from the plaza next to the park office. (☎973 62 41 05. Taxis run July-Sept. 15 9am-8pm; June 9am-6pm. Call for service in winter.) Espot taxis go to: Estany de Sant Maurici (20min., €4.40); Estany de Ratera (40min., €14.50); Estany d'Amitges (50min., €18); Estany Negre (1hr., €20). There is a four-person minimum.

▐ ACCOMMODATIONS

Since camping is not permitted within park borders, *refugios* (mountain cabins with bunks, a kitchen, and bathrooms) are the only option for wilderness adventurers planning to stay more than one day; mattresses are provided, just make sure to bring your own sheets or a sleeping bag. Reserve several days (or months for July-Aug.) in advance for a spot. Note that not all the *refugios* are open year-round; check their status with the park office. Hot showers are about €2 for 5min.

INSIDE THE PARK

Refugio de Ernest Mallafré (☎973 25 01 18, in winter 973 25 01 05), a 15-minute walk from the information point near the Estany de Sant Maurici. One of the more popular *refugios* because of its proximity to the lake. Be prepared to squeeze in. 28-person capacity. €11.80 per night, €32.30 including dinner and breakfast. Cash only. ❶

Refugio d'Amitges (☎973 25 01 09, in winter *973* 25 00 07; www.amitges.com), near Estany de Amitges, 1½hr. away from Estany St. Maurici. 60-person capacity. €12.50 per night. MC/V. ❶

Refugio de Josep María Blanc (☎973 25 01 08, in winter 934 23 23 45; www.jmblanc.com), recently renovated, near Estany Negre de Peguera. 60-person capacity. €12.50 per night. ❶

Refugio de Estany Llong (☎973 29 95 45, satellite phone 00 882 1650 1000 90), next to Estany Llong, a 30min. walk from the park taxi stop on the Boí side. Spacious *refugio* with 47-person capacity. €6.50 per night. Breakfast €4.50, dinner €13. Lunch available from 2-4pm. Open June 1-Oct. 15 and during *Semana Santa*. Cash only. ❶

Refugio de Ventosa i Calvell (☎973 29 70 90, in winter 934 50 09 66; www.refugiventosa.com), in the northern portion of the park on the Boí side, next to Estany Negre de Boí. 80-person capacity. €12.50 per night. ❶

OUTSIDE THE PARK

These refugios are in the areas surrounding the national park. Though not officially part of the park, they are still somewhat-protected natural reserves.

Refugio de Colomers (☎973 25 30 08, in winter 64 05 92), on the north side of the park by Lac Major de Colomers. 40-person capacity. No showers. €11.40 per night. ❶

Refugio dera Restanca (☎608 03 65 59; www.restanca.com), north of Refugio de Ventosa i Calvell next to Lac dera Restanca. 80-person capacity. ❶

Refugio de Saboredo (☎973 25 30 15, in winter 973 25 24 63), north of Refugio d'Amitges across the Serra de Crabes. No showers. 21-person capacity. ❶

Refugio de Colomina (☎973 25 20 00, in winter 973 68 10 42; www.colomina.casacota.net), south of the park, near the Estany de Mar 50-person capacity. ❶

Refugio del Gerdar (☎973 25 01 70, in winter 973 60 74 40 50; www.refugigerdar.com), north of the park. 25-person capacity. Breakfast, dinner included. €28. ❶

Refugio Pla de la Font (☎619 93 07 71), just north and a little west of Espot near the Coll de Foguerix. 20-person capacity. ❶

FREE REFUGIOS (OUTSIDE THE PARK)

These *refugios* are unguarded and unattended throughout the year. Check with the park office before you leave to make sure they're open.

Refugio Gerber "Mataró," above the Estany Gerber, is unattended and free. It can be reached in about 3hr. from C-28. 16-person capacity. ❶

Refugio Besiberri, just northeast of Besiberri Nord, is unattended and free. It can be reached in about 2hr. from N-230 at La Contesa, 2km south of the Vielha tunnel. 16-person capacity. ❶

⬛ HIKING

Free maps from the park information offices in Espot and Boí list well-defined itineraries, but explorers may want to drop the extra cash to buy the more detailed *Editorial Alpina* map (€9). For more detailed hiking info, contact the park **tourist offices** (Espot ☎973 62 40 36, Boí 69 61 89). Check trail conditions and weather with a park office before heading out.

BOÍ SIDE

⬛ **El Valle de Dellui** (*Ruta* #3; 4½hr., moderate difficulty). A more difficult trail to Estany Llong. Beautiful hike among alpine meadows and glacial lakes. For the best views of both sides of the park, climb the 450m. up to the pass of **Portarró de Espot** (2424m). From the Portarró pass, a side trail leads up the **Pic del Portarró** (2736m), with a 360° panorama (3hr. from parking lot, moderate difficulty due to elevation gain).

Ruta de la Nutria (*Ruta* #1 on tourist office map for Boí side hikes; 1¾hr., low difficulty). Leaves from the main public parking lot and park taxi stop, heading along the **Ribera de Sant Nicolau** and its waterfalls to the last information booth at the Aigüestortes, passing **Estany de Llebreta** on the way.

Camino de Estany Llong (*Ruta* #2; 45min., low difficulty). Heads from the Aigüestortes to **Estany Llong** and its *refugio*.

ESPOT SIDE

⬛ **Hike across the park** (5½hr., moderate difficulty due to length and elevation gain) from **Estany de Sant Maurici to Aigüestortes**. A good day's hike, leading over the Portarró. Stunning views on both sides of the park; make sure to reserve a bed for the night at the Refugio de Mallafré or Refugio de Estany Llong, depending on your direction.

Ruta del Isard (*Ruta* #1 on hiking map from Espot side. 1¼hr., low difficulty.). Well-traveled trail leads from the last parking lot before the park entrance to the **Estany de Sant Maurici**. A pleasant hike through flowery meadows and evergreen forests.

El mirador del Estany de Sant Maurici (*Ruta* #2; 2½hr., low difficulty). Circular route with great view of the lake and valley. Runs around the lake to the **Cascada de Ratera** (waterfall) and the **Estany de Ratera,** before looping back.

To get to the **Estany de Amitges** and the popular **Refugio d'Amitges** (*Ruta* #3; 1¾hr., low difficulty to Estany de Ratera, moderate difficulty continuing on to Amitges), start at the Estany de Sant Maurici and continue up the trail past **Estany de Ratera.**

The **Portarró de Espot** (*Ruta* #4; 2½hr., moderate difficulty due to steepness and elevation gain) is also accessible from Estany de Sant Maurici.

Carros De Foc trail; Famous multi-day, circular route through the entire park. Stops at all the park's *refugios* along the way. Be sure to reserve beds in advance. (Trail open early June to late September, for more information check www.carrosdefoc.com.)

ESPOT
☎973

The gateway to the eastern half of the park and the best point of entrance coming from Barcelona, the tiny town of Espot is comprised mostly of rustic restaurants and quiet accommodations for the weary hiker. Those with cars can park at the last parking lot, just outside the park entrance.

Casa Peret de Peretó ❶ and **Camping Solau ❷** run a joint establishment, offering spacious, sunny rooms with private baths. Solau also features 22 campsites. From the center of town, walk uphill; follow the sign at the arched stone bridge. (☎973 62 40 68. Singles €15; doubles €30; Aug. add €5; campsites €4.40 per person, per tent, and per car. Cash only.) **Residència Casa de Pagés Felip ❷** has comfortable rooms and private baths. From the park office, follow the main road for two blocks and then take a left; the *residencia* is up the hill behind Hotel Roya. (☎973 62 40 93. Laundry available. Singles, doubles, and triples €20 per person.) Located 1km down the park entrance road on the right, **Camping Vora Parc ❶** offers the closest camping to the park, with secluded campsites along the riverbank, and a swimming pool. (☎973 62 41 05; www.voraparc.com. Electricity €4,10. Reception open daily 8·30am 11pm. €5 per person, tent, and car. Children 6-14 €4.50, under 6 free. MC/V.) For fresh food made from local ingredients, try **L'Avet de St. Maurici ❷**, near the Hotel Saurat. (☎973 62 41 62; www.hotelsaurat.com. *Menú del día* with appetizer, main course, dessert, and bottle of wine €15. Open daily 1-11pm, closed Oct. MC/V.) Gourmet diners will appreciate **Restaurant Juquim ❷**, on Pl. Sant Marti, which serves *javalí* (warthog) and shepherd's egg soup on a €15 *menú del día* that includes plenty of wine and a dessert. (☎973 62 40 09. Entrees €6-9. Sandwiches €3-4. Open daily 1-5pm and 8-11pm, in winter closed Su. MC/V.)

Buses stop within 7km of Espot, on highway C-13 at the La Torrassa crossing. The nearest stop from La Seu d'Urgell is at **La Guingueta d'Aneu** (via Sort), about 9km from Espot, with service to Barcelona (5½hr.; June 15-Sept. 30 M-F 7:35am and 1:42pm, Sa-Su 1:42pm; Oct. 1-June 14 M-F 7:35am and 2:32pm, Sa-Su 2:32pm; €26) and Lleida (3hr., M-F 5:33am and 7:36am, Sa 5:33am). From La Guingueta you can either walk to Espot (2½hr.) or call the jeep service. (☎973 62 41 05 or 62 41 32. €10-12 to Espot.) The extremely helpful **park information office** (on the right as you enter Espot) provides brochures on accommodations around Espot, itineraries, maps, and trekking advice. (☎973 62 40 36. Open June-Sept. daily 9am-1pm and 3:30-6:45pm; Oct.-Apr. M-Sa 9am-2pm and 3:30-6pm.) The local **bank,** with 24hr. **ATM,** is **La Caixa,** next to the park office. (Open M-F 11am-2pm.) The **police** can be reached at ☎088; firemen ☎085. There is a **supermarket** on the left across the main bridge uphill from the info office. (☎973 62 40 51, 62 40 23, or 62 40 22. Open M-Sa 9am-1:30pm and 4:30-8:30pm.)

HOW TO EAT IN ARANESE

Weary travelers arriving in the Val D'Aran might be slightly perplexed by the unfamiliar words they suddenly see on street signs. Gone is familiar *castellano* Spanish, or even *catalán*. Instead, the region has its own language, Aranese.

Geographically isolated from the rest of Spain and Catalunya for centuries, the inhabitants of the Val D'Aran developed their own language. Full of "th" and "r" sounds, Aranese has a pleasant, soft inflection.

To avoid any embarrassing encounters with unwanted body parts on your plate, here's a quick survival guide to eating out in Aranese:

If you want to sink your teeth in to some ham, then you're after, *pernilh*. If you're more of a lamb person, ask for *anèth*. If it's chicken you want, *polhastre* will get you your wish. Fish can be ordered in a snap by asking for the day's selection of *peish*.

For a more vegetarian-oriented diet, why not go for a salad with mushrooms, onions, and peppers, an appetizing *anciam damb misharnons e cebas e pebas*. For eggs, go for the tongue-twisting *ueus*.

Finally, for dessert, ice cream sounds so much better as *gelat*. When asked if you'd like some *haragues*, or strawberries, on top, you can turn them down politely with a brief *non*, or nod enthusiastically and simply say *oc*.

BOÍ ☎973

Despite the nearby ski resort in **Taüll**, tiny Boí hasn't lost its country charm. The village's cobblestone streets wind their way through low arches and plazas, and the town's Romanesque church has been awarded UNESCO World Heritage Site status. Boí is the most convenient base for exploring the western half of the park, and its main road is full of stores and accommodations catering to tourists' needs.

Green RCPs *(Residèncias Casa de Pagés)* indicate the local residences offering lodging for travelers. **Casa Rural Marco ❷**, is the best deal in town, with pleasant rooms with shared bathrooms. Make a left as you exit the park info office and follow the *"habitaciones"* sign. (☎973 69 61 61; www.ribagorcarural.com. €15. Cash only.) **Hostal Fondevila ❷**, to the right of the main road through Boí, has well-kept rooms with baths and plenty of social space. (☎ 973 69 60 11. Breakfast €7. Dinner €15. Reception 8am-11pm. Wheelchair accessible. Singles €25; doubles €45; triples €65. MC/V.) **Camping Taüll ❶**, is uphill about 4km on the main road just before Taüll. Inquire at the reception office or call for staff-led hikes (€15-30) in the Parc Nacional or canyoning excursions (€35-50). (☎973 69 61 74. Reception daily 9am-2pm and 5-8pm. Electricity €6. €4.50 per person, per car, and per tent; €4 per child. Bungalows for 2-3 people €60; 4 people €90; 6 people €90-100; 8 people €120; 10 people €150; all with private bathrooms and kitchen, some with shower. Min. stay 5 nights in Aug.; closed Oct. 15-Nov. 30. For guided tour reservations call ☎973 69 61 42.) For a welcome reprieve from typical mountain fare, ▧**Creperie Ca La Pepa ❷**, in the upper end of Boí, has delicious variations on the classic thin pancake. (☎973 69 63 12. On the highway towards Taüll, in the last building out of town on the right. Sweet crepes €4-6; savory €6-9.50. Open Su, W-Sa 1pm-siesta and 8:30pm-closing.) **Restaurante Pey ❸**, Pl. Treijo, 3, has tasty entrees like roasted chicken. (☎973 69 60 36. *Menú* including bottle of wine €13. Open daily 1-4pm and 8-10pm. AmEx/MC/V.) There is a **supermarket** to the left of the village church. (Open M-Sa 9am-1:30pm and 5-8:30pm, Su 9am-1:30pm.)

Public transportation from the east to Boí is inconvenient but possible. From Vielha, take the bus (M-F 1pm) to Boí via Pont de Suert (1¼hr., returns to Vielha between 8:30-9am, €4.21). Taxis run from Boí to the national park and other towns in the area. (☎973 69 63 14 or ☎629 20 54 89, to Aigüestortes €4.40, to Pont de Suert €23.) Boí's park info office is near the bus stop on the *plaça*, inside the old stone building. Look for the signs for *Casa del Parc*. (☎973 69 61 89;

www.parcsdecatalunya.net. Open daily June-Sept. 9am-1pm and 3:30-6:45pm; Oct.-May 9am-2pm and 3:30-6pm.) There is a 24hr. Caixa Catalunya ATM on the main road through town. Reach the Mossos d'Esquadra (*català* police) at ☎973 69 08 15 (located in Pont de Suert). For medical emergencies call ☎973 69 10 85.

VAL D'ARAN

Roughly translated as "valley of the valley," the Val d'Aran is anything but redundant. Cut off from the rest of Spain by some of the Pyrenees' highest mountains. the verdant Val D'Aran has a rich history of self-government and cultural independence, outstanding within a principality as autonomous as Cataluña. Today it contains some of the best skiing in Spain, as well as a multitude of other outdoor options during the rest of the year.

VIELHA   ☎973

The capital and biggest town of Val d'Aran, Vielha (pop. 4500) combines the serenity of its small old quarter with the bustling activity of commercial thoroughfares.

⌨ TRANSPORTATION AND PRACTICAL INFORMATION. Alsina Graells (Lleida office ☎973 27 14 70) runs buses from Vielha to Barcelona (6hr.; M-F 5:30, 9:15am, 1:30pm, Sa 5:30am and 1:30pm, Su 5:59am and 1:30pm; €28-33) via Lleida (3hr.); Boí (1hr.; 1pm, return 8:30am; €4.21); Baqueira via Salardú (20-30min.; 9-13 daily 8am-8:25pm, return 5-13 daily 7:55am-9:40pm; €0.90). For a **taxi,** call ☎973 64 01 95. Rent **bikes** and **skis** at **Bodysport,** Aptos. Sapporo II, down the main road toward Salardú. (☎973 64 04 44. Bikes €15 per 4hr., €20 per day. Ski, boots and poles rental €16 per day, discounts for multiple-day rentals. Ski and snowboard lessons also offered. Open M-Sa 10:30am-1:30pm and 5:30-8:30pm. MC/V.) The **tourist office,** C. Sarriulèra, 10, is one block upriver from Pl. de Gléisa and gives out several free maps and information pamphlets, including hiking and biking maps for the entire valley. (☎973 64 01 10; www.torismearan.org. Open daily 9am-9pm.) **ATMs** pepper the main thoroughfare, Av. Castièro. Local services include: a drop-off **laundromat, Jonerih,** in the Complejo Elurra commercial building, a 10min. walk down Pas d'Arró towards Baqueira, on the left (☎973 64 09 54; €13 90 for up to 4kg; open M-Sa 10am-2pm and 5-8pm); **Mossos d'Esquadra** (local police; ☎973 35 72 85) and **Guardia Civil** (☎973 64 00 05); **Farmàcia Palá,** C. de Sentin, 2, across the river from Pl. de Gléisa about one block down on the left before the traffic rotary (☎973 64 25 85; open daily 9am-10pm); **Hospital Val d'Aran** (☎973 64 00 06); **Internet** access at **Biblioteca Generau de Vielha,** Av. Garona, 33, on the left side of the Riu Garona facing Baqueira, inside the gigantic Palai de Geu (☎973 64 07 68; 30min. free, €0.50 every 15min. thereafter; open M, W, F-Sa 3-9pm, Tu and Th 9am-3pm); the **post office,** C. Sarriuléra, 6, by the tourist office (☎973 64 09 12; open M-F 8:30am-2:30pm, Sa 9:30am-1pm). **Postal Code:** 25530.

⌨ ACCOMMODATIONS AND FOOD. Budget travelers can put their feet up at the elegant **Hotel El Ciervo ❸,** Pl. Sant Orenç, 3. (☎973 64 01 65; fax 64 20 77. Jacuzzi bath €9. Closed June-Sept. Singles €30-45; doubles €45-72. MC/V.) Several other inexpensive *pensiones* fill the end of C. Reiau, off Pg. Libertat. **Pensión Casa Vicenta ❷,** C. Reiau, 3, is a great deal, with quiet rooms, private bathrooms, and a comfy common area. (☎973 64 08 19; casavincenta@teleline.es. Closed parts of May, June, Oct.-Nov. Breakfast €12. Singles €20; doubles €35; triples €45. Cash only.) Another good budget option is **Pensión Busquet ❷,** C. Major, 11. The modest, homey *pensión* has wooden floors and shared bathrooms. (☎973 64 02 38. Singles €22; doubles €33. Cash only.) **◼Eth Breç ❶,** Av. Castièro, 5, beneath Hotel d'Aran, serves incredible pastries (€1-3) and teas and has free **Internet** access. (☎973 64 00 50. Open daily 8:30am-1:30pm and 4-8:30pm. MC/V.) You can buy groceries at **Bona Compra Supermarket,** Pas d'Arro, 46, on the road towards Baqueira. (Open daily 9:30am-1:30pm and 4:30-8:30pm. MC/V.)

◙Ⅺ SIGHTS AND OUTDOOR ACTIVITIES. Vielha welcomes many hikers and skiers to its lively streets. In Pl. d'Era Gléisa, the **Gléisa de Sant Miquéu de Vielha,** a simple 12th- to 13th-century Romanesque church facing the tourist office, contains the famous exquisitely carved statue **Crist de Mijaran.** (Open daily 11am-8pm.) The **Muséu dera Val d'Aran,** C. Mayor, 26, explains the Aranese culture and language. (☎973 64 18 15. Open Tu-Sa 10am-1pm and 5-8pm, Su 11am-2pm. €2, students €1.) **Camins del Pirineu,** Av. Pas d'Arró, 5, is a great place to go for organized outdoor activities. The staff leads hikes and multi-day **treks** into the nearby mountains, including the Parc Nacional Aigüestortes i Estany Sant Maurici (from €20 for a full-day hike) as well as **rafting, horseback-riding, canyoning,** and **paragliding trips.** They also rent **mountain bikes** (half-day €15, full-day €22). Ask about the tough but popular half-day bike trip (€33) to Camino Real/Vielha-Les. (☎973 64 24 44.) **Palai De Geú,** Av. Garona 33, has a swimming pool, sauna, and sizable ice skating rink. (☎973 64 28 64. Ice rink open M-F 5:30-8:45pm, Sa 4:30-9pm, Su noon-2pm and 4:30-8pm. €6.20, skate rental €3.80. Pool and sauna open M-F 8:30am-9:30pm, Sa 11am-2p and 4:30-9pm, Su 11-2pm and 4:30-8pm. €6. MC/V.)

BAQUEIRA-BERET AND SALARDÚ ☎973

Baqueira-Beret is Spain's most fashionable ski resort; currently, about 80 alpine trails and a few cross-country ones wind down the peaks at four different *estaciones.* For skiing info and reservations, contact the **Oficeria de Baqueira-Beret.** (☎973 63 90 00; www.baqueira.es. €39 per day for over 2000 hectares of mountain terrain, including the most off-piste terrain in the Pyrenees.) While in town, don't miss the recently restored 16th-century murals on the ceiling of Salardú's 13th-century **Església de Sant Andreu** and its incredible garden view. During July and August and in the off-season, Baqueira-Beret is mostly shut down.

While Baqueira and Beret themselves don't have much in the way of budget accommodations, a few reasonably priced options can be found along the streets of picturesque **Salardú,** just 4km down the highway from Baqueira. The rooms of **Pensión Montaña ❷,** C. Major, 8, provide a rustic setting with wooden beds. (☎973 64 41 08. Breakfast €3.75. Singles €25-28; doubles €28-45; triples €34-51. Cash only.) The **Auberja Era Garona (HI) ❶,** Ctra. de Vielha, is a 5min. walk up the highway from Salardú towards Baqueira. The enormous Auberja has plenty of dorm rooms and boasts a gigantic patio and a game room/discoteca. (☎973 64 52 71; www.eragarona.com. Breakfast included. Private bath €3. Linen €3. Laundry €3.70. Internet €3.50 per hour. Reception 8am-11:30pm. Quiet policy 10:30pm-8am. €19.55-23.45 per person, under 25 €16-19.75. MC/V.) You haven't really eaten in style until you've hit **Eth Cabilac ❸,** C. Mayor, 14, next door to Pensión Montaña. (☎973 64 42 78. *Menú* €16, special *"Aromas del Valle" menú* €24. Entrees €7-15. Open daily 1-3:30pm and 8:30-10:30pm. AmEx/MC/V.) Just down the street from the church is **El Horno ❶,** C. Sant Andreu, 4, whose pastries you can smell a block away. (☎636 32 58 20. Pastries €0.80-€1.20. Orange juice €1. Open M-Sa 10:30am-1pm and 5-8pm, Su 10:30am-1pm.)

Salardú's **tourist info office** is uphill from the bus stop on and to the right on C. des Estudis. (☎973 64 01 10. Open daily 10am-1pm and 4-7pm. Closed June 15-July 3.) If arriving by public bus, take the stairs next to Refugi Rosta to get to the main *plaça,* on C. Major. Both Baqueira and Salardú have 24hr. **ATMs** scattered throughout town. Salardú has a **pharmacy,** C. Major, 4 (open M and W-F 11:30am-2pm). For **medical emergencies,** call ☎973 64 00 46.

SORT

The town of Sort (pop. 2000), tucked away in the heart of the *català* Pyrenees, is a mecca for lovers of whitewater rafting and canyoning. Sort's relative accessibility makes it a good gateway to the nearby Parc Nacional d'Aigüestortes i Estany de Sant Maurici in the summer and to various ski resorts in the area in winter. The town's gushing river is regulated to improve rafting conditions, and numerous companies offer excursions on its waters. **Alta Ruta,** Av. de la Pallars, 15, leads guided rafting, climbing, canyoning, horseback riding, and mountain biking trips. (☎973 62 08 09; www.altaruta.com. Rafting €20-69 depending on length. Canyoning €32-60.) A popular nearby ski resort is **Port Ainé,** accessible by taxi from the Rialp bus stop (10min. from Sort). It features 44km of trails and €30 per day lift passes (☎902 19 01 92; www.port-aine.com. Trails open Dec.-Apr.) Backcountry and cross-country skiers can find a mix of steep and flat trails at **Tavascan,** accessible from the Llavorsí bus stop. (☎973 62 30 79. Trails open Dec.-Mar. €15 per day, €20 holidays, €8.50 per day cross-country only.)

Sort's popularity can make cheap lodging hard to come by; reserve well in advance for weekends in June and during July and August. A good budget option is the **Can Josep ❸,** Ctr. La Seu d'Urgell, 12, a friendly *residencia* across the river from town on the road to La Seu. (☎973 62 01 76. Breakfast included. Singles €29; doubles €52; triples €61. MC/V.) Another is **Hospedatge Les Collades ❷,** C. Major, 5, which has new hotel-style rooms with adjoining bathrooms. (☎973 62 11 80. Singles €20; doubles €40. MC/V) Camping is available at **Noguera Pallaresa ❶,** on Av. de la Generalitat on the way out of town, but reservations are highly recommended (☎973 62 08 20). Sort is home to a string of bars and cafes along Av. del Pallars. **▨Rock Cafe Escalarre ❷,** Av. del Pallars, 39, has a great selection of hamburgers, pizzas, and pastas named after musicians. (☎973 62 06 94. Occasional live music. Open Tu-Su 10-1am. MC/V.) If you prefer to prepare your own meals, there is a **supermarket,** Can Kiko, on C. Major, 15 (open M-Sa 10am-2pm and 5-8pm).

To get to La Seu d'Urgell, call and reserve a spot on the shuttle (☎689 49 57 77 for the morning bus or 610 47 71 57 for the afternoon bus; M-F 7:45am and 5:30pm, Sa 7:45am; €3.20). **Alsina Graells** buses leave Barcelona for Sort. (4½-5hr.; Oct. 1- June 14 7:30am, 2:30pm; June 15-Sept. 31 7:30am. Return Oct.10-June 14 M-F 8:03am and 2:55pm, Sa-Su 2:55pm; June 15-Sept. 31 M-F 8:03am and 2:10pm, Sa-Su 2:10pm.) The cheapest option to the Parc Nacional d'Aigüestortes i Estany de Sant Maurici is the **Alsina Graells** bus towards Esterri d'Aneu. Get off at the turnoff to Espot, at the covered La Crossarra gas station (M-F 12:36, 2:51pm, Sa-Su 12:36pm, in summer daily also 7:05pm; €2.75). From there, you can call a jeep taxi (☎973 62 41 05, 9am-6pm, €10). Buses to Sort deliver travelers to the junction between Av. de la Verge Montserrat and Av. Comtes del Pallars. Both feed into Av. de la Generalitat, which follows the river. Most shops and services are on Av. de Pallars or Generalitat. The town's **tourist office,** Av. Comtes del Pallars, 2, is to your left up Av. del Pallars with your back to the bus station. (☎973 62 10 02. Open July-Sept. 5 M-Sa 9am-8pm, rest of year M-Sa 9am-3pm). Other services include **emergency medical care** (☎061 or ☎973 62 01 63); police, **Mossos d'esquadra** (☎088). There are several 24hr. **ATMs** throughout town. Caixa Catalunya has one on Pl. Major, above the tourist office. The **post office** is at the corner of C. del Doctor Muxi i Monroset and Av. de la Diputacio, across from the Hotel Pessets. (☎902 19 21 97. Open M-F 8:30am-2:30pm, Sa 9:10am-1pm.) **Postal Code:** 25560.

LA SEU D'URGELL   ☎973

La Seu (pop. 12,000), a peaceful town nestled between two rivers, was an important political center in the Middle Ages and still retains its religious significance.

More recently, it hosted the 1992 Olympic kayak and canoe events. La Seu also serves as Spain's gateway to the tiny Pyrenean country of Andorra, just a few kilometers to the north. Budget accommodations, a relaxed atmosphere, and a very pleasant series of parks make this a good base for exploring the region.

TRANSPORTATION. The **bus station** (☎973 35 00 20) is located on Av. de J. Garriga i Massó at the end of town nearest to Andorra, about 400m from the town center. To get to the main plaza from the bus station, walk left down Av. de J. Garriga i Massó until you come to the traffic rotary at the intersection with Av. de Pau Claris, where both become C. De Sant Ot. Continue two blocks to the main plaza, Pl. de Catalunya. (Bus information open M-F 9am-1pm and 3-7pm, Sa 9am-12:15pm and 3-7pm, Su 3-7pm.) **Buses** run to: Andorra la Vella (40min.; M-Sa hourly 7am-8pm, Su 5 per day 7:45am-6:30pm; €2.65); Barcelona (3hr., 9 per day 6:30am-7:40pm, €20.50); Lleida (2½hr.; M-Sa 6am and 4:20pm, Su 9am and 4:20pm; €14.15); Puigcerdà (1hr., M-F 7:30, 9:15am, 12:15, and 7pm, Sa-Su 9:15am, 12:15, and 7pm, €5.60.) A shuttle runs to Sort (1½hr., 10:30am and 7:30pm, €3.20; call in advance to reserve, morning van ☎689 49 57 77, afternoon van ☎610 47 71 57).

ORIENTATION AND PRACTICAL INFORMATION. The main road in La Seu is **Avinguda de Pau Claris,** which runs north to the highway toward Andorra and becomes C. de Sant Ot to the south, leading to the main plaza **Passeig de Joan Brudieu** and to Parc Olímpic del Segre. The historic district is to the left of Av. de Pau Claris facing the Passeig, the new center of town. The main **tourist office,** Av. de les Valls d'Andorra, 33, is inconveniently located at the very edge of town, just before the start of the highway to Andorra; ask your bus driver to drop you off here so you don't have to back-track uphill from the bus station. From the center of town, head up Av. de Pau Claris, veering left at the fork onto Av. de les Valls d'Andorra. (☎973 35 15 11; www.turismeseu.com for info on accommodations and outdoor activities. Open July-Aug. M-Sa 9am-8pm, Su 10am-2pm; Sept.-June daily 10am-2pm and 4-6pm.) More convenient (but less helpful) guidance is available at the **Oficina del Consel Comarcal,** Pg. Joan Brudieu, 15 (☎ 973 35 31 12. Wheelchair accessible. Open M-F 10am-2pm and 5-8pm, Sa 11am-2pm and 5-8pm.) They also have **Internet** access downstairs (first 15min. free, €0.40 every 30min. thereafter, €0.30 for students). Local services include: **banks** and 24hr. **ATMs** lining C. de Sant Ot; **municipal police** (☎973 35 04 26); **Mossos d'Esquadra** (emergencies ☎088, non-emergencies 973 36 00 73); and the **hospital** on C. de Sant Ot, beyond the Pg. Brudieu (☎973 35 00 50). The **post office** is on C. de Josep Zulueta at Av. del Salória. (☎973 35 07 24. Open M-F 8:30am-2:30pm, Sa 9:30am-1pm.) **Postal Code:** 25700.

ACCOMMODATIONS AND FOOD. Conveniently located near the center of town, the **Alberg Centre Residencial i de Serveis ❶,** C. Sant Joan de La Salle, 51, on the corner of C. Zulueta, was originally built to house Olympians in 1992. Today, it houses both a school and an *alberg* (youth hostel) in the same building. Clean dorm-style setup with larger-than-usual rooms and hallway bathrooms. (☎973 35 38 16. Breakfast €2; full board €13. Sept.-June dorms €14; July-Aug. €16. Cash only.) The **Alberg de la Seu d'Urgell (HI) ❷,** also known as La Valira, at C. Joaquim Viola, 57, offers a good deal for dorm rooms. Head toward town from the bus station on Av. de J. Garriga Massó, and take a right at the traffic rotary. (☎973 35 38 97. Dorms €14.85-€17.30. €2 extra for non HI members. Cash only.)

La Seu has plenty of fairly priced eating options, most of them concentrated around C. de Sant Ot and Pg. Brudieu. The homey family **Restaurant Conigó ❷,** C. De Sant Ot, 3, serves excellent sandwiches (€3-4), pizzas (€4-6), and fresh pastas (€7-8). (☎973 35 10 43. Open daily 7am-1am. MC/V.) The popular **Bar El Piano ❶,**

Pl. de la Carme, dominates local nightlife. It serves Spanish bar food in a cheerful, smoky atmosphere. (☎973 35 41 04. Live music Th. Open 9am-1am, F later. Cash only.) For a cutting-edge dining experience, head to **Miscela ❸**, Av. Claris, 24, which has ornately decorated dishes and a creative menu. Try some homemade pasta (€10) with the blissfully flavorful *porcini ceps* sauce, and finish it off with the absurdly rich hot chocolate souffle (€5.75). Gluten-free and vegetarian options are available. (☎973 35 46 20. Open daily 1-3:45pm and 9-10:45pm. MC/V.) Enjoy a hearty dinner at the tavern-style dining room at **Mesón Teo ❸**, Av. de Pau Claris, 38, where medieval weapons line the walls. (☎973 35 10 29. *Menú* €12. Entrees €6-16. Open M-Th 1-4pm and 8:30-10:30pm, F-Sa 1-4pm and 8:30-11:30pm. MC/V.)

◪ SIGHTS. The 12th-century **Catedral d'Urgell** is the only preserved Romanesque cathedral in Cataluña. The cloister has a meditative atmosphere aided by projectors and dramatic music. The oldest piece in the connected **Museu Diocesá d'Urgell** is a set of 10th-century illustrations of the apocalypse known as *Beatus*. (☎973 35 32 42. Reception desk has a very informative pamphlet. Cathedral and museum open June-Sept. M-Sa 10am-1pm and 4-7pm, Su 10am-1pm; Oct.-May daily 10am-1pm, cathedral only 4-6pm. €3, under 25 €2.50.) Inquire at the tourist office for details on other workshops, including a number of popular **cheese tours** (☎973 36 05 52). Die-hard whitewater fans and novices alike converge on the **◪Parc Olímpic del Segre** (open June-Sept. 8am-8pm, Oct.-May 8am-7pm), which was constructed to host the canoe and kayak events for the 1992 Barcelona Olympic Games and now serves as a pleasant riverside park. (Trips €11-35 per person per hour, including canoe or kayak, equipment, and drinking water; classes €32 per hour.) The park also rents mountain bikes. (☎973 36 00 92; www.parcolimpic.com. Open M-F 10am-7pm, Sa 10am 2pm and 4-7pm, Su 10am-2pm. ½-day €17.50, full-day €24.)

ANDORRA

The tiny Principat d'Andorra (pop. 80,000) bills itself as *El País dels Pirineus*, the country of the Pyrenees. The natural beauty of its towering and dramatic mountainous surroundings is closely rivaled by the artificial glitz, busy highways, and gaudy billboards of its flashy capital, Andorra la Vella. According to legend, Charlemagne founded Andorra in AD 784 as a reward to the valley's inhabitants for having led his army against the Moors. For the next 12 centuries, the country was the rope in a four-sided tug-of-war between the Spanish counts of Urgell, the French counts of Foix, the Spanish bishop of Urgell, and the king of France. Not until 1990 did the country create a commission to draft a democratic constitution, adopted on March 14, 1993. Upon entering Andorra, tourists say goodbye to the quiet sleepy towns of the Spanish Pyrenees, to the siesta, and to "mañana"; Andorra is one hundred percent shopping-filled capitalist action.

⬛ TRANSPORTATION

The only way to get to Andorra is by car or bus. The train from Spain goes as far as Puigcerdà, and buses connect to Andorra through the town of La Seu d'Urgell. The gateway from France is Pas de la Casa (Andorra). Take the train to Hospital-et-pres-l'Andorre or La Tour de Carol (or Ax-les-Thermes in summer), and then the bus to Andorra. Upon exiting Andorra, you may be required to stop at customs for a brief search. **Driving** in Andorra la Vella is an adventure for some, a nightmare for others. Road signs are confusing, and navigating the crowded, twisting streets can prove a maddening chore for the most patient driver.

International Buses: Catch international buses to destinations other than La Seu d'Urgell at either of the two offices (separated by a fence) at **Estació Central d'Autobusos,** C. Bonaventura Riberaygua, in **Andorra la Vella. Autocars Julia\Nadal** (☎902 40 50 40, www.autocaresjulia.es) goes to **Madrid** (9hr.; W and Su 1:30pm, F 10pm; return Th and F 10pm, Tu 10:30am; €50) and **Barcelona** (3hr.; daily 8 per day, 6:15am-10:15pm; return daily 8 per day 6:15am-11:15pm, also stops at Barcelona Airport; €23.50). **Novatel** (☎376 80 37 89) has service to **Barcelona** (3hr.; daily 5, 8, 10am, 12:30, and 3:15pm; €26). **Alsina Graells** has buses to downtown **Barcelona** (3½hr., daily 9 per day 6am-7:15pm, €26). **La Seu d'Urgell** is accessible hourly on a **La Hispano-Andorra** bus (☎376 82 13 72, www.andorrabus.com; 30min.; M-Sa hourly 8am-9pm, Su 5 per day 8:15am-7:15pm; €2.65) departing from Pl. de la Rotonda, across from the tourist office, also stops in Pl. Giullemó.

Intercity Buses: Efficient intercity buses connect the villages along the 3 major highways that converge in Andorra la Vella. The tourist office provides a very helpful bus schedule. Since most towns are only 10min. apart, the outlying cities can be seen in a day via public transportation (€0.70-1.70).

ANDORRA LA VELLA ☎ 376

Andorra la Vella (pop. 20,760), the capital, is anything but *vella* (old). Remnants of the city's past, however, make for quirky contrasts to shiny new electronics and sporting goods stores. After doing a little shopping, escape to the countryside for a walk in the mountains.

■ 🛈 **ORIENTATION AND PRACTICAL INFORMATION.** Coming from Spain, visitors first pass through Sant Julía de Lòria and then reach the tiny road, Santa Coloma, that runs directly into Andorra la Vella. The main thoroughfare, **Avinguda Santa Coloma,** becomes **Avinguda Príncep Benlloch** several blocks into the city, becoming **Avinguda Meritxell** at Pl. Príncep Benlloch before continuing on as the highway to the northeast. There are several **tourist offices** scattered throughout Andorra la Vella, including one at the junction of C. Dr. Vilanova and C. Prat de la Creu and the Oficina d'Informacio i Turisme located on the Pl. de la Rotonda (☎376 82 71 17; open Sept. 10-June 30 M-F 9am-1pm and 3-7pm, Sa 9am-1pm and 3-

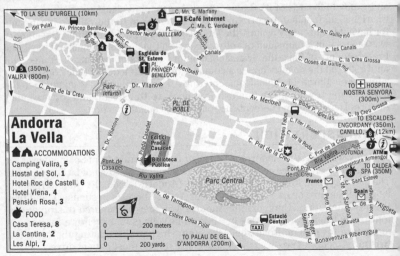

Andorra La Vella

🏠🏠 ACCOMMODATIONS
Camping Valira, **5**
Hostal del Sol, **1**
Hotel Roc de Castell, **6**
Hotel Viena, **4**
Pensión Rosa, **3**

🍴 FOOD
Casa Teresa, **8**
La Cantina, **2**
Les Alpi, **7**

8pm, Su 8am-1pm, July 1st-Sept. 9 M-Sa 9am-9pm, Su 9am-7pm). Andorra La Vella connects with the next town, Escaldes, but if you can't walk between them, the information office there will direct you to bus stops. At any one of the tourist offices, the multilingual staff offers free *Sports Activities* and *Hotels i Restaurants* guides. Local services include: 24hr. **ATMs** located directly across from the info office on Pl. Rotonda; **weather and ski conditions** from **Ski Andorra** (☎376 80 52 00); **taxi** service (☎376 86 30 00 or 376 82 80 00); **medical emergency** (☎116); **police** (emergencies ☎110, non-emergencies 376 87 20 00); and **Hospital Nostra Senyora de Meritxell** (☎376 87 10 00). **Internet** access is available at the public **library,** in the Edifici Prada Casadet on the C. Prat de Creu and C. Prada Casadet (☎376 82 87 50; open M-F 10am-8:30pm, Sa 10am-1pm; July-Aug. M-F 8:30am-7pm; €1.50 per 1hr.) and **E-Cafe,** corner of C. Marfany and C. la Llacuna, walk C. Marfany from the Pl. Guillemó (open daily 8am-12:30am; €1.20 per 30min.). **Laundry** at **Tintoreria Cris** on Mn. Cinto Verdaguer, 5 (☎376 82 37 05; open M-F 9:30am-1:30pm and 4-8pm; €12.75 for up to 6kg). The **Spanish post office** is at C. Joan Maragall, 10. (☎376 82 02 57. Lista de Correos upstairs. Open M-F 8:30am-2:30pm, Sa 9:30am-1pm.)

> **PHONE CALLS FROM ANDORRA.** Collect calls to most countries—including the US—are not possible. Buy an STA (Servei Telefonica Andorra) *teletarjecta* (telecard) at the tourist office for calls within the country (€3-6). Ask for an international calling card for calls out of the country, since the domestic STA card will only get you a few minutes. To call Andorra from Spain or France, you must dial the international code (☎376) first. For directory assistance, dial ☎111 or 119 (international).

ACCOMMODATIONS AND FOOD. At the lower end of the budget, the quiet **Pensión Rosa ❷,** Antic C. Major 18, offers well-kept rooms with shared bathrooms. (☎376 82 18 10. Breakfast €3. Singles €17.68; doubles €29.12; triples €44; quads €58. MC/V.) The basic **Hostal del Sol ❷,** Pl. Guillemó, 3, provides small, simple rooms with big, well-scrubbed hall baths. (☎376 82 37 01. Singles €15.60-20; doubles €30.16. MC/V.) Swanky **Hotel Viena ❸,** C. de la Vall, 32, has an open, friendly ground floor lounge with a bar, pool table, and foosball table beneath a television. Their big rooms include bathroom, shower, TV, telephone, and a small porch. (☎376 82 92 33; Internet access €0.50 per 20min. Singles €30; doubles €35; triples €43. AmEx/MC/V.) You don't exactly rough it at shaded **Camping Valira ❶,** Av. de Salou, behind the Estadi Comunal d'Andorra la Vella, which has satellite TV, showers, a restaurant, laundry, and a pool. (☎376 72 23 84; www.campvalira.com. Wheelchair accessible. €5 per person, per tent, and per car.)

Casa Teresa ❸, C. Bonaventura Armengol, 11, has phenomenal spaghetti (€6.75) and a variety of delicious dishes, including large, creative pizzas (€6-7) and fish and meat entrees (€9-17). (☎376 82 64 76. *Menú* €9. Open daily 8am-10pm. Kitchen open 12:30-3:30pm and 8-11pm. Bar open 8am-10pm. MC/V.) **Les Alpi ❸,** is as convenient and urban as it gets. (☎376 80 81 00. Open daily noon-3:30pm and 8-10:30pm. *Catalana* meat dishes €8-18. MC/V.) For herbivores itching to try paella, **La Cantina ❷,** on Pl. Gulliermó, has a delicious vegetarian version (€10.50), and also serves pastas and pizzas (€7-8). (☎376 82 30 65. MC/V.)

SIGHTS. Canillo's colossal **Palau de Gel d'Andorra,** on Cta. General, is a recreational complex with swimming pool, ice-skating rink ("ice disco" by night), gym, tennis, and squash courts. Brace yourself on Fridays for ■ice-rink go-carts. (☎376 80 08 40. €5.90-8.70 for each activity, or €13.30 for 1 day. Go-carts €14. Equipment rental €3.30-4.50. Open daily 10am-10:30pm; each facility has its own hours.)

Nowhere is the uniquely Andorran contrast of old and new better on display than at the **Santuari de Meritxell**, perched on the hills 2km from Canillo toward Andorra la Vella. The original Romanesque chapel was completely remodeled in the 18th century, only to burn down in 1972. The new chapel, designed by *català* architect Ricardo Bofill, is an ultra-modern building that strives to incorporate disparate elements of Andorra's past. To get there, either ask the bus driver to be let off at the entrance on the way to Canillo, about 200m from the actual *santuari*, or hike over from Canillo (25min.). Walk along the highway toward Andorra until you see the monastery on the hills; from there either hike up the hill from the footpath or continue on the paved road 500m ahead. (☎376 85 12 53. Open M and W-Su 9am-1pm and 3-6pm. Inquire about summer guided tours. Free.)

⚑⚑ HIKING AND THE OUTDOORS. An extensive network of hiking trails traverses Andorra. The free, multilingual, and extremely helpful tourist office brochure *Mountain Activities* includes 41 hiking itineraries, 9 mountain biking itineraries, and even several rock-climbing routes, as well as bike rental services and cabin and refuge locations. Most trailheads can be accessed using Andorra's public transportation system. La Massana is home to Andorra's tallest peak, **Pic Alt de la Coma Pedrosa** (2942m). For organized hiking trips, try the **La Rabassa Sports and Nature Center** (☎376 32 38 68; www.campdeneudelarabassa.ad), in the parish of Sant Julía de Lòria. In addition to *refugio*-style accommodations, the center has mountain biking, guided hikes, horseback riding, and field sports. Vertical enthusiasts may want to try **Bosc Aventura's** treetop activities (☎376 385 077) or **via ferrade**, a series of metal ladders, cables, and bridges that allow novices to accomplish traverses and climbs of dramatic mountain terrain. The **tourist office** in Canillo (☎376 75 36 00) and outfitters like **Natura I Aventura** (☎376 349 542) offer guided trips (€30-40). The same outfitters also offer guided **descents of river canyons.**

⛷ SKIING. With five outstanding resorts, Andorra offers skiing opportunities galore from December to April; lift ticket prices range from €38-55. **Ski Andorra** provides a 5-day pass to all sites (€157-168). Vall Nord is composed of resorts: **Pal** (☎376 878 000), 10km from La Massana, is accessible by bus from La Massana (5 per day; 8:45am-7:45pm, return 9:10am-5:05pm; €1) and nearby Arinsal (☎376 73 70 20), which is also accessible from Andorra la Vella by bus (every hour; 8:15am-8:45pm, return 8:25am-8:45pm; €1). On the French border, **Grand Valire** (☎376 80 10 60) is the valley's highest resort at 2050m, with 53 slopes, more than any other resort, totaling 100km. It is accessible by bus from Andorra la Vella (4 per day 9am-6:45pm, return 9:30am-7:45pm; €4.70). The more horizontal **La Rabassa** (☎376 75 97 98 or 38 75 58) is Andorra's only cross-country ski resort. If you want someone else to propel you, try taking the ▨**sled dogs.** More recently added winter activities include snowshoeing, snowmobiling, and heli-tours. Andorra's tourist office publishes a winter edition of *Ski Andorra*, a guide of all things related to skiing in the valley. Call **SKI Andorra** (☎376 80 52 00; www.skiandorra.ad) or the tourist offices for info on reservations, prices, and transportation.

ARAGONESE PYRENEES

Aragón claims 90km of Pyrenean grandeur, keted by the Río Gallego in the west, and the Río Nobuera in the east. This fertile region birthed the Kingdom of Aragón in the mid 9th century and remained unconquered through the tempestuous Middle Ages. The most popular entry point for the Aragonese Pyrenees is Jaca, the former military capital of the medieval kingdom of Aragón and a stop in the historic Camino de Santiago. From the nearby towns of Aínsa and Torla, most travelers head to the deep green meadows and pure white snowfields of the Parque Nacional de Ordesa. In the east, Benasque draws serious mountaineers to the highest peaks in the Pyrenees, while the western valleys of Ansó and Hecho are peaceful farm valleys ideal for less-strenuous mountain rambling or scenic bicycle tours. In summer, make sure to stop by the **Pirineos Sur** international cultural festival, which features a host of concerts, markets, and foods from all over the world. (☎974 49 01 96; www.pirineos-sur.com.)

JACA   ☎974

Many centuries ago, the town of Jaca (pop. 14,000) served as a refuge for weary pilgrims crossing the Pyrenees on the Camino de Santiago. Today, it serves as a perfect base for excursions to the Camino de Santiago and Pyrenees in summer and to the nearby ski resorts in winter.

▊ TRANSPORTATION. RENFE trains leave from the station, 1km from the *ciudadela* (fortress) at the end of Av. Juan XXIII (☎902 24 02 02; open daily 9am-1pm and 4-8pm) to Zaragoza (3¼hr.; 3 per day 7:45am, 3:45 and 6:40pm; €10.25-13.20) via Huesca (2hr., €6.25-7.30). **Alosa buses** (☎902 21 07 00; www.alosa.es) run to Pamplona (2¼hr.; M-F 8:15am and 1:45pm, Sa 8:15am, Su 11am and 7pm; €6.61), Sabiñánigo (20min., 6-9 per day 8:15am-7:15pm, €1.35), and Zaragoza (2hr., 6-9 per day 8:15am-7:15pm, €11.78). From Sabiñánigo, **Empresa Hudebus** (☎974 21 32 77) goes to Torla (1hr.; July-Aug. 11am and 6:30pm, Sept.-June 11am; €2.85), near Ordesa and Aínsa. **Josefa Escartín buses** (☎974 36 05 08) go to Ansó (1½hr., M-Sa 6:30pm, €3.37) via Hecho (45min., €2.67) and Siresa (1hr., €2.80). Get a **taxi** (☎974 36 28 48 or 659 644 332) on the Plaza Cortes de Aragón, where Av. Regimiento Galicia becomes Primer Viernes de Mayo.

▊ ORIENTATION. The two major sites of interest in Jaca are the massive **ciudadela** and the **parte viejo**, divided by **Avenida Regimiento Galicia**, which turns into **Primer Viernes de Mayo.** Buses drop passengers on Av. Jacetania, at the northern edge of the *parte viejo.* A city bus runs every hour from the **train station** to the center of town.

▊ PRACTICAL INFORMATION. The staff at the **tourist office,** Plaza de San Pedro 11-13, near the cathedral, speak English and will give you more tourist literature than you can carry. (☎974 36 00 98; www.jaca.es. Open July-Aug. M-Sa 9am-9pm, Su 9am-3pm; Sept.-June 9am-1:30pm and 4:30-7:30pm.) **Alcorce Aventura,** Av. Regimiento de Galicia, 1, organizes hiking, rock climbing, canyoning, and rafting trips. (☎974 35 64 37; www.alcorceaventura.com. Guided hiking trips from €21 per day; rafting from €36.50, 3-4 person min. Bike rentals €15 per ½-day, €25 per full day. Also has ski and snowboard rentals. Open daily June-Sept. 10am-1:30pm and 5-8:30pm; Oct.-May M-Sa 10am-1:30pm. MC/V.) For ski conditions, call **Teléfono Blanco** (☎976 20 11 12) or the tourist office. Local services include: **Banco IberCaja,** Av. Jacetania 22-24, across Pl. Biscos from the bus station (open Oct.-Apr. M-W and F 8:15am-2:30pm, Th 8:15am-1:45pm and 5:15-7:30pm; May-Sept. M-F 8:15am-2:30pm) with a **24hr. ATM; police,** C. Mayor, 24 (☎974 35 57 58); **medical services** at **Centro de Salud,** Pl. de la Constitución, 6 (☎974 36 07 95); **Internet** access at **Ciber Civa,** on Av. Regimiento de Galicia (☎974 35 67 75. €2 per hour. Open M-Sa 11am-1:30pm and 5-11pm, Su 5:30-10pm); **public library** at **Biblioteca Municipal,** C. Levante 4 (☎974 35 55 76; open M 5-9pm, Tu-F 11am-1pm and 5-9pm, Sa 10:30am-1:30pm; July-Sept. also M 11am-1pm) has **Internet** access, first 30min. free, also has free Wi-Fi; and the **post office,** C. Pirineos, 8 (☎974 35 58 86; open M-F 8:30am-2:30pm, Sa 9:30am-1pm). **Postal Code:** 22700.

ACCOMMODATIONS AND FOOD. Jaca's hostels and *pensiones* cluster around C. Mayor and the cathedral. The funky ■La Casa del Arco ❷, C. San Nicolás, 7, provides cozy rooms in an old stone house. (☎974 36 44 48. Reserve ahead. Breakfast €4. Singles with shared bath €18-20; doubles with private bath €50. Cash only.) A more conventional budget option is the quiet **Hostal Alpina ❷**, C. Mayor 57, with basic, spacious rooms with bathrooms. (☎974 36 07 00. Reception at the nearby Hotel La Paz, C. Mayor 41. Closed Nov. Doubles €40-44. MC/V.) Another budget option is the **Hostal Somport ❸**, C. Echagaray, 11, which has doubles with shared bathrooms. (☎974 36 34 10. Singles €25-35; doubles €45-50. MC/V.) **Hotel Bucardo ❸**, Av. de Francia, 13, has bright, large rooms with private baths and a relaxing common room. From the bus station, walk along Av. Jacetania toward the *ciudadela* (fortress), and turn right onto Av. de Francia. (☎974 36 01 00; www.lospirineos.com/bucardo. Breakfast included. Singles €29-40; doubles €43-53.60; triples €53.20-63.80. AmEx/MC/V.) To reach the old-fashioned, slightly dim rooms of **Hostal Paris ❸**, C. San Pedro, 5, from the bus station, head toward the cathedral. (☎974 36 10 20; www.jaca.com/hostalparis. Breakfast €2.75. Reception open 7am-midnight. Closed May and Nov. Singles €25; doubles €38; triples €52. July 15-Sept. 15 and *Semana Santa* €25/35. MC/V.)

Bocadillos fill the menus on Av. Primer Viernes de Mayo, and locals fill the cafes on Pl. de la Catedral. ■Restaurante Vegetariano El Arco ❶, C. San Nicolás, 74, on the second floor of the Casa del Arco, serves a refreshingly original all-vegetarian *menú* (€11). Try the *cebolla asada con pisto y roquefort* (roasted onions with mixed vegetables in Roquefort sauce). (Open M-Sa 1-3pm and 8:30-11:30pm. Appetizers €5. Entrees €7. Cash only.) A good lunch option is the popular and busy **Restaurante Asador Biarritz ❸**, Av. Primer Viernes de Mayo, 12, which has a satisfying, excellent lunch *menú* (€10.75). (☎974 36 16 32. Open daily 1-3:45pm and 8-11:30pm. AmEx/MC/V.) **Supermercado ALVI**, C. Correos, 9, sells groceries. (Open M-Sa 9:30am-2pm and 5:30-8:30pm. MC/V.)

SIGHTS AND FESTIVALS. The whole western side of Jaca is dominated by the pentagonal **ciudadela** (fortress), a military fortification from the 16th century constructed during the reign of Felipe II. Though today it is a tourist attraction, the complex is still the site of the Command and Headquarters of the 64th Galicia High Mountain Regiment, the oldest regiment in the Spanish military. The park is free and open at all times, but to get inside the *ciudadela*, you must take a guided tour. (☎974 36 30 18. Open Tu-Su 11am-2pm and 5-8pm. Group reservations available. €10, students €8, price includes entry to military miniatures museum.) A number of sights recall Jaca's medieval grandeur, notably the **Catedral de Jaca**, begun in the 11th century and one of the first Romanesque buildings of its kind in Spain. The adjoining **Museo Diocesano** houses one of the most important collections of medieval art in Europe. (Pl. de la Catedral, across the street from the bus station. Museum currently undergoing renovations; cathedral open daily 8am-1:30pm and 4-8pm. Group visits M-F 9:30-10am, noon-1:30pm, 4-6:30pm; Su 4-6:30pm.) If you arrive in Jaca during the spring and summer months, you're almost certain to stumble across a fiesta of some sort. The biggest celebrations are the **Primer Viernes de Mayo**, held on the first Friday in May to celebrate the 8th century triumph of the Christian army over the Moors, and the week-long **Fiestas de Santa Orosia y San Pedro**, held annually from the June 24-29 in honor of the city's patron saints. During the festival, religious ceremonies, cultural performances, and varied musical concerts take place throughout the day and late in to the night.

DAYTRIP FROM JACA: ■MONASTERIO DE SAN JUAN DE LA PEÑA. It's hard to imagine walking to the secluded, spectacular **Monasterio de San Juan de la**

Peña today, let alone 10 centuries ago when construction began. The monastery is purposefully difficult to reach; an alleged Holy Grail, now stored in the cathedral at Valencia, was concealed here for three centuries. Determined hermits hid the *monasterio viejo* (old monastery), high in a canyon 22km from Jaca and maintained such extreme isolation that both the church and the chalice were kept safe from invading Moors over the centuries. The 17th-century *monasterio alto* (upper monastery) sits 1.5km uphill; it is currently undergoing renovations and will reopen as the **Centro de Interpretación de los Reyes de Aragón. (☎974 35 51 19;** www.monasteriosanjuan.com. Open June 1-July 14 10am-2pm and 3-8pm; July 15-Aug. 31 daily 10am-8pm; Sept.-Oct. 10am-2pm and 3:30-7pm; Nov.-March 15 Tu-Su 11am-2pm and 3:30-6pm; March 16-May 31 daily 10am-2pm and 3:30-7pm. €10, €8 for students, includes entrance to church in Santa Cruz de la Seró and parking lot shuttle.) **Taxis (☎**974 36 28 48 or 609 34 44 66) will make the journey for €25 each way, or will add €3 for every 15 minutes they wait for you. In July or August, park at the lot above the monastery; a shuttle transports visitors every 30min. from the *monasterio alto* to the *monasterio viejo* (1.5km). The adventurous can catch a **bus** from Jaca to Pamplona and ask to be dropped at the intersection with the monastery road (CN 240, km 295). From there, it's a 7km hike.

VAL D'ECHO

Just northwest of Jaca, the craggy Val d'Echo and its hamlets are a relatively untouched wilderness and a great place to get away from it all. The only bus service to this picturesque valley is the **Autocares Escartín** bus (☎974 36 05 08) that leaves Jaca (M-Sa 6:50pm), stopping at Hecho (7:30pm) and Siresa (7:40pm) before continuing to Ansó (8pm, €3.35). Every morning except Sunday, the bus returns from Ansó (6:30am). **Taxis** are available at ☎974 37 50 20 or 620 14 38 48. Outside of the towns, check out the new **El Megalitismo Pirináico,** Ctra. de Oza, km 8, a museum devoted to the ancient stone constructions of the megalithic period. (From Hecho, take the highway to Oza and look for the sign at km 8. ☎629 07 85 13 or 619 71 06 24. Call ahead for opening schedule. €2.)

HECHO (ECHO)   ☎974

Hecho (pop. 700) is the valley's geographical and administrative center. *Casas rurales* (rural guest houses), marked with a green CR sign, provide enjoyable company in an intimate atmosphere. Look for the white building in the Plaza Fuente, where **Casa Blasquico ❹,** Pl. Fuente, 1, provides a friendly, family atmosphere. (☎974 37 50 07. Closed Sept. 7-15 and Dec. 22-26. Breakfast €5. Doubles €45-49. IVA not included. MC/V.) Downstairs, the acclaimed **Restaurante Gaby ❹** serves out-of-this-world dishes, specializing in wild game. (Breakfast €5. Entrees €10-20. Reservations required. Open daily 1:30-3:30pm and 8:30pm-last customer.) The modern **Hotel de la Val ❸,** Ctra. Selva de Oza, on the way out of Hecho towards Siresa, has incredible views of the countryside and comfortable common areas. (☎974 37 50 28; www.hoteldelaval.com. Breakfast €6. Singles €30-35; doubles €37-49. IVA not included. MC/V.) At the entrance to Hecho from Jaca, the well-kept sites and bunks of **Camping Valle de Hecho ❶,** Ctra. Pte. la Reina a Hecho, km 22, are just a short walk from town down the main road to Huesca. The campsite has a swimming pool, laundry, bar, and supermarket. (☎974 37 53 61. Reception 8:30am-11pm; check in first caravan on the left if office is locked. €3.74 per person, per tent, and per car. Bunks in refugio €7. Bar/restaurant open 8:30am-midnight. Supermarket open 8:30am-9:30pm. IVA not included. AmEx/MC/V.)

Restaurante Lo Foratón ❸, above the gas station on C. Cruz Alta on the way out of Hecho towards Siresa, is a good choice for basic meat and fish dishes. (☎974 37 52 47. Open daily 1-3pm and 9-10pm. *Menú del día* €12. MC/V.) For a smaller, simpler meal, Subordán ❶, on the Pl. Fuente, fills up at lunch and dinner with locals eager for dishes like mushroom crepes (€4) and basic tapas and sandwiches (€3-4). (☎974 37 50 65. Open daily 8:30am-1am. Cash only.)

The **tourist office** is in the Pallar d'Agustín, a renovated farmhouse that houses the **Museo de Arte Contemporáneo.** Look for the modern sculptures on the main road toward Ansó. (Both open June Th-Su 10am-1:30pm and 5:30-7pm; July M 5:30-8pm, Tu-Sa 10am-1:30pm and 5:30-8pm, Su 10am-1:30pm; Aug.-mid Oct. daily 10am-1:30pm and 5:30-8pm, Su closed in afternoon. Free.) The staff at the **Ayuntamiento** in Pl. Conde Xiquena (next to Pl. Alta, off C. Mayor) upstairs in the office (M-F 8am-3pm) or down in the library (M-F 6-8pm) will also answer questions. The hiking experts of **Compañía de Guías Valle de Echo** lead trips and rent crosscountry skis. (☎974 37 52 18 or 609 85 08 43; www.guiasdehecho.com. Call ahead for info.) Local services include: **bank** with 24hr. **ATM** on Pl. Alta, above the church plaza, off C. Mayor (open May-Sept. M-Tu and Th-F 8:15am-2:30pm; Oct.-Apr. same except Th 8:15am-1:30pm and 5:15-7:30pm); **police** at the **Guardia Civil** (☎974 37 50 04); **pharmacy** on the road from Ansó (☎974 37 51 02; open M-F 10am-1:30pm and 6-8:30pm); free **Internet** access at the **Telecentro,** high on the C. Mayor (☎974 37 53 78; open M-F 10am-noon and the **library**); and the **post office,** Pl. Alta, off C. Mayor (open M-F 8:30am-2:30pm, Sa 9:30am-1pm). **Postal Code:** 22720.

VAL D'ANSÓ

The little town of Ansó lies just down the road from Jaca in one of the most appealing valleys in the Pyrenees. Lucky hikers might even see one of Spain's very last endangered brown bears peeking out from behind one of the region's trees. Travelers stop in cobblestoned Ansó before heading up the valley to Zuriza (also accessible from Izaba in Navarra), the departure point for the valley's best hikes.

ANSÓ   ☎974

Just east of Navarra, the cobblestone streets and matching houses of Ansó (pop. 500) give the sleepy town a gentle warmth. In an old movie theater, the **Centro de Interpretación de la Naturaleza,** C. Santa Bárbara, 4, houses permanent displays on the flora and fauna of Ansó and surrounding valleys. (☎974 37 02 10. Open Sa-Su 10am-2pm; mid June-Aug. also daily 4-8pm; Sept.-Apr. also 3-6pm. Free.)

Though its owner may be the town's former mayor, ■**Posada Magoria** ❹, C. Milagro, 32, is the perfect place to avoid getting down to business. With a meticulously tended garden, a covered porch overlooking the quiet Río Verál, and a dining room boasting delicious vegetarian meals, Magoria is idyllic. (☎974 37 00 49. Breakfast €6. Dinner €12. Doubles €48-53. Cash only.) Though **Hostal Aisa** ❷, next to the *Ayuntamiento,* has been around for over 120 years, its big rooms are furnished with modern amenities and have bathrooms, TVs, and great views. (☎974 37 00 09. Singles with bath €22; doubles €40-42; triples €54. MC/V.) The **restaurant** downstairs has breakfast (guests only) for €3. (Open daily 8am-10:30pm. *Hostal* and restaurant both closed Dec.-Feb.)

Josefa Escartín buses (☎974 36 05 08) leave from Jaca to Ansó (1½hr., M-Sa 6:50pm, €3.35) via Hecho (1hr.) and return to Jaca (M-Sa 6:30am). The **tourist office** is on Pl. Domingo Miral. (☎974 37 02 25. Open mid-June to Sept. 15 daily 10am-2pm and 4-8pm.) During the rest of the year, call the **Ayuntamiento,** which also has a **library** with free **Internet** access. (☎974 37 00 03. Library open M and Th July-Aug. 6:30-8:30pm; Sept.-June 6-8pm; ask for the key at the *Ayuntamiento* outside of regular hours. *Ayuntamiento* open M-Sa 8am-3pm.) The **Guardia Civil** is at ☎974 37 00 04. There is a 24hr. **ATM** on C. Mayor, in the **Ibercaja** branch (open M noon-2:30pm, W and F 8:15am-2:30pm). To get to the **pharmacy,** walk down C. Mayor from the bus stop, and take the right after Altemira (☎974 37 00 37 or 696

66 78 42; open M-F 10am-1:30pm and 5:30-8pm). Next to the tourist office is the **post office.** (Open M-F 10-10:45am.) **Postal Code:** 22728.

ZURIZA ☎974

In the northern part of the Valle de Ansó (15km north of Ansó itself) lies Zuriza, little more than a single camping location. Surrounding terrain alternates between the shallow hills and valleys of the campsite and the steep summit of southwestern **Ezcaurri.** Many hikers use the area as a base for the arduous trek to **Sima de San Martín,** a gorgeous trail along the French border. To get there, drive from Zuriza 12km towards Izaba until you come to the Izaba-Belagua crossroads. Take the road to Belagua, north along the Río Belagua. After 12km of smooth terrain and a 2km ascent, you'll approach the French border and will see signs for the trail.

Camping Zuriza ❶ provides a **supermarket, hostel,** and **pub/restaurant** where you can get info and maps (€4-7.50) of nearby trails. (☎974 37 01 96. Campsite €3.75 per person, €3.20 per child, €3.20 per tent, €3.75 per car. IVA not included. Hostel bunks €10; doubles €29, with bath €39. *Menú* €12. MC/V.) Alternatively, exhausted campers and hikers can find accommodations and extensive hiking possibilities in the nearby 96-bed **Refugio de Linza ❶,** only 5km from Zuriza. (☎974 34 82 89. Breakfast €3. Dinner €13. Dorms €12.) From the *refugio,* it's a reasonable and well-marked day hike (7hr. round-trip) to the summit of **Mesa de los Tres Reyes** (2444m), one of the highest peaks in the region, which spans the borders of France, Navarra, and Aragón.

PARQUE NACIONAL DE ORDESA ☎945

The well-maintained trails and impressive waterfalls of ⬛**Parque Nacional de Ordesa y Monte Perdido** draw hikers out of crowded *refugios* and through the park, cutting across forests, escarpments, and snow-covered peaks. If you're lucky, you might just catch a glimpse of an endangered *quebrantahueso,* or bearded vulture, the largest bird of prey in the Pyrenees. The park is located just south of the French border, and includes the canyons and valleys of Ordesa, Añisclo, Escuaín, and Pineta. Huge crowds descend into Ordesa through the village of **Torla** in July and August, and traipse along the park's diverse trails all year.

🖪 **TRANSPORTATION.** All **trains** along the Zaragoza-Huesca-Jaca line stop in Sabiñánigo. **Alosa** (☎974 48 00 45; www.alosa.es) runs a **bus** between Sabiñánigo and Jaca (20min.; M-Sa 8 per day 7:35am-9:20pm, Su 8 per day 10:20am-10:35pm; €1.35) From there, buses run to Torla (55min.; July-Aug. 11am, 6:30pm; Sept.-June M-Sa 11am, Su 5pm; €2.78). During *Semana Santa* and from June 30-Sept. 16 and from Oct. 12-14, a **shuttle** runs between Torla and Ordesa (15min.; June 28-Aug. every 15min. 6am-7pm; *Semana Santa,* Sept.-Oct. 6am-6pm; last trip back from Ordesa to Torla July-Aug. 10pm, *Semana Santa* and Oct. 8:30pm, Sept. 9pm; €2.40; round-trip €3.40). When the shuttle is running, cars are prohibited from entering the park. (Parking lot in Torla €0.72 per hour. 9am-8pm; overnight parking free; 20% discount after first 24hr.) In the low season, those without a car will have to either hike the 8km to the park entrance or catch a **jeep taxi** (☎630 418 918; www.ordesataxi.com; €15). The company also offers van tours for up to 8 people. Buses leave Torla for Sabiñánigo (1hr.; daily 3:30pm, Su also 6:25pm, July-Aug. also daily 8pm; €2.88) and Aínsa (1¼hr., daily at noon, €2.95).

 STREET SMARTS. Don't try to drive off the main road in any of the towns near the park, especially Torla. The narrow, steep streets were not designed with cars in mind. Just park and walk; your car's suspension will thank you.

E [?] ORIENTATION AND PRACTICAL INFORMATION. C. A Ruata is the main cobblestone road that passes through Torla. The park **visitors center** is 1.8km beyond the park entrance. The shuttle stops here on the way to the **pradera**, the parking lot within the park (3km farther on). (Open daily Mar.-Dec. 9am-2pm and 4-7pm.) There is also a smaller **park info center** in Torla, across the street from the bus stop. (☎974 48 64 72. Open July-Sept. M-F 8am-3pm, Sa-Su 9am-2pm and 4:30-7pm; Oct.-June M-F 8am-3pm.) You can pick up free maps and the **Senderos Sector Ordesa** trail guide from the park info center, or the indispensable *Editorial Alpina* guide (€8) in town. For more information on Torla head to the **tourist office** on Pl. Aragón at the end of C. Fatas. (☎974 48 63 78. Open June-Sept. and *Semana Santa* M-Sa 10am-1:30pm and 5-9pm, Sun 5-9pm.)

Across from the pharmacy on C. Ruata, **Compañía Guías de Torla** organizes rafting (€40), canyoneering (€35-60), and year-round mountaineering (€35-60) expeditions. (☎974 48 64 22; www.guiasdetorla.com. Open daily 9am-2pm and 5-8pm; extended hours July-Aug. MC/V.) In neighboring **Broto** (4km from Torla), **Aventuras Pirenaicas,** Av. de Ordesa, 13, offers rafting (€42) and canyoneering (€40) trips. (☎974 48 63 92; www.ordesa./netaventuraspirenaicas. Open daily 10am-2pm and 5-9pm.) **Internet** and **Wi-Fi** access is free at the Torla **tourist office**. Local services include: **Guardia Civil** (☎974 48 61 60); a **pharmacy,** between Restaurant la Brecha and Refugio l'Atalaya (☎974 48 62 06; open M-F 10am-1:30pm and 5-8pm); and the **post office,** Pl. de la Constitución (open M-Sa 9-11am). **Postal Code:** 22376.

[?] ACCOMMODATIONS AND CAMPING. Torla has the most budget accommodations in the area, but they fill up fast in July and August—reserve ahead. The funky, if slightly cramped, **▨Refugio L'Atalaya ❶,** C. Ruata, 45, is budget traveler heaven. (☎974 48 60 22. Kitchen access. Open *Semana Santa*-Oct. Bunks €9 per person. €25 half-board. Restaurant and bar open daily 7-11:30pm. MC/V.) Named for Ordesa's best-known poet, **Refugio Lucien Briet ❶,** C. Ruata, two doors down from L'Atalaya, has bunks with partitions. (☎974 48 62 21; www.refugiolucien-briet.com. Sheets €3. Bunks €9, half board €25; doubles with bath €37. Basic kitchen with sink and tables available. Cash only.) Across from the tourist office, **La Casa de Laly ❸,** C. Fatas, has a cozy B&B atmosphere and friendly owners. (☎974 48 61 68. Breakfast €3.25. Curfew 12:30am. Oct.-June singles or doubles €25, with bath €30. July-Aug. €30/35. Cash only.) **Camping San Antón ❶,** closest to the park, also rents 4-person bungalows and 4-6-person apartments. (☎974 48 60 63. Camping open *Semana Santa*-Sept. €3.50-4.10 per person, per car and per tent, €3.30 per child; €4.30 per large tent. Electricity €3.30-4.10. Bungalows and apartments open year-round.) Within the park, the only option is **▨Refugio Góriz ❶,** a 5-6hr. hike from the **Pradera.** Be sure to reserve ahead. (☎974 34 12 01. Breakfast €4.80. Dinner or lunch €14. Basic kitchen available. Bunks €12.) There is a free campsite behind the refugio, though tents must be taken down in the morning.

[?] FOOD. Most accommodations serve dinner (€13-15) and include a simple breakfast. On weekends and during the busy summer months, the understaffed restaurants in Torla struggle to handle the hordes of tourists. For the cheapest *menú* in town (€13.40), check out **Restaurant La Brecha ❸,** C. Ruata. (☎974 48 62 21. Cash only.) Up C. Fatas, off Pl. Aragón, **Restaurante Bar El Rebeco ❸** serves a satisfying *menú* (€15) in three dining rooms. (☎974 48 60 66. Open daily June-Oct. 15 and Semana Santa 1-3pm and 8-10pm. MC/V.) **Pizzeria-Bocatería Santa Elena ❶,** C. Furquieto, offers a friendly, casual setting and cheap, hearty eats. In addition to pizzas (€5.50-7), the pizzeria offers a selection of salads (€3-3.50) and *bocadillos* (€3-4), as well as huge glasses of beer for €3. (☎974 48 63 59. Open daily 1:30-3pm and 8-11pm. July-Sept. extended hours. Cash only.) **Supermercado**

Torla is close to the end of C. Ruata furthest from the tourist office. (☎974 48 61 63. Open daily 9am-2pm and 5-8:30pm. MC/V.) The undisputed king of the Torla nightlife scene is the lively **Pub Arco Iris,** on C. Fatas, where tourists and a few locals mingle, drink, and dance the night away. (☎974 48 64 52.)

 HIKES. A main trail runs up the Río Arazas to the foot of Monte Perdido and **Refugio Góriz.** Passing through evergreen forests and a spectacular open valley, and with three spectacular waterfalls within 1hr. of the trailhead, it's the most practical and rewarding hike, especially for inexperienced hikers who don't mind crowded pathways. The full round-trip hike from the *pradera* to the *Refugio* takes about 8-9hr., but worthwhile points lie between the two for hikers interested in a shorter excursion. A 6-7hr. round-trip hike leads to the busy **Cola de Caballo** (horse tail), one of the most photographed waterfalls in the park, with an excellent view of the open valley and snow-capped Monte Perdido in the distance. A trek to the **Gradas de Soasa** waterfall is about 5hr. round-trip. The ■**Cascadas de Estrecho,** a breathtaking waterfall that drops 30m through a narrow chute, has viewing platforms both at the base and above, and makes for a 2hr. round-trip hike. For experienced hikers, **Sendero Faja Pelay,** along the ridge above the main valley path, is a good day hike that also reaches the Cola de Caballo. From the parking lot at the Pradera de Ordesa, take the trail right, across the Río Arazas, and follow the signs for Senda de los Cazadores. The trail includes the steep snake-like path, **Senda de los Cazadores,** and the beautiful lookout point at **Calcilarruego.** Return via the main valley path along the Río Arazas (7-8hr. round-trip).

> ❗ Check for weather conditions at the park office (☎974 48 64 72 or 24 33 61); the park can be dangerous in the snow or rain. The descent of the Senda de los Cazadores is treacherously steep, so returning to the Pradera on the Faja Pelay path is not encouraged.

To see the impressive **Cascada de Cotatuero,** which drops nearly 200m from the Cotatuero glacier, it's a more difficult 4hr. round-trip hike. Take the left-hand trail that breaks away from the main trail at the Virgen de Pilar monument. Arrive early, especially July-August, as the park is flooded with visitors by noon.

L'AINSA (AÍNSA)   ☎974

A thousand years ago, romantic Aínsa (pop. 1700) was the capital of the Kingdom of Sobrarbe (later incorporated into Aragón). Aínsa's hilltop old neighborhood provides a perfect combination of medieval charm and panoramic views. In 1181, priests consecrated the **Iglesia de Santa María,** at the lowest part of Plaza Mayor. The church and adjoining cloister are free and open to the public, with recordings of Gregorian chants available for €1. Across the plaza lies the 11th-century **castillo,** which houses a modern **Eco Museo** with explanations about the geology, flora and fauna of the Central Pyrenees, as well as an area with injured animals. (☎974 50 05 97. Open June-Sept. daily 10am-2pm and 5-9pm; Oct.-May Tu-Sa 9am-2pm and 4-7pm. Wheelchair accessible. €2.50, €2 for groups of 20 or more.) The annual **Festival Músicas de Europa** draws artists from across Europe in late July or August. (For info., call the Aínsa tourist office ☎974 50 07 67; www.festivales.aragon.es.)

The cheapest place to spend the night is the **Hostal Pirineos ❸,** C. Sobrarbe, 15, near the bus stop, which has large rooms with a view and huge private baths. (☎974 50 02 71; www.pirinei.com/hostalpirineos. Breakfast €4. Singles €24-35; doubles €34-48; triples €51-62. AmEx/MC/V.) **Camping Aínsa ❶,** Ctra. Aínsa-Campo, 1.5km, has a swimming pool, supermarket, bar, and restaurant. (☎974 50 02 60; www.campingainsa.com. Open *Semana Santa*-Oct. 15 €4.65 per person, per car, and per tent; July-Aug. €4.80. Electricity €3.30-4.10. Restaurant open July-Aug. 9am-11pm. MC/V.) Across from the tourist office, **Cafetería Dos Ríos ❶**, Av. Central, 4, offers stone-oven pizzas and Spanish classics in a diner-like setting. Its *platos combinados* (€7-8) are the best deal in town. (☎974 50 09 61. Open daily 8am-12:30am. MC/V). For a quick bite, the cafeteria at **Hotel Sanchez ❶** serves up *bocadillos* and tapas. (Open daily 6:30am-midnight. Internet access €0.20 per 8min. MC/V.) For groceries, head to **Supermercado Alvi**, Av. de la Sobrarbe, 15. (☎974 50 00 18. Open daily 9am-2pm and 4-8:30pm; Oct.-June closed Su.)

Alosa (☎974 21 32 77; www.alosa.es) runs daily buses from Sabiñánigo to Aínsa (2 hr.; 11:45am, return 2:30pm; €6) stopping in Torla (1hr., €3), and from Aínsa to Barbastro (1hr.; M-Sa 7am, returns 7:45pm; July-Aug. also 2:45pm from Aínsa and 11am from Barbastro; €4.50), where buses connect to Benasque (2hr., M-F 11, 11:30am and 5:20pm; €7). Buses stop in front of Hotel Sanchez on Av. Sobrarbe. To get to the **pueblo viejo**, walk past the post office to find a set of stairs. There is a regional **tourist office** by the castle. (☎974 500 512. Open July-Aug. daily 9am-9pm; Sept.-June M-Tu 10am-2pm and 4-7:30pm, W-Su 10am-2pm and 4:30-8pm) and a local one in the new part of Aínsa, on Av. Pirenáica, 1, at the highway crossroads, visible from the bus stop. (☎974 50 07 67; open daily 10am-2pm and 4-8pm.) A **pharmacy** is on Av. Sobrarbe just before the bridge. (☎974 50 00 23; open M-Sa 9:30am-2pm and 4:30-8:30pm, Su 10am-2pm.) **Internet** access is at the **library**, C. los Murros, 2, on the top floor of the big brick building at the base of the old quarter. (☎974 50 03 88. €1.50 per hour. Open M-F 10am-1:30pm and 4-8pm.) The **post office** is on Av. Sobrarbe, down the street across from the tourist office towards the old town. (☎974 50 00 71; open M-F 8:30am-2:30pm, Sa 9:30am-1pm.) **Postal Code:** 22330.

VALLE DE BENASQUE ☎974

The Valle de Benasque is a haven for hard-core hikers, climbers, and skiers. Countless trails wind through the mountains, and the area teems with *refugios*, allowing for longer expeditions. With its many excursion companies and nearby trailheads, the mellow town of **Benasque** (pop. 2160) is an excellent base for outdoor activities. Casual hikers are often scared off by the valley's reputation for serious mountaineering—the Pyrenees' highest peaks, including awe-inspiring Mt. Aneto (3404m), are here—but relaxing walks are within every visitor's reach.

🖪🖫 TRANSPORTATION AND PRACTICAL INFORMATION. Alosa (☎974 21 07 00; www.alosa.es) runs buses to Zaragoza (4 hr.; M-Sa 6:45am and 3pm, Su 3pm, return M-Sa 9am and 3:30pm, Su 9am; €16.35); to Lleida (4 hr.; M-Sa 6:45am and 3pm, Su 3pm, return M-Sa 9:30am and 4pm, Su 9:30am; €12); and to Barcelona (8hr.; M-Sa 6:45am and 3pm, Su 3pm, return M-Sa 7:30am and 1pm, Su 7:30am; €19.38). From June 28-Sept. 10, the shuttle bus **Pirineos 3000** makes frequent runs from the town to the trailhead parking lots of Senarta (€2, round-trip €3) and La Besurta (€5, round-trip €8). During the rest of the year, call 4X4 **Taxis** at (☎608 93 04 50). To get to the **tourist office**, C. San Sebastián, 5, face Hotel Aragüells at the main bus stop and walk one block down the alley between the BBVA bank and the building with the KHURP sign. The office has a map of the town, basic hiking maps for the area, and Internet access. (☎974 55 12 89; www.turismobenasque.com. €1 per 15min. Open daily 9:30am-1pm and 4:30-8pm.) The **bank**, on the Av. los Tilos, next to Hotel Aragüells, has a 24hr. **ATM.** (☎902 24 24 24. Open M-F 8:30am-2pm, Sa 8:30am-1pm.) In case of a **medical emergency**, call ☎974 55 21 38. For the **Guardia Civil**, call ☎974 55 10 08. A **pharmacy** is at Av. de Francia, 38, about 2 blocks past the BBVA. (☎974 55 28 10. Open M-F 10am-2:30pm and 5-8:30pm, Sa 10am-2pm and 5-9pm.) **Laundry** can be done at the **Lavandería Ecologica**, near the pharmacy on C. Francia (☎974 55 15 04. Up to 5kg €10.50, up to 10kg €13.50.

Opening hours change throughout the year). The **post office,** Pl. del Ayuntamiento, is in the *Ayuntamiento* across from the church. (☎974 55 20 71. Open M-F 8:30am-2:30pm, Sa 9:30am-1pm.) **Postal Code:** 22440.

▓ ACCOMMODATIONS. Benasque has no true budget hostels, but the reasonably priced modern hotels on the main road won't break the bank. The centrally located **Hotel Avenida ❹,** Av. de Los Tilos, 14, is one of the cheapest options in town. Comfortable rooms with private baths, TVs, and friendly service make this a good base for your journeys. (☎974 55 11 26; www.h-avenida.com. From the bus station, cross the street towards town, and walk past hotel Aragüells. Wi-Fi available in rooms. Singles €32-40; doubles €39-65. MC/V.) Those with strong legs can head 3km up the highway toward France, where **Camping Aneto ❶** serves as a convenient starting point for a day's hike, with a mountain setting complete with, playground, TV lounge, and bar-restaurant. (☎974 55 11 41; www.campinganeto.com. Heated pool and supermarket July-Aug. Rooms with shared kitchen, living room, and bath €15 per person year-round. *Semana Santa,* Christmas, and July-Aug. camping €4.90 per person, per car, and per tent; otherwise €4.40. 2-person bungalows €70-82. MC/V.) **Free camping** is also available inside the park in Senarta. Inquire at the park office about current regulations. (☎974 55 20 66.)

❐ FOOD. At lively **La Pizzeria ❷,** C. Los Huertos, delighted customers commend the chef's lasagna (€7-8) as well as his pizzas (€7-9), which feature local mushrooms. (☎974 55 15 76. Open daily 1-3:30pm and 7-11pm. MC/V. Credit card minimum €20.) Electronic music blends with the cigarette smoke of locals and Wi-Fi addicts at **Bar Borda Roldanet ❶,** Av. Francia, just before C. de Luchon, where sandwiches (served all day) are €3-4 and tapas are €1-6. Signs from C. Ministro Cornel off Pl. del Ayuntamiento will lead you to **Pub-Terraza Les Arkades ❸,** a stone building built in 1647. (☎974 55 12 02. *Menú* €12. Restaurant open daily June 22-Oct. 12 1-4pm and 8-11pm; bar open 5:30pm-3:30am.) Stock up at **Supermercado Aro Rojo,** C. Molino. From the highway, take Av. de los Tilos one block and then left onto C. Molino. (☎974 55 28 79. Open M-Sa 9:30am-2:30pm and 5-9pm, Su 10-2pm.)

▓ OUTDOOR ACTIVITIES. For mountaineering courses and guided excursions, try **Compañía de Guías Valle de Benasque** on Av. de Luchón, 19. (☎974 55 13 36; www.guiasbenasque.com. Mountaineering, rock climbing, rafting, paragliding, and canyoneering start at €50. Open daily 4-9pm.) A number of forest trails lead from Benasque, including an easy hike to the nearby village of **Cerler** (1hr.) and a longer hike to the **Valle de Estos** (3hr. by foot, 1½hr. by bike; moderate difficulty). The park info office and the tourist office have free maps of excursions by foot and bike, but serious hikers should buy an additional guide at one of the bookstores in town. Benasque serves as the entry point to the **Parque Natural de Posets-Maladeta,** with numerous snow-covered peaks above 3000m, and 13 of the southernmost glaciers in Europe. The **Centro de Visitantes** is about 1km down the road to Campo from Benasque. (☎974 55 20 66. Open late June-mid-Sept. daily 10am-2pm and 4-8pm; late Sept.-early June Sa-Su 10am-2pm and 4-8pm.)

Experienced hikers can take the 4hr. hike to the Lago de Cregüeña, the highest lake in the area at 2657m. Start out early from Benasque and hike 8km uphill on the valley road toward France, or take a shuttle to Senarta. From Senarta, turn right onto the trail off the main road and climb up, following the falls of the Río Cregüeña. The sometimes steep ascent twists through glens, but never strays far from the river's edge. Another longer, though less-tiring route (5hr. one-way from Senarta) leads to the **Lagos de Vallibierna** (2432m and 2484m) from Senarta. Take the GR-11 along the river up the Valle de Vallibierna to the **Refugio de Vallibierna.** From there, look for the signs to the lakes, which lie another 2hr. up. Those wishing to scale **Mount Aneto** (3404m), the highest of the Pyrenees, can pick up gear next door to the Compañía (p. 471) and head out at 5am from the **Refugio de la Renclusa ❶**. To reach the *refugio*, take the main road (follow the signs to France) north 14km until the paved road ends at Besurta, or take a shuttle; from there it is a 30min. hike to the *refugio*. (☎974 55 21 06. Open Apr.-Sept. Reserve ahead.) Hiking in the Benasque valley does not require a permit, but the park office encourages all who wish to ascend peaks above 3000m to bring proper equipment (piolet, crampons, rope, winter garments). In case of accidents, call ☎112. For less-strenuous wandering, head in the opposite direction down the main road and follow signs to **Forau de Aigualluts,** a lovely pond at the base of a waterfall (40min.). Trails can be impassable in winter, so ask at the tourist office in advance.

NAVARRAN PYRENEES

The Navarran Pyrenees mark the peaceful transition from bare mountaintops to forested slopes, pastoral farmlands, and a maritime environment. The many hamlets scattered throughout the mountains and the impressive Selva de Irati forest make for a good escape from the craziness of Pamplona during San Fermín. The first Roman road connecting Hispania and Gallium (modern day France) passed through here, setting a trend for mountainside meandering that culminated in the Camino de Santiago. Higher peaks dominate the eastern Valle de Roncal, while the mountain slopes to the west allow access to the area's streams, waterfalls, and meadows. Mist obscures visibility at high altitudes to create a dreamy atmosphere (or nerve-racking driving conditions). The Navarran Pyrenees are difficult to traverse using public transport, but daytrips to Roncal, Ochagavía, and Roncesvalles from Pamplona are possible.

 COZY CASAS. Navarra's rural lodging houses are comfy budget options (€15-30 per person; for information call ☎948 20 65 40, or pick up a copy of the *Guía de alojamientos de turismo rurales* in any of Navarra's tourist offices).

RONCESVALLES ☎948

The first stop in Spain on the Camino de Santiago, the mist-shrouded town of Roncesvalles rests amid miles of thickly wooded mountains. Folklore buffs come to this tiny town (pop. 28) in search of French hero Roland, Charlemagne's favorite soldier, who died nearby in the Battle of Roncevaux in AD 778. The remains of the troops supposedly rest in the 12th-century **Capilla de Sancti Spiritus (Silo de Carlomagno)**, with the bones of pilgrims who died en route to Santiago de Compostela. The church buildings known as the **Colegiata** includes the 13th-century French Gothic **Iglesia Colegial** and the adjoining cloister and museum. Behind the cloister, the **tombs** of King Sancho El Fuerte (the Strong) and his bride rest in solitary splendor, lit by the stained-glass windows of the **Capilla de San Agustín.** (☎948 79 04 80. Church of St. Mary open daily 9am-9pm. Free. Chapel, cloister, museum, silo, and Church of St. James open June-Sept. daily 10am-2pm and 3:30-7pm; Oct.-May 10am-2pm and 3:30-5:30pm. €3.90 for the whole complex, students and under 25 €3. English audioguide €10.)

There is an *albergue* in Roncesvalles with lodging for pilgrims only—enter the **Oficina de Peregrinos** adjoining the monastery to obtain your "official pilgrim" status by paying €1; remember that it's disrespectful to become official just to get cheap lodging. (☎948 76 00 00. Reception M-Sa 10am-1:30pm and 4-7pm, Su 10am-1:30pm and 4-6pm.) The **Albergue de Peregrinos ❶**, the first building on the left across from the Silo, provides basic *refugio*-style lodging for pilgrims. (Reception

4-10pm. Sheets and blanket €5. Curfew 11pm. Checkout by 8am.) **La Posada ❸,** the first building on your right entering town from the Spanish side, has basic rooms with private bath. (☎948 76 02 25. Restaurant open 1-3:30pm and 8-10pm. *Menú* €16, for pilgrims €8; served 7-8:30pm, reserve before 7pm daily. Bar open 8:30am-10:30pm. Closed Nov. May-Oct. doubles €50. MC/V.) Accommodations are more plentiful and cheaper in nearby **Burguete,** 3km away and accessible by car or by a 20-min. walk on the first part of the Camino de Santiago. The main street, C. San Nikolas, is lined with *casas rurales, hostales,* and restaurants. Not much has changed at **Hostal Burguete ❸,** C. San Nikolás, 71 (founded in 1880), since Hemingway wrote and rested here on his way back to Paris from Pamplona; the hostal is still owned and run by the same family. (☎948 76 00 05. *Menú* €14. Restaurant open daily 1:30-3pm and 8:30-10pm. All rooms with bathroom. Breakfast included all year except Aug. Curfew 11:30pm. Wheelchair-accessible. Singles €31; doubles €42. MC/V.) Tasty Navarran dishes (vegetarian options available) are served up nightly at the professional **Restaurante Loizu ❸,** C. San Nikolas, 13. (☎948 76 00 08. *Menú* €15.50. Open daily 1-3:30pm and 8:30-11pm. Closed Jan. MC/V.)

Autobus Artieda buses (☎948 30 02 87) run between Pamplona and Roncesvalles via Burguete. (1½hr.; Sept.-June M-F 6pm, Sa 9:30am; €4.20; return buses M-F 9:20am, Sa noon. July-Aug. buses run from Pamplona M-F 10am and 6pm, returning 8:30am and 11:30am; Sa 9:30am and 4pm, returning 8am and noon.) Call ☎670 616 190 or 609 44 70 58 for **taxis.** A **tourist office** in the mill uphill from Casa Sabina Hostería provides information on the sights of Roncesvalles and the Camino de Santiago. (☎948 76 03 01. Open *Semana Santa*-Oct. 12 M-Sa 10am-2pm and 4-7pm, Su 10am-2pm; otherwise M-F 10am-2pm and 2:30-5pm, Sa-Su 10am-2pm.) An **ATM** is inside the lobby of La Posada, as well as **Internet** access (€1 per 18min.) In Burguete, 2km south, **Caja Navarra** has more services (ATM open 24hr., bank open M-F 8:30am-2:15pm). Burguete also has a **post office** on C. Roncesvalles (open M-F 9-10am). **Postal Code:** 31640.

OCHAGAVÍA (OTSAGABIA)   ☎948

At the confluence of the Ríos Anduña, Zatoia, and Salazar is picturesque Otsagabia (pop. 600). The mountains surrounding the town offer some of Navarra's best hiking, trout fishing, and cross-country skiing. At 17,000 hectares of uninterrupted woods, the nearby **Selva de Irati** (Irati forest) is one of the most extensive forests in Europe and the most popular outdoor attraction in the region. The tourist office in Ochagavía sells trail maps of the Irati forest (€2) and gives out free descriptions of hikes. The lake is also accessible by car from Orbaitzeta. Most trailheads are only accessible on foot or by **taxi** (☎620 27 02 41). **Cross-country skiers** can enjoy two circuit trails that originate down the same highway in **Pikatua. Ekia,** on the plaza across the river from the info office, does everything from caving (€30) to canyoneering (€30-36). (☎696 89 99 95; www.ekiapirineo.com.)

Inquire at the tourist office for accommodations or look for the "CR" signs advertising *casas rurales.* The cheerful and well-maintained ▧**Casa Pistolo ❷,** Iribarren, 2, has 2nd-floor bedrooms with a shared bathroom and a comfortable common room with tables and a TV. Entering town from Pamplona, make your first left and look for the sign on the right. (☎948 89 05 97. Breakfast €4. Singles €18; doubles €28. Cash only.) Follow the blue "parking" signs across the river from the main road to get to ▧**Kixkia ❷,** C. Urrutia. With huge cider casks embedded in the far wall, long wooden tables, and plenty of well-prepared typical Navarran dishes, Kixkia is a perfect example of the area's *sidrerías* (cider houses). (☎948 89 05 17; www.kixkia.com. Entrees €8-16. *Menús* €9-24. Open July-Oct. daily 1:30-4pm and 8:30-10:30pm; Dec.-June Sa-Su only. MC/V.) Another excellent dining option is the **Restaurante Auñamendi ❸,** Plaza Dr. Gurpide 1, which has quick, no-nonsense service and serves a tantalizing selection of appetizers and fish and meat entrees. (☎948 89 01 89. Entrees €7-13. *Menú* €14. Open daily 1-3:30pm and 8:30-11pm. Closed mid-Sept. to mid-Oct. MC/V.)

The **tourist office**, on the main road, Ctra. Aísaba, uphill from the riverside fountain, has slow but free **Internet** access. (☎948 89 06 41; fax 948 89 06 79. Open June 15-Sept. 15 M-Sa 10am-2pm and 4:30-8:30pm, Su 10am-2pm; Sept. 16-June 14 daily 10am-2pm, F-Sa also 4:30-7:30pm.) The **nature center** in the same building (Centro de Interpretación de la Naturaleza) has info on flora and fauna (entrance €1.20).

VALLE DE RONCAL

Carved by the Río Esca, the Valle de Roncal (pop. 1500) is a handsome valley covered by dark pine groves and winding trails that stretches south from the French border. White beech forests and ochre tiled roofs balance out the color palette. Open pastures ensure that the area's famous cows continue to produce top-quality milk used to make the valley's famous cheese. Livestock aside, the Valle de Roncal offers travelers intimate towns, cozy *casas rurales*, and prime hiking trails. Go to www.vallederoncal.es for more information.

RONCAL ☎948

Smack in the center of the Valle de Roncal, diminutive **Roncal** (pop. 300) prides itself on two things: its famed *queso Roncal*, a sharp, sheep's milk cheese, and its world-renowned tenor, Julián Gayarre (1844-1889). **Casa Museo Julián Gayarre,** on C. Arana, occupies the singer's birthplace, showcasing the tenor's ▓**preserved larynx.** (☎948 47 51 80. Open Tu-Su 11:30am-1:30pm and 4-6pm. €1.80; seniors and students €1.60; under 12 free.) **Casa Villa Pepita ❶,** Po. Julián Gayarre, 4, just before the bridge toward Pamplona and near the *Ayuntamiento*, is wonderfully homey. (☎948 47 51 33. Breakfast €3.50, other meals €11.50. Singles €13.50; doubles €27, with bath €35. Cash only.) **Hostal Zaltua ❸,** C. Castillo, 23, right across the river, offers comfortable rooms with private bath and TV. (☎948 47 50 08. Singles €31-35; doubles €42. MC/V.) Go to **Panadería Lus ❷,** C. Iriondoa, 3, down the path next to Caja Navarra, for wine and a taste of one of the five varieties of the lauded Roncal cheese. (☎948 47 50 10. Open daily July-Aug. 9am-2pm and 5-8pm; Sept.-June 9:30am-2pm and 5-7:30pm.) Find groceries at **Autoservicio a Mano.** (☎978 47 51 82. Open M-Sa 9:30am-1:30pm and 4:30-7pm, Su 9:30-11am.) **La Tafallesa buses** (☎948 22 28 86) run to Pamplona (2hr., M-F 7am, €7.67).

The **tourist office** on Roncal's main road, Po. Julián Gayarre, near the exit towards Izaba, has English-speaking staff and **Internet** access for €1 the first 15min. and €0.50 every additional 15min. (☎948 47 52 56; fax 47 53 16. Open June 15-Sept. 15 M-Sa 10am-2pm and 4:30-8:30pm, Su 10am-2pm; Sept. 16-June 14 M-Th and Su 10am-2pm, F-Sa 10am-2pm and 4:30-7:30pm.) Local services include the **Guardia Civil** (☎948 47 50 05) and a **pharmacy,** next to the tourist office (☎948 47 51 52; open M-F 10am-2pm and 5-7:30pm, Sa 10am-2pm).

ISABA (IZABA) ☎948

Izaba (pop. 500) draws hikers and skiers north of Roncal to explore the surrounding cliff-studded mountains. A stunning hike along the GR-11 (a trail that links the Atlantic to the Mediterranean) leaves from Izaba and climbs to Zuriza in the Valle de Hecho (15.6km, 5-6hr.) The ascents from Collado Argibiela to Punta Abizondo (1676m) and Peña Ezkaurre (2047m) are shorter but steeper. Another hike, also along the GR-11, leads from Izaba to neighboring Otsagabia, in the Valle de Salazar (21.4km, 5-6hr. one-way). For more routes in the area, ask at the tourist office. Ski trails run north of Izaba at the **Estación de Ski Larra-Belagua**, km 12, 20, and 24 on NA-1370, the highway towards France (call the **tourist office** ☎948 89 32 51; open Tu-Sa 10am-2pm and 5-8pm, Su 10am-2pm). For skiing lessons, try the local

Escuela de Esqui de Fondo (☎948 89 32 66). A festival featuring dancing and games of *pelotas*, a local variation of polo, runs July 25-28 in honor of Santiago. Izaba merrily celebrates San Cipriano, its patron saint, on September 16.

On the north side of town, next to a parking lot, is ◼**Hotel Ezkaurre ❹**, Garagardoya, 14. Bask in the garden out back or sit down for a board game in the common room. (☎948 89 33 03. July-Sept. 15 singles €37; doubles €50; Oct.-June €31/42. MC/V.) The sunny rooms and beautiful woodwork are complemented by the **restaurant ❷** downstairs. Bedraggled backpackers appreciate the generous portions. (Breakfast €4, *menú* €11; lodgers only. Restaurant open daily 8:30-10:30am and 8:30-10pm.) **Albergue Oxanea ❶**, C. Bormapea, in a stone house, offers wooden bunks and a TV lounge with VCR and board games. (☎948 89 31 53. Breakfast €2.40. Meals €10. Sheets €2. Dorms €9.) **Camping Asolaze ❶**, 6km up the road toward France, has campsites, a restaurant, store, bunk beds, and a wheelchair-accessible private bungalow. (☎948 89 30 34; www.campingasolaze.com. Breakfast €4. *Menú* €11. Laundry €3.50. Camping €4 per person, per tent, and per car; €3.50 per child. Dorms €9.50. 4-person bungalow €75; 6-person €85. Electricity €3.90. Closed Nov. 15-30. MC/V.) Stock up at **Coviran Supermercado** on C. Mendigatxa. (☎948 89 31 91. Open 9:30am-1:30pm and 4-8pm; July-Aug. extended hours.) **La Tafallesa buses** (☎948 22 28 86) run to Pamplona (2hr., M-F 7am, €7.67), stopping 7km down the road in Roncal along the way.

THE PYRENEES

ARAGÓN, LA RIOJA, AND NAVARRA (NAVARRE)

 To the south of the Pyrenees lie the provinces of Aragón, La Rioja, and Navarra, a collage of semi-desert and lush countryside: a hybrid of Mediterranean and Continental climates. Regional delights lie in every direction; to the south, a collection of sun-baked towns and flaxen plains are scattered with fine examples of ornate *mudéjar* architecture. In the center, prosperous Zaragoza is Aragón's capital and the fifth largest city in Spain. Out west, Logroño offers travelers a taste of urbanism infused with Santiago's pilgrim culture—and the chance to taste La Rioja's famed wines. Pamplona, the capital of Navarra, is preceded by its reputation thanks to Ernest Hemingway's famous novel, *The Sun Also Rises*. The Ebro, Spain's largest river, ties these three distinct regions together.

HIGHLIGHTS OF ARAGÓN, LA RIOJA, AND NAVARRA

TOAST yourself for a week at **Teruel's** liquor fest (p. 484).

CAVE in to the temptation of the dripping grottoes of the **Parque de la Piedra** (p. 483).

SPLASH fellow travelers at the Batalla del Vino wine fight in **Haro** (p. 490).

ABANDON your sanity and run with the bulls in **Pamplona** (p. 492).

ARAGÓN

Aragón's harsh climate, coupled with the region's strategic location, has lent it a martial history. Established as a kingdom in AD 1035 and united with enterprising Cataluña in 1137, Aragón forged a Mediterranean empire. But when Felipe II marched into Zaragoza in 1591, he brought the region to its knees. Economic decline followed political humiliation, and as eyes turned to the New World, Aragón's people moved to the coast in search of wealth. Today, Aragón is back on its feet, and having gained state autonomy in 1982, it continues to expand its political influence, along with its appeal for travelers and Spaniards alike. When the beach towns of the Mediterranean coast and the wide avenues of Barcelona are flooded by summer crowds, Aragón serves as a relaxing getaway.

ZARAGOZA ☎976

The charm of lively Zaragoza (pop. 700,000), the political and cultural center of Aragón, lies in its relative obscurity. Augustus founded the city in 24 BC as a retirement colony for Roman veterans (ruins of the public baths still remain), lovingly naming it Caesaraugusta, after himself; the name was eventually blurred to Zaragoza. Many of the major plazas and leafy boulevards have been converted into modern, tourist-friendly sights with luxury shopping, but take heart: there are still plenty of places unaffected by tourism. With mostly free museums, awe-inspiring cathedrals, and the World Expo 2008 on its way, Zaragoza provides a more intimate alternative to Spain's better-known famous cities. For the best place to perfect that Spanish lisp, look no further than "Tharagotha."

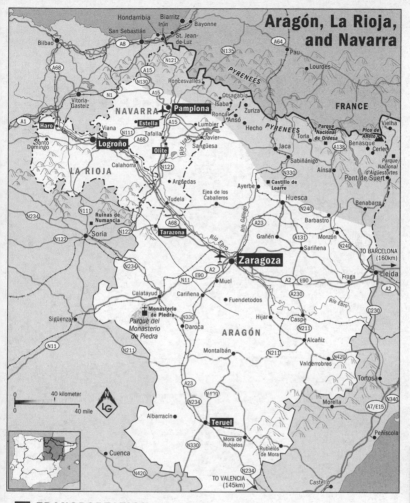

Aragón, La Rioja, and Navarra

TRANSPORTATION

Flights: Zaragoza Airport (☎976 71 23 00). **Iberia** (www.iberia.com) has flights to other parts of Spain and nearby international destinations. **Agreda Automóvil** (☎976 22 93 43) runs **buses** to and from the airport, stopping at Po. de Pamplona, Pl. de San Francisco, the Cámara de Comercio on Po. Isabel la Católica, and Vía Hispanidad, 100. Airport buses leave from Po. de Pamplona (25min.; M-F 6 per day 10:45am-9:45pm, Sa 4 per day 6am-2pm, Su 4 per day 10:45am-9pm; return M-F 6 per day 8:45am-11pm, Sa 6:30pm, Su 11:30pm; €1.80). **Taxi** to the airport approx. €14.

Trains: Estación Zaragoza-Delicias, C. Rioja, 33 (☎902 24 02 02). Open daily 5:30am-midnight; if closed, entrance only with pre-purchased ticket (booth open daily 5:30am-11pm, advance tickets sold 8am-10pm). Trains to: **Barcelona** (4hr., 8 per day 8am-

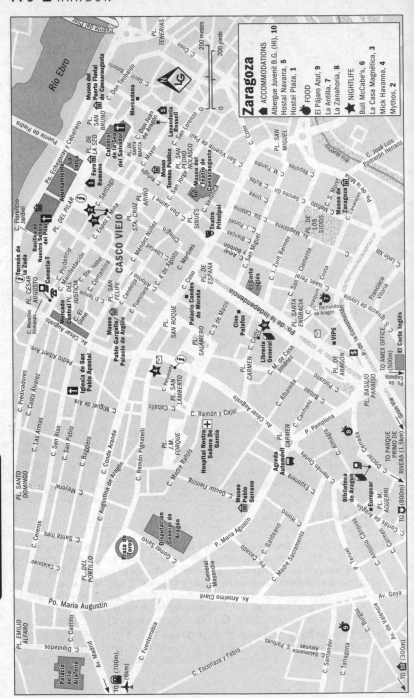

7:30pm, €20-36); **Logroño** (2¼hr., 3-4 per day 6:30am-7:30pm, €9.50-19.50); **Madrid** (3hr.; M-F 15 per day 12:48am-10pm, Su 13 per day; €22-42); **Pamplona** (2¼ hr., 6 per day 6:30am-9:15pm, €9.50); **San Sebastián** (4-5hr., 2 per day 11am-4:33pm, €22-26.50); **Teruel** (3hr., 3 per day 8:10am-7:20pm, €9.20); **Valencia** (6hr., 2-3 per day 12:33am-3:45pm, €16.50-38.50). **AVE** or **Altair** high-speed trains go to: **Guadalajara** (1¾hr., 6 per day 7am-9:25pm, €37); **Lérida** (1hr., 11 per day 6:40am-10:46pm, €24); **Madrid** (2hr., 12 per day 6:45am-10pm, €43).

Buses: Various bus companies dot the city, each with private terminals. **Agreda Automóvil,** Pa. María Agustín, 7 (☎ 976 22 93 43; www.agredasa.es). As of summer 2008 all buses will run from Delicias Station. Make sure to confirm schedule details online or at the ticket window. To **Barcelona** (3¾hr., 18-21 per day 12am-10:45pm, €12.60); **Madrid** (3¾hr., 18-21 per day 12:15am-9:45pm, €13.23); and **Soria** (2½hr.; M-Sa 3 per day 7:30am-4:30pm, Su 9am-2:30pm; €9).

Public Transportation: TUZSA buses, Po. Independencia 24-26. (☎976 59 27 27; www.tuzsa.es. open M-F 9:30am-2pm and 5-8pm; phone information daily 6am-11pm) cover the city (7am-midnight; €0.80, 10-ride pass €4.65; tickets available at the office or on the bus). Nighttime service (BUHO) limited to 7 lines; up to 45min. waits. Bus #51 runs from the train station past the bus station to Pl. Basilio Paraíso on Po. de la Constitución. Bus #23 runs down Av. César Augusto past Pl. Pilar, through Pl. España, then south of Po. Constitución. Bus #21 runs down C. San Vicente de Paúl to Pl. España, Pl. Paraíso, and then toward Palacio de la Aljaferia.

Taxis: Radio-Taxi Aragón (☎ 976 38 38 38) and **Cooperative** (☎976 75 15 15 or 976 42 42 42). Train station to Pl. del Pilar €6-8.

Car Rental: Europcar, C. Hernán Cortés, 31 (☎976 23 23 63). Second location in RENFE station. From €60 per day or €229 per week. Many discounts offered. 21+. Under-25 fee €6 per day. Open M-F 8am-1:30pm and 4-8pm, Sa 9am-1pm.

■✚🔢 ORIENTATION AND PRACTICAL INFORMATION

Five spokes radiate from **Plaza Basilio Paraíso.** Facing the center of the plaza with the IberCaja bank building at your back, the spokes are (moving clockwise): Po. de Sagasta; Po. Gran Vía, which becomes Po. Fernando el Católico; Po. Pamplona, which leads to Po. María Agustín and the **train station;** Po. de la Independencia, which ends at **Plaza de España** (at the bottom of the *casco viejo,* or old quarter); and Po. de la Constitución, (the top border of La Zona). Most tourist attractions are in the *casco viejo,* close to the river; **Plaza del Pilar,** the tourist hub, is a block from the water. To head downtown, take the #51 bus, which stops just outside the station. The areas around the university (corner of Pamplona and Gran Vía), as well as **C. Espoz y Mina,** are full of small cafes and bars where students and locals sip drinks and eat one *bocadillo* after another.

Tourist Office: Pl. del Pilar (☎976 39 35 37; www.turismozaragoza.com). Friendly, multilingual staff offer a free **map** and brochures. The *Guía de servicios turísticos de Aragón* has information on accommodations and services for the whole region. The Zaragoza Card (€12) waives all museum admission fees for 24hr. Open daily Sept.-Mar. 10am-8pm; Apr.-Oct. 9am-9pm. **Branches** in the train station (☎976 32 44 68; open daily 10am-8pm) and in the Torreón de la Zuda (☎976 20 12 00; open daily 10am-8pm, Jan. 7-Easter 10am-2pm and 4:30-8pm). **Tourist bus** (☎902 20 12 12 or 976 20 12 00. 1hr.; daily July-Aug. every 15min 10:45am-8pm; Sept.-Oct. Sa and Su every 15min. 10:45am-8pm. Night tours July 9:30 and 11pm, Aug. also 10pm, Sept.-Oct. 17 9:30pm; day €4, night €5.50; children under 5 free, over 65 half-price). Tickets on sale on the bus and in tourist offices; night bus tickets at the Pl. de Pilar office before 7pm.

Currency Exchange: Banks line Po. de la Independencia, with **ATMs** everywhere. **Banco Santander Central Hispano,** Pl. de Aragón, 6 (24hr. ☎902 24 24 24) has good rates on traveler's checks with no commission on AmEx Travelers Cheques. Open M-F 8:30am-2pm, Sa 8:30am-1pm.

Luggage Storage: Train station (small €3, large €4.50 per 24hr.). Open 7am-11pm. Agreda Automóvil bus station, Po. María Agustín, 7. €1.20, open M-F 10am-1:30pm and 4-7:30pm, Sa 10am-1:30pm.

English-Language Bookstore: Librería General, Po. de la Independencia, 22 (☎976 22 44 83). 5 levels with modest English selection in the basement. Open M-Sa 10am-1:30pm and 5-8:30pm.

Laundromat: Lavandería Rossell, C. San Vicente de Paúl, 29 (☎976 29 90 34). Wash and dry small load €7, medium €9.80, large €13. Open M-F 8:30am-1:15pm and 4:45-8pm.

Police: Emergency (☎092), all other calls (☎ 976 72 41 11), on C. Domingo Miral and in train station lobby.

Medical Services: Emergency (☎112). **Hospital Universitario Miguel Servet,** Av. Isabel la Católica, 1 (☎976 76 55 00). **Ambulancias Cruz Roja,** C. Sancho y Gil, 8 (☎976 22 48 80).

Internet Access: Conecta-T, C. Murallas Romanas, 4 (☎976 20 59 79). €0.80 per 30min. on flat-screen computers. International calls €0.13 per min. to US. Open M-F 10am-11pm, Sa-Su 11am-11pm; **Biblioteca de Aragón,** C. Doctor Cerrada, 22 (☎976 71 50 26; http://portal.aragon.es). Has 9 free Internet terminals, but expect a wait. Open M-F 8:30am-8:30pm, Sa 9:30am-2pm.

Post Office: Po. de la Independencia, 33 (☎902 19 71 97). **Faxes** upstairs; Locutorio (cheap long-distance calls) downstairs. Open M-F 8:30am-8:30pm, Sa 9:30am-2pm. **Postal Code:** 50001.

▐ ACCOMMODATIONS

Small hostels and *pensiones* line the narrow streets of the central *casco viejo* (old town), especially within the rectangle bounded by C. Alfonso I, C. Don Jaime I, Pl. de España, and Pl. del Pilar. Be wary the week of October 12, when Zaragoza celebrates the *Fiesta de la Virgen del Pilar*. Make reservations as early as possible and expect to pay up to double the rates listed below. Reservations are essential during *Ferias* (trade shows; www.feriazaragoza.com; Feb.-Apr.).

Hostal Navarra, C. San Vicente de Paúl, 30 (☎976 29 16 84). Comfortable rooms with sink, some with balconies. TV lounge. Convenient location near nightlife in La Zona. Singles €20, with bath €30; doubles €38; triples €45/55. MC/V. ❷

Hostal Plaza, Pl. del Pilar, 14 (☎976 29 48 30; fax 976 29 48 39). Upstairs from the Plaza in a prime location. Modern baths, TV, and phone in the 13 cozy rooms; interior rooms have A/C. Singles with shower and sink or toilet €25, larger with full bath €35; doubles €45; triples €60. AmEx/MC/V. ❸

Albergue Juvenil Baltasar Gracián (HI), C. Franco y López, 4 (☎976 71 68 80; central reservation line 902 08 89 05). Quite out of the way, but a real deal. 50 beds in rooms of 2, 4, and 8. Sheets and breakfast included. Reception 7am-midnight. HI card required. Dorms €9.90-€14. MC/V. ❶

▐ FOOD

Zaragoza is the self-proclaimed tapas capital of Spain. Check out the tourist-office pamphlet, *Guía de Tapas*, for details and information on this tasty tradition. The staple food of Zaragoza are *bocadillos*, and visitors are never far from a salty snack and a cold *tubo* (beer on tap). The side streets flanking C. Don Jaime I and Pl. de Santa Marta positively brim with tapas bars, restaurants, and *cervecerías* (breweries, such as **Domino, El Lino,** and **Cervecería Marpi**). Fresh fruits, meats, cheeses, and vegetables are stashed in the **Mercado Central,** a long green building on Av. César Augusto off Pl. del Pilar. (Open M-F 9am-2pm and 5-8pm, Sa 9am-2pm.) Stock up on groceries at **Mercadona,** C. San Vicente de Paúl, 42 (☎976 20 57 83. Open M-Sa 9:30am-9:30pm. MC/V.), or at the supermarket in **El Corte Inglés,** Po. de Sagasta, 3. (☎976 21 11 21. Open M-Sa 10am-10pm. AmEx/MC/V.)

📰 **La Zanahoria,** C. Tarragona, 4 (☎976 35 87 94). One of a handful of vegetarian restaurants in all of Aragón, Zanahoria has dished up fresh salads (€4-6), quiches (€7), and soup (€4-6) for over 25 years. Food served in the colorful dining room by the owner himself. *Menú* €10. Open Tu-Sa 1:30-4pm and 9-11:30pm, Su 1:40-4pm. MC/V. ❷

El Pájaro Azul, C. Doctor Cerrado, 8 (☎976 23 93 83). The perfect place for a beer (€1.50) and *bocadillos* (€1-3) in the afternoon or early evening, the Pájaro sports blue tiled walls, salty *jamón serrano*, and a diverse crowd of students and locals. Like any *bocadillo* place worthy of the name, this one's cheap, so try anything that catches your eye from the clear glass case on the bar. Open daily 7am-11pm. Cash only. ❶

La Antilla, C. Hernando de Aragón, 1 (☎976 23 87 83), off Pl. Santa Engracia just across the street from the church when walking from Po. Independencia. Look for the orange sign. Has great *bocadillos* (€3.70) and *tostadas* (€2.10-2.90) with smoked ham, egg, peppers, and cheeses. Slightly upscale crowd packs in for lunch, but space at the bar turns over quickly. Open daily 7am-1am. AmEx/MC/V. ❶

🔘 SIGHTS

AROUND PLAZA DEL PILAR. A sweeping square bordered by buildings that range from Baroque to ultramodern, Pl. del Pilar alone offers enough to satisfy any traveler. The beautiful basilica, flanked on one side by a dignified Goya statue-fountain and on the other by a modernist angular fountain, presides over the square. It's the perfect place to begin a city tour or simply sit and feed pigeons all day.

🔲 BASÍLICA DE NUESTRA SEÑORA DEL PILAR. Zaragoza's defining landmark was built to replace temples destroyed by fires in 1443 and again in 1515. The structure was built around the **Sacred Pillar of the Virgin,** which has never moved from its original location and now supports a statue of Mary. Many of the walls feature frescoes by Goya, who was commissioned to paint the church's cupolas. Three bombs (two of which are now on display) were dropped on the basilica during the Spanish Civil War in 1936, but they failed to explode, purportedly due to divine intervention ("low-flying planes" to skeptics). The **Museo del Pilar** inside the basilica exhibits the glittering *Joyero de la Virgen* (Virgin's jewels), including a gold crown inlaid with jewels from every region of Spain and preliminary paintings of the ceiling frescoes. The one absolute must-see is the breathtaking 🔲**panorama** of Zaragoza from one of the towers (access from rear). Nowhere else is the collision of ultra-ancient and ultra-modern more visible than in a view of the Iber-Caja building tower over the *casco viejo*, with Roman ruins peeking out from behind modern fountains, or 21st-century wind power next to 10th-century farms. *(Pl. del Pilar. Basílica open daily in summer 5:30am-9:30pm; in winter 5:30am-8:30pm. Free. Museum ☎976 29 95 64. Open daily 9am-2pm and 4-6pm. €1.50. Elevator open June-Aug. M-Th and Sa-Su 9:30am-2pm and 4-7pm; Sept.-May M-Th and Sa-Su 9:30am-2pm and 4-6pm. €2.)*

CATEDRAL DE LA SEO DEL SALVADOR. This equally beautiful but less imposing Romanesque cathedral was constructed in the latter half of the 12th century, but reworked in Gothic style between 1316 and 1319. Inside, the jaw-dropping alabaster high altarpiece (1434) has the tomb of the first Archbishop of Aragón embedded in it. *(Pl. de la Seo, to the right when facing the Basílica. Entrance through the back, on C.*

Palafox. ☎ 976 20 07 52. Open May-Oct. M-F 10am-2pm and 4-7pm, Sa 10am-1pm and 4-7pm, Su 10am-noon and 4-7pm; Nov.-Apr. closes at 6pm. Last entrance 30min. before closing.)

BEYOND PLAZA DEL PILAR

MUSEO PABLO GARGALLO. Dedicated to one of the most influential Aragonese sculptors (1881-1934) of the 1920s, the Museo Pablo Gargallo houses 170 of his works in the graceful Palacio de los Condes de Argillo, built in 1670. The building's layout and bright interior reinforce Gargallo's commitment to space as a sculptural medium. The collection also holds drawings, jewelry, and pieces shaped for use in sculptures, providing insight into Gargallo's artistic process. *(Pl. San Felipe, 3. ☎ 976 72 49 22. Open Tu-Sa 10am-2pm and 5-9pm, Su 10am-2pm. Closed indefinitely for renovations. Free.)*

PALACIO DE LA ALJAFERÍA. The turrets, towers, and great halls of this impressive palace are an architectural documentary of the history of Aragón and Spain. In its long history, Aljafería was host to Muslims, Catholics, and even monarchs. The palace's oldest standing structure, the **Troubador Tower,** is emblematic of the palace's original defensive purposes. Sheltered within this site is the exquisitely detailed **Taifal Palace,** built in the *omeya* style, an influence of 9th-century Muslim palaces. When Alfonso I el Batallador (The Warrior) took Zaragoza from the Muslims in 1118, the Aljafería was Christianized, but the influence of Islamic art and architecture still lingers. In 1492, **El Palacio de los Reyes Católicos** was erected by Fernando and Isabel. Visitors are free to go upstairs into the palace and enjoy room after immaculate room. *(C. Diputados. Take bus #21, 51, or 33 until you reach the massive compound. ☎ 976 28 96 83. Open Apr. 15-Oct. 15 daily 10am-2pm and 4:30-8pm; Oct. 16-Apr. 14 M-Sa 10am-2pm and 5-8pm, except Th and F mornings, Su 10am-2pm. Guided tours in English. €3, students and seniors €1, under 12 free.)*

MUSEO PABLO SERRANO. This modern building houses 150 bronze sculptures by the rhythm-and-space-obsessed *aragonés* Pablo Serrano (1908-1985). Look for *Gran pan partido* (Big Sliced Bread) and sculptural reinterpretations of works by Picasso, Velázquez, and Goya. Serrano's distorted busts of famous writers make parts of the exhibit a "who's who" of Spanish literature, with Machado, Cela, Velasquez and others all in attendance. *(Po. María Agustín, 20. Catch #21 bus from Pl. España. ☎ 976 28 06 59. Open Tu-Sa 10-2pm and 5-8pm, Su and holidays 10-2pm. Free.)*

MUSEO DEL TEATRO DE CAESARAGUSTA. The ruins of this 1st-century Roman theatre were dug up unexpectedly by Zaragozans in 1972. To protect the archaeologically important structure, it has been covered by a trussed hemispherical roof and interlaced with suspended footpaths, and is accompanied by a museum. Those interested in the Christian and Jewish history of Zaragoza will not be disappointed by exhibits that recount, among other oddities, the system of locking doors that kept Jews out of the Christian neighborhoods during Easter in the 13th century. *(Calle San Jorge 12. ☎ 976 20 50 88. Open Tu-Sa 10am-9pm, Su 10am-2pm. €4.)*

 NIGHTLIFE AND FESTIVALS

The nightlife scene in Zaragoza is limited almost entirely to weekends—many bars don't bother to open until Thursday or Friday. Most locals begin their nights in swanky **La Zona,** the streets bounded by Po. de la Constitución, C. León XIII, Po. de las Damas, and Camino de las Torres, between Plaza Del Pilar and downtown. Partiers craving flashing lights and thumping music should head over to C. Espoz y Mina near Pl. del Pilar, or small streets north of Pl. San Felipe like C. Temple, C Contamina, and C. Sta Isabel, for a variety of venues. Party like a god at **Mythos,** C. Espoz y Mina, 19, a throwback to the hip 5th century. (Beer €3. Mixed drinks

€5.50. Open Th 11pm-3:30am, F-Sa 11pm-4:30am.) Alternatively, go to its neighbor, **La Casa Magnética,** a sometime dance club with black lights and a bar suspended from the ceiling. (Beer €2. Mixed drinks €4.50. Open Tu-Th 7pm-late, F-Su 8pm-late.) For a taste of home, stop by **Bull McCabe's,** C. Cádiz, 7. This Irish pub has two floors, pizza, and five TV screens. (☎976 22 50 16. Open until 2:30am, food until 10:30pm. Cash only.) **Gay bars** and **discotecas** are in and around the west side of the *casco viejo.* Guys from their late teens and up start the night at **Mick Havanna,** C. Ramón Pignatelli, 7, which sports zebra-striped wallpaper, a long bar, and numerous television screens. (☎976 28 44 50. Open daily 5pm-3am.)

🗺 DAYTRIPS FROM ZARAGOZA

Ask at the Zaragoza tourist office for info on excursions like the Ruta del Vino (wine route) and the Ruta de Goya. Students of the Romanesque should inquire about visits to the **Cinco Villas** (Five Villages).

🗺 PARQUE DEL MONASTERIO DE PIEDRA

Aragón Tours buses, Estación Delicias (☎976 21 93 20; www.aragon-tours.com), leave from Zaragoza (2¾hr.; July to mid-Oct. daily 9am, return 5pm; mid-Oct. to June M, Th, Sa, Su only; round-trip €17.16). Park open daily July-Sept. 9am-8pm (or until dark); Oct.-June 9am-6pm. ☎976 84 90 11; www.monasteriopiedra.com. Open July-Sept. 10:15am-1:15pm and 3:15-7:15pm; Oct.-June 10:15am-1:15pm and 3:15-5:15pm. Park, monument, museum, and presentation €11, under 12 and seniors €7.50; monument only €6.

In the heart of semi-arid central Spain, 100km southwest of Zaragoza, the Parque del Monasterio de Piedra seems like a mirage: a blur of greenery, waterfalls, and ponds fill the park. At the orders of Alfonso II of Aragón, who sought to extend the influence of Catholicism in this region, the monastery was constructed in the late 12th century by Cistercian monks over 23 years from remnants of a Moorish castle. After 700 years and many wars, a second state order forced its abandonment in 1835. The monastery was auctioned off and is still privately owned. It currently serves as a three-star hotel and a wine museum (once the monastery's cellar). A tour through the monastery takes you past translucent alabaster windows (which admitted light but prevented views of the tempting world outside the monastery), and other ingenious architectural ploys of the monks. Don't miss the park's highlight, La Gruta Iris (Iris Grotto), the narrow, dripping system of caverns behind the 53m Cascada Iris (Iris Waterfall). The waterfall is part of the Río Piedra, a calcium-rich stream that, according to legend, once turned everything it touched into stone. For a treat, visit at sunset.

TARAZONA

Therpasa (☎976 22 57 23, at Delicias Station) runs buses from Zaragoza (1hr., 6 per day 8am-8:30pm, €5.90) and Soria (1hr., 6 per day 7:30am-8pm, €4.45). Tarazona station (☎976 64 11 00), is on Av. Navarra, near Pl. San Francisco.

Tarazona (pop. 11,000) is, without doubt, one of the best cities in which to get lost. The winding streets at the base of this ancient Roman city are lined with one-room *panaderías* (bakeries), cafes, and markets. In the old Jewish Quarter, iron lanterns hang from the walls, and the streets open onto small green plazas.

Known as the "Mudéjar City," Tarazona was ruled by Romans, Visigoths, and Muslims. Legend has it that Hercules himself helped build it. The town makes a nice daytrip from Zaragoza, especially during **Las Fiestas de Cipotegato** (Aug. 27–Sept. 1). The festivities begin at noon on the 27th, when a jester, clad in a red, green, and yellow harlequin suit, is released into the crowd from the Ayuntamiento. After being pelted with tomatoes, he makes his way through the city. Once he completes his route, the jester's identity is triumphantly revealed before the townsfolk. The next six days are ablaze with activities, including *encierros*, bullfights, concerts, and dances honoring San Atilano, Tarazona's patron saint. At other times of the year, you can visit the **Ayuntamiento** (Pl. de España) and admire its beautiful 16th-century facade.

Tarazona's centerpiece is its hulking 13th- and 15th-century **cathedral**, under renovation until August 2008, when it is expected to reopen in time for the Expo 2008 in Zaragoza. The brick towers, belfry, lantern, and plasterwork in the inner cloister and ceiling are fine examples of *mudéjar* work. From the cathedral, follow signs for Soria and Zaragoza down C. De Los Laureles, then take your first right and enter the yellow, octagonal **Plaza de Toros Vieja**. Erected in the 18th century, the bullring included private residences with built-in balconies for watching *corridas* (bullfights). Now renovated, it houses offices and a *taberna* (bar/restaurant). Tarazona was also the occasional residence of Aragón's kings until the 15th century. The current **Palacio Episcopal** (exit the bullring on the side opposite the entrance, cross the river, and follow the signs) was their home; before that, it was a Muslim palace. Opposite the Palacio Episcopal, in the heart of **El Cinto** (the medieval quarter), rises the 12th-century **Iglesia de Santa Magdalena,** with its *mudéjar* tower. (Open in summer M-F 8pm, Sa 7pm, Su 11:30am; in winter M-F 7pm.) Entrance across from the Palacio, on the Plaza del Palacio. From Santa Magdalena's stairs, there is a wonderful panoramic view of the cathedral and the bullring. Many travelers with cars drive the 10min. to the nearby **Monasterio de Veruela**, while those without take a Therpasa bus to Vera and follow the signs.

The **tourist office,** Pl. de San Francisco, 1, is on the opposite side of the river from most of the *casco viejo*. Make sure to stop by and get their excellent *Plano-Guía*, or combination map and guide. (☎976 64 00 74. Open July-Aug. M-F 10am-1:30pm and 4:30-7pm, Sa-Su 10am-1:30pm and 4:30-8pm; Sept.-June Sa-Su closes at 7pm. Tours by reservation; €5.) **Banco Santander Central Hispano,** in Pl. San Francisco, charges no commission and has a 24hr. **ATM.** (Open Apr.-Sept. M-F 8:30am-2pm; Oct.-Mar. M-F 8:30am-2pm, Sa 8:30am-1pm.) The **police station** is on Pl. de San Francisco (☎976 64 16 91).

TERUEL ☎978

Teruel (pop. 31,000), the small capital of southern Aragón, seduces visitors with its history of tragic love and rich cultural exchange. Muslims, Jews, and Christians lived and worked here together between the 12th and 15th centuries, and this pluralism is still evident today: the city's ubiquitous *mudéjar* architecture mixes Arabic patterns with Gothic and Romanesque styles. The town's welcoming narrow streets and tucked-away plazas belie its cosmopolitan past. The modern city adjoining is the busier counterpart to the winding streets of the *casco antiguo*. An easy stopover between Valencia and Zaragoza, Teruel doesn't reach its prime until July, when citizens celebrate the resilience of their *torico* (iron bull) in a seven-day liquor fest.

⎚ TRANSPORTATION. Trains depart from Camino de la Estación, 1 (☎902 24 02 02), downstairs from Po. del Óvalo, to **Valencia** (2½-3¾hr.; 3, 8am, 6:45pm; €9.20-10.60) and **Zaragoza** (2½hr.; 6:45, 11:52am, 6:17pm; €11.25). **Buses** depart from the station on Ronda de Ambeles (☎978 61 07 89; www.estacionbus-teruel.com), opposite the *casco antiguo* from the train station. **Abasa** (☎978 83 08 71) goes to **Barcelona** (5½-6½hr., M-Sa 8am, €23). **Jiménez** runs to **Zaragoza** (3hr.; M-Sa 6-7 per day 7am-11pm, Su 3 per day 2:15-7pm; €8). **Samar** (☎978 60 34 50) goes to **Cuenca** (2hr.; M-Sa 11:45am, Su 9:30pm; €8.20) and **Madrid** (4½-5hr.; M-F 4 per day 7:30am-5pm, Sa-Su 7:30am, 1:30, 5pm; €16.50). For a **taxi,** call ☎978 61 75 77.

❇️🔢 ORIENTATION AND PRACTICAL INFORMATION. With your back to the train station, the *casco antiguo* lies at the top of a postcard-worthy staircase, perched on a hilltop. Modern Teruel is to the right over the bridges joining two hills. Unless you are extra-adventurous, or are drawn to suburban housing, you should probably not leave the *casco antiguo*. The center of the *casco antiguo* is affectionately known as **Plaza del Torico** for the tiny bull statue perched atop a column in the street. The plaza, C. Nueva, and Pl. de Tomás Bretón also house a handful of *Modernista* buildings by Pablo Monguió, a Gaudí follower. To reach Pl. del Torico from the **train station,** go up the staircase from the park in front and walk down C. Nueva, the street that runs straight from the stairs; it ends in Pl. del Torico. From the **bus station,** a purple sign to your left points to a small street. Take it, and make a right at the intersection with the blue "Sony" sign.

The **tourist office** is on C. San Francisco in a large, modern Gobierno de Aragón building. To get there from the train, turn left immediately after scaling the stairs. From Pl. del Torico, follow C. Salvador and turn right on C. San Francisco. Most useful are their *itinerarios*, walking routes through the *casco antiguo*, which feature guides to *modernista* buildings and the *mudéjar* towers throughout the city. (Free guided tour in Spanish or English; www.turismoaragon.com. Open M-Sa 9am-2pm and 4:30-7pm, July 1-Sept.15 until 8pm; Su 10am-2pm and 4:30-7pm.) **Banco Santander Central Hispano** is at Pl. del Torico, 15. (Open M-F 8:30am-2:30pm; Oct.-May also Sa 8:30am-1pm.) **Internet, international calls, fax,** and Western Union **money transfers** are available at **Mister Phone** down the stairs at C. Ramón y Cajal, 15. (☎978 61 77 39. Internet €0.50 per 15min. Open M-Sa 11am-2pm and 5:30-9:30pm, Su 5:30-10pm.) The **post office,** C. Yagüe de Salas, 19, can also send **faxes.** (☎902 927 927. Open M-F 8:30am-8:30pm, Sa 9:30am-2pm.) **Postal Code:** 44001.

🔢🔲 ACCOMMODATIONS AND FOOD. Lodgings are scarce during August and *Semana Santa* and impossible during the fiesta in early July—reserve months in advance. Thought to be the oldest hostel in all of Spain, **Fonda del Tozal ❷,** C. Rincón, 5, promises the rustic charm and comfort of a *casa rural* complete with tiled floors and skeleton keys. Guests will enjoy the impressive stable-turned-bar downstairs. (☎978 61 02 07. Doubles €27-33, with bath €38-45; triples €37-42/48-55. Extra bed €9. Cash only.) To get to **Hostal Aragón ❷,** C. Santa María, 4, head in the direction the *torico* statue faces and take the first left as you leave Pl. del Torico. Friendly owners keep spacious rooms, some with TV. (☎978 61 18 77. Singles €20, with bath €25; doubles €29-43; triples with bath €51. MC/V.) Teruel is famous for its cured ham, *jamón de Teruel*, featured in tapas bars, **Rokelín** ham stores, and restaurants; there are several in the town (C. Comandante Foreta, 9, C. Rincón, 2, and C. Joaquin Costa, 33). The *Rokelín* tapas bar on C. Ramón y Cajal off Pl. del Torico serves trays of fresh ham, cheese, salads, and sandwiches (€3-12). For a quick bite in an enviable location (albeit a slightly touristy one), check out the giant *bocadillos* (€3.50-16), *patatas bravas*, and salads (€4-10) at **Bar Gregory ❶,** Po. del Ovalo, 6, overlooking the city staircase. (☎978 60 05 80. Liters of *cerveza* or *sangria* €5-7. Open daily 7-1am. MC/V.) Lovers of all things Italian will appreciate the pastas (€5.40-7.20) and crisp specialty pizzas (€7-10), along with local wines, served at the cozy **Los Caprichos ❷,** C. Caracol, 1, from Pl. del Torico, two blocks up C. Hartzenbusch on the right. (☎978 60 03 30. Takeout available. Open Tu-Su 1:30-4pm and 8:30-11:30pm. MC/V.) Of course, you can always skip a meal and stuff yourself with assorted goodies from pastry shops, including **Pastelería Sanz ❷,** C. Ramón y Cajal, 2, half a block from the plaza, which has flawless croissants. (Open M-F 8am-2pm and 5-8pm, Sa 9am-2pm and 5:30-8:30pm, Su 10am-2pm. Cash only.) If your sweet tooth is under control, however, there is a **market** on Pl. Domingo Gascón; from Pl. del Torico, take C. Joaquín Costa for two blocks. (Open M-F 9:30am-2pm and 5-7pm, Sa 9am-2pm.) During the summer, Thursdays and Fridays bring a flock of fresh fruit and vegetable stands to Los Arcos 9am-2pm; follow Ronda Damaso Torán a few blocks downhill to the left.

◐ **SIGHTS.** The mother of all Teruel's *mudéjar* monuments is the 13th-century **Catedral de Santa María de Mediavilla.** The vast aesthetic difference between the two chapels is noteworthy—the gilding of the Baroque **Capilla de la Inmaculada,** dating from the 18th century, is brilliant compared to the more subdued, though intricately detailed, wooden carvings of the 16th-century *retablo mayor* (altar). What brings the cathedral fame, however, is the intricate *techumbre mudéjar,* a decorative red-and-blue ceiling displaying clear Islamic influences in scenes of religious imagery, animals, and even vegetables. Behind the cathedral in the Episcopal Palace is the **Museo de Arte Sacro,** exhibiting religious paintings by local artists, carvings, and sculptures from medieval to Baroque origin. (☎978 61 80 16. Cathedral open daily 11am-2pm and 4-7pm; May-Sept. open until 8pm. Call ahead for free guided tours in Spanish. Museum open M-Sa 10am-2pm and 4-8pm. Cathedral and museum €3, students and seniors €2.) Muslim artisans built the brick-and-glazed-tile **Torres Mudéjares** between the 12th and 15th centuries; the tourist office offers a walking tour that hits them all. The most intricately designed of the towers is the 14th-century **Torre del Salvador,** which rises above C. del Salvador and literally straddles the street, a striking green and white welcome to the city. Climb 122 steps through several chambers, many packed with intricate model cities, to the bell tower and its panoramic views. (☎978 60 20 61; www.teruelmudejar.com. Open Tu-Su 11am-2pm and 4-8pm, M 11-2pm. Closed July 10-13. €2.50, ages 6-12 and seniors €1.80.) According to local legend, in 1217 Teruel's Diego Marcilla died from heartache after the love of his life, Isabel Segura, was married off to a wealthy nobleman. After his funeral, Isabel gave her dead lover a kiss and collapsed dead on top of his body. Teruel's famous love story is kept alive at the colorful **Mausoleo de los Amantes,** a recently renovated tomb connected to the modernist and *mudéjar* **Iglesia de San Pedro.** The church has a 14th century structure, but was designed by 20th-century local artist Salvador Gisbert. It accompanies the **Torre San Pedro,** Teruel's first *mudéjar* tower. Ask about guided tours of the Tower and especially the *Ándito,* a tiny path around the outside of the church providing close-up views of the magnificent 19th century stained glass windows. (☎978 60 83 98. Open daily 10am-2pm and 4-8pm; last entry 30min. before closing. €7 for the Conjunto Amanto: San Pedro, its tower, and the tomb/museum.)

▓ **FESTIVALS.** Teruel's most renowned celebration is the **Fiestas del Ángel,** also known as *La Vaquilla* (the heifer). The 10-day celebration takes place from the F-Su closest to the **Fiesta del San Cristóbal** (July 10), usually the second weekend of July. The festivities are in loving honor of the town square's little *torico* (he wears an honorary red handkerchief for the week). The second guest of honor is Santa Emerenciana, the patron saint of Teruel. Traditional attire is worn for the *corridas,* puppet parades, public picnics, fireworks, and, of course, the continuous liquored-up nighttime celebrations (Su-Tu dawn). Teruel's population quadruples for this celebration, so plan accordingly. Sept. 10-17 brings the **Feria del Jamón,** when ham producers set up stands to advertise their mouth-watering delicacies.

LA RIOJA

La Rioja is synonymous with great wine. The Ebro tributary Río Oja, from which the region's name is derived, trickles through the countless vineyards and wineries that characterize the region. "Rioja" is an internationally acclaimed family of wines with an 800-year-old tradition; the '94, '95, '01, and '02 grapes received the highest ratings possible, and since 1991, it has been the only Spanish wine to earn the coveted *Calificada* rating. The best *bodegas* (wine cellars) draw from the lands in western Rioja Alta, around the town of Haro. Try to stay sober enough to walk at least part of the Camino de Santiago, which passes through much of the region. The Camino towns take great pride in their role in the pilgrimage and show hospitality to pilgrims and tourists alike. The smallest of Spain's provinces, La Rioja offers a relaxed atmosphere and varying terrain—the Sierra mountains, with tranquil fields at the feet of their towering peaks, line the region's southern border.

LOGROÑO   ☎941

Logroño (pop. 140,000), the capital city of La Rioja, is the best place to enter the region's vineyard towns, loosely known as the *"Ruta de Vino,"* or wine route. The city's first priority has always been its *bodegas:* in 1635, the mayor banned carts from streets next to wineries "for fear that the vibration caused by these vehicles might affect the wine." But Logroño offers more than just wine; it calls itself Spain's first commercial city, boasting a long tradition of arts, theater, and food. The mayor himself wrote the city's best tapas guide. Logroño's name dates as far back as the 10th century and comes from *"illo Gronio"* (the passageway), the gate-like rock elevations along the Río Ebro. Many castles guarded the crucial *puente de piedra* (stone bridge) over the Ebro, as Logroño was a prized target for conquest. Though the town is home to several stops on the Camino de Santiago, these days Logroño offers little but commerce for the culture-hungry tourist. Delicious local specialties, however, are sure to satisfy the heartiest appetite.

▐ TRANSPORTATION

Trains: RENFE, Pl. de Europa (☎902 24 02 02), off Av. de España on the south side of town, southeast of the bus station. Info open daily 7am-11pm, advance tickets 9am-9pm. To: **Barcelona** (7hr., 3 per day 12:46pm-4:04am, €32-43); **Bilbao** (4hr., 2-3 per day 4:20am-6:48pm, €21-26); **Burgos** (2hr., 2-3 per day 4:20am-6:40pm, €21-27); **Madrid** (4hr., M-Sa 8am, €49.80); **Vitoria-Gasteiz** (1½hr., M-F 7pm, €7.20); **Zaragoza** (2-2½hr.; M-F 6-7 per day 1:41am-8:10pm, Sa-Su 4:04am-8:10pm; €10.20-22).

Buses: Av. de España (☎941 23 59 83), on the corner of C. del General Vara de Rey and Av. de Pío XII. More

LOOT OF THE VINE

As the old saying goes, behind every great grape is a great non-governmental regulatory agency. Nowhere does that maxim hold more true than in La Rioja wine country, where every bottle is strictly controlled by the Consejo Regulador: referee of the reds and watchdog of the whites.

The Consejo began some 100 years ago, when growers and bodega-owners decided that they needed to a way to differentiate between the real, more expensive Rioja wine and the average Vino de Mesa (table wines) that competed with them.

The first order of Consejo business was the development of a sacrosanct labeling system for every Rioja bottle. The little rectangle on the back of the *rosado* you bought at a vineyard certifies it as genuine Rioja product. The rectangle on the bottle that came with your €9 *menú* is puny by comparison, saying only "vino de mesa," and lacking the shiny silver stamp.

Today, the Consejo polices the industry like an over-protective mother, shutting down growers and *bodegas* that fail to comply with an intricate set of rules.

Caught growing grapes in April? Vineyard producing more wine per acre than allowed? These infractions mean trouble, because a sanction from the Consejo is a wine business death sentence. You may find, though, that the distinctions matter less and less with each glass you drink.

convenient than trains for nearby destinations. Info M-Sa 6am-11pm, Su 7am-11pm. To: **Barcelona** (6hr., 5 per day 12:40am-3:30pm, €25); **Burgos** (2hr.; M-Sa 6-7 per day 8:30am-7:30pm, Su 3 per day 11am-9:45pm; €7); **Madrid** (4hr.; M-Th and Sa 6 per day 6:45am-7pm, F 10 per day 6:45am-10pm, Su 12 per day 9:30am-10pm; €19-45); **Pamplona** (2hr.; M-Sa 5 per day 7am-7pm, Su 3 per day 10am-4:30pm; €7); **Santo Domingo de la Calzada** (1hr.; M-F 11 per day 7:15am-8pm, Sa 7 per day 8:30am-7:30pm, Su 3 per day 11am-9:45pm; €3); **Soria** (1½hr., departure times same as Madrid, €7); **Vitoria-Gasteiz** (2hr.; M-F 6 per day 7am-8pm, Sa 4 per day 10am-8pm, Su 5 per day 10am-9:30pm; €8); **Zaragoza** (2hr.; M-Th and Sa 6 per day 6:45am-7pm, Su 4 per day 10:30am-9pm; €6-11).

Public Transportation: All local buses (☎941 20 27 77) run to Gran Vía del Rey Juan Carlos I at the intersection with C. del General Vara de Rey, 1 block from Parque del Espolón. **Info booth** at the bus station. Buses #1 and 3 pass the bus station. €0.56.

Taxis: Stands at the bus station (☎941 23 75 29) and Parque del Espolón (☎941 22 42 99). **Radio Taxi** (☎941 50 50 50). **ENO-Taxi** offers fixed prices on round trips.

Car Rental: Europcar, Pl. de Europa (☎941 51 23 41), to the left in the same building when exiting the train station.

✈ 🛈 ORIENTATION AND PRACTICAL INFORMATION

Gran Vía del Rey Juan Carlos I is Logroño's main east-west road. The token border between the old and new towns, **Po. del Espolón,** also the city's central park, runs one block north of Gran Vía. The *casco antiguo* (old quarter) lies between the park and the Río Ebro on the far north side of the city. To reach the park (and the regional tourist office, located in the park by C. del General Vara de Rey) from the **train station,** angle left on Av. de España, directly across from you with your back to the station. This will lead to the **bus station** (the next major intersection), where you turn right on C. del General Vara de Rey, which leads north to the park and the *casco antiguo* on your left (8min.).

Tourist Office: C. Portales, 39. (☎941 27 33 53; www.logroturismo.org). Two blocks to the right from Sagasta or 2 blocks to the left from C. del General Varda. Tours of the *casco antiguo* available, call for more information. English, French, and German spoken. Open June-Oct. M-F 9am-2pm and 5-8pm, Sa 10am-2pm and 5-8pm, Su 10am-2pm; Nov.-May M-Sa 10am-2pm and 4-8pm, Su 10am-2pm.

Currency Exchange: Banco Santander Central Hispano, Muro Francisco de la Mata, at Parque del Espolón. **ATM** inside. Open Apr.-Sept. M-F 8:30am-2pm; Oct.-Mar. M-F 8:30am-2pm, Sa 8:30am-1pm.

Luggage Storage: At **bus station.** €2 per locker. Open M-Sa 6am-11pm, Su 7am-11pm. At **train station** (€3). Open 24hr.

English-Language Bookstore: Santos Ochoa, C. de Sagasta, 3 (☎941 25 86 22) has a decent selection of books in English, and offers coffee and free Wi-Fi in a comfortable room upstairs. Open M-F 10am-1:45pm and 5-8:30pm, Sa 10:30am-2pm. MC/V.

Police: C. Ruavieja (☎092), near Iglesia de Palacio.

Medical Services: Hospital San Pedro, Plaza de San Pedro s/n (☎941 29 75 00). Follow Av. de La Paz away from the *casco antiguo,* and go right 5 blocks after the *Ayuntamiento.*

La Rioja Public Library, C. Merced, 1 (☎941 21 13 82; www.blr.larioja.org) has 2 terminals for public use on the top floor; drop by for 10min.

Post Office: C. Pérez Galdós, 40. From the bus station, turn left and walk 5 blocks. Open M-F 8:30am-8:30pm, Sa 8:30am-12pm. **Postal Code:** 26002.

ℾ ACCOMMODATIONS

For budget accommodations, the *casco antiguo* is the best bet. The neighborhood is chock-full of hostels and pensions of varying levels of affordability. Try C. San Juan, the second left past Parque del Espolón from the stations, or C. San Agustín and C. Laurel. Reservations are crucial for fiesta week near September 21.

Fonda Bilbaína, C. Capitán Eduardo Gallarza, 10, 2nd fl. (☎941 25 42 26). Take C. de Sagasta into the *casco antiguo*, turn left onto C. Hermanos Moroy and then right on C. Capitán Eduardo Gallarza. Bright rooms with high ceilings, wood floors, sinks, and big beds. Ask for a room with a balcony. Singles €26; doubles €30 MC/V. ❸

Pensión Sebastián, C. San Juan, 21 (☎941 24 28 00). Accessible from C. Muro del Carmen or C. Hermanos Moroy. Convenient location, colorfully decorated rooms, and friendly owner. Shared bath. Good social space. Doubles €30. Cash only. ❷

Hostal Niza, C. Capitán Eduardo Gallarza, 13 (☎941 20 60 44; www.hostalniza.com), a block before Bilbaína. A great deal for doubles. 16 rooms with TV, A/C, new baths, coffee and cookies, hair dryers, and (in some) DVD players. Doubles €60.20, for individual use €42.80, for 3 with extra bed €80.25. AmEx/MC/V. ❹

Residencia Universitaria (HI), C. Caballero de la Rosa, 38 (☎941 26 14 22). From C. del General Vara de Rey, turn right on Muro de Cervantes, which becomes Av. de la Paz. After 7 blocks, turn left on C. Caballero de la Rosa and walk 3 blocks. Rooms have public phone and 2 common rooms with TV. Doubles with bunks and private bath; rooms usually not shared. Breakfast included. Sheets €2.86. €8.15 per person. ❶

Asociación Riojana, Ruavieja, 32 (☎941 26 02 34; www.asantiago.org). Exclusively for pilgrims hiking the Santiago trail. Provides 88 beds in rooms of 24 for almost nothing. Lights out 10pm, laundry, free Internet, bag storage available. €3. ❶

◖ FOOD

Logroñeses take their grapes seriously—wine is the beverage of choice. C. Laurel and C. San Juan brim with bars and cafes. The **Mercado de Abastos** offers meat, fresh fruit, and vegetables in a building on C. Capitán Eduardo Gallarza. (Open M-F 8-2pm and 5-8pm, Sa 8-2pm) For **groceries,** head to **Champion,** Av. La Rioja 14-16, at C. Miguel Villanueva. (☎941 22 99 00. Open M-Sa 9am-9:30pm. AmEx/MC/V.)

◪ Juan & Juan, C. Albornoz, 5 (☎941 22 99 83). Brothers Juan Marcos and Juan Manuel opened this intimate restaurant 1 year ago. The lunch *menú* (€9) has good table wine, creative fries, and clever takes on local specialties like *lomo a la plancha* (pork loin). You'll be shocked you aren't paying twice the price. *Menús* €9-11. Open Tu-Sa 1:30-4pm and 9-closing, Su 1:30-4pm. MC/V. ❷

Bar De La Tortilla "Mere," Travesía de San Juan, 2 (☎941 23 07 16). Family-owned restaurant known for a variety of tapas, often involving tortillas in various guises. More adventurous diners order the fried lamb's ears, and toast with a local Rioja wine. Open Tu-Su 10am-3pm and 7pm-midnight. ❷

En Ascuas, C. Hermanos Moroy, 22 (☎941 24 68 67; www.enascuas.com). White tablecloths and rustic decor offset large black-and-white pictures and a window into the grill. Delicious appetizers (€3-13) and salads (€4.43-7). Fish entrees €7.50-14. Open Tu-Su 1:30-3:30pm and 8:30-11:30pm. D/MC/V. ❷

◔ SIGHTS

Aside from the beautiful **Parque del Espolón,** the numerous shopping streets, and the shop-and cafe-lined walkways of Av. de Juan, Logroño offers a few more historically significant attractions. In an 18th-century Baroque palace, the **Museo Provincial de La Rioja** has a collection of art, mostly religious works, spanning the last eight centuries. The museum also hosts a rotating contemporary art exhibit. (Pl. San Agustín, 23, along C. Portales. ☎941 29 12 59. Closed indefinitely for renovations. Free.) The twin towers of the 19th-century **Catedral de Santa María de La Redonda,** that hides a well-protected Michelangelo inside, dominate Pl. del Mercado in the *casco antiguo*. (Open M-Sa 8am-1pm and 6:30-8:45pm, Su 9am-2pm and 6:30-8:45pm. Free.) To get to **Iglesia de Santiago El Rea,** take C. Sagasta towards the river and make a left on C. Barriocepo. A mandatory stop on the Camino de Santiago, it is home to the Virgen de la Esperanza and a gleaming gold altar. (Open daily 8:15am-1:15pm and 6:30-7pm.) To walk a small stretch of the **Camino de Santiago,** face the river and make a right on C. Ruavieja (the oldest street in the city and part of the Camino) then follow it to the water and over the bridge. Walk through **Parque del Ebro** along the river for a view of the *casco antiguo* and the Ebro.

🎭🎆 NIGHTLIFE AND FESTIVALS

Logroño **nightlife** begins in the densely packed bars along C. Laurel in the *casco antiguo*. After midnight it moves to C. Portales along Pl. del Mercado, C. de Sagasta, and C. Carnicerías. The central blocks of C. Herreros are packed with bars with outside tables. Two of the best spots are the elegant, artsy **Traz Luz,** C. Portales, 71 (☎947 21 41 94. Open M-Th 9am-10pm, F-Sa 5:30pm-3am) and the sophisticated but inviting **Noche y Día,** C. Portales, 63 (☎949 20 64 06; www.nochedia.com. Open M-Th 7:30-2am, F-Sa 7:30-2:30am.) A block away, on C. Sagasta, 9, **La Granja** features a long curved bar and uber-modern barstools. (☎941 23 02 62. Open M-Th 8am-10:30pm, F-Sa 8am-3am.) Head down to the dark and friendly **cafe Casablanca,** Av. de Portugal, 30. Adorned with posters and photos from the film, a drink at this bar may be the start of a beautiful evening. (☎941 22 09 45. Drinks €5.50. *Pinchos* €1.50. Coffee €1. Open M-Th 8:30-1am, F-Sa 9am-2:30am.) The **Fiestas de San Bernabé** (June 8-11) feature the procession of the *Virgen Esperanza* from Iglesia Santiago to the cathedral, along with revelry and fireworks. The biggest party in town begins the week of September 21 for the **Fiestas de San Mateo,** and that same week, locals celebrate the grape harvest with the **Fiestas de la Vendimia,** when they make an offering of wine to the Virgin of Valvanera, patron saint of La Rioja, accompanied by bullfights and plenty of regional street food.

🚊 DAYTRIP FROM LOGROÑO

🍷 HARO

*RENFE trains (☎947 34 80 52) connect Logroño to Haro. (40min.; daily 7:36am and 7pm, also M, W, F 2:30pm; €3.40. Return trains run M-F 8:55am, 9:47pm; €3.40.) **Jimenez** (☎941 23 12 34) runs buses from Logroño to Haro. (1hr.; M-F 7 per day 7:30am-8pm, Sa 4 per day 10:15am-8pm, Su 3 per day 10:15am-8:30pm; €2.62. Return buses M-F 6 per day 7:45am-8:30pm, Sa 3 per day 8:45am-6pm, Su 3 per day 8:45am-7pm.)*

Haro (pop. 12,000) is the heart of La Rioja's wine industry, thanks to its grape varieties, climate, and soil. No fewer than seventeen *bodegas* occupy a fertile stretch of land just across the River Tirón. Many offer tours and tastings, making Haro a high-priority stop for both the connoisseur and the curious. Haro gets festive on June 29, the day of San Pedro, when participants spray wine at innocent bystanders during the 🍷**Batalla del Vino.**

Most wineries offer tours of their facilities between 9am and 2pm, but you can pick up a complete list of their schedules at the tourist office. Tours typically include a tasting, and reservations—just a quick phone call will do—are almost always required. The large **Bodegas Muga,** which produces the most popular Spanish wine in the US, offers a detailed, enjoyable tour of its facility, including its 14,000 barrel cellar (maximum 12 per tour). They also sell bottles from €4 to €70. The bodega is a 10-minute walk across the Río Tirón.To get there, cross the bridge and bear right, then go under the train tracks and they're straight ahead. (☎941 31 04 98; www.bodegasmuga.com. Tours M-F 10am in English, 11am and noon in Spanish. €5. MC/V.) **Bodegas C.V.N.E. (Compañía Vinícola del Norte de España)** also offers tours in English. (☎941 30 48 09; visitas@cvne.com. Call ahead to reserve a spot.) If the samples just aren't enough, hit up the numerous **wine shops** on C. Santo Tomás and find a quiet spot back on the winery side of the river, or take a bottle to the flower-filled **Jardines de la Vega,** on C. Virgen de la Vega, three blocks up from the tourist office. Most shops charge €1.40-3 (and *way* up) per bottle, but *jarreros* (Haro locals) insist that any bottle less than €2.80 isn't worth drinking. The government-run **Centro de Interpretación del Vino de La Rioja,** Av. Bretón de los Herreros, 4, has sleek trilingual (English, French, and Spanish) exhibits, with lots of multimedia, detailing everything you could possibly want to know about the production, tasting, and packaging of wine, and the many cultural activities in La Rioja that revolve around it. Whether you find the museum a nice complement to a winery tour or total overkill will depend on your enthusiasm for the subject matter. (☎941 31 05 47. Open Mar.-Oct. M-Sa 10am-2:30pm and 3:30-7pm, Su 10am-2pm. Call for hours for Nov.-Feb. €3, seniors/under 16 €2, children under 6 free.)

There are numerous food options in this same area, most of them identical to each other. For large portions of salads, pizzas, pasta, and *platos combinados* (€6-10), try **Popy's ❷,** C. Arrabal, 3, right off Pl. de la Paz. (☎941 30 35 74. Open Tu-Th 7:30-11:30pm, F 7:30-11:45pm, Sa-Su 1-3:30pm and 7:30-11:45pm.)

To reach **Plaza de la Paz** from the **train station,** turn left and take the road downhill, bear right for a while and then left across the river, and follow C. Navarra uphill to the plaza (15min.); look for white signs to *"centro ciudad."* From the **bus station,** follow signs to *centro ciudad* along C. la Ventilla, around the corner to the left from where the bus leaves you. You will reach Pl. de la Cruz six blocks from the station; there, veer left on C. Arrabal, which leads straight into Pl. de la Paz. The **tourist office,** in Pl. Florentino Rodríguez on C. de la Vega, provides a list in English of all the *bodegas* and tours. Take curving C. Virgen de la Vega from the corner of Pl. de la Paz; the office is in the plaza to the left around the bend, in the stone building. (☎941 30 33 66. Open July-Sept. 20 M-Sa 10am-2pm and 4:30-7:30pm; Sept. 21-June Tu-Sa 10am-2pm and 4-7pm.) Other services include: **municipal police** (☎941 31 01 25); **guardia civil** (☎941 31 09 99); **cruz roja (red cross)** (☎941 31 11 71); **centro de salud** (☎941 31 05 39); **taxis** (☎941 31 01 07).

NAVARRA (NAVARRE)

Navarra is a historically independent kingdom that formed in the Middle Ages from eastern segments of the Basque country as a wedge against aggressive neighbors. The religiously and politically conservative region is known for siding with the fiercely Catholic Nationalist forces in the Spanish Civil War, but Navarrans also throw the country's wildest parties—Pamplona's **Fiestas de San Fermín** (July 6-14) is undoubtedly the most (in)famous. Aside from summer partying, Navarra is the entry point to Spain of the **Camino de Santiago** and home to pastoral mountain villages known for artisanal cheese-making and quality hiking and cycling.

ARAGÓN, LA RIOJA, AND NAVARRA

PAMPLONA (IRUÑA) ☎948

El encierro, the Running of the Bulls, *la Fiesta de San Fermín*, utter debauchery: call it what you will, the outrageous festival of the city's patron saint is the principal reason people come to Pamplona (pop. 200,000). *San Fermín* is rightly touted as the biggest and craziest festival in all of Europe. The famous *encierro*, the daily running of the bulls from July 7-14, draws visitors from around the world. Ever since Ernest Hemingway immortalized the chaos of *San Fermín* in *The Sun Also Rises*, visitors have come to witness and experience the legendary spectacle, and drink themselves silly while they're at it. At the bull ring, Hemingway's bust welcomes fans to the eight-day extravaganza of dancing, dashing, and of course, drinking—no sleeping allowed.

Although *San Fermín* may be the city's most irresistible attraction, Pamplona's lush parks, Gothic cathedral, massive citadel, and winding *casco antiguo* enter-

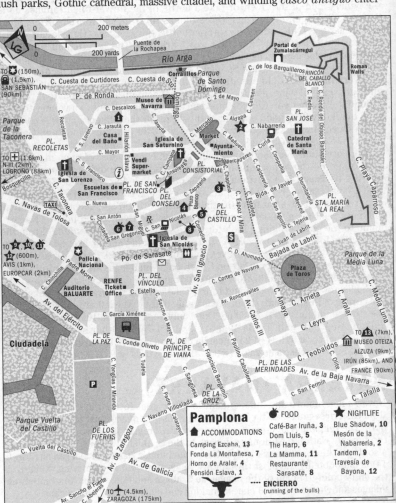

Pamplona

♠ ACCOMMODATIONS

Camping Ezcaba, **13**
Fonda La Montañesa, **7**
Horno de Aralar, **4**
Pensión Eslava, **1**

♥ FOOD

Café-Bar Iruña, **3**
Dom Lluis, **5**
The Harp, **6**
La Mamma, **11**
Restaurante
  Sarasate, **8**

★ NIGHTLIFE

Blue Shadow, **10**
Mesón de la
  Nabarrería, **2**
Tandem, **9**
Travesía de
  Bayona, **12**

---- **ENCIERRO**
(running of the bulls)

tain visitors in the off-season—but beware of the post-*San Fermín* recovery period, when many stores and restaurants close for one to two weeks. Despite being the capital of Navarra, Pamplona's roots are actually Basque; the area was settled long before the Roman "founders" arrived and named the city after Pompey the Great. Pamplona is a fiercely independent city awash with Basque pride.

⌐ TRANSPORTATION

Flights: Aeropuerto de Noaín (☎948 16 87 00; www.aena.es), 6km from town. Accessible only by taxi (€9). **Iberia** (☎948 31 71 82) to **Barcelona** and **Madrid**. **Spanair** (☎902 13 14 15; www.spanair.com) flies to **Palma** and **Tenerife**. **TAP-Air Portugal** (☎902 10 01 45; www.flypga.com) flies to **Lisboa**.

Trains: Estación RENFE, Av. de San Jorge (☎902 24 02 02). Bus #9 from Po. Sarasate (20min., €1). Info daily 6am-10pm. **Ticket office**, C. Estella, 8 (☎948 24 02 02). Open M-F 9am-1:30pm and 4:30-7:30pm, Sa 9:30am-1pm. Trains are not the best option, as Pamplona is not well connected by rail and the station is far from the city center. To: **Barcelona** (6-8hr., 3 per day 12:31pm-12:57am, from €33); **Madrid** (3¾hr., 4 per day 7am-7pm, €50.20); **Olite** (35min.; M-Sa 4 per day 9:25am-8:10pm, Su 7:05pm; €2.50); **San Sebastián** (1½hr., 2-3 per day 5:36am-6:42pm, €14.20-18.50); **Vitoria-Gasteiz** (1¼hr., M-Sa 4 per day 8:45am-7:40pm, €4-11); **Zaragoza** (2hr., 4 per day 12:32pm-12:57am, €10.20-16.70).

Buses: Estación de Autobuses at C. Conde Oliveto and C. Yangüas y Miranda. **La Burundesa** (☎948 22 17 66; www.laburundesa.com) to **Bilbao** (2hr.; M-Sa 6 per day 7am-8:30pm, Su 5 per day 9am-8pm; €12.45) and **Vitoria-Gasteiz** (1½hr.; M-F 11 per day 7am-9pm, Sa 8 per day 7am-8:30pm, Su 6 per day 9am 9pm; €0.50-7.10). **Conda** (☎948 22 10 20; www.conda.es) to **Madrid** (5hr.; M-Sa 6 per day 1:30am-6:30pm, F midnight-9:30pm, Su 10 per day 1:30am-9:30pm; €25.24) and **Zaragoza** (2-3hr., 9-12 per day 7:15am-8:30pm, €11-12). **La Estellesa** (☎948 22 22 23) to **Estella** (1hr.; M-Sa 12 per day 7:30am-8:30pm, Su 4 per day 10am-7pm; €3.32) and **Logroño** (1hr.; M-Sa 5 per day 7:30am-7pm, Su 4 per day 10am-7pm; €7). **La Tafallesa** (☎948 22 28 86) to **Olite** (50min.; M-F 3 per day 8:15am-9pm, Sa 6 per day 9:30am-8:30pm, Su 1 and 8:30pm; €2.84). **La Veloz Sangüesina** (☎948 87 02 09) to **Sangüesa** (M-Sa 3 per day 1-8pm, Su 8:15pm; €3.30). **Vibasa** (☎948 10 13 63) to **Barcelona** (6-8hr., 4-5 per day 8:05am-5:15pm, €24). **La Roncalesa** (☎948 22 20 79 or 943 46 10 64) runs to **San Sebastián** (M-F 14 per day 7am-10:45pm, Sa-Su 11 per day 8:15am-10:45pm; €6.14).

Taxis: Teletaxi (☎948 23 23 00) or **Radiotaxi** (☎948 22 12 12); stand at Parque de la Taconera at the intersection of C. Navas de Tolosa and C. Taconera.

Car Rental: Europcar, Hotel Blanca Navarra, Av. de Pío XII, 43 (☎948 17 25 23). Take bus #4-1, 4-2, or 15 from Po. Sarasate and get off after the traffic circle past the *Ciudadela*. 21+. Open M-F 8:30am-1pm and 4-7:30pm, Sa 9am-1pm. AmEx/MC/V. **AVIS**, C. Monasterio de la Oliva, 29 (☎948 17 00 36) and at airport (☎948 16 87 63). Open M-F 8am-1pm and 4-7pm, Sa 9am-1pm. Airport hours coincide with arrivals (M-F morning and evening, Sa morning, Su evening). AmEx/MC/V.

✴❼ ORIENTATION AND PRACTICAL INFORMATION

Pamplona is a relatively small city, and most sites are generally accessible on foot. The **casco antiguo**, in the northeast quarter of the city, contains almost everything of interest. The wide-open **Plaza del Castillo** is Pamplona's center. To reach it from the **bus station**, turn left onto Av. Conde Oliveto, then left after two blocks at Pl. Príncipe de Viana onto Av. de San Ignacio (second from the left), which runs into the plaza. From the **train station,** take bus #9 to Pl. de las Merindades and head up Av. Carlos III, passing the bullring on your right, until the plaza at the end. North of Pl. del Castillo, the Baroque **Ayuntamiento** is a helpful marker in the swirl of medieval streets, but it's still easy to get lost—pick up a free map at the tourist office. The **ciudadela** is outside of the *casco antiguo,* just 5min. up Av. del Ejercito from the bus stop. The **Río Arga** runs beneath the *casco antiguo* to the north.

Tourist Office: C. Hilarión Eslava, on Pl. San Francisco (☎848 420 420; www.turismo.navarra.es). Aside from maps and info on the region, accommodations, food, and culture, the staff offers a crucial minute-by-minute **San Fermín Fiesta Programme** guide that lists every event, and another guide to the *encierro* with relevant bank schedules and info on transportation, Internet access, laundry, showers, and luggage storage. Info also available at www.pamplona.net. Ask about private guided tours. English and French spoken. Open during *San Fermín* daily 8am-8pm; July-Aug. M-Sa 9am-8pm, Su 10am-2pm; Sept.-June M-Sa 10am-2pm and 4-7pm, Su 10am-2pm.

Currency Exchange: Banco Santander Central Hispano, Pl. del Castillo, 21 (☎948 20 86 00), has an **ATM** and will exchange American Express travelers checks commission-free. Open *San Fermín* July 9-13 9:30am-noon; April-Sept. M-F 8:30am-2pm; Oct.-Apr. M-F 8:30am-2pm, Sa 8:30am-1pm. Note that hours are reduced right after *San Fermín*—make sure to get money before the weekend.

Luggage Storage: At the **bus station.** Bags €2 per day, large packs €3 per day. Open M-Sa 6:15am-9:30pm, Su 6:30am-1:30pm and 2-9:30pm. Closes for *San Fermín,* when the **Escuelas de San Francisco,** the big stone building at the end of Pl. San Francisco, opens instead from July 4 at 8am to July 16 at 2pm). Lines are long, and you must have passport or ID. €3.20 per day and each time you check on luggage. Open 24hr.

Laundromat and Public Baths: Casa del Bano, C. Eslava, 9, (☎948 22 17 38). Drop-off laundry service (€10.40 wash and dry) open M-Sa 8:30am-8:30pm. Showers (€3.10) open M-Sa 8:30am-8:30pm, Su 9am-1pm. No laundry service during *San Fermín.* Showers open daily 8am-9pm.

Municipal Police: C. Monasterio de Irache, 2 (☎092 or 948 42 06 40). **National Police,** C. General Chinchilla, 3 (☎091).

Pharmacy: FarPlus, C. San Nicolás, 76 (☎948 21 07 04). Open M-F 9am-1:30pm and 4:30-7:30pm, Sa 9:30am-1:30pm. **Late-night pharmacy** on some nights, rotates daily. All pharmacies post location for that evening.

Medical Services: Hospital de Navarra, C. Irunlarrea (☎948 42 22 22, medical emergencies 112), at the corner with Av. de Pío XII. The **Red Cross** sets up stands at the bus station and along the *corrida* during *San Fermín.* The **Ambulatorio Solchaga** is in the Pl. de Toros year-round.

Internet Access: At the library on Pl. San Francisco. Free Internet access for up to an hour with a sign-up sheet. Open Sept.-June M-F 8:30am-8:45pm, Sa 8:30am-1:45pm; July-Aug. M-F 8:30am-2:45pm. Kuria.net, C. Curia, 15 (☎948 22 30 77). Look for the big yellow sign. First 10min. €0.50, 1hr. €2.50. During *San Fermín* €4.50 per hour. Open July-Aug. daily 10am-10pm; Sept.-June closed Su. Locutorio San Nicolás, C. San Nicolás, 37. Ice cream (€1-2) and location may make up for slow connections and lines. €2 per hour. Open daily 11am-11pm.

Post Office: Po. de Sarasate, 9 (☎948 20 68 40). Open M-F 8:30am-8:30pm, Sa 9:30am-2pm; July 6th 9am-2pm; closed July 7th. **Postal Code:** 31001.

▶ ACCOMMODATIONS AND CAMPING

If you think you're going to get a good night's sleep on a budget during *San Fermín,* think again. Unless you've booked a hotel room at least five months in advance, start fluffing up your sweatshirt: it's going to be your pillow on the park grass or a *pensión* floor. Some early birds may be lucky enough to secure space at campgrounds, or the few hostels that don't take reservations; they may be the only affordable option, and buses run back and forth all day and night (the tourist office has a schedule). Expect to pay rates up to four times the listed prices in most budget hotels. Many who can't find rooms (or never planned on finding them at all) sleep outside on the lawns of the park around the *Ciudadela*, Pl. de los Fueros, and Pl. del Castillo, or along the banks of the river. Those who choose this risky option should store their luggage or, at the very least, sleep on top of it. Try to stay in a large group or near other tourists.

 HOSTEL HASSLES? During *San Fermín,* the tourist office offers a real-time list of available accommodations in the city, but don't expect to find much during the first 2 or 3 days. Check the newspaper *Diario de Navarra* for *casas particulares* (guest homes), although some advertisers are hesitant to let anyone other than Spanish speakers into their home; look for advertisements posted on the streets in the days leading up to the festival. These temporary accommodations generally run between €40-60.

During the rest of the year, finding a room in Pamplona is no problem. Hostels line busy C. San Nicolás and C. San Gregorio, off Pl. del Castillo, as well as the parallel C. Zapatería and C. Nueva, off Pl. de San Francisco. On weekends, expect plenty of noise on these streets; rabble-rousing in Pl. del Castillo and the surrounding streets may make it difficult to sleep. Most hostels have different prices for *temporada alta* (before, after, and during *San Fermín*), *temporada media* (usually only July and Aug., but sometimes June or Sept.), and *temporada baja* (the rest of the year). The price icons below reflect *temporada media* prices.

Pensión Eslava, C. Hilarión Eslava, 13, 2nd fl. (☎948 22 15 58). Not as crowded as other *pensiones* and relatively quieter, but still inside the *casco antiguo*. Big, very basic rooms, some with balconies. Shared baths. *San Fermín* doubles €100. Otherwise singles €10-15 depending on length of stay; doubles €20-30. Cash only. ❶

Fonda La Montañesa, C. San Gregorio, 2 (☎948 22 43 80), down C. San Nicolás a block from Po. de Sarasate. Rooms in an old building share hall baths. This is one of the cheapest options in the city, so don't expect much. Gets very noisy on weekend nights. No reservations. *San Fermín* singles €50; doubles €100. Otherwise singles €15; doubles €30. Cash only. ❶

Horno de Aralar, C. San Nicolás, 12 (☎948 22 11 16). Five fresh, spotless rooms with TV, fan and full bath above an upscale, homey restaurant. During *San Fermín* all rooms €200. Otherwise singles €35; doubles €45. V. ❸

Camping Ezcaba (☎948 33 03 15; www.campingezcaba.com), in Eusa, 7km down the road to Irún. Take city bus line 4-V (dir.: Oricaín) from Pl. de las Merindades (4 per day, during *San Fermín* 26 per day). Hop off at the final stop; ask the driver or follow other backpackers on the moderate walk to the campground. Fills fast during *San Fermín,* but frequent 24hr. transportation makes it worth it. *San Fermín* prices €9 per person, €8 per tent. Otherwise €4.50 per person, €4.76 per tent and €4.23 per car. MC/V. ❶

FOOD

Tiny neighborhood cafe-bars advertise hearty *menús:* try the side streets near C. Jarauta, C. Descalzos, near Po. de Ronda, and the area above Pl. San Francisco. C. Navarrería and Po. de Sarasate are lined with numerous *bocadillo* bars. Many cafes and restaurants raise their prices during *San Fermín* and then close for one to two weeks to recover. The nicely renovated **market,** C. Mercado, is to the right of the Casa Consistorial, down the stairs. (Open M-Th 8am-2pm, F 8am-2:30pm and 4:30-7:30pm, Sa 8am-2:30pm.) **Vendi Supermarket** is at the corner of C. Hilarión Eslava and C. Mayor. (☎948 22 15 55. Open during *San Fermín* M-Sa 9am-2pm; otherwise M-F 9am-2pm and 5:30-7:30pm, Sa 9am-2pm. MC/V.)

■ **Restaurante Sarasate,** C. San Nicolás, 19 (☎948 22 57 27), above a seafood store. Mellow atmosphere. Organic, flavorful vegetarian dishes include both typical as well as more innovative options. Vegan and gluten-free dishes available. Try one of the delicious mixed fresh fruit juices (€1.30). Lunchtime *menú* €10.50, F-Sa night and Su *menú* €16. During *San Fermín,* pure capitalism wins over culinary preferences and the restaurant also serves more typical meat and fish dishes. Open M-Th and Su 1-4pm, F-Sa 1-4pm and 8:30-11pm. V. ❸

■ **Café-Bar Iruña,** Pl. del Castillo (☎948 22 20 64). This former casino that Hemingway made famous in *The Sun Also Rises* proudly puts its history on display. From the antique decor of the elegant interior to the Hemingway quotes on the menu, you'll be reminded that this is no ordinary cafe. The reasonably-priced *menú* (€12) is the only option for table dining. Drinks and *bocadillos* at the bar, terrace seating on the famed plaza. During *San Fermín* bar only. Open M-Th 8am-11pm, F 8am-2am, Sa 9am-2am, Su 9am-11pm. Food served 1-3:30pm and 8-10:30pm. MC/V. ❸

La Mamma, C. Monasterio de la Oliva (☎948 26 29 96), a 15min. walk away from the old city through the Parque de la Taconera. Less touristy than most restaurants, this trattoria serves up fresh pasta (€9-10) and enormous calzones (€10). Dining room decorated with pictures of old Italian movie stars. Open M-F 1:30-3:30pm and 9-11pm, Sa-Su 1:30-3:30pm and 9pm-midnight. AmEx/MC/V. ❸

Dom Lluis, C. San Nicolás, 1 (☎948 22 17 31). At C. San Nicolás and Pl. del Castillo, the location could not be better. Filling €10.50 *menú del día* with choices among paella, salad, *lomo, cordero,* and other traditional dishes. At night, Dom Lluis packs in a crowd of all ages. Open M-Th 8:30am-midnight, F-Sa 8:30am-4am. Cash only. ❷

The Harp, C. San Gregorio. Come for a lively dose of the English language and Irish breakfasts, along with moderately priced imported beers and a welcoming atmosphere. Often open late nights when everything else is closed. *Menú* €9-13. Open M-Th and Su 10am-1am, F-Sa 10am-3am. MC/V. ❷

⬤ SIGHTS

■ **MUSEO OTEIZA.** Although it is only accessible by car or bus, this unique, modern museum is worth the short drive. It houses Basque sculptor Jorge Oteiza's 1650 sculptures and 2000 "experimental" pieces. *(C. de la Cuesta, 7, in Alzuza, 9km northeast of Pamplona. Río Irati buses go to Alzuza M-Sa 8:45am and 1:30pm, Su 4 and 7:30pm; return buses M-Sa 9:30am and 2:15pm, Su 4:20 and 7:55pm; €1.20. ☎948 33 20 74; www.museooteiza.org. Open June-Sept. Tu-Su 11am-7pm; Oct.-May Tu-F 10am-3pm, Sa-Su 11am-7pm. €4, students and retired €2, under 12 free. Free.)*

CATHEDRAL AND CHURCHES. Carlos III and his wife Queen Leonor are entombed in an alabaster mausoleum in the recently restored 16th to 18th-century Gothic **Catedral de Santa María.** *(Pl. San José. ☎948 22 29 90. Open during San Fermín 10am-2pm; closed July 7 and 11; otherwise M-F 10am-2pm and 4-7pm, Sa 10am-2pm. Guided tours, including church, cloister, and Museo Diocesano, M-F 7 per day, Sa 3 per day. €4.15, groups €3.15 per person, children €2.50.)* The 13th-century Gothic **Iglesia de San Saturnino,** C. Ansoleaga, 4, which served both religious and defensive purposes in the city's past, is near the *Ayuntamiento.* *(☎948 22 11 94. Open 9:30am-12:30pm and 6-8pm; July 6, 7, and 13 9:30am-1:30pm and 6:30-8pm. Free.)* The

Romanesque 12th-century **Iglesia de San Nicolás,** in Pl. San Nicolás, is also close by. *(C. San Miguel, 15.* ☎948 22 12 81. *Open daily 9am-12:30pm and 6-8:30pm. Modified hours during San Fermín. Inquire about guided tours in the summer. Free.)* For a peek at the *San Fermín,* head to **Iglesia de San Lorenzo,** also known as Capilla *San Fermín,* near the tourist office. *(C. Mayor, 74.* ☎948 22 53 71. *Open M-F 8am-12:30pm and 6:30-8pm, Sa 8am-1pm. Modified hours during San Fermín. Free.)*

MUSEO DE NAVARRA. This museum, atop Pamplona's highest hill, showcases art and artifacts from prehistoric to present. The museum's four floors contain iron-age relics, Roman mosaics, medieval pieces, and a collection of 14th- to 20th-century works, including Goya's portrait of the Marqués de San Adrián. Ask for an information leaflet in English. *(Up C. Santo Domingo from Pl. Consistorial.* ☎948 42 64 92. *Open Tu-Sa 9:30am-2pm and 5-7pm, Su 11am-2pm; San Fermín closed July 7-14. €2, students €1, under 18 and retired free, Sa afternoons and Su mornings free.)*

▓ CIUDADELA. Felipe II built the pentagonal *Ciudadela* in an effort to secure the city from attack. Today, it's part of a grassy park that hosts a *San Fermín* fireworks display and free exhibits and concerts during the summer. Its impressive **walls** reputedly discouraged even Napoleon from invading. For a scenic walk to the *Ciudadela* from the *casco antiguo,* find C. Redín at the far end of the cathedral plaza. A left turn follows the walls past the **Portal de Zumalacárregui** and along the **Río Arga.** Bear left through the gardens of the **Parque de la Taconera**—where deer, swans, and peacocks roam—until reaching the Ciudadela. If you're in the city during *San Fermín,* you can get a glimpse of the bulls in their corrals from the lookout point at **Portal Nuevo,** at the northern end of the park. *(To get to the walls directly from Pl. del Castillo, follow Po. de Sarasate to its end, then take a right onto C. Navas de Tolosa. Take the next left on C. Chinchilla; you'll see the entrance at the end of the street, 2 blocks down Av. del Ejército.* ☎948 22 82 37. *Park open M-Sa 7:30am-9:30pm, Su 9:30am-9:30pm. Exhibits open M-Sa 6:30-9pm, Su noon-2pm. Entire ciudadela closed July 6-14. Free.)*

◗ NIGHTLIFE

There is (night)life after *San Fermín,* and it's not difficult to find. **Plaza del Castillo** is the social heart of Pamplona, with outdoor seating all around the beautifully lit plaza. Revelers of all ages gather at bars in the *casco antiguo* to demonstrate their vocal abilities: singing, shouting, and any other type of loud carousing are the norm. Bar-hopping down C. San Nicolás and C. San Gregorio is a favorite nighttime activity, as is drinking at the bars on C. Caldererería, C. San Agustín, and C. Jarauta. The down-to-earth **Mesón de la Nabarrería,** C. Nabarrería, 15, near the cathedral, draws crowds day and night to dance to a funky mix of Spanish and American music and to enjoy the cheap beer. (☎948 21 31 63. Open July-Aug. M-Th and Su 10am-2am, F-Sa noon-4pm and 6:30pm-2:30am; Sept.-June M-Th and Su noon-4pm and 6:30pm-midnight, F-Sa noon-4pm and 6:30pm-2:30am. Open all night during *San Fermín.*) If you don't mind the trek, follow the example of claustrophobes and college students who escape the cramped streets of the *casco antiguo* to the bars in Barrio San Juan on Av. de Bayona. You'll find more dancing and partying at **Travesía de Bayona,** a small plaza of bars and discotecas off Av. de Bayona, just before it forks into Monasterio de Velate. The best bars are **Blue Shadow** (☎948 27 51 09) and **Tandem,** Tr. de Bayona, 3 and 4, both of which have good dancing, big crowds, and friendly bartenders. (Beer €3.50. Mixed drinks €6. Blue Shadow open Th-Sa 9pm-3:30am. Tandem open Th-Sa 6pm-6am.) Av. de Bayona also boasts the most stylish and pricey of nightspots.

IN RECENT NEWS

SAN FERMÍN EXPOSED

A mass of flesh running through the streets of Pamplona may sound like old news, but for the past five years, the bare hides have not belonged only to the bulls. Since 2002, the international organization People for the Ethical Treatment of Animals, or PETA, has annually held the "Running of the Nudes," a clothes-free march through the streets of Pamplona to protest the treatment of the bulls throughout San Fermín.

Exactly 24hr. before the official San Fermín festivities start, the minimally clad marchers gather near the lower corrals where the bulls are kept. Due to controversy, the authorities in Pamplona have permitted the mock run to proceed only under the condition that the marchers are not fully exposed. These are no meek tree-huggers, however; the participants have since made an art form of stripping down as much as possible.

Carrying anti-bullfighting signs in multiple languages and shouting slogans such as *"Fiesta Si! Corrida no!"* (Yes to the party! No to Bullfights!) or *"La cultura no es tortura"* (Culture isn't torture), the participants walk through the center of Pamplona, passing by masses of curious spectators. The march quickly becomes an all-out party in the spirit of the *fiesta*.

Full video highlights, complete with a sexiest runner spotlight and details about PETA's campaign can be found at www.runningofthenudes.com.

FIESTA DE SAN FERMÍN (JULY 6-14)

No limits, no lethargy, and no liability make Pamplona's ◪**Fiesta de San Fermín**—known to English-speakers as "The Running of the Bulls"—Europe's premier party. At no other festival will you witness mayhem quite like this nine-day frenzy of parades, bullfights, dancing, fireworks, concerts, champagne-spraying, and wine. *Pamploneses*, clad in white with *fajas* (red sashes, about €5) and *pañuelos* (bandannas, €1.50-5), cram in innumerable hours of merry-making, displaying impossible levels of physical stamina and alcohol tolerance envied by even the hardiest of partiers. From the moment the fiesta starts on July 6th until the moment it ends on July 14th, the party doesn't let up for even a second.

Around 10am on July 6th, the whole city crowds around the **Casa Ayuntamiento** and the adjacent streets in anticipation of the mayor's noontime appearance. If you plan to get in to the square, arrive no later than 10:45am. While they wait, the people in the square spray each other with various alcoholic drinks, sing fiesta chants, and have massive food fights. The residents who live in the buildings above the square also join in the fun, throwing down buckets of water and other goodies, such as giant beach balls, on the masses below. If you're planning to be in the plaza, don't expect to remain dry or clean by the end. As the midday hour approaches, the mass sings and chants *"San Fermín!"* raising *pañuelos* (bandannas) high above their heads. As the mayor emerges, fires the awaited *chupinazo* from the balcony, and screams "People of Pamplona! Long live *San Fermín!"* in Spanish and *Euskera* (Basque), a howl explodes from the sea of waving red triangles in the plaza below. Champagne (and corks) rains down along with eggs, ketchup, mustard, wine, flour, and yellow *pimiento*. Within minutes, the streets of the *casco antiguo* flood with improvised singing and dancing troupes, and the streets stay crowded for the remainder of the fiesta. The *peñas*, Pamplona's cele-

> ❗ **FERMÍN FAUX PAS.** Don't commit the faux pas of wearing your *pañuelo* before the first *chupinazo* (rocket blast); tie it around your wrist to keep it safe. The plaza gets unbearably packed; wear closed-toed shoes and prepare to get up close and personal with fellow revelers. Some of them may try to pick your pockets and others may require medical attention for suffocation or cuts from the broken glass. Claustrophobics and agoraphobics should avoid the square.

brated social clubs, lead the hysteria. At 5pm on the 6th day and at 9:30am every other day, they are joined by the *Comparsa de Gigantes y Cabezudos*, a troupe of beloved *gigantes* (giant wooden monarchs) and *zaldikos* (courtiers on horseback). *Kilikis* (swollen-headed buffoons) run around chasing little children and hitting them with play clubs. These misfits, together with the city band and church and town officials, escort a 15th-century statue of San Fermín on his triumphant procession through the *casco antiguo*, serenading him with a *jota*, the local folk song. The statue is brought from the Iglesia de San Lorenzo at 10am on July 7, the actual *Día de San Fermín;* in exchange for this promenade, he is asked to protect the runners of the *encierro*, who sing to him before their fateful sprint.

THE RUNNING OF THE BULLS

The *encierro* (running of the bulls), is the highlight of *San Fermín*. The ritual dates back to the 14th century. It served the practical function of getting the bulls from their corrals to the bullring until someone decided it would be fun to run in front of—not behind—the bulls. The city authorities originally tried to ban the dangerous habit, but eventually decided that if they couldn't beat the masses, they should join them, and made the *encierro* an official part of *San Fermín*. These days, the first and grandest *encierro* of the festival is at 8am on July 7 and is repeated every day for the next week. Hundreds of bleary-eyed, adrenaline-charged runners flee from large, horned bulls, as bystanders cheer from barricades, windows, and balconies.

A rocket marks the release of the bulls and another announces that all the bulls have left the enclosure into the 846m course, as runners scurry ahead of them. Both the bulls and the mob are dangerous; in recent years, overcrowding has resulted in the bulls getting blockaded by the masses. The course has three sharp turns, which the bulls often have difficulty cornering; when their legs slide out from under them, they falter, creating a heaping pile of bull. Avoid outside corners to prevent getting crushed under said pile, and be especially careful at the Mercaderes-Estafeta corner. Bulls separated from the herd tend to be more nervous and aggressive, often turning against the flow of the crowd and attacking runners. After the final, dangerous, downward-sloping stretch, the run cascades through a perilously narrow opening (where a large proportion of injuries occur), and pours into the bullring amid shouts and cries from spectators. After the bulls have been rounded into their pens inside the Pl. de Toros, young bulls with protective padding on their horns are released into the ring to "play" with the mass of people.

NO BULL. If you're planning to run, don't bring anything except for your rolled-up newspaper. Those with backpacks, cameras or anything of the sort will be thrown out of the course by the police.

The safer alternative is to watch the *encierro* from the bullring or the sidelines. Music, waves, chanting, and dancing pump up spectators until the headline entertainment arrives. Bullring spectators should arrive at 6:45am at the latest. Tickets for the *grada* (free) section are available at 7am in the bullring box office (July 7, 8, and 14, €5.50, July 9-13, €4.50). You can watch for free, but the free section is overcrowded, and it can be hard to see and breathe. To watch from the sidelines, arrive by 6:15am or earlier, as the fences get unbearably packed. One of the best places to sit is the wall over C. Santo Domingo, right near the beginning of the run.

Tickets to the daily **bullfights,** every evening at 6:30pm, are incredibly hard to get, as over 90% of the tickets belong to season ticket-holders. The remaining few are sold every evening for the next day's fight. You can try your luck by lining up at the bullring ticket office before 8:30pm every evening, from the 7th of July onwards, or just buy scalped tickets (€40 and up). For detailed prices of face-value tickets, if you're lucky enough to get them, check www.feriadeltoro.com.

> **TICKET TIP.** Cheaper, more subdued spectacles occur in the days preceding and following *San Fermín*—bargain with the scalpers outside the bullring for the best price (€5-13, much higher on *San Fermín*). Although the *sol* (sunny) section can get hot, it is cheaper, closer, and generally more fun. The *peñas* (local social clubs) add to the fun, loudly making their opinion known on the *toreador's* performance.

THE PARTYING OF THE PARTICIPANTS

Right after the first rocket goes up on July 6th, the insanity spills in to the streets, gathering steam until nightfall, when it explodes with singing in bars, dancing in alleys, spontaneous parades, and a no-holds-barred party in Pl. del Castillo, which quickly becomes a huge open-air dance floor. If you don't want to stick out like a sore thumb, the attire for this dance-a-thon includes sturdy, closed-toed shoes (there's glass everywhere), a white T-shirt and pants or skirt (soon to be wine-soaked), a red *pañuelo* (bandana), and a cheap bottle of champagne (to spray, of course—don't pay more than €3). Cheap white clothes are available at countless stands throughout the city. English speakers often congregate where C. Estafeta hits Pl. de Toros, at an outdoor consortium of local discotecas.

After each night's hedonistic carnival, the new day's party begins (or ends) each day at 6am, when bands with shrill trumpets march down the streets. The city eases the transition with tamer concerts, outdoor dances, a mule-and-horse procession, a rural sports festival, fun fairs, bull leaping and swerving demonstrations in the bullring, and other such performances. To catch an important event that doesn't involve binge-drinking, check out the Pamplona Cathedral Choir's performance of the Vespers, a religious song for the occasion, at 8pm on July 6 in the chapel of *San Fermín*. Also, don't miss the fireworks competition that takes place every night at 11pm over the *Ciudadela*. After the first few days of *San Fermín*, crowds thin out, and the atmosphere goes from Olympic-level citywide debauchery to a more distilled, experts and locals-only flavor of insanity. The festivities culminate at midnight on July 14 with the singing of *Pobre de mí: "Pobre de mí, pobre de mí, que se han acabado las Fiestas de San Fermín"* (Poor me, poor me, the festivals of *San Fermín* have ended).

OLITE   ☎948

Olite (pop. 3000) was once the home of Navarran kings, and it still retains a regal air. Olite's ▨**Medieval Palacio Real** was the 15th-century home of Carlos III (1387-1425) and one of the most luxurious European palaces of its time. Although the town's 1937 restoration was far from subtle, the palace's six airy towers, countless spiral staircases, endless halls, and gardens exude so much ancient lore that persons of all ages will be tempted to believe in fairy tales again. (☎948 74 00 35. Open M-F 10am-7pm, *Semana Santa* and holidays 10am-8pm. Guided tours in English and Spanish Sa-Su every hour; €2.80, over 65 and ages 6-13 €1.40; under 5 free.) Olite's appeal extends beyond its courtly past; it holds the title of wine capital of Navarra. The ▨**Museo del Vino,** Pl. de los Teobaldos, 4, has information and exhibits on everything you'd ever want to know about wine. From Bar Orly, head up R. de San Francisco. (☎948 74 12 73. Open Easter-Oct. 12 M-Sa 10am-2pm and 4-7pm, Su 10am-2pm; Oct. 13-Easter M-F 10am-5pm, Sa-Su 10am-2pm. €3.50; ages 6-13 and over 65 €1.50; under 5 free.)

Olite's courtly airs are preserved in its high prices. **Restaurante Gambarte ❷**, C. R. del Seco, 15, off Pl. de Carlos III, has inexpensive rooms above the popular restaurant, which attracts a ravenous lunch crowd for a filling two-course *menú* (€10). (☎948 74 01 39. Restaurant open M-Th 1-3:30pm, F-Su 1-3:30pm and 8:30-10:30pm. Meat and fish entrees €12-15. Vegetarian options are limited. Singles €20; doubles €25. MC/V.) **Camping Olite ❶** is 2km outside of town heading west on Carretera N-115 toward Peralta, at km 2300. (☎948 74 10 14. €2.70 per person and per car, €2.40 per child, €3 per tent, bunks €8.40-13. AmEx/MC/V.) At **■ Casa Vidaurre, Obredor Artesano ❶**, C de la Estación, 3, the Vidaurre family makes pastries, cakes, and candies from family recipes more than 100 years old. (☎948 74 05 79. Desserts from €1.20. Coffee €1.10. Open Tu-Su 7:30am-3pm and 4:30-10pm. MC/V.) Supermarkets line C. Mayor off Pl. de Carlos III, including **Coviran Supermarket,** C. Mayor, 9. (☎948 74 00 66. Open daily 9:30am-1:30pm and 5:30-8pm. MC/V.)

Trains (☎948 56 21 44) run to Pamplona (40min.; M-Th and Sa 3 per day 7:58am-3:55pm, F 4 per day 7:58am-5:40pm, Su 3 per day 1:05pm-7:39pm; €3.10) and Zaragoza (1½hr.; 5:17pm, Su also 7:39pm; €7.55). To get from the station to Plaza de Carlos III, take C. de la Estación to Bar Orly at highway N-121, walk through the archway to the left, and follow R. de San Francisco to Plaza de Carlos III. Conda (☎948 22 10 26) and La Tafallesa (☎948 22 28 86) both run **buses** to Pamplona (M-Sa 16-19 per day 6:45am-8pm, Su 7 per day 8:45am-8pm). **Taxis** Comarca (☎948 74 01 43) are available at the end of R. de San Francisco, before Pl. de Carlos III. The **tourist office** is in Pl. Teobaldos. (☎948 74 17 03; www.navarra.es. Open Apr.-Sept. M-F 10am-7pm, Sa 10am-2pm and 4-7pm, Su 10am-2pm; Oct.-Mar. M-F 10am-5pm, Sa-Su 10am-2pm.) Local services include: **Banco Santander Central Hispano,** R. de Medios, 4 (☎902 24 24 24; open M-F 8:30am-2pm, in winter also Sa 8:30am-1pm); **Centro de Salud** (☎948 74 17 01) at the opposite end of R. de Medios from Pl. de Carlos III; **Internet** access at Cyber Camelot, R. de Medios, 4, off Pl. de Carlos III (€2.50 per hr.; open M-Sa 11am-1pm and 7-11pm, Su 11am-2pm and 7pm-11pm); and the **post office,** R. Portillo, 3, on the other side of Pl. Carlos from the palace (☎948 74 05 82; open M-Sa 8:30-11am). **Postal Code:** 31390.

ESTELLA ☎948

Hiding between the cities of Logroño and Pamplona, charming Estella (pop 14,000) lies nestled in a bend of the Río Ega, surrounded by mountains all around. With characteristic walking sticks in hand, and sometimes telltale backpacks, pilgrims traversing the Camino de Santiago have been descending on Estella since the town's founding in 1090. Sancho Ramírez reworked the route to include this historic town because the medieval pilgrim found "good bread, excellent wine, and an abundance in meat and fish" when he arrived in Estella. Cathedrals in Estella are some of the region's most undiscovered. The town is also a great alternative if you can't find accommodations in Pamplona for *San Fermín*.

▐ TRANSPORTATION. La Estellesa **buses** (☎948 55 01 27) leave from the station (☎948 32 65 09) on Pl. de la Coronación to: **Logroño** (1hr.; M-Sa 8-10 per day 8:30am-8pm, Su 8 per day 10:45am-8:30pm; €3.87); **Pamplona** (1hr.; M-Sa 14 per day 7am-8pm, Su 5 per day 11am-8pm; €3.32); **San Sebastián** (1½-2¼hr., 3-6 per day 11am-8pm, €9.29); **Zaragoza** (2½hr., M-Sa 8:30am, €12.71); **Vitoria-Gasteiz** (1hr.; M-F 3 per day 8:30am-8:45pm, Sa 4 per day 8:30am-8:45pm, Su 2 per day 4:15-9pm; €3.20). Check the second page of the local newspaper, *Noticias* (€1), for daily schedules and destinations. **Teletaxi Estella** can be reached 24hr. at ☎948 55 00 01.

◢▐ ORIENTATION AND PRACTICAL INFORMATION. Calle San Andrés/Baja Navarra runs north-south from the bus station on Pl. de la Coronación to the Plaza de los Fueros, while **Paseo de la Inmaculada** runs east-west from **C. Dr. Huarte de San Juan/Avenida de Yerri** to the Puente del Azucarero. **Calle Mayor/Zapatería/Ruiz**

ARAGÓN, LA RIOJA, AND NAVARRA

de Alda/Espoz y Mina, runs parallel to Po. de la Inmaculada and is the main commercial hub. Estella is an atypical town in that its historic neighborhood is not found in the city center. The river divides the city disproportionately; the older sites and the tourist office are on the smaller south side. To reach the bridge to the tourist office and old city from the bus station, turn your back to the station and walk left across the parking lot. Then follow C. Sancho el Sabio to the river and cross the bridge. Make a left at the rotary, walk one block, and the **Plaza de San Martin** and the Renaissance Fuente de los Chorros will be on the right.

To reach the **tourist office,** C. San Nicolás, 1, walk across Pl. de San Martín towards the building with the wooden doors and flags. Turn right onto the street just in front of it—the tourist office is the fifth archway on your right. It provides a very good map of the city and listings of prices, hours, and locations for accommodations, restaurants, and museums. (☎948 55 63 01; oit.estella@cfnavarra.es. Open daily in summer 10am-2pm and 4-7pm; in winter M-F 10am-5pm, Sa-Su 10am-2pm.) The **police,** Po. de la Inmaculada, 1 (☎092), are in the red building with wooden doors. The entrance is on C. Sancho el Fuerte, around the corner to your left when facing the station. **Medical services** (☎948 55 62 87) are at the opposite end of Po. de la Inmaculada, near C Dr. Huarte de San Juan, and at the **Hospital Comarcal** (☎848 43 50 00). ☎**112** (only valid in Navarra) will reach police, fire, and ambulance services, and provide information on late-night pharmacies. The **library,** C. Ruiz de Alda, 34-36, provides free **Internet** to patient patrons; drop by to reserve a 30min. slot. (☎948 55 64 19. Open June-Sept. M-F 8:30am-2:30pm; Oct.-May M-F 9am-9pm.) **Locutorio Los Andes,** C. Gustavo de Maetzu, 2, off Po. De La Immaculada, has six terminals and cheap long-distance. €2 per hour. Open daily 11am-3:30pm and 5-11pm. The **post office** is at Po. de la Inmaculada, 5. (☎948 55 17 92. Open M-F 8:30am-2pm and 4-7:30pm.) **Postal Code:** 31200.

▐▌ ACCOMMODATIONS AND FOOD. Estella is a good place to catch some shut-eye during *San Fermín*. Reservations are advisable then and during its own *encierro* (running of the bulls) the first week of August and the first few weeks of September. Many bars offer upstairs rooms for the night at affordable rates— check around Pl. de los Fueros and Pl. de Santiago, or consult the map in the pedestrian zone of C. Baja Navarra. Straight out from the bus station, follow C. San Andrés to C. Mayor, found at the end of the pedestrian zone of C Baja Navarra, and go left two blocks to ▐**Pensión San Andrés ❷,** C. Mayor, 1. Clean, quiet rooms have TVs, and some even come with refrigerators and microwaves. Balconies overlooking the peaceful plaza below become exhilarating lookout points during the *encierro*. (☎948 55 41 58. Singles €20, with bath €30; doubles €30/38; triples with bath €45; quads with bath €60. MC/V.) Turning to the left after visiting the tourist office, it's 1km (20min.) down the river and past the factory to **Camping Lizarra ❶,** C. Ordoiz; let the Pamplona bus driver know where to stop. The grounds include a supermarket, pool, laundry, playground, money exchange, horseback riding, fishing, a 300-bed hostel, and a bar. (☎948 55 17 33; www.campinglizarra.com. Open year-round. €4.92 per person, €4.12 per child; €4.81 per tent; €13.42 per *parcela* (site), €8.60 per smaller site; hostel bunks €8.02. MC/V.)

Estella is known throughout the region for its *gorrín asado* (roast piglet, also called *gorrín de Estella*). The overwhelming portions of juicy regional food served upstairs at ▐**Restaurante Casanova ❸,** C. Nueva s/n, are sure to slow any pilgrim's progress. Entering Pl. de los Fueros from C. Baja Navarra, take the immediate left and look for the black and yellow sign. Ask to sit upstairs. (☎948 55 28 09. *Menú* M-F €11, Sa-Su €18. Fish and meat entrees €6.50-20. Tu-Su 1-3:30pm and 8-11pm. MC/V.) **Asador Astarriaga ❸,** Pl. de los Fueros, 12, offers Navarran fare such as *gorrín* (€13) and various other meat entrees (€11-16), leaving diners to decide whether an idyllic outdoor plaza setting is worth the price of the food. (☎948 55 08

02. Fish entrees €11-20. *Menú* M-F €13.30, F-Sa €24.40. Open M-Th 1-4pm and 8-10:30pm, F 1-4pm and 9-11pm, Sa 1:30-4pm and 9-11pm, Su 1:30-4pm. MC/V.)

◉ 🔎 **SIGHTS AND ENTERTAINMENT.** Next to the tourist office, a representation of the medieval French hero Roland jousts with Farragut the Moor on the columns of the 12th-century **Palacio de los Reyes de Navarra,** the city's self-proclaimed "architectural jewel" and now the **Museo Gustavo de Maetzu.** Inside, nine galleries of the works of painter Gustavo de Maetzu, who spent his last years in Estella, accompany rotating modern exhibitions. (☎948 54 60 37; fax 948 55 32 57. Open Tu-Sa 11am-1pm and 5-7pm, Su 11am-1:30pm. Free.) The 12th-century **Iglesia de San Miguel** commands a view of Estella from the hilltop Pl. de San Miguel, to the right after crossing the Puente del Azucarero from the tourist office. Its ornate stone portal depicts San Miguel fighting dragons, weighing souls, and taking care of celestial business. Exit at the door opposite the entrance to catch some more dazzling stone arches. Opposite the tourist office, the late Romanesque-early Gothic **◣Iglesia de San Pedro de la Rúa,** with its picturesque, half-destroyed cloister garden, towers above Calle de la Rúa. This church has been largely undiscovered by tourists, and is all the more magical for it. Tours of the San Pedro de la Rúa and San Miguel churches are available and leave from the tourist office (30min.; about 7 per day after masses; €2.30, both churches €3.60; pilgrims €2.10/3.35; children €2/3) as well as a general monuments visit (☎948 55 00 70. Tours daily 12:15 and 5:15pm €3.85, pilgrims €3.50, children €3.15).

During the week of July 16-20, the city's more enthusiastic residents dress up in medieval garb for **Semana Medieval,** featuring parades, concerts, an Arab Market with food and crafts in Pl. de Santiago, theater performances, a roaming storytelling character, and even a jousting match. The week long **Fiestas de la Virgen del Puy y San Andrés** kick off the Friday before the first weekend in August, featuring an *encierro* (running of the bulls) of baby bulls (less ferocious than Pamplona's), kiddie entertainment, a fair, Navarrese dancing, and *gaitas* (traditional instruments of northern Spain similar to bagpipes, but without the bags).

PAÍS VASCO (EUSKADI)

As the Basque saying goes, "Before God was God and the rocks were rocks, the Basques were Basque." The País Vasco is officially composed of the provinces Gipuzkoa, Álava, and Vizcaya, but the Basque homeland, *Euskal Herria*, extends into Navarra and southwestern France. The region boasts one of the most varied landscapes in Spain, from verdant hills to industrial wastelands, from quaint fishing villages to the glittering coastal cities of Bilbao and San Sebastián. The people are marked by their deep attachment to the land and immense cultural and national pride. However, it is *euskera*, a language unrelated to any other in Europe, that binds and quite literally defines them. Even the Basque name for themselves, *Euskaldinuak*, means "speakers of *euskera*."

The Basques are thought to have descended from the first Europeans, whose arrival predated that of the Indo-European tribes. Their culture and genes have gone relatively undiluted despite Roman incursions, medieval interference, and finally Spanish abolition of *fueros*, medieval grants of semi-autonomy. The Basques enjoyed a brief return to independence under the Second Spanish Republic, but the Republican defeat in the Spanish Civil War ushered in the Fascist rule of General Francisco Franco, who oppressed the Basques and banned *euskera* and other forms of cultural self-expression. In 1968, in response to such injustices, the organization *Euskadi ta Askatasuna* (ETA; "Basque Country and Freedom") began a terrorist movement that persists today. Anti-ETA sentiment is now quite strong among Basques, but many also argue that the methods employed to suppress ETA undermine free speech and disregard human rights. Street protests and graffiti continue to call for amnesty for political prisoners.

Today, most Basques share a desire to preserve their cultural identity. Although *castellano* is the predominant language, *euskera* has enjoyed a resurgence since Franco's death. Traditions like *cesta punta* or *pelota vasca* (known outside Spain as the deathly fast sport of jai alai) continue to thrive. Basque cuisine is some of Iberia's finest, including *bacalao a la vizcaína* (salt cod in tomato sauce) and dishes *a la vasca* (in parsley steeped white wine sauce). Tapas, considered a regional specialty, are called *pintxos* (PEEN-chos); locals wash them down with *sidra* (cider) and the local white sparkling wine, *txakoli*. Famous chefs, including Juan Mari Arzak, hail from this region.

HIGHLIGHTS OF PAÍS VASCO

BASQUE in the seaside splendor of **San Sebastián** (p. 504).

ADMIRE your reflection (and some art) in the **Museo Guggenheim** in Bilbao (p. 518).

PAVE the road to peace in resilient **Guernica** (p. 519).

IMPROVE your groove at **Vitoria-Gasteiz's** International Jazz Festival (p. 522).

SAN SEBASTIÁN (DONOSTIA)   ☎943

San Sebastián (pop. 180,000) glitters on the shores of the Bay of Biscay. An elaborate, Romantic-style boardwalk, great waterfront palaces, and wide golden beaches give the city an air of gentility but mask the 21st-century edge found in its boutiques, surf-shops, and nightclubs. Ever since Queen Isabel II made Playa de la Concha popular in the mid 19th century, the city has been a fashionable vacation venue for much of Europe's aristocracy. Still, its cosmopolitan air doesn't interfere with its strong sense of regional culture. San Sebastián once stood as one of

País Vasco (Euskadi)

Golfo de Viscaya

Costa Vasca

Costa Cantábrica

FRANCE

TO SANTANDER (40km)

Plentzia
Bermeo
Mundaka
Hondarribia
Hendaye

Getxo
BI631
BI2238
Zumaia
San Sebastián

Bilbao
Ondarroa
Zarautz
Irún

Barakaldo
BI2235
Guernica
A8
Hernani

VIZCAYA
Eibar
GUIPÚZCOA

Durango
Tolosa
A15
N121A

E5
Arrasate-
Mondragón
N1

A68
GI627

CANTABRIA
Amurrio
N240
N130

A625

N1

Salvatierra
Pamplona

Vitoria-
Gasteiz
Campezo
NAVARRA

ÁLAVA
Estella

Miranda de Ebro
N124

A1
N111

Haro
Laguardia

TO BURGOS (40km)
N120
N232
Logroño
A15

E804 A68

Spain's great ports, but much of it was destroyed during the 1813 Peninsular War when an invading Anglo-Portuguese force dislodged Napoleon and set fire to the city. The ruined walls were finally torn down in 1864, amid the construction of a more modern city replete with French architectural influences. Today, San Sebastián draws tourists old and young to bathe and surf in its beaches, hike its mountains, and enjoy its lively and friendly atmosphere.

TRANSPORTATION

Flights: Airport in Hondarribia (☎943 66 85 00; www.aena.es), 22km east of the city. **Iberia** (☎943 66 85 21; www.iberia.es) flies to **Madrid. Air Nostrum** (☎902 40 05 00; www.airnostrum.es) **Barcelona, Málaga, Palma di Mallorca,** and **Sevilla. Interurbanos buses** to Hondarribia pass by the airport (45min.; every 20-30min. M-Sa 7:35am-9:45pm, July-Aug. also Su 8:45am-9:45pm; €1.75). A new airport shuttle goes to and from the bus platform at Pio XIII with each flight (€3). A **taxi** to the airport costs €27.

Trains: San Sebastián has 2 train stations.

Estación de Amara, Euskotren (www.euskotren.es), runs to: **Bilbao** (2½hr., hourly 5:47am-8:47pm, €6); and **Hendaye, France** (every 30min., €1.35).

Estación del Norte, RENFE (☎902 24 02 02; www.renfe.es), Po. de Francia. Info open daily 7:30am-11pm. To: **Barcelona** (8-8½hr.; June-Aug. daily 10:45am, Oct.-May M-F and Su also 11pm;

PAÍS VASCO

CANTABRIAN SEA

TO MONTE ULIA (1km)

GROS

TO (20km)

Playa de la Zurriola

Pukas Surf Club
Bici Rent Donosti

C. Gran Vía
C. Zabaleta
P. DE CATALUÑA
San Francisco
Secundino Esnaola
C. Miracruz
Wash & Dry

C. Usandizaga
C. Colón
C. Peña y Goñi

Club Vasco de Camping
Chillida-Leku

Cuesta de Aldaconea
Camino de Cencorrónea

Puente de la Zurriola

C. Ramón M. Lili

P. de Francia

Estación del Norte (RENFE)

Virgen del Carmen

RÍO URUMEA

Puente de Santa Catalina
Puente de María Cristina

P. de los Fueros

Parque Cristina Enea

P. de Salamanca

C. Aldamar

C. San Juan

P. Nuevo

Castillo de Santa Cruz de la Mota

SEE INSET

PARTE VIEJA

P. DE LA CONSTITUCIÓN

PL. DE SARRIEGI

Alameda del Boulevard

P. Rep. Argentina

Bus to Museo Chillida-Leku

C. Oquendo
C. Aldamar
C. Elcano
C. Peñaflorida
Garibai
C. Hernani
C. Echaide
C. Idiaquez
C. Andía
C. Bergara
C. Getaria
C. Fuenterrabia
C. Loiola

PL. DE GIPUZKOA

CENTRO

Av. de la Libertad

C. Reyes Católicos
C. Urbieta
C. Easo
C. Urdaneta

Catedral del Buen Pastor

PL. DE BILBAO

C. Prim

P. del Árbol de Guernica

TO (200m)

C. San Martín
C. San Marcial
C. Arrasate
C. Loiola

PL. DEL BUEN PASTOR

C. Moraze

PL. EASO

Estación de Amara (Euskotren)

AMARA VIEJO

C. de Manterola
C. Triunfo
PL. ZARAGOZA
C. San Bartolomé
C. Zubieta

Bahía de la Concha

Parque de Aldefoi Eder

San Jerónimo

PL. DE CERVANTES

TO MUSEO CHILLIDA-LEKU (4km), MUSEUM OF SCIENCE (6km), PALACIO DE AETE (600m)

Monte Urgull

Cementerio de los Ingleses

Aquarium

Isla de Santa Clara

Playa de la Concha

P. de la Concha

Cuesta de Aldapeta

C. de Aldapeta

Parte Vieja

P. de Salamanca

Santa María del Coro

Museo de San Telmo

PL. ZULOAGA

C. Sta. Corda
C. Sorazu
San Juan
C. 31 de Agosto
C. Juan de Bilbao
C. Iñigo
C. Esterlines
C. Embeltran
C. F. Calbetón
C. Mayor

PL. DE LA CONSTITUCIÓN

San Jerónimo

Alameda del Boulevard

Mercado de la Brecha

C. Euskal Herria
San Vicente
General Jauregi
C. Pescadería
C. San Lorenzo
PL. DE SARRIEGI

Narrica

Ctra Escape

C. R. Regente

PL. LASALA

C. Bentea

C. Korruko Andra Mari

C. Compañado

C. Angel

Ayuntamiento

Palacio de Miramar

Parque del Palacio Real de Miramar

Playa de Ondarreta

ANTIGUO

Monte Igueldo

Funicular

PL. DEL FUNICULAR

Monte Igueldo

TO (5km)

Av. de Zumalacárregui
Av. de Satrustegui
C. Infante Jaime
Av. de Brunet
Av. de Pamplona Inunea
Camino de Igara
Av. de Matia

TO (5km)

San Sebastián (Donostia)

200 meters

200 yards

€37.10-48.70); **Burgos** (3hr., 4 per day 8:32am-10:37pm, €21); **Hendaye, France** (45min., 4 per day 6:34am-8:43pm, €8.20-10.80); **Madrid** (7-8hr.; 8:32am, 10:37pm; €36-47.70. Express train 5hr., 5:21pm, €55); **Salamanca** (6½hr.; M-F and Su 8:32am, 10:20pm; €31.20); **Vitoria-Gasteiz** (1¾hr.; M-Sa 8 per day 6:57am-10:37pm, Su 7 per day 8:32am-10:37pm; €8-15).

Buses: San Sebastián has a bus platform and a series of ticket windows around the corner, though not everything is under 1 roof. Av. de Sancho el Sabio, 31-33, and Po. de Vizcaya, 16. Most open June-Aug. daily 8am-9pm.

ALSA, Po. de Vizcaya, 16 (☎902 42 22 42), to **Santander** (3hr., 8 per day 8:10am-12:20am, €12.09)

Continental Auto, Av. de Sancho el Sabio, 31 (☎943 46 90 74; www.continental-auto.es) to: **Madrid** (6hr., 7-10 per day 7:15am-12:30am, €30) and **Vitoria-Gasteiz** (1¾hr., 8 per day 7:15am-12:30am, €7). **Interbus**, Pl. Gipuzkoa (☎943 64 13 02; www.interbus.es) to **Hondarribia** (45min.; every 20-30min. 7:45am-10:05pm, July-Aug. also Su 8:45am-10pm; €1.75.) and **Irún** (35min., every 15-30min., €1.60).

La Burundesa, Po. de Vizcaya, 16 (☎943 46 23 60; www.laburundesa.com), to **Vitoria-Gasteiz** (1½hr., 7-8 per day 8:30am-8:30pm).

La Estellesa, Po. de Vizcaya, 17 (☎943 47 01 15; www.laestellesa.com), to **Logroño** (2½hr., 4 per day 8:30am-8:15pm, €11.97-13.66).

La Roncalesa, Po. de Vizcaya, 16 (☎943 46 10 64), to **Pamplona** (1hr., 6-10 per day 7am-9:15pm, €6.20).

Transportes PESA, Av. de Sancho el Sabio, 33 (☎902 10 12 10; www.pesa.net), to **Bilbao** (1¼hr.; M-F every 30min. 6:30am-10pm, Sa hourly 7:30am-10pm, Su hourly 8:30am-10pm; €8.95).

Vibasa, Po. de Vizcaya, 16 (☎943 45 75 00; www.vibasa.es), to **Barcelona** (7hr., 3 per day 7:20am-11:40pm, €28).

Public Transportation: Local Buses (☎943 00 02 00; www.dbus.es). Maps and schedule at the tourist office. **Bus #16** goes from Alameda del Boulevard to campground past Mt. Igueldo and beaches (€1.10).

Taxis: Vallina (☎943 40 40 40) and **Donostia** (☎943 46 46 46).

Bike Rental: Bici Rent Donosti, Po. de la Zurriola, 22 (☎655 72 44 58; bicirent-donosti@yahoo.es). Provides bike trail maps. Bikes €12 per 4hr., €20 per day. Tandem bikes €6 per 1hr., €20 per 4hr., €36 per day. Also sells second-hand bikes. Call ahead for mopeds. Open July-Sept. daily 10am-9pm; Oct.-June 10am-2pm and 4-8:30pm.

✦🛈 ORIENTATION AND PRACTICAL INFORMATION

The **Río Urumea** splits San Sebastián down the middle, with the **parte vieja** (old town) to the east, and **El Centro** (the new downtown) to the west, separated by the wide pedestrian **Alameda del Boulevard**. The famed **Playa de la Concha** is to the west of El Centro, starting just beneath Alameda del Boulevard. The **RENFE train station** and the neighborhood **Gros** lie on the east side. Intercity **Buses** stop in the south of the city on the west side of the river.

Tourist Office: Centro Municipal de Atracción y Turismo, C. Reina Regente, 3 (☎943 48 11 66; www.sansebastianturismo.com), on the edge of the *parte vieja*. English, French, and German spoken. Open June 15-Aug. M-Sa 9am-8pm, Su 10am-2pm; July-Aug. also Su 3:30-7pm; Oct.-May M-Sa 9am-1:30pm and 3:30-7pm, Su 10am-2pm.

Hiking Information: Club Vasco de Camping, C. Iparraguirre, 8 (☎943 27 18 66; www.vascodecamping.org). Local mountaineering and hiking club organizes and coordinates excursions. Info on hiking opportunities in País Vasco. Open M-F 6-8:30pm.

Luggage Storage: At the **RENFE train station** (€3 per day; buy tokens at the ticket counter). Open daily 7am-11pm. Also at **Donosti@Net,** C. Narrika, 3, at the end of Pl. Sarriegi in the *parte vieja*, for €3 per 4hr. or €6 per day. Open daily 9am-11pm; Oct.-May 9am-9pm.

Laundromat: Wash & Dry, Iparraguirre, 6 (☎943 29 31 50). On the east side of the river, over Puente de Santa Catalina. Lines are long in high season. Coin-operated washer and dryer available daily 8am-10pm. €6 wash, €6 dry, €0.50 detergent. Drop-off and pickup service available M-F 9:30am-1pm and 4-8pm, €20.

Police: Policia Municipal, C. Easo, 41 (☎092).

Medical Services: Casa de Socorro, C. Bengoetxea, 4 (☎943 44 06 33). Services only available to EU citizens, but others should come here to be redirected to a private clinic, or call ☎112 in an emergency.

Internet Access: Zarr@net, C. San Lorenzo, 6 (☎943 43 33 81). €2 per 1hr. Also sells **phone cards.** Open M-Sa 10am-10pm, Su 4-10pm. Also at the **Biblioteca Central,** Pl. Ajuntamiento, facing the huge Casa Consistorial. Free Internet access up to 45min.; sign up at front desk. Open M-F 10am-8:30pm, Sa 10am-2pm and 4:30-8pm. *Locutorios* outside the center also tend to have better prices.

Post Office: C. Urdaneta (☎902 19 71 97), behind the cathedral. Open M-F 8:30am-8:30pm, Sa 9:30am-2pm. **Postal Code:** 20006.

ACCOMMODATIONS AND CAMPING

Small *pensiones* are scattered throughout the noisy *parte vieja*. For a more restful night's sleep farther from the action, look for *hostales* and *pensiones* on the outskirts of El Centro. In July and August, *completo* (no vacancy) signs begin to appear in many doorways. Particularly tight times are during *San Fermín* (July 6-14) and *Semana Grande* (week of Aug. 15); September's film festival is not much better. To make matters worse, many *pensiones* don't take reservations in summer. Come early in the day and be prepared to shop around, as finding a room may take some time. Solo travelers should be prepared to pay for a double; single rooms are virtually impossible to come by. The tourist office has a list of all registered accommodations in the city and a booking service for a charge, though many of the cheapest *pensiones* are not registered with the office.

PARTE VIEJA

Brimming with reasonably priced *pensiones* and restaurants, the *parte vieja* is where the younger backpackers go for a night's rest (or more accurately, a night's partying). Its proximity to Playa de la Concha and the port makes this area a prime nightspot; scores of places offer a night's sleep above loud *pintxos* (tapas) bars. Call in advance for reservations, and expect to deal with some noise.

▓ **Pensión Amaiur,** C. 31 de Agosto, 44, 2nd fl. (☎943 42 96 54; www.pensionama-iur.com). Facing the Iglesia de Santa María; look for the building with flower-covered balconies on your right. Virginia, the owner, offers 13 beautiful rooms in a historic, warmly-decorated house. 7 common baths and 2 tidy kitchens with microwave and fridge. Study room with travel info, public phone, and Internet access (€1 per 18min.). English spoken. Singles €24, with balcony €42; doubles €35/60; triples €54/80; quads €65-95. AmEX/MC/V. ❷

▓ **Pensión San Lorenzo,** C. San Lorenzo, 2 (☎943 42 55 16; www.pensionsan-lorenzo.com), off C. San Juan by the mercado. This sunny hostel features a helpful owner and rooms with kettle, toaster, fridge, and private baths. Internet access €1.50 per 1hr. or bring your laptop for free Wi-Fi. Singles €20 (only available Oct.-May); doubles €28-50. Cash only. ❷

Pensión Boulevard, Alameda del Boulevard, 24, 2nd fl. (☎943 42 94 05; www.pen-sionboulevard.com). All rooms come with balcony, mini-fridge, TV, and bath. Ask for a room with a view of the square and boulevard. Doubles €45-75. Cash only. ❸

Pensión Larrea, C. Narrica, 21, 2nd fl. (☎943 42 26 94; www.pensionlarrea.com). Welcoming owner. Every room has a small balcony. Shared bath. Microwave and fridge for communal use. Internet access €1 per 18min. July-Aug. singles €28; doubles €50; triples €70; Sept.-June €20/38/48. Cash only. ❸

OUTSIDE THE PARTE VIEJA

These accommodations tend to be quieter than those in the *parte vieja*, but are still close to the port, beach, bus, and train stations, no more than 10min. from the old city by foot. This area also has some of the city's most elegant boulevards and buildings.

Pensión La Perla, C. Loiola, 10, 2nd fl. (☎943 42 81 23; www.pensionlaperla.com), on the pedestrian street directly in front of the cathedral. English spoken. Rooms come with private bath with bathtub, beautiful wooden floor, and balcony. Free Internet and Wi-Fi. Very quiet, central location. Singles €25-35; doubles €35-55. Cash only. ❸

Pensión Añorga, C. Easo, 12 (☎943 46 79 45; www.pensionanorga.es). Quiet *pensión* for travelers in search of a peaceful night's sleep. Spacious, spotless rooms have wood floors and comfy beds. Some rooms have fridges. Wi-Fi access. Singles with shared bath €24-42; doubles with private bath €38-66. Cash only. ❹

Albergue Juvenil la Sirena (HI), Po. Igueldo, 25 (☎943 31 02 68), 3min. from the beach. Bus #16 runs to Po. Igueldo, right in front of the *albergue* (hourly 7:30am-10pm, €1). Clean 2- to 4-person rooms, multilingual staff. Laundry and kitchen available. Breakfast included. Sheets €2.65. Max. 3-night stay if full. May-Sept. €15, 26+ €18. Reduced prices Oct.-Apr. €2 extra without HI or ISIC cards. MC/V. ❷

Camping Igueldo (☎943 21 45 02; www.campingigueldo.com), 5km west of town atop Monte Igueldo. Bus #16 ("Barrio de Igueldo-Camping") runs between the site and Alameda del Boulevard (hourly 7:30am-10pm, €1). Min. 5-night stay. *Parcelas* (spot for 2 people with room for car and tent) June 16-Sept. 15 and *Semana Santa* €28.20, extra person €4.40; electricity €3.50. Sept. 16-June 15 *parcelas* €19-25. Fully equipped family-size bungalows €60-85. MC/V. ❷

█ FOOD

Pintxos (tapas), chased down with local *sidra*, are a religion here; bars line the streets in the *parte vieja*, where arrays of enticing tidbits on toothpicks cover countertops everywhere. In the harbor, many places serve tangy sardines with slightly bitter *sidra*. The modern **Mercado de la Bretxa**, in an underground shopping center, sells everything from fresh produce and meat to *pintxos*. The huge supermarket inside offers a choice of groceries (open M-Sa 8am-9pm, though most vendors take lunch 3-5pm).

PARTE VIEJA

Juantxo, C. Esterlines, 6 (☎943 42 74 05), main entrance off C. Embeltran, 6. The bread definitely makes the sandwich. Try the *filete* with onions, cheese, and peppers (€2.90). Wide selection of excellent *bocadillos* (€3-3.50), *pintxos* (€1.20-3), and *raciones* (€3-5). Open M-Th 9am-11:30pm, F-Su 9am-1:45am. Cash only. ❶

Café Santana, C. Reina Regente, half a block toward the river from the tourist office. *Pintxos* (€1.40-2.40) all nicely labeled. Open July-Sept. daily 7am-10pm; Oct.-June M-Sa 7am-10pm, Su 7am-3pm. MC/V. ❶

Va Bene, Alameda del Boulevard, 14 (☎943 42 24 16). Frequented by tourists and locals alike. The place to go for high-quality, low-price hamburgers and hot dogs served in the tradition of the best American diners. Norman Rockwell prints make for a retro setting inside. Burgers €2.75-4.75. Open daily 11am-1am. Cash only. ❶

La Capricciosa, C. Fermín Calbetón, 50 (☎943 43 20 48). A busy Italian place in the *parte vieja* with brick walls and a diner atmosphere. Pizzas €6-9, are their specialty.

Open July-Aug. daily 1-3:30pm and 8:30-11:30pm; Sept.-June M-Tu and Th 9-11am and 1:30-3pm, F-Su 9-11:30am and 1:30-3:30pm. ❷

OUTSIDE THE PARTE VIEJA

Kursaal, Po. de la Zurriola, 1 (☎943 00 31 62; www.restaurantekursaal.com). Modern and trendy, in a glass cube across the river from the *parte vieja*. Treat yourself to an elegant gourmet lunch on their breezy patio. The chef is a legend among locals. Cafeteria *menú* (from €18.50) served M-F 1-3:30pm. Entrees €20-30. Open W-Sa 1-3:30pm and 8:30-10:30pm, Tu and Su 1:30-3:30pm. Aug. open daily 1:30-3:30pm and 8:30-10:30pm. AmEx/MC/V. ❹

Restaurante Tsi Tao, Po. de Salamanca, 1 (☎943 42 42 05; www.tsitao.com). A rare opportunity for sushi lovers to satisfy their craving in Spain. Tasty and filling Asian cuisine in an uber stylish setting. Try the green tea flan. Reserve ahead. Lunch *menú* €13. Open daily 1-3:30pm and 8:30-11pm. AmEx/MC/V. ❸

Caravanseraí Café, Pl. del Buen Pastor (☎943 47 54 18), near the cathedral. Chic and artsy, without pretentious prices. Fabulous vegetarian appetizers and entrees (€4-10). Entrees €6-10. €0.60 surcharge for patio dining. Open M-Th 8am-midnight, Sa-Su 10:30am-11:30pm. AmEx/MC/V. ❷

⚲ SIGHTS

San Sebastián's sights, while impressive on their own, are nothing compared to the splendor of the city as a whole. The best way to absorb it all is on an evening stroll along Playa de la Concha, which has breathtaking views of Santa Clara, the Estatua del Sagrado Corazón, and the city's skyline.

▧ MUSEO CHILLIDA-LEKU. The Museo Chillida-Leku houses a large collection of the works of Eduardo Chillida, San Sebastián's contemporary art guru. His stone and steel sculptures are spread throughout a peaceful, spacious outdoor garden; pieces are hidden around every turn of the path. The 16th-century farmhouse at the center, a spectacular construction of huge wood beams and arching stone restored by the sculptor himself, now houses some of Chillida's earliest pieces. *(Bo. Jauregui, 66. 15min. from the town center. Autobuses Garayar, line G2, leave from C. Oquendo every 30min. daily 7am-10pm, €1.20. By car, take N-1 out of San Sebastián south toward Vitoria-Gasteiz. Turn toward Hernani on GI-2132. Museum is on the left. ☎943 33 60 06; www.museochillidaleku.com. Open July-Aug. M-Sa 10:30am-8pm, Su 10:30am-3pm; Sept.-June Tu-Su 10:30am-3pm. Daily tours and audioguides. €8, under 12 and seniors €6, under 8 free.)*

▧ MONTE IGUELDO. San Sebastián's mountains afford spectacular views, but those from Monte Igueldo win hands down. On a sunny day, the countryside meets the ocean in a line of white and blue, and Isla de Santa Clara floats in the blue of the bay. The sidewalk toward the mountain ends just before the base of Monte Igueldo, next to Eduardo Chillida's spectacular sculpture *El Peine de los Vientos* (Wind Comb) by the raging sea. If you're interested in taking the quick route to the summit, try the #16 bus or the funicular. On top of the hill you'll find an 18th-century tower with a dazzling ▧ **panoramic view** of the sea, mountains, and city. *(☎943 21 02 11. Open July-Sept. daily 10am-10pm; Oct. and Jan.-May M-F 11am-6pm, Sa-Su 11am-8pm; Apr.-June M-F 11am-8pm, Sa 11am-10pm, Su 10am-10pm. Funicular runs every 15min. July daily 10am-9pm; Aug. 10am-10pm; Sept.-Nov. and May-June 11am-8pm; Nov.-Apr. noon-6pm. €1.20. Tower open daily 10am-9pm. €2. Mar.-Oct. opening hours depend on weather.)*

MONTE URGULL. Across the bay from Monte Igueldo, the paths on Monte Urgull wind through shady woods, monuments, and stunning vistas of the old town and fishing port below. The fortified hills served as a major defense base for the city until the 19th century; today, visitors can absorb its history, as well as some local art, at the **Castillo de Santa Cruz de la Mota,** which tops the summit with 12 cannons, a chapel, and the statue of the *Sagrado Corazón de Jesús. (Paths lead to the summit from Po. Nuevo; the official Subido al Castillo starts at the end of Pl. de Kaimingaintxo, past the Iglesia de Santa María toward Santa Clara. Entire park open May-Sept. 8am-9pm; Oct.-Apr. 8am-7pm. Castillo and exhibitions open daily 8am-1:30pm and 5-8pm. Free.)*

MUSEO DE SAN TELMO. The Museo de San Telmo resides in a former Dominican monastery and houses magnificent collections of Basque art, funerary relics, prehistoric Basque artifacts, dinosaur skeletons, and more recent anthropological exhibits. Especially impressive is the converted church, hung with monumental tapestries of Basque traditions like whaling and navigation in Republican style. *(Pl. Zuloaga, 1. ☎943 48 15 80; www.donostiakultura.com. Open Tu-Sa 10:30am-1:30pm and 4-7:30pm, Su 10:30am-2pm. Free.)*

PALACES. When Queen Isabel II started vacationing here in the mid-19th century, fancy buildings sprang up like wildflowers. A visit to the palaces and a glance at their view will make you turn green with envy. The **Palacio de Miramar** has passed through the hands of the Spanish court, Napoleon III, and Bismarck. *(Between Playa de la Concha and Playa de Ondarreta. Open daily June-Aug. 8am-9pm; Sept.-May 8am-7pm. Free.)* The other royal residence, **Palacio de Aiete,** is also closed to the public, but surrounding trails in the adjacent garden are not. *(Follow Cuesta de Aldapeta or take bus #19 or 31. Grounds open daily June-Sept. 8am-9pm, Oct.-May 8am-7pm. Free.)*

AQUARIUM. If you can't stand to eat any more of your finned friends, watch over 5000 of them, including sharks and sea turtles, in the aquarium's spectacular underwater tunnel. The second floor holds a coral and conch collection. *(Po. del Muelle, 34, on Pl. de Carlos Blasco de Imaz. Arrows point the way from the port. Look for the big "Aquarium" sign. ☎943 44 00 99; www.aquariumss.com. Open July-Aug. daily 10am-9pm, Apr. 8-June 30 and Sept. M-F 10am-8pm, Sa-Su 10am-9pm; Mar. 1-Apr.7 M-F 10am-7pm, Sa-Su 10am-8pm. €10, students and seniors €8, children €6.)*

◢ BEACHES

The gorgeous **Playa de la Concha** curves from the port to **Pico del Loro,** the promontory home of the Palacio de Miramar. The flat beach virtually disappears during high tide. Sunbathers jam onto the smaller and steeper **Playa de Ondarreta,** beyond Miramar, and surfers flock to the bigger waves of more exposed **Playa**

THE LOCAL STORY

AND ALL THAT JAZZ

Despite being known for their steadfast loyalty to regional traditions and their rich age-old cultural heritage, every July the Basque people show that they are also quite capable of bringing in some of the best the outside world has to offer, when they host not one, but two world-class jazz festivals. The festivals take place in San Sebastián, the glittering jewel of the Basque coastline, and in Vitoria-Gasteiz, the sophisticated but laid-back capital.

Both festivals annually bring in a wealth of top-tier musical talent: some of Vitoria's headline performers last year were Norah Jones, McCoy Tyner, and Ornette Coleman, while San Sebastián brought in Elvis Costello, Chick Corea, and Sly and the Family Stone. Both also complement more established artists with plenty of smaller concerts given by up-and-coming jazz musicians.

Vitoria's festival tends to focus on modern and traditional jazz, while San Sebastián's branches out to other genres such as soul, rock, and funk. Both provide plenty of free entertainment, with outdoor performances, marching bands and free live shows in bars.

For more information on the Vitoria-Gasteiz festival, visit www.jazzvitoria.com; for San Sebastián's check out www.jazzaldia.com. The best tickets cost about €40, while the younger ensembles go for about €25. Season tickets to all the main concerts cost €100-136.

de la Zurrida, across the river from Mt. Urgull. Picnickers head for the alluring **Isla de Santa Clara** in the bay. (☎943 00 04 50. Motorboat ferry (5min.) departs from docks behind *Ayuntamiento* June-Sept. every 30min. Round-trip €3.25.)

Several sports-related groups offer a variety of activities and lessons. For **kayaking,** call the **Federación Gipuzkoaka de Piragüismo,** Po. de la Concha, 18. (☎943 44 51 03. €6 per hour. Open July-Aug. M-F 10am-12:30pm and 4-7pm.) Surfers should check out the **Pukas Surf Club,** Av. de la Zurriola, 24, or the hut on the beach, for expert info, lessons, and rentals. The store manufactures its own surf boards and offers courses at various levels for €65. (☎943 32 00 68; www.pukassurfeskola.com. Surfboard rental €25 per day, fins €3 per hour, wetsuits €20 per 2 days. Guided surfing €37 per hour. Open M-Sa 9:30am-8pm. MC/V.) For general information on all sports, pick up a copy of the *UDA-Actividades Deportivas* brochure at the tourist office.

▣ ❀ NIGHTLIFE AND FESTIVALS

The *parte vieja* pulls out all the stops in July and August, particularly on C. Fermín Calbetón, three blocks in from Alameda del Boulevard. During the year, when students outnumber backpackers, nightlife tends to move beyond the *parte vieja.* Keep an eye out for coupons, but be aware that some deals are too good to be true.

San Sebastián is a great city for cultural events and festivals. Highlights of the year are the internationally renowned, week-long **Jazzaldia** jazz festival in late July and the equally prestigious **International Film Festival** in late September. During both, ticketed events take place alongside free street performances. For more traditional celebrations, try the **Semana Grande,** held annually the week around August 15th, when the entire city heads to the streets for shows, parades, concerts, and a nightly international fireworks competition over the Concha beach. Reserve ahead if you're planning on visiting the city during any of these events.

> **Ostadar,** C. Fermín Calbetón, 13 (☎943 42 62 78). This lively little bar is among the most popular places for tourists and locals to dance to the best mixes in the *parte vieja.* Cheap beer and trendy, chilled-out decor. Beer €2. Mixed drinks €5. Open daily 5pm-3am. Cash only.

> **Zibbibo,** Pl. de Sarriegi, 8 (☎943 42 53 34). Packed with young tourists in the *parte vieja,* Zibbibo is practically a disco, just on a smaller scale. Blend of Top 40 and Euro-techno. "Grande" sangria €5.50. 2-pint Heineken €5. Happy hour daily 7-9pm and 10-11:30pm. Open M-W 4pm-2:30am, Th-Sa 4pm-3:30am. AmEx/MC/V.

> **Bideluze,** Pl. Gipuzkoa, 14 (☎943 42 28 80). For a relaxed evening out, this cafe has chill music, good coffee (€1.50), and plush red chairs. *Bocadillos* €4-7. Open M-F 8am-1am, Sa 9am-2am, Su 11am-1am. Cash only.

> **Bebop Bar,** Po. de Salamanca,1 (☎943 42 89 69). A good alternative to the more conventional bars, with occasional live jazz performances, salsa nights and funk and groove DJs. Open daily 7pm-3am. MC/V.

HONDARRIBIA   ☎943

Hondarribia (pop. 13,600), less than 1hr. east of San Sebastián by bus, is a relaxing getaway from its popular and glitzy neighbor. A perfect mix of small mountain town charm and wide open sea views, the city's ancient fortifications are largely intact, preserving much of the old town for quiet walks among cobblestone streets and inviting restaurants. Along the waterfront, old wharfs and new shops mingle along a beautiful walkway. In the peak days of summer, crowds of vacationers from Madrid and Barcelona flock to the beach, but it's usually calm through June.

🔁 TRANSPORTATION AND PRACTICAL INFORMATION. The **airport,** on **Gabarrari Kalea** (☎943 66 85 00), is serviced by **Iberia** (☎943 42 35 86) and lies within walking distance of the town center; it also acts as the airport for San Sebastián. Green-and-white **Interbus buses** (☎943 64 13 02; www.interbus.com.es) run from San Sebastián's Pl. Guipuzkoa to Hondarribia via Irún (45min.; every 20-30min. M-Sa 7:35am-9:45pm, Su 8:45am-9:45pm; return buses to San Sebastián every 20-30min. M-Sa 6:45am-9:15pm, Su 7:45am-9:15pm; €1.75). Pay onboard and get off at the stop in front of the post office at Pl. San Cristóbal. **AUIF buses** go to Irún (10min.; every 15min. M-F 6am-10:30pm, Sa 11:30am-5:30pm; €1). **Taxi** service offered by **Donostia** (☎943 46 46 46; to San Sebastián €35). The **tourist office, Bidasoa Turismo,** Jabier Ugarte Kalea, 6, is right off Pl. San Cristóbal; from the bus stop walk across the plaza. (☎943 64 54 58; www.hondarribiaturismo.com. Open July-Sept. M-F 10am-7:30pm, Sa-Su 10am-2pm and 4-8pm; Oct.-June M-F 9:30am-1:30pm and 4-6:30pm, Sa-Su 10am-2pm. English spoken. Gives out maps of town and hiking trails in the region.) Local services include: a **bank, Caja Laboral/Kutxa,** San Pedro Kalea, 9, across from the post office (open M-F 8:15am-2:15pm; **ATM** open 6:30am-10:30pm); 24hr. **ATMs** on C. San Nicolas; and the **police,** Mayor Kalea, 10 (☎943 30 21 86). The **post office** is at Pl. San Cristóbal, 1. (☎943 64 12 04. Open M-F 8:30am-2:30pm, Sa 9:30am-1pm.) **Postal Code:** 20280.

🏠 ACCOMMODATIONS. The tiny **Hostal Txoko Goxoa ❹,** Margolari Etxenagusia, lies in the other direction from Pl. San Cristóbal. From the tourist office, head up Jabier Ugarte Kalea, and take the second right onto Juan Laborda Kalea. Follow it uphill, then downhill, then take a right at the city's old walls. The friendly English-speaking owner will greet you and show you to your airy, relaxing room with spotless private bath and TV. (☎943 64 46 58, www.txokogoxoa.com. Breakfast €5. Singles €36-46; doubles €55-69. Closes for 2 weeks in October. MC/V.) **Camping Jaizkibel ❶** is 1km from town on Ctra. Guadalupe toward Monte Jaizkibel and can be reached by car or foot. The campground has hot showers, a cafeteria, a restaurant, and laundry. (☎943 64 16 79. Reception 9am-10pm. €4.40 per person, per tent, and per car. Bungalows €50-68. Laundry €3.50. No reservations. MC/V.)

🍴 FOOD. Several **markets** spill onto San Pedro Kalea, three blocks inland from the port. Stock up at **Solbes,** Santiago, 2. (☎943 64 70 10. Open daily 9am-2:30pm and 5:30-9:30pm. MC/V.) Eat like royal royalty at ⬛**Antontxo ❸,** Santiago Kalea, 47, where you'll find generous portions served in an old farmhouse. Bright yellow and blue wall decorations and reliefs celebrating traditional Basque culture bring the dining room to life. The *rabo de buey* (oxtail; €14) is amazing. (☎943 64 00 59. Entrees €12-20. Open Tu-Sa 1-3:30pm and 8-11pm, Su 1-3:30pm. MC/V.) For a more affordable meal, head to the straightforward **Alcanadre Bar ❷,** C. San Pedro, 26. The down-to-earth eatery has a user-friendly and extensive menu of sandwiches, fish, meat, and *platos combinados.* (☎943 64 27 72. Entrees €7-10. Open daily 10am-11:30pm. MC/V.)

◼🏃 SIGHTS AND OUTDOOR ACTIVITIES. The stone-and-timber *casco antiguo,* ringed by a sturdy wall of rock and mortar and centered around Carlos V's imposing palace in Pl. de Armas (now a *parador nacional* called El Emperador—peek inside to catch a glimpse of the luxury, state-run hotel), provides welcome relief from Coppertone fumes. The **Parroquía de Nuestra Señora de la Asunción,** also in Pl. de Armas, is a lovely 15th-century church where Louis XIV of France married María Teresa of Spain. There are several possible excursions from Hondarribia. **Monte Jaizkibel,** 6km up Monte Jaizkibel Etorbidea, guards the **Santuario de Guadalupe** (open for Su mass at 9:30am). Hiking the mountain affords incredible views of the coast; on a clear day you can see as far as Bayonne, France. **Rekalde Boats** (☎639 61 78 98) shuttle travelers across the bay to **Hendaye,** a French town with a bigger beach. The boats leave from the pier at the end of Domingo Egia Kalea, off La Marina (10min.; every 30min. 10am-1am, return every 30min. 10:15am-12:45am; €1.50). Inquire about a number of other excursions by boat and guided tours of the town. Sick and tired of being above sea level? Head to **Centro de Buceo Scuba Du,** C. Ramón Iribarren, 23, where the knowledgeable staff offers scuba lessons and rents equipment. (☎943 64 23 53; www.divescubadu.com. English and French spoken. 20min. guided exploration of sea floor. Week-long open-water certification course €400. Open Tu-Sa 10am-1pm and 4:30-8pm, Su 10am-1pm.)

BILBAO (BILBO) ☎944

Bilbao (pop. 354,000) is a city transformed. Over the last decade, it has made a technological, cultural, and aesthetic turnaround. The economic engine of the Basque country and a major shipbuilding center since the 1700s, Bilbao, known as "Botxo" to Basques, was an important trade link between Castilla and Flanders. Bilbao has diversified from its industrial roots by appealing to tourists with its forward-thinking architecture, busy shopping streets in the *casco viejo*, and pleasant green spaces. Its incredibly efficient public transportation, built around the futuristic subway system and the recently overhauled international airport, remains the envy of other big cities. Frank Gehry's Guggenheim Museum, whose graceful gleaming curves embody the spirit of the new Bilbao, has powerfully fueled the city's rise to international cultural prominence. Enjoy Basque cuisine, summer festivals, and unforgettable art in this booming tourist destination.

◪ TRANSPORTATION

Flights: Airport (☎944 86 96 64; www.aena.es), 12km from Bilbao. Serviced by many European budget airlines flying to different cities in Spain and Europe. To reach the airport take **BizkaiBus** (☎902 22 22 65) marked Aeropuerto from Termibus, or Pl. Moyúa in front of the Hacienda building (line A-3247; 25min., every 30min. 5:25am-9:55pm; €1.10). Buses return from airport to Pl. Moyúa (every 30min. 6:15am-midnight). **Taxis** to Pl. Moyúa cost approx. €18.

Trains: Bilbao has 3 train stations.

Ferrocarriles Vascongados/Eusko Trenbideak (FV/ET): Estación de Atxuri, Cl. Atxuri, 8 (☎902 54 32 10; www.euskotren.es). Trains to **San Sebastián** (2¾hr.; 17-18 per day M-F 5:57am-8:34pm, Sa-Su 6:57am-8:34pm), via **Guernica.**

FEVE: Estación de Santander, C. Bailén, 2 (☎944 25 06 15; www.feve.es). To: **León** (7hr., 2:30pm, €19.80) and **Santander** (3hr.; 8am, 1, 7:30pm; €7). Also offers extensive local service.

RENFE: Estación de Abando, Pl. Circular, 2 (☎902 24 02 02). M: Abando. To: **Barcelona** (9-10hr.; July-Aug. daily 10:05am, 10:25am, Sept.-June daily 10:05am, M-F 10:25pm; €38.40-50.50); **Madrid** (6hr.; daily 8:55am, M-F and Su also 11pm; €38.50-43.80); **Salamanca** (5½ hr., 2pm, €28.20). **Info booth** open in summer daily 7:30am-10:30pm; in winter 9:30am-1:30pm and 4:30-8pm.

Buses: The following companies are based at the **Termibús terminal,** C. Gurtubay, 1 (☎944 39 52 05). M: San Mamés. **Info booth** open M-F 7am-10pm, Sa 8am-9pm, Su 9am-10pm.

ALSA: (☎902 42 22 42; www.alsa.es). To: **Barcelona** (7hr.; 3 per day 7am-3:15pm, F and Su also 11:30pm; €39.49); **A Coruña** (7-8hr., 6am, F and Su also 10:15pm, Su 2:30pm, €43-56.50); **Santander** (1¼hr.; every 30-60min. 6am-11:30pm, also 1:45am; €6.25-9); **Zaragoza** (4hr.; 7 per day 6:30am-8:45pm, F and Su also 4:30 and 9:30pm; €18.51).

Bilbao

▲ ACCOMMODATIONS
Pensión de la Fuente, 7
Pensión Ladero, 6
Pensión Mardones, 5
Pensión/Hostal
Méndez, 9
Residencia Blas de
Otero, 12

● FOOD
Agape, 13
New Inn Urrestarazu, 2
Restaurante-Bar Zuretzat, 1
Restaurante Peruano Aji
Colorado, 11
Restaurante Vegetariano
Garibolo, 10

♦ NIGHTLIFE
Alambique, 3
The Cotton Club, 8
Karachi, 4

Continental Auto: (☎944 27 42 00). To: **Burgos** (2hr.; M-Sa 7-10 per day 6:30am-8:30pm, Su 7 per day 8:30am-10:30pm; €10.49) and **Madrid** (4-5hr.; M-F 10-18 per day 9am-1:30am, Su hourly 8am-1:30am; €24.54).

PESA: (☎902 10 12 10; www.pesa.net). To **San Sebastián** (1¼hr.; M-F hourly 6:30am-10pm, Sa-Su every 30-60min. 7:30am-10pm; €8.65).

La Unión: (☎944 27 11 11). To: **Haro** (1hr.; M-F 5 per day 9:15am-8:25pm, Sa 4 per day, Su 3 per day 8:30am-7:30pm; €8.05); **Logroño** (1¾hr., 4-6 per day 8:30am-7:30pm, €11.35); **Pamplona** (2hr.; July-Sept. M-Sa 6 per day 7am-8:30pm, Su 5 per day 8:30am-8pm; Oct.-June M-Th and Sa 7:30am-7pm, F 7:30am-8pm, Su 11am-8pm; €12.10); **Vitoria-Gasteiz** (1hr.; M-F every 30min. 6am-10pm, Sa hourly 7am-10pm, Su hourly 7:30am-9:30pm except 9:30am; €5.15).

Public Transportation: If you'll be in Bilbao for a few days, buy a pre-paid Creditrans pass for €5, €10, or €15 at metro ticket machines, ONCE booths, or most kiosks. The card is a convenient way to pay for all Bilbao public transportation on Bilbobús, BizkaiBus, EuskoTran, the metro, and the funicular. All fares on these lines discounted with the card.

Bilbobús runs 23 lines across the city (daily 6am-11:30pm; M-F €0.90, Sa-Su €1). Signs at most stops list the complex schedules.

BizkaiBus (☎902 22 22 65) connects Bilbao to the suburbs and the airport. 20% discount on fares with Creditrans. Leaves daily from in front of Estación de Abando to **Guernica** (lines A-3514 and A3515; 45min.; M-F every 15min. 6:15am-10pm, Sa every 30min. 6:30am-10:30pm, Su every 30min. 7:30am-10:30pm.)

EuskoTran, C. Buenos Aires, 9 (☎902 54 32 10), runs brand-new, fast, comfortable tram-trains on a circuit in Bilbao. When walking in the city, make sure to avoid the tracks, which often run next to the sidewalk. Service now reaches from the Termibus station to Atxuri (€1; Creditrans €0.40).

Metro (☎944 25 40 00 or 944 25 40 25; www.metrobilbao.net). Ultra-modern. Though it only has 2 lines, one on each side of Bilbao's river, it will quickly get you just about anywhere you need to go in and around the city. Look for 3 interlocking red circles to find entrances, and **hang on to your ticket after entering**—you'll need it again to exit. Travel within 1 zone €1.25, 2 zones €1.40, 3 zones €1.50. Trains run daily every 15min. 6am-10:30pm, also every 30min. F 10:30pm-2am, Sa 10:30pm-6am hourly.

Taxis: Teletaxi (☎944 10 21 21). **Radio Taxi Bilbao** (☎944 44 88 88).

Car Rental: Europcar, C. Licenciado Poza, 56 (☎944 42 22 26). 21+ with passport and valid driver's license. Open M-F 8am-1pm and 4-7:30pm, Sa 9am-1pm. Airport **branch** (☎944 71 01 33). Open daily 7:30am-11:30pm.

■✦▮ ORIENTATION AND PRACTICAL INFORMATION

The Ría de Bilbao runs through the city and separates the historic **casco viejo** to the east and the newer parts of town to the west. The train stations are directly across the river from the **casco viejo,** while the bus station is considerably farther west. **Gran Vía de Don Diego López de Haro** connects three of Bilbao's main plazas, heading east from **Pl. del Sagrado Corazón,** through central **Pl. Federico Moyúa,** and ending at **Plaza Circular.** The **Guggenheim Museum** is in the middle of the northern part of the newer, western bank, about a 20min. walk from the **casco viejo.**

Tourist Office: Oficina de Turismo de Bilbao, central branch at Pl. Ensanche, 11 (☎944 79 57 60; www.bilbao.net/bilbaoturismo). Provides information on city transportation, accommodations, museums, and restaurants. Open M-F 9am-2pm and 4-7:30pm; *Semana Grande* (mid-Aug.), Sa-Su 9am-2pm and 4-7:30pm. **Branch** at **Teatro Arriaga** (open July-Aug. M-Sa 9:30am-2pm and 4-7:30pm, Su 9:30am-2pm; Sept.-June Tu-F 11am-6pm, Sa 11am-7pm, Su 11am-2pm), also near the **Guggenheim,** Abandoibarra Etorbidea, 2. English spoken. Open Tu-F 11am-6pm, Sa 11am-7pm, Su 11am-2pm; July-Sept. M-Sa 10am-7pm, Su 10am-6pm. All 3 offices offer guided walking tours of the old quarter and of the newer Ensanche-Abandoibarra (Sa-Su 10am for old quarter, noon for newer neighborhood, €4.) The tourist office also runs an accommodations booking service for a fee, call for information.

Currency Exchange: Caja Laboral, Pl. Circular. 24hr. **ATM.** Open M-F 8:30am-2:15pm and 4:15-7:45pm; Oct-Mar. Sa 8:30am-1:15pm; June 15-Sept. 30 closed F afternoons.

Luggage Storage: In **Termibús terminal,** lockers €1; inside €1 per bag. Open M-F 7am-10pm, Sa-Su 8am-9pm.

English-Language Bookstore: Casa del Libro, Alameda de Urquijo, 9 (☎944 15 32 00), next to New Inn Urrestarazu. English, French, and Italian best-sellers and classics; find Grisham next to Gogol. Open M-Sa 9:30am-9pm. AmEx/MC/V.

Municipal Police: C. Luis Briñas, 14 (☎092).

Medical Services: Hospital Civil de Basurto, Av. Montevideo, 18 (☎944 00 60 00). For emergencies **Servicio Medico de Urgencias** (☎902 21 21 24).

Internet Access: Biblioteca Municipal, C. Bidebarrieta, 4 (☎944 15 09 15) has part-time free Wi-Fi, Internet access, and library card with sign-up. Open Sept. 16-May 31 M 2:30-8pm, Tu-F 8:30am-8:30pm, Sa 10am-1pm; July M-F 8:30am-7:30pm; Aug. M-F 8:30am-1:45pm; June Tu-F 8:30am-7:30pm, Sa 10am-2pm.

Post Office: Alameda de Urquijo, 19 (☎944 70 93 38). Open M-F 8:30am-8:30pm, Sa 9:30am-2pm. **Postal Code:** 48008.

▐▗ ACCOMMODATIONS

During **Semana Grande** (Aug. 17-25) rates are higher than those listed below. **Plaza de Arriaga** and **Calle Arenal,** near the *casco viejo,* have budget accommodations, while upscale options pepper the river and new city off **Gran Vía.**

Pensión Méndez, C. Sta. María, 13, 4th fl. (☎944 16 03 64). Bright, very cheerful rooms with firm beds and spacious balconies. Singles €25; doubles €35; triples €50. MC/V. ❷ The affiliated **Hostal Méndez,** C. Sta. María, 13, 1st. fl. (☎944 16 03 64). is pricier, but more comfortable than the neighboring *pensión.* Newly renovated rooms have windows, full bath, and TV. Many have balconies. Singles €38-40; doubles €50-55; triples €65-70. MC/V. ❹

Residencia Blas de Otero, C. de las Cortes, 38 (☎944 34 32 00). A university dorm that rents out rooms in summer. All rooms como with desk, full kitchenette and private bathroom. Free Internet in lobby, and 24hr. guard. Laundry machines (€3 wash and dry) and game room in basement. Location can be somewhat dangerous at night; make sure to walk back in a group. Singles €35; doubles €47. MC/V. ❸

Pensión Ladero, C. Lotería, 1, 4th fl. (☎944 15 09 32). Recently renovated shared baths, rooms with TV, some with balcony. Two very large triples, and several considerably smaller doubles, though all well-appointed. Singles €23; doubles €35; triples €52. No reservations. Cash only. ❷

Pensión de la Fuente, C. Sombrerería, 2 (☎944 16 99 89). Quiet, comfortable rooms with basic amenities. Doubles differ in size, and some include porches. TV €2. Singles €22; doubles €32-36, with bath €45. Extra bed €12. Cash only. ❷

▐ FOOD

Restaurants and bars in the *casco viejo* offer a wide selection of local dishes, *pintxos,* and *bocadillos.* The new city has even more variety. **Mercado de la Ribera,** on the riverbank by C. Pelota, is the biggest indoor **market** in Spain; it's worth a trip just to see the endless counters of every type of freshly caught fish imaginable and the rows of equally fresh vegetables (open M-Th and Sa 8am-2pm, F 8am-2:30pm and 4:30-7:30pm). **Champion** supermarket, Pl. Santos Juanes, is past Mercado de la Ribera. (Open M-Sa 9am-9pm. AmEx/MC/V.) **El Corte Inglés,** Gran Vía, 7-9, in Pl. Circular, has a supermarket. (☎944 25 35 00. Open M-Sa 10am-9pm. AmEx/MC/V.)

PAÍS VASCO

Restaurante Peruano Ají Colorado, C. Barrenkale, 5 (☎944 15 22 09). This intimate restaurant specializes in traditional Andean *ceviche* (marinated raw fish salad; €9.95-12.75), and also serves up excellent, filling Peruvian mountain dishes. M-F lunch *menú* €12. Open Tu-Sa 1:30-4pm and 9-11pm, Su 1:30-4pm. MC/V. ❸

Agape, C. Hernani, 13, (☎944 16 05 06). Easy to overlook in its hole-in-the-wall location, the stylish Agape serves up creative modern Spanish cuisine in its snazzy interior. Fills with a local lunch crowd eager to try out the specials on the daily *menú* (€9.50). Open Tu 1-4pm, W-Sa 1-4pm and 8-11pm. MC/V. ❷

Restaurante Vegetariano Garibolo, C. Fernández del Campo, 7 (☎944 22 32 55). Delicious, creative vegetarian fare, but get here early; seating is limited and the line is long. *Menú* €11. Open M-Th 1-4pm, F-Sa 1-4pm and 9-11:30pm. MC/V. ❷

New Inn Urrestarazu, Alameda de Urquijo, 9 (☎944 15 40 53). As its English-Basque name suggests, this has both authentic local cuisine and American fare. Try the Idiazábal cheese (€5.55) or onion rings (€5), and wash them down with an imported beer. Open M-Th 7:30am-10pm, F-Sa 7am-midnight, Su 10am-10pm. Cash only. ❶

Restaurante-Bar Zuretzat, C. Iparraguirre, 7 (☎944 24 85 05), near the Guggenheim. The walls are lined with helmets signed by the workmen who built the Guggenheim from 1993 to 1997. High-quality seafood. Don't miss the incredibly sweet cinnamon rice pudding (€3.20). *Menú* €10-12. Open daily 7:30am-11pm. MC/V. ❷

👁 SIGHTS

▨ MUSEO GUGGENHEIM BILBAO. Lauded in the international press with every superlative imaginable, Frank Gehry's Guggenheim, opened in 1997, has catapulted Bilbao straight into cultural stardom. Visitors are greeted by Jeff Koons's *Puppy*, a dog composed of 70,000 live flowers standing almost as tall as the museum. The undulating shapes and flowing forms of the building itself are undoubtedly its main attraction. Sheathed in mute titanium, tan limestone, and fluid glass, the US$122 million building is said to resemble an iridescent fish, ship, or a blossoming flower. The dramatically spacious interior features a towering atrium and a series of unconventional exhibition spaces, including a colossal 130m by 30m hall with *The Matter of Time*, a massive permanent installation of curving steel plates by Richard Serra. Especially endearing is the mammoth 30ft. high metal spider lovingly called *"Maman,"* (mommy). Don't be surprised if you are asked to take your shoes off, lie on the floor, walk through mazes, or even sing during your visit to the eccentric exhibits. For those who find modern art hard to swallow, a handy multilingual audioguide provides good commentary and explanations, some by the artists themselves. *(Av. Abandoibarra, 2. ☎944 35 90 80; www.guggenheim-bilbao.es. Open July-Aug. daily 10am-8pm; Sept.-June Tu-Su 10am-8pm. Free guided tours Tu-Su 11am, 12:30, 4:30, 6:30pm. Sign up 30min. before tour at the info desk. Wheelchair-accessible. Museum €12.50, students and seniors €7.50, under 12 accompanied by adult free. Restaurant open Tu-Su 1-3:15pm, W and Sa also 9-10:30pm. Menú €19-24. Adjacent cafeteria open Tu-Su 9am-9pm, July-Aug. also M. First-floor cafe open Tu-Su 9am-9pm.)*

MUSEO DE BELLAS ARTES. Although it can't boast the name recognition of the Guggenheim, the Museo de Bellas Artes wins the favor of locals. The museum has an impressive collection of 12th- to 20th-century art, featuring excellent 15th- to 17th-century Flemish paintings and works by El Greco, Zurbarán, Goya, Gauguin, Francis Bacon, Velázquez, and Mary Cassatt, as well as canvases by Basque artists. A separate section showcases contemporary art, with works by Basque sculptors Chillida and Oteiza. *(Pl. del Museo, 2. Take C. Elcano to Pl. del Museo or bus #10 from Pte. del Arenal. ☎944 39 60 60, guided visits 39 61 37. Open Tu-Sa 10am-8pm, Su 10am-2pm. €5.50, students and seniors €4, under 12 free. W free.)*

OTHER SIGHTS. The best view of the Guggenheim, the city, the surrounding landscape, and the perfect place for a picnic is atop **Monte Artxanda,** north of the old town and equidistant from the *casco viejo* and the Guggenheim. *(Funicular 3min., every 15min. M-F 7:15am-10pm; additional service June-Sept. Sa 7:15am-11pm, holidays 8:15am-11pm. €0.80, cheaper with Creditrans. Wheelchair-accessible lift €0.25.)*

 WAVE WATCH. Ask at the tourist office for information on neighboring beaches. The break attracts local and tourist crowds of surfers near the Bay of Biscay.

NIGHTLIFE AND ENTERTAINMENT

Bilbao has a thriving bar scene. In the *casco viejo*, revelers spill out into the streets to sip their *txikitos* (chee-KEE-tos; small glasses of wine), especially off of Barrenkale, one of the seven original streets from which the city of Bilbao has grown. The action in the *casco viejo* tends to die down around 2am. Then, teenagers and 20-somethings fill C. Licenciado Poza on the west side of town, especially between C. General Concha and Alameda de Recalde, where a covered alleyway connecting C. Licenciado Poza and Alameda de Urquijo teems with bars and loud, flashy discotecas. Mellow **Alambique,** Alda. Urquijo, 37, provides elegant seating and chance for conversation under chandeliers and photos of old Bilbao. (☎944 43 41 88. Beer €2-3. Open M-Th 8am-2am, F-Sa 8am-3am, Su 5pm-3am.) **The Cotton Club,** C. Gregorio de la Revilla, 25 (entrance on C. Simón Bolívar, around the corner from the metro stop), decorated with over 30,000 beer bottle caps, draws a huge 30-something crowd on Friday and Saturday nights, while the rest of the week is a little more low-key. A DJ spins Thursday at 11pm and Friday through Saturday at 1am; live music is on intermittent Thursdays during the college term. (☎944 10 49 51. Beer €3. Over 100 choices of whiskey; mixed drinks €6. Rum €6. Open M-Th 5pm-3:30am, F-Sa 5pm-6am, Su 6:30pm-3:30am.) Soccer fans can find staunch supporters of the Atleti at **Karachi,** Alda. Urquijo, 27, as well as a welcoming laid-back atmosphere in which to linger over a drink or a smoke. (☎944 05 01 91. Open M-Sa in summer 5pm-1:30am, in winter 10am-1am.)

The massive fiesta in honor of *Nuestra Señora de Begoña* takes place during **Acto Nagusia,** a nine-day party in late August, with fireworks, concerts, theater, bullfighting—you name it. Pick up a *Bilbao Guide* from the tourist office for event listings. Street theatre takes over the Pl. Arriaga in mid-July. Documentary filmmakers from all over the world gather for a week in December for the **Festival Internacional de Cine Documental y Cortometraje de Bilbao.** Contact the tourist office for specific information and ticket sales, or visit www.zinebi.com/fant. During the summer, the municipal band offers free **concerts** every other Sunday morning at the bandstand in Pl. Arriaga, Parque del Arenal in winter. Catch some **fútbol** at an Athletic de Bilbao match at **Campo de San Mamés.**

GUERNICA (GERNIKA)

Founded in 1366, Guernica (pop. 16,000) long served as the ceremonial seat of the Basque country. Representatives from all seven Basque provinces met in Guernica's *Casa de Juntas*, and under a nearby oak tree Castilian monarchs ritually swore to uphold the *fueros*, ancient laws guaranteeing Basque autonomy. Guernica is currently home of the parliament of Bizkai, and occasionally hosts ceremonial meetings of the entire Basque parliament.

TRANSPORTATION AND PRACTICAL INFORMATION. Trains (☎902 54 32 10; www.euskotren.es) connect Guernica to Bilbao (45min.; M-F every

THE TRAGEDY OF GUERNICA

Billing itself today as a "City of Peace," Guernica was once the site of one of the most horrifying displays of absolute warfare. The historic Basque town was almost entirely wiped out on April 26, 1937, as bomb after bomb was dropped on the town for more than 3hr., until over 100,000 lb. of explosives had been unloaded on the battered buildings.

The bombardment was carried out at the behest of Generalissimo Francisco Franco by the German Condor Legion, eager to test out its new strategy of carpet-bombing civilian populations to achieve quick military victories. The Spanish leader-to-be wanted to make an example out of Guernica and to nip any potential Basque uprising in the bud. While the town itself had no real strategic military significance, both Franco and the Germans had something to gain from the utterly demoralizing blow it delivered.

Survivors from that Monday, a market day, recall being chased in the fields and forced into their homes by machine-gun fire, only to have the buildings above them torn apart by the bombs moments later. One woman recalled fires burning in the town for three days after the bombardment. When it was all over, over three quarters of the town had been destroyed, leaving only the *Casa de Juntas* (the Biscayan assembly chamber), the church of Santa Maria, and the symbolic oak tree of Guernica untouched. Hun-

30min. 6:15am-10:56pm except 9:45pm, Sa-Su hourly 7:15am-10:15, last at 10:56pm; €2.25, round-trip €3.80). **BizkaiBus** (☎902 22 22 65) sends more convenient and more frequent **buses** from Bilbao's Estación Abando to Bermeo and Lekeitio via Guernica. (Lines A-3514 and A3515. 45min.; buses leave from Hdo. Amezaga in front of RENFE station M-F every 15min. 6:15am-10pm, Sa every 30min. 6:30am-10:30pm, Su every 30min. 7:30am-10:30pm. Return buses M-F every 30min. 6:15am-9:45pm; €2.15, Creditrans €1.65.) Taxi services include **Tele Taxi** (☎944 10 21 21) and **Radio Taxi Bizkai** (☎944 44 88 88). There is free **Internet** access at the former waiting lounge next to the bus stop (open M-F 9am-1pm and 4-8pm). To reach Guernica's multilingual **tourist office**, Artekalea, 8, from the train or bus station, cross the street and head right onto Geltoki Pl. Then walk up C. Adolfo Urioste, past C. 8 de Enero, and turn right onto Barrenkalea. Turn left at the alley marked by signs. The office is at Artekalea, 8. (☎946 25 58 92; www.gernika-lumo.net. Open July-Aug. M-Sa 10am-7pm, Su 10am-2pm; Sept.-June M-Sa 10am-2pm and 4-7pm, Su 10am-2pm.) **Ipar Kutxa**, C. Pablo Picasso, 3, has a 24hr. **ATM**. **Farmacia Ledo R. Boyra Navea**, is at Artekalea, 1. (☎946 25 11 76. Open M-F 9am-1:30pm and 4:30-8pm, Sa 9am-1:30pm.) The **post office**, C. Iparragirre, 26, is two blocks to the left of the main bus stop on C. Iparragirre; turn right at C. Alhóndiga. (☎946 25 03 87. Open M-F 8:30am-2:30pm, Sa 9:30am-1pm.) **Postal Code:** 48300.

⌧ ▣ ACCOMMODATIONS AND FOOD. Although Guernica's main attractions can be seen in a daytrip from Bilbao, accommodations are available for those looking to spend a relaxing night away from the city. Sit on the terraces at ▨**Akelarre Ostatua Pensión ❹**, Barrenkalea, 5, and enjoy the panoramic views of Guernica. The new rooms are clean and large, with TV, phone, and private bath. From the train station, walk up C. Adolfo Urioste and take a right onto Barrenkalea. (☎946 27 01 97; www.hotelakelarre.com. Free Internet and Wi-Fi. Breakfast included. Reception 9am-1pm and 6-9pm. Wheelchair accessible. High season singles €45; doubles €60. Low season €27-32/35-42. 10% discount with a stay of 2 nights or more. AmEx/MC/V.) The *pensión* is affiliated with the **Albergue Gernika Aterpetxea ❶**, Kortezubi Bidea, 9, across the river toward Lekeito. (☎685 75 22 86; alberguegernika.com. Sheets €2.50. Towels €1.20. Reception 4-9pm. Breakfast €3. €13 per person.) Alternatively, head next door to **Hotel Boliña ❹**, Barrenkalea, 3, for rooms with bath, phone, and TV. (☎946 25 03 00; www.hotelbolina.com. Breakfast

included. Singles €48; doubles €65. AmEx/MC/V.)
Downstairs from the hotel is **Restaurante Boliña ❷**,
which draws a large local crowd with a classy low-
key vibe, friendly waitstaff, and huge portions of delicious food. (☎946 25 03 00. *Menú* M-F 1-3:30pm €9.
Open daily 9am-10:30pm. AmEx/MC/V.) For local
lunchtime atmosphere, step away from the shopping
streets to **Bar Gernika ❷**, C. Industria, 12, which
serves €9 lunch *menús*, €18 on the weekends,
including exquisite Basque fish dishes, and original
pintxos. From the train station, walk up C. Adolfo
Urioste and take C. Pablo Picasso left until it
becomes C. Industria. (☎946 25 07 78. Open M-Sa
noon-midnight, Su 1-4pm. MC/V.)

🈶 🎌 **SIGHTS AND FESTIVALS.** In January 2003,
after a complete overhaul, the modest Gernika
Museoa reopened its doors as the 🏛**Guernica Peace
Museum**, in Pl. Foru, 1, across from the town hall.
From the train station, walk 2 blocks up C. Adolfo
Urioste and turn right onto Artekalea. A board near
the entrance displays a quote from Gandhi's dic-
tum: "There is no road to peace, peace is the road."
The museum includes a powerful exhibit recreating the bombing (in Spanish). (☎946 27 02 13. Free
guided tours at noon and 5pm. Open July-Aug. Tu-
Sa 10am-8pm, Su 10am-2pm; Sept.-June Tu-Sa
10am-2pm and 4-7pm, Su 10am-2pm. €4, students
and seniors €2. First Su of every month free.) The
historical focus of Guernica is 🌳**El Árbol,** inside the
gates of the **Casa de Juntas,** up C. Adolfo Urioste
from the train station and on the left, past the
Museo de Euskal Herria. Encased in stone columns, the 300-year-old oak trunk is the most important symbol for the Basques and marks the former
political center of the País Vasco. The old tree is
not the original *Árbol*, but its oldest preserved
descendant. Today, the Vizkaya General Assembly
meets in the Casa, which is open to the public,
along with an adjoining room with a stained-glass
ceiling. (☎946 25 11 38; www.jjggbizkaia.net. Open
daily June-Sept. 10am-2pm and 4-7pm; Oct.-May
10am-2pm and 4-6pm. Free.) Nearby is the **Parque
de los Pueblos de Europa.** Eduardo Chillida's dramatic sculpture **Gure aitaren etxea** (Our Father's
House), a monument commissioned for the 50th
anniversary of the city's bombing, stands in a quiet
corner of the park. To get to the park from the bus
station, follow C. Adolfo Urioste; at the top, follow
the arrow to the right. (Open daily June-Aug. 10am-
9pm; Sept.-May 10am-7pm. Free.) Paintings and
artifacts on display inside the **Museo de Euskal Herria,** C. Allende Salazar, 5, document Basque history,
culture, language and folklore. The extensive col-

dreds had been killed in the attack
and many thousands more injured.
In just a few hours, Guernica had
been transformed in to a smoldering
shell of its former self.

Guernica was rebuilt over the following five years, but it has since
remained an almost universal symbol for the atrocities of warfare and
indiscriminate killing. Many pictures, sketches, and paintings have
attempted to capture this nightmarish day. In a painting now at the
Guernica Peace Museum (see left),
Sofía Gandarias depicts women
holding dead children underneath
the words *"y del cielo llovía sangre"*
(and from the sky rained blood).
Picasso's famous masterpiece,
Guernica, which now hangs in
Madrid's Reina Sofía (p. 127), chill
ingly captured the unspeakable
horror of that day, and brought
Guernica's tragedy lasting widespread international recognition.
When asked by a German ambas-
sador, "Did you do this?" Picasso
answered simply, "No, you did."

Today, however, Guernica is looking to move beyond its devastating
past, and to become a herald of
peace and reconciliation throughout
the world. In 1989, the town
received a public apology from the
president of Germany for his country's role in the attack, and it has
since adopted the motto "renunciar
a olvidar, renunciar a la venganza"
(not forgetting, not seeking vengeance). Once the setting for some
of humanity's darkest moments,
Guernica is now looking to light the
way for the rest of the world.

lection of historical maps of the Basque country, the oldest dating from the 16th century, is not to be missed. The building itself, the Palacio Alegra, is an impressive 18th-century mansion that survived the 1937 air raid. (☎946 25 54 51. Audio tour included. Open Tu-Sa 10am-2pm and 4-7pm, Su 11am-3pm. €3, under 26 and over 65 €1.50.) The tourist office rents historic **audio guides** (€2.50).

The biggest fiesta of the year honors **San Roque** (Aug. 14-18). From June-October, a special **market day** is held the first Saturday of every month in the Pl. del Mercado; there are also two major market days the first and last Mondays of October. On these days, as well as at smaller weekly markets every Monday morning, vendors sell everything from fine chocolates to freshly grilled emu.

VITORIA-GASTEIZ ☎945

While most tourists flock to San Sebastián and Pamplona, the hidden cosmopolitan gem of Vitoria-Gasteiz (pop. 229,000) lies only an hour away. This city, the capital of Basque Country, is threaded with green lines of trees and long pedestrian walkways, and the music of street performers drifts about the elegant avenues on many a summer night. The relaxing pace of the city nurtures a thriving arts scene; numerous posters advertise live shows and jams, and one of the most prestigious jazz festivals in the world is held here every summer. Plenty of hiking and biking await visitors here as well. The city has a progressive and feisty attitude, evident in everything from the politically charged graffiti art to its public bicycles, free for all to use. Vitoria-Gasteiz's hyphenated name testifies to its regional ties; founded as Villa de Nueva Victoria by King Sancho VI of Navarra in 1181 over the small Basque village of Gasteiz, the city regained its original name centuries later when the Basques recovered regional autonomy in 1979. Spray-painted road signs with "Vitoria" crossed out are evidence of continuing loyalty to Basque roots today.

⌐ TRANSPORTATION

Flights: Aeropuerto Vitoria-Foronda (☎902 40 47 04; www.aena.es), 9km outside town. Flights to Mallorca, London and Dublin. Accessible May-Oct. by **La Union** bus from the bus station (☎944 76 50 07; www.laburundesa.com. €3). Otherwise, only by car or taxi (approx. €17). Info open M-F 8am-2:15pm. **Iberia** (☎902 40 05 00). Info open daily 6am-midnight.

Trains: RENFE, Pl. de la Estación (☎902 24 02 02). Info open daily 7am-10:30pm. To: **Barcelona** (7hr., 4:22pm, €35.70); **Burgos** (1½hr., 10 per day 7:20am-1:15am, €7.85-18.80); **Logroño** (1½hr., 8:10am, €7.60); **Madrid** (5½-7hr., 5-6 per day 6:10am-12:30am, €29.40-53); **Pamplona** (1hr., 4-5 per day 6:10am-7:05pm, €4.25-15.10); **San Sebastián** (1¾hr., 8 per day 4:24am-7:37pm, €8.50-19.40).

Buses: C. los Herrán, 50 (☎945 25 84 00). Bus #2 goes from the bus station to C. Florida, but it's probably easier to walk, as buses come infrequently and stops are poorly marked. Open M-F 8am-8pm, Sa-Su 9am-7pm. **ALSA** (☎945 42 22 42; www.alsa.es) to: **Barcelona** (6½-7hr., 3 per day 7am-11:25pm, €35.49) and **Zaragoza** (3hr.; M-Th and Sa 5 per day 7:30am-9:30pm, F and Su 7 per day 7:30am-10:30pm; €14.71). **Burundesa** (☎948 26 46 26; www.laburundesa.com) to **Pamplona** (1½hr.; M-F 11 per day 6:30am-9pm, Sa 9 per day 7am-9pm, Su 6 per day 9am-9pm; €6.50-7.10). **Continental Auto** (☎945 28 64 66; www.continental-auto.es) to **Burgos** (1½hr., 8 per day 6:45am-2:05am, €6.93); **Madrid** (4½-5hr.; M-Sa 9 per day 6:45am-2:05am, Su 11 per day 8:45am-2:05am; €22.41-34); and **San Sebastián** (1½hr.; M-Th and Sa 6 per day 5am-11:30pm, F and Su 7 per day 5am-1:30am; €7.30). **La Unión** (☎945 26 46 26; www.laburundesa.com) to **Bilbao** (1hr.; M-F every 30min. 6am-10pm, Sa every 30min. 7:30am-10pm, Su 14 per day 8:30am-9:30pm; €5.30).

Vitoria-Gasteiz

🏠 **ACCOMMODATIONS**
Camping Ibaya, **7**
Hotel Dato, **8**
Hotel Iradier, **11**
Pensión Amaia, **3**
Pensión Araba, **6, 9, 12**

🍴 **FOOD**
Club Colonial, **4**
Museo del Órgano, **13**
El Siete, **2**
La Taberna de Los
    Mundos, **5**

⭐ **NIGHTLIFE**
The Man in the Moon, **10**
Sherezade, **1**

Public Transportation: Tuvisa Buses (☎945 16 10 54) cover the city and suburbs (7am-10pm, €0.80). A **tourist train** makes a 45min. loop of major landmarks, departing from Pl. de la Virgen Blanca (July-Sept. hourly 11:30am-1:30pm and 5-8pm; €4, children €3).

Taxis: Radio Taxi (☎945 27 35 00). 24hr. service to Vitoria and surrounding areas.

Car Rental: Europcar, C. Adriano VI, 29 (☎945 20 04 33). 21+. Open daily 9am-1pm and 4-7:30pm, Sa 9am-1pm. Airport **branch** (☎16 36 44). Open M-F 1:30-2:45pm.

Bike Rental: Free from tourist office and civic centers. Open July-Sept. daily 10am-7pm; Oct.-June M-Sa 10am-7pm, Su 11am-2pm.

✳🛈 ORIENTATION AND PRACTICAL INFORMATION

The medieval **casco viejo** is the almond-shaped core of Vitoria-Gasteiz, with its three oldest streets: Fray Zacarias Martinez, Santa Maria and Las Escuelas in the highest and most central part of town. **Plaza de la Virgen Blanca,** directly beneath them, is the focal point of the town.

Tourist Office: Pl. del General Loma, 1 (☎945 16 15 98; www.turismo.vitoria-gasteiz.org). **Guided tours** of the casco viejo (11:30am) and other sights (5:30pm) leave from the office. July-Sept. daily; €5, min. 2 people. For tours in languages other than Spanish reserve in advance with the tourist office. **Bike tours** are also available (2-

3 per month, inquire at tourist office for details; €7). Open July-Sept. daily 10am-7pm; Oct.-June M-Sa 10am-7pm, Su 11am-2pm.

Currency Exchange: Banco Santander Central Hispano, Pl. del Arca, 1-3 (☎945 14 24 00). 24hr. **ATM.** Open May-Sept. M-F 8:30am-2pm; Oct.-Apr. M-F 8:30am-2pm, Sa 8:30am-1pm.

Luggage storage: At the **bus station.** €1 per item per day, €2 large items. Open M-Sa 8am-8pm, Su 9am-7pm.

Laundromat: Autoservicio Lavanderia Rico Valle, C. Luis Heinz, across from the Parque de Florida. Open daily 7am-10pm, holidays 9am-10pm. 8kg wash €5; 30min. dry €2. Detergent included.

Police: C. Olaguíbel (☎092).

Medical Services: Osakidetza Servicio Vasco de Salud, Av. de Santiago, 7 (☎945 24 44 44), off C. de la Paz. Open M-F 5pm-midnight, Sa 2pm-midnight, Su 9am-midnight. **Hospital General de Santiago,** C. Olaguíbel, 29 (☎945 00 76 00). For **Pharmacy** information call ☎945 23 07 21. Emergencies call ☎112.

Internet Access: Ponte Cómodo.com, C. los Herrán, 37 (☎945 27 28 41). €2.40 per hour. **Photocopying** €0.15 per page. Open M-F 10am-8pm, Sa 11am-8pm.

Post Office: C. Postas, 9 (☎945 15 52 41). Open M-F 8:30am-8:30pm, Sa 9:30am-2pm. **Lista de Correos** on C. Nuestra Señora del Cabello. **Postal Code: 01001.**

▐ ACCOMMODATIONS AND CAMPING

Vitoria-Gasteiz is loaded with deluxe options, but a growing number of budget accommodations are beginning to appear along the main streets of C. Francia and C. de la Paz, leading away from the bus station. If you plan to come during the Jazz Festival (July 16-21) or the *Fiestas de la Virgen Blanca* (Aug. 4-9), make reservations at least one week in advance.

▨ Hotel Dato, C. Dato, 28 (☎947 14 73 05; www.hoteldato.com). An impressive stone sculpture greets you at the entrance to this luxurious establishment. Rooms with large crown wall-pieces and curtains set over every bed make you feel like royalty. Wi-Fi available. Singles €31-34.10; doubles €44-48.40, with glassed-in terrace €50-55; triples €59-64.50. AmEx/MC/V. ❸

Hotel Iradier, C. Florida, 49 (☎945 27 90 66; www.hoteliradier.com). Ring buzzer to enter. Big blue and yellow rooms with brand new mattresses. All very modern, some with balconies, all with private bath, TV, and phone. Singles €34; doubles €55; triples €70. AmEx/MC/V. ❸

Pensión Araba, C. Florida, 25, 1st fl. (☎945 23 25 88). Attractive rooms, thoughtfully decorated with TV, some with VCR. Parking available. Apartments available at a separate location on C. Iradier and C. Independencia; ask at reception at C. Florida. Wi-Fi available. Singles €35; doubles with bath €40. Cash only. ❸

Pensión Amaia, C. La Paz, 15 (☎945 25 54 97). Conveniently located. Well-maintained, clean rooms come with TV and private bath. Rooms overlooking the main street can be slightly noisy. Parking available. Singles €25; doubles €38. ❷

Camping Ibaya, Ctra. Nacional, 102 (☎945 14 76 20), 4km from town toward Madrid. Follow Portal de Castilla west from the new cathedral. Restaurant, hot showers. Electricity €3. Open year-round. €3.50 per person, per tent, and per car. MC/V. ❶

◖ FOOD

You can't go wrong in the *casco viejo*. The area around Pl. de España has *pintxos* (tapas) galore, many marked with *"pintxos €1"* signs in the evening. Get your groceries at **Carrefour Express,** C. General Álava, 10. (Open M-Sa 9:15am-

9:45pm.) **El Corte Inglés,** on C. de la Paz, has a supermarket downstairs. (☎945 26 63 33. Open M-Sa 10am-10pm. AmEx/MC/V.)

■ **Museo del Órgano,** C. Manuel Iradier, 80 (☎945 26 40 48), on the corner just before the Pl. de Toros. Locals line up at lunch for fresh, filling vegetarian cuisine. Make sure to go for the unlimited and delightfully tasty salad bar. M-F 4-course *menú* €12. Open M-F 1-4pm. MC/V. ❸

El Siete, C. Cuchillería, 3 (☎945 27 22 98). Popular with locals in search of traditional food—and lots of it. 38 varieties of sandwiches (€2.50-3.60). *Pintxos* €1.35-1.50. *Menú* M-F 1-4pm €10-13. Open M-Th and Su 9:30am-12:30am, F-Sa 10:30am-3am or later. Cash only. ❷

Club Colonial, C. de Postes, 44 (☎945 13 48 09). Attracts a lively after-work crowd with brightly colored lights and a huge wall map at one end. Extensive list of sandwiches and *pintxos. Platos combinados* (€7.50-8.50) and *bocadillos* (€3.25-4.50). Open M-Th 7:30am-11pm, F 7:30am-1:30am, Sa 7:30am-2am, Su 12:30-10:30pm. MC/V. ❷

La Taberna de Los Mundos, C. de la Independencia, 14 (☎945 13 93 42). Serves affordable, mouth-watering sandwiches (€4-4.50) in a friendly, neighborhood-haunt atmosphere. Wi-Fi access €3. *Menú* €10. Open M-Th 8:30am-midnight, F 8:30am-1am, Sa 10:30am-1am, Su 11:30am-midnight. MC/V. ❷

👁 SIGHTS

The tree-lined pedestrian walkways of the new city and steep narrow streets of the *casco viejo* make for pleasant strolls. **Plaza de la Virgen Blanca** is the focal point of the *casco viejo* and site of Vitoria-Gasteiz's fiestas. Beside Pl. de la Virgen Blanca is the broad, arcaded **Plaza de España,** which marks the division between the old and new towns. **Los Arquillos,** a series of arches that rise above Pl. de España, were designed by architect Justo Antonio de Olaguíbel and constructed from 1787 to 1802 to connect the *casco viejo* with the rapidly growing new town below. **◪El Anillo Verde,** a ring of parks and grassy promenades entirely encircling the city, makes for a beautiful afternoon walk, bike ride, or bird-watching sojourn.

VITORIA-GASTEIZ FOR POCKET CHANGE. The capital of Basque Country may have its share of fancy accommodations and ritzy restaurants, but it can also be a delight for budget travelers. Start your day off with a satisfying combo breakfast at the **Taberna de Los Mundos** (€3.30), then head over to the tourist office and rent a **free bike.** Go for a spin down the shady **Po. de la Senda** and stop in for a free visit at the grand **Museo de Bellas Artes.** Then, head back towards town, buy a picnic lunch at the supermarket, and spend the rest of the afternoon in the gorgeous and peaceful **Salburua park.**

MUSEUMS AND CATHEDRALS. The rotating permanent collection at ◪**Artium,** the city's contemporary art museum, boasts multimedia works and paintings by 20th-century greats such as Dalí, Picasso, and Miró. You're nearly guaranteed to see something shocking as you walk through the unconventional exhibits. The two galleries on the bottom floor feature regular multimedia exhibitions by prominent contemporary artists. *(C. de Francia, 24. ☎945 20 90 00; www.artium.org. Open Tu-Su 11am-8pm. €4.50; students, seniors, and ages 14-17 €2.20; under 14 free. W by donation, proceeds from which are used to make annual acquisitions.)* Many of the *casco viejo's* Renaissance *palacios* are open to the public as museums. The gorgeous **Palacio de Augusti** houses the **Museo de Bellas Artes,** with works by regional artists. The permanent collection contains Spanish art from the 17th to 19th centuries and marvellous Basque art from the mid-19th to the mid-20th centuries. *(Po.*

Fray Francisco de Vitoria, 18. ☎945 18 19 18. Open Tu-F 10am-2pm and 4-6:30pm, Sa 10am-2pm and 5-8pm, Su 11am-2pm. Free.) At the other end of town, the spacious, modern **Centro Cultural Montehermoso** sits in the stately 16th-century **Aguirre Palace,** C. Fray Zacarias Martinez, 2, at the highest point of the *casco viejo* and overlooking the city. Rotating exhibits, cinematic events, and courses on visual art are held throughout the year. Free concerts are held during the jazz festival. From Pl. de la Virgen Blanca, walk up the stairs to C. Correría, and follow the street until you see stairs on your right. The **Centro Cultural** is at the end of the stairs. *(Open Tu-F 11am-2pm and 6-9pm, Sa 11am-2pm and 5-9pm, and Su 11am-2pm.)* The 🎴**world's largest deck of playing cards,** recognized by the Guinness Book of World Records, weighs 10kg and measures 94 by 61.5cm, and you'll find it (along with 23,000 other decks of cards and more information than you could ever want on their production) at the unusual and architecturally magnificent **Museo Fournier del Naipe (Playing Card Museum).** *(C. de la Cuchillería, 54. ☎945 18 19 18. Tours can be booked W and F mornings. Open Tu-F 10am-2pm and 4-6:30pm, Sa 10am-2pm, Su 11am-2pm. Free.)* The apse of the 20th-century neo-Gothic **Catedral Nueva,** in the *casco viejo*, hosts the **Museo Diocesano de Arte Sagrado,** an extensive collection of religious artifacts from Basque churches, including canvases by El Greco and Ribera. *(C. Monseñor Cadena y Eleta. ☎945 15 06 31.)* The 14th-century **Catedral de Santa Maria,** Canton de San Marcos is under renovation, but can be seen via a guided tours of the restoration works. *(☎945 25 51 35. Open 11am-2pm and 5-8pm. €3.)*

🎭 🌺 NIGHTLIFE AND FESTIVALS

After nightfall, the *casco viejo* lights up. Bars line C. Cuchillería ("La Cuchi"), C. Herrería ("La Herre"), C. Zapatería ("La Zapa"), and C. San Francisco, where university and high school students revel on the weekends. A slightly older crowd gathers in the bars along C. Dato. For intimate socializing, crash 🪔**Sherezade,** C. Correría, 42, a sumptuous Moroccan tea room with intoxicating ambience. Sip a kiwi shake (€1.80) or hot tea with fresh herbs blended to order (€1.50) and let your creative juices flow—crayons and paper are provided. (☎945 25 58 68. Coffee €1-1.50. Open daily July-Sept. 6-11pm; Oct.-June 5-10:30pm.) For a chance to catch a conversation in English, try **The Man in the Moon,** C. Manuel Iradier, 7. (☎945 15 71 80. W Pop Quiz night in English, Th jazz night. Open M-Th 8am-11pm, F 8am-2am, Sa 11am-3am, Su 4-11pm.)

Vitoria hosts countless cultural, music, and sports festivals throughout the year. For info on **theater** and special events, pick up the free monthly *Gidatu* at the tourist office. Jazz grooves in the city the third week of July at the **Festival de Jazz de Vitoria-Gasteiz.** Tickets cost €15-35, but there are free street performances. Call or visit the **Asociación Festival de Jazz de Vitoria,** C. Florida, 3, for specific info (☎945 14 19 19; www.jazzvitoria.com). On July 24-25, *Las Blusas* (The Blouses) hold their own festival with wine, music, and games. The blue shirts represent the old shepherds that used to live in Vitoria. Rockets and a massive gathering in the square mark the start of Vitoria's biggest, craziest party of the year, the **Fiesta de la Virgen Blanca** (Aug. 4-9), at 6pm on August 4th in Pl. de la Virgen Blanca. After the rockets go off, one of the greatest spectacles of the fiesta takes place, when a doll of a Basque youth in traditional garb and holding an open umbrella, called **El Celedón**, descends Mary Poppins-style from the top of the tower of church of San Miguel to the crowd in the square.

ASTURIAS AND CANTABRIA

Asturias and Cantabria are a far cry from familiar sun-and-tapas Spain. These tiny northern regions, tucked between País Vasco and Galicia, are distinguished by endless greenery, precipitous ravines, and jagged cliffs. The impassable peaks of the Cordillera Cantábrica halted the advance of the Moors, making Asturias and Cantabria the stronghold of the Visigoth Christians, who left behind a trail of pre-Romanesque churches. Cut off from the rest of Spain during Moorish rule of the country, today the Asturians and Cantabrians take pride in their states' preservation of "true Spain." It was the Asturian hero Don Pelayo who officially launched the *Reconquista* in AD 722 from the Picos hamlet of Covadonga, a campaign which lasted until the fall of Granada in 1492. Today the heir to the Spanish throne is titled the Príncipe de Asturias. Asturias and Cantabria retain some of their separation from Spain proper—the endless, rough terrain has limited the number of rail lines through the regions, leaving lone roads to wind along the steep mountain sides and scalloped shore. These two little territories also maintain cultures that differ from the rest of Spain— they have their own languages, drinking customs, and a unique way of life.

Despite their shared landscape and location, Asturias and Cantabria have distinct personalities. Asturias draws hearty mountaineers looking to reach new heights in its national parks, while Cantabria, with world-class resort towns of Santander and Comillas, appeals to Spain's vacationing elite. Cuisine also distinguishes the two regions. Asturias is famous for its apples, strong cheeses, wholesome fresh fruit, and *arroz con leche* (rice pudding), and true Asturians can be recognized by the way they take their cider, poured from several feet above and downed immediately. Cantabrian cuisine comes from the mountains and the sea, with *cocido montanés* (bean stew) and *marmita* (tuna, potato, and green pepper stew) as popular delicacies. In both regions, no matter what's on the menu, the portions are always generous and filling.

HIGHLIGHTS OF ASTURIAS AND CANTABRIA

RELAX on the renowned Península de Magdalena in **Santander** (p. 548).

PARQUE yourself on the peaks of the **Picos de Europa** (p. 538).

SWIG some of Asturias's famous *cidra* in **Oviedo** (p. 528).

BURY your feet in the silky sand of **Comillas** (p. 556).

ASTURIAS

Mountain ranges and dense alpine forests define the Asturian landscape. Though Asturias never fell to the marauding Moors, today tourists invade to take advantage of the booming adventure tourism industry in the Parque Nacional Picos de Europa. The wide swaths of sand and lively waves in Gijón draw swarms of beachgoers, but plenty of quiet, cliff-lined coves lie just off the beaten path, where tropical and alpine vegetation mingle and await the lucky visitor.

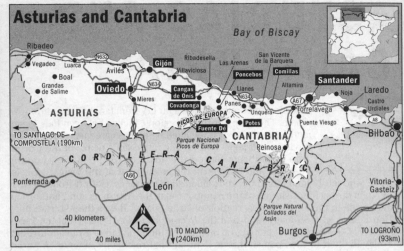

Asturias and Cantabria

Bay of Biscay

Ribadeo
Vegadeo Luarca
● Boal
Grandas
de Salime **Oviedo**
ASTURIAS
Avilés
Mieres
Ribadesella Las Arenas San Vicente
de la Barquera
Gijón
Villaviciosa
Poncebos **Comillas**
Altamira
Santander
Noja Laredo
**Cangas
de Onis**
Covadonga Llanes
Panes
PICOS DE EUROPA
Unquera
Potes
Castro
Urdiales
Torrelavega
Puente Viesgo
CANTABRIA
Reinosa
Bilbao
Fuente Dé
*Parque Nacional
Picos de Europa*
TO SANTIAGO DE
COMPOSTELA (190km)
C O R D I L L E R A   C A N T Á B R I C A
Ponferrada ●
León
A66
*Parque Natural
Collados del
Asón*
Vitoria-
Gasteiz
0   40 kilometers
0   40 miles
TO MADRID
(240km)
Burgos
TO LOGROÑO
(93km)

OVIEDO   ☎958

Although the city of Oviedo (pop. 200,000) has faded into the background of Spanish political life, its bustling old quarter, immense park, spectacular art museum, and endless shopping are more than enough to keep visitors busy for several days. Oviedo's name comes from the Latin *urbis* (city), and for a few centuries, it was the most important city in Spain. As a haven from Moorish attacks, Oviedo became the epicenter of the *Reconquista* and was made the capital of the Kingdom of Asturias around AD 810. If the urban scene isn't for you, the mountains on the horizon, with majestic Monte Naranco minutes away and the Picos de Europa beyond, allow you to explore the countryside.

█ TRANSPORTATION

Flights: Aeropuerto de Ranón/Aeropuerto Nacional de Asturias (☎985 12 75 00), in Avilés, 28km from Oviedo. **Alsa** runs buses from the station to the airport M-F every hour 6am-11pm, €5.80. **Aviaco** (☎985 12 76 03) and **Iberia** (☎985 12 76 07) fly to **Barcelona, London,** and **Madrid.**

Trains: Both **RENFE** and **FEVE** serve Oviedo from **Estación del Norte,** Av. de Santander.

FEVE (☎985 29 76 56), 3rd fl. Info open daily 7am-9:30pm. To: **Bilbao** (7-8hr., 9am, €19.80); **El Ferrol** (6½hr.; 7:47am, 2:47pm; €18.60) via **Ribadeo** (4hr., €9.65); **Llanes** (2hr., 4 per day 9:05am-6:55pm, €6.70); **Santander** (4½hr.; 9:05am, 3:35pm; €12.70).

RENFE (☎902 24 02 02), 1st fl. Pay attention to the type of train; a slow local train through the mountains can double your travel time. Info open daily 8am-9pm. To: **Barcelona** (12-13½hr.; daily 10:57am, M-F and Su also 7:34pm; €46-47) via **Burgos** (5-6hr., €24); **Gijón** (30min.; M-F every 30min, Sa-Su every hour 5:18am-10:39pm; €2.40); **León** (2-2½hr.; M-F 7 per day 7:34am-11pm, Sa-Su 5 per day Sa 9:50am-11pm, Su 9:50am-7:53pm; €7-16); **Madrid** (6-9hr.; M-F Su 9:50am, 4:25, 11pm, Sa 9:50am, 4:25pm; €38-44) via **Valladolid** (4hr., €27-31).

Buses: Information open daily 7am-10:30pm. **ALSA** (national) and **Económicos/EASA** (regional) buses run out of the station on C. Pepe Cosmen (☎902 49 99 49). Open daily 6:30am-12:30am.

ALSA (☎902 422 242). To: **Barcelona** (12hr.; 8:30am, 7:30pm; €48); **Burgos** (3¾hr.; 8:30am, 7:30pm; €15.69); **La Coruña** (4½-6¾hr.; M-Sa 4 per day 6:30am-4:30pm, Su 6:30am-7pm;

€20-31); **León** (1½hr., 9-12 per day 12:30am-10:30pm, €7.82); **Logroño** (6hr.; 8:30am, 7:30pm; €21-23). **Madrid** (5-5½hr.; M-Sa 11-13 per day 12:30am-7:30pm; €29-46); **San Sebastián** (6-8hr.; M-Sa 6 per day 1am-5:45pm, Su 7 per day 1am-9:45pm; €23-41); **Santander** (3-4hr.; M-Th, Sa 9-11 per day 1am-8:45pm, F, Su 11-12 per day 1am-9:45pm; €12-20); **Santiago de Compostela** (5½-7hr.; 4 per day M-Sa 6:30am-4:30pm, Su until 7pm; €26-34); **Valladolid** (3-4hr.; M-Sa 5 per day 12:30am-6:30pm, Su 6 per day 12:30am-8pm; €16.61); **Vigo** (7-9hr.; 6:30am, 3:30pm; €34).

Económicos/EASA (☎985 29 00 39). To: **Arenas de Cabrales** (2hr.; M-F 4 per day 10:30am-6:30pm, Sa-Su 10:30am, 6:30pm; €7.85); **Cangas de Onís** (1-1½hr.; M-F 13 per day 6:30am-9:30pm, Sa-Su 7-8 per day 8:30am-9:30pm; €5.55); **Covadonga** (1¾hr.; M-F 3 per day 8:30am-3:30pm, Sa-Su 3 per day 12:15pm-4:30pm; €6.35); **Llanes** (1½-2hr.; M-F 15 per day 8:30am-9pm, Sa-Su 12 per day 8:30am- 7:30pm; €8.55).

Public Transportation: Strict times vary, but **TUA** (☎985 22 24 22) runs **buses** daily from between 6 and 7am until between 10 and 11pm (€0.85). All stops have bus maps. #4 runs from the train station down C. Uría, turning off just before Campo de San Francisco. #2 goes from both stations to the hospital. #2, 5, and 7 run from the train station along C. Uría to the old city. #10 also runs from Campo de San Francisco and C. Uría up to Monte Naranco.

Taxis: Radio Taxi Ciudad de Oviedo (☎985 25 00 00). 24hr. service. €3-4 from the stations to the old city.

Car Rental: Hertz, C. Ventura Rodríguez, 4 (☎985 26 39 05; reservations 902 402 405). From €45 per day. 200km limit. 23+, must have had license for 2 years; ages 23-25 €8 extra per day. Open M-F 9am-1pm and 4-7:30pm, Sa 9:30am-noon. AmEx/MC/V.

◢■ 🔃 ORIENTATION AND PRACTICAL INFORMATION

The train station is at the top of **Calle Uría,** the city's main passage. Follow it downhill from the station to the city center and *casco viejo,* with the park, **Campo de San Francisco** on your right. The **cathedral** is down C. San Francisco from C. Uría. From the bus station, turn right out of the main entrance and walk up the road, which will bring you C. Uria in front of the train station.

Tourist Office: Regional Office, C. Cimadevilla, 4 (☎985 21 33 85). Open daily 10am-7pm. **Municipal Office,** C. Marqués de Santa Cruz, 1 (☎985 22 75 86). Open daily 10am-2pm and 4:30-7pm.

Currency Exchange: Banco Santander Central Hispano, C. Pelayo Esq. Alonso Quintanilla (☎985 24 24 24). **Branch,** C. Uría, 1 (☎985 10 60 00), across the street from the park. Both open Apr.-Sept. M-F 8:30am-2pm; Oct.-Mar. M-F 8:30am-2pm, Sa 8:30am-1pm.

Luggage Storage: Lockers at the **RENFE station** (Open daily 7am-11pm. Medium €3 per day, large €4.50) and the **bus station** (Open daily 6:30-12:30am. €2 per day.).

English-Language Bookstore: Librería Cervantes, C. Dr. Casal, 9 (☎985 20 77 61). The English book section is located on the 2nd fl. Open M-Sa 10am-1:30pm and 4:15-8:15pm. MC/V.

Laundromat: C. Emilio Alarcos Llorach, 1. (☎985 08 88 66). Open daily 9am-10pm.

Police: Municipal, C. General Yague (☎985 11 34 77), across the street from Hotel Reconquista. Main office located on the Carretera del Rubín. **Guardia Civil** (☎985 28 02 04), also located on the Carreterra del Rubín, next door to the municipal office.

24hr. Pharmacy: Farmacia Dr. Luis Gómez Prado, C. Magdalena, 17. (☎985 20 30 84)

Medical Services: Hospital Central de Asturias, C. Calvo Sotelo. (☎985 10 61 00) **Emergencies:** 112.

Internet Access: Laser Internet Center, C. San Francisco, 9 (☎985 20 00 66). €1 per 20min., €3 per hour. Open M-F 9:30am-12:30am, Sa-Su 11am-midnight. **Ciber Cafe**

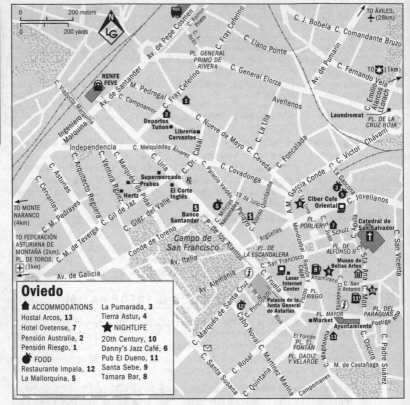

Oviedo

🏠 ACCOMMODATIONS
Hostal Arcos, **13**
Hotel Ovetense, **7**
Pensión Australia, **2**
Pensión Riesgo, **1**

🍎 FOOD
Restaurante Impala, **12**
La Mallorquina, **5**

La Pumarada, **3**
Tierra Astur, **4**

⭐ NIGHTLIFE
20th Century, **10**
Danny's Jazz Café, **6**
Pub El Dueno, **11**
Santa Sebe, **9**
Tamara Bar, **8**

Oriental, C. Jovellanos, 8 (☎985 20 28 97). €1.50 per 30min., €2.20 per hour, €3.90 per 2hr. Open M-F 8am-1am, Sa-Su 9am-3am.

Post Office: C. Santa Susana, 18 (☎985 20 88 82). **Lista de Correos, fax,** and **photocopying.** Open M-F 8:30am-8:30pm, Sa 9:30am-2pm. **Postal Code:** 33007.

📷 ACCOMMODATIONS

Although *pensiones, hostales,* and *hoteles* pack the new city on C. Uría, C. Campoamor, and C. Nueve de Mayo, cheap accommodations aren't easy to find, especially in July and August. Most rooms are clean and many are in restored buildings, offering comfort and convenience at a higher price than nearby cities.

Hostal Arcos, C. Magdalena, 3, 2nd fl. (☎985 21 47 73). Minutes away from the grand cathedral. Vibrant paint colors and photos of Oviedo at its finest adorn the walls of this romantic, friendly hostel. Most rooms have TVs and a few come with chandeliers. Singles €25, with bath €30; doubles €35. Cash only. ❷

Pensión Australia, C. Campoamor, 14, 2nd fl. (☎985 22 22 67). Centrally located between the train station and the park. Expansive rooms come with a TV and big windows. Clean, common bathroom and cozy living room. Laundry free. Singles €22; doubles €35; triples €40. Shared bath. Cash only. ❷

Pensión Riesgo, C. Nueve de Mayo, 16 (☎985 21 89 45; pensionriesgo@hotmail.com). Doilies, heavy curtains, and mismatched bedspreads decorate this *pensión*. Handicapped accessible. Singles €15; doubles €26-28, with shower €28-30. Cash only. ❷

Hotel Ovetense, C. San Juan, 6 (☎985 22 08 40; www.hotelovetense.com). Well-maintained but small rooms just steps away from the main plaza. Full bath, satellite TV, phone, and Wi-Fi access. Restaurant and *sidrería* (cider bar) downstairs. Reserve ahead in summer. July-Sept. singles €37; doubles €52; triples €62; quads (2 doubles with shared bathroom) €85; Oct.-June €30/45/57/75. AmEx/MC/V. ❹

⬦ FOOD

If you have only enough euros for one drink in Oviedo, be sure to try ⬚**sidra** (cider) by the bottle (€1.50-3.60). For the best experience, head to the wood-beamed **sidrerías** (cider houses), where waiters pour from above their heads and expect you to swallow in one gulp. *Sidrerías* line C. Gaconga—"The Boulevard of Cider"—and cheap restaurants can be found on C. Fray Ceferino between the bus and train stations. The indoor **market** at Pl. el Fontán (open M-Sa 8am-8pm) and **El Corte Inglés,** C. Uría, 15 (open M-Sa 10am-8pm), sell produce and groceries.

⬚ **Tierra Astur,** C. La Gascona, 1 (☎985 20 25 02). Wooden *terraza* and cavernous interior, complete with a faux meat market. The perfect place to down bottle after bottle of *sidra* (€2.60) with traditional Asturian meat and cheese platters (€3.60-12). Also features a wide selection of salads and generous fish entrees (€3-18). Open daily 1-4:30pm and 8-12:30pm. AmEx/MC/V. ❸

Restaurante Impala, C. Noval, 10 (☎985 22 01 56). Huge portions of fresh Asturian fare for reasonable prices. 4-course *menú* includes wine and bread. (M-F €7, Sa-Su €9). Open Su-Th 8am-11pm, F-Sa until 1am. MC/V. ❷

La Mallorquina, C. Milicias Nacionales, 5 (☎985 22 40 75; www.la-mallorquina.net). This restaurant has a glass terrace and the feel of a Parisian cafe. Magnificent range of cakes, pastries, and chocolates. Salads (€7-12), sandwiches (€2-5), and combined plates (€9). Open daily 7am-11pm. AmEx/MC/V. ❷

La Pumarada, C. Gascona, 8 (☎985 20 02 79). Down the street from Tierra Astur. Popular for its Asturian entrees and sidra-soaked atmosphere. Waiters pour the cider by holding the bottle high over their heads and every table has a bucket in front of it to catch the spills. Tapas €5-13. Entrees €7-20+. Open daily 9am-12am. MC/V. ❸

◉ SIGHTS

⬚**CATEDRAL DE SAN SALVADOR.** A recent renovation restored Oviedo's 14th-century Gothic cathedral to its original splendor. The **Capilla de Santa María del Rey Casto,** which contains the royal pantheon, was chosen by Alfonso II el Casto in AD 802 to house the remains of Asturian monarchs and Christian relics rescued from the Moors. In this chapel, also look for the statue of San Pedro holding a metal key in his hand. According to legend, if you make three wishes and turn the key around three times, one of the wishes will come true. The cathedral complex includes pristine cloisters, the famous **crypt** of Santa Leocadia, which holds the remains of the martyrs Eulogio and Leocadia, and a *cámara santa* (holy chamber) containing several enormous golden and jeweled crosses. The highlights of the church **museum,** a Bible from the 12th century and a modern painting of Mother Teresa, warrant the entrance fee. (*Pl. de Alfonso II. ☎985 22 10 33. Cathedral open July-Sept. daily 9am-8pm; Oct.-June M-F 10am-1pm and 4-8pm, Sa 10am-1pm and 4-6pm. Su mass 10, 11am, noon, 1, 6:30pm. Museum open July-Sept. daily 10:15am-8pm (last visit*

7:15); Oct.-June 10:15am-1pm and 4-7pm. Cathedral free. Cámara santa €1.50. Museum (including cloisters and crypt) €3, children €1.50. Th evening free.)

■ **MONTE NARANCO.** Take an afternoon away from the hustle and bustle of Oviedo and venture into the Picos by way of Monte Naranco. Not only does the mountain make for a pleasant half-day hike, but it also showcases some of Asturias' oldest sites. The recreational palace **Santa María del Naranco** and the royal church of **San Miguel de Lillo,** located on the side of Monte Naranco, both built in the 9th century, represent some of the first European attempts to blend architecture, sculpture (including human representations), and murals after the fall of the Roman Empire. The style was developed under **Alfonso II** (789-842) and refined under his son Ramiro I, for whom the Ramirense style is named. The guided tour around the two ancient buildings will tell you all about the construction and use of the two buildings when Asturias was the last defense against the Moors. The top of Monte Naranco is approximately a 4km hike from the center of Oviedo. Bus #10 takes you near the top, but the walk up the mountain should take no more than two hours; the municipal tourist office has maps of the suggested walking route. Although the main trail is a bit steep, the path brings you through some of the beautiful greenery around Oviedo and allows you a glimpse of the majestic mountains surrounding the city. *(From C. Uría, take bus #10 toward the train station. Daily 8:30am and every hour. 9:40am-9:40pm, €0.75. ☎985 29 56 85. Both structures open Apr.-Sept. Tu-Sa 9:30am-1pm; 3:30-7pm, M-Su 9:30am-1pm; Oct.-March Tu-Sa 10am-12:30pm, 3-4:30pm, Su-M 10am-12:30pm. €3, children €2. M free, but no guide.)*

■ **MUSEO DE BELLAS ARTES.** The three beautifully maintained buildings of the Museo de Bellas Artes in the Palacio de Velarde display one of the best public art collections in Spain. In addition to the Klimt-esque work of Herme Anglada Camaresa, highlights include 18 pieces of the original Retablo de Santa Marina and works by Goya, Velázquez, and Picasso—there is also an entire room on the first floor full of saint portraits by El Greco. The museum guide (€1) is useful. *(C. Santa Ana, 1, just up from Pl. de Alfonso II. ☎985 21 30 61. Open July-Aug. Tu-Sa 10:30am-2pm and 4-8pm, Su 10:30am-2pm; Sept.-June Tu-F 10:30am-2pm and 4:30-8:30pm, Sa 11:30am-2pm and 5-8pm, Su 11:30am-2:30pm. Free.)*

🔊 NIGHTLIFE

The streets south of the cathedral, especially C. Mon and the areas around Pl. Riego, Pl. el Fontán, and Pl. el Paraguas, teem with noisy *sidrerías* and clubs. Mid-week nightlife in Oviedo is pretty tame, but from Thursday to Saturday the discotecas and bars keep the music pumping all night long. **Pub El Dueno,** C. Mon 15, has both a laid-back bar and disco-dance club feel, and is popular with younger crowd (Beer €2.50-3. Drinks €4.50. Open M-W and Su 10:30pm-3:30am, Th till 4:30am, F-Sa until 5:30am). For suave music and a bit of an older feel, head to **Tamara Bar,** where posters from the 40s and mood lighting lend sophistication to an evening out. (Beer €2.50. Open W-Th 9pm-3am, F-Sa until 5am.) After a few *chupitos* (shots) and *copas* (mixed drinks), most students head to one of the clubs near the Pl. Riesgo. **20th Century,** C. Mon, 12, features pop music and 70s decor, while **Santa SeBe,** C. Altamirano, 6, has more of a psychedelic feel. Both clubs pick up after 2am and are popular with locals. (Beer €2,20-2.50. Mixed drinks €3.50-5. Open weekends 11pm-5:30am. 20th century also open M-F 11pm-3:30am.) At **Danny's Jazz Café,** C. La Luna, 11, between C. Alcalde M. García Conde and C. Jovellanos, Nat King Cole and Miles Davis LPs fill the walls. A lively spot even mid-week. Live music is an occasional treat. (☎985 21 14 83. Beer €2.20. Mixed drinks €3.60. Open daily 10:30pm-3:30am.) Wine connoisseurs follow **la**

ruta de los vinos (the wine route) from bar to bar along C. El Rosal (mixed drinks €1.80-3.60). For about 10 days around Sept. 21, Oviedo throws a **fiesta** with concerts and processions in honor of its patron saint, San Mateo.

🎿 OUTDOOR ACTIVITIES

Though not the best base for hiking in the Parque Nacional Picos de Europa (p. 538), Oviedo is definitely the place to stock up on gear and supplies, as shops within the park and in gateway towns can be prohibitively expensive. A good first stop is the ■**Federación Asturiana de Montaña,** Av. de Julián Clavería, 11, near the bullring and university, a 30min. walk from the city center, or take bus #2 (dir.: Hospital) from C. Uría. From the bus stop go into green gate for the Federación Deportivos del Principado de Asturia, enter the building through the second door on the right and go up to the second floor. This office is in charge of all outdoor activities in the national park and can direct visitors to branches throughout the area. It organizes excursions and provides guides and advice on weather and the best hiking routes. Instructors for everything from paragliding to kayaking are available. The office also provides information on the best places to gear-up in Oviedo. (☎985 25 23 62; www.fempa.net. Open M-Th 10am-2pm.)

GIJÓN ☎985

Gijón (pop. 275,000) may harbor nine beaches along its shoreline, but sand, sun, and sea are not the only reasons to visit this lively coastal city. Both an industrial port and a seaside resort, Gijón (Xixón in the local dialect) has made the transition to a modern city while remaining solidly connected to its history. The reconstructed Roman wall still stands, and the name of Gijón's most famous citizen, Gaspar Melchor de Jovellanos, an illustrious 18th-century thinker and close friend of Diego Velázquez, adorns many of the city's main buildings. Old cobblestone streets wind up from the Plaza del Marques and the Plaza Mayor to the Cimadevilla—once the site of the Roman city and today a hotbed of fantastic restaurants and booming nightlife.

🚍 TRANSPORTATION

Airport: Aeropuerto de Asturias (☎985 127 500 or 902 400 500) is 14km from Gijón toward Avilés in the Ranon (Castrillon). **ALSA** buses (☎985 12 76 00) run from the bus station to the airport (45min.; M-F hourly 6am-11pm, Sa-Su 9 per day 6am-10pm; €11).

Trains: Gijón has 2 train stations, **Estación FEVE-RENFE**, C. Álvarez Juárez and **Estación Jovellanos RENFE**, C. Sanz Crespo (☎985 17 02 02). **RENFE:** (☎985 98 13 63). To **Barcelona** (13hr.; daily 10:30am, M-F and Su also 7:05pm; €47), **Madrid** (6-7hr.; daily 9:20am, 3:55pm, M-F, Su also 9:30pm; day trains €40, night train €46), and **Oviedo** (35min.; M-F every 30min., Sa-Su every hour 6am-11:20pm; €2:40). **FEVE:** (☎985 34 24 15). To **Avilés** (40min., every 30min. 6:20am-10:30pm, €1.35) and **Cudillero** (1½hr.; M-F 13 per day 6:22am-7:32pm, Sa-Su 8 per day 7:32am-8:32pm; €2.50).

Buses: (☎985 35 75 82), Av. Magnus Blikstad at Av. Llanes. Info open daily 9am-2pm, 4-8pm. Runs **ALSA** buses to: **Barcelona** (12-13hr.; 8am, 7pm; €49); **Bilbao** (5hr.; 9-11 per day M-Th 12:14am-7:15pm, F-Su until 9:15pm, Sa until 5:15pm; €19-32); **Madrid** (5½hr., 11-14 per day 1am-11:59pm, €31-46); **Oviedo** (1hr.; M-Sa every 30min. 6:30am-10:30pm, Sa night also hourly, Su every 30min. 7am-10:30pm; €1.80); **Ribadesella** (1¾hr., 8-11 per day 12:14am-8pm, €5.45-6.36); **San Sebastián** (6½hr.; 6-8 per day M-Sa 12:14am-5:15pm, Su until 9:15pm; €25-43); **Santander** (2½-3½hr.; 10-12 per day M-Th and Sa 12:14am-8:15pm, F-Su until

9:15pm; €13-22); **Villaviciosa** (1hr.; M-F every hour 6:30am-10:30pm, Sa-Su 13 per day 8am-10:30pm; €2.40).

Taxis: Radio Taxi, Antolín de la Fuente Cla, 4 (☎985 14 11 11).

✳ 🔁 ORIENTATION AND PRACTICAL INFORMATION

The high headland of the peninsula known as **Cimadevella** marks the edge of the old town, which centers around the Plaza Mayor. The main beach to the east **(Playa de San Lorenzo)** and the **Puerto Deportivo** dock to the west sandwich the more modern downtown; the **Jardines de Begoña,** public gardens, lie to the south. To reach the municipal tourist office from the train station, exit through the main entrance directly in front of the ticket gates and head straight onto C. Álvarez Garaya. Take the first left onto C. de Felipe Menéndez and follow the street to the ocean—the dock in front of you is where the tourist office is located.

Tourist Offices: Municipal office (☎985 34 17 71), on the big dock in the Puerto Deportivo. Listings of accommodations, beaches, restaurants, museums, and festivals. Open daily July-Sept. 9am-10pm; Oct.-June 9am-8pm. 2 smaller summer offices at Playa de San Lorenzo (open Apr.-Nov. 10am-2pm and 4-8pm) and Pl. de los Campinos (open July-Sept. 10am-2pm and 4-8pm), next to the Jardines de Begoña.

Laundromat: Lavarama, C. Dindurra, 3. Open M-F 9am-1:30pm and 4-8pm.

Police: Municipal Police Station, San Jose, 2 (☎985 18 11 00).

24hr. Pharmacy: Farmacia Begoña (☎985 34 25 18), next to the Teatro de Jovellanos.

Medical Services: Health center, C. Donato Argüellas (☎985 14 30 30), 300m east of the Teatro Jovellanos. The nearest hospitals are **Hospital de Jove** (☎985 32 00 50) and **Hospital de Cabueñes** (☎985 18 55 00). **Ambulance:** ☎1006.

Internet access: InterMedia, C. Salustio Regueral, 4 (☎985 17 50 13), near Jardines de la Reina. From main tourist office, cross the street and follow C. Felipe Mendez until 3rd left (C. Cervantes). Turn onto C. Cervantes and follow until right turn, followed immediately by a left turn onto C.Salustio Regueral—the shop will be up the street on your left. €1.60 per hour. Open M-F 10:30am-2pm and 4:30-8:30pm; Sa 11am-1:30pm and 4:30-7:30pm.

Post Office: Pl. Seis de Agosto, s/n. (☎985 17 78 06). Open M-F 8:30am-8:30pm, Sa 9:30am-2pm. **Postal Code:** 33206.

🏠 ACCOMMODATIONS AND CAMPING

Expensive hotels fill the streets near the stations and along the beach, while a few reasonably priced hostels are scattered through town.

🏨 **Hospedaje Don Pelayo,** San Bernardo, 22 (☎985 34 45 50; www.hostaldonpelayo.com). 17 spacious, colorful rooms just 1 block from the beach. 2 comfortable common lounges with couch and flowers. Shared bath. Doubles €40; triples €55. MC/V. ❷

Hostal Manjon, Pl. de Marques, 1, 2nd fl. (☎985 35 23 78), between Playa de San Lorenzo and Playa de Poriente overlooking the plaza. Rooms are spacious, though the linoleum floors and mismatched furniture leave something to be desired. Pleasant all the same, particularly for the price. Singles €20-36; doubles €35-47, with bath €37-49. Prices increase in the summer. Cash only. ❸

Hostal Covedonga, C. La Libertad, 10, 3rd fl. (☎985 34 16 85; www.hostalpensioncovadonga.com). Salmon-pink walls, modern rooms, and friendly staff lend a welcoming vibe. Singles €20, with bath €35; doubles €35; triples €45. All doubles and triples have private bath. MC/V. ❷

Hotel Albor, Pl. Estación de Langrea, 2 (☎ 985 34 75 89), next to the train station. Standard rooms with dark paneling and satellite TV. All rooms have full bath and TV. Cafe downstairs. Inexpensive Sept.-June, but very pricey during summer. Sept.-June singles €35; doubles €45. July-Aug. up to €70/100. MC/V. ❸

Camping Deva-Gijón (☎985 13 38 48), exit A-66 Salida Deva from Cta. N-632, 4km east of the city. Pools, tennis court, restaurant, and lounge make this campground seem like a hotel. €5.50 per person, €5.40 per tent, €5.50 per car. Cash only. ❶

⚡ FOOD

The tourist office hands out the *Guía de Empresas*, which lists restaurants, *sidrerías*, and bars in city. Local specialties include delicious seafood dishes such as clam and mussel paella. In restaurants, *sidra* is sold by the bottle (€2-8). For groceries, try **Mercados Oblanca**, C. Corrida, 3. (Open M-F 9am-2pm and 5-8:30pm, Sa 9am-2pm. AmEx/MC/V.)

La Zamorana, Hermanos Felgueroso, 38-40 (☎985 38 06 32). Located south of the Jardines de Begoña, La Zamora is one of the best *sidrerías* in town. Excellent seafood, including trout and paella. Prices match the quality of the service at this classy joint. Entrees €12-20, special plate of the day €12-15. Open Tu-Su noon-4:30pm and 7:30pm-12:30am. MC/V. ❸

La Casona, Pl. de Jovellanos, 1 (☎985 34 18 20). Situated in the center of old Gijón at the center of the plaza up the hill from the water. Delicious seafood as well as a selection of salads and cheeses. Beautiful view of the ocean. *Menú* €9. Entrees €9-12. Open daily in summer 1-4pm and 8-noon. Cash only. ❷

La Farándula, C. Marques de San Estehen, 7 (☎984 29 03 33). This cross between sexy wine bar and fancy restaurant is pricey, but has the ambience and popularity to back it up. Entrees €7-16, meats €13-20. Open daily noon-4pm and 7pm-last customer. MC/V. ❸

Café Dindurra, Paseo Begoña, 11 (☎985 35 26 14), next to the Teatro Jovellanos. One of the snazzier cafes in the Jardines de Begoña, with over 18 different specialty coffees (€3.25-4.25), as well as various types of tea. Sandwiches €3-6. *Raciones* €2-9. Open Su-Th 8-12:30am, F-Sa until 2am. MC/V. ❷

 SALUD! The quality of an establishment's *sidra* can be measured by the server's style of pouring. Generally, the higher they hold the bottle over their heads and the farther down and more horizontally they hold the glass, the better the *sidra* is. Remember to down your glass quickly, in true Asturian style, to get all the good fizz at the top. Watch your shoes, as servers often care more about the height of their pour than the amount they spill.

👁 🎯 SIGHTS AND BEACHES

TERMAS ROMANAS. Located directly under the Campo Valdés, the 1st-2nd century Roman baths, discovered in 1903 and opened as a museum in 1990, are the most impressive remains of the fortified Roman city that originally sat on the Cimadevilla. Other parts of this ancient city include sections of the old wall that have been reconstructed. *(Campo Valdés, underground at the old town end of the Playa de San Lorenzo. ☎985 18 51 51. Open July-Aug. Tu-Sa 11am-1:30pm and 5-9pm, Su and holidays 11am-2pm and 5-8pm; Mar.-June and Sept. Tu-Sa 10am-1pm and 5-8pm, Su and holidays 11am-2pm and 5-8 pm; Oct.-Feb. Tu-Sa 10am-1pm and 5-8 pm, Su and holidays 11am-2pm and 5-7pm. €2.40, EU citizens, students, and seniors €1.40.)*

MUSEO EVARISTO VALLE. The museum houses the works—and conch collection—of Asturian painter Evaristo Valle (1873-1951), a major Spanish Postimpressionist, in the former residence of Valle's niece, María Rodríguez. The mansion's century-old garden, with some 16,000 sq. mi. of greenery and 120 species of fauna, is no less impressive than the artist's works. *(On Camino de Cabueñes, 261, in the nearby town of Somio. Take bus #10 from Gijón. ☎ 985 33 40 00. Open May-Oct. Tu-Sa 5-8pm, Su noon-2pm; Nov.-Apr. Tu-Sa 4-6pm, Su noon-2pm. €3, students €1.80.)*

MUSEO DEL FERROCARRIL DE ASTURIAS. Situated in the late 19th-century North Station, this museum is dedicated to preserving the history of trains and railways in Asturias and examining their effects on the region. A visit allows you not only to explore the old station but also to step inside some of the old-fashioned trains scattered all over the museum. *(In the old Estación del Norte, in front of the Playa de Poniente. ☎ 985 30 85 75. Open July-Aug. Tu-Sa 10am-2pm and 5-9pm, Su and holidays 11am-2pm and 5-9pm; Sept.-June Tu-Sa 10am-2pm and 4-8pm, Su 11am-2pm and 4-8pm. €2.40, students, retired persons and people younger than 16 €1.40.)*

CENTRO CULTURAL CAJASTUR AND PALACIO REVILLAGIGEDO. Gijón's modern art museum has contemporary exhibitions that rotate once a month—with free admission, it's worth a visit. *(Plaza del Marqués, 2. ☎ 985 34 69 21; revillagigedo@cajastur.es. Open July-Aug. Tu-Sa 11am-1:30pm and 4-9pm, Su and holidays noon-2:30pm; Sept.-June Tu-Sa 10:30am-1:30pm and 4-8pm, Su noon-2:30pm. Free.)*

BEACHES. When the sun is shining the beaches are the place to be in Gijón. The city's main beach, **Playa San Lorenzo,** located to the east of the old quarter, attracts hordes of eager sunbathers, but it virtually disappears at high tide. On the other side of the Puerto Deportivo, the **Playa de Poniente** is sheltered by breakwaters, resulting in gentler waves and a more relaxed—though still crowded—atmosphere. To reach the Playa de Poniente, simply walk past the dock where the tourist office is with the old quarter behind you; the long stretches of sand will be obvious almost immediately. Past San Lorenzo a series of beaches string out at the foot of the cliffs and isolated from the hustle above. While rougher and rockier, these beaches still offer a serene break. At the top of the day, hike up the hills of the Cimadevilla for a view of the coastline and city at sunset; at the top of the hill, the majestic Elogio del Horizonte, created by Basque sculptor Eduardo Chillida in 1990, looks out to the Atlantic's endless horizon.

CANGAS DE ONÍS   ☎985

During the summer months, when the streets are packed with mountaineers and vacationing families, it can seem like the sole purpose of Cangas (pop. 3500) is to help travelers spelunk, hike, and hang-glide. The town's accessibility by bus makes it a useful and ideal base for exploring Parque Nacional Picos de Europa; those seeking more extensive treks move on to towns within the park such as Posada de Valdeón, Sotres, or Poncebos. With all the hubbub about the Picos, however, it is easy to forget that Cangas has its own claim to fame. For 70 years, it was the first capital of what would come to be the country of Spain, founded in AD 718 by Don Pelayo when his victory over the Moors marked the beginning of the *Reconquista*. Between arranging adventures, take a break to explore the legacies left behind by Pelayo and the previous Paleolithic, Celtic, and Roman inhabitants.

⌸ TRANSPORTATION. ALSA, Av. de Covadonga, 18 (☎ 985 84 81 33), in the Pícaro Inmobiliario near the tourist office, has **buses** to: Arenas de Cabrales (30min.; M-F 4 per day noon-8pm, Sa-Su noon, 8pm; €2.35); Covadonga (20min.;

M-F 5 per day 8:45am-5pm, Sa-Su 4 per day 10:45am-6pm; €1.10); Gijón (2hr., daily 5:42 and 8:10pm, €5.95-6.95); Madrid (7hr., daily 12:20am, €28.95); Oviedo (1½-2hr.; M-F every 1-2hr. 6:15am-9:15pm, Sa-Su 7 per day 8:15am-9:15pm; €5.35); Valladolid (5hr., 12:20am, €15.93). For a taxi, call **Radio Taxi.** (☎985 84 87 97 or 84 99 99; 24hr.) Otherwise taxis are next to the *Ayuntamiento*, off Av. Covadonga. Rent cars at **EuropCar,** C. San Pelayo, 17. (☎985 94 75 02. Open Tu-Sa 9:30am-1:30pm and 4:30-7:30pm, Su 10am-2pm. MC/V.)

⊞⚑ ORIENTATION AND PRACTICAL INFORMATION. The main street in Cangas de Onís is **Avenida de Covadonga.** The **tourist office,** Jardines del Ayuntamiento, 2, is in the Plaza del Ayuntamiento across from the bus stop and has information about the town, accommodations, and adventure tourism offices located in other park border towns. (☎985 84 80 05. Some English spoken. Open *Semana Santa*-Oct. daily 9am-10pm; Nov.-*Semana Santa* M-Sa 10am-2pm and 4-8pm, Su 10am-3pm.) Local services include: **ATMs** all along Av. Covadonga; library, Casa de Cultura, C. La Carcel, 13, with **Internet** access, art exhibitions, and evening concerts (☎985 84 86 01; www.cangasdeonis.com; open M-F 10:30am-1pm and 5:30-10:30pm); laundromat, HigienEc Tintorería, C. Rey Fruela, 1 (☎985 94 74 71; open Tu-Sa 10am-2pm and 4-8pm, Su 10am-2pm); the **municipal police** at Av. de Covadonga, 21, in the *Ayuntamiento* (☎985 84 85 58); **pharmacy,** Farmacia Riera, Av. de Castilla (☎985 84 80 38; open daily 9am-2pm and 4:30-7:30pm); **health center,** adjoining the Casa de Cultura at C. de la Cárcel, 13 (☎985 84 85 71); and **Internet** access in the same building as the **post office,** Av. Constantino González, to the right off Av. de Covadonga heading toward the bridge. (☎985 84 81 96. Open M-F 8:30am-2:30pm, Sa 9:30am-1pm.) **Postal Code:** 33550.

▐☖ ACCOMMODATIONS AND FOOD. There are many mid-range hotels in Cangas, and cheaper *pensiones* abound along Av. Covadonga. **Pension Principado ❷,** Av. Covadonga, 6, 4th fl., has comfortable rooms with TV and hall bath. (☎985 84 83 50 or 667 983 185. Doubles €30, with bath €35. Cash only.) **Sidreria Lo de Fidel ❷,** C. San Pelayo, 9, feeds locals in an unpretentious atmosphere for good prices. (☎985 84 87 58. *Sidra* €2.20. *Menú* €8. Open in summer daily 9am-11pm; in winter closed M.) **Los Robles ❸,** C. San Pelayo, 8 (☎985 84 90 15), serves a €9 lunch *menú* and delicious fish and meat dishes (€14-19) in an elegant setting. (Open daily 8am-4pm and 8-11:30pm. MC/V.) Choose from sandwiches (€3), pasta and pizza (€6.20), and paella (€7.50) at **Cafetería Reconquista ❶,** Av. de Covadonga, 6. (Open daily 8am-11:30pm. MC/V.) For a do-it-yourself-meal, try **Alimerka Supermercado,** Av. de Covadonga, 13 and Av. de Castillo, 16. (☎985 84 94 13. Both open M and Su 9am-2pm, Tu-Sa 9am-9:30pm. MC/V.)

◎⚐ SIGHTS AND EXCURSIONS. At the far end of Av. de Covadonga is the **Puente Romano,** an ancient bridge with an ornate golden cross hanging from the main arch, particularly beautiful at night. From the bridge, follow Av. de Covadonga into town, turn left onto C. Constantino González, and cross the river to reach the **Capilla de Santa Cruz.** This Romanesque chapel, built in AD 737, sits atop the town's oldest monument, a Celtic *dolmen* (monolith) dating from 3000 BC, which can be seen from the chapel's cave. (☎985 84 80 05. Open M-Th 10am-2pm and 4-7pm, F-Sa 10am-2pm and 4-7:30pm. Free.) **Cueva del "Buxu"** (BOO-shoo) offers an intimate glimpse into the lives of Cangas's Paleolithic residents, whose few preserved drawings depicting deer and horses date from over 15,000 years ago. To reach the cave, follow the main road to Covadonga for 3km until the signs for the Cueva del Buxu and Cardes, the closest town, direct you left. Cardes is up the hill about 600m, and the path to the cave starts in front of Bar Buxu. From the bar, it's about 1km to the actual cave. Buses to Arenas de Cabrales, Covadonga, and Llanes run near the cave; ask to be dropped off at the **Cruce de Susierra.** Call ahead and arrive before 9:30am, as only 25 people are admitted each day. (☎608 17 59 67 or 985 94 00 54. Open W-Su 9am-1pm and 3-5:30pm. €3, children €1, W free.)

At **La Grandera Zoo,** up Highway AS-114 about 4km toward Soto, gray bears *(osos sardos)*, Iberian wolves *(lobos)*, wild boars *(jabalí)*, Iberian lynx, and 200 other native species can be viewed from the comfort of a short, flat path. (☎985 94 00 17; www.zoolagrandera.com. Open daily 11am-8pm; Nov.-Mar. closed M. €6, children €4.) Those with wheels will want to head south from Cangas on highway N-625, which winds along the Río Sella. This route heads through Santillan and Sames, finally coming to the awe-inducing **Desfiladero de los Beyos,** an 11km gorge with wet rocks and blossoming beech trees.

🏔 **OUTDOOR ACTIVITIES.** Cangas de Onís is the perfect place to arrange outdoor activities, but you must reserve at least two days ahead of time, three to five days from June to August. There are several outfitters in town, but all are closed from December to February. **Cangas Aventura,** Av. de Covadonga, 17, sets up expeditions, including *barranquismo* (canyoneering; €36), canoeing (€23), horseback riding (€15 per 1hr., €25 per 2hr.), and hiking. (☎985 84 92 61; www.cangasaventura.com. Open daily 9:30am-10pm. MC/V.) Prices include equipment, a guide, transportation to and from Cangas, and sometimes a bag lunch. The **Centro de Aventura,** C. Puente Romano, 6, is also the site of **Escuela Asturiana de Piraguismo**. Paragliding courses run €270, but a single tandem flight is only €42. Kayaking, whitewater rafting, canyoneering, and hydrospeed are also available, starting at a reasonable €23. (☎985 84 12 82; www.piraguismo.com. MC/V.) **Deportes Tuñón,** C. San Pelayo, 31, sells hiking boots (€40-129), backpacks (€20-180), and other gear for conquering the Picos. (☎985 94 70 61. Open daily 10am-1:30pm and 4:30-8:30pm. MC/V.)

PARQUE NACIONAL PICOS DE EUROPA

The twisted limestone folds of the Picos de Europa emerged 300 million years ago, creating a mountain range of chaotic beauty and formidable border between the Asturias and Cantabria regions and the rest of Spain. Founded in 1918 as the Parque Nacional de Covadonga, Spain's first national park grew into the second largest national park in Europe, spanning three *macizos* (groups of mountains) and three provinces. The ancient crags and summits of the Picos de Europa shelter some of Europe's most elusive endangered species. The scrub-spotted peaks also lure thousands of outdoor enthusiasts to the caves and caverns carved by centuries of glacial activity and the backcountry trails that trace the contours of the mountains. Highlights include the remote and regal Naranjo de Bulnes (p. 545), the sparkling Lagos de Covadonga (p. 543), and the astounding but crowded 13km walk along the Cares Gorge (p. 545).

◼ TRANSPORTATION

Getting to the Picos is much easier than getting around them. The most important towns within the park are **Covadonga** (accessible from Cangas by bus or car), **Posada de Valdeón** (accessible only by car from Potes through Portilla de la Reina), and **Poncebos** (accessible from Arenas by bus or car). **ALSA buses** link Cangas de Onís (p. 536) and Arenas de Cabrales (p. 538), the gateways in the west and the north, to towns just inside the park's borders. In summer, these buses run from Arenas to Panes as well. **La Palomera buses** link Potes, the gateway in the east, with Panes to the north, and during July and August, with Fuente Dé to the south.

Picos de Europa

It is much more efficient to travel by **car,** as buses run infrequently and irregularly and make many stops. By car, approach from either Oviedo or Santander via the **E70** (A8), which connects to the N625 (to Cangas de Onís) and the N621 (to Potes). Route **AS-114** runs along the northern edge of the Picos from Cangas de Onís through Arenas de Cabrales and on to Panes, where it intersects Route N-621. N-621 runs 50km south and west to Potes, where a branch leads to Fuente Dé. If you don't plan on hiking the dusty roads and mountains, it is sensible to visit the base towns as daytrips for a day or so; otherwise, the many *refugios* and *albergues* within the park provide adequate stops for multi-day treks into the interior.

⬛✚🛈 ORIENTATION AND PRACTICAL INFORMATION

Part of the larger Cordillera Cantábrica, the Picos de Europa consist of three *macizos* (massifs): the **Occidental (Cornión),** the **Central (Urrieles),** and the **Oriental (Ándara).** The highest peak, Torre Cerredo (2648m), rises out of the Central *macizos.* Several rivers wind through the park; the four largest, which mark the borders between the different *macizos,* are the Sella, Dobra, Cares, and Duje. The **Garganta del Cares** (Cares Gorge) cuts a line between the Macizo Oriental and Macizo Central, the latter of which holds the park's most popular trails and famous peaks: the treacherous **Peña Vieja** (2613m) and **Pico Tesorero** (2570m), the stark **Llambrión** (2642m), and the mythic **Naranjo de Bulnes** (Picu Urriellu; 2519m). Part of the Picos' allure is that many of the highest areas are relatively easily accessible for the average hiker, with well-marked trails and plenty of *refugios.* There are also many guided hiking options for more difficult ascents and lengthier excursions. The **park info office** in Tama can be reached at ☎942 73 81 09. Another office in Arenas de Cabrales can be reached in the summer at ☎985 84 64 84. For more information, visit www.picoseuropa.net.

⬛ ACCOMMODATIONS

The most convenient and comfortable accommodations are in Cangas de Onís, Arenas de Cabrales, and Potes. For multi-day hikes, the **refugios** and the **albergues** in the towns within the park, are the best option for staying overnight in the backcountry. *Refugios* provide shelter in the mountains in the form of dorm-style bunks (sometimes mattresses or sheets; a few rent blankets or sleeping bags) and most cost €6-8 per night and accept cash only. They are often known by several names, and the larger ones, such as Vegarredonda and Vega de Urriellu, generally have better amenities. All of the park offices have lists of the *refugios*. Before embarking on any hikes in the park, consult the list of *refugios* below, many of which also double as **ranger stations** in spring and fall. The stations are often unmanned in the winter, though there is at least one building per region open for winter hikers. For more information, inquire at the park info office.

 CAMPING CORRECTLY. While you may see tents pitched out by *refugio*s in the Picos, camping outside of campgrounds is not officially allowed. According to park rules, tents can be pitched at dawn, but must be taken down by nightfall. Save yourself fines and embarrassment, and either stick to the official campsites or arrange for *refugio* accommodations.

There are only four private **campgrounds** ❶ inside the park (at Caín, Santa Marina, Soto de Valdeón, and Fuente Dé), and they are all in the southern half. There is also a free campsite with no services next to Lago Enol near Covadonga. In addition, many towns close to the park borders, including Cangas and Arenas de Cabrales, have campsites. Prices for camping are €3-5 per person, car and tent; call in advance to see if sites are open and spots are available, though reservations are generally not accepted. Other lodging options include **albergues** (dorm-style hostels, usually in ancient buildings with several basic services, shared bathrooms and beds with sheets; towels are not included) and **casas** (buildings with bunks, hot water, and stoves); these, however, are also only in or near towns, and nonexistent farther out in the mountains. In all cases, bring a sleeping bag. Towns within the park also have **pensiones, hostels, hotels,** and **rooms** in private homes; look for *camas* and *habitaciones* signs (typically €35-45 per double). For detailed information on all of the refugios in Asturias, check www.fempa.net/refugios.

MACIZO OCCIDENTAL

▨ **Casa Municipal de Pastores/Vega de Enol** (alt. 1100m), overlooking Lago Enol, accessible from the Lagos de Covadonga road by car. Shower and meals. 10 beds. No telephone. Open year-round. Bunks €8. Cash only. ❶

Vegarredonda (☎985 92 29 52; alt. 1410m), south of Lake Enol. Accessible from Lake Enol via Mirador del Rey and Pozo del Aleman (1½hr.). Blankets, shower, and meals. 68 spots. Open year-round. Bunks €9. Cash only. ❶

Marqués de Villaviciosa/Vega de Ario (☎639 81 20 69 or 650 90 07 60; alt. 1630m), by Vega de Ario southeast of Lago Enol. Open year-round. 40 bunks. Little water available during winter. Meals available. Accessible from Lago Ercina (2½hr.). Open May-Oct. Bunks €9. Cash only. ❶

Vegabaño (☎699 63 32 44; alt. 1340m), in the southwest corner of the park. 25 bunks. Shower and meals. Open year-round. Accessible from Soto de Sajambre (1hr.). Bunks €9. Cash only. ❶

Ordiales (alt. 1750m), at the Ordiales lookout, 30-45min. from Vegarredonda. 4 bunks. No rangers in residence. Houses the remains of the Marques de Villaviciosa, who was instrumental in founding the park. Free access. Cash only. ❶

El Frade (alt. 1700m) near the Pico del Frade in the southwest of the park. Accessible from Posada de Valdeón or Refugio Vegabaño. 8 bunks. Unattended, free access. ❶

MACIZO CENTRAL

▨ **Delgado Úbeda/Vega de Urriellu** (☎985 92 52 00; www.picuurriellu.com; alt. 1953m), by Vega de Urriellu. 96 spots, open year-round with rangers in residence. Accessible from Sotres via Pandebano and Vallejo (4hr.), from Fuente Dé's *teleférico* via Collado Horcados Rojos and Jou de los Boches (4hr.). Also accessible from Poncebos via Bulnes and Camburero by foot (5-6hr.). Open all year. Reservations recommended in peak summer months. €7 per night, half-board €22. Cash only. ❶

▨ **Toño Odriozola/Hotel de Áliva** (☎942 73 09 99; alt. 1670), in the Puertos de Áliva. 24 hotel-style doubles with private bath in a beautiful valley. A 2-star hotel masquerading as a *refugio*. Open June-Sept. Land Rover ride to and from and top *teleférico* station included. Doubles €78, with breakfast and dinner €91. MC/V. ❺

Cabaña Verónica (☎942 73 00 07; alt. 2325m), near Pico Tesorero. The highest *refugio* in Spain, this tiny igloo-shaped cabin is placed right on the edge of the ridge looking southeast. 4-6 spots. Guarded all year. No water in vicinity, but bottles and other drinks for sale, as well as basic meals. Accessible from Espinama via Aliva and Covarrobles (5-6hr.) and from the upper Fuente Dé *teleférico* station (2hr.). €8 per person, dinner €10. Cash only. ❶

El Redondo/Fuente Dé (☎942 73 66 99; alt. 1085m), 100m above the *teleférico* parking lot, in the campsite. 16 bunks. No reservations. Open May-Oct. €5 per person, €3 per child. Cash only. ❶

Diego Mella/Collado Jermoso (☎636 99 87 27; alt. 2060m), next to Collado Jermoso, in the southern central part of the park. 28 bunks. Guarded May-Oct. Sleeping bags for rent and meals provided. Accessible from Fuente Dé via Tornos de Liordes; also from Cabana Veronica via Tiro Callejo or via Tiros de Casares (4hr., difficult). Open May-Oct. Bunks €6. Cash only. ❶

José Ramón Lueja/Jou de Los Cabrones (☎985 92 52 00; alt. 2034m), by Jou de los Cabrones. 24 bunks. Open May-Oct. Meals and drinks offered. Blankets for rent. Accessible from Poncebos via Bulnes, Amuesa, and Cuesta de Trave (5hr.); from Vega de Urriello via Collada Arenera (3½hr.); from Cabana Veronica via Horcada de Don Juan and Jou Cerredo (4½hr.). Bunks €9 a night. Cash only. ❶

La Terenosa (alt. 1315m), near the Collado Pandébano en route to Vega de Urriellu. 30 spots. Open May-Oct. No meals. Accessible from Poncebos via Sotres and Collado Pandebano, or from Picu Uriellu. No rangers in residence. Free access, keys are in first cabin coming from Pandebano. ❶

MACIZO ORIENTAL

Casetón de Andara (☎671 404 277; www.casetondeandara.iespana.es; alt. 1725m), by Vegas de Andara and Pica del Mancondiú. Accessible from Bejes (3hr.), also from Potes via Hito de Escarand via Ctra. Sotres-Treviso (1½hr.). 18 bunks. Meals available. No water in vicinity. Open July-Oct. Sa-Su. ❶

◢ OUTDOORS

While many visitors opt for organized bus tours and guided trips from the base towns, the beauty of the Picos—and the variety of the landscape—are best appreciated on foot. The many *refugios* scattered throughout the park facilitate long treks, and a decent network of roads allows for good access for day-hikes. For multi-day routes, consult one of the Picos de Europa park offices. These offices also arrange **free guided day hikes** (min. 3 people) departing from various base towns in the park from July-Sept. Simply show up at the departure point at the listed time to participate; consult the park office for the most up-to-date schedule. The hikes listed at the end of this section are arranged according to the nearest trailhead or town. Before embarking on any hike, get a map that has all trails clearly marked. Locals use the *Ediciones Adrados* maps (1:25,000), available in bookstores and some tourist offices.

Note that while the gateway towns may appear well developed in tourism, much of the Picos remains untamed, and few amenities are available within the park proper. Non-technical hiking is possible from May to September, and the best times to visit the Picos are July and August. In spring, it is colder, and storms and snow are still a real possibility; September weather can be equally unpredictable. During July and particularly August, make reservations at least a week in advance if you plan to stay in the gateway cities to the park (Cangas de Onís, Arenas de Cabrales, and Potes).

For information on adventure tourism outings, see **Cangas de Onís** (p. 536), **Arenas de Cabrales** (p. 538), and **Potes** (p. 546).

HIKE NUMBER/NAME	DIFFICULTY	DURATION	SCHEDULE	DEPARTURE POINT
Northwest Sector (by Cangas de Onís)				
A-1 **Lagos de Covadonga**	Low	3hr.	Tu-W and F 10:30am	Buferrera parking lot at the lakes
A-2 **Belbín**	Medium	3½hr.	M 9:45am	Buferrera parking lot at the lakes
A-3 **Fana-Covadonga**	Medium	4hr.	Tu 9:30am	Covadonga, at the highway towards the lakes
A-4 **Orrial**	Medium	4hr.	W 9:30am	Buferrera parking lot at the lakes
A-5 **El Toyeyu**	Medium	3½hr.	Th 9:30am	Lago Ercina (Vega La Tiese)
Northeast Sector (by Arenas de Cabrales)				
B-1 **Monte Camba**	Medium	4hr.	M and F 10am	Plaza de Tielve
B-2 **Bulnes**	Medium	4hr.	Tu, Sa 10am	Info booth at Poncebos
B-3 **Minas de Ándara**	Medium-High	4½hr.	W, Su 10am	Hoyo del Tejo, between Sotres and Tresviso
B-4 **Peña Maín**	High	6hr.	Th 9:30am	Sotres—Main Plaza
Southeast Sector (Liébana—by Potes and Fuente Dé)				
C-1 **Horcados Rojos**	Medium/High	4hr.	M 10am	Fuente Dé at the upper *teleférico* station
C-2 **Hayedo de las Ílces**	Low	4hr.	Tu 10am	Plaza at Espinama
C3 **Monte Acebo**	Medium	5hr.	W 10am	Mogrovejo (Entrance to village)
C-4 **Brez-Canal Arredondas**	Low	4hr.	Th 10am	Brez (Entrance to village)
C-5 **Entorno de Fuente Dé**	Low	3hr.	F 10am	Fuente Dé (Info office near parking lot)
C-6 **Sierra de Bejes**	Low	4hr.	Sa 10am	Bejes (Entrance to village)
C-7 **Espinama-Áliva**	Medium	5½hr.	Su 10am	Plaza at Espinama
Southwest Sector (by Sajambre and Valdeón)				
D-1 **Fuente Oscura**	Medium	4hr.	M 9:30am	Posada de Valdeón park info booth
D-2 **Majada Vieja**	Medium	4½hr.	Tu 9:30am	Sta. Marina de Valdeón-Plaza

HIKE NUMBER/NAME	DIFFICULTY	DURATION	SCHEDULE	DEPARTURE POINT
D-3 **Monte Piergua**	Medium	4½hr.	W 9:30am	Posada de Valdeón park info booth
D-4 **Majada de Vegabaño**	Medium	4½hr.	Th 9:30am	Soto de Sajambre-School building
D-5 **Llarellampo**	Low	4hr.	F 9:30am	Oseja de Sajambre (Ayuntamiento)
D-6 **El Odrón**	Low	4hr.	Sa 10am	Posada de Valdeón park info booth
D-7 **Colladín Redondo**	Low	3½hr.	Su 10am	Posada de Valdeón park info booth

ASTURIAS AND CANTABRIA

HIKING

▧ LAGOS DE COVADONGA

These mountain lakes are accessible from Cangas de Onís and Covadonga. ALSA buses (☎902 42 22 42) run from Covadonga to Lago Enol in the summer (30min.; July 8 per day 10am-6pm, Aug., 1st half of Sept. every 10-15min. 10am-6:30pm; returns July 8 per day 11am-7pm, Aug., 1st half of Sept. every 10-15min. 10am-7pm; €1.80). During Semana Santa, Aug., and early Sept., it is prohibited to drive up with private cars to the lakes. Visitors need to park in one of the many parking lots between Cangas and Covadonga and take the ALSA bus from there. Find a complete schedule with all parking lots and bus stops at any tourist or park information office. During the rest of the year, access to the lakes is open. From Lago Enol (alt. 1060m), it is a 1km climb or 5min. drive to Lago Ercina (alt. 1108m). In Covadonga, buses leave from the basilica to follow a road lined with pastures and precipitous cliffs; the right side of the bus has the best views en route. Alternatively, Turataxis runs shuttles several times daily between the lakes and the basilica. (20min., schedule varies, €10 depending on group size.)

The **Lagos de Enol y Ercina** sparkle between the peaks of the mountains past Covadonga. The **Centro de Visitantes Pedro Pidal**, a short climb up from the lower parking lot, has an exhibit laden with sound and water effects, recreating the natural conditions in the park. Extensive info on the Lagos region and on the entire park, including geology, flora, and fauna, is available. The center also provides info on hikes and *refugios* in the entire park. (Open *Semana Santa* to Dec. daily 10am-6pm. Free.) Free **guided hikes** around the lakes depart from the Buferrera parking lot. Just below Lago Ercina is a path through the former **Minas de Buferrera.** In August, the pastures surrounding the lakes feel like a crowded beach with picnicking families. Hit the trails to ditch the crowds. To see both lakes in all of their splendor, head to the aptly named **Mirador de Entrelagos** (between the lakes). A short climb up from the Lago Ercina parking lot, the lookout has great views of both lakes and of the mountains surrounding them. Don't forget your camera.

Two especially good hikes, at a slightly higher level of difficulty, take travelers east from the lakes to the **Vega de Ario,** which offers a panoramic view of the Urrieles Mountains (7hr. round-trip, medium-high difficulty), or south to the **Mirador de Ordiales,** a vantage point overlooking the Pico de las Vidriosas, Río Dobra, and a terrifying gorge (7-8hr. round-trip, high difficulty). Alternatively, head west 2km to the **Mirador del Rey** lookout point (1hr. round-trip), where you can see the **Bosque de Pome.** The ▧**Casa Municipal de Pastores ❶,** just past Lago Enol on the road to the Mirador del Rey in the Vega de Enol, has 10 spots year-round and provides meals, hall bath, and bunks, as well as a view of the lake. Bring your own sleeping bag. (Accessible by car. €8.)

COVADONGA

The sanctuary of Covadonga is accessible only through Cangas, on the Bustio-Arriondas route. ALSA buses (☎ 902 42 22 42; www.alsa.es) run from Cangas (20min.; M-F 5 per day 8:45am-5pm, Sa-Su 3 per day 10:35am-6pm; €1) and back (20min.; M-F 5 per day 9am-5:30pm, Sa-Su 4 per day 10am-6pm; €1.15). Buses stop at the Hospedería, uphill at the basilica, and in front of the ALSA window on Av. Covadonga in Cangas.

"This little mountain will be the salvation of Spain," Don Pelayo, the first King of Asturias, prophesied to his Christian army in AD 722, gesturing to the rocky promontory above what is now Covadonga. The mountain soon became the site of the first successful battle in the *Reconquista*, although legend claims that it was not geography but the intervention of the Virgin Mary that made victory over the Moors possible. Today, Covadonga is one of Asturias's most important historical and religious sites. At its center, the candlelit **Santa Cueva grotto,** where the Virgin appeared to Pelayo, contains the King's remains. (Open daily in summer 9am-8pm; in winter 9am-7pm. Free.) Under the cave, to the right of the water, is the **Fountain of Seven Spouts,** which blesses young girls with marriage and fertility. A **monument** to King Pelayo, built in 1964 and inscribed with the above famous sentence, stands in the Basilica square. Below the Grand Hotel is the **San Fernando Collegiate Church** (constructed 1585-1599), the oldest building in town, which houses the tombs of two abbots from the 11th century. Visitors are not allowed inside. The **Museo de Covadonga,** next to the bus stop above the cave, has explanations in Spanish on the history of Covadonga, and displays the treasures—including Romantic paintings of the kings of the *Reconquista*, swords, books, and jewelry—donated to the Virgin over the years. Make sure to see the sparkling crowns of Our Lady of Covadonga and the Baby Jesus, encrusted with gold, platinum, pearls, sapphires, and rubies. (☎ 985 84 60 96. Open in summer daily 10:30am-2pm and 4-7pm; in winter 10:30am-2pm and 4-6:30pm. €3, children €2.) From there, head to the **Basílica de Covadonga,** a neo-Romanesque basilica built in 1901, whose red and white marble towers provide a marvelous contrast against the lush backdrop of the mountains; the best view is from the road up. (Open daily in summer 9am-8pm; in winter 9am-7pm. Free.)

Cangas offers cheaper accommodations, but it's hard to resist the friendly atmosphere and stunning views of the mountains at the **Hospedería del Peregrino** ❸, on the main road next to the bus stop below the basilica. All rooms are carpeted and have sinks; bathrooms are shared. The **restaurant** ❷ downstairs offers an €11.95 *menú* that includes half a bottle of Rioja wine served in a spacious dining room. (☎ 985 84 60 47; www.picosdeeuropa.net/peregrino. Singles €25.25-39.59; doubles with hall bath €36.38-55.10. Reserve ahead in summer. Closed Nov.-Mar. MC/V.) At **El Huerto del Ermitaño** ❹, savor local dishes like baked *jabalí* (wild boar, €15) to the tune of the Cueva's waterfall just across the road. (Halfway up the hill to the basilica. ☎ 985 84 60 97. Entrees €17-32. *Menú* €15. July-Sept. open daily 11am-11pm. Oct.-June open M-W and F-Su 11am-4pm.)

Covadonga's info booth, at the top of the hill, has details in English on local accommodations and the sanctuary. (☎ 985 84 60 35. Open Tu-Su 10am-2pm and 4-7:30pm. Closed Jan. and first half of Feb.)

PONCEBOS

Poncebos is accessible from Arenas de Cabrales and Cangas de Onís. ALSA buses run from Arenas (15min., end of July to early Sept. 6 per day 9:30am-7pm, €1.15) and arrive at the Restaurante-Bar Garganta del Cares. Return 9 per day 10am-7:30pm. From Cangas, there is 1 bus a day (1¾hr., 9:30am, €8.25). By car, take AS-114 from Panes to Las Arenas; cross the river where the signs point to Poncebos onto AS-264. Taxis (☎ 985 84 51 77 or 985 84 64 87) also go to Poncebos at almost any time of day (€5-6).

Poncebos, a cluster of buildings just within the park's borders, about 6km from Arenas, is the starting point for many of Arenas's hiking trails. The walk to the main trailhead from Arenas threads through the feet of surrounding mountains; tight, winding roads make some corners dangerous. To stay overnight in Poncebos, try **Hostal Poncebos ❸**, downhill through the tunnel from the main intersection. The *hostal* has both newer, remodeled rooms with bathrooms or older, simpler ones with half baths. (☎985 84 64 47. Singles €23-31; doubles €20-35; with bath and TV €45-60. MC/V) Otherwise, head to **Hotel-Restaurante-Bar Garganta del Cares ❸**. (☎985 84 64 63. Breakfast included. Singles €25-38; doubles with TV and bath €40-62. MC/V.)

The famous 12km ⬛**Ruta del Cares** is an easy 3hr. one-way hike along a trail that can be done in either direction from Caín to Poncebos. The trail itself is carved along a water canal straight into the cliffside, which drops 200m from the trail down to the Río Cares below. A longer alternative is to include the stretch from **La Posada del Valdeón** to Caín. Stay overnight in Caín at either **Hostal La Ruta ❹** (☎987 74 27 02; www.hostallaruta.com; closed Oct. 1 to *Semana Santa;* singles €37; doubles with bath and TV €50), or **La Posada del Montañero ❸** (☎942 31 86 50; doubles €40). The **Poncebos-Bulnes** route, a medium difficulty 1hr. hike, follows the Río Tejo to **Bulnes,** a small village seemingly frozen in time, except for the Coca Cola signs and New Age bar chairs. An underground funicular also connects Bulnes with Poncebos. The ride takes 7min. (☎985 84 68 00. Arrive early for tickets. Open daily July-Sept. and *Semana Santa* 10am-8pm, otherwise 10am-12:30pm and 2-6pm. €13.93, round-trip €17.42.) Pamper yourself at **La Casa del Chiflón ❹**, which has 14 beds, a bar, hot showers, guides, weather reports, and meals. (☎985 84 59 43; www.casadelchiflon.com. One-week advance reservations suggested. Breakfast included. Open *Semana Santa* to Nov. and around Christmas. Singles €30-40; doubles €50-59; triples €61-70; quads €72-80. MC/V.) A simpler option in Bulnes is the basic **Albergue Peña Maín ❶**, which provides dorm-style bunk accommodations at €9 a night. (☎985 84 59 39. Open Mar.-Jan. Cash only.)

The park service offers free **guided hikes** to Bulnes on Tuesdays and Saturdays at 10am (4hr.; departs from the small information hut on Poncebos's main highway). The ⬛**Poncebos-Collado Pandébano-Naranjo de Bulnes (Mt. Urriellu)** route, a must-see killer 17km hike (8-10hr. round-trip), showcases the park's mountain streams and peaceful green pastures, and leads to the saddleback Collado Pandébano, and eventually to the foot of the Picos's most famous mountain, **Naranjo de Bulnes,** named for its sunburnt orange face.

EXPERTS ONLY. From Bulnes, make sure to take the path marked to Pandébano; the other path to Urriellu through the Canal de Balcosin is not well-marked and is treacherously steep. This second option should only be attempted by experienced hikers looking for a challenge.

Most climbers choose to start the Urriellu hike in **Sotres,** the highest town in the Picos, and continue from there (5hr. round-trip). For accommodations in Sotres itself, try the friendly ⬛**Albergue Peña de Castil ❶**, which has dorm-style bunks, with every four beds separated by a wall or curtain partition. Each bed also has a personal light and electric socket, and there is plenty of hot water for showers. (☎985 94 50 70 or 629 82 02 26. Breakfast €3. Curfew midnight. Silence 11pm-7am. €14 per person. MC/V.)

If you have a car and are coming from Sotres, consider driving up part of the way to Pandebano, as the first part of the path is a wide dirt road. There are two *refugios* in the Naranjo de Bulnes area: ⬛**Refugio Vega de Urriellu/Ubeda ❶** (☎985 92 52 00), at the foot of the Naranjo, and **Refugio Jou de Los Cabrones/**

Lueje ❶ (☎ 650 78 03 81). It's worth going beyond the **Poncebos-Camareña** path to **Puertos de Ondón,** where the view is gorgeous.

POTES

La Palomera buses (☎ 942 88 06 11 or 50 30 80) travel to Fuente Dé July-Aug. (45min.; M-F 8am, 1pm, July 16-Aug. 17 also 8pm; Sa-Su 1pm; €1.40) and back (M-F 8:45am, 5pm, July 16-Aug. 17 also 8:45pm; Sa-Su 5pm). During the rest of the year, buses run to Espinama, 4km below Fuente Dé (40min., M-F 1pm, €1.10) and back (M-F 9am and 2:10pm). Buses also go to Santander (2½hr.; July-Aug. M-F 7, 9:30am, 5:30pm, Sa-Su 5:30pm; Sept.-June M-F 7, 9:30am, 5:30pm, Sa 9:30am, 5:30pm, Su 5:30pm; €6.63) via Panes (40min., connection available to Cangas de Onis and Arenas de Cabrales) and Unquera (1hr.). There are 2 taxi stops in town, one about 100m toward the town center from the tourist office on Pl. de la Serna and the other across town on C. Dr. Encinas.

A Potes (pop. 2000) tourist brochure prophesies *"Y volverás"* (you will return), and you probably will—despite a touristy veneer, Potes's ancient cobblestone streets, arches, and main street arcade contain a fair amount of charm, and the town's unbeatable location allows easy access to the heart of the Picos.

Urdón, 15km north of Potes on the road to Panes, is the start of a challenging 6km (2½hr.) hike to **Tresviso,** a tiny town where chickens outnumber humans. A 3km uphill hike from the tourist office toward Fuente Dé and left at the intersection with the Hwy. 885 is the **Monasterio de Santo Toribio de Liébana,** which protects the *Lignum Crucis,* reportedly the largest surviving piece of the true cross. (Open daily in summer 10am-1pm and 4-7pm; in winter 9am-1pm and 3:30-7pm. Free.) In town, the recently restored **Molino del Palacio,** behind the library, offers a look at a functional flour mill dating to at least 1468. (Open daily 4:30-8:30pm.)

The tourist office has a list of the outfitters in town. **EuroPicos,** San Roque, 6, a couple of blocks past the bridge on the main road toward Panes, leads trips on horseback (€20 per 1½hr., €30 per 3hr.), canyon descents (€30-42), mountain biking (€25 per day), and other activities. (☎ 942 73 07 24; www.europicos.com. Open daily July-Aug. 9am-9pm; Sept.-June 10am-1pm and 5-8pm. AmEx/MC/V.) **Extreme Factory,** C. Sol, 1, by the bridge in the middle of town, offers paragliding (€95, includes transportation) and bungee jumping in addition to the other outdoor activities. (☎ 942 73 06 19; www.extremefactoryliebana.com. Open daily Aug. 10am-10pm; Mar.-July and Sept.-Nov. 10am-2pm and 4:30-8:30pm. MC/V.)

Several hostels are scattered on C. Dr. Encinas and on C. Cántabra, a side street. The beautiful **█Casa Cayo ❸,** C. Cántabra, 6, a right off C. Dr. Encinas when walking into town from the bus stop, with exposed rafters and bright white walls, has the feel of a country cottage in the middle of town. All the rooms are spacious and immaculate with TV, phone, and bath. There's also a cozy lounge with a big TV. (☎ 942 73 01 50. Closed Dec. 23-March 1. Singles €30; doubles €50. MC/V.) The **█restaurant ❷** downstairs serves delicious meat and fish dishes; try the incredibly tender veal cutlet (€11) with a shot of *urquijo,* the Spanish version of grappa, distilled with herbs. (Open M-Sa 1-4pm and 8-11pm.) If you're looking for a clean, relatively cheap place to stay without extra creature comforts, try **Hostal Lombraña ❸,** right in the center of town, next to the bridge over the river. Most of the rooms have private bathrooms, while several share a hall bath. (☎ 942 73 05 19. Doubles €23-31, with bath €25-35.50. Cash only.) The closest campsite is **Camping La Viorna ❶,** about 1km up the Hwy. 885 toward Monasterio Santo Toribio, which has a res- taurant-bar, supermarket, and pool. (☎ 942 73 20 21. Open *Semana Santa* to Oct. 30. €3.50-3.80 per person, per car, and per tent. MC/V.) **La Isla,** N621, km 3, on the way to Fuente Dé, is a shadier campsite with a flatter, if slightly longer, walk from town, and a pleasant bar/restaurant with a terrace right on the Rio Deva's edge. (☎ 942 730 896. Pool, hot showers, and market. Hiking maps sold at reception. In summer €3.95 per person, per car, and per tent. In winter €3.65.) Potes can feed plenty of hungry hikers, and despite its touristy status, it can do so cheaply; C. Dr. Encinas, C. Cántabra, and C. San Cayetano are packed with restaurants, tapas bars, and cafeterias. For crispy pizzas made on special locally made bread, try **Cafe de Picos,** C. Palacios, 22 (☎676 86 58 24. Open July-Aug. 9am-11:30pm; Sept.-June 9am-11pm, closed Tu. Cash only.) Supermarket **El Árbol** is across the street from the bus station and tourist office. (☎942 73 05 26. Open in summer daily 9am-9pm; in winter M 9:30am-8:30pm, Tu-Sa 9:30am-2pm and 5-8:30pm. MC/V.) The local sherry-like sweet wine, *tostadillo,* is available at the **bodega de las telaranas,** on C. Independencia, downhill and toward town from the library. (Glasses €0.80. Bottles €3.50. Open in summer M-F noon-8pm; in winter Sa-Su noon-6pm. Cash only.)

The **tourist office,** in the bus station, has info on adventure tourism, local hikes, *refugios,* and accommodations. (☎942 73 07 87. Open daily 10am-2pm and 4-8pm.) The **Sotama** park office and visitor's center, in nearby Tama (3km) on the road to Panes, has more extensive information on the national park, as well as an extensive exhibit on the geology, flora and fauna of the park with informative signs in perfect English. (☎942 73 81 09. Open daily July-Sept. 9am-8pm; Oct.-June 9am-6pm.) Local services include: **Banco Santander Central Hispano,** C. Dr. Encinas, with a 24hr. **ATM** (☎902 24 24 24; open M-F 8:30am-2pm, Oct.-Mar. Sa 8:30am-1pm); **Guardia Civil** (☎942 73 00 07), on C. Obispo off C. Dr. Encinas; **Farmacia F. Soberón,** C. Palacios, 2 (☎942 73 00 08; open daily 9:30am-9:30pm); **Centro de Salud** (☎942 73 03 60) on C. Eduardo García de Enterría; **Internet** access at **CyberLiebana,** in the arcade off of C. Dr. Ercinas (☎942 75 80 41; €2 per hour; open daily from 11am or noon to 2:30am) or at the **Biblioteca Municipal,** C. Independencia, 22, across the park from the church (free; open M-F from 8am-2pm); **post office,** Pl. de la Serna, a block from the tourist office on the main road (open M-F 8:30am-2:30pm, Sa 9:30am-1pm). **Postal Code:** 39570.

FUENTE DÉ

Fuente Dé is only accessible July-Aug. from Potes on La Palomera buses (☎942 88 06 11 or 50 30 80; 30min.; M-F 8am, 1, 8pm, Sa-Su 1pm; €1.40; return M-F 8:45am, 5, 8:45pm, Sa-Su 5pm). The bus stops in front of the Parador de Fuente Dé, just below the teleférico (cable car) base. During other months, take the bus to Espinama and walk the rest of the way to Fuente Dé (4km).

Only 33km from Potes, the ⬛**Teleférico de Fuente Dé** is well worth an excursion. The goose bump-inducing *teleférico,* the third-largest cable car system in the world, jets 800m to the mountain top (1834m) in less than 4min., at some points going up along an almost vertical rock-face. The upper station is ideally located for multiple hikes in to the heart of the central *macizo* (massif). (☎942 31 89 50 or 902 21 01 12; www.cantur.com. Open daily July-Aug. 9am-8pm; Sept.-June M-F 10am-6pm, Sa-Su 10am-8pm. €7.50, round-trip €14, under 8 €3.) A zig-zagging trail ascends just left of the cable car (2½hr.) for those up for a brutal but dramatic hike. Be aware, though, that the path is not well-marked along the entire route. At the top, there are also many hikes along 4WD tracks and trails toward *refugios* and the high peaks of the eastern *macizo.* From Fuente Dé itself, there are many possible hikes. From the cable car's lower station, the **Somo Waterfall Route** (11.5km, 4½hr.) swings through the Berrugas cattle sheds, the soft Bustantivo meadows, and on to the Somo waterfall. The *teleférico* is a great starting point for exploring the Macizo Central. From the upper station, follow the main path until the first fork. From there, you can head left (north) to **Mt. Urriellu, Naranjo de Bulnes,** via the tiny Cabana Veronica and Horcados Rojos; (5hr., medium to high difficulty), or turn right to get to the Hotel-Refugio de Aliva (40min., low difficulty) and continue to **Poncebos** via **Sotres** (3hr. from Refugio Áliva to Sotres and 5-6hr. descending from Sotres to Poncebos, low difficulty). The path from ⬛**Refugio de Áliva to Sotres** winds through gorgeous alpine valleys, passing through the abandoned stone walls and ruins of Las Vegas del Toro. Sotres itself, a 1km detour from the main walking path, is a town frozen in time at the foot of the mythic peaks. Hikers wearied by a day's descent can find rustic lodging with spectacular views at Fuente Dé's **El Redondo Camping ❶**, just above the base of the *teleférico*. A small gnome garden at the entrance sets the relaxed tone for the campsite. (☎942 73 66 99; www.elredondopicosdeeuropa.com. Open May-Oct. Bar, market, and hot showers. Reception daily 9am-9pm. No reservations. €5 per person, €3 per child, €6 per site. Electricity €3. Cash only.) A higher, more expensive option is to spend the night at **Refugio/Hotel de Áliva ❹** (1666m), the most expensive and luxurious *refugio* in the park, located 3km from the top of the *teleférico* (40min., all-terrain jeep ride €3 each way). All 24 doubles come with full bath and heat in winter; there is also a restaurant and cafeteria on site. (☎942 73 09 99. Doubles €78; triples €92, with dinner and breakfast €85 or €99. MC/V.)

CANTABRIA

From the spectacle of Santander's El Sardinero beaches to the pristine provincial park of Oyambre, it's the coast that makes Cantabria famous. Though it has yet to see the resort build-up of Spain's more famous southern shores, the region's beach towns, declared by some to have the world's cleanest surfing water, are by no means untouched or secluded. Cantabria also has hiking in the Picos de Europa, Paleolithic cave drawings, and renowned architecture, including Gaudí's El Capricho and the 12th-century Colegiata de Santa Juliana in Santillana del Mar.

SANTANDER   ☎942

Life in Santander (pop. 185,000) begins and ends with one thing: the beach. Every summer, beautiful coastline and miles of spotless, soft, sandy beaches play host to thousands of tourists looking to catch up on their tan. Palm trees

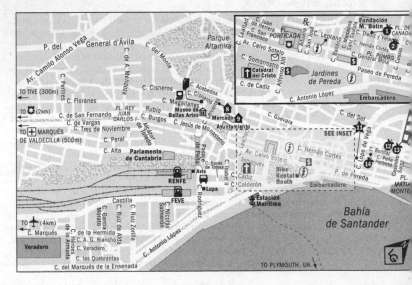

rub shoulders with pines, pasty Brits bake next to bronzed Spaniards, and the hustle and bustle of the city center is easily forgotten on a stroll down El Sardinero's vine-filled boardwalks. Santander became fashionable thanks to royal attention; King Alfonso XIII summered in the early 20th century on Peninsula La Magdalena, and hotels now occupy the summer palaces of his court in El Sardinero. While definitely a well-visited destination, Santander is far more relaxed than the frenetic beaches in the Costa del Sol or Islas Canarias, and in the weeks in between its big summer festivals, the crowds thin a little. With a mountainous horizon and cliff-top lighthouses, Santander is the Bay of Biscay at its best.

TRANSPORTATION

Flights: Aeropuerto de Santander, Av. de Parayas (☎942 20 21 00; www.aena.es), in nearby Camargo (5km away). Serviced by many European budget airlines, including **Ryanair.** Accessible by taxi (€15); buses run from bus station to airport every 15-30min. 6:30am-10:45pm (€1.50).

Trains: FEVE (☎942 20 95 22; www.feve.es) and **RENFE** (☎902 24 02 02; www.renfe.es), Pl. de las Estaciones. RENFE serves distant destinations to the south, as Santander is the terminus of a national rail line; take a regional FEVE train to cities east or west of Santander. RENFE info open daily 7:30am-10pm; station open 5am-12:30am. RENFE goes to **Madrid** (6-8hr.; M-F 3 per day 8:10am-11pm, Sa 2 per day 8:10am, 3:45pm, Su 4 per day 8:10am-11pm; €26.65-37.40), **Valladolid** (3-4½hr., 5-8 per day 8:10am-11pm, €14.35-25.40) and **Palencia** (2-3½hr., 5-8 per day 8:10am-11pm, Sa 8:10am-8:05pm; €11.30-22.30). FEVE goes to: **Bilbao** (2¾hr., 3 per day 8am-7pm, €7) and **Oviedo** (4½hr.; 9:10am, 4:10pm; €12.50).

Buses: C. Navas de Tolosa (☎942 21 19 95; www.santandereabus.com). Info open daily 8am-10pm.

ALSA (☎902 42 22 02; www.alsa.es) goes to: **Barcelona** (8-9hr.; 9am, 9pm; €46.02); **Bilbao** (1½hr.; every 30-60 min. 6am-9:30pm, also 3:30am; €6.25-12.25); **León** (3½-6½hr.; 8:30am, F, Su also 8pm; €15.83); **Oviedo** (3hr.; 6-9 per day 7:15am-8pm and 3:30am, F, Su

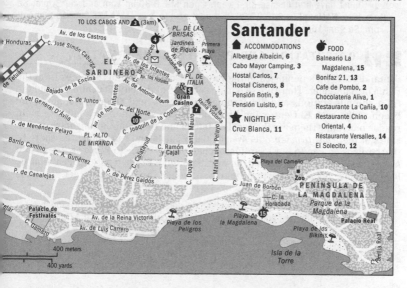

Santander

🏠 **ACCOMMODATIONS**
Albergue Albaícin, 6
Cabo Mayor Camping, 3
Hostal Carlos, 7
Hostal Cisneros, 8
Pensión Botín, 9
Pensión Luisito, 5

⭐ **NIGHTLIFE**
Cruz Blanca, 11

🍴 **FOOD**
Balneario La
  Magdalena, 15
Bonifaz 21, 13
Cafe de Pombo, 2
Chocolatería Aliva, 1
Restaurante La Cañia, 10
Restaurante Chino
  Oriental, 4
Restaurante Versalles, 14
El Solecito, 12

also 10:15pm; €12.21-20.77); **Palencia** (3hr., 3 per day 8:30am-8:15pm, €8.65); **San Sebastián** (2½-3hr.; 9-11 per day 6am-8:30pm, Su also 11:59pm; €12.09-22) and **Vitoria-Gasteiz** (2½hr., 4 per day 8am-7pm, €18.66).

Continental Auto (☎902 33 04 00; www.continental-auto.es) goes to: **Madrid** (6hr.; M-Sa 6 per day 12:30am-7pm, Su 8 per day 12:30am-11:59pm; €25.78-35); and **Burgos** (4hr.; M-Sa 5 per day 8am-12:30am, Su 6 per day 12:30am-8pm; €9.84-10.48).

La Cantabrica (☎942 72 08 22) runs buses to **Comillas** (1hr., €3.30) through **Santillana del Mar** (40min.; Sept.-June M-F 4 per day 10:30am-7:15pm, Sa-Su 3 per day 11:30am-8:30pm; July-Aug. M-F 7 per day 8:30am-9:30pm, Sa-Su 5 per day 10:30am-9:30pm; €2.10). Buy tickets onboard.

Palomera (☎942 88 06 11) runs buses to the town of **Potes** in the **Picos de Europa** during July-Aug. (2½hr.; M-F 3 per day 10:30am-5pm, Sa 10:30am, 3:15pm, Su 10:30am). Call in advance for groups larger than 6 people. Continuing service also available to **Fuente De** during July and Aug., call for information.

Ferries: Brittany Ferries, Estación Marítima (☎942 36 06 11; www.brittany-ferries.com), by the Jardines de Pereda. Reserve 2wk. ahead in summer. Info open M-F 9am-7pm. To **Plymouth, UK** (20½hr., 2 per week, €89-134 plus €8 for a seat). **Los Reginas,** C. Embarcadero (☎942 21 67 53; www.losreginas.com), by the Jardines de Pereda, runs to **Pedreña, Somo,** and the **Playas del Puntal** (15min., every 30min. 7:50am-8:30pm, round-trip €3.70), and runs **tours** of the bay (1hr., July-Oct. 13 per day 11:15am-8:30pm per day, €7.50).

Public Transportation: Transportes Urbanos buses (☎942 20 07 71) run throughout the city (July-Aug. roughly 6am-11pm, Sept.-June 6am-10:30pm; night buses hourly midnight-6am; €1). Buses #1, 4, 7, 9, 13, and 14 run from the *Ayuntamiento* stop (buses coming from El Sardinero stop in the plaza; buses stop by Foot Locker) to El Sardinero on Po. de Pereda and Av. de la Reina Victoria, stopping at Pl. de Italia and Jardines de Piquío. #15 runs from the RENFE station to El Sardinero. The tourist office gives out free schedules.

Taxis: (☎942 33 33 33 or 36 91 91). 24hr. service to greater Santander. Taxis wait outside the train and bus stations, on C. Vargas, and near the *Ayuntamiento.* The tourist office has a map with all taxi stops throughout the city.

Car Rental: Avis (☎942 22 0 25), in the RENFE parking lot, Pl. de los Estaciones. 21+, must have had license for 1 year. Open M-F 8:30am-1pm and 4-7:30pm, Sa 9am-1pm. **National** (☎942 22 29 26), right next to Avis. Open M-F 9am-1pm and 4-7pm, Sa 9am-1pm, Su 10am-1pm.

■✦❷ ORIENTATION AND PRACTICAL INFORMATION

Santander sits on a peninsula in the Bay of Biscay; its southern shores form the Bahía de Santander. There are two main sections of the city: **El Centro,** around the train and bus stations and the Jardines de Pereda, and **El Sardinero,** along the beach to the east. El Centro and El Sardinero are separated by a hill. The main roads connecting them are the **Tunel de Tetuan** and the main thoroughfare, which starts at the *Ayuntamiento* as **Avenida Calvo Sotelo** and runs along the shore to the Jardines de Piquío in El Sardinero, changing its name to **Paseo de Pereda** and **Avenida de la Reina Victoria** along the way. Santander's famed park, **La Península de la Magdalena,** sits at the eastern tip of Santander. The best way to get around is by bus or the free bikes loaned out by the tourist office.

Tourist Office: Regional office inside Mercado del Este (☎942 31 07 08), open June-Sept. daily 9:30am-1pm and 1:30-7pm. Oct.-May daily 9am-2pm and 4-9pm has info on sights in Cantabria. **Municipal office** in Jardines de Pereda (☎942 20 30 00; www.ayto-santander.es). Open daily July-Aug. 9am-9pm; Sept.-June M-F 8:30am-7pm, Sa 10am-2pm. **Branch** in El Sardinero, across from the grand casino, open July-Aug. daily 10am-9pm; June M-F 10am-7pm, Sa-Su 10am-2pm. Both branches, as well as a booth on the Peninsula de La Magdalena rent out ◼ **free bicycles** for 4hr. Open daily July-Aug. 10am-7pm; Sept.-June 10am-2pm and 4-6pm. Closed Nov.-Jan.

Currency Exchange: Banco Santander Central Hispano, on Av. Calvo Sotelo. **Branch** at Pl. de Italia. Open May-Sept. M-F 8:30am-2pm, Oct.-Apr. also Sa 8:30am-1pm. 24hr. **ATMs** abound.

Luggage Storage: Lockers at the **bus station** bottom level (€2.40 per day). Open daily 6am-midnight. For large items M-F 7am-10pm, Sa 7am-1am. Passport or local ID required.

Police: Pl. Canadio (☎092).

Hospital: Hospital Universitario Marqués de Valdecilla, Av. de Valdecilla, 25 (☎942 20 25 20). For emergencies call ☎061.

Pharmacy: Farmacia Lavin y Camus, C. Hernán Cortés, 2 (☎942 21 12 69). 24hr. In El Sardinero, **Somacarrera,** Pl. de Italia, 1 (☎942 27 05 96), underneath the Gran Casino. Open daily 10am-1:30pm and 4:30-8pm. For locations of late-night pharmacies, call ☎942 22 02 60 or check the schedule at any pharmacy.

Internet: Up to 1hr. free at the **Biblioteca Pública,** C. Gravina 4 (☎942 21 15 50) July-Aug. M-F 8:15am-1:45pm, Sept.-June daily 8:15am-2:45pm and 3:30-9:30pm. Also at **Divernet Informática,** C. Cisneros, 29 (☎942 24 14 25). English spoken. €2 per hour. Open M-Sa 9:30am-2pm and 4-8:30pm, Su 4-9:30pm.

Post Office: Av. Alfonso XIII (☎942 36 55 19). Open M-F 8:30am-8:30pm, Sa 9:30am-2pm. **Branch** in El Sardinero on Av. Castaneda. Open M-F 8:30am-8:30pm, Sa 9:30am-1pm. **Lista de Correos** and **fax. Postal Code: 39080.**

▛ ACCOMMODATIONS AND CAMPING

In July and August, especially during the big festivals, you'll need to reserve ahead. The train and bus stations are filled with *pensión* hawkers, but beware: many rooms are far from the beaches. Lodgings are concentrated on Pl. de la Esperanza, across from the train station on C. Rodríguez, and along Av. de los Castros in El Sardinero.

EL SARDINERO

Lodging in El Sardinero is available along the busy Reina Victoria, overlooking the bay and close to the beaches and promenade; there are also a few quieter *pensiones* along Av. de las Castros. From the *Ayuntamiento* in the center, ask bus drivers to drop you off at El Piquío (Hotel Colón).

◼ **Pensión Luisito,** Av. de los Castros, 11 (☎942 27 19 71). Well-kept, well-lit rooms and an incredibly friendly owner will make you feel right at home. Many have spacious balconies, and some overlook the garden and a slice of the sea. Room sinks, hall baths. Open July-beginning of Sept. Singles €24.50; doubles €42.25. Breakfast €2.67. Cash only. ❸

◼ **Hostal Carlos,** Av. de la Reina Victoria, 135 (☎942 27 16 16). This building, a designated historical site where King Alfonso XIII put up his favorite barons, has sunny rooms with hardwood floors. English and French spoken. Breakfast €3.40. Singles €36-55; doubles €52-61; triples €62-85. AmEx/MC/V. ❹

Cabo Mayor Camping, Av. del Faro (☎942 39 15 42; www.cabomayor.com). On the scenic bluff of Cabo Mayor, 3km from Playas Primera and Segunda. From the *Ayuntamiento,* take bus #1, 9, or 15 to "Av. del Faro," 7 stops after El Piquío. Turn left on Av. del Faro and follow it 10min. into the Cabo. Or, head north along coastal Av. de Castañeda, bear right at the rotary, and then turn left onto C. Gregorio Marañón; Av. del Faro is on the right. Pool, currency exchange, supermarket, bar, and tennis courts. Reception 8am-11pm. Open Apr.-Oct. €5 per adult and per tent, €4.50 per car. Electricity €3. Cash only. ❶

EL CENTRO

The city center has the advantage of being near cheap food, convenient transportation, a pleasant portside *paseo*, and busy nightlife. North of the *Ayuntamiento* and Av. de Calvo Sotelo is a tranquil collection of restaurants, shops, and bars. Pl. Santa Lucia is the nucleus of several blocks of bars and nightclubs that spill into the streets on weekends.

Pensión Botín, C. Isabel II, 1, 1st fl. (☎942 21 00 94; www.pensionbotin.com). The committed owners have over 20 years' experience keeping guests happy. Immaculate, homey rooms, some with balconies overlooking the market behind the *Ayuntamiento*. All rooms have TV, brand-new private showers, and sink. Singles €34-40; doubles €43-56; ask about rates for rooms of up to 5 people. ❹

Hostal Cisneros, C. Cisneros, 8, 1st fl. (☎942 21 16 13). Cozy rooms have clean wooden floors, overlooking the nearby streets. Some have a covered balcony. Singles (only Sept.-June) €18; doubles €32-47. Cash only. ❷

Albergue Albaicín, Fco. Palazuelos 21-23, (☎942 21 77 53 or 676 70 97 02). A school that converts classrooms into dorm-style bedrooms in the summer; probably your only chance to write on a blackboard from your bed. On the hill above El Centro, it has stunning views of the bay, but be prepared to huff it up a steep climb. Breakfast included. Coin-operated laundry machines available. Bunks in 10-bed mixed or single-sex dorm €17. ❶

🗒 FOOD

EL SARDINERO

El Sardinero is packed with ice cream stands and expensive restaurants. To get more value for your euro, head to the city center, where good, cheap food is plentiful. The best grocery option is **Diferente,** C. Joaquín de la Costa, 28, in the **Hotel Santemar** shopping complex. (☎942 281 782. Open M-F 9am-2:30pm and 5:30-9:30pm, Sa 9am-2:45pm and 5:45-9:30pm, Su 9:30am-3pm. AmEx/MC/V.)

Balneario La Magdalena, C. la Horadada (☎942 03 21 07), on Playa de la Magdalena. Bar and restaurant perched above the beach, with a delectable menu of meat (€12-17) and fish (€13-17). Lunch *menú* €15. Open daily 9am-midnight. MC/V. ❸

Restaurante Chino Oriental, Pl. las Brisas, on the corner of Av. de los Castros (☎942 27 32 30). Ornate Chinese balustrades welcome you to the 2nd fl., with big glass windows looking out to the sea and an €8.50 *menú*. Open daily 12:30-4pm and 7:30pm-midnight. MC/V. ❷

Restaurante La Cañia, Joaquín Costa, 45 (☎942 27 04 91). Touristed restaurant with reasonably priced fare—rare for El Sardinero. Good selection of fish and seafood and helpful wait-staff. *Pintxos* €1-1.50. Fish €7.50-15. Su *menú* €16. Open daily noon-4pm and 8pm-midnight. ❸

EL CENTRO

Seafood restaurants crowd the *Puerto Pesquero* (fishing port), grilling up the day's catch at the end of C. Marqués de la Ensenada. Across the street from the bus station towards the water, **Lupa,** C. Calderon de la Barca, 8, sells groceries. (☎900 20 03 28. Open M-Sa 9am-9pm, Su 9:30am-2:30pm.)

▨ El Solecito, C. Bonifaz, 19 (☎942 36 06 33, takeout 32 51 18). The plates are the only square things in this artsy hole-in-the-wall bistro. Autumn leaves, African masks, and intimate booths make for a unique dining experience. Try the incredibly tender *croquetas de solomillo* (sirloin croquettes; €6) or their large selection of pastas (€7-

10). Pizzas €6-13. *Menú* €12. Open M-Th and Su 1-4pm and 8-11:30pm, F-Sa 1-4pm and 8pm-12:30am. MC/V. ❷

Café de Pombo, C. Hernán Cortés, 21 (☎942 22 32 24). On Pl. de Pombó, behind the central Banco de Santander, in a building once home to Cuban national hero José Martí. Coffee, pastries, ice cream, crepes, sandwiches—all delicious, all huge, all €1-5, served out on the square or in an elegant dining area that conjures up images of literary haunts. Open daily 8am-1am. Cash only. ❶

Restaurante Versalles, C. Peña Herbosa, 15 (☎942 21 58 65). Serves authentic dishes in a homey, unassuming atmosphere with quiet upstairs seating. Conscientious waitstaff give helpful advice on the menu, ranging from the local specialty of *rabas* (square-cut fried calamari) to peasant-style bean stews. *Menú* €11. Open M, W-Th, and Su 10:30am-midnight, Tu and F-Sa 10:30am-2am. Cash only. ❷

Restaurante Bonifaz 21, C. Bonifaz, 21 (☎942 22 74 85), 2 doors down from El Solecito. Cozy back-room restaurant fills with locals during lunchtime. Great selection of fish (€12-19). Menu €12. Meat dishes €8-19. MC/V. ❸

◉ SIGHTS

Assuming you're not fast asleep on the beach, the best way to experience Santander is to wander the beaches and peninsulas. The tourist office has a list of 1-2hr. walking tours, which are a good way to get to know the city itself. On a rainy day, head indoors to the free museums and churches.

▨ PENÍNSULA DE LA MAGDALENA. Although it can feel a bit like an amusement park at times, La Magdalena is Santander's prime attraction and one of the most beautiful parts of the city. The entire peninsula is filled with palms and pines and is ringed by bluffs plunging into the sea along slender, calm beaches. Crowds of people line the main walkways, but you can find peace and quiet among the paths in the middle or in a secluded, romantic nook along the cliffs. The park's crowning landmark is the **palacio,** a modern, neo-Gothic mansion that Alfonso XIII used as a summer home. Today, the palace hosts the elite Universidad Internacional Menéndez Pelayo's summer sessions on oceanography. You may find yourself exchanging grunts with the sea lions at the mini-zoo, which also houses penguins and seals. A **tourist train** runs past the zoo, an adjacent display of historic ships, and through the rest of the peninsula. (☎942 29 10 44 or 639 51 36 72. €2.05.) Walking, however, is the best way to explore, and the 2km path ends with tasty incentives: snack stands and bars flank the park's entrance. (☎942 27 25 04. *Park open daily June-Sept. 8am-10pm; Oct.-May 8 9am-8:30pm. The palace has no scheduled visiting hours, during winter months inquire at tourist office.)*

▨ LOS CABOS. More peninsular parks lie just north of the El Sardinero beaches. While Cabos Menor and Mayor lack the man-made attractions and action of La Magdalena, their bluffs and secluded beaches make for a more peaceful setting. Cabo Menor, the southernmost of the two, houses Santander's golf course and another mini-zoo; it also has postcard-worthy views of Cabo Mayor's 19th-century lighthouse. From Pl. de Italia, walk up Av. de Castañeda past Glorieta del Dr. Fleming, and turn right onto Av. de Pontejos, which turns into Av. del Faro and takes you toward the capes. There are great views from the path around the cliffs encircling the Cabos. To reach it, follow Av. García Lago to the end of Playa la Segunda and look for stairs that lead up to the top of the peninsula. *(Parque Municipal de Mataleñas on Cabo Menor open 9am-9pm.)*

CATEDRAL DE SANTA MARÍA DE LA ASUNCIÓN. Built in the 13th century, Santander's Gothic cathedral is often called the city's first monument. The

THE CAVES AT ALTAMIRA

Aside from being blessed with beautiful green countryside and miles of pristine beaches, the Cantabrian coast is also home to one of the most significant sites of prehistoric art in the world. The cave of Altamira, discovered in 1879, was one of the first caves of its kind to be found. Altamira's prehistoric cave drawings date back to between 15,000 to 18,000 years ago. The drawings, done with charcoal and ochre and ingeniously incorporating the cracks and curves of the rock into the pictures, mainly depict animals—primarily bison and horses—and mysterious symbols whose meaning is forever lost. They are so exquisite that they once led Picasso to say "After Altamira, everything is decadence."

Throughout the 70s and 80s, Altamira became one of the most visited tourist attractions in Spain. The throngs of tourists that turned up to see Altamira, however, began to threaten the survival of the caves and the drawings, and eventually, the actual cave was indefinitely closed to all but preservation specialists and archaeologists. Today, visitors are not allowed into the original cave, but can instead visit the "neocave," an exact replica of the original cave and drawings. The neocave was created using the original drawing materials, and is accurate down to the last microscopic crack and bump in the rock. The neocave

remains of the heads of martyred Roman soldiers Emeterio and Celedonio are kept in the crypt below the cathedral in two 16th-century silver reliquaries formed in the image of their faces. After dropping into the guillotine basket in AD 300 in La Rioja, the heads were brought to Santander in the 8th century for safekeeping during the Moorish invasion, where they were kept in the ruins of an oven. These ruins have now been excavated, and you can see them through a section of glass flooring below the church. The relics are occasionally taken out for religious processions. *(Pl. del Obispo José E. Eguino, behind the post office and Banco España. ☎942 22 60 24. Open M-F 10am-1pm and 4-8pm, except during mass at 11-11:30am and 6:30-7pm, Sa 10am-1pm and 4:30-8pm, Su 10am-1:30pm and 5-9pm. July-Aug. free tours in Spanish by appointment.)*

MUSEO DE BELLAS ARTES. Devoted to the eclectic works of local artists, Santander's Museo de Bellas Artes houses an impressive permanent collection, uniquely organized according to themes from Hollywood movies. Modern photographs share wall space with canvases from classic artists such as Goya, but the majority of the works are by local artists, featured in rotating exhibitions on the ground floor. Art history buffs will enjoy the collection of 20th-century pieces. *(C. Rubio, 6. ☎942 20 31 20. From the Ayuntamiento, walk up C. Jesús de Monasterio and turn right onto C. Cervantes. Open June 16-Sept. 14 M-F 10:45am-1pm and 6-9pm, Sa 10:30am-1pm; Sept. 15-June 15 M-F 10:15am-1pm and 5:30-9pm, Sa 10am-1pm. Free.)*

🢔 BEACHES

In Santander, every day is a beach day: rain or shine, locals flock to the beach as soon as work gets out and spend the late afternoon and evening soaking up the last rays of sun. Whichever beach you choose, it's hard to go wrong in Santander: the sand is always silky, soft, and clean. The waves, however, can get very rough; with the raging wind, it's not uncommon for five-foot breakers to crash onto the beach. Calmer water and rockier beaches can be found on the bay side. The best and most popular beaches are undoubtedly ▨**Playas Primera y Segunda** in El Sardinero. Not only does the sand go on forever, but the EU has declared these one of its "blue flag" cleanest beaches. Primera and Segunda are also hangouts for Santander's surfing crowd, which emerges during and after rain. Crowds rush to the calmer waters on the southern shore of La Magdalena. Rock-framed **Playa de Bikinis** is the most secluded and the haunt of Santander's guitar-strumming teens. To escape the beach-going hordes, either head across the bay by ferry to **Playas Puntal, Somo,** and **Loredo,** which line a narrow peninsula of dunes, or hike up to the remote beaches of Los Cabos where ⊠**Playa de Mataleñas** and **Playa de los Molinucos** await you without throngs of people (or lifeguards).

🅿 🎶 NIGHTLIFE AND FESTIVALS

Santander's nightlife revolves around multiple epicenters and has a definite schedule. Dinner lasts roughly from 10pm until midnight or 1am at places like **Cruz Blanca,** C. Lope de Vega, 5, where you can have a table with its own beer tap (€6 per liter) to warm up for the evening. (☎942 08 47 00. Open M-Th and Su 9am-11:30pm, F-Sa 9am-1:30am. MC/V.) After that, people begin to carry drinks from bars into outdoor spaces like the **Pl. Santa Lucia.** Try nearby Australian-themed **El Dorado,** C. Hernan Cortes, 18 (open daily noon-5am). In El Sardinero, try Pl. de Italia, which also hosts the **Gran Casino** (18 to gamble, pants and shoes required). By 2am on a weekend, Pl. Santa Lucia, C. Rio de la Pila, and C. Casimior Sainz are filled with waiters desperately trying to recover glasses before patrons flock to nightclubs for the last stops of the night. The night isn't dead until you've had ⊠**chocolate con churros** (€2), a traditional Spanish breakfast of hot chocolate so thick, it's used as more of a dipping sauce than a drink. Treat that early morning hangover at **Chocolateria Aliva ❶,** C. Daoiz y Velarde, 7, which starts serving churros at 5am on weekends. (☎942 22 20 49. Open M-F 7am-12:30pm and 5:30-10pm, Sa-Su 5am-12:30pm and 5:30-10pm. Cash only.)

The huge, month-long **Festival Internacional de Santander** in August brings crowds of people and myriad classical music and dance performances to town, many held in the city's historic churches. For more info, contact the **Oficina del Festival,** Palacio de Festivales de Cantabria (☎942 21 05 08; www.festivalsantander.com), on C. Gamazo. For a younger, more contemporary scene, try the **Santander Summer Festival** (mid-August), which brings rock, pop and techno to the beaches. (Check www.santandersummerfestival.com for info and tickets.) The **Semana Grande** festival takes place the third week of July on the El Sardinero promenades, with bathers clad in swimsuits. That same week, the *barrio pesquero* celebrates the **Virgen del Carmen,** patron saint of men of the sea.

also has several exhibits recreating what life was like in the cave during prehistoric times. Make sure to check out the computerized description of how the neocave was made; the process of replicating the old cave is almost as impressive as the original paintings themselves.

In addition visitors can see the newly erected Altamira museum, which has modern, interactive exhibits on the history and culture of prehistoric humans, as well as on the methods used by archaeologists today to unravel that past. The museum, with well-written explanatory signs in both English and Spanish, is a must for any archaeology buff, or anyone interested in learning about prehistoric life. Despite the fact that its main attraction is closed to the public, Altamira is definitely worth a quick daytrip if you are in the area.

Altamira is accessible only by car, 10min. away from Santillana Del Mar. Take the A67 to Santillana del Mar and from there, follow the brown signs to Altamira. Museum open daily June-Sept. 9:30am-7:30pm; Oct.-May 9:30am-5pm. €2.40. Sa afternoons, Su free. Entrance to the neocave is timed, make sure to pick up a timeslot card from the reception desk. For more information, call ☎942 81 80 05, or visit www.museodealtamira.mcu.es.

ASTURIAS AND
CANTABRIA

🔀 DAYTRIP FROM SANTANDER

🏛 COMILLAS

La Cantábrica (☎942 72 08 22) buses depart from the main bus station in Santander. (1hr.; July-Aug. M-F 7 per day 8:30am-9:30pm, Sa-Su 5 per day 10:30am-9:30pm; Oct.-June M-F 4 per day 10:30am-7:15pm, Sa-Su 3 per day 11:30am-8:30pm; €3.30. Return to Santander July-Aug. M-F 7 per day 7am-7:45pm, Sa-Su 5 per day Sa-Su 10am-8pm; Oct.-June M-F 4 per day 7am-5:30pm, Sa-Su 3 per day 10am-7:15pm.) The bus stop is at the bottom of the hill across from the Palacio de Sobrellano.

The coast of Comillas (pop. 2500), with gorgeous green hills rolling in to the sea, boasts an intoxicating landscape. From desolately calm inlets to the wind-swept swaths of sand on the Bay of Biscay, the beaches of Comillas are the main attraction, drawing everyone from Spanish nobles to foreign visitors. This small resort town's central beach, **Playa Comillas,** is an expanse of silky sand; on windy days, 10-foot breakers pound the shores.

From the main bus stop, follow C. Marqués de Comillas uphill into town. At the top of the hill, turn left onto C. los Infantes, which will turn into C. Antonio Garelly. Follow this road down through the tunnel to arrive at the parking lot and the beach's main entrance. Heading in the opposite direction on C. Marqués de Comillas from the bus stop will bring you, 4km later, to **Playa Oyambre,** an equally beautiful but uncrowded and less-developed beach.

Comillas is also known for its architectural attractions. Most notable, and amusing, is 🏛 **El Capricho,** Gaudí's summer palace, built between 1883-1885. While it's not open to tourists, most visitors are content to see the swirling turrets, sunflower facades, and gingerbread-esque windows from outside. Behind the palace, a quiet corner contains a statue of a sitting Gaudí, looking up and admiring his whimsical work. From the bus stop, you can see the colorful palace on the hill; follow the footpath across the street for a closer view. One way to get a look inside El Capricho is to eat in its **restaurant ❸.** (Reservations ☎924 72 03 65. Entrees €16-20. *Menú* €21. Open in summer M-Sa 1-4pm and 9-11:30pm, Su 1-11pm; in winter Tu-Sa 1-3:30pm and 4-7pm, Su 1-3:30pm. MC/V). Next to it on the same hill are the neo-Gothic **Palacio de Sobrellano,** designed by *català* architect Doménech i Montaner (open May-Sept. daily 10am-9pm), and the **Capilla-Pantheon,** containing furniture designed by Gaudí. (Open May-Sept. daily 10:30am-9pm; Oct.-Apr. W-Su 10:30am-1:30pm and 4-7pm. Entrance to both only by guided tours. Tickets sold 5min. before each tour; €6 for the chapel and palace). From the lawn of the *Palacio,* you can see the impressive facade of the **Universidad Pontificia** (closed to the public). Comillas goes up in a blaze of fireworks, goose-chasing, and dancing in the days surrounding July 15th during the town's **Fiesta de Cristo del Amparo.**

Comillas Aventura will take care of all your active sporting needs, with bike rentals, surf rentals and lessons, paintball, canyoning, and horseback riding. (☎625 61 14 49. Open daily 9:30am-1:30pm and 6-9pm). The **tourist office** is at Pl. Joaquín de Piélago, 1, two blocks from the main bus stop. (☎942 72 25 91. Open July-Aug. M-Sa 9am-9pm, Su 10am-4pm and 4-8pm; Sept.-June M-F 9am-2pm and 4-6pm, Sa 11am-2pm and 4:30-6:30pm, Su 11am-2pm.)

GALICIA (GALIZA)

If, as the Galician saying goes, "rain is art," then there is no area more artistic than northwestern Spain. Often veiled in a silvery mist, this province of fern-laden woods, slate-roofed fishing villages, and endless beaches has earned a reputation as a land of magic with tales filled with witches, fairies, and buried treasure. The Celts stopped in during their trip to Ireland around 900 BC, and ancient *castros* (fortress-villages), inscriptions, and *gaitas* (bagpipes) attest to the Celtiberian past. The rough terrain has historically hampered trade, but ship building, auto manufacturing, and even renowned fashion labels are contributing to the region's gradual modernization and development. Tourists have begun to visit even the smallest towns, and Santiago de Compostela, the terminus of the Camino de Santiago, continues to be one of the world's most popular backpacking destinations.

Galicians speak *gallego*, the linguistic link between Castilian and Portuguese. While newspapers and street signs alternate languages, most conversations are conducted in Spanish. Regional cuisine features *caldo gallego* (a vegetable broth), *vieiras* (scallops), *empanadas* (stuffed turnovers), and *pulpo a gallego* (boiled octopus). Regionalism in Galicia doesn't cause the stir it does in the País Vasco or Cataluña, but you still may see graffiti calling for *"liberdade"* (liberty).

GALICIA

HIGHLIGHTS OF GALICIA

PROGRESS with other pilgrims on the way to **Santiago de Compostela** (p. 557).

WATCH your step at the edge of the world, **Cabo Finisterre** (p. 564).

GULP down the fiery local concoction during the Fiesta de San Xuan in **Vigo** (p. 566).

MARVEL at Hercules' strength in his lighthouse in **A Coruña** (p. 578).

SANTIAGO DE COMPOSTELA   ☎981

For hundreds of years, visitors to Santiago de Compostela (pop. 94,000) have arrived with sore feet, aching shoulders, and tears of joy in their eyes. The final stop on the Camino de Santiago, an 800km pilgrimage through northern Spain that ends in the cathedral housing the remains of St. James, this haunting city bursts with symbols honoring the pilgrims' presence, from cross-emblazoned pastries to the scallop-shell jewelry. Though the city is geared towards the hundreds of people who arrive by foot every year, Santiago has much to offer for those who come by train or bus as well. Contagious chatter and excitement, the smell of sweet almond cakes, and the eerie strains of Celtic bagpipes and flutes fill the city's crooked Baroque streets, welcoming travelers to this sun-blessed spot.

▐ TRANSPORTATION

Flights: Aeropuerto Lavacolla (☎981 54 75 00), 10km toward Lugo. Buses leave for the airport from the bus station and the C. Doutor Teixeiro (6:40am-10:30pm, €1.55). Schedule in the daily El Correo Gallego (€0.75) and at the tourist office. **Iberia,** R. do Xeneral Pardiñas, 36 (☎981 57 20 24). Open M-F 9:30am-2pm and 4-7pm.

Trains: R. do Hórreo (☎902 24 02 02). Info daily 7am-11pm. To: **Bilbao** (10¾hr., 9:04am, €41) via **León** (6½hr., €29) and **Burgos** (8hr., €36); **A Coruña** (1hr.; M-F 17 per day 6:50am-11:33pm, Sa 14 per day 6:50am-10:25pm, Su 13 per day 7:45am-11:33pm;

€5.05); **Madrid** (8hr.; M-F and Su 1:37, 10:35pm, Sa 9:54am, 10:35pm; €43-67); **Vigo** (2hr., M-F 17 per day 6:15am-9:37pm, €5.55-7.70) via **Pontevedra** (1-1½hr., €3.75-5.05).

Buses: Estación Central de Autobuses, R. de Rodríguez (☎981 54 24 16), a 20min. walk from downtown. Bus #5 goes from the station to the Pr. de Galicia (10min.; M-F every 16 min. 6:40am-10:40pm, Sa every 20min. 7am-3pm, every 30min. 3-10:30pm, Su every 30min. 7:30am-10:30pm; €0.90). Info open daily 6am-10pm. **ALSA** (☎981 58 61 33, reservations 902 42 22 42). Open daily 6:30am-9pm. To **Madrid** (8-9hr.; Sa 5-6 per day 6am-9:30pm, Su 4 per day 9:45am-9:30pm; €39.04-55.50, round-trip €65-110), **San Sebastián** (13½hr.; 8:30am, 6pm; €54, round-trip €102), and **Bilbao** (11¼hr.; 8:30am, 6, 9:15pm; €45, round-trip €67). **Arriva/Finis-terre** (☎981 58 85 11) to **Finisterre** (2½hr.; M-F 7 per day 8am-7:30pm, Sa 3 per day 8am-4:30pm, Su 3 per day 9am-6:30pm; €11). **Castromil** (☎981 58 97 00). To: **A Coruña** (1½hr.; M-F 6:50am, hourly 8am-10:30pm, Sa 12 per day 9am-10:30pm, Su 11 per day 10am-10:30pm; €7); **El Ferrol** (2hr.; 8-10 per day 7:30am-8pm, Sa until 10pm; €8.90); **Noia** (1hr.; 8:15am, hourly 10am-10pm, Sa 9 per day 10am-10pm, Su 7 per day 10am-8pm; €3); **Vigo** (2hr.; M-F hourly 9am-10pm, Sa hourly 9am-1pm and 5-9pm, Su 9 per day 10am-9pm; €8) via **Pontevedra** (1½hr., €5.15).

Public Transportation: Local buses (☎981 58 18 15). Bus #6 to the train station (7:20am-11pm), #4 to the campgrounds (7am-10:30pm), and #5 to the bus station.

In the city center, almost all buses stop at Pr. de Galicia, where there are 2 stops, one on the R. do Dr. Teixeiro side and one along R. de Montero Ríos. Except for #6, buses run daily 7:30am-10:30pm every 20-30min. €0.90.

Taxis: Radio Taxi, (☎981 569 292) at the bus station and Pr. de Galicia. Stand outside Zara in Pr. de Galicia. 24hr. Late-night service near clubs in Pl. Roxa.

Car Rental: Avis (☎981 59 04 09), at the train station. 23+, must have had license for 1 year. Open M-F 9am-1:15pm and 4-7pm, Sa 9am-12:45pm, Su 9:30am-12:30pm. From €86 per day for 350km, €450 per week 25 and under €10.50 extra per day. Discounts for longer rentals. **Autos Brea,** Gomez Ulla, 8 (☎981 56 26 70), 23+, must have had license for 2 years. Open M-F 9am-1:30pm and 4-8pm, Sa 9am-1pm and 4-7pm, Su 10am-1pm. Rents cars for €60 per day. Insurance included (deposit required).

◀🛈 ORIENTATION AND PRACTICAL INFORMATION

Santiago centers around **Pr. de Obradoiro** and the renowned **Catedral de Santiago de Compostela.** The cathedral marks the center of the old city, on a hill above the new city. The **train station** is at the southern end of town. To reach the old city from the station, take bus #6 to **Praza de Galicia** or walk up the stairs across the parking lot from the main entrance, cross the street, bear right onto R. do Hórreo, and continue uphill for 10min. The **bus station** is at the town's northern end. The walk is 20min.; exit the bus station, walk up R. de Anxel Casal and turn left at the roundabout on to R. da Pastoriza, which becomes R. dos Basquinos, R. de Santa Clara, and then R. de San Roque. Follow the road left on or R. das Rodas, which becomes R. de Aller Ulloa, R. da Virxe da Cerca, and R. da Ensinanza, which leads to Pr. de Galicia; or take bus #5 to Pr. de Galicia (5min.). In the old city, three streets lead to the cathedral: **Rúa do Franco, Rúa do Vilar,** and **Rúa Nova.**

Tourist Office: Municipal Office, R. do Vilar, 63 (☎981 55 51 29; www.santiagoturismo.com). English, French, German, Portuguese, Finnish, Swedish, Danish and Italian spoken. Open June-Sept. 9am-9pm; Oct.-May 9am-2pm, 4-7pm. **Regional Office,** R. do Vilar, 30 (☎981 58 40 81), provides information about Galicia and daytrips from Santiago. Open M-F 10am-8pm, Sa 11am-2pm and 5-7pm, Su 11am-2pm. Info about guided tours of Santiago. **Oficina Xacobeo,** (☎981 58 40 81) also located at R. do Vilar, 30, provides information about the Camino de Santiago. Open M-F 10am-8pm. There is also another tourist office located closer to the train station at the Pza. de Galicia. Open M-F 10:30am-1:30pm.

Currency Exchange: Banco Santander Central Hispano, Pr. de Galicia, 1 (☎981 58 61 11). Open May-Sept. M-F 8:30am-2pm; Oct.-Apr. M-F 8:30am-2pm, Sa 8:30am-1pm. **Western Union** services and 24hr. **ATM** outside.

Religious Services: Mass in the cathedral M-F 9:30am, noon, and 7:30pm (vespers); Sa 9:30am, noon, 6, 6:30pm (vespers) Su 10am, noon, 1, 6, and 7:30pm (vespers). **Special pilgrim's mass** at noon featuring the *botafumeiro* (a gigantic incense burner).

Laundromat: ServiLimp, C. Rosalía de Castro, 33 (☎981 59 24 08). 4½kg of laundry €7.80. Open M-F 9:30am-1:30pm and 4-8pm, Sa 10am-2pm.

Police: Pr. do Obradoiro, 1 (☎981 54 23 23).

24hr. Pharmacy: Farmacia R. Bescanses, Pr. do Toural, 1 (☎981 58 59 90).

Hospital: Hospital Clínico Universitario, Tr. da Chupana (☎981 95 00 00), 2km west of town.

Internet Access: CyberNova 50, R. Nova, 50 (☎981 57 51 88). 26 fast computers. €1.20 per hour. Open M-Sa 9am-midnight, Su 10am-midnight.

Post Office: R. Orfas, 17. (☎981 58 12 52). **Lista de Correos** and **fax** at R. do Franco, 6. Open M-F 8:30am-8:30pm, Sa 9am-noon. **Postal Code:** 15703.

GALICIA

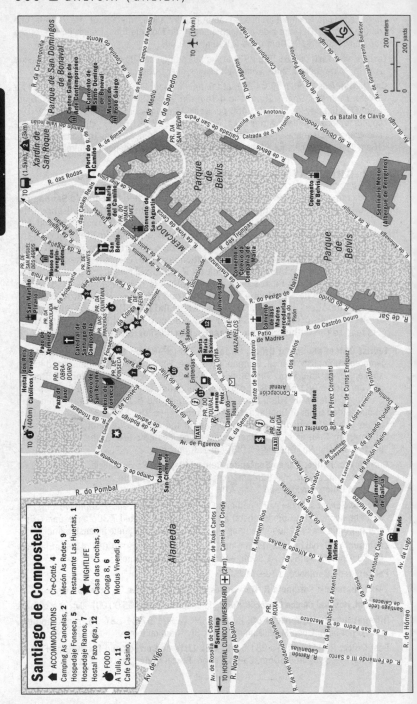

Santiago de Compostela

♦ ACCOMMODATIONS
Camping As Cancelas, **2**
Hospedaje Fonseca, **5**
Hospedaje Ramos, **7**
Hostal Pazo Agra, **12**

♦ FOOD
A Tulla, **11**
Cafe Casino, **10**

Cre-Cotté, **4**
Mesón As Redes, **9**
Restaurante Las Huertas, **1**

★ NIGHTLIFE
Casa das Crechas, **3**
Conga 8, **6**
Modus Vivendi, **8**

▐▊ ▐▊ ACCOMMODATIONS AND CAMPING

The liveliest and most popular rooms are on R. do Vilar and R. da Raíña. Youthful celebration may filter up into your room if you are staying in the old city, so consider staying in another part of the city (or wearing earplugs) if you need quiet.

▩ Hospedaje Ramos, R. da Raíña, 18, 2nd fl. (☎981 58 18 59), above O Papa Una restaurant. In the center of the *ciudad vieja*, these well-lit, modern rooms have private baths and sound-proof windows. Some rooms have views of the cathedral. Reserve 2 week ahead in summer. Singles €22; doubles €35. Cash only. ❷

Hospedaje Fonseca, R. de Fonseca, 1, 2nd fl. (☎646 937 765). Colorful rooms with floor-to-ceiling windows that let in lots of sun. Common kitchen with TV. Shared baths. Sept. 16-June singles, doubles, and triples €15 per person. July-Aug. singles €20; doubles €30. Cash only. ❷

Hostal Pazo Agra, R. da Calderería, 37 (☎981 58 35 17). Rich colors, beautiful fixtures, and an old-fashioned feel characterize this *hostal*. Rooms have high ceilings, glass doors opening onto balconies, some with shared bath and TV. Reception in *hostal* or in Restaurante Zingara, Cardenal Payá, 2, just around the block. May-Oct. singles €26; doubles €36. Nov.-Apr. €18/22. MC/V. ❸

Camping As Cancelas, R. 25 de Xullo, 35 (☎981 58 02 66). 3km north of the cathedral. Take #4 from R. da Senra, 1 block off Pr. de Galicia as you head toward it. Laundry, supermarket, and pool. Reception 8am-11pm. July-Aug. €5.25 per person, €5.50 per car and tent; Sept.-June €4 per person, car, and tent. Electricity €3.60. MC/V. ❶

▐ FOOD

Santiago's restaurants are worth the trek, but be wary of exorbitant prices. **Rúa da Raíña** is the best street for delicious, affordable meals, and **Rúa do Franco** has excellent tapas bars. **Rúa do Vilar** and **Rúa Nova** are also good options. In the new city, look near **Pr. Roxa.** Santiago is famous for its excellent seafood, so be sure to try paella or *mejillones* (mussels) before you leave. End your meal with a *tarta de Santiago*, a rich almond cake emblazoned with a sugary St. James cross. The best bakery in town, **Confitería El Coral,** R. Dr. Teixeiro, 32, has a tantalizing selection of homemade chocolate, ice cream, and pastries. (☎981 56 20 10. Open daily 9:30am-2:30pm and 4:30-9pm.) The **mercado** near the Convento de San Agustín is a sight in its own right. (Open M-Sa 8am-2pm.) **Supermercado Lorenzo Froiz,** Pr. do Toural, is one block from Pr. de Galicia. (Open M-Sa 9am-10pm. MC/V.)

▩ A Tulla, R. de Entrerúas, 1 (☎981 58 08 89). Almost literally a hole in the wall, this tiny family restaurant is accessible only through a tiny, easily-missed alley between R. do Vilar and R. Nova. To get there from R. do Vilar, look for the alley to the right of Consorcio de Santiago, underneath the overhang labeled "Casa del Doctor." Entrees €6.50-8.50. *Menú* €11.80, vegetarian *menú* €9. Open M-Sa 1-4pm and 8:30pm-midnight. MC/V. ❷

Restaurante Las Huertas, R. das Hortas, 16. (☎981 561 979). Right down the street from the cathedral, Las Huertas satisfies a craving for elegance. Excellent fresh-made paella for 2 with a bottle of *albariño* (a white wine) €26. *Menú del día* €9. Entrees €9-12+. Open daily 1-4pm and 9-11:30pm. MC/V. ❷

Cre-Cotté, Pr. de Quintana, 1 (☎981 57 76 43). Rich crepes (€5.80-8.50) and an extensive selection of salads (€6.50-7.50) served either on the beautiful terrace next to the cathedral or in the lemon-colored, welcoming dining room. *Menú* €11.50. Open July-Aug. 1pm-midnight; Sept.-June 1-4:30pm and 8:30pm-midnight. AmEx/MC/V. ❷

Mesón As Redes, R. da Raíña, 17 (☎981 576 822). Over half the options at this laid-back restaurant are under €5 and can serve as a full meal—this includes *raciones,* *tablas*, Spanish *tortillas*, pastas, seafood, hamburgers, sandwiches, and even heaping *platos combinados*. Open M-Th noon-4:30pm and 8pm-midnight, F-Su noon-4:30pm and 7pm-1am. Cash only. ❶

Café Casino, Rúa de Vilar, 35 (☎981 57 75 03). With deep arm chairs, dark wood working, stained glass and a cavernous interior, this coffee shop wouldn't be out of place in a medieval castle. Delicious coffee drinks (€2-3) as well as wide selection of desserts (€2.50-5) fit to make anybody's mouth water. Open daily 9am-11:30pm. ❶

🜚 SIGHTS

■ CATEDRAL DE SANTIAGO DE COMPOSTELA. This Romanesque masterpiece, a terminus of Christian pilgrimage since the 10th century, not only symbolizes Santiago, but the entire Camino and the Catholic religion. The 9th-century discovery of James the Apostle's relics gave rise to a chapel, and then to two pre-Romanesque churches. The current cathedral, which faces east into Pr. do Obradoiro, was erected in 1075. On any summer day, pilgrims recently unburdened from their backpacks fill the plaza, gazing for hours upon the cathedral's magnificent moss-covered walls and ornate spires. The Baroque **Obradoiro Facade**, built in the 18th century dominates the square of the same name, which means "workshop" in *gallego*; it was here that stonemasons worked during its construction. Many consider Maestro Mateo's **Pórtico de la Gloria,** set in the Obradoiro facade, the crowning work of Spanish Romanesque sculpture. This apocalyptic 12th-century amalgam of angels, prophets, saints, sinners, demons, and monsters is a compendium of Christian theology, and includes scenes of the Final Judgement. From the southern **Praza das Praterías**, recognizable by the sea horse, enter the cathedral through the Romanesque arched double doors. To the west of the cathedral the Pórtico Real and Porta Santa face **Praza da Quintana**. To the north, a blend of Doric and Ionic columns, rebuilt after a fire in the 18th century, grace **Praza da Inmaculada**, which mixes Romanesque and Neo-classical styles. Inside the cathedral, the revered **remains of St. James** (Santiago) lie beneath the high altar in a silver coffer, while his bejeweled bust, polished by the embraces of thousands of pilgrims, rests above it. The **botafumeiro**, a silver censer used in religious rituals, swings during High Mass and liturgical ceremonies. Older than the towers that house them, the **bells** of Santiago were stolen in 997 by Moorish invaders and transported to Córdoba. When Spaniards later conquered Córdoba, they had their revenge when they forced Moors to carry the bells back. (☎981 58 35 48. Open daily 7am-9pm. Free.)

MUSEUM AND CLOISTERS. The museum enables visitors to tour the cathedral, the Treasury and Relics, the Cloister, the Tapestry room, the Archaeology rooms and the Chapter house, the Cripta del Pórtico de la Gloria, Palacio de Gelmínez, the library, and the archives. Inside the museum are manuscripts from the *Codex Calixtinus* and Romanesque remains from one of many archaeological excavations conducted in the cathedral. The museum also has an extensive collection of coins from Santiago, dating as far back as the 1300s. The 12th-century *Codex*, five volumes of manuscripts of the stories of the Apostle James, includes travel information for early pilgrims. (☎981 58 11 55. Museum open June-Sept. M-Sa 10am-2pm and 4-8pm, Su and holidays 10am-2pm; Oct.-May M-Sa 10am-1:30pm and 4-6:30pm, Su and holidays 10am-1:30pm. €5, students, retired persons and pilgrims €3; includes entrance to crypt. Pamphlets for tour of the museum available in German, English, French, Italian, and Portuguese)

■ MUSEO DAS PEREGRINACIÓNS. This three-story Gothic building is full of creatively displayed historical info about the Camino and other pilgrimages from all over the world. It also includes statues of the Virgin as a pilgrim carrying the baby Jesus, illustrations of the different routes to Santiago, and exhibits on the rituals of pilgrimage and the iconography of Santiago. *(R. de San Miguel, 4. ☎ 981 58 15 58; www.mdperegrinacions.com. Open Tu-F 10am-8pm, Sa 10:30am-1:30pm and 5-8pm, Su 10:30am-1:30pm. €2.40, students, seniors and children €1.20, pilgrims free. Special expositions and most of the summer free.)*

PAZO DE RAXOI. Facing the grand cathedral and set against a backdrop of clear sky, the facade of the Pazo de Raxoi majestically completes the square. Once a royal palace, it now houses the *Ayuntamiento* and the office of the president of the *Xunta de Galicia* (Galician government). At night, floodlights illuminate the remarkable bas-relief of the 844 Battle of Clavijo, during which, according to legend, Santiago helped to fight off the Moors. *(Across Pr. do Obradoiro, facing the cathedral.)*

CENTRO GALLEGO DE ARTE CONTEMPORÁNEO. The expansive galleries and rooftop *terraza* of the sparkling Centro Gallego de Arte Contemporáneo (CGAC) house cutting-edge exhibitions of boundary-bending artists from around the world, including photo exhibitions, sculptures, and paintings. The top of the *terraza* has incredible views of all of Santiago. *(R. de Ramón del Valle Inclán. Next to the Museo de Pobo Gallego. ☎ 981 54 69 29; www.cgac.org. Open Tu-Su 11am-8pm. Free.)*

MUSEO DE POBO GALLEGO. A Galician folk museum where you can find out everything you ever wanted to know about traditional Galician living. Exhibits on ship building, pottery, house construction, and *gaitas* (the Galician bagpipe) fill the rooms branching off three intertwining spiral staircases. *(Inside the Convento de Santo Domingos de Boneval. ☎ 981 58 36 20; www.museodopobo.es. Open Tu-Sa 10am-2pm and 4-8pm, Su 11am-2pm. Free.)*

MONASTERIO DE SAN MARTIÑO PINARIO. Once a religious center almost as prestigious as the cathedral, this huge monastery of 20,000 square ft., built between the 17th and 18th centuries, is a mixture of Romanesque cloisters, Plateresque facades, and Baroque sculpture. *(In Pr. de San Martiño Pinario.)*

🎷 NIGHTLIFE

Many begin the night by hopping from one tapas bar to another. The best street for tapas is ▧ **Rúa do Franco,** with popular options including **A Taberna do Bispo** (Franco, 37), **Casa Rosalía** (Franco, 10)**, and Xantares** (Franco, 40). If you'd rather boogie with local students, try the bars and clubs off Pr. Roxa.

THE LOCAL STORY

SHELLS BY THE SEASHORE

If you're anywhere on the Camino de Santiago, you're likely to find yourself surrounded by scallop shells—on roadways, doorways to lodgings, backpacks, and maybe even one or two on yourself. The scallop shell is a symbol of the ancient pilgrimage, but its use dates back to pre-Christian times.

Long before the Romans and the Christians settled in what are today Spain and Portugal, the Iberian Peninsula was populated by various tribes, including the Celts (known in Spain as the Castros). Before the route became a Christian pilgrimage to St. James' remains in the Cathedral of Santiago de Compostela, it was a pagan route. One theory claims that the route was part of a pagan fertility ritual and the scallop shell the symbol of fertility. Another suggests that the shell, symbolic of the setting sun which it resembles, was part of a Celtic death pilgrimage through northern Spain, westwards with the setting sun to Cabo Fisterra and the Costa de Morta—the End of the World and the Coast of Death.

During the Middle Ages, when the route became increasingly popular for devout Christians, pilgrims would bring back Galician scallop shells as proof that they completed their journey. Today, the scallop shell continues to point the way towards Santiago.

Casa das Crechas, Vía Sacra, 3 (☎981 57 61 08). A cavernous, witchcraft-themed drinking hole, alive with good cheer. Renowned for live jazz and Galician folk concerts. Call ahead for schedule. Beer €2. Open daily in summer noon-4am; in winter 4pm-3am.

Conga 8, R. da Conga, 8 (☎981 58 34 07). Salsa, merengue, and Spanish pop music mix keep the basement dance floor crowded. Popular hangout for locals around 3am. Beer €1.80. Mixed drinks €4. Open daily 10pm-5am.

Modus Vivendi, Pza. Feixóo, 1 (☎981 57 61 09). A hot spot on the Santiago scene, with a darkened interior and psychedelic decoration. Listen to the rock music while chatting with both locals and foreigners in the cramped, but cozy, interior. Beer €2. Mixed drinks €4.20. Open Su-Th 6:30pm-3am, F-Sa until 4:30am.

♪ ❀ ENTERTAINMENT AND FESTIVALS

The local newspaper *El Correo Gallego* (€0.75) and the free monthly *Compostela Capital* list art exhibits and concert information. Consult any of three local monthlies, *Santiago Días Guía Imprescindible, Compostelán,* or *Modus Vivendi,* for updates on the live music scene. One of the city's biggest festivals, **Fiestas de la Ascensión,** forty days after Easter Sunday, features concerts, a famous cattle market, and the consumption of many octopi in the Santa Susana oak grove. The city celebrates the **Día de Santiago** (July 25) for a full two weeks (July 15-31), in a celebration called *Apóstolo;* on the night of the 24th, a Pontifical Mass is held in the cathedral during **Las Vísperas de Santiago.**

➋ DAYTRIPS FROM SANTIAGO DE COMPOSTELA

The northern part of the Rías Baixas hides undiscovered hamlets frequented only by pilgrims. These small towns make good daytrips from Santiago, although buses in this area tend to make frequent stops, so travel can be slow.

■ CABO FINISTERRE (CABO FISTERRA)

Arriva/Finisterre buses run from Santiago to Fisterra (2½hr.; M-F 7 per day 8am-7:30pm, Sa 3 per day 8am-4:30pm, Su 3 per day 9am-6:30pm; €11, round-trip €21.40) and back (M-F 4 per day 7:50am-4:30pm, Sa 3 per day 10:30am-4pm, Su 3 per day 9:45am-6pm). The bus stop is near the Albergue de Peregrinos, 50m uphill from the water.

After arriving in Santiago, many pilgrims decide to continue on for as far as their feet and the land will take them; the windswept shores of Fisterra, once believed to be the end of the world, is their final stop. Jutting out precariously from the infamously rocky Costa de la Muerte ("Coast of Death"; Costa da Morte in Gallego), Cabo Fisterra was, for centuries, a crucial port for all naval trade along the Atlantic. Today, the lonely, peaceful town, Spain's last stop before the "New World," still feels like the end of the earth. The 45min. trail up to the lighthouse from the center of town reveals a truly breathtaking view. The best **beach** in the town is on the flat isthmus that connects the peninsula with the mainland. The beaches are powdery and wide, the waters calm but frigid. Either walk 4km along the road to Santiago or take the bus and ask to stop. The 1½hr. hike from the port up **Monte San Guillermo** cuts through heather-covered mountainside and commands incredible views of the sea. At the top of the cliffs, pilgrims burn their clothes and throw the ashes into the wind, as a ritual for cleansing their souls after the long journey. The mountain also hosts Fisterra's famous bed-shaped **fertility rocks.** Couples having problems conceiving are advised to make a go of it on the rocks under a full moon (harvest moons are even better). On another hill on San Guillermo are **As Pedras Santas,** two large boulders that slide effortlessly side-to-side if you press the right spot.

If you miss the last bus back to Santiago, you can stay at **Hospedaje López ❷**, R. de Carrasqueira, 4. The clean, inexpensive rooms with shared baths all have views of the coast. From the bus stop, cross the street and walk uphill; when you reach the post office turn left onto the narrow street, C. Carrasqueira; the hostel has gnomes in the front yard. (☎981 74 04 49. Singles €15; doubles €20.) For delicious and inexpensive seafood, try the numerous cafes and restaurants lining the Paseo del Puerto, right on the ocean. **Bodegón O Casón ❷**, Paseo del Puerto s/n, is a good stop—eat fresh seafood while enjoying fantastic views of the harbor and cove (☎981 74 02 66. *Menú del día* €9. Open daily 11:30am-3pm and 7:30-11pm). The **Albergue de Peregrinos**, C. Real, 2, has brochures and tourist info. From the bus stop, facing the water, turn right. (☎981 74 07 81. Open Sept.-May M-F 11am-2pm and 5-10pm, during summer open later.) Nearby, **Bazar de Artesanía da Costa da Morte** also has maps and info on bike rentals. (☎981 74 00 74. Bikes €4 per hour, €12 per day. Open M-Sa 10am-1:30pm and 5-9pm.)

▨O CASTRO DE BAROÑA (PORTO DO SON)

To reach these two towns, you'll need to make a connection in Noia. Castromil (☎981 58 90 90) runs buses from Santiago to Noia (1hr.; M-F 13 per day 8:15am-10pm, Sa 8 per day 10am-10pm, Su every 2hr. 10am-8pm; €3). From Noia, Hefsel buses stop at Porto do Son and O Castro de Baroña (in front of Café-Bar O Castro) en route to Riveira (30min.; M-F 14 per day 6:50am-9:30pm, Sa 7 per day 8am-9pm, Su 10 per day 9am-10pm; €1.60). Be sure to tell the bus driver where you're going, as the stop for Castro is easy to miss. From the bus stop at Castro, follow signs to the fortress, downhill toward the water. Catch the bus home across the road from Café-Bar O Castro.

One of Galicia's best-preserved coastal Celtic villages, O Castro de Baroña lies 19km south of Noia. The seaside remains of a 5th-century Celtic **fortress** cover the neck of the Isthmus, ascending to a rocky promontory above the sea; circular foundations are all that remain of the 1500-year old structures, but they make for a tangled, snaky vista from the area's highest point. Waves crash against the rocky sides of the little peninsula, giving the remains of the fortress a lonely, peaceful feeling. The bluff descends to the soft sands of an excellent crescent **beach**, where clothing is *"prohibido,"* but don't be intimidated by the hostile graffiti denouncing those who don swimsuits; beachgoers are friendly and some cover their bodies as well. For those who need a shower and a bed, **Café-Bar O Castro ❸**, Lugar Castro de Baroña, 18, in the Castro de Baroña bus stop), offers a few spotless rooms under the care of a very nice owner. (☎981 76 74 30.) Still, since the rooms are 2km away from the bus stop, you are probably better off staying in neighboring Porto do Son—there are inexpensive accommodations scattered around the bus stop.

MUROS AND LOURO

Castromil runs buses between Santiago and Muros (2hr.; M-F 11 per day 8:15am-9pm, Sa 8 per day 10am-10pm, Su every 2hr. 10am-8pm; €5.90) via Noia. Arriva buses run from Muros to Cee via Louro— make sure to tell the bus driver where you're going (M-F 8 per day 7:30am-7pm, Sa 6 per day 8am-9pm, Su 5 per day 8:30am-5:30pm; €1). The bus station is to the right of the Hotel Muradana (when facing the ocean), across the street from the harbor.

Tucked into the arm of a large cove, Muros is a small but lively fishing village. In 1970, it was recognized as a historical site for its traditional Gothic architectural design, sailor houses, and bite-size plazas. The main road in the town is the Av. de Castelao, which runs right along the coast from the ayuntamiento to the town's outskirts. 4km away in Louro are some of the most secluded soft sand beaches in all Galicia. The combination of the two towns makes an ideal daytrip—Muros, with its transportation facilities, accommodations, and restaurants, provides the amenities necessary for a day in the surf at Louro. From Muros, after roaming the old city's winding streets, visitors can take the **Paseo Marítimo** (to the right, facing the water) to Louro, with views of cobalt waters on the way. The first beach in Louro, **Playa San Francisco,** is less than 3km from Muros.

Stay overnight right on the beach at **A Vouga Camping ❶,** which has a restaurant, bar, hot showers, and a small market. (☎981 82 76 07. Reception 9am-11pm. Reserve a few days in advance. €3.15 per person, €3.15 per tent, €17-20 per site, depending on size. Electricity €2.40. AmEx/MC/V.) If you'd like to stay in Muros, try **Hospedaje A Vianda ❷,** Av. de Castelao, 47. White-washed walls, linen sheets, and ceiling lanterns make up this plain but pleasant *hospedaje.* Some rooms have a view and a TV, and all have shared baths. Book ahead during the summer months, as this place fills up. (☎981 82 63 22. Reserve a month ahead for Aug. stays. Doubles €30, with view €36; triples with shared bath €36. Cash only.) Cheap cafes can be found off Pl. de Pescadería or along the harbor on Av. de Castelao. Huge pizzas (€6-8), salads (€2-6), and sandwiches are available at ship-themed restaurant **A Darsena ❷,** Av. Castelao, 11. (☎981 82 76 64. Open daily noon-5pm and 8pm-1am). Another tasty option is **Bar Encontos ❷,** Pl. Pescadería, 15 (☎981 76 20 26. *Bocadillos* €2-4, tapas €4-10. Open daily 11am-8pm). For **bike rentals,** restaurant and hotel **Muradana** (☎981 82 68 85) on R. Castelao, 99, rents mountain bikes for €2.50 per hour. The **police,** C. Curro de Praza, 1, are reachable at ☎981 82 72 76. The **Ayuntamiento** at the end of the Ave. de Castelao has tourist information.

RÍAS BAJAS (RÍAS BAIXAS)

According to Galician lore, the Rías Baixas (Low Estuaries) were formed by God's tremendous handprint, with each river stretching like a finger through the land. The deep bays, sandy coves, and calm, cool waters have lured vacationing Spaniards for decades. While not nearly as cool or rainy as their Galician neighbors, the Baixas are blessed with an ocean wind that provides a refreshing respite from the scorching heat (and hordes of tourists) of central and southern Spain. Due to its proximity to Portugal, there's also greater cultural fluidity in this part of Spain; the Gallego is stronger here, the accents thicker and the people more diverse. It all adds to the charm, however, in this unique part of Galicia.

VIGO   ☎986

Spanish poet José María Álvarez once wrote that "Vigo does not end, it goes on into the sea." Sure enough, the downward sloping streets are packed with restaurants, shops, and people right up to the waterfront. Often called Spain's door to the Atlantic, Vigo (pop. 300,000) began as an unobtrusive fishing port. With the arrival of the Citröen manufacturing plant it exploded into the biggest city in Galicia, putting its neighbors to shame with its liveliness and nightlife; Vigo's countless and diverse bars and clubs keep thumping into the wee hours of the morning. Its increasing popularity among European travelers has prompted extensive construction projects to expand pedestrian space near the city center and the marina. Vigo is also a good launching pad for exploring the many beach towns and rocky islands that surround the city.

▐ TRANSPORTATION

Flights: Aeropuerto de Vigo, Av. del Aeropuerto (☎986 26 82 00), 15km from the city center. The local bus #9 runs regularly from R. Urzáiz near R. Colón to the airport (€1). **Iberia** (☎986 26 82 28) and **Air Europa** (☎986 26 83 10) have offices at the airport. Daily flights to **Barcelona, Bilbao, Madrid,** and **Valencia.**

Trains: RENFE, Pr. de la Estación (☎902 24 02 02), off R. Urzáiz. Open daily 7am-11pm. To: **A Coruña** (2½hr.; M-F 15 per day 5:50am-8:55pm, Sa-Su 12 per day 5:50am-8:55pm; €8.90-11.20); **Madrid** (8-9hr.; M-F and Su 1:20, 10:20pm; Sa 9:30am, 10:20pm; €44); **Pontevedra** (30min.; M-F 20 per day 5:50am-9:40pm, Sa 13-14 per day 5:50am-8:55pm, Su 13-14 per day 5:50am-9:40pm; €2.60); **Santiago de Compostela** (2hr.; M-F 17 per day 5:50am-9:40pm, Sa-Su 13-14 per day Sa until 8:55pm, Su 5:50am-9:40pm; €5.65-7.70); **Tui** (35min.; 7:45am, 7:32pm; €2.50).

Buses: Estación de Autobuses, Av. de Madrid (☎986 37 34 11), on the corner of R. Alcalde Gregorio Espino. Info daily 8am-10pm. **ATSA** (☎986 61 02 55) to: **Bayona (Baiona)** (50min.; M-F every 30min.-1hr. 7am-1:30pm, every 15-30min. 2pm-10:15pm; Sa-Su every 15-45min. Sa 7:30am-10:30pm, Su 8am-11pm; €2.10); **La Guardia (A Guardia)** (1½hr.; M-F every 30min.-1hr. 7:30am-9:30pm; Sa 12 per day 8:30am-9:30pm, Su 6 per day 10am-9:30pm; €4.80); **Túy (Tui)** (45min.; M-F every 30min.-1hr. 7:30am-9:30pm, Sa 10 per day 8:30am-9:30pm, Su 4 per day 10am-9:30pm; €2.80). Buy tickets on board. **Auto-Res** (☎902 02 09 99; www.auto-res.net) to: **Madrid** (6½-8hr.; 7-6 per day 8:30am-11pm; €32-39, round-trip €57-68).

Ferries: Estación Marítima de Ría, R. As Avenidas (☎986 22 52 72; www.marde-ons.com), past the nautical club on the harborside walkway. To: **Cangas** (20min.; M-F every 30min. 6:30am-10:30pm, Sa-Su hourly 6:30am-10:30pm; €3.90 round-trip); **Islas Cíes** (45min.; July-Aug. 8 per day 10am-7pm (weather-dependent, check schedule), Sept.-June 4 per day 11am-7pm; round-trip €17.50, children €6); **Moaña** (30min.; M-F every 30min.-1hr. 6:30am-10:30pm, Sa-Su hourly 6:30am-10:30pm; €3.70 round-trip).

Taxis: Central Radio Taxi, at Porta do Sol (☎986 47 00 00). About €0.50 per km.

Car Rental: Europcar Ibérica, Pl. de la Estación, s/n, (☎986 22 91 61; www.europcar.com), at the train station. 21+, must have had license at least 1 year. Open M-F 8am-1:30pm and 4-7:30pm, Sa 9am-1:30pm. From €68 per day.

✦ 🛈 ORIENTATION AND PRACTICAL INFORMATION

Gran Vía, the main thoroughfare, stretches south to north from Pr. de América through Pr. de España and ends on the very steep slope of **R. Urzáiz.** A left turn downhill onto R. Urzáiz leads to C. Príncipe, Pta. do Sol, and into the **casco antiguo.** As you exit the train station onto R. Ur

áiz (upstairs from the main entrance), go right two blocks to reach Gran Vía. Keep walking on R. Urzáiz for 10min. and bear right at the fork onto C. Colón to reach the waterfront. To reach the **municipal tourist office,** bear left at the fork with C. Colón to stay on R. Urzáiz, which becomes R. Príncipe. At the Porto do Sol, continue up the street. Turn right directly after the Pr. de Princesa and pass through the Pr. de la Constitución onto R. do Triunfo. Make a left onto R. da Palma and then a right to pass through Pr. a Pedra. Go down the stairs in front of you to street level and the office is on your right. The city center is a 25min. walk from the bus station. Exit right uphill along **Av. de Madrid.** When you arrive at a large rotary, make a right on Gran Vía at Pr. de España, leading to the intersection with R. Urzáiz. It's easier to take bus #12a, or 12b from Av. de Madrid in front of the bus station to Gran Vía, R. Urzáiz, or R. Colón (€1).

Tourist Office: Regional branch, R. Cánovas de Castillo, 22 (☎986 43 05 77; www.turgalicia.es). Open July-Aug. M-F 9:30am-2pm and 4:30-7:30pm, Sa 10am-1:30pm and 4:30-7:30pm, Su 10am-1:30pm; Sept.-June M-F 9:30am-2pm and 4:30-6:30pm, Sa 10am-1:30m. **Vigo branch,** Teofilo Llorente, 5 (☎986 22 47 57; www.turismodevigo.org). Open daily June 15-Oct. 15 10am-2pm and 4-7:30pm; winter M-Sa 10am-2pm, and 4-7:30pm, Su 10am-2pm. There are also tourist info huts scattered throughout the city, including the Porto do Sol and train station, most open June-Oct. daily 10am-2pm and 4-7:30pm.

Currency Exchange: Banco Santander Central Hispano, R. Urzáiz, 2 (☎902 24 24 24). Open Apr.-Sept. M-F 8:30am-2pm; Oct.-Mar. M-F 8:30am-2pm, Sa 8:30am-1pm. 24hr. **ATM** outside.

Luggage Storage: At the **bus station** (€2 per day; open daily 6:30am-midnight, buy tokens at the information stand (open daily 8am-10pm).

English-Language Bookstore: Casa del Libro, C. Velázquez Moreno, 27 (☎986 44 16 79), downhill off C. Príncipe. Open M-Sa 9:30am-9:30pm. Books in English on 2nd fl.

Police: Pr. do Rei (☎092).

Pharmacy: Jose Luis Charro Pharmacy, R. Urzaia, 176 (☎986 27 29 86).

Medical Services: Hospital Xeral, R. Pizarro, s/n (☎986 81 60 00). **Ambulance:** ☎061.

Internet Access: Sereo Cyber's, Pr. de Princesa, 3 (☎986 22 36 35), by the bus stop. €1.80 per hour. Open M-F 9am-midnight, Sa 10am-midnight, Su 11am-midnight

Post Office: Lista de Correos and **fax.** Open M-F 8:30am-8:30pm, Sa 9:30am-2pm. **Postal Code:** 36201.

ACCOMMODATIONS

Most accommodations are near the train station on R. Alfonso XIII. Reserve ahead in summer and visit the ATM before checking in, as some places ask for payment upon arrival instead of departure.

■ **Hostal Ría de Arosa,** R. Cervantes, 4, 2nd fl. (☎986 43 50 96). At the very end of R. Cervantes, so the noise of nightlife is less noticeable. Beautiful rooms with white fixtures and lemon-colored walls. All have TV, some have balconies. Spotless hall baths. July-Aug. singles €18; doubles €25. Sept.-June €15/20. Cash only. ❷

Hostal Ría de Vigo, R. Cervantes, 14, 1st fl. (☎986 43 72 40), a left off R. Alfonso XIII, 4 blocks down from the station. Wooden-framed beds in cheerful rooms with private bath, TV, some with balconies over R. Cervantes. July-Sept. singles €21; doubles €31. Oct.-June €19/26. Cash only. ❷

Ancla Dorada Hostal-Residencia, C. Irmandiños, 2 (☎986 43 66 07), near the train station off R. Cervantes. Yellow walls, old photos of Vigo, and wrought-iron beds make this hostel feel like home. July-Aug. single €30; double €34; triple €55, with bathroom €34/38/60. Sept.-June €24/28/48, with bathroom €28/30/55. MC/V. ❸

Hospedaje La Estrella, C. Martín Codax, 5 (☎986 22 50 35), a left off R. Alfonso XIII, 3 blocks down from the station. Basic but large rooms in this antique apartment building come complete with TV and clean bath. Singles €20, with bath €25; doubles €25/35. Reserve at least 2 weeks ahead in summer. Cash only. ❷

FOOD

Gran Vía and C. Venezuela, four streets uphill from R. Urzáiz off Gran Vía, brim with bright cafeterias and terrazas. Many seafood restaurants and *pulperías* (octopus stands) lie around the **As Avenidas** boardwalk by the water, near the touristy *casco antiguo*. For 24hr. cheap, hot food visit **Ecos Cafetería 1 ❷,** R. Urzáiz, 25. (☎986 22 34 81. Combined plates €6-14, sandwiches €2-4.) For groceries, hit **Supermercado Froiz,** R. do Uruguai, 14 (open M-Sa 9:30am-9:30pm).

■ **Restaurante Lamari,** Pl. de la Piedra (☎986 22 32 43). The seafood is so fresh you can see the boats that pull it in from the restaurant's terrace. Low key ambience and high-quality food. Entrees €4-12+ (prices vary with market price), mostly fish and shellfish. Open daily 1-4pm and 8pm-midnight. MC/V. ❷

Restaurante Don Quijote, C. Late, 4 (☎986 22 93 46). Enjoy savory *pulpo* (octopus; €10) while sitting on the raised platforms of the outdoor terrace with views of the harbor below. *Menú del día* €10. Open daily 1-4pm and 8pm-midnight. MC/V. ❷

Estrella de Galicia, Pl. de Compostela, 17, near the harbor. Doubles as a warehouse-style bar. Inexpensive dishes including *Plato del mes* €8.50 and *filloas*, crepe pockets stuffed with deliciousness (€6-6.50). Open daily 12:30-4pm and 8pm-midnight. ❶

Cafetería El Coral, R. Ecuador, 71 (☎986 41 07 19), on the corner of C. Ecuador and C. Cuba. This informal cafetería is a good spot for a cup of coffee or a cheap meal. *Platos combinados* €6-10. Open daily 7am-midnight. Cash only. ❶

🔋 NIGHTLIFE

Vigo loves to party. The area around **R. Areal** and **R. Concepción Arenal** is jam-packed with discotecas, nightclubs, and bars playing the latest Spanish hits for trendy crowds. Near the train station—on **R. Cervantes, R. Lepanto,** and **R. Churruca,** in particular—are dark, smoky bars and clubs with great music, decor, dancing, and a curiously common 70s theme.

Black Ball, R. Churruca, 8. A throwback complete with disco balls, life-size star trek posters, and psychedelic lighting. Black Ball is the spot for disco dancing, a quirky crowd, and cheap mixed drinks (€5). Beer €3. Open July-Aug., Dec. Tu-Sa 12:30-4:30am; Sept.-Nov., Jan.-June Th-Sa 12:30-4:30am.

El Monstruo de un Solo Ojo, C. Cervantes, 18 (www.myspace.com/elmonstruodeunsoloojo). A funky club that stays true to its name, with the one-eyed monster cartoons strewn all over the walls. Regular summertime concerts/promotional parties with mostly rock and punk bands. Beer €3. Drinks €5. July-Aug. open M-W 11:30pm-3am, Th-Sa till 4:30am; Sept.-June open Th-Sa 11:30pm-4:30am.

Kenzo Café, R. Arenal, 40 (www.kenzocafe.com). A dark pub decorated with African masks and gin bottles right off the wharf. Beer €1.90. Open daily 7am-3am.

👁 🌸 SIGHTS AND FESTIVALS

The original settlement of Vigo was founded on the slopes of **Mt. Castro.** At the top lie the remains of a massive fortress (which, of course, is now an expensive restaurant). You'll forget you're in the confines of the city when you reach the very top of the *monte.* The view is definitely worth the climb and gives an idea of the city's gradual expansion. To get to the park, walk up the Gran Via from R. Uzaia and turn right at R. Venezuela. Continue for six blocks; the park is on the left. The **Museo Municipal de Vigo "Quiñones de León,"** Parque de Castrelos, s/n, is also worth checking out. The museum houses artwork from a variety of ages and movements, and an impressive archaeological collection. If the art isn't enough to draw you, visit the museum just to explore the *pazo* (palace) itself, which dates from the 18th century. Getting to the museum is a 45min.-1hr. walk from city center; head up the Gran Vía from R. Urzaíz, straight through the rotary at the Pr. España and downhill to the Pr. America. Turn left onto Av. de Castrelos, and after the stone entrance to the Parque Municipal, turn left onto Carretera O Pazo. The museum is up the hill on your right. (☎986 29 50 70; www.museodevigo.org. Open Tu and Th-F 10am-1:30pm and 5-8pm, W 10am-8pm, Sa 5-8pm, Su 10am-1:30pm. Free.) Popular museums include the **Museo de Arte Contemporáneo de Vigo** (C. del Príncipe, 54; open Tu-Sa 11am-9pm, Su 11am-3pm; €3, students, seniors €2; W free.) and the **Museo del Mar de Galicia.** (☎986 24 76 91. Av. Atlántida, 160. Open June-Sept. Tu-Th 10am-2pm and 5-10pm, F-Sa 10am-2pm and 5-11:30pm, Su 10am-10pm; Oct.-May Tu-Th 11am-8pm, F-Sa 11am-11:30pm, Su 10am-9pm. €6, students €3.)

Watch for the magical **Fiesta de San Xuan** on June 23, when neighborhoods light huge cauldrons of *aguardiente* (firewater) to make an infusion called *la queimada*, which consists of *aguardiente*, coffee, lemon, and sugar; revelers pass around the sweet mixture while dancing among bonfires on the beach or in the streets. You can catch a similar display, as well as concerts and processions, during the **Fiestas del Cristo de la Victoria** in the end of July and beginning of August.

▶ DAYTRIPS FROM VIGO

█ ISLAS CÍES (ILLAS CÍES)

Ferries make the 14km trip between Estación Marítima in Vigo and the islands. (45min.; July-Aug. 8 per day 10am-7pm, Sept.-June 4 per day 11am-7pm; round-trip €17.50, children €6.) Book round-trip tickets early in the day, as they do sell out.

The Romans called them the "Islands of the Gods," and it is easy to believe that the deities happily left Olympus to spend their weekends in the Illas Cíes. Guarding the mouth of the Ría de Vigo, two connected islands—**Illa de Monte Agudo** (a.k.a. **Illa del Norte**) and **Illa do Medio** (a.k.a. **Illa del Faro**)—offer irresistible beaches and cliffside hiking trails for travelers. The islands were declared a national park in 1980; only 2200 people are allowed in per day, ensuring wide stretches of uncrowded beach. The ferry drops off at **Playa de Rodas,** a pristine beach with fine white sand. For smaller, more secluded spots, head right on the trail from the tourist office juncture to **Area de Figueiras** (300m), another gorgeous white-sand beach with sheltered waters. If you continue to walk left, you will find more beaches, coves, and rocky lookouts. There are four main trails that traverse the two islands, from pristine beaches to rocky cliffs. A 4km hike to the left of the dock on the main path leads to a bird observatory and two lighthouses with breathtaking views. Along the same trails lies the park campground, which includes a restaurant and supermarket (open 10am-9pm). You can stock up at the market before a hike to the **Faro de Cíes,** the big lighthouse on the southern tip of the island.

If you plan to spend the night, you can **camp ❶** on the island. Facilities include a small market, bar, baths, and hot showers. (Reservations ☎ 986 43 83 58. Reception 8:30am-10pm. Open June-Sept. and *Semana Santa.* Camping €6.50 per person, €5.10 per child 3-12, €6.65-6.85 per tent. IVA not included.) Before leaving Vigo, be sure to make reservations and get a *Tarjeta de Acampado* in the **Camping Office** (☎ 986 43 83 58; open daily 8:30am-1pm and 2:30pm-7pm) at the Estación Marítima. If you plan on staying, stock up on food in Vigo, as prices on the island are higher. To get to the **tourist office** (open June daily 11:30am-2:15pm and 4:30-8pm; July-Sept. 10am-8pm), just follow the trail from the dock (50m). The tourist office has information on hikes around the island and beach locations.

LA GUARDIA (A GUARDA)

ATSA Buses (☎ 986 61 02 55) return to Vigo (1½hr.; M-F every 30min.-1hr. 5:45am-8pm, Sa 12 per day 7am-8pm, Su 6 per day 8:30am-8pm; €4.30) or Tui from the bus stop at the corner of C. Domínguez Fontela and C. Concepcíon Arenal (45min., M-F every 30min.-1hr., 5:45am-8pm, Sa 9 per day 7am-8pm, Su 4 per day 8:30am-8pm; €2.55) Buy tickets on the bus.

A Guarda (pop. 10,000), between the mouth of the Río Miño and the Atlantic Ocean, thrives on an active fishing industry and the 500,000 tourists who annually make their way up its mountain, **█ Monte Santa Tecla.** The town itself does not have much to offer; most visitors skip it and head off to scale the majestic peaks. From the bus stop, turn right onto C. Domínguez Fontela and right again onto C. José Antonio. From C. José Antonio, bear right uphill onto C. Rosalía de Castro, which continues to the top (3.5km). Alternatively, 5min. up the road, take the steps off to the left that mark the start of a shorter, steeper pedestrian pathway through the woods (3km). The highlight of the climb is the ruins of a pre-Roman **Celtic castle,** which you will come upon three quarters of the way up the mountain. Originally occupied between 600-200 BC, it was a walled town with gates; the foundations of houses, ovens, water canals, and many dwellings of a circular shape are still apparent today. A **chapel** dedicated to Santa Tecla, the patron saint of headaches and heart disease, is near the peak of the mountain. A small archeological museum displaying Celtic objects from the excavations is near the chapel. Cured worshippers gave the wax body parts inside (hearts, heads, and feet) as gifts. (Open Mar.-Nov. daily 11am-2pm and 4-7:30pm. Free.) For a bite to eat in town there are a number of decent, albeit expensive, restaurants along the harbor next to the tourist office. A Guarda's **tourist office** is by the harbor on the left side of the crescent. (☎986 61 45 46. Open daily noon-3pm and 5-8pm.)

TÚY (TUI)

The train station (☎986 60 08 13) on Av. Concordia sends trains to Vigo (40min.; 11:08am, 10:28pm; €2.35), but it's much more convenient to travel by bus. An ATSA bus (☎986 61 02 55) from Vigo stops on C. Calvo Sotelo at Hostal Generosa and returns on the other side of the street (45min.; M-F every 30min.-1hr. 6:30am-8:45pm, Sa 9 per day 7:45am-8:45pm, Su 4 per day 9:15am-8:45pm; €2.60).

While the medieval border town of Tui (pop. 16,000), situated by the Río Miño, marks the border with Portugal, it's more notable for its *casco antiguo* and views of the Río Miño valley. The old city's centerpiece is the **cathedral,** constructed in 1120, which houses the first Gothic *portico* in Iberia and the relics of San Telmo, patron saint of fishermen. One ticket gets you into both the cathedral and the **Museo Diocesano.** Constructed in 1756, the building was originally a hospital for pilgrims and now shelters regional religious art. (Museum ☎986 60 31 07. Cathedral and museum open July-Sept. daily 11am-2pm and 4-9pm; Oct., Apr.-June 11am-2pm and 4-8pm; Nov.-Mar. 11am-1:30pm and 4-7pm. €2.)

To spend a night in Tui, head to the bright, high-ceilinged rooms at **Hostal La Generosa ❷,** P. Calvo Sotelo, 37. (☎986 60 00 55. Singles €18; doubles €25. Cash only.) ⬛**Pizzeria di Marco ❶,** C. Seijas, serves pizza and pasta (€5.20-10) on a quaint patio. (☎986 60 36 85. Open daily 1-4pm and 8pm midnight. MC/V.) **Supermercado Frolz,** on Av. Corredoira, has groceries. (Open M-Sa 9:30am-9:30pm. MC/V.) To get to the **regional tourist office** on R. Colón, continue on Po. de Calvo Stelo from the bus stop and turn right onto R. Augusto González Besada (☎986 60 17 89. Open July-Aug. M-F 10am-2pm and 5-7pm, Sa-Su 10am-2pm and 5-6:30pm; Sept.-June M-F 9:30am-1:30pm and 4:30-6:30pm, Sa 10am-2pm.) The **municipal tourist office** (☎986 60 70 27; open July-Sept.) is in Pl. de la Inmaculada. Local services include: **Banco Santander Central Hispano,** R. Augusto Gonzales Besada, 7 (open May-Sept. M-F 8:30am-2pm; Oct.-Apr. M-F 8:30am-2pm, Sa 8:30am-1pm), with a 24hr. **ATM** outside; the **police** in the *Ayuntamiento* in Pl. de la Inmaculada (☎986 60 36 77); medical Centro Salud on R. Lugo (☎986 60 18 00); **Internet** access at Info-Tui Cafe, Tr. Foxo, 1 (☎986 60 41 90, €2 per hour; open M-F 9am-midnight, Sa 10:30am-midnight); and the **post office,** R. Martínez Padín, 12 (Lista de Correos and Western Union; open M-F 8:30am-2pm, Sa 9:30am-1pm). **Postal Code:** 36700.

BAYONA (BAIONA)

ATSA buses run to Vigo (50min.; every 30min. M-F 6am-9:15pm, Sa 6:30am-9:30pm, Su 7am-10pm; €1.95).

In March 1493, Columbus returned from the New World to Bayona (pop. 10,000), a small beach town with exquisite views of the Islas Cíes, making it the first Iberian town to receive word of the Americas. The town boasts a reconstructed version of the famous globe-trotting ship, **La Caravela Pinta,** which sits in the harbor, and reenacts the landing every March. (Open daily 10am-8:30pm. €1.) The entire town is surrounded by blustery Atlantic beaches, and the golden sand is perfect for lounging. The 2km pedestrian Po. Alfonso IX loops along the shore. As you get off the bus, walk along Po. Alfonso IX to your right for 15-20min. to get to the enormous crescent-shaped stretch of sand at **Praia Ladeira.** To your left, the path leads to the shell-filled **Praia Concheira** and loops around the fortress to the rocky and quieter **Praia de los Frailes.** The path goes along the water around the 16th-century **Fortress of Monte Real,** now a *parador* which stands just above the beaches and offers a great view of the islands below.

Hospedaje Kin ❷, R. Ventura Misa, 27, is inexpensive and convenient. (☎986 35 56 95. Open *Semana Santa* and July-Aug. Singles €20; doubles €35; either with bath €50. Cash only.) Excellent seafood restaurants are on the marina front in Pl. Pedro de Castro and on the parallel street behind it, Ventura Misa. **Restaurante Refugio ❶,** is no exception. A rare economic find, the restaurant boasts a variety of salads (€2-4) and seafood dishes from €4-8. (☎986 35 52 39. Open daily noon-4pm and 8pm-12:30am.) For **Internet** access, head to **Euris Cyber Cafe.** (☎986 35 54 63. €1.50 per 30min. Open daily 10:30am-2:30pm and 5:30-9:30pm.) The **tourist office** provides maps and walking routes. Once off the bus, with your back to the water, head right on Po. Alfonso IX until the road bends; it's in a small glass building. (☎986 68 70 67; www.baiona.org. Open daily Nov.-Mar. 10am-2pm and 3-7pm; Apr.-June and Sept.-Oct. 10am-2pm and 4-8pm; July-Aug. 10am-3pm and 4-9pm.)

RIBADAVIA

The train station is on R. Estación (☎988 47 03 08). Trains run to Ribadavia from Vigo (4 per day 6:40am-10:20pm). Trains to Vigo (1hr., 4 per day 6am-8:43pm, €5.65). The bus station is on R. San Francisco (☎988 21 32 40). Buses from Vigo to Ribadavia (M-F 5 per day 8:30am-7pm, Sa-Su 4 per day 8:30am-6:30pm). Buses to Vigo leave from the bus stop just across the bridge, Ponte de San Francisco, in front of "Auto Industrial" (M-F 7per day 9:30am-9pm, Sa 9:30, 11:30am, 1:14pm, Su 9:10am, 1:45pm; €6.85).

Ribadavia (pop. 5700) is most famous for its remarkable Jewish history, exquisite wines, and international theater festival in mid-July. During the 11th century, the town's Jewish population blossomed, only to disperse and flee to Portugal during the 15th-century Inquisition. The old synagogue stood in Pl. de la Magdalena; the beautiful Iglesia de Sta. María Magdalena now sits in its place at the intersection of C. Puerta Nueva de Arriba and C. Puerta Nueva de Abajo. The **Jewish Information Center of Galicia** is located above the tourist office in Pr. Maior and houses a fascinating **museum** outlining the history of the Jewish population of the area. (Museum open July-Sept. M-Sa 10:30am-2:30pm and 5:30-7:30pm, Su 11am-2:30pm; Oct.-June M-Sa 10am-2pm and 4:30-7pm, Su 11am-2:30pm.) The tourist office provides information about guided tours and hikes. Other highlights of historic Ribadavia include the 15th-century **castillo,** immediately above Pr. Maior, which has an auditorium for theater and music performances in the summer.

To spend the night, seek out **Hostal Plaza ❷,** Pr. Maior, 15. Rooms have fans, TV, phone, and bath, and most face the square. (☎988 47 05 76. Ground fl. restaurant. Singles €25; doubles €35; triples €45. Cash only.) For groceries, head to **Supermercado Froiz,** R. Progreso, near the old quarter opposite Sergy's Hair Design. (Open M-Sa 9am-2:30pm and 4:30-9pm. MC/V.) For a more substantial meal, head to **Latino Restaurante ❷,** C. García Penedo, 5, which also has a bar downstairs. (☎988 47 22 37. *Menú de la casa* €8. Open daily 1-5pm and 9pm-midnight.) The **tourist office** is on Pr. Maior, 7. (☎988 47 12 75; www.ribadavia.com. Open July-Sept. M-Sa 10am-3pm and 5-8pm, Su 10:30am-3pm; Oct.-June M-Sa 9:30am-2:30pm and 4-7pm, Su 10:30am-3pm.) Local services include: **Banco Santander Central Hispano** on the corner of R. Progreso and R. Salgado Moscoso (☎902 24 24 24; open May-Sept. M-F 8:30am-2pm; Oct.-Apr. M-F 8:30am-2pm, Sa 8:30am-1pm), with a 24hr. **ATM** outside; the **police,** on R. Redondela (☎ 650 45 00 70); a **pharmacy,** García Carrera, on R. Progreso (☎ 988 47 00 77; open in summer 9am-1:30pm and 4-8pm, in winter 9am-1:30pm and 4-7:30pm); and the **post office,** next to the police station on R. Redondela (open M-F 9:30am-2:30pm, Sa 9:30am-1pm). **Postal Code:** 32400.

CANGAS

Ferries run between Vigo's Estación Marítimo and Cangas approximately every 30min. (20min., daily 6:30am-10:30pm, round-trip €3.90.) Cangas also sends ferries to Islas Cíes and back. Departs Cangas (July-Sept. 10:15am, 12:15, 4:15, and 6:15pm; returns 1:15, 5:15, and 7:15pm; round-trip €17.50) Check station for confirmation, as frequency of ferries depends on weather.

Cangas is a quiet coastal town with an uncrowded beach and a charming *casco antiguo.* The town is speckled with churches, statues, crosses, and *gallego* architecture, of which the quaint *casa marinera,* **"Casa de Patín,"** in the old city, is a perfect example. The **Paseo Marítimo** is a pleasant stroll along the coast of Cangas, beginning at the port and ending in the golden-sand beach, **Praia de Rodeira.** During July and August, open air-markets and many small festivals fill the streets. If you wish to spend the night, **Camping Limens ❶,** Praia de Limens, is a good option. (☎ 986 30 46 45; administracion@campinglimens.com. Electricity €3.74. €5.09 per person, €5.09 per tent.) For a bed, seek out the **Hostal Belén ❹,** C. Antonio Nores, 12. (☎ 986 30 00 15. July-Aug. all rooms €40. Sept.-June €30.) Inquire at the **tourist office,** on the port with the bus station and Estación Marítima (M-F 10am-2pm and 4:30-8:30pm) about current festivals. The tourist office also offers free guided tours (M-F 11am) through the *casco antiguo.* Local services include: **Banco Santander Central Hispano,** across the street from the bus/ferry stations (☎ 986 30 07 36; M-F 8:30am-2pm, Sa 8:30am-1pm); **police,** Av. da Castelao, s/n (☎ 986 30 30 31); **youth information center,** C. Real, with **Internet** access (☎ 986 39 21 71); **women's information center,** R. Andalucía, 3, in the Xoia building (☎ 986 39 22 68).

PONTEVEDRA ☎ 986

According to legend, Pontevedra (pop. 80,000) was founded by the Greek archer Teucro as a place to convalesce after his Trojan War exploits. Greek origins notwithstanding, Pontevedra is a typical Galician city. The old city—filled with palm trees, flowering balconies, stately cathedrals, and squares lined with traditional arcaded *gallego* buildings—is calm and inviting. At night, the plazas and countless outdoor cafes fill with people enjoying wine and tapas. There isn't too much to see in Pontevedra itself, but it makes a good base for exploring nearby beach towns.

▐ TRANSPORTATION

Trains: R. de Estación (☎ 902 24 02 02), a 20min. walk southeast of the old city. Info open daily 7:30am-10pm. To: **A Coruña** (2-3hr.; M-F 15 per day 6:22am-9:18pm, Sa-Su 12 per day 6:22am-9:18pm; €11.10) via **Santiago** (1-1½hr., €5.05); **Madrid** (11hr.; M-F and Su 12:35, 9:30pm, Sa 8:45am, 9:30pm; €45); **Vigo** (20-35min.; M-F 20 per day 7:30am-10:57pm, Sa-Su 13-14 per day Sa 7:52am-10:57pm, Su 8:54am-10:57pm; €2.60).

Buses: Av. Alféreces Provisionales (☎ 986 85 24 08). Info open daily 8am-10pm. To: **A Coruña** (2½hr.; M-F 9 per day 6:45am-9pm, Sa 8 per day 9am-9pm, Su 7 per day 9am-9pm; €11.35); **Cambados** (1hr.; M-F 10 per day 8:15am-8:35pm, Sa 4 per day 9:30am-8:35pm, Su 3 per day 12:15-8:35pm; €2.60); **El Grove/La Toja** (1hr.; M-F every 30min. 7:45am-10pm, Sa-Su 11 per day 9:30am-10pm; €3.60) via either **La Lanzada** or **Villalonga,** check schedule; **Madrid** (8hr., 6-7 per day 9am-11pm, €31-39); **Santiago** (1hr.; M-F every 1hr.-1½hr. 6:45am-9pm, Sa 11 per day 8am-8pm, Su 9 per day 9am-9pm; €5); **Vigo** (1hr.; M-F every 20min.-1hr. 7am-10:50pm, Sa 16 per day 9:30am-10pm, Su 14 per day 10:50am-10pm; €2.40).

Taxis: Radio Taxi (☎986 86 85 85). 24hr. From the stations to town €3-4.

Car Rental: Avis, R. da Peregrina, 49 (☎986 85 20 25). 23+, must have had license for 1 year. From €60 per day for 350km. Ages 23-25 add €12 per day for insurance. Discounts for longer rentals. Open M-F 9am-1:15pm and 4-7pm, Sa 9am-12:45pm.

✦🛈 ORIENTATION AND PRACTICAL INFORMATION

Six streets branch out from **Praza da Peregrina,** the main plaza connecting the new city and the casco antiguo. The main streets are **R. Oliva, R. Michelena, R. Benito Corbal,** and **R. da Peregrina.** Pr. de Galicia is a 5min. walk from Pr. da Peregrina; from Pr. da Peregrina, head down R. da Peregrina and veer right at the first fork on R. Andrés Muruais. **Pr. de España** is a five minute walk up R. Michelena from the Pr. da Peregrina. The train and bus stations, located across from each other, are about 1km from Pr. da Peregrina. From the train station, walk straight out of the station to the rotary and continue straight onto **C. Calvo Soleto.** From the bus station, turn left out of the station onto C. Calvo Soleto. Follow the road straight to the intersection and continue straight through the rotary onto Av. de Vigo, which will become R. da Peregrina. Stay on this road until the Pr. da Peregrina—you will see a church on your right when you have reached the plaza.

Tourist Office: R. General Gutiérrez Mellado, 1 (☎986 85 08 14). From Pr. da Peregrina, get on R. Michelena and take the 1st left onto R. General Gutiérrez Mellado. English spoken. Open July-Aug. M-F 10am-2pm and 4-6pm, Sa 10am-12:30pm; Sept.-June M-Sa 10am-2pm and 4:30-7:30pm, Su 10am-2pm. **Branch** in a wooden hut on Pr. de España. Open May-Nov. 10am-1:30pm and 4:30-7:30pm, more hours in July and Aug.

Currency Exchange: Banco Santander Central Hispano, R. Michelena, 26. (☎986 85 61 50). Open M-F 8:30am-2pm, Oct.-March also Sa 8:30am-1pm. 24hr. **ATM** outside.

Luggage storage: At the **bus station,** on the top floor across from information Lockers €2 per day.

Police: C. Ingeneiro Rafael Aresas s/n, under the *pazo cultura* (☎986 83 30 80).

Pharmacy: Farmacia C. Carballo, R. Oliva, 30 (☎986 85 13 69). Open daily 9:30am-10pm.

Hospital: Ambulatorio, Rúa de Maestranza (☎986 85 27 99). Emergencies ☎061.

Internet Access: Doble Clik, C. Virgen del Camino, 21 (☎986 86 63 85), just off R. da Peregrina, €2 per hour. Open daily 10am-midnight.

Post Office: R. Oliva, 19 (☎986 85 16 77). **Lista de Correos, fax,** and **Western Union** services available. Open M-F 8:30am-8:30pm, Sa 9:30am-2pm. **Postal Code: 36001.**

🏠 ACCOMMODATIONS

The most reasonably priced accommodations are in the *casco antiguo.* Reservations are necessary in August, when Spaniards head to coastal towns and cities.

Casa Maruja, Av. de Santa María, 12 (☎986 85 49 01). From Pr. da Peregrina, walk up R. Michelena through Pr. de España and turn right onto R. Mestre Mateo. Most rooms in this very friendly family-run *pensión* have pleasant views of the old city. Rooms are sparsely decorated, but spacious. Private bath and TV. June-Sept. 15 singles €25; doubles €38. Sept. 16-May €20/30. MC/V. ❷

Pensión Santa Clara, R. de Santa Clara, 31, 1st fl. (☎986 84 68 20). A few blocks away from the Pr. da Peregrina, this *pensión* has friendly management and plain, comfortable rooms with TVs. Shared bathroom. June-Aug. singles €20; doubles €30. Sept.-May €18/25. ❷

⬛ FOOD

Pontevedra prides itself on seafood. Tiny bars crowd the streets around Pr. da Peregrina. C. Figueroa, Pr. da Leña, Pr. de Verdura and C. San Sebastián harbor some of the most popular *marisquerías* and tapas bars. For groceries, try **Gadis Supermercado**, Av. de Vigo, 8. (Open M-Sa 9:30am-3pm and 5-9:30pm. MC/V.)

Bodegón Micota, R. da Peregrina, 4 (☎986 85 59 17). This basement *bodega* serves Spanish renditions of global classics like fajitas (€9-10), *kebaps* (€9.50-15), omelettes (€7.50-9), and fondue (€13-15.50). The tables are filled with locals and the walls are decorated in true bodega fashion with wine bottles. Open daily noon-4:30pm and 7:30pm-midnight. MC/V. ❸

La Algueria Mudéjar, C. Churruchaos, 2 (☎986 84 12 58). On the other side of the *Ayuntamiento* from Pr. de España. Rowdy Spanish tapas bar meets the Middle East. Extensive wine selection. Entrees €8-11+. Glass of wine €1-2.80. Open daily 1:30-4pm and 8:30pm-midnight. MC/V. ❸

A Casa do Lado, Pr. da Leña, 3 (☎986 86 02 25). Directly across from the Museo de Pontevedra in the pleasant and secluded Pr. da Leña, this tapas joint keeps the customers happy with new spins on typical spanish cuisine. Creative *croquetas* (€5-8). Open M-Th 1:30-4pm and 8-11:30pm, F-Sa 1:30-4pm and 8pm-midnight. MC/V. ❷

El Alcázar, C. Peregrina, 16 (☎886 21 48 12). An inexpensive eatery with hearty portions. Friendly, informal atmosphere. *Menú del día* €7.50, entrees €5-11. MC/V. ❷

⬛ SIGHTS

Pontevedra's primary sight is the extensive **⬛Museo de Pontevedra**, R. Pasantería, 10. From Pr. da Peregrina, walk up Po. de Antonio Odriozola, which runs between the gardens and Pr. da Ferrería. Bear left at the fork; this road eventually curves into R. Pasantería and leads to the museum right on the Pr. da Leña. The *museo* occupies exhibits religious sculptures in a crypt-like basement, models of a traditional Galician kitchen and ship interior, and contemporary art. One of the houses is devoted to pre-historical artifacts from Spain's ancient inhabitants, including the Romans, Iberians, Visigoths and Castros. (☎986 85 14 55. Open June-Sept. Tu-Sa 10am-2:15pm and 5-8:45pm, Su 11am-2pm; Oct.-May Tu-Sa 10am-1:30pm and 4:30-8pm, Su 11am-2pm. Free.) The moss-covered 13th-century Gothic **Ruinas do Convento de Santo Domingos** are in Pr. de España. (Open July-Aug. Tu-Sa 10am-2pm and 5-8:30pm. Free.) The **Basílica de Santa María a Maior**, Av. de Santa María, 24, features a 16th-century door that depicts versions of Mary. From Pr. de España take Av. de Santa María, 24, downhill to the left of the *Ayuntamiento*. (☎986 86 61 85. Open daily 10am-1pm and 5-9pm.)

⬛⬛ NIGHTLIFE AND ENTERTAINMENT

Sunny days bring a crowd to the white-sand **beaches** in the coves of nearby Marín. **Monbus** buses make the journey from the outer corner of Pr. de Galicia on Av. Augusto García Sánchez (30min., every 15min., €1.90). Buses leaving from the bus station to Cangas also stop in Marín (M-F 7:35am and hourly 9:15am-9:30pm, Sa 11 per day 9:15am-9:30pm, Su 9 per day 10:10am-9:30pm; €1.90). From the bus stop in Marín, facing the water, head left on C. Angusto Miranda around the military school and up the hill. To reach both beaches, turn right on C. Tiro Naval Janer, continue for 15min., and exit right at the turn-off. The first beach is **Playa Porticelo**; another 10min. on the same path brings you to the larger **Playa Mogor**.

GALICIA

At night, you'll find bar after pub after *taparía* on the triangle of streets made by R. Princesa, R. Paio Gómez Charino, and R. Tetuán. Pr. de Vendura also hosts a crowd of pleasant terraced bars. A local crowd chows on late night tapas and drinks at the popular **Café Universo,** in the neighboring Pr. Méndez Núñez, 1. (☎986 86 59 53). The many candles flickering at the chic **Pub Liceus,** C. Manuel Quiroga, 20, make for an intimate evening. (Beer €3, drinks €4.50. Open F-Sa 11pm-3am.) The festival of Santiaguiño del Burgo (July 25) is marked by religious processions throughout Pontevedra, and La Peregrina (the second week of August, peaking on Su) brings films, concerts, loads of honey, and bullfights to the city.

◪ DAYTRIPS FROM PONTEVEDRA

Buses run frequently to all nearby towns. The towns can also be reached easily from Santiago de Compostela.

◩ CAMBADOS

26km from Pontevedra. Plus Ultra buses run from Pontevedra to the bus station in Cambados near Pr. Concello (1hr.; M-F 10 per day 8:15am-8:35pm, Sa 4 per day 9:30am-8:35pm, Su 3 per day 12:15-8:35pm; €2.60). The return schedule is posted on bus station window.

Visitors to harborside Cambados (pop. 15,000) will enjoy the views of sweeping vineyards, orchards, and a glass of renowned *albariño* wine accompanying a platter of fresh shellfish. Begin at the **Palacio de Fefiñanes,** a 16th-century palace-turned-*bodega* that brims with giant, sweet-smelling barrels of *albariño*. Although the majority of the palace is closed due to reconstruction, you can still tour the bodega and sample some of the vineyard's wine (€3). With your back to the tourist office, turn left and head for the park to your right. At the end of the park, bear right onto C. Príncipe. At the plaza bear right onto R. Real, which will bring you to the Pl. de Fefiñanes and the *palacio*. (☎986 54 22 04. Open for visits Apr.-Oct. Tu-Su 10am-2pm and 4-8pm.) To reach the river, walk straight down Po. os Olmos (on the right facing the museum gate), cross the main street, and continue walking until you hit the water and see the **Torre de San Sadorniño.** The remains of this 12th-century fortification stand on a seemingly dissolving island connected to the mainland by a tiny bridge. The **Museo Etnográfico do Vino** on Avenida da Pastora, 104, is the first wine museum in Galicia. (☎986 52 61 19. Open Tu-Su 10:30am-2pm and 5-8pm.) From the tourist office, walk straight up Av. de Villarino and then take your first right onto R. San Francisco. Stay straight onto Av. da Pastora, which will bring you to the museum. Directly behind the museum in a graveyard stand the 15th-century **Ruinas de Santa Marina**.

The first weekend in August brings in famous poets and politicians for the town's well-known **wine festival.** The culinary specialities, including shellfish and cheese, are just an excuse to keep sampling the *albariño*, whose vines peek out from backyard fences and porch rooftops throughout Cambados. Most of the celebrations take place on Paseo de la Calzada, with additional feasts in the courtyard behind the Fefiñanes *bodega*. To feast otherwise, try **Raxeria Martinez Mariscos ❷**, at C. Real, 16, which serves traditional Galician fare and delicious seafood and salad options for those who have overdosed on tentacles. Be sure to try some of the local wine. (☎676 33 01 34. *Menú* €8. Open daily 11am-noon. AmEx/MC/V.) **Moldes Supermercado,** Pr. Ramon Cabanillas, will meet your grocery needs. (Open M-Sa 9:30am-2pm and 5-9:30pm.)

Visitors may find it helpful to start at the **tourist office.** With your back to the bus station and the water, walk left. The office, a small, glass building, will be on the left. Inquire here about *La Ruta del Vino*. (☎986 52 07 86. Open July-Sept. M-F

10am-2pm and 4:30-8pm, Sa-Su from 10:30am; Oct.-June M-F 10am-2pm and 4:30-7:30pm, Sa-Su from 10:30am.) Three **ATMs** are across the street from the tourist office. The **police** can be reached at ☎986 52 40 92.

EL GROVE (O GROVE) AND LA TOJA (A TOXA)

Monbus (☎902 15 87 78) runs buses from Pontevedra to O Grove (1½hr.; M-F every 30min.-1hr. 7:45am-10pm, Sa-Su 9-11 per day 9:30am-10pm; €3.60); an equal number return (20-22 per day 6:30am-8pm). Buses also run from Santiago (€6) via Cambados (M-F 4 per day 7:30am-6pm, Sa-Su 8:45am, 6pm; €2.05). Schedules are posted in the O Grove bus station (☎986 680 411).

The self-pro-claimed "Paraíso de Marisco" (Shellfish Paradise), O Grove, a tranquil fishing wharf west of Pontevedra, offers access to pleasant hiking trails and secluded white sand beaches. The island of A Toxa, O Grove's fancy neighbor across the bridge, is dotted with elegant summer homes, a country club, a golf course, and a casino, and it is watched over by a series of flags and security guards. Besides being noted worldwide for its soap production (made from native salts in the spas), A Toxa is a popular destination for couples looking to tie the knot. A fish auction is held in O Grove weekdays from 5-6:30pm in the Lonja building, directly behind the **mercado** (next to the tourist office). The market itself sells fresh fish, fine cheeses, organic breads, and honey (open M-Sa 9am-2pm). Fridays also provide a chance to peruse clothing, local food, and crafts at the waterside **moving market** (9am-2pm)—like a traveling circus, the market moves from town to town each day of the week. The town's popular **seafood festival** during the first two weeks of October draws flocks of visitors. For a night's rest in O Grove, look on C. Castelao or Av. Teniente Domínguez, but most accommodations are expensive (€30-40 per night). The **tourist office,** Pl. de Corgo, 1, has information on boat rides and beaches. (☎986 73 14 15. June-July 15 10am-2pm and 4-7pm; July 16-Oct. 10am-8pm; Nov.-Dec. 10am-2pm and 4-7pm.)

LA LANZADA (A LANZADA)

Buses run frequently between Pontevedra and O Grove (1hr.; M-F every 30min. 7:45am-10pm, Sa-Su 9-11 per day 9:30am-10pm; €3.60) via either A Lanzada (45min-1hr., €2.90) or Villalonga—check schedule for bus information for A Lanzada.

A Lanzada, between Pontevedra and O Grove, is best known for its magnificent beaches. Unlike many other beach towns in coastal Spain, however, the backdrop to the sands isn't high-rises and shlocky beach stalls, but beautiful government-protected sand dunes. The bus drops off across the street from Playa de La Lanzada, and there is really no reason to walk much further. Pl. de La Lanzada is a massive stretch of soft sand sheltered by cliffs and dunes. (Lifeguards are on duty daily July-Sept. 11am-8pm.) Weekends throughout the summer are quite crowded, but on weekdays, the massive beach is relatively empty. If you walk left for 1km (facing the water) along the highway by the beach, you will arrive at Capilla de La Lanzada, a Roman chapel that offers spectacular views of the beach and sea. Continue walking, and you will find many more beautiful, less crowded beaches. The only **cafe** on the beach serves up cheap sandwiches, tapas and drinks. (Open daily July-Sept. 10am-9pm.) The bus route from La Lanzada to Pontevedra is lined with beaches, most of which are public; look out the window as you travel, and ask to stop when you see a beach you like. Beware of the undertow, which locals report is stronger than usual. The last Sunday of August brings **Nueve Olas,** a festival of fertility; people gather by the beach for food, drink, bonfires, and festivity.

RÍAS ALTAS

If you're one to fall asleep during train rides, be sure to stay awake during the trek through the breathtaking valleys and magical pine forests of Rías Altas. Thick fogs and misty mornings have kept the Rías Altas secret from most visitors. With the exception of A Coruña, the area's busy capital, the Rías Altas seem to have been nearly forgotten by tourism, and that's the very reason to visit: residents of the tiniest of coastal towns heartily welcome travelers, and visitors who make it here have miles of green estuaries and secluded beaches all to themselves.

LA CORUÑA (A CORUÑA)   ☎981

Unlike most of its Galician neighbors, A Coruña (pop. 260,000) is a big city, complete with high-rises, expressways, and urban sprawl. At the same time, A Coruña maintains natural beauty and quirky charm. The center is a maze of narrow alleys that teem with raucous bars and popular *marisquerías* (seafood restaurants). The miles of harborside walks echo with Galician legend and lore: Greek hero Hercules supposedly built the lighthouse, and the city's nickname, the Crystal City, refers to the blinding sunset reflected on rows of tightly packed windows. As any proud *coruñese* will tell you, Santiago might be the northwest's most popular city, but A Coruña is the real Galicia.

▉ TRANSPORTATION

Flights: Aeropuerto de Alvedro (☎981 18 72 00), 8km south of the city. Served by **Air Europa** (☎981 18 73 08), **ERA** (☎981 18 72 86), **Spanair** (☎902 13 14 15), and **Iberia** (☎981 18 72 54). Daily flights to **Madrid, Lisboa,** and **Paris** via **Barcelona** and **London.** Bus from the airport to the bus station is run by **ASICASA** (☎981 231 234) from 6:45am-10:45pm.

Trains: Estación San Cristóbal, Av. Joaquín Planells Ríera s/n (☎902 24 02 02). Info open daily 7am-10:30pm. **RENFE** To: **Barcelona** (15-16hr.; daily 6pm; M, Th-F, Su also 7:05am; €49-64); **Madrid** (8½-11hr.; daily 9:30pm, M-F and Su also 12:45pm, Sa also 9am; €45); **Santiago** (1hr.; M-F 20 per day 6:10am-9:52pm, Sa-Su 16 per day, Sa 6:20am-9:30pm, Su 6:20am-9:52pm; €3-13); **Vigo** (2hr.; M-F 15 per day 6:10am-7:50pm, Sa-Su 12 per day 6:20am-7:50pm; €9-12) via **Pontevedra** (€8-11).

Buses: C. Caballeros (☎981 23 96 44).

ALSA/Enatcar (☎902 42 22 42) to: **Madrid** (8½hr.; M-Sa 5-6 per day 7am-10:30pm, Su 6 per day 10am-10:30pm; €37-55); **Oviedo** (4½-6¾hr., 4-5 per day 9am-7pm, €20-31); **San Sebastián** (14hr., 2-3 per day 9:30am-7pm, €49-62) via **Santander** (10hr., €34-48).

Castromil (☎981 23 57 59) to: **Santiago** (50-90min.; M-F every 30min. 6:30am-10:20pm, Sa every hr 6:30am-10:20pm, Su 6:30am and hourly 10am-10pm; €6.35) and **Vigo** (2-2½hr.; M-F 9 per day 8am-8:15pm, Sa 8 per day 8am-8:15pm, Su 6 per day 11am-8:15pm; €13.50) via **Pontevedra** (1½-2hr., €11.35).

IASA-Arriva (☎981 18 43 35) to: **Betanzos** (40min.; M-F every 30min. 6:30am-10:30pm, Sa-Su hourly 6:30am-10:30pm; €2.50); **El Ferrol** (45min.; M-F hourly 7:30am-9:30pm, Sa 6 per day 8:30am-8:30pm, Su 8 per day 10:30am-8:30pm; €3.10); **Ribadeo** (4hr.; M-F 8 per day 8am-4pm, Sa 5 per day 8am-4pm, Su 3 per day 8am-2:30pm; €12.90); **Viveiro** (3½hr.; M-Sa 6-7 per day 6:30am-7pm, Su 4 per day 11:30am-7pm; €12.70) via **Betanzos.**

Public Transportation: Red **Compañía de Tranvías de La Coruña** buses (☎981 25 01 00) run frequently (6:15am-midnight, €0.85). Buy tickets on board. The night bus, **Buho,** runs F-Sa hourly 12:30am-4:30am.

Taxis: Radio Taxi (☎981 24 33 33) and **TeleTaxi** (☎981 28 77 77). Both 24hr. Train and bus stations to the *ciudad vieja* €5.

A Coruña

ACCOMMODATIONS
Pensión La Alianza, 6
Pensión Las Rías, 12
Pensión Roma, 11

FOOD
Créperie Petite Bretagne, 10
La Bottega, 8
La Casa de las Tortillas, 2
Otros Tiempos, 7

NIGHTLIFE
Kántaro, 4
Lavtrec, 1
Ocaciraehe, 5
Rochester, 9
Sol Pirámide, 13
Xxele, 3

Car Rental: Autos Brea, Av. Fernández Latorre, 110 (☎981 23 86 45). 21+, must have had license for 1 year. From €60 per day with unlimited mileage. Open M-F 9am-1pm and 4-7pm, Sa 9am-2pm.

✈ 🛈 ORIENTATION AND PRACTICAL INFORMATION

A Coruña sits on a narrow peninsula between the Atlantic Ocean and the Ría de A Coruña. The new city stretches across the mainland; the peninsula encompasses the *ciudad vieja* (old city). Beaches are on the Atlantic side and the harbor is on the river. **Avenida de la Marina** runs along the harbor and leads past the obelisk and the tourist office to **Puerta Real,** the entry into **Plaza de María Pita** and the *ciudad vieja*. From the bus station, take bus #1 or 1a to the **tourist office** at the Puerta Real stop. To get buses from the train station to the *ciudad vieja*, exit from the main entrance of the train station on Pr. San Cristóbal, cross the plaza, and walk right on R. de Outeiro. At the rotary, turn left onto R. Estaciones and follow the pedestrian paths over the highway. The bus station and stop for buses #1 and 1a are across the parking lot from the pedestrian stairs. Bus #14 connects the center with the monuments along **Paseo Marítimo.**

Tourist Office: Regional Office, Av. de la Marina (☎981 22 18 22; www.turgalicia.es). English spoken. Info on regional travel and daytrips from A Coruña. Open M-F 10am-2pm and 4-7pm, Sa 11am-2pm and 5-7pm, Su 11am-2pm. **Turismo A Coruña** (☎981 18 43 43; www.turismocoruna.com), in a glass building in a corner of Pl. María Pita. Open M-F 9am-8:30pm, Sa 10am-2pm and 4-8pm, Su 10am-2pm.

Currency Exchange: There are many banks throughout the city. **Banco Santander Central Hispano,** C. Cantón Grande, 4 (☎981 18 88 44), next to Banco Popular. Open M-F 8:30am-2pm; Oct.-Mar Sa 8:30am-1pm. There is another **Banco Santander Central Hispano** on C. San Andres, by the Fuente de Santa Catalina, next to Hostal Las Rías.

English Book Store: Librería Universal, Galerias Centro Real, 86-1a (☎981 22 96 45). In a small shopping center right off the C. Real, it's the only all-English book store in town. Open Sept.-June M-F 10am-1:30pm and 5-8pm, Sa 10am-1:30pm; July-Aug. M-F 10am-1:30pm. MC/V.

Laundromat: Surf, C. Hospital San Roque, 35 (☎987 20 44 20). Wash and dry up to 6kg for €10. Open M-F 9:30am-1:30pm and 4:30-8pm.

Police: Municipal, C. Miguel Servet (☎981 18 42 25).

24hr. Pharmacy: C. del Torre, 54 (☎981 20 38 42).

Medical Services: Ambulatorio San José, C. Comandante Fontanes, 8 (☎981 22 60 74).

Internet Access: One of the cheaper cafes is **Cyber,** C. Zalaeta, 13 (☎981 20 38 41). Speedy connections. €0.80 per 30min., €1.30 per hour. Open daily 10am-midnight.

Post Office: C. Alcalde Manuel Casas (☎981 22 51 75). **Lista de Correos** and **fax** service. Open M-F 8:30am-8:30pm, Sa 9:30am-2pm. **Postal Code:** 15001.

◪ ACCOMMODATIONS

Most accommodations are near the *ciudad vieja,* on C. Riego de Agua and R. Nueva. Reservations are necessary during August due to the month-long festival.

▨ Pensión Roma, R. Nueva, 3 (☎981 22 80 75). Spotless, sunny rooms with TV, phone, and bath. Very clean and comfortable. Large kitchen and dining room. 24hr. reception. Internet access. Rooms rarely available from Sept.-June—they are rented out by local students. July singles €26; doubles €42; triples €62. Aug. €36/52/74. MC/V. ❸

Pensión Las Rías, C. San Andrés, 141, 2nd fl. (☎/fax 981 22 68 79). With private bath, TV, and phone, these spacious rooms come at a bargain. The friendly owner is happy to help. July-Aug. singles €27; doubles €43. Sept.-June €20/32. Cash only. ❸

Pensión la Alianza, C. Riego de Agua, 8, 1st fl. (☎981 22 81 14), next to Pl. María Pita. An eclectic assortment of paintings cover the hallways and smallish rooms of this old-fashioned but charming *residencia.* Staff is very friendly. Be sure to request a room with a window. Singles €18; doubles €30. MC/V. ❷

◪ FOOD

The streets around C. Estrella, C. de la Franja, and C. la Galera teem with cheap seafood restaurants and cafes. The area around Av. Rubine off Playa de Riazor is fancier. If you're looking for something cheaper, Pl. María Pita is full of inexpensive tapas bars with glass-enclosed outdoor terraces. The **Mercado San Agustín** is in the oval building on Pr. San Agustín, near the old town. (Open M-Sa 8am-3pm.) For groceries, stop by **Supermercado Gadis,** just off C. del Orzán. (Open daily M-Sa 9am-4:30pm and 5:30-10pm.)

▨ La Bottega, C. Olmos, 25 (☎981 91 46 76). An intimate interior with walls covered by sea-themed paintings. Wide variety of crepes (€6-9), salads (€5-8), creative omelettes, and delicious meat and fish dishes. Non-smoking section. Most dishes are well under €10. Open M-Th 1:30-4:15pm and 8pm-12:15am, F-Sa until 12:45am. AmEx/MC/V. ❷

▨ La Casa de las Tortillas, C. del Orzán, 5 (☎981 22 67 18). A cross between a cave and odd clock shop, the friendly La Casa offers sangria (€10) and dozens of creative varieties of *tortilla española* (€5-9). Open M and W-Su 8:30pm-12:30am. MC/V. ❸

Otros Tiempos—Cervecería-Jamonería, C. la Galera, 54 (☎981 22 93 98). While funky music plays in the background and the lively local crowd chats it up, fill up on hearty *raciones* (€3-11), sandwiches (€2.60-4.50), and empanadas (€4-6). Wide selection of beer €2-3. Open M-Tu and Th-Su noon-4pm, 8pm-midnight. MC/V. ❶

Créperie Petite Bretagne, C. Riego de Agua, 13-15 (☎981 22 48 71). A romantic restaurant right off the Pl. de María Pita serving crepes, stuffed with everything from mozzarella and sausage to decadent chocolate (€5-9). Open daily 1:30-4:30pm and 8:30pm-12:30am. MC/V. ❶

SIGHTS

A Coruña lacks many of the historic monuments dotting other towns, but it has phenomenal attractions along Po. Marítimo. To visit them all in one day, start from Playa del Orzán and follow waterside Po. Marítimo to the major museums and Torre de Hércules. The route begins at the start of Po. Marítimo, near Puerta Real, and ends at Pl. del Orzán. (Trolleys daily every 30min. noon-9pm; €1. A €12 *bono* ticket allows same-day admission to all 3 museums; details at www.casaciencias.org.)

▓ TORRE DE HÉRCULES. A Coruña's major landmark, the Torre de Hércules stands on a hill overlooking the city, looming over rusted ships at the peninsula's end. The tower dates from the 2nd century BC, but was renovated in Neoclassical style in 1790. Legend has it that Hercules erected the tower, the world's oldest working lighthouse, over the remains of his defeated enemy, Geryon. After taking a look at the tower's ancient foundations in the basement of the lighthouse, climb the 234 steps to the top of the tower for stunning views of the city and bay. A sculpture park, Hercules's Garden, surrounds the Tower. *(Av. de Navarra, s/n. On Po. Marítimo, a 20min. walk from Puerta Real (or a 5min. trolley ride). From C. Millán Astray, turn left onto C. Orillamar, which turns into Av. de Navarra and brings you to the tower. ☎ 981 22 37 30. Open daily July-Aug. 10am-9:45pm; Sept.-June 10am-6:45pm. €2, children and seniors €1.)*

▓ MUSEO DE BELAS ARTES. This superb museum displays classic Spanish, French, Italian, and Flemish art from the Renaissance to the 20th century. Its magnificent new building, lit by a skylight and stone-set windows, is a renovated convent. Includes works by Murilla, Sorolla, Rubens, and Tintoretto, sketches by Goya (an entire room is devoted to his works), and a Picasso. It also houses the work of *gallego* artists. *(Rua Zalaeta. ☎ 981 22 37 23. Open Tu-F 10am-8pm, Sa 10am-2pm and 4:30-8pm, Su 10am-2pm. Free.)*

▓ AQUARIUM FINISTERRAE. Also known as the Casa de los Peces, this aquarium is A Coruña's magnificent homage to the sea. Over 200 species of local marine life are displayed in vast tanks, while the downstairs room features interactive exhibits on marine ecosystems from all over the world. Don't miss Nautilus, an enormous, eerie aquarium in the basement that recreates Jules Verne's adventure in *20,000 Leagues Under the Sea*. *(On Po. Marítimo at the bottom of the hill from the Torre de Hércules. Bus #14 from the Puerta Real. ☎ 981 18 98 42. Open July-Aug. daily 10am-9pm; Sept.-June M-F 10am-7pm, Sa-Su 10am-8pm. €10, children, seniors and holders of Carnet Joven or ISIC cards €4.)*

MUSEO DOMUS. The Domus, also called the Casa del Hombre (House of Man), is a natural history and science museum in one, with interactive exhibits on human cultures and anatomy. Watch "blood" spurt from a model heart, hear "Hello, I love you" in over 30 languages, and spend hours playing with microscopes and other gizmos. Exhibits are in Spanish, but many, like the ▓**childbirth video,** need no translation. *(C. Santa Teresa, 1, on Po. Marítimo between aquarium and Playa Orzán. ☎ 981 18 98 40. Open daily July-Aug. 11am-9pm; Sept.-June 10am-7pm. €2, children, seniors and holders of either Carnet Joven or ISIC cards €1. IMAX €1.20; check at ticket booth for schedule.)*

CASA DE LAS CIENCIAS. Located in the beautiful Parque de Santa Margarita, the kid-friendly Casa de las Ciencias is designed for hands-on learning about physics, geology, and the environment. Fun models prompt visitors to ponder the rules of the natural world. The planetarium plays videos with music, images, and of course, the stars. There are also several exhibits about the environment and natural world, including a chicken hatchery and insect-holding geospheres—look out for the *cucaraches* (cockroaches). The four-story building features a giant Foucault's pendulum and a planetarium. *(Parque Santa Margarita. ☎ 981 18 98 44; www.casaciencias.org.*

Open daily July-Aug. 11am-9pm; Sept.-June 10am-7pm. Casa €2, children and seniors €1. Planetarium €1. Check show schedules. Sept.-June planetarium open only weekends.)

BEACHES

A Coruña's best beaches are the long, narrow ▨ **Playa del Orzán** and **Playa de Riazor** that flank Po. Marítimo on the Atlantic side of the peninsula. On weekends, the sand along these calm waters is packed with people, but crowds thin out on weekdays. Small, secluded beaches, including **Playa del Matadero, Playa de San Amaro,** and **Playa das Lapas,** hide farther down Po. Marítimo near Torre de Hércules, although these tend to be a little more rocky and have a bit more seaweed.

NIGHTLIFE

In the early evening, *coruñeses* linger in Celtic pubs throughout the *ciudad vieja,* bar-hopping around C. del Orzán, C. del Sol, and the mess of streets near C. de la Franja and C. de la Florida. **XXele,** C. del Orzán, 11, spills an edgy, local crowd out onto the street, but keeps its flavored *chupitos* (shots), including chocolate and *perfecto amor* safely in their glasses. (Beer €1.20. Chupitos €1.20. Open Tu-W 7pm-1:30am, Th-Sa 7pm-3:30am.) Popular Celtic pubs include **Rochester,** C. de la Franja, 61, where posters from Ireland plaster the walls and Irish stouts flow from the taps, but the crowd inside certainly isn't foreign. (Beer €1.20. Open Su-Th 7:30pm-1:30am, F-Sa until 2:30am). The tightest squeeze is **Ocacivache** on C. Orzan, 28, a darkened pub/dance bar with a hippie feel that specializes in *queimada,* a traditional Galician spirit. A reenactment of an ancestral ceremony used by medieval witches to ward off evil spirits is performed every Thursday night (☎981 91 47 33). When bars die down around 2am, **discotecas** pick up along the two beaches and on C. Juan Flórez. **Sol Pirámide,** C. Juan Flórez, 50, plays dance music loud enough to rouse the dead. (Open daily 1-6am). Locals pack the small dance floor of **Kántaro,** C. del Sol, 21. (Open Th-Sa midnight-5am.) Across the street, **Lautrec** has its walls plastered with old movie posters and draws crowds with electronica. (Open M-Th 1am-5am, F-Sa until 5:30am.)

FESTIVALS

Party-hardy *coruñeses* spend the month of August celebrating **Las Fiestas de María Pita,** with concerts, parades, and medieval fairs. To kick off the events, the city holds a mock naval battle in the harbor on July 31 to honor María Pita, the woman who single-handedly rallied a defense against the invading army of Sir Francis Drake in 1589 after the town's men had fled the port in fear. Although **La Noche de San Juan** (June 23) is celebrated in many parts of Europe, A Coruña greets the occasion with particular fervor since it coincides with the opening of sardine season. Locals light bonfires with *aguardiente* (firewater) before spending the night leaping over flames and gorging on sardines. Risk aside, the rite is supposed to ensure fertility. If you drop an egg white in a glass of water on this night, it will supposedly assume a form symbolic of your future spouse's occupation.

THE NORTHERN COAST

If you want to leave the beaten path, this is the place to do it. The rainy Rías Altas are Spain's unknown treasures—nowhere else will you find such dense forests, dramatic cliffs, and striking beaches all together. Half the enjoyment of the trip is just getting there; the rail lines and lonely highways snake past endless forests and majestic ocean views—just make sure you stay awake to see the views. Public transportation is reliable, but renting a car can be more convenient.

VIVEIRO

The FEVE train (☎ 982 55 07 22; www.feve.es) leaves Viveiro for Ferrol (4 per day 7:53am-7:22pm, €5.20) and Oviedo (10am, 5:10pm, €13.30). Arriva buses (☎ 982 56 01 03) from Viveiro connect to: A Coruña (4hr.; M-F 8 per day 6:15am-7:45pm, Sa 4 per day 8am-7:45pm, Su 3 per day 11:15am-7:45pm; €12.70); El Ferrol (2¼hr.; M-F 8 per day 6:15am-7:45pm, Sa 4 per day 8am-7:45pm, Su 3 per day 11:15am-7:45pm; €8); Ribadeo (1½hr.; M-F 6 per day 9:15am-8pm, Sa noon-4:45pm; €5.20); Santiago (3hr.; M-F 5 per day 6:15am-3pm, Sa 11:15am, Su 3pm, 6:15pm, change over in Ferrol; €16.90).

A tranquil old port poised between forest and sea, **Viveiro** (pop. 16,000) is known for its pristine beaches and fresh seafood—especially octopi. In the historic city center, the **Concepcionistas Monastery** and the **Santa María del Campo Church** both exhibit Romanesque urban architecture. For a dose of natural beauty, head 5km away from Viveiro, to 🏖**Playa de Area**, which stretches for 1km and forms the only set of sand dunes in the district or test out one of the numerous hiking trails that weave their way around the countryside. The local bus company, Autobuses de Viveiro (☎982 55 11 17), runs buses between the towns and beaches. See bus station for details on schedules and costs.

For information on **camping ❶** on the beach, call ☎982 56 00 04. (€3.75 per person, €3.75 per tent.) The tourist office has information on popular local hikes. If you choose to stay in town, **Fondo Nuevo Mundo ❷**, C. Teodoro de Quirós, one block uphill from Pr. Maior, has wood-paneled rooms, most with sun-filled balconies, and modern, tidy common baths. (☎982 56 00 25. Singles €15; doubles €30. Cash only.) Also reasonably priced is **Hostal Mayfre ❸**, C. Nicolás Cora, 68, which has cozy doubles and singles. They rent by the room, so the prices are optimal for groups but overpriced for solo travelers.(Sept.-June €25, July-Aug. €50.) Head to popular 🍽**Restaurant O Muro ❸**, C. Margarita Pardo de Cela, 26, a pizzeria-*pulpería* (octopus eatery) combo, for friendly service and delicious food. (☎982 56 08 23. Open daily 1-4 pm and 9pm-2:30am. Dishes €7-16. Pizza €8-12. Cash only.) **Fontenova ❷**, Pr. Mayor, 16, is a cafeteria and ice cream store serving rich coffee and chocolate drinks, sandwiches (€2-3), a wide variety of teas, crepes (€2-4), and of course, ice cream (☎982 55 19 60. Open Su-Th 8:30am-noon, F-Sa open later.)

Though Viveiro is a beautiful spot throughout the summer, July is a particularly good time to visit. Horses undergo a ritual tail- and mane-cutting ceremony at **Las Rapas das Bestas** festival, which takes place the 1st Sunday of July in the nearby town of Candaoso. The second weekend of July, Galicia's youth pitch tents out on the beaches of Ortiguera, 36km from Viveiro, for the town's **Celtic Music Festival.** A special bus runs from A Coruña to Ortiguera Wednesday through Sunday.

Autos Galicia, in the bus station on Alcade López Perez, rents cars. (☎649 90 31 19. From €56 per day. 25+, must have had license for 2 years. Open M-F 9am-1:30pm and 4-7:30pm, Sa 9am-1:30pm.) Viveiro's **tourist office,** Ave. Ramón Canosa, s/n, has town maps and information. (☎982 56 08 79. Open M-Sa 11am-2pm, 4:30-7:30pm.) Local services include: **banks** along the water on Av. de Marina; **police** (☎982 56 29 22) on Pl. Mayor, 1; the **Centro de Salud** (☎92 56 12 01) on Av. Ramón Canosa; **Internet** access at **Ciberfox,** C. Nicolas Cora Montenegro, 68; and the **post office** (☎982 56 08 23. Open M-F 8:30am-2:30pm, Sa 9:30am-1pm), Av. Ramón Canosa. **Lista de Correos** and **fax** available. **Postal Code:** 15176.

LUARCA

FEVE trains leave Luarca's station (☎ 985 64 05 52), a 1km walk uphill from the town, for El Ferrol (2 per day 9:56am, 5:03pm; €12.70) and Oviedo (3 per day 7:07am, 12:23pm,

GALICIA

7:32pm; €6). ALSA buses run from the bus station (☎ 985 64 03 51) to Oviedo (2½hr.; M-F 8 per day 6:20am-8pm, Sa-Su 5 per day 9:30am-8pm; €15) and Santiago de Compostela 5:30pm. ALSA info open M-F 8:30am-12:45pm, Su 5:15-9:15pm.

Nestled between jagged cliffs and the Mar Cantábrico, Luarca (pop. 5270) is a small fishing village that provides a day of beachside relaxation, either in the sand or at the bar. The most popular attraction is the **Aula del Mar,** C. Villar, a museum run by **CEPESMA,** an organization dedicated to the protection and rehabilitation of marine animals. The museum is full of preserved sea creatures and relics from the old whaling industry, including a frightening collection of giant squid, all caught off the coast of Luarca. (☎ 985 64 04 47; www.cepesma.com. Open M-F 11am-1pm and 4-8pm, Sa-Su 11am-2pm and 4-9pm, €1.50.) **Playa de Luarca,** the local beach, is a short, clearly marked walk from the town center. To stretch your legs and enjoy a spectacular view of Luarca and its coast, head up to the top of one (or both) of the cliffs that surround the town.

There are a few expensive hotels in Luarca, but for the most part the accommodations are pretty cheap and offer great amenities for their price. The centrally located **Hotel Oviedo ❷,** C. El Crucero, 3, offers spacious rooms with TV and bathrooms. Steamy showers come with massage settings. A bar is downstairs. (☎ 985 64 09 06; singles €20; doubles €40. MC/V). Try this little fishing village's local fare at **Sidrería El Faro ❸,** Paseo del Muelle, 25, which serves up delicious, fresh seafood for the adventurous eater. Located right on the waterfront with a fantastic view of the harbor and cliffs at sunset. (☎ 985 64 20 70. Tapas and raciones €3-12. Open daily 1-4:30pm and 8-11pm, in winter closed W.). For groceries and fresh fruit try **Frutería Gemo,** Pl. de la Constitución.

The **tourist office,** Oficina Municipal de Turismo de Luarca, is on C. Los Caleros, 11. (☎ 985 64 00 83; turismo@ayto-valdes.net. Open Oct.-June Tu-F 10am-2pm and 4:30-6:30pm, Sa 10:30am-2pm, 5-7pm, Su 12-2pm; July-Sept. longer hours.) Local services include: **Banco Herrero,** on C. Párroco Camino (☎ 902 33 11 33. Open M-F 8:30am-2pm, Oct.-March also open Sa 8:15am-1pm); the **police** (☎ 985 47 07 08); **Internet** access is available at **Ciber California,** C. Ramón Asenjo, 8. (☎ 985 640 229; €2.40 per hour, 15min. for €0.60. Open M-F 10:45am-1:30pm and 5-10:30pm, Sa 10:45am-1:30pm and 5-10pm, Su 5-10:30pm.) **Farmacia Mittel Brum,** C. de Ramón Asenjo, 30 (open daily 9am-1:30pm and 4-7:30pm) rotates with four other pharmacies to stay open 24hr. The **post office** is on C. de Ramón Asenjo (open M-F 8:30am-2:30pm, Sa 8:30am-1pm). **Postal Code:** 33770.

LAS ISLAS CANARIAS

 Las Islas Canarias have captivated imaginations for millennia with their natural wonders, from the snowy peak of Mount Teide to the fiery volcanoes of Timanfaya. Homer and Herodotus referred to the islands as gardens of astounding beauty, and the lost civilization of Atlantis was said to have left only these seven islands behind when it sank into the ocean. The Spanish spoken here bears stronger resemblance to Cuban or Puerto Rican Spanish, and *canario* fare is marked by a heavy Mediterranean influence. Rural village traditions, dialects, and names like Tenerife are remnants of the pre-Spanish Guanche culture that thrived prior to the 1402 Spanish conquest and subsequent development of plantation economies. Many beautiful coastlines (mostly in the south of each island) are now marred by ugly tourist developments catering primarily to Europeans; do whatever you can to avoid them. Las Islas Canarias reward anyone who steps off the beaten path.

HIGHLIGHTS OF LAS ISLAS CANARIAS

WASH away pollution on the islands' **beaches** (p. 611).

SPLASH in the sweet waves of Playa Jandía in **Fuerteventura** (p. 609).

FISH with your bare hands on a scuba dive in **Morro Jable** (p. 612).

CRASH one of the rollicking festivals in **Puerto de la Cruz** (p. 597).

GETTING THERE

Located off the western coast of Morocco, the Canarias are a 2½-3½hr. flight from mainland Spain. Competitive fares make flying the best option. Many airlines fly direct from mainland Spain, Portugal, and northern Europe. **Air Europa** (24hr. ☎902 40 15 01; www.aireuropa.com) and **Spanair** (☎902 13 14 15; www.spanair.com) fly to the islands (round-trip €150-360). **Iberia** (24hr. ☎902 40 05 00; www.iberia.com) flies from Madrid and Barcelona to Gran Canaria, Fuerteventura, Tenerife, and Lanzarote (round-trip €170-350). Flights from Madrid are the cheapest and most frequent. Airfares during January and February are the most expensive, but a one-way ticket in summer should cost no more than €115.

GETTING AROUND

INTER-ISLAND TRANSPORT

BY PLANE. Binter Canarias (☎902 39 13 92; www.binternet.com) has daily flights connecting almost all islands, and trips to Morocco on certain days of the week. The number of flights per day varies by season; check the website. From Gran Canaria flights go to: **Fuerteventura** (40min.; €63.50); **La Gomera** (40min.; €86.50); **Lanzarote** (45min.; €70.50); **La Palma** (50min.; €86.50); **Tenerife Norte** (40min.; €55.50); **Tenerife Sur** (35min.; €55.50).

BY BOAT. Fred Olsen runs jetfoils throughout the islands. (☎902 10 01 07; www.fredolsen.es. MC/V.) **Naviera Armas** runs ferries. (☎902 45 65 00; www.naviera-armas.com. MC/V.) **Garajonay Exprés** (☎902 34 34 50; www.garajonayexpres.com) runs jetfoils between Tenerife and La Gomera, often for the best price.

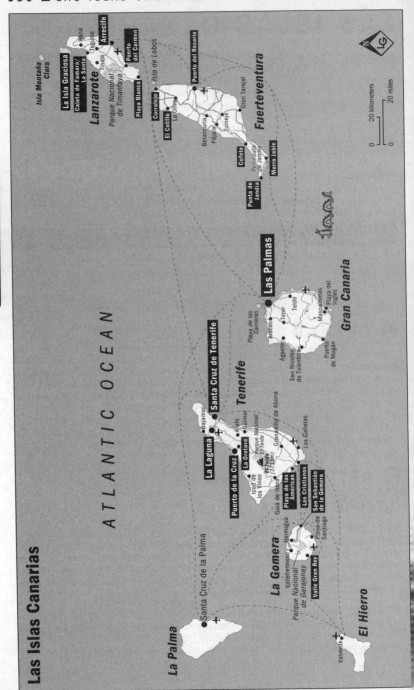

Las Islas Canarias

ATLANTIC OCEAN

La Palma

Santa Cruz de la Palma

La Gomera

Vallehermoso Hermigua
Parque Nacional
de Garajonay
Valle Gran Rey Playa de
Santiago
San Sebastián
de la Gomera

El Hierro

Valverde

Tenerife

La Laguna
Bajamar
Tacoronte
Güímar
La Orotava
Puerto de la Cruz
Icod de
los Vinos
Guía de Isora
Santa Cruz de Tenerife
Parque Nacional
▲ El Teide
El Teide
(3718m)
Granadilla de Abona
Las Galletas
**Playa de las
Américas**
Los Cristianos

Gran Canaria

Las Palmas
Playa de las
Canteras
Arucas
Teror Telde
Agaete Playa del
Inglés
San Nicolás Maspalomas
de Tolentino
Puerto
de Mogán

Lanzarote

Isla Montaña
Clara
La Isla Graciosa
**Caleta de Famara/
La Santa**
Haría
Teguise **Arrecife**
Tinajo
Parque Nacional
de Timanfaya
**Puerto
del Carmen**
Playa Blanca
El Cotillo **Corralejo** Isla de Lobos
La Oliva
Puerto del Rosario

Fuerteventura

Betancuria
Pájara Antigua
Gran Tarajal
Cofete
Península
de Jandía **Morro Jable**
**Punta de
Jandía**

0   20 kilometers
0   20 miles

Jetfoils are faster but cost almost twice as much—consider taking them on longer voyages. Prices for ferries and jetfoils vary with accommodations; travelers can choose between a reclinable *butaca* (similar to bus seat) and, on especially long trips, a *camarote a compartir* (dorm bed). All ferries carry cars. The offices at each city's ports list timetables and fares, although it is much easier and faster to check them on the Internet. Arrive at least 1hr. before departure to buy your ticket. Substantial student discounts are available.

ORIGIN	DESTINATION	LENGTH	FREQUENCY	TIME	PRICE
(FO) denotes Fred Olsen. (NA) denotes Naviera Armas. Fuel surcharge is not included in some prices.					
Arrecife (NA)	Las Palmas	5hr.	Tu-Th, Sa	Tu, Th, Sa 11am; W 10am	€29
Arrecife (NA)	Santa Cruz, Ten.	7-10hr.	W and F	10:15 am	€34
Corralejo (NA)	Playa Blanca	25-35min.	5-7 per day	daily 8am-8pm	€13
Corralejo (FO)	Playa Blanca	30min.	5-7 per day	M-F 7:45am-7pm, Sa-Su 9am-7pm	€12-15
Las Palmas (NA)	Arrecife	7-12hr.	M-F	11:50pm	€32
Las Palmas (NA)	Morro Jable	3hr.	1 per day	M-Sa 7:10am, Su 2pm	€30
Las Palmas (NA)	Puerto Rosario	7hr.	M-F	11:30pm	€32
Las Palmas (NA)	Santa Cruz, Ten.	3½hr.	M-Tu and Th-F 2 per day, W 3 per day, Sa-Su 1 per day	M 8am and 4pm, Tu, Th, F 7am and 4pm, Sa-Su 7am	€11-29
Las Palmas (FO; leaves from Agaete; free bus leaves C. Luis Morote, 4, for Agaete 1hr. prior to departure)	Santa Cruz, Ten.	1½hr.	M-F 8 por día, Sa-Su 6 per day	M-F 6:30am-8:30pm, Sa-Su 8am-8:30pm	€34
Los Cristianos (NA)	San Sebastián	1½hr.	M-Tu, Th-F, and Su	6:30 pm, 6:15 pm on F and Su	€19
Los Cristianos (FO; bus available from the bus station in Santa Cruz; leaves 30min. prior to departure)	San Sebastián	40min.	M-Sa 5 per day, Su 4 per day	daily 8:30am-8:30pm,	€20-25 €5.30 extra for bus
Morro Jable (NA)	Las Palmas	3hr.	1 per day	7pm	€30
Playa Blanca (NA)	Corralejo	30min.	5-7 per day	daily 7am-7pm	€13
Playa Blanca (FO)	Corralejo	30min.	M-F 7per day, Sa-Su 5 per day	M-F 7:10am-6pm, Sa-Su 8:30am-6pm	€13-15
Puerto del Rosario (NA)	Las Palmas	6½hr.	Tu-Sa	noon	€33
San Sebastián (FO)	Los Cristianos (bus available to Santa Cruz upon arrival)	40min.	4 per day	7am-6:30pm	€18-21 €5.30 extra for bus
Santa Cruz, Ten. (NA)	Arrecife	7-13hr.	Tu and Th	10pm	€36
Santa Cruz, Ten. (NA)	Las Palmas	3½hr.	1-3 per day	M, Tu, W, F noon and 10pm, Th 3am, noon, 10pm, Sa-Su 10pm	€14
Santa Cruz, Ten. (NA)	Morro Jable	6hr.	1 per day	3:00 am	€37
Santa Cruz, Ten. (NA)	Santa Cruz, La Palma	7hr.	W and F	W-11:50pm, F 11pm	€20

INTRA-ISLAND TRANSPORT

Outside of Gran Canaria and Tenerife, **public transportation** is sparse. Dependency on public transportation will leave you in one of the abysmal capital cities of the smaller islands, where buses run only to and from the main bus station. Renting a **car** (€30-50 per day) is a cost-effective investment for groups.

CAR RENTAL. CICAR (Canary Islands Car; ☎928 82 29 00; www.cicar.com), with 40 offices throughout the islands, is the best option for car rental, with economy cars at €30 per day. Certain offices arrange for free pickup upon arrival. Other reliable companies include: **Auto-Reisen** (☎922 26 02 00; www.autoreisen.es; €26 per day); **Avis** (☎902 18 08 54 or 902 13 55 31; www.avis.es; €30-65 per day); **Betacar/Europcar** (☎922 37 28 82; www.betacar.biz; €46 per day, €50 per 2 days); **Felycar** (☎900 21 10 40 or 928 81 90 91; www.felycar.com; €40 per day); **Hertz** (☎902 14 37 89; www.hertz.es; €41 per day).

GRAN CANARIA   ☎928

Often called the "miniature continent," Gran Canaria has a geographical variety rivaling that of countries hundreds of times its size. The relatively small island played a key role in the Age of Exploration—it was the last safe port en route to the Americas, and claims Christopher Columbus as one of its former inhabitants. Since then, Gran Canaria has been a major destination for modern-day adventurers. Unfortunately, the coastline has all the trappings of an island paradise, but is loud, busy, and, in some places, downright industrial. Las Palmas, the capital, has museums and the famous Playa de las Canteras, but European tourists flock to the south, reveling in Gran Canaria's sunshine. Head toward the interior mountain towns to catch a rare glimpse of the local culture. Explore beyond the beach—it will still be there when you're ready for it.

LAS PALMAS   ☎928

The urban mecca of the Canarias, Las Palmas (pop. 400,000) is not exactly a natural paradise. Overbearing buildings dominate an otherwise tranquil landscape, while electrical towers dot the sides of a nearby dormant volcano. The north boasts a beach and roaring nightlife, but spend your days in the south, where the historic district holds the Canarias' best museums and most tranquil walks.

▐ TRANSPORTATION

Flights: (Info ☎928 57 90 00). **Buses** (*guaguas*) run from the airport to Parque de San Telmo's **Estación de Guaguas** (#60; 20min.; hourly on the hr. and every 45min. 6am-1:30am; €1.95). Connecting buses run from San Telmo to **Santa Catalina** every 15min. after arrival from airport (#12 and 13; 15min.; 6am-1:30am; €1).

Buses: Estación de Guaguas (☎928 36 83 35; www.guaguas.com), on the sea side of Parque de San Telmo. Office open M-F 7am-8:30pm, Sa-Su 8am-1pm. **Líneas Global** (☎902 38 11 10; www.globalsu.es) connects Las Palmas to the rest of the island's bus lines, some of which run long into the night. For those exploring extensively by bus, the blue **tarjeta insular** prepaid pass (€15) gives a 25% discount on rides less than 11km, 22% on rides longer than 11km, and 30% on intercity buses. Bus schedules change on weekends, especially on Su; pick up a timetable in the ticket office. To: **Arucas** (#202, 205, 206, 209, and 234; 1hr.; every 30min. 6am-1:30am; €1.60-2.15); **Faro-Maspalomas** (#5, 30, and 32; 1hr.; every 20min., 24hr. between all 3; €5.15);

Playa de las Canteras
Po. de las Canteras

C. Luis Morote
Sgto. Llagas
Parque de Santa Catalina
Museo Elder
PL. RAMÓN FRANCO
Av. Alcalde Juan Rodríguez Doreste

Muelle de Rivera Oeste
El Muelle de Las Palmas de Gran Canaria
Hertz
CICAR
Muelle de Sta. Catalina
Muelle de la Luz
Transmediterránea

C. Nicolás Estévanez
PL. ALBAREDA
C. Franchy Roca
Simón Bolívar
C. León y Castillo

C. Gral Bassas
C. Thomas Miller
C. Martínez de Escobar
C. Isla de Cuba
Presidente Alvear
General Vives

SANTA CATALINA
PL. FARRAY
C. Bernardo de la Torre
C. L. Fernández Navarro
Cirilo Moreno
C. Montevideo
C. Ruiz de Alda
C. Juan Manuel Durán

Naval Base

Tomás A. Edison
C. Olof Palme
PL. DE ESPAÑA
Av. José Mesa y López

C. Portugal
C. Secretario Padilla
C. Fernando Guanarteme
C. República Dominicana
Av. Mesa y López
C. Jesús Ferrer Gimeno

C. Néstor de la Torre
C. Galicia
C. Gen. Más de Gaminde
C. Menéndez y Pelayo
Barcelona
Po. de Chil

C. Pío XII
C. Valencia
C. Alemania
C. Luis Antúnez

Playa de Alcaravaneras

C. Habana
Estadio Insular
C. Leopoldo Matos

Puerto de la Luz

C. Bogotá
Quintana

C. Hnos. García de la Torre
PL. MILITÓN
C. Maestro Valle
C. García del Castillo

Muelle Deportivo

C. Alcalde L. Fasnao Ferrer
C. Antonio María Manrique
C. Manuel Benítez Inglot
C. Benítez Inglot
C. Batllón Lorenzo

Rafael Ramírez
PL. JULIO ANTONIN
Jardines Alonso Quesada
Lope de Vega
Po. de Chil
Lord Byron

Jardín de Buenavista

CIUDAD JARDÍN

Av. Alcalde José Ramírez
Av. León y Castillo
Bentencourt

Ayuntamiento

ATLANTIC OCEAN

TO SANTA CRUZ DE TENERIFE, SANTA CRUZ DE LA PALMA

Naviera Armas

TO MORRO JABLE, PUERTO DEL ROSARIO

C. Luis Benítez Inglot
AV. de Escaleritas
C. Joaquín Blume
C. Agustín de Zurbarán
C. Sedeño

Pío XII
C. Hidalgo
C. Beethoven
Parque Doramas

Pueblo Canario/
Museo Néstor
Jardines del Rubió
Jardín Zoológico

C. Fco.-P. González Díaz

C. Prolongación AV. de Escaleritas
C. Obispo Pomo
C. Eduardo Benítez

C. Ruiz de Zárate
C. Juan Ramón Jiménez
C. Carlos Bisenty
C. Echegaray
Av. Juan XXIII
C. Álvarez de Castro

Av. de Juan XXIII
Policlínica
Gobierno Canario

C. Benítez Inglot
C. Henry Dunant

Vía de Enlace

C. Sor Simona
C. Mariucha
C. Pablo Penagullas
C. Federico Viera
C. Zaragoza

P. de Lugo
LUGO
P. de Tomás Morales
C. Carvajal
Pamochamosos
C. Molinos de Viento
Av. León y Castillo
C. 13 de Noviembre
C. Luis Doreste Silva
Av. Marítima del Norte

C. S. Monsalud
P. de Chil
P. de San Antonio
PL. DON BENITO

C. D. Pío de Coronado
C. Agustina de Aragón

C. Galo
C. Doctor Waksman
C. Rabadán
C. Venegas
C. Arrieta
C. Alonso Alvarado

PL. FUENTE LUMINOSA

400 meters
0   400 yards

N LG

C. Murga
C. Cebrián
C. Peojo

Biblioteca Pública
C. Muelle de las Palmas
Parque de San Telmo

C. Bravo Murillo
C. Buenos Aires
C. Domingo J. Navarra

TRIANA

C. Primero de Mayo
C. Dr. Juan de Padilla
C. Juan E. Doreste
C. Viera
C. Cano
C. Mayor de Triana
C. Francisco Gourie
C. Rafael Cabrera
Av. de Canarias

Castillo de San Francisco
Hospital Militar

TO PLAYA DEL INGLÉS (53km),
(2km),
(18km)

PL. CAIRASCO
C. San Nicolás Remedios
C. Calvo Sotelo

SEE INSET

C. Matteses
PL. CAIRASCO
C. San Nicolás Remedios
PL. HURTADO MENDOZA
C. Calvo
Cotelo

Pelegrina
C. Mendizábal
Mercado de Vegueta
Ermita S. Antonio Abad
Casa de Colón
Los Balcones
CAAM

Herrería
C. Colón
Catedral de Santa Ana
C. Espíritu Santo
C. Dr. Chil
Museo Canario

TO IGLESIA PLAZA DE SANTO DOMINGO (.5km)

VEGUETA

Puerto de Mogán (#1; 1½hr.; every 20min. 5am-7pm, also 8:30, 9:30, 10:30, 11:30am; €7.35); **Puerto Rico** (#91, hourly 6:15am-8:15pm; €6.35); **Teror** (#216 and 229; every 30min. 6am-11:30pm; €1.95).

Public Transportation: Local Buses, the so-called *guaguas*, are yellow buses (€1.10) that travel within the city. Stops are frequent. When in doubt, hop on bus #1 (24hr.), which runs north to south from Muelle de la Luz to Teatro Pérez Galdós, passing Parque de Santa Catalina and Parque de San Telmo. 10-ride **bono** passes (€5.80) available at tobacco shops or at the main bus station in Parque de Santa Catalina. **Guaguas Municipales,** Cebadal C. de Arequipa (☎928 44 65 00).

Ferries: Naviera Armas (☎902 45 65 00; www.naviera-armas.com) ferries depart from Muelle León y Castillo. Tickets can be purchased at docks 1hr. before departure. **Fred Olsen** (☎902 10 01 07; www.fredolsen.es) ferries to **Tenerife** depart from **Agaete.** A free bus leaves Parque de Santa Catalina 1hr. before the ferry leaves. Buy your ferry tickets and board the bus at the Fred Olsen office in the northwest corner of the park. Tickets also sold at travel agencies for small fee. See **Inter-Island Transport,** p. 585.

Taxis: Radio Taxi (☎928 46 18 18).

Car Rental: CICAR (airport ☎928 57 93 78, Las Palmas 928 27 72 13). **Hertz** (☎928 57 95 77; www.hertz.es) has offices at the airport, in the jetfoil office at Muelle de Santa Catalina, and scattered around the island.

Bike Rental: Burbujita, General Vives, 49 (☎928 22 68 12 or 928 48 42 04 for surf shop; www.burbujita.com), offers adventure packages and bike rental. Open M-F 9am-1:30pm and 3-6pm.

■ 🛈 ORIENTATION AND PRACTICAL INFORMATION

Guaguas (buses, pronounced WAH-WAHs) are the easiest way to get around Las Palmas. The city is divided into a series of districts, connected by a major highway and avenues running north to south along the east coast. **Calle León y Castillo** cuts through the city center. **Playa de Las Canteras** and **Muelle de la Luz** frame the fast-paced north end of the city, which is packed with accommodations, bars, discos, and sex shops. Farther south through a series of residential neighborhoods lies **Triana,** a shopping district close to the city's main bus station. **Vegueta,** the city's historical district, branches south from there, with classic, brightly colored facades, winding streets, and intricately painted street markers. At night, walk along well-lit C. Mayor de Triana to get from Vegueta to the bus station. Buses #1, 12, and 13, run between **Parque de Santa Catalina** and Vegueta. Use common sense and caution after dark in the northern area of the city and La Isleta, north of Santa Catalina.

The **tourist office, Patronato de Turismo,** C. León y Castillo, 17, in Vegueta, has an invaluable website with information on Gran Canaria updated more frequently than the available brochures. (☎928 21 96 00; www.grancanaria.com. Open M-F 8am-3pm.) For **currency exchange** try **Banco Santander Central Hispano,** C. de Franchy Roca, 4, across from the police station in Parque de Santa Catalina. No commission for transactions less than €600. (☎902 24 24 24. Open M-F 8:30am-2pm, Sa 8:30am-1pm.) Other services include: **police,** Parque de Santa Catalina (local ☎928 26 05 51 or national 902 10 21 12); **hospital** at **Hospital Insular,** Pl. Dr. Pasteur (☎928 44 40 00); free **Internet access** at the **Biblioteca Pública del Estado Las Palmas de Gran Canaria,** C. Muelle de Las Palmas, by San Telmo station. (☎928 43 23 43; www.culturadecanarias.com; open Oct.-June M-F 9am-9pm, Sa 10am-2pm and 5-8pm; July M-F 9am-8pm; Aug.-Sept. M-F 9am-2pm) and the **Biblioteca Insular,** Pl. Hurtado de Mendoza, 3, in Vegueta (☎928 38 26 72; free Internet daily 9am-8:30pm. Library open 24hr.); and the **post office,** Av. Primero de Mayo, 62. (☎928 36 13 20; open M-F 8:30am-8:30pm, Sa 9:30am-2pm.) **Postal Code:** 35007.

ACCOMMODATIONS

Without advance notice, it's nearly impossible to find lodging during high season (Dec.-Feb., especially during *Carnaval*). ■Hotel Madrid ❸, Pl. Cairasco, 4, the oldest in the Canarias, became a local landmark after Gen. Francisco Franco slept in room #3 on the eve of the Spanish Civil War. Family-run, Hotel Madrid is far and away the best value in the city. (☎928 36 06 64. Singles with bath €30; doubles €40. AmEx/D/MC/V.) Pensión Perojo ❷, C. Perojo, 1, has the trappings of the Old World: a wrought-iron staircase, ornate ceiling molding, and pastel colors. (☎928 37 13 87. Singles €20; doubles €23. Cash only.)

FOOD

Las Palmas serves up international cuisine, but almost all kitchens closes between 3:30 and 8:30pm. Restaurante "La Alquitara" ❷, C. Domingo J. Navarro, 9, relieves you from tourist fare with *canario* and Basque food (€8-11). (☎928 38 49 59. Open daily 9am-2am. AmEx/MC/V.) Casa Montesdeoca ❸, C. de Montesdeoca, 10, serves Spanish entrees (€10-18) in a romantic courtyard where wooden shutters give way to antique paintings. (☎928 33 34 66. Open M-Sa 12:30-4pm and 8pm-midnight. AmEx/D/MC/V.) For groceries, head to Mercado de Vegueta, on C. Mendizábal, (☎928 33 41 29. Open M-Th 6:30am-2pm, F-Su 6:30am-3pm.)

SIGHTS

Las Palmas's sights, many of which are in the historic neighborhood Vegueta, can be easily explored in a day. The old district's colonial and Neoclassical architecture and open markets provide a respite from the commercial buildings in the new city. Keep a map handy, but don't get frustrated. Though small, tortuous passages make precise navigation difficult, the museums are so tightly packed together that precision is hardly necessary. From the Parque San Telmo Bus Station, head down C. Mayor de Triana and cross C. Lentini to enter the historic neighborhood. C. Mayor de Triana's lamppost-lined footpath is the best-lit route home at night.

CASA DE COLÓN. The museum, part of which was assembled to replicate life on the Santa Maria, contains artifacts from early transatlantic voyages, including an extensive collection of old maps and ship logs written by Columbus himself. Artifacts from pre-Colombian cultures are in the crypt. Don't miss the parrots in the courtyard, but don't waste your breath talking to them either—they won't talk back. (*C. de Colón, 1.* ☎928 31 23 73; www.grancanariacultura.com. Open M-F 9am-7pm, Sa-Su 9am-3pm. Free.)

MUSEO CANARIO. This collection provides a comprehensive background to the Canarias' pre-conquest history. The most impressive exhibit is a corridor lined with more Cro-Magnon skulls, skeletons, and mummies than are usually found in a B-grade horror flick. Did we mention that they talk? (*C. Dr. Verneau, 2.* ☎928 33 68 00; www.elmuseocanario.com. Open M-F 10am-8pm, Sa-Su 10am-2pm. All exhibits in Spanish. Inquire about guided tours in Spanish. €3, students €1.20.)

CATEDRAL DE SANTA ANA. This 16th-century Gothic cathedral is the most important example of artistic design in all of the islands. After four centuries of planning and construction, the building is a mix of different architectural styles. With an extra €1.50, you can scale the tower for a great view of the city. (*C. Obispo Codina, 13.* ☎928 31 49 89. Open M-F 10am-5pm, Sa 10am-2pm. €3, under 12 free.)

☞ BEACHES

The waters along **Playa de Las Canteras** are protected during low tide by a natural reef, turning the ocean into a tranquil swimming pool. Surfers and windsurfers head to the far extremes where waves and wind are plentiful. **Buceo Canarias by Medusa,** C. Bernardo de La Torre, 56-58, specializes in diving courses and equipment rental. Some tours take you to a sunken ship. (☎928 26 27 86; www.buceo-canarias.com. €22 per dive, €40 with equipment. 2-week certification course €300. Open M-Sa 11am-2pm and 5-9pm.)

♫ ENTERTAINMENT

El Muelle de Las Palmas de Gran Canaria, Muelle de Santa Catalina (☎928 32 75 27), right across from the Parque Santa Catalina, is an enormous glittering edifice with over 60 shops, 30 restaurants, a movie theater, a bowling alley, and outdoor discotecas. It has even been voted the best shopping center in Europe.

Nightlife isn't the main draw of Las Palmas, but www.laspalmastonight.com lists hip local hangouts. Most popular spots (including karaoke bars) are located near **Parque de Santa Catalina,** but be careful at night. Take advantage of year-round outdoor terraces on **Pl. de España** and along **Po. de las Canteras. Palacio Latino,** C. Luis Morote, 51, is a typical discoteca. (Cover €6, includes 1 drink. Open F-Su midnight-5:30am.) **Pequeña Habana,** C. Fernando Guanarteme, 45, sizzles with salsa. (Classes Th-F 9-11pm. Open Th-Sa 11pm-4am. ☎638 24 32 66 for salsa classes.)

TENERIFE   ☎922

The imposing peak of El Teide jutting up from Tenerife's center makes the island easy to spot. At 3718m, the mountain is the third largest volcano on earth, and towers over a diverse and beautiful landscape. Microclimates have generated the island's ever-changing flora and terrain— marked by lush gardens in the north, dry beaches to the south, and volcanic spectacles in the interior.

SANTA CRUZ DE TENERIFE

Santa Cruz, or, as it is officially called, the "Very Loyal, Noble, Unconquered, and Highly Beneficial City, Port, and Fortress of Santa Cruz de Santiago de Tenerife," lives up to its pretentious title. The first shots of the Spanish Civil War rang out here; Francisco Franco, then the General-in-Chief of the Canarias, went on to establish the oppressive regime in Spain that endured for nearly four decades. Since the general's time, the city has become one of the busiest ports in Spain. The bustling energy of Santa Cruz makes for a pedestrian paradise, with sunlight streaming by day and romantic street lamps lighting the way by night.

⬚ TRANSPORTATION

Flights: There are 2 airports on Tenerife. National flights land at the northern airport, **Los Rodeos** (☎922 63 56 35; www.aena.es), commonly known as Tenerife Norte, 6km west of Santa Cruz. From Los Rodeos, buses #102, 107, and 108 run to town (25min.; every 20min. 6am-10:15pm, €1.20). International flights arrive in the south, at the **Reina Sofía airport** (☎922 75 90 00; www.aena.es), Tenerife Sur. From Reina Sofía, buses #111 and 341 head to town (1½hr.; every 30 min. 6:50am-10:45 pm, also 1, 1:30, 5am, and 11:45pm; €5.20). **Iberia** (Los Rodeos ☎922 63 58 55, Reina

Sofía 922 75 91 15, Central 902 40 05 00; www.iberia.com), **Spanair** (Los Rodeos ☎922 63 58 19, Reina Sofía 922 75 91 50, Central 902 13 14 15; www.spanair.com), **Air Europa** (Los Rodeos ☎922 63 59 35, Los Cristianos 922 63 59 55, Central 902 40 15 01; www.aireuropa.com), and **Binter Canarias** (Los Rodeos ☎922 63 56 44, Central 902 39 13 92; www.binternet.com) all fly to the island.

Buses: TITSA (☎922 53 13 00; www.titsa.com) serves all towns from the **Estación de Guaguas**, Av. Tres de Mayo, 57, down Av. José Antonio Primo de Rivera, which becomes Av. de la Constitución, from Pl. de España. Open daily 6:30am-10pm. Some lines do not run in summer; call ahead or check online for info. To **Los Cristianos/ Playa de las Américas** (#110 and 111. 1hr.; every 30min.-1hr. 5:30am-9:30pm, last bus at 2:30am; €6.50-6.90) and **Puerto de la Cruz** (#101 and 102 have stops, #103 runs direct; 45min.-1hr.; every 30min.-1hr. 6am-9:30pm, also 1:15, 1:45, 4:15am, 10:15, 11:15pm; €3.60). If you plan on using buses often, buy a prepaid **bonobus ticket** (Card Titsa; €12), which gives a 30% discount on cost of individual tickets on short rides and 50% for distances greater than 20km. For passengers who return within 2hr., the return trip is free. One ticket valid for group use.

Metro: Tranvía (☎902 075 075; www.metrotenerife.com) serves Santa Cruz and La Laguna, making 20 stops between the 2 cities. Trains come about every 15 min. and cost €1.25 per ride.

Ferries: Fred Olsen (Santa Cruz Riviera Port ☎922 29 00 11, Los Cristianos 79 05 56, Central 902 62 82 00, info 10 01 07) runs a free bus (☎922 21 92 44) from the main station to Los Cristianos for trips to La Gomera 1½hr. prior to departure. Arrive at the station early. **Naviera Armas** (Santa Cruz ☎922 53 40 50, Los Cristianos 922 79 61 78, Central 902 45 65 00). See **Inter-Island Transport,** p. 585, for more info.

Taxis: Radio Taxi (☎922 21 00 59).

Car Rental: Local offices include **Auto-Reisen** (☎922 26 02 00), **Avis** (☎922 24 12 94), and **CICAR** (☎922 29 24 25). See **Intra-Island Transport,** p. 588.

> **ROLLING CHEAP.** If you plan to spring for a rental car, make reservations before arriving. It will save you a 100% walk-in fee.

ORIENTATION AND PRACTICAL INFORMATION

Santa Cruz is easily navigable on foot. The port city branches out from **Plaza de España** by the large clock tower. Across from Pl. de España is **Plaza de la Candelaria;** C. de Castillo runs perpendicular to the water from here into the commercial district. Av. José Antonio Primo de Rivera and Av. Francisco La Roche originate in Pl. de España and run along the waterfront, separating the port and the city. To get to Pl. de España from the **ferry terminals,** turn left onto Av. Francisco la Roche/Av. Anaga, and follow it to the plaza (10min.). From the **bus station,** head right down Av. Tres de Mayo toward the water and take a left on Av. José Antonio Primo de Rivera, continuing on to the plaza (15min.).

The **tourist office,** Pl. de España (☎ 922 23 95 92; open M-F 9am-6pm, Sa 9am-1pm) also has a kiosk in Pl. de Candelaria (☎922 53 11 07). To get to the **police,** Av. Tres de Mayo, 72, follow Av. Tres de Mayo past the intersection with Av. La Salle; the station is on the left. (☎922 60 60 92). Other services include: **Farmacia La Marina,** C. de la Marina, 7, 1 block from Pl. de España. (☎922 24 24 93; open M-F 8am-8pm, Sa 9am-1:30pm); **Hospital Universitario de Canarias,** Urbanización Ofra, in La Laguna, north of Santa Cruz (☎922 67 80 00; take bus #013, 015, 136, or Tranvía, stop at Hospital Universitario); **Internet access** at **Tóp Anaga,** Av. Francisco la Roche/Av. Anaga, 11, next to the 24hr. convenience store. (☎922 28 24 96; €1 per

30min. Open daily 9am-midnight); and **post office:** Pl. de España (☎922 53 36 29; cash only; open M-F 8:30am-8:30pm, Sa 9:30am-2pm). **Postal Code:** 38002.

ACCOMMODATIONS

Pensiones and hostels in Santa Cruz tend to be less desirable than one- and two-star hotels. Affordable accommodations are scattered on C. de Castillo and C. Bethencourt Alfonso. It's a bit of a hike to ⊠**Pensión Casablanca ❷,** C. Viera y Clavijo, 15, but the price is right. Quiet, festively painted rooms have shared baths. (C. Bethencourt Alfonso becomes C. Pérez Galdós and then C. Viera y Clavijo. ☎922 27 85 99. Singles €15-25; doubles €21-35. Cash only.) Centrally located **Hotel Anaga ❸,** C. Imeldo Seris, 19, offers basic rooms with white walls and bedding, antique keys, pictures on the walls, TV, and phone. (Off C. General Gutiérrez. ☎922 24 50 90. Singles €28; doubles €46; triples €57. AmEx/D/MC/V.)

FOOD

Bars and restaurants crowd Pl. de España, but **Av. Francisco la Roche/Av. Anaga** has better deals (*menús* from €6). For a more sophisticated evening, grab some tapas at any of the nightlife spots on **C. Antonio Dominguez Alfonso,** a street known more commonly by its old name, **La Noria. La Hierbita ❷,** C. del Clavel, 19 serves delicious, amazingly priced *canario* specialties including fresh fish (€2.75-9), local wines, and homemade desserts. (☎922 24 46 17; www.lahierbita.com. *Menú* €7. Open M-Sa noon-4:45pm and 8pm-12:30am. D/MC/V.) Huge, delicious specialty crepes come hot off the griddle at **Creperia la Bohème ❶,** C. Emilio Calzadilla, 8. (☎922 29 62 96. Savory crepes €3-6, sweet €2-5, with fruit or ice cream €3-6. Open daily 1-5pm and 7-11:30pm. Cash only.) Fill up on the *ropa vieja* (goat, mutton, potatoes, and peppers) at **Bodeguita Canaria ❷,** C. Imeldo Seris, 18. (☎922 29 32 16. Entrees €5-11. Open M-F 10am-1am, Sa 1-4pm and 8-11pm. AmEx/D/MC/V.)

SIGHTS AND ENTERTAINMENT

The greatest sights in Santa Cruz are outside the city limits along lookout points off the main highway. Renting a car allows you to explore the hidden treasures that encircle the city. Especially enchanting are the forested trails of the **Anaga headlands** and the black sand beaches of **Almáciga.** Walk along the promenade by the port to get a close look at the **Auditorio de Tenerife.** Finished in 2003, it was designed to look like a tidal wave crashing over a large ship, or, depending on your angle, a small version of the Sydney Opera House. Facing the water, head right from Pl. de España. The ticket office is on Av. Constitución, 1. (☎922 56 86 02; www.auditoriodetenerife.com. Box office open M-F 10am-2pm, 5pm-7pm.) **Parque Municipal García Sanabria** doubles as a garden and open-air sculpture museum with some avant-garde works by Pablo Serrano and Rafael Soto. (From Pl. del Príncipe de Asturias, follow C. El Pilar uphill to the Parque.) The **Museo de la Naturaleza y el Hombre,** C. Fuente de Morales, 1, off C. San Sebastián, details everything from prehistoric marine biology to Guanche burial practices.(☎922 53 58 16; www.museosdetenerife.org. Open Tu-Su 9am-7pm. €3, students €1.50. 50% discount with bonobus pass. Su free. Audio tours in English €3.)

BEACHES

Some of the best beaches in Tenerife are accessible by frequent buses leaving from the main station. If you're in the area, check out the small black sand beaches of **Almáciga** (bus #246) and **Benijo** (bus #246). For surfers, there is a good swell at

Almáciga, even in the summer. With hairpin turns along the mountainous Anaga countryside, the drive (or bus ride) is an adventure in itself. **Las Teresitas** (bus #910, 246, or 247), with sand imported from the Sahara, is closest to the city center. Those who want to tan in more intimate areas can head to **Las Gaviotas** (bus #245), a nude beach. Trekkers should pick up a guide of hiking trails from the tourist office. With proper planning, you can get off a bus high up in the Anaga mountains and hike down to the black sand beaches. For an easy hike, set out from **La Laguna** (bus #014 or #015) and head out toward **Casa Carlos,** pass through the **Laurel Forest,** and finish by relaxing by the sands of **Roques de Anaga** and **Roque Taborno** (3hr.).

NIGHTLIFE

The real nightlife hot spot is in the old city along **C. Antonio Dominguez Alfonso,** commonly known as **La Noria.** Navigate to the bar at **Bulan,** C. Antonio Dominguez Alfonso, 35, through dozens of plush rooms, all adorned in a South Asian decor. (☎922 27 41 16. Beer €2-2.50. Mixed drinks €4. Open M-Tu and Su 12:30-2am, F-Sa 12:30-3am. AmEx/D/MC/V.) **Mojos y Mojitos,** C. Antonio Dominguez Alfonso, 38 has walls made of psychedelic kaleidoscope panels. (☎922 28 16 41. Tapas €5-10. Mojitos €6. Artisan wines €7-11. Open M-W and Su 11am-1am, Th-Sa 11am-4:30am. AmEx/D/MC/V.) The laid back and funky **Tasca Sáffron & Porron,** C. Antonio Dominguez Alfonso, 36, has ample outdoor seating. (☎922 15 18 67. Beer €1.50. Mixed drinks €3.50. Open Tu-Sa 1:30-4:30pm and 8pm-midnight, Su 1:30-4:30pm. AmEx/D/MC/V.

DAYTRIPS FROM SANTA CRUZ

LA LAGUNA
The Estacion de Guaguas (#015 from Santa Cruz) and the Tranvía (stop at la Trinidad) both stop outside the historic district on opposite sides of the city.

San Cristobal de la Laguna is a historical masterpiece of architecture, education, and *la marcha* (fiesta). Today, it pulses with energy from the 30,000 students studying at the Universidad de La Laguna. The most interesting sights are a series of 18th century mansions that showcase the architectural eccentricities of bygone *Canarios.* Free **walking tours** in English leave the tourist office daily at 11:30am. In the Pl. Santo Domingo, across from the Post Office, the **Iglesia Ex-Convento de Santo Domingo** is a beautiful convent that houses temporary exhibitions. The church also holds the red-stone fountain used to baptize the founder of São Paulo, Josè de

THE LOCAL STORY

CLASH OF THE CANARIOS

Ferocious, dirt-covered men in cloth diapers and T-shirts fly through the air in a combination of sumo wrestling and acrobatic maneuvers. So goes the aboriginal tradition of *lucha canaria* (Canarian Wrestling). Derived from a similar sport among African Berber tribes, *lucha canaria* was popularized in the Canaries by the ancient Guanche people of Tenerife. Every year during the principal festival in each village, one group of fighters would square off against another group from a nearby tribe.

The competition takes place in the *terrero,* an uncovered, circular area of earth or sand. Here, fighters use different maneuvers to knock their competitor onto the ground or out of the ring. The acceptable *mañas* involved in this intricate sport fall into three categories: *mañas de aggare,* grasping any part of the opponent's body to unbalance him; *mañas de desvío,* the avoidance of incoming attacks; and *mañas de aggare,* the use the momentum of incoming attacks to unbalance the opposing *luchador.*

Unlike their beefy Asian counterparts, bigger doesn't always mean better for Canarian wrestlers. In this sport smaller fighters have been known to throw vastly larger players. Today, the Federación Regional de Lucha Canaria has institutionalized the festival game, creating teams and interscholastic leagues.

Anchiete. A 10min. walk outside of town from the Estación de Guaguas, **Hostal Berlín ❷**, C. Marcelino Perdomo Reyes, 1, offers the only budget option in town. (☎922 25 50 43; hostalberlin@hotmail.com. Singles €20; doubles €25.) There are many restaurants in the historic district of La Laguna. Try **L'Amuse Bouche ❸**, C. Santo Domingo, 26, for French-Canary fusion. (☎922 63 39 16. Open Tu-Sat, 1:30-3:30pm and 8:30-11:30pm. Entrees €12-18. AmEx/MC/V.) Just uphill from the University, a series of bars and clubs form a triangle of nocturnal hedonism in the **Zona Cuadrilátero,** bordered by three streets: C. Elias Sierra Rafols, C. María del Cristo Ossuna, and C. Dr. Antonio González. The free map provided at the **tourist office,** C. Obispo Rey Redondo, 1 is quite useful. (☎922 60 11 06. Open M-Sa 9am-6pm.) For **Internet** access, head to Reicona Services, C. Santo Domingo, 12, which offers computers, Wi-Fi, or cable connection for €0.50 per hour.

LOS CRISTIANOS AND PLAYA DE LAS AMÉRICAS

Buses run from stops on Av. Juan Carlos in Los Cristianos to: El Teide (#342; 9:15am; €10.45); Puerto de la Cruz (#343; 4 per day 10am-5:45pm; €11.80); Reina Sofía airport (#487; hourly 7:20am-9:20pm; €2.20); Santa Cruz (#110 and 111; every 30min. 6am-10pm, also 11:15pm, 12:30, 4:30am; €6.70). In Playa de las Américas, buses stop along Av. Rafael Puig Lluvina. Buses #342, 416, 441, 442, 450, 467, 470-73, and 487 link Playa de las Américas and Los Cristianos. Ferries leave from Los Cristianos, connecting Tenerife to the western islands. Fred Olsen (☎922 79 02 15; www.fredolsen.es) runs ferries to Santa Cruz, San Sebastián, and Valverde. Garajonay Express (☎922 78 80 14) runs a ferry to San Sebastián de la Gomera.

Playa de las Américas and Los Cristianos serve as bases for exploring other shores in the south, including the windsurfing mecca, Playa del Médano. The azure waters and tan visitors of Playa de las Vistas in Los Cristianos brighten the gray expanse. Water Sports & Charters monopolizes the water sports centers on several beaches around Playa de las Américas. (☎922 71 40 34. Sailing €20 for 2hr. Booking office open daily 9am-7pm.) Keep an eye out for the open air market at the port in Los Cristianos, which offers crafts, clothing, and memorabilia. (Su 9am-2pm.) One option for accommodations is **Pensión La Playa ❷**, C. Paloma, 9. From Av. General Franco, turn uphill onto C. Estocolmo; C. Paloma is the first left. The basic rooms have warm, orange walls, a striped curtain motif, shared bath, and are near the beach. (☎922 79 22 64. Singles €18; doubles €25; triples €30. Cash only.) Find huge portions at good prices at **Bar El Cine ❶**, C Juan Bariajo, 8, across from the port on C. General Franco. The seafood is fresher than the sunburns of the clientele. (☎609 10 77 58. Entrees €5-7.50. Open daily noon-10pm. Cash only.) A modern hangout, **Don Chicharro ❶**, C. Av. General Franco, 9, has cheap tapas, fruit drinks, and milkshakes. (☎922 75 20 58. Open M-Sa 9am-midnight. Cash only.) **Nightlife** centers on Playa de las Américas, where lights and beer (€2-5) await in abundance. The Verónicas complex caters to a very British crowd and offers a strip of pubs and discos under a dazzling array of neon. In front of the Hotel Conquistador is **Metropolis,** Paseo Marítimo, (☎922 79 73 59; www.discotecametropolis.com), a sleek discoteca with two massive dance floors blasting house music and salsa. (Open daily 10:30pm-6am. Free salsa lessons on Tu and Th at 11pm. Cover F €6, Sa €10, includes one drink. MC/V.) To reach the **tourist office** from Los Cristianos bus stop, walk downhill on Av. Juan Carlos and go right onto Av. de Amsterdam; it's on your left in the Centro Cultural. (☎922 75 71 37. Open M-F 9am-3:30pm.) Local services include: **banks,** near Pl. Carmen and Av. General Franco in Los Cristianos (most open M-F 9am-2:30pm.); **police,** in the Centro Cultural in Los Cristianos (☎922 72 55 62); and **Internet** access at **Ciber World,** Av. Suecia, 25, off of Pl. del Carmen. Wi-Fi connection available. (☎922 79 30 35. €2 per hour. Open M-Sa 8am-11pm, Su 5-11pm.) The **post office** is on C. Perez Valero off C. Sabadeños. (☎922 79 10 56. Open M-F 8:30am-8:30pm, Sa 9:30am-1pm.) **Postal Code:** 38650.

PUERTO DE LA CRUZ   ☎922

The battlements of Puerto de la Cruz circle towering hotels, painted villas, and steep streets. One of the more enjoyable urban spots on the islands, this port town (pop. 25,000) brims with European tourists showing off their new tans. Once a capital of the wine trade and an important 17th-century connection to the New World, Puerto de la Cruz draws a mix of sailors and tourists; the steep streets bustle with European visitors, curios and electronics shops, and African vendors.

☐☑ TRANSPORTATION AND PRACTICAL INFORMATION. From the main **bus station** on C. del Pozo, 1 (☎922 38 18 07), buses leave for: La Orotava (#101, 345, 350, 352, 353; 25min.; every 30min.-1hr. 6:30am-1:10am; €1.20); Playa de las Américas (#343; 1hr.; 4 per day 9am-5:45pm; €10.80); Santa Cruz (#101 makes stops, 102 and 103 are direct; 1-2hr.; every 30min. 6:15am-9:40pm, also 12:45, 3:15, 4:45am, 11pm; €3.70). There is also a bus for the **Teide National Park** every morning (9:15am); be sure to get there early. Puerto de la Cruz expands from Playa San Telmo past **Plaza del Charco,** reaching the sands of Playa Jardín. To get to Pl. del Charco from the bus station, turn right onto C. del Pozo as you exit, continue onto C. Dr. Ingram, and turn left onto C. Blanco (10min.). The **tourist office** is on Pl. Europa. From Pl. del Charco, head toward the port on C. Blanco and turn right onto C. Santo Domingo; the office is on the left at the far end of the plaza. (☎922 38 60 00. Open July-Sept. M-F 9am-7pm, Sa 9am-noon; Oct.-June M-F 9am-8pm, Sa 9am-1pm.) Local services include: **police,** on Pl. Europa (☎922 37 84 48); **pharmacy** at **Farmacia Machado,** on Pl. del Charco (☎922 38 38 19; fax 30 47 17; open M-Sa 9am-9pm); and free **Internet** access at the **Biblioteca Pública Municipal,** Augustín Bethencourt, 11A. (Open M-Sa 9:15am-9pm.) The **post office** is at C. del Pozo, 14, across from the bus station. (☎922 38 58 05. Open in summer M-F 8:30am-2:30pm, Sa 9:30am-1pm; in winter M-F 8:30am-8:30pm, Sa 9:30am-1pm.) **Postal Code:** 38400.

⬛TIP   **BONUS CASH.** If you plan to make use of public transportation, buy one of the €12 prepaid bonocards, available for purchase in all bus stations. The discounts will cut your costs in half.

⬛⬛ ACCOMMODATIONS AND FOOD. *Pensiones* are particularly comfortable and plush in Puerto de la Cruz—reserve in advance. For hotel-quality rooms with balconies, comfy chairs, ornate headboards, and full baths at budget prices, head to **Pensión Rosa Mary ❶,** C. San Felipe, 14. (☎922 38 32 53. Doubles €30. Discount offered for multi-night stay. Cash only.) For smaller rooms of similar quality, try **Pensión los Geranios ❷,** C. del Lomo, 14. From Pl. del Charco, turn left on C. San Felipe, right on C. Pérez Zamora, and left on C. del Lomo. (☎922 38 28 10. Breakfast €3. Doubles €27. Cash only.)

Menus in at least six different languages line all of the main plazas, while restaurant staff aggressively court potential customers. **⬛La Rosa di Bari ❷,** C. del Lomo, 23, is a tranquil and tasty break from the neon flare of Puerto Cruz. (Open Tu-Su 12:30-2:45pm and 6:30-11pm. AmEx/MC/V.) The cavernous barn doors of **Meson Charco Cha Paula ❶,** C. de Valois, 2, reveal some of the cheapest *canario* specialties in town. Try the *conejo al ajillo* (rabbit in garlic sauce; €6). (☎922 38 07 30. Open daily noon-midnight. Cash only.)

◙ SIGHTS. Advertisements for **Loro Parque,** a (self-proclaimed) "must-see" of the Canarias, are everywhere. The park is home to Europe's largest dolphinarium, as well as marine mammal shows and a penguin exhibit. The bright yellow kiddie-train that shuttles children and their parents to the park is emblematic of the target audience. (Shuttle picks up by Hotel Catalonia Las Vegas on **Playa Martiánez** and leaves every 20min. from 9am. Last shuttle leaves park at 6:45pm. Taxi €6. ☎922 37 69 01; www.loroparque.com. Open daily 9am-5pm. €24, under 11 €15.60.) The small **Museo Arqueológico,** C. del Lomo, 9, features exhibits on the processes and ceremonies used by the prehistoric natives to produce pots, urns, jewelry, and decorations. (☎922 37 14 65. Open Tu-Sa 10am-1pm and 5-9pm, Su 10am-1pm. €1, students €0.50. Th free.) Far more interesting are the city's botanical gardens, the **Jardin de Aclimatación de La Orotava,** C. Retama, 2. Be sure to check out the *Dama de Noche* (Lady of the Night) with its peach-colored lampshade flowers and thorny-barked Bottle Tree. The centerpiece is a towering **ficus tree;** the upper branches drop down tendrils that become trunks with roots of their own. To reach the gardens, climb from Playa de San Telmo onto C. la Hoya and continue onto C. Calzada de Martiánez until you reach Av. Marqués Villanueva del Prado. Follow the road past the Canary Centre; the gardens are on your left. (30-40min.) The climb is very steep, and it may be worth taking the €2 taxi ride up; buses to La Orotava and Santa Cruz pass by as well. (☎922 38 35 72. Open daily Apr.-Sept. 9am-7pm; Oct.-Mar. 9am-6pm. €3.) For beaches, **Playa Jardín** is preferable to the smaller, black-sand **Playa Martiánez.** The amusing **Lago Martiánez** is a nature-themed water park with saltwater pools and waterfalls designed by César Manrique. (Open daily 10am-7pm. €3.30, under 10 €1.10.)

⬛⬛ NIGHTLIFE AND FESTIVALS. Beware of the overpriced discotecas on C. Generalisimo, where a drink can cost upward of €6. To salsa without dishing out a fortune on drinks, go to **Azúcar,** C. Iriarte, 1, at the intersection of C. Dr. Ingram and C. Blanco. This Cuban-themed bar and local favorite spins salsa, merengue; and other Latin beats. (Drinks €3.40-4. Open Tu-Su 10pm-4am.) Tourists are also drawn to the **Fiestas de Julio,** two drunken weeks of live performances and festive meals centered around the July 16 **Fiesta de la Virgen del Carmen,** in which an image of the saint is paraded through town and into the ocean.

⬛ DAYTRIPS FROM PUERTO DE LA CRUZ

⬛ PARQUE NACIONAL EL TEIDE

Bus #348 departs from the main station in Puerto de la Cruz at 9:15am and returns from the Parador de Turismo of El Teide at 4pm. (2hr., one-way €4.80.) Renting a car provides flexibility and allows exploration of the wildly different but equally beautiful views from the eastern (Puerto de la Cruz) and western (Los Cristianos) access roads.

Towering 3718m over Tenerife, Spain's highest peak presides over a vast, unspoiled expanse of rock formations and unique wildlife and a view of the entire archipelago. El Teide itself forms the northern ridge of a much larger volcano that erupted millions of years ago. The last eruption was in 1798, but the Teide-Pico Viejo complex in the summit crater is still active. For now, over 400 species inhabit the almost otherworldly terrain; watch out for the **Lagarto Tizón,** a stone-camouflaged lizard, the endangered **Teide violets,** and the exotic **Teide bugloss,** a magenta, cone-shaped plant, both native species.

The bus makes its first stop in the park at **El Portillo Visitor's Center** (38300 El Portillo), which offers comprehensive park maps and a short, excellent video on the history and geology of El Teide in three different languages. (☎922 35 60 00. Open daily 9am-4:15pm.) It stops next at the base of Montaña Blanca, before arriving at the **teleférico** (cable car), which climbs the final 1000m almost all the way to El Teide's peak. (Open daily 9am-4pm; €20.) Hikes to the summit require a permit, early start, and strong legs, but a worthwhile view of the entire island that awaits at the top. To get a permit, apply in person at least two days in advance at the **Oficinas del Parque,** C. Emilio Calzadilla, 5, in Santa Cruz. (☎ 922 29 01 29. Open M-F 9am-2pm. Free.) The office also offers **free guided hikes** that depart daily. The last stop is **Parador de Turismo,** located near the stately **Roques de García** (2140m), rock chimneys and remnants of volcanic eruptions. Though tourists crowd the lookout, you'll be alone on the trail (an easy 2hr. hike), which has fantastic views of the bizarre rock formations. Next to the Parador is the newer **Cañada Blanca** visitors center, where hikers can get advice and directions on nine different routes. (☎ 922 37 33 91. Open 9am-4:15pm.)

LA OROTAVA

Buses #101, 350, and 353 run from Puerto de la Cruz's main bus station (30min., every 30min.-1hr. 5:30am-1:25am, €2.20).

The small town of La Orotava, named for the valley of banana plantations that spreads out below, was once the richest and largest of Tenerife's nine Guanche fiefdoms, and it finally fell to the conquistadors in 1496. In the 17th and 18th centuries, Spanish, Italian, and Flemish nobility resided here, leaving elegant squares, botanic gardens, and churches renowned for their facades. Plan for a weekday jaunt—most establishments here are closed on weekends.

The tourist office map lists over 15 sights. Though it would take a full day to see them all, the following walking tour should take only 2hr. From the **bus station,** head uphill on C. Alfonso Trujillo and turn right onto Av. Emilio Luque Moreno, which becomes Av. José Antonio and then Carrera del Escultor Estévez. Continue past Pl. de la Constitución to the **tourist office,** C. Carrera del Escultor Estévez, 2. (☎ 922 32 30 41. Open M-F 8:30am-6pm.) From the tourist office, turn left down C. Tomás Zerolo to find **Iglesia de Santo Domingo,** whose chapel contains several notable paintings. Next door is the **Museo Iberoamericano de Artesanía** C. Tomás Zerolo, 34, which houses handicrafts of Spain and Latin America. (☎ 922 32 33 76. Open M-F 9am-6pm, Sa 9am-1pm. €2.10.) Next, **Iglesia de la Concepción,** off C. Cologan, is a national artistic monument and perhaps the Canarias' most graceful Baroque building. (Open daily 9am-1pm and 4-7pm. Free.) From the church, go uphill on C. Tomás Pérez and right on Carrera del Escultor Estévez to the Neoclassical **Palacio Municipal** and the **Plaza del Ayuntamiento.** The cobblestones in the plaza are the result of regal egotism—Alfonso XIII ordered the streets paved before he visited. Just up C. Tomás Pérez, the sensory explosion of **Hijuela del Botánico** offers celestial walkways through tropical flora and a fine specimen of the **drago tree,** a long-living species considered sacred by the Guanche people. Exiting the Hijuela, cross the street into the **Jardines de la Quinta Roja** with more formal terraced gardens with fountains and views of the sea. The **Pl. de la Constitución** boasts a few small restaurants, but none are especially noteworthy.

LA GOMERA ☎ 922

La Gomera, only 45min. from Tenerife by boat, is worlds away in scenery and spirit. Many believe the island, with its rocky gorges, sleepy beaches, and mountain passes, possesses the most blessed landscape in all the *Canarias.* Surrounded by banana and avocado plantations and cooled by a constant breeze, the island's capital, San Sebastián, is unspoiled by city skylines or daytrippers from Tenerife. La Gomera's crown jewel is the spectacular Parque Nacional de Garajonay, the last remaining refuge in the world of laurisilva forests, which died out elsewhere millions of years ago. Rent a car: limited schedules and gut-wrenching rides make buses the territory of the truly hardy traveler.

SAN SEBASTIÁN DE LA GOMERA ☎922

The town's main claim to fame is Christopher Columbus's brief stay. He passed through the islands on his way to the "New World." Modern-day explorers breeze through this sleepy San Sebastián on their way to beaches in the south, but the town is also a calm base for exploring the rest of La Gomera.

⌐ TRANSPORTATION

Flights: Most people arrive via ferry from Tenerife, but the island's **airport** (☎922 87 30 13) has a few daily flights from Tenerife's northern airport, Los Rodeos, and Gran Canaria.

Buses: Servicio Público Regular has limited service on the island. There's a bus stop by the ferry station on the port; 3 lines branch out across the island (up to €5, depending on destination). Buses also stop at the **Estación de Guaguas** (☎922 14 11 01), in San Sebastián on the corner of Av. de Colón and Av. del Quinto Centenario. Line 1 to **Valle Gran Rey** (M-Sa 4 per day 11am-9:30pm, Su 11:00am, 6:30pm; €5) via **Parque Nacional de Garajonay** (€2, 1hr.). Line 2 to **Vallehermoso** (M-Sa 5 per day 9:30am-9:30pm, €4.50) via **Hermigua** (€2.50) and **Agulo** (€3). Line 3 to **Alajeró** (M-Sa 4 per day 11:30am-9:30pm, Su 11:30am, 6:30pm; €4) via **Playa Santiago** (€3.50) and the island's **airport** (€4).

Ferries: Fred Olsen (☎902 10 01 07) runs daily ferries to **Los Cristianos** and **El Hierro** (see **Inter-Island Transport**, p. 585). Garajonay Exprés (☎922 87 21 18, Central 902 34 34 50; www.garajonayexpres.com) runs a passenger ferry to **Los Cristianos** and **Tenerife** with bus service to **Santa Cruz, Tenerife, Playa de Santiago,** and **Valle Gran Rey** (45min.; 3 per day 9:40am-8:40pm; €3.38, students €2.70). Ferries are cheaper and faster than buses.

Car Rental: CICar (☎922 14 17 56; open M-Su 8am-7pm) and **Hertz** (☎922 87 04 61; open M, W, F 8am-7pm; Tu, Th, Sa-Su 8:30-11:30am and 1:30-6:30pm), both in the port terminal. 21+. AmEx/MC/V.

Taxis: ☎922 87 05 24.

✦? ORIENTATION AND PRACTICAL INFORMATION

Navigating San Sebastián is not difficult. From the port, **Paseo de Fred Olsen** becomes **Avenida de los Descubridores** and runs along the entire coast, intersected midway by **Calle Real,** also known as **Calle Medio,** at **Plaza de las Américas,** the town's social center. To get to the plaza from the **port,** turn left on Po. de Fred Olsen; the plaza is on the right (5min.). If you arrive after sunset, consider taking a quick taxi into town (€2), as the streets aren't clearly marked and are difficult to manage in the dark. **Buses** stop at the port, meeting most ferries. If you're driving, turn left out of the port onto Po. de Fred Olsen, take the third right onto **Avenida del Quinto Centario** and left at the gas station onto Ctra. General de Sur (TF-713) to head out of town toward **Valle del Gran Rey.** Use extreme caution driving on the island; there are numerous blind corners, hairpin turns, and mountain passes.

Tourist Office: C. Real, 4 (☎922 14 15 12 or 07 02 81; www.gomera-island.com), behind Pl. de las Américas in the Casa de la Aguada. Open M-Sa 9am-1:30pm and 3:30-6pm, Su 10am-1pm. **Park Service,** Ctra. General de Sur (TF-713), 6 (☎922 87 01 05). Go left on Av. de Colón from C. Real and across the bridge, following signs to Valle Gran Rey; the office is on the right at the 2nd bend. Open M-F 8am-3pm.

Currency Exchange: Banco Santander Central Hispano, C. Real, 7 (☎922 87 07 55 or 922 87 07 56). 24hr. **ATM.** Open M-F 8:30am-2pm, Sa 8:30am-1pm. Banks line Pl. de las Américas.

Laundromat: Lavandería HECU, C. Real, 76 (☎922 14 11 80). Open M-Sa 9am-2pm, 5:30-8pm. €4.50 cold water wash, €9 cold wash and dry; €6.30/10.80 with hot water.

Police: Pl. de las Américas, 4 (☎922 14 15 72), in the *Ayuntamiento*.

Pharmacy: Pl. de la Constitución, 14 (☎922 14 16 05). Open M-F 9am-1:30pm and 5-8pm, Sa 9am-1:30pm.

Hospital: Nuestra Sra. de Guadalupe (☎920 14 02 00). From Pl. de las Américas, walk away from the port, turn right onto Av. del Quinto Centenario, left across the bridge, and take the 1st right.

Internet Access: The best option is the artsy café **El Rincón del Poeta,** Av. de Colon, 8 (☎606 94 45 62). €2 per hr. Wi-Fi available. Open M-Sa 9:30am-2pm, 5pm-midnight.

Post Office: C. Real, 60 (☎922 87 10 81). Open M-F 8am-3pm, Sa 9:30am-1pm. **Postal Code:** 38800.

ACCOMMODATIONS

San Sebastián's budget accommodations are more affordable than anywhere in the Canarias. *Pensiones* offer double rooms in old *Canario* homes; most have hall baths. *Pensión* signs hang outside doors on C. Real. Victor, who knows just about everyone in town, tirelessly cares for **Pensión Victor ❷,** C. Real, 23, housed in a 350-year-old building with flower beds and vines along the patio. (☎607 81 32 01 or 607 51 75 65; fax 922 87 13 35. Singles €18; doubles €20-25. Discounts for longer stays. MC/V.) Farther from the Pl. de las Américas than Victor, the **Pensión Colombina ❷,** C. Ruiz Padrón, 83 has comfortable, simple rooms with private bath, some with balcony. (☎922 87 12 57. Singles €20; doubles €25. Cash only.) At the **Pensión Colón ❷,** C. Real, 59, tiled floors and spacious rooms surround a quiet courtyard. (☎922 87 02 35. Singles €20; doubles €25. Cash only.)

FOOD

San Sebastián is filled with authentic *canario* restaurants and cheap tapas bars. Be sure to stop in on a bakery selling *dulces gomeros* (Gomeran sweets) in the plaza. **Bar-Restaurante Casa del Mar ❷,** Po. de Fred Olsen, 1, serves *bacalao a la vizcaína* (cod in tomato and zucchini sauce with local potatoes; €8.50) and an assortment of seafood dishes. (☎922 87 03 20. Entrees €5-9. Open daily 1-3pm and 7-10:30pm.) **Bar-Restaurant Rosa ❷,** C. Virgen de Guadalupe, 2, off Pl. de la Constitución, dishes up healthy portions of typical *canario* seafood and meat fare to a local crowd. (☎922 77 38 69. Entrees €7-10. Open daily 11am-4pm and 6:30-11pm.) For a more upscale feel, try **Marques de Oristano ❷,** C. Real 24, a gourmet restaurant, grill, and *pastelería* set inside an airy stone room with high ceilings and generous wooden windows. (☎922 87 29 09. Entrees €6.20-10.50. Grill open M 8am-11pm, Tu-Sa 1:30-4pm and 8-11pm. Gourmet restaurant open Tu-Sa 1:30-4pm and 8-11pm. AmEx/MC/V.) For a quick bite on the way to the bus station, try **Los Descubridores ❶,** on the corner of C. Ruiz de Padrón and the Parque de la Torre, which offers cheap tapas, sandwiches, and fresh fruit juices and shakes for €1.50-3.40. (☎922 87 17 94. Open Tu-Su 9am-11pm.) Buy groceries at **Hiper Trebol** in the market complex at the intersection of C. Colón and Av. del Quinto Centenario, underneath the bus station. (☎922 87 13 66. Open M-Sa 9am-9pm, Su 9am-3pm. MC/V.)

SIGHTS

The city's motto reads "de aquí partió Colón," or "Columbus left from here." Accordingly, the few sights in San Sebastián focus on this famous foreigner, Italian-born Cristóbal Colón (Christopher Columbus). Before he set out for the 'New World,' Columbus prayed at the **Iglesia Nuestra Senora de la Asunción**, C. Real, across from the intersection of C. República de Chile. (☎922 87 03 03. Open before mass M-F 6pm, Sa-Su 11am and 6pm.) The **Torre del Conde,** a rather stumpy 15th-century fort, peers out over the coast from a small park. In 1488, Beatriz de Bodadilla, Columbus's love interest, bolted herself inside as she watched the citizens take control of the port. (Open M-F 10am-1pm and 4-7pm. Free. Park open in summer daily 9am-9pm; in winter daily 9am-8pm.) The tourist office is inside **La Casa de la Aguada,** C. Real, 4, featuring the **Pozo de la Aguada,** the well from which Columbus drew water to "baptize the Americas." Although there is a small patch of sand in front of Pl. de las Américas, **Playa de la Cueva,** a little black beach, is a slightly better bet, offering more sand, calmer waters, and on a clear day, a view of Tenerife. From Pl. de las Américas, follow Po. de Fred Olsen toward the port and curve left away from the wharf.

🛈 DAYTRIP FROM SAN SEBASTIÁN

◪ PARQUE NACIONAL DE GARAJONAY

Take the bus (line #1) to Valle Gran Rey and get off at Pajarito (M-Sa 4 per day 11am-9:30pm, Su 11:30am and 6:30pm; €2); bear right, and the trailhead is 1km up the road. A car greatly facilitates exploration of the park, offering several more points of entry, but several of the best trails are accessible by bus.

Blanketed in thick mist and fog that produces a "horizontal rain" year-round, Garajonay National Park sustains some of the last **laurisilva forests** on earth. The park maintains numerous trails, most originating from **Contadero.** From there it's about 1.7km climb through ferns, myriad streams, and dripping plants up to the **Alto de Garajonay,** a moderate climb well worth the stunning mountaintop view. For the less athletically inclined, the drive up is almost as stunning as the hikes— giant, precariously placed rocky remnants of past volcanic activity, **Los Roques,** line the roadside. The **visitors center** is in **Agulo,** 9km outside the park. The center provides maps, guides to flora and fauna, and info on the park's hikes. (☎922 80 09 93. Open daily 9:30am-4:30pm.) To get there, take bus #2 from San Sebastián (45min., M-Sa 5 per day 9:30am-9:30pm) and get off at the Las Rosas stop (the center is about 2km away). The **Park Service,** Ctra. General del Sur (TF-713), 6, in San Sebastián, has the same info. (☎922 87 01 05. Open M-F 8am-3pm.) The Agulo office makes reservations that are required for the **free guided tours** (spring/summer Sa 10:30am, fall/winter Sa 10am). They meet in the visitors center in La Laguna Grande and are in Spanish only. (Open daily 8:30am-4:30pm.)

VALLE GRAN REY   ☎922

"The Valley of the Great King," a string of five tranquil towns connected by sandy beaches and terraced banana farms, is a far cry from the busy port cities of the Canarias. The small towns provide a nice break from the glitz of the islands, offering bohemian comforts and keeping tourists content with sunbathing, cliff-exploring, water sports, and the feel of an authentic fishing village.

🯇 TRANSPORTATION. Garajonay Exprés runs passenger ferries (p. 587) to **Playa de Santiago, San Sebastián,** and **Los Cristianos.** Bus #1 runs from San Sebastián to Valle Gran Rey's five small villages: **La Calera, Borbalán, Vueltas, La Puntilla,** and **La Playa,** in that order. (2hr.; M-Sa 4 per day 11am-9:30pm, Su 11:30am and 6:30pm; €5.) **Taxis** are at ☎922 80 50 58. Although Valle Gran Rey is small enough to travel by foot, exploration is possible with cheap top-end bike rental at **Bike Station Gomera,** La

Puntilla, 7, which organizes excursions (€34 and up; book a day in advance) and €12 shuttle service to **La Laguna**, 1260m uphill. (☎922 80 50 82; www.bike-station-gomera.com. Beach cruisers €7 per day. Hard tails €13. Full suspension €18. Discounts for multi-day rentals. Open M-Sa 9am-1pm and 5-8pm.)

🔢🔢 ORIENTATION AND PRACTICAL INFORMATION. La Calera sits up higher in the valley, while La Playa, La Puntilla, and Vueltas are on the shores below; Borbalán is between La Calera and Vueltas. The five are geographically aligned in a triangular form less than a kilometer long. Street signs and numbers are pretty much nonexistent, but the area is easy to navigate. The **tourist office**, C. Lepanto, is located in La Playa. From the La Playa's bus stop, face the beach, head right on the main road, and turn left on C. Noria. From the port, bear right and follow the major road along the coast. (☎922 80 54 58. Open in summer M-Sa 9:30am-1:30pm; in winter M-Sa 9am-1:30pm and 4-6:30pm, Su 10am-1pm.) Local services include: a **medical center**, C. Las Orijamas beyond C. La Calera (☎922 80 70 05); an **Internet cafe**, Cyber Dragon, just outside the port off C. Vueltas (☎922 80 70 29; open M-Sa 11am-2pm and 6-9pm); a **pharmacy**, Farmacia Celina, on the main road in Borbalán (☎922 80 59 19; open M-Su 9am-2pm and 5-9pm); farther up the street, away from the port, is a 24hr. **ATM** and the **post office** (☎922 80 57 30; open M-F 8:30am-2:30pm, Sa 9:30am-1pm). **Postal Code:** 38870.

📱📱 ACCOMMODATIONS AND FOOD. The few *pensiones* in the area primarily offer doubles. Apartments provide more amenities and are widely available; the owner of the **San José ❸**, next to the tourist office in La Playa, rents apartments with kitchens and new floors. (☎922 80 53 31. Doubles €27; quads €35.) At the fork in the road before entering La Playa, **Pension Las Jornadas ❷**, has simple rooms with private bath or shower. (☎922 80 50 47; fax 80 52 54. Singles €18; doubles €20. Price increases after 3 days.)

If you're staying in La Playa looking for good eats, don't miss the mouth-watering tapas (€3-5) at **Tasca Mango ❷**, Po. de Las Palmeras, 2. (☎922 80 53 62. Open M-Sa for dinner. Kitchen closes at 10:30pm.) In Vueltas, walking along the Av. Marítimo, 1min. from the port, lies **Tambara Cafe ❶**, decorated with a Moroccan-themed tiled interior (☎646 511 090, www.tambaracafe.com. Open M-Tu and Th-Su 9am-midnight.) For a town favorite, try **Restaurante El Puerto ❶**, right in the port at the end of Av. Marítimo. Try the medregal, a local fish, for €6. (☎922 80 52 24. Open M-Tu and Th-Su 1-3:45pm and 6-10pm.) For groceries, try **Albatros Supermercado**, left out of the tourist office. (Open M-F 7:30am-9:30pm. MC/V.)

📷 BEACHES AND OUTDOOR ACTIVITES. Walking from village to village is an enjoyable stroll past colorful awnings and families with children wading in clear blue waves. The most popular beaches here are **Playa de Argaga** and **Playa las Arenas,** a short walk left of Vueltas when facing the beach. The sandy **Playa de Calera** and **Playa de Puntilla**, which stretch left from La Playa, have calm waters. The nude beach **Playa del Inglés** is popular, but don't shy away for fear of a crowd; there are dozens of personal tanning "cubbies" built with volcanic stones to accommodate your desire for pseudo-privacy. With your back to the tourist office, walk to the right, take the first right, and follow the road, as it becomes dirt, to the beach (10min.). For scuba diving, try **Fisch & Co.**, La Playa, Apt. 99, which heads out every day at 9am. (☎922 80 56 88; www.fischco.com. Dive with equipment €35. Taster's lesson €38. 5-day certification course €375. Open M-Th and Sa-Su 9am-7pm.) **Gekko Tours,** La Playa, 2, offers hiking, biking, and scuba booking. There are also computers in the back with Internet for €1 per 30min. The South African owner, Charles, has answers to all questions Canaria. (Open daily 10am-2pm and 6-9pm).

LANZAROTE
☎928

Volcanic activity from 300 years ago left Lanzarote barren and dry, with an unusual crater-like landscape created by lava flow. Driving through the island takes you from one arid landscape to another—cacti, cinder cone, sandy beach, and quaint, isolated towns that could be at home on the surface of the moon. When visiting, do not rely on public transportation—as on Fuerteventura, the vast majority of the island's sights can be accessed only by car or infrequent buses. In order to avoid exorbitant charges and endless frustration, the best choice is to rent a car, pick up an island map at any tourist office, and start exploring.

ARRECIFE
☎928

For the most part, visitors to Arrecife (pop. 51,000) see little more than the airport. A stopping point en route to the beaches in the south, Lanzarote's capital city has little to see in itself, but is a useful base for daytrips.

▙▐ TRANSPORTION AND PRACTICAL INFORMATION. All flights land at the **Aeropuerto de Lanzarote** (☎928 84 60 00), 6km west of Arrecife. From the airport, bus #4 runs to **Playa Reducto** at the edge of town (25min.; every 30min. M-F 7:20am-10:50pm, Sa-Su 8:50am-10:50pm; €0.90). The green and white **Arrecife Bus** (☎928 81 15 22) runs to: Cruce de César Manrique (#7 and 9; 10min.; M-F 6 per day 6:40am-7pm, Sa-Su 3-4 per day 7am-9pm; €0.95); Playa Blanca (#6; 1hr.; M-F 12 per day 6am-8:15pm, Sa-Su 6-8 per day 6:50am-7:40pm; €2.75); Puerto del Carmen (#2; 40min.; M-F every 20min. 6:20am-11:20pm, Sa-Su every 30min. 6:20am-11:20pm; €1.30); and various other destinations. **Naviera Armas** (☎902 22 02 25) runs ferries to: Las Palmas (5hr., 4 per week, €32), Puerto Rosario (2-3hr., W 10am, €15); and Santa Cruz de Tenerife (7-10hr., 4 per week, €36). Discounts apply for those under 26 or over 60. **Taxis** (☎928 80 31 04, 81 27 10, or from the airport 52 22 11) run where buses do not, though the service number changes with each town, so make sure to call ahead to find out. The major commercial thoroughfare and shopping district of town, **C. León y Castillo**, divides the city, running perpendicular to the coast, and is directly across from the **castle,** or Puente de las Bolas. To get from the **bus stop** at Playa Reducto to C. León y Castillo, head toward the castle, following the coastline toward the city, and take a left. Av. Fred Olsen becomes Av. Dr. Rafael Glez Negrin until you get to the marina, where it hugs the boardwalk (15min.). The **tourist office** is on Blas Cabrera Felipe (☎928 81 17 62; www.turismolanzarote.com. Open July-Sept. 8am-2pm; Oct.-June 8am-3pm.) Local services include: **police,** Av. Vargas, 6 (☎928 81 13 17), along the coast past C. León y Castillo on the right; **pharmacy,** C. León y Castillo, 13 (☎928 81 10 93; open M-F 9am-1pm and 5-8pm, Sa 9am-1pm); and **Internet** access at **Recreativos Lanzarote** (☎928 80 04 02; open 8am-10:30pm), at C. León y Castillo and C. Emilio Ley, is €0.50 for 20min. The **post office** is on C. Av. de la Marina, 8. (☎928 80 06 73. Open M-F 8:30am-8:30pm, Sa 9:30am-1pm.) **Postal Code:** 35500.

▙▐ ACCOMMODATIONS AND FOOD. Budget accommodations are rare in Arrecife. If you need a place to crash for the night, head first to **Pension Cardona ❸,** C. 18 de Julio, 11. The pleasant owner provides bright, high-quality, and exceptionally clean rooms. From Av. Dr. Rafael Glez. Negrin, parallel to the water, take a right onto C. 18 de Julio, and it's on your right at the end of the street. (☎928 81 10 08; fax 81 10 12. Laundry. Singles €27; doubles €33. Cash only.) Cafes abound along the coast and up C. León y Castillo, but the *pastelerías* are particularly noteworthy. **Pastelería La Salud ❷,** C. León y Castillo, 37, has over 40 years of experience serving cheap and oh-so-delicious pastries. (☎928 81 18 48. Open M-Sa

8:30am-9pm. Cash only.) Artsy **Café Gernika ❶**, C. Gines de Castro, 4, provides cheap breakfast (hot chocolate and a croissant for €3) and a tiled interior combining French and Spanish influences. It is the first right off of C. León y Castillo. (☎928 81 65 02. Open M-F 8am-8pm, Sa 9am-3pm. Cash only.) For staples, head across the street to the ground floor of the **Atlántida Shopping Complex**, where there is a **HiperDino** supermarket. (☎928 80 10 09. Open M-Sa 9am-9pm.)

SOUTHERN LANZAROTE

PUERTO DEL CARMEN   ☎928

Puerto del Carmen, a stop on many packaged tours, is flooded with British tourists. **Avenida de las Playas** crams in an incredible number of restaurants, bars, and bazaars. Though lined with signs of tourism's ugliness, the city has done its best to beautify its beaches with volcanic rock and plants. **Playa Grande** and **Playa del Baranquillo** are both off of Av. de las Playas. Offshore reefs offer some of the islands' best **scuba diving**. For more information, try **Centro de Buceo Atlantica**, on Playa Grande across from the McDonald's on Av. de las Playas. (☎660 46 99 58. Offers PADI certification. 1 dive €26. Open M-Sa 10am-5pm.)

In the center of the old town, bright, tasteful rooms with beautiful bathrooms and ocean views make **Pensión Magec ❷**, C. Hierro, 11 a great deal and a good base for those without cars. (☎928 51 51 20; www.pensionmagec.com. Singles €22, with shower €30; doubles €25/30. MC/V.) To eat away from the crowd of Brits and Dubliners, try the fish (€7.50-10.50) at **Mardeleva ❷**, C. Los Infantes, 10. (☎928 51 06 86. Open M-Sa noon-3pm and 8pm-11:30pm. MC/V.)

The white-and-green **Arrecife Bus** (arrecifebus.com) runs between Arrecife and Puerto del Carmen, stopping along Av. de las Playas (#2; 40min.; M-F every 20min. 6:20am-11:20pm, Sa-Su every 30min. 6:20am-11:20pm; €1.40). Bus #6 runs to Playa Blanca from the Biosfera (40min.; M-F 10 per day 6am-9:30pm, Sa-Su 6-8 per day 6:50am-7:30pm; €2.50). **Fred Olsen** (☎902 10 01 07; www.fredolsen.es) and **Naviera Armas** (☎902 45 65 00, in Corralejo 928 86 70 80; www.navieraarmas.com) also run free buses for clients to Playa Blanca to meet ferry departures. The **tourist office** is at Av. de las Playas near the beach. (☎928 51 33 51; www.puertodelcarmen.com. Open July-Sept. M-F 10am-4pm; Oct.-June slightly less.) Local services include: **Cyber cafes** and **pharmacies** on Av. de Las Playas; **Hospital General** (☎928 59 50 00); and the **post office**, C. Manguía, 2. (☎928 51 03 81. Open M-F 8:30am-2:30pm, Sa 8:30am-1pm.) **Postal Code:** 35510.

PLAYA BLANCA   ☎928

A mid-size city not yet completely destroyed by tourist traffic, Playa Blanca, at the bottom tip of Lanzarote, is best experienced for a day or en route to somewhere else. If you have a car, stop by **Playa de Papagayo**, one of the most famous beaches on the island. From Ctra. Playa Blanca, follow the road until you reach the end. Turn left on Av. de Papagayos and continue until you reach the beach (10min.). If you need a place to stay, try **Apartamentos Gutiérrez ❹**, Pl. Nuestra Señora del Carmen, 8. Rooms are clean, large, pretty, and a great deal for more than one person. (☎636 37 28 93. Singles €36; doubles €40; triples €45; quads €50. Cash only.) For groceries, head to **Supermercado SPAR**, on C. Limones, on the corner of El Varadero. (☎928 51 91 36. Open M-Sa 8am-10pm, Su 8am-2pm and 4-10pm.)

Buses run from Arrecife to Playa Blanca (#6; 1hr.; M-F 12 per day 6am-8:15pm, Sa-Su 6-8 per day 6:50am-7:40pm; €2.75), and from Puerto del Carmen (#6; 40min.; M-F 8 per day 6:20am-8:35pm, Sa-Su 6-8 per day 7:15am-8:05pm; €2.50). **Pharmacy** on Av. Papagayo, 15. (☎928 51 84 73. Open M-Sa 9am-9pm.) A **tourist**

office is located in the port (☎928 51 90 18; open M-F 9am-1:30pm) and another is on C. El Varadero, down the street from the bus stop. (☎928 51 90 18. Open M-F 8am-8pm.) The **post office** is farther down El Varadero.

WESTERN LANZAROTE

⬛PARQUE NACIONAL DE TIMANFAYA   ☎928

No public transportation runs directly to the park, though you can take line 6 to Yaiza, and a cab from there to the park for €15. If taking a cab, arrange a set time and price with the driver for service to and from the park. For a more flexible experience, renting a car is highly recommended. ☎928 84 00 57. Park open daily 9am-5:45pm; last bus leaves at 5pm, last car enters park at 3:45pm. €8.

Known as the **Montañas del Fuego** (Fire Mountains), the barren landscape of Lanzarote's national park still shows evidence of the six-year explosion that began in 1730, with copper *hornitos* (mud volcanos) and blackened folds of solidified lava carved into the loose soil. Exploring the park solo is prohibited. Instead, there is a trilingual 35min. **bus tour.** The light orange buses leave from the main parking lot in front of El Diablo Restaurant. Don't worry—the frequent explosions of steam

 THE RIGHT SEAT. If you take the park's bus tour, make sure to grab a seat on the right. Unlike your fellow wayfarers on the left, you'll actually get a glimpse of the views you came so far to see.

aren't vehicle malfunctions, only the magic tricks of **Islote de Hilario's** geothermal heat. Legend has it that the hermit **Hilario,** who lived here with his lone camel, planted a fig tree whose fruit was consumed by the underground fires; today, park employees demonstrate the effects of the 600°C temperatures below the earth, unleashing jets of steam from the ground and setting brush on fire.

Free **walking tours** along the 3.5km Termesana trail can be arranged in advance through the Spanish National Park State Network. They are limited to two groups of seven people per day and must be arranged in advance—at least two weeks ahead of time—with the **visitors center** in Mancha Blanca, where they begin. (5min. from park main entrance. Take the road from Yaiza to Tinajo. Center located at km 11.5. ☎928 84 08 39; www.mma.es. Tours M, W, F 10am. Reservations via phone or email. Open daily 9am-5pm.) The **⬛Caldera Blanca** is staggeringly gorgeous, but climb it in the morning so you don't melt.

Volcanic heat seeping up from the earth roasts the sizzling chicken breasts on the grill at **El Diablo ❹**, the restaurant that now occupies the islote. Designed by local artist César Manrique and constructed using only stone, metal, and glass to withstand the high temperatures, the restaurant has the best panoramic view of the island, extending from the arid mountains to the azure sea. (☎928 84 00 57. Entrees €9-20. Open daily noon-6:45pm. AmEx/MC/V.)

CALETA DE FAMARA AND LA SANTA

Though located less than an hour from Arrecife, Famara beach could be a completely different island. Caleta de Famara, a town so tiny it is solely managed by almost three families, attracts sun-soakers and thrill-seekers alike by its proximity to world-class surf breaks. About 15-20min. to the west by car or bus is the surf town of La Santa, where hard-nosed wave-riders dominate the water and championship cyclists conquer the roads.

⬛🎏 **ORIENTATION AND PRACTICAL INFORMATION.** It is possible to reach Famara and La Santa by bus, though the schedules are extremely restrictive; a car allows for much more flexibility and time to explore. Take the #20 bus from

Arrecife to La Caleta de Famara (M-F, 4 per day 7am-5pm). To La Santa, catch a local bus.) The highway is the main drag in both towns and cannot be mistaken for anything else. In Caleta de Famara it is also called **Avda. El Marinero,** and in La Santa, **C. Encarnación.** Facing the water, the beach lies to the right of Famara and to the left of a set of terraced, Manrique-esque bungalows. In La Santa, face the coast and head right to find most of the friendly waters. **Internet** can be found in either town for a reasonable price. In Famara, heading toward La Santa, at the very end of the highway, in **Caleta Surf Action Center,** Avda. El Marinero, 128. (☎619 35 63 93. €1 per hr. Open M-Sa 10am-1pm and 4-8pm.) In La Santa, head to **Locutorio-Bazar La Santa,** next to Sense Surf and across the main drag from Pro Bike. (€0.20 for computer use and then €0.04 per min. after that.)

⚐ ACCOMMODATIONS. Inquiring about rooms in one of many surf shops or supermarkets on your own is entirely feasible and frequently practiced. Packaged deals are possible at **Club La Santa ❸,** Avda. Krogager, which occupies a good portion of La Isleta, just to the north of La Santa. (☎59 99 95 4430; www.clublasanta.com. Triples €75-86 in the low season. AmEx/MC/V.) For apartments in Caleta de Famara, try **Apartamentos Nano ❷.** Apartments are clean and well-kept, and depending on your luck, close to the beach. (☎928 52 86 50. For 1-2 nights, €36 per night; 1 week €30 per night; and 2 weeks €24 per night.)

❑ FOOD. For groceries head to **Supermercado Otila** on the Av. El Marinero on the right just as you pass the beach. (Open in summer daily 8am-10pm; during the rest of the year 8am-2pm and 5-9pm. Cash only.) **El Risco ❸,** C. Montaña Clara, 30, overlooks a rocky shore and for upscale prices offers a stunning view of Famara beach, Isla Graciosa, and the mountains overhead. Try the fresh fish for €8.50-10.50. (☎028 52 85 50. Open M-W and F-Su 12:30-10pm. MC/V.) **Restaurante La Santa ❷,** on the main strip, across from Pro Bike, is a fun, no-frills roadside restaurant. (☎928 84 03 53. Entrees run about €8. Open daily noon-midnight. MC/V.)

🏔 OUTDOOR ACTIVITIES. The beautiful stretch of coastline just to the northwest of Famara, known as **◼Playa Famara,** caters to everyone, from lazy afternoon sunbathers to surfing afficionados. Don't forget your sunscreen and a towel—though the beach has beginner-friendly break, there is no shade or cheap beach bazaar here. For lessons try the **Costa N-Oeste Surf School,** Avda. El Marinero, just off the highway on the left as you pass Famara Beach and enter town. (☎620 95 60 64 or 649 38 14 80. Half-day surf €25, full day surf €40, and full day kite surf €95.) If you're ready to hit the waves on your own, rent a board for €9 and a wetsuit for an extra €3. (Open daily 10am-1pm and 4-8pm. MC/V.) The **Caleta Surf Action Center,** Avda. El Marinero, 128, is a surf shop, Internet cafe, gym, and training center all rolled into one. (☎619 35 63 93. Boards start at €10 per day. Open daily 10am-1pm and 4-10pm. Hours subject to change. MC/V.) To connect to your inner om, **Lanzarote Yoga,** behind C. Islote in the Community Center, offers "yoga integral" classes that are both a great stretch and a light workout. (☎606 76 92 70. She teaches five times a week in Famara, Tu 7, 9:30am, 7pm; Th 9:30am and 7pm. €9 per class or 4 classes for €30. Cash only.) Inundated with jolly European cyclists, **Pro Bike,** C. Encarnación, 14, in La Santa on the main road, is geared toward expert cyclists. (☎928 84 01 03. Open Tu-Su 10am-2pm and 5-8pm. AmEx/MC/V.)

NORTHERN LANZAROTE

LA ISLA GRACIOSA   ☎928

If you're looking to escape the south, head all the way up to La Isla Graciosa (pop. 650), a small island spread below the dramatic northern cliffs. The isolated beaches and barren volcanic landscapes are worth a day of exploring. The more adventurous can **rent bikes** from **La Graciosa Bike,** Av. Virgen del Mar (☎928 84 21 38; €8 per day), or **Natural Bike** (☎928 84 21 42; €7-9 per day) within the town itself and head for ▓**Playa de las Conchas,** a perfect white-sand paradise, with crystal clear water and hardly any visitors. Call well in advance for space at **Pension Enriqueta ❶,** Mar de Barlovento, 4. (☎928 84 20 51. Doubles €20. Cash only.) **Camping** is allowed in the *zona de acampada* on Playa de Salao; facing the town from the harbor, walk left along the coast and around the point. Apply ahead for a permit (☎928 84 59 85). **Líneas Romero,** C. García Escámez, 11, runs daily ferries between Orzola and La Isla Graciosa. (☎928 84 20 55; www.lineas-romero.com. From Orzola: 20min.; July-Sept. 5 per day 10am-6:30pm; Oct.-June 3 per day 10am-5pm. From La Isla Graciosa: July-Sept. 5 per day 8am-6pm; Oct.-June 3 per day 8am-4pm. Round-trip €18, children €10.)

EASTERN LANZAROTE

Welcome to a giant César Manrique museum! Lanzarote's most famous sights were designed by this local artist, legendary throughout Las Islas Canarias for his participation in Spain's new-wave abstract art movement and his environmental contributions to the archipelago. The **Centros de Arte, Cultura, y Turismo** are all influenced or created by Manrique. Outside Teguise, restaurant/bar **LagOmar** was a Manrique design, and in the Parque Nacional de Timanfaya, take note of Manrique's **El Diablo** restaurant. To explore fully, rent a car.

▓**FUNDACIÓN CÉSAR MANRIQUE.** This fabulous two-story house, once home to the famous artist, was constructed over five large volcanic bubbles and lava caves in the late 1960s, resulting in a series of strange and incredible subterranean chambers and rooms connected by volcanic passageways. Lava, cooled after hundreds of years now appears mid-ooze, frozen in time, covering the windows of the upstairs gallery. *(6km north of Arrecife. Take the highway to Tahiche and turn onto Taro de Tahiche, off C. San Bartolomé. Alternatively, take bus #7 from Arrecife to Teguise and ask to be let off at the Fundación (6 per day 8am-8pm, Sa-Su 3-4 per day 7:30am-8pm; €0.95). A taxi from Arrecife costs approximately €5.50. ☎928 84 31 38; www.fcmanrique.org. Open July-Oct. daily 10am-7pm; Nov.-June M-Sa 10am-6pm, Su 10am-3pm. €8, under 12 free.)*

MUSEO INTERNACIONAL DE ARTE CONTEMPORÁNEO. Once an 18th-century fortress built to defend the island from pirates, this small museum was revitalized by Manrique in 1975. The original castle is a work of art itself, and showcases rotating exhibits and a permanent collection of geometric and abstract works affixed to the fort and hanging in the restaurant below. *(40min. walk to the west of Arrecife, off Av. Naos; taxis from Arrecife cost €3.60 and are safer than walking after dark. ☎928 81 23 21 and 80 06 16. Open daily 11am-9pm. Restaurant open 1-10:45pm. Free.)*

JAMEOS DEL AGUA. Built into subterranean tubes formed by volcanic activity 3000-4500 years ago, the Jameos del Agua is now a visitable underground chamber that houses a lagoon. Keep an eye out for the tiny white phosphorescent blind crabs unique to the Jameos. An auditorium built into the grotto holds the Festival de Música Visual de Lanzarote every October. *(On the northeastern coast 4km north of Arrieta. Take #9 bus from Arrecife to Cruce de Jameos; 30min.; M-F 7:40, 10:30am, 3:30pm; Sa-Su 7:40am and 3:30pm; €2.75. Taxi from Arrecife €26. ☎928 84 80 20. Open Tu and F-Sa 10am-6:30pm. Restaurant open Tu and F-Sa 7:30-11:30pm. Bar open 10am-6:30pm. Folk music performances Tu and F-Sa 7:30pm-2am. No casual attire. €8 during the day, €9 at night.)*

LA CUEVA DE LOS VERDES. This fantastic series of caves was formed by the volcanic eruption of nearby Corono thousands of years ago. The subterranean chambers were used by Canarios as refuge from pirate attacks in the 17th century.

The caves' coloring and texture are stunning, ranging from smooth basalt to porous red oxide-rich stone. The 40min. mandatory tour conducted in English and Spanish will make any tourist feel like a veritable spelunker; it runs every 20min. *(500m inland from Jameos del Agua. From Jameos del Agua, walk straight out of entrance up the center road to the parking lot; entrance is on your left. #9 bus from Arrecife (30min.; M-F 7:40, 10:30am, 3:30pm; Sa-Su 7:40am and 3:30pm; €2.50). Taxis from Arrecife run about €26. ☎928 84 84 84; fax 928 84 84 61. Open daily 10am-6pm, last entrance 5pm. €8.)*

MIRADOR DEL RÍO. Manrique's Mirador del Río is yet another magnificent example of architecture melting into the landscape. The building remains hidden from view until you've almost reached it, and the breathtaking view from over 1400 ft. makes you feel as though you are hovering over La Isla Graciosa. *(At the northern tip of the island, 7km north of Máguez. Accessible by the #7 bus to Plaza de Haria, and then a cab. Taxis from Arrecife cost €30. ☎928 52 65 48; fax 928 52 65 50. Mirador open daily 10am-6pm, last entrance 5:45pm. Bar-cafe open daily 10am-5:45pm. €4.70.)*

JARDÍN DE CACTUS. Constructed in the style of a Roman amphitheater, Manrique's prickly paradise boasts 1420 species of spiky, flowering, many-armed, and globular cacti from around the world, as well as a 24 ft. cactus sculpture. Visitors can tour a traditional windmill that locals occasionally use to grind barley for *gofio* (cereal). *(Off the highway in Guatiza. If not driving, catch the bus from Arrecife or the roundabout near Fundación César Manrique. From Arrecife take bus #7 or 9; M-F 3-6 per day 7:40am-8pm, Sa-Su 2-3 per day 7:40am-8pm; €1.30. ☎928 52 93 97. Open daily 10am-6pm. Bar open 10am-5:45pm. €5.)*

FUERTEVENTURA   ☎928

Locals will tell you that when *canarios* need a vacation they come to Fuerteventura. Boasting unparalleled aquamarine waters and empty coastlines, the second-largest island in the Canarias archipelago was named for the strong winds that whip along its western coast and make it an ideal location for surfing, wind sports, and scuba diving. Car rental is a must for those venturing to Fuerteventura on their own, as buses connect only to major cities.

PUERTO DEL ROSARIO   ☎928

Until 1957, Fuerteventura's whitewashed capital was known as Puerto de Cabras (Goats' Harbor). The goats knew what was good for them when they migrated out of the city, which has since become the junkyard of the Canarias. The town is trying to pull itself back up by its boot-straps, but for now, don't plan on staying in Puerto del Rosario (pop. 21,000) for more time than it takes you to leave. If you're stuck for the night, **Hostal Residencia Tamasite ❷**, C. León y Castillo, 9, has spectacularly clean rooms on the waterfront. From the bus station, head downhill on Av. de la Constitución, take a left onto C. León y Castillo, and head all the way to the water. All have TV, phone, and bath with shower. (☎928 85 02 80; fax 85 03 00. Singles €27; doubles €36. Cash only.) Food in Puerto del Rosario is equally basic; *cafeterías* are scattered along Av. Primero de Mayo and C. León y Castillo. A good one is **Tanguaro V ❶**, Pl. España, 7. From C. León y Castillo, turn right onto C. Fernández Casteñeyra; there's a nice view and great *churros*. (☎928 85 10 86. Sandwiches €1.50-2.50. Burgers €2. Combo plates €5.50-9. Open M-Sa 7am-11pm. Cash only.) Flights land at **Aeropuerto Fuerteventura** (☎928 85 12 50), and **Naviera Armas** (☎902 45 65 00) runs ferries to and from Las Palmas (see **Inter-Island Transport**, p. 585). **Tiadhe buses** run from Avda. de la Constitución, off of C. León y Castillo (☎928 85 21 66) to: the **airport** (#3 Caleta de Fuste bus and #10 Morro Jable bus; 20min.; M-F every 30min. 6:30am-10:30pm, hourly 10pm-midnight, Su hourly 7am-midnight; €2.50); Cor-

LAS ISLAS CANARIAS

ralejo (#6; 45min.; daily every 30min. 7am-6:30pm, hourly 7-11pm; €3.15); El Cotillo (#7, 40min., 3 per day 10am-7pm, €4.65); Morro Jable (#1 and 10; 2hr.; M-F hourly 6:30am-5:30pm, also 7, 8:30, 10:30pm; Sa hourly 9am-10:30pm, Su 10 per day 9am-8:30pm; €8.70). For a **taxi,** call ☎928 85 00 59. The **tourist office** (☎928 53 08 44) is brand new, where C. León y Castillo hits the roundabout at the port. Local services include: **police,** C. Fernández Castañeira, 2 (☎928 85 06 35); **pharmacy** on C. León y Castillo, 63 (☎928 85 01 97; open M-F 8:30am-1pm and 5-8pm, Sa 8:30am-1pm); a **hospital** on Ctra. Aeropuerto (☎928 53 73 99); free **Internet** access at **Bazar Locutorio Sahara,** Av. de la Constitución, 4 (☎928 53 85 50; open daily 9:30am-9pm.); and the **post office,** Av. 23 de Mayo, 76. (☎928 85 04 12. Open M-F 8:30am-8:30pm, Sa 9:30am-1pm.) **Postal Code:** 35600.

CORRALEJO ☎928

Corralejo's center is a zoo of northern European families, car rental shops, and restaurants, all blaring with neon light that makes even the green *farmacia* cross hard to distinguish. Toward the beach, however, a tight-knit community of Spaniards and ex-pats make their home. Southward, sunbathers and water sports enthusiasts will appreciate protected sand dunes and crystal oceans.

⊏ TRANSPORTATION. Fred Olsen and **Naviera Armas** run daily **ferries** to **Playa Blanca, Lanzarote** (see **Inter-Island Transport,** p. 585). To reach the center from the **port,** follow the stone walkway around the port, take a right on C. General García Escámez and turn left onto C. la Milagrosa, then turn left to reach **Avenida Nuestra Señora del Carmen** (10min.). **Tiadhe** runs **buses** from the station on Av. Juan Carlos I (☎928 85 21 66), off C. Lepanto, to **El Cotillo** (#8, 35min., hourly 9am-9pm, €4.55) and **Puerto del Rosario** (#6; 45min.; M-Sa every 30min. 7am-6:30pm, except 1:30 and 5pm, Su hourly 7am-9pm; €3.60). For a **taxi,** call ☎928 53 74 41 or hail one by Supermercado Los Corales.

⊟▨ ORIENTATION AND PRACTICAL INFORMATION. All activity extends along **La Calle Principal,** once referred to as **Avenida General Franco,** where tourists walk from the southern sand dunes to their hotels in the north, by the port. The **tourist office** is in Pl. Pública, off the end of Av. General Franco nearest the port. (☎928 86 62 35. Open summer M-F 8am-2pm, Sa-Su 9am-2pm.) There is a smaller branch in the main building at the port. Local services include: **police,** Po. Atlántico, 7 (☎928 86 61 07), near the intersection with Av. General Franco; **pharmacy,** Av. General Franco, 46 (☎928 53 55 62; open M-F 9am-1:30pm and 5-9pm, Sa 9am-1:30pm); and **Internet** access at Goticom, C. Gravina, 17, a left off Av. General Franco when heading toward the port (☎928 86 62 19; €2 per hr.; open M-Sa 10am-midnight). The **post office** is on C. Isaac Peral, 35 (☎928 53 50 55; open M-F 8:30am-2:30pm, Sa 9:30am-1pm). **Postal Code:** 35660.

▛▟ ACCOMMODATIONS AND FOOD. Graffitied ocean murals cover the walls of **Hotel Corralejo ❸,** C. Delfin, 1, off of Ntra. Sra. del Carmen, with pleasant rooms and generous common space. (☎928 53 78 27. Rooms €25-45. Cash only.) You can also rent reasonably priced, beautiful apartments from the **Dive Center Corralejo ❹,** C. Nuestra Sra. del Pino, 22. (☎928 53 59 06. €35-45 per night. Open M-Sa 8:30am-6:30pm. MC/V.) Easily the best deal in town, and a local take-away favorite (with a small outside terrace), is ▨**Da Uli ❶,** C. Crucero Baleares, one block toward the port and parallel to the Quicksilver and Red Shark surf shops. You won't pay much more than €5 for a full meal here, but the food is worth a US$1 million. (Open M-W and F-Su noon-11pm. MC/V.) **Cafe Lounge ❸,** C. Pulpo, 6, just behind the port, is a drink and dinner spot popular with local anglophones. Mondays features a €10 all you can eat BBQ. (☎928 86 64 73; www.cafe-lounge.com. Open M-W and F-Su 5pm-2am. MC/V.) For standard supplies, try **Supermercado Los Corales,** C. Principal, 40. (☎928 86 70 43. Open daily 9:30am-midnight.)

⚅ 🎵 NIGHTLIFE AND ENTERTAINMENT. Nightlife in Corralejo is a parade of tipsy tourists and lively locals. Going on its 14th year, **Oink!,** C. Commercial Atlántico, bottom floor, ocean side, is a lively surf bar with great music. Beer runs €1.80 and mixed drinks €4. Endear yourself to the owner, Jay, by ordering a shot of Jägermeister for €2. (Open daily 8pm-2:30am.) **Kiss Kiss Bang Bang,** C. Commercial Atlantico, bottom floor and also ocean side, is another surf-crowd/local hangout. (☎639 91 82 07. Open M-F 9pm-2:30am, Sa-Su 10pm-3am.) The **Fiestas del Carmen,** beginning July 16 and lasting two weeks, make for a lively visit. During the festival, decidedly unholy events such as volleyball competitions and outdoor dances help celebrate the town's patron saint before she is led on a parade through the port.

⚄ 🏄 BEACHES AND ACTIVITIES. The main attraction in Corralejo is the **Parque Natural de Corralejo y Lobos,** which contains protected, Sahara-sized sand dunes and beaches. For those without cars, the dunes are accessible via the #6 bus bound for Puerta Rosario; ask to stop at Los Hoteles (every 30min. 7am-6.30pm, hourly 7-11pm; €0.90). If you're interested in surf, head to **🏄Red Shark Fuerteventura,** C. Juan Sebastián El Cano, 32B, right around the corner from Quiksilver, before anywhere else. Its specialty is kite surfing lessons, but Red Shark also has a weekly fitness schedule, including yoga and boxing, and rents conventional surf supplies. (☎928 86 75 48; www.redshark-fuerteventura.com. From the roundabout near the clock tower on C. Principal, turn uphill on C. San Juan Sebastián, take the second right onto C. Juan Sebastián El Cano. €95 per day. Rent equipment separately for €35 per day, or a surfboard for €12 per day. Store also has free Wi-Fi. Open daily 9:30am-1pm and 6-9:30pm. MC/V.) **Dive Centro Corralejo,** C. Nuestra Señora del Pino, 22, offers dive trips, lessons, and equipment rental. PADI-associated, this place has been around forever, and is the most professional and well-equipped in the Canarias. (☎928 53 59 06. Open M-Sa 8:30am-6:30pm. MC/V). **Catamarán Celia Cruz** rigs daily trips on glass-bottomed catamarans to nearby Lobos Island. (☎639 14 00 14. €10-12 per person, ½-price for under 12, under 4 free.) **Ventura Surf,** in the Apartamentos Hoplaco complex on the C. Principal, on the left side of the beach, rents windsurfing equipment (€40 per day)

GIVING BACK

MAKING WAVES

Surfer Wim Geinaert came to Fuerteventura in search of the elusive "perfect wave" on the "perfect beach." However, what he found was far from pristine; much of the coastline was marred by unsightly amounts of litter.

To fight for the beach, Geinaert decided to start the Clean Ocean Project. Based on the island, the organization has launched several awareness campaigns to educate tourists and locals on the consequences of human impact on nature. The organization distributes trashcans and sponsors beach clean-ups all over the island, including Punta Blanca, Playa de la Lajita, and El Cotillo. Volunteers help by collecting hundreds of bags of trash in the name of preserving some of nature's most valuable assets.

If traipsing around in the sand with gloves and a trashbag isn't your idea of fun, then you can support the Project with a flair for fashion. The Clean Ocean Project stores, located throughout Fuerteventura, sell environmentally friendly clothing and use the proceeds to finance their clean-ups or to fund relief efforts elsewhere. Items include wallets made from recycled juice cartons and T-shirts advertising their environmental mission.

For more information on upcoming events, news, and clothing stores, visit www.cleanoceanproject.org or email info@cleanoceanproject.org.

and offers a 3hr. beginner's course (€75) and a 9hr. course (€129) for extra assistance. (☎928 86 62 95; www.ventura-surf.com. Open daily 10am-6pm.)

▶ DAYTRIP FROM CORRALEJO

EL COTILLO

Bus #8 runs to Corralejo (40min., every 2hr. 8am-7pm, €3.75). From Puerto del Rosario, follow the FV10 all the way to the coast, bearing left before La Olivia. El Cotillo is at km 37. Bus #7 runs to Puerto del Rosario (40min., 3 per day 6:45am-5pm, €4.55).

Still uncorrupted by the sprawl of tourism, this tiny fishing village is a surfers' heaven. From September to April beaches just south of town sport world-class waves, and nearby lagoons make the spot a top destination for more laid-back bathers year-round. The town's center is the old harbor, a short walk down and around the hill from the bus stop. If you've come to play, head to the only surf shop in town, **Montaña y Mar,** C. Reyes Católicos, which rents out surfboards, bodyboards, and wetsuits, as well as bikes. (☎610 31 69 86. Boards and wetsuits €5-12.50. Bikes €7.50 per day, €40 per week; includes helmet, lock, and map. Open 10am-noon and 5-7pm, or inquire at **The Last Resort,** next door.) If you plan on staying longer than a day, head for ▓**La Gaviota ❷**, C. Juan Betencourt, 14, perched on a cliff above the old harbor, which appears as an old pirate ship. (A skull and crossbones flag marks the spot.) Three-night stays are required. (☎928 53 85 67. Doubles €35-42, extra bed €10. Cash only.) Those looking for a more conventional hotel experience should try **Hotel Maríquita Hierro ❸**, C. Maríquita Hierro, 1, by the main bus stop, for standard rooms, some with views and all with bath, TV, phone, A/C, mini-fridge, breakfast, and use of a rooftop pool. (☎928 53 85 98; www.usarios.lycos.es/fuertehotels. Singles €28-35; doubles €45-47. Extra bed €9.50. MC/V.) Enjoy seating overlooking the harbor and Fuerteventuran specialities like *vieja a la plancha* (grilled parrot fish) with *papas arrugadas* ("wrinkled" potatoes with chunks of salt) at **Restaurante Playa ❷**, Muelle Viejo de Cotillo. (Seafood plates €7-11. Open M-W and F-Su 1-5:30pm.) **El Roque de Los Pescadores ❷**, C. Caleta, 2, specializes in fresh fish plates. (☎928 53 87 13. Entrees €8-11. Open daily 11am-10:30pm. MC/V.) **The Last Resort Bar/Cafe ❶**, C. Reyes Católicos, is a colorful place to grab a drink and catch British League rugby on the tube. (☎678 47 24 42. Beer €1.50. Mixed drinks €3. Open M-F 10am-last customer, Sa-Su noon-last customer.)

MORRO JABLE   ☎928

Bordered by the deep blue currents of Playas de Cofete and Barlovento, and the calm, turquoise bright, and sunny waters of the Playa de Sotavento, the Península de Jandía is 70km of heaven. The picture-perfect peninsula has transformed the fishing village of Morro Jable into a hothouse of accommodations and food.

⧉ TRANSPORTATION. There is no designated bus station in town. **Tiadhe** buses (☎928 85 21 66) stop at the Centro Comercial de Cosmo before terminating on C. Gambuesas in Morro Jable. **Buses** run to Costa Calma (#5; 1hr.; M-Sa 12 per day 8:30am-12:15am, Su 7 per day 9:30am-12:15am; €2.25) and Puerto del Rosario (#1, 2hr., 8-14 per day 6am-10:30 pm, €7.75; #10 direct, 1¼hr., 3 per day 6:30am-3:45pm, €7.50). **Taxis** (☎928 54 12 57) gather at the port and outside the Centro Comercial de Cosmo. A ride to one of the two main *playas* of Jandía costs €3. Car rental dealers are behind the tourist office in the Apartamentos El Matorral. **Orlando** rents 4WD vehicles for navigating the peninsula's rough dunes. (☎928 53 50 24. From €35 per day. 21+. Open M-F 8am-1pm and 4-7pm. AmEx/V.)

⬛🔢 ORIENTATION AND PRACTICAL INFORMATION. Morro Jable hugs the beach, most notably the **Playa de la Cebada** and the **Playa del Matorral**. **Avenida Jandía**, which becomes **Avenida del Saladar**, connects the east and west sides of the city center. Most hotels and restaurants line these two streets; the town's roads inevitably lead to the beach. The **tourist office**, Av. del Saladar, is in the Centro de Comercial Cosmo, local 88. (☎928 54 07 76. Open M-F July-Sept. 8am-2pm; Oct.-June 8am-3pm.) Local services include: **police**, Peatonal Atlántida, 1 (☎928 54 10 22); the **Centro Médico Jandía**, at the Jandía Beach Center, Urb. Solana (☎928 54 15 43 or 54 04 20; open 24hr.); and **Internet** access at **Videoclub Canal 15**, C. del Carmen, 41, parallel to C. Maxorata. (☎928 16 60 30. €2 per hour. Open daily 10am-midnight.) The **post office** is on the corner of C. Buenavista and C. Gambuesas. (☎928 54 03 73. Open M-F 8:30am-2:30pm, Sa 9:30am-1pm.) **Postal Code:** 35625.

🔢💠 ACCOMMODATIONS AND FOOD. Budget accommodations can be found around the town center, most notably along C. Maxorata and C. Senador Velázquez Cabrera, two parallel streets that lead to the sea. A short walk from the beach, **Hostal Omahy ❷**, C. Maxorata, 47, has small, clean rooms some with balcony. (☎928 54 12 54. Reserve ahead. Doubles with bath €25.) Restaurants in the area are tailored to the tourist crowds; Italian bistros, dime-a-dozen seafood joints, and German *konfiterias* line the beach. **Ristorante Mattarello ❷**, Avda. Tomás Gurrea, 2, is a quiet Italian nook just along the beach, as far toward the port before the road ends. Delicious pumpkin and orange soup for €5.50. (☎928 54 08 04. Entrees €8.50-10.50. Open Tu-Su 12:30pm-11pm. MC/V.)

💠🔢 BEACHES AND ENTERTAINMENT. The main attractions on the peninsula and in Morro Jable are fierce tanning and water sports in the welcoming ocean. Morro Jable's ▦**beaches** are lined with bodies—from gorgeous to ghastly—in various states of undress from early morning to late night. The most pristine *playas* on the peninsula are those in the south along Playa de Sotavento, followed by those in Playa de Batihondo and Playa del Matorral, close to the city center. If you get a chance, take a walk up the coast from Morro Jable to Costa Calma—empty shores and awe-inspiring horizons will make it well worth the long walk. Unbelievably calm waters, and truly fantastic marine ecosystems make Morro Jable a prime location for nearly every **water sport**. Stiff breezes off the peninsula's southern tip justify the innumerable **windsurfing** and **kitesurfing** schools that set up camp on the beach (the coast has hosted the World Championships for Professional Windsurfing during the last two weeks of July every year since 1985). Windsurfing and kitesurfing lessons are available at many of the kiosks that line the beach, while others offer jet skiing, wakeboarding, and boating excursions. For the most part, late-night activity revolves around the resorts on Av. del Saladar and the bars found in the **Centro Comercial de Cosmo** and the **Centro Comercial de Faro Atlantida**.

🔢 DAYTRIP FROM MORRO JABLE

PLAYA DE COFETE AND PUNTA DE JANDÍA

From Morro Jable, head toward the port. Before turning downhill to the left, the turnoff is well marked: Punta de Jandía and Playa de Cofete. Turn right. It is about 16km to the point, and about halfway, there will be another, not so well-marked sign marking the turn right and uphill, toward Cofete. Try to head out early; the later you go, the more congested the small road becomes, and it takes exponentially longer to pass.

For the patient and adventurous who want to get far, far away from the crowds and wade in decidedly wilder waters, the southern shores of the Peninsula are well worth it. The waters on this side of the peninsula are turbulent, violent, and have cross-currents. Rip tides are dangerous, especially for unaccustomed ocean swimmers. Be careful not to be swept to Morocco. Unless you possess a burning desire to contract skin cancer, bring sunscreen. There's not a bit of shade in sight. Camping is unofficially practiced, but it's best to make this a day-trip. If you're here for the beaches, skip the Faro (lighthouse) on the **Punta de Jandía** and head straight uphill for **Playa de Cofete.** These beaches are exclusively accessible by rental car—4WD is highly recommended and easy to come by, though the traditional, toonish little European cars will, if in good shape, be just fine. If you're driving on your own, take every precaution—brakes, gas, drinking water, etc. The views on the way are stunning, but keep your eyes on the road! Cofete's access route is a slow-going, stomach-churning, one-lane, dirt road that hovers precariously at points over a long drop into the ocean below. Once you arrive, the Playa de Cofete is isolated and beautiful. There are few restaurants, so it is advisable to pack a lunch. And then walk—for miles. **Playa de Barlovento** is farther north and a considerably longer drive. Driving on the sand is a bad idea; your car may get stuck, and worse, you will be trampling a pristine natural environment. Park at the bottom of the road to the beach and walk.

PORTUGAL

Portugal wears the ornaments of modernity and the artifacts of the past with equal elegance. The European country with the oldest established border, Portugal reached great heights as a superpower during the Golden Age of Vasco da Gama's maritime discoveries, but plummeted to lows as a vassal under the Moors, the Spanish, and finally the French. These extremes of fortune have contributed to the Portuguese concept of *saudade*, a yearning for people, places, and times that are gone, an idea that finds its greatest expression in the musical style *fado*. *Saudade* may be stitched into the soul of the nation, but Portugal is a lively country with pulsing cities, animated festivals, and a fervent passion for soccer. From the quiet forests of Douro and Minho to the rollicking coastal culture of the Algarve, cosmopolitan Lisboa to the sun-drenched, castle-dotted interior towns, discover Portugal's hidden treasure troves of landscapes, art, and architecture. Portugal has something to offer every traveler, including a sense of *saudade* when it comes time to leave.

HISTORY

In the 14th and 15th centuries, Portugal ruled a wealthy empire that stretched from America to Asia and was one of the most powerful nations in the world. While the country's international prestige diminished with the Spanish invasion in 1580, the Portuguese people's pride did not, and the nation did not rest until they regained independence in 1640. Today national pride is as strong as ever: one need look no further than the emotional fanfare surrounding the 2004 European Football Championship, and the 2006 World Cup semifinals for evidence. Modern Portugal, a country with a stable democracy, a growing economy, and a vibrant culture has proven the strength of its national character.

EARLY HISTORY (8000 BC-AD 469). Settlement of Portugal began around 8000 BC when neolithic tribes arrived from Andalucía in search of hotter climates. The traditions of these hunters and fishermen evolved into the Megalithic culture that emerged in 2000 BC and left its mark in the many necropolises scattered across the Beira Alta. During the first millennium BC, several tribes began to populate the Iberian Peninsula, including the **Celts**, who settled in northern Portugal and Galicia in the 9th century BC, and the **Phoenicians,** who founded fishing villages in the Algarve. The **Greeks** and **Carthaginians** soon followed in 600 BC, settling the southern and western coasts. The Romans gained control of Portugal in 140 BC and integrated the region into the Iberian province of Lusitania, which included the whole of Portugal and parts of western Spain. Six centuries of Roman rule ensued.

GIMME MOORS (469-1139). Rome's decline in the AD 3rd and 4th centuries had a heavy impact on the Iberian Peninsula. In the wake of diminished Roman power, the **Visigoths,** a tribe of migrating Germanic people, crossed the Pyrenees in 469 and

8000 BC
Neolithic tribes settle in Portugal.

1000 BC
Portugal's love affair with *bacalhau* (cod) officially begins with the arrival of Phoenician fishermen.

200 BC
Romans invade the Iberian Peninsula, gaining control of Portugal half a century later.

AD 469
Visigoths cross the Pyrenees and invade Iberia.

AD 711
The Moors settle in the area they called the *al-Gharb* (Algarve).

AD 718
The *Reconquista* begins.

1139
Dom Afonso Henriques declares Portuguese independence from Spain and crowns himself king.

1279-1325
Dinis I reigns and writes copious amounts of poetry in the newly developed Portuguese language.

1386
The Treaty of Windsor is signed, assuring centuries of cooperation between Britain and Portugal.

1492
Columbus reaches America.

1495-1521
Dom Manuel I the Fortunate reigns.

1498
Vasco da Gama lands in India.

1500
Pedro Álvares Cabral claims Brazil for Portugal.

dominated the peninsula for the next two centuries. In 711, Muslims (also known as the **Moors**) invaded Iberia, toppling the Visigoth monarchy. Muslim communities were established along the southern coast, which they called the *al-Gharb* (Algarve). After nearly 400 years of rule, the Muslims left a significant legacy of agricultural advances, architectural landmarks, and linguistic and cultural trends.

THE CHRISTIAN RECONQUISTA AND THE BIRTH OF PORTUGAL (1139-1415). Though the *Reconquista* officially began in 718, it didn't pick up steam until the 11th century, when Fernando I united Castilla and León, providing a strong base from which to reclaim territory for the Christians. At the same time, Portugal was fighting for its own sovereignty. The groundwork for this sovereignty was laid in the Battle of São Mamede in 1128, when **Dom Afonso Henriques (Afonso I)** declared independence from Castilla y León. The following year, after the victory over the Muslims in Ourique, Afonso named himself the first king of Portugal. Dom Afonso Henriques' legacy, the boundary between Spain and Portugal, is the oldest established border in Europe.

With the help of Christian military groups like the Knights Templar, the new monarchy battled Muslim forces, capturing Lisboa in 1147. By 1249, the *Reconquista* under **Afonso III** had defeated the last remnants of Muslim power with campaigns in the Alentejo and the Algarve. The Christian kings, led by **Dinis I** (1279-1325), promoted the Portuguese language above Spanish, and, with the **Treaty of Alcañices** (1297), settled border disputes with neighboring Castilla, asserting Portugal's identity as the first unified and independent nation in Europe.

João I (1385-1433), the first king of the House of Aviz, ushered in a period of unity and prosperity. Dom João increased the power of the crown, establishing a strong base for future Portuguese expansion and economic success. The Anglo-Portuguese alliance, secured with the **Treaty of Windsor** (1386) and his marriage to Phillipa of Lancaster, influenced Portugal's foreign policy well into the 19th century.

PORTUGAL SAILS THE OCEAN BLUE (1415-1580). The 15th century was one of the greatest periods in maritime travel history and in Portuguese history. Under the leadership of João's son, **Prince Henry the Navigator,** Portugal became a world leader in maritime science and exploration. Portuguese adventurers captured the Moroccan city of Ceuta in 1415, discovered Madeira (and scurvy) in 1419, happened upon the uninhabited Açores in 1427, and began to exploit the African coast for riches. Lagos became Europe's first slave market in 1441. In 1488, **Bartolomeu Dias** opened the route to the East and paved the way for Portuguese entrance into the spice trade when he rounded Africa's Cape of Storms, later renamed the Cape of Good Hope.

The Portuguese monarchs may have rejected **Christopher Columbus,** but they funded a number of other momentous voyages. In 1497, they supported **Vasco da Gama,** who led the first European naval expedition to India. Successive expeditions put numerous East African and Indian colonies under Portu-

Portugal

N LG

Vila Nova de Cerveira
Minho
Parque Nacional da Peneda-Gerês
Valença do Minho
Caminha
MINHO
Viana do Castelo
Lima
SERRA DO GERÊS
Parque Natural de Montesinho
Cávado
Caldas de Gerês
Bragança
Costa Verde
Barcelos
Braga
Guimarães
Tâmega
Amarante
TRÁS-OS-MONTES
Mirandela
Parque Natural do Alvão
Vila Real
Miranda do Douro
DOURO LITORAL
Porto
Espinho
SERRA DO MARÃO
DOURO ALTO
Parque Natural do Douro Internacional
Douro
Ovar

ATLANTIC OCEAN

Aveiro
BEIRA ALTA
Viseu
BEIRA LITORAL
Luso
Buçaco
Mondego
SERRA DA ESTRÊLA
Guarda
Manteigas
Parque Natural da Serra da Estrela
Sabugal
Coimbra
Sortelha
Costa Da Prata
Figueira da Foz
Conímbriga
Zêzere
SERRA DA GARDUNHA
Monsanto
BEIRA BAIXA
Leiria
Castelo Branco
Nazaré
Batalha
São Martinho do Porto
Alcobaça
Fátima
Ilhas Berlengas
Caldas da Rainha
Tomar
Cabo Carvoeiro
Óbidos
SERRA DE AIRE
Tejo
Peniche
ESTREMADURA
RIBATEJO
Castelo de Vide
Marvão
SERRA DE SÃO MAMEDE
Santarém
Crato
Portalegre
Ericeira
Vila Franca de Xira
Mafra
SPAIN
Sintra
Queluz
Cascais
Lisboa
Estoril
ALTO ALENTEJO
Estremoz
Elvas
Parque Natural de Arrábida
Évora Monte
SERRA DE OSSA
Setúbal
Évora
Cabo Espichel
Tróia Peninsula
Sesimbra
Costa Azul
Alcácer do Sal
Baia de Setúbal
Sines
Santiago do Cacém
Beja
SERRA DE ADIÇA
Guadiana
BAIXO ALENTEJO
Miro
Costa Dourada
Mértola
SERRA DE MONCHIQUE
Lagos
Silves
ALGARVE
Tavira
Cabo de São Vicente
Portimão
Albufeira
Sagres
Faro
Vila Real de Santo António
Olhão
Golfo de Cádiz

0   50 kilometers
0   50 miles

PORTUGAL

1519

Portuguese-born explorer Magellan sets sails around the globe on Spain's dime.

1580-1598

Spaniard Felipe II reigns as King of Portugal.

1588

Portugal is dragged into Spain's conflict with England, and their armadas suffer a crushing defeat.

1640

The House of Bragança reasserts independence from Spain.

1706-1750

João V plunders Brazil to pay for the construction of new palaces in Portugal.

1755

A massive earthquake rumbles across Portugal, destroying Lisboa and killing up to 100,000.

1807

The royal family flees upon learning that Napoleon's forces are approaching the border.

1828-1834

Sibling rivalry peaks in the War of Two Brothers.

guese control. (The colonies were less than thrilled about this, as revolts would soon prove.) Three years after da Gama's voyage, **Pedro Álvares Cabral** claimed Brazil for Portugal, establishing a far-flung empire. Portugal's international power peaked during the reign of **Dom Manuel I the Fortunate** (1495-1521). Known as "the King of Gold," Manuel controlled vast tracts of land and the riches these lands contained. One of the greatest feats of Portuguese navigation occurred at the end of his rule, when Fernão de Magalhães, known as **Magellan**, completed the first circumnavigation of the globe in 1521.

BRING ON THE BRAGANÇA (1580-1801). Competition from other commercial powers with alternative routes to the east eventually took a toll, and the House of Aviz lost its predominance in 1580. The Habsburg King of Spain, **Felipe II**, then claimed the Portuguese throne, and the Iberian Peninsula was briefly ruled by one monarch. Over the course of the next 60 years, the Habsburgs dragged Portugal into several ill-fated wars, including the Spanish Armada's crushing loss to England in 1588. King Felipe tended to neglect "that other country" which he ruled, and Portugal soon lost the bulk of its once-vast empire. In 1640, however, the **House of Bragança** engineered a nationalist rebellion against the unfortunate monarch. After a brief struggle, the House of Bragança assumed control, asserting Portuguese independence from Spain. To secure sovereignty, the Bragança dynasty went to great lengths to reestablish ties with England. In 1661, Portugal ceded Bombay to England, and the marriage of Catherine of Bragança to England's Charles II cemented the Portuguese-British alliance. Nearly half a century later, **João V** (1706-1750) restored a measure of prosperity for Portugal, if not Brazil, using newly mined gold and diamonds from the colony to finance massive building projects, including the construction of extravagant palaces. The bulk of the architecture did not survive the momentous **earthquake of 1755**, which devastated Lisboa and southern Portugal. Fires, started by the overturned votive candles in churches, raged throughout the city, eventually killing over 60,000 people. Despite the widespread damage, dictatorial minister **Marquês de Pombal** was able to rebuild Lisboa.

NAPOLEON'S CONQUEST (1807-1910). Napoleon took control of France in 1801 and set his sights on the rest of Europe. When he reached Portugal six years later, his army encountered little resistance. The Portuguese royal family opted for flight over fight and escaped to Brazil. **Dom João VI** returned to Lisboa in 1821, only to face an extremely unstable political climate. Amidst turmoil within the royal family, João's son **Pedro** declared Brazil's independence, becoming the country's first ruler. The **Constitution of 1822**, drawn up in Portugal during the royal family's absence, severely limited the power of the monarchy. After 1826, the **War of the Two Brothers** (1826-1834) between constitutionalists (supporting Pedro, the new king of Brazil) and monarchists (supporting Miguel, Pedro's brother) divided the country over the question of the Portuguese throne. Eight gory years later, Pedro's daughter **María II** (1834-1854) ascended the throne at the tender age of 15. The next 75 years were marked by continued tension between liberals and monarchists.

SUPER SALAZAR (1910-1970). Portugal spent the early years of the 20th century trying to recover from the political discord of the 19th. On October 5, 1910, the king, 20-year-old **Dom Manuel II,** fled to England in search of amnesty. The new government that replaced Dom Manuel II, known as the **First Republic,** earned worldwide disapproval for its expulsion of the Jesuits and other religious orders, while conflict between the government and labor movements heightened domestic tensions. Portugal's decision to enter **World War I** on the side of the Allies proved economically fatal and internally divisive, despite the eventual victory. The weak republic teetered and eventually fell in a 1926 military coup. General **António Carmona** took over as leader of the provisional military government and, in the face of financial crisis, appointed **António de Oliveira Salazar,** a prominent economics professor, as minister of finance. In 1932, Salazar became prime minister, but soon devolved into a dictator. His *Estado Novo* (New State) granted suffrage to women, but did little else to end the country's authoritarian traditions. While Portugal's international economic standing improved, the regime laid the cost of progress squarely on the shoulders of the working class, the peasantry, and colonial subjects in Africa. A terrifying secret police (PIDE) crushed all opposition to Salazar's rule, and African rebellions were quelled in bloody battles.

YOU SAY YOU WANT A REVOLUTION (1974-2000). The slightly more liberal prime minister **Marcelo Caetano** continued the unpopular African wars after Salazar's death in 1970. In just a few years, international disapproval of Portuguese imperialism and the army's dissatisfaction with colonial entanglements led **General António de Spinola** to call for decolonization. On April 25, 1974, a left-wing military coalition calling itself the Armed Forces Movement overthrew Caetano in a quick coup. This **Revolution of the Carnations** sent citizens dancing into the streets, and put a "Rua 25 de Abril" in nearly every town in Portugal. The Marxist-dominated armed forces granted civil and political liberties and withdrew claims on the country's African colonies by 1975, resulting in the immigration of over 500,000 refugees.

The socialist government nationalized several industries and appropriated large estates in the face of substantial opposition. The country's first elections, in 1976, put the charismatic socialist prime minister **Mario Soares** into power. When a severe economic crisis hit, Soares instituted "100 measures in 100 days" to shock Portugal into shape. The year 1986 brought Portugal into the European Community (now the European Union), ending its age-old isolation from northern Europe. Despite challenges by the newly formed Social Democratic Party (PSD), Soares won the election in 1986, becoming the nation's first civilian president in 60 years. Soares was eventually replaced by the Socialist former mayor of Lisboa, **Jorge Sampaio,** in 1996.

1839
Construction begins on Sintra's Palácio da Pena.

1869
Portugal abolishes slavery.

1916
Portugal joins the Allies in World War I.

1917
Three children claim to see an image of the Virgin Mary in Fátima.

1932
António de Oliveira Salazar begins to serve his 36 years as prime minister and dictator.

1974
Caetano is overthrown in the Carnation Revolution.

1976
Elections are held in Portugal for the first time in history. Mario Soares becomes prime minister.

1986
Portugal joins the European Community.

1988
Marathoner Rosa Mota takes the gold for Portugal in the 1988 Olympic Games.

PORTUGAL

CURRENT EVENTS

2002
Jose Manuel Durão Barroso becomes prime minister and oversees the change from the *escudo* to the euro.

2004
Portugal hosts the **European Football Championship;** much drunken cheering ensues.

The **European Union** declared Portugal a full member of the EU Economic and Monetary Union (EMU) in 1999, and the nation continues its quest to catch up economically with the rest of Western Europe. In 1999, Portugal ceded Macau, its last overseas territory, to the Chinese. Portugal and Indonesia have agreed to cooperate over the reconstruction of East Timor, an ex-Portuguese colony.

Jorge Sampaio returned to the presidency after the January 2001 parliamentary elections, but Socialist prime minister **António Guterres** resigned in December of 2001, just after overseeing Portugal's successful transition to the euro. President Sampaio then appointed Socialist Democrat **Jose Manuel Durão Barroso** as prime minister to represent the newly merged parties. Barroso resigned the post in July 2004, accepting the presidency of the European Union. **Pedro Santana Lopez,** of the same party, took his place until **José Sócrates,** the leader of the Socialist party, became the new prime minister in March 2005. The presidential elections of 2006 named **Aníbal Cavaco Silva,** who had lost to President Sampaio in the 1996 presidential elections, as the next leader of Portugal.

In 2004, Portugal hosted the **European Football Championship.** As a result, local transportation, such as the Lisboa metro system and national rail lines, was vastly improved. Despite these signs of success, Portugal continues to encounter challenges to its economy. In 2005, a severe drought hit the Algarve region, hampering agricultural projects and tourism, which together account for more than 60% of Portugal's employment. The worst drought in 60 years also resulted in wildfires that raged uncontrollably, exacerbated by a water shortage and high temperatures.

FURTHER READING. These books are useful additional resources on the history and culture of Portugal.

A Concise History of Portugal, by David Birmingham (1993). An amazing quantity of historical and cultural information in one volume.

Prince Henry 'the Navigator', by Peter Russell (2000). A debunking of numerous preconceptions about one of Portugal's most misunderstood leaders.

Journey to Portugal, by José Saramago (1990). A literary examination of Portugal from the Nobel Prize-winning author.

PEOPLE AND CULTURE

LANGUAGE

Although this softer sister of Spanish is closely related to the other Romance languages, modern Portuguese is an amalgamation of diverse influences. The majority of Portuguese is derived from Latin, but the Moorish occupation also left Arabic influences on the language. A close listener will also catch echoes of Italian, French, and even English and Slavic languages. Portugal's global escapades spread the language to other regions, from Brazil in South America to Macau in China. Today, Portuguese (the world's 6th most-spoken language) unites over 200 million people worldwide, most of them in Portugal, Brazil, Mozambique, and Angola. Some may be heartened to know that English, Spanish, and French are widely spoken throughout Portugal, especially in tourist-oriented locales. The Let's Go **Phrasebook** (p. 760) contains useful phrases in Portuguese, and the **Glossary** (p. 766) lists terms used in this guide.

RELIGION

Though the constitution mandates that there is no state religion in Portugal, roughly 85% of the Portuguese population is Roman Catholic. A major force in shaping Portugal's history, the Catholic Church is still a respected and powerful influence in modern-day Portugal; attendance is high at Sunday masses, and festivals honoring patron saints (*romarias*) are celebrated everywhere. Portugal is also home to communities of Protestants, Jehovah's Witnesses, and Mormons, as well as 35,000 Muslims and a mere 700 Jews.

FOOD AND DRINK

The Portuguese season their dishes with the basics of Mediterranean cuisine: olive oil, garlic, herbs, and sea salt, and dishes can be spicy. Cumin and coriander are especially popular. Pork, potatoes, and pastries are the Holy Trinity of Portuguese cuisine and are available everywhere, but each region has its own distinctive culinary traditions.

LOCAL FARE

LISBOA AND THE NORTH. The cuisine of Northern Portugal reflects its geography. Open ocean and lush forests provide for delicious seafood, game, and produce. Small farms produce succulent sausages, as well as distinctive *queijos* (cheeses) such as **Serra da Estrela,** which is made in the region of the same name (p. 753). This cheese is so soft that it is typically eaten with a spoon. The availability of excellent produce means that *sopas* (soups) are usually made from local vegetables. Common varieties include *caldo de ovos* (bean soup with hard-boiled eggs), *caldo de verdura* (vegetable soup), and the famous *caldo verde* (a potato and kale mixture with a slice of sausage and olive oil). Portugal's delectable *broa* (cornbread) is at its best in this region. For dessert, dine on *pasteis de nata* (custard tarts) in **Belém** (p. 654), *queijadas da Sapa* (cheese tarts) in **Sintra** (p. 660), and egg yolk-based sweets just about everywhere.

FROM THE ROAD

LOOKING BACK

Portugal emerged from Antonio de Oliveira Salazar's dictatorship (1932-1974) far behind much of Europe. Although physical results of the dictatorship remain evident in broken windows, unpaved roads, worn-down buildings, and murals of political slogans, the effects on the people are not as easy to see or understand.

Chatting with a senior citizen gave me insight into how life has changed for older generations. Sitting at an oak table in a century-old house with my octogenarian friend, Maria, I was shocked to learn that a mere 15 years ago her town, only an hour's drive from Lisbon, had no running water, no electricity, and no paved roads. Living in the grasp of a harsh dictatorship, she said, was like living in another universe.

Before democracy, many citizens, including Maria, did not realize other religions besides Catholicism existed. The opening of the political sphere has allowed for more religious freedom, but progress has been slow. Even though it has been decades since Salazar ruled, marriages sanctioned by non-Catholic churches were only recently recognized by the state. The process of understanding and accepting others is in many ways just beginning in Portugal. Older generations are curious about how younger generations understand the world and about where they will guide it. — *Illiana Quimbaya*

A SWEET GUIDE

You've probably found yourself ogling the glass display case of Portugal's many pastelarias wondering which tempting treat to pick. Wonder no more with this quick guide to carbohydrate heaven.

Altreia: a sweet and simple treat from Northern Portugal made of pasta cooked with eggs and sugar topped with cinnamon.

Arroz-doce: sweet rice. There are many variations of this rice pudding, so try it in different places!

Bolinhos: little balls of cake filled with cream and/or dried fruit .

Bolinhos de Jerimu: pumpkin, egg, and Port wine fried to sweet perfection. Yum.

Dolce de Ovos: Aveiro's small sweets made of egg yolks and sugar.

Pão-de-ló: the Portuguese version of sponge cake.

Pastel de Natas: petit pastries filled with cinnamon cream, also known as pastel de Belém.

Pastel de Santa Clara: star-shaped puffs filled with almond flavored cream from the northeast.

Rabanadas: thick slices of bread soaked in milk (or wine), tossed in sugar, and fried.

Pão de Deus: sweet bread topped with a pineapple and coconut concoction. Add butter and the bread melts in your mouth while the shredded coconut gives a slight crunch. God's bread indeed.

ALGARVE. Miles of coastline mean that fresh seafood forms the core of the cuisine in this area. While *bacalhau* (cod) is undoubtedly the fish of choice for most Portuguese, *choco grelhado* (grilled cuttlefish) and *peixe espada* (swordfish) are also excellent. The more adventurous should try the *polvo* (boiled or grilled octopus) and *lulas grelhadas* (grilled squid). In **Lagos** (p. 667), dishes served *em cataplana* (in clam-shaped steaming dish) are an expensive treat. For the more economically savvy, *caldierada* is fish stew that is sure to satisfy the traveler. Marzipan made with almonds from local groves are reminders of the region's Moorish legacy. The Algarve is also known for its oranges and figs. For something different, try *pêras* (pears) drenched in sweet port wine and served with raisins and hazelnuts on top. *Pastelarias* (bakeries) are in most towns, and provide a cheap and tasty breakfast.

ALENTEJO. The arid plains of central Portugal lend themselves to ranching rather than farming. Pork, chicken, and beef appear on most menus, often combined in *cozida à portuguesa* (boiled beef, pork, sausage, and vegetables), or served with heavy sauces and other embellishments. True connoisseurs add a drop of *piri-piri* (chili pepper sauce) to their *cozida* (meat and vegetable stew). This sauce also adds a kick to *frango assado* (roast chicken), which competes with *bacalhau* (cod) for the title of Portugal's favorite dish. A more expensive delicacy is roasted *cabrito* (goat). Hearty bread-based soups like *açorda à Alentejana* (Alentejan stew) round out the menu, and are often a meal in themselves. But no matter what you order, leave room for *batatas* (potatoes), prepared countless ways, which accompany every meal.

DRINKS

The exact birth date of Portuguese wine is unknown, although 5000 BC is often used as an estimate. It may not be an international star, but the quality and low cost of Portuguese *vinho* (wine) is truly astounding. The best of them all, *vinho do porto* (port), pressed by foot from the red grapes of the **Douro Valley** (p. 720) and fermented with a touch of brandy, is a dessert in itself. When chilled, white port can be a snappy aperitif, while ruby or tawny port makes a classic after-dinner drink. The island of Madeira produces its own popular wine, which is heated for six months before bottling. Sparkling *vinho verde* comes in either red or white—its name refers to the wine's age, rather than the color. Excellent local table wines include Colares, Dão, Borba, Bairrada, Bucelas, and Periquita. If you can't decide, experiment with the *vinho de casa* (house wine), either the *tinto* (red) or the *branco* (white). Tangy *sangria* comes filled with fresh orange slices and makes a budget meal festive at a minimal expense. Your Portuguese drinking vocabulary should contain the terms: *claro* (new wine), *espumante* (sparkling wine), *rosado* (rose wine), *vinho de mesa* (table wine), and *vinho verde* (young wine).

Bottled Sagres, Cristal, and Super Bock are excellent beers. If you don't ask for it *fresco* (cool), it may come *natural* (room temperature). A tall, slim glass of draft beer is a *fino* or an *imperial*, while a larger stein is a *caneca*. To sober up, order a *bica* (espresso), a *galão* (coffee with milk, served in a glass), or a *café com leite* (coffee with milk, served in a cup).

MEALS AND DINING HOURS

Portuguese eat their hearty midday meal—*almoço* (lunch)—between noon and 2pm and *jantar* (dinner) between 8pm and midnight. Breakfast in Portugal is typically a small affair—a pastry from a *pastelaria* (bakery) and *cafezinho* (espresso) from a cafe suffices for *pequeno almoço* (breakfast). If you get the munchies between 4 and 7pm, snack bars sell *sandes* (sandwiches) and sweet cakes. It is advisable to make reservations when dining in some of the more upscale city restaurants. A full meal costs €6-15, depending on the restaurant's location and quality. *Meia dose* (half-portions) cost more than half-price but are often more than adequate. The ubiquitous *prato do dia* (special of the day) or *ementa* of appetizer, bread, entree, dessert, and beverage will satisfy even the largest appetite. Standard pre-meal bread, butter, cheese, and *pâté* may be served without your asking, but these pre-meal munchies are not free (€1-3 per person). You may appreciate them, however, since chefs start cooking only after you order; be prepared to wait. Smoking is still generally accepted in most establishments, although there has been a recent move to institute no smoking zones. Signs stating *"proibida fumar"* (no smoking) mark these areas. A ban on public smoking was enacted in May 2007 but was revised shortly after and instead will come into effect in January 2008.

CUSTOMS AND ETIQUETTE

The Portuguese are generally friendly, easygoing, and receptive to foreign travelers. Even if your Portuguese is a little rusty, a wholehearted attempt at speaking the native tongue will be appreciated.

TABOOS. Shorts and flip-flops may be seen as disrespectful in some public establishments and rural areas, even during a heat wave. Though dress in Portugal is more casual in the hot summer months than in the cold of winter, strapless tops on women and collarless t-shirts on men are generally unacceptable. Skimpy clothes are always a taboo in churches, as are tourist visits during masses or services. Do not automatically assume that Spanish will be understood by the Portuguese; while many Portuguese do speak Spanish, one of the best ways to offend a local is to tacitly suggest that Portugal is part of Spain.

PUBLIC BEHAVIOR. On any list of Portuguese values, politeness would be at the top. Be sure to address a Portuguese as *senhor* (Mr.), *senhora* (Ms.), or *senhora dona* (Mrs.) followed by the first name. To blend in, it's a good idea to be as formal as possible upon first meeting. Introduce yourself in detail, giving more than just your name. You'll be welcomed openly and made to feel at home if you mention who you are, where you're from, and what you are doing in Portugal. Don't be surprised if you get pecked on both cheeks by younger Portuguese, but handshakes are generally the standard introductory gesture.

TIPPING. In restaurants, a service charge (*serviço*) of 10% is usually included in the bill. When service is not included, it is customary to leave 5-10% as a tip. It is also common to barter in markets.

THE ARTS

ARCHITECTURE

PREHISTORIC ARCHITECTURE. The largest prehistoric remains in Portugal can be found at Valverde (p. 684), near Évora. These dolmens, ancient tombs, complement the town's later architectural styles manifest in the Celtic round stone houses, Roman forums, and the temple of Diana. Romanesque cathedrals can also be found in Lisboa (p. 645), Porto (p. 720), and Coimbra (p. 740), and Alcobaça (p. 706) and Batalha (p. 710) display examples of Gothic-style monasteries.

MANUELINE STYLE. Portugal's signature **Manueline** style celebrates the prosperity and imperial expansion of Dom Manuel I's reign (p. 616). Manueline works merge Christian images and maritime motifs, such as shells, coral, waves, fish, anchors, and ropes. Their lavish ornaments reflect a hybrid of Gothic, Plateresque, and Moorish influences. The **Torre de Belém** (p. 655), an elaborate expression of Manueline style, was built by King João II as a defense fortress. Close seconds are the **Mosteiro dos Jerónimos** (p. 655) in Belém and the **Mosteiro Santa Maria de Vitória** (p. 711) in Batalha, both grand testaments to Portugal's imperial success.

AZULEJOS. Few Moorish structures survived the Christian *Reconquista*, but their style influenced later Portuguese architecture. One of their most beautiful (and popular) traditions is the colorfully painted ceramic tiles **(azulejos)** that grace many walls and ceilings. These ornate tiles, carved in relief by the Moors, later took on Flemish designs. Contrary to popular belief, their name comes not from the color, *azul* (blue), but rather from the Arabic word *azulayj* (little stone). Lisboa's **Museu Nacional do Azulejo** (p. 649) showcases *azulejo* collections.

PAINTING AND SCULPTURE

THE AGE OF DISCOVERY. The **Age of Discovery** (1415-1580) was an era of vast cultural exchange with Renaissance Europe and beyond. Flemish masters like **Jan van Eyck** brought their talent to Portugal, and many Portuguese artists polished their skills in Antwerp, Belgium. One result of this exchange was the emergence of a group of painters known as the **Lisbon School**, which included Dom Manuel's favorite High Renaissance artist **Jorge Afonso**. Afonso created realistic portrayals of human anatomy, and today his best works hang at the **Convento de Cristo** in Tomar (p. 717) and the **Convento da Madre de Deus** in Lisboa (p. 649). In the late 15th century, the talented **Nuno Gonçalves** led a revival of the primitivist school, which is characterized by simple forms rendered in bold, primary colors.

THE BAROQUE ERA. Portuguese Baroque art featured even more diverse styles and themes. Wood-carving became extremely popular in Portugal during the Baroque period. **Joachim Machado** carved elaborate crèches (figurines of the nativity) in the early 1700s. On canvas, portraiture was by far the most impressive of genres in Portugal. The prolific 19th-century artist **Domingos António de Sequeira** depicted historical, religious, and allegorical subjects using a technique that would later inspire French Impressionists. Many of Sequeira's works can be found in Mafra (p. 658) and throughout palaces and churches in Lisboa (p. 645). Portugal has also seen its share of sculptors as well as carvers and painters. Porto's prominent **António Soares dos Reis** brought his Romantic sensibility to 19th-century Portuguese sculpture. His work went largely unappreciated in his lifetime, however, and the sculptor committed suicide.

RECENT WORKS. In the 20th century, Cubism, Expressionism, and Futurism trickled into Portugal despite Salazar-instituted censorship. More recently, the late **Maria Helena Vieira da Silva** won international recognition for her abstract works, and the master **Carlos Botelho** gained international renown for his wonderful vignettes of Lisboa life until his death in 1982.

LITERATURE

THE RENAISSANCE. Portuguese literature blossomed during the Renaissance, most notably in the letters of **Francisco de Sá de Miranda** (1481-1558) and the poetry of **António Ferreira** (1528-1569). **Luís de Camões** (1524-1580) celebrated Vasco da Gama's sea voyages to India in Portugal's greatest epic, *Os Lusíadas* (*The Lusiads;* 1572), modeled on the *Aeneid.*

19TH-CENTURY REBIRTH. Imperial decline made the literature of the 17th and 18th centuries less triumphant than that of earlier eras. The 19th century, however, saw a dramatic rebirth with poet **João Baptista de Almeida Garrett** (1799-1854), the leader of the romantic movement in Portugal and a twice-exiled political liberal. Political thinkers dominated the crop of literary intelligentsia in the **Generation of 1870,** shifting literature from romantic to realist. The most visible influence on this shift was novelist and life-long diplomat **José Maria Eça de Queiroz.** He conceived a distinctly Portuguese social realism and documented 19th-century Portuguese society, sometimes critical of its bourgeois elements. His most famous work was *O Crime do Padre Amaro* (*The Sin of Father Amaro;* 1876).

PESSOA AND THE MODERN TRADITION. Fernando Pessoa (1888-1935), Portugal's most famous writer of the late 19th and early 20th centuries, wrote in English and Portuguese under four different names: Pessoa, Alberto Caeiro, Ricardo Reis, and Alvaro de Campos; each alias is associated with a different writing style. His semi-autobiography, *Livro do Desassossego* (*The Book of Disquiet;* 1982) is his only prose work, posthumously compiled and viewed as a modernist classic.

RECENT WORKS. Portugal's literary tradition continues to thrive in the contemporary era, as writers like **Miguel Torga** have gained international fame for their satirical novels. **José Saramago,** winner of the 1998 Nobel Prize for Literature, is without a doubt Portugal's most important living writer. His work, written in a realist style and laced with irony, has achieved new acclaim in the post-Salazar era, dominating in all genres from the dystopian parable of *Blindness* (1998) to the historical fiction of *Baltasar and Blimunda* (1987). The end of the dictatorship also saw the emergence of female writers. In *Novas Cartas Portuguesas* (1972), collectively written by Maria Barreno, Maria Horta, and Maria Velho da Costa, the three female protagonists expose the mistreatment of women in a patriarchal society. Other acclaimed post-Salazar authors include **António Lobo Antunes** and **José Cardoso Pires.** Antunes is known for his scattered form and psychoanalytic themes. Pires's works often comment on the repression of the Salazar regime, and his novel *Balada da Praia dos Cães* (*Ballad of Dogs' Beach;* 1986) exposes the terror of Salazar's secret police.

MUSIC

FADO. Fado (FAH-doo) is a musical tradition unique to Portugal, identified with a sense of *saudade*, meaning pining or nostalgia. Literally translated as "fate," *fado* is characterized by tragic, romantic lyrics and mournful melodies. Supposedly,

PORTUGAL

> **FURTHER READING.** For Portuguese classics, check out **Literature** (p. 625). The more famous works have been translated into English.
> **The Lusiads,** by Luís de Camões (1558). Chronicles Portuguese exploration during the Age of Discovery.
> **The Last Kabbalist of Lisbon,** by Richard Zimler (1998). A murder mystery that explores the world of Portugal's 16th-century Jewish mystics.
> **The History of the Siege of Lisbon** and **All the Names,** by José Saramago (1989, 1997). A subversive and allegorical perspective on Portuguese history by a Nobel laureate.

these songs of longing were originally sung by fishwives whose husbands were at sea. Lisboa and Coimbra are now the most active centers for this tradition, but the two regional styles vary sharply. Lisboa's singers tend to be female, and the songs are up-tempo, while almost all *fado* singers in Coimbra are male and the tunes are more maudlin. Solo ballads, accompanied by the *guitarra* (a flat-backed guitar like a mandolin), appeal to the romantic side of Portuguese culture. **Amália Rodrigues** (1920-1999) gained international renown as a singer of *fado* and Portuguese folk music. **Mariza,** Portugal's answer to Madonna, continues the tradition today.

CLASSICAL. Apart from its folk tradition, the music of Portugal has yet to achieve international fame. Portuguese opera peaked with **António José da Silva** (1705-1739), a victim of the 1739 Inquisition. The Renaissance in Portugal led to the development of pieces geared for solo instrumentalists and vocals. Coimbra's **Carlos Seixas** thrilled 18th-century Lisboa with his genius and contributed to the development of the sonata. **João Domingos Bomtempo** (1775-1842) introduced symphonic innovations from abroad and established the *Sociedade Filarmónica,* modeled on the London Philharmonic, in Lisboa in 1822.

Although the Portuguese Civil War decreased funding and stifled experimentation, folk music and dancing are still popular in rural areas. In the late 19th century, **Joly Braga Santo** led a modern revival of Portuguese classical music. The Calouste Gulbenkian Foundation in Lisboa has also kept Portuguese music alive, sponsoring a symphony orchestra since 1962 and hosting local folk singers (including Fausto and Sérgio Godinho), ballets, operas, and jazz festivals. The **Teatro Nacional de São Carlos,** with its own orchestra and ballet company, has further bolstered Portuguese music. The Teatro has spawned a group of talented young composers, including **Filipe Pires, Antonio Vitorino d'Almeida,** and **Jorge Peixinho,** all of whom have begun to make their mark in international competitions. Today, pop artists of Portuguese descent, like Nelly Furtado, have gained recent and international acclaim.

THE MEDIA

Portugal's most widely read daily newspapers are *Público* (www.publico.pt), *Diário de Notícas* (www.dn.sapo.pt), and *Jornal de Notícas* (www.jn.sapo.pt). If you haven't mastered Portuguese, check out *The News* (www.the-news.net), Portugal's only online English-language newspaper. Those interested in international news stories can also pick up day-old foreign papers at larger newsstands.

Portuguese TV offers four main channels: the state-run Canal 1 and TV2, and the private SIC (Sociedade Independente de Communicação) and TVI (TV Independente). Couch potatoes can also enjoy numerous cable channels, most of which air Brazilian and Portuguese soap operas and subtitled foreign sitcoms.

SPORTS

Futebol is the game of choice for just about all Portuguese sports fans. Team Portugal has had its moments in the sun—the national team took second in the 2004 European Championships and garnered a third-place finish in 2000 at the European Championship with the help of Luis Figo and goldenboy Cristiano Ronaldo. However, the team has also fallen short at crucial moments, such as the World Cup 1998 qualification matches and in the semi-finals of the World Cup in 2006. Portugal hosted the 2004 European Championship in which Greece emerged victorious over Portugal in the final match. Lisboa's **Benfica,** with some of the world's best players, including American sensation Freddy Adu, has not only an avid Portuguese fan base, but also a substantial international following.

Native Portuguese have also made names for themselves in long-distance running; marathon queen **Rosa Mota** dominated her event during the 1980s. For recreation other than jogging and pick-up soccer, the Portuguese often turn to the sea. Wind, body, and conventional **surfers** make waves along the northern coast; **snorkelers** and **scuba divers** set out on mini-explorations to the south and west.

NATIONAL HOLIDAYS

The following table lists the national holidays for 2008.

DATE	FESTIVAL
January 1	*Dia do Ano Novo* (New Year's Day)
January 6	*Dia do Reis* (Epiphany)
February 20	*Carnaval* (Carnival)
March 14-23	*Semana Santa* (Holy Week)
March 20	*Senhor Ecce Homo* (Maundy Thursday)
March 21	*Sexta-feira Santa* (Good Friday)
March 23	*Páscoa* (Easter)
April 25	*Dia de 25 Abril* (Liberation Day)
May 1	*Dia do Trabalhador* (Labor Day)
May 22	*Corpo de Deus* (Corpus Christi)
June 10	*Dia de Camões* (Portugal Day)
August 15	*Assunção* (Feast of the Assumption)
October 5	*Dia da República* (Republic Day)
November 1	*Dia de Todos Santos* (All Saints' Day)
December 8	*A Conceição Imaculada* (Feast of the Immaculate Conception)
December 25	*Festa de Natal* (Christmas)
December 31	*Noite Velha* (New Year's Eve)

LISBOA

At sunset, the scarlet glow cast over the Rio Tejo is matched by the ruby red shimmer inside your glass of *vinho do porto*. Welcome to Lisboa. A magnificent history has left its mark upon this ancient city: illustrious bronze figures stand proud in open plazas, Roman arches and columns inspire reverence in passersby, while a towering 12th-century castle watches over Lisboa from atop one of the city's infamous seven hills. Lisboa is quickly becoming one of the most talked-about capitals in Europe, a feat driven by cutting-edge fashion, flourishing art and music scenes, and relentlessly enthusiastic nightlife. Graffiti breathes life into the time-worn walls of Bairro Alto and Santa Catarina, and at night the cobblestone sidewalks echo with the pounding heartbeat of local clubs. A monumental past may fill every corner of the city, but Lisboa is thriving in the present. Immigrants and visitors from all around the world give Lisboa an international feel that is hard to come by anywhere else in Portugal. Crowds of unique people—street performers, break dancers, and peddlers of various sorts—line the streets of Baixa and Bairro Alto, giving the city its distinctive and complex flavor.

Complexity in its composition is not new to Lisboa. Half a dozen civilizations claim parenthood of the city, beginning with the Phoenicians, Greeks, and Carthaginians. The Romans arrived in 205 BC and ruled for 600 years; under Julius Caesar, Lisboa became one of the most important port cities in Lusitania. In 1255, Lisboa was made the capital of the kingdom of Portugal. The city, along with the empire, reached its zenith at the end of the 15th century, when Portuguese navigators pioneered explorations of Asia, Africa, and South America during the Age of Discovery. A terrible earthquake on November 1, 1755, catalyzed the nation's fall from glory—close to one-fifth of the population died and two-thirds of Lisboa was destroyed in the resulting fires. Immediately, the Prime Minister Marquês de Pombal began a massive reconstruction effort, an overhaul that explains the contrast between the neat, grid-like layout of Baixa and the hilly mazes of surrounding areas. Twentieth-century Lisboa saw plenty of change, as new technologies complemented the traditions of the past. The temples, castles, and cathedrals left behind by centuries of prior civilizations are an essential part of the city's character, but crowded plazas, buzzing cafes, and blaring discotecas are proof that Lisboa has a pulse very much its own.

✈ INTERCITY TRANSPORTATION

BY PLANE

All flights land at **Aeroporto de Lisboa** (☎218 41 35 00, 41 37 00 for departures and arrivals) near the city's northern edge. Major **airlines** have offices at Pr. Marquês de Pombal and along Av. da Liberdade. The cheapest way into town is by bus; walk out of the terminal, turn right, and go straight across the street to the bus stop, marked by yellow metal posts with arrival times of incoming buses. Take bus #44 or 45 (15-20min., every 12-15min. 6am-midnight, €1.50) to Pr. dos Restauradores; the bus stops in front of the tourist office, located inside the Palácio da Foz. The express **AeroBus** #91 runs to the same locations (15min.; every 20min. 7:45am-8:15pm; €1.50, TAP passengers free); it's a good option during rush hour. The bus stop is in front of the terminal exit. A **taxi** downtown costs about €10 (plus a €1.60 baggage fee) at low traffic hours, but you're billed by time, not distance. Beware that some drivers may try to keep your change or take a longer route.

Lisboa and Vicinity

ATLANTIC OCEAN

Bahia de Setúbal

Parque Natural da Arrábida

Península de Tróia

TIP **PRE-PAY YOUR WAY.** Ask at the airport **tourist office** (☎218 45 06 60; open 7am-midnight) about the **voucher** program, which allows visitors to pre-pay for cab rides from the airport (M-F €15, Sa-Su €18).

BY TRAIN

Train service in and out of Lisboa routinely confuses newcomers, as there are three stations in Lisboa and one across the river in Barreiro, each serving different destinations. Buses, although more expensive and toilet-free, are faster and more comfortable. The two train lines with service to Cascais and Sintra (and stops along the way) are reliable. Contact **Caminhos de Ferro Portugueses** for further info. (☎808 20 82 08; www.cp.pt. Open daily 7am-11pm.)

Estação do Barreiro (☎213 47 29 30), across the Rio Tejo. Travels south. Accessible by ferry from the Terreiro do Paço dock off Pr. do Comércio (30min., every 30min., €2). Trains go to **Pinhal Novo** (25min., every 25min., €1.30) and **Setúbal** (20min., every 30min., €1.75). To get to **Évora** and **Lagos,** take a train to **Pinhal Novo** station and transfer. From Pinhal Novo, trains go to **Lagos** (3½hr., 5 per day 9:04am-8:04pm, €12-17) and **Évora** (1½hr.; 2 per day 7:09, 8:30pm; €7).

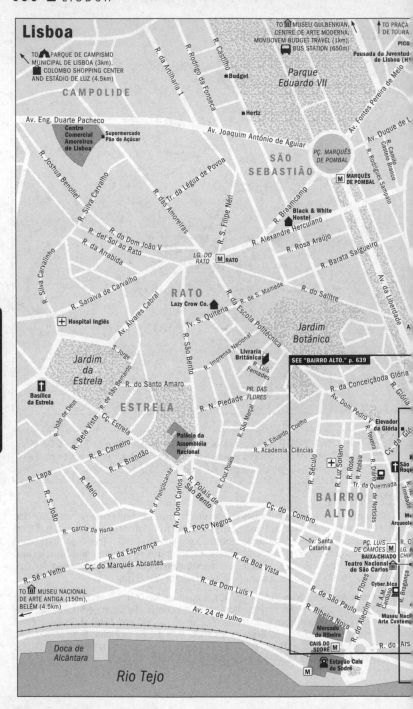

Lisboa

LISBOA

TO ⛺ PARQUE DE CAMPISMO
MUNICIPAL DE LISBOA (3km),
■ COLOMBO SHOPPING CENTER
AND ESTÁDIO DE LUZ (4.5km)

TO 🏛 MUSEU GULBENKIAN,
CENTRE DE ARTE MODERNA,
MOVIJOVEM BUDGET TRAVEL (1km),
🚌 BUS STATION (650m)

TO PRAÇA
DE TOURA

PICO

Pousada da Juventude
de Lisboa (H

CAMPOLIDE

R. da Artilharia 1

R. Rodrigo da Fonseca

R. Castilho

■ Budget

Parque Eduardo VII

Av. Fontes Pereira de Melo

Av. Eng. Duarte Pacheco

Centro Comercial Amoreiras de Lisboa

Supermercado Pão de Açúcar

■ Hertz

Av. Joaquim António de Aguiar

R. das Amoreiras

R. da Tr. da Légua de Povoa

SÃO SEBASTIÃO

PÇ. MARQUÊS DE POMBAL

Av. Duque de L

R. Camilo Castelo Branco

R. Rodrigues Sampaio

Ⓜ **MARQUÊS DE POMBAL**

R. Joshua Benoliel

R. Silva Carvalho

R. do Dom João V

R. del Sol ao Rato

R. da Arrábida

R. S. Filipe Néri

Black & White Hostel

R. Braamcamp

R. Alexandre Herculano

R. Rosa Araújo

R. Barata Salgueiro

Av. da Liberdade

R. Silva Carvalinho

R. Saraiva de Carvalho

Av. Álvares Cabral

LG. DO RATO Ⓜ **RATO**

RATO

Lazy Crow Co.

Tv. S. Quitéria

R. da Escola Politécnica

R. de S. Mamede

R. do Salitre

➕ **Hospital Inglês**

R. São Bento

R. Imprensa Nacional

Jardim Botánico

A

Jardim da Estrela

S. Jorge

R. de São Bernardo

Livraría Británica

R. Luís Fernades

SEE "BAIRRO ALTO." p. 639

R. da Conceiçãoda Glória

R. Glória

✝ **Basílica da Estrela**

R. João de Deus

R. Bela Vista

Cç. Estrela

R. do Santo Amaro

ESTRELA

PR. DAS FLORES

R. N. Piedade

R. São Marçal

Av. Dom Pedro V

R. Teixeira

Elevador da Glória

Cç. da Gló

São Roqu

R. B. Carneiro

R. A. Brandão

Palácio da Assembléia Nacional

R. Eduardo Coelho

R. Academia Ciências

R. Século

R. Luz Soriano

R. Rosa

R. Atalaia

➕ R. Diário

Tr. da Queimada

R. de Notícias

Trindade

M

Arqueole

R. Lapa

R. Meio

R. d Franciscanas

R. Dom Carlos I

R. Polais de São Bento

R. Cou Polais

Cç. do Combro

BAIRRO ALTO

R. C
LG.
CHI

R. S. João

R. Garcia da Horta

R. Poço Negros

Tv. Santa Catarina

PÇ. LUIS DE CAMÕES Ⓜ

BAIXA-CHIADO

R. da Esperança

Cç. do Marquês Abrantes

R. da Boa Vista

Teatro Nacional de São Carlos 🏛

Cyber.bica

R. Flores

R. Bragança

R. Sé o Velho

R. de Dom Luís I

R. de São Paulo

R. de Alecrim

R. A.M. Cardoso

Museu Nacl Arte Contemp

TO 🏛 MUSEU NACIONAL
DE ARTE ANTIGA (150m),
BELÉM (4.5km)

Av. 24 de Julho

R. Ribeira Nova

Mercado da Ribeira

R. do Ars

CAIS DO SODRÉ Ⓜ

🚉 **Estação Cais do Sodré**

Ⓜ

Doca de Alcântara

Rio Tejo

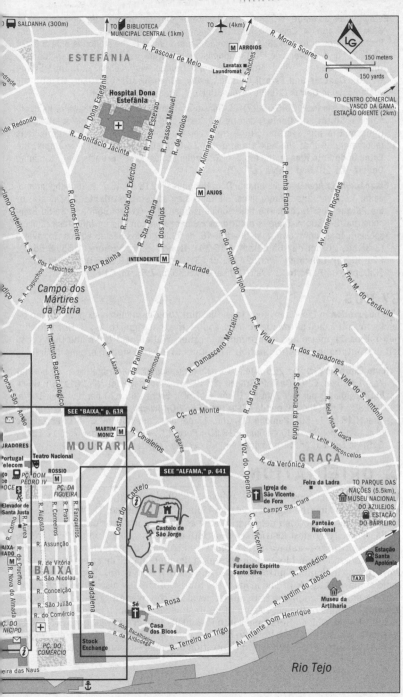

SALDANHA (300m)

TO BIBLIOTECA
MUNICIPAL CENTRAL (1km)

TO ✈ (4km)

R. Morais Soares

N
LG

0   150 meters
0   150 yards

ESTEFÂNIA

R. Pascoal de Melo

M ARROIOS

Lavatax ■
Laundromat

R. F. Sanches

TO CENTRO COMERCIAL
VASCO DA GAMA,
ESTAÇÃO ORIENTE (2km)

ande
o

ide Redondo

R. Dona Estefânia

Hospital Dona
Estefânia

R. Bonifácio Jácinta

R. Escola do Exército

R. José Estevão

R. Passos Manuel

R. de Arroios

Av. Almirante Reis

R. Penha Franca

Av. General Roçadas

R. Frei M. do Cenáculo

riano Cordeiro

A. S. A. dos Capuchos

R. Gomes Freire

Paço Rainha

R. Sta. Bárbara

R. dos Anjos

M ANJOS

M MANJOS

R. do Forno do Tijolo

ndico

S. A. Capuchos

Campo dos
Mártires
da Pátria

R. Instituto Bacteriológico

R. S. Lázaro

R. da Palma

R. Benformoso

INTENDENTE M

R. Andrade

R. Damasceno Monteiro

R. A. Vidal

R. dos Sapadores

R. Vale do S. António

R. da Graça

R. Senhora da Glória

R. Bela Vista à Graça

R. Leite Vasconcelos

SEE "BAIXA," p. 638

JRADORES

Portugal
Telecom

Teatro Nacional

MARTIM
MONIZ M

R. Cavaleiros

MOURARIA

Cç. do Monte

Cç. do Monte

R. Lagares

GRAÇA

go
ce
OCE

DOM
PEDRO IV

ROSSIO M

PÇ. DA
FIGUEIRA

SEE "ALFAMA," p. 641

Costa do Castelo

R. Voz do Operário

R. da Verónica

Igreja de
São Vicente
de Fora

Campo Sta. Clara

Feira da Ladra

TO PARQUE DAS
NAÇÕES (5.5km),
MUSEU NACIONAL
DO AZULEJOS,
ESTAÇÃO
DO BARREIRO

Elevador de
Santa Justa

R. Áurea

R. Prata

R. Correeiros

R. Fanqueiros

Costa do Castelo

Castelo de
São Jorge

Panteão
Nacional

BAIXA-
HADO M

R. do Crucifixo

R. Augusta

R. Assunção

R. de Vitória

R. São Nicolau

R. Conceição

R. da Madalena

ALFAMA

Fundação Espírito
Santo Silva

C. S. Vicente

Estação
Santa
Apolónia

R. Nova do Almada

BAIXA

R. São Julião

R. do Comércio

Sé

R. A. Rosa

R. Remédios

TAXI

Ç. DO
NICIPO

PÇ. DO
COMÉRCIO

Stock
Exchange

R. dos Bacalhoeiros

R. da Alfândega

Casa
dos Bicos

R. Terreiro do Trigo

R. Jardim do Tabaco

Museu da
Artilharia

eira das Naus

Av. Infante Dom Henrique

Rio Tejo

LISBOA

Estação Cais do Sodré (☎213 47 01 81), just beyond the end of R. do Alecrim, a 5min. walk from Baixa. M: Cais do Sodré. Take the metro or bus #36, 45, or 91 from Pr. dos Restauradores or tram #28, from Estação Santa Apolónia. The station is across R. 24 de Julho, on the river side. To the monastery in **Belém,** take trains labeled "Cascais Todos" or "Oeiras," which stop in: Belém (10min., every 15min. 5:30am-1:30am, €1.20); **Cascais** and **Estoril** (40min., every 30min. 5:30am-1:30am, €1.60); the youth hostel in **Oeiras** (20min., every 30min. 5:30am-1:30am, €1.30).

Estação Rossio (☎213 46 50 22), M: Rossio or Restauradores. Travels west. Its destinations, **Sintra** and **Queluz,** can be reached using metro connections to other stations or the bus system. Since these metro connections are changing, it is recommended that you ask a metro agent which station to use. For example, the **Estação de Sete Rios** on the top fl. of M: Jardim Zoológico sends trains every 15min. to **Queluz** (€1.20) and **Sintra** (€1.60).

Estação Santa Apolónia, Av. Infante Dom Henrique (☎218 88 40 25). Runs the international, northern, and eastern lines. All trains stop at **Estação Oriente** (M: Oriente) by the **Parque das Nações.** The ticket office is open M-F 7:20am-9pm and Sa-Su 8am-noon and 2-4:30pm. There is a **currency exchange** station and an **info desk** (English spoken). To go downtown, take bus #9, 46, or 59 to Pr. dos Restauradores. To: **Aveiro** (3-3½hr., 20 per day 6am-9pm, €16-24); **Braga** (5hr.; 5:55am, 1:55, 6:55pm; €21.50-30); **Coimbra** (2½hr., 24 per day 5:10am-9pm, €16-22.60); **Madrid** (10hr., 10:05pm, €60); **Porto** (3-4½hr., 20 per day 5:55am-7:55pm, €19-29.50).

BY BUS

The **bus station** in Lisboa is close to the Jardim Zoológico metro stop, but it can be tricky to find. Once at the metro stop, follow the exit signs to Av. C. Bordalo Pinheiro. Exit the metro and go around the corner. Walk ahead 100m and then cross left in front to the Sete Rios station. The stairs to the bus station are on the left.

Rede Expressos (☎707 223 344; www.rede-expressos.pt). To: **Braga** (5hr., 13 per day 7am-12:15am, €17); **Castelo Branco** (2½-3½hr., 8 per day 8am-7pm, €11.20); **Coimbra** (2½hr., 25 per day 7am-12:15am, €11.50); **Évora** (2hr., 20 per day 7am-10pm, €10.80); **Faro** (4hr., 16 per day 7am-1am, €16.50); **Lagos** (4-5hr., 16 per day 7:30am-1am, €16.50-17.50); **Peniche** (1½-2hr., 13 per day 7am-7:30pm, €7.30); **Portalegre** (4½hr., 13 per day 7:30am-6pm, €12.50); **Porto** (3½-4hr., 19 per day 7am-12:15am, €16) via **Leiria** (2hr., €9); **Tavira** (5hr., 10 per day 7am-1am, €16.50-17.50).

■ ORIENTATION

The city center has three neighborhoods: shop-filled **Baixa** (the low district), night-life-rich **Bairro Alto** (the high district), and hilly, winding **Alfama.** The latter, Lisboa's famous medieval Moorish neighborhood, was the lone survivor of the 1755 earthquake. The city's oldest district is a labyrinth of narrow alleys, unmarked streets, and *escandinhas*—stairways that only seem to lead to more unmarked streets. Expect to get lost, and lost again without a detailed map. The street-indexed **For Ways** maps (including Sintra, Cascais, and Estoril) are good, though expensive (sold at newsstands; €5). The maps at the tourist offices are also reliable, and free.

The suburbs extending in both directions along the river are some of the fastest-growing sections of the city. Areas of interest several kilometers from downtown include: **Belém,** which offers a peek into Portugal's 16th-century glory days (p. 654), **Alcântara,** whose docks are home to Lisboa's party scene, and the **Parque das Nações** (p. 654), the site of the 1998 World Exposition and many daytime attractions.

Lisboa Metro

BLUE — Gaivota
YELLOW — Girassol
GREEN — Caravela
RED — Oriente

THE BAIRROS (NEIGHBORHOODS) OF LISBOA

BAIXA

Baixa, Lisboa's old business hub, is the center of town, with restaurants and trendy apparel stores lining the streets. The grid begins at **Praça Dom Pedro IV** (better known as **Rossio**) and ends at **Praça do Comércio** on the **Rio Tejo**. The *praças* (squares) function as decorative bookends to new Lisboa, which was rebuilt after the earthquake of 1755 destroyed most of the city. If Mr. Richter's scale had been available back then, records show that this quake would have tipped 8.9. Pr. do Comércio was actually built on the site of the former Royal Palace, which toppled in the quake, and hence bears the nickname *Terreiro do Paço* (the Palace Lot). Expect to meet many travelers in Baixa; the main Portuguese tourist office makes Rossio the city's tourist hub. Linked to Rossio is **Praça dos Restauradores,** a central transit point and the main drop-off for buses from the airport. Pr. dos Restauradores lies just above Baixa, and from it, **Avenida da Liberdade** runs uphill to the business district around **Praça do Marquês de Pombal.**

BAIRRO ALTO

Bairro Alto is Lisboa's most famous neighborhood, but it means something different to everyone. To hundreds of natives, the upper floors and laundry-covered balconies are home. To shopping enthusiasts, it's one of Europe's fashion capitals. To art lovers, it's a must-see for *fado*, and to night owls, it's the best place to party. Cobblestone sidewalks line low-budget cafes filled with locals enjoying f *bacalhau assado* (grilled codfish), and graffiti-covered walls separate the quirky shops selling shoes and T-shirts with rare designs. Bairro Alto has budget delights as well, such as the bargain-filled shopping center at the end of **Rua Garrett,** and better yet, the beautiful churches and museums around **Chiado.** At night, *fado* houses present Portuguese songs over fine meals and red wine. After the show, fans congregate in the streets outside and enter one of the many bars between **Rua do Norte** and **Rua da Atalaia.** Get your *caipirinha* in a plastic cup so you can take it with you as you wander from place to place; the night never ends in Bairro Alto.

SÃO SEBASTIÃO

Located north of Baixa, São Sebastião, with its department stores and scores of strip malls, offers a more modern setting than much of Lisboa. Those in search of culture need not avoid São Sebastião; it also has two of the finest museums in all of Portugal, legacies of oil tycoon Calouste Gulbenkian.

ALFAMA

Alfama, Lisboa's medieval quarter, was the lone neighborhood to survive the infamous 1755 earthquake. The fine layer of dust that has settled over the blue, green, and rose-toned *azulejos* (ceramic tiles) adorning the buildings increases Alfama's sense of timelessness. The Castelo de São Jorge is the focal point of this neighborhood. Around it, layers of houses, shops, and restaurants descend to the Rio Tejo. Between Alfama and Baixa is the Mouraria (Moorish quarter), which was ironically established by Dom Afonso Henriques after the expulsion of the Moors in 1147. This labyrinth of alleys, small stairways, and unmarked streets is a challenge to navigate, so be careful after nightfall. Though the hike through Alfama's streets is half the fun, visitors can also hop on historic tram #28 from Pr. do Comércio (€1.20), which winds past most of the neighborhood's sights.

GRAÇA

If the climb to Graça doesn't take your breath away, the incredible *miradouros* (lookout points) you'll find there will. The neighborhood is one of the oldest in Lisboa, and in addition to great views of the city and river, Graça offers several impressive historical sights that keep tourists trekking up its hilly streets day after day. Graça is a mainly residential area, easily accessible by tram (#28, €1.30), making it a quick and convenient daytrip from Baixa or Bairro Alto. Even if your stay is short, you won't want to leave town without grabbing a bite to eat. Graça is known for its amazing Brazilian cuisine, due to its large population of São Paulo expats.

▣ LOCAL TRANSPORTATION

Lisboa and its surrounding areas have an efficient public transportation system with subways, buses, trams, and funiculars run by **CARRIS** (☎213 61 30 00; www.carris.pt). Use it to full advantage—no suburb takes longer than 1½hr. to reach. If you plan to stay in Lisboa for any length of time, consider a *passe turístico*, good for unlimited travel on all CARRIS transports. Passes are available for one and five days (€3.35/13.50). CARRIS booths, located in most network train stations and the busier metro stations (e.g., M: Restauradores), sell multi-day passes. (Open daily 8am-9pm.)

Buses: €1.30 within the city; pay on the bus. Exact change not required.

Metro: (☎213 50 01 00; www.metrolisboa.pt). €0.75 per ride, round-trip €1.30, unlimited daily use ticket €3.35, 10 tickets €10.45. Covers downtown and the modern business district with 4 lines. A red "M" marks metro stops. Trains run daily 6:30am-1am, though some stations close earlier.

Trams: €1.30. Many date from before WWI. Line #28 is great for sightseeing in Alfama and Mouraria (stop in Pr. do Comércio). Line #15 heads from Pr. do Comércio and Pr. da Figueira to Belém, Av. 24 de Julho, and Docas de Santo Amaro.

Funiculars: €1.30. Funiculars link the lower city with the residential areas in the hills. Elevador da Glória goes from Pr. dos Restauradores to Bairro Alto (3min., every 5min.).

Taxis: Rádio Táxis de Lisboa (☎218 11 90 00), **Autocoope** (☎217 93 27 56), and **Teletáxis** (☎218 11 11 00). Along Av. da Liberdade and Rossio. Luggage €1.60.

Car Rental: Agencies have offices at the airport, train stations, and downtown; contact them for specific locations. **Avis,** Av. Marechal Craveiro Lopes, 2 (☎217 54 78 21;

www.avis.com.pt); **Budget,** R. Castilho, 167B (☎213 86 05 16; fax 213 55 69 20); **Hertz,** R. Castilho, 72A (☎213 81 24 30; www.hertz-europe.com).

⑦ PRACTICAL INFORMATION

TOURIST AND FINANCIAL SERVICES

Tourist Office: Palácio da Foz, Pr. dos Restauradores (Portugal line ☎213 46 63 07, Lisbon line ☎213 46 33 14). M: Restauradores. The largest tourist office, with info for all of Portugal. Open daily 9am-8pm. The **Welcome Center,** Pr. do Comércio (☎210 31 28 10), is the main office for the city. Sells tickets for sightseeing buses and the Lisboa Card, which includes transportation and entrance to most sights, as well as discounts at various shops, for a flat fee (1-day €14.85, 2-day €25.50, 3-day €31; children age 5-11 €7.50/12.75/15.50). English spoken. Open daily 9am-8pm. An **airport branch** (☎218 45 06 60) is by the baggage area. English spoken. Open daily 7am-midnight. For info, look for kiosks that read "Ask me about Lisboa" in Santa Apolónia, Belém, and other locations.

Budget Travel: Movijovem, R. Lúcio de Azevedo, 29 (☎707 20 30 30; www.pousadasjuventude.pt). M: São Sebastião. Make reservations at Hostelling International youth hostels all over Portugal. Open daily 9am-7pm.

Embassies: See **Embassies and Consulates,** p. 11.

Currency Exchange: Banks are open M-F 8:30am-3pm. **Cota Câmbios,** Pr. Dom Pedro IV, 41 (☎213 22 04 80). Open daily 9am-8pm. Sells 2hr. phone cards to the US and European land lines for €5. **Western Union** inside for money transfers. The main post office, most banks, and travel agencies also change money. Exchanges line the streets of Baixa. Ask about fees first—they can be exorbitant.

LOCAL SERVICES

English-Language Bookstore: FNAVC, Armazéns do Chiado, 4th fl., R. do Carmo, 2 (☎213 22 18 00). Large section just for English books, but they can be found throughout the store in the regular sections as well. Open daily 10am-10pm.

Libraries: Biblioteca Municipal Central, Palácio Galveias (☎217 97 13 26). M: Campo Pequeno. Open July 15-Sept. 15 M-F 2-7pm, Sa 11am-6pm; otherwise M-F 10am-7pm, Sa 11am-6pm. **Biblioteca Municipal Camões,** Largo do Calhariz, 17 (☎213 42 21 57). Free Internet access. Open July 15-Sept. 15 M-F 1-7pm, 2nd and 4th Sa of every month 1-8pm; Sept. 16-July 14 M-F 10am-7pm, 2nd and 4th Sa 11am-6pm.

Shopping Centers: Armazéns do Chiado, (☎213 21 06 00) at the end of R. Garrett. Food court at the top. Open daily 10am-8pm. **El Corte Inglés,** Av. António Augusto de Aguiar at Av. Duque d'Ávila (☎213 71 17 00; www.elcorteingles.pt). M: São Sebastião. Portugal's first branch of the Spanish department store has everything. Open M-Th 10am-10pm, F-Sa 10am-11:30pm. MC/V. **Colombo,** Av. Lusíada (☎217 11 36 00; www.colombo.pt), in front of Benfica stadium. M: Colégio Militar-Luz. Over 400 shops, a 10-screen cinema (adult ticket €5), and a small amusement park. Open daily 10am-midnight. **Centro Comercial Amoreiras de Lisboa,** Av. Eng. Duarte Pacheco (☎213 81 02 00; www.amoreirs.com), near R. Carlos Alberto da Mota Pinto. M: Marquês de Pombal. Take bus #11 from Pr. dos Restauradores. Towers house 383 shops, including a huge **Pão de Açúcar** supermarket and cinema. Open daily 10am-11pm. **Centro Comercial Vasco da Gama,** Av. Dom João II (☎218 93 06 00; www.centrovascodagama.pt). M: Oriente. Open daily 10am-midnight.

Laundromats: Lavatax, R. Francisco Sanches, 65A (☎218 12 33 92). M: Arroios. Wash, dry, and fold €3 per kg. Open M-F 9am-1pm and 3-7pm, Sa 8:30am-1pm.

Lavanderia Clin, R. de São João da Praça, 5-7 (☎218 86 64 44) in Alfama. Wash, dry, and fold €5 per kg. Open M-F 8:30am-5pm, Sa 9am-1pm.

EMERGENCY AND COMMUNICATIONS

Police: Tourism Police Station, Palácio Foz in Restauradores (☎213 42 16 24; lsbetur@psp.pt), and at R. Capelo, 13 (☎213 46 61 41 or 42 16 34). English spoken.

Late-Night Pharmacy: ☎118 (directory assistance). 24hr. pharmacy rotates. Look for the green cross at intersections, or check listings at **Farmácia Azevedos,** Pr. Dom Pedro IV, 31 (☎213 43 04 82), at the base of Rossio in front of the metro.

Medical Services: Dial ☎112 in case of emergency. **Hospital de Saint Louis,** R. Luz Soriano, 182 (☎213 21 65 00; fax 46 02 21) in Bairro Alto. Open daily 9am-6pm. **Hospital de São José** (☎218 84 10 00 or 261 31 28 57), R. José António Serrano.

Telephones: Portugal Telecom, Pr. Dom Pedro IV, 68 (☎808 21 11 56). M: Rossio. Pay the cashier after your call or use a phone card. Also has **Internet** access. (€1.30 for first 30min., €0.75 per 15min. after that.) Office open daily 8am-11pm. Portugal Telecom **phone cards** (50 units €3) available at the office or at bookstores and stationers. Local calls cost at least 2 units. Minutes per unit vary. PT cards should only be purchased for local use; better deals on non-local calls can be found elsewhere, such as at **Casa Viola,** R. Augusta, 110, in Baixa (2hr. calling card to the US €5).

Internet Access: Portugal Telecom (see above). **Cyber.bica,** R. Duques de Bragança, 7 (☎213 22 50 04), in Bairro Alto. €0.75 per 15min. Open M-Sa 11am-midnight. Two fun cyber cafes in Bairro Alto also double as bars: **Web C@fé,** R. Diário de Notícias, 126 (☎213 42 11 81). Friendly couple behind the bar will keep you entertained if none of your buddies are online. €0.75 per 15min. Open daily 4pm-2am. **Blue Net Cafe,** R. da Rosa, 165 (☎213 473 095). €1 for 30min. Mixed drinks €3. Beer €1.20. M-F 11am-midnight, Sa-Su 3pm-midnight. Cash only.

Post Office: Main office, Pr. dos Restauradores (☎213 23 87 00). Open M-F 8am-10pm, Sa-Su 9am-7pm. To avoid the lines, go to the **branch,** Pr. do Comércio (☎213 22 09 20). Open M-F 8:30am-6:30pm. Cash only. **Postal Code:** 1100.

▐ ACCOMMODATIONS

Pensões and budget hotels abound in Lisboa, but room quality may vary significantly—ask to see the room before paying. During the summer, expect to pay €20-30 for a single and €35-45 for a double, depending on amenities. You can usually find a room in the summer with little or no notice, but you may want to book in advance during mid-June, due to the **Festa de Santo Antonio.** In the low season, prices generally drop €5 or more, so try bargaining. Many establishments only have rooms with double beds, and charge per person. Backpacking hostels are relatively new to the accommodation scene in Lisboa, with most opening their doors within the last year or two. They are very similar in set-up: mixed four- to eight-person dorms, shared bathrooms, a common living room, and almost always free Internet access. They do differ slightly in amenities, but all are comfortable and run €18-20 in the summer. Due to online booking, they fill up fast; reserve ahead.

Several hotels are in the center of town on Av. da Liberdade, while cheaper *pensões* can be found in Baixa and Bairro Alto. Avoid those surrounding Rossio: while they're very convenient, they're usually around €10 more than the norm. Look around Baixa's R. da Prata, R. dos Correiros, and R. do Ouro (R. de Aurea) for cheaper accommodations. Most of the backpacking hostels are near Bairro Alto. Lodgings near Castelo de São Jorge are quieter and closer to the sights, but much more difficult to reach. Be careful at night, especially in the winding streets of Alfama and in Bairro Alto; many streets are poorly lit. Bairro Alto is generally safe until the bars close at 4am, but it pays to be alert.

ACCOMMODATIONS BY PRICE

A Alfama **B** Baixa **BA** Bairro Alto **E** Elsewhere			
UNDER €15 (❶)		🏚 Lisbon Lounge Hostel (637)	B
Pque. Mun. de Camp. de Monsanto (637)	E	🏚 Lisbon Poets Hostel (640)	B
Casa de Hóspedes (641)	A	Luar Guest House (640)	BA
		🏚 Oasis Backpackers Mansion (640)	BA
€15-25 (❷)		Pensão Beira Mar (641)	A
Albergo Odisseo (640)	B	Pensão Estrela (641)	A
Black and White Hostel (642)	E	Rossio Plaza (640)	B
Casa de Hóspedes Globo (640)	BA		
Duque (640)	B	**€26-35 (❸)**	
🏚 Easy Hostel (637)	B	🏚 Pensão Ninho das Águias (640)	A
Goodnight Backpacker's Hostel (640)	B		
Lazy Crow & Co. (640)	E		

CAMPING

Camping is popular in Portugal, but campers can be prime targets for thieves. Stay at an enclosed campsite and ask ahead about security. There are 30 campgrounds within a 45min. radius of the capital. The only one in Lisboa proper is **Parque Municipal de Campismo de Monsanto ❶**, on the road to Benfica. Take bus #14 to Parque Florestal Monsanto. (☎217 62 31 00; fax 62 31 06. Pool and supermarket. 24hr. reception. July-Aug. €5 per person, €5-6 per tent, €3.50 per car. Prices slightly lower Sept.-June. High season 2-6 person bungalows available with small kitchen, TV, and heating €60-100; low season €40-60.)

BAIXA

Dozens of pensions are located around the three connected *praças* that form the heart of downtown Lisboa. Staying in this area is convenient, as it's a great home base for visiting sights. On the other hand, Baixa's prices are often noticeably higher (by €10-20) than other neighborhoods, particularly during the summer. Most *pensões* are on the top floors of buildings, a hassle for luggage-laden travelers. Keep your head up (literally) when looking for a place to stay in Baixa, as *pensões* are often poorly advertised and easy to miss. If you didn't reserve ahead in summer, it's usually possible to track something down. Hostels are an alternative to *pensões*, and have more amenities, are less expensive, and are generally nicer than *pensões*. Due to online booking, however, they fill up fast in the summer.

🏚 **Lisbon Lounge Hostel,** R. de São Nicolau, 41, 2nd fl. (☎/fax 213 46 20 61). M: Rossio or Baixa-Chiado. One look at the Lisbon Lounge and you'll think you've entered a 5-star hotel. Features a central living room, lounge areas on each floor, free breakfast, Wi-Fi, ultra-secure magnetic card access, and lockers. Hungry for more? Dinner is available for a mere €6. 4-8 person dorms €20; double room with shared bath €54. Cash only. ❷

🏚 **Easy Hostel,** R. de São Nicolau, 13, 5th fl. (☎218 86 42 80). Centrally located in the middle of Baixa. Great living room area for hanging out with fellow travelers. Bright and airy rooms with 4-6 beds. Recent upgrades include a new floor, soundproof walls, ceiling fans, and combination door locks. The elevator makes life at Easy that much easier. Free breakfast with freshly baked bread. Wi-Fi. €18 per night. Laundry €3. Cash only. ❷

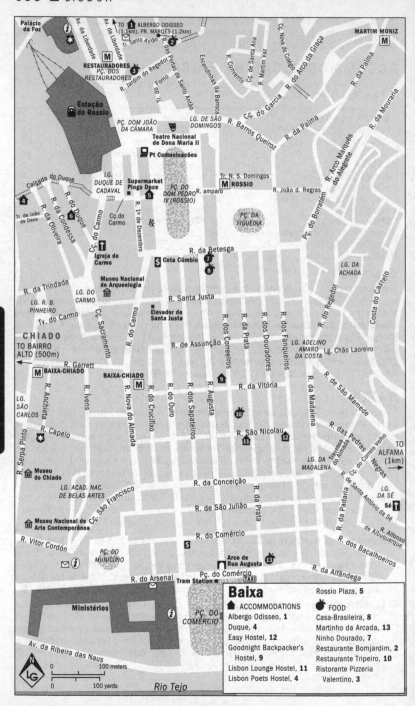

LISBOA

Palácio da Foz

TO (1.1km), PR. MARQÊS (1.2km)
ALBERGO ODISSEO

Av. da Liberdade

Tr. Santo Antão

MARTIM MONIZ
M

RESTAURADORES
M
PÇ. DOS
RESTAURADORES

R. das Portas de Santo Antão

R. Jardim do Regedor

Forno

Tr. do Forno

Escadinhas da Barroca

R. do Convento

Cç. de Santa Ana

R. Martim Vaz

Cç. Nova do Colégio

R. do Arco da Graça

R. da Palma

R. da Mouraria

Estação do Rossio

Calçada do Duque

LG. DUQUE DE CADAVAL

Supermarket
Pingo Doce

PÇ. DOM JOÃO DA CÂMARA

LG. DE SÃO DOMINGOS

Teatro Nacional de Dona Maria II

Pt Comunicações

R. Barros Queiroz

Cç. do Garcia

R. da Palma

R. Arco Marquês do Alegrete

PÇ. DO DOM PEDRO IV (ROSSIO)

Tr. N. S. Domingos
M ROSSIO

R. amparo

R. João d. Regras

R. do Borratém

PÇ. DA FIGUEIRA

Tr. de João de Deus

R. da Condessa

R. da Oliveira

R. do Duque

Cç. do Carmo

Cç. do Carmo

R. 1º de Dezembro

Igreja do Carmo

Museu Nacional de Arqueologia

LG. DO CARMO

R. da Betesga

S Cota Cûmbio

LG. DA ACHADA

R. da Trindade

LG. R. B. PINHEIRO

Tv. do Carmo

Cç. Sacramento

R. do Carmo

R. Santa Justa

Elevador de Santa Justa

R. de Assunção

R. dos Correeiros

R. da Prata

R. dos Douradores

R. dos Fanqueiros

R. do Regedor

Costa do Castelo

LG. ADELINO AMARO DA COSTA

Lg. Chão Laoreiro

CHIADO
TO BAIRRO ALTO (500m)

R. Garrett

M BAIXA-CHIADO

BAIXA-CHIADO
M

R. Nova do Almada

R. do Crucifixo

R. do Ouro

R. dos Sapateiros

R. Augusta

R. da Vitória

R. da Madalena

R. de São Mamede

LG. SÃO CARLOS

R. Anchieta

R. Ivens

R. Capelo

R. Serpa Pinto

Museu do Chiado

LG. ACAD. NAC. DE BELAS ARTES

Museu Nacional de Arte Contemporânea

R. Vitor Cordón

R. de Conceição

R. de São Julião

R. do Comércio

R. da Prata

R. São Nicolau

LG. DA MADALENA

Travessa do Almada

Cç. do Correio velho

R. das Pedras Negras

TO ALFAMA (1km)

R. de Santo António da Sé

R. da Padaria

LG. DA SÉ
Sé

R. Afonso de Albuquerque

R. dos Bacalhoeiros

Cç. de São Francisco

PÇ. DO MUNICÍPIO

Arco de Rua Augusta

PÇ. do Comércio
TAXI

R. da Alfândega

R. do Arsenal

Tram Station

Ministérios

PÇ. DO COMÉRCIO

Av. da Ribeira das Naus

N
LG

0   100 meters
0   100 yards

Rio Tejo

Baixa

🏠 ACCOMMODATIONS
Albergo Odisseo, 1
Duque, 4
Easy Hostel, 12
Goodnight Backpacker's Hostel, 9
Lisbon Lounge Hostel, 11
Lisbon Poets Hostel, 4

Rossio Plaza, 5

🍴 FOOD
Casa-Brasileira, 8
Martinho da Arcada, 13
Ninho Dourado, 7
Restaurante Bomjardim, 2
Restaurante Tripeiro, 10
Ristorante Pizzeria Valentino, 3

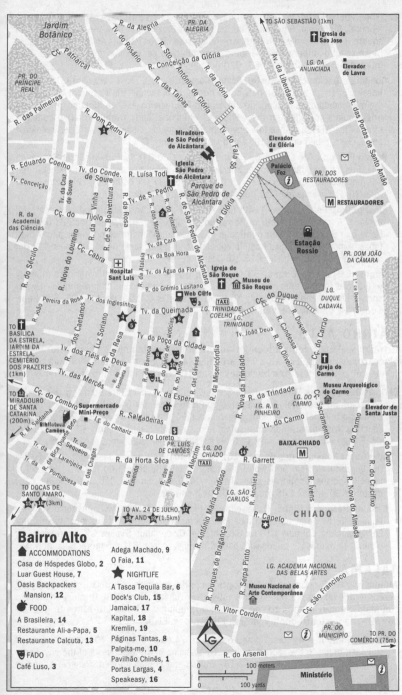

LISBOA

Bairro Alto

🏠 ACCOMMODATIONS
Casa de Hóspedes Globo, **2**
Luar Guest House, **7**
Oasis Backpackers
  Mansion, **12**

🍎 FOOD
A Brasileira, **14**
Restaurante Ali-a-Papa, **5**
Restaurante Calcuta, **13**

🎭 FADO
Café Luso, **3**

Adega Machado, **9**
O Faia, **11**

⭐ NIGHTLIFE
A Tasca Tequila Bar, **6**
Dock's Club, **15**
Jamaica, **17**
Kapital, **18**
Kremlin, **19**
Páginas Tantas, **8**
Palpita-me, **10**
Pavilhão Chinês, **1**
Portas Largas, **4**
Speakeasy, **16**

Lisbon Poets Hostel, R. do Duque, 41, 2nd fl. (☎213 46 10 58; www.lisbonpoetshostel.com). M: Rossio. Situated in the outskirts of Baixa, away from the hustle of Rossio square. Young, friendly staff and cozy lounge, the Lisbon Poets is not a typical *pensão*. Close co-ed quarters provide a great opportunity to get to know fellow travelers. Free Internet and Wi-Fi. Breakfast €3. €20 per person. AmEx/MC/V. ❷

Goodnight Backpacker's Hostel, R. dos Correeiros, 113, 3rd fl. (☎213 43 01 39). M: Rossio. To get to this brand-new co-ed hostel, walk through the storefront, go through the mirrored doors, and climb up the *azulejo*-lined staircase. Cheerful atmosphere, with bright colors splashed on the walls and whimsical Andy Warhol art. Two common rooms, free Wi-Fi, a smoke-free environment, single sex bathrooms, and free breakfast and lockers. 8-bed dorms €19; 4-bed €20. Cash only. ❷

Rossio Plaza, Cç. do Carmo, 6, 3rd fl. (☎213 42 60 04). M: Rossio. Great Bohemian feel. Community guitar, incense, and living room encourage mingling. Breakfast, Internet, and lockers. Co-ed rooms with 4-6 beds. Single sex bathrooms. Weekdays until June 30 €18; weekends €20. July-Aug. €20. Cash only. ❷

Albergo Odisseo, Tv. Larga, 1, 4th fl. (☎213 57 41 98; www.albergoodisseo.com), M: Avenida. A few blocks north of Baixa, on top of a hill. Strategically located between Baixa and Bairro Alto, near numerous bus lines and a metro stop. Lower prices than those of many of the Baixa hostels but almost all of the same perks. Doubles €22 per person; quad, €18; 6 beds, €17.50. Cash only. ❷

Duque, Calçada do Duque, 53 (☎213 46 34 44; duquelisboa@yahoo.com). Very well-priced for the area, with plain but spotless rooms. Five cheap singles. Owner speaks English and French. July 15-Sept. 15 singles €20-25; doubles €32-36. Sept. 16-July 14 €20/30. Cash only. ❷

BAIRRO ALTO

If you're seeking a central location for nightlife entertainment, there is no better place to stay than Bairro Alto. The area has several great budget accommodations where you can meet fellow backpackers and hit the bars and clubs together.

Oasis Backpackers Mansion, R. de Santa Catarina, 24 (☎213 47 80 44; www.oasislisboa.com). M: Baixa-Chiado, exit Largo do Chiado. The best place to stay in Lisbon, the Oasis is a backpacker's dream: gorgeous building, free Internet access, free breakfast, spacious living room, individual safes, and extremely clean. Laundry €6. M-Sa dinner €5. F free Portuguese lessons. €20 per person for a mixed dorm. Cash only. ❷

Luar Guest House, R. das Gáveas, 101 (☎213 46 09 49; www.pensaoluar.com). Follow the beautiful *azulejo* and wood staircase to brightly decorated rooms. The staff is friendly and the location is great. Laundry €10/6kg. Singles €15, with shower €20; doubles €30; triples €45; quads €60. Cash only. ❷

Casa de Hóspedes Globo, R. Teixeira, 37 (☎213 46 22 79; www.pensaoglobo.com). Popular for its great nightlife location. Rooms with phone and TV; most have bath. English spoken. Laundry €10 for 6kg. Internet €2 per hour. Singles €25; doubles €30; triples with bath €40; quads with bath €50. High season €10-15 more. Cash only. ❷

ALFAMA

Alfama has few accommodations options and less price competition, but staying here is a nice change of pace (especially after Baixa). The steep, unmarked streets can make each trip back to the *pensão* a grueling workout, but hikes frequently pay off with postcard-quality views of downtown Lisboa.

Pensão Ninho das Águias, Costa do Castelo, 74 (☎218 85 40 70). Climb the spiral staircase to get to the reception desk. Offers some of the best views of the city, especially from rooms #5, 6, and 12-14. English and French spoken. Reserve ahead in

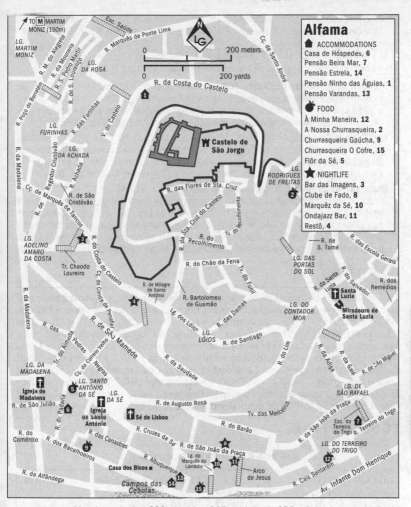

Alfama

🏠 **ACCOMMODATIONS**
Casa de Hóspedes, **6**
Pensão Beira Mar, **7**
Pensão Estrela, **14**
Pensão Ninho das Águias, **1**
Pensão Varandas, **13**

🍅 **FOOD**
À Minha Maneira, **12**
A Nossa Churrasqueira, **2**
Churrasqueira Gaúcha, **9**
Churrasqueira O Cofre, **15**
Flôr da Sé, **5**

⭐ **NIGHTLIFE**
Bar das Imagens, **3**
Clube de Fado, **8**
Marquêz da Sé, **10**
Ondajazz Bar, **11**
Restô, **4**

LISBOA

summer. May-Aug. singles €30; doubles €45, with bath €50; triples (some with bath) €60. Sept.-Apr. prices drop by €5. Cash only. ❸

Pensão Beira Mar, Largo Terreiro do Trigo, 16 (☎218 86 99 33; beira@iol.pt), near the Sta. Apolonia train station. Avoid the 4-story climb by entering through the back where there are only 2 flights of stairs. Brightly decorated rooms include a shower, TV, and sink. Free Internet, munchies, and breakfast. Living room and kitchen for guest use. Reservations by fax or email only. June-Aug. singles €20-35; doubles €30-40; triples €45; quads €60. Oct.-May prices drop by €5. Cash only. ❸

Casa de Hóspedes, R. da Padaria, 38 (☎218 86 77 10). One of the better deals in Alfama; clean floors and bathrooms. Owned by a friendly couple. Very well located near many of the district's sights. Open June-Aug. doubles €30; triples €45. Cash only. ❶

Pensão Estrela, R. dos Bacalhoeiros, 8 (☎218 86 95 06; pensaoestrela@hotmail.com). Don't be put off by the ancient, dilapidated staircase; the rooms it leads are quite nice and have basic amenities, including TV. Some look out onto the water. Spanish spoken. June-Sept. Singles €20-25; doubles €35-40; triple €53. Oct.-May €15/30-35/45. ❷

OUTSIDE THE CITY CENTER

Three high-quality, inexpensive hostels lie outside the city center.

Pousada de Juventude de Lisboa (HI), R. Andrade Corvo, 46 (☎213 53 26 96). M: Picoas. Exit the metro station onto R. Andrade Corvo; the hostel will be in front of you, marked by a large banner. Large rooms. Breakfast included; lunch and dinner €6 each. HI card required. Reserve ahead. Dorms €16; doubles with bath €43. MC/V. ❷

Lazy Crow & Co., Tv. Santa Quiteria, 12 (☎ 213 90 90 20). M: Rato. From the station, go down S. Bento, turn on first right. Big pink house; ring the crow doorbell. Spacious mixed dorms, free Internet access, as well as a nice common area for hanging out. Breakfast included. Check-in after 2pm. Singles €17; doubles €44. MC/V. ❷

Black and White Hostel, R. Alexandre Herculano, 39 (☎ 213 46 22 12) M: Marquês de Pombal. From the station, walk away from the statue down Av. da Liberdade. Take a right on R. Alexandre Herculano and the hostel is 2 blocks down on your left. Rock bottom prices for a stay at one of the most artistic hostels in town—rooms are boldly painted with murals of psychedelic spirals and abstract creatures. Quick walk to both Baixa and Bairro Alto. Free Internet and breakfast. Mixed dorms €14-18. Cash only. ❷

◪ FOOD

Calorie-counters beware: Lisboa has some of the cheapest, most irresistible restaurants of the western European capitals, not to mention the best wine. A full dinner costs about €9-11 per person and the *prato do dia* (daily special) is often only €4-6. Between lunch and dinner, snack on cheap, filling, and addictively delicious Portuguese pastries. Lisboa boasts almost as many *pastelarias* as Spain has tapas bars, and abounds with seafood specialties such as *pratos de caracois* (snail dishes), *creme de mariscos* (seafood chowder with tomatoes), and *bacalhau cozido com grão e batatas* (cod with chickpeas and boiled potatoes, doused in olive oil). For a more diverse food selection, head up to the winding streets of Bairro Alto where you'll find many international restaurants.

FOOD BY TYPE

A Alfama **B** Baixa **BA** Bairro Alto **G** Graça

INTERNATIONAL		Restaurante Tripeiro (643)	B ❷
Restaurante Ali-a-Papa (644)	BA ❸		
Restaurante Calcuta (644)	BA ❷	**CAFES**	
▨ Ristorante-Pizzeria Valentino (644)	B ❷	A Brasileira (644)	BA ❷
		Bar Cercamoura (644)	G ❶
PORTUGUESE		Casa-Brasileira (644)	B ❶
▨ À Minha Maneira (644)	A ❷	Esplanada Igreja da Graça (645)	G ❶
A Nossa Churrasqueira (644)	A ❶	▨ Flôr da Sé (644)	A ❶
▨ Churrasqueira Gaúcha (644)	A ❷	Ninho Dourado (643)	B ❷
Churrasqueira O Cofre (644)	A ❷	O Pitéu (644)	G ❷
Martinho da Arcada (643)	B ❹	Pastelaria Estrela da Graça (645)	G ❶
Restaurante Bomjardim (643)	B ❷		

SUPERMARKETS

Pingo Doce, R. 1 de Dezembro, 81-83 (☎213 24 73 30). Just outside of the Pr. do Dom Pedro IV. A branch of Portugal's major supermarket chain. Open daily 8:30am-9pm.

Mercado da Ribeira, Av. 24 de Julho (☎213 46 29 66). M: Cais de Sodré. Accessible by bus #40 or tram #15. This vast market complex is over a century old and located inside a warehouse just outside Estação Cais do Sodré. Go early for the freshest selection of fruit, fish, and a variety of other foods. Prices on produce can't be beat. Open Tu-Sa 5am-2pm for produce, M-Sa 5am-7pm for flowers. Cash only.

Supermercado Mini-Preço, R. do Loreto. Open M-Sa 9am-8pm, Su 9:30am-1:30pm and 3:30-7:30pm. Also on R. de São Paulo, 80. Open M-Sa 9am-8pm.

Supermercado Pão de Açúcar, Amoreiras Shopping Center de Lisboa, Av. Duarte Pacheco (☎213 82 66 80). Take bus #11 from Pr. dos Restauradores or Pr. da Figueira. Open daily 9am-11pm.

BAIXA

There are a ton of restaurants along R. dos Correeiros and on R. das Portas de S. Antão, but the revolving menu stands in nine different languages should tip you off to their tourist orientation. Those with menus in Portuguese tend to serve the more affordable meals.

▨ **Ristorante-Pizzeria Valentino,** R. Jardim do Regedor, 37-45 (☎213 46 17 27). Portugal's very own *Italia* in the Pr. do Restauradores. Watch the chefs prepare a variety of dishes in the open kitchen. Keep your eyes peeled for famous Portuguese players; they've been known to frequent Valentino's. Try the crunchy crusted Pizza Caprese (€8.50). Entrees €7-19. Pizzas €4-10. Open daily noon-midnight. AmEx/MC/V. ❷

Martinho da Arcada, Pr. do Comércio, 3 (☎218 87 92 59). Enjoy the one of a kind ambience at the oldest restaurant in Lisboa, founded in 1782. Guests can read poems by Portuguese poet Fernando Pessoa, a regular during his lifetime. Outside seating available. Fish options less expensive than grilled meats or chicken. Entrees €17-35. Open M-Sa noon-3pm and 7-10:30pm. AmEx/MC/V. ❹

Casa-Brasileira, R. Augusta, 267-269 (☎213 46 97 13). A great place to grab some food and a pastry while sightseeing. Cheap sandwiches (€3), pizza (€2-4), and fruit smoothies (€1.25-1.75). Menu of the day (sandwich, fries, and a freshly squeezed smoothie or an ice cold beer) for €4.50. Open daily 7am-1am. Cash only. ❶

Ninho Dourado, R. Augusta, 278 (☎213 46 97 39). Situated in the heart of Baixa. Pleasant outdoor seating, a huge menu, and decent prices. Daily specials offer a complete meal (plate of the day, drink, dessert, and coffee) for €6. Sandwiches €3-4. Pizzas for two €8. Entrees €8. Open daily 6am-2am. Cash only. ❷

Restaurante Bomjardim, Tr. Santo Antão, 12 (☎213 42 43 89). The self-proclaimed "king of chicken" serves up hearty portions of scrumptious fried, baked, and roast chicken (€9.20) both indoors and under the umbrellas outside. Other grilled meats €8-11. Open daily noon-11:30pm. AmEx/MC/V. ❷

Restaurante Tripeiro, R. dos Correeiros, 70A (☎213 42 25 12). This chatty, cheerful restaurant has been a Baixa favorite for almost 30 years. Specializes in fish with piles of veggies on the side. Entrees €6-13 (though some as much as €50). Open M-Sa 9am-3pm and 6-midnight. Cash only. ❷

BAIRRO ALTO

The narrow streets of Bairro Alto are lined with bars, restaurants, and the famous *casas de fado*. Prices range from modest to supremely immodest, as in the *casas*. Budget eaters and those searching for veritable Portuguese food should not be discouraged by Bairro Alto's expensive international eateries; though it may be a treasure hunt to find the cheap, traditional restaurants, it's worth the extra effort. You can find nicer restaurants on the water in the **Docas de Santo Amaro** area.

A Brasileira, R. Garrett, 120-122 (☎213 46 95 41). M: Baixa-Chiado. A former stomping ground of early 20th-century poets and intellectuals, this cafe almost doubles as a tourist sight. Poet Fernando Pessoa was once a frequent patron, and his statue now sits at his regular chair. Restaurant downstairs serves up platters of Portuguese food. Entrees €6-13. Sandwiches €2-5. Open daily 8am-2am. AmEx/MC/V. ❷

Restaurante Calcuta, R. do Norte, 17 (☎213 42 82 95; www.calcuta1.com), near Lg. Camões. Listen to Indian music in an relaxing atmosphere while you enjoy Calcuta favorites like the *prawn masala* (€9.50). Offers a wide selection of vegetarian options (€6.50-7.50). Open M-F noon-3pm and 6-11pm, Sa-Su 6-11pm. AmEx/MC/V. ❷

Restaurante Ali-a-Papa, R. da Atalaia, 95 (☎213 47 41 43). Serves generous helpings of Moroccan food in a quiet atmosphere; dishes include couscous and tangine. Vegetarian-friendly. Entrees €9-14.50. Open M and W-Sa 7pm-12:30am. AmEx/MC/V. ❸

ALFAMA

The winding streets of Alfama conceal a number of small and simple restaurants, often packed with locals. The Rua da Padaria and the area surrounding its intersection with Rua dos Bacalhoeiros offers the cheapest options in Lisboa.

▨ **À Minha Maneira,** Largo do Terreiro do Trigo 1 (☎218 86 11 12; www.a-minha-maneira.pt). Once a bank, the old vault has been revamped into a wine closet. Various meat and fish dishes. Free Internet access and printing. Entrees €8-15. Open daily 11am-11pm. Cash only. ❷

▨ **Churrasqueira Gaúcha,** R. dos Bacalhoeiros, 26C-D (☎218 87 06 09). Affordable Portuguese food cooked to perfection in a comfortable, cavernous setting. The best restaurant on a street already packed with great deals. Incredibly fresh meat, poultry, and fish. No vegetarian options. Open M-Sa 10am-midnight. AmEx/MC/V. ❷

▨ **Flôr da Sé,** Largo Santo António da Sé, 9-11 (☎218 87 57 42). This *pastelaria* is extremely clean, brightly lit, and serves quality food at some of the lowest prices in Lisboa. The lunchtime *prato do dia* (€4) is scrumptious, and the wide selection of desserts and candies taste as good as they look. Open M-F and Su 7am-8pm. Cash only. ❶

Churrasqueira O Cofre, R. dos Bacalhoeiros, 2C-D (☎218 86 89 35). A display case shows what's available—mostly meat but also some grilled seafood. Breezy outdoor seating in summer. Entrees €5-11. Open M-Sa noon-4pm and 7-11pm. AmEx/MC/V. ❷

A Nossa Churrasqueira, Lg. Rodrigues de Freitas, 2 (☎218 86 66 02). A quality budget restaurant in the heart of Alfama serving hearty portions. Chickens rotate over flaming coals behind the counter. Entrees €7-11. Open Tu-Su noon-9:30pm. Cash only. ❷

GRAÇA

Good, cheap eats abound on the small streets of Graça. Things heat up after dark when the lovely views are no longer the main attraction, and the thumping beats of music take center stage.

O Pitéu, Lg. da Graça, 95-6, (☎218 87 10 67). Next door to Pastelaria Estrela da Graça. *Azulejo*-lined walls and wine-inspired decorations. The restaurant serves a few Brazilian dishes in addition to traditional Portuguese dishes of fish, chicken, pork, and steak. Entrees €8-12. Open daily noon-3pm and 7-10:30pm. Cash only. ❷

Bar Cercamoura, Largo das Portas do Sol, 4 (☎218 87 48 59). Take the #28 tram up the hill from the stop on R. da Conceição. Hop off when you see the statue and the gorgeous view on the right; the bar is on your left. Cozy, leather-covered interior and airy outdoor seating are perfect for kicking the night off. Snacks €1-4. Beer and wine €2-3. Cocktails €5. Open daily noon-2am. Cash only. ❶

Esplanada Igreja da Graça, Lg. da Graça. Walk 1 stop uphill beyond the Panteão Nacional to the Lg. da Graça, then follow the Lg. da Graça to the left. This *miradouro* has a perfect view of Lisboa. Sandwiches €2-4.25. Tea €1.50. Open daily 11:30am-3am. ❶

Pastelaria Estrela da Graça, 98 Lg. da Graça (☎218 87 24 38), 1 tram stop above the Panteão Nacional. The mouth-watering pastries, candy, cakes, and lunch entrees, like the delectable grilled salmon (€5), are well worth a stop. Open daily 7am-10pm. Cash only. ❶

◎ SIGHTS

Three thousand years of history have made Lisboa into a rare and fascinating aesthetic timeline. Moorish **azulejos** (painted tiles) adorn the Alfama district; the 12th-century **Sé** cathedral maintains a tough Romanesque stone facade, contrasting with the elaborate Manueline monastery in Belém, which features excessive ornamentation reflective of Portugal's glory during the Age of Discovery. The neoclassical design of Praça do Comércio's triumphal Roman arch marks a return to simpler forms, as it's the product of the Marquês de Pombal's post-earthquake planning. But Lisboa's beauty speaks of the present as well, from the sleek and modern Parque das Nações to the expressive, graffitied streets of Bairro Alto.

Those planning to do a lot of sightseeing in a few days should consider purchasing the Welcome Center's "Lisboa Card" for a flat fee (see **Tourist Office,** p. 635). Museums and many sites are closed on Mondays and free on Sundays before 2pm.

BAIXA

Although Baixa claims few historical sights, the lively pedestrian traffic and dramatic history surrounding the neighborhood's three main *praças* make it a monument in its own right. Beware the thousands of softly cooing pigeons spoiled by countless statues of distinguished leaders on which to make their marks.

AROUND ROSSIO. Begin your tour of 18th-century history Lisboa at its heart: **Rossio,** or **Praça Dom Pedro IV** as it is more formally known. The city's main square was once a cattle market, public execution stage, bullring, and carnival ground. Today, it is the domain of tourists and ruthless local drivers circling Pedro's enormous statue. Another statue, this one of Gil Vicente, Portugal's first great dramatist (see **Literature,** p. 625), peers from atop the **Teatro Nacional de Dona Maria II** (easily recognized by its large, Parthenon-esque columns) at one end of the *praça*.

AROUND PRAÇA DOS RESTAURADORES. In **Praça dos Restauradores,** a giant obelisk celebrates Portugal's hard-earned independence from Spain in 1640 after 60 years of Spanish rule. The obelisk is accompanied by a bronze sculpture of the "Spirit of Independence" and is a constant reminder of the centuries-old Spanish-Portuguese rivalry. The tourist office and shops line the *praça* and C. da Glória, the hill that leads to Bairro Alto. Pr. dos Restauradores is also the start of **Avenida da Liberdade,** one of Lisboa's most elegant promenades. Modeled after the boulevards of 19th-century Paris, this mile-long thoroughfare ends at **Praça do Marquês de Pombal.** There, an 18th-century statue of the Marquês still keeps watch over the city he whipped into shape 250 years ago.

AROUND PRAÇA DO COMÉRCIO. After the earthquake of 1755 leveled this section of Lisboa, the Marquês de Pombal designed the streets to serve as a conduit for goods from the ports on the Rio Tejo to the city center. The grid formed perfect blocks, with streets designated for specific trades: *sapateiros* (shoemakers), *douradores* (gold workers), and *bacalhoeiros* (cod merchants) each had their own avenue. Although much has changed over the last 250 years, Baixa remains a commercial center. The roads lead to **Praça do Comércio,** on the banks of the Tejo.

DISTANCE: 1 mi.

DURATION: 2hr.

WHEN TO GO: Tu or Sa for the Feira da Ladra

Much of Lisbon was destroyed in the 18th century by a massive earthquake. The most interesting and well-preserved structures are located in the hillier areas of Alfama and Graça. To save yourself a 2+ hour hike uphill, start the walking tour with a ride in one of the city's historically preserved trams. From Praça do Comércio take tram #28 (€1.30) up to the Igreja de São Vicente de Fora.

1. IGREJA DE SÃO VICENTE DE FORA. Built between 1582 and 1629, the Igreja, like many in Portugal, is ornately decorated with gold leafing, large archways, and stained-glass windows. The sacristas, covered with beautiful Sintra marble, are a sight to see. This house of worship is particularly interesting because it's dedicated to Lisbon's real patron saint, St. Vincent.

2. FEIRA DA LADRA. On Tuesdays and Saturdays between 7am and 4pm you will find a pleasant surprise behind the large church structure: the Feira da Ladra, a flea-market style fair that sells everything from souvenirs to used shoes to beautiful African necklaces.

3. PANTEÃO NACIONAL. Around the corner is the stunning Panteão Nacional. The Panteão was intended to be a church but the town ran out of money before it could be completed. Seized by the government, it was turned into a monument documenting and honoring the forefathers of Portugal.

4. BAR CERCAMOURA. From the Panteão Nacional follow the tram tracks downhill. Window shop or stop at variety of unique antique stores on either side of the street. About ½ mi. downhill there is a great view of Lisboa's skyline. Take a break at the Bar Cercamoura before heading onward.

5. SÉ DE LISBOA. The small but impressive Sé lacks the splendor of Lisboa's grander cathedrals, but its sheer age and wonderful location make for an enjoyable visit.

6. CASTELO DE SÃO JORGE. Follow the signs to the castle. At the top of the small hill you'll find the entrance to the Castelo de São Jorge. Constructed during the 5th century by Visigoths, the castle was later taken over by the Moors and finally by the royal family of Portugal. Today, it stands as a series of stone walls with amazing views of Lisboa.

LISBOA

Today, Pr. do Comércio, with its 9400 lb. statue of **Dom João I,** serves as a wide and inviting space between the Tejo's many boats and the city's crowds of people.

BAIRRO ALTO

■ MUSEU ARQUEOLÓGICO DO CARMO. Located under the skeletal arches of an old church destroyed in the 1755 earthquake, this partially outdoor museum allows visitors to get close to historical relics like a 16th-century coat of arms. Check out the two Peruvian mummies and the Egyptian sarcophagus inside. *(Largo do Carmo. Open M-Sa 10am-7pm. €2.50, students €1.50, under 14 free.)*

CEMITÉRIO DOS PRAZERES. At the cemetery, hundreds of small family mausoleums are lined together, forming a genuine city of the dead. Many of these minibuildings have broken doors or glass pane windows, allowing you to see inside (if you want to). Watch out, some of the older ones have broken coffins too! Go early if you're squeamish, since coffins might seem creepy in the evening. *(Pr. S. João Bosco. ☎213 96 15 11. Take tram #28 to the end of the line, in the opposite direction as you would the castle, €1.30. Open daily Oct.-Apr. 9am-5pm; May-Sept. 9am-6pm.)*

ELEVADOR DE SANTA JUSTA. This historic elevator built in 1902 inside a Gothic wrought iron tower, once served as transportation up to Bairro Alto, but now takes tourists up 45m to the top. There is a small cafe where visitors can have a drink while enjoying a view of the city. Avoid the elevator on weekends—there's a huge line. *(Runs daily 10am-1pm and 2-6pm. €1.40, €2.60 round-trip.)*

BASÍLICA DA ESTRELA. Directly across from the Jardim da Estrela, the Basílica da Estrela dates back to 1796 and casts an imposing presence over the *Praça.* Its dome, poised behind a pair of tall belfries, towers over surrounding buildings to take its place in the Lisboa skyline. Half-mad Dona Maria I promised God anything and everything if she were granted a son. When a baby boy was finally born, she built this church, and today, architecture aficionados are grateful. Ask to see the 10th-century nativity. *(Pr. da Estrela. Accessible by metro or tram #28 from Pr. do Comércio. ☎213 96 09 15. Open daily 7:45am-8pm. Free.)*

IGREJA DE SÃO ROQUE. When the Catholic church decided to bring Sr. Roque's bones and other relics to Lisboa from Spain in the 1500's, they had not intended to build a church in his name. But when the pesky rodents and their epidemic-inducing germs then afflicting Lisbon miraculously disappeared upon his arrival, Sr. Roque became a *São* (saint); a Jesuit church with all the bells and whistles of the era was quickly built in his honor. Inside, the **Capela de São João Baptista** (fourth from the left) blazes with agate, lapis lazuli, and precious metals. Considered a masterpiece of European art, the chapel caused a stir upon its installation in 1747 because it took three ships to transport it from Rome, where it was built. The ceiling is covered entirely by a magnificent painting portraying scenes from the life of Jesus. *(Lg. Trindade Coelho. ☎213 23 53 83. Open daily 8:30am-5pm, holidays 8:30am-1pm.)*

PARKS. Across from the Basílica on Lg. da Estrela, the wide paths of the **■ Jardim da Estrela** wind through flocks of pigeons, happily quacking ducks, and lush flora. *(M: Rato. With your back to the metro stop, follow R. Pedro Álvares Cabral, the 2nd road from the left in the traffic circle, for 10min. Open daily 6am-midnight.)* More greenery awaits uphill along R. Dom Pedro V at the **Parque Príncipe Real,** which connects to the **Jardim Botánico.** For a good view, head to the **Parque de São Pedro de Alcântara.** The Castelo de São Jorge in Alfama occupies the cliff opposite the park, and Bairro Alto twinkles below.

SÃO SEBASTIÃO

■**MUSEU CALOUSTE GULBENKIAN.** Perhaps Portugal's biggest fan ever, native Armenian Calouste Gulbenkian liked the country so much when he visited in 1942 that he stayed in the same hotel in Lisboa for 13 years, until his death in 1955. In his will, the billionaire left his extensive art collection (some of it purchased from the Hermitage in St. Petersburg, Russia) to Portugal. The collection is divided into sections of ancient art—Egyptian, Greek, Roman, Mesopotamian, Islamic, and Oriental—and European pieces from the 15th to 20th centuries. Highlights include the Egyptian room, Rembrandts, Monets, Renoirs, Rodins, Manets, and a collection of ancient coins. *(Av. Berna, 45. M: São Sebastião. From the main entrance of El Corte Inglés, follow the main road, Av. Augusto Antonio de Aguiar, downhill until you see the sign for the "Fundação Calouste Gulbenkian." Take a right up the staircase, climb another set of stairs, and the Museu is across the parking lot. Bus #16, 26, 31, 46, 56. ☎217 82 30 00; www.gulbenkian.pt. Open Tu-Su 10am-5:45pm. €3, pass for both the Gulbenkian and the CAMJAP €5. Free for students, teachers, and seniors everyday; free on Su.)*

CENTRO DE ARTE MODERNO. Though not as famous as its neighbor, this museum contains an extensive modern collection promoting Portuguese talent from the late 19th century to the present. The center also places an emphasis on works from Portugal's former colonies across the globe. Don't miss the sculpture gardens that separate the two museums. *(R. Dr. Nicolau Bettencourt. M: São Sebastião. From the main entrance of El Corte Inglés, follow the steep Rua Marquês de Fronteira downhill, take a left before the palace, the Ministério do Exército; the Centro will be on your right about 200m farther. Bus #16, 26, 31, 46, 56. ☎217 82 34 74. Open Tu-Su 10am-5:45pm. €3. Free for students, teachers, and seniors. Su free for general public.)*

ALFAMA

■**CASTELO DE SÃO JORGE.** Built in the 5th century by the Visigoths and enlarged 400 years later by the Moors, this castle was converted into a playground for the royal family between the 14th and 16th centuries. The towers and castle walls allow for spectacular views of Lisboa and the ocean. *(☎218 80 06 20; www.egeac.pt. Open daily Mar.-Oct. 9am-9pm; Nov.-Feb. 9am-6pm. €5, students €2.50, with Lisboa card €3.50, under 10 or over 65 free.)*

LOWER ALFAMA. The small white **Igreja de Santo António** was built in 1812 over the saint's alleged birthplace. The construction was funded with money collected by the city's children, who fashioned altars bearing saintly images to place on doorsteps. The custom is reenacted annually on June 13, the saint's feast day and Lisboa's biggest holiday, which draws out thousands and involves a debaucherous festival the night before. The church is located on R. da Alfândeo, which begins two blocks away from Pr. do Comércio and connects Baixa and lower Alfama. *(Veer right when you see Igreja da Madalena in Lg. da Madalena on the right. Take R. de Santo António da Sé and follow the tram tracks. ☎218 86 91 45. Open daily 8am-7pm. Mass daily 11am, 5, and 7pm.)* In the square beyond the church is the 12th-century ■**Sé de Lisboa.** The cathedral's interior lacks the ornamentation of the city's other churches, but its age and treasury make it an intriguing visit. *(☎218 86 67 52. Open daily 9am-7pm except during mass, held Tu-Sa 6:30pm, Su 11:30am and 7pm. Free. Treasury open M-Sa 10am-5pm. €2.50, students €1.50. Cloister open daily May-Sept. 2-7pm; Oct.-Apr. M-Sa 10am-6pm, Su 2-6pm. €2.50, students €1.25.)*

GRAÇA

■**PANTEÃO NACIONAL.** The National Pantheon was originally meant to be the Igreja da Santa Engrácia; the citizens of Graça started building the church in 1680 to honor their patron saint. Their ambitions outstripped their finances, however, and they abandoned the project before completing the dome, leaving a massive hole in the top. General Salazar's military regime eventually took over construction, dedicating it as the National Pantheon, a burial ground for important statesmen, in 1966. In a twist of irony, when democracy was restored in 1975, the new government relocated the remains of prominent anti-Fascist opponents to the building and prohibited those who had worked with Salazar from entering. The dome juts out from amongst the other old buildings of Graça, providing an amazing view of Lisboa from the outdoor terrace. Highlights include the tombs of presidents as well as cenotaphs (honorary tombs for people buried elsewhere) for explorers. The Pantheon also houses the remains of Amália Rodrigues, the queen of *fado*. *(To reach the Panteão, take the #28 tram from R. Do Loreto or R. Garrett. ☎ 218 81 53 20 or 218 81 53 29; fax 218 86 73 17. Open Tu-Su 10am-5pm. €2, seniors €1.)*

IGREJA DE SÃO VICENTE DE FORA. Built between 1582 and 1629, the Igreja is dedicated to St. Vincent, Lisboa's patron saint, though Lisboa tends to celebrate its adopted patron saint, St. Antony, much more. Ask to see the *sacristia* (chapel) with its inlaid walls of Sintra marble. *(From the bottom of R. dos Correeiros in Baixa, take bus #12 or tram #28. ☎ 218 82 44 00. Open daily 10am-6pm except for mass. Mass Tu and F 9:30am, Sa 9:30am, Su 10am. Free. Chapel open Tu-Su 10am-5pm. €2.)*

FEIRA DA LADRA. Every Tuesday and Saturday between the Panteão and Igreja de São Vicente, local venders hit the streets in the early morning for the Graça "thieves market." Merchants bring piles of goods, from Beatles paraphernalia to African sculptures, and passersby are encouraged to make an offer. Get steals on old wristwatches and cameras, dig through piles of jewelry, or admire handmade chandeliers and crucifixes. *(Tu and Sa 8am-late afternoon.)*

MUSEU NACIONAL DO AZULEJO. Housed within the 16th-century Convento da Madre de Deus, this museum is devoted to the art of the *azulejo* (ceramic tiles), which was first introduced by the Moors (see **Architecture**, p. 624). A Manucline doorway leads into the Baroque interior embellished with oil paintings and a huge variety of *azulejos*. *(R. Madre de Deus, 4. East of Alfama in Xabregas. From Pr. do Comércio, just next to the giant arch, take bus #104 or 105. The museum is next to the Igreja Madre de Deus. ☎ 218 10 03 40; www.mnazulejo-ipmuseus.pt. Open Tu 2-6pm, W-Su 10am-6pm. Last entrance 5:30pm. €3; under 25, seniors, and teachers €1.50. Free Su before 2pm.)*

🎭 ENTERTAINMENT

Agenda Cultural and *Follow Me Lisboa*, free at the tourist office and at kiosks in the Rossio on R. Portas de Santo Antão, have information on concerts, *fado*, movies, plays, and bullfights. They also have lists of museums, gardens, and libraries.

FADO

A mandatory experience for anyone visiting the city, Lisboa's trademark entertainment is the traditional tear-jerking *fado*, an expressive art combining elements of singing and narrative poetry (see **Music**, p. 625). *Cantadeiras de fado*, cloaked in black dresses and shawls, relate emotional tales of lost loves and faded glory. Numerous *fado* houses lie in the small streets of **Bairro Alto** and near R. de São João da Praça in **Alfama**. Some have both *fado* and folkdance performances. To avoid shelling out, explore nearby streets; various bars and small venues often offer free shows with less notable performers. Book in advance, especially on weekends, and arrive at fado houses 30-45min. early. Minimum consumption requirements tend to run €10-20, but ask ahead of time as they may

LISBOA

only apply to the second show, which starts around 11pm. The following places may be touristy, but they feature Portugal's top names in *fado*.

■ **Café Luso,** Travessa da Queimada, 10 (☎213 42 22 81; www.cafeluso.pt). Pass below the club's glowing neon-blue sign to reach *fado* nirvana. Open since 1927, Lisboa's premier *fado* club combines the best in Portuguese music, cuisine, and atmosphere. *Menú* €25. Entrees €22-29. Min. €20. Late night show, drink min. €15. *Fado* 9-10:30pm. Reservations are a good idea F and Sa nights. Open M-Sa 8pm-2am. AmEx/MC/V. ❹

■ **O Faia,** R. Barroca, 56 (☎213 42 67 42). Performances by famous *fadistas* like Anita Guerreiro and Lenita Gentil, as well as some of the finest Portuguese cuisine available, make O Faia worth your time and money. 4 singers. Entrees €23-30. Min. €17.50, includes 2 drinks. *Fado* starts at 9:30pm. 2nd show starts at 11:30pm. Open M-Sa 8pm-2am. AmEx/MC/V. ❹

Adega Machado, R. do Norte, 91 (☎213 22 46 40; fax 46 75 07). Founded in 1937, Machado is one of the larger *fado* restaurants and features some of the best known *cantadeiras* and guitarists. The many portraits and wall decorations make this cavernous bar warm and inviting. Slightly older crowd. A typical meal, including drinks, is €35. Min. drink charge €16. *Fado* starts at 9:15pm. Open Tu-Su 8pm-3am. AmEx/MC/V. ❹

THEATER, MUSIC, AND FILM

Teatro Nacional de Dona Maria II, Pr. Dom Pedro IV, stages performances of classical and foreign plays. (☎213 47 22 26. Tickets €3.50-10.) At Lisboa's largest theater, **Teatro Nacional de São Carlos,** R. Serpa Pinto, 9, near the Museu do Chiado in Bairro Alto, **opera** reigns from late December to mid-June, and the **Orquestra Sinfonica Portuguesa** plays from December to July. (☎213 25 30 45. Tickets €7-60. Open M-F 1-7pm and performance days 1pm until 30min. prior to shows.)

The **São Jorge movie theater,** Av. da Liberdade, 175 (☎213 10 34 00) is one of the oldest in Portugal. Daily shows are held between 2:30pm and 9:30pm. Ten-screen cinemas are also located in the **Amoreiras** (☎213 81 02 00; M: Marquês de Pombal), the **Colombo** shopping center (☎217 11 36 00; M: Colegio Militar Luz), and on the top floor of the **Centro Vasco da Gama** (☎218 93 06 01; M: Oriente). The largest theater, with 14 screens, is part of the new **El Corte Inglés** shopping complex (☎213 71 17 00; M: São Sebastião). American films are shown with Portuguese subtitles. Movies cost about €7; special matinee shows are slightly less.

BULLFIGHTING

Portuguese bullfighting differs from the Spanish variety in that the bull is typically not killed in the ring, a tradition that dates back to the 18th century. These spectacles take place most Thursdays from late June to late September at ■**Praça de Touros de Lisboa,** Campo Pequeno. (☎217 93 21 43. Open daily 10pm-2am.) The newly renovated *praça* doubles as a shopping center during the day, and at night also features the distinctly Portuguese *toureio equestre,* or horseback bullfighting. Aficionados should include **Santarém** (p. 664) in their travel plans—it's the capital of Portuguese bullfighting and hosts the most celebrated *matadores.*

FUTEBOL

Futebol is the lifeblood of many a Portuguese citizen. *Futebol* fever became an epidemic during the 2006 World Cup, and after a month of nail-biting, shop-closing, crowd-gathering soccer mania, the Portuguese team returned from Germany national heroes after reaching the semifinal round for the first time in 40 years. These days, the Portuguese get riled up for the popular Euro Cup and regional games. Portugal's two most renowned teams are in Lisboa: **Benfica** and **Sporting,** both of which feature some of the world's finest players. (Benfica at Estádio da

Luz. ☎707 200 100; www.slbenfica.pt. M: Colégio Militar-Luz. Ticket office open daily 10am-7pm. Sporting at Alvalade Stadium. ☎707 20 44 44; www.sporting.pt. M: Campo Grande. Ticket office open M-F 10am-7pm.) Benfica made headlines in April with its magical rise to the semifinal round of the 2006 UEFA Champions League, the most prestigious club tournament in Europe, for the first time in over a decade. Benfica and Sporting are bitter rivals—be careful whom you support, since both have diehard fans who won't care that you're "just a tourist." Check the ABEP kiosk in Pr. dos Restauradores or the newspaper *A Bola* for games.

NIGHTLIFE

Bairro Alto is the first place to go for nightlife, especially before 2am. **R. do Norte, R. do Diário de Notícias,** and **R. Atalaia** which run parallel to each other pack many small bars and clubs into three short blocks, making bar-hopping as easy as crossing the street. Several gay and lesbian establishments lie in this area, as well as in **Rato** near the edge of Bairro Alto, past Pr. Príncipe Real. The options near the water are larger, flashier, and more diverse. The **Docas de Santo Amaro** host a strip of waterfront bars, clubs, and restaurants, while the Av. 24 de Julho and the parallel R. das Janelas Verdes (Street of Green Windows), in the **Santos** area, have some of the most popular clubs and discotecas. Newer expansions include the area along the river across from the **Santa Apolónia** train station, home to glitzy club **Lux.** The Bairro Alto bar scene is very casual, but at clubs, jeans, sandals, and sneakers are generally not allowed—some places have uptight fashion police at the door. Inside, beer runs €3-5. Some clubs also charge a cover (generally €5-20), which usually gets you two to four free drinks. There's no reason to show up before midnight; crowds flow in around 2am and stay past dawn.

BAIRRO ALTO

From tiny bars to punk clubs to posh *fado* restaurants, the Bairro Alto and nearby districts can't be beat for nightlife entertainment.

BAIRRO ALTO AND NORTH TO THE JARDIM BOTÁNICO

A Tasca Tequila Bar, Tr. da Queimada, 13-15 (☎919 40 79 14). A great place to go on a slow weekday night, this Mexican bar is always full. The bartenders don't forget to have a good time themselves while serving up some

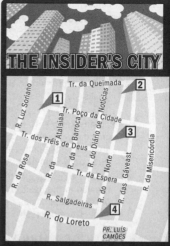

THE INSIDER'S CITY

ALTO FASHION

Bairro Alto features some excellent (if eccentric) shopping.

1 **Maomao Shop,** R. da Rosa, 85 (☎213 46 06 56). It's highly unlikely the Chairman would have approved. To describe its clothes as colorful is an understatement. (Open M-Sa 2pm-midnight. Cash only.)

2 **Agência 117,** R. do Norte, 117 (☎ 213 46 12 70). Cutoff tees and chic retro shirts and dresses beckon from this style hub in the heart of Bairro Alto's fashion world. (Open M-Sa 2pm-midnight. MC/V.)

3 **Bad Bones,** R. do Norte, 85 (☎213 46 08 88). Walk in to up your cool factor with a body piercing; if you want a tattoo, call ahead. (Open M-Sa 11am-11pm, Su 2-7pm. Cash only.)

4 **Diesel Lisboa,** Pr. Luís Camões, 30 (☎213 42 19 80). The Lisboa shop has cool house music and two floors of the chic Italian label. (Open M-Sa 11am-9pm. AmEx/MC/V.)

potent mixed drinks at the T-shaped counter. Mixed drinks €5. Open M-Sa 6pm-2am.

▨ Pavilhão Chinês, Dom Pedro V, 89 (☎213 42 47 29). Ring the doorbell and a red-vested waiter ushers you into this classy establishment, where the walls and ceilings drip with collection pieces. Good place to chill or play pool, but if you're looking for loud music and dancing, it's not the place for you. Open daily 6pm-2am.

Palpita-me, R. Diário de Notícias, 40-B (www.palpita-me.com). Sing out of tune to your favorite hits from the 80s and 90s at this karaoke bar smack in the center of it all. Drinks are on the cheaper side (beer €1.50, whiskey €4) and there is frequently live music. Open M-Sa 10pm-4am. Cash only.

Páginas Tantas, R. Diário de Notícias, 85 (☎213 46 54 95). This classical jazz bar provides a quiet and cool retreat from the wild street parties of Bairro Alto. A diverse group of young professionals sips on the bar's specials during Happy hour (9-11pm). Open daily 9pm-4am. AmEx/D/MC/V.

Portas Largas, R. da Atalaia, 105 (☎213 46 63 79), at the end of Tr. da Queimada. Located in the heart of Bairro Alto, Portas Largas is one of the district's most popular bars. A combination of gay and straight crowds keeps this place full every night of the week. Open daily July-Sept. 7pm-3:30am; Oct.-June 8pm-3:30am.

SOUTH OF BAIRRO ALTO: AVENIDA 24 DE JULHO AND SANTOS

It is best to take a cab (€6 from Rossio) to these clubs due to their distance and the danger in walking alone at night—the E-15 line stops at 1am.

Jamaica, R. Nova do Carvalho, 6 (☎213 42 18 59). M: Cais do Sodre. This small club is famous for playing 80s music. Packed until the early morning. Women get in free, but it's usually €6 for guys (plus 3 free beers). Be careful when you leave the club; it's not the safest neighborhood late at night. Open Tu-Sa 10:30pm-6am.

Kapital, Av. 24 de Julho, 68 (☎213 95 71 01). The classiest club in Lisboa has a ruthless door policy that makes admission a competitive sport. Don't expect to get in, especially if you're an unaccompanied male or if it's clear you're a tourist. For the best chance, go with regulars and dress nicely. Cover €10-20. Open M-Sa 11pm-6am.

Kremlin, Escandinhas da Praia, 5 (☎213 95 71 01; www.kremlin-k.com), off Av. 24 de Julho. Run by the same management as Kapital, but a more mixed crowd including Kapital rejects and migrants. Come nicely dressed. Rave music and ambience. Cover usually €7 for women, €12 for men. Open W-Th midnight-7am, F-Sa midnight-9am.

WEST OF BAIRRO ALTO: DOCAS DE SANTO AMARO

To get to the clubs and bars on the Docas, take the E-15 electric car from the Praça do Comércio to the Alcantara-Mar stop and then walk or take a cab from there. It's cheap (€6) to take a cab straight from Rossio. Should you choose to walk, be forewarned that the docks can be dangerous at night and the bars are a long, uncertain walk away. The only way back is a cab, as the E-15 stops at 1am.

▨ Dock's Club, R. da Cintura do Porto de Lisboa, 226 (☎213 95 08 56). A €4-6 cab ride from the taxi station in Bairro Alto. This huge club plays great hip-hop, latino, and house music, and starts to fill up around 2am. Two bars inside and one outside if you need to cool off (or dry off). On famous Tu nights girls get in free and receive 4 free drinks (men pay €12 and get 2 free drinks). Open Tu-Sa 11pm-6am.

▨ Speakeasy, Docas de Santo Amaro (☎213 90 91 66; www.speakeasy-bar.com), between the Santos and Alcântara stops, near the river. More of a concert with waiters and beer than a bar. A premier jazz and blues center with nightly live shows. Older crowd. Beer €3. M night jazz. Open M-Sa 9pm-4am, restaurant 8-11pm. Cash only.

ALFAMA

■ **Restô,** R. Costa do Castelo, 7 (☎218 86 73 34). Don't be surprised to see a flying trapeze or tight-rope act—Restô is on the grounds of a government-funded clown school, Chapitô. Upstairs serves Argentine steaks (€13) and Spanish tapas (€4-8). Huge patio. Open daily 7:30pm-1:30am. Lunch noon-3pm, dinner 7pm-midnight. Cash only.

Clube de Fado, R. S. João da Praça, 92/94 (☎218 88 26 94; www.clube-de-fado.com). A relaxed alternative to the *fado* scene in Bairro Alto, Clube de Fado's rustic wood and stone parlor takes you back to the days of a less hectic Lisboa. Entrees €16-22. Min. €7.50. Open daily 8pm-2am; *fado* starts at 9:30pm. AmEx/MC/V.

Ondajazz Bar, Arco de Jesus, 7 (☎ 919 18 48 67). Visit the Ondajazz Bar to see a wide selection of on-stage performances including jazz, blues, and poetry readings. W open mic. €6 drink min. Open Tu-Th 9pm-2am, F-Sa 9pm-3am.

Marquês da Sé, Lg. do Marquês do Lavrádio, 1 (☎218 88 02 34). *Fado* under vaulted ceilings and lit by candles perched along the walls. A little on the pricey side (€20 drink min., entrees €17-24) but well worth it. Reservations recommended. Open daily 8pm-2am; *fado* starts at 9:30pm. AmEx/MC/V.

Bar das Imagens, Calçada de Marquês de Tancos, 11-13 (☎218 88 46 36). Tasty finger foods and Brazilian "mocktails" (€3.50) get the crowd pumped for the specially made house *caipirinhas* (€5). Open M-Sa noon-1am, Su 3-11pm. Cash only.

GRAÇA

■ **Lux/Frágil,** Av. Infante D. Henrique A, Cais da Pedra a Sta. Apolonia (☎218 82 08 90). Take a taxi (€6 from Chiado) to the area across from the Sta. Apolónia train station to get to this enormous 3-fl. complex. One-of-a-kind view from the roof of what fans call "the perfect nightclub." A high-tech lighting system and awesome music playing all night long. Bouncers are selective, so dress extra nice and say "please." Arrive after 2am. Min. consumption usually €15. Open Tu-Sa 10pm-6am. AmEx/MC/V.

❀ FESTIVALS

Those who love to mingle with locals will want to visit Lisboa in June. Open-air *feiras*—festivals of eating, drinking, live music, and dancing—fill the streets. After savoring *farturas* (huge Portuguese pastries whose name means "abundance") and Sagres beer, join in traditional Portuguese dancing. On the night of June 12, the streets explode into song and dance in honor of St. Anthony during the **Festa de Santo António.** Banners are strung between streetlights and confetti falls in buckets during a parade along Av. da Liberdade. Young crowds pack the streets of Alfama and the neighborhood of Santa Catarina, and grilled *sardinhas* (sardines) and *ginja* (wild cherry liqueur) are sold everywhere. Lisboa also has a number of commercial *feiras*. From late May to early June, bookworms burrow for three weeks in the outdoor **Feira do Livro** in Parque Eduardo VII, behind Pr. Marquês de Pombal. The **Feira Internacional de Lisboa** occurs every few months in the Parque das Nações; in July and August, the **Feira de Mar de Cascais** and **Feira de Artesanato de Estoril** (celebrating famous Portuguese pottery) take place near the casino. Year-round *feiras* include the **Feira de Oeiras** (sells antiques on the fourth Sunday of each month) and the **Feira de Carcanelos** (sells clothes Th 8am-2pm) in Rato. Packrats should catch the **Feira da Ladra,** a large flea market, whose name literally means "thieves' fair" (don't be surprised if your stolen watch turns up there). Held behind Igreja de São Vicente de Fora in Graça (Tu 7am-1pm and Sa 7am-3pm; take tram #28, €1.30).

LISBOA

OUTER DISTRICTS

▨ PARQUE DAS NAÇÕES

*From Lisboa, take the metro to M: Oriente at the end of the red line. The station has esca-
lators to the park's main entrance, through the Centro Vasco da Gama shopping center.
(☎ 218 93 06 01; www.centrovascodagama.pt. Open daily 10am-midnight.) Alternatively,
city buses #5, 10, 19, 21, 25, 28, 44, 50, 68, 114, 208, and 210 all stop at the Oriente
station (€1.30). Parque das Nações (☎ 218 91 93 93; www.parquedasnacoes.pt).*

Until the mid-1990s, this area was a muddy wasteland consisting of a few rundown factories and warehouses along the banks of the Tejo. Today, after millions
spent preparing for the 1998 World Exposition, the Parque das Nações (Park of
Nations) is a masterpiece in civil engineering. Much more than a park, the region
is quickly becoming a small city, with residential areas to the north and south. Visitors can find map kiosks outside the Centro Vasco da Gama shopping mall. On the
way in, look around the **Estação Oriente**, an attraction in itself. Santiago Calatrava,
Spain's most famous contemporary architect, designed its arches.

▨ OCEANÁRIO. The park's biggest attraction, this enormous oceanarium has
interactive sections showcasing the four major oceans, recreating their allure right
down to the sounds, smells, and climates. All of these connect to the main tank,
which has over 470 different species of fish, sharks, and other sea creatures. Visitors can get within arm's length of playful sea otters and penguins. (☎ *218 91 70
02/06; www.oceanario.pt. Open daily Apr.-Oct. 10am-7pm; Nov.-Mar. 10am-6pm. €10.50, under
12 €5.25, over 65 €5.75. Families with children get in together for €25.)*

CABLE CARS. Gondolas connect the ends of the park and offer visitors a bird's
eye view of the park and Rio Tejo. (☎ *218 95 61 43. 8min.; June-Sept. M-F 11am-8pm,
Sa-Su 10am-9pm; Oct.-May, M-F 11am-7pm, Sa-Su 10am-8pm. €3.50 one-way, €5.50
round-trip; under 14, over 65 €1.80/€3 round-trip.)*

PAVILHÃO DO CONHECIMENTO. The "Pavilion of Knowledge" is an interactive
science and technology museum with permanent and temporary exhibits that
explore both scientific and cultural phenomena. Free Internet access at the
Cib@rcafé. Check out the Exploratoria, modeled after the exploratorium in San
Francisco. (☎ *218 91 71 00; www.pavconhecimento.pt. Open Tu-F 10am-6pm, Sa-Su
11am-7pm. €6; under 17, over 65 €3.)*

OTHER SIGHTS. Several pavilions are scattered throughout the park, including
the International Fairgrounds, with rotating exhibits throughout the year, the
Atlantic Pavilion, which hosts many big concerts, and the Virtual Reality Pavilion,
with rides that challenge the senses. The 145m **Torre Vasco da Gama** is the tallest
building in Lisbon, and its 21st-century architecture draws visitors from far and
wide. The entire city can be seen from the top of this observation tower.

BELÉM

*Visitors can reach Belém by tram, bus, or train. By tram, take #15 (toward Algés) and get off
at the Mosteiro dos Jerónimos stop, 1 stop beyond the regular Belém stop. Take bus #714
from Pr. Figueira or Pr. do Comércio (40min., €1.30). Alternatively, take the train from
Estação Cais do Sodré. To start at the Padrão dos Descobrimentos, exit the station by taking
the overpass toward the water. To begin at the Mosteiro dos Jerónimos, exit the overpass to
the right, then go through the public gardens to R. de Belém.*

The Age of Discovery began in Portugal, and there is no greater tribute to its pio-
neering spirit than the sea front of Belém. Explorers like Vasco da Gama and
Prince Henry the Navigator launched their famous 15th-century voyages from its

sands. Today, visitors come from around the world to pay their respects to the architectural magnificence and seafaring glory that awaits in Belém. It's not just a rich history that makes Belém worth your while. The town is also famous for its delicious custard-filled pastries, *pasteis de Belém*. These desserts, with a recipe perfected at the nearby monastery, have been served in their original form at ◙**Pasteis de Belém ❶**, R. de Belém, 84-92, since the restaurant's 1837 opening. (☎213 637 423; www.pasteisdebelem.pt. Open daily 9am-11pm.) If wandering the shores has left you with an empty stomach, stop in at **Pão Pão Queijo Queijo ❶**, R. de Belém, 124. This small, quaint locale is perfect for a quick bite, serving delicious pitas (€3-4), sandwiches (€3-4), and entrees (€6.55) (☎213 62 33 69). Try avoiding its peak lunchtime hours (1-3pm). Additional seating upstairs. (Open M-Sa 8am-midnight, Su 8am-8pm.)

◙**MOSTEIRO DOS JERÓNIMOS.** Established in 1502 in commemoration of Vasco da Gama's ground-breaking expedition to India, the Mosteiro dos Jerónimos is a gorgeous structure designed with minute Renaissance detail and ornate Gothic construction. It was recognized for its beauty in the 1980s, when it was granted UNESCO World Heritage status. Note the anachronism on the main church door: Prince Henry the Navigator mingles with the Twelve Apostles on both sides of the central column. The symbolic tombs of Luís de Camões and navigator Vasco da Gama lie in opposing transepts. (☎213 62 00 34. Open May-Sept. Tu-Su 10am-6:30pm; Oct.-Apr. Tu-Su 10am-5:30pm. Last admission 30min. before closing. Church free, cloister €4.50.) Directly across from the church lies the Museu Nacional de Arqueologia. This five room museum explores Portugal's ancient past through prehistoric ruins and evidence of Roman influence. Check out the treasure room—it is full of priceless works of gold and silver from thousands of years ago. Also notable is the Egyptian archaeology room that features several sarcophagi. (☎213 62 00 00, fax 213 62 00 16. Open Tu 2-6pm, W-Su 10am-noon and 2-6pm. €3, students, teachers, and seniors €1.50. Lisboa card holders get in free. Cash only.)

◙**PADRÃO DOS DESCOBRIMENTOS.** Along the river and directly across from the Mosteiro is the Padrão dos Descobrimentos, built in 1960 to celebrate the 500th anniversary of Prince Henry the Navigator's death. The enormous monument is shaped like a cross and features Henry in front of a line of celebrated compatriots (among them Vasco da Gama and Diogo Cao) as they look out across the Rio Tejo. The view is better than that from the Torre, and there's an elevator that transports visitors 50m up to the narrow roof top. The Padrão also hosts temporary art exhibits. (Across the highway from the Mosteiro. ☎213 03 19 50. Open May-Sept. Tu-Su 10am-7pm; Oct.-Apr. 10am-6pm. Last admission 30min. before closing. €2.50; students and seniors €1.50.)

TORRE DE BELÉM. The best-known tower in all of Portugal, the Torre de Belém is a stone fortress sitting on the banks of the Rio Tejo. Built under Manuel I from 1515 to 1520 as a military stronghold, the Torre has since served several functions, including a stint as Portugal's most famous political prison. The tower is a powerful symbol of Portuguese grandeur and offers photo ops in every direction. Images of this UNESCO World Heritage site can be found in just about every postcard stand in Lisboa. (A 10min. walk from the monastery, with the water on your left. Take the overpass by the gardens to cross the highway. Open May-Sept. Tu-Su 10am-6:30pm; Oct.-Apr. Tu-Su 10am-5:30pm. Last admission 30min. before closing. €3; under 25 and seniors €1.50.)

CENTRO CULTURAL DE BELÉM. Contemporary art buffs will bask in the glow of this luminous complex, which could best be described as a modern Mayan fortress. With three pavilions holding rotating world-class exhibitions and a huge auditorium for concerts and performances, the center provides the only modern entertainment in a sea of imperial landmarks. You'll also find the **Museu Design** inside, which features a timeline collection of furniture from the 1940s to the

LISBOA

1990s. The CCB holds a wide variety of performances, ranging from puppet shows to plays, orchestral music, and even Indonesian music and dance. (☎213 61 24 00; www.ccb.pt. Ticket office is open daily 1-7:30pm. Museu Design ☎213 61 28 00. Open Tu-Su 10am-7pm, last entrance 6:15pm.)

SETE RIOS. Home to one of Lisboa's major transportation centers, Sete Rios also happens to house over 250 species of plants and animals in the neighboring Jardim Zoológico. A combination of a zoo, a botanical garden, and a carnival, the complex offers much for visitors to do. Fountains and open air stores decorate the majority of the complex just outside of the zoo entrance. A string of restaurants lie within the grounds serving traditional Portuguese cuisine and that of former colonies as well. To the right of the main gate is a mini-carnival for kids and kids at heart. Ask at the information booth for ride schedules and prices, as they change frequently.

JARDIM ZOOLÓGICO. A trek into the actual zoo brings opportunities to play with dolphins, pet fuzzy bunnies, admire flat-headed turtles, and view a diverse assemblage of creatures. In addition to the dolphin shows there are various other scheduled events to check out, such as the feeding of the flamingos and an aviary show featuring numerous free-flying birds. The recently remodeled monkey facility has a beautiful waterfall near which chimps, gorillas, and apes swing around playfully. Near the dolphin tanks you can board a cable car that will dangle you above the homes of some of the larger animals. Before you exit take a stroll through the mini-botanical garden. (☎217 23 29 10; www.zoo.pt. Open daily April-Sept. 10am-8pm; Oct.-Mar. 10am-6pm. €14.50, seniors €12, children €11. Children 11 and under with a paying parent, free. Lisboa card holders receive a discount of €1.50-2. MC/V.).

⚡ DAYTRIPS FROM LISBOA

CASCAIS

Trains from Lisboa's Estação Cais do Sodré (☎213 42 48 93; M: Cais do Sodré) head to Cascais (30min., every 20min. 5:30am-1:30am, €1.60). Take the "SAAP," which has fewer stops. Scott URB has a bus terminal in downtown Cascais, underground next to the blue glass tower of the shopping center by the train station. Buses #417 (40min., every 50min. 6:30am-7:50pm) and the more scenic #403 (60-80min., every 75min.) go from Cascais to Sintra for €3.20. To visit Praia de Guincho, a popular windsurfing beach, considered by many to be best on the coast, take the circular route bus #405/415 to the Guincho stop (22min., every 1-2hr. 7:15am-7:40pm, €2.40).

Cascais is a beautiful beach town, serene during the low-season, but brimming with vacationers in the summer. **Praia da Ribeira, Praia da Rainha,** and **Praia da Conceição** are especially popular with sunbathers. To reach Praia da Ribeira, take a right upon leaving the tourist office and walk down Av. dos Combatentes de Grande Guerra until you see the water. Facing the water, Praia da Rainha and Praia da Conceição are to your left. Those in search of less crowded beaches should take advantage of the ⚡**free bike rentals** offered at two kiosks in Cascais (one is in front of the train station, by the McDonald's, the other is in the parking lot of the Cidadela fortress, up Av. dos Carlos I). All you need is a passport or driver's license and your hotel information, and you can use the bikes from 8am to 6:30pm. Ride along the coast (to your right if facing the water) and check out the ⚡**Boca de Inferno** (Mouth of Hell), so named because the cleft carved in the rock by the Atlantic surf creates a haunting sound as waves pummel the cliffs. (About 1km outside Cascais, a 20min. walk up Av. Rei Humberto de Itália.) For some shade, head to the expansive **Parque Municipal da Gandarinha** and hang with the wandering peacocks. The park is a family getaway, as it has a playground, a mini-zoo, and children's library. (Open daily 8:30am-7:45pm.) When the sun sets, nightlife picks up on **Largo Luís de Camões,** the main pedestrian square.

There are several restaurants on Av. dos Combatentes de Grande Guerra, between the tourist office and the ocean. The best is **Restaurante Dom Manolo ❷,** which serves mussels, salmon, and chicken. (☎214 83 11 26. Entrees €5-11. Open daily 10am-midnight. MC/V.) For a rawer taste of the sea, head to **Sushi eXpress ❷,** R. Dra. Iracy Doile, 9A. Located just around the corner from the shopping mall in the direction of the beach, the restaurant serves up Japanese-style noodles, sushi, sashimi, and a host of other Japanese favorites. The restaurant only has three tables, so most customers take their meals to go. (☎214 86 74 28; sushiexpress@gmail.com. Rolls €4-10. Sushi/Sashimi boxes €7-16. Cash only.) The nautically decorated **Golfinho Pizzeria and Cybercafe ❷,** to the left of the McDonald's, serves pizzas, sandwiches, and other lunch entrees between €6-12. (☎214 84 01 50. Internet €6 per hour. Open M-Sa 9:30am-midnight. MC/V.) Sleeping in Cascais is costly unless you stay at the hostel; try using Lisboa (a 30min. train ride away) as your base. Alternatively, nearby Oeiras has a pousada da juventude (HI youth hostel). If you do stay, the best place to crash is ⁜**Cascais Beach Hostel ❷,** R. da Vista Alegre, 10, located a hop and skip away from the beach, major transportation points, and the main shopping center. Co-ed rooms with four to seven beds are clean and decorated with splashes of lime green. A shared kitchen, free Internet, luxurious common room with flat-screen TV, swimming pool, and sunbathing deck round out the experience. (☎309 90 64 21; www.cascaisbeachhostel.com. Co-ed dorms Apr. 15-Nov. 15 €20. Nov. 16-Apr. 14 €18. Double rooms €49, with bath, €69. AmEx/MC/V.) Another, more expensive option is **Residencial Valbom ❹,** Av. Valbom, 14. (☎214 86 58 01; fax 214 86 58 05. July-Sept. singles €55-60; doubles €70-75. Apr.-June and Oct. €50-55/65-70. Nov.-Mar. €35/40. AmEx/MC/V.)

To get to the **tourist office,** Av. dos Combatentes de Grande Guerra, 25, exit the train station through the ticket office and look for the big McDonald's arches across Lg. da Estação. To the right of McDonald's is Av. Valbom; the office is a yellow building with "turismo" in big letters at the end of the street. The staff speaks English, Spanish, and French. (☎214 86 82 04. Open in summer M-Sa 9am-8pm, Su 10am-6pm; in winter M-Sa 9am-7pm, Su 10am-6pm.)

SESIMBRA

Buses run from Lisboa's Praça da Espanha bus shelter #2 (40-50min.; M-F every 30min. until 8:10pm, Sa-Su hourly until 7:40pm; €3.45, round-trip €6.20). Returning to Lisboa buses depart from the TST station on Av. da Liberdade just up the street from the library (€3.45, round-trip €6.20).

Just across the Rio Tejo from Lisboa, nestled in the center of the Costa Azul lies the gorgeous beach town Sesimbra. Appropriately referred to as a *mar de emoções* (sea of emotions), Sesimbra offers visitors a mixture of natural beauty, live entertainment, rich history, and some of the freshest seafood around. The popular **Praia da California** is constantly dotted with sun-worshipping tourists and locals. Keep your eyes open for famous soccer players; many *futbolistas* own beachside apartments in this charming town. Visitors come to Sesimbra to take advantage of the local golf scene, or to explore the rich marine life located just off shore. **Aquarama** offers glass-bottom boat tours of the reefs surrounding Sesimbra's beaches. Trips leave daily from Sesimbra's port. (☎965 26 31 57. Call ahead for reservations. €15 adults, children €9.) Av. dos Naúfragos is a pleasant place to relax on summer evenings when it's closed off to non-pedestrian traffic and bands play lively music on the streets.

Seafood in Sesimbra is as fresh as it gets. The local docks provide much of the fare that area restaurants serve. For a fresh bargain try **O Coral ❷,** Lg. Almirante Gago Coutinho, 8. Though non-seafood options are available, vegetarian fare is

LISBOA

extremely limited. (☎212 23 36 04. Daily specials €5-9. Open M and W-Su noon-3pm and 6-11pm. AmEx/MC/V.) Just around the corner is Sesimbra's neighborhood pizzeria, **Pizzaria Fratello ❷**, R. Prof. Dr. Fernandes Marques, 15. Large vegetarian salads are available for just under €5. Crunchy pizzas run €3-7 for individual size and €7-11 for family size. Be sure to try their tantalizing mango mousse (€2). (☎936 29 44 11. Open M-Tu and Th-Su 11am-3pm and 6-11pm. Oct.-May no lunch except on national holidays. Cash only.) Beds in Sesimbra, as in many other beach towns, can be extremely expensive; it's usually cheaper to stay in one of Lisbon's budget accommodations. If the sirens of white sand beaches and bright blue waters beckon you to stay, however, try **Casa Garcia ❺**, Tv. Xavier da Silva, 2. The large, clean rooms are located less than 300 ft. from the beach. Although the rooms are simply decorated, you cannot beat the price. Ask for a room on a higher floor to get a good view of the water. (☎212 23 32 27. High season doubles €60; triples €70. Low season €30/50. Cash only.)

The **tourist office** is located on Av. Marginal and has information about attractions in the Costa Azul region. (☎212 28 85 40. Open daily June-Sept. 9am-8pm; Oct.-May 9am-12:30pm and 2-5:30pm.) Local services include: the **police** (☎212 23 02 69) located near Lg. Gago Coutinho and the local **hospital** (☎212 23 36 92), 1 block away from Lg. 5 de Outubro in the direction away from the water. (☎212 28 81 41. Open M-F 9am-12:30pm and 2:30-6pm.) For free, fast **Internet** access try the local **library** housed in the old theatre building on Av. da Liberdade, across the street from the bus station. (Open Tu-F 9:30am-5:30pm, Sa 10am-6pm.) The local **post office** is just off of R. D. Sancho. **Postal Code**: 2970.

MAFRA

Mafrense buses, labeled with a green and white "M," run from Lisboa's Campo Grande and stop in the square across from the palace (the "Mafra Convento" stop). Buses from Mafra serve Lisboa (1-1½hr.; hourly M-F 5:26am-9:20pm, Sa 5:30am-8:44pm, Su and national holidays 6:19am-9:51pm; €1.80) and Ericeira (20min.; hourly. M-F 7:36am-12:32am, Sa 7:36am-12:20pm, Su and national holidays 8:05am-12:33am; €1.70). Don't take the train from Lisboa's Estação Santa Apolónia unless you're up for the 7km walk to Mafra; cabs are rare by the station. To return to Ericeira, walk down Terreiro de D. J. V and veer left. Continue down Av. 25 de Abril. The stop is on the right-hand side of the road about 50 ft. from the gas station.

Mafra is a tiny country village with an enormous claim to fame: the ▨**Palácio Nacional de Mafra**. Built by Dom João V as a "hunting palace," the building took 50,000 workers 30 years to build. The stunning Baroque monastery has its own hospital-chapel hybrid, where patients' bed curtains were pulled back for mass. There is also the chilling **Sala de Penitência** (Penance Room), where the Franciscan monks performed self-flagellation—notice the whip on the wall and the skull above the bed. The **Sala do Trono** (Throne Room), where the king gave his speeches, is covered with murals representing his eight ideal virtues. The **Sala da Caça** (Hunting Room) is decorated with antlers and heads of all kinds—the chairs, the tables, and even the chandelier are all made of elk antlers. The most impressive space is the palatial **biblioteca** (library) containing 40,000 16th-18th centuries volumes, many of which were bound by the monks. The monks were quite serious about the preservation of books and brought a colony of bats into the library to eat insects and other would-be book destroyers; a few bats still come out from the ancient bookshelves at night. (☎261 81 75 50. Open M and W-Su 10am-5pm, last entrance at 4:30pm. Daily 1hr. tours in English and Portuguese 11am and 2:30pm. €4, students and seniors €2, under 14 free; Su before 1:30pm free. Palácio tickets sold in the room to the left of the main palace steps. Basílica open daily 10am-1pm and 2-5pm. Free.) For a quality bargain meal, try the cozy, wood-adorned **A Toca da Raposa ❷**, R. 1 de Dezembro, 6. From the palace entrance, cross the street to the shops, go up

R. J. M. Costa one block and turn right. Serves up a variety of fresh Portuguese dishes, though vegetarian options limited. Try their traditional Mafrense bread. (☎261 81 51 22. Entrees €6.50-10. Open M-Su noon-2:30pm, W-Sa 7-9:30pm.)

The **tourist office** is inside the palace compound, to the right of the large church entrance. In addition to maps, the office offers 10min. of free **Internet** access. (☎261 81 71 70; www.cm-mafra.pt. Open daily 9:30am-1pm and 2:30-6pm.)

ERICEIRA

Mafrense buses run from Lisboa's Campo Grande; the bus for Ericeira leaves from the leftmost part of the waiting area (1½hr., hourly 6:30am-11:40pm, €4.70). Get off at the bus station. Buses run from Ericeira to Lisboa (1½hr.; M-F hourly 5:10am-9:03pm, Sa 5:10am-8:20pm, Su 6:00am-9:35pm; €4.40), via Mafra (25min., €1.60), and to Sintra (50min., €1.80).

Ericeira is a pleasant fishing village whose white sand beaches were the departure point of Dom Manuel II, the last king of Portugal, when he was exiled in 1910. A small cliff covered in white-washed houses now overlooks the famous shores that are invaded by surfers every summer. Beachgoers quickly find their way to nearby **Praia do Norte** (a.k.a. Praia do Algodio), a long beach to the right of the port, and **Praia do Sul** to the left. Although the waves close to town are great for novices, experienced surfers head past Praia do Norte to the more pristine **Praia de São Sebastião, Praia da Ribeira d'Ilhas** (site of a former World Surfing Championship), or **Praia dos Coxos** (Crippled Beach) beyond Ribeira d'Ilhas. There are several shops within town that give surfing lessons and rent out boards. If you've never surfed, contact licensed **NaOnda Surfschool,** whose teachers are lifelong surfers and speak English. It's a 2km walk from Ericeira; head left from the port. (☎916 00 90 04; www.ericeirasurf.com. Lessons 2hr. per day for 3 days €59, children €39. Prices include wetsuit and board rental. Private lessons €25 per hour. Max. 3 people. Board €15 per day, wetsuit €7 per day. Open daily 10am-6pm.) For an adrenaline rush on land, call **Tres Ondas,** which offers guided mountain bike rides. (☎261 81 98 38. €30 for bike, helmet, and 3hr. tour. Max. 4 people. Rides depart from the post office on R. Prudêncio Franco da Trindade. Rides Tu-F 4:30pm, Sa 10am.) You might have trouble finding a cheap room in summer; check with the tourist office for a list of rooms in private homes. ⊠**Hospedaria Pedra Dura ❷,** Rua Dr. Eduardo Burnay, 28, has eight newly renovated rooms with private baths, impeccable decor, and great location. Warm colors adorn the beds and rugs of each room. When facing the tourist office, go up the road on the right-hand side. (☎261 86 21 62; Doubles Sept. 1-June 15 €30-35; June 15-July 15 €40; July 15-Aug. 31. €50. Reservations recommended in the summer. MC/V.) The cheapest option is **Hospedaria Bernardo ❶,** R. Prudêncio Franco da Trindade, 11, which has a hotel-style *residencial* with amenities. Skylights brighten each room. Each has TV, table, and chairs. (☎261 86 23 78; hospedariabernardo@iol.pt. *Residencial* singles €25-30; doubles €35-40; triples €40-45. Prices drop €5-10 Sept.-May. Reservations recommended in Aug.) Seafood restaurants and several bars can be found along **R. Dr. Eduardo Burnay,** which runs from Pr. da República. Ericeira is home to the second-oldest discoteca in Portugal, **O Ouriço,** R. Capitão João Lopes, 9, at the entrance to Praia dos Pescadores. This beachfront club, whose name means "hedgehog," opened in 1960 and still packs in locals every night. (☎261 86 21 38. Open daily 11pm-6am.)

To get to the **tourist office,** R. Dr. Eduardo Burnay, 46, from the bus station, cross the road (EN 247-2), turn left, and walk uphill. At the top of the hill, follow the signs for the Centro and go right on R. Prudêncio Franco da Trindade. Go straight until Pr. da República; the tourist office is at the opposite end of the square. (☎261 86 31 22. Open M-F 10am-1pm and 2:30-6:30pm, Sa 10am-1pm and 3-10pm, Su 10am-1pm and 3-7pm.)

LISBOA

SINTRA ☎ 219

Deep in the misty Serra mountains lies the enchanting city of Sintra, home to ancient castles, fairy-tale palaces, and verdant gardens. For centuries, sultans, monarchs, and wealthy noblemen were drawn by the area's haunting beauty, and they left a trail of opulence and grandeur behind them. Today, Sintra is Portugal's pride and joy, and tourists from around the world scour the city, eager to absorb every detail and uncover every secret. If travelers part ways with Sintra after a day or two, it is because they know they'll be back.

▐ TRANSPORTATION

Trains: Estação de Caminhos de Ferro, Av. Dr. Miguel Bombarda (☎219 23 26 05). To Estação Sete Rios in **Lisboa** (35min., daily every 10min. 5:06am-12:56am, €1.60). From the train station, take the subway to downtown Lisboa.

Buses: ScottURB buses (☎214 69 91 00; www.scotturb.com), on Av. Dr. Miguel Bombarda, run to **Cascais** (#417 or 403; 40min., daily hourly 6:30am-8:35pm, €3.25) and **Estoril** (#418; 40min., daily every 45-50min. 6:12am-11:23pm, €3.25). **Mafrense** buses, 500m up the street away from Vila, on Av. Dr. D. Cambournac, go to **Ericeira** (50min., daily hourly 7:15am-8:25pm, €1.80).

▨ **Horse-drawn Carriages: Sintratur,** Largo Rainha D. Amélia (☎219 24 12 38; www.sintratur.com). Fixed routes or pay by the hr. Carriages, drivers, and horses for hire wait in the Praça da República. To **Quinta da Regaleira** and back (30min., €30); **Monserrate** and back, including a 30min. stop on the grounds for a quick picnic (1½hr., €70). Carriages available daily Apr.-Sept. 10am-6pm.

✴▮ ORIENTATION AND PRACTICAL INFORMATION

Situated in the mountains 25km northwest of Lisboa and 12km north of Cascais, Sintra has three main sections. Excursions to the area by bus or train begin in the modern **Estefânia,** where several banks and budget accommodations can be found. **São Pedro de Sintra,** farther uphill, has more shops and municipal offices. Sintra is made famous by its heart, **Sintra-Vila,** better known as the **Historic Center** and home to most of the town's fantastic sights. The Historic Centre can be reached via the long and bending **Volta do Duche.** The 15min. walk from **Estefânia** is scattered with statues and fountains like bread crumbs for sight-hungry tourists. To get to the Historic Center, take a left out of the train station onto Av. Dr. M. Bombarda and follow it down 150m. At the intersection, take the curving road to the left (Volta do Duche), which passes the **Parque da Liberdade** and leads to the edge of the Historic Centre, where shops begin to appear again. Stay to the right, and the **Palácio Nacional de Sintra** should be visible on the right. The **tourist office** is straight ahead. Sintra is navigable by foot, but a few sights lie outside (and uphill from) the town center. The ScottURB bus line #434 sells day tickets to most of these places (€4.00). Pay on the bus, which departs in front of the main train station every 15min. (9:35am-7:05pm) and then stops in the Historic Centre. From there, the bus will head to the **Castelo dos Mouros** and then **Palácio da Pena.** On the way back down the mountain, the bus stops in front of the **Museu Brinquedo** (Toy Museum).

Tourist Office: Pr. da República, 23 (☎219 23 11 57; fax 23 87 87), in the Historic Center. Open daily June-Sept. 9am-8pm; Oct.-May 9am-7pm. **Branch** in the train station (☎219 24 16 23) with the same hours. English, French, and Spanish spoken.

Police: R. João de Deus, 6 (☎219 23 07 61), next to the train station.

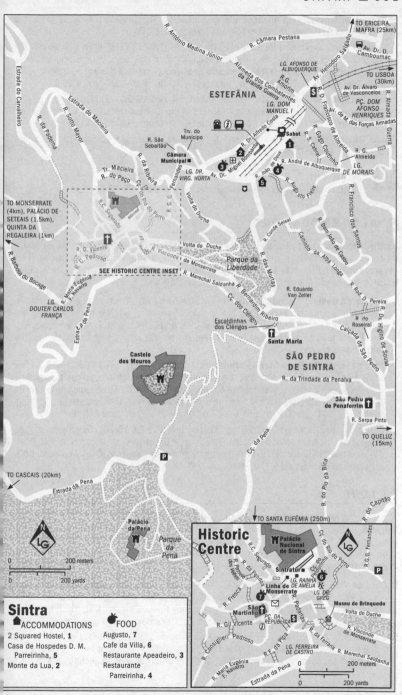

Sintra

ACCOMMODATIONS
2 Squared Hostel, **1**
Casa de Hospedes D. M.
Parreirinha, **5**
Monte da Lua, **2**

FOOD
Augusto, **7**
Cafe da Villa, **6**
Restaurante Apeadeiro, **3**
Restaurante
Parreirinha, **4**

Pharmacy: Farmácia da Misericórdia de Sintra, Lg. Dr. Gregório d'Almeida, 2 (☎/fax 219 23 03 91). Open M-F 9am-7pm, Sa 9am-2pm. MC/V.

Medical Services: Centro de Saúde, R. Dr. Alfredo Costa, 34, 1st fl. (☎219 10 66 80; fax 24 42 38). Open M-F 8am-6pm, emergency care only 6-9:30pm; Sa-Su and holidays 10am-7:30pm. **Hospital Fernando Fonseca (Amadora-Sintra)** in nearby Amadora (☎214 34 82 00). 20min. by train (every 10min. 5am-12:50am, €1.20).

Internet Access: Sabot, R. Dr. Alfredo Costa, 74 (☎219 23 08 02). Just across the street from the main train station, to the right of the Chinese restaurant. €1 per 15min., €2.50 per hr. CD burning for €1.80 (CD included). Open daily 11-2am.

Post Office: Pr. da República, 26 (☎219 10 67 91). Open M-F 9:30am-12:30pm and 2:30-6pm. **Postal Code:** 2710.

 SAVE YOUR STAMPS. Many post offices in Portugal sell pre-stamped postcards for international postage, saving you up to €0.75 per card.

ACCOMMODATIONS

Sintra begs you to stay for as long as you can afford, but accommodations can be more expensive than in nearby towns or Lisboa, a 45min. train ride away. The central tourist office has a list of private accommodations, but prices are similar to the *residenciais* (singles €35-40; doubles €40-50).

2 Squared Hostel, R. João de Deus, 68 (☎219 24 61 60). The best budget accommodation in Sintra, this hostel also has a cafe downstairs. Brightly painted rooms are spacious and open. Some face the train station and can be loud. Free Internet access. Reserve ahead by phone. English spoken. Dorms (usually single-sex) €15; double with shared bath €20. Cash only. ❶

Casa de Hóspedes Dona Maria Parreirinha, R. João de Deus, 12/14 (☎219 23 24 90; www.dmariaparreirinha.com). Exit the train station and go left around the tracks. *Azulejo*-decorated hallways, immaculate tile floors, and cable TV. Most rooms have private baths. Free parking available. Some English spoken. Singles €30, with bath €35; doubles €35/40; triples €45; quints €60. €5-10 less in winter. Cash only. ❸

Monte da Lua, Av. Miguel Bombarda, 51. (☎/fax: 219 24 10 29). Directly across the street from the train station. Extremely well-located *residencial* offers rooms with heat, TV, and telephone for competitive prices. High-season doubles €40, with bath €50. Low-season doubles €35/€45. Cash only. ❸

FOOD

Pastelarias and restaurants crowd the end of **Rua João de Deus** and **Avenida Heliodoro Salgado.** In the old town, **Rua das Padarias** (near the Palácio Nacional) is lined with lunch spots. On the 2nd and 4th Sundays of every month, take bus #433 from the train station to nearby São Pedro (15min., €1.30) for the spectacular **Feira de São Pedro,** featuring cheap local cuisine, as well as music, clothes, flowers, and antiques.

▨ **Café da Villa,** Calçada do Pelourinho, 8 (☎967 09 13 96). In the main square in front of the Palácio Nacional. Decorated with colorful flags and paintings of famous faces like the Dalai Lama. Offers a variety of internationally themed meals (€8), which include 3 courses and a drink. Great after-hours hangout. Open daily noon-2am. AmEx/MC/V. ❷

▨ **Restaurante Parreirinha,** Rua João de Deus, 43 (☎ 219 23 12 07). Behind the train station. A welcome change from the dark, antiquated café-bars of the city. New stainless-steel appliances, a flat-screen TV, and cinnamon-colored tablecloths make for a modern look. Variety of fish and wine. Daily special €6; entrees €7-10. No vegetarian options. Open M-Sa noon-4pm and 7-11pm. MC/V. ❷

Restaurante Apeadeiro, Av. Miguel Bombarda, 3A (☎219 23 18 04). From the flag on the wall to the hanging *futebol* (soccer ball) over the bar, this is a classic Portuguese cafe experience. Try the freshly grilled sardines. Entrees €7-13. Few vegetarian options. Open M-W and F-Su 11am-3pm and 7-10pm. AmEx/MC/V. ❷

Augusto, Rua da Pendôa, 11 (☎219 24 63 05). From the tourist office, make a left facing the post office and curve around under the arch. Augusto is on the left. Budget eaters can feast here: soup, bread, plate of the day, drink, dessert, and *cafezinho* for only €6.50. Some vegetarian entrees. Open daily noon-2am. Cash only. ❶

SIGHTS

█ QUINTA DA REGALEIRA. A UNESCO World Heritage sight, this turret-studded palace was built in the early 1900s by Brazilian Antonio Monteira and flamboyant Italian architect Luigi Manini. Quinta's gardens, wells, grottoes, and towers follow mythological and historical themes, rendered in a fascinating amalgam of Manueline, Gothic, and Renaissance styles. The **Poço Iniciatico** (Initiation Well) was inspired by the secret rituals performed by the famous Knights Templar. *(To get to the Quinta da Regaleira, turn right out of the tourist office and follow R. Consiglieri Pedroso as it turns into Rua M. E. F. Navarro. 15min. walk. ☎219 10 66 50; regaleira@mail.telepac.pt. Open daily Oct. and Feb.-Apr. 10am-6:30pm, last entrance 6pm; April-Sept. 10am-8pm, last entrance 7pm; Nov.-Jan. 10am-5:30pm, last entrance 5pm. Unguided visits €5, students and seniors €4. Guided tours at 10:30, 11am, noon, 2:30, 3:30pm; €10, students and seniors €8.)*

> **TIP**
>
> **LIGHT IT UP.** To add some adventure to your experience at Quinta da Regaleira, bring a flashlight—there are several unmarked (and unlit) grottoes that are fun to explore, if you dare.

█ PALÁCIO DA PENA. Built in the 1840s by Prince Ferdinand of Bavaria, husband of Portugal's Dona Maria II, this royal retreat embraces romantic and fantastic style with its excessive detail. The prince, nostalgic for his native country, rebuilt and embellished the ruined monastery with the assistance of a Prussian engineer, combining the artistic heritages of both Germany and Portugal. The result is a colorful Bavarian castle decorated with Arabic minarets, Gothic turrets, Manueline windows, and a Renaissance dome. *(Bus #434 runs to the palace from outside the tourist office. All-day bus pass €4. ☎219 10 53 40; www.parquesdesintra.pt. The area surrounding the palace, Parque da Pena, is open daily June-Aug. 9am-8pm; Sept.-May 9am-7pm. €4.50, children and seniors €2.50. Palace €8, children and seniors €6. Open daily 10am-5:30pm. Tickets for both attractions are sold until 1hr. before closing. Guided tours in English, Portuguese, and Spanish; €4.50, €3 per person in groups of 10 or more.)*

█ CASTELO DOS MOUROS. Built in the 8th century by the Moors, this ancient castle rests along the side of the Serra mountains. It was abandoned during the Moorish retreat to the south in 1147, but fortunately, Dom Fernando II made some much-needed repairs in the 19th century. A steep climb up the walls will reward you on a clear day with unmatched views of the Ribatejo plains and the breathtaking contrast between natural rock formations and manmade walls. *(About 1km below the Palácio da Pena. Bus #434 departs from outside the tourist office and stops at the castle. All-day bus pass €4. ☎219 23 73 00; www.parquesdasintra.pt. Open daily June-Sept. 9am-8pm, last entrance 7pm; Oct.-May 9:30am-5pm, last entrance 4pm. €4.50,* *seniors and under 17 €2.50, families (2 children, 2 adults) €10, 4 tickets €12. Guided tours €4.50, €3 per person in groups of 10 or more.)*

PALÁCIO NACIONAL DE SINTRA. The palace, also known as the Paço Real or Palácio da Vila, dominates Pr. da República. Once a summer residence for Moorish sultans and their harems, the Palácio da Vila was taken over by the Portuguese following the Muslim defeat. The conquest is illustrated in the paintings of Portuguese noblemen gunning down Moorish soldiers. The palace and gardens were built in two stages: Dom João I built the main structure in the 15th century, and Dom Manuel I amassed the best collection of *azulejos* (glazed tiles) in the world a century later. The palace has over 20 rooms, including the *azulejo*-covered Sala dos Árabes and the gilded Sala dos Brasões. Some of the palace's greatest treasures are overhead; look up at the ceiling to see the royal coat of arms surrounded by the armorial bearings of 72 noble families, elaborately painted animals, and various other artistic treasures. The palace is marked by a bird theme: doves symbolizing the Holy Spirit line the walls of the Capela, swans grace the Sala dos Cisnes, and on the ceiling of the Sala das Pegas magpies symbolic of the ladies-in-waiting hold a piece of paper proclaiming D. João I's motto—*"por bem,"* or "for good." *(Lg. da Rainha Dona Amélia. ☎219 10 68 40; www.ippar.pt. Open M-Tu and Th-Su 10am-5:30pm. Last entrance 5pm. €4, seniors and students €2; Su and holidays before 2pm free.)*

MONSERRATE. Located about 4km from the center of Sintra, Monserrate is well worth a visit for those staying in town for more than a day. This sprawling estate is known for its gentle, quiet botanical gardens shaded by towering sequoias and gigantic tropical ferns. The Moghul-style mansion, with its burnt-orange roof modeled on Brunelleschi's Dome in Florence, is a classic example of Portuguese Romanticism. Designed by the English architect John T. Knowles in 1858, the estate became a refuge for eccentric English aristocrat William Beckford following scandalous publicity regarding his homosexual affairs. *(To get to Monserrate, catch the small green train, Linha de Monserrate, ☎214 66 26 03, beside the Palácio Nacional in Pr. da República. 25 min., hourly, €5 round-trip. Monserrate ☎219 23 73 00 or 10 78 06. Open daily summer 9am-8pm; winter 9:30am-6pm. Last entrance 1hr. before closing. €4.50, children and seniors €2.50, families (2 adults, 2 children) €10, 4 tickets €12. Guided tours €4.50, €3 for groups of 10 or more.)*

SETÚBAL ☎265

There's no question about it, Setúbal is a port city—you can smell it in the air and see it on the menus. But unlike the coastal developments in the Algarve, Setúbal leaves travelers with more options than just beaches and *bacalhau* (cod). The wild dolphin population in the Reserva Natural do Estuário do Sado offers a relaxing opportunity to commune with some of Mother Nature's perkiest creatures. If you're fleeing from campy tourist traps in a quest to discover the real Portugal, Setúbal will more than oblige with central city squares full of traditional *lojas* (shops), cobblestone streets, and, of course, statues of Portuguese statesmen. A compact city, Setúbal takes no more than a day or two to visit, but it makes a good base for daytrips as well.

◧ TRANSPORTATION. Trains leave from either Estação Praça de Quebedo, which is the most convenient to the city center, or Estação de Setúbal (☎265 52 68 45), in Pr. do Brasil (a 10min. walk down the same street) and Estação do Barreiro (50min., every 30min. 5am-noon, €1.40), where you transfer to a boat to get to Lisboa. **Buses** leave from Av. 5 de Outubro, 44 (☎265 52 50 51). From the tourist office, walk up R. Santa Maria to Av. 5 de Outubro and turn left; the station is about 2 blocks down on the right, in the building with "Rodoviária" written vertically down the front. Buses go to: Évora (2½hr.; 10:25am, 12:15, 5:10pm; €9.50); Faro (4hr., 3:05pm, €15.40); Lisboa's Praça de Espanha (1hr., 17 per day 6:55am-9pm, €5); Sesimbra (45min., 9 per day 7:20am-8pm, €2.60). **Transado**, Doca do Comércio (☎265 23 51 01), off Av. Luísa Todi at the waterfront's end, sends **ferries** to Tróia (15min.; every 30min.; €1.25, ages 5-10 €0.50, under 5 free). **Rádio Táxi** (☎265 23 33 34) is at Av. Luísa Todi and by the bus and train stations.

⚎ 🛈 ORIENTATION AND PRACTICAL INFORMATION.

Setúbal's spine is **Avenida Luísa Todi,** a wide boulevard parallel to the Rio Sado. Farther inland from Luísa Todi is **Avenida 5 de Outubro,** and between the two major roads lies a dense district of shops and restaurants centered around the **Praça de Bocage. Avenida da Portela** runs perpendicular to Av. 5 de Outubro, past the train and bus stations.

The regional **tourist office** is **Posto de Turismo da Costa Azul**, on Tr. Frei Gaspar, just off Av. Luísa Todi near Lg. da Misericórdia. (☎265 53 91 30. English, French, and Spanish spoken. Open May-Sept. M-Sa 9:30am-7pm, Su 9:30am-12:30pm; Oct.-Apr. M-Sa 9:30am-6pm.) There is a convenient **municipal branch** at R. Santa Maria, 2-4. From the bus station, turn left and walk two blocks down Av. 5 de Outubro; take a right on R. Santa Maria and the office will be on the right. (☎265 52 44 02. Open M-Sa 9:30am-12:30pm and 2-6pm, Su 2-6pm.) **Banks** line Av. Luísa Todi. (All open M-F 8:30am-3pm.) **Agência de Cambios Central,** Av. Luísa Todi, 226, has currency exchange. (☎265 54 80 40. Open M-Sa 9am-7pm.) The **police** are at Av. Luísa Todi and Av. 22 de Dezembro (☎265 52 20 22). Local services include: **Hospital São Bernardo,** R. Camilo Castelo Branco (☎265 54 90 00); **laundry** at **Lavanderia Donini,** R. Oliveira Martins, 17 (☎265 52 71 54; open M-F 9am-1pm and 3-7pm, Sa 9am-1pm, €3 per kg); **Farmácia Normal do Sul,** Pr. de Bocage, 135 (☎265 52 84 50; open M-Sa 9:30am-6:30pm); **Internet** access at **Cybertody,** R. São Cristóvão, 7 (follow the sign for Residencial Bocage off Av. Luísa Todi; ☎265 22 12 54; €1.65 per hour; open M-F 11am-midnight, Sa-Su 2:30pm-midnight) and **Sobicome,** Av. Luísa Todi, 333 (☎936 73 54 06; €3 per hour with student ID; open daily 3pm-4am); and **post office** at **Ctt Correios,** Praça de Bocage (☎213 55 35 05; open M-F 9am-12:30pm and 2:30-6pm). **Postal Code:** 2900.

🛏 🍴 ACCOMMODATIONS AND FOOD.

There are a few good *pensões* along Av. Luísa Todi and near Pr. de Bocage. Alternatively, ask at either tourist office for a list of *quartos* in private houses. ⚑**Pousada da Juventude de Setúbal (HI) ❶,** Lg. José Afonso, has clean, cozy rooms, a common room with TV, and a friendly multilingual staff. It also offers 30min. free Internet access. Facing the river, walk right on Av. Luísa Todi until you reach a large plaza on the left with a salmon-colored building in the center. Cut in front of the building to the parking lot; the *pousada* is the building ahead with the two-story glass tower. (☎265 53 44 31; fax 53 29 63. Reception 8am-noon and 6pm-midnight. Check-out noon. Dorms €9; doubles €20, with bath €24. HI discount €2. AmEx/MC/V.) **Residencial Bocage ❸,** R. São Cristóvão, 14, off Av. Luísa Todi, has fully loaded suites without fully loaded prices. Recently renovated rooms include bath, phone, TV, A/C, and breakfast. The front desk staff is extremely helpful and friendly. (☎265 54 30 80. Jan.-Mar. singles €26; doubles €34. Apr.-July €30/42. Aug. €37/49. Sept. €28/39. Oct.-Dec. €26/34. AmEx/MC/V.) **Pensão O Cantinho ❶,** Beco do Carmo, 1-9, is in an alley off Av. Luísa Todi behind Lg. do Carmo, near the police station. Spacious rooms above the restaurant have private baths and are the cheapest in town. (☎265 52 38 99. Reserve ahead in summer. Singles €10-15; doubles €20. Cash only.)

Seafood places line Av. Luísa Todi just up the street from Doca do Comércio; you can watch as they cut and fry your fish on sidewalk grills. Pick up **groceries** and fresh baked goods at **Supermercado Mini-Preço,** Av. Cinco de Outubro, 72. (Open M-Sa 9am-8pm.) For a sit-down meal, try **Duarte Dos Frangos ❸,** Av. Luísa

Todi, 285, across the plaza from the youth hostel. Chatty locals and a friendly staff makes the place warm and welcoming. (☎265 52 26 03. Fish and meat entrees €5.50-14. Open daily noon-3pm and 7-10:30pm. Cash only.) If you are interested in trying Setubal's famed specialty, *choco frito* (fried cuttlefish), **Novo 10 ❸,** Av. Luísa Todi, 422-426, is one of the best seafood restaurants around. Even non-seafood lovers should find something to their taste on the extensive menu. The beef (€8-12) is among the best in town. (☎265 52 54 98. Open M-Tu and Th-Su noon-midnight. AmEx/MC/V.)

◨ ☗ **SIGHTS AND FESTIVALS.** The town's most impressive sight, the 16th-century ☗**Forte de São Filipe,** sits just outside the city. Designed by Italian engineer Filipe Terzi, the fortress was built during the Spanish occupation of Portugal in 1582 and took almost 20 years to finish. The star-shaped fortress is now a luxury *pousada* (around €250 a night), but anyone is free to explore it. During the last week of July and first week of August, the **Feira de Santiago** in Lg. José Afonso brings a carnival, folk music, and enormous outdoor market. Coinciding with the fair, Portuguese bullfighting, which spares the bull, takes over the Pr. dos Touros by the train station.

Setúbal's best **beaches** are **Praia Figueirinha** and **Praia Galapos** (buses run from the main station to Figueirinha, 20min., round-trip €2.80), while **Vertigem Azul,** Av. Luísa Todi, 375 (☎265 23 80 00; www.vertigemazul.com) offers dolphin-watching daytrips (€30, children €20) in addition to kayaking, snorkeling, and jeep tours. (Prices around €15 per hour.) Planeta Terra, Praça General Luís Domingues, 9, rents street, hybrid, and mountain bikes starting at €8 per day. (☎919 47 18 71; www.planetaterra.pt. Delivery available. Reserve ahead.)

ALGARVE AND ALENTEJO

The Algarve and the Alentejo form a striking contrast. The Alentejo's small villages, seemingly stuck in another time, provide an escape from the Algarve's heavily touristed beaches and wild nightlife. Nearly 3000 hours of annual sunshine have transformed the Algarve from a fishermen's backwater town into one of Europe's favorite vacation spots. In July and August, visitors mob its resorts, packing bars and discos from sunset until long after sunrise. Still, the Algarve isn't all about excess. The region between Faro and the Spanish border remains relatively untouched, and, to the west of Lagos, towering cliffs shelter pristine beaches. Life slows down even more as you enter the Alentejo, where arid plains punctuated by olive trees, two-toned cork trees, and fields of wheat and sunflowers stretch to the horizon in a display of endless shades of yellow. This vast region appeals to travelers in search of relaxation, history, and plenty of wine. The Algarve and Alentejo provide visitors with the best of both worlds, with only a short drive in between.

HIGHLIGHTS OF ALGARVE AND ALENTEJO

SPELUNK in the grottoes and sea cliffs of **Lagos** (p. 667).

CHANNEL the spirit of Prince Henry the Navigator at his outpost in **Sagres** (p. 674).

FEEL it in your bones at Évora's **Capela dos Ossos** (p. 680).

STORM the walls of the 13th-century castle in **Marvão** (p. 689).

ALGARVE

Behold the Algarve: a vacationland where happy campers from the world over bask in the sun. Off the sands, the geometric design and minaret-style chimneys of Algarve's old houses reveal a strong Arab influence. While regional crafts specialize in basket-weaving, the Algarve's most perfect craft is its delicious seafood—local favorites include flavorful *sardinhas assadas* (grilled sardines) and the creamy *caldeirada* (seafood chowder). Almonds and figs also make their way into most regional cooking, especially in divine desserts like *figos cheios*. In the winter, the resorts empty and wildlife of a different sort arrives, as roughly one-third of Europe's flamingos migrate to the wetlands surrounding Olhão.

LAGOS
☎ 282

Lagos (pop. 17,500) has a way of making visitors want to stay forever; just ask any one of the innumerable expatriate bartenders, surf guides, or restaurant owners. As the Algarve's capital for almost 200 years, Lagos launched many of the *caravels* (sailing ships) that brought Portugal power and fortune in the 15th and 16th centuries. Today, the city is immersed in another, equally profitable golden age—that of tourism. While the 20-somethings recuperate from the previous night, the 40-plus crowd comes out in the morning and lingers until dinner time, perusing storefronts, taking dolphin tours, and relaxing in the sunny plazas.

◪ TRANSPORTATION

To reach Lagos from northern Portugal, you must go through Lisboa; trips originating in the east generally transfer in Faro.

Trains: (☎282 76 29 87). Over the footbridge and behind the marina. To: **Beja** (3¼hr.; 6:57am and 12:19pm; €9.80 and €17.30); **Évora** (5-5½hr.; 6:57am and 12:19pm; €14.50 and €21.60) via Faro; **Lisboa** (3½-4½hr., 7 per day 6:11am-6:12pm, €15.50); **Silves** (40min., 1:39pm, €1.70); **Vila Real de Santo António** (3hr., 7 per day 7:03am-7:04pm, €6.50) via Faro.

Buses: The EVA bus station (☎282 76 29 44), off Av. dos Descobrimentos, is just before R. Porta de Portugal (when walking into town) and across the channel from the footbridge to the marina and train station. To: **Albufeira** (1¾3hr., 6 per day 7am-5:15pm, €4.35); **Faro** (2½hr., 6 per day 7am-5:15pm, €4); **Lisboa** (5hr., 6 per day 5:30am-6:15pm, €15); **Sagres** (1hr., 16 per day 7:15am-8:30pm, €3.05).

Taxis: Lagos Central Taxi (☎282 76 24 69). 24hr. service to Lagos and environs.

Car Rental: 21+ for cars, 16+ for mopeds.

Auto Jardim, Travessa do Ferro de Engomar (☎282 76 94 86). Cars from €91.50 per 3 days, tax and insurance not included. AmEx/MC/V.

Luzcar Rent-a-Car, Lg. Portas de Portugal, 10 (☎282 76 10 16). July-Sept. cars from €200 per week including tax and insurance; Apr.-June and Oct. €150; Nov.-Mar. €130. Baby seat and roof rack included. AmEx/D/MC/V.

Motorent, R. Victor Costa Silva, 8B (☎282 76 97 16; fax 282 48 34 95). Rents bikes (€20 per 3 days), scooters (€50 per 3 days), and motorcycles (€110 per 3 days). 18+, 25+ for motorcycles; license required. AmEx/MC/V.

■✦🛈 ORIENTATION AND PRACTICAL INFORMATION

Running the length of the channel, **Avenida dos Descobrimentos** carries traffic to and from Lagos. From the **train station,** walk through the pink marina and cross the pedestrian suspension bridge; turn left onto Av. dos Descobrimentos. From the **bus station,** walk straight until Av. dos Descobrimentos and turn right. **Praça Gil Eanes** is the center of the old town and extends into Lg. Marquêz de Pombal, where the **tourist office** is located. Follow R. Silva Lopes to R. General Alberto da Silveira to reach the grotto-lined beach of **Praia Dona Ana.**

Tourist Office: Municipal office (☎282 76 41 11), on Lg. Marquêz de Pombal. Open M-Sa 10am-6pm.

Currency Exchange: Cotacâmbios, Pr. Gil Eanes, 11 (☎282 76 44 52). Open M-F 9am-9pm, Sa-Su 9am-6pm.

English-Language Bookstore: The Owl Story, Marreiros Neto, 67 (☎ 282 79 22 89). Limited selection of English novels and travel guides. Open M-F 10am-7pm and Sa 10am-2pm.

Laundromat: Lavanderia Míele, Av. dos Descobrimentos, 27 (☎282 76 39 69). Wash and dry €7 per 5kg. Open M-F 9am-1pm and 3-7pm, Sa 9am-1pm.

Library: R. Dr. Julio Dantas. Open Tu-W 10am-6pm, Th 10am-8pm, F 10am-6pm, Sa 10am-1pm; closed Su and M and the month of Aug. Free **Internet access** upstairs.

Police: R. General Alberto da Silveira (☎282 76 29 30).

Pharmacy: Farmácia Silva, R. 25 de Abril, 9 (☎282 76 28 59). 9am-1:30pm and 3-7:30pm. Ask at any one of the many pharmacies for a pamphlet listing the hours and locations of all the pharmacies in Lagos.

Medical Services: Hospital Distrital de Lagos, R. Castelo dos Governadores (☎282 77 01 00).

Internet access: Snack Bar Ganha Pouco, 1st right after the footbridge coming from the bus station. Internet access (€2.50 per hour; €0.50 per fax. Open 10am-7pm) and a full array of drinks and munchies. Several bars in Lagos have computers; check along R. Lançarote de Freitas. Free access also found in the **Library.**

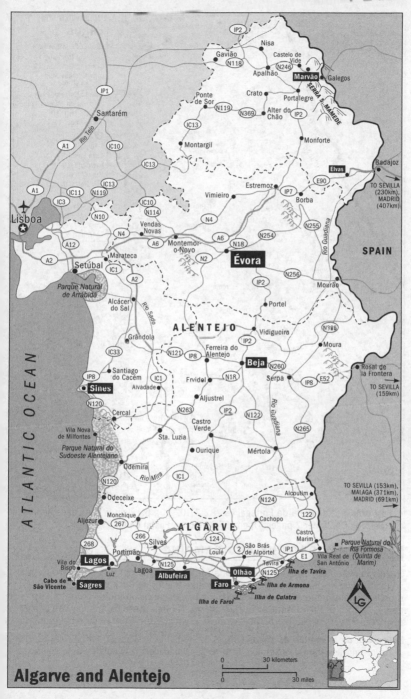

Algarve and Alentejo

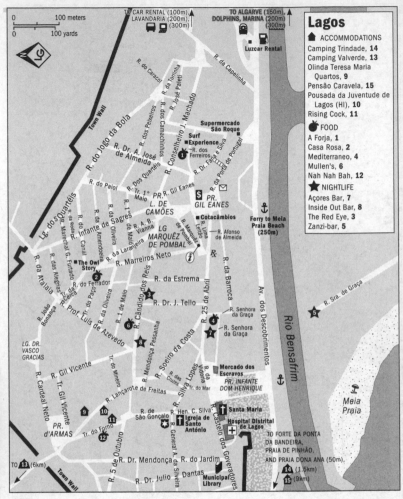

Lagos

🏠 ACCOMMODATIONS
Camping Trindade, **14**
Camping Valverde, **13**
Olinda Teresa Maria
 Quartos, **9**
Pensão Caravela, **15**
Pousada da Juventude de
 Lagos (HI), **10**
Rising Cock, **11**

🍎 FOOD
A Forja, **1**
Casa Rosa, **2**
Mediterraneo, **4**
Mullen's, **6**
Nah Nah Bah, **12**

⭐ NIGHTLIFE
Açores Bar, **7**
Inside Out Bar, **8**
The Red Eye, **3**
Zanzi-bar, **5**

Post Office: R. da Porta de Portugal (☎282 77 02 50), between Pr. Gil Eanes and the river. **Fax** €4.25 per 2 pages. Open M-F 9am-6pm. **Postal Code:** 8600.

🏠 ACCOMMODATIONS AND CAMPING

In July and August, budget accommodations fill up quickly; reserve more than a week in advance. Some accommodations, like the **Rising Cock,** set aside a limited number of last-minute rooms. Locals trying to rent rooms in their homes will probably greet you at the station or in the streets. Though these rooms may be a little out of the way, they can be the best deals in town at €10-15 per person in summer.

🛏 **Pousada da Juventude de Lagos (HI),** R. Lançarote de Freitas, 50 (☎282 76 19 70; lagos@movijovem.pt). Personable staff and social lodgers congregate in the courtyard and bar-hop together at night. Internet access (€1 per 15min.), a kitchen, and a TV room with billiards and foosball. For July-Aug. book through the **Movijovem** office (☎217 23 21 00). Breakfast included. June 16-Sept. 15 dorms €16; doubles with bath €43. Sept. 16-June 15 €11/30. Cash only. ❷

■ **Rising Cock,** Travessa do Forno, 14 (☎969 41 11 31; www.risingcock.com). Legendary among backpackers and spring-breakers. Social, college-like atmosphere. Mrs. Ribeiro, referred to by guests as "Mama," makes free breakfast. Upstairs patio, huge common room with big-screen TV, DVD library, and free Internet access and Wi-Fi. Coed rooms with lockers; most have bathrooms. Reserve ahead. Prices vary by season. In summer single bed in mixed dorm €22-25. AmEx/MC/V. ❷

Olinda Teresa Maria Quartos, R. Lançarote de Freitas, 37, 2A 1st and 2nd fl. (☎282 08 23 29; www.quartosolinda.pt.vu). Home converted into a crowded hostel with low prices and a dorm-style atmosphere. Doubles or dorms with shared fridge, terrace, and bath. Mid-July-Sept. 16 dorms €16; doubles €43; offseason €11/30. Cash only. ❷

Pensão Caravela, R. 25 de Abril, 8 (☎282 76 33 61), just up the street from Pr. Gil Eanes. 16 small but well-located rooms with half-baths, some with balconies. Singles €25, with bathroom €30; doubles €35/37.50; triples €50. Cash only. ❸

Camping Trindade (☎282 76 38 93), just outside town. Follow Av. dos Descobrimentos toward Sagres. €3.50 per person, €4.50 per tent, €4.80 per car. ❶

Camping Valverde (☎282 78 92 11), 6km outside Lagos, 1.5km west of Praia da Luz. Restaurant and pool. Showers free. €6 per person, €5 per tent, €4.50 per car. AmEx/MC/V. ❶

⬡ FOOD

The cheapest dining options in Lagos are the local indoor produce market on Av. dos Descobrimentos and **Supermercado São Roque,** R. da Porta de Portugal, 61 (☎282 76 28 55; open July-Sept. M-F 9am-8pm, Sa 9am-7pm; Oct.-June M-F 9am-7:30pm, Sa 9am-7pm). Eateries on R. de Silva Lopes and R. 25 de Abril tend to be more expensive.

■ **Casa Rosa,** R. do Ferrador, 22 (☎282 18 02 38). The friendly staff at this Australian/ American restaurant will engage the daring in an intense game of Connect Four. Various vegetarian options. Entrees €5-7.50. All-you-can-eat spaghetti or vegetarian bolognese €7 daily. The 40cl strawberry daiquiris (€4.50) are a sweet start or finish to any meal. Free Internet access for diners. Open daily 5pm-midnight. ❶

■ **A Forja,** R. dos Ferreiros, 17 (☎282 76 85 88). Few traditional Portuguese restaurants exist in Lagos, but locals swear by A Forja, known affectionately as "Blue Door." Serves Algarvian seafood; look for a placard outside listing specials, like the tremendous plate of *pato* (duck). Entrees €5-15. Open daily noon-3pm and 6:30-10pm. Cash only. ❷

Mediterraneo, R. Senhora da Graça, 2 (☎282 76 84 76). Mediterranean and Thai cuisine, including enticing tapas (€2-7.50) and great seafood. The town's most enticing vegetarian options. Entrees €8.50-14.50. Open Tu-Sa 7pm-until late. Cash only. ❷

Mullen's, R. Cândido dos Reis, 86 (☎282 76 12 81). A unique combination of great Portuguese and international cuisine, stereotypical Irish pub atmosphere, and live jazz. Try the duck in orange sauce and the spicy *frango grelhado* (grilled chicken). Entrees €7.50-12. Bar open daily 11pm-2am; restaurant open 6-10:30pm. ❷

Nah Nah Bah, Travessa do Forno, 11. Owner personally prepares dishes and chats with customers nightly. Try The Nah Nah Bird with the "legendary" Nah Nah chips (€7). Reggae beats (sometimes with live DJ) and cabana-feel keep the relaxed vibe alive well into the night. Entrees €6.50-8. Open 7pm-2am. ❷

WHAT'S IN A CHIMNEY?

Christmas aside, most cultures don't pay much attention to the hard working smokestacks above their houses. The chimney is somewhat of a neglected child—one of the least glamorous parts of the house, it's associated with soot, bats, and sad, exploited chimneysweeps. Not so in Portugal's Algarve region, where the chimney is celebrated as an artistic symbol. It is the baby of the family, lavished with attention.

From the delicate filigree patterns on some to the simple, elegant designs on others, each Algarvian chimney is a unique work of skilled artisanship. In fact, when building a chimney, stonemasons traditionally ask the house owners, *"Quantos dias quer de chaminé?"* ("How many days worth of chimney would you like?").

Most traditional Algarvian country houses boast two chimneys, emphasizing the divide between function and ornamentation. The simpler of the two was traditionally in the "oven room," where the family ate, while the more intricate one was above the kitchen, used on special occasions. While chimneys throughout the Algarve provide a welcome variation on the region's unpolished beauty, it's the Algarvian critters that call them their homes who are truly lucky—without a doubt, they are living in style.

SIGHTS AND BEACHES

Lagos, manufactured into one continuous Spring Break city, has nearly lost track of its historic past. The few mementos that remain can be seen in under two hours on a lazy afternoon walk back from the beach. The **Forte da Ponta da Bandeira**, a 17th-century fortress with maritime exhibitions and tiled chapel, overlooks the marina. It is the site of Lagos' traditional Banho 29 (Bath 29) festivities; in ancient times, locals traveled to the waters of Lagos and purified themselves in the sea at midnight on August 29. The date has been transformed to an annual debaucherous and celebratory rave. (☎282 76 14 10. Open Tu-Su 9:30am-12:30pm and 2- 5pm, €2, students €1, under 13 free.) Also near the waterfront is the former **Mercado dos Escravos** (slave market). Legend has it that the first sale of African slaves in Portugal took place here in 1441. One block from Pr. Infante Dom Henrique is **Igreja de Santo António.** The church is home to a museum containing artifacts ranging from the Neolithic age to the Republic. (Open Tu-Su 9:30am-12:30pm and 2-5pm. Entrance €2.20, seniors, students, under 18 €2.10.) The waterfront and marina offers jet-ski rentals, scuba diving lessons, sailboat and dolphin-sighting trips, and motorboat tours of the **coastal rocks and grottoes.** Lagos's **beaches** are undeniably seductive. A 4km blanket of flat, smooth sands (crowded in summer but bare in the sunny low season) lines the well-known **Meia Praia,** across the river from town. To get there, hop on the 30-second ferry near Pr. Infante Dom Henrique (€0.50). For abrupt cliffs that plunge into the sea and smaller, less-crowded beaches and caves, keep the ocean to your left and follow Av. dos Descobrimentos toward Sagres to **Praia de Pinhão** (20min.). Five minutes farther down the coast lies **Praia Dona Ana,** with sculpted ochre cliffs and grottoes that appear on half of all Algarve postcards.

WATER ACTIVITIES

If you want to take a break from sunbathing and venture further into the ocean, Lagos offers a variety of water sports and tours—from scuba diving to surfing to (booze) cruising.

Algarve Dolphins, Marina de Lagos, 10 (☎282 7646 70; www.bomdia-boattrips.com). 1½hr. of dolphin-watching in the ocean in high-speed rescue boats. The best deal for spotting wildlife, tours leave every hour from the Lagos Marina (look for the red *Bom Dia* sign). Actual dolphin sightings are not guaranteed, so check with people getting off boats or pay a little extra to cruise until the dolphins come to you. Tickets €30, €35 for guaranteed sightings. BBQ-Cruise and Family Fishing packages available (€25-48).

Grotto Boat Tours, Av. dos Descobrimentos, on the marina side. Companies set up shop on Av. dos Descobrimentos and over the footbridge near the marina offering tours of the cliffs and grottoes as well as a chance to dive into the teal waters. Most tours 45min., from €10. Easy to haggle if you have a group. Smaller boats are preferable, as they can get into rock caves and under sea bridges. *Bom Dia* offers a 2hr.r tour for €17-21.

Surf Experience, R. dos Ferreiros, 21 (☎282 76 19 43; www.surf-experience.com). 1- or 2-week surfing trips including lessons, transportation, and accommodations in a decked-out surf house in Lagos. All levels welcome. Daytrips when space available. Board and wet suit rental €75/114. Apr.-Nov. 1 week with board €525, 2 weeks €881; Dec.-Mar. €473/836.

The Booze Cruise, (☎969 41 11 31). A 4hr. afternoon boat ride around Lagos' coast. You're certain to get vertigo, whether from looking up at the dizzying heights of the cliffs or the all-you-can-drink bar (don't touch your drink with your right hand or you may be forced to down a beer bong). Not for those looking for a tour—anchor drops about an hour in. €35, all inclusive. Booking available through The Rising Cock and Joe's Garage.

NIGHTLIFE

Lagos's young crowd flocks from the beaches to the bars as the sun dips below the horizon. On alternate Sundays from 4-10pm, coteries of local workers from Lagos's bars and restaurants come to **Bahia Beach Bar** on Meia Praia for live music and volleyball. In town, the area between **Praça Gil Eanes** and **Praça Luis de Camões** is filled with cafes. **Rua Cândido dos Reis, Rua do Ferrador,** and the intersection of **Rua 25 de Abril, Rua de Silva Lopos,** and **Rua Soeiro da Costa** are the bar and club scene mecca. The streets get busy around 10pm, and serious pedestrian traffic hits at midnight. Drinks are relatively cheap, and bars boast an abundance of specials.

Inside Out Bar, R. Cândido dos Reis, 119. Inside Out is an insomniac's dream come true. Things don't pick up until a little after 2am, when most of the other bars close. The house specialty is the barely-legal Fishbowl (€25). Outfitted with a pool table, an extensive drink menu, and entertaining staff, it's a shame this bar ever has to close. Beer: bottles €2, pints €3. Shots €1-3. Mixed drinks €4.50-5.50. Open daily 8pm-4am.

Zanzi-bar, R. 25 de Abril, 93. Another "2 o'clock" stop, Zanzi-bar is always packed. The back room has a few tables for a more intimate setting. Scan the crowd for waiters and waitresses from local restaurants. Shots €2.50-3. Beer €2-3. Open daily 8pm-4am.

The Red Eye, R. Cândido dos Reis, 63. Brits and Aussies flood in around midnight for the classic rock, cheap liquor, and casual pool games. Mostly a pick-up scene. Free shot with first drink. Beer €2-3. Mixed drinks €3.50-5. Shots €2.50. Jug of *sangria* €10. Happy hour with €5 2-pint mixed drinks 8-10pm. Open daily 8pm-2am.

Açores Bar, R. Sra. da Graça, 12. A Portuguese twist on the mainly anglophone-run bar scene, owned by a couple from the Açores. The multi-level bar allows for more breathing room than most surrounding establishments can claim, although the population explodes around 1am. €8 liter of *sangria*. Reggae music nightly. Open daily 3pm-2am.

DAYTRIP FROM LAGOS

PRAIA DA ROCHA

To reach Praia da Rocha from Lagos, take the bus to Portimão (40min., 10 per day 6:11am-8:19pm, round-trip €5) and get off at the Praia da Rocha stop.

A short jaunt from Lagos, locals and tourists agree that Praia da Rocha is the best beach the Algarve has to offer. With vast expanses of big surf, scabrous red cliffs, and secluded coves, Praia da Rocha's reputation is well-deserved reputation, and the crowds attest to this fact. The **tourist office**, at the end of R. Tomás Cabreira, offers maps and lists of accommodations and restaurants. (☎282 41 91 32. Open May-Sept. daily 9:30am-7pm; Oct.-Apr. M-F 9:30am-12:30pm and 2-5:30pm, Sa-Su 9:30am-12:30pm.)

SAGRES   ☎282

Marooned atop a windy plateau at the southwesternmost point in Europe, Sagres (pop. 2500) was considered the end of the world for centuries. It was here that Prince Henry's famous school of navigation organized exploratory voyages to the far reaches of the globe. While large tour groups and upscale vacationers are discouraged by its desolate location and relative lack of recreation, Sagres' picturesque beaches, friendly locals, and lively nightlife make it a perfect destination for travelers in search of a stress-free day. Sagres, with access to both southern and western coasts, is rapidly becoming one of Europe's prime surfing grounds.

🖅🖪 TRANSPORTATION AND PRACTICAL INFORMATION. EVA buses (☎282 76 29 44) run from **Lagos** (1hr.; 14 per day M-F 6:10am-7:35pm, Sa 9 per day 6:10am-7:10pm, Su 7 per day 7:15am-7:10pm; €3.05). Buses also run to Lisboa (5¼hr., daily July-Sept. 4pm, €15). When arriving in Sagres use the tourist office on Av. Comandante Matoso as a signpost for when to get off; the actual stop, Escola, is easy to miss, as are the following two stops in Sagres. Schedules are posted to the left of door of the **tourist office.** The office offers practical and recreational pamphlets in English, including maps, regional information, and suggestions for golfing and enjoying the surf. (☎808 78 12 12; www.visitalgarve.pt. Open Tu-Sa 9:30am-12:30pm and 1:30-5:30pm.). The **police** are in Vila do Bispo (☎282 63 91 12). **Turinfo,** located in the lobby of Pensão Residencial D. Henrique (across from the restaurant A Conchincha in Pr. da República) offers **Internet** access (€0.10 per minute), **bike rental** (€6 per ½-day, €9.50 per full-day), info on **surfing/adventure tours,** scuba advice, **luggage storage** (€0.70 per hour), **laundry** (€8.50 for up to 5kg), and **currency exchange** (☎282 62 00 03; 24hr. reception. Tourist desk open weekdays 9am-4pm. Internet available daily 9am-midnight .) Other local services include: **banks and ATMs** along Av. Comandante Matoso, and across from the post office and at the **Alisuper** (supermarket); a **pharmacy** on R. Comandante Matoso, at the corner of R. Jaime Conde (☎282 62 48 50; open M-F 9am-2pm and 3-7pm, Sa 9am-1pm and 5pm-7pm, Su 11am-1pm and 5pm-7pm); a **post office** on the right-hand side of Av. Comandante Matoso when walking toward Praia da Baleeira (☎707 26 26 26; open M-F 9am-12:30pm and 2-5:30pm); ▓**Freeride Surfcamp,** or Casa Azul, with a blue-tiled hub on Pr. da República offers surf lessons and packages starting at €350 (including free pickup from Lagos bus and train stations). For surfers of all levels. (☎282 62 42 45; www.freeridesurfcamp.com); free **Internet** access at Água Salgada and neighbor O Dromedário (see **Sights and Entertainment,** p. 675).

🖪🖸 ACCOMMODATIONS AND FOOD. Finding a bed in Sagres is not hard; windows everywhere display multilingual signs for rooms. Singles and doubles range from €15-30, and triples from €25-40, with lower rates in winter. Use caution if considering the offers of residents at the bus station; prices tend to run a little higher than those on Av. Comandate Matoso and rooms could be outside the main city. To stay within city limits, try **Atalaia Apartamentos ❷,** on R. Patrão António Faustino, just off the main drag. The spacious beach-themed rooms match the blue and yellow painted tiles adorning the hallway. The apartments boast full kitchen, bath, living room, and terrace. (☎282 62 46 81. July-Sept. doubles €40, Oct.-June doubles €30. July-Sept. 2-person apartments €60, 3-4-person apartments €80-90. Apr.-June €40/50-60; Oct.-Mar. €30/40-50.) Sagres strictly forbids open-air **camping** due to its strong winds. Campers can legally get their fix of the outdoors at the isolated **Orbitur Campground ❶**, 2.5km toward Cabo de São Vicente, just off ER 268 and about a 25min. walk to the lesser-known Praia do Belixe. (☎282 62 43 71; fax 62 44 45. Reception 8am-10pm. June-Aug. €4.30 per person, €4.60 per tent, €3.80 per car. Sept.-May €4.10/4.30/3.40.) For groceries, try **Alisuper**, a larger supermarket on R. Comandante Matoso (☎282 62 44 87; open daily 9am-8pm). **❷O Dromedário Bistro ❷**, on R. Comandante Matoso, is a Moroccan-inspired haven for vegetarians and meat-lovers alike. With an extensive bar, constant stream of early 90s American pop/rock, and free Internet (ask the bartender for the code), this hip restaurant/bar is a gem. Try the hearty crepes (€2.40-5.30), inventive sandwiches (€2.10-6.70), and any one of the array of fresh fruit juices and shakes (€2-3.50). The bar is a night hot spot, especially on Karaoke Thursdays. (☎282 62 42 19; www.dromedariosagres.com. Restaurant open daily 10am-midnight. Bar open daily in winter until 2am; in summer 3am.)

❻❼ SIGHTS AND ENTERTAINMENT. Near town, the ❽**Fortaleza de Sagres** divides the famed Ponta de Sagres that grips both coasts of the jutting peninsula with its far-reaching walls. The fort, once home to Prince Henry the Navigator, is an integral part of every visit to Sagres, not for its history but for the seascape it looks out upon. (Open daily May-Sept. 9:30am-8pm; Oct.-Apr. 9:30am-5:30pm. Closed May 1 and Dec. 25. €3, under 25 €1.50.)

Several swimmer-friendly **beaches** fringe the peninsula, the most prominent of which is **Marota**, at the bottom of the road from the town center. Craggy rock formations bookend this sandy crescent. Mareta is popular for its length and isolation, but remember that Sagres is known for its windiness, and this beach is no exception. Less than a mile up the coast from Praia da Baleeira is **Praia de Martinhal**, widely-acclaimed for its windsurfing. Less windy **Praia da Belixe** is located 3km outside of town on the way to Cabo de São Vicente.

With the last traces of sunlight snuffed out, rock music and crowds fill the lively **Rosa dos Ventos** in Pr. da República. (☎282 62 44 80. Beer €1-2. Mixed drinks €3-5. Famous *sangria* €5.50. Open M-Tu and Th-Su 10am-2am.) Another hot spot is **Água Salgada**, on R. Comandante Matoso, pulsing with house and dance mixes spun by a live DJ. Free Wi-Fi, card games, and a foosball table in the back room provide entertainment off the dance floor. (☎282 62 42 97. Beer from €1.50. Cocktails €4.50-5. Shots €2. Open daily 10am-4am. Sept.-May closed Tu.) Next door is **O Dromedário** (see **Accommodations and Food,** p. 674), where trendy young locals let loose. A projector screen plays surf movies while the DJ keeps the party moving with the likes of Lynyrd Skynyrd and REM. Burgers, crepes, and specials available. (☎282 62 42 97. Beer €1-2. Daiquiris and coladas €3.50-5. Open daily in summer 10pm-3am; in winter Th and Su 10am-2am, F-Sa 10am-4am.)

ALBUFEIRA   ☎289

Sandwiched between two hills, Albufeira's landscape is covered in sprawling hotel and condominium developments. The lively international nightlife includes such stellar (impersonation) performances as the Rolling Stones and Neil Diamond. But don't let the hype and glamour of Swedish hotels and English pubs scare you off; you are in the Algarve, and that means fabulous beach space. Soak it up, especially since your hotel is most likely only a 5min. walk from the shore.

TRANSPORTATION. EVA buses (10min., hourly 7:05am-8:20pm, €1.50) connect the **train station** (☎289 57 26 91) and **bus station** (☎289 58 97 55) to the town center 6km away. Trains to: Faro (1hr., 8 per day 7:17am-11:10pm, €5); Lagos (1hr., 8 per day 7:38am-9:17pm, €4); Lisboa (3-5½hr., 5-7 per day 6:06am-6:28pm, €13.50); Olhão (1hr.; M-F 9 per day 7:17am-10:31pm, Sa-Su 6-7 per day 8:13am-10:31pm; €2.20); Vila Real de Santo António (1½-2¼hr., 7-9 per day 8:13am-10:31pm, €5). The EVA bus station is in nearby Caliços. **Buses** head to: Faro (40min., 7 per day 7:05am-6:35pm, €3.60); Lagos (1½hr., 6 per day 8:50am-6:25pm, €4.35); Lisboa (3½-4hr., 4 per day, 9:20am-7:50pm; 6 per day M-F 7:05am-7:50pm, €15). Or grab a ride from **Táxi Rádio** (☎298 58 32 30).

ORIENTATION AND PRACTICAL INFORMATION. Albufeira spreads along the Atlantic, with **R. Latino Coelho, R. Bernardino Sousa, and R. da Bateria** bordering the coast. **R. 5 de Outubro** and **Av. da Liberdade** run perpendicular to the ocean and separate the town's busy cafe- and bar-filled section to the east from the slightly calmer area to the west. From the new bus station, it is at least a 20min. trek to the town center. Take the blue or green line (not the 40min. city-sweeping red line) of the Giro city bus from the station to Av. da Liberdade (every 20min. 9am-8pm, €1.50). To reach the **tourist office**, R. 5 de Outubro, 8, follow Av. da Liberdade downhill to Tr. 5 de Outubro and take a right. Turn left when this small street intersects R. 5 de Outubro. The staff offers maps and info on water sports, including fishing and scuba diving. (☎289 58 52 79. Open M-F 9:30am-12:30pm and 1:30-5:30pm.) Local services include: **banks,** surrounding the tourist hub Lg. Eng. Duarte Pacheco; **police** (☎289 58 33 10) on Av. 25 de Abril; **Farmácia Piedade** (☎289 51 22 54) on R. João de Deus, open daily until 7:30pm and posts listings of on-call pharmacies; **Centro de Saúde** in nearby Caliços (☎289 59 84 00). **Internet** access can be found in the Shopping Center California, R. Cândido dos Reis, 1. (☎289 00 15 33. €1.50 per 30min. Open daily 10am-midnight.) The **post office** is next to the tourist office on R. 5 de Outubro. (☎289 58 08 70; fax 58 32 30. Open M-F 9am-12:30pm and 2:30-6pm.) **Postal Code:** 8200.

ACCOMMODATIONS AND FOOD. Most lodgings in Albufeira are booked solid by package tours from late June through mid-September. To find a room, head to R. Cemitério Velho, R. do Saco, R. Igreja Nova, and R. Igreja Velha; looking expectantly at anyone around and saying "Quartos?" will automatically start the room process. Some of the rooms can be far away from the center–make sure to see the room before agreeing to anything, settle on a price, and get a receipt for your stay. **Pensão Dianamar ❸**, R. Latino Coelho, 36, is close to the beach but removed from the commotion. It features a charming courtyard, kitchen, TV lounge, and bright, white rooms with bath. (☎289 58 78 01. Breakfast included. July singles €28-35; doubles €38-45. Aug. €30-40/50-65. June and Sept. €25-30/35-43. Mar.-May and Oct. €20-25/30-33. Closed Nov.-Feb.) Open-air camping is illegal, but travelers can pay for **Parque de Campismo de Albufeira ❶**, 2km outside town on the road to nearby Ferreiras. With a stone moat, three swimming pools, restaurant, tennis courts, supermarket, and a dance club, it's more like a resort than a campground. (☎289 58 76 29; fax 58 76 33. May 16-Sept. €5.20 per person, €4.70 per car, €5.30 per tent. Oct.-May 15 50% discount. AmEx/MC/V.)

For fresh produce and seafood, check out the **mercado municipal.** Follow R. da Figueira from the main bus station and take a right onto Es. Vale Pedras. (Open Tu-Su 8am-1pm; Th offers the most variety.) R. 5 de Outubro offers ample options with many inexpensive, fast-service eateries. Alternatively, **O Zuca ❶**, Travessa de Malpique, is a rare local eatery. A wide variety of Algarvian entrees (read: no vegetarian options) range €5-9.50. Try the cilantro-garnished *carapau* for a truly traditional and delicious eating experience. (☎289 58 87 68. Open M-Tu and Th-Su noon-3pm and 6:30-10:30pm.) For a tapas experience made colorful by the witty staff, head to **Al'Face ❶**, R. Latino Coelho, 14. This Havana-inspired cafe doubles as a bar at night and serves a variety of tapas (€3-4) against a backdrop of Cuban and reggae beats. (☎289 50 13 24. Open daily 11am-2pm and 6pm-2am. AmEx/MC/V.)

◪ BEACHES. The constant stream of tourists that flows into Albufeira empties into the city's spectacular spread of **beaches,** ranging from the popular **Galé** and **São Rafael** (4-8km toward Lagos) to the chic local favorite **Falésia** (10km toward Faro), both accessible by car, taxi, or bus. Check the tourist office for seasonal schedules. To get to the centrally located **Inatel beach** from the main square, Lg. Eng. Duarte Pacheco, follow Av. 25 de Abril to its end and continue down R. Gago Coutinho until you hit sand. Beautiful, but packed **Praia de Albufeira** awaits through the gate to the tourist office.

⎗ ENTERTAINMENT. Bars and restaurants line all the town's streets, but all you really need to do for a great night out is head for R. Cândido dos Reis where the young, lively crowd hangs out. Locals recommend **Atrium Bar,** R. Cândido dos Reis, 7, especially for no-holds-barred karaoke. (Karaoke nightly 9pm-4am. Beer €3.50. Mixed drinks €6-7.50. Light food served until 11pm. Open daily 6pm-4am.) **Classic Bar,** R. Cândido dos Reis, 10, is a rocking spot with elaborately concocted drinks. You're sure to blend in with the anglophone clientele. (☎289 51 20 75. Beer €2-3. Mixed drinks €5-7.50. Open daily June-Sept. noon-4am; Oct.-May noon-midnight.)

FARO   ☎289

Stepping off the bus in Faro (pop. 55, 000), visitors are greeted by McDonald's arches and a run-of-the-mill chain sandwich shop. Don't let these sights discourage you, however; a few blocks down, the street spills out into a square overlooking a tightly-packed marina, the lifeline of the city for centuries. Visitors can take advantage of a pedestrian shopping district, museums of all sorts, a quiet historical neighborhood in the *cidade velha* (old city), and beaches on the estuary's island.

▐ TRANSPORTATION

Flights: Aeroporto de Faro (☎289 80 08 00, flight info 80 08 01; www.ana.pt/portal/page/portal/ana/aeroporto_faro), 4km west of the city, has a **car rental, tourist info booth, bank, police station,** and **post office.** Open daily 10am-midnight. Buses #14 and 16 run there from opposite the bus station (20min.; M-F 18 per day 7:10am-8:40pm, Sa-Su and holidays 12 per day 8am-7:30pm; €1.30). AEROBUS also provides a shuttle service from the airport into the city center June-Oct. Check with the airport beforehand to make sure the shuttle is operating.

Trains: Lg. da Estação (☎289 82 64 72), near the center of town next to the bus station, not to be confused with a secondary station in Faro 2km away. Free **Internet** access available at 2 kiosks. To: **Albufeira** (30min., 5 per day 6:45am-6:05pm, €1.90); **Beja** (2½hr.; M-F 3 per day 9:10am-3:32pm, Sa-Su 9:10am and 2:10pm; €10); **Évora** (4½-6hr.; M-F and Su 3-4 per day 6:45am-4:04pm, Sa 6:45 and 9:10am; €13); **Lagos** (1½hr., 9 per day 7:12am-8:11pm, €16.85); **Vila Real de Santo António** (1hr., 11 per day 7:34am-11:25pm, €5.50).

Buses: EVA, Av. da República (☎289 89 97 00. Open daily 7am-11pm). To: **Albufeira** (1hr.; M-F 15 per day 6:30am-7:15pm, Sa-Su 9 per day 7:20am-6:45pm; €3.50); **Beja** (3-3½hr., 5 per day 8:30am-5pm, €10); **Huelva** (3½hr.; 8:20am, 3:35pm; €8); **Lagos** (2hr., 7 per day 8am-5:30pm, €4.30); **Olhão** (20min., every 20-40min. 7:15am-8:35pm, €1.57); **Tavira** (1hr., 11 per day 7:15am-7:30pm, €2.50); **Vila Real de Santo António** (1½hr., 9 per day 7:15am-6:20pm, €3.70). **Renex,** Av. da República

ALGARVE AND ALENTEJO

(☎289 81 29 80), provides long-distance service to **Braga** (8½hr., 9 per day 5:30am-1:30am, €22.50) and **Porto** (7½hr., 6-13 per day 5:30am-1:30am, €22) via **Lisboa** (4hr., 9 per day, €15). €2-2.50 discount with ISIC.

Taxis: Táxis Rotáxi (☎289 89 57 95). Beige, poorly marked taxis gather near Jardim Manuel Bívar (by the tourist office) and at the bus and train stations.

✴ ☊ ORIENTATION AND PRACTICAL INFORMATION

Faro's center, like the storks that trim its skyline, nestles against the **Doca de Recreio**, a marina lined with luxurious ships and bordered by the **Jardim Manuel Bívar** and **Praça Dr. Francisco Gomes**. The lively, walkable shopping district is tucked between Pr. Ferreira de Almeda and R. da Misericórdia, near the entrance to the old city. From the train or bus stations, turn right and follow Av. da República toward the harbor. Enter the **cidade velha**, or old city, with its ancient walls and cathedral, through the **Arco da Vila**, a stone passageway next to the tourist office on the far side of the garden bordering Pr. Dr. Francisco Gomes.

Tourist Office: R. da Misericórdia, 8 (☎289 80 36 04). From the bus or train station, turn right down Av. da República along the harbor, then left at the garden. English and French spoken. Open daily May-Sept. 9:30am-12:30pm and 2-7pm; Oct.-Apr. 9:30am-12:30pm and 2-5:30pm. **Regional office,** Av. 5 de Outubro, 18-20 (☎289 80 04 00). Open M-F 9am-7pm.

Currency Exchange: Cotacâmbios, R. Dr. Francisco Gomes, 26 (☎289 82 57 35). Open daily June-Sept. 9am-8pm; Oct.-May 9am-7pm.

Laundromat: Sólimpa, R. Batista Lopes, 30 (☎289 82 29 81). Wash and dry €7 for 4kg, €1.75 per additional kg. Open M-F 9am-1pm and 3-7pm, Sa 9am-1pm.

Police: R. Polícia da Segurança Pública (☎289 82 20 22).

Pharmacy: Farmácia Caminé, R. Dr. F. Gomes, 14 (☎289 82 22 77). Open M-F 9am-8pm, Sa 9am-1pm.

Hospital: R. Leão Penedo (☎289 89 11 00), just north of town across from the old soccer stadium. **Centro de Saúde** (☎289 83 03 00). Open daily 8am-8pm.

Internet Access: Free at the **Instituto Português de Juventude,** next to the youth hostel (☎289 89 18 20). Max. 30min. Open M-F 9am-8pm.

Post Office: Lg. do Carmo (☎289 89 25 90), across from Igreja do Carmo. Open M-F 8:30am-6:30pm, Sa 9am-12:30pm. **Postal Code:** 8000.

 THE EASY TICKET. Many banks, post offices, and Internet cafes operate on a system that assigns customers numbered tickets and calls them up in order. Look out for ticket machines and keep an eye on what locals are doing—you'll save yourself some embarrassment.

☊ ACCOMMODATIONS

Lodgings surround the bus and train stations, as well as the pedestrian streets of R. Vasco de Gama, R. de Santo Antonio, and R. Conselheiro Bivar. Most of the low-end budget *pensões* are plain but adequate.

Pousada da Juventude (HI), R. Polícia de Segurança Pública (☎289 82 65 21; faro@movijovem.pt). A 15min. walk from the bus station. From the tourist office, follow R. da Misericórdia as it turns into R. Alexandre Herculano, then Brites de Almeida. Pass through Lg. do Pé da Cruz onto R. da Trindade, then take the 1st right onto R. da PSP.

Large patio and TV common room are great spots to trade stories. Basic, industrial-looking interior and shared bathrooms, but still the best deal in town. Free breakfast. July-Aug. dorms €13; doubles €28, with bath €36. Sept.-June €9/22/25. AmEx/MC/V. ❶

Pensão Emília, R. Reitor Teixeira Guedes, 21 (☎289 80 19 62). Tiled facade, large windows, and dark wood furnishings contribute to the pension's Old World charm. Oct.-June singles €15; doubles €25. Prices vary July-Sept. call ahead. Cash only. ❷

Pensão-Residencial Oceano, Tr. Ivens, 21, 2nd fl. (☎289 82 33 49). From Pr. Dr. Francisco Gomes, head up R. 1 de Maio. A little out of the way, but rooms are pleasant and have bath, phone, and TV. July-Sept. 15 singles €40; doubles €50; triples €65. Sept. 16-June €25/35/45. AmEx/MC/V. ❹

Residencial Madalena, R. Conselheiro Bívar, 109 (☎289 80 58 06), close to the train and bus stations. Follow R. Gil Eanes to R. Infante Dom Henrique and take a right. 21 simply decorated rooms, some with TV. Breakfast €2.50. July-Sept. 15 singles €35, with bath €50; doubles €50/60. Sept. 16-June €20/25/35/40. Cash only. ❸

▟ FOOD

Pizzerias and sandwich shops abound along **Rua Conselheiro Bívar** and **Praça Dr. Francisco Gomes,** but be wary of overpriced pre-made meals. The true Faro flavor comes out a few blocks from the shopping district, where you'll find restaurants that cater to local families. At the **market** in Lg. Dr. Francisco Sá Carneiro fishermen peddle the day's catches. (Open daily 7am-3pm.) The **Supermercado Garrafeira Rui,** Praça Ferreira de Almeida, 28, boasts the city's best selection of port wine. (☎289 82 15 86. Open M-F 10am-7pm.) Always a quick, cheap option, the **Alisuper** grocery store, Lg. de Carmo, is to the right when facing the church. (☎289 82 49 20. Open M-Sa 8:30am-8pm, Su 9am-1pm. AmEx/MC/V.)

▨ **Restaurante São Domingo,** R. da Trindade, 10. Serving local fish and meat dishes, this small restaurant is recommended and frequented by locals. Entrees €5.50-8. Bottle of house wine €4. Open daily 10am-midnight. Cash only. ❶

O Gargalo, Lg. Pé da Cruz, 30 (☎289 82 42 64). Flip to the back page of the menu for an extensive list of gourmet pizzas (€8-9). order the homemade mozzarella-covered garlic bread as a starter; a small feeds two people while leaving enough room for the gigantic main course (€2.50, large €5). Open daily 10am-midnight. ❷

GIVING BACK

STATELY STORKS

A hollow clatter fills the air. Guarding your eyes from Faro's afternoon sun, you see a monstrous bearded silhouette atop a woody perch. Meet the white stork, a migratory bird native to Europe, the Middle East, South Africa, and west-central Asia.

Year after year, the storks come to Faro and construct grandiose nests, sometimes creating abodes more than 2m in diameter. Some nests, built on manmade structures since the Middle Ages and expanded annually, have been used for centuries.

Increased pollution, pesticide use, and wetland drainage have endangered the foragers' eating and breeding grounds, leading to population decline, especially in Western Europe. Catch-and-release efforts yielded semi-domesticated storks that forego migration to feast on the abundant fish and shellfish in Faro's marina and beaches. Locals welcome these prehistoric-looking neighbors, but the birds' tendency to nest on power lines—a tendency that led to the electrocution of a stork and the subsequent blackout of the all southern Portugal in 2000—is inauspicious for avian and human residents alike. As such, the Sociedade Portuguesa para o Estudo das Aves (SPEA) has initiated volunteer groups to monitor and help move nests located on or near power lines. *E-mail spea@spea.pt or call ☎213 22 04 30 and get involved!*

VISA VIDA

In Faro's Cemitério dos Judeus you may notice a small plaque thanking Dr. Aristides de Sousa Mendes, the former Portuguese consul, for helping Jews escape Nazism. Though the one-sentence note is easily overlooked and the significance of the 18 cypresses planted in the doctor's honor easily missed, the doctor's sacrifice is etched in the hearts of the 33,000 people he helped flee from Hitler's persecution.

Sent by neutral Portugal to Bordeaux, France at the outbreak of WWII, de Sousa Mendes happened upon one Rabbi Kruger, who explained how Jews were being tormented and killed by the Nazis. Torn between the obligations of his conscience and his post, de Sousa Mendes chose the former, hand-writing and stamping over 30,000 visas with the Rabbi's help.

Portuguese emissaries, hearing of these "backdoor" visas, forcibly removed the consul from his post; even as he was being dragged back to Portugal de Sousa Mendes stopped the driver at the sight of thousands more pleading for aid.

De Sousa Mendes was shunned for jeopardizing the nation's neutrality, and lived in poverty for the rest of his life with his wife and 14 children, but he had no regrets. "If thousands of Jews can suffer because of one Catholic [Hitler]," he said, "then surely it is permitted for one Catholic to suffer for so many Jews."

O Ribatejano, R. São Luis, 32A (☎289 81 21 10; www.ribatejano.net). A rare gem in carnivorous Portugal. Chef whips up protein-conscious vegetarian platters delicious enough to rival classic fare. Entrees €4.60-9. Open daily 7-11pm. Cash only. ❶

Mister Frango, R. Cruz das Mestras, 51 (☎289 82 84 44). From R. Santo António, turn left on R. Portugal and follow it 2 blocks. The name—and the mouth-watering aroma—says it all: *Frango assado* (roast chicken) as only the Portuguese can make it. Secondary door for picnic-style dining and a €6.50 meal of a salty half-chicken, bed of fries, drink, and dessert or coffee. Open daily noon-2:30pm and 7-10:30pm. Cash only. ❶

Crepería, Pr. Ferreira d'Almeida, 27, at the end of R. 1 de Maio. Gourmet options from basic ham/tomato/cheese to the house specialty: kiwi, pineapple, banana, orange, and chantilly cream (€1.80-7). Also serves a few pasta dishes and many vegetarian options. Open M-Sa Oct.-June 8:30am-8pm; July-Sept. 8:30am-midnight. Cash only. ❶

🖸 SIGHTS

Faro's *Vila-Adentro,* a medley of ornate churches and museums punctuated by shops selling local handicrafts and houses of multi-generational families, is an uncorrupted haven for those looking for a slice of the Old World. As you walk through the **Arco da Vila,** look to the right to see the city's only remaining Moorish door. At the end of a sweltering day, seek refuge in the **Jardim Alameda João de Deus,** next door to the Pousada da Juventude, where you can relax under lush tropical greenery. (Open daily 8am-8pm. Mini-golf €0.27.)

🖼 CAPELA DOS OSSOS. The Capela dos Ossos (Chapel of Bones) in the courtyard of the **Igreja de Nossa Senhora** was built to commemorate the monks who were formerly buried behind the church. Brace yourself before you look up; the walls and ceiling were constructed with over 1245 skulls and countless other bones. (*Lg. do Carmo.* ☎289 82 44 90. Open May-Sept. M-F 10am-1pm and 3-6pm, Sa 10am-1pm; Oct.-Apr. M-F 10am-1pm and 3-5pm, Sa 10am-1pm. Su mass 8:30am. Chapel €1, church free.)

CATEDRAL (SÉ). A narrow road climbs up from the Arco da Vila to a square lined with orange trees and blindingly white buildings, home to Faro's cathedral, a compilation of Roman, Moorish, and Catholic architecture. The original Roman frame sits within the expanded cathedral walls, and its main altar, ablaze with multi-levels of gilded icons, is sandwiched between two Moorish chapels. The tower is easy to climb and provides a fantastic vantage point to admire the town's seascape and landscape peppered with stork nests. The small museum displays a limited selection of religious artifacts, but Sr. Zacariah, who often hangs out by the cathedral's gate, will tell you the church's history more comprehensively than any museum. *(☎289 80 66 32. Open M-F 10am-6pm, Sa 10am-1pm. Museum €3.)*

CEMITÉRIO DOS JUDEUS. One of a few Jewish cemeteries left in Europe, this cemetery is dedicated to the memory not only of those buried within, but also to the courageous Dr. Aristides de Sousa Mendes (see p. 680), who helped Jews escape Nazism. The scattered marble gravestones were restored in 1952 and serve as symbols of one community's long, often painful, history. *(R. Leão Penedo, between the hospital and the soccer stadium. A 20min. walk from the tourist office. Cemetery and small museum open M-F 9:30am-12:30pm. Free.)*

◪ ◙ BEACHES AND NIGHTLIFE

Faro's sandy beach, **Praia de Faro,** hides on an islet off the coast with the **Parque Natural da Ria Formosa** on one side. Take bus #16 from the bus station, the stop in front of the tourist office, or under the blue bus sign near Pousada da Juventude. From Faro, you can also explore Portugal's southernmost point, the beautiful **Ilha Deserta;** boats leave from Faro's central pier. (www.ilha-deserta.com. 30min.; 4 per day 10am-4:15pm, last return from the island at 6pm; €7.) Sidewalk **cafes** crowd the pedestrian walkways off the garden in the town center, and several **bars** liven R. Conselheiro Bívar and its side streets in July and August (the bar scene is pretty dead for the rest of the year). **O Conselheiro,** in the middle of R. Conselheiro Bívar, is a great chill-out spot with a youthful ambience, a pool table, and excellent music that often turns the bar into a dance floor. (Beer €1.50. Mixed drinks €4-5.50. Karaoke W, F. 18+. Open daily 10pm-4am. AmEx/MC/V.) Alternatively, just a couple of streets away, you can toast to revolution at **Chessenta Bar,** R. do Prior, 24. (☎918 74 58 37. Beer €1.50. Mixed drinks €3-5. Open daily 10pm-4am. Cash only.)

OLHÃO ☎289

Olhão (ol-YOWN, pop. 31,000), though it blatantly caters to tourism, takes pride in its status as the largest, most productive fishing port in the Algarve. The port stretches along the coast, paralleled by a strip of pork and fish restaurants nearly as long and twice as welcoming. The buildings are peeling and the historic sights are few, but the region's natural beauty, friendly locals, bird sanctuary, and necklace of unspoiled islands (see **Daytrips,** p. 683) make the port town worth a trip.

▣ TRANSPORTATION. The **train station** is on Av. dos Combatentes da Grande Guerra, one block from Av. da República. (☎289 72 17 00. Open daily 6am-9pm.) **Trains** run to Faro (10min., 9-16 per day 6:37am-9:40pm, €1); Tavira (30min., 6-16 per day 8:16am-12:04am, €1.55); Vila Real de Santo António (1hr., 10-11 per day 8:45am-12:33am, €2.90). The **bus station** is on R. General Humberto Delgado, one block from Av. da República. (☎289 70 21 57. Open M-F 7am-7:30pm, Sa 7:05am-12:40pm and 1:30-6:30pm, Su and holidays 7:45am-12:40pm and 1:30-6:30pm.) **EVA buses** run to Faro (20min., 13 per day 7:35am-7:50pm, €1.50); Tavira (40min., 11 per day 8:15am-8:30pm, €2); Vila Real de Santo António (1hr., 9 per day 8:55am-8pm, €3.25).

▦ ◪ ORIENTATION AND PRACTICAL INFORMATION. To reach the **tourist office** from the train station, turn left onto Av. dos Combatentes da Grande

Guerra and take a right onto **Avenida da República** past the Palácio da Justiça (5min.). From the bus station, turn right down R. General Humberto Delgado and then take another right onto Av. da República. Once on Av. da República, go straight until you reach Olhão's main church. Here, Av. da República splits into three streets—take the middle path, R. do Comércio, which turns into a pedestrian street. Continue as far as possible, following the street right as it turns into R. da Lagoa. After a block, the street becomes a little plaza, Lg. Sebastião Martins Mestre, and the tourist office (8A) is directly opposite the Câmara Municipal. Its English-speaking staff has maps and ferry schedules. (☎289 71 39 36. Open M-F 9:30am-1pm and 2-5:30pm.) Free **Internet** access is at **Olhão Internet** on Tr. do Gaibeu, at the end of R. Téofilo Braga. (☎289 70 10 40. 30min. limit. Open M-F 10am-10pm, Sa 10am-8pm.) **Lavanderia Olhanese**, R. Téofilo Braga, 54, across from Pensão Bela Vista, does laundry for €2 per kg, with a 4kg min. (☎289 70 26 41. Open M-F 9am-1pm and 3-7pm, Sa 9am-1pm.) Other services include: **police**, R. 5 de Outubro, 178 (☎289 71 07 70); local **Centro de Saúde**, off R. Antero Nobre (☎289 70 02 60); **Farmácia Rocha**, R. do Comércio, 120 (☎289 70 30 85), with a list of all of Olhão's pharmacies, their numbers, and their hours; and the **post office** at Av. da República, 17 (☎289 70 06 03; open M-F 8:30am-6pm). **Postal Code:** 8700.

⌂⍁ ACCOMMODATIONS AND FOOD. To live like a king on a pauper's budget, head to ▧ **Pensão Bicuar ❷**, R. Vasco de Gama, 5, which has dark wood furnishings, chairs upholstered in red velvet, a kitchen, and a terrace with a magnificent view. All rooms have a shower and sink; toilets are available in ensuites. From the tourist office, retrace back to R. do Comércio. (☎289 71 48 16; www.pension-bicuar.net. Reception 9am-midnight. Singles €25; doubles €35; ensuite toilet €45; special backpacker doubles €30. Discount for longer stays. Cash only.) **Pensão Bela Vista ❷**, R. Teófilo Braga, 65-67, feels like a home away from home. From the tourist office, turn right onto R. Teófilo Braga. Bright rooms, each with a double and single bed. A/C, cable TV, and marble bathrooms add to your comfort. (☎289 70 25 38. July-Aug. singles €25, with bath €35; doubles €40/45. Sept.-June singles €20/30, doubles €35/40. Cash only.) Olhão's year-round campground is the **Parque de Campismo dos Bancários do Sul e Ilhas ❶**, off the highway outside of town and accessible by the green and yellow lines of the local "CircuitOlhão" buses (6-13 per day 7:15am-7:45pm, €0.80) which stop at the bus station and in front of the gardens near the church on Av. 5 de Outubro. The campground includes a swimming pool, tennis court, supermarket, Internet access, bar, and restaurant. (☎289 70 03 00; www.sbsi.pt. Showers included. Laundry €4 per load. Electricity €1.50 per kW. June and Sept. €3.40 per person, €2.60-4 per tent, €2.75 per car. July-Aug. €4/3-4.50/ 3.30. Jan.-May and Oct.-Dec. €2.20/1.75-2.20/1.70. AmEx/MC/V.)

Supermercado São Nicolau, R. General Humberto Delgado, 62, is up the block from the bus station. (Open M-Sa 8am-8pm.) The town **market** is housed in two red brick buildings adjacent to the city gardens on R. 5 de Outubro, along the river near Pr. Patrão J. Lopes. (Open daily 9am-12:30pm and 2-5:30pm.) Many eateries on Av. 5 de Outubro, including **Restaurante O Bote ❷**, Av. 5 de Outubro, 122, serve the daily catch fresh off the boat. Enjoy the must-have tomato-herb salad (€1.50). Although meat is offered, seafood is the star here—try the traditional entrees (€5.50-10), like the scabbard fish. (☎289 72 11 83. Open M-Sa 11am-4pm and 7pm-midnight. Cash only.) Leave room for dessert at **Olhão Doce ❶**, R. do Comércio, 107. The glass display case has an astonishing variety of carefully prepared local pastries, all under €3. (Open M-Sa 8am-8:30pm. Cash only.)

🔖 DAYTRIPS FROM OLHÃO

🏝 ILHAS ARMONA, CULATRA, AND FAROL

Ferries go to Armona (30min.; July-Aug. 13 per day M-F 7:30am-8pm, Sa-Su 8am-8pm; June and Sept. M-F 9 per day 7:40am-7:30pm, Sa-Su 11 per day 8am-7:30pm; Oct.-May 3 per day 8:30am-5pm; last return July-Aug. 8:30pm, June 8pm; €2.60). Another fleet serves Culatra (45min.; June-Aug. every 2hr. 7am-7:30pm, Sept.-May 4 per day 7am-6:30pm, last return June-Aug. 8pm; €2.40) and Farol (1hr.; June-Aug. every 2hr. 7am-7:30pm, Sept.-May 4 per day 7am-6:30pm; last return June-Aug. 8:20pm; €3.20).

Long expanses of uncrowded, sandy beach and a glistening blue-green surf surround the islands off Olhão's coast. **Ilhas Armona** and **Culatra,** the two major islands, and then **Farol,** trailing the far end of Culatra, are convenient daytrips from Olhão. Armona's and Farol's cottages house mostly vacationers, while Culatra remains a fishermen's village. Farol is easily the most beautiful of the islands, but none of the three has the volume of tourists seen in other sections of the Algarve. The islands and sandbars just offshore fence off the Atlantic, creating the Parque Natural da Ria Formosa, an important 80km lagoon and wetland habitat home to an impressive variety of sea creatures and bird life. During the winter, roughly one-third of Europe's flamingo population can be found here. Bungalows are available in Armona at **Camping Orbitur ❶**, on the central path 5min. from the dock, and are best for a family or group of friends willing to exchange the 30min. ferry for a late-morning sleep-in. (☎289 71 41 73. July-Aug. min. stay 4 nights; Sept.-June min. 2 nights. Cheapest bungalow sleeps 4; in summer €43-56, in winter €30-41. Cash only.) While in Armona, check out the international **Restaurante Santo António ❷** at the entrance to the beach 15min. from the dock, down the central path, popular for its specialty: grilled *chocos* (large squid) caught right off the island's coast. (☎289 70 65 49. Meals €8-11. Open Apr. 15-Sept. 15 9am-11pm. Cash only.)

QUINTA DE MARIM

Only local buses stop within reasonable walking distance of Quinta de Marim. Rodoviária buses go to the town of Marim, but will leave you stranded on the highway, far from the park. Local CircuitOlhão buses drop you at "Parque de Campismo," and then it's a 3min. walk over the train tracks to the park's main gates. Take the green line from the bus station or across from the gardens near the church on Av. 5 de Outubro (10min.; M-F 13 per day 7:15am-7:15pm, Sa 6 per day 8:15am-1:15pm; €0.80). To get back to Olhão, take the yellow line, which stops across the street from the green line in front of the campground (10min.; M-F 13 per day 8:30am-8:30pm, Sa 7 per day 8:30am-2:30pm; €0.80). Reception/front gate open M-F 8am-8pm and Sa-Su 10:30am-6pm (☎289 70 02 10). Visitors center open M-F 9am-5:30pm. €1.50 per person, students and under 18 €0.75.

A serene, isolated escape to nature, **Quinta de Marim** was created in 1987 as a representative sample of the larger **Ria Formosa Natural Park.** An internationally-recognized protected wetland, the park provides a haven for many endangered birds and fish. On the 3km walking trail, you'll find salt marshes, sand dunes, fields, and pine forests, as well as paths through blooming rhododendron bushes. The park, originally created for conservation and educational purposes, is now suffering from governmental neglect; funds are being diverted to other projects. The bird specialists, however, are not deterred by the decrease in funding. The hospital is still fully functional and, though prolonged human contact tames the birds and is detrimental to their redistribution, the doctors gladly oblige eager visitors looking for a more hands-on experience. Visitors can also play with the two champion 🔖**Portuguese water dogs** in the park's kennel. (Open M-F 11am-1pm and 2-4pm.)

ALENTEJO

Vast golden plains spotted with giant stone castles and tiny red-roofed villages cover the region between the Tagus and the Algarve. A sharp contrast to the commotion of Lisboa or the wilds of the Algarve, the Alentejo graces travelers with a more stately, historical setting. Évora, Elvas, and other remarkably well-preserved towns lie in the Alto Alentejo, while Beja remains the only major town on the seemingly endless Baixo Alentejo plain. The region is known primarily for its cork; more than two-thirds of the world's supply comes from here, and the local villages specialize in cork handicrafts. The area is best in the spring; fiery temperatures can turn the Alentejo into an oven in summer.

ÉVORA   ☎266

Évora (pop. 55,000) is the capital and largest city of the Alentejo region. The historical center is completely enclosed by ancient walls, housing palaces, churches, and Roman ruins. The city is also famous for its chilling medieval approach to recycling (see **Capela dos Ossos,** p. 686). Across the city, mock burials decorate the sidewalks in lieu of benches. During the school year, University of Évora (UÉ) students enliven the town, especially during the *Queima das Fitas* (Burning of the Ribbons), a week-long graduation celebration during the last week of May with live music, dancing, and drunken merriment. The town remains surprisingly active during the summer, despite the absence of most students and the locals' inclinations to vacation on the coast.

⌐ TRANSPORTATION

Trains: Lg. da Estação de CP, at Av. dos Combatentes de Grande Guerra (☎266 70 21 25 or 808 20 82 08; www.cp.pt). Service to **Beja** (1½hr., 5 per day 5:55am-7:10pm, €6.40-11.40), **Faro** (5hr.; 6:22am, 12:44pm; €12.80-19.80), and **Lisboa** (2½hr., 4-6 per day 5:55am-7:10pm, €11.10).

Buses: Av. São Sebastião (☎266 76 94 10), 300m outside the town wall. More convenient schedules than trains. Buses go to: **Beja** (1½hr.; 6 per day 8:45am-10:45pm, F also 11:15pm; €7); **Braga** (8-10hr.; 8 per day 6am-8:45pm, Su also 9:30pm; €20) via **Porto** (6-8½hr.; 10 per day 6am-8:45pm, Su also 9:30pm; €19); **Castelo Branco** (2-3hr., 6 per day 6am-5pm, €11.90); **Elvas** (1½hr.; 12:15am, 1:45, 5, 9:05pm; €9.50); **Faro** (4hr.; 8:45am, 2:30, 5:15pm; €13.50); **Lisboa** (2hr.; 20 per day 6am-8:45pm, Su also 9:30pm; €10.80); **Portalegre** (1½hr., 5 per day 1:30-8:15pm, €10); **Setúbal** (1¾hr.; 8:30, 10:15am, 2pm; €9.50).

Taxis: (☎266 73 47 34). 24hr. taxis wait in Pr. do Giraldo.

✴🛈 ORIENTATION AND PRACTICAL INFORMATION

To reach **Praça do Giraldo** from the **bus station** (15min. walk), turn right up Av. São Sebastião, keeping the small white wall to the right, and continue straight when it turns into R. Serpa Pinto at the city wall. Follow this road into Pr. do Giraldo, the center of the city. All major sites are a short walk from this square. No direct bus connects the **train station** to the center of town. By foot, go up Av. Dr. Baronha and continue straight as it turns into R. da República at the city wall. To avoid either walk, hail a taxi (€3).

Tourist Office: Pr. do Giraldo, 73 (☎266 77 70 71; www.cm-evora.pt/guiaturistico). Staff speaks English, French, and Spanish and provides maps and lists of restaurants.

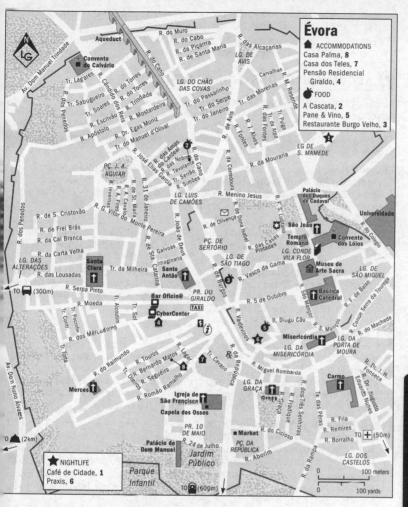

Évora

⌂ ACCOMMODATIONS
Casa Palma, **8**
Casa dos Teles, **7**
Pensão Residencial
Giraldo, **4**

🍴 FOOD
A Cascata, **2**
Pane & Vino, **5**
Restaurante Burgo Velho, **3**

★ NIGHTLIFE
Café de Cidade, **1**
Praxis, **6**

Self-guided audio tours of the city €2, due back before 5pm. Wheelchair accessible. Open daily May-Oct. 9am-7pm; Nov.-Apr. 9am-6pm.

Currency Exchange: 24hr. **ATM** outside the tourist office. Several banks line Pr. do Giraldo, all open M-F 8:30am-3pm.

Police: R. Francisco Soares Lusitano (☎266 70 20 22).

Pharmacy: Farmácia Galeno, R. da República, 34 (☎266 70 32 77). Open M-F 9am-1pm and 3-7pm.

Hospital: Hospital do Espírito Santo, Lg. Senhor Jesus da Pobreza (☎266 74 01 00 or 266 75 84 24), near the city wall and the intersection with R. Dr. Augusto Eduardo Nunes.

Internet Access: CyberCenter, R. dos Mercadores, 42 (☎266 74 69 23). 20 high-speed computers. €2 per hour. Open M-F 10:30am-11pm, Sa-Su 2-10pm. **Bar Ofi-**

cin@, R. Moeda, 27 (☎266 70 73 12). Only 1 computer, so expect to wait. €0.50 per 10min., €2.50 per hour. Open Tu-F 8pm-2am, Sa 9pm-2am.

Post Office: R. de Olivença (☎266 74 54 80; fax 74 54 86). **Posta Restante** and **fax.** Open M-F 8:30am-6pm. **Postal Code:** 7999.

ACCOMMODATIONS AND CAMPING

Most accommodations cluster on side streets off Pr. do Giraldo and are well-advertised. They're crowded in the summer, especially during graduation in May and the *Feira de São João,* the celebration of Évora's patron saint (June 18-30). Private *quartos,* about €25-30 per double, are pleasant summer alternatives to the crowded *pensões;* check with the tourist office for listings.

■ **Casa Palma,** R. Bernardo Matos, 29A (☎266 70 35 60). Located right off Pr. da República. The house is over 100 years old and looks like an antiques market. The grandmotherly owner keeps it in excellent shape and offers reasonable prices for petite rooms on the top floor. Singles €15-25; doubles €30-35. Cash only. ❷

Casa dos Teles, R. Romão Ramalho, 27 (☎266 70 24 53), 1 block off Pr. do Giraldo. The friendly dog gives this private home a welcoming feel. Many spacious rooms are decorated with pictures from around town. Reserve ahead. June-Sept. singles €25; doubles €35, with bath €40; triples €37/40. Oct.-May €5 less. Cash only. ❷

Pensão Residencial Giraldo, R. dos Mercadores, 27 (☎266 70 58 33). Spacious, comfortable rooms have TV and carpeting. Clean rooms with A/C make for a refuge from the streets outside. Reserve ahead. In summer singles €25, with bath €35; doubles €35/45; triples €55. In winter €5-10 less. Cash only. ❷

FOOD

Restaurants are scattered near Pr. do Giraldo, especially along **Rua dos Mercadores the** and the small streets off **Rua 5 de Outubro,** but many are tourist-oriented; to find inexpensive local favorites, wander away from the center and the main sights. The **market,** near Pr. da República, sells crafts and regional goods as well as cheese and produce. (Open Tu-Su 7am-1pm.)

■ **Restaurante Burgo Velho,** R. de Burgos, 10 (☎266 70 58 58). A couple of blocks off Pr. Giraldo lies a fine example of *alentejano* cuisine. Cozy and quiet, "Old City Restaurant" offers an intimate dining experience with excellent service and large, well-presented portions. Entrees €4.50-9. Open M-Sa noon-3pm and 7-10pm. AmEx/MC/V. ❷

Pane & Vino, R. Diogo Cão, 22 (☎266 74 69 60). This popular corner restaurant's classic, thin-crust pizzas are too good to be missed. Pizzas and pasta (€6-9). Open Tu-Su noon-3pm and 7-11pm. AmEx/MC/V. ❷

A Cascata, Tr. do Tavolante, 23 (☎965 82 21 38). You won't find anything cheaper. Small selection, but entrees are only €3-4 for lunch, €4.50-7 for dinner. Complete meal with soup, bread and olives, fish or meat, dessert, and coffee €10. Open M-Sa 11:30am-3pm and 6:30-10:30pm. Cash only. ❶

SIGHTS

■ **CAPELA DOS OSSOS.** Few places on earth rival the Capela dos Ossos in spookiness. The "Chapel of Bones" warmly welcomes visitors: *"Nós ossos que aqui estamos, pelos vossos esperamos"* (We bones that are here are waiting for yours). In order to provide a hallowed space to reflect on the profundity of life and death, three Franciscan monks built this chapel from the remains of over 5000 anonymous bodies buried in surrounding churches. The walls are covered in neatly piled bones and skulls, while the three founders lie enclosed in stone sarcophagi. For thrills and chills, check out the preserved corpse hanging from one of the chapel's walls, then go give mom a call: legend has it that the body is a son cursed by his mother for disobedience and cruelty. *(Pr. 1 de Maio. Follow R. da República from Pr. do Giraldo, then take a right into Pr. 1 de Maio; enter the chapel through the door of the Convento de São Francisco to the right of the church steps. ☎266 70 45 21. Open M-Sa May-Sept. 9am-12:50pm and 2:30-5:45pm; Oct.-Apr. 9am-12:50pm and 2:30-5:15pm. An audio tour plays in several languages inside the chapel. €1.50, students €1, €0.50 more for camera use—well worth it.)*

BASÍLICA CATEDRAL. Built during the 12th century, the Basílica Catedral, also known as the Sé, looms over Évora with its two giant asymmetrical towers like a mad scientist's castle. Inside, however, its ornate carvings and splendid architecture are similar to those of other European cathedrals. Climb the cloisters' stairs to see the view of Évora from the cathedral's terrace or tour the **Museu de Arte Sacra.** *(From the center of Pr. do Giraldo, head to the end of R. 5 de Outubro. Cathedral open daily 9am-12:30pm and 2-4:30pm. €1. Cloisters open daily 9am-noon and 2-4:30pm. Museum open Tu-Su in summer 9am-4:30pm; in winter 9am-12:30pm and 2-4:30pm. Cloisters and museum €3, students €2.50. Cloisters and cathedral €1.50, cathedral only €1. July to mid-Sept. ticket includes visit to the tower.)*

TEMPLO ROMANO. Enormous and well-preserved columns of an ancient Roman temple sit in a spacious square at the highest point of the city, perpetual reminders of Évora's long history as a city of great influence. The small temple was built in the first century from local granite, but walled up in the Middle Ages and used as a slaughter house. It is widely believed, despite a lack of historical evidence, that the small temple was built in honor of the goddess Diana. *(Open daily 24hr.)*

IGREJA DE SÃO JOÃO DE EVANGELISTA AND PALÁCIO DE DUQUES DE CADAVAL. Also known as the Convento dos Loíos, the Igreja faces the Templo Romano. The church and ducal palace are owned by the Cadaval family, who restored the buildings with their personal fortunes in 1957-58. The interior of the church is covered with dazzling *azulejos*, and a beautiful cloister with an outdoor cafe is open to tourists. The main part of the convent is now used as a luxury *pousada* for guests looking for a unique overnight experience. *(Lg. Conde do Vila Flor. ☎266 74 43 00 connects you to the neighboring restaurant. Open Tu-Su 10am-12:30pm and 2-6pm. In winter closes at 5pm. €3, €5 for church and next-door exhibition hall.)*

⚑ NIGHTLIFE

Évora's nightlife is fueled largely by the students from the university, who fill the bars after midnight and then move on to the clubs. Wednesday nights are student nights at most establishments, so expect larger crowds. The cafes in Pr. do Giraldo are great for socializing and stay busy until around midnight. **Praxis,** R. Valdevinos, is the only nightclub in town, boasting four different bars and two floors for dancing. (☎933 35 57 82. Beer €1.50. Mixed drinks €4-6. Min. consumption €7 for men, €5 for women. Open daily 11pm-4am.) A warehouse-like bar/cafe, **Café de Cidade,** R. das Alca Carias, 1, swarms with local crowds. (☎266 78 51 63. Beer €1.20. Mixed drinks €3.50. Tu and Th live jazz. Open M-Sa 11am-2am. AmEx/MC/V.)

ELVAS   ☎268

Elvas (pop. 25,000) is located 13km from the Spanish border, and is surrounded by fields of vineyards. The quiet, hilly town has an inviting main square and narrow, steep cobblestone streets leading to the fortified city walls. To walk into the old portion of town is to find a lost time capsule: the traditional architecture is straight out of the 19th century. The city pulses with the vibe of a border town; mixed conversations of Portuguese and Spanish, affectionately referred to by locals as Portanhol, fills the streets. Elvas's main sight, the ◼Aqueduto da Amoreira, clearly visible from many kilometers away, marks the entrance to the city. Begun in 1498 and not finished until 1622, the colossal structure is Europe's largest aqueduct—its 843 arches extend almost 8km. The **castelo**, above Pr. da República, has a pleasant view of the aqueduct and the infinite rows of olive trees on the horizon; a stairwell to the right of the entrance leads up to the castle walls. (Castle open daily 9:30am-1pm and 2:30-5:30pm. €1.50; seniors and ages 14-25 €0.75, under 14 free.) The **Igreja de Nossa Senhora da Assunção**, better known as the **antiga Sé**, in Pr. da República, was designed by Francisco de Arruda, who was also the mind behind the great aqueduct. The *Igreja* features 17th-century *azulejos*. (☎268 62 59 97. Open M-F 10am-12:30pm and 2-5:30pm. Mass Su 6pm. Free.)

António Mocisso e Garcia Coelho ❷, R. Aires Varela, 15, is one of the most reasonably priced accommodations in town. From the tourist office, take a right out of the *praça* and then the first left; go left at the end of the street and reception is on the right. The small rooms have TV, A/C, and private baths. Reservations are recommended June-Sept. (☎268 62 21 26. Breakfast included. Check-in after noon. Singles €20; doubles €30; triples €40; quads €50. Cash only.) For camping, the **Parque de Campismo ❶** is ideal. From the bus station, follow the road that leads toward the aqueduct until the park's sign. (☎268 62 89 97. Reception daily 9am-6pm. €2.80 per person, €2.50 per car or tent. Cash only.) Fresh fish, fruit, and vegetables abound at the **mercado municipal** on Av. de São Domingos (open M-Sa 7am-1pm). ◼**O Lagar ❷**, R. Nova da Vedoria, 7, is considered the best restaurant in Elvas. Try the *bife da vitela à Lagar* (€10.50), a succulent layering of veal steak with cheese and ham in between. (☎268 62 47 93. Entrees €6.50-13.50. Open M-W and F-Su noon-4pm and 7-11pm. AmEx/MC/V.) Fans get their fill of *Frango assado* (grilled chicken) at **Canal 47 ❶**, R. dos Sapateiros, 16. Exit Pr. da República on R. dos Sapateiros next to Banco Espírito Santo, and follow the curving road to the left. Get your half-chicken to go for only €2; dine in and it's €4. (☎268 62 35 93. Entrees €3.50-7. Open M and W-Su 10am-3pm and 6-10pm. Cash only.)

The nearest **train station** (☎808 20 82 08; www.cp.pt) is in **Fontaínhas** (3km) and runs to Badajoz, Spain (17min., 12:08pm, €1.20). Service is infrequent. **Taxis** (☎268 62 22 87 or 266 73 06 90) provide the only transport to town (€5). The **bus station** (☎268 62 28 75), at the entrance of the city, is the best option, with buses going to: Beja (2½-3½hr.; M-Sa 6:40am, Su 4:30pm; €11.80); Castelo Branco (4hr.; 8:30am, 1pm; €15.50); Évora (1½hr.; 6:40, 8:30am, 6:30pm; €9.50); Faro (6½hr.; 6:40am, 4:30pm; €16); Lisboa (3hr., 8 per day 6:40am-6:30pm, €13); Portalegre (1½hr.; 8:30am, 1pm; €11). Buses stop at the entrance to the city walls. The **tourist office** is in **Praça da República**. From the bus station, take a right and go through Lg. da Misericórdia; continue up to R. da Cadeia, and after a series of fountains take a left into Pr. da República—the office is on the right (5min. walk). (☎268 62 22 36. Open Apr.-Oct. M-F 9am-7pm, Sa-Su 10am-12:30pm and 2-5:30pm; Nov.-Mar. M-F 9am-5:30pm, Sa-Su 10am-12:30pm and 2-5:30pm.) The **Banco Espírito Santo** (☎268 63 92 40; open M-F 8:30am-4:30pm) is in Pr. da República, in front of the tourist office, and has a 24hr. **ATM**. Other local services include: **police,** R. André Gonçalves (☎268 63 94 70); **Farmácia Moutta,** directly behind the tourist office (☎268 62 21 50; open daily 9am-1pm and 3-7pm); **Hospital de Santa Luzia,** Estrada Nacional, 4 (☎268 63 76 00). For **Internet** access, **Informontagem,** R. João de Casqueiro, 2, is around the corner from the museum on R. da Carreira (☎960 19 03 16; €0.50 per 10min., €0.75 per 30min., €1.50 per hour). The tourist office offers

5mln. of free Internet access. The **post office,** Lg. da Misericórdia, 1, is one block behind the tourist office. (☎268 63 90 33. Open M-F 9am-6pm.) **Postal Code:** 7350.

🔖 DAYTRIP FROM ELVAS: MARVÃO. This Portuguese candidate for UNESCO World Heritage status is one of the Alentejo's best-kept secrets. The ancient walled town of Marvão (pop. 185) floats like an island over the vast expanse of the Alentejo plains; in fact, it is the highest town in Portugal. The hills and meadows of the Parque Natural de São Mamede only add to the village's appeal. Almost all of the town's whitewashed houses are enclosed by ancient walls that have protected the village for nearly 700 years—before the walls' construction, Marvão was repeatedly seized. Marvão's noteworthy 13th-century 🔲**castelo,** atop the ridge at the west end of town, contains a museum of archaic weaponry, but the real highlight is the breathtaking view of the Alentejo's arid plains. Remnants dating as far back as the Paleolithic era are on display at the Museu Municipal, near the castle in the Igreja de Santa Maria. (☎245 90 91 32. Open daily 9am-12:30pm and 2-5:30pm. €1, students €0.75.) From Elvas, take the train to Portalegre (50min.; 5:30am, 3:07pm; €2.84), or a bus from Castelo Branco (1¼hr.; 10:45am, 2:30pm; €9) or from Évora (1¼hr.; 1:30, 5pm; €10) and a bus to Marvão (50min.; M-F 7:05am, 1:10pm; €1.60-5). The bus will drop you off just outside the town wall. Enter through a gate and walk up R. Cima until you see the stone whipping post in Pr. Pelourinho. From here, R. Espírito Santo leads toward the *castelo* and the tourist office. (☎245 99 38 86. Open Aug.-Sept. M-F 9am-7pm, Sa-Su 10am-12:30pm and 2-7pm; Oct.-July daily 9am-12:30pm and 2-5:30pm.)

BEJA   ☎284

The stunning landscape alone—seemingly endless stretches of burnt grass punctuated by olive trees, vineyards, cattle, and half-stripped cork trees—makes it worth traveling to Beja (pop. 35,000). The town's winding cobblestone streets bear the footprints of the likes of Julius Caesar and Arab poet Al-Mu'Tamid. Beja has grown into a small, modern town relatively untouched by tourism and still steeped in tradition; the sounds of late-afternoon *bocce* games echo through the squares. Though Beja can be seen in a day, it is a convenient base for a tour of the villages nearby and can serve as a calm hiatus from the hurried rhythm of traveling.

📠 TRANSPORTATION. Trains run from the **station** (☎284 32 61 35), just outside the historical center on Lg. da Estação, to: Évora (1½hr., 7 per day 6:22am-6:44pm, €8.10); Faro (3½hr.; 8:53am, 1:55pm; €8) via Funcheira; Lisboa (2½-3hr., 5 per day 8:10am-7:10pm, €8.50). Timetables and destinations can be found on the schedule cards opposite the ticket window. The **bus station** (☎284 31 36 20), open M-F 6:30am-8:30pm and Su 7:30am-8:30pm, is on R. Cidade de São Paulo, across from Av. do Brasil. Most attendants speak English. **Buses** to: Faro (3½hr., 3 per day 10:10am-7pm, €11.50); Lagos via Albufeira (3hr., 3:30pm, €11.90); Lisboa (3½hr., 6 per day 7:45am-3pm, €11.50) via Évora (3½hr., 4 per day 6:45am-6pm, €8); Portoalegre (5hr., 3 per day 11:30am-6pm, €7.05-11.50); Serpa (35min., 7 per day 6:50am-6:20pm, €2.88); Sines via Santiago de Cacém (3hr., 4:20pm, €5.55).

⬛🔲 ORIENTATION AND PRACTICAL INFORMATION. The **tourist office,** R. Capitão J. F. de Sousa, 25, provides free but unreliable **Internet** access, comprehensive city and regional maps (also available at nearly every tourist stop in the city), and information pamphlets about Beja and other villages in the Alantejos. To get to the tourist office from the train station, take a left out of the station and then a right onto the main road, Lg. da Estação. At the rotary, go straight up R. Pedro Victor and straight again up R. Frei Manuel do Cenáculo. Continue uphill onto R. D. Nuno Álvares Pereira with the park (Jardim Gago Coutinho e S. Cabral) on your left. Take a right at the rotary onto R. Portas de Mertola and a left onto R. de Mertola. Turn right onto the pedestrian street R. J.F. de Sousa; the tourist office is about 200m up the street on the right. (☎ 284 31 19 13. Open M-Sa 10am-1pm and 2-6pm.) Other local services include: **banks** (open M-F 8am-3pm); **ATMs** near the bus station and on R. de Sousa across from the tourist office; **luggage storage** at the bus station on weekdays (€2 per day); **laundry** at **Lavanderia Baldeira**, R. Dr. Brito Camacho, 11 (☎ 284 32 99 57; open M-F 9:30am-1pm and 3-7pm, Sa 9:30am-1pm); **police** on R. D. Nuno Álvares Pereira (☎ 284 32 20 22 or 32 20 23), a 2min. walk from the tourist office across R. Portas de Mertola; **taxis**, convenient for daytrips to surrounding towns, with hubs at the bus station and Lg. Conde de Boavista; several **pharmacies** in the historical center, including Farmácia J. A. Pacheco, R. Capitão J. F. de Sousa (☎ 284 32 25 01; open M-F 9am-8pm, Sa 9am-1pm); free **Internet** access can be found at the Instituto Português da Juventude (☎ 284 32 14 94; open M-F 9am-12:30pm and 2-6pm), next to the Pousada de Juventude de Beja on R. Professor Janeiro Acabado. Black-and-white and color printing €0.35-0.50, discount with student card. The library, on R. Luís de Camões, also offers free Internet access. (☎ 284 31 19 00. Open M 2:30-11pm, Tu-F 9:30am-12:30pm and 2:30-11pm, Sa 2:30-8pm). To get to the **post office,** Lg. dos Correios, take a left from the tourist office and a right onto R. Infantaria. Posta Restante and fax (€4.50 per page) are available. (☎ 284 32 21 11. Open M-F 8:30am-12:30pm and 2:30-6:30pm.) **Postal Code:** 7800.

⌂🏠 ACCOMMODATIONS AND FOOD. Most accommodations are located within a few blocks of the tourist office or the bus station, like the **Pousada de Juventude de Beja (HI) ❶**, R. Professor Janeiro Acabado. From the front of the bus station, turn left, and then left again on R. Cidade de São Paulo, then right on R. Professor Janeiro Acabado; the hostel is on the left. The government-run inn boasts impeccably clean rooms with lockable cabinets; quads and sextets are available, as well as doubles. It includes a common room is complete with TV and foosball table, a laundry room, and a kitchen. (☎ 284 32 54 58; beja@movijovem.pt. Breakfast included. Reception 8am-midnight. July-Aug. dorms €11; doubles with bath €30.) Marked by a two-story vine of fuschia flowers, the three-star **Residencial Bejense ❸**, R. Capitão J. F. de Sousa, 57, is just steps from the tourist office. On the other side of a stunning doorway, 24 spotless rooms await, all with marble bathrooms, TVs, phones, A/C, and tiny balconies. (☎ 284 31 15 70; residencial-bejense@sapo.pt. Breakfast included. Singles €27.50; doubles €37.50-42, with 3rd bed €50. AmEx/MC/V.) The **Parque de Campismo Municipal de Beja ❶**, Av. Vasco da Gama, offers the security of an enclosed campground and modern amenities such as free showers, a bar, bathrooms, and cheap electricity (€1.75). (☎ 284 31 19 11. Reception 8am-11pm. Oct.-Apr. €1.15 per adult, €0.80 per tent; May-Sept. €2.29/1.60. 10% discount with student ID and up to 25% discount for extended stays.)

The **Mercado 25 de Abril,** in Lg. do St. Amaro next to the castle at the end of town, has a small selection of local produce. (Open M-Sa 6am-1:30pm.) Head to the ▩**Casa de Pasto O Saiote ❶**, R. de Biscainha, 6, for filling portions of no-frills, classic *Alentejano* fare amidst locals. Leaving the tourist office, turn left and walk nearly to the end of the block; R. de Biscainha is a small side street on the right. Try the *carne de porco à l'Alentejana* (pieces of pork in a light, buttery sauce) and some of the local wine. (☎ 284 32 92 89. Entrees €5-7.50. Open M-Sa noon-3pm and 7-10pm.) For a quick, greasy, and delicious bite of chicken or for one of the deepest baskets of fries in Portugal (€2), pop by **Restaurante O Frangote ❶**, R. Cidade de São Paulo, 7, right next to the bus station. (☎ 284 31 04 20. Sandwiches from €1.75. Entrees €4-6. Open M-F 9:30am-10pm, Sa 9:30am-3pm.) One of Beja's few vegetarian options, **Restaurante Sabores do Campo ❶**, R. Professor Bento de Jesus Caraça, 4, is a self-serve, cafeteria-style cafe that features creative offerings, including tofu de fricassé and *"bacalhau" com natas*, a meatless take on the traditional codfish plate. (☎ 284 32 02 67. Open M-Th 9am-8pm, F 9am-5:30pm.)

⬛ **SIGHTS.** At the center of the historic area lies the **Convento de Nossa Senhora da Conceição**, at Lg. de Conceição. Take a right from the tourist office and walk down Pr. Diogo Fernandes de Beja. Go right on R. Dr. Brito Camacho, through Lg. de São João to Lg. da Conceição; the convent is on the right. The convent is known in French and Portuguese literary circles as the site of an illicit love affair between Sister Mariana Alcoforado and Noël Bouton, a French Marquis who enlisted to reorganize the Portuguese army in 1665. The romance is chronicled in the 1669 book *Cartas Portuguesas* (Portuguese Letters), widely considered a fictional work, though a 2007 book by Myriam Cyr attempted to reassert the authenticity of these five letters of lust and betrayal. (☎ 284 32 33 51. Open Tu-F 9:30am-12:30pm and 2-5:15pm, Sa-Su 9:30am-12:30pm. €2, students €1, Su free. Closed on holidays. Ticket includes the **Museu Regional de Beja**, on the 2nd fl. of the convent.)

One block downhill from the Convento-Museu is the 13th-century **Igreja de Santa Maria da Feira**, Lg. de Santa Maria. Briefly transformed into a mosque during the Moorish invasion, the church's geometrical body houses heavy-set columns that distinguish three naves. The sobering altars display elaborate *talha dourada* carvings, while the retable within the Chapel of the Blessed Sacrament features Renaissance paintings of the Last Supper. (Open daily for mass 6-6:30pm and Su noon. Free.) Take a right out of the Igreja, cross Lg. de Santa Maria, and take R. Dr. Aresta Branco until you see the **Castelo de Bej**, founded by the Celts as a fortified village around 40 BC and later transformed into a Roman fortress. The surrounding ramparts, turrets, and single tower are all that remain. (Castle open May-Sept. Tu-Su 10am-1pm and 2-6pm; Oct.-Apr. 9-11:30am and 1-3:30pm. Free. Tower open 10am-12:30pm and 2-5:30pm. Buy tickets for tower at reception in the castle. €1.35, students €0.71.)

SINES ☎ 269

Tiny Sines (pop. 16,000) is a seaside town still steeped in Portuguese tradition. Its port, which inspired native-son **Vasco da Gama** with a passion for the sea, remains the lifeline of the city, providing a source of fresh seafood for the local restaurants. Sines is also making a name for itself with its renowned World Music Festival (in late July) and its new Arts Center. From the unmistakably salty air to the impossibly narrow cobblestone streets and the

LOCAL LEGEND

NAUGHTY, NAUGHTY NUN

You are a nun, living a life of piety and devotion—until you have a passionate, scandalous affair with a dashing French army official. What do you do when he leaves, never to return? Establish a genre of literature, of course!

That's what Beja's Mariana Alcofonado did, anyway. While living in the Convento de Nossa Senhora da Conceição in the 17th century, Mariana became enveloped in an illicit romance with the French Marquis of Chamilly, Noel Bouton, who was fighting in the War of Portuguese Restoration (1640-1668). When Bouton was called back to France, Mariana wrote him a series of five love letters, collected and edited in 1669 as *Les Lettres Portugaises*. Since then, the letters have been edited in more than 30 languages and are considered a landmark work of literature.

Besides the steamy details, Mariana's self-reflection and earnestness in expressing her undying love set a precedent for sentimentalism in literature, later reflected in works such as Samuel Richardson's *Pamela* (1740). Although there has always been the question of the letters' authenticity, even today Mariana's story continues to capture readers' imaginations—recently, novelist Katherine Vaz published *Marianna* (2004), yet another attempt to imagine the life of one of the most passionate nuns of all time.

bronzed De Gama overlooking the Atlantic, Sines offers an authentic maritime Portuguese experience.

⬛ TRANSPORTATION. The **bus station**, R. Julio Gomes da Silva, (☎269 63 22 68), is an easily missed small, green shed-like office with "Rodoviária Alentejo" written on it. Plan ahead, since most trips out of Sines involve multiple transfers and departures are infrequent. **Buses** are the only way in and out of town and go to: Beja (3hr., M-F 8:20am, €3.15) via Santiago de Cacém; Lagos (3hr., 10:15am, €10.40); Lisboa (2¾hr.; schedules vary, roughly 3 per day 5:30am-10:30am; €10.60); Setúbal (2hr., 3pm and 6pm, €9.40). The station (with free public bathrooms) is open M-F 7am-1pm and 3-6:30pm, Sa-Su 7:45-11am and 3-6pm.

⬛⬛ ORIENTATION AND PRACTICAL INFORMATION. Everything in Sines centers around the castle and its surroundings. A few shops line R. Serpa Pinto and R. Francisco Luís Lopes, both pedestrian walkways a block away from the castle. The **tourist office** is located right next to the castle, at the corner of R. Teófilo Braga, and offers pamphlets, maps, and other essential information in Portuguese, French, and English. From the bus station, go through Pr. da República, take R. Marquês de Pombal, and go straight until Lg. Afonso Albuquerque; there, take a left and go straight until the castle. (☎269 63 44 72. Open daily 10am-1pm and 2-6pm.) Other local services include: **banks** and **ATMs** around Pr. da República and the castle; **police,** Av. General Humberto Delgado (☎269 63 22 54 or 269 63 66 11); **hospital** (Centro de Saúde), R. Julio Gomes da Silva, across from the bus station (☎269 63 21 72); **laundry** at **Lavanderia Varanda**, R. Francisco Luís Lopes, 47, (☎269 63 23 88; open M-F 9am-1pm and 3-7pm, Sa 9am-1pm); **Farmácia Atlântico,** on Pr. da República (☎269 63 00 10; open M-F 9am-1pm and 3-7pm). The **library** is found in the **Sines Center for the Arts,** R. Cándido dos Reis, 49, and offers free **Internet** access. From the castle, take R. Teófilo Braga and turn right at Pr. Tomás Ribeiro. The two modern buildings made of pink granite at the end of the street are the Sines Center; the library is in the left wing. (☎269 86 00 80; open M 2-8pm, Tu-F 10am-8pm.) Public **Internet** access is also available at the **post office** in Pr. Tomás Ribeiro. (Open M-F 9am-6pm.) **Postal Code:** 7520.

⬛⬛ ACCOMMODATIONS AND FOOD. As word has gotten out about Sines' charm, truly affordable accommodations have become more scarce. Most accommodations in Sines take advantage of the limited tourist season, upping prices by an average of 10% during July and early August. Less than a block away from the castle, **Pensão Carvalho ❷**, R. Gago Coutinho, 27, Guests buzz into the pensão and should make note of the unposted 1am curfew. Ask to use the second-floor terrace for a coastal panorama; the view itself is worth the cost of the stay. (☎269 63 20 19. Singles €20, with bath €30; doubles €30/38. Prices slightly lower Sept.-May. Cash only.) Though a pricier option, **Residencial Veleiro ❺**, R. Sacadura Cabral, 19-A, offers sea views from 12 of its 14 rooms, each of which is equipped with full bathroom and balcony. (☎269 63 47 51; www.residencialveleiro.com. Breakfast included. Sept.-May singles €55; doubles €65. June-Aug. €70/75. MC/V.)

Sines offers both typical *Alentejano* meat-based dishes and an excellent variety of freshly-caught seafood. Strict vegetarians beware: you may have to survive on dessert, fruit, and wine during your stay. **⬛Churrasqueira Regional ❶**, R. António Aleixo, 18, serves excellent grilled cuisine, *churrasco* (gently-grilled meat) style. Be prepared to wait around 40min. for the delicious *frango assado* (roast chicken; €5) and reward your patience with a slice of the revered *chorlote*, a four-layer chocolate mousse cake soaked in rum and topped with whipped cream. (☎269 08 70 95. Open M-Sa noon-3pm.) Tucked away from the city center, **⬛Restaurante A Nau ❶**, R. Marquês de Pombal, 103-B, is a pleasant place to dine alongside local families and seasoned travelers at one of the five extra-long picnic tables. Try the grilled sardines—if you don't mind dealing with bones (or fish heads), and don't miss the true steal: the *prato do dia* (€7), which includes an entree, bread, a bottle of wine, and *espresso*. Outdoor seating and takeout available. (☎269 08 76 51. Open daily 12:30pm-midnight. Cash only.)

◙ **SIGHTS.** Famous Portuguese navigator **Vasco da Gama** was born in the keep of the **Castelo de Sines,** but the arresting stature of the *castelo* gives way to a deserted courtyard. Don't let this discourage you; if you cross the courtyard to the right wall and climb the ramparts you will be rewarded with a breathtaking ocean panorama. (Open daily 10am-noon and 2-6pm. Free.) Turn the corner to find the **Igreja Matriz,** a 14th-century church that was rebuilt during the 18th century. A ceiling painting of a crucifix and life-size figure of Nossa Senhora Dores (Our Lady of Pains) sets the reflective tone. Inside, the sound of the ocean reverberates against the walls, partially composed of Visigothic stones left over from a primitive chapel previously built on the same site. Outside, a bronze Vasco gazes over the open seas. (Open daily 9am-6pm. Summer mass daily 6:30pm and 7pm, Su 9:30, 11am; winter, mass daily 6:30pm, Su 9:30, 11am.) Outside of Sines's historic center sits the quiet **Igreja de Nossa Senhora das Salas.** Rebuilt in 1529 under the commission of Vasco da Gama himself, the chapel's origins are unknown. It is believed that the Byzantine Princess D. Vetácia founded the chapel after falling in love with Sines in 1336. Unpretentious in size and architecture, the chapel's exterior tells nothing of the prizes it shelters. A deep gilded altar, intricate blue tiling, and multiple domes are backdrop to a variety of relics that fill the church. Don't miss the back room to the left of the altar where part of Santa Ursula's skull is displayed. The *igreja* is difficult to find: walk away from the castle along Av. Vasco de Gama with the ocean on your left for about 2min. The church will be visible on the hills to your right. If you reach a guarded parking lot, you've gone too far. (☎269 63 60 65; dphadb@sapo.pt. Open W-Su 10am-12:30pm and 2:30-6pm.) A recent addition to Sines, the **Centro de Artes de Sines,** located on R. Cândido does Reis, 49, holds rotating exhibitions and houses the municipal library. It is the only truly modern architecture in town and is worth a visit, if just for its unusual granite and glass composition. (☎269 80 00 80; www.centrodeartesdesines.com.pt. Open daily 2-8pm.) Praia Sines, also known as Praia Vasco da Gama, stretches along Av. Vasco da Gama. Lifeguard, bathrooms, and beach bar make for comfortable sea-side excursions. The beach's firm, soft sand and indigo waters are undeniably beautiful; still, Sines is a port, and debris and refuse from ships and nearby fisheries collect near the beach wall.

ALGARVE AND ALENTEJO

RIBATEJO AND ESTREMADURA

 Some of the greatest treasures of Portugal can be found in the region just north of Lisboa. The Ribatejo is often referred to as the "Heart of Portugal" for its central location and its essential agricultural production. With the ornate monasteries in Alcobaça and Batalha, the fairy-tale town of Óbidos, and the hallowed sanctuary at Fátima (one of the largest Catholic pilgrimage destinations in the world), Ribatejo boasts some of the country's finest sights, not to mention most exquisite beaches. Nearby, serrated cliffs and whitewashed fishing villages line Estremadura's Costa de Prata (Silver Coast), where the beaches rival those of the Algarve. Throughout the two regions, festivals of food, bullfighting, and local crafts are prevalent.

HIGHLIGHTS OF RIBATEJO AND ESTREMADURA

PUSH your limits surfing **Super-tubos,** a famously unforgiving beach break (p. 702).

RECHARGE with a short trip to beautiful and relaxing **Nazaré** (p. 703).

WORSHIP the mysterious ways of the Virgin Mary at **Fátima** (p. 712).

HAUNT the stomping grounds of the Knights Templar at **Convento de Cristo** (p. 717).

SANTARÉM   ☎243

Nicknamed the "balcony over the Tagus," Santarém (pop. 60,000) is a 3000-year-old city known for its ancient churches affiliated with the Knights Templar, traditional festivals, and the best view of the Tejo in all of Portugal. From religious festas in the winter months to bike "festivals" in the fall and a commemoration of national theatre in the spring, this small city is constantly in celebratory mode. The prime time to visit Santarém is in the first days of June, when the city holds its Feira Nacional de Agricultura, a renowned festival featuring eight days of bullfighting, good food, and wild celebration in old tradition.

▐ TRANSPORTATION

Trains: Station, Estrada da Estação (☎243 32 11 99), 2km outside town. **Bus** service to and from the station (10min.; M-F every 45min. 6:50am-7:45pm, Sa 4 per day 8am-1:30pm; €1.10). To: **Coimbra** (2hr.; M-Sa 15 per day 6:25am-8:45pm, Su 8:43am-8:45pm; €13.60); **Faro** via **Lisboa's Estação do Barreiro** (4hr., 4 per day 7am-6pm, €22.90); **Lisboa's Sta. Apolónia** (1hr., 48 per day 5am-11pm, €4.90); **Portalegre** (3hr.; 8:50am, 6pm; €17); **Porto** (4hr., 15 per day 6:45am-9:45pm, €16); **Tomar** (1hr., 17 per day 6:15am-10:20pm, €4.90).

Buses: Rodoviária do Tejo, Av. do Brasil (☎243 33 32 00). To: **Braga** (5½hr., 5 per day 10:45am-6:45pm, €15.20); **Caldas da Rainha** (1½hr., 2-3 per day 7:20am-7:15pm, €4.80); **Coimbra** (2hr., 5 per day 10:45am-6:45pm, €10.90); **Faro** (7hr.; M-F 10 per day 7:45am-7pm, Sa 10:30am-4:30pm, Su 10:30am-7pm; €17); **Leiria** (1½hr., 4 per day 10:45am-6:45pm, €9.70); **Lisboa** (1hr.; M-F and Su 7 per day

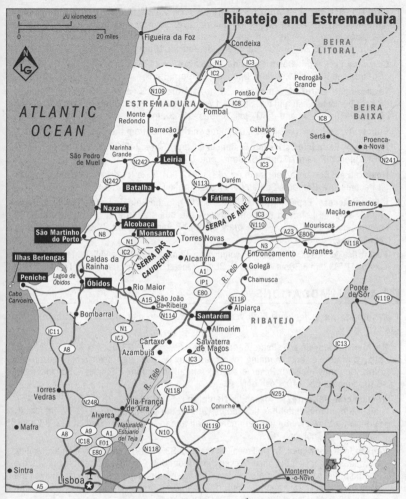

Ribatejo and Estremadura

10:45am-7pm, Sa 10:45am-4:30pm; €6.20); **Óbidos** (1½hr., 4 per day 7:20am-2:45pm, €4.60) via **Caldas Rainha; Porto** (4hr., 5 per day 10:45am-6:45pm, €14); **Nazaré** (2hrs.; M-F 7:30am, €4.60).

Taxis: Scaltaxis (☎ 243 33 29 19) has a stand across the park from the bus station.

✈ 🛈 ORIENTATION AND PRACTICAL INFORMATION

The historic center is made up of narrow grid-like streets typical of old Portuguese cities. The main square is the **Praça Sá da Bandeira.** From there, **Rua Serpa Pinto** and **Rua Capelo e Ivans** run through the core of old Santarém. **Avenida Sá da Bandeira** marks the outer edge of the historic center, and meets **Avenida Afonso Henriques** at the large shopping center. Av. Afonso Henriques runs to the newer part of the city, passing the bullfighting stadium in **Praça de Touros.**

Tourist Office: R. Capelo e Ivens, 63 (☎243 30 44 37; pturismo.santarem@mail.telepac.pt). Maps and informative brochures on accommodations and transportation. Friendly staff speaks English, French, and Spanish. Open M 9am-1:30pm and 2-5:30pm, Tu-F 9am-7pm, Sa and Su 10am-12:30pm and 2:30-5:30pm.

Currency Exchange: Caixa Geral de Depósitos (☎243 33 30 07), at R. Dr. Texeira Guedes and R. Capelo e Ivens. Open M-F 8:30am-3pm.

Laundromat: Tinturaria Americana, R. João Afonso, 15 (☎243 32 35 02). Charges €4.62 per kg to wash and dry. Specify if you don't want your clothes ironed *(passeado)*. Open M-F 9am-1pm and 2:30-7pm, Sa 9am-12:30pm.

Police: Av. do Brasil (☎243 32 20 22), down the street from the bus station.

Pharmacy: Farmácia Veríssimo, R. Capelo e Ivens, 72 (☎243 33 02 30, fax 243 33 02 36). Open M-F 9am-7:30pm, Sa 9am-1pm.

Hospital: Av. Bernardo Santareno (☎243 30 02 00). Take R. Alexandre Herculano until it becomes Av. Bernardo Santareno. English spoken.

Internet Access: Esp@ço Net (☎243 32 53 11), in the Sala de Leitura Bernardo Santa Reno, a public library in the park between the bus station and the police station. 9 computers, max. 40min. Free. Library open M-F 9am-8pm, Sa 9:30am-1pm; Internet access M-F 10am-6:30pm.

Post Office (☎243 30 97 00) on the corner of Lg. Cândido dos Reis and R. Dr. Texeira Guedes. Open M-F 8:30am-6:30pm, Sa 9am-12:30pm. Closed Su and holidays. **Postal Code:** 2000.

⌂ ACCOMMODATIONS

Accommodation prices are high year-round and increase during the Ribatejo fair in early June.

Residencial Muralha, R. Pedro Canavarro, 12 (☎243 32 23 99; fax 32 94 77). Simple, comfortable, and charming rooms, all with TV and large *azulejo*-covered private bath. Centrally located. Reserve a week ahead in summer. Singles €25, with bath €30; doubles €35/40. Cash only. ❷

Residencial Beirante, R. Alexandre Herculano, 5 (☎243 32 25 47; fax 33 38 45). This 42-room mini-hotel has tidy rooms with all the perks: phone, A/C, TV, breakfast, and even a blow-dryer in the bathrooms. Call ahead in summer. Singles €30-35; doubles €35-40. Cash only. ❸

Pensão José Rodrigues, Tr. Do Froes, 14 (☎ 962 83 79 09), marked by a small hanging *"Dormidas"* sign. Half the price of everything around it. Gigantic footprint rugs mark the way to spotless rooms decorated with pastel-flowered bedspreads. In some doubles the toilet stands feet away from the bed, offering no bathroom privacy. Singles €15, with shower €20; doubles with shower €30. Cash only. ❷

FOOD

Many small, traditional eateries hide in the narrow streets around R. Capelo e Ivens and R. Serpa Pinto. The municipal **market,** in the pagoda on Lg. Infante Santo near Jardim da República, sells fresh produce. (Open M-Sa 6am-2pm.) The somewhat pricey **Supermercado Minipreço,** R. Pedro Canavarro, 31, is on the street leading from the bus station to R. Capelo e Ivens. (Open M-Sa 9am-8pm.)

🍽 **Adiafa,** Campo E. Infante da Câmara (☎243 32 40 86), out by the bullfighting stadium. A giant restaurant that looks like a barn on the inside. Try their *sopa de legumes* (€1.50), the best around. Entrees €8-13. Open daily 10am-9:30pm. AmEx/MC/V. ❷

Santarém

🔺 ACCOMMODATIONS
Pensão José Rodrigues, **5**
Residencial Beirante, **1**
Residencial Muralha, **4**

🍴 FOOD
A Caravana, **3**
Adiafa, **6**
O Saloio, **2**

⭐ NIGHTLIFE
Cavalariça 1, **7**

A Caravana, R. Capelo e Ivens, 28 (☎243 33 26 38). One of the best places for lunch, with cafeteria-style entrees cooked fresh for takeout (€4). Also a sit-down restaurant with glass-covered tables showcasing a variety of seeds and beans. Entrees €6-10. Open M-Sa 9am-7pm. Cash only. ➋

O Saloio, Tr. do Montalvo, 11 (☎243 32 76 56), off R. Capelo e Ivens. This local favorite serves a variety of meat and a mean *caldeirada* (monster fish stew). No vegetarian options. Entrees €5-10. Open M-F 9:30am-9pm, Sa 9:30am-4pm. Cash only. ➋

👁 SIGHTS

PORTAS DO SOL. Large Moorish walls surround this tranquil park of flowers and fountains high above the Rio Tejo and the Alentejo plains. Climb the stone steps and take in the timeless beauty of the surrounding countryside. Don't be surprised if you're the only one enjoying the actual view; the park seconds as Santarém's prime lovers' rendezvous. A quiet cafe, a large birdcage, and a playground are also enclosed by the ancient castle walls. (*Take R. Serpa Pinto to R. São Martinho, past the Torre das Cabaças and stay right as the road becomes Av. 5 de Outubro after the abandoned Art Deco theater. Open daily June-Aug. 9am-10pm; Sept.-May 9am-6:30pm. Free.*)

PRAÇA VISCONDE DE SERRA PILAR. Centuries ago, Christians, Moors, and Jews gathered for social and business affairs in this *praça*. *(Take R. Serpa Pinto from Pr. Sá da Bandeira.)* The 12th-century **Igreja de Marvila,** off the *praça*, was revamped in the late 17th century with traditional ornamentation of the era. Don't be fooled by the simplicity of the exterior; the *azulejo*-covered interior is dazzling, as is the Manueline entrance. *(Open Tu-Su 9am-12:30pm and 2-5:30pm. Free.)* The early Gothic minimalism of nearby **Igreja da Graça** contrasts with Marvila's exuberance; construction began in 1380 on the orders of the first earls of Ourém, and the cloister dates back to the 16th century. Within the church, in the **Capela de São João Evangelista,** lies Pedro Cabral, the explorer who "discovered" Brazil and one of the few to live long enough to return to his homeland. *(Open Tu-Su 9am-12:30pm and 2pm-5:30pm. Free.)*

TORRE DAS CABAÇAS. The medieval Torre das Cabaças (Tower of the Gourds) was named after the eight earthen bowls installed in the 16th century to amplify the sound of the bell's ring. Today the tower serves as the **Museu de Tempo.** The interior walls of the tower are peppered with clocks and sundials from different times and civilizations. Buy tickets across the street at the small **Museológio de Arqueologia e Arte Medievais,** which has a hearty collection of medieval pots, pans, and jugs, and an exhibit comparing Christian and Muslim influences on Santarém. *(Take R. Serpa Pinto to São Martinho, past Pr. Visconde de Serra Pilar. Open W-Su 9am-12:30pm and 2-5:30pm. Tower €1, Archaeology Museum €2, both €2.50; under 25 €0.50/1/1.25.)*

■ ■ NIGHTLIFE AND FESTIVALS

Most of the fun in Santarém takes place outside the historic center. Every other Sunday, bargain shoppers flock to the large market in front of the bullfighting stadium, where they sift through mounds of inexpensive merchandise, from clothes to furniture to pets. (Open 7am-2pm.) This is also the location of the annual Festival Nacional de Gastronomia, a giant celebration of Portuguese cuisine in late October or early November. Better known is the Feira Nacional de Agricultura (a.k.a. Feira do Ribatejo), a ten-day extravaganza of markets, bullfighting, and farmers racing tiny horses. The party starts the first week of June and continues until the 11th or 13th. When there is no BBQing or horseback riding to be done, however, Santarém can seem a little lethargic, especially in comparison with Lisboa. Pubs can be found along **R. Pedro de Santarém**, beside the shopping center, a road which leads to the bullfighting stadium in Pr. de Touros. If you want to dance, try **Cavalariça 1**, in the buildings behind the Adiafa restaurant, near the stadium. This little disco is a local favorite. (Open Tu-W 11pm-2am, Th-Sa 11pm-4am.)

ÓBIDOS   ☎262

Resting in the palm of a 12th-century castle, Óbidos, a tiny village of 200 residents is completely enclosed by massive walls; the walls seem to have sequestered Óbidos away from passing time as well. The residents are extremely friendly, only adding to Óbidos' undeniable charm. As wonderful as it is to live in a castle, however, the lifestyle doesn't leave much room for anything but tourism, and the narrow and winding streets are crammed with small shops selling handcrafts, souvenirs, and *ginjinha*, a delicious cherry liquor. The bulk of the commercial activity takes place along **Rua Direita,** the street to the left after entering the town, which passes through the central square and heads toward the castle. The castle itself—now a luxury *pousada* (inn)—is open only to guests, but everyone is free to walk the scenic 1.5km of its walls. (☎262 95 50 80.)

Doubles €250. Reservations required 1-2 months in advance.) The **Igreja de Santa Maria,** to the right of the post office in the central *praça*, is decorated with a unique juxtaposition of *azulejos* and oil canvases of religious scenes painted by the famous 17th-century female artist, Josefa de Óbidos. The church's decorations make it a unique place to visit. Built in 1148 by the order of Portugal's first king, Dom Afonso Henriques, the church was the site of the wedding of 10-year-old Dom Afonso V to his 8-year-old cousin, Isabel. (Open daily Apr.-Sept. 9:30am-12:30pm and 2:30-7pm; Oct.-Mar. 9:30am-12:30pm and 2:30-5pm. Free.)

There are several private rooms for rent in Óbidos, as advertised by signs around R. Direita, but it may be difficult to find a low price. Cheaper rooms can be found outside of the castle walls in the surrounding town. **Residencial Alcaidaria Mor ❷,** Pç. Dr. Azeredo Perdiagão, 6-8, is an inexpensive place to stay, but you'll probably want to take a taxi from the castle entrance, as the *residencial* is located 2 km away. (☎262 96 99 48. Singles €20; doubles €25. Cash only.) There are a few centrally located bargain options. ⬛**Milena ❷,** to the right of the Igreja de Santa Maria, is away from the tourist hustle and bustle. The two breezy bedrooms with private bath are decorated to make you feel at home. (☎919 18 25 63. Singles €25; doubles €35. Cash only.) Restaurants (most with tourist-oriented menus and prices) and several markets can be found on R. Direita. Save a few euros for Óbidos's signature *ginjinha*; stores on R. Direita sell bottles for €5-8.50, and shots for €1-2. **1° Dezembro ❶,** right off of R. Direita, 45, has a large selection of cheap meals (€2-6), including omelettes, burgers, pizza, and steak. Spacious patio seating makes it a popular lounging area. (☎262 95 92 98. Open daily 8:30am-9pm. MC/V.) Down the road on the right is **O Conquistador ❸,** R. Josefa D'Óbidos, 20, marked by a large shield above the door. If you're feeling brave, try the stewed hare with white beans (€12.50) or the poached partridge (€10.50). (☎ 262 95 95 28. Entrees €9-16. Open M and W-Su noon-3pm and 5-10pm. AmEx/MC/V.)

Buses stop at the town gate (make sure you pay attention to the stop—it is not clearly marked) and are more convenient than trains. Connections go to Caldas da Rainha (10min.; M-F 23 per day 7:30am-7:06pm, Sa 7 per day 7:30am-8:20pm, Su 5 per day 8:36am-8:20pm; €1.20), Lisboa (1¼hr.; M-F 7 per day 7:05am-6pm, €5.20; Sa-Su 5-7 per day via Caldas da Rainha, €6.20), and Peniche (40min.; M-F 10 per day 9:40am-7:40pm, Sa 7 per day 8:10am-7:40pm, Su 5 per day 9:40am-7:40pm; €2.45). The **tourist office** is a small white cottage near the entrance to the castle; from the bus stop, go up the steps, turn left, and walk about 100m. The office is on the left. The staff speaks English, French, and Spanish, and has luggage storage and bus schedules. (☎262 95 92 31; fax 95 55 01. Open May-Sept. daily 9:30am-7:30pm; Oct.-Apr. M-F 9:30am-5:30pm, Sa-Su 9:30am-12:30pm and 1:30-5:30pm. 2hr. audio tour of the city €5, each additional hour €3. Bike rentals also available.) Free **Internet** access is available at **NET,** on R. Direita near the plaza. Check out the preserved ancient granary while you surf the net. (Open daily June 21-Sept. 21 M-F 10am-7pm, Sa and Su 11:30am-6:30pm.)

PENICHE

☎262

Whether lured by rolling waves, beautiful beaches, or delicious seafood, vacationers to Peniche (pop. 27,000) have one thing in common: a love for the ocean. From decor to cuisine, natives and visitors alike can't seem to get enough of the sea. Peniche is also home to some fantastic rock formations, a 16th-century fortress, and the Berlengas Islands Natural Reserve. After a leisurely, sun-filled day, surfers, nature-lovers, and history buffs mingle together in the local cafes and bars. Endowed with the best of it all, Peniche makes the perfect weekend getaway.

⌐ TRANSPORTATION

Buses: Peniche is accessible only by bus. The **station** (☎968 90 38 61) is on R. Dr. Ernesto Moureira, on an isthmus outside the town walls. Wait until the bus gets to the station to exit. Buses run to: **Alcobaça** (1¾hr., 2:45pm, €8); **Leiria** (2hr., 3 per day 7am-6pm, €9.70) via **Caldas da Rainha** (1hr., 10 per day 8am-7:40pm, €2.80); **Lisboa** (1½hr., 6 per day 7am-6:30pm, €7.40); **Nazaré** (1½hr.; 7am, 2:45, 6pm; €7.60); **Porto** (6hr., 11 per day 6am-6:30pm, €14); **Santarém** (1½hr., 7 per day 6am-6:30pm, €12) via **Caldas da Rainha.**

Taxis: (☎262 78 26 87; 78 29 10) in Pr. J. Rodrigues Pereira and Lg. Bispo Mariana.

◢✳ ☑ ORIENTATION AND PRACTICAL INFORMATION

A giant wall and a small waterway divide Peniche in half. From the bus station, visitors must cross a small bridge to enter the city center. Tracing the inside of this wall is **Rua Alexandre Herculano,** which passes the tourist office and the central square, **Praça Jacob Rodrigues Pereira.** The wall ends at **Avenida do Mar,** which continues along the water toward the docks and the fortress, lined with seafood restaurants and bars. Paralleling Av. do Mar two streets inland is **Rua José Estévão,** where numerous *residenciais* can be found. This street and those nearby it fill with loud music and bar-hoppers until the wee hours of the morning.

Tourist Office: R. Alexandre Herculano (☎262 78 95 71) The office is located in the small park on R. Alexandre Herculano. Reservations for camping and bungalows can be made in the tourist office. Bus schedules are also available. English spoken.

Banks: Caixa Geral de Depósitos, on R. Alexandre Herculano across from the tourist office. Open M-F 8:30am-3pm. 24hr. **ATMs** line R. Alexandre Herculano and Av. do Mar.

> **TIP** **CASH WITHDRAWAL.** If you're staying in Peniche over the weekend bring a good amount of cash. The city is popular with foreigners and locals so ATMs usually run out of cash by Saturday afternoon.

Police: R. Heróis Ultramar (☎262 78 95 55). From the tourist office, go right on R. Alexandre Herculano, then left on R. Arquitecto Paulino Montez, past the post office. Turn left on R. Heróis Ultramar.

Pharmacy: Farmácia Higiênica, R. António Conceição Bento, 21 (☎262 78 24 15). From the tourist office, turn onto R. Alexandre Herculano, left onto R. Arquitecto Paulino Montez, and right on R. António da Conceição Bento. Open M-F 9am-8pm.

Hospital: R. Gen. Humberto Delgado (☎262 78 19 00). From the tourist office, turn right and take the first left onto R. Arquitecto Paulino Montez; walk past the post office, then take a right onto R. Gen. Humberto Delgado. English spoken.

Internet Access: Free Internet access is available at **Espaço Internet,** R. Dr. João Matos Bilhau (☎969 19 58 95), around the corner from the police station. Call ahead to make sure computers are available for public access. Open M-Sa 10am-1pm and 3-10pm, Su 10am-noon and 3-8pm.

Post Office: R. Arquitecto Paulino Montez, 53 (☎262 78 00 61). From the tourist office, turn right on R. Alexandre Herculano, left on R. Arquitecto Paulino Montez, and walk 3 blocks. **Posta Restante** and **fax.** Open M-F 9am-6pm. **Postal Code:** 2520.

⌂ ☂ ACCOMMODATIONS AND CAMPING

Peniche's budget accommodations are often located above restaurants of the same name; look for signs to find a *residencial* on Av. do Mar. Rooms in private homes are the best budget options, but ask to see them first and inquire about amenities.

■ **Residencial Marítimo,** R. António Cervantes, 14 (☎262 78 28 50). Colorful hallways and bedrooms add to the cheery atmosphere. Rooms are on the smaller side but come packed with amenities—42-channel TV, private, beautifully tiled bathroom, free Internet access, and a great location. Reserve ahead. Sept.-May singles €20; doubles 35. June-Aug. €25/45. Cash only. ❷

■ **Vasco da Gama,** R. José Estévão (☎262 78 19 02). Look for the big flashy sign designed to draw in passerby. Cable television and free breakfast make up for the plain decoration of the rooms. Central location. High-season singles €30; doubles €40. Low-season €20/€35. Cash only. ❸

Residencial Aviz, Pr. Jacob Rodrigues Pereira, 2 (☎262 78 21 53). Centrally located with unbeatable prices. Singles €11, with bath €20; doubles €20/30. Cash only. ❶

Peniche Praia Municipal Campground, Estrada Marginal Norte (☎262 78 34 60; www.penichepraia.pt). On the opposite side of the peninsula. Located across the street from Peniche's rock formations. Laundry €6. Hot showers and swimming pool free. €3.40, child ages 5-9 €1.70, under 5 free; €3.40-4.25 per tent depending on size, €3.40 per car. Bungalow for 2 people high/mid/low season €65/49/33. Cash only. ❶

⚫ FOOD

The restaurants lining Av. do Mar serve excellent, freshly-grilled seafood and have great views of the water. Despite the multilingual menus, the prices are reasonable and plenty of locals mix in with tourists. Peniche's *sardinhas* (sardines) are reputedly the best in Portugal, as are the seafood *espetadas* (skewers). The outdoor cafes on Praça Jacob Rodrigues Pereira are lively, even on Sundays when the rest of town is quiet. The **market,** on R. António da Conceição Bento, stocks produce. (Open Tu-Su 7am-1pm.)

■ **Ristorante Il Boccone,** Av. do Mar, 4 (☎ 262 78 24 12). Fantastic pizza (€5-8) and enormous pasta dishes (€6-8.50) provide a welcome reprieve from seafood. Great sangria (€3.50). Open daily noon-11pm. AmEx/MC/V. ❷

Adamastor, R. Alexandre Herculano, 70 (☎ 964 94 20 41). This small seafood joint offers up a tasty tourist menu for only €6. Included is the plate of the day, bread, a drink, dessert, and coffee. Sandwiches and salads start at €1.50. If you're in the mood to spend a little more, the seafood tank in the back of the room offers the opportunity to pick your dinner. Open daily 10am-2pm. Cash only. ❷

Java House, Lg. da Ribeira, 14 (☎ 918 66 91 88). Craving a mocha frappuccino? The frozen *café frappe* (€2.40) and house specialty, the *café moka* (€1.50), are the closest things you'll find in Portugal. Fully stocked bar at night. Shots €1.50. Mixed drinks €3. Open daily June-Aug. 8am-4am; Sept.-May M-Th 9:30am-2am F-Su 9:30am-4am. ❷

Restaurante Kate Kero I, Av. do Mar, 90 (☎ 262 78 14 80). Seafood lovers of the world unite! Kate Kero I serves up some of the most inexpensive seafood on Av. do Mar. Entrees (€6-20) include a side of boiled potatoes and a hearty helping of salad. Save room for a delicious dessert (€1.50-3.25). Open daily noon-11pm. MC/V. ❸

⚫ SIGHTS

FORTALEZA. António Salazar, Portugal's longtime dictator from 1932 to 1968, chose Peniche's formidable 16th-century fortress as one of his four high-security political prisons. Today it houses the **Museu de Peniche,** the highlight of which is a chilling tour of the cells of Salazar's prison, including replicas of the torture room and interrogation chamber. Outside the museum, a small exhibition traces the Fascist dictatorship and underground resistance from the seizure of power in 1926 to the coup that toppled the regime on April 25, 1974. *(Campo da República, near the dock* *where boats leave for the Ilhas Berlengas. Fortaleza open Tu 2-5:30pm, W-F 9am-12:30pm and 2-5:30pm, Sa-Su 10am-12:30pm and 2-5:30pm. Free. Museum ☎www.cm-peniche.pt. Same hours as Fortaleza. Last entrance 30min. before closing. €1.45, under 16 free.)*

BEACHES. For sun and surf, head to any of the town's three beaches. They are within walking distance, but bikes can be rented for the day from several local shops (€4-5 per day). The windy **Praia de Peniche de Cima,** along the north crescent, is the highlight of the three, with beautiful white sand and warm water. *(From the tourist office, take a right on R. Alexandre Herculano, cross the bridge over the river, take a left on R. da Ponte Velha, and continue 10-15min. to the ocean. Once at the water, Praia de Peniche de Cima is 300m to your right.)* About a half-hour walk further, Praia de Peniche de Cima merges with another beach at Baleal, a small fishing village very popular with tourists, especially surfers and body boarders. The southern **Praia do Molho Leste** marks the entrance to **Super-tubos;** also known as the "Portuguese Pipeline" (after the famous Hawaiian break), Super-tubos is perfect for watching daring surfers risk bodily injury on the unforgiving beach break. *(Praia do Molho Leste is over the river by the rotary at the end of Av. do Mar; cross the bridge and follow the coastline around the Porto de Pesca (15min.); Praia do Molho Leste is just after the jetty.)* Beyond Super-tubos lies crowded **Praia da Consolação,** a favorite of Portuguese families on weekend getaways. The strange humidity and hot rocks at this beach supposedly cure bone diseases. Watch out for elderly visitors seeking relief from their afflictions, often wearing nothing but a hopeful smile.

◢ NIGHTLIFE

Peniche may seem sleepy during the day, but the town's nightlife gets going after dinner and continues until late at night, especially during the summer. The area by the docks has some great bars, as do the streets around R. José Estévão.

▨ **Três Ás,** Lg. da Ribeira, 12 (☎262 18 96 77). A wooden sea-inspired decor gives this cafe a classy ambience popular with young locals. Três Ás has 2 bars and patio seating, but still manages to stay full every night in the summer. Shots €2-3. Mixed drinks €3. Sandwiches €1.20-2. Open M-F 10am-2am, Sa and Su 9am-4am. Cash only.

Bar No. 1, R. Afonso Albuquerque, 14, off R. José Estévão just after the church. On Saturday, the friendly owner gets on the turntables after 10pm, taking advantage of his big bar and turning it into a rocking dance floor. The bar also exhibits local art. Beer €1. Shots €1-1.50. Mixed drinks €3. Open daily noon-2am.

▨ FESTIVALS

For daytime party-seekers, Peniche's biggest festival starts the first weekend in August, when boats festooned with flags and flowers parade into the harbor to launch the two-day **Festa de Nossa Senhora da Boa Viagem,** celebrating the protector of sailors and fishermen. The town lets loose with carnival rides, live entertainment, wine, and seafood, continuing the festivities that begin two weeks before the launch. If you're lucky, you'll be in town during early June for the **Sabores do Mar** festival when Peniche enjoys an eight-day celebration of all things seaworthy, including discounts for specialty dishes made by local seafood restaurants.

◣ DAYTRIP FROM PENICHE

▨ ILHAS BERLENGAS

Several companies operate boats from Peniche's public dock, near the fort at the end of Av. do Mar. Viamar ferry (☎262 78 56 46, fax 78 38 47. Ticket booth open 8:30am-

nnnn and 3 5:30pm), offers 1 or 2 crossings per day. (40min.; July-Aug. 9:30am and 4:30pm; returns 11:30am and 6:30pm; May 15-June and Sept. 1-15 departs 10am, returns 4:30pm. Same-day round-trip ticket €18, ages 5-12 €10, under 5 free.) Other companies have smaller boats, and though they post schedules, they will leave when full. If they don't fill up by the scheduled departure time, they will send you off on the big Viamar boat. Smaller boats have earlier and more frequent return times. To stay overnight, buy an €11 ticket each way. Arrive 15-30 min. in advance. Reserve camping 3-4 days in advance at the tourist office in Peniche (☎262 78 95 71; tent for 2 people €9.25, 3 people €13, 4 people €16.50). The crossing is notoriously rough; expect to witness or experience sea sickness.

The main island of Berlengas is not easily missed; its enormous orange face looms large off the coast of Peniche. The inspiration for Alfred Hitchcock's *The Birds*, the rugged Ilhas Berlengas (the main island and the smaller surrounding Farilhões, Estelas, and Forcados) are inhabited by thousands of screeching seagulls. The **Reserva Natural da Berlenga** is also home to wild black rabbits, lizards, and a very small fishing community. Unfortunately for visitors, the reserve is off-limits to non-researchers, and hikers risk serious institutional fury by stepping off the paths. Nevertheless, the real prize of the islands is the collection of wild rock formations. Deep gorges, natural tunnels, and pebble-strewn caves carve through Berlenga, begging to be explored. Bring a pair of hiking shoes and a walking stick if you plan to hike; several of the trails are quite steep and strewn with small rocks. At the docks, kayaks are rented by the hour (single €4; doubles €6). The main path (2km) goes up past the lighthouse to the other side of the island, where the formidable 17th-century fortress **Forte de São João Batista ❶** sits out in the crystal clear water. Accessible by bridge, it now functions as a hostel with a small cafe inside. (☎918 61 41 90. No running water. Reception 11am-2pm, and 6-8pm. Singles €11.) The fortress walls have openings that form mini-patios perfect for sunbathing and offer unbeatable views of the water. Outside the fortress, small motorboats offer tours of the caves (20min.; €3). The main beach lies in a small cove by the landing dock. For those willing to brave the cold, the beach has an accessible cave beside it and a jumping board off the dock.

NAZARÉ ☎262

Home to a beautiful stretch of golden sand and calm turquoise water, Nazaré (pop. 16,000) has become one of the Ribatejo's main tourist attractions. In true postcard fashion, the beaches are lined with hundreds of small colorful tents that help visitors escape the hot summer sun. In Nazaré, tourism is a big business dominated by women dressed in traditional black scarves and aprons who offer rooms, sell snacks and souvenirs, and rent beach tents to tourists. Still, the town's relaxed feel begs tourists to return year after year for a peaceful vacation under the warm Portuguese sun. At night Nazaré is just as busy as it is during the day. Local bars and cafes stay crowded all night, and the beach comes alive again in the early morning.

▐ TRANSPORTATION

Buses: Av. Vieira Guimarães (☎967 44 98 68), perpendicular to Av. da República. More convenient than trains (6km away). To: **Alcobaça** (20min., 11 per day 7:10am-7:10pm, €2); **Batalha** (50min., 6 per day 7:10am-6:45pm, €3.30); **Caldas da Rainha** (1¼hr., 10 per day 6:30am-7:25pm, €3.10); **Coimbra** (2hr.; 4 per day M-Sa 6:25am-7:25pm, Su 8:25am-7:25pm; €10.20); **Fátima** (1½hr., 3 per day 7:10am-5:10pm, €4.50); **Leiria** (1¼hr., 5 per day 7:10am-6:45pm, €3.30); **Lisboa** (2hr.; M-Th 6 per day 6:50am-6:40pm, F and Su 9 per day 6:50am-7:40pm, Sa 5 per day

6:50am-4:40pm; €8.30); **Porto** (3½hr.; M-Sa 4 per day 6:25am-7:25pm, Su 7 per day 8:25am-7:25pm; €12.50);

Taxis: Praça de Taxi (☎262 55 13 63).

◈▪ 🛈 ORIENTATION AND PRACTICAL INFORMATION

All of the action in Nazaré takes place near the beach, mainly along **Avenida da República,** which follows the coastline. The avenue runs past the two main squares, **Praça Dr. Manuel de Arriaga** and then **Praça Sousa Oliveira,** before ending at the cliffs. From there, the funicular runs up the side of the mountain, connecting the two levels of Nazaré. **Sítio,** the old town, forms the second story of the city, and its position 100m above the water has kept it calmer and more traditional than the beach area below. The downtown area is grid-like and easily navigable by foot. To get to the tourist office from the bus stop, take a right out of the station toward the beach and then another onto Av. da República; the office is a 5min. walk along the shore and lies between the two plazas.

Tourist Office: (☎262 56 11 94), beachside on Av. da República. Provides maps and info. English spoken. Open daily July-Aug. 9am-9pm; Sept. and Apr.-June 9:30am-1pm and 2:30-7pm; Oct.-Mar. 9:30am-1pm and 2:30-6pm.

Bank: Major banks lie on and around Av. da República. **Millennium BCP,** Av. Manuel Remígio (☎262 56 90 02), right on the beach. Open M-F 8:30am-3:30pm.

Laundromat: Lavanderia Belmatic, Av. Manuel Remígio Solmar, Loja 2 (☎ 911 08 72 16). Walk down Av da República away from the cliffs. Turn left on Av. Manuel Remígio Solmar. Self serve wash and dry. €5 to wash up to 8kg of clothing, €2 to dry up to 8kg of clothing. Ironing and tailoring services also available. Open M-Sa 9am-9pm.

Police: (☎262 55 12 68) Station is at the corner of R. Sub-Vila and Av. Vieira Guimarães near the bus station.

Pharmacy: Farmácia Sousa on R. Mouzinho de Albuquerque, 30 (☎262 56 12 21). Up the street from Pr. Sousa Oliveira. Open M-Th 9am-7pm, F 9am-8pm, Sa 9am-1pm.

Medical Services: Hospital da Confraria da Nossa Senhora de Nazaré (☎262 55 01 00), in the Sítio district on the cliffs above the town center. **Centro de Saúde** (☎262 56 91 20), Urbanização Caixins, in the new part of town. Go down Av. Da República, which becomes Av. Manuel Remígio. Turn left on R. das Hortas, almost to the end. Open M-F 9am-1pm and 2-6pm.

Internet Access: Centro Cultural, Av. Manuel Remígio (☎262 56 19 44), on Av. da República. Max. 30min. Free. Open Sept.-July 14 M-F 9:30am-1pm and 2-7pm, Sa 3-7pm. July 15-Aug. M-F 10am-1pm, 3-7pm and 9pm-midnight, Sa 3pm-7pm and 9pm-midnight. For late-night Internet access try **Online,** Pr. Sousa Oliveira (☎262 18 78 67), up the set of stairs beside the Caixa General Bank. 16 computers, all with big comfy leather chairs. €1.50 per 30min., €2 per hr., €5 per 3hr. Open Sept.-June M-Sa 2pm-11pm; July-Aug. M-Sa 11am-midnight, Su 2pm-midnight.

Costa Pareiro e Silva, Av. Vieira Guimarães, 12 (☎262 08 46 41), on the same road as the bus station at the intersection with Av. da República. €1 per 30min. Open daily 10am-1am.

Post Office: Av. da Independência Nacional, 2 (☎262 56 91 00). From Pr. Sousa Oliveira, walk up R. Mouzinho de Albuquerque. **Posta Restante** and **fax.** Open M-F 9:30am-12:30pm and 2:30-6pm. **Postal Code:** 2450.

▌ ACCOMMODATIONS AND CAMPING

Nazaré is inhabited by the most aggressive room-hawkers in Portugal; they swarm arriving buses at the station and line Av. da República, offering their homes to tourists and locals alike. Bargain with the same aggressive attention they use to court you. Agree on a price before seeing the room, but don't settle the deal until afterward. In summer, take nothing over €30.

Hospedaria Ideal, R. Adrião Batalha, 98 (☎262 55 13 79), just after Pr. Dr. Manuel. Six rooms with high ceilings, mirrors, and comfortable beds. Clean bathroom with retro linoleum is shared. July-Aug. singles €20; doubles €25-30; triples €35-40. Sept.-June €15/20/30-35. Cash only. ❷

Vila Turística Conde Fidalgo, Av. da Independência Nacional, 21-A (☎262 55 23 61). Choice of rooms with TV and mini-fridge or private apartments with TV, kitchen, refrigerator, microwave, and bath. Laundry €5. July-Aug. singles €30; doubles with kitchen €45; Sept.-June €20/30. Cash only. ❸

Vale Paraíso, Estrada Nacional, 242 (☎262 56 18 00; www.valeparaiso.com), 2.5km out of town in a wooded area. Take the buses to Alcobaça or Leiria (10min.; 12 per day 7am-7pm; €1.60). Swimming pools, restaurant, supermarket, showers, Internet (€2 per 30min., €3 per hour), and laundry (€7). June-Sept. 14 €4.20 per person, €3.60-5.30 per tent, €3.50 per car; Sept. 15-May €3.10/2.70-3.90/2.90. Bungalows Oct.-Mar. €15.50 for 2 people, €20.50 for 3-4 people; Apr.-May and Sept. €23/31; June July 14 €33/41; July 15-Aug. €56/63.50. AmEx/MC/V for purchases over €150. ❶

■ FOOD

For groceries, check out the municipal market in the huge warehouse across from the bus station. (Open daily 6:30am-2pm.) Supermarkets, like **Minipreço,** line R. Sub-Vila, parallel to Av. da República. (Open daily 9am-9pm.)

▨ **Casa Marquês,** R. J. B. de Sousa Lobo, 37 (☎ 262 10 20 22) Facing Pr. Dr. Manuel Arriaga, go right. Generous portions of succulent seafood at a bargain. The cook has prepared the house specialty, *caldeirada* (fish stew; €8), for almost 30 years. Entrees €6-12.50. Open daily 8am-5pm and 7pm-11:30pm. Cash only. ❷

▨ **Pastelaria Batel,** R. Mouzinho de Albuquerque, 2 (☎262 55 11 47), and on Av. Vieira Guimarães. The best-known pastry shop in Nazaré, and the place to try sweet local specialties. All pastries €0.75. Try the *tamares* (little boats with custard filling capped in chocolate), *sardinhas* (flaky pastry, not fish), or the *nazarenos* (almond pastry). Open daily June-Aug. 7am-2am; Sept.-May closed on W. Cash only. ❶

O Borgas, R. Mouzinho de Albuquerque, 4 (☎262 57 91 03), near Pr. Sousa Oliveira. *Bife na lage,* seasoned steak grilled on a heated rock at the diner's table, is the house specialty (€10). Complete tourist menu for €11.50 (plate of the day, bread, a drink, dessert, and coffee). Vegetarian options include grilled vegetables, various soups, and salad. Entrees €10-12.50. Open daily 8am-4pm and 6pm-2am. MC/V. ❷

◗ ♫ BEACHES AND ENTERTAINMENT

Nazaré's main attraction is its stretch of beautiful beach where locals spend their days playing volleyball, racquetball, and of course, soccer. The colorful tents that ornament the golden beach can be rented from the women sitting in front of them along Av. da República (€6 per day, €35 per wk.). After catching some rays, take the **funicular** (3min.; every 15min. 7:15am-9:30pm, every 30min. 9:30pm-midnight; €0.85), which runs from R. Elevador off Av. da República to the **Sítio,** the cliff top area of Nazaré. For centuries, all of Nazaré stood on the Sítio, well above the dangerous tide below. The charming, uneven cobbled streets, weathered buildings, and breathtaking views provide the perfect site for a picnic.

On Saturday afternoons in May and June, locals dress in traditional outfits and haul fishing nets out of the water, using an old-fashioned technique in an event

LOCAL LEGEND

THE REAL CORPSE BRIDE

When Prince Dom Pedro took one look at his wife's lady-in-waiting, Inês de Castro, it was (forbidden) love at first sight. Upon discovering this illicit amor, Dom Pedro's father, King Alfonso, condemned the affair and had Inês exiled to a convent in Coimbra. The prince's wife soon died in childbirth, however, and Pedro and Inês continued their affair for the next decade. The prince's plans for a wedding were cut short: his father had Inês killed for fear that her and Pedro's children would eventually claim the throne. Dom Pedro, in retaliation, waged war against the king until his mother convinced him to put the civil strife to an end.

Two years later, Dom Pedro took the throne; he had his wife's assassins tracked down and brought to the public courtyard. There he watched as their hearts were torn from their living bodies. He then set about making his children rightful heirs to the throne. In a shocking announcement, Dom Pedro ordered a posthumous matrimonial ceremony to take place. Five years after her death, Inês was removed from her grave and dressed like a queen. Dom Pedro forced the court to kneel before her corpse and kiss her rotting hand. He had his own tomb built opposite hers, and on it reads *"Até ao fim do mundo"* (until the end of the world).

known as **Arte Xávega**, named after the style of boat used. An exciting fish auction, open to the public, follows. During the summer, look for late-night **folk music** gatherings on the beach. **Bullfights** are also popular; Nazaré features *corridas* on various summer weekends (usually Sa 10pm; tickets from €10). Bullfights occur the first three Saturdays in July and August and the first week of September. Inquire at the tourist office for exact times, dates, and prices.

◪ DAYTRIPS FROM NAZARÉ

ALCOBAÇA

Buses are the best way to reach Alcobaça. The bus station on Av. Manuel da Silva Carolino (☎262 58 22 21) offers service to: Batalha (30min., 7 per day 7:30am-7:10pm, €2.50); Leiria (1hr., 6 per day 7:30am-7:10pm, €3.10); Lisboa (2hr.; M-F 2 per day, Sa-Su 1 per day 6:30am-3pm; €8.30); Nazaré (25min., 11 per day 7:30am-7:40pm, €1.70).

Visitors from around the world travel to this tranquil hillside town to stand inside the ◪**Mosteiro de Santa Maria de Alcobaça**, the largest church in Portugal. This enormous abbey was founded in 1153 by Portugal's first king, Dom Afonso Henriques, following his removal of the Moors from Santarém. In an attempt to secure Christianity in the region, the king granted the land to Cistercian monks. To appease him, the monks built a monastery spanning over 200m in length, the largest building of the Cistercian order in all of Europe. It was also the first Portuguese edifice constructed using Gothic techniques. Today, all that remains of the original facade are the pointed-arched doorway and the rose window above it. In the sanctuary of the church lie the tombs of Portugal's most famous star-crossed lovers, Dom Pedro I and his wife, Inês de Castro. Surrounding the monastery's cloisters are numerous Gothic rooms, most notably the **Sala dos Monges** (Monks' Hall), and the immense *azulejo*-covered kitchen and refectory, where the monks could roast more than six oxen at a time. The neo-Gothic **Royal Pantheon** and the **Hall of Kings.** If you can manage it, time your visit to coincide with the religious opera concerts held M-F at 11am and 3pm. (☎262 50 51 20. Open daily Apr.-Sept. 9am-7pm; Oct.-Mar. 9am-5pm, Su before 2pm free. Last entrance 30min. before closing. €4.50, students 14-25 €2.25, under 14 free.)

To escape the international swarm flowing in and out of the monastery, take a 5min. hike to the **Castelo de Alcobaça** and check out the ruins of a 12th-century castle. The remaining stone walls provide a serene retreat for crowd-weary travelers and an incredible panoramic view of the surrounding area. Be careful, though, as the climb up the walls is easier than the descent. From R. D. Pedro V, turn right on R. Alexandre Herculano. At the end of the street go left, following the *"castelo"* sign. Continue through the intersection as the road becomes R. do Castelo, passing the Igreja da Misericórdia on the left. About 200m up the hill the road splits; there will be a dirt trail to your left, marked by another *"castelo"* sign. The **Museu da Vinha e do Vinho,** a 10min. walk from the bus station, houses a comprehensive 10,000 piece exhibit about the history and methods of Portugal's wine industry. While not a wine-tasting tour, the exhibit is participatory and may involve free samples. (☎262 58 22 22; info@ivv.min-agricultura.pt. Open M-F 9am-12:30pm and 2-5:30pm. Weekend visits for groups available with reservation. €1.50, students €0.75.) Turn right out of the bus stop and left on Av. dos Combatentes de Grande Guerra, away from the monastery. Continue straight on the road, around two rotaries. The museum is 300m past the second.

Alcobaça makes a great daytrip, but should you spend the night, **Pensão Corações Unidos ❷,** R. Frei António Brandão, 39, off Pr. 25 de Abril, has 35 rooms decorated in a rustic style with private bathrooms. Buffet breakfast is included. (☎262 58 21 42. Reception 8am-midnight in the restaurant below. July-Sept. singles €20; doubles €40. Oct.-June €15/30. AmEx/MC/V.) The **tourist office** is on the corner of Pr. 25 de Abril, across from the hulking monastery. Turn right out of the bus station and right again onto Av. dos Combatentes de Grande Guerra, following the road as it becomes R. D. Pedro V and curves around the monastery. The tourist office is at the end of the strip of shops, across from the monastery. (☎262 58 23 77. English, Spanish, and French spoken. 15min. free Internet access. Open daily May-July and Sept. 10am-1pm and 3-7pm; Aug. 10am-7pm; Oct.-Apr. 10am-1pm and 2-6pm.)

SÃO MARTINHO DO PORTO

Buses run to Nazaré (20min., M-F 10 per day 7:04am-7:54pm, €1.70). Schedules are posted in the tourist office. The bus stops on the main road leading into São Martinho do Porto, R. Conde de Avelar.

A stroke of geological good fortune for beachgoers, São Martinho do Porto is a bay almost entirely enclosed by coastline. Millennia of crashing surf hollowed out the area to form a 3km semi-circle of gorgeous, breezy beach. Rolling hills and steep cliffs extend outward, leaving only a small opening for the sea to enter. São Martinho do Porto's tranquil water, red-roofed houses and palm-studded hillside give it a Mediterranean charm that remains untainted by tourists during the year.

If a tiring day at the beach calls for a night of quality relaxation, then **Residencial Atlântica ❹,** R. Miguel Bombarda, 6, just up the road from the tourist office, is the town's best bet. Spotless rooms decorated in a nautical theme come complete with cable TV, a small veranda, private bathroom, and a buffet breakfast. Some of the larger rooms also include a mini-fridge. Avoid staying here in August, when prices rise steeply. (☎262 98 01 51; fax 98 01 63. Reserve ahead for July and Aug. July 15-Aug. doubles €80; Sept.-March €30-35; Apr.-July 14 €35-45. AmEx/MC/V.) For something cheaper, try the **Pensão Americana ❸,** R. D. José de Saldanha, 2, about 20m from the bus stop on the corner of R. Conde de Avelar. While not as nice as the Atlântica, you'll be hard-pressed to find anything cheaper. The 25 rooms are decorated with dark wood furniture and pastel bed linens, making for an inviting and relaxing environment. All rooms come with a private bathroom, TV, and buffet breakfast at the restaurant/bar below. Rooms for 3+ persons come with a full-sized bath tub. (☎262 98 91 70; fax 98 93 49. June singles €30; doubles €45; triples €55; quads €65. July €35/50/65/80. Aug. €40/65/80/100. Sept.-May €25/40/50/60. AmEx/MC/V.) If the beach doesn't provide enough entertainment, give **Bar do Tico ❶** a try. Less than a year old, this cafe/bar has already won over the locals with its cheap food, cool interior, and outdoor foosball table. (☎919 13 93

62. Sandwiches €1.30-3.50, fish/meat dishes €3.50-8.50. DJ after 10pm. Open June-Sept. 9am-4am; Oct.-May 2pm-2am. AmEx/MC/V.)

The bus stop is on R. Conde de Avelar, which runs just parallel to the beach. To get to the tourist office, Lg. Vitorino Fróis, stay on this road and head toward the hills in the opposite direction from the bus (if facing the water, the hills are to the right). The tourist office is on the right. There, visitors can find a list of private rooms, which are generally the cheapest accommodation options. (☎262 98 91 10. English, French, and Spanish spoken. Free Internet access for 15min. Open Tu-Su May-Sept. 10am-1pm and 3-7pm; Oct.-Apr. 10am-1pm and 2-4pm.)

LEIRIA   ☎244

An ancient castle towers over this city of 120,000, while a *futebol* stadium sparkles below. In Leiria, Portugal's two great passions, history and soccer, rival one another for veneration. Situated between Lisboa and Coimbra, Leiria was a strategic point during Dom Afonso Henriques's campaign against the Moors, culminating in its recapture in 1135. Today, the city is one of Portugal's most important economic centers. Its streets lined with trendy boutiques and filled with people from all over Portugal make for a diverse urban center basking in a regal past.

▐ TRANSPORTATION

Trains: The train station is 3km outside town (☎244 88 20 27). Buses run to the train station from a stop along Av. 25 Abril, the street beside the garden connecting the tourist office and the bus station. The stop is a green post marked *"urbana."* (15min.; every 45min. M-F 7:22am-7:32pm, Sa 7:22am-4:42pm; €1. Ask the tourist office for an exact schedule.) To **Coimbra** (2hr., 6 per day 8:55am-9:20pm, €4.50-7); **Figueira da Foz** (1hr., 3 per day 7am-9:20pm, €4.90); **Lisboa** (1¾hr., 6 per day 7:20am-8:40pm, €4.90-10.40).

Buses: The bus station (☎244 81 57 17), off Pr. Paulo VI, across the park from the tourist office. Ticket office in back. Most convenient transport out of Leiria. Express buses are usually twice the price of regional buses. To: **Alcobaça** (50min.; M-F 6 per day 7:10am-6:30pm, Sa-Su 7:10am, 2:25pm; €2.60); **Batalha** (20min., 13 per day 7:10am-7:10pm, €1.57-2.60); **Coimbra** (1hr., 11 per day 7:15am-2am, €8); **Fátima** (1hr., 12 per day 8am-7:25pm, €2.73-5); **Figueira da Foz** (1½hr., 8 per day 7:45am-7:25pm, €5); **Lisboa** (2hr.; 13 per day M-F 6am-11pm, Sa 7am-11pm, Su 7:45am-11pm; €8.70); **Nazaré** (1hr., 8 per day 8am-7:20pm, €2.60-6.60); **Porto** (3½hr., 10 per day 7:15am-2am, €12); **Santarém** (2hr., 3 per day 10:30am-5:15pm, €4.50-10); **Tomar** (1hr.; 6:45am, 6pm; €3.60).

Taxis: Many gather at the Jardim Luís de Camões (☎244 81 59 00 or 88 15 50).

▐✻▐ ORIENTATION AND PRACTICAL INFORMATION

The Jardim Luís de Camões is at the center of Leiria, surrounded by *pensões* and restaurants. Just off the garden is **Praça Rodrigues Lobo,** the heart of the historical center, between the Jardim Luís de Camões and the castle. It is surrounded by cozy cafes, and at night the bars fill with local students. The castle is a 10min. climb from the Praça.

Tourist Office: (☎244 84 87 70; fax 84 87 79), in the Jardim Luís de Camões, across the park from the bus station The office has maps, accommodations lists, and a ▧ **model of Batalha's monastery** made entirely of sugar, egg whites, and water. Free short-term luggage storage and **Internet** access (15min. limit). English, French, and Spanish spoken. Open daily May-Sept. 10am-1pm and 3-7pm; Oct.-Apr. 10am-1pm and 2-6pm.

Laundromat: Ecosec Lavanderia, (☎244 83 36 38) on Beco de São Francisco. From the bus station, walk away from the tourist office on Av. Heróis de Angola, take a left at the theater on Cor. T. Sampaio and take a right on Beco de São Francisco. €4 per kg, shirts and pants €3.80. Open M-F 9am-6pm.

Police: Lg. São Pedro (☎244 84 52 00), by the castle.

Hospital: Hospital de Santo André (☎244 81 70 00), on R. Olhalvas, on the way to Fátima. For non-emergencies, go to the closer **Centro Saúde Dr. Arn. Sampaio** (☎244 81 78 20), R. Dr. Egas Moniz, a 10min. walk from the tourist office.

Internet Access: Convenient (and free) service at **Espaço Internet,** Lg. de Santana (☎244 81 50 91), in the Mercado Sant'Ana. 12 computers with fast connections. 1hr. time limit when people are waiting; the afternoon gets crowded. Identification (passport, driver's license) required to use a computer. Open M-F 9am-7:30pm and 8-11pm, Sa 2-7pm. Access also free at **Biblioteca Municipal Afonso Lopes Vierira,** Lg. Cândido dos Reis, 6, beside the Pousada de Juventude. Open M 1-6pm, Tu-F 10am-6pm.

Post Office: Downtown office (☎800 20 68 68), Av. dos Combatentes da Grande Guerra, between the tourist office and the youth hostel. Label Posta Restante mail "Estação Santana." Open M-F 8:30am-12:30pm and 2-6pm. **Main office,** Av. Heróis de Angola, 99 (☎244 84 94 00), past the bus station toward the mall. Open M-F 8:30am-12:30pm and 2-6:30pm, Sa 9am-12:30pm. **Postal Code:** 2400.

■ ACCOMMODATIONS

Pousada da Juventude de Leiria (HI), Lg. Cândido dos Reis, 7 (☎244 83 18 68). From the bus station, walk across the garden and cross the street to the plaza with fountains. Take a right after the Caixa Geral de Depósitos building, and follow to the end. (If there is construction going on, follow the metal wall down the street.) Take a left on Lg. Cândido dos Reis, and the *pousada* is ahead on the left. An old bishop's residence, now with guest kitchen, TV room, and library. Wi-Fi and breakfast included. Single sex dorms €11; doubles €26, with bath €28. HI card required. AmEx/MC/V. ❶

Rooidenclal Dom Dinis, Tr. Tomar, 2 (☎244 81 53 42; fax 82 35 52). Turn left after exiting the tourist office, cross the bridge, walk 2 blocks, and make a left up the hill at the Residencial's sign. 25 neatly decorated rooms with private bathrooms, phone, and cable TV. In a quiet part of town, but still near the action. Large lounge area with comfy couches. Internet access available. Breakfast included (8-10am). July-Aug. singles €25; doubles €38; triples €50. Sept.-June €22.50/34/45. AmEx/MC/V. ❷

Pensão Residencial Leiriense, R. Afonso de Albuquerque, 6 (☎244 82 30 54; fax 82 30 73). Off Pr. R. Lobo. Bright, slightly undersized rooms with private bath and phone. Great location for hitting up the bars around the area. Check-out noon. In summer singles €25; doubles €38; in winter €24/36. Cash only. ❷

■ FOOD

The **Mercado Municipal,** on Av. Cidade de Maringá, near the stadium and beside the river, sells fresh fish and produce. (Open Tu and Sa 8am-1pm.) Groceries and fresh bread are available at Leiria's convenient **Pingo Doce,** Av. Heróis de Angola, 69, just past the bus station. (Open daily 9am-9pm.)

Cervejaria Camões, Jardim Luís de Camões (☎244 83 86 28) behind the tourist office. French-inspired steaks, served in a pan with a delicious choice of sauces, are the house specialty. Vegetarians can chow down on one of many creative salads. Budget friendly daily specials for only €5. Entrees €6-13. Open daily 10am-2am. AmEx/MC/V. ❷

Restaurante Monte Carlo, R. Dr. Correia Mateus. Practically thievery—guests at the Monte Carlo get the highest quality seafood for the lowest prices in town. Entrees €5-9. Open Tu-Su noon-10:30pm. AmEx/MC/V. ❶

Docevida, Centro Comercial D. Dinis, 6, 7th fl. (☎244 82 78 46), down the street from the Mercado Sant'Ana. For lunch, the only thing cheaper is the university cafeteria. Self-service Portuguese meal for €3. Open daily noon-3pm and 7-10pm. AmEx/MC/V. ❶

👁 📷 SIGHTS AND BEACHES

Leiria's most significant monument is the giant **Castelo de Leiria,** visible throughout the city and particularly stunning late at night, when it is completely lit up against the dark mountainside. Built by Dom Afonso Henriques after he snatched the town from the Moors, this granite fort presides atop the crest of a volcanic hill on the north edge of town. One of the castelo's highlights is the **Torre de Menagem** (Homage Tower) which houses rusty swords, chain mail armor, and artifacts found on-site. The **Sala dos Namorados** (Lovers' Hall) sets the stage for medieval courting—don't miss the beautiful view of the town and river from the terrace. The gigantic and colorful **Estádio Doutor Magalhães Pessoa,** built especially for two Euro Cup 2004 soccer games, is also easily visible. From the main square, walk toward the bus station on Lg. 5 de Outubro. Turn left on Lg. das Forças Armadas, just after the Banco de Portugal. Follow the signs past the austere **Sé** (cathedral) and zigzag up to the castle. (*☎ 244 81 39 82. Castle open Apr.-Sept. M-F 9am-6:30pm, Sa-Su 10am-6:30pm; Oct.-Mar. M-F 9am-5:30pm. Sa-Su 10am-5:30pm. Tower open Tu and Su 10am-noon and 1-5pm. €2.50, students, children, and seniors €1.25).*

Nearby beaches are accessible via buses running from the station to **Praia de Viera** (45min.; 9 per day 7am-7:30pm, last return 6:30pm; July-Sept. 14; €2.30); **Praia Pedrógão,** popular with locals and lined with stately residences (1hr.; 5 per day 9:15am-6pm, last return 7:30pm; €2.40); and the more secluded **São Pedro de Muel** (45min.; 4 per day 8:50am-4:30pm, last return 7:15pm; €2). Check for the exact schedules at the bus station in Leiria, as they are subject to change.

BATALHA   ☎244

Batalha (pop. 7500), a small, sleepy city just outside of Leiria, does not attract much tourist attention, but there are two spectacular reasons not to miss this town. The first is the gigantic Mosteiro de Santa Maria da Vitória, which rivals Belém's Mosteiro dos Jerónimos in its commanding splendor, and second, the equally impressive caves in the nearby park.

📧 TRANSPORTATION

Buses stop in Lg. 14 de Agosto de 1385 across the street from the monastery, near the supermarket. Inquire at the tourist office for info or call the bus station in Leiria (☎244 81 15 07). Buses to: **Leiria** (16 per day 7:15am-7:45pm, €1.57); **Lisboa** (2hr., 5 per day 7:25am-6:10pm, €6.60); **Nazaré** (1hr., 5 per day 7:32am-6:50pm, €2.90) via **Alcobaça** (45min., €2.30); **Tomar** (1½hr.; 8:05am, noon; €2.90) via **Fátima** (40min., €1.60).

🔆 🔽 ORIENTATION AND PRACTICAL INFORMATION

The **tourist office** is on Pr. Mouzinho de Albuquerque along R. Nossa Senhora do Caminho, next to the monastery. The staff speaks English, French, and Spanish and offers maps and bus information as well as lists of accommodations, free short-term luggage storage, and 15min. of free Internet access. (☎244 76 51 80. Open daily May-Sept. 10am-1pm and 3-7pm; Oct.-Apr. 10am-1pm and 2-6pm.) The **police** (☎244 76 51 34) are on R. Mouzinho de Albuquerque, across the street from the bus stop. The **Centro de Saúde** (medical center; ☎244 76 99 20) is on Estrada da Freiria. **Internet** access is available on one computer at **Cafeteria Online,** R. Nossa Senhora do Caminho, down the sidewalk behind the tourist office, in the opposite direction of the rotary. (€2 per 30min., €2.50 per hour.) The **post office,** in Lg. Papa Paulo VI near the freeway entrance, has a fax machine (€2.30 per page) and **Posta Restante.** (☎244 76 91 00; fax 76 91 06. Open M-F 9:30am-1pm and 2:30-6:30pm.) **Postal Code:** 2440.

🛏🍴 ACCOMMODATIONS AND FOOD

Pensão Vitória ❶, well-located on Lg. da Misericórdia next to the bus stop, has four standard rooms, each with one double bed. Grocery store, bus stop, and sites are all within a 5min. walk. (☎244 76 56 78. Reception 9am-11pm in the restaurant below. Singles/doubles €20. Cash only.) **Gládius Quartos ❸,** Pr. Mouzinho de Albuquerque, 7, has three bright, airy blue and white rooms, all with TV and bath. Two rooms have a view of the plaza and the gorgeous monastery. (☎244 76 57 60. Reception 9am-11pm. Singles €20; doubles €30; triples €40, but negotiable. Cash only.) The **restaurant** below Pensão Vitória offers large portions of specials for €5-8 and *frango assado na brasa* (grilled chicken). (Open daily 9am-midnight.) **Bassani ❶,** Lg. 14 de Agosto, 7, sits across from the bus stop, offering over 30 pizza varieties, vegetarian options, and meal combos for €3-4. Locals of all ages crowd into the small foyer, waiting in line to get a slice of pie. (☎244 76 53 33. Open daily 9:30am-3pm and 5:30-10pm. Cash only.)

🔆 SIGHTS

The 📷**Mosteiro Santa Maria da Vitória,** a UNESCO World Heritage site, puts Batalha on the map, and for good reason. Its flamboyant facade soars upward in Gothic and Manueline style, opulently decorated and crowned in dozens of spires. Construction began in 1386 to fulfill Dom João I's promise to the Virgin Mary: he promised to build an enormous monument in her honor if the Portuguese were victorious against Castilian invaders at the Battle of Aljubarrota. The **Capela do Fundador,** the pantheon of João I and the Avis dynasty, lies immediately to the right of the church, housing the elaborate sarcophagi of Dom João I, his English-born queen Philippa of Lancaster, and their famous son Prince Henry the Navigator. Just outside the pantheon entrance rests a far simpler tomb: that of the man who saved Dom João I's life in the Battle of Aljubarrota. Through the 15th-century **Claustro de Dom Afonso V** is the mosteiro's highlight, the **Capelas Imperfeitas** (Unfinished Chapels). Jealous of his predecessor's impressive pantheon, Dom Duarte commissioned the construction of an equally impressive pantheon to house his remains and those of his progeny; unfortunately, construction of the mosteiro dos Jerónimos in Belém drained resources and interest, leaving the elegant Renaissance chapel roofless. Today the mosteiro houses a tomb of unknown soldiers from WWI, under constant guard by military officials. There is also a professional school of stone carving that does demonstrations on how some of the mosteiro's ornate sculptures were made. (Open daily Apr.-Sept. 9am-6pm; Oct.-Mar. 9am-5pm. €4.50, under 25 and seniors €2.25, under 14 and Su before 2pm free.)

A 20min. drive outside town brings you to a spelunker's paradise: a series of spectacular underground *grutas* (caves) in Estremadura's natural park. The **Grutas de Mira de Aire,** with a river 110m below ground level, are the deepest and the largest in all of Portugal. They are so popular that 3 million people visited them within the first 10 years of their opening. The nearby **Grutas de Santo António** and **Alvados**, with their numerous washed-out caverns and sandcastle-like limestone formations, are equally impressive. The easiest way to get to the caves is by **taxi** (€30-40 roundtrip including waiting time). Be sure to set the price with the taxi driver before you head out. It is possible to take a **bus**, but set aside a whole day, as the bus schedules from Batalha require careful planning and involve several hours of layover. Check with the **tourist office** to confirm schedules. (☎244 44 03 22 or 249 84 18 76. Grutas de Mira de Aire open daily July-Aug. 9:30am-8:30pm; June and Sept. 9:30am-7pm; Oct.-Mar. 9:30am-5:30pm; Apr.-May 9:30am-6pm. €3.50, students and seniors €2.50. Grutas de Santo António and Alvados open daily Sept.-May 10am-5pm; June-Aug. 10am-8pm. Tickets for one cave €4.80, children €3. Combination tickets can be purchased for €8/3. Last tickets for both attractions sold 30min. before closing.)

FÁTIMA ☎249

Until May 13, 1917, when the Virgin Mary appeared to three local peasant children, Fátima (pop. 8,000) was just a quiet sheep pasture. Today, every year over 4 million Catholics make pilgrimages to the town to see the stunning *santuário* built to honor the miracle. A sign at the entrance of the *santuário* complex states in several languages, "Fátima is a place for adoration; enter as a pilgrim." Only France's Lourdes rivals this site in popularity with Catholic pilgrims; the miracles believed to have occurred here attract an endless international procession of religious groups. The plaza in front of the church, larger than St. Peter's Square in the Vatican, floods with pilgrims on the 12th and 13th of each month. These pilgrims have created a large tourism industry in Fátima—there are over 10,000 beds for visitors in the various hotels and *residenciais*.

▐ TRANSPORTATION

Trains: The **Caxarias** station (☎808 208 208; www.cp.pt), 10km out of town, is closer than the Fátima station, 22km away. Caxarias to: **Coimbra** (1½hr., 15 per day 5:10am-9:15pm, €6.40-10.10); **Lisboa** (2½hr., 12 per day 4:15am-8:37pm, €8.20-12.25); **Porto** (2-3hr., 15 per day 5:15am-9:15pm, €13.40-24); **Santarém** (1½hr., 16 per day 7am-4:15am, €4.90-7.60). **Buses** run between Caxarias and Fátima (30min., 5 per day 7:40am-5:20pm, €2) and the Fátima train and bus stations (45min., 7 per day 7:40am-6:45pm, €2.67).

Buses: Av. D. José Alves Correia da Silva (☎249 53 16 11). To: **Batalha** (30min., 3 per day 9am-6:25pm, €1.57); **Coimbra** (1½hr., 16 per day 7:45am-9:30pm, €8); **Leiria** (35min., 13 per day 7:45am-8pm, €2.67-5); **Lisboa** (1½-2½hr., 11-19 per day 7am-8pm, €8.70); **Nazaré** (1½hr., 8:45am-7:45pm, €3.50-8.70); **Porto** (2-3½hr., 4 per day 7:45am-7:40pm, €12); **Santarém** (1hr., 5 per day 7:30am-5:45pm, €10); **Tomar** (1¼hr.; M-Sa 3 per day 8:30am-2:35pm, Su 8:30am-2:15pm; €2.98).

Taxis: Next to the bus station (☎49 53 11 93 or 249 53 38 16).

▐▌ ORIENTATION AND PRACTICAL INFORMATION

Fátima is essentially a religious monument surrounded by souvenir shops; all activity centers around the basilica complex. The **Santuário de Fátima** is the huge, open *praça* in the middle of everything, filling with visitors on special occasions and on the 12th and 13th of each month. Directly below it, a new 9000-seat church set to open in October 2007 is under construction. **Av. Dom José Alves Correia da Silva** is below the Santuário, beginning near the bus station. It runs past the lower end of the complex to the **tourist office**, which is situated in a lovely stone building with a wooden roof. From the bus station, go right and walk approximately 10min.; the office is on the right.

Tourist Office: (☎249 53 11 39). Free **Internet** access (15min. limit). English, French, and Spanish are spoken. Open daily June-July and Sept. 10am-1pm and 3-7pm; Aug. 10am-7pm; Oct.-May 10am-1pm and 2-6pm. The Santuário has its own information office (on the left side when facing the basilica; ☎249 53 96 23) with temporary **luggage storage**. Every day at 6:30am it posts the day's schedule of masses. English, French, and Spanish spoken. Open M-Sa 9am-6pm, Su 9am-5pm.

Banks: Several major banks have branches along the commercial center of R. Jacinta Marto. Most open 8:30am-3pm.

Police: Av. D. José Alves Correia da Silva (☎249 53 05 80), past the bus station.

Medical: Centro de Saúde (☎249 53 18 36) on R. Jacinta Marto, near the bus station.

Internet: Space Net on the 3rd floor of the **Museu da Vida do Cristo** complex has self-service coin-operated Internet access. €0.50 per 15min. Open daily 9am-11pm.

Post Office: R. Cónego Formigão (☎249 53 90 80) Open M-F 8:30am-6pm. **Postal Code:** 2495.

ACCOMMODATIONS AND FOOD

Scores of *residenciais* and hotels surround the basilica complex. During the grand pilgrimages on the 12th and 13th from May to October, the crowds are so big that they fill the entire plaza, an amazing feat given its mammoth size. Understandably, prices tend to vary greatly. Saturday stays are usually €5-10 more than weekday stays, and it's best to reserve a week ahead, and a month ahead on summer weekends and holidays. The newly renovated █ **Residencial Aleluia ❸**, Av. D. José A. C. Silva, 120, down the street from the bus stop on the lower corner of the complex, has chic rooms with hardwood floors, suede bedspreads, and leather couches. The *residencial* also offers dormitory-style rooms with shared baths on the top floor. (☎249 53 15 40; www.residencialaleluia.com. Breakfast €3. Lunch/dinner buffets €10. Singles €25-30; doubles €30-35; triples €36-42. Dorms €10 per person or €15 for a double. Prices go up €5 on summer weekends and during all of August. AmEx/MC/V.) Another budget option is **Residencial São Francisco ❷**, R. Francisco Marto, 100, near the Santuário. The rooms are plainly decorated but quiet and well furnished. All come with TV, phone, and private bath. (☎249 53 30 17; fax 53 20 28. Breakfast included. Reception 8am-midnight. Singles €22.50; doubles €37.50; triples €42.50. Cash only.)

Restaurants and snack bars cluster in between souvenir shops along R. Francisco Marto, R. Santa Isabela, and R. Jacinta Marto. Close to the wax museum on the left side of the Santuário, the upstairs **O Terminal ❷**, R. Jacinta Marto, 24, offers the biggest portions of traditional Portuguese food for the best prices in town. (☎249 53 19 77. Open daily 10am-3:30pm and 6-9:30pm. Cash only.) On the other side of the Santuário, well-established **Restaurant Alfredo ❷**, R. Francisco Marto, 159 CV, serves huge plates and is always filled with locals. Their *bacalhau no forno* (oven-broiled cod) is a house specialty. Limited vegetarian options. (☎249 53 12 49. Down the stairs past the corner Millennium BCP bank. Entrees €6-10. Open daily noon-3pm and 7-10pm. MC/V.) Rock bottom budget needs can also be met at the **Pingo Doce** supermarket on Av. D. José A. C. da Silva. (From the bus station, go to the left. Open daily 8:30am-9pm.)

👁 SIGHTS

■ **SANTUÁRIO DE FÁTIMA.** This modern holy sanctuary is visually overwhelming. The sanctuary itself is comprised of an open plaza, surrounded by a large chapel and other small buildings. Many of the devout travel the length of the plaza on their knees, all the way from the cross to the *capelinha*, praying for divine assistance or giving thanks to the Virgin Mary.

 THE 2000-YEAR-OLD VIRGIN. In 2000, after decades of fervent speculation, the Vatican disclosed the closely-guarded "third secret" revealed to the children of Fátima. The Virgin is said to have prophesied the 1981 assassination attempt on Pope John Paul II and the fall of the Soviet Union. The Pope credited the Virgin with saving his life and had the bullet placed in her crown.

At the end of the plaza rises the **Basílica do Rosário** (erected in 1928), featuring a crystal cruciform beacon atop the tower's seven-ton bronze crown. Inside are the tombs of the three "seers," or witnesses of the apparitions. Francisco and Jacinta died as children, and lie in opposing naves. Lúcia, the third and oldest child, died in 2005 at the age of 97 after serving as a devout nun for over 70 years. Her tomb was placed beside Jacinta's in February 2006. *(Open daily 7:30am-10:30pm. Mass daily at 7:30, 9, 11am, 3, 4:30, and 6:30pm. Free.)* To the left is the **Capelinha das Aparições,** the first of the buildings to be constructed, where a statue of the Virgin now stands in the exact location where the miracles are said to have taken place. Sheltered beneath a metal and glass canopy, the *capelinha* was built in 1919 and continues to house "Perpetual Adoration," which consists of several masses in various languages during the day and a fire, continuously fueled by the candles of visitors. *(International mass Th 9am. Candlelight procession daily Apr.-Oct. 9:30pm.)*

MUSEUMS. The **Museu de Cera** (Wax Museum) gives a comprehensive history of Fátima and the miracles that made it famous, taking visitors through 31 unnervingly realistic wax scenes. *(R. Jacinta Marto. ☎249 53 93 00; www.mucefa.pt. Open daily Apr.-Oct. 9:30am-6:30pm; Nov.-Mar. M and Sa 9am-5:30pm, Tu-F and Su 10am-5pm. €5, under 12 €3.)* The **Museu Fátima 1917 Aparições**, with its visual and sound effects and descriptions of the legend, is a similar but more dramatic version of the wax museum. The audio guide is available in English, Portuguese, Spanish, French, Italian, and German. *(R. Jacinta Marto below ground level in the J.P. II building. To the left of the basilica, follow the signs to the underground complex across the street from Hotel Fátima. ☎249 53 28 58; www.museuaparicoes.com. Open daily Apr.-Oct. 9am-7pm; Nov.-Mar. 9am-6pm. €3, under 12 €1.50.)* The **Museu de Arte Sacra e Etnologia** exhibits Catholic icons from various centuries and cultures, showcasing the interplay between local people and the Catholic religion. *(R. Francisco Marto, 52. ☎249 53 94 70; fax 53 94 79. Open Tu-Su Apr.-Oct. 10am-7pm; Nov.-Mar. 10am-5pm. €2.50, seniors and students €1.50.)* Fátima's newest museum, the **Museu do Vida de Cristo,** traces the life of Jesus from conception to resurrection in 33 scenes. The shiny, white-marbled modern complex also houses a mini-shopping center where wine, religious artifacts, and other small trinkets can be purchased. *(Rua Francisco Marto. ☎249 53 06 80; www.vidadecristo.pt. Open daily 9am-7pm. €6, children under 12 €3.50.)*

Fátima's ■**Grutas da Moeda** (Moeda Caves) offer a refreshing change from the religious sites and are just as beautiful and more budget-friendly than the caves near Batalha. The **Grutas da Moeda** are easily accessible. Discovered in 1971 by two hunters chasing a fox, the caves lie 45m below the surface. Several stunning limestone formations and an underground waterfall make the caves a relaxing place to visit. Bring a rain jacket if you go in the winter, as cave showers are frequent. (☎244 70 43 02 or 244 70 38 38. Call ☎800 20 56 18 from the tourist office to schedule a free pick-up. Be advised that the number does not work outside of the tourist office. Caves open daily July-Sept. 9am-7pm; April-June. 9am-6pm; Oct.-Mar. 9am-5pm; last tickets sold 30min. before closing. €5, children 6-12 €2.50.)

TOMAR   ☎249

Visitors come to Tomar (pop. 20,000) to walk wide-eyed through the castle, fortress, convent, and several beautiful gardens that make up the Convento de Cristo. In 1160, Dom Afonso Henriques enlisted the Knights Templar to build a fortified castle at Tomar, then the weak spot between Lisboa and Coimbra. When the Knights fell out of favor with the Pope 200 years later, sheepish Portuguese royalty quickly founded a new religious order and gave them the Templar's property, resulting in today's unique collage of menacing medieval walls and ornate architecture. The rest of the town lazes beside the Rio Nabão, stirring only every four years for the Festival dos Tabuleiros (due again in June 2011).

⌐ TRANSPORTATION

Trains: Av. dos Combatentes da Grande Guerra (☎808 20 82 08; www.cp.pt). Tomar is the northern end of a minor line, so most destinations require a transfer at Entroncamento or Lamarosa; ask about this when purchasing your ticket and pay attention to the stops. Ticket office open M-F and Su 5:30am-8:30pm and 9:30-10:30pm, Sa 5:30am-8:30pm. To: **Coimbra** (2½hr., 12 per day 5:45am-8pm, €8.20); **Lisboa** (2hr., 16 per day 5am-10pm, €8.20); **Porto** (4½hr., 11 per day 5:44am-8pm, €17.05-23.50); **Santarém** (1hr., 16 per day 5am-10pm, €4.90).

Buses: Rodoviária Tejo, Av. dos Combatentes da Grande Guerra (☎968 94 35 50). Beware: express buses are twice the price of regular buses. To: **Coimbra** (2½hr., 7am, €9.50); **Fátima** (30min., 4 per day 7:50am-5:20pm, €2.98-5.20); **Figueira da Foz** (4½hr., 7am, €9.40); **Leiria** (1hr.; M-F 7:15am, 5:45pm, Sa 7am; €3.10); **Lisboa** (2hr., 3 per day 9:30am-4:45pm, €6.50); **Nazaré** (1½hr., 6 per day 7:30am-5:20pm, €5.50); **Porto** (4hr., 7am, €11.60); **Santarém** (1hr., 12:30pm, €4.70).

Taxis: Taxis wait by the bus and train stations and across the river on R. Santa Iria. ☎249 31 23 73 or 917 81 68 19 to schedule a pick up.

✷⑦ ORIENTATION AND PRACTICAL INFORMATION

The Rio Nabão divides Tomar into eastern and western banks. Almost everything travelers need—the train and bus stations, accommodations, and sights—can be found on the western bank around the checkered **Praça da República**. Running from this main square to the river is **Rua Serpa Pinto**, which ends at the ancient **Ponte Velha** (Old Bridge) and becomes **Rua Marquês Pombal** on the other side of the water. **Avenida Dr. Cândido Madureira** parallels R. Serpa Pinto a few streets away, starting at the main **tourist office** and running into the **Ponte Nova** (New Bridge), the second bridge connecting the halves of Tomar. The bus and train stations sit side by side on **Avenida dos Combatentes da Grande Guerra** at the edge of town.

Tourist Office: Av. Dr. Cândido Madureira (☎249 32 24 27; www.tomartourism.com). From the bus/train station, head down Av. General Bernardo Faria, which runs parallel to the river toward the city past several municipal buildings. Turn left 3 blocks later onto Av. Cândido Madureira. Short-term **luggage storage** available. English, Spanish, and French spoken. Open daily from 10am-1pm and 2-6pm.

Laundromat: 5 á Sec (☎249 32 35 31), inside Supermercado Modelo. From Pr. da República, take R. Serpa Pinto and go straight for about 1.5km; the Supermercado will be on your right after passing the McDonald's. €4 per kg for towels and sheets. Wash, dry, and iron €2.30 for shirts, €2.95 for pants. Next day service. Open daily 9am-9pm.

Police: R. Dr. Sousa (☎249 31 34 44).

Pharmacy: Farmácia Central, R. Marquês de Pombal, 18 (☎249 31 23 29). From Pr. da República, take R. Serpa Pinto and cross the bridge; it will be on your left. Open M-F 9am-7:30pm, Sa 9am-1pm.

Hospital: Hospital Nossa Senhora da Graça, Av. Dona Maria de Lourdes Melo e Castelo (☎249 32 01 00), on the other side of the river (25min. walk).

Internet Access: Espaço Internet, R. Amorim Rosa, 33 (☎249 312 291), across the river. From Ponte Velha, make a right onto R. Amorim Rosa. From Ponte Nova make a left. Free. 30min. limit only enforced if people are waiting. Open M-Sa 9:30am-8pm.

Post Office: Av. Marquês de Tomar (☎249 31 04 00; fax 31 04 06), across from Parque Mouchão. **Posta Restante** and **fax machine** available. Open M-F 8:30am-6pm, Sa 9am-noon. **Postal Code:** 2300.

ACCOMMODATIONS

Finding accommodations is a problem only during the Festival dos Tabuleiros. **R. Serpa Pinto** is lined with great, quality lodging, while cheaper options lie closer to the bus and train stations.

Residencial União, R. Serpa Pinto, 94 (☎249 32 31 61; fax 32 12 99), halfway between Pr. da República and the bridge. One of the nicest budget accommodations Tomar has to offer, in an elegant 106-year-old house decorated with antique furniture. 28 cozy rooms have satellite TV, phone, regal red carpet, and private bath. Breakfast included. Internet access (first 5min. free, €0.50 per 10min. afterwards). Reserve ahead. Singles €22.50; doubles €32.50; triples €40. Cash only. ❷

Residencial Luz, R. Serpa Pinto, 144 (☎249 31 23 17; www.residencialluz.com). 14 tidy, snug rooms, most with private bath, TV, and phone. Quite a bargain if you don't mind a tiny bathroom. Common room with satellite TV and movies in English. Internet €2.40 per hr. May 16-Sept. singles €19; doubles €32.50; triples €35; quads €60. Oct.-May 15 €17.50/25/35/45. Cash only. ❷

Residencial Cavaleiros de Cristo, R. Alexandre Herculano, 7 (☎249 32 12 03 or 249 32 10 67; fax 32 11 92). One street to the right of Pr. da República (if facing the castle). Rooms decorated in a steel-gray Egyptian motif have satellite TV, minibar, A/C, central heat, phone, and tile bathroom. Breakfast included. In summer singles €35; doubles €49; in winter €26.50/41. AmEx/MC/V. ❸

FOOD

Tomar is home to some of the cheapest, most delectable restaurants in Portugal. Around Pr. da República a full meal can be enjoyed for under €5. Still, there is no better place for a picnic than the lush **Parque do Mouchão,** in the center of the river near **Ponte Velha.** The market, on the corner of Av. Norton de Matos and R. Santa Iria, provides all but the red-checked blanket. (Open Tu and Th-F 8am-2pm. Flea market on F.) Several **mini-markets** line the side streets between the tourist office and Pr. da República. Supermarket **Ponto Fresco,** Av. Dr. Cândido Madureira, 56, is on the same street as the tourist office. (Open daily 9am-1:30pm and 3-8pm.)

Piri/Piri, R. dos Moinhos, 54 (☎249 31 34 94). Make a right off R. Serpa Pinta, one street from the river. One of the friendliest places in town. Pick from the list of daily speɩɩals ui Portuguese cuisine (€4.95; half-plate €3.95) and add a half-bottle of red wine (€1.50). Entrees €4.50-6. Open daily noon-3pm and 7-11pm. Cash only. ❶

Salsinha Verde, Pr. da República, 19 (☎249 31 65 63), to the left of town hall. While the *pratos do dia,* like the baked chicken, are only €3.50, the real steal is the *ementa económica,* a full meal consisting of soup, an entree, dessert, and coffee for only €5.50. Other entrees €5-8. Open daily 8:30am-4pm and 7pm-midnight. Cash only. ❶

O Siciliano, R. Voluntários da República, 164 (☎249 32 43 88), across the river from R. Serpa Pinto; take a left at the first real intersection. This welcoming little restaurant promises a stomach-stuffing Italian meal. Delicious pasta entrees (€6-10) and massive pizzas (€6.50-10). Open M-Sa noon-2:30pm and 7-11pm. Cash only. ❷

◎ 🏵 SIGHTS AND FESTIVALS

Tomar is known throughout the world for its 🏛**Convento de Cristo,** an architectural treasure filled with peaceful cloisters, stunning domes, and beautiful, winding staircases. From the tourist office, take a right and follow the road until you see a steeper stone path to the left. It's a 3min. climb to the convent. A UNESCO World Heritage site, the convent's first structure was built by the Moors during the 9th century as a defense from insistent invaders. The attempt failed, and after the defeat of the Moors, the Knights Templar fortified the stronghold in 1160. One of the more impressive aspects of the convent is the area that surrounds its entrance; *azulejo*-covered benches beckon visitors to sit in the garden and admire the views of the nearby national forest. Upon entering the castle walls, an ornate canopy protects the high altar of the **Templo dos Templares,** modeled after the Holy Sepulchre in Jerusalem. Below stands the **Janela do Capítulo** (chapter window), a tribute to the Age of Discovery. Further into the complex lies one of Europe's masterpieces of Renaissance architecture: the **Claustro dos Felipes.** The *claustro* honors Felipe II of Castilla, crowned here as Felipe I of Portugal during Iberia's unification (1580-1640). Stairs spiral upward to views of the **Terraço da Cera.** From the terrace you can see the **Claustro da Santa Bárbara** where gargoyles alternately cough up spurts of water into a fountain. The nearby **Charola** (oratory) was built in the second half of the 12th century and was the original Templar church. (☎249 31 34 81; convento.cristo@ippar.pt. Open daily June-Sept. 9am-6pm; Oct.-May 9am-5pm. Last entry 30min. before closing. €4.50, under 25 and seniors €2.25.)

The **Museu Luso-Hebraico Abraáo Zacuto** is the most significant reminder of Portugal's historical importance to the European Jewish community. This synagogue was built between 1430 and 1460 and abandoned in 1496 when the Jews faced exile or conversion to Christianity. It is the oldest Jewish temple in Portugal, and it became the town prison in 1516. Over the years, it was converted first into a Catholic chapel, then a food storage space, and finally an urban barn. Today, it houses a small museum of international Jewish history, with a collection of tombstones, inscriptions, and objects from around the world. (R. Dr. Joaquim Jaquinto, 73. Open daily 10am-1pm and 2-6pm. Free. Donations welcome.)

Around the 20th of October, during the **Feira de Santa Iria,** handicrafts, folklore, *fado,* and raisins (for the Raisin Fair) fill Tomar. Since 1984, Tomar has also celebrated the **Feira de Artesanato** (Crafts Fair) during the first half of May. The biggest party in Tomar, however, is the **Festa dos Tabuleiros,** a religious festival celebrating the Holy Spirit that takes place in mid-June once every four years (next scheduled for 2011). Six thousand people swarm the town for a week to watch young girls walk in a 4km procession bearing the traditional 40 lb. *tabuleiro* (tray) stacked on their heads. The tabuleiro consists of flowers and 30 loaves of bread, symbolizing the 30 pieces of silver that sold Christ to the Romans.

CASTELO BRANCO ☎272

The capital of the Beira Baixa province, Castelo Branco (literally "White Castle") is the largest city for miles, but it's more a transportation hub and a base for day-trips than a tourist destination itself. However, in over 700 years, the city has managed to create more than a few worthwhile tourist sites. The most popular are the **castle** ruins, of which there are just enough left to determine that the castle was not, in fact, white. The ruins lie a steep 10min. climb from the center, but visitors are free to climb the 12th-century **walls** and **towers** for a spectacular view of the surrounding towns (and countries, on a clear day). The nearby **Miradouro de St. Gens** offers magnificent views as well. Down in the city, the highlight is the **Jardim do Paco,** formerly the gardens of the Bishop's estate, now speckled with small allegorical statues, including Death and Hell in the far corners of the main garden. (☎272 34 05 00. Open daily July-Aug. 9am-7pm; Sept.-June 9am-5pm. €2.)

Residencial Arraiana ❷, Av. 1 de Maio, 18, has sparsely decorated, average-sized rooms. Rooms feature a small yet clean private bath, TV, A/C, balconies in some rooms, and even a mini-bar. From the tourist office, go left on Al. da Liberdade and continue straight as it becomes Av. 1 de Maio. (☎272 34 16 34, ext. 7. Breakfast included. Singles €20-25; doubles €40; triples €50. AmEx/MC/V.) **Restaurante Kalifa ❷,** R. Cadetes de Toledo, 10, around the corner from the tourist office and down a ramp from Av. Nuno Alvares, has served traditional Portuguese favorites for 25 years. (☎272 34 42 46. Entrees €4-14. Open daily 7am-midnight. AmEx/MC/V.) For groceries, hit **Pingo Doce,** Av. 1 de Maio, 60. (Open daily 8:30am-9pm.)

Rede Expressos buses, R. Rod. Rebelo, are just down the street from the central square. Buses run to: Coimbra (3hr.; 6:30, 7:30am, 2:30, 4:15, 4:45pm; €11); Elvas (3½hr.; M-Sa 10:45am, 2:15, 6pm, Su 6pm; €15.80); Guarda (1¾hr.; M-Sa 8 per day 8am-9:34pm, Su 9am-9:34pm; €8:50); Lisboa (2½-3½hr., 8 per day 5am-6:36pm, €11.20); Porto (4hr., 8 per day 6:30am-4:47pm, €14.40). **Taxis** (☎272 341 539) are on Av. Nuno Alvares, around the corner from the tourist office. Castelo Branco's backbone is a continuous street with several names: the **Alameda da Liberdade** runs the length of the main square, **Praça do Município,** and then becomes **Avenue 1 de Maio** as it leaves the town center. The corner of the square, in front of the municipal building, also marks the point of departure for the hike to the hilltop **castle.** In the other direction, Al. de Liberdade becomes **Rue das Olarias** and runs past the cathedral to **Largo da Sé,** and then to the **Jardim do Paco.** The **tourist office** is in a kiosk on the top level of the main square just off of Al. da Liberdade. From the bus station, exit the station toward the tunnel across the street, take a right onto R. do Saibreiro, take your first left, walk a block, and turn right onto R. S. da Piedade; the office is at the end on the right, across from the white rocks that spell out Castelo Branco. Its multilingual staff provides short-term **luggage storage.** (☎272 33 03 39. Open M-F 9:30am-7:30pm, Sa-Su 9:30am-1pm and 2:30-6pm.) **Banks** and 24hr. **ATMs** line Al. da Liberdade; for **currency exchange** go to **Millennium BCP,** Al. da Liberdade, 19. (☎707 50 24 24. Open M-F 8:30am-3:30pm.) **Farmácia Nuno Alvares** is on Av. 1 de Maio, 83. (☎272 34 14 45; www.farmacianunoalvares.com. Open M-F 9am-12:30pm and 2:30-7pm. Weekend pharmacy opening schedules available.) The **Hospital Amato Lusitano** (☎272 00 02 72) is on R. da Granja. The **police** (☎272 34 06 22), R. de S. Jorge, are next to the government building at the corner of the main square. **Internet** access is at **Cyber Centro,** through the courtyard of the yellow building on Av. G. H. Delgado, the street parallel to Al. da Liberdade on the other side of the square. (Open M-F 9am-11pm. Students €0.70 per hour, non-students €1.)

The **post office,** R. da Se, €30/32, is across from the cathedral. (☎272 34 00 30. Open M-F 8:30am-6:30pm, Sa 9am-12:30pm.) **Postal Code:** 6000.

MONSANTO

A tiny village carved into the peak of a granite mountain, Monsanto would warrant a daytrip even without its amazing ▧**castle ruins.** Deemed "the most Portuguese village in Portugal" in 1938, Monsanto captures the Portuguese spirit with its stone houses, friendly residents, and incredible sweeping views of the countryside. Starting from the town's center, the 15th-century **Igreja de São Salvador,** walk uphill and follow the pedestrian signs to the castle. The ruins are one of the most beautiful sites in Portugal. The 12th- and 13th-century Roman-inspired ▧**Capela de São Miguel** and the empty **graves** carved into the rock by its entrance are of particular interest. Cross the short path to the left of the castle, just after the Capela de São Miguel, to see the **Capela de São João,** a ruined chapel overgrown with vegetation. Due to patchy bus service, trips usually require overnight stays. **Casa da Maria ❷,** Av. Fernando Ramos Rocha, 11, is on the street leading into town, about 50m down from the bus stop. Dona Maria and her English-speaking husband Erizo rent out the house to visitors. The town is tiny, so just ask around for them or try calling. (Dona Maria ☎965 62 46 07, Erizo 966 44 36 63. TV, A/C, kitchen, 2 bathrooms. €25 per person per night. Cash only.) The **restaurant ❷** serves typical Portuguese plates, and some not-so-typical ones, like the vegetable tart (€12.50), in a classy setting. (☎277 31 44 71. Entrees €10-15. Open daily 1-3pm and 7:30-10pm.) The **bus** to Monsanto leaves from Castelo Branco's bus station (1½hr.; M-F 5:15pm, returns to Castelo Branco M-Sa 6:15am, Su 2:20pm; €4.50). The drop-off and pickup spot is in a small parking lot on top of a steep hill. From there, it's a short walk to anywhere in town, including the tourist office. Just follow the signs up the road, past the church and to the left. Be aware: there is only one bus per day from Monsanto, and it often leaves very early in the morning. Alternatively, buses can be taken to Adeia do Bispo, and from there a taxi is around €14. There is a **tourist office** uphill from the central church that provides maps and info. Unfortunately, it may be closed by the time the bus from Castelo Branco arrives at 6:45pm. English, French, and Spanish are spoken. **Internet** access is available (☎277 31 46 12. Open daily in summer 10am-1pm and 2-6pm; in winter 9:30am-1pm and 2-5:30pm.)

THE NORTH

As new buildings and modern flair come to Europe, many lament the loss of the "old country," as if the last century's big cities and big governments squashed the soul of the continent. This march of progress must have lost its beat when it neared the north of Portugal, where ancient narrow streets, ornately decorated buildings, green mountains, and peaceful vineyards stretch for miles, unaltered by time. In addition to sweet wine, the region is also famous for its memories of yester-year; history buffs go to the North to retrace the steps of Lusitania's ancestors. With ample opportunities for hiking, camping, and relatively untamed forestry, the region is also paradise for nature-lovers. A visit to the North is indispensable. After all, though wine can be shipped, Portugal's finest countryside cannot.

HIGHLIGHTS OF THE NORTH

CRAWL through Celtic ruins on Monte de Santa Luzia in **Viana do Castelo** (p. 736).

MARVEL at the elaborate **Capela de São Miguel** in **Coimbra** (p. 740).

BELIEVE your favorite childhood fairy tale in the enchanting **Buçaco Forest** (p. 745).

HIKE a misty mountain top in the medieval town of **Sortelha** (p. 752).

DOURO AND MINHO

The region of the Douro and Minho rivers is wine country—the purples, blues, and greens of the stretching vineyards and *quintas* (wine estates) are worthy of a Keats ode. The major cities of this region, Porto and Braga, are enchanting as well. With age-old buildings, lively festivals, tall medieval towers, and amazing shopping, these metropolis areas provide numerous opportunities for adventure.

PORTO (OPORTO)   ☎ 22

Stunning edifices rise up from the bustling city squares of Oporto (pop. 263,000) with an elegance reminiscent of Paris or Prague. Portugal's second largest city, commonly referred to as Porto, is brimming with small shops and residences that seem to be on the brink of toppling into the Rio Douro. Once a magnificent Roman trade center, Porto still retains its thriving commercial industry, focusing predominantly on the production, sale, and most importantly, consumption, of port wine. Visitors to Porto usually come to admire the breathtaking monuments of its medieval glory days, but it's the busy shopping centers, friendly bars and cafes, and overall warmth and vivacity of this big city that keeps them around.

⌐ TRANSPORTATION

Flights: Aeroporto Francisco de Sá Carneiro (☎229 43 24 00), 13km from downtown. The recently completed metro E (violet line) goes to the airport and is the fastest and cheapest option (25min., €1.35). Buses #601 and 87 run to the airport from R. do Carmo, but make multiple stops (1hr., €1.50). The **aerobus** (☎225 07 10 54) from Av. dos Aliados near Pr. da Liberdade is more efficient (40min., every 30min. 7am-7pm,

THE NORTH

Northern Portugal

€4, free for TAP passengers). Buy tickets onboard. **Taxis** are even quicker (15-20min., €18-20). **TAP Air Portugal,** Pr. Mouzinho de Albuquerque, 105 (☎226 08 02 31), flies to major European cities, with 6 daily shuttles to **Lisboa** (35min., €100-150).

Trains: Trains arriving in Porto stop at **Estação de Campanhã** (☎808 20 82 08; www.cp.pt), on R. da Estação, before entering the station in the town center, **Estação de São Bento** (☎808 20 82 08), Pr. Almeida Garrett. Trains leaving S. Bento will run to Campanhã first (5min., every 5-10min. 5:35am-12:40am, €1). From **Estação de Campanhã** trains run to: **Aveiro** (1hr., 47 per day 5:45am-1:35am, €2-12.50); **Braga** (1hr., 26 per day 6:20am-10:35pm, €2-12.50); **Coimbra** (1½-2hr., 24 per day 6:05am-1:35am, €12-16.10); **Lisboa** (3½-4½hr., 18 per day 6:15am-1:35am, €15.60-28.60); **Madrid** (11-12hr., 10pm, €64; change at Entroncamento); **Viana do Castelo** (1½-2hr., 11 per day 6am-8:35pm, €4.35-7); **Vigo,** Spain (4hr.; 8:05am, 6:05pm; €12.80).

Buses: Several companies operate in the downtown area.

Internorte, Pr. Galiza, 96 (☎226 05 24 20) has service to **Madrid** (10hr.; daily 9am and 9:30am, also M-F and Su 9pm; €43-44), as well as other international cities. Book 3 days ahead. Open M-F 9am-12:30pm and 2-6:30pm, Sa 9am-12:30pm and 2-4pm, Su 9am-12:30pm and 2-5:30pm.

Rede Expressos, R. Alexandre Herculano, 366 (☎222 00 69 54; www.rede-expressos.pt). To **Braga** (1¼hr., 10 per day 10am-4:30am, €5); **Bragança** (3-5hr., 7 per day 9:15am-7:30pm, €10:40); **Coimbra** (1½hr., 11 per day 6:45am-12:45am, €10.20); **Lisboa** (4hr., 11 per day 7:15am-12:45am, €16); **Viana do Castelo** (1¾hr., 4 per day 11am-10:30pm, €6.40).

Renex, Campo Mártires da Pátria, 37 (☎222 00 33 95), has express service to **Lagos** (8½hr., 6 per day 7:30am-1:15am, €24) via **Lisboa** (3½hr., 12 per day 7:30am-1:15am, €29) and **Vila Real de Santo António** (9½hr., 3 per day 9am-5pm, €44).

Rodonorte, R. Ateneu Comercial do Porto, 25 (☎222 00 56 37 or 00 43 98), to **Vila Real** (1¾hr.; M-F 16 per day 7am-9:20pm, Sa-Su 7 per day 7am-9:20pm; €6.40) via **Amarante** (1hr., €5.20).

Transdev, R. Dr. Alfredo Magalhães, 94 (☎222 00 26 60), 2 blocks from Pr. da República, has buses to **Braga** (1hr.; M-F 17 per day 7:30am-8pm, Sa-Su 5-6 per day 10am-6pm; €4).

Public Transportation: A €0.50 rechargeable **Andante** card must be purchased before using the metro, trams, and some buses. It can be purchased with an individual ticket or beforehand at the tourist office, at many small kiosks throughout the city, or at the **STCP** office, Pr. Almeida Garrett, 27 (open M-F 8am-7:30pm, Sa 8am-1pm). Transportation ticket prices determined by a zone system; each zone is an additional fare. Most of Porto is in 1 zone, and 2 trips on the metro or tram are €1.60 and €6.80 for 10 trips. A single bus fare is €1.30. The best option for those planning to moving around a lot is an unlimited EURO ticket (1-day €4, 3-day €9; available onboard or at the tourist office), which is valid for all STCP buses and trams, the Aerobus, and the metro. All buses operate between 6am-9pm, half operate until 1am, and a handful run 1-5am. Tram operates 9:15am-7:15pm. Metro 6am-1am.

Taxis: Av. dos Aliados and along the river in Ribeira. Ask for a quote beforehand, and make sure the taxi has a meter. Luggage €1.60 extra. **Radiotáxis,** R. de Alegria, 1802 (☎225 07 39 00).

✦❷ ORIENTATION AND PRACTICAL INFORMATION

Porto's heavy traffic and chaotic maze of one-way streets fluster travelers who come by car. The city center is easy to navigate, however: hillside **Praça da Liberdade** is joined to **Praça General Humberto Delgado** by **Avenida dos Aliados,** forming a long, open, and easily recognizable main square. The liveliest part of the city during the day surrounds the gigantic **Mercado do Bolhão** and includes the main pedestrian thoroughfare, **R. de Santa Catarina,** packed with stores and cafes as well as a large shopping center. Along the Río Douro, directly below the city center lies the **Ribeira** district, where much of Porto's sights and nightlife are located on steep sidestreets. The two-level **Ponte de Dom Luís I** spans the river, connecting Ribeira to **Vila Nova de Gaia** and its many port wine cellars. Down the river from Ribeira (5km), the **Foz** district has many popular beaches and older nightclubs, but the **industrial area,** 4-5km northwest of the city center, has the best discotecas in Porto.

Tourist Office: Main office, R. Clube dos Fenianos, 25 (☎223 39 34 70; www.portoturismo.pt). Staff speaks English, French, German, Italian, and Spanish. Offers maps and general info about Porto. Open M-F 9am-6:30pm, Sa-Su 9:30am-6:30pm. **Ribeira branch,** R. Infante Dom Henrique, 63 (☎222 06 04 12); same hours and services. **ICEP (National Tourism) office,** Pr. Dom João I, 43 (☎222 05 75 14). Open Nov.-Mar. M-F 9am-7pm, Sa-Su 9:30am-3:30pm; Apr.-Oct. M-F 9am-7:30pm, Sa-Su 9:30am-3:30pm. **Airport branch** (☎229 41 25 34). Open daily Jan.-Mar. 8am-11pm; Apr.-Dec. 8am-11:30pm.

Budget Travel: Abreu Jovem, Av. dos Aliados, 221 (☎222 04 35 80). Between Pr. da Liberdade and the main tourist office. English-speaking staff offers advice and student rates. Open M-F 9am-12:30pm and 2:30-6:30pm, Sa 9am-12:30pm.

Porto

▲ ACCOMMODATIONS
Andarilho Oporto Hostel, 4
Camping Prelada, 14
Oporto Poets Hostel, 15
Pensão Duas Nações, 8
Pensão Grande Oceano, 12

● FOOD
Café Guarany, 10
Café Majestic, 13
Capoeira Central dos Leões, 9

Confeitaria Império, 11
O Caçula, 7

★ NIGHTLIFE
Bar Arcos Ribeira, 17
Discoteca Swing, 1
Mais Food, 3
O Muro, 18

▣ WINE TOURS
Sandeman, 5
Solar do Vinho do Porto, 6
Taylor's, 2
Vinhos da Quinta, 16

Rio Douro

THE NORTH

Currency Exchange: Portocâmbios, R. Rodrigues Sampaio, 193 (☎222 00 02 38). Open M-F 9am-6pm, Sa 9am-noon. **ATM** on Av. dos Aliados.

Laundromat: NorSec, Via Catarina, 115, 1st fl. (☎222 00 31 32), in the shopping center on R. de Santa Catarina. Go down the stairs, and NorSec is in the back on the left. €5 per kg wash and dry. Open daily 10am-10pm.

Police: R. Clube dos Fenianos, 11 (☎222 08 18 33).

Pharmacy: Farmácia Souza Soares, R. de S. Catarina, 141 (☎222 00 21 45). 3 blocks from Pr. G. H. Delgado at R. Formosa. Posts 24hr. pharmacy list. Open M-F 9am-8pm, Sa 9am-7pm.

Hospital: Hospital de Santo António (☎222 07 75 00), on R. Alberto Aires Gouveia.

Internet Access: Laranja Mecânica, in a small shopping center off R. de Santa Catarina, 274; €0.50 per 15min., €1.30 per hour. Open M-Sa 10am-midnight, Su 3pm-11pm. **Sid@Internet,** R. Santa Catarina, 72. 2nd fl. €0.90 per hour 10am-7pm, €0.60 per hour 7pm-1am. Open M-F 10am-1am, Sa-Su noon-midnight.

Post Office: Pr. Gen. Humberto Delgado (☎223 40 02 00). **Fax,** phone, and **Posta Restante.** Financial services closed after 6pm. Open M-F 8:30am-7:30pm, Sa 9:30am-3pm. **Postal Code:** 4000.

⊓ ACCOMMODATIONS

Expensive *pensões* congregate around Av. dos Aliados. The best deals are around Pr. Filipa de Lancastre or near the *mercado* on R. de Fernandes Tomás and R. Formosa. Prices dip in the low season, so try bargaining.

▨ **Oporto Poets Hostel,** Tv. do Ferraz, 13 (☎ 223 32 42 09). The hippest place to stay in Porto, with 6-to 8-bed orange-splashed co-ed dorm rooms. Check out the nighttime view from the patio while enjoying a beer from the mini-bar and a fresh grilled sausage from the barbecue. Laundry €5, with dry €7. High season dorms €20; doubles €44. Low season €18/40. Cash only. ❷

Andarilho Oporto Hostel, R. da Firmeza, 364 (☎222 01 20 73; www.andarilhohostel.com). Co-ed rooms of 6, 8, or 10 beds are large enough to do several cartwheels in. Bright, huge living area just off the patio garden. Laundry €4, with dry €6. Free breakfast and Internet access. High season €20 per person; low season €18. Cash only. ❷

Pensão Duas Nações, Pr. Guilherme Gomes Fernandes, 59 (☎222 08 16 16). Bedroom walls painted bright colors for an upbeat feel. Rooms are well-furnished, though modestly decorated. Reception until 2am. Laundry €7. Internet access €1 per 30min. Singles €14, with bath €22.50-25; doubles €23-25; triples €36; quads €46. Cash only. ❶

Pensão Grande Oceano, R. da Fábrica, 45 (☎222 03 87 70; www.pensaogrande-oceano.com). Well-kept rooms have private bath and TV. 4- to 5-person room at a reduced per person price. Singles €20; doubles €25-30. Cash only. ❷

Camping Prelada (☎228 31 26 16), on R. Monte dos Burgos, in Quinta da Prelada, 4km from the town center and 5km from the beach. Bus #300, 50, and 87 from Pr. da Liberdade (only #50 runs at night). Free hot showers, electricity, and baths. Reception 8am-midnight. €3 per person, €3-3.50 per tent, €2.60 per car. Cash only. ❶

◲ FOOD

Quality budget meals can be found near Pr. da Batalha on **R. Cimo de Vila** and **R. do Cativo.** Places selling *bifanas* (small pork sandwiches) line R. Bomjardim. Ribeira is popular for high-quality, affordable riverside dinners. Local *azeitarias* (olive houses) offer a fantastic selection of olives. Adventurous eaters can try the city's specialty, *tripas à moda do Porto* (tripe and beans). Supermarket **Pingo Doce** is on R. de Sa de Bandeira, 387, two blocks from Pr. G. H. Delgado. (Open M-Sa 8:30am-8:30pm, Su 9am-8pm.) The ⬛**Mercado de Bolhão** has an enormous selection of fresh bread, cheese, meat, and olives. (Open M-F 8am-5pm, Sa 7am-1pm.)

⬛ **O Caçula,** R. do Bonjardim, 20 (☎222 05 59 37; www.ocacula.com). The only restaurant in town where a fancy 3-course meal can be enjoyed for only €5.50. Delicious vegetarian options. Free Wi-Fi. Open M-Sa noon-3pm and 7pm-last customer. MC/V. ❶

⬛ **Café Majestic,** R. de Santa Catarina, 112 (☎222 00 38 87). One of the best replicas of 19th-century bourgeois opulence—it was originally called Elite Café—this Titanic-inspired restaurant is the oldest and best known in the city. Entrees €9-16. Sandwiches €5-13. Elaborate pastries €4-6. Open M-Sa 9:30am-midnight. AmEx/MC/V. ❷

Capoeira Central dos Leões, Pç. Guilherme Gomes Fernandes, 9 (☎222 05 11 85). Large portions for a small budget; ¼ of a chicken with generous side of fries goes for a mere €2.30, while a whole chicken is €7.20. Save room for the creative and yummy desserts (layered strawberry ice cream cake, €2.50). Delivery available. Cash only. ❶

Café Guarany, Av. dos Aliados, 85 (☎223 32 12 72; www.cafeguarany.com). Right on Pr. da Liberdade. Features live weekend entertainment, from piano to *fado* to Cuban music. Best for coffee and dessert (€2-3). Duck with port wine €15. Sandwiches €3.50-9. Salads €6-10. Entrees €6-14. Open daily 9am-midnight. AmEx/MC/V. ❷

Confeitaria Império, R. de Santa Catarina, 149-151 (☎222 00 55 95). This *pastelaria* has a huge selection of excellent pastries and lunch specials (€3-5). Open M-Sa 7:30am-8:30pm. A new **branch** at R. de Fernandes Tomás, 755, is the largest self-service cafe in the city and has a wide selection of personal pizzas (€2.50-4). ❶

⊙ SIGHTS

For most travelers, the first brush with Porto's fine artwork is the Estação de São Bento, a monastery-turned-collection of *azulejos*, which display ancient forms of transportation. Up Av. dos Aliados in Pr. Gen. Humberto Delgado, the formidable **Câmara do Porto** (City Hall) attests to Porto's late 19th-century prosperity.

⬛**PALÁCIO DA BOLSA.** The elegant Palácio da Bolsa (Stock Exchange) is one of Porto's most visited sites, as it is essentially one tremendous work of art. It was built over the ruins of the Convento de São Francisco, after the convent was destroyed by fire in 1832. The construction took 60 years longer than expected due to the painstaking task of making the enormous granite staircase. The pinnacle of embellishment is the golden **Sala Árabe** (Arabian Hall), designed by Portuguese artists with the sole intention of impressing potential foreign investors. The green crests on the ceiling proclaim "Allah above all," and its gold and silver walls are covered with the oddly juxtaposed inscriptions "Glory to Allah" and "Glory to Dona Maria II," the Catholic queen. (*R. Ferreira Borges.* ☎223 39 90 00. *Open daily Apr.-Oct. 9am-7pm; Nov.-Mar. 9am-1pm and 2-6pm. Last tour 30min. before closing. Multilingual tours every 30min. €5, students €3. Tour of palace and wine cellars across the river €6/4. Palace and a bus tour of Porto €12. Palace and a Port wine cruise €12. Palace tour, bus tour, and wine cruise for €20.*)

IGREJA DE SÃO FRANCISCO. The Gothic and Baroque eras of ecclesiastical architecture favored gilded wood, but they outdid themselves here. At one point, there were between 400 to 600kg of gold on the chapel's walls and altar, all donated by rich families trying to buy their way into paradise. Check out the giant family tree tracing Christ's genealogy, starting from the loins (literally) of a statue of Jesse of Bethlehem, father of King David. Next door, a museum showcases religious art from the 16th-18th centuries; in the basement of the museum lies the *Ossário*, the mass burial grounds for Porto's poor. The cavernous catacombs have several individual graves belonging to the benefactors. *(R. Infante Dom Henrique. ☎ 222 06 21 00. Open daily in summer 9am-8pm; in winter 9am-5pm. €3, students €2.50.)*

MUSEU NACIONAL DE SOARES DOS REIS. A former royal residence and Portugal's first art museum (founded in 1833), Soares dos Reis houses a collection of 19th-century Portuguese painting and sculpture, much of it by Soares dos Reis, often called Portugal's Michelangelo. It features works by other great Portuguese artists, like Marquês de Oliveira. *(R. Dom Manuel II, 44. ☎ 223 39 37 70. Open Tu 2-6pm, W-Su 10am-6pm. Last entrance 5:30pm. €3, seniors and students €1.50. Su until 2pm free.)*

SÉ. On the hilltop slightly south of the train station stands Porto's imposing Romanesque *Sé* (cathedral). Built in the 12th-13th centuries, the Gothic, *azulejo*-covered cloister was added in the 14th century. Shining with solid silver and plated gold, the **Capela do Santíssimo Sacramento,** to the left of the high altar, was used as the bishop's study. During the Napoleonic invasion, townspeople whitewashed the altar to prevent vandalism. *(Terreiro da Sé. ☎ 222 05 90 28. Open M-Sa 9am-12:30pm and 2:30-7pm, Su 2:30-6pm. Closes 1hr. earlier from Nov.-Mar. Cloister €2.)*

MUSEU DE ARTE CONTEMPORÂNEA. This world-renowned museum houses rotating exhibits of contemporary international paintings, architecture, photography, and sculpture. Its 44 colossal acres of manicured gardens, fountains, and old farmland, tumbling down toward the Douro River, are also easy on the eyes. *(R. D. João de Castro, 210. ☎ 226 15 65 00. Several km out of town, on the way to the beach. Bus #78 leaves from Av. dos Aliados; ask the driver to stop at the museum; 30min., return buses run until midnight. Apr.-Sept. museum open Tu-F 10am-7pm, Sa-Su 10am-8pm; Oct.-Mar. Tu-Su 10am-7pm. Park Tu-Su 10am-7pm. Museum and park €5, park only €2.50. Su before 2pm free.)*

IGREJA E TORRE DOS CLÉRIGOS. The 18th-century **Igreja dos Clérigos** is decorated with Baroque and Rococo carvings. The highlight of the church is its **Torre dos Clérigos,** the city's tallest landmark and the tallest tower in Portugal, topping out at over 75m. The spectacular view of the Rio Douro valley doesn't come easily though; it involves 225 spiraling steps. *(R. dos Clérigos. ☎ 222 00 17 29. Church open M-Sa 8:45am-12:30pm and 3:30-7pm, Su 10am-1pm and 8:30pm-10:30pm. Tower open daily Apr.-Oct. 9:30am-1pm and 2:30-7pm; Nov.-Mar. 10am-noon and 2-5pm. Tower €2, church free.)*

JARDINS DO PALÁCIO DE CRISTAL. Beautiful gardens lie outside the Palácio do Cristal (Glass Palace), which is not, in fact, made out of glass. Take a gander at the geese, swans, ducks, peacocks, and fountains, while enjoying a stroll through the lush vegetation. *(R. Dom Manuel II. ☎ 226 05 70 80. Open daily until dark.)*

■ NIGHTLIFE

The heart of Porto's nightlife is **Ribeira.** Summer crowds leave outdoor cafes at 2am and head to neighboring bars or more distant clubs. The Ribeira's narrow, poorly lit streets can be unsafe at night, so don't go alone. Nightlife in Porto is tough without a car, as most clubs are along the river in **Foz** and in the industrial zones. Bus #500 runs until 1am from the São Bento train station to the beach at Matosinhos, passing Foz along the way. Bus #200 also runs past Foz to the beach until 1am, but begins at Pr. da Liberdade. A taxi to Foz from downtown costs €4-5. To get to the clubs in the industrial center, take the metro to Viso, which runs until 1am, as does bus #201 from Pr. da Liberdade to Viso. A taxi ride is €5-6.

Discoteca Swing, Pr. , 766 (☎ 226 09 00 19). A staple of Porto's nightlife for over 25 years, Swing is at its most swinging at around 2 or 3am. Beer €2-3. Mixed drinks €6-

8. Su ladies' night includes 2 free drinks. W-Th no cover, F-Su €2.50-10, but usually €5. Open W-Su midnight-6am. AmEx/MC/V.

Bar Arcos Ribeira (Bar AR), R. dos Canastreiros, 58. Just off Pr. da Ribeira, under the archway. This unassuming local bar draws a mixed crowd. Try the bartender's specialty: a flaming mix of Gold Strike, Sapphire, and absinthe (€1.75), or the bucket-sized mixed drinks for €5. Beer €0.70-1. Open daily 8:30pm-2am, F-Sa 8:30pm-4am.

O Muro, Muro dos Bacalhoeiros, 87-88 (☎222 08 34 26), upstairs from a pedestrian street along the water off Pr. de Ribeira. A tiny yet remarkable restaurant during the day, O Muro attracts night owls with a great view of the river and complimentary snacks with a beer (€1-4.50). Open Tu-Su noon-2am.

Mais Food, R Gonçalo Cristóvão, 323 (☎222 01 13 82). A trendy cafe featuring white and lime green leather couches and a large circular bar, Mais Food serves *tostas* (€4) and small plates (€5-7) during the day, but puts on its bar face at night with a DJ and fun lighting. Open M-Sa 7am-2am. Cash only.

🎵 WINERIES

No visit to Porto is complete without one of the city's famous wine-tasting tours. They are incredibly cheap (€1-3) if not free, and take about 30min. Wine tasting is most prevalent across the river, in Vila Nova de Gaia, where 17 large port lodges reside, and tours there often include visits to the wine caves below. To get there, walk across the bottom level of the Ponte de D. Luiz I in Ribeira. It's best to visit the wineries from noon-2pm when most tourists head away from the tours for lunch.

▨ Vinhos de Quinta, R. Fonte Taurina, 89 (☎222 08 92 57). A small, non-profit wine shop dedicated to small, lesser-known port wine producers. The owners serve samples for a fee of €2.50-10. Prices are rock bottom (about half off of retail, €2.50-70) and all proceeds go to farmers in the Douro. Open Tu-Su 11am-6pm. Wine shop open Tu-Su 11am-7pm. Bar open in summer daily 11am-11pm.

Solar do Vinho do Porto, R. Entre Quintas, 220 (☎226 09 47 49). Go around the Palácio de Cristal to the end of R. de Entre Quintas. Enjoy a fine glass of port on the swanky outdoor terrace of a former manor house. Limited snack menu including cheesecake (€3). Port €1-20. Open M-Th 2pm-8pm, F-Sa 2pm midnight. AmEx/MC/V.

Sandeman, Lg. Miguel Bombarda, 3 (☎233 74 05 00, fax 233 74 05 94), just off Av. Diogo Leite. Founded by a Scottish merchant 2 centuries ago, Sandeman now offers a tourist-friendly dive into the world of port. Lively tours every 20min. €3. Open Mar.-Oct. daily 10am-12:30pm and 2-6pm; Nov.-Feb. M-F 9:30am-12:30pm and 2-5:30pm.

Taylor's, R. do Choupelo, 250 (☎223 74 28 00; www.taylor.pt). Walk along the river and make a left on R. Afonso III. Go right as it splits and take the stairs to R. do Choupelo. Taylor's will be on the left. Taylor offers expert wine knowledge, outdoor gardens (complete with peacocks), and free tours and tasting. Tours every 20-30min., last tour 5pm. Open July-Aug. M-Sa 10am-6pm; Sept.-June M-F 10am-6pm. AmEx/MC/V.

🎊 FESTIVALS

For two weeks in February, Porto hosts the **Fantasporto Film Festival**, screening international fantasy, sci-fi, and horror flicks for crowds of film enthusiasts. Early June brings the **Festival Internacional de Teatro de Expressão Ibérica,** which stages free performances of Portuguese and Spanish drama. Porto's biggest party, however, is the **Festa de São João** (June 23-24), when locals storm the streets for free concerts, folklore, *fado,* and (of course) wine. The festival is rooted in paganism: the balloons symbolize sun worship, people jump over bonfires three times for good luck, and women roll around in the morning dew to ensure fertility.

BRAGA
☎**253**

Elegant fountains and open plazas welcome visitors to Braga (pop. 166,000), the "Portuguese Rome." Nine centuries ago it was the nation's religious capital and the seat of Portugal's archbishops. Though Braga has lost much of its religious influence over time, it still remains a devout city, and it is home to Portugal's Catholic University. It was in Braga that the 1926 coup paved Salazar's path to power, and the city retains conservative tendencies. Nonetheless, Braga is on the cultural edge, boasting of innovative restaurants, a flourishing art scene, and the best *Semana Santa* celebration in Portugal. Braga also makes a great base for daytrips to the lush natural beauty nearby.

⌸ TRANSPORTATION

Trains: The recently renovated train station, **Estação da Braga** (☎808 20 82 08; www.cp.pt), is 1km from Pr. da República. Take R. do Souto and pass through the town gate; the station is 400m to the left. Trains run to: **Lisboa** (4-5½hr., 12 per day 5:07am-10:07pm, €21.50-30), **Porto** (45-60min., M-F 26 per day 5:07am-10:07, €2-12.50), and **Vigo, Spain** via **Nine** (4hr., trains leave Nine 8:49am and 7:52pm, €14).

Buses: The bus station is the **Central de Camionagem,** R. General Norton de Matos (☎253 20 94 00; offices open M-Sa 6am-8pm, Su 9am-9pm), a few blocks north of the city center. **Rodoviária (REDM)** runs to **Guimarães** (1hr.; every 30min. M-F 6:35am-8:05pm, Sa hourly 7:10am-7:10pm, Su 8 per day 8:10am-6:40pm; €2.55). **Rede Expressos** runs to: **Coimbra** (3hr., 6 per day 6am-11:30pm, €11.50); **Faro** (12-15hr.; June-Sept. 6 per day 6am-11:30pm, Oct.-May 3 per day 11am-7pm; 7am and 7pm buses are direct, 11hr.; €25); **Lisboa** (5¼hr., 10-11 per day 6am-11:30pm, €17); **Porto** (1¼hr., 25 per day 6am-11:30pm, €5). **Hoteleira do Gerês** runs to **Caldas de Gerês** from terminal #18 in the bus station (1½hr.; M-F 11 per day 7:05am-8pm, Sa 9 per day 8am-8pm, Su 6 per day 8am-7:10pm; €3.50).

Taxis: ☎253 68 32 28 or 61 19 92. Next to the train and bus stations, in Largo de S. Francisco, and next to Pr. da República.

⊞⍰ ORIENTATION AND PRACTICAL INFORMATION

Braga's focal point is the **Praça da República,** a large central square. The tourist office is at the corner of the square and marks the start of the large **Avenida da Liberdade.** Across the plaza from the tourist office is the enormous **Braga Shopping** center, where visitors can find a grocery store and even a place to stay among the various shops and cafes. Pedestrian thoroughfare **Rua do Souto** begins at the tourist office corner of Pr. da República, eventually becoming R. Dom Diogo de Sousa and then R. Andrade Corvo, before leading to the train station. To get to Pr. da República from the bus station, take a right onto the commercial street with your back to the station. Continue straight under the overpass onto Pr. Alexandre Herculano, then take R. dos Cháos straight into the square.

Tourist Office: Av. da Liberdade, 1 (☎253 26 25 50; www.cm-braga.com.pt/turismo), in Pr. da República. Open June-Sept. M-F 9am-7pm, Sa-Su 9am-12:30pm and 2-5:30pm; Oct.-May M-Sa 9am-12:30pm and 2-6:30pm.

Budget Travel: Tagus, Pr. Municipal, 7 (☎253 21 51 44). Open June-Sept. M-F 9am-7pm, Sa 10am-1pm; Oct.-May M-F 9am-1pm and 2:30-6pm.

Currency Exchange: Caixa Geral de Depósitos, Pr. da República (☎253 60 01 00), next to Café Astória. Open M-F 8:30am-3pm. ATM outside.

Braga

▲ ACCOMMODATIONS
Pensão Grande Residência
Avenida, 9
Pousada da Juventude da Braga
(HI), 2
Hotel Residencial Avenida, 4

◆ FOOD
Abade de Priscos, 1
Anjo Verde, 10
Churrasqueria da Sé, 11
Rangoli, 5

★ NIGHTLIFE
Black Shoe Cafe, 6
Café Astória, 8
Insólito Bar, 7
Populum, 3

THE NORTH

Laundromat: Lavandaria Confiança, R. D. Diogo de Sousa, 46 (☎253 21 69 07). Wash and dry €2.50 per kg. Open M-F 9am-1:30pm and 3-8pm, Sa 9am-2pm.

Police: R. dos Falcões, 12 (☎253 20 04 20).

Pharmacy: Farmácia Cristal, Av. da Liberdade, 571 (☎253 26 23 21). Open M-F 9am-7:30pm, Sa 9am-1pm.

Hospital: Hospital de São Marcos, Lg. Carlos Amarante, 6e (☎253 20 90 00). From the tourist office, walk down Av. da Liberdade away from Pr. da República and make a right onto R. 25 de Abril. The hospital is on the right.

Internet Access: Espaço Internet Braga, Pr. Conde de Agrolongo, 177 (☎254 26 74 84). 10 computers. Free. 1hr. limit if people are waiting; go early to avoid a crowd. Open M-F 9am-7:15pm, Sa 9am-1pm. The **Instituto Português de Juventude,** next to the youth hostel on R. Santa Margarida, has free Internet access. Open M-F 9am-8pm. **Videoteca Municipal,** R. do Raio, 2 (☎253 26 77 93). Free. Connection fast and stable. 1hr. limit. Open M-F 9am-12:30pm and 2-6pm, Sa 10am-12:30pm and 2-5pm.

Post Office: Av. da Liberdade (☎253 20 03 60). For **Posta Restante,** indicate "Estação Avenida." **Phone, fax,** and other services. Open M-F 8:30am-6pm. **Postal Code:** 4700.

ACCOMMODATIONS AND CAMPING

■ **Pousada da Juventude de Braga (HI),** R. Santa Margarida, 6 (☎/fax 253 61 61 63). Taxi from train station €5. 8- to 10-bed dorms are smallish, but have a friendly atmosphere and a convenient locale. Large living area with pool table. Free breakfast and communal kitchen. Reception 8am-noon and 6pm-midnight. Lockout noon-6pm, but bag drop-off possible. Dorms €9; doubles with bath €22. AmEx/MC/V. ❶

Pensão Grande Residência Avenida, Av. da Liberdade, 738, 2nd fl. (☎253 60 90 20; www.residencialavenida.net). Handsome rooms with phone and TV. Some rooms have bathrooms large enough for the ■ **Brady Bunch** to share. Breakfast included. June-Aug. singles €22.50-30, with bath and A/C €35; doubles €30/40; triples €40/50. Sept.-May singles €20/25; doubles €25/30; triples €35/40. MC/V. ❷

Hotel Residencial Avenida, Av. Central, 27 (☎253 61 63 63). In the Braga Shopping Mall. 48 comfortable rooms with A/C and private bath. Breakfast included. Internet €1 per 30min. July-Sept. singles €37; doubles €47; triples €60. Oct.-Feb. €28/38/45. Mar.-June €33/40/50. Rooms on the top floor are €5-10 cheaper. MC/V. ❹

Camping Parque da Ponte (☎253 27 33 55), 2km down Av. da Liberdade from the center, next to the stadium and municipal pool. Buses every 20min. 6:30am-11pm. €2.50 per person, €2 per car, €1.70-2.50 per tent. Electricity €1.50. Cash only. ❶

FOOD

Braga is one of the more visitor-friendly places to eat in Portugal, offering a wide variety of cuisines at reasonable prices. Modest local restaurants on the busy streets near the train and bus stations serve cheap *pratos do dia* (plates of the day) starting at €2. More upscale Portuguese dining can be found in Campo das Hortas. Supermarket **Pingo Doce** is in the basement of Braga Shopping. (Open daily 10am-11pm.) The **market** is in Pr. do Comércio. (Open M-Sa 7am-3pm.) Try the *pudim do Abade de Priscos,* a pudding flavored with caramel and port wine.

■ **Anjo Verde,** Lg. da Pr. Velha, 21 (☎253 26 40 10). Dine like a star at one of Portugal's few strictly vegetarian restaurants. Meals are only €6.50, with a large selection of specials for €5. Open M-Sa noon-3:30pm and 7:30-10:30pm. Cash only. ❶

■ **Rangoli,** R. dos Capelistas, 59, 2nd fl. (☎253 21 55 05). Rangoli has taken the traditional family-run Indian restaurant and given it a makeover, offering guests colorful an delicious favorites in a young and stylish atmosphere. Many vegetarian options. Weekday lunch special €5.25. Open M-Sa noon-3pm and 7-11pm. MC/V. ❶

Churrasquería da Sé, R. D. Paio Mendes, 25 (☎253 26 33 87). Serves delicious, generous portions of meat and fish entrees to lunch crowds in a classy atmosphere (€7-13). *Prato do dia* €5-7. Open M-Tu and Th-Su 9:30am-9:30pm. Cash only. ❷

Abade de Priscos, Pr. Mouzinho de Albuquerque, 7, 2nd fl. (☎253 27 66 50). Named after a priest from the early 1900s who is still considered Portugal's best chef. The menu is small but the food is outstanding. Open M 7:30-10pm, Tu-Sa noon-3pm and 7:30-10pm. Closed last 3 weeks of June and last week of Dec. Cash only. ❷

🔘 SIGHTS

▨IGREJA DO BOM JESUS. Crowning a hillside 5km outside of town stands one of Portugal's most impressive religious sanctuaries and Braga's most famous landmark. The 18th-century church was built in an effort to recreate Jerusalem in Braga, providing Iberian Christians with a pilgrimage site closer to home. The 20-25min. walk up the staircase, which many devout Christians tread on their knees during the May Pilgrimage to Bom Jesus, represents the progression of a spiritual journey and the ascent to heaven. The staircase passes the 14 Stations of the Cross, fountains representing the five senses ("smell" spouts water through a boy's nose), and the staircase of three virtues, *"Fé, Esperança, e Caridade"* (faith, hope, and charity). Alternatively, the 285m climb can be made in an antique cable car, in use since 1882 (daily 8am-8pm, every 15min., €1). Behind the church is a small and peaceful lake where visitors can rent paddle boats (€1.50 per 15min.). *(Buses labeled "#02 Bom Jesus" depart at 10 and 40min. past the hour in front of Farmácia Cristal, Av. da Liberdade, 571. Buses stop at the bottom of the stairway; the last bus from Bom Jesus leaves at 9pm, Su 7pm. €1.25.)*

CATEDRAL. Braga's **Sé**, Portugal's oldest cathedral, has undergone a series of renovations since its construction in the 11th and 12th centuries. Today, it's a glorified graveyard: the **Capela dos Reis** (Chapel of the Kings) houses the 12th-century stone sarcophagi of the parents of Dom Afonso Henriques, as well as the all-too-accessible mummified remains of the 14th-century archbishop Dom Lourenço Vicente. The cathedral has a collection of *cofres cranianos* (brain boxes), one of which contains the 6th-century cortex of São Martinho Dume, Braga's first bishop. The treasury showcases the archdiocese's most precious paintings and relics. *(☎253 26 33 17. Mass daily 5:30pm. Open to visitors Tu-Su 9am-noon and 2-6:30pm. Cathedral free. Treasury and chapels €2.)*

MUSEU REGIONAL DE ARQUEOLOGIA DOM DIOGO DE SOUSA. Braga's newest museum focuses on the rich Roman history of the area. Artifacts collected during the excavation of the Roman ruins scattered around Braga are on display for visitors to enjoy. Check out the collection of ancient coins and everyday objects (combs, toothpicks, etc.). To get to the museum walk down R. do Souto away from the tourist office. Take a left on R. do Matadouro and follow it until it becomes R. dos Bombeiros Voluntários just past Lg. Paulo Orósio. The museum will be on your left. *(☎253 27 37 06; www.mdds.ipmuseus.pt. Open Tu-Su 10am-5:30pm. €3.)*

📔 NIGHTLIFE

Locals and travelers of all ages head to ▨**Populum,** off Pr. Conde de Agrolongo. The cavernous bar and discoteca's dance floors are always at full force with Top 40 hits or merengue and salsa. (☎253 61 09 66. Beer €2. Mixed drinks €4. Min. consumption for men €5, after midnight €10; women €5, W free. Open Th-Sa 10pm-5am. Closed Aug.) The upstairs bar of **Café Astória,** Pr. da República, 5, next door

ABORTION AUTHORIZED

Portugal recently removed its long-standing restrictions on abortion, once the strictest in the EU. Previously, abortions were only permitted in cases of rape or health risk to the mother. Still, there were an estimated 23,000 clandestine abortions annually. According to the new law, women are now allowed to receive abortions at private clinics or for free at their local hospital up to 10 weeks into their pregnancies.

Portugal hasn't shut its ears to the voices of dissenters. Doctors are permitted to register as conscientious objectors and refrain from personally performing abortions. If there is no willing physician in a hospital, the law requires that women be given access to a doctor in another hospital. All women who do opt to terminate their pregnancies must participate in a three-day "reflection period" before the operation takes place and mandatory classes on contraception education following the procedure.

The law was put into effect in the summer of 2007 following a national referendum in February. Of the 43.61% registered voters who participated, nearly 60% said "Yes" to the proposal. Removing the restrictions was an interesting move for Portugal, which also began its turn at the head of the EU's rotating presidency in July of 2007.

to Café Vianna, is a popular student hangout after midnight during the school year. (☎966 08 36 97. Beer €1. Open daily 8am-2am. Nearby is the **Insólito Bar,** Av. Central, 47, between Pr. da República and the youth hostel. Student artwork on the walls and occasional live music in the yard attracts a university crowd. (☎253 61 71 51. Beer €1. Mixed drinks €3.50. Min. consumption M-Th €1, F-Sa €2.50. Open M-Sa 10pm-6am. Closed Aug.) The area around Pr. do Comércio between Tr. do Carmo and R. Alferes Ferreira is quite dangerous at night; be cautious after dark. The black and white **Black Shoe Café,** Av. Central, 11, is designed as a tribute to the late 1950s, and is covered with faces from the era. €2.50 gets guests a traditional New York City shoe-shining and a coffee. (☎253 61 61 18. Open M-Th and Su 8am-midnight, F-Sa 8am-midnight. Cash only.)

🎊 FESTIVALS

Nowhere in Portugal is there a better Easter celebration than in Braga, where endless *Semana Santa* processions trace the city, some somber and hooded, others upbeat and musical. Each parish church brings a cross to the neighborhood doorstops to be kissed by the residents inside. Families signal that the cross is welcome by leaving flowers outside their front door; it doesn't take long before Braga is literally a bed of roses. Another popular festival is the **Festa de São João,** a week-long celebration culminating with the night of June 23. Traditional folk music, good food, colorful lights, and general revelry take over Av. da Liberdade and Lg. São João da Ponte. Don't be surprised to see locals running around beating each other on the head with 🔨**toy hammers;** few seem to remember the bizarre ritual's origin, but older folks relate that it's a tribute to São João, Protector of the Head. The **Festival de Teatro de Braga** takes place in the first week of July and celebrates the art of theatre with shows all across the city in open air plazas. Toward the end of July and the beginning of August the streets of Braga are filled with music as the **Festival de Música Tradicional** (Festival of Traditional Music) takes over the city.

🚌 DAYTRIPS FROM BRAGA

GUIMARÃES
Several lines of buses, including Transdev and REDM (☎253 20 94 01), run from Braga to Guimarães (1hr.; M-F 20 per day 6:35am-8:05pm, Sa 12 per day 7:10am-7:10pm, Su 8 per day 8:10am-6:40pm; €2.55) and return

(1hr., M-F 20 per day 6:35am-8:05pm, Sa 12 per day 7:10am-7:10pm, Su 8 per day 8:10am-6:40pm; €2.55).

Portugal's original capital, Guimarães (pop. 60,000) claims to be the birthplace of the nation. The city was the hometown of the first king of Portugal, Dom Afonso Henriques, and the site of his first court in the 12th century. Besides its historical significance, Guimarães is famous for its wild and decorative saints celebration, the **Festas Gualterianas** during the 1st week of August. The town is home to one of the country's most gorgeous palatial estates, the **Paço dos Duques de Bragança** (Ducal Palace), modeled after the manors of northern Europe. The museum inside includes furniture, silverware, tapestries, and weapons. Don't miss the elaborate floor-to-ceiling Pastrana tapestry replicas in the **Sala dos Pasos Perdidos** (Hall of Lost Footsteps), or the large display of archaic weaponry in the **Sala das Armas,** including swords, daggers, and armor nearly 600 years old. (☎253 41 22 73. Palace open M-F 9:30am-6:30pm, Sa-Su 9am-7:30pm. Last entrance 30min. before closing. €3, ages 15-25 and seniors €1.50. Su before 2pm free.)

Near the palace is the **Igreja de S. Miguel do Castelo,** the small Romanesque chapel in which Dom Afonso was baptized. On the floor are the tombs of warriors who fought alongside him at the nation-founding Battle of Ourique. Just up from the church is the great **Castelo de Guimarães,** built as a fort in the 10th century under Countess Mumadona Dias, who had been recently widowed and was looking to protect her nearby monastery and residence from Moorish attacks. Visitors scramble up the small stairs of the castle's central tower, the **Torre de Menagem,** which works hand in hand with the arduous climb to leave viewers breathless. The outline of this castle appears on the Portuguese coat of arms. (☎253 41 22 73. Church and castle open M-W 9:30am-5:30pm, Th-Su 9:30am-6:30pm. Free. Torre de Menagem open Tu-Su 9:30am-1pm and 2:30-5:30pm. €1.50, ages 14-25 €0.75. Last entry to all sites 30min. before closing.)

Even the view from the Torre can't match the one from the top of **Monte da Penha,** which looms over the city and is home to an excellent campsite, several picnic areas, and mini-golf. A **teleférico,** (cable car) starting from Lg. das Hortas makes the 400m climb to the top. Take a right out of the tourist office, and at the rotary take the second right (R. José Sampaio). Make another right onto R. Rei do Pegu and follow it to the cable car station. At the top of the mountain, boulders line the pathways leading to *miradouros* (lookouts) at the Santuário de Penha and at the Monumento a Pio IX. (☎253 51 50 85. Open M-F 10am-7pm, Sa-Su 10am-8pm. Last ticket 30min. before closing. €2.30, round-trip €3.60.)

TELEFÉRICO OR TAXI? If you plan on taking camping equipment up Monte da Penha it's best to invest in a taxi; the teleférico does not go all the way up to the campsite.

For an authentic Portuguese meal with local company, head off the beaten path to the family-run **Restaurante O Pinguim ❷,** Tr. do Picot. From Av. Conde Magaride, head straight until reaching Lg. Navarros de Andrade. Go around the rotary and up Av. Humberto Delgado. Make a left onto R. Picoto up the hill; the restaurant is off to the left as the street starts to curve right. (☎253 41 81 82. Entrees €6-11. Open Tu-Su 8am-10:30pm; serves meals 11:30am-3:30pm and 7-10:30pm.) Cheap accommodations can be found at the **Pousada de Juventude de Guimarães (HI) ❶,** Complexo Multifuncional de Couros, Lg. do Cidade. From the tourist office, go right on Alameda S. Dâmaso. Make a right before the *"pousada"* sign and follow the road as it curves down and around to the youth hostel. (Breakfast included. Lockout noon-6pm, but bag drop-off available. Single-sex dorms €13; doubles with bath €36 in high season; €11/30 in low season. AmEx/MC/V.)

THE NORTH

The main **tourist office** is on Alameda de São Dâmaso, 83, and the staff speaks English, French, and Spanish. (☎253 41 24 50. Open M-F 9:30am-12:30pm and 2-6:30pm.) A second tourist office on Pr. de Santiago has longer hours. (☎253 51 87 90. Open M-F 9:30am-6:30pm, Sa 10am-6pm, Su 10am-1pm.) The **bus station** (☎253 51 62 29) is in the Guimarães Shopping complex, on Alameda Mariano Felgueiras. To get to the main tourist office from the bus station, go right on the large street in front, Av. Conde Margaride. Walk uphill, and turn right at the intersection onto R. Paio Galvão. Follow it past Lg. do Tournal to its end; the tourist office is on the left. From the **train station** (☎253 41 23 51) it is a 10min. walk to the tourist office. Go left on Av. D. João IV from the station, and then right on Av. Afonso Henriques; the office will be on the right. The **police** are on Alameda Alfredo Pimenta (☎253 51 33 34) and the **hospital** on R. dos Cutileiros (☎253 54 03 30).

BARCELOS

REDM buses (☎253 80 83 00) run from Braga to Barcelos (40-50min.; M-F 14 per day 7:15am-7:10pm, Sa 8 per day 7:15am-7:10pm, Su 6 per day 8:35am-7:10pm; €2.10) and return from Av. Dr. Sidónio Pais, 245, across the street from the marketplace (the Campo da República) near the rotary and outside the REDM office (M-F 15 per day 7am-7:20pm, Sa 8 per day 7:40am-7:20pm, Su 6 per day 7:40am-7:20pm; €2.10).

Barcelos's fame is rooted in a legend dating back to the Middle Ages. A Galician traveler was wrongly accused of theft and taken to the gallows while his rich accuser sat down for dinner. Just before the boy was to be hung, the chicken on the nobleman's plate stood up and crowed, proclaiming the boy's innocence. The legendary "Barcelos cock" has been a national icon ever since, and much of the town's touristic appeal is centered on the famous rooster. Barcelos has also made a name for itself by hosting one of the largest weekly markets in Europe—vendors come on Thursdays to sell everything from produce and ceramics to live animals and furniture. The market, the **Feira de Barcelos,** was inaugurated in 1412 by Dom João I. Vendors begin arriving at the huge **Campo da República** late Wednesday night, and by 8am on Thursday the market is going at full force; the lively vendors don't leave until 5pm (7:30pm in summer). The **tourist office** is to the right of the bus station when facing away from the church, behind the Torre da Porta Nova, part of the town's original 15th-century wall and the only remaining tower of the three that once marked the entrance to the ancient city. (☎253 81 18 82; fax 82 21 88. Short-term **luggage storage.** Open Mar. 15-Sept. 30 M-F 9:30am-6pm, Sa 10am-1pm and 2-5pm, Su 10am-1pm and 2-4pm; Oct. 1-Mar. 14 M-F 9:30am-5:30pm, Sa 10am-1pm and 2-5pm.) Local services include the **police** (☎253 80 25 70) on Av. Dr. Sidónio Pais and the **hospital** (☎253 80 92 00) on Lg. Campo da República.

 COCK-A-DOODLE-DOO. Bent on taking home one of Portugal's national icons? The infamous ceramic cocks generally cost 50% less in Barcelos.

PARQUE NACIONAL DA PENEDA-GERÊS

Portugal's northern border with Spain is a sight to behold: a dark, quiet forest spread over the rugged mountains and picturesque rivers, punctuated by faint hiking trails. A crescent-shaped nature reserve, the ⬛**Parque Nacional da Peneda-Gerês** became Portugal's first protected area in 1971. The park consists of the northern Serra da Peneda and the southern Serra do Gerês, and it provides refuge for the endangered Iberian wolf. The base for travelers is Vila do Gerês (also called Caldas do Gerês), a spa town that draws hordes in late summer. From here, visitors can explore the park's many relaxing villages, turquoise waters, tree-covered mountains, and Iron Age artifacts. Activities range from hikes by abandoned monasteries to adrenaline-powered water sports to pampering in the thermal waters.

TRANSPORTATION AND PRACTICAL INFORMATION. Empresa Hoteleira do Gerês (☎253 26 20 33) runs **buses** between Braga and Gerês, terminal #18 in Braga's bus station (1½hr.; M-F 11 per day 7:05am-8pm, Sa 7 per day 8am-7:10pm, Su 6 per day 8am-7:10pm; return 1½hr.; M-F 11 per day 6:30am-6:30pm, Sa 6 per day, Su 5 per day 7:15am-6:30pm; €3.60). Gerês is essentially a 500m one-way street loop, running beside the water. The tourist office is at the far end of the loop, uphill from the bus stop. Next to the tourist office is a two-lane highway which continues 13km to Spain. To catch the bus back to Braga, you must be on the side of the loop that leads traffic away from the tourist office.

To get to the **tourist office** from the bus stop, walk uphill along Av. Manuel Francisco da Costa; the office is off the rotary at the end of the mini-shopping center. The staff speaks English, French, Italian, and Spanish and provides info on activities in the national park as well as **luggage storage.** (☎253 39 11 33; fax 39 12 82. Open M-W and F-Sa 9am-12:30pm and 2:30-6pm.) The **police** (☎253 39 11 37) are off Av. Manuel Francisco da Costa, and the **Red Cross** (☎253 39 16 60) is on Cha de Ermida. The **Espaço Internet** in the Biblioteca Municipal on Av. Manuel Francisco da Costa, across from the spa, has free **Internet.** (☎253 39 17 97. Open M-F 9:30am-1pm and 2-5:30pm, Sa 9am-12:30pm.) The **post office** is off the rotary that leads into the center. (☎253 39 00 10; fax 39 00 16. Open M-F 9am-12:30pm and 2-5:30pm.)

ACCOMMODATIONS AND FOOD. There are plenty of accommodations in Gerês, from fancy hotels to budget *pensões*. Try **Residencial Ribeiro ❷**, R. Miguel Torga, 101, where the nicest owner in town offers beautiful rooms with private bathrooms and free breakfast. From the bus stop, head down the street until the road splits off at the ice cream shop and goes downhill. Take it to the bottom, and then follow the signs left. (☎253 39 19 09. Singles €25; doubles €35; triples €45. Cash only.) A comparable option is **Pensao Residencial o Horizonte de Gerês ❸**, R. de Arnaçó, 19, near the bus stop returning to Braga. Simply decorated rooms come with a TV and private bath. (☎253 391 260. Breakfast included. Singles €25-30; doubles €35-40; triples €45-50. Cash only.) For camping, try **Camping Vidoeiro ❶**, 1km up the road from the tourist office and 250m beyond the park office. (☎253 39 12 89. Reception 8am-noon and 3-7pm. Open May 15-Oct. 15. €2.15 per person; €1.90-2.40 per tent; €2.40 per car.) Meals are served at the *pensões* throughout town. A small **supermarket** is on the way into town, across from the post office. (Open M-Sa 8am-12:30pm and 2:30-7pm, Su 8am-noon.) **Restaurants** line Av. Manuel Francisco da Costa, near the bus stop. For a filling meal, try **Geresiana ❷**, located just down the street from the tourist office, across from the spa. The *menú* (€8) includes a choice of fish, chicken or pork served with soup, a drink, and dessert. Entrees run €7-12. Come early for lunch though; the place is small and is packed from 1-2pm. (☎253 39 12 26. Open M-Sa 10am-10pm. Cash only.)

HIKING AND OUTDOOR ACTIVITIES. The main **park office** is in **Braga**, on Av. António Macedo. (☎253 20 34 80; fax 61 31 69. Open M-F 9:30am-12:30pm and 2:30-5:30pm.) The Gerês **branch**, on Av. Manuel Francisco da Costa, is a white building 1km uphill from the tourist office, near the campgrounds. (☎253 39 01 10. Open in summer daily 9am-noon and 2-5:30pm; in winter M-F 9am-noon and 2-5:30pm.) Casual visitors tend to stick to the manageable but scenic southern trails, while dedicated hikers head north. The popular **Trilha da Preguiça** (Lazy Trail; 5km) begins 3km north of Gerês proper, on the right side of the highway, and follows the Rio Gerês. Another hike follows the road from the tourist office to Spain 10km farther toward **Portela do Homem,** a town with a river pool in the **Minas dos Carris** valley. The tourist and park offices can recommend additional hikes.

As the name suggests, the main attraction of **Caldas do Gerês** (Gerês hot springs) is its spa, owned by **Empresa das Águas do Gerês,** on Av. Manuel Francisco da Costa, 133, as are the large hotel, restaurant, and park next to the tourist office. The spa complex (the pink building in the center of town) contains therapeutic waters. (☎253 39 11 13; www.aguasdogeres.com. Open May-Oct. M-Sa 8am-noon and 4-6:40pm.) For spa services, go to the office, a yellow building across from Hotel das Águas do Gerês. (30min. full-body massage €20. Sauna €7.50. Whirlpool €6. Open M-Sa 8am-noon and 2:30-5:30pm.) To the left of the tourist office, **Parque das Termas** has mineral waters, jogging trails, three pools, and canoe rentals. Purchase tickets at the booth inside. (☎253 39 11 13; fax 39 11 84. Park open 9am-7pm. Entrance €1, under 12 €0.50. Free if staying at the hotel. Pool open daily July-Sept. 10am-7pm; M-F €4, Sa-Su €6; May-June 9am-6pm; €4, under 12 €2. Tennis €3 per hour. Canoeing €3 per 30min.)

Geresmont, R. de Arnaçó, 43, has a variety of outdoor activities, including paintballing, rope climbing, and off-roading. (☎919 61 77 73; www.geresmont.com.) South of Gerês, the **Miradouro do Gerês** overlooks the **Caniçada** reservoir—beware the mass migration of weekend picnickers. The village of **Rio Caldo,** at the base of Caniçada reservoir just 8km south of Gerês, offers canoeing and waterskiing through **Água Montanha Lazer.** (☎253 39 17 79; www.aguamontanha.com. Single canoe €4 per hour, €13 per ½-day, €19 per day. Double canoe €7/21/32. 5-person motorboat €35/95/125. Waterskiing €35 per 20min., €90 per hr.)

VIANA DO CASTELO   ☎258

Viana do Castelo (pop. 37,000), a town nestled among mountains and overlooking the sea, is a real-life postcard, with trees in the plazas and potted plants lining the cobblestone streets. The surrounding hilltops and the nearby Monte de Santa Luzia offer unparalleled views of the fertile landscape and the sea. Viana is mainly a beach resort, but it also has a lively historic district, unique culinary specialties, and intriguing architecture, including a bridge designed by Gustave Eiffel. The town's buildings, some of the best preserved in all of Portugal, are an intriguing mix of Baroque, Art Deco, and Revivalist styles. The antiquity of the architecture combined with the tranquility of the sea make Viana more than worth a visit.

▎▊ TRANSPORTATION

Trains: The station (☎258 82 13 15) is at the top of Av. dos Combatentes da Grande Guerra, under the Santa Luzia hill. Trains to **Porto** (2hr., 11-14 per day 5:34am-8:23pm, €7), **Valença do Minho** (1hr.; M-F 9 per day 7:33am-9:34pm, Sa-Su 7 per day 8:46am-7:35pm; €2.90), and **Vigo,** Spain (2½hr.; 9:35am, 7:35pm; €8.15).

Buses: The new bus station is next to the train station in the basement of the new mall. Enter the mall to the left of the train station, go up the escalators, across the 1st floor, and then down the set of escalators on the opposite side of the mall. **Transdev** runs to **Braga** (1½hr.; M-F 8 per day 7am-6:35pm, Sa 6 per day 6:50am-6:35pm, Su 4 per day 8:20am-6:35pm; €3.70). **Linhares** also runs to **Braga** (1½hr.; M-F 6:30, 9am, 2:25, 5:55pm; €3.70). **A.V. Minho** runs to **Porto** (2hr.; M-F 4 per day 7:15am-5:30pm, Sa 6 per day 7:30am-5:30pm, Su 4 per day 7:30am-6:30pm; €4.60). **Avic** runs to **Lisboa** (5½hr.; M-F 8am, 12:30pm, Sa 7am, Su 6:15pm; €14.50) and **Valença do Minho** (1hr., M-F 3 per day 5:25-11:25pm, Sa-Su 5:25, 11:25pm; €4).

Taxis: Táxis Vianenses (☎258 82 66 41). About €0.75 per km.

◢✦ ▎⁊ ORIENTATION AND PRACTICAL INFORMATION

Wide **Avenida dos Combatentes da Grande Guerra** runs from the train station to the port. Most accommodations and restaurants are on or near the Avenida. Facing the ocean, the **historic center** stretches left of the *avenida* around the **Praça da República**. **Templo de Santa Luzia** is above the town, behind the train station. Beaches, sights, and stations are all within a 10min. walk from Pr. da República.

Tourist Office: Rua Hospital Velho, s/n (☎258 82 26 20; turismo.viana@rtam.pt). From the train, take the 4th left on R. da Picota and then a right. Open May-July, Sept. M-F 9:30am-1pm and 2-6pm, Sa 9:30am-1pm and 2:30-6pm, Su 9:30am-1pm; Aug. M-F 9:30am-7pm, Sa 9:30am-1pm and 2:30-6pm, Su 9:30am-1pm; Oct.-Apr. M-F 9:30am-1pm and 2-5:30pm, Sa 9:30am-1pm and 2:30-5:30pm, Su 9:30am-1pm.

Currency Exchange: Banco Santander, Av. dos Combatentes da Grande Guerra, 332 (☎258 82 88 97), near the train station. 24hr. **ATM** outside. Open M-Sa 8:30am-3pm.

Bookstore: Livraria Bertrand, R. Sacadura Cabral, 32 (☎258 82 28 38). English fiction, travel guides, and Portuguese classics. Open M-Sa 9am-7pm. MC/V.

Police: R. de Aveiro (☎258 82 20 22).

Pharmacy: Farmácia Almeida, R. João da Costa, 34 (☎258 82 25 20). Open daily June-Aug. 9am-10pm; Sept.-May 9am-8pm. Check the door for a listing of rotating 24hr. pharmacies.

Hospital: Centro Hospitalar Alto Minho, Estrada Sta. Luzia (☎258 80 21 00).

Internet Access: Free at the **Biblioteca Municipal** on Lg. 5 de Outubro, s/n (☎258 80 93 02), right off Av. dos Combatentes da Grande Guerra near the water. 5 computers. ID required. Strict 30min. limit. Open M-F 9:30am-12:30pm and 2-7pm, Sa 9:30am-12:30pm. For faster connections, try **Pekim Online,** R. General Luis do Rego, 121. €1 per hour. Open daily noon-midnight.

Post Office: Av. dos Combatentes da Grande Guerra (☎258 80 00 84). **Posta Restante, fax,** and **Western Union.** Open M-F 8:30am-6pm, Sa 9am-12:30pm. **Postal Code:** 4900.

▐ ACCOMMODATIONS AND CAMPING

▨ **Pousada de Juventude de Viana do Castelo (HI),** R. de Límia (☎258 80 02 60; fax 80 02 61), on the marina, off R. da Argaçosa and Pr. da Galiza. Dorm-style rooms with spacious communal bathrooms. Internet €5 per hour. Breakfast included. Laundry €2.50. Reception 8am-midnight. Reserve ahead. July-Aug., festivals dorms €13; doubles €30, doubles with bathroom €38. Sept.-June €11/26/32. ❶

Residencial Viana Mar, Av. dos Combatentes da Grande Guerra, 215 (☎/fax 258 82 89 62), 2min. from the train station. Large, homey rooms with cable TV, sink, and mirror. Lounge has bar, TV, and stereo. Breakfast included. June-July rooms with shower €35, with full bathroom €40. Aug.-Sept. €40/60. Oct.-May €25/35. AmEx/MC/V. ❸

Residencial Laranjeira, R. General Luis do Rego, 45 (☎258 822 261), just off Av. dos Combatentes da Grande Guerra. Yellow, darkened rooms have a hotel feel. June-Sept. singles with shower €37.50, with bath €42.50; doubles €50/55. Oct.-May €29/34/38/43. AmEx/MC/V. ❹

Orbitur (☎258 32 21 67; www.orbitur.pt), at Praia do Cabedelo. Catch a Trans-Cunha "Cabedelo" bus from Lg. 5 de Outubro. See tourist office for details on bus schedule. A well-equipped campsite. Free showers. July-Aug. €4.60 per person, €5 per tent, €4.20 per car. Sept.-June €4.30/4.60/3.60. ❶

▐ FOOD

Food is more than just fuel in Viana do Castelo. Local specialities include *arroz de sarabulho* (rice cooked with blood and served with sausages and potatoes) and *bacalhau à Gil Eanes* (cod cooked with milk, potato, onion, garlic, and oil). Most budget restaurants lie off Av. dos Combatentes da Grande Guerra. The **municipal**

market is on Av. Capitão Gaspar de Castro. With your back to the train station, go left and walk for 3min. (Open M-F 7am-7pm, Sa 7am-1pm.) A weekly **market** with produce, fresh fish, ceramics, live birds, and flowers is held Fridays from dawn to dusk off Av. Campo do Castelo. For groceries, go to **Modelo Bonjour Supermercado** in the mall by the train station. (☎258 10 05 40. Open daily 9am-11pm.)

▨ **Restaurante Dolce Vita,** R. Poço, 44 (☎258 82 48 60), at the corner of Pr. da Erva, across the square from the tourist office. Italian-style restaurant with brick-oven pizzas (€4.50-6.25) and a variety of pasta dishes (€4.50-6). Open daily May-Oct. noon-3pm and 7:30-10:30pm; Nov.-Apr. noon-3pm and 7-10pm. MC/V. ❶

Restaurante Glamour, R. da Bandeira, 185 (☎258 82 29 63). Choose from a small menu of fish and meat entrees and an extensive wine menu in this sleek, contemporary restaurant upstairs from the bar. Entrees €10-13. Open daily 7:30pm-2am. Bar open 10pm-2am. MC/V. ❷

Restaurante Camelo, Estação Viana Shopping (☎258 83 90 90), 2nd fl. Located in the mall food court, but the outside terrace, with gorgeous views of the city, ocean, and mountains beyond will make you forget your surroundings. Try the delicious traditional food from the city, including *arroz de Galo* (€9). Entrees €7-12. AmEx/MC/V. ❷

Restaurante Marisqueira, R. General Luis do Rego, 38 (☎258 82 32 25). A great place for traditional Portuguese food at reasonable prices. Full 3-course meal for €8. Entrees €9-12. Half portions €7-8. Open daily noon-3pm and 7-10pm. Cash only. ❷

A Matriz, R. do Tourinho, 5 (☎258 82 60 69), on the corner with R. Sacadura Cabral. Enjoy the excellent fish and meat dishes at this quaint, quiet hole-in-the-wall. Entrees €6-12. Open daily 11am-4pm and 7-11pm. ❷

◔ SIGHTS

The ▨**Monte de Santa Luzia,** overlooking the city, is guarded by the **Monumental Templo de Santa Luzia.** Conceived by the same architect who designed the Sacre Coeur in Paris, this early 20th-century church is nothing brilliant to look at, but the valley views are. Behind the *templo* are the **ruins** of a Celtic village, including circular foundations and a village wall. Although the elevator to the top offers a chance to sit back and enjoy the views on your way up, don't shy away from the half-hour hike to the top of the monte—the moss-covered stairwells and pretty views make it a pleasant journey. (*Templo* open daily June-Aug. 8am-7pm; Sept.-May 8am-5pm. Mass Sa 4pm, Su 11am and 4pm. Free. Elevator every 15min. Open daily June-Sept. 8am-8pm; Oct.-May 8am-6pm. €2, €3 round-trip.) For a less strenuous activity, check out the **Museu de Traje** in Pr. da República, which displays the traditional attire of the region. (☎258 80 01 71. Open Tu-Sa June-Sept. 10am-1pm and 3-7pm; Oct.-May 10am-1pm and 3-6pm. €2, students €1.)

◔ BEACHES

Sunbathers, swimmers, and windsurfers fill the beaches of Viana do Castelo and its neighboring towns. **Praia Norte,** at the end of Av. do Atlântico, is an easy 15min. walk to the west edge of town, and has two natural swimming pools (although frigid water and a rocky beach discourage beach activity). **Praia da Argaçosa** is a small beach covered with sunbathers on Rio Lima next to the marina. A ferry runs to **Praia do Cabedelo,** a great beach for surfing and windsurfing (7min.; hourly, ask tourist office for details; €1). A 10min. train ride north of Viana leads to Afife's **Praia do Bico,** frequented by surfers, where the acclaimed surfing school **Escola Zurf** offers lessons and equipment rentals. (☎966 22 10 92; www.surfingviana.pt. Lessons June to mid-Sept. €20 per person in group, €40 private. Surfboards €15 per 3hr., €20 per day; bodyboards, wetsuits, and bikes €10 per 3hr., €15 per day; fins €5/10.) The **Praias de Âncora, Moledo,** and **Caminha** are farther north.

THE NORTH

NIGHTLIFE AND FESTIVALS

The cafes and bars around Pr. da República fill up in the evening. The most popular place in Viana is **Bar Glamour,** R. da Bandeira, 183, down the street from the plaza and away from the main avenue. With white-mod furniture, colorful tapestries hanging from the ceiling, and a stage set for the next hip band, this bar combines chic and modern with an eclectic twist. (☎ 258 82 29 63. Open July-early Sept. daily 10:30pm-4am; late Sept.-June Tu-Sa 10:30pm-4am. Drinks €4.) Viana's biggest festival is the annual **Festa de Nossa Senhora da Agonia,** celebrated with processions, parties, and performances in the plaza on August 20 and the weekend closest to August 20th. ▨**The Feira do Livro,** held for most of July in the Jardim Público, promotes literary arts and culture in Viana. Though the focus is on books, the festival also includes nightly musical events, art displays, a merry-go-round and bumper cars for children, and several booths selling pastries and snacks.

DAYTRIP FROM VIANA DO CASTELO

VALENÇA DO MINHO

The cheapest and most convenient way to reach Valença do Minho is by train. Trains leave from Viana do Castelo (M-F 9 per day 7:33am-9:34pm, Sa-Su 7 per day 8:46am-7:35pm; €2.90). From the train station, walk through the rotary in front and take a right at the end of the street. Up this hill is another rotary with a large fountain; cross it and make your way uphill until you see the fortaleza. The tourist office is at the base of this hill; to get there, continue straight after the rotary until you see the wooden house on your left.

Valença's sizeable ▨**fortaleza,** whose 13th-century walls were once used to keep outsiders out, is now what brings them in. Wide-eyed tourists, bustling locals, eager vendors, and patient cars jumble together in the *fortaleza's* streets, infusing the tiny walled-in town with uninterrupted movement and a provincial quality. The hilltop location also offers panoramic views of the neighboring countryside and Río Minho, and the canons and remains of the fortress provide the young at heart with hours of fun. The entirety of the old town is encircled by the fortress—within its walls are a number of beautiful churches and countless market streets. Just outside the walls is **El Puente Internacional,** built in 1886. The iron bridge stretches across the Río Minho from Valença to Túy (p.572), uniting Spain and Portugal. Staying the night in Valença may not be necessary, but if you stay, head to ▨ **Pensão Rio Minho ❷,** Largo da Estação, s/n, right next to the train station. The rooms, complete with TV and bathroom, are cozy and have an antique feel. Some have balconies. (☎ 251 80 92 40. July singles €20; doubles one bed €35, two beds €45. Aug.-Sept. 15 €25/40/50. Sept. 16-June €20/30/40). The **tourism office,** Av. de Espanha 4930, is located right below the fortaleza. (☎ 251 82 33 29. Open M-Sa May-Sept. 9:30am-12:30pm and 2:30-6pm; Oct.-Apr. 9:30am-12:30pm and 2-5:30pm).

THE THREE BEIRAS

The Three Beiras region offers a versatile sampling of the best of Portugal: the pristine beaches of the coast, the rich greenery of the interior, and the ragged peaks of the Serra da Estrela. The Costa da Prata (Silver Coast) encompasses the wild nightlife of Figueira da Foz and passes through Aveiro on the way to Porto. The countryside is dotted with red-roofed farmhouses surrounded by expanses of corn, sunflowers, and wheat. A mecca for youth since the days in which it boasted the only university in Portugal, Coimbra hosts an opinionated, lively population; its nightlife and gorgeous architecture continue to attract young people. Still undisturbed by tourists, the region retains a wealth of Portuguese traditions.

COIMBRA ☎ 239

The crown jewel of the three Beiras, Coimbra is a rollicking city of 200,000, but it possesses the vibe of a metropolis many times its size. Backpackers and local college students roam the graffiti-lined streets and provide a youthful exuberance rare in the Portuguese interior. For centuries, the Universidade de Coimbra was the only university in Portugal, attracting young men from the country's elite. Though universities now abound in Portugal, Coimbra's university district maintains its historical appeal. Visitors may be surprised to see the outer facade of the university in a state of disrepair. The city's preservation efforts seem to be aimed at the old white buildings' interior, so be sure to visit the indoor splendor.

▐ TRANSPORTATION

Trains: (Info ☎808 20 82 08; www.cp.pt). **Estação Coimbra-A (Nova)** is 2 blocks from the lower town center, on the river. **Estação Coimbra-B (Velha)** is 3km northwest of town. Regional trains stop first in Coimbra-B, then continue to Coimbra-A, departing in reverse order. Long-distance trains stop in Coimbra-B only; take a connecting train to Coimbra-A to reach the city (4min., right after trains arrive, €1.08 or free if transfer). To: **Braga** (2-3hr., 16 per day 5:45am-8:40pm, €10-20); **Figueira da Foz** (1¼hr., 20 per day 5:20am-12:10am, €1.81); **Lisboa's Sta. Apolonia** (2-3hr., 17 per day 5:45am-2:40pm, €12-30); **Porto** (1-2hr., 14 per day 8am-10:55pm, €6.90-20).

Buses: Joalto (Formerly AVIC), R. Joâo de Ruão, 18. Bus stops are in front of the Coimbra-A train station. (☎239 82 01 41; www.joalto.pt.) To: **Condeixa** (25min., 6-30 per day 7:05am-11:30pm, €1.79) and **Conímbriga** (30min.; departs M-F 9:05, 9:35am, returns 1, 6pm; Sa-Su departs 9:35am, returns 6pm; €1.95). **RBL** (☎239 85 52 70; www.rede-expressos.pt), at the end of Av. Fernão de Magalhães and a 15min. walk past Coimbra-A. To: **Évora** (4-6hr., 9 per day 2:15am-7:30pm, €14.40); **Faro** (8-9hr., 14 per day 6:15am-2:10am, €21); **Lisboa** (2½hr., 18 per day 6:15am-2:15am, €11.50); **Luso** and **Buçaco** (45min.; M-F 5 per day 7:35am-7:30pm, Sa 9am; €2.82); **Porto** (1½hr., 14 per day 7am-3am, €10.20).

Public Transportation: SMTUC buses and street cars (☎239 81 02 47; www.smtuc.pt). One-way on the bus €1.50; 3-trip ticket €1.80; 1-day pass €2.80; book of 11 €6. Sold at vending machines in Lg. da Portagem, Pr. da República, and in local shops such as mini-markets and bookstores.

Taxis: Politaxis (☎239 49 90 90), outside Coimbra-A and the bus station.

Car Rental: Avis (☎239 83 47 86, reservations toll-free 800 20 10 02; www.avis.com), in Coimbra-A. 21+. From €80 per day. Manual transmission only. Open M-F 8:30am-12:30pm and 3-7pm. AmEx/MC/V.

◼◼ ORIENTATION AND PRACTICAL INFORMATION

Coimbra's steep, cobbled streets rise in tiers above the Río Mondego. The main pedestrian thoroughfare runs from **Praça 8 de Maio** to **Largo da Portagem** by the river and the tourist office. It starts as **Rua Visconde da Luz** and becomes **Rua Ferreira Borges** as it nears the water. This road forms a triangle region with the **Rio Mondego** called **Baixa,** which is the most central of the three major parts of town and the location of the Coimbra-A train station, as well as dozens of great restaurants and accommodations. The historical **university district** looms atop the steep hill overlooking Baixa. On the other side of the university, the area around **Praça da República** is home to cafes, a shopping district, and the youth hostel.

Tourist Office: Regional office, Lg. da Portagem (☎239 48 81 20; www.turismo-centro.pt). English, French, and Spanish spoken. Open June 10-Sept. 14 daily 9am-7pm; Sept. 15-

Coimbra

▲ ACCOMMODATIONS
Pousada da Juventude de Coimbra (HI), **5**
Residência Solar Navarro, **10**
Residencial Vitória, **7**

● FOOD
Café Santa Cruz, **2**
Porta Romana, **3**
Restaurante Adega Paço do Conde, **6**
UC Cantina, **8, 9**

★ NIGHTLIFE
A Capella, **4**
Diligência Bar, **1**
Quebra Club, **11**

THE NORTH

Rio Mondego
Parque de Santa Cruz
Jardim Botânico
UNIVERSIDADE DE COIMBRA

June 15 M-F 9:30am-5:30pm, Sa-Su 10am-1pm and 2:30-5:30pm. **Municipal office,** Lg. Dom Dinis (☎239 83 25 91). Open M-F 9am-6pm, Sa-Su 9am-12:30pm and 2-5:30pm. Also at Pr. da República, next to the cafe (☎239 83 32 02). Open M-F 10am-6:30pm.

Budget Travel: Tagus (☎239 83 62 05; coimbra@viagenstagus.pt) inside the A.A.C. building on R. Padre António Vieira. Sells ISIC cards. Open M-F 9:30am-6pm.

Currency Exchange: Montepio Geral, Lg. da Portagem (☎239 85 17 00 or 82 80 31). €5 commission above €50. Open M-F 8:30am-3pm.

Laundromat: Lavandaria Lucira, Av. Sá da Bandeira, 86. Wash and dry €5.90 per 6kg (full machine), €2 for 1kg. Specify if you don't want your clothing ironed (*passada*). Open M-Sa 9am-1pm and 3-7pm, Su 9am-1pm.

Police: Local police, R. Olímpio Nicolau Rui Fernandes (☎239 85 13 00). **Serviço de Estrangeiros** (tourist police), R. Venâncio Rodrigues, 25 (☎239 82 40 45).

Pharmacy: Farmácia Universal, Pr. 8 de Maio, 32 (☎239 82 37 44), in the center of town. Open M-F 8am-7pm, Sa 8am-1pm.

Hospital: Hospital da Universidade de Coimbra (☎239 40 04 00), at Pr. Professor Mota Pinto and Av. Dr. Bissaya Barreto. Take bus #6 or 29.

Internet Access: Espaço Internet, Pr. 8 de Maio, 38. This free, city-run service is popular, so expect a 15-30min. wait. Passport or driver's license required. Open M-F 10am-8pm, Sa-Su 10am-10pm. **Sp@cenet,** Av. Sá da Bandeira, 67 (☎239 83 98 44). €2 per hour. Open M-Sa 10am-midnight, Su 2pm-midnight.

Post Office: Estação Central, Av. Fernão de Magalhães, 223 (☎239 85 07 70). **Posta Restante** and fax. Open M-F 8:30am-6:30pm. **Municipal Office,** Lg. D. Dinis (☎239 85 17 60). Open M-F 9am-6pm, Sa 9am-noon. **Branch office,** Pr. da República (☎239 85 18 20). Open M-F 9am-6pm. **Postal Code:** 3000.

ACCOMMODATIONS

Accommodations are packed on Av. Fernão de Magalhães. Their bright and flashing signs make the area between the Largo das Olarias and the Coimbra-A train station seem like a mini Vegas strip. The youth hostel is a 15min. walk or short bus ride away from the city center.

Residencial Vitória, R. da Sota, 11-19 (☎239 82 40 49; fax 84 28 97). Convenient location next to the train station. Friendly staff, and newer rooms with bath, phone, cable TV, breakfast, and A/C. In summer singles €30; doubles €45; triples €60. In winter €25/40/50. Older rooms without amenities are roomy and comfortable, with shower, sink, and TV. Breakfast (€2.50). Singles €15; doubles €25. AmEx/MC/V. ❷

Pousada da Juventude de Coimbra (HI), R. Henrique Seco, 14 (☎239 82 01 14). Off R. Lourenço Azevedo, to the left of Parque de Santa Cruz. At the end of the road, take the 2nd right, or take the #6 bus from in front of the train station. Get off 2 stops after Pr. da República, on R. Pedro Monteiro, which runs parallel to R. Henrique Seco just one street up. Kitchen, TV room (with pool table and foosball), and impeccable bathrooms. Breakfast included. 24hr. bag drop-off. High season dorms €11; singles with bath €16; doubles €26, with bath €28. Low season €9/14/24/26. AmEx/MC/V. ❶

Residência Solar Navarro, Av. Emídio Navarro, 60-A, 2nd fl. (☎239 82 79 99). Rock-bottom prices, large rooms, and high ceilings. Ensuite bathrooms. Singles €15; doubles, triples, and quint €12.50 per person. Cash only. ❷

FOOD

The side streets below Pr. do Comércio, the areas around R. Direita off Pr. 8 de Maio, and the university side of Pr. da República all have bargain eats. Restaurants offer local favorites: steamy portions of *arroz de lampreia* (rice with eel) and *cabrito* (young goat). The cheapest meals are at the **UC Cantinas** (full meal for under €2), the university student cafeterias, on the right side of R. Oliveiro Matos and up the stairs near Lg. Dom Dinis. You'll need an ISIC card. For groceries stock up at **Mercado Dom Pedro V** on R. Olímpio Nicolau Rui Fernandes (open M-Sa 8am-1pm). The large supermarket **Pingo Doce**, is on R. João de Ruão, 14, a 3min. walk up R. da Sofia from Pr. 8 de Maio (☎239 85 29 30; open daily 8:30am-9pm).

Restaurante Adega Paço do Conde, R. do Paço do Conde (☎239 82 56 05). Adored by locals. A variety of fish and meat options for €5. The giant restaurant is partly indoors, partly outdoors and covered by a tin roof, and the entrance is marked by a large archway. Entrees €4-13. Open M-Sa 11:30am-3pm and 7-10:30pm. MC/V. ❷

Porta Romana, R. Martins de Carvalho, 8/10 (☎239 82 84 58), tucked away behind Café Santa Cruz. Large pasta entrees for €6-8 and pizzas for €4-7. Half portions of local cuisine from €4.50. Try the Fettucine Fantasia, with Roquefort cheese, cream sauce, and ham (€6.50). Open daily 10am-2am. Cash only. ❶

Café Santa Cruz, Pr. 8 de Maio, 5 (☎239 83 36 17; www.cafesantacruz.com). Formerly part of a church, this is the city's most famous cafe. A vaulted ceiling and carved wooden chairs distinguish the dining space. Sandwiches €1.60-3. Open M-Sa 8am-midnight. Cash only. ❶

🜚 SIGHTS

OLD TOWN. Take in Coimbra's old town sights by making the steep 15min. climb from the river up to the university. Begin at Pr. 8 de Maio and the **Igreja de Santa Cruz.** The 16th-century church boasts an enormous center dome and *azulejo*-lined walls, though the centerpiece is the tomb of Dom Afonso Henriques, Portugal's first king. *(☎239 82 29 41. Open M-Sa 9am-noon and 2-5:45pm, Su 4-6pm. Check the schedule at the main door for mass times. Sacristia with royal tombs €2.50, students and seniors €1.50.)* The ascent continues to the ancient **Arco de Almedina**, a remnant of the Moorish town wall, one block uphill from Lg. da Portagem. The gate leads past several university bookstores to the aptly named R. Quebra-Costas (Back-Breaker Street). Up a narrow stone stairway looms the 12th-century Romanesque **Sé Velha** (Old Cathedral). *(Open M-Th 10am-6pm, F 10am-2pm, Sa 10am-5pm. Cathedral free. Cloister €1, students €0.75.)* Follow the signs to the 16th-century **Sé Nova** (New Cathedral), whose part-classic and part-Baroque style exterior was completed for the resident Jesuit community. Bring sunglasses; the gilded main altar can be blinding at certain times of day. *(☎239 82 31 38. Open Tu-Sa 9:30am-12:30pm and 2-6:30pm. Free.)*

UNIVERSIDADE DE COIMBRA. Though many buildings have since been constructed from reinforced concrete, the original law school retains its spot on the architectural dean's list. Enter through the **Porta Férrea** (Iron Gate), off R. São Pedro, to the **Pátio das Escolas,** which sports an excellent view of the city. The staircase to the right leads up to the **Sala Grande dos Actos** or **Sala dos Capelos** (Graduates' Hall), where portraits of Portugal's kings (6 of whom were born in Coimbra) hang below a 17th-century ceiling; this is where graduates receive their diplomas. The magnificent 🜚**Capela de São Miguel,** adorned with intricate *talha dourada* carvings (especially the organ), is a sight to behold. *Azulejos*, gold, silver, paintings, or carved wood line every surface; almost no floor, wall, or ceiling space is left uncovered. At the end of the row of buildings is the oldest library in Portugal, the **Biblioteca Joanina,** which overwhelms visitors with gold-trimmed extravagance. The portrait of Louis XV stares at viewers from every angle, making sure they don't snatch any of the library's 300,000 ancient books. A small army of bats keeps the books bug free. The library's oldest book, a marriage guide for young men, dates back to 1523. (☎ *239 85 98 84. Open daily Mar. 13-Oct. 9am-7:20pm; Nov.-Mar. 12:10am-5:30pm. Tickets to all of the university sights can be purchased outside the Porta Férrea, in the Biblioteca Dom João V. General ticket €6, seniors €3, students €4.20. The Sala dos Capelos and Biblioteca Joanina are each €3.50, seniors €1.75, students €2.45. There is a limit to how many people can be in the library at a time, so expect a 15-20min. wait.)*

▐ NIGHTLIFE

After dinner, the outdoor cafes surrounding Praça da República buzz until 2am, after which crowds move on to the bars and clubs farther afield. The scene is best October through July, when the students are around. **Figueira da Foz** (p. 746), an hour away, offers more options and makes a popular night trip. Many take the train, party all night, and return in the morning.

■ **A Capella,** R. Corpo de Deus (☎ 239 833 985). From Pr. 8 de Maio, take R. V. da Luz for about 100m and make a sharp U-turn to the left on R. Corpo de Deus. A Capella is tucked off the road to the left. Built in 1364, A Capella is now a small late-night cafe and the best place to hear Coimbra-style *fado*. Mixed drinks €4-5. Performances at 9:30, 10:30, and 11:30pm. Cover €10, includes 1 drink. Open daily 1pm-3am.

Diligência Bar, R. Nova, 30 (☎ 239 82 76 67). Touristy during the summer, yet still intimate and pleasant. *Fado* performed by students and regulars after 10pm. Entrees €9-11. Sangria €9.50 per jug. Min. consumption €5. Open daily 6pm-2am. AmEx/MC/V.

Quebra Club, P. Verde do Mondego (☎ 239 82 16 61; www.quebracostas.com). On the riverside in the park, 300m from the Ponte de Santa Clara toward the bridge. Specializing in salads during the day, this artistic joint blasts jazz and funk to a crowd in their 20s and 30s. Admire the modern art and enjoy the cool river air. Beer €1-3. Mixed drinks €4-5. Open M-Th and Su noon-2am, F-Sa noon-4am. AmEx/MC/V.

❀ FESTIVALS

Students run wild during the **Queima das Fitas** (Burning of the Ribbons), Coimbra's infamous week-long festival in the first or second week of May. The festivities begin when graduating seniors set fire to narrow ribbons, gifts from friends and family to commemorate their graduation; they then receive wide, ornamental replacement ribbons. The fun continues with nights of music and food in the streets of Coimbra. The **Festas da Rainha Santa,** in the first week of July, brings live choral music to the streets and the city's largest fireworks display to the sky. During even-numbered years, there are two processions of the statue of Rainha Santa (one at the beginning, one at the end) which reflect the festival's religious roots. Old ladies line the streets hours before the event to claim their spot on the sidewalk. The firework-punctuated **Feira Popular** in the second week of July involves a giant fair full of games and carnival rides that keep the people across the river laughing and screaming all night. (Entrance €1, rides €2.)

▐ DAYTRIPS FROM COIMBRA

CONÍMBRIGA

Joalto (buses are either marked Joalto or AVIC) buses (☎ 239 23 87 69) run from Coimbra (30min.; M-F 9:05 and 9:35am, Sa-Su 9:35am; €1.95; return M-F 1 and 6pm, Sa-Su 6pm). The buses from Coimbra leave from the first bus stop on the left when facing the train station. The buses going to Conímbriga are often marked as Condeixa so be sure to confirm the destination with the bus driver. Buses run more frequently to Condeixa, 2km from Conímbriga (25min.; M-F every 30min. 6:30am-7:30pm, Sa noon,

1pm; €1.79). Come on a weekday morning and leave at 1pm, or trek 25-30min. to Condeixa. The bus stop is across from the tower of the church. Taxis (☎ 239 94 12 43; about €4) are more expensive but a secure bet.

The **Ruínas de Conímbriga** is Portugal's largest preserved Roman site. Already a prosperous village prior to their arrival, the Romans transformed Conímbriga into a thriving metropolis in the second half of the 1st century BC. Unfortunately, the enormous town wall wasn't enough to protect the city from barbarian invasion after the fall of the Empire, and by the end of the AD 5th century, Conímbriga was abandoned. What remains are intricate floor mosaics and crumbling walls in the shape of the rooms they once divided. (Open daily Mar.-Sept. 9am-8pm; Oct.-Feb. 9am-6pm. Ticket office closes 30min. before the ruins. €3; seniors, under 25, and students €1.50; under 14 free. Su before 2pm free.) The ticket for the ruins includes the **Museu Monográfico de Conímbriga,** which displays artifacts, the oldest dating back to the Bronze Age in the 10th century BC. (☎ 239 94 91 10; www.conimbriga.pt. Open Tu-Su Mar.-Sept. 10am-8pm; Oct.-Feb. 10am-6pm.)

 BRIGA YOUR OWN LUNCH. Conímbriga only has one, very overpriced restaurant. To save some dough bring a picnic lunch to enjoy outside the ruins.

BUÇACO FOREST AND LUSO

Buses run from Coimbra to Luso (45min.; M-F 7:35am, 12:30, 3:30, 5:30, 7:30pm, Sa 9am; €2.82) and continue to Viseu. Buses to Coimbra depart a few blocks from the Luso tourist office, by the fountain in front of the bathrooms. (45min.; M-F 7:38, 9:03am, 2:30, 6:38pm, Sa 10:38am; €2.82.) To get to the palace and convent, walk straight up the hill from the bus stop, past the souvenir stands. At the end, a green national park sign will direct you up the stone steps to a dirt trail, which eventually runs into the road. Stay on the road until you reach a pond on the right and a stairway with a stream down its center. Take the steps up and turn left at the top. You'll reach a small parking lot; the road on the left goes to the hotel. It's a 25min. uphill climb from the bus stop to the palace. (☎ 231 93 91 33; fax 93 90 07. Open M-F 9am-7pm, Sa-Su 10am-1pm and 3-5pm.)

Nature lovers have never had it so good. Buçaco is home to Portugal's most revered forest, a 105 hectare hiking wonderland and national monument since 1943. Urban Portuguese have escaped to the forest for centuries: Benedictine monks settled the Buçaco area in the 6th century, established a monastery, and remained in control until the 1834 disestablishment of all religious orders. The forest owes its fame to the Carmelites, who arrived here barefoot and set on a life of seclusion nearly 400 years ago. Selecting the forest for their *desertos* (isolated dwellings for penitence), the Carmelites planted over 700 exotic types of trees and plants brought from around the world by missionaries. In the center of the forest, adjoining the old Carmelite convent, is Dom Carlos's exuberant **Palácio de Buçaco.** Now a luxury hotel, the building is an attention-grabbing display of neo-Manueline architecture. The *azulejos* depict scenes from Camões' *Os Lusíadas,* the great Portuguese epic about the Age of Discovery (see **Literature,** p. 625). (☎ 231 93 92 26. *Palace interior open to guests only. Convent open Tu-Sa 9am-12:30pm and 2-5:30pm.*) In the forest itself, landmarks include the lovely **Fonte Fria** (Cold Fountain), the **Vale dos Fetos** (Fern Valley), and the **Porta de Rainha** (Queen's Gate). A 1hr. hike along the Via Sacra leads past 17th-century chapels and the **Obelisco á Batalha do Buçaco** (Battle of Buçaco Monument) to a sweeping panorama from the **Cruz Alta.** If you find yourself addicted to the natural beauty of Luso, **Pensão Astória ❷,** down the street from the tourist office, has sparkling, modest rooms. (R. Emidio Navarro. ☎ 231 93 91 82. High season singles €25; doubles €40. Low season €20/30.)

Stop at Luso's **tourist office,** R. Emidio Navarro, 136, downhill from the bus stop, to pick up detailed maps outlining the different hikes and routes, ranging from a

1hr. nature walks to a 3hr. historical hike. Free **Internet** access available. (☎231 93 91 33. Open July 1-Sept. 15 M-F 9am-7pm, Sa-Su 10am-1pm and 3pm-5pm; Sept. 16-June 30 daily from 9:30am-12:30pm and 2-6pm.) Relax at **Termas do Luso**, a spa situated over natural hot springs in Luso. The spa offers reasonably priced massages (€17 for 30min.) and a wide variety of other services. (R. Apartado, 1. ☎231 93 79 10. www.termasdoluso.com. Electrotherapy, starting at €5.15; thermal baths, also starting at €5.15. Open M-Sa 8am-noon and 4-7pm, Su 8:30am-10am). Fill your bottle with free natural spring water near the spa entrance.

FIGUEIRA DA FOZ

Two words describe this city: bars and beaches. Figueira da Foz (pop. 62,000) appeals to young pilgrims in search of the vacation Holy Land. When Pedro Santana Lopes, former Portuguese Prime Minister, was mayor of Figueira da Foz, he set out to transform it into a major tourist destination. The plan was successful, and the town now hosts bevies of sun-seekers from Portugal, Spain, and abroad. As if that weren't enough, Figueira's infamous casino makes losing money an art.

⌐ TRANSPORTATION

Trains run from Coimbra (70min.; M-Sa 20 per day 5:20am-12:10am, Su 6:17am-12:10am; €1.81). Most trains from the Figueira station go through Coimbra (1½hr., 20 per day 6:20am-11:25pm, €1.81) en route to Aveiro (1½-2½hr., 15 per day 6:45am-9:50pm, €6.71), Lisboa (3-4¼hr., 11 per day 6:20am-6:40pm, €5-22), and Porto (2¼-3½hr., 15 per day 6:45am-9:50pm, €7.71-12.31). From the Figueira station, it's a 25min. J-shaped walk to the tourist office and beach. Keep the river on your left until reaching the beach, and then follow the road around the corner to the tourist office. For those who want to save their energy for the waves, the local **Joalto bus** (or **AVIC**) goes to the center and can drop you off on R. Miguel Bombarda (7min., every 30min. until midnight, €0.95).

✹ 🛈 ORIENTATION AND PRACTICAL INFORMATION

The heart of Figueira da Foz is shaped like a triangle, with the **Rio Mondego** and the **Praia da Figueira da Foz** meeting at a virtual right angle at the small Santa Catarina fortress. From the fortress, **Av. Foz do Mondego** runs along the river past the **Jardim Municipal**, the **Lg. Luís de Camões**, and the **Pr. 8 de Maio** before changing names and hitting the train and bus stations. **Av. 25 de Abril** starts at the fortress, heads the opposite direction along the beach, and passes the tourist office. At the heart of this triangular shape is the **Casino Figueira**, whose sheer enormity necessarily makes it the center of all the action. It sits on the corner of **R. Bernardo Lopes**, which parallels the beach four blocks inland, and **R. Cândido dos Reis**, three blocks up from the river. Four blocks inland and parallel to Av. 25 de Abril, **R. Bernardo Lopes** is lined with semi-affordable hostels and restaurants, and is the heart of the city's nightlife. The city's action is between the casino and the beach.

The **tourist office**, Av. 25 de Abril, 24, is next to Hotel Atlântico, the tallest building around, underneath the patio facing the beach. (☎233 42 26 10. Open July-Aug. daily 9am-midnight; Sept.-June M-F 9am-12:30pm and 2-5:30pm, Sa-Su 10am-12:30pm and 2:30-6:30pm.) For a **laundromat**, follow R. Cândido dos Reis in the direction opposite the beach, pass the casino, and on the right will be **Tinturaria Figueirense**, R. Cândido dos Reis, 15. (Wash and dry €3.50 per kg. Open M-F 9am-1pm and 3-7pm, Sa 9am-1pm.) The **police** are on R. Joaquim Carvalho (☎233 40 75 60). One block from R. Bernardo Lopes, you'll find **Farmácia Praia**, R. da Liberdade, 100. (☎233 42 21 83. Open M-F 9am-1pm and 3-7pm.) Take the "Gala" or "Hospital" bus (from in front of the market on R. 5 de Outubro; €0.95) or catch a taxi (approx. €5) to the **Hospital Distrital de Figueira da Foz,** across the river in the Gala district (☎233 40 20 00). Near the end of Av. 25 de Abril is the **Internet** cafe **Webgest,** Av. 25 de Abril, 34. (☎233 42 03 28. €0.70 per 15min., €2 per hour. Open daily 10:30am-11pm.) Free **Internet** access at the casino is available for 30min. after registering with the front desk. The **post office,** on R. Miguel Bombarda, is two blocks up from the tourist office and a block to the left. (☎233 40 23 30. Open M-F 9am-12:30pm and 2-6pm.) **Postal Code:** 3080.

ACCOMMODATIONS AND FOOD

Accommodations are plentiful on R. Bernardo Lopes and R. Miguel Bombarda, but while prices are reasonable in the early summer, everything doubles (at least) after mid-July. Unless you win at the casino, staying in Coimbra is a safer bet. Comfortable **Pensão Residencial Bela Figueira ❷,** R. Miguel Bombarda, 13, is two short blocks from the tourist office, and only a couple blocks from the beach. The rooms are modest in decoration but meticulously clean. (☎233 42 27 28. Breakfast included. High season singles €15-17.50; doubles €20-25. Low season €20-25/35-40. AmEx/MC/V.) **Pensão Residencial Central ❷,** R. Bernardo Lopes, 36, can house you two doors down from the massive casino complex. Rooms are large and airy, with ensuite bathrooms. (☎233 42 23 08; www.pensaocentral.nafigueira.com. Breakfast included. Oct.-May singles €20; doubles €30; triples €45; quads €60. June and Sept. €25/35/45/55. July €30/50/60/70. Aug. €35/60/70/80. Guests receive a 10% discount on all meals eaten at the owner's restaurant, Lisfoz. Cash only.)

Eating in Figueira da Foz can be expensive, especially around the casino. Prices drop down the river in the small streets past the Jardim Municipal. At ◨**Restaurante Andaluz ❷,** R. Maestro David de Sousa, 110, warm platefuls of Portuguese food, especially seafood, are served in the dark, rustic wood interior. (☎233 42 04 54. *Pratos do dia* €7.50. Beer €1. Open M and W-Su noon-3pm and 7-10pm. Bar open until midnight. AmEx/MC/V.) For cheap local favorites, **Sporting ❸,** above the public garden in the Lg. Dr. Pereira das Neves, serves a varied meal (soup, salad, fish or meat or a mix, drink, and dessert) for €7.50, with wine included during the week. (☎233 43 48 82. Open daily noon-3pm and 7-11pm.) If you fancy a picnic on the beach, the large local **market** beside the public garden between Av. Foz do Mondego and R. Dr. Francisco A. Dinis is a fun place to fill your picnic basket. (Open June-Sept. 15 daily 7am-7pm; Sept. 16-May M-Sa 7am-4pm.) Alternatively, try **Supermercado Ovo,** on the corner of R. Francisco António Dinis and R. Bernardo Lopes. (☎233 42 43 24. Open M-Sa 8:30am-1:30pm and 3-8pm, Su 9am-1pm.)

SIGHTS AND FESTIVALS

The popular **casino complex,** on R. Dr. Calado, at the corner of R. Bernardo Lopes, is always the center of entertainment. Entrance is free, and many non-gambling locals hang out (nap) in the leather couches in front of the flat screen or relax in the bar. The beautiful **Salão Nobre** holds shows ranging from Latin dance to vocal performances. (☎233 40 84 00; www.casinofigueira.com. Open daily 3pm-3am.) Just up from the public gardens on R. 5 de Outubro, the **Museu Municipal Dr. Santos Rocha,** R. Calouste Gulbenkian, in Parque Abadias, displays ancient coins, medieval weapons, the once popular fashions of Portuguese nobility, and a large collection of Portuguese sculpture. (☎233 40 28 40. Open June-Sept. 15 Tu-Su 9:30am-5:15pm; Sept. 16-May Tu-F 9:30am-5:15pm, Sa-Su 2:15-5:15pm. €1.20, seniors €0.70.) Nearby is the looming **Centro de Artes e Espetáculos,** home to the majority of summer entertainment. Ask the tourist office for a schedule of programs or check the website. (☎233 40 72 00; www.cae.pt. Tickets from €10, movies €4.) On

R. Joaquim Sotto Mayor, the continuation of R. da Liberdade parallel to the beach, the modest exterior of **Palácio Sotto Mayor** conceals an unexpected extravagance within; lavish green marble columns line the main hallway, works by Portuguese artists like António Ramalho adorn the palace, and gold leaf covers the ceiling. (☎ 233 42 21 21. Open June-Aug. Tu-Su 2-6pm; Sept.-May Sa-Su 2-6pm. €1.)

The drunken shenanigans that normally characterize Figueira's party life take on a more religious tone with the **Festa de São João**, usually starting in mid-June and continuing through the first week of July. The party includes the biggest display of fireworks in the area and a somber procession where the sea receives the official blessing of the Catholic Church. On the night of June 23, the eve of the ▧**Dia de São João,** crowds of locals dance in the streets and on the beach, gleefully bonking each other on the head with plastic hammers. After the fireworks display finishes at 1am, crowds congregate around bonfires along the beach until the 5am *banho santo* (holy bath), when the brave take a dip in the ocean.

◤ NIGHTLIFE

Figueira da Foz nightlife begins much later than in neighboring cities. Most bars stay open until 4am, and clubs don't even open until 2 or 3am. Even the tourist office stays open until midnight. **Rua Acadêmico Zagalo,** parallel to the beach one street over from the casino, is lined with casual bars. For Latin music and close-quarter dancing, try the colorful **Cantina San Lourenço,** R. São Lourenço, 12, on the other side of the casino. (Open Tu-Su 7:30pm-4am.) Ease your late-night hunger pains around the corner at the **Cocktail Bar,** Tr. São Lourenço, 4, where the huge sandwiches and juicy burgers barely fit on the tiny tables. (Open daily until 6am.) Grab a Bacardi (€4.50) at the never-lonely Cuban bar **Havana,** R. Cândido dos Reis, 86. (☎ 233 43 48 99. Open daily 5pm-4am. DJ after 11pm. Shots €1.80. Mixed drinks €4.50.) Then make your way to **Bergantim,** R. Dr. António Lopez Guimarães, 28, the best club in town. DJ plays pop and rock music for a wild crowd on Friday and Saturday nights. (☎ 233 42 38 85. Open Tu-Sa. Doors open at 2am.)

AVEIRO ☎234

Small, tranquil canals detailed with footbridges and gondola-like *moliceiros* (curved boats) wind through the historic heart of Aveiro (pop. 80,000), the "Venice of Portugal." The Ria de Aveiro, which spans 65 sq. km, surrounds the city, but Aveiro has access to the sea at only one point, Barra. Many come to Aveiro to delight in its classic architecture, delicious pastries, and the Museu de Aveiro, the convent where the canonized princess Santa Joana once lived. Visited primarily by European tourists, Aveiro is still a hidden treasure for many Americans.

▛ TRANSPORTATION

Trains: Lg. Estação (☎ 234 38 16 32), end of Av. Dr. Lourenço Peixinho. To: **Braga** (2hr., 21 per day 4:42am-9:15pm, €6-17.50); **Coimbra** (1hr., 32 per day 6:12am-2:27am, €5-13.50); **Lisboa** (5hr., 19 per day 6:50am-2:27am, €13-25); **Ovar** (20min., 28 per day 5:45am-11:30pm, €1.65); **Porto** (45min., 47 per day 5:45am-11:30pm, €2).

Ferries: TransRia (☎ 234 33 10 95; fax 33 15 61) ferries depart for the beach at **São Jacinto** from the dock next to the bus stop at Barra (15 per day M-F 6:30am-1am, Sa-Su 7:25am-1am; last return at 1am; €1.05 one-way). Take the bus across the canal from the tourist office to the stop at the rotary in Barra. (20min.; 13 per day M-F 7:10am-12:45am, Sa-Su 8:25am-12:45am; bus and ferry €2.60 one-way.)

Taxis: Near the train station on Av. Lourenço Peixinho and along the canal in Pr. Humberto Delgado (☎234 42 37 66).

⚡ 🛈 ORIENTATION AND PRACTICAL INFORMATION

The heart of Aveiro is split by the **Canal Central** and its parallel street, **Avenida Dr. Lourenço Peixinho,** which runs straight from the train station to **Praça Humberto Delgado,** a big rotary fed by eight different streets. The **tourist office** is next to this intersection, off to the right from the train station. The fishermen's quarter, **Beira Mar,** is behind the tourist office, between the canal and the river; its central square, **Praça do Peixe,** is surrounded by restaurants. The residential district, where Aveiro's monuments lie, is on the other side of the Canal Central. From Pr. Humberto Delgado, **Rua Coimbra** runs past **Praça de República** and **Praça Marquês de Pombal** before intersecting the large **Rua Miguel de Bombarda,** that leads to the museum and the youth hostel.

Tourist Office: R. João Mendonça, 8 (☎234 42 07 60 or 234 42 36 80; fax 42 83 26). From the train station, go straight on Av. Dr. Lourenço Peixinho until you reach the bridge and Pr. Humberto Delgado (15min.); the tourist office will be just past the intersection on the right. English, French, and Spanish spoken. Staff provides information, maps, and bus, ferry, and train schedules. Open daily 9am-8pm.

Currency Exchange: Banks lining Av. Dr. Lourenço Peixinho are generally open M-F 8:30am-3pm. **ATMs** can be found on Av. Dr. Lourenço Peixinho, Pr. Humberto Delgado, and Pr. Marquês de Pombal.

Laundromat: Lavanderias Popular, Pr. 14 de Julho, 6 (☎234 42 39 53). €3-3.50 per kg. Open M-F 9am-12:30pm and 2:30-7pm, Sa 9am-1pm.

Police: Pr. Marquês de Pombal (☎234 42 20 22).

Pharmacy: Farmácia Central, R. dos Mercadores, 26/28 (☎234 42 38 70). Around the corner from the tourist office. Open M-F 9am-7pm, Sa 9am-1pm.

Hospital: Hospital Distrital de Aveiro, Av. Dr. Artur Ravara (☎234 37 83 00), near the park across the canal from the tourist office.

Internet Access: Aveiro Digital, (☎234 37 16 66) in Pr. da República behind the statue of José Estévão. Free. Sign up and hang around until your name is called. 30min. limit. Open M-F 9am-8pm, Sa 10am-7pm. **Instituto Português da Juventude,** in the same building as the youth hostel. Free Internet access. Open daily 9am-8pm.

Post Office: Main office, Pr. Marquês de Pombal (☎234 38 08 40), across the canal and up R. Coimbra. Open M-F 8:30am-6:30pm, **Branch,** Av. Dr. Lourenço Peixinho, 169B (☎234 38 04 90), 2 blocks from the train station. Open M-F 8:30am-6:30pm. **Postal Code:** North of the canal 3800, south 3810.

⌂ ACCOMMODATIONS AND CAMPING

Inexpensive *pensões* line the streets of the old town, north of Pr. Humberto Delgado, and on the side of the canal with the tourist office; look for signs for *quartos* or *dormidas*. Prices generally fall in winter. The youth *hostal* is the best budget option, a 15-20min. walk from the tourist office on R. das Pombas.

🔲 **Residencial Palmeira,** R. de Palmeira, 7-11 (☎234 42 25 21). Newly renovated rooms, all with dark wood furniture, cable TV, sparkling hardwood floors, bath, and hair dryer. Free Internet access. Breakfast included. Reserve ahead for summer weekends. June-Sept. singles €30; doubles €40; triples €50. Oct.-May €20/30/40. MC/V. ❸

Pensão Estrela, R. José Estévão, 4 (☎/fax 234 42 38 18). Well-located *residencial* with a family atmosphere and a huge winding staircase. Rooms are modestly decorated but cleaned meticulously. Breakfast included. July-Aug. singles €30; doubles €40. Sept.-May €20/25. Cash only. Across the street, **Hospedaria dos Arcos,** R. José Estevão, 47 (☎ 234 38 31 30), owned by family members of Estrela, offer similar accommodations for about €5 less. Cash only. ❸

Pousada da Juventude de Aveiro (HI), R. das Pombas, 96 (☎234 42 05 36). On the backside of the yellow building. Simpler than most *pousadas* and far from the center, but its prices can't be matched. Big breakfast included. Reception 8am-noon and 6pm-midnight. Lockout noon-6pm. Dorms €9; doubles €18, with bath €22. Cash only. ❶

Camping Municipal de São Jacinto (☎/fax 234 33 12 20), in São Jacinto. Take the bus to Barra (20min., 21 per day 7:10am-12:45am, €1.60), and then the ferry to São Jacinto (16 per day 6:15am-11:50pm; €1, round-trip €1.70). Provides basic amenities, including free hot showers and baths. Electricity €0.75. Reception 8am-7pm. Open Jan.-Nov. €1.84 per person, €1.02 per tent and per car. ❶

◗ FOOD

Aveiro is famous for its *ovos moles* (sweetened egg yolk wrapped in paper-thin casings), which are traditionally packed into small decorative wooden barrels. For something a little more substantial, check out the seafood restaurants which circle the fish market off Pr. do Peixe (Fish Square) in the old town, a few blocks behind the tourist office. **Supermercado Pingo Doce,** R. Batalhão de Caçadores, 10, is across the canal from the tourist office, slightly hidden on the left. (☎234 38 60 42. Open daily 9am-10pm.)

Restaurante Zico, R. José Estévão, 52 (☎234 42 96 49), off Pr. Humberto Delgado. A friendly, diner-like restaurant marked by a dramatic yellow Z, Zico cooks up delicious plates of typical Portuguese cuisine. Entrees €6-11, half portion €5-6. Open M-Sa 8am-midnight. Kitchen closed from 5-6pm and after 11pm. Cash only. ❷

Pizzico Pizzaria, Lg. da Pr. do Peixe, 24 (☎234 42 45 09). An Italian menu in the middle of "Fish Square," a stylish interior, friendly staff, and plates that are works of art all make Pizzico stand out. Entrees €8-12. Open daily noon-11pm. Cash only. ❷

A Gruta Snack-Bar, R. de Luis Cipriano, 25 (☎234 42 24 35). So cheap you'll leave feeling guilty. Complete meal, including soup, bread, classic Portuguese fish or meat entree, dessert, and coffee for €4.50. Open M-Sa 11am-10pm. Cash only. ❶

◗ SIGHTS

The old town's main attraction is the ◪**Museu de Aveiro,** Av. Sta. Joana Princesa. The museum, housed in the former Mosteiro de Jesus, honors the devout princess who retreated to the monastery in 1472 despite her father, King Afonso V's objections. In the **Sala do Túmulo de Santa Joana,** *azulejo* panels depict the story of her life, and beneath the magnificent gilded Baroque ceiling lies one of the most famous works of art in Portugal—Santa Joana's Renaissance tomb, supported by the heads of four angels. (☎234 42 32 97. Open Tu-Su 10am-5:30pm. €2, students and seniors €1, under 14 free. Su before 2pm free.) Another popular attraction is the 16th-century **Igreja da Misericórdia** in Pr. República, across the canal and a block uphill from the tourist office. The striking blue *azulejos* cover much of the wall space. (☎234 42 67 32. Open M-F 10am-12:30pm and 2:30-5pm.) Also worth a look are the traditional Aveiro **salt pans** that lie along the city's edge. A visit to this ocean-side factory shows you how salt is removed from the water. The salt pans were a source of wealth for the city until the 16th century, when storms raised the sand bars and blocked off access to the sea for nearly 200 years.

BEACHES AND ENTERTAINMENT

The beach towns near Aveiro boast beautiful sand dunes. **Barra** and **Costa Nova** can be reached by bus from the central canal or train station stops (20min., M-F 21 per day 7:05am-12:40am, €1.60). Distant beaches, like the pine-scented natural reserve at the **Dunas de São Jacinto** (10km), are accessible by ferry (see **Ferries,** p. 748).

At night, head to Beira Mar, where the bars around **Praça do Peixe** overflow with people. From the *praça*, follow the small canal to the Canal de S. Roque, which runs parallel to the lagoon and is lined with great places to bar hop. For live Latin music, head to the always popular **Azúcar&Salsa,** Cais de São Roque, 82, down the canal, just after the small white bridge. Wednesdays are salsa nights. (☎234 42 21 11. Open Tu-Su until 2am.) For dancing, check out **Club 8,** Cais do Paraíso, 19. From the tourist office, cross Pr. Humberto Delgado and go right along the canal. Where the canal splits, take the bridge over the left arm of the canal and go left. (☎914 03 58 18. Open W-Th midnight-4am, F-Sa midnight-6am.)

DAYTRIP FROM AVEIRO

OVAR

The train station (☎808 20 82 08; www.cp.pt) in Ovar is on Lg. Serpa Pinto, off R. António Coentro de Pinho (20min., 28 per day 5:45am-11:30pm, €1.65).

There's not much to do here except hang out at the beach but no one seems to mind. To get to the beach, **Praia do Furadouro,** catch a bus at the stop by the gardens up the road from the tourist office (5min., every 30min. 6:15am-7:30pm, €1). Alternatively, **free bikes** are available at Bicicleta Interurbana de Ovar, behind the public library at the end of R. Gomes Freire where the road splits. (Open M-Sa from 7am-9pm. ID required.) If you're lucky, you'll arrive in time for the **Feira de Doce Tradicional**, a ten-day celebration of everything sweet. Usually held during the first week of July, the event entices pastry buffs from all around. Ovar's most famous pastry is its *pão-de-ló de Ovar* (collapsed sponge cake), supposedly made the same way since a nun concocted the recipe over 300 years ago. Those who want a taste should check out **Confeitaria Progresso ❶**, R. Elias Garcia, 32, before the tourist office. (☎256 57 20 78. Open M-F 9am-7pm, Sa 9am-1:30pm.)

The **tourist office,** on R. Elias Garcia, has maps and info about accommodations and transport. It also offers free **luggage storage.** From the train station, head straight up the street, through the traffic circle on Pr. São Cristóvão, and take R. do Bom Reitor (the 2nd left, across the rotary), following it straight as it becomes R. Gomes Freire. When it splits, go right on R. Elias Garcia. The office is ahead on the left. (☎256 57 22 15; fax 58 31 92. Open W-Su 10:30am-1:30pm and 3-7pm.)

GUARDA   ☎271

A granite stronghold situated over 1km above sea level, Guarda (pop. 27,000) is Portugal's highest city. Whether it's the chilly temperatures created by the altitude or the icy feel of the cathedral and Gothic architecture, things are much colder here. Guarda's residents have survived centuries of physical isolation and notoriously harsh winters. Two of the town's epithets, *fria* (cold) and *fuerte* (strong), allude to this legacy. Don't be fooled by the cool breeze; Guarda's inhabitants are some of the warmest in Portugal. Guarda offers visitors relaxation, countryside, and a few remnants of centuries past. The **Sé** cathedral is a confused blend of architectural styles, which is hardly surprising since it took 150 years to complete. (☎271 22 32 02. Open Tu-Su 9am-noon and 2-5pm. Free.) The nearby **Museu da Guarda,** has an archaeological and ethnographic collection as well as regional painting and sculpture. (☎271 21 34 60; www.ipmuseus.pt. Open Tu-Su 10am-12:30pm and 2-5:30pm. €2, students, teachers, and seniors €1. Su until 12:30pm free.) It's also worth scrambling up the rocks to the castle ruins for a 360° view; from Pr. Luis de Camões take R. Miguel Alarcão and go right at Lg. João Soares.

Inexpensive *pensões* and *residenciais* aren't hard to come by around Pr. Luis de Camões, but they can fill up quickly on weekends. ⊠**Residencial Filipe ②**, R. Vasco da Gama, 9, has well-decorated, average-sized rooms, all equipped with TV, phone, unique paintings, and spotless private bathrooms. It's only a block from Pr. Luis de Camões, 200m ahead of the public park. (☎271 22 36 58/9; fax 22 14 02. Breakfast included. Singles €20; doubles €30; triples €40. AmEx/MC/V.) Just down the street is **Pensão Aliança ②**, R. Vasco da Gama, 8-A, which has comparable rooms for a few euros less. (☎271 22 22 35. Breakfast included. Singles €16, with A/C €25; doubles €25/40; triples €30/50; quads €40/60. MC/V.) Traditional restaurants abound in the historical district; the oldest and best is ⊠**Restaurante A Floresta ②**, R. Francisco de Passos, 40, where you can try Guarda's *morcelas torradas* (barbecued black pudding) in the stone-walled interior. (☎271 21 23 14. Entrees €5-10. Open daily noon-4pm and 7-11pm. MC/V.)

Buses depart Guarda from Centro Coordenador de Transportes, R. António Sérgio (☎271 22 15 15), a 10min. walk from town. **Rede Expressos** runs to: Braga (4-5hr.; M-F 5 per day 8:10am-6:40pm, Sa 8:10am, 2:20, and 6:40pm, Su 6 per day 10:45am-6:40pm; €12.50); Coimbra (3hr.; M-F 4 per day 6:15am-6:40pm, Sa 8:05am, Su 4 per day 10:45am-6:45pm; €10.60); Faro (9-10hr.; 9 per day M-F 6:15am-6pm, Sa-Su 7am, 2:15pm; €20.50); Lisboa (4½hr.; M-F 8 per day 7am-6:45pm, Sa 4 per day 8:05am-6:45pm, Su 8 per day 8:10am-6:40pm; €13.50); and Castelo Branco (1¾hr.; 11 per day M-Th 7am-7:25pm, F-Su 7am- 10:45pm; €8:50). **Taxis** (☎271 22 18 63 or 271 23 91 63) to town cost about €3. The tourist office and Guarda's cathedral lie on either side **Praça Luis de Camões**. To get to the plaza from the bus station, exit from the upper level and turn right onto R. do Nuno Alvares Pereira, walking uphill for several blocks. Continue straight past Jardim José de Lemos on your left. At the peak of the park, continue straight until you reach Residencial Filipe, and then go left onto R. do Comércio, just past the white church. An open square will be ahead on the left; the **tourist office** is around the corner, and has free **Internet** access and city and regional maps. (☎271 20 55 30. Open daily 9am-12:30pm and 2-5:30pm.) **Internet** access is also available at **CyberCentro Guarda** located directly across the tourist office on the other side of the Pç. Luis de Camões. (☎271 23 22 50. €1 per hour. Open M-F 9am-10pm.) The bank **Millennium BCP** is next door to Residencial Filipe and has a 24hr. **ATM** outside. (☎271 20 51 60. Open M-F 10am-3:30pm.) Local services include **Hospital Distrital,** on Av. Rainha D. Amelia (☎271 20 02 00 or 271 22 21 33) and the **police,** on Lg. Frei Pedro (☎271 22 20 22). The **post office,** Lg. São João de Deus, 24, behind the Museu da Guarda, can send and receive faxes. (☎271 20 00 30. Open M-F 8:30am-6pm, Sa 9am-12:30pm.) **Postal Code:** 6300.

◪ **DAYTRIP FROM GUARDA:** ⊠**SORTELHA.** Sortelha is a ghostly medieval village seemingly in the middle of nowhere. The town's name literally means "ring," a name chosen for the fortified 13th-century castle walls that enclose the old town. Inside, the cobblestone streets wind like snakes, creating a labyrinth reminiscent of Lisboa's Alfama district; indeed, both were founded during the Arabic occupation. Fortunately, the area is so small that it is nearly impossible to get lost. Among the town's highlights are its castle, whose ruins perch on the edge of a dangerously steep cliff. The castle walls run the perimeter of the village—the vertigo-immune are free to meander the edges. In the center is Igreja da Nossa Senhora das Neves, also known as the Igreja Matriz, with its beautiful Arabic *mudéjar*-style ceiling (open Su 10am-noon). Sortelha's best party is on August 15, the Festa de Santo António; the celebration sometimes includes a bullfight.

By the castle gate is **Dom Sancho I ❸**, Lg. do Corro, which advertises "medieval food" and isn't far off the mark; the menu draws heavily on meat and other staples that haven't changed much in the last few centuries. Vegetarian options are limited to salad. (☎271 38 82 67. Entrees €11-17. Open Tu-Sa 10am-10pm, Su 10am-3pm. Cash only.) The **tourist office** is in a kiosk to the left after entering the castle gate. (☎271 38 81 98. Open in summer daily 10am-1pm and 2-6pm; in winter M-F 10am-noon and 2-5pm.) V. Monteiro **buses** to nearby Sabugal leave from platform 9 of the Guarda bus station (1hr.; M-F 5 per day 10:15am-6pm, Sa 12:15pm, return M-F 6:45am-1:30pm, Sa 8:30am; €2.88). From the bus station in Sabugal, take a taxi to Sortelha. (Alternatively, a one-way bus heads into town Tu and Th 1:30pm.) **Taxis** (☎271 38 81 82) gather in town, a 3min. walk from the bus station. Exiting the station through the cafe, go to the intersection on the right, then take a left onto Av. dos Bombeiros Voluntarios. 50 meters later, take a right at the fire station and walk into Lg. da Fonte, where taxis congregate in the center. A ride to the castle gate in Sortelha is about €11. You can ask the driver to return to the castle to pick you up a few hours later for no extra charge.

PARQUE NATURAL DA SERRA DA ESTRELA

With craggy, barren mountains lining the horizon and emerald green rivers that flow through timeworn glacial valleys, **Parque Natural da Serra da Estrela** has attracted thousands of visitors since its establishment in 1976. Several hiking trails run north-south through the park, passing several small stone villages along the way. The three main **trails** are T1 (indicated with a solid red line), T2, and T3 (both marked with solid yellow lines). These three trails pass through the mountain ranges, rivers, and villages, and each covers a distance of about 80-90km. Six shorter trails—T11, T12, T13, T14, T31, and T32—marked with dotted lines, branch off the main routes.

Manteigas provides an opportunity to do several **day hikes** on portions of the trails that pass through the town. These include walking up a gradual incline along the **Rio Zezere** towards **Albergaria**, 14km south of Manteigas, as well as a more challenging 12km hike to the stunning **Poço de Inferno** waterfall. The weather in the park is erratic at best, snowfall often obscures the trail markers in winter, summer heat can be scorching, and rain is frequent. Check with the offices about weather conditions and be sure to bring extra waterproof layers and sunscreen.

In recent years, the park has also been home to several other adventure sports such as **skiing, kayaking, mountain climbing, rapelling,** and **mountain biking.** Near Manteigas, **SkiParque,** Relva da Reboleira, leads excursions into the mountains or through the Rio Zezere, and fills its slopes between December and March. (☎275 98 28 70; www.skiparque.pt. Open M-F 9am-5pm, Sa-Su 10am-8pm. Guided hikes €20-40 per day, kayaking €6 per hour, €17.50 per ½-day; horseback riding €50 per ½-day; mountain biking €12.50 per hour. Ski slopes ½-day €25, full day €30.) **UniversoTT,** R. Almirante Gago Coutinho, 10, operates directly out of Guarda and provides similar services like rapelling, dirt biking, and canoeing. (☎271 08 44 00; www.universott.pt.) The most popular skiing spot is **Torre,** a €15-20 cab ride from Manteigas. (☎275 31 47 08. Slopes open Nov. to mid-Apr.) **Parapente** (hang gliding) is also popular; Serra da Estrela hosted the Parapente World Cup in the summer of 2005. **Escola Parapente,** located in the SkiParque Complex between Manteigas and Belmonte, offers lessons for beginners and experts. (☎275 98 28 70; www.skiparque.pt. 700m descent with 1-2 people €30-32 per hour.)

The cheapest beds in Manteigas are at **Pensão Serradalto ❷**, R. 1 de Maio, upstairs from the **restaurant ❷**, about 50m from the gas station, with bright rooms overlooking the valley and impeccable baths. (☎275 98 11 51. Breakfast included. Singles €25; doubles €35; triples €50. Restaurant open daily noon-3pm and 7-

11pm. Entrees €7-13. Cash only.) **Camping** in the park is prohibited, except at designated sites. Consult the information offices in Guarda or Manteigas about campsites or cabins in the park. You can also camp at **SkiParque ①**, located off the main road 6km from Manteigas. (Taxis from Manteigas €5-6. €4.25 per person, €2-2.50 per tent, €2 per car.) The best **restaurant** in Manteigas is **☒A Cascata ②**, R. 1 de Maio, behind the gas station and down a staircase; enjoy their regional specialties. (☎275 98 21 39. Entrees €7-12. Open M-Sa noon-3pm and 7-9:30pm. Cash only.)

Buses from platform 1 of the Guarda bus station to the gas station in Manteigas run infrequently and only on weekdays (1½hr.; M-F 11:30am, 5pm, return to Guarda M-F 7am, 12:50pm; €3.20). The **Parque Natural da Serra da Estrela information office** in **Guarda,** R. D. Sancho, 1, has books and detailed topographic maps of the park, with clearly illustrated trails and points of interest (☎271 22 54 54). Alternatively, the first place to get info in **Manteigas** is the information center across the street from the gas station where the bus arrives and departs. Both offices sell the invaluable *Discovering the Region of the Serra da Estrela* (€4.20), which includes maps and detailed descriptions of all trails, including altitude changes, walking times, and landmarks along the way. (☎275 98 00 60; fax 98 00 69. Both offices open M-F 9am-12:30pm and 2-5:30pm.)

TRÁS-OS-MONTES

The country's roughest and most isolated region, Trás-Os-Montes ("beyond the mountains") is a land of extremes. Inhabitants describe their seasons as "nine months of winter and three months of hell." With rugged landscapes and radical seasonal weather, a visit to this remote area of Portugal can be difficult but it is definitely rewarding. The unique cultures that have sprung up in the isolated hamlets and the landscapes sweeping off into the middle distance are more than memorable. Rocky hilltops give way to fields of corn, followed by arid stretches of olive groves. Residents have cared for the land intimately, leaving vast expanses of wilderness that visitors can enjoy. Trás-Os-Montes has long been home to Portugal's political and religious exiles. Dom Sancho I practically had to beg people to settle here after he incorporated it into Portugal in the 12th century, and it was here that the Jews chose to hide during the Inquisition. The Jews created the area's famous vegetarian sausages—abstaining from the region's delicious meat products in efforts to keep kosher would not have gone unnoticed. Despite the tough conditions in their region, *trasmontanos* are possibly the friendliest people in the country. Transportation is sparse and distances between villages can be vast; expect to spend hours on rickety buses. The difficulty in travelling through the region is not without its benefits, however, as today, Trás-Os-Montes remains one of the last outposts of traditional Portugal.

BRAGANÇA   ☎273

Wedged in a narrow valley between two steep slopes, Bragança (pop. 37,000) is a wilderness outpost and the perfect base for exploring the Parque Natural de Montesinho, which extends into Spain. Its isolation is what makes Bragança special; it provides the chance to experience some of Portugal's best scenery as well as a unique and hospitable culture that has thrived in this remote location.

▬ TRANSPORTATION

The nearest **train** station is in **Mirandela,** 1½hr. from Bragança by bus. The **bus** station (☎273 300 450) is at the top of Av. João da Cruz, on Rua da Estação. **Rodonorte** (☎273

30 01 80; www.rodonorte.pt) runs to **Braga** via **Mirandela** and **Vila Real** (4-5hr.; M-W 5 per day 6am-3:30pm, Th-F 6-8 per day 6am-5pm, Sa 8am, Su 3 per day 2-5pm; €12.50, students €11.20). **Rede Expressos** (☎273 33 18 26; www.rede-expressos.pt) runs to: **Coimbra** (5hr.; M-Sa 6-7 per day 6am-7pm, Su 7 per day 6am-9:30pm; €12.50); **Lisboa** (8hr.; M-Sa 9-10 per day 6am-7pm, Su 14 per day 6am-9:30pm; €16.50); **Porto** (3hr.; M-Sa 9-10 per day 6am-7pm, Su 14 per day 6am-9:30pm; €10.40); **Vila Real** (2hr.; hourly 6am-8:15pm, Su until 9:30pm; €8.50); **Madrid** via **Zamora, Spain** (5hr.; Tu and F 1:30, Su 5:45pm; €42) **Santos** (☎273 30 01 80; www.santosviagensturismo.pt) goes to **Lisboa** via **Vila Real** and **Coimbra** (8hr.; M-F 5 per day 6am-4pm, Sa 4 per day 8:30am-4pm, Su 8 per day 8:30am-9:30pm; €16, students €14.40). **Taxis** (☎273 32 20 07) are at Av. João da Cruz, near the post office and bus station.

◢◪ ❷ ORIENTATION AND PRACTICAL INFORMATION

The bus station is located blocks from the center of town. With your back to the station (facing bus slots), walk left along R. da Estação. Turn left below the rotary and walk over the bridge. You will soon come to a grassy, plaza-like street, Av. João da Cruz. Turn right. When you get to the post office, bear left onto downward-sloping **R. Almirante dos Reis,** which leads to more budget *pensões* and the **Praça da Sé** at the heart of the old town. To reach the **fortress,** on the hill west of Pr. da Sé, take R. dos Combatentes da Grande Guerra; bear right at the fork, and continue uphill to enter through the opening in the walls.

Tourist Office: Av. Cidade de Zamora (☎273 38 12 73). From Pr. da Sé, take downward sloping R. Abilio Beca; take the left at the fork with R. Combatentes da Grande Guerra and the second left on R. Marqués. R. Marqués will turn into Av. Cidade de Zamora, a two-sided street with a barrier in the middle. Cross to the side with the Cepsa gas station and continue straight for 100m. The tourist office is on the corner to your left. From the bus station, instead of turning right at Av. João da Cruz, continue straight until you reach R. de Santo António. Continue straight downhill, and turn right at the rotary. The office is downhill on the corner to your right. Has short-term **luggage storage.** Open Tu-Su 10am-12:30pm and 2-6pm.

Currency Exchange: Caixa Geral, R. Almirante dos Reis (☎27331 08 00), opposite the post office on the corner. Also has 24hr. **ATM.** Open M-F 8:30am-3pm.

Police: (☎273 30 34 00), on R. Dr. Manuel Bento.

Medical Services: Centro Hospitales do Nordeste, Av. Abade de Baçal (☎273 31 08 00), before the stadium on the road to Vinhais.

Internet Access: available at the **Biblioteca Municipal,** Pr. Mercado, just off Pr. da Sé (☎273 30 08 51; open M-F 9am-12:30pm and 2-7pm; max. 1hr.) and at **CyberCentro** (☎273 33 19 32), 2nd floor of the *mercado municipal.* €1 per hour, students €0.72 per hour. Open M-Sa 10am-11pm, Su 2pm-8pm.

Post Office: (☎273 32 21 49), on the corner of R. Almirante dos Reis and R. 5 de Outubro. Western Union. Open M-F 8:30am-5:30pm, Sa 9am-12:30pm. **Postal Code:** 5300.

◪ ◪ ACCOMMODATIONS AND CAMPING

Cheap *pensões* and *residenciais* line Pr. da Sé and R. Almirante dos Reis.

▨ **Pensão Poças,** R. Combatentes da Grande Guerra, 200 (☎273 33 14 28), just off Pr. da Sé. Central location. Large and charming rooms in an old building. Reception in *restaurante* below. Singles €12.50, with bath €15; doubles €25 (all with full or half bath); triples €30 (all without bath). AmEx/MC/V. ❶

THE NORTH

Pousada de Juventude–Bragança (HI), Forte de São João de Deus (☎273 30 46 00, fax 30 46 01), off Av. 22 de Maio. A 15min. walk from town center. Plain, bunk-bed style dorms with balconies. Breakfast included. Laundry €3. Internet €5 per hour. July-Aug. dorms €11; doubles €26, with bath €32. Sept.-June €9/22/28. AmEx/MC/V. ❶

Pensão Rucha, R. Almirante Reis, 42 (☎273 331 672). This tiny hostel is in a great location, so call ahead to book a room. Small, simple white rooms with spacious shared bathrooms. June-Aug. singles €15; doubles €25. Oct.-May €15/22. Cash only. ❷

Parque de Campismo Municipal do Sabor, 6km from town on the edge of the Parque Natural de Montesinho, on the road to Portelo (☎273 32 26 33). The yellow STUB bus #7 to Meixedo passes nearby, leaving from the Caixa Geral de Depósitos on Av. João da Cruz (10min.; M-F 12:43, 2:09, 6pm; return to Bragança 1:34, 2:36, 6:26pm; €1.10). Playground, cafe, and swimming lagoon. Reception 8am-midnight. May-Oct. €2 per person, €1.50-2 per tent, €1.50 per car. 6-person cabin €50. Electricity €2. ❶

🍽 FOOD

The region is celebrated for its *presunto* (cured ham) and *salsichão* (sausages), as well as the local delicacy, *alheiradas (*sausages made with bread and various meats). You can find these and fresh produce at the stores that surround the **mercado municipal**, several blocks up from Pr. da Sé (see directions to CyberCentro; open M-Sa 8am-7pm, Su 8am-1pm.)

🍴 **Solar Bragançano,** Pr. da Sé, 34, 1st fl. (☎273 32 38 75; www.solar-braganca.com). Enjoy a first-class meal in an elegant dining room complete with chandeliers, linen tablecloths and classical music overlooking Pr. da Sé. Entrees €8.50-12.50+. Menú €14. Open Jan.-Oct. daily noon-3pm and 6-11pm. Nov.-Feb. closed M. AmEx/MC/V. ❸

Restaurante Dom Fernando, Cidadela, 197 (☎273 32 62 73). Located in the heart of the old citadel; enter the walls and turn right. This rustic restaurant has numerous meat dishes, fish, and omelettes. Entrees €4-9. Tourist *menú* €12. Open daily 9am-10pm. ❷

Restaurante Poças, R. Combatentes da Grande Guerra, 200 (☎273 33 14 28), off Pr. da Sé, serves bread, *pâté,* and black olives with meals. Popular with the local crowd, the two floors of this restaurant fill with eager patrons. Entrees €4-9+. Salads €3-4. Open 9am-11pm; meals served noon-3pm and 8-11pm. AmEx/MC/V. ❷

👁 SIGHTS

Bragança's major sites are concentrated in the citadel on the hill above the town. From the Pr. da Sé continue down R. Combatentes da Grande Guerra; bear right at the fork and head upwards to the fortress' walls. The 12th-century **castelo** watches quietly over the town; a silent reminder of the city's regal past. The castle's **Museu Militar** has a wide range of military paraphernalia that traces Portugal's military history, from medieval treaties with Spain to Portuguese efforts in WWI and African campaigns. (Open July Tu-Su 9am-6pm; Aug. daily 9am-6:30pm; Sept.-June Tu-Su 9am-12:45pm and 2-5:45pm. €1.50, Su mornings free.) The **pelourinho** (pillory) in the square behind the castle has a granite pig at its base, a vestige of pagan ideology; sinners and criminals were bound there in the Middle Ages. The **Domus Municipalis,** behind the church across the square from the castle, once served as the city's municipal meeting house. The **Igreja de Santa Maria** is a nice surprise; the gray stone exterior betrays nothing of the colorful Baroque display of carved wood inside, or the vividly painted ceiling. (Open daily 9am-6pm. Free.) The **Museu Ibérico da Máscara e do Traje,** located right across the street from the *castelo,* which features an extensive collection of traditional dress and masks from the Trás-os-Montes region and neighboring provinces. The colorful suits and fierce masks are unlike anything you would think to find in this seemingly somber region of Portugal. (Open Tu-Su 10am-12:30pm and 2-6pm. Free).

■ ✿ NIGHTLIFE AND FESTIVALS

A popular hangout, especially after 1am on weekends, is **Klaustrus Cafe,** Pr. da Sé, 16, located underground off the Pr. da Sé. A local crowd chills out in this low-lighted and relaxed bar. (☎273 33 34 59. Beer €1. Open daily 8pm-2am.) The most important festival is the mid-August **Festa de Nossa Senhora das Graças,** which includes concerts, art exhibits, and ceramics fairs. It culminates in fireworks the night of the 21st and religious processions the following day (the patron's day). For a week in mid-May, the **Festa do Estudante** celebrates students' graduation from the university; music groups perform in Pr. da Sé and other public spaces.

■ DAYTRIP FROM BRAGANÇA

PARQUE NATURAL DE MONTESINHO. The ▧Parque Natural de Montesinho covers 290 sq. mi. between Bragança and the Spanish border. Old mountain paths lead through rolling woodlands of oak, chestnut, pine, and cherry past the Rio Sabor. *Pombais pombales* (pigeon lofts) dot the landscape, and the park is home to many rare and endangered species, including the Iberian wolf, royal eagle, and black stork. You may be fortunate enough to arrive during the ▧**Festa dos Rapazes,** a Christmas-time rite of passage for village boys. Outdoor activities include horseback riding, trout fishing, and hiking. Horseback riding can be arranged in França (☎273 91 91 41; call ahead). Plenty of mapped hiking routes are available in the park information office in Bragança. If you have only one day, the most worthwhile trip is to **Rio de Onor,** a village near the northeast corner, on the Spanish border. Here the Portuguese and Spanish have lived together for centuries, intermarrying and even speaking their own dialect, *rionorés.* A subtle stone post, with a "P" for "Portugal" on one side and an "E" for "España" on the other, marks the border. Villagers cross into Spain for groceries and back into Portugal for coffee at **Cervejaria Preto,** the only bar in town. There are also several small towns which can serve as starting points for hiking trails. See the park tourism office for more information. Getting to the park is difficult without a car and only worthwhile if you have a specific activity in mind. Taxis to the park run €20 one-way depending on your destination; arrange ahead for pick-up in the park. For the **information office** in Bragança, R. Cónego Albano Falcão, 5, walk downhill from the tourist office on Av. Cidade de Zamora, take the first left onto a paved street and the first left again; it's at the end of the street on the right. Park trails are unmarked, but the office has maps and can help plan hikes. (☎273 30 04 00; fax 38 11 79. Open M-F 9am-12:30pm and 2-5:30pm.) If you plan on going for a hike in the park, add an extra hour to your time calculation; the trails in park aren't well marked and take longer to complete than would seem. The office rents out traditional houses, known as **Casas Abrigos ❷.** (☎273 38 12 34. Doubles €40; quads €80. Houses are fully equipped with kitchen and bathroom.)

VILA REAL ☎259

Vila Real (pop. 25,000) overlooks the deep gorges of the Corgo and Cabril Rivers in the foothills of the Serra do Marão. The **Parque Natural do Alvão** is Portugal's smallest natural park, but this pine-covered paradise, only 15km north of Vila Real, offers excellent hiking. Vila Real's most visited site is the ▧**Casa de Mateus,** an 18th-century manor house designed to reflect symmetry and repetition wherever possible. (☎259 32 31 21. Open daily June-Sept. 9am-7:30pm; Oct. and Mar.-May 9am-1pm and 2-6pm; Nov.-Feb. 10am-1pm and 2-5pm. Ticket to gardens €4. Gardens and guided tour of manor house and chapel €7.)

Tr. de S. Domingos, next to the Cathedral on Av. Carvalho Araújo, is full of cheap *pensões*. ■**Residencial S. Domingos ❷,** Tr. de S. Domingos, 33, offers charming, old-fashioned rooms with private bath, cable TV, and phone. (☎259 32 20 39; fax 32 20 39. Singles €15; doubles €25; triples €30. Cash only.) ■**Churrasquería Real ❷,** R. Teixeira de Sousa, 14, located on a quiet street off the main thoroughfare, serves grilled meat and fish dishes to local crowds. (☎259 32 20 78. Entrees €4-12.50. Open M-Sa 9am-11pm. Cash only.) A **supermarket** is in the basement at the corner of Av. 1 de Maio and R. Nova, around from **Espaço Internet** (open M-Sa 9am-8pm). The cafes along **Av. Carvalho Araújo** and the square offer several nightlife options.

Trains (☎808 20 82 08) run from Av. 5 de Outubro to **Porto** (4½hr., 4-5 per day 7am-7:15pm, €10.20). From the train station, it's a 5min. walk to the town center; head up Av. 5 de Outubro, cross the bridge onto R. Miguel Bombarda, take the third left onto R. Roque da Silveira (labeled as Largo V. de Almeida on pharmacy wall), and then bear left until you hit Av. 1 de Maio. **Buses** are a quicker option. **Tamega** runs buses to Agarez, a small town at the entrance of the park. (☎259 32 29 28. To Vila Merin via Agarez 30min.; M-F 7 per day 7am-7:15pm; return trips to Vila Real M-F 7 per day 7:25am-7:40pm, Sa 8am; €1.47.) To reach the Tamega station from the Vila Real station on R. Don Pedro Castro, take a left out of the station onto R. Don Pedro Castro. When you come to a wall of barriers on your left, continue on the sidewalk and turn left onto Av. Cidade de Orense. At the end of the barriers, turn left into the parking lot, which serves as the Tamega station. **Rede Expressos buses,** R. D. Pedro de Castro, are located in the main bus station in town. Buses run to: Bragança (2hr., 7-12 per day 8:30am-11pm, €8.50), Lisboa (6½hr.; M-Th 7 per day 8am-5:45pm, F 8 per day 8am-7:15pm, Sa 4 per day 10:15am-5:45pm, Su 8 per day 10:15am-11:15pm; €15.50), and Porto (1¾hr.; M-F 14 per day 6:25am-8:30pm, Sa 8 per day 8am-7pm, Su 8 per day 8am-11pm; €6.40). **Taxis,** including **Rádiotáxi Expresso** (☎259 32 15 31), gather along Av. Carvalho Araújo.

Most activity centers around **Av. Carvalho Araújo,** which forms a T with **Largo Conde Amarante** and **Avenida 1 de Maio**. The **tourist office** is on Av. Carvalho Araújo, 34. (☎259 32 28 19; www.rtsmarao.pt. Short-term luggage storage. Open Oct.-May M-Sa 9:30am-12:30pm and 2-6pm; June-Sept. M-F 9:30am-7pm, Sa-Su 9:30am-12:30pm and 2-6pm.) To reach the tourist office, turn right out of the bus station and continue down R. D. Pedro de Castro onto Av. Carvalho Araújo, a street separated in the middle by a grassy barrier. Cross to the left side of the street, and the tourism office is down on the left. Local services include: **Caixa General de Depósitos,** Pr. Luís de Camões, at the end of Av. Carvalho Araújo (open M-F 8:30am-3pm); **Lavandaria Miracorgo,** R. Camilo Castelo Branco, 33-33A, on a small street off Av. 1 de Maio (☎259 37 28 16; open M-F 8am-1pm and 2-7pm, Sa 8am-1pm); **police,** (☎259 33 02 40), at the end of Lg. Conde Amarante; **Farmácia Almeida,** Av. Carvalho Araújo, 41-43 (☎259 32 28 74; open daily 8:30am-7:30pm); **Hospital Distrital Vila Real,** Av. da Noruega (☎259 30 05 00; from Lg. Conde Amarante, follow the road as it becomes Av. da Noruega); free **Internet** access at **Espaço Internet,** Av. 1 de Maio (open M-F 10am-2pm and 4-7pm), 150m down Av. 1 de Maio; the **post office,** Av. Carvalho Araújo, across and up the street from the tourist office (☎259 33 03 00; open M-F 8:30am-6pm, Sa 9am-12:30pm). **Postal Code:** 5000.

APPENDIX

CLIMATE

In the following charts, the first two columns for each month list the average daily minimum and maximum temperatures in degrees Celsius and Fahrenheit. The rain column lists the average number of days of rain in that month.

SPAIN	JANUARY			APRIL			JULY			OCTOBER		
	°C	°F	Rain	°C	°F	Rain	°C	°F	Rain	°C	°F	Rain
Barcelona	6-13	43-55	5	11-18	52-64	9	21-28	70-82	4	15-21	59-70	9
Bilbao	7-12	45-54	16	10-15	50-59	13	16-22	61-72	11	12-18	54-64	14
Madrid	2-9	36-48	8	7-18	45-64	9	17-31	63-88	2	10-19	50-66	8
Santiago de Compostela	7-13	45-55	19	9-16	48-61	12	15-22	59-72	8	12-19	52-66	14
Sevilla	6-15	43-59	8	11-24	52-75	7	20-36	68-97	0	14-26	57-79	6

PORTUGAL	JANUARY			APRIL			JULY			OCTOBER		
	°C	°F	Rain	°C	°F	Rain	°C	°F	Rain	°C	°F	Rain
Faro	9-15	48-59	9	13-20	55-68	6	20-28	68-82	0	16-22	61-72	6
Lisboa	8-14	46-57	15	12-20	52-68	10	15-25	59-77	2	14-22	57-72	9
Porto	5-13	41-55	18	9-18	48-64	13	15-25	59-77	5	11-21	52-70	15

TIME DIFFERENCES

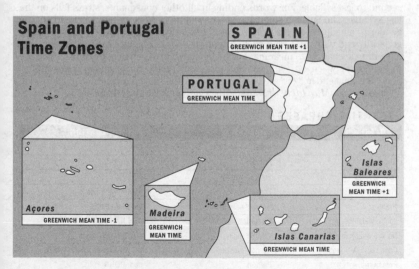

Spain and Portugal Time Zones

SPAIN
GREENWICH MEAN TIME +1

PORTUGAL
GREENWICH MEAN TIME

Islas
Baleares
GREENWICH
MEAN TIME +1

Açores
GREENWICH MEAN TIME -1

Madeira
GREENWICH
MEAN TIME

Islas Canarias
GREENWICH MEAN TIME

MEASUREMENTS

Spain and Portugal use the metric system. The basic unit of length is the **meter (m)**, which is divided into 100 **centimeters (cm)**, or 1000 **millimeters (mm)**. One thousand meters make up one **kilometer (km)**. Fluids are measured in **liters (L)**, each divided into 1000 **milliliters (mL)**. A liter of pure water weighs one **kilogram (kg)**, divided into 1000 **grams (g)**, while 1000kg make up one metric **ton**.

1 in. = 25.4mm	1mm = 0.039 in.
1 ft. = 0.30m	1m = 3.28 ft.
1 yd. = 0.914m	1m = 1.09 yd.
1 mi. = 1.609km	1km = 0.62 mi.
1 oz. = 28.35g	1g = 0.035 oz.
1 lb. = 0.454kg	1kg = 2.205 lbs.
1 fl. oz. = 29.57ml	1mL = 0.034 fl. oz.
1 gal. = 3.785L	1L = 0.264 gal.

SPANISH PHRASEBOOK

Each vowel has only one pronunciation: *a* ("ah" in "father"); *e* ("eh" in "pet"); *i* ("ee" in "eat"); *o* ("oh" in "oat"); *u* ("oo" in "boot"); *y*, by itself, is pronounced the same as the Spanish *i* ("ee"). Most consonants are the same as in English. Important exceptions are: *j* ("h" in "hello"); *ll* ("y" in "yes"); *ñ* ("ny" in "canyon"); and *r* at the beginning of a word or *rr* anywhere in a word (trilled). *H* is always silent. *G* before *e* or *i* is pronounced like the "h" in "hen;" elsewhere it is pronounced like the "g" in "gate." *X* has a bewildering variety of pronunciations; depending on dialect and word position, it can sound like the English "h," "s," "sh," or "x." *B* and *v* have similar pronunciations. Spanish words receive stress on the syllable marked with an accent. In the absence of an accent mark, words that end in vowels, *n*, or *s* receive stress on the second to last syllable. For words ending in all other consonants, stress falls on the last syllable. The Spanish language has masculine and feminine nouns, and gives a gender to all adjectives. Masculine words generally end with an *o*, feminine words generally end with an *a*. Pay close attention—slight changes in word ending can have drastic changes in meaning. For instance, when receiving directions, mind the distinction between *derecho* (straight; more commonly *recto*) and *derecha* (right). Sentences that end in *?* or *!* are also preceded by the same punctuation upside-down: *¿Cómo estás? ¡Muy bien, gracias!* ("How are you? I'm fine, thanks!")

ESSENTIAL PHRASES

ENGLISH	SPANISH	PRONUNCIATION
Hello.	Hola.	OH-la
Goodbye.	Adiós.	ah-dee-OHS
Yes/No.	Sí/No.	SEE/NO
Please.	Por favor.	POHR fah-VOHR
Thank you.	Gracias.	GRAH-thee-ahs
You're welcome.	De nada.	DEH NAH-dah
Do you speak English?	¿Habla inglés?	AH-blah EEN-glace
I don't speak Spanish.	No hablo español.	NO AH-bloh ehs-pahn-YOHL
Excuse me.	Perdón.	pehr-DOHN
I don't know.	No sé.	NO SAY
Can you repeat that?	¿Puede repetirlo?	PWEH-deh reh-peh-TEER-lo

SURVIVAL SPANISH

ENGLISH	SPANISH	ENGLISH	SPANISH
Again, please.	Otra vez, por favor.	Could you speak more slowly?	¿Podría hablar más despacio?
What (did you just say)?	¿Cómo?/¿Qué?	How are you?	¿Cómo está?
I don't understand.	No entiendo.	Where is (the bathroom)?	¿Dónde está (el baño)?
What is your name?	¿Cómo se llama?	Is the store open/closed?	¿La tienda está abierta/cerrada?
How do you say (dodgeball) in Spanish?	¿Cómo se dice (dodgeball) en español?	I'm sick/fine.	Estoy enfermo(a)/bien.
Good morning/Good night.	Buenos días/Buenas noches.	I am hungry/thirsty.	Tengo hambre/sed.
How much does it cost?	¿Cuánto cuesta?	I am hot/cold.	Tengo calor/frío.
It's/That's fine.	Está bien.	I want/I would like...	Quiero/Me gustaría...
That is very cheap/expensive.	Es muy barato/caro.	Let's go!	¡Vámonos!
What's up?	¿Qué pasa?/¿Qué tal?	Stop/that's enough.	Basta.
Who?	¿Quién?	What?	¿Qué?
When?	¿Cuándo?	Where?	¿Dónde?
Why?	¿Por qué?	Because.	Porque.
Maybe.	Tal vez.	Look!	¡Mira!
See you later.	Hasta luego.	OK/Yes/Fine.	Vale.

ON ARRIVAL

ENGLISH	SPANISH	ENGLISH	SPANISH
I am from (the US/Europe).	Soy de (los Estados Unidos/Europa).	What's the problem, sir/madam?	¿Cuál es el problema, señor/señora?
I have a visa/ID.	Tengo una visa/identificación.	I lost my passport/luggage.	Se perdió mi pasaporte/equipaje.
I will be here for less than six months.	Estaré aquí por menos de seis meses.	I have nothing to declare.	No tengo nada para declarar.
I don't know where that came from.	No sé de dónde vino eso.	Please do not detain me.	Por favor no me detenga.

GETTING AROUND

ENGLISH	SPANISH	ENGLISH	SPANISH
How can you get to...?	¿Cómo se puede llegar a...?	On foot.	A pie.
Does this bus go to (San Sebastián)?	¿Este autobús va a (San Sebastián)?	What bus line goes to...?	¿Cuál línea de buses tiene servicio a...?
Where is (El Cid) street?	¿Dónde está la calle (El Cid)?	From where/when does the bus leave?	¿De dónde/cuándo sale el autobús?
Can you let me know when we get to...?	¿Me podría avisar cuando lleguemos a...?	Could you tell me what time it is?	¿Podría decirme qué hora es?
I'm getting off at...	Me bajo en...	How far/near is...?	¿Qué tan lejos/cerca está...?
Can I buy a ticket?	¿Podría comprar un boleto?	Can you take me to (the train station)?	¿Podría llevarme a (la estación de tren)?
How long does the trip take?	¿Cuánto tiempo dura el viaje?	The flight is delayed/cancelled.	El vuelo está atrasado/cancelado.
Round-trip/one-way.	Ida y vuelta/ida.	Is it safe to hitchhike?	¿Es seguro hacer autostop?
I am going to the airport.	Voy al aeropuerto.	I'm lost.	Estoy perdido(a).
I'm in a hurry!	¡Tengo prisa!	Please let me off at (the zoo).	Por favor, déjeme en (el zoológico).

ENGLISH	SPANISH	ENGLISH	SPANISH
I would like to rent (a car).	Quisiera alquilar (un coche).	Where can I check e-mail?	¿Dónde se puede che-quear el correo elec-trónico?
How much does it cost per day/week?	¿Cuánto cuesta por día/semana?	Are there student dis-counts available?	¿Hay descuentos para estudiantes?

DIRECTIONS

ENGLISH	SPANISH	ENGLISH	SPANISH
(to the) right	(a la) derecha	(to the) left	(a la) izquierda
next to	al lado de/junto a	across from	en frente de/frente a
straight ahead	recto/derecho	turn (command form)	doble
near (to)	cerca (de)	far (from)	lejos (de)
above	arriba/ encima	below	abajo
traffic light	semáforo	corner	esquina
street	calle/avenida	block	cuadra

ACCOMMODATIONS

ENGLISH	SPANISH	ENGLISH	SPANISH
Is there a cheap hotel around here?	¿Hay un hotel económico por aquí?	Are there rooms with win-dows?	¿Hay habitaciones con ventanas?
Do you have rooms avail-able?	¿Tiene habitaciones libres?	I am going to stay for (four) days.	Me voy a quedar (cuatro) días.
I would like to reserve a room.	Quisiera reservar una habitación.	Are there cheaper rooms?	¿Hay habitaciones más baratas?
Can I see a room?	¿Podría ver una habit-ación?	Do they come with pri-vate baths?	¿Vienen con baño pri-vado?
Do you have any singles/doubles?	¿Tiene habitaciones sim-ples/dobles?	Does it have (heating/A/C)?	¿Tiene (calefacción/aire acondicionado)?
I need another key/towel/pillow.	Necesito otra llave/toalla/almohada.	My bedsheets are dirty.	Mis sábanas están sucias.
The shower/sink/toilet is broken.	La ducha/pila/el servicio no funciona.	I'll take it.	Lo acepto.
There are cockroaches in my room.	Hay cucarachas en mi habitación.	Who's there?	¿Quién es?
They are biting me.	Me están mordiendo.	Dance, cockroaches, dance!	¡Bailen, cucarachas, bailen!

EMERGENCY

ENGLISH	SPANISH	ENGLISH	SPANISH
Help!	¡Socorro!/¡Ayúdeme!	Call the police!	¡Llame a la policía/los carabineros!
I am hurt.	Estoy herido(a).	Leave me alone!	¡Déjame en paz!
It's an emergency!	¡Es una emergencia!	They robbed me!	¡Me han robado!
Fire!	¡Fuego!/¡Incendio!	They went that-a-way!	¡Se fueron por allá!
Call a clinic/ambulance/doctor/priest!	¡Llame a una clínica/una ambulancia/un médico/un padre!	I will only speak in the presence of a lawyer.	Solo hablaré en la pres-encia de un abogado(a).
I need to contact my embassy.	Necesito comunicarme con mi embajada.	Don't touch me!	¡No me toque!

HEALTH

ENGLISH	SPANISH	ENGLISH	SPANISH
I feel bad/worse/fine/better.	Me siento mal/peor/bien/mejor.	I need to speak to a doc-tor.	Necesito hablar con un médico.

ENGLISH	SPANISH	ENGLISH	SPANISH
I have a headache.	Tengo un dolor de cabeza.	I have a stomachache.	Me duele el estómago.
I'm sick/ill.	Estoy enfermo(a).	Here is my prescription.	Aquí está la receta médica.
I'm allergic to Spain.	Soy alérgico(a) a España.	I think I'm going to vomit.	Creo que voy a vomitar.
What is this medicine for?	¿Para qué es esta medicina?	I haven't been able to go to the bathroom in (four) days.	No he podido ir al baño en (cuatro) días.
Where is the nearest hospital/doctor?	¿Dónde está el hospital/médico más cercano?	I have a cold/a fever/diarrhea/nausea.	Tengo gripe/una calentura/diarrea/náusea.

INTERPERSONAL INTERACTIONS

ENGLISH	SPANISH	ENGLISH	SPANISH
What is your name? (informal)	¿Cómo te llamas?	Pleased to meet you.	Encantado(a)/Mucho gusto.
Where are you from?	¿De dónde es usted?	I'm (twenty) years old.	Tengo (veinte) años.
This is my first time in Spain.	Esta es mi primera vez en España.	I have a boyfriend/girlfriend/spouse.	Tengo novio/novia/esposo(a).
Do you come here often?	¿Viene aquí mucho?	I love you.	Te quiero.
Do you have a light?	¿Tiene fuego?	No hash for me, thanks.	No hachís para mí, gracias.
Let's dance. All night.	Bailemos. Toda la noche.	I had the very same dream!	¡Tuve el mismo sueño!
Would you like to go out with me?	¿Quieres salir conmigo?	Why not?	¿Porqué no?

NUMBERS, DAYS, AND MONTHS

ENGLISH	SPANISH	ENGLISH	SPANISH	ENGLISH	SPANISH
0	cero	20	veinte	last night	anoche
1	uno	21	veintiuno	weekend	(el) fin de semana
2	dos	22	veintidos	morning	(la) mañana
3	tres	30	treinta	afternoon	(la) tarde
4	cuatro	40	cuarenta	night	(la) noche
5	cinco	50	cincuenta	month	(el) mes
6	seis	100	cien	year	(el) año
7	siete	1000	mil	early/late	temprano/tarde
8	ocho	1 million	un millón	January	enero
9	nueve	Monday	lunes	February	febrero
10	diez	Tuesday	martes	March	marzo
11	once	Wednesday	miércoles	April	abril
12	doce	Thursday	jueves	May	mayo
13	trece	Friday	viernes	June	junio
14	catorce	Saturday	sábado	July	julio
15	quince	Sunday	domingo	August	agosto
16	dieciseis	today	hoy	September	septiembre
17	diecisiete	tomorrow	mañana	October	octubre
18	dieciocho	day after tomorrow	pasado mañana	November	noviembre
19	diecinueve	yesterday	ayer	December	diciembre

EATING OUT

ENGLISH	SPANISH	ENGLISH	SPANISH
breakfast	(el) desayuno	lunch	almuerzo
dinner	(la) comida/cena	drink (alcoholic)	bebida (trago)
dessert	(el) postre	bon appetit	buen provecho
fork	(el) tenedor	knife	cuchillo
napkin	(la) servilleta	cup	copa/taza
spoon	(la) cuchara	Do you have hot sauce?	¿Tiene salsa picante?
Where is there a good restaurant?	¿Dónde hay un restaurante bueno?	Table for (one), please.	Mesa para (uno), por favor.
Can I see the menu?	¿Podría ver la carta/el menú?	Do you take credit cards?	¿Aceptan tarjetas de crédito?
This is too spicy.	Es demasiado picante.	Disgusting!	¡Guácala!/¡Qué asco!
I would like to order (the eel).	Quisiera (el congrio).	Delicious!	¡Qué rico!
Do you have anything vegetarian/without meat?	¿Hay algún plato vegetariano/sin carne?	Check, please.	La cuenta, por favor.

CATALAN/BASQUE/GALLEGO PHRASEBOOK

ESSENTIAL PHRASES

ENGLISH	CATALAN	BASQUE	GALLEGO
Hello.	Hola.	Kaixo.	Ola.
Goodbye.	Adéu.	Agur.	Adeus.
Yes/No.	Sí/No.	Bai/Ez.	Si/Non.
Please.	Si us plau.	Mesedez.	Por favor.
Thank you.	Gràcies.	Eskerrik asko.	Graciñas.
You're welcome.	De res.	Ez horregatik.	De nada.
Do you speak English?	Parles anglès?	Ingelesez hitz egiten al duzu?	Falas inglés?
I don't understand.	No ho entenc.	Ez dut ulertzen.	Eu non entendo.
Excuse me.	Perdoni.	Barkatu.	Perdóeme.
I don't know.	No sé.	Ez dakit.	Eu non sei.
Can you repeat that?	Pot repetir?	Errepikatu ahal duzu hori?	Pode repetilo?
Where is...?	On és...?	Non dago...?	Onde está...?
Who/What/When/Why	quem/que/quando/porque	nor/zer/noiz/zergatik	quen/que/cando/por qué
How do I get to (Madrid)?	Com puc arribar a (Madrid)?	Nola joaten da (Madril) era?	Como vou a (Madrid)?
Do you have any rooms available?	Teniu alguna habitació disponible?	Badaukazu logelik?	Ten habitacións?
Help!	Ajuda!	Lagundu!	Axuda!
What is your name?/My name is...	Com et dius?/Em dic...	Nola duzu izena?/ ...dut izena.	Como te chamas?/Me chama...
Let's be friends.	Estiguem amics.	Izan dezagun lagunak.	Sexamos amigos.

NUMBERS

	CATALAN	BASQUE	GALLEGO		CATALAN	BASQUE	GALLEGO
1	u/una	bat	un/unha	20	vint	hogei	vinte
2	dos/dues	bi	dous/dúas	30	trenta	hogeita hamar	trinta

	CATALAN	BASQUE	GALLEGO		CATALAN	BASQUE	GALLEGO
3	tres	hiru	tres	40	quaranta	berrogei	corenta
4	quatre	lau	catro	50	cinquanta	berrogei hamar	cincuenta
5	cinc	bost	cinco	60	seixanta	hirurogeita	sesenta
6	sis	sei	seis	70	setanta	hirurogeita hamar	setenta
7	set	zazpi	sete	80	vuitanta	larogei	oitenta
8	vuit	zortzi	oito	90	noranta	larogeita hamar	noventa
9	nou	bederatzi	nove	100	cent	ehun	cen
10	deu	hamar	dez	1000	mil	mila	mil

PORTUGUESE PHRASEBOOK

Portuguese words are often spelled like their Spanish equivalents, but their pronunciation can be quite different. In addition to regular vowels, Portuguese has nasal vowels as in French; vowels with a *tilde* (ã, õ, etc.) or before an *m* or *n* are pronounced with a nasal twang. At the end of a word, *o* is pronounced "oo" as in "room," and *e* is sometimes silent (usually after a *t* or *d*). The consonant *s* is pronounced "sh" or "zh" when it occurs before another consonant. The consonants *ch* and *x* are pronounced "sh," although the latter is sometimes pronounced as in English; *j* and *g* (before *e* or *i*) are pronounced "zh"; *ç* sounds like "es". The combinations *nh* and *lh* are pronounced "ny" as in "canyon" and "ly" as in "billion."

ESSENTIAL PHRASES

ENGLISH	PORTUGUESE	PRONUNCIATION
Yes/No.	Sim/Não.	seem/now
Hello.	Olá.	oh-LAH
Good day/afternoon/night.	Bom dia/tarde/noite.	bom DEE-ah/TARD/NOYT
Goodbye.	Adeus.	ah-DAY-oosh
Please.	Por favor.	pohr fa-VOHR
Thank you.	Obrigado(a).	oh-bree-GAH-doh/dah
Sorry/Excuse me.	Desculpe.	dish-KOOLP-eh
Do you speak English?	Fala inglês?	FAH-lah een-GLAYSH?
I don't understand.	Não entendo.	now ehn-TEHN-doh
Where is...?	Onde é...?	OHN-deh ch...?
How can you get to...?	Como vou para...?	COH-moo VOH-oo PAH-rah?
How much does this cost?	Quanto custa?	KWAHN-too KOOST-ah?
Do you have a single/double room?	Tem um quarto individual/duplo?	tem oom KWAR-too EEN-dee-vee-doo-WAHL/DOO-ploh?
That is very cheap/expensive.	É muito caro/barato.	eh MUY-toh CAH-roh/bah-RAH-toh
Help!	Socorro!	soh-KOH-roh!
Who/What	quem/que	KEHM/KEH
When/Why	quando/porque	KWAN-do/pohr-KAY
I want/would like...	Eu quero/gostaria...	EH-oo KER-oh/gost-ar-EE-uh
What is your name?/My name is...	Como se chama?/O meu nome é...	COH-mo seh SHA-mah?/oh MEH-oo NO-meh eh...
I am (twenty) years old.	Eu tenho (vinte) anos.	EH-oo TEN-yo (VIN-teh) anyos

NUMBERS, DAYS, AND MONTHS

ENGLISH	PORTUGUESE	ENGLISH	PORTUGUESE	ENGLISH	PORTUGUESE
0	zero	20	vinte	last night	ontem à noite
1	um/uma	21	vinte-um/uma	weekend	(o) fim-de-semana
2	dois/duas	22	vinte-dois/duas	morning	(a) manhã
3	três	30	trinta	afternoon	(a) tarde
4	quatro	40	quarenta	night	(a) noite
5	cinco	50	cinquenta	month	(o) mês
6	seis	100	cem	year	(o) ano
7	sete	1000	um mil	early/late	cedo/tarde
8	oito	1 million	um milhão	January	Janeiro
9	nove	Monday	segunda-feira	February	Fevereiro
10	dez	Tuesday	terça-feira	March	Março
11	onze	Wednesday	quarta-feira	April	Abril
12	doze	Thursday	quinta-feira	May	Maio
13	treze	Friday	sexta-feira	June	Junho
14	catorze	Saturday	sábado	July	Julho
15	quinze	Sunday	domingo	August	Agosto
16	dezasseis	today	hoje	September	Setembro
17	dezassete	tomorrow	amanhã	October	Outubro
18	dezoito	day after tomorrow	depois de amanhã	November	Novembro
19	dezanove	yesterday	ontem	December	Dezembro

GLOSSARY

In the following glossary we have tried to include the most useful Spanish and Portuguese terms, particularly words we use in the text and those that you will encounter frequently in menus. Non-Castilian words are specified as **C** (Catalan), **B** (Basque), or **G** (Gallego), respectively.

SPAIN: TRAVELING

abadía: abbey
abierto: open
ayuntamiento/ajuntament (C): city hall
albergue: youth hostel
alcazaba: Muslim citadel
alcázar: Muslim palace
arena: sand
autobús/autocar: bus
avenida/avinguda (C): avenue
bahía: bay
bakalao: Spanish techno
bandera azul: blue flag, EU award for clean beaches
baños: baths
barcelonés: of Barcelona
barrio viejo: old quarter
biblioteca: library
billete/boleto: ticket
buceo: scuba diving
cabo: cape
cajero automático: ATM

calle/carrer (C): street
cambio: currency exchange
capilla: chapel
casa particular: lodging in a private home
caseta: party tent for Sevilla's *Feria de Abril*
castillo/castell (C): castle
catedral: cathedral
cerrado: closed
carretera: highway
casco antiguo/viejo: old city, old district
chocolate: chocolate or hash
churrigueresco: ornate Baroque architecture style
ciudad vieja/ciutat vella (C): old city
colegio: high school
consigna: luggage storage
Correos: post office
corrida: bullfight
cripta: crypt
cuarto: room
encierro: running of the bulls

entrada: entrance
ermita/ermida (C): hermitage
escuela: (elementary) school
estación: station
estanco: tobacco shop
estanque: pond
estany (C): lake
extremeño: of Extremadura
fachada: facade
feria: outdoor market, fair
ferrocarriles: trains
fiesta: holiday or festival
fuente/font (C): fountain
gallego: of Galicia
gitano: gypsy
glorieta: rotary
iglesia/església (C)/igrexa (G): church
IVA: value-added tax
jardín público: public garden
judería: Jewish quarter
librería: bookstore
lista de correos: poste restante
litera: sleeping car (in trains)

llegada: arrival
madrileño: Madrid resident
madrugada: early morning
manchego: from La Mancha
mercado/mercat (C): market
mezquita: mosque
mirador: lookout point
monestir (C): monastery
monte: mountain
mosteiro (G): monastery
mozárabe: Christian art style
mudéjar: Muslim architectural style
muelle/moll (C): wharf, pier
murallas: walls
museo/museu (C): museum
oficina: office
palacio/palau (C): palace
parador nacional: state-owned luxury hotel
parte viejo: old town
paseo, Po./passeig, Pg. (C): promenade, stroll
pico: peak
plateresque: architectural style noted for its facades
playa/platja (C): beach
plaza/plaça, Pl. (C)/praza, Pr. (G): square, plaza
puente: bridge
quiosco: newsstand
rastro: flea market
real: royal
REAJ: the Spanish HI youth hostel network
Reconquista: the Christian reconquest of the Iberian peninsula from the Muslims
refugio: shelter, refuge
reina/rey: queen/king
retablo: altarpiece
ría (G): estuary
río/riu (C): river
rua (G): street
sacristía: part of the church where sacred objects are kept
sala: room, hall
salida: exit, departure
selva: forest
Semana Santa: Holy Week, leading up to Easter Sunday
sepulcro: tomb
seu (C): cathedral
sevillana: type of flamenco
SIDA: AIDS
sierra/serra (C): mountain range
Siglo de Oro: Golden Age
sillería: choir stalls
tienda: shop, tent
tesoro: treasury
torre: tower
universidad: university
v.o.: *versión original,* a foreign-language film subtitled in Spanish
valle: valley
zarzuela: Spanish light opera

SPAIN: FOOD AND DRINK

a la plancha/a brasa: grilled
aceite: oil
aceituna: olive
adabo: battered
agua: water
aguacate: avocado
aguardiente: firewater
ahumado/a: smoked
ajo: garlic
al horno: baked
albóndigas: meatballs
alioli: *català* garlic sauce
almejas: clams
almendras: almonds
almuerzo: midday meal
alubias: kidney beans
anchoas: anchovies
anguila: eel
arroz: rice
arroz con leche: rice pudding
asado: roasted
atún: tuna
bacalao: salted cod
bacón: (American) bacon
bistec: steak
bocadillo: sandwich
bodega: wine cellar
bollo: bread roll
boquerones: anchovies
brasa: chargrilled
cacahuete: peanut
café con leche: coffee w/milk
café solo: black coffee
calabacín: zucchini
calamares: calamari, squid
caldereta: stew
caldo gallego: white bean and potato soup
calimocho: red wine and cola
callos: tripe
camarones: shrimp
caña: beer in a small glass
canelones: cannelloni
cangrejo: crab
caracoles: snails
carne: meat
cava (C): sparkling white wine
cebolla: onion
cena: dinner
cerdo: pig, pork
cereza: cherry
cervecería: beer bar
cerveza: beer
champiñones: mushrooms
choco: cuttlefish
chorizo: spicy red sausage
chuleta: chop, cutlet
chupito: shot
churros: fried dough sticks
cocido: cooked, stew
conejo: rabbit
coñac: brandy
copas: drinks
cordero: lamb
cortado: coffee with little milk

croquetas: fried croquettes
crudo: raw
cuba libre: rum and cola
cuchara: spoon
cuchillo: knife
cuenta: the bill
desayuno: breakfast
dorada: sea bass
empanada: meat/fish pastry
ensaladilla rusa: vegetable salad with mayonnaise
entremeses: hors d'oeuvres
escabeche: pickled fish
espagueti: spaghetti
espárragos: asparagus
espinacas: spinach
fabada asturiana: bean soup with sausage and ham
flan: crème caramel
frambuesa: raspberry
fresa: strawberry
frito/a: fried
galleta: cookie
gambas: prawns
garbanzos: chickpeas
gazpacho: cold tomato soup with garlic and cucumber
ginebra: gin
guindilla: hot chili pepper
guisantes: peas
helado: ice cream
hielo: ice
horchata: sweet almond drink
horneado: baked
huevo: egg
jamón dulce: cooked ham
jamón ibérico: Iberian ham
jamón serrano: cured ham
jatetxea (B): restaurant
jerez: sherry
langosta: lobster
langostino: large prawn
leche: milk
lechuga: lettuce
lenguado: sole
lomo: pork loin
manzana: apple
manzanilla: dry, light sherry
mayonesa: mayonnaise
mejillones: mussels
melocotón: peach
menestra de verduras: vegetable mix/pottage
menú: full meal with bread, drink, and side dish
merienda: tea/snack
merluza: hake
migas: fried breadcrumb dish
mojito: white rum and club soda with mint and sugar
morcilla: blood sausage (black pudding)
mostaza: mustard
muy hecho: well-done (steak)
naranja: orange
natillas: creamy milk dessert
navajas: razor clams
paella: rice and seafood dish
pan: bread

pasa: raisin
pastas: small sweet cakes
pastel: pastry
patatas bravas: potatoes w/
spicy tomato sauce and mayo
patatas fritas: French fries
pato: duck
pavo: turkey
pechuga: chicken breast
pepino: cucumber
picante: spicy
pimienta (negra): (black)
pepper
pimiento (rojo): (red) pepper
piña: pineapple
pintxo (B): Basque for tapa
plancha: grill
plátano: banana
plato del día: daily special
plato combinado: entree and
side dish
poco hecho: rare (steak)
pollo: chicken
pulpo: octopus
queso: cheese
rabo de toro: bull's tail
ración: small dish
rebozado: battered and fried
refrescos: soft drinks
relleno/a: stuffed
sal: salt
salchicha: pork sausage
sangria: red wine punch
seco: dried
servilleta: napkin
sesos: brains
setas: wild mushrooms
sidra: (alcoholic) cider
solomillo: sirloin
sopa: soup
taberna: tapas bar
tapa: bite-sized snack
tenedor: fork
ternera: beef, veal
terraza: patio seating
tinto: red (wine)
tocino: (Canadian) bacon
tomate: tomato
tortilla española: potato fri-
tatta
tortilla francesa: omelette
tostada: toast
trucha: trout
trufas: truffles
tubo: tall glass of beer
txakoli (B): fizzy white wine
uva: grape
vaca, carne de: beef
vaso: glass
verduras: green vegetables
vino: wine
vino blanco: white wine
vino tinto: red wine
xampanyería (C): champagne
bar
yema: candied egg yolk
zanahoria: carrot
zarzuela de marisco: shellfish
stew

zumo: fruit juice

PORTUGAL: TRAVELING

alto/a: upper
autocarro: bus
bairro: neighborhood, district
baixo/a: lower
berrões: stone pigs found in
Trás-Os-Montes
bicicleta de montanha:
mountain bike
bilhete: ticket
bilheteria: ticket office
câmara municipal: town hall
camioneta: long-distance bus
capela: chapel
casa de abrigo: shelter-
house, usually in parks
castelo: castle
centro de saúde: state-run
medical center
chegadas: arrivals
cidade: city
claustro: cloister
construção: construction
conta: bill
coro alto: choir stall
Correios: post office
cruzeiro: large stone cross;
cruise
Dom, Dona: courtesy titles,
usually for kings and queens
domingo: Sunday
entrada: entrance
esquerda: left (abbr. E, Esqa)
estação rodoviária: bus station
estrada: road
feriado: holiday
floresta: forest
fortaleza: fort
grutas: caves
horario: timetable
igreja: church
ilha: island
intercidade: inter-city train
lago: lake
largo: small square
ligação: connecting bus/train
livraria: bookstore
miradouro: lookout
mosteiro: monastery
mouraria: Moorish quarter
mudança: switch/change
palácio: palace
paragem: stop
partidas: departures
pelourinho: stone pillory
pensão (s.), pensões (pl.):
pension(s)/guesthouse(s)
ponte: bridge
porta: gate/door
posto de informações turísti-
cas: tourist office
pousada da juventude: youth
hostel
pousada: guest house
praça: square
praça de touros: bullring

praia: beach
PSP: Polícia de Seguranca
Pública, the local police force
quarta-feira: Wednesday
quarto de casal: room with
double bed
quinta-feira: Thursday
quiosque: kiosk; newsstand
rés do chão (R/C): ground
floor
residencial: guesthouse,
more expensive than pensões
retábulo: altarpiece
ribeira: stream
ria: narrow lagoon
rio: river
romaria: pilgrimage-festival
rua: street
sábado: Saturday
saída: exit
sé: cathedral
segunda-feira: Monday
selos: stamps
sexta-feira: Friday
terça-feira: Tuesday
termas: spa
tesouraria: treasury
tourada: bullfight
velho/a: old
vila: town

PORTUGAL: FOOD AND DRINK

açorda: thick soup with bread
and garlic
adega: wine cellar, bar
aguardente: firewater
alface: lettuce
alho: garlic
almoço: lunch
ameijoas: clams
Antiqua: aged grape brandy
arroz: rice
arrufada de Coimbra: raised
dough cake with cinnamon
assado: roasted
azeitonas: olives
bacalhau: cod
bacalhau à Brás: cod with
scrambled eggs and fried
potatoes
bacalhau à Gomes de Sá:
cod with olives, herbs, and
hard-boiled eggs
bacalhau à transmontana:
cod braised with cured pork
balcão: counter in bar or café
(also balcony)
batata: potato
batido: milkshake
bem passado: well done
(steak)
bica: espresso
bifinhos de vitela: veal filet
with wine sauce
bitoque de porco: pork chops
bitoque de vaca: steak
bolachas: cookies

branco: white (wine)
cabrito: kid (goat)
café com leite: coffee with milk, in a mug
café da manhã: breakfast
caldeirada: shellfish stew
caldo: broth/soup
caldo verde: kale soup
camarões: shrimp
caneca: pint-size beer mug
caracóis: snails
carioca: coffee with hot water; like American coffee
carne: meat
carne de vaca: beef
cebola: onion
cerveja: beer
chocos: cuttlefish
chouriço: sausage
churrasco: BBQ
churrasqueira: BBQ house
cogumelos: mushrooms
conta: bill
couvert: cover charge added to bill for bread
cozido: boiled
cozido no forno: baked
doce: sweet
ementa: menu
ervilhas: green peas
esacalfado: poached
espadarte: swordfish
espetadas: skewered meat served with melted butter

esturjão: sturgeon
fatia: slice
feijão: bean
frango: chicken
frito: fried
galão: coffee with hot milk
garrafa: bottle
gasosa: soda
gelado: ice cream
grão: chickpeas
grelhado: grilled
guisado: stewed
hambúrguer no prato: hamburger patty with fried egg
imperial: draft beer
jantar: dinner
lagosta: lobster
lampreia: lamprey
laranja: orange
legumes: vegetables
leitão: suckling pig
linguado: sole
linguiça: very thin sausage
lula: squid
maçã: apple
manteiga: butter
mariscos: shellfish
massapão: marzipan
mexilhões: mussels
ovo: egg
padaria: bakery
panado: breaded
pão: bread
pastelaria: pastry shop

pasteis de nata: custard tarts
peru: turkey
pimentos: peppers
polvo: octopus
porco: pork
posta: slice of fish or meat
prato do dia: dish of the day
presunto: ham
queijo: cheese
recheado: stuffed
salmão: salmon
sande/sanduíche: sandwich
seco: dry
sobremesa: dessert
sopa juliana: soup with shredded vegetables
suco: juice
tasca: bistro/cafe
tigelada: egg custard
tinto: red (wine)
tomatada: rich tomato sauce
tosta: grilled cheese
tosta mista: grilled ham and cheese sandwich
toucinho do ceu: rich cake made with pumpkin, egg-yolk, and bacon-drippings
uva passa: raisin
vinho de casa: house wine
vinho verde: young, sparkling wine
vitela: veal

INDEX

ABOUT LET'S GO

NOT YOUR PARENTS' TRAVEL GUIDE

At Let's Go, we see every trip as the chance of a lifetime. If your dream is to grab a machete and forge through the jungles of Costa Rica, we can take you there. If you'd rather bask in the Riviera sun at a beachside cafe, we'll set you a table. We write for readers who know that there's more to travel than sharing double deckers with tourists and who believe that travel can change both themselves and the world—whether they plan to spend six days in Mexico City or six months in Europe. We'll show you just how far your money can go, and prove that the greatest limitation on your adventures is not your wallet, but your imagination.

BEYOND THE TOURIST EXPERIENCE

To help you gain a deeper connection with the places you travel, our fearless researchers scour the globe to give you the heads-up on both world-renowned and off-the-beaten-track attractions, sights, and destinations. They engage with the local culture only to emerge with the freshest insights on everything from local festivals to regional cuisine. We've also opened our pages to respected writers and scholars to hear their takes on the countries and regions we cover, and asked travelers who have worked, studied, or volunteered abroad to contribute first-person accounts of their experiences. In addition, we increased our coverage of responsible travel and expanded each guide's Beyond Tourism chapter to share more ideas about how to give back while on the road.

FORTY-EIGHT YEARS OF WISDOM

Let's Go got its start in 1960, when a group of creative and well-traveled students compiled their experience and advice into a 20-page mimeographed pamphlet, which they gave to travelers on charter flights to Europe. Four and a half decades later, we've expanded to cover six continents and all kinds of travel—while retaining our founders' adventurous attitude toward the world. Laced with witty prose and total candor, our guides are still researched and written entirely by students on shoestring budgets, experienced travelers who know that train strikes, stolen luggage, food poisoning, and marriage proposals are all part of a day's work.

THE LET'S GO COMMUNITY

More than just a travel guide company, Let's Go is a community. Our small staff comes together because of our shared passion for travel and our desire to help other travelers see the world the way it was meant to be seen. We love it when our readers become part of the Let's Go community as well—when you travel, drop us a postcard (67 Mt. Auburn St., Cambridge, MA 02138, USA), send us an e-mail (feedback@letsgo.com), or post on our forum (http://www.letsgo.com/connect/forum) to tell us about your adventures and discoveries.

For more information, visit us online: www.letsgo.com.

GET CONNECTED & SAVE WITH THE HI CARD

An HI card gives you access to friendly and affordable accommodations at over 4,000 hostels in over 60 countries, including across Spain & Portugal. Members also receive complementary travel insurance, members-only airfare deals, and thousands of discounts on everything from tours and dining to shopping, communications and transportation.

Join millions of HI members worldwide who save money and have more fun every time they travel.

 Hostelling International USA

MAP APPENDIX

MAP LEGEND

▪ Point of Interest	✈ Airport	⛪ Convent/Monastery	⛷ Ski Area
■ Accommodation	⌂ Arch/Gate	⚓ Ferry Landing	℞ Pharmacy
▲ Camping	$ Bank	(N-I) Highway Sign	✛ Police
🍎 Food	☂ Beach	✚ Hospital	✉ Post Office
■ Shopping	🚌 Bus Station/Stop	▢ Internet Café	✡ Synagogue
🏛 Museum	♜ Castle	📖 Library/Bookstore	♥ Theater
● Sight	✝ Church	Ⓜ M Metro Station	ⓘ Tourist Office
★ Nightlife	⚑ Consulate/Embassy	⛰ Mountain	🚉 Train Station

Park	Water	Beach	⠿ Pedestrian Zone	The Let's Go compass always points NORTH
			⠿ Stairs	